D0869484

# MEDIEVAL LITERATURE IN TRANSLATION

*Edited by*
Charles W. Jones

DOVER PUBLICATIONS, INC.
Mineola, New York

Published in Canada by General Publishing Company, Ltd., 30 Lesmill Road, Don Mills, Toronto, Ontario.

## Bibliographical Note

This Dover edition, first published in 2001, is an unabridged republication of the work originally published in 1950 by Longmans, Green and Co., New York.

## Library of Congress Cataloging-in-Publication Data

Medieval literature in translation / edited by Charles W. Jones.
    p. cm.
  Originally published: New York : Longmans, Green, 1950.
  Includes bibliographical references.
  ISBN 0-486-41581-3 (pbk.)
    1. Literature, Medieval—Translations into English. I. Jones, Charles Williams, 1905–

PN667 .J6 2001
808.8'994'0902—dc21

00-064492

Manufactured in the United States of America
Dover Publications, Inc., 31 East 2nd Street, Mineola, N.Y. 11501

# PREFACE

The frontispiece of the eighteenth-century DuCange represents the attitude of the Age of Reason toward medieval literature. It shows Rome ablaze while barbarians feed the flames with books and *Latinitas* lies aswoon. Later readers have learned that *Latinitas* did not die in the Middle Ages, but much later — perhaps in the Age of Reason, perhaps more recently. From the time of the Romantic Revival they have rediscovered, one by one, the medieval giants on whose shoulders we stand. From Thomas Carlyle to Dorothy Sayers, poet and prose writer, journalist and scholar, pedant and antiquarian, have turned Boethian. The useful Farrar and Evans *Bibliography* lists 3839 translations from medieval literature into modern English, and more appear annually.

But though we may thank the romantics for adjusting our sights, we have suffered from their weakness. Wherever the Revival occurred, it was nationalistic. For that reason it distorted medieval literature even as it revived interest. The Germans "discovered" the *Nibelungenlied* (though it had never been lost) because it was German; the French "discovered" the *Chanson de Roland,* resting comfortably in an English library; and Walter Scott turned the troubadour Richard, who spoke English infrequently if at all, into a lasting symbol of English monarchical benevolence. There were no nations in the Middle Ages. Geographical boundaries were provincial; linguistic cleavage followed the watersheds, not treaties; and over all the West moved the Benedictines and Franciscans, the Latin language, the minstrels and the *vagantes.* Yet even today, because of the Revival, Old English, Old French, or Old German literature is read as a self-contained unit. I hope that this book will contribute to breaking down such insulation, even though I have had to bow to tradition in grouping some of the contents.

There are those to whom anthologies, abridgments, and scissors-and-paste are hateful. Sometimes I am of their humor; but not with respect to medieval literature. From the first, the medieval author wrote to have his book excerpted. Many of the authors represented here were themselves editors of *florilegia.* I do not remember an important medieval work that does not exist in abridged, expanded, or revised state in a fair share of the extant manuscripts. A medieval literary work was built like a Gothic cathedral, where one can pray in a chapel when he cannot commune in the nave. Like the opprobrious medieval scribe, I have often altered the punctuation and even the diction without acknowledgment and at my own caprice, though usually with an authoritative text to guide me. I have omitted footnotes and other deterrents to readers' flights of imagination everywhere that they were not thought necessary by medieval readers; but I have followed the Provençal bookmakers in interspersing little *vidas,* or introductions, which I hope are no more superfluous than theirs. This volume, then, is medieval in form, if not in format.

Translators would be the last to say that any literature can survive in translation. Translation distills away more than the precious life-blood of a master spirit. I presume that only in times of decadence need this point be labored. But since many languages are the possession of but a few people, and even when a man has the ability to read a second and a third tongue, he infrequently grasps the living idiom, translation serves its purpose. It distorts direct communication little more than does the two-dimensional screen or the flat-tone record.

There is no canon of medieval literature, no list of the hundred best works. The choice here is entirely my own. A reader may question even the implicit definition of both *medieval* and *literature*. No doubt I have excluded works of science, theology, and philosophy that many would include; I have no doubt that the chronological or geographical limits will disturb some readers. One may well ask why, for instance, I have omitted Cynewulf, Chrétien, or the *Mab-inogion;* why I include German lyrics but not Portuguese, Icelandic literature but not Arabic; why much of the *Nibelungenlied* but little of *Beowulf* or *Parzival*. Why does the literal, prosaic, and (in a kindly sense) colorless Norton translation of Dante's *Comedy* stand near the loose, rhymed version of *The Romance of the Rose?* I have chosen what worked best with my students, with whom I have been reading medieval literature for some years. Authors and publishers have been generous: in no instance have I been prevented from reproducing a translation I felt was essential. I have excluded Middle English literature because it does not need translation, and handy and inexpensive anthologies of that literature are available with which to supplement this volume. I have excluded Italian literature written after Dante because it is not really a part of this unit; the reader will find it represented in Professor Blanchard's *Prose and Poetry of the Continental Renaissance in Translation,* in this series. In brief, this book has all the shortcomings of an anthology. It is not amiss to quote from Master Bede, who twelve centuries and more ago prefaced a similar work with the words: *Cui displicet vel superfluum videtur, quod haec rogatu fratrum undecumque collegi uniusque libelli tenore conclusi, dimittat ea legenda, si qui velint, et ipse de communibus patrum fontibus quae sibi suisque sufficere arbitretur hauriens mecum nihilominus debita fraternitatis intemerata iura custodiat.*

I have sharpened my wits on the whetstone of my friends' criticism. I mention Professor Robert A. Pratt, and especially Professor Thomas G. Bergin, who helped me where I felt most ignorant, spotted some blunders, and composed some delightful improvements. Some of my colleagues, named in the proper places, have translated lyrics for the volume. In assisting me, my wife has combined the virtues of Beatrice and Griselda. Last, I thank Mr. Robert L. Straker of Longmans, Green and Company for help beyond that normally given to an editor.

CHARLES W. JONES

# CONTENTS

# CONTENTS

# CONTENTS

# CONTENTS

# CONTENTS

## MAPS

# MAPS

## *Key to Towns, Cities, and Provinces*

[NOTE: Names of countries or provinces are added after the name of the town only as a means of assisting the reader when he is consulting this map. They do not indicate medieval political relationships.]

1. Aachen (Aix-la-Chapelle) Germany
2. Abbeville France
3. Aix in Provence Savoy
4. Albi Provence
5. Albreth Provence
6. Alençon Normandy
7. Alhambra Moorish Spain
8. Amiens France
9. Ancona Italy
10. Andelot France
11. Angers France
12. Aquinum Italy
13. Arezzo Italy
14. Argenteuil France
15. Arles Provence
16. Armagh Ireland
17. Assisi Italy
18. Athelney England
19. Autun France
20. Auxerre France
21. Avignon Provence
22. Avranches Normandy
23. Badon Hill England
24. Barfleur Normandy
25. Bath England
26. Bayeux Normandy
27. Beaune France
28. Beauvais France
29. Bechlaren (?) Austria
30. Belcaire Provence
31. Benevento Italy
Bern (*see* Verona)
32. Berne Swabia
33. Besançon Burgundy
34. Biaucaire Provence
35. Blois France
36. Bobbio Liguria
37. Bologna Lombardy
38. Bouillon France
39. Boulogne Artois
40. Bourdeaux Provence
41. Breslau Poland
42. Brétigny France
43. Brunanburh (?) England
44. Burgos n. Spain
45. Cadiz Moorish Spain
46. Caen Normandy
47. Caerleon Wales
48. Cahors Provence
49. Calais Artois

50. Camel Cornwall
51. Campaldino Tuscany
52. Candé Brittany
53. Canterbury England
54. Capraia Tuscany
55. Capua Italy
56. Carcassonne Provence
57. Carmarthen Wales
58. Carthage Morocco
59. Casentino Tuscany
60. Casseres Provence
61. Cassino Italy
62. Ceuta Morocco
63. Chalons Burgundy
64. Chartres France
65. Chartreuse Savoy
66. Chiassi (r) Tuscany
67. Chimay France
68. Chinon France
69. Citeaux Burgundy
70. Clairvaux Burgundy
71. Cluny Burgundy
72. Cologne Germany
73. Compostella n. Spain
74. Corbeil France
75. Cordova Moorish Spain
76. Coucy France
77. Crecy Artois
78. Cremona Lombardy
79. Darmstadt Germany
80. Devon (shire) Cornwall
81. Dijon Burgundy
82. Dublin Ireland
83. Dundalk Ireland
84. Emain Ireland
85. Empoli Tuscany
86. Erfurt Germany
87. Eschenbach Germany
88. Este Lombardy
89. Faenza Lombardy
90. Fano Italy
91. Florence Tuscany
92. Fulda Germany
93. Gaeta Italy
94. Gandersheim Germany
95. Gargano (mt) Italy
96. Genoa Liguria
97. Gloucester England
98. Gorgona Tuscany
99. Granada Moorish Spain

(*continued on page xx*)

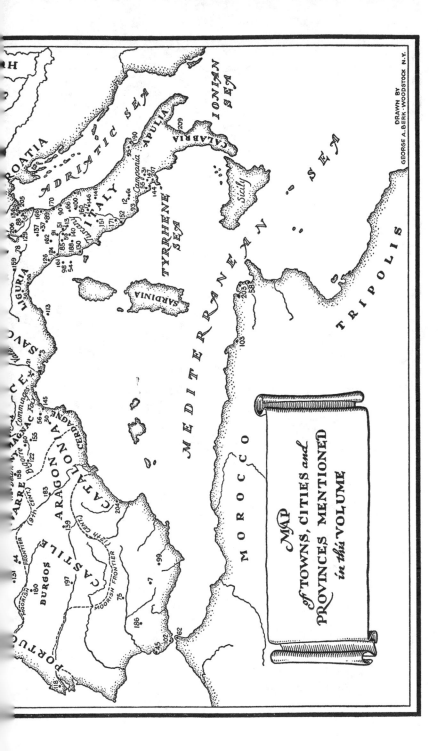

MAP
of TOWNS, CITIES and
PROVINCES MENTIONED
in this VOLUME

DRAWN BY
GEORGE A. BERK · WOODSTOCK N.Y.

xvii

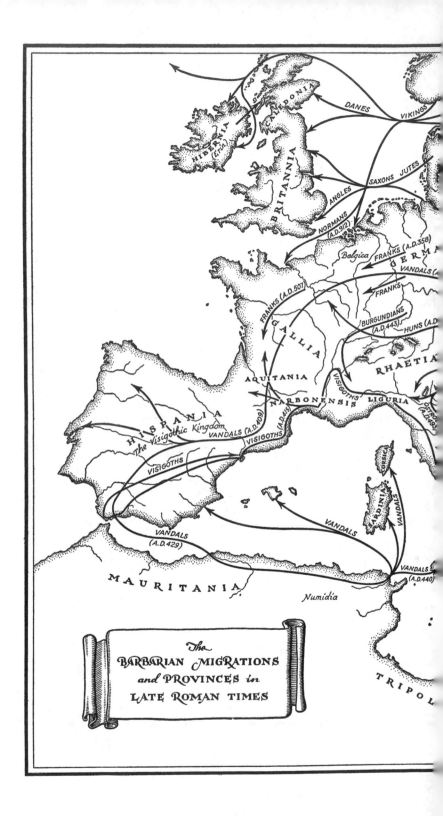

The
BARBARIAN MIGRATIONS
and PROVINCES in
LATE ROMAN TIMES

ARDS (A.D.568)

HUNS

GOTHS (BEFORE A.D. 214)

HUNS    (4th CENT.)

Scythians

JM

Ostrogoths

PANNONIA

AVARS (A.D.562)

Visigoths

OSTROGOTHS (A.D.488)

(A.D.41)

VISIGOTHS (A.D.39)

THRACIA

VISIGOTHS

VISIGOTHS (A.D.378)

61)

EGYPT

DRAWN BY GEORGE A. BERK · WOODSTOCK · N.Y.

100. Gubbio   Italy
101. Hastings   England
102. Hercules (Columns of)   Moorish Spain
103. Hippo Regius   Morocco
104. Iona   Albany
105. Islay (is)   Albany
106. Jarrow   England
107. Jersey (is)   Normandy
108. Langres   Neustria
109. Laon   France
110. Lausanne   Burgundy
111. Leicester   England
112. Le Mans   Normandy
113. Lerins (is)   Savoy
114. Liath Manchan   Ireland
115. Limoges   Provence
116. Lincoln   England
117. Lindisfarne (is)   England
118. Lisbon   Portugal
119. Llandaff   Wales
120. Loch Etive (?)   Albany
121. London   England
122. Lourde   Provence
123. Lubeck   Germany
124. Lucca   Tuscany
125. Lucerne   Burgundy
126. Lunigiana   Tuscany
127. Lyons   Burgundy
128. Mainz   Germany
129. Mantua   Lombardy
130. Maremma   Tuscany
131. Medina   n. Spain
132. Meissen   Germany
133. Melun   France
134. Metz   Neustria
135. Milan   Lombardy
136. Mira, La   Lombardy
137. Modena   Lombardy
138. Moleme   Neustria
139. Molina   n. Spain
140. Montaperti   Tuscany
141. Montauban   Provence
142. Namur   Artois
143. Nantes   Brittany
144. Naples   Italy
145. Narbonne   Provence
146. Nocera   Italy
147. Nola   Italy
148. Nursia   Italy
149. Orléans   France
150. Orthez   Provence
151. Orvieto   Italy
152. Ostia   Italy
153. Oxford   England
154. Padua   Lombardy
155. Pamiers   Provence
156. Paris   France
157. Passau   Bavaria
158. Pau   Provence
159. Pavia   Lombardy
160. Perugia   Italy
161. Pisa   Tuscany
162. Pistoia   Tuscany
163. Poitiers   France
164. Prague   Germany
165. Provins   France
166. Ravenna   n.e. Italy
167. Reichenau   Swabia
168. Rennes   Brittany
169. Rheims   France
170. Rimini   n.e. Italy
171. Rome   Italy
172. Romney   England
173. Roncesvalles   n. Spain
174. Rouen   Normandy
175. St. Asaph   Wales
176. St. Fiacre   France
177. St. Gall   Swabia
178. St. Gildas   Brittany
179. St. Michel   Brittany
180. Salamanca   n. Spain
181. Salisbury   England
182. Salzburg   Bavaria
183. Saragossa   n. Spain
184. Sempach   Swabia
185. Sens   France
186. Seville   Moorish Spain
187. Shaftesbury   England
188. Siena   Tuscany
189. Silchester   England
190. Sipontus   Italy
191. Soissons   France
192. Southampton   England
193. Strassburg   Burgundy
194. Thanet, Isle of   England
195. Thiers   Provence
196. Tintagel   Cornwall
197. Toledo   Castile
198. Totnes   Cornwall
199. Toulouse   Provence
200. Tours   France
201. Trèves (Trier)   Neustria
202. Troyes   France
203. Utica   Morocco
204. Valenciennes   Artois
205. Venice   n.e. Italy
206. Verona (Bern)   Lombardy
207. Vesuvius (mt)   Italy
208. Vienne   Savoy
209. Vivarium   s. Italy
210. Wear (r)   England
211. Whitby   England
212. Winchester   England
213. Wissant (is)   Brittany
214. Worms   Germany
215. Würzburg   Germany
216. Xanten   Germany
217. York   England
218. Zurich   Swabia

# I. THE CHRISTIAN TRADITION

The Christian literary tradition began in Hellenic Asia Minor in the days of persecution before the Edict of Constantine (A.D. 311). After the period of writings eventually included in the canon of the New Testament came a period of apocryphal writings and works of the Fathers of the Church, that is, of clergy who wrote books of instruction, theological tracts, Christian biographies either factual or idealized, histories of the Church, hymns and antiphons, and the like. The primary languages were Greek, Coptic (Egyptian), and Syrian. Not until the third century did Christianity become firmly enough established in the West to develop a notable literature in Latin, and only after the Church became a ward of the Empire early in the fourth century did Latin literature become really Christianized. The four great Latin Fathers, Ambrose, Jerome, Augustine, and Gregory, all wrote after A.D. 350.

The selections that follow have been chosen, not to give a proportioned view of Christian teaching, but to acquaint the reader with cardinal passages and works on which medieval literature depends. Those who use this book are advised to read, in addition to the selections given here, the following passages in the New Testament: Luke I, 26–39 (Annunciation); II, 1–34 (Nativity); Matthew V–VII (Sermon on the Mount); Mark XIV, 10–16, 20 (Crucifixion, Resurrection, Ascension); John I, 1–18 (Divinity of Christ); Acts II, I Thess. IV, 14–V, 3 (Holy Ghost, Second Advent, Formation of the Church); Acts VII, 54–VIII, 4, IX, 1–31 (Stephen, Paul); Romans VIII, 28–30 (Predestination, Election); I Cor. XIII (Faith, Hope, Charity); XV, 12–50 (Eternal Life); Gal. IV, 1–6, 22–31, V, 13–23 (New Law and New Jerusalem); Eph. II, 18–22 (Communion and Intercession of the Saints); VI, 10–20 (Arming of the Christian Warrior); Col. II, 8, I Tim. I, 3–11, II Tim. II, 16–17 (Secular Literature); II Tim. III (Christian Ministry); Hebrews XI, I–XII, 2 (Faith and the Patriarchs); I Peter II, 13–18 (Right of Kings); II Peter II, 4, Jude I, 6 (Fall of the Angels); II Peter III, 7–18, Revelation, esp. XII (Millennium and Last Judgment).

Until the Council of Nicaea (A.D. 325), called by the Emperor Constantine, Christians lived under fear of persecution as opponents of the religion of the state. In consequence, the literature of this ante-Nicene period is characterized by anonymity, an enigmatical form of writing, and a considerable amount of prophecy and apocalypse in anticipation of better days. Moreover, since the Gospels were not theological but a record of Christian experience, dogma and doctrine had to be established, and much of the literature was created to support and disseminate some particular theological view. At the time of the Nicene Council, the Church was torn between Arianism and Orthodoxy; largely through the efforts of Bishop Athanasius and his supporters the orthodox view prevailed.

Almost immediately began a period of historical writing, for the clergy, now freed from its illegal position, felt the need to explain its status to the world. The increase in number of converts and the new problems arising from its official position forced increased organization. The bishops' sees had been small; but now emerged the *metropolitan,* eventually an archdiocese. Four "apostolic sees" came to be viewed as arbiters in dogma and canon law: Constantinople, Antioch, Alexandria, and Rome. For the first three, Greek was the ecclesiastical language; for Rome, Latin.

Through the fourth century, most Christian literature was at least inspired by the East; but as literacy declined with the decline of state power in the West, fewer ideas were imported from the Greek and Hebrew world, and fewer works were translated. In the fifth and sixth centuries, communication between Latin and Greek churches came to be limited to envoys and ambassadors. The Latin-speaking people of the West no longer depended upon eastern churches for their knowledge of Christianity and for literature acceptable to Christians; but already a vast mass of liturgy, Christian history, doctrine, story, and legend from the Orient had come into the West. It is a vital element in medieval literature.

# APOCRYPHAL NEW TESTAMENT

A group of writings composed during the first five centuries of the Christian Era, generally called the Apocryphal New Testament, is made up of spurious gospels, acts, epistles, or visions of St. Mary, the disciples, apostles, or other figures of the New Testament. Their authors' purpose in writing under the assumed names of New Testament personages was to enlist respect; usually the pretence was that a work, hidden in apostolic days, had just been brought to light. A modern editor and translator, Montague Rhodes James says: "As religious books they were meant to reinforce the existing stock of Christian beliefs: either by revealing new doctrines — usually differing from those which held the field; or by interpreting old ones — again, usually in a fresh sense; or by extolling some special virtue, as chastity or temperance; or by enforcing belief in certain doctrines or events, e.g. the virgin birth, the resurrection of Christ, the second coming, the future state — by the production of evidence which, if true, should be irrefragable. . . . Not a few of the stories are notable and imaginative, and have been consecrated and made familiar to us by the genius of mediaeval artists. But the authors do not speak with the voices of Paul or of John, or with the quiet simplicity of the three first Gospels. It is not unfair to say that when they attempt the former tone, they are theatrical, and when they essay the latter, they are jejune." The works varied in popularity in antiquity as well as during the Middle Ages and recent times.

One of the most popular, though consistently condemned or cited with disapproval by Church writers from St. Augustine on, is the *Apocalypse* or *Vision of Paul,* which stimulated western writers to create visions of the afterlife and specifically influenced Dante in the composition of his *Comedy* (cf. Inferno ii, 28). It was subjected to numerous revisions, adaptations, and paraphrases in verse and prose, as homilies or romances; versions exist in Greek, Latin, Syriac, Coptic, Arabic, Armenian, and Slavic.

The work opens with a prologue describing the alleged discovery of the text, and then narrates the vision of Paul of Tarsus who "while I was in the body, was caught up into the third heaven." The vision falls into six parts: (1) an appeal of creation to God against man; (2) a report of the angels to God about men; (3) a description of the deaths and judgments of the righteous and of the wicked; (4) a vision of Paradise; (5) a vision of Hell and Paul's intercession; (6) a second vision of Paradise. The selections that follow are translated from what is generally regarded as the oldest Latin version.

## THE  VISION  OF  PAUL

Anonymous (3rd cent.?)

[From *The Ante-Nicene Christian Library*, Additional
Volume, edited by Allan Menzies; T. & T. Clark, Edinburgh, 1896.]

In the consulship of Theodosius Augustus the Younger and Cy-
negius, a certain nobleman then living in Tharsus, in the house which
was that of Saint Paul, an angel appearing in the night revealed to
him, saying that he should open the foundations of the house and
should publish what he found, but he thought that these things were
dreams.

But the angel coming for the third time beat him and forced him to
open the foundation.   And digging he found a marble box, inscribed
on the sides; there was the revelation of Saint Paul, and his shoes in
which he walked teaching the word of God.   But he feared to open
that box and brought it to the judge; when he had received it, the
judge, because it was sealed with lead, sent it to the Emperor Theodosius, fearing lest it might be something else; which when he had
received the emperor opened it, and found the revelation of Saint
Paul; a copy of it he sent to Jerusalem, and retained the original
himself.

While I was in the body in which I was snatched up to the third
heaven, the word of the Lord came to me saying: "Speak to the people: Until when will ye transgress, and heap sin upon sin, and tempt
the Lord who made you?   Ye are the sons of God, doing the works
of the devil in the faith of Christ, on account of the impediments
of the world.   Remember therefore and know that while every creature serves God, the human race alone sins.   But it reigns over every
creature and sins more than all nature.

The creature is subject to God, but the human race alone sins.
For this cause, therefore, ye sons of men, bless the Lord God unceasingly, every hour and every day: but more especially when the
sun has set: for at that hour all the angels proceed to the Lord to
worship him and to present the works of men, which every man
has wrought from the morning till the evening, whether good or evil.
And there is a certain angel who proceeds rejoicing concerning the
man in whom he dwells.   When therefore the sun has set in the
first hour of night, in the same hour the angel of every people and
every man and woman, who protect and preserve them, because
man is the image of God: similarly also in the matin hour which
is the twelfth of the night, all the angels of men and women go up
to God to worship God and present every work which each man
has wrought, whether good or evil.   Moreover every day and night
the angels show to God an account of all the acts of the human race.

To you, therefore, I say, ye sons of men, bless the Lord God without fail all the days of your life."

Therefore at the appointed hour all the angels whatever, rejoicing at once together, proceed before God that they may meet to worship at the hour determined. And behold suddenly it became the hour of meeting, and the angels came to worship in the presence of God, and the spirit proceeded to meet them: and there came a voice and said: "Whence come ye, our angels, bearing the burdens of tidings?"

They answered and said: "We come from those who have renounced this world for the sake of thy holy name, wandering as pilgrims, and in caves of the rocks, and weeping every hour in which they inhabited the earth, and hungering and thirsting because of thy name, with their loins girded, having in their hands the incense of their hearts, and praying and blessing every hour, and restraining and overcoming themselves, weeping and wailing above the rest that inhabit the earth. And we indeed, their angels, mourn along with them: whither therefore it shall please thee, command us to go and minister, lest others also do it, but the destitute above the rest who are on earth."

And there came the voice of God to them saying: "Know ye that now henceforward my grace is appointed unto you, and my help, who is my well-beloved Son, shall be present with them, guiding them every hour; ministering also to them, never deserting them, since their place is his habitation."

When therefore these angels had retired, behold other angels came to adore in the presence of honour, in the assembly, who wept; and the spirit of God proceeded to meet them, and there came the voice of God and said: "Whence come ye, our angels, bearing the burdens of the ministry of the tidings of the world?"

They answered and said in the presence of God: "We have arrived from those who called upon thy name, and the impediments of the world made them wretched, devising many occasions every hour, not even making one pure prayer, nor out of their whole heart, in all the time of their life; what need, therefore, is there to be present with men who are sinners?"

And there came the voice of God to them: "It is necessary that ye should minister to them, until they be converted and repent: but if they do not return to me I will judge them."

Know therefore, sons of men, that whatever things are wrought by you, these angels relate to God, whether good or evil.

And I said to the angel: "I wished to see the souls of the just and of sinners going out of the world."

And the angel answered and said unto me: "Look down upon the earth."

And I looked down from heaven upon the earth, and saw the whole world, and it was nothing in my sight and I saw the sons of men as though they were naught, and a-wanting, and I wondered and said to the angel: "Is this the greatness of men?"

And the angel answered and said unto me: "It is, and these are they who do evil from morning till evening."

And I looked and saw a great cloud of fire spread over the whole world, and I said to the angel: "What is this, my Lord?"

And he said to me: "This is injustice stirred up by the princes of sinners."

I indeed when I had heard this sighed and wept, and said to the angel: "I wished to see the souls of the just and of sinners, and to see in what manner they go out of the body."

And the angel answered and said unto me: "Look again upon the earth."

And I looked and saw all the world, and men were as naught and a-wanting; and I looked carefully and saw a certain man about to die. And the angel said to me: "This one whom thou seest is a just man."

And I looked again and saw all his works, whatever he had done for the sake of God's name, and all his desires, both what he remembered, and what he did not remember; they all stood in his sight in the hour of need. And I saw the just man advance and find refreshment and confidence, and before he went out of the world the holy and the impious angels both attended; but the impious found no place of habitation in him. The holy took possession of his soul, guiding it till it went out of the body. And they roused the soul saying: "Soul, know thy body whence thou goest out, for it is necessary that thou shouldst return to the same body on the day of the resurrection, that thou mayest receive the things promised to all the just."

Receiving therefore the soul from the body, they immediately kissed it as familiarly known to them, saying to it: "Do manfully, for thou hast done the will of God while placed in the earth."

And they led him along till he should worship in the sight of God. And when they had ceased, immediately Michael and all the army of angels, with one voice, adored the footstool of his feet, and his doors, saying at the same time to the soul: "This is your God of all things, who made you in his own image and likeness."

Moreover the angel returns and points him out saying: "God, remember his labours; for this is the soul whose works I related to thee, doing according to thy judgment."

And the spirit said likewise: "I am the spirit of vivification inspiring him; for I had refreshment in him, in the time when I dwelt in him, doing according to thy judgment."

And there came the voice of God and said: "In as much as this man did not vex me, neither will I vex him; for according as he had pity, I also will have pity. Let him therefore be handed over to Michael, the angel of the Covenant, and let him lead him into the Paradise of joy, that he himself may become co-heir with all the saints."

And after these things I heard the voices of a thousand thousand

angels, and archangels, and cherubim, and twenty-four elders saying hymns, and glorifying the Lord and crying: "Thou art just,
O Lord, and just are thy judgments, and there is no acceptance of
persons with thee, but thou rewardest unto every man according to
thy judgment."

And the angel said unto me: "Hast thou believed and known,
that whatever each man of you has done, he sees in the hour of
need?"

And I said: "Yes, sir."

And he saith to me: "Look again down on the earth, and watch
the soul of an impious man going out of the body, which vexed the
Lord day and night, saying: 'I know nothing else in this world,
I eat and drink, and enjoy what is in the world; for who is there
who has descended into hell, and ascending has declared to us that
there is judgment there!'"

And again I looked carefully, and saw all the scorn of the sinner,
and all that he did, and they stood together before him in the hour
of need; and it was done to him in that hour, in which he was
threatened about his body at the judgment, and I said: "It were
better for him if he had not been born."

And after these things, there came at the same time the holy angels
and the malign and the soul of the sinner, and the holy angels did
not find a place in it. Moreover the malign angels cursed it; and
when they had drawn it out of the body, the angels admonished it
a third time, saying: "O wretched soul, look upon thy flesh, whence
thou camest out; for it is necessary that thou shouldst return to thy
flesh in the day of resurrection, that thou mayest receive the due
for thy sins and thy impieties."

And after these things it was presented, that it might worship
in the sight of God, and an angel of God showed him God who
made him after his own image and likeness. Moreover his angel
ran before him saying: "Lord God Almighty, I am the angel of
this soul, whose works I presented to thee day and night, not doing
according to thy judgment."

And the spirit likewise said: "I am the spirit who dwelt in it
from the time it was made, in itself moreover I know it, and it has
not followed my will: judge it, Lord, according to thy judgment."

And there came the voice of God to it and said: "Where is thy
fruit which thou hast made worthy of the goods which thou hast
received? Have I put a distance of one day between thee and the
just man? Did I not make the sun to arise upon thee as upon the
just?"

But the soul was silent, having nothing to answer. And again
there came a voice saying: "Just is the judgment of God, and there
is no acceptance of persons with God, for whoever shall have done
mercy, on them shall he have mercy, and whoever shall not have
pitied neither shall God pity him. Let him therefore be handed
over to the angel Tartaruch, who is set over the punishments, and

let him place him in outer darkness, where there is weeping and gnashing of teeth, and let him be there till the great day of judgment."

And after these things I heard the voice of angels and archangels saying: "Thou art just, Lord, and thy judgment is just."

And he took me down from the third heaven, and led me into the second heaven, and again he led me on to the firmament and from the firmament he led me over the doors of heaven: the beginning of its foundation was on the river which waters all the earth. And I asked the angel and said, "Lord, what is this river of water?" And he said to me, "This is Oceanus!" And suddenly I went out of heaven, and I understood that it is the light of heaven which lightens all the earth. For the land there is seven times brighter than silver.

And I said, "Lord, what is this place?"

And he said to me, "This is the land of promise. Hast thou never heard what is written: Blessed are the meek: for they shall inherit the earth? The souls therefore of the just, when they have gone out of the body, are meanwhile dismissed to this place."

And I said to the angel, "Then this land will be manifested before the time?"

The angel answered and said to me, "When Christ, whom thou preachest, shall come to reign, then, by the sentence of God, the first earth will be dissolved and this land of promise will then be revealed, and it will be like dew or cloud, and then the Lord Jesus Christ, the King Eternal, will be manifested and will come with all his saints to dwell in it, and he will reign over them a thousand years, and they will eat of the good things which I shall now show unto thee."

And I looked around upon that land and I saw a river flowing of milk and honey, and there were trees planted by the bank of that river, full of fruit: moreover each single tree bore twelve fruits in the year, having various and diverse fruits: and I saw the created things which are in that place and all the work of God, and I saw there palms of twenty cubits, but others of ten cubits: and that land was seven times brighter than silver. And there were trees full of fruits from the roots to the highest branches, of ten thousand fruits of palms upon ten thousand fruits. The grape-vines moreover had ten thousand plants. Moreover in the single vines there were ten thousand thousand bunches and in each of these a thousand single grapes: moreover these single trees bore a thousand fruits. And I said to the angel, "Why does each tree bear a thousand fruits?"

The angel answered and said unto me, "Because the Lord God gives an abounding flood of gifts to the worthy, because they also of their own will afflicted themselves when they were placed in the world doing all things on account of his holy name."

And again I said to the angel, "Sir, are these the only promises which the Most Holy God makes?"

And he answered and said to me: "No! there are seven times greater than these. But I say unto thee that when the just go out of the body they shall see the promises and the good things which God has prepared for them. Till then, they shall sigh, and lament saying: Have we emitted any word from our mouth to vex our neighbour even on one day?"

I asked and said again: "Are these alone the promises of God?"

And the angel answered and said unto me: "These whom you now see are the souls of the married and those who kept the chastity of their nuptials, containing themselves. But to the virgins and those who hunger and thirst after righteousness and those who afflicted themselves for the sake of the name of God, God will give seven times greater than these, which I shall now show thee. Follow me and I will lead thee into the City of Christ."

And he was standing on the Acherousian Lake and he put me into a golden ship and angels as it were three thousand were saying hymns before me till I arrived at the City of Christ. Moreover those who inhabited the City of Christ greatly rejoiced over me as I went to them, and I entered and saw the City of Christ, and it was all of gold, and twelve walls encircled it, and twelve interior towers. And there were twelve gates in the circuit of the city, of great beauty, and four rivers which encircled it. There was, moreover, a river of honey and a river of milk, and a river of wine and a river of oil.

And I said to the angel: "What are these rivers surrounding that city?" And he saith to me: "These are the four rivers which flow sufficiently for those who are in this land of promise. The river of honey is called Fison, and the river of milk Euphrates, and the river of oil Gion, and the river of wine Tigris. Such therefore they are for those who when placed in the world did not use the power of these things, but they hungered for these things and afflicted themselves for the sake of the Lord God, so that when these enter into this city the Lord will assign them these things on high above all measure."

I indeed entering the gates saw trees great and very high before the doors of the city, having no fruit but leaves only, and I saw a few men scattered in the midst of the trees, and they lamented greatly when they saw anyone enter the city. And those trees were sorry for them and humbled themselves and bowed down and again erected themselves. And I saw and wept with them and I asked the angel and said: "Sir, who are these who are not admitted to enter into the City of Christ?"

And he said to me: "These are they who zealously abstained day and night in fasts, but they had a proud heart above other men, glorifying and praising themselves and doing nothing for their neighbours. For they gave some friendly greeting, but to others they did not even say hail! and indeed they shewed hospitality to those only whom they wished, and if they did anything whatever for their neighbour they were immoderately puffed up."

And I said: "What then, sir? Did their pride prevent them from entering into the City of Christ?"

And the angel answered and said unto me: "Pride is the root of all evils. Are they better than the Son of God who came to the Jews with much humility?"

But I went on while the angel instructed me, and he carried me to the river of honey, and I saw there Isaiah and Jeremiah and Ezekiel and Amos, and Micah and Zechariah, the minor and major prophets, and they saluted me in the city. Moreover he led me outside the city through the midst of the trees and far from the places of the land of the good, and put me across the river of milk and honey; and after that he led me over the ocean which supports the foundations of heaven. The angel said unto me: "Dost thou understand why thou goest hence?" And I said: "Yes, sir."

And he said to me, "Come and follow me, and I will show thee the souls of the impious and sinners, that thou mayest know what manner of place it is."

And I proceeded with the angel and he carried me by the setting of the sun, and I saw the beginning of heaven founded on a great river of water, and I asked: "What is this river of water?" And he said to me: "This is Ocean which surrounds all the Earth."

And when I was at the outer limit of Ocean I looked, and there was no light in that place, but darkness and sorrow and sadness: and I sighed.

And I saw there a fervent river of fire, and in it a multitude of men and women immersed up to the knees, and other men up to the navel, others even up to the lips, others moreover up to the hair. And I asked the angel and said: "Sir, who are those in the fiery river?"

And the angel answered and said to me: "They are neither hot nor cold, because they were found neither in the number of the just nor in the number of the impious. For those spent the time of their life on earth passing some days in prayer, but others in sins and fornications, until their death."

And I asked him and said: "Who are these, sir, immersed up to their knees in fire?"

He answered and said to me: "These are they who when they have gone out of church throw themselves into strange conversations to dispute. Those indeed who are immersed up to the navel are those who, when they have taken the body and blood of Christ, go and fornicate and did not cease from their sins till they died. Those who are immersed up to the lips are the detractors of each other when they assemble in the church of God; those up to the eyebrows are those who nod approval of themselves and plot spite against their neighbour."

And I saw on the north a place of various and diverse punishments full of men and women, and a river of fire ran down into it. Moreover I observed and I saw pits great in depth, and in them several souls together, and the depth of that place was as it were three thousand cubits, and I saw them groaning and weeping and saying: "Have pity on us, O Lord!" and none had pity on them. And I asked the angel and said: "Who are these, sir?"

And the angel answered and said unto me: "These are they who did not hope in the Lord, that they would be able to have him as their helper."

And I asked and said: "Sir, if these souls remain for thirty or forty generations thus one upon another, if they were sent deeper, the pits I believe would not hold them."

And he said to me: "The Abyss has no measure, for beyond this it stretches down below him who is down in it. And so it is, that if perchance anyone should take a stone and throw it into a very deep well and after many hours it should reach the bottom, such is the Abyss. For when the souls are thrown in there, they hardly reach the bottom in fifty years."

I, indeed, when I heard this, wept and groaned over the human race. The angel answered and said unto me: "Why dost thou weep? Art thou more pitiful than God? For though God is good, He knows also that there are punishments, and He patiently bears with the human race, dismissing each one to work his own will in the time in which he dwells on the earth."

And he carried me south and placed me above a well, and I found it sealed with seven seals: and the angel who was with me said to the angel of that place: "Open the mouth of the well that Paul, the well-beloved of God, may see, for authority is given him that he may see all the pains of hell." And the angel said to me: "Stand afar off that thou mayest be able to bear the stench of this place."

When therefore the well was opened, immediately there arose from it a certain hard and malign stench, which surpasses all punishments; and I looked into the well and I saw fiery masses glowing in every part, and narrow places, and the mouth of the well was narrow so as to admit one man only. And the angel said unto me: "If any man shall have been put into this well of the abyss and it shall have been sealed over him, no remembrance of him shall ever be made in the sight of the Father and His Son and the holy angels."

And I said: "Who are these, sir, who are put into this well?"

And he said to me: "They are whoever shall not confess that Christ has come in the flesh and that the Virgin Mary brought him forth, and whoever says that the bread and cup of the Eucharist of blessing are not this body and blood of Christ."

And I looked to the south in the west and I saw there a restless worm and in that place there was gnashing of teeth; moreover the worms were one cubit long, and had two heads, and there I saw men and women in cold and gnashing of teeth. And I asked and said, "Sir, who are these in this place?"

And he said to me: "These are they who say that Christ did not rise from the dead and that this flesh will not rise again."

And I asked and said: "Sir, is there no fire nor heat in this place?"

And he said to me: "In this place there is nothing else but cold and snow," and again he said to me: "Even if the sun should rise upon them, they do not become warm on account of the super-abundant cold of that place and the snow."

But hearing these things I stretched out my hands and wept, and sighing again, I said: "It were better for us if we had not been born, all of us who are sinners."

But when those who were in the same place saw me weeping with the angel, they themselves cried out and wept saying, "Lord God have mercy upon us!" And after these things I saw the heavens open, and Michael the archangel descending from heaven, and with him was the whole army of angels, and they came to those who were placed in punishment and seeing him, again weeping, they cried out and said, "Have pity on us! Michael the archangel, have pity on us and on the human race, for on account of thy prayers the earth standeth. We now see the judgment and acknowledge the Son of God! It was impossible for us before these things to pray for this, before we entered into this place; for we heard that there was a judgment before we went out of the world, but impediments and the life of the world did not allow us to repent."

And Michael answered and said: "Hear Michael speaking! I am he who stands in the sight of God every hour. As the Lord liveth, in whose sight I stand, I do not intermit one day or one night praying incessantly for the human race, and I indeed pray for those who are on the earth; but they do not cease doing iniquity and fornications, and they do not bring to me any good while they are placed on earth; and ye have consumed in vanity the time in which ye ought to have repented. But I have always prayed thus and I now beseech that God may send dew and send forth rains upon the earth, and now I desire until the earth produce its fruits and verily I say that if any have done but a little good, I will agonise for him, protecting him till he have escaped the judg-ment of penalties. Where therefore are your prayers? Where are your penances? Ye have lost your time contemptuously. But now weep and I will weep with you and the angels who are with me with the well-beloved Paul, if perchance the merciful God will have pity and give you refreshment."

But hearing these words they cried out and wept greatly, and all said with one voice: "Have pity on us, Son of God!"

And I, Paul, sighed and said: "O Lord God! have pity on thy creature, have pity on the sons of men, have pity on thine image."

And I looked and saw the heaven move like a tree shaken by the wind. Suddenly, moreover, they threw themselves on their faces in the sight of the throne. And I saw twenty-four elders and twenty-four thousand adoring God; and I saw an altar and veil and throne, and all were rejoicing. And the smoke of a good odour was raised near the altar of the throne of God, and I heard the voice of one saying: "For the sake of what do ye our angels and ministers intercede?"

And they cried out saying: "We intercede seeing thy many kindnesses to the human race."

And after these things I saw the Son of God descending from heaven, and a diadem was on his head. And seeing him those who were placed in punishment exclaimed all with one voice saying: "Have pity, Son of the High God! Thou art He who shewest refreshment for all in the heavens and on earth, and on us likewise have pity, for since we have seen Thee, we have refreshment."

And a voice went out from the Son of God through all the punishments saying: "And what work have ye done that ye demand refreshment from me? My blood was poured out for your sakes, and not even so did ye repent. For your sakes I wore the crown of thorns on my head; for you I received buffets on my cheeks, and not even so did ye repent. I asked water when hanging on the cross and they gave me vinegar mixed with gall; with a spear they opened my right side; for my name's sake they slew my prophets and just men. And in all these things I gave you a place of repentance and ye would not. Now, however, for the sake of Michael the archangel of my covenant and the angels who are with him, and because of Paul the well-beloved, whom I would not vex, for the sake of your brethren who are in the world and offer oblations, and for the sake of your sons, because my precepts are in them, and more for the sake of mine own kindness, on the day on which I rose from the dead, I give to you all who are in punishment a night and a day of refreshment forever."

And they all cried out and said, "We bless thee, Son of God, that Thou hast given us a night and a day of respite. For better to us is a refreshment of one day above all the time of our life which we were on earth, and if we had plainly known that this was intended for those who sin, we would have worked no other work, we would have done no business, and we would have done no iniquity: what need had we for pride in the world? For here our pride is crushed which ascended from our mouth against our neighbour; our plagues and excessive straitness and the tears and the worms which are under us, these are much worse to us than the pains which we have left behind us."

When they said thus, the malign angels of the penalties were angered with them, saying: "How long do ye lament and sigh? for ye had no pity. For this is the judgment of God who had no pity. But ye received this great grace of a day and a night's refreshment on the Lord's Day for the sake of Paul the well-beloved of God who descended to you."

[tr. ANDREW RUTHERFORD]

# ATHANASIUS, BISHOP OF ALEXANDRIA

Monasticism attached itself to the Church as an adopted child in the fourth century. Groups of ascetic cenobites existed in the East before Christ; Philo, for instance, describes in detail the life of the Essenes, a Hebrew brotherhood formed in the second century B.C. But the notion of renouncing the world to adopt an eremitical life as, to use Montalembert's phrase, a "war against nature," struck fire when the Roman world sank into profligacy (*luxuria*). The first Christian solitaries (*monachi*) practiced their ascetic life in cells near home, but shortly sought out the desert places in Asia Minor, notably in the region of Antioch, and in Egypt. They were especially stimulated by the mystical teachings of the Neo-platonic schools of Alexandria. It was natural that, as the number of "Desert Fathers" increased, they should form communities and set themselves under rules and chosen teachers. Monasticism from the first was characterized by excessive abstraction from external objects, rigorous chastisement of the flesh through fasting and flagellation, and a kind of torpid idleness. These traits, not unsuited to the semitropical South and East, led to extremes as monasticism during the next century swept like a tidal wave through the West, engulfing Italy, France, and Spain and even becoming, in the fifth century, the pattern of Irish ecclesiastical organization.

From the fifth to the twelfth centuries, monasticism is a distinguishing feature of western life and thought. As the ancient world sank into economic and political chaos, the poor monastic communities, established in wilderness or on marginal land, formed stable islands — centers from which the arts of peace were disseminated. Because western literature during that period is over-whelmingly monastic in inspiration and creation, what is peculiar to monasticism is peculiar to the literature. As monasticism came from the East, it brought eastern images, tales, and literary forms; as it was a reaction against nature, so the literature expressed either abhorrence, indifference, or distortion of nature.

Anthony was among the earliest of the Desert Fathers, the list of whom includes the renowned names of Pachomius, Simeon Stylites, Hilarion, and finally Jerome. Nothing is now known of Anthony except what is stated in the *Life*. Though a few modern scholars have questioned the attribution, from earliest times the *Life* has been considered the work of Athanasius (296?-373), Bishop of Alexandria; of him the church-historian William Bright has said, "We shall not be extravagant if we pronounce his name to be the greatest in the Church's post-apostolic history." This work is one of the first examples, if not the first, of a saint's life. Its form was achieved by fusing elements from oriental biblical narrative, the classical panegyric, and the early Christian martyrology. Very shortly translated into Latin by Evagrius, it spread with monasticism through the West and became the pattern for the most popular form of creative literature during the next several centuries. Imitations and adaptations can be numbered in thousands. Through this *Life* and others that were shortly composed, readers learned to look upon the saint's life as an entertaining book of manners, yielding the exaltation and edification of romance, not as theological doctrine. Features here found for the first time, which shortly became conventional, are the saint's struggles with anthropomorphic demons and with Satan, the saint's equanimity illustrated by miraculous anecdote, the communion with beasts in the wilderness, the transcription of the saint's didactic speeches, the honors conferred by secular rulers, and the saint's calm anticipation and realization of death. Though this popular form can be traced, in its effects, throughout modern romantic literature, the best-known derivative is Flaubert's *Temptations of St. Anthony*.

## LIFE OF ST. ANTONY

### Athanasius of Alexandria (?) (A.D. 296?–373)

[From *Bibliotheca Sacra*, Vol. I, 1844.]

The life and discipline of our holy father Antony, written and sent to the monks in foreign lands, by our father in God, Athanasius, Bishop of Alexandria.

#### HIS EARLY LIFE — COMMENCES HIS MONASTIC CAREER

Antony was by birth an Egyptian. His parents were noble and sufficiently wealthy and, being Christians, brought up their son in their own faith. During his early childhood, he was kept at home, seeing nothing but his parents and their house. In his boyhood and as he grew up, he would not go to school because he wished to avoid associating with other boys. His sole desire was to be, as is said of Jacob, a plain man, dwelling in his own house. He used to attend church with his parents, and when there he was not listless while a boy nor disdainful when a young man; but he was obedient to his parents and attentive to the reading and careful to treasure up the instruction in his breast. Again, though his parents were in easy circumstances, he never importuned them for different and dainty food nor sought pleasure in such gratifications, but was content with what he found and asked for nothing more.

When he was about eighteen or twenty years of age, his parents died, leaving to his care their house and his only sister, who was yet very small. Not six months after the death of his parents, he was going to church as usual, and his thoughts dwelt upon the Apostles' leaving all and following the Saviour, and those mentioned in the Acts, who sold their possessions and brought the price and laid it at the Apostles' feet, to be distributed among the poor, and upon the hopes laid up for them in Heaven. In the midst of these reflections he entered the church, just as that passage in the Gospels was read where the Lord says to the rich man, "If thou wilt be perfect, go and sell all that thou hast, and give to the poor, and come and follow me, and thou shalt have treasure in Heaven." Antony considered his recollections of the saints as from God and the reading as addressed to himself, and immediately left the church and made over his patrimony, consisting of three hundred *arurae* [more than a hundred acres] of fertile and pleasant land, to the people of his village, to prevent them from molesting at all either himself or his sister. His personal property he sold for a large sum of money which he gave to the poor, reserving only a little for his sister.

Entering the church again, he heard our Lord saying, in the Gospel, "Take no thought for the morrow." He could stay no longer, but went out and distributed the remainder of his property to the poor. Having entrusted his sister to some known and faithful virgins to be brought up in a nunnery, he devoted himself with circumspection and firmness to an ascetic life before his own house; for monasteries were not then common in Egypt, nor had any monk at all known the great desert; but every one who wished to devote himself to his own spiritual welfare performed his exercises alone not far from his own village.

Now there was at that time in a neighboring village an old man who had lived a monastic life from his youth. Antony saw him and was filled with pious emulation. At first he took up his abode in places in the vicinity of the village; and if he heard of any one remarkable for Christian attainments, he would go and seek him out, like the wise bee, and he never returned until he had seen him and obtained from him some provisions to support him on the way to virtue. Therefore remaining here at first, he established his mind so as not to turn again toward his patrimony nor remember his relatives, but to have all his desires and zeal for rigor in his asceticism. Accordingly, he labored with his hands; for he had heard, "If any will not work, neither shall he eat." Part of the proceeds of his labor he spent for bread, and gave the remainder to the poor. And he prayed constantly, having learned that he ought to pray without ceasing in secret. And he was so attentive to the reading that nothing of the Scriptures fell from him to the ground, but he retained all; so that at last his memory served him instead of books.

Conducting himself thus, Antony was beloved by all. To the devout men to whom he went he paid the utmost deference, and learned the peculiar excellences of character and practice in each: the gentleness of one, the prayerfulness of another, the meekness of another, the philanthropy or the vigils or the studious habits of another. He would admire another's endurance of suffering and fasting and sleeping upon the ground, or observe another's mildness and long-suffering; while he marked the piety toward Christ and love for each other which all displayed. Thus he would return richly laden to his own cell, and labor to make his own all the several graces which he had found. He had no contest with those of his own age, except only not to seem second to them in virtue; and this he did so as to grieve no one, but to cause all to rejoice in him. And the villagers and the pious men with whom he had conversed, seeing him such, called him the friend of God, and they loved him, some as a son, others as a brother.

### HIS CONFLICTS WITH THE DEVIL

But the devil, the envier and enemy of all good, could not bear to see such a purpose in so young a man, and accordingly tried his old arts upon him. At first he assayed to turn him aside from his ascetic life by suggesting recollections of his estate or care for his sister, and his rank and the love of money and of glory, and the various gratifications of the appetites and other delights of life; and he added the hardship and toil attendant upon virtue and the feebleness of his body and the long life before him. In fine, he raised a great dust of thoughts in his mind, aiming to turn him from his holy purpose. But the adversary found that, so far from being able to shake Antony's resolution, he was himself defeated by his constancy, vanquished by his strong faith, and falling before his ceaseless prayers. His next reliance was upon "the force which is in the navel of his belly," and in this he greatly confided. He assailed him, as he is wont first to assail the young, harassing him by night and so besetting him by day that any one who saw him might perceive the conflict which was going on between them: the one suggesting impure imaginations, the other repelling them by prayer; the one inciting the passions, the other blushing and defending himself by faith and prayer and fasting. The wretched devil would assume, by night, the form and imitate the deportment of a woman, to tempt Antony; but he would put out the coal of his temptation by reflecting upon Christ and the nobility which He gives and the spirituality of the soul. Again, the adversary would suggest the sweetness of pleasure, to which Antony, like one grieved and enraged, opposed the threat of the fire and the worm, and thus came off unharmed. So that all these attempts resulted in the confusion of the adversary. For he who thought to be like unto God was baffled by a youth, and he who gloried over flesh and blood was overthrown by a man in the flesh; for he had the aid of the Lord who took the flesh for us and hath given to the flesh the victory over the devil, so that every true soldier of His may say, "Not I, but the grace of God that is with me."

At last, failing in this assault upon Antony and finding himself thrust out of his heart, the dragon gnashed with his teeth, as it is written; and, as if beside himself, assumed the form of a boy as black as his own nature, and falling before him he no more assailed him with imaginations; for the deceiver had been cast out. But using a human voice, he said, "I have deceived and overcome multitudes, but I find the temptations which prevailed with them too weak for thee." Antony asked, "Who art thou that sayest this to me?" He replied, in a woeful voice, "I am the friend of fornication. My charge is to tempt and incite the young to this sin, and I am called the spirit of fornication. How many who wished to live correctly have I led astray, and how many who struggled to keep the body in subjection have I overcome by my enticements! It was on my account that the prophet rebuked those who had fallen, saying, 'The spirit of whoredoms hath caused them to err; for by me were they caused to stumble.' I am he that hath so often assailed thee and so many times been foiled by thee." Then Antony gave thanks to the Lord and took courage and said to the demon, "Thou art most worthy of contempt; for thou art black in soul and weak as a child. I have no more care for thee, for the Lord is my helper and I will rejoice over my enemies." Hearing this, the black one fled in terror at his word, not daring longer to be near the man.

This was Antony's first victory over the devil, or rather the glorious work, in Antony, of that Saviour who condemned sin in the flesh that the righteousness of the law might be fulfilled in us, who walk not after the flesh but after the spirit. Still, Antony did not conclude that the demon was vanquished and relax his watchfulness, nor did the adversary desist from his machinations. For he prowled about like a lion seeking some occasion against him. But Antony had learned from Scripture that many are the wiles of the devil and he was zealous in his practice of the ascetic life, considering that though the devil had failed to lead his heart astray by sensual pleasure, he would constantly be laying new snares in his way; for the devil loves sin. Accordingly, he reduced and subjected his body more and more, lest having prevailed over some temptations he should yield to others.

He resolved to adopt a more rigorous life. Many were astonished at him, but he bore the labor easily, for the ardor of his soul, enduring for a long time, had wrought in him such an excellent temper that a little incitement from others produced great zeal in him. Such were his vigils that he often passed the whole night without sleep; this he did not merely once but so frequently as to be an object of astonishment. He used to eat but once in the day, after sunset, and often he would fast for two and even four days. His food was bread and salt and his drink water only. But we need not speak of meat and wine, for nothing of the kind is found among other ascetics. His bed was a small rush mat, but he usually slept upon the bare ground. He would not be anointed with oil because he said that young monks should be in earnest in their asceticism; instead of seeking emollients for the body, they should train it to hardship, remembering the words of the apostle, "When I am weak then am I strong." For he used to say that the powers of the mind were most vigorous when the pleasures of the body were most under restraint.

Thus constrained, Antony retired to some tombs at a distance from the village and, having directed one of his friends to bring him bread at long intervals, he entered one of the tombs, which was closed by his friend, and he was left alone. This was more than the adversary could bear. He was afraid that by degrees Antony would fill the desert with asceticism. He came upon him one night with a host of demons and beat him until he lay upon the ground speechless from his sufferings. His tortures, as he said afterwards, were such as no blows by men could inflict. But by the Providence of God, for the Lord never overlooks those who trust in Him, his friend came the next day to bring his bread; and upon opening the entrance and finding him lying upon the ground as if dead, he took him up and carried him to the church in the village and laid him on the ground. Many of Antony's relatives and the people of the village sat down by him as if he were dead. But about midnight he came to himself; and being aroused and finding all asleep except his friend, he beckoned him to come to him and requested him to carry him back to the tombs without awaking any one.

He was accordingly carried back by the man and the door closed as usual, and he was left alone again. Finding himself unable to stand on account of the blows, he lay down and prayed; and after the prayer he cried out, "Here am I Antony. I flee not your blows. And should you even inflict more, nothing shall separate me from the love of Christ." Then he sang, "Though a host should encamp against me, my heart shall not fear." Thus thought and said our ascetic.

But the enemy of all righteousness, astonished at Antony's daring to come after his flagellation, called his dogs together and said, "You see that we have not been able to stop this man either by the spirit of lust or by flagellation; but he is bold against us. We must vary our mode of attack." For it is easy for the devil to assume different shapes for his wicked purposes. Then in the night, they made such a din that the whole place seemed to be shaken, and the demons appeared to break the four walls and rush in upon all sides in the shapes of wild beasts and reptiles; and in a moment the place was full of lions, bears, leopards, bulls, serpents, asps, scorpions and wolves, all acting according to their several natures, — the lion roaring and striving to come upon him, the bull thrusting at him with his horns, the serpent creeping about but unable to reach him, and the wolf being held back in the act of springing upon him. In fine, the noises of all the shapes were dreadful and their rage terrific.

Under these assaults and tortures, Antony suffered cruel pains of body, but his soul was fearless and vigilant. And as he lay groaning from his corporeal tortures, he would deride the fiends, crying, "If ye had any power, it would be enough for one alone of you to come upon me; but now that the Lord hath made you weak, ye think to terrify me by your numbers. Your assuming the forms of brutes is proof enough of your feebleness." And again he would confidently exclaim, "If ye are strong, if ye have received any power against me, come upon me at once. But if powerless, why do ye attempt in vain to alarm me? For our trust in the Lord is a seal and wall of protection." After many assaults, the demons gnashed their teeth at him, being themselves more imposed upon than he.

And the Lord did not forget the conflict of Antony, but came to his relief. Raising his eyes, he saw as it were the roof opened and a ray of light coming down upon him. Instantly the demons vanished; his bodily pain left him, and his habitation was whole again. Antony, feeling the relief, breathing again and free from pain, thus addressed the vision: "Where wast thou? Why didst thou not appear at first to deliver me from my agony?" A voice replied: "I was not away but was here, Antony, a witness of thy conflict; and since thou hast endured and not yielded, I will always be thy helper, and will make thy name known everywhere." Hearing this, he rose up and prayed, and found himself even stronger in body than before. He was at this time nearly thirty-five years of age.

The next day he went out yet more full of pious zeal, and coming to an old man, he asked permission to live with him in the desert. Rejected here, on account of his youth and the novelty of his request, he went at once to the mountain. But again the adversary, seeing his zeal, sought to ensnare him by putting in his way the appearance of a great silver plate. Antony saw the artifice of the wicked one and stood, and, looking at the plate, exposed the demon that was in it thus: "Whence a plate in the desert? This is no beaten road; there is not a traveller's footstep here. Besides, the plate is too large to fall without being observed, and if any one had lost it, he would have turned back and found it without fail in such a desert place. This is an artifice of the devil. But thou shalt not thus catch me, thou devil. This go with thee to perdition." As Antony said this, it vanished like smoke before the fire.

Thus he lived a solitary ascetic life for nearly twenty years, never going out and rarely seen by any one. At last, as many were anxious to imitate his practice, his friends came and threw down and broke through the door, and Antony came forth like an initiated and inspired man from some sacred recess. Now, for the first time he was seen out of the castle by those who came to him; and they who saw him were astonished to find his condition of body the same as before. He had neither grown corpulent from inactivity nor become emaciated by fastings and combats with demons. He was just as they had known him before his withdrawal. The state of his mind also was perfect; for he was neither depressed by sorrow nor unduly excited by joy — not inclined to laughter, nor to sadness. He was not embarrassed at the sight of the crowd, nor elated by the honors they paid him. He was always the same, his whole deportment regulated by reason and natural propriety. Therefore the Lord healed through him many who were suffering from diseases of the body and delivered others from demons. The Lord, too, gave him grace in speaking and thus he consoled many who were in sorrow and reconciled others who were at variance, charging all to prefer none of the things of this world before love to Christ. As he discoursed upon and enjoined the remembrance of good things to come and the love of God towards us, who spared not His own Son, but gave Him up for us all, many were induced to assume the ascetic life; so that from that time, there were monasteries among the mountains and the desert was peopled with monks, who left their all and enrolled themselves as citizens of the heavenly community.

His visitation of the brethren made it necessary for him to cross the canal of Arsinoë, which was full of crocodiles. Defended only by prayer, he and all with him entered and passed it in safety. On his return to the monastery, he resumed his former observances. By frequent conversations, he increased the zeal of those who were already monks and led many others to love the monastic life; and in a short time, by his persuasions, many monasteries were established, over all of which he presided as a father.

### ANTONY'S DISCOURSE TO THE MONKS

All the monks once came to him, as he was proceeding, and requested to hear a discourse from him; and he addressed them in the Egyptian language as follows:

"The Scriptures are sufficient for instruction. Still it is well to exhort and comfort each other in the faith. You then, as children, should tell your father what you have learned, and I, as your elder in years, will share with you the fruits of my knowledge and experience.

"And, first, let it be the aim of us all, having begun, not to yield nor to be disheartened in our labors, not to say we have spent a long time in this monastic life; but rather, as beginning anew from day to day, let us add to our ardor. For the whole life of man is exceedingly brief compared with the ages to come. All our time here is as nothing to the eternal life. In this world, everything is sold for its value, and one gives equal for equal; but the promise of eternal life is purchased at a trifling expense. For it is written, 'The days of our years are threescore years and ten, and if by reason of strength they be fourscore years, yet is their strength labor and sorrow.' If, then, we persevere in the ascetic life for the whole fourscore years or even an hundred, our reign shall not be just an hundred years, but for the hundred we shall reign for ages of ages. And for our conflicts upon earth, we shall receive our promised inheritance, not on earth but in the heavens. And again, for this corruptible body which we lay aside, we shall receive an incorruptible."

And he said that the evil spirits often appeared such as the Lord described the devil to Job, saying, "His eyes are like the appearance of the morning star; out of his mouth go burning lamps and sparks of fire leap forth. From his mouth goeth the smoke of a furnace burning with a fire of coals; his breath is coals and a flame goeth out of his mouth." When the guileful prince of devils appears in this shape, he strikes terror by his great swelling words, as again the Lord explained to Job in these words, "For he esteemeth iron as straw and brass as rotten wood, and he esteemeth the abyss of hell as a pot of ointment, and he regardeth the abyss as a path," and by the prophet, "The enemy said, I will pursue, I will overtake," and again by another, "The whole earth will I seize in my hand like a nest and as eggs that are left will I take it." Thus, to lead astray God's worshippers, they vaunt and proclaim what they will do. "But neither here is there any occasion for us who are faithful to fear his phantoms or to regard his words. For he lies, and speaks no truth at all. Though he speaks and boasts so much and so boldly, he was drawn as a dragon with a hook by the Saviour, and as a beast of burden he suffered a halter upon his nose, and as a run-away he was bound with a ring in his nostrils, and his lips were pierced with a chain, and he has been tied by the Lord like a sparrow, to be sported with by us. He and his fellow demons are to be trodden under foot by us Christians, like scorpions and serpents. A proof of this we find in our following our loyal pursuits in spite of him.

"And since I have become a fool in expounding these things, receive also this for your safety and intrepidity and believe me, for I lie not. Once, some one in the monastery knocked at my door. And going out I saw one who appeared large and tall. When I inquired, 'Who art thou?' he replied, 'I am Satan.' So I said, 'What, then, are you here for?' He said, 'Why do the monks and all the other Christians falsely accuse me? Why do they curse me every hour?' But I said, 'Why, then, do you molest them?' 'It is not I that trouble them,' said he, 'but they trouble themselves; for I am become weak. Have they not read, that the spears of the enemy utterly fail, and thou hast destroyed cities? No longer have I a place, a weapon, a city. Everywhere they have become Christians. And finally, even the desert is filled with monks. Let them look to themselves, and not curse me without cause.' Then admired I the grace of the Lord, and said to the devil, 'Although you are always a liar and never speak the truth, yet for this once, though not willingly, you have uttered the truth. For Christ has come and made you weak, and prostrated and stripped you.' On hearing the name of the Saviour, and not being able to abide its burning, he vanished."

### MONKS BECOME NUMEROUS — THEIR HABITS

Thus spake Antony, and all were delighted. And in some the love of virtue was increased, and the sluggishness of some was removed, while the former opinion of others was changed; and all were led to despise diabolical machinations and wonder at the gift of discerning spirits which was conferred by the Lord upon Antony. Then were the monasteries in the mountains, as tabernacles, filled with holy choirs, singing, studying the word, fasting, praying, exulting in the hope of things to come, and laboring for the purpose of giving alms, and living in love and harmony with each other. And in truth it was to look upon as a secluded region of godliness and honesty. For there was there neither the unjust nor the injured nor any complaint of the taxgatherer. There was a multitude of ascetics, but their desire for virtue was one. So that whoever saw the monasteries and such order among the monks might exclaim, "How goodly are thy dwellings, O Jacob, thy tabernacles, O Israel; like shady valleys, and like a garden by the river side, and like tents which the Lord hath pitched, and like cedars by the waters."

### ANTONY SEEKING MARTYRDOM IN ALEXANDRIA — HIS RETURN

After this, the persecution of the church under Maximin took place. And when the holy martyrs were taken to Alexandria, he left his monastery and followed them, saying, "Let us also go, that we may contend if called to it, or may see them in the conflict." He had, indeed, a strong desire to be a martyr; but not wishing voluntarily to surrender himself, he ministered to the confessors in the mines and prisons. He was also very active at the tribunal, encouraging to boldness those who were on trial and receiving the martyrs and accompanying them till their end. The judge, therefore, when he saw the fearlessness and zeal of Antony and his companions, commanded that none of the monks should appear at the tribunal or even remain in the city. Accordingly, all the rest thought it best to hide themselves that day; but Antony, on the contrary, only took care to wash his cloak and the next day to stand in an elevated situation and appear conspicuous to the perfect. While all wondered at this, and the judge saw him as he passed by with his guard, Antony stood unagitated, showing the boldness of us Christians; for, as I have said, he longed to become a martyr. He seemed grieved, therefore, at not being martyred; but the Lord preserved him for the benefit of us and of others, that he might be to many a teacher in the ascetic life which he had learned from the Scriptures; for many, simply by seeing his example, hastened to follow his system. Again he now ministered as usual to the confessors and, as though bound with them, was incessant in kind offices.

But when the persecution had finally ceased and the blessed Bishop Peter had suffered martyrdom, Antony departed and again retired to his monastery and was there daily a martyr to his conscience and fighting the battles of faith. He even increased the severity of his ascetic practices; for he fasted continually and had his inner garment of hair cloth and his outer of leather, which he kept till his death. He never washed his body with water to cleanse it from filth nor his feet, and even abstained from putting them in water except from necessity. But no one ever saw him unclothed; nor did any one ever see the naked body of Antony till at his burial after death.

After he had retired and determined to pass his time without either going abroad or admitting anybody, one Martian, a commander of soldiers, came and occasioned some disturbance to Antony. For he had a daughter possessed of a devil; and as he remained a long time knocking at the door and entreating him to come and pray for the child, though he would not open the door he bent down from above and said, "O man, why dost thou cry to me? I also am a man as thou art. But if thou believest on Christ whom I serve, go and pray as thou believest, and it shall be done." And immediately he believed and called upon Christ and departed, with his daughter cleansed of the devil. And many other things were performed through him by the Lord, who has said, "Ask and it shall be done unto you"; for many of the suffering, as he would not open the door, slept without the monastery and, believing and praying sincerely, were cleansed.

### ANTONY RETIRES TO A MOUNTAIN IN THE DESERT

But as he saw himself thronged by a multitude and not left to the retirement he desired, and apprehensive lest, from what the Lord was doing by him, either himself should become elated or some one else should think of him above what he was, after deliberation he started to go into Upper Thebais, among those who were ignorant of him. And having received some bread of the brethren, he sat down on the bank of the river, looking out, if some vessel should pass along, to go on board and ascend with them. But while contemplating these things, a voice from above said to him, "Antony, whither art thou going? and wherefore?" But listening unmoved (as he had often been thus addressed), he answered saying, "As the multitudes will not allow me to be quiet, I desire to go into Thebais, because of the many interruptions I suffer from those here, and especially because they demand of me what is above my power." But the voice said to him, "Shouldst thou go up to the Thebais, or even go to the herds of cattle, as thou art thinking to do, thou wouldst have to endure more and twice as severe labor. But if thou wouldst be truly quiet, retire now into the interior of the desert." And when Antony said, "And who will show me the way? for I am not acquainted with it," he immediately pointed out to him some Saracens who were about to travel that way. Antony accordingly went to them and requested that he might accompany them into the desert. As though by the command of Providence, they readily received him. And after journeying three days and three nights with them, he came to a very high mountain. And under the mountain there was most transparent water, sweet and very cold, and a plain around and a few neglected palm-trees.

Antony therefore, as if moved by God, loved the place. For it was the one indicated by him that had spoken to him on the bank of the river. Having, therefore, received some bread from his fellow-travellers, he remained alone in the mountain, with no other one there; for, regarding it as his proper home, he took permanent possession of the place. And the Saracens, seeing Antony's resoluteness, purposely passed that way and gladly brought him bread. He also then derived some little and meagre solace from the palm-trees. But afterwards the brethren, learning of the place, as children mindful of a father, were careful to send to him. But when Antony saw that some were fatigued with toil in bringing him bread, he considered with himself how he might spare the monks this labor, and desired some of those who came to him to bring him a mattock and an axe and a little wheat.  And having received these, he surveyed the region around the mountain and found a very small fit place and, having ample means for irrigation, he cultivated and sowed it.  And doing this year by year, he thence derived his bread, rejoicing that he should thus be troublesome to no one and that he kept himself from being a burden in any respect.  But afterwards, seeing that some still came, he cultivated a very few vegetables [cabbages perhaps], that the visitant might have some little refreshment from the fatigues of the hard journey.  At first the wild beasts of the desert, coming for water, often injured his crop and his ground.  But he, gently taking one of the beasts, said to them all, "Why do you injure me, when I have not injured you?  Depart, and, in the name of the Lord, come not near this place again."  And from that time, as if fearing the injunction, they approached the place no more.

### HIS CONFLICTS WITH THE DEVILS AND HIS VISIT TO THE MONKS

A few days after, as he was at work, for he thought it good to labor, some one standing at the door pulled the cord of his work, for he was making baskets which he gave to those who came to him in exchange for what they brought him.  Rising up, he saw a beast resembling a man as far as the thighs, but it had legs and feet like an ass.  Antony only crossed himself and said, "I am the servant of Christ.  If you were sent against me, see, I am here."  But the beast with his demons fled so fast that he fell down and died.  But the death of the beast was the fall of the demons.  They employed every means to induce him to leave the desert, and they could not.

Being once asked by the monks to come down and visit them and their abode for a while, he went with the monks who came to him.  A camel carried their bread and water, for the whole of that desert is dry and there is no potable water at all except in that mountain in which was his retreat and from whence they procured water.  The water failing while on their journey and the heat being intense, they were all in danger.  For wandering about in those places, they were unable either to find water or to proceed further, but they lay upon the ground, in despair for themselves, and permitted the camel to go loose.  But the old man, seeing them all in danger, greatly sorrowing and groaning, going a little way from them, bending his knees and stretching out his hands, prayed; and immediately the Lord caused water to come forth where he had been praying.  And thus all drank and were refreshed; and filling the skins, they sought the camel and found him, for the halter happening to get wound around a stone, he was thus detained.  After leading him to drink, they placed the skins upon him and proceeded uninjured.

When he came to the outer monasteries, all, as if beholding their father, embraced him. He, as though he had brought supplies to them from the mountain, entertained them with words and imparted what was useful. And on the other hand, there was joy in the mountains, and a zeal for progress, and consolation from their mutual faith. He therefore also rejoiced as he beheld the alacrity of the monks, and his sister now old and still a virgin and presiding over other virgins.

### ANTONY IN HIS MOUNTAIN

After some days, he again went into the mountain, and many at length came to him; and some who had infirmities ventured to go in. On all the monks who came, he was continually pressing the injunction to trust in the Lord and love Him, and to keep themselves from sordid views and carnal pleasures, and, as it is written in the Proverbs, not to be beguiled in satiating the appetite; likewise to flee vain glory and to pray alway, to sing both before and after sleep, and to repeat over the precepts in the Scriptures; and to reflect on the deeds of holy men, in order that the soul, reminded of the commandments, might be attuned to their zeal. And especially did he urge them continually to regard that saying of the Apostle, "Let not the sun go down upon your wrath," and to consider it as spoken in common of all the commands, so that neither upon your wrath nor upon any other sin should the sun go down; for it is proper and necessary that neither the sun should accuse us of wickedness by day nor the moon of sin by night or even of an improper desire.

A man called Fronto, belonging to Palatium, afflicted with a sad disorder (for he devoured his own tongue and was in danger of injuring his eyes), came into the mountain and entreated Antony to pray for him. And when he had prayed, he said to Fronto, "Depart, and thou shalt be healed." But as he obstinately remained there for days, Antony continued to say, "Thou canst not be healed while remaining here; depart, and as thou comest into Egypt, thou shalt see a sign wrought in thee." He believed and departed. And as soon as he came in sight of Egypt, his disorder ceased and the man was well, according to the word of Antony which he had learned of the Saviour in prayer.

Likewise a certain virgin, from Busiris of Tripolis, had a sore and very loathsome disease; for her tears and the mucus from her nose and the moisture from her ears, falling on the ground, immediately became worms. She was also paralytic and her eyes were unnatural. Her parents, hearing of some monks who were going to Antony, and believing on the Lord who healed one of the bloody flux, asked leave to accompany them with their daughter. But they refused; and the parents remained with their child out of the mountain, with Paphnutius the confessor and monk. The monks entered; and as they were about to speak of the virgin, Antony anticipated them and described both the disease of the child and how she journeyed with them. Then they requested that the parents and child might be allowed to come. This, indeed, he would not permit, but said, "Go, and, if she is not dead, you shall find her healed; for this achievement is not mine, that she should come to me, a pitiable man, but the healing is of the Saviour, who exhibits His mercy in every place towards those who call upon Him. The Lord has therefore granted her prayer, and His kindness has shown me that He will heal the virgin's disease where she is." The miracle accordingly took place; and going forth they found the parents rejoicing and the maid healed.

Many other such things a multitude of the monks have harmoniously testified to have been done by him. And still these things do not appear so astonishing as some others. For once, when about to eat and having risen to pray about the ninth hour, he perceived himself wrapt in spirit; and, what is strange, while standing, he saw himself as it were out of himself and as if conducted away in the air by some beings; and then some odious and frightful ones, standing in the air and wishing to prevent his passing through. But as his conductors opposed them, they asked if he was not amenable to them. And as they wished to take an account from his birth, Antony's conductors prohibited it, saying to them, "The things from his birth the Lord hath expunged; but from the time he became a monk and consecrated himself to God, it is proper to take the account." And when they had made accusations and could not prove them, the way became free and unobstructed to him. And immediately he saw himself as it were coming and standing in himself, and he was again Antony entire. Then, forgetting to eat, he remained the rest of the day and the whole night groaning and praying. For he was amazed as he saw against how many we have to wrestle and by what labors one has to pass through the air; and he remembered that to this belongs what the Apostle said, "Against the prince of the power of the air." For in this the enemy has power, in fighting and attempting to prevent those who are passing through. And therefore he especially admonishes, "Take unto you the whole armor of God, that ye may be able to withstand in the evil day, that the enemy may be ashamed, having no evil thing to say of you." But, having learned these things, let us remember the saying of the Apostle, "Whether in the body I know not, or out of the body I know not; God knoweth." Paul, however, was caught up to the third heaven, and, having heard unspeakable words, descended; but Antony saw himself go up to the air and contend until he appeared free.

He enjoyed likewise this blessing, that, being alone in the mountain, if he was at any time in doubt about what he was seeking to know, it was revealed to him by Providence in answer to prayer; and he was, as it is written, "Blessed, being taught of the Lord." Accordingly, after these things, having had a discussion with some who came to him, in regard to the transition of the soul after death, and what kind of a place it will have, on the following night one called to him from above and said, "Antony, arise and come forth and see." So he arose (for he knew to whom he should give ear); and looking up, he saw one, tall, ugly, and terrific, standing and reaching to the clouds, and some ascending and having as it were wings; and he saw him stretching forth his hands, and some hindered by him, and others flying above, and finally passing through, and borne upward free of care. At such, therefore, the huge one gnashed his teeth; but over the fallen he rejoiced. And immediately the voice came to Antony, "Understand what thou hast seen." And his understanding being opened, he perceived it to be the transit of souls, and the huge one standing there to be the enemy who envies the faithful and seizes such as are accountable to him and prevents them from passing through, but is not able to detain those who have not confided in him and who pass above him. Having again seen this, and being as it were reminded, he daily strove the more to attain to the things that are before.

These things, however, he did not willingly relate; but as he remained long in prayer and wonder with himself, those present inquired and pressed him, and he was compelled to declare them, as a father that could not hide them from his children. He considered also his own consciousness clear and that the recital would be profitable to them, as they would perceive the fruit of the ascetic life to be good and visions to be often the solace of labors.

In regard to his disposition, he was patient of evil and humble in spirit. And being so, he respected extremely the canon of the church and wished every clergyman to take precedence of himself in honor. For he was not ashamed to bow his head to the bishops and presbyters; and if a deacon came to him in order to be benefited, he discoursed indeed on what was profitable, but conceded to him in regard to prayer, not blushing himself to learn. And often he made inquiries and desired to hear from those present, and confessed himself benefited if one said anything profitable. His countenance, likewise, possessed a great and wonderful charm; and this gift he also derived from the Saviour. For if he was present in a multitude of monks and any one not acquainted with him before wished to see him, he would pass by the rest and run immediately to him, as though drawn by his looks. Not, however, that he excelled others in height or breadth, but in the placidity of his features and the purity of his soul. For, his soul being calm, the organs of his external senses were tranquil, as from the joy of the soul the countenance is cheerful, and from the motions of the body the state of the soul is perceived, according to what is written, "When the heart rejoices the countenance blooms; but when in sorrow, it is gloomy." Thus Jacob perceived that Laban was meditating a plot against him, and said to his wives, "Your father's countenance is not as it was yesterday and the day before." Thus Samuel recognized David, for his eyes were charming and his teeth white as milk. So, too, was Antony known; for, his soul being serene, he was never ruffled, and his mind being joyful, his countenance was never gloomy.

He was also very wonderful in regard to faith and piety. For he never communed with those schismatics the Miletians, having known their perversity and apostasy from the beginning. Nor did he have familiar intercourse with the Manichaeans or any other heretics, except so far as to admonish them to turn to godliness, thinking and declaring their friendship and familiarity to be injurious and ruinous to the soul. So likewise did he abhor the heresy of the Arians, and warned all neither to go nigh them nor hold their corrupt doctrine. Accordingly, when some of the Ariomaniacs came to him, on examining and finding them impious, he drove them from the mountain, saying "Their words were worse than the poison of serpents."

### ANTONY CALLED TO ALEXANDRIA TO OPPOSE THE ARIANS

And when the Arians at one time falsely asserted that he thought with them, he was grieved and indignant at them. Whereupon, being requested by the bishops and all the brethren, he came down from the mountain and entering Alexandria he publicly denounced the Arians, pronouncing this the last heresy and the precursor of Antichrist. He taught the people that the Son of God was not a creature, nor made out of nothing; but that the Word and Wisdom of the Father's essence is eternal. "And therefore it is impious to say, There was a time when he was not; for the Word was always coëxistent with the Father. Therefore have no communion with the most impious Arians; for light hath no communion with darkness. For you who worship aright are Christians; but they, as they call him a creature who is from the Father and is the Word and Wisdom of God, differ nothing from the heathen who worship the creature rather than God the Creator. But believe that even the whole creation is indignant at them, because the Creator and Lord of all, in whom all things exist, Him they reckon among things created."

All the people therefore rejoiced, as they heard the heresy that is hostile to Christ anathematized by such a man. And all belonging to the city ran together to see Antony. The heathen, too, and even those whom they call their priests came to the church, saying, "We wish to see the man of God," for so was he called by all. For then and there the Lord, through him, cleansed many from devils and healed such as were injured in mind. Many of the heathen also requested though only to touch the aged man, believing they should be benefited. And positively, in those few days as many became Christians as one might see converted in a year. And when some, supposing him annoyed by the multitudes, were turning all away from him, he undisturbed said, "There are not more of them than the devils with whom I contend in the mountain."

### HIS INTERVIEWS WITH PHILOSOPHERS

Antony was very intelligent; and, what is wonderful seeing he was unacquainted with letters, he was a sagacious and ready-witted man. For at a certain time while in the exterior mountain, two Greek philosophers came to him, thinking themselves able to tempt him.  Knowing the men by their countenance, he went out to them and said by an interpreter, "Why, O philosophers, have you been at so much pains to come to a fool?"  And upon their replying that he was no fool but very wise, he said to them, "If you have come to a fool, your labor is useless; but, if you think me wise, be as I am, for it is proper to imitate what is good; and if I had gone to you, I would have imitated you.  But as you have come to me, be like me; for I am a Christian."  But they, astonished, departed; for they saw that even the devils stood in fear of Antony.

Again, when others of the same sort came to him in the exterior mountain, thinking to make sport of him because he had not learned letters, Antony said to them, "But what say ye? which is first, mind or letters? and which is the cause of the other, the mind of letters, or letters of the mind?"  And upon their replying, that the mind was first and the inventor of letters, Antony said, "To one, then, who has a sound mind, letters are not necessary."  This struck with surprise both them and those that were present.  So they departed, astonished at having seen such sagacity in an illiterate man.  For though he had lived and grown old in the mountain, his manners were not rude but graceful and polite.  His discourse, too, was seasoned with divine salt, so that no one would envy, but all who came would rather rejoice in him.

And again others came who were esteemed wise among the Greeks, and requested of him an account of our faith in Christ; and undertook to reason about the preaching of the divine Cross, intending to ridicule it.  After waiting a little and compassionating them for their ignorance, Antony said, through an interpreter who translated his language adroitly: "Which is the more excellent, to profess the Cross, or to ascribe adultery and the corruption of children to those you call gods?  For our profession is a proof of courage and a sign of contempt of death; but yours, of lustful passions.  And then, which is better, to say that the Word of God did not change, but remaining the same assumed for the salvation and benefit of men a human body so that, partaking in human birth, He might make men partakers of the divine and intellectual nature — or to liken the Deity to irrational animals and from this to worship quadrupeds and reptiles and images of men?

"But in respect to the Cross, which of the two would you pronounce the more noble, to endure the Cross through the machinations of vile men and not to shrink from death whenever or however inflicted, or to relate fables about the wanderings of Isis and Osiris and the plots of Typhon and the flight of Saturn and the devouring of children and concerning parricides? for this is your wisdom!  But why do not you who ridicule the Cross admire the Resurrection? for those who mention the one, have described also the other.  Or why, having mentioned the Cross, are you silent about the dead raised to life and the blind restored to sight and the paralytics healed and the lepers cleansed and the walking on the sea and the other signs and wonders which show Christ to have been no longer man but

God? Plainly you seem to me unjust to yourselves, and not in-
genuously to have read our Scriptures. But read ye, and see that
the things which Christ did, prove Him to be God coming for the
salvation of men.

"But relate now, for yourselves, your own principles. But what
would you mention of brutes, except their ferocity and want of
reason? But if, as I hear, you would affirm that these things are
said by you mythically, and you explain the rape of Proserpine as
allegorically signifying the earth; and the limping of Vulcan, fire;
and Juno, the air; and Apollo, the sun; and Diana, the moon; and
Neptune, the sea; nevertheless you do not worship God, but serve
the creature rather than God the Creator of all. But if you have
fabricated such things because creation is beautiful, you should have
been content with admiring without deifying the things made, that
you might not give the honor of the Creator to things created. You
transfer the honor of the architect to the house he has made, or
that of the general to the army. What, now, do you say to these
things, that we may know if the Cross has anything deserving of
ridicule?

"These signs are enough to show that the faith in Christ is the
only true one for piety. Behold, now, you disbelieve and seek formal
reasoning. But, as says our teacher, we do not expound in persuasive words of Grecian wisdom, but rely upon faith, which clearly
precedes a nice arrangement of proofs. Behold! here are persons
vexed with devils"; for some were coming to him who were troubled
by demons. And conducting them into the midst, he said, "Now by
your syllogisms and by whatever art you please, even magic, do you,
calling upon your idols, either cleanse these men or else if you
cannot do it give up your contest with us and witness the power
of the Cross of Christ." Having said this, he called upon Christ
and sealed twice or three times the sufferers with the Sign of the
Cross. And immediately the men stood whole and in their right
mind and also praising God. And the so-called philosophers wondered and were truly amazed at the sagacity of the man and at the
miracle wrought. But Antony said, "Why wonder at this? It is
not we who did it, but Christ, who does such things by those who
believe on Him. Believe, therefore, also yourselves, and you shall
see that ours is not the art of words, but faith which works by love
in Christ; which, if you shall have, you will no longer seek demonstrations by words, but will regard faith in Christ enough for you."
These were the words of Antony. But they wondering at this departed, having embraced him and confessed themselves benefited by
him.

### CONSTANTINE WRITES TO ANTONY

A report concerning Antony even reached the kings. For Constantine the Augustus and his sons Constantius and Constans the
Augusti, learning these things, wrote to him as to a father and begged
to receive answers from him. But he neither placed much value on

the writings nor was delighted with the letters, but was the same as before the kings wrote to him. But when the letters were brought to him, he called the monks and said, "Wonder not if the king writes to us, for he is a man; but rather wonder that God has written his law to men, and has spoken to us by his Son." He therefore wished not to receive the letters, saying that he knew not how to reply to such letters. But being urged by the monks, because the kings are Christians and that they might not be offended by such a neglect, he consented to the reading; and wrote back, commending them for worshipping Christ, and counselled them respecting salvation and not to regard present things as great but rather to remember the judgment to come and to know that Christ is the only true and eternal king. He also entreated them to be humane and mindful of justice and of the poor. And they rejoiced on receiving his letter. Thus was he dear to all, and all wished to regard him as a father.

### HIS LAST ADDRESS TO THE MONKS — HIS DEATH

It is proper both for me to relate and for you, who greatly desire it, to hear how Antony closed his life; for in this also is he worthy of zealous imitation. On his customary visit of inspection to the monks in the exterior mountain, being premonished by Providence of his death, he said to the brethren, "I am now making my last examination of you, and I marvel whether we shall again see each other in this life. It is time for me to go hence, for I am nearly an hundred and five years old." On hearing this, they wept, and clasped and kissed the aged man. But he, as though departing from a foreign to his own city, conversed joyfully and admonished them not to be dilatory in their labors nor discouraged in the ascetic life, but to live as though dying daily; and, as I have said before, to strive earnestly to guard the soul from impure thoughts, and to have zeal for holy men, but not to go near the schismatic Miletians, for you know their evil and unhallowed purpose, nor to have any communion with the Arians, for their impiety is manifest to all; neither be terrified, [said he], if you see the judges favoring them, for their vain show shall cease and is mortal and of short duration. Therefore rather keep yourselves, and hold to the tradition of the fathers and above all to the pious faith in our Lord Jesus Christ, which you have learned from the Scriptures, and have often been reminded of by me.

And as the brethren would constrain him to remain with them, and die there, he refused, for many reasons which he silently indicated, and especially because the Egyptians, though accustomed to perform funeral rites and to wrap in linen the bodies of the pious dead, and especially those of the holy martyrs, yet do not hide them under ground but place them on couches and keep them in their houses with themselves, thinking by this to honor the departed.

Knowing this custom and fearing they would thus treat his body, he took leave of the monks in the outer mountain and hasted away;

and having entered the inner mountain where he was accustomed to abide, in a few months he became ill. And calling those who were with him (for there were two who remained within, following the ascetic life for fifteen years and ministering to him because of his advanced age), he said to them, "If ye care for me and remember me as a father, suffer none to take my body to Egypt, lest they place it in their houses; for on this account I have come into the mountain and come here. And ye know how I always reproved those who do this, and urged them to cease from such a practice. Bury therefore my body and hide it under ground. And let this direction about myself be kept a secret, so that none but yourselves may know the place. For, at the resurrection of the dead, I shall again receive it from the Saviour, incorruptible. Divide my raiment and give to Athanasius the Bishop one sheep-skin and the cloak in which I am wrapped, which he gave to me new, but which has become old in my possession; and to Bishop Sarapion give the other sheep-skin; and yourselves may have my sackcloth. Finally, children, farewell; for Antony departs and is with you no more."

When he had said these things and they had embraced him, stretching out his feet, and seeing as it were friends coming to him, and being delighted on account of them (for he appeared joyful in countenance as he was lying), he died and was gathered to his fathers. And they, as he had given them commandment, adjusted and wrapped his body, and hid it in the earth; and to this day, no one knoweth where it is hid except those two only. And they who respectively received the sheep-skins from the blessed Antony and the cloak worn out by him keep them as a great treasure; for when they see them they behold as it were Antony, and when wrapped in them, with joy they bear about as it were his admonitions.

Therefore read these things to the other brethren, that they may learn what the life of a monk ought to be and may be persuaded that our Lord and Saviour Jesus Christ honors those who honor Him; and that He not only conducts to the kingdom of heaven those who serve Him to the end, but that even here those who are hid and are anxious for seclusion He causes to become everywhere known and celebrated, both as a reward of their virtue and as a benefit to others. And if it will be of use, read this also to the pagans, that thus they may at least know that our Lord Jesus Christ is God and the Son of God, and also that the Christians who truly serve Him and piously believe on Him not only show that the demons, whom the pagans suppose to be gods, are no gods, but even tread them under foot and expel them as deceivers and corrupters of men. In our Lord Jesus Christ, to whom be glory forever and ever. Amen.

[tr. RALPH EMERSON]

# AUGUSTINE, BISHOP OF HIPPO

In the patristic period, from the Nicene Council (A.D. 325) to the collapse of the Roman Empire in the West at the end of the sixth century, a prolific Latin literature from the pens of great Christian leaders shaped the Latin Church. Foremost among these author-prelates were: Ambrose, Bishop of Milan from A.D. 374 to 397; Jerome, translator of the Bible, who died in Bethlehem in the year 420; Augustine, Bishop of Hippo, not far from ancient Carthage, who died in 430 as the Vandals, who had swept through France, Spain, and Algeria, were approaching the city; and Gregory, Bishop of Rome, who died in 604. The writings of these four, who composed in a wide variety of forms, helped to change western idiom and literature quite as much as to develop Christian theology. All four had comparatively aristocratic parents and studied in the Roman schools of rhetoric which trained public servants. There the formalized studies consisted largely of imitation of classical models which could not express the new concepts flowing in from Palestine, Asiatic Greece, and Persia. Moreover, the aristocratic language lacked appeal for the masses whom these writers and orators wanted as an audience. So the Fathers learned to express the fresh new poetry and imagery of Christianity in a diction and syntax largely drawn from the colloquial language of the plebs. The writings of these men, thoroughly trained in the old and inspired by the new, set the pattern for medieval Latin language and literature.

The two most widely read works of Augustine today were also the most popular in the Middle Ages. *The City of God,* begun about A.D. 413 after the earthshaking sack of Rome by Alaric the Goth, was not completed until A.D. 425. Augustine began it as a polemic against those not yet converted to Christianity, who were asserting that the foresaking of pagan gods brought on the calamity. Though he kept to a single theme — the parallel development of the City of God and the City of Man — his habits of writing at odd moments snatched from the busy day of leading his people in a time of stress resulted in a work loosely constructed, journalistic, and often self-contradictory. Nevertheless, its twenty-two books have probably been more influential in western religious thought than any other except the books of the Bible.

The much shorter *Confessions,* in thirteen books, is a spiritual autobiography, which Augustine wrote in the year 397 to detail the steps of his conversion. He concludes the story with the death of his mother, following the conversion, in 387. There are many reasons to believe that Augustine did not exaggerate the waywardness of his youth. He may have inherited his violence and tendency to excess from his irreligious father Patricius, a *vir curialis,* or member of the local senatorial class, who occupied the then unenviable, pauperizing office of tax collector. His mother, Monica, a devout Christian, patiently watched her son move from error to error.  His sins were many.  As he pursued his course of education in North Africa, he attached himself to heresy after heresy, for nine years espousing Manichaeism, an adaptation of Zoroastrianism imported from the Orient.  When he had completed his formal schooling, he moved with his concubine and son to Rome in 383, to set himself up as a teacher of rhetoric.  But success in his profession eluded him and he changed to Milan, hoping for appointment to a lucrative post.  There Monica joined him.  Milan was at that time almost the seat of Empire, the crossroads for the main routes north and south, east and west.  Ambrose, who as Bishop was to make the great Emperor Theodosius, stripped of his royal insignia, publicly beg pardon of the Church with groans and tears, was then involved in a struggle with the Empress Justina, who advocated Arianism.  The passage from the *Confessions* given here describes in part Augustine's conversion, Ambrose's kindliness and personal magnetism, and one of the great forward steps in western literature — the introduction of eastern hymnody into the West.

## CONFESSIONS

### Augustine of Hippo (A.D. 354–430)

[From *The Works of Aurelius Augustine*, Vol. xiv, edited by Marcus Dods, translated by J. G. Pilkington; T. & T. Clark, Edinburgh, 1876.]

#### BOOK V

*Chapter XIII.  He is sent to Milan, that he, about to teach Rhetoric, may be known by Ambrose.*

When, therefore, they of Milan had sent to Rome to the prefect of the city, to provide them with a teacher of rhetoric for their city, and to despatch him at the public expense, I made interest through those identical persons, drunk with Manichaean vanities, to be freed from whom I was going away — neither of us, however, being aware of it — that Symmachus, the then prefect, having proved me by proposing a subject, would send me.  And to Milan I came, unto Ambrose the bishop, known to the whole world as among the best of men, Thy devout servant; whose eloquent discourse did at that time strenuously dispense unto Thy people the flour of Thy wheat, the gladness of Thy oil, and the sober intoxication of Thy wine [cf. Ps. iv, 7, and civ, 15].  To him was I unknowingly led by Thee, that by him I might knowingly be led to Thee.  That man of God received me like a father, and looked with a benevolent and episcopal kindliness on my change of abode.  And I began to love him, not at first indeed as a teacher of the truth — which I entirely despaired of in Thy Church — but as a man friendly to myself. And I studiously hearkened to him preaching to the people, not with the motive I should, but, as it were, trying to discover whether his eloquence came up to the fame thereof or flowed fuller or lower than was asserted. I hung on his words intently, but of the matter I was but as a careless and contemptuous spectator. I was delighted with the pleasantness of his speech, more erudite yet less cheerful and soothing in manner than that of Faustus. Of the matter, however, there could be no comparison; for the latter was straying amid Manichaean deceptions, whilst the former was teaching salvation most soundly. But "salvation is far from the wicked," [Ps. cxix, 155] such as I then stood before him; and yet I was drawing nearer gradually and unconsciously.

*Chapter XIV. Having heard the Bishop, he perceives the force of the Catholic faith, yet doubts, after the manner of the modern Academics.*

For although I took no trouble to learn what he spake, but only to hear how he spake (for that empty care alone remained to me, despairing of a way accessible for man to Thee), yet, together with the words which I prized, there came into my mind also the things about which I was careless; for I could not separate them. And whilst I opened my heart to admit "how skillfully he spake," there also entered with it, but gradually, "and how truly he spake!" For first, these things also had begun to appear to me to be defensible; and the Catholic faith, for which I had fancied nothing could be said against the attacks of the Manichaeans, I now conceived might be maintained without presumption; especially after I had heard one or two parts of the Old Testament explained, and often allegorically — which then I accepted literally, I was "killed" spiritually [cf. I Cor. xiii, 12, and II Cor. iii, 6.] Many places, then, of those books having been expounded to me, I now blamed my despair in having believed that no reply could be made to those who hated and derided the Law and the Prophets. Yet I did not then see that for that reason the Catholic way was to be held because it had its learned advocates, who could at length and not irrationally answer objections; nor that what I held ought therefore to be condemned because both sides were equally defensible. For that way did not appear to me to be vanquished; nor yet did it seem to me to be victorious.

Hereupon did I earnestly bend my mind to see if in any way I could possibly prove the Manichaeans guilty of falsehood. Could I have realized a spiritual substance, all their strongholds would have been beaten down and cast utterly out of my mind; but I could not. But yet, concerning the body of this world and the whole of nature which the senses of the flesh can attain unto, I, now more and more considering and comparing things, judged that the greater part of the philosophers held much the more probable opinions. So, then, after the manner of the Academics (as they are supposed), doubting of everything and fluctuating between all, I decided that the Manichaeans were to be abandoned. Judging that, even while in that period of doubt, I could not remain in a· sect to which I preferred some of the philosophers; to which philosophers, however, because they were without the saving name of Christ, I utterly refused to commit the cure of my fainting soul. I resolved, therefore, to be a catechumen in the Catholic Church, which my parents had commended to me, until something settled should manifest itself to me whither I might steer my course.

### BOOK VI

*Chapter I. His mother having followed him to Milan declares that she will not die before her son shall have embraced the Catholic faith.*

O Thou, my hope from my youth, where wert Thou to me, and whither hadst Thou gone? For in truth, hadst Thou not created me and made a difference between me and the beasts of the field and fowls of the air? Thou hadst made me wiser than they, yet did I wander about in dark and slippery places, and sought Thee abroad out of myself, and found not the God of my heart; and had entered the depths of the sea, and distrusted and despaired finding out the truth. By this time my mother, made strong by her piety, had come to me, following me over sea and land, in all perils feeling secure in Thee. For in the dangers of the sea she comforted the very sailors (to whom the inexperienced passengers, when alarmed, were wont rather to go for comfort), assuring them of a safe arrival because she had been so assured by Thee in a vision. She found me in grievous danger through despair of ever finding truth. But when I had disclosed to her that I was now no longer a Manichaean, though not yet a Catholic Christian, she did not leap for joy as at what was unexpected although she was now reassured as to that part of my misery for which she had mourned me as one dead, but who would be raised to Thee, carrying me forth upon the bier of her thoughts, that Thou mightest say unto the widow's son, "Young man, I say unto thee, arise" [Luke VII, 12–15], and he should revive, and begin to speak, and Thou shouldest deliver him to his mother. Her heart, then, was not agitated with any violent exultation, when she had heard that to be already in so great a part accomplished which she daily, with tears, entreated of Thee might be done — that though I had not yet grasped the truth, I was rescued from falsehood. Yea, rather, for that she was fully confident that Thou, who hadst promised the whole, wouldst give the rest, most calmly and with a breast full of confidence she replied to me, she believed in Christ, that before she departed this life, she would see me a Catholic believer. And thus much said she to me; but to Thee, O Fountain of mercies, poured she out more frequent prayers and tears, that Thou wouldest hasten Thy aid and enlighten my darkness. She hurried all the more assiduously to the church and hung upon the words of Ambrose, praying for the fountain of water that springeth up into everlasting life [John IV, 14]. For she loved that man as an angel of God, because she knew that it was by him that I had been brought, for the present, to that perplexing state of agitation I was now in, through which she was fully persuaded that I should pass from sickness unto health after an access, as it were, of a sharper fit, which doctors term the "crisis."

*Chapter II. She, on the prohibition of Ambrose, abstains from honouring the memory of the martyrs.*

When therefore, my mother had at one time — as was her custom in Africa — brought to the oratories built in the memory of the saints certain cakes and bread and wine and was forbidden by the door-keeper, so soon as she learnt that it was the bishop who had forbidden it she so piously and obediently acceded to it that I myself marvelled how readily she could bring herself to accuse her own custom, rather than question his prohibition. For wine-bibbing did not take possession of her spirit nor did the love of wine stimulate her to hatred of the truth as it doth too many both male and female, who nauseate at a song of sobriety, as men well drunk at a draught of water. But she, when she had brought her basket with the festive meats, of which she would taste herself first and give the rest away, would never allow herself more than one little cup of wine, diluted according to her own temperate palate, which, out of courtesy, she would taste. And if there were many oratories of departed saints that ought to be honoured in the same way, she still carried round with her the selfsame cup, to be used everywhere; and this, which was not only very much watered, but was also very tepid with carrying about, she would distribute by small sips to those around; for she sought their devotion, not pleasure. As soon, therefore, as she found this custom to be forbidden by that famous preacher and most pious prelate, even to those who would use it with moderation, lest thereby an occasion of excess might be given to such as were drunken, and because these, so to say, festivals in honour of the dead were very like unto the superstition of the Gentiles, she most willingly abstained from it. And in lieu of a basket filled with fruits of the earth, she had learned to bring to the oratories of the martyrs a heart full of more purified petitions, and to give all that she could to the poor; that so the communion of the Lord's body might be rightly celebrated there, where, after the example of His passion, the martyrs had been sacrificed and crowned. But yet it seems to me, O Lord my God, and thus my heart thinks of it in thy sight, that my mother perhaps would not so easily have given way to the relinquishment of this custom had it been forbidden by another whom she loved not as Ambrose, whom, out of regard for my salvation, she loved most dearly; and he loved her truly, on account of her most religious conversation, whereby, in good works so "fervent in spirit" [Rom. XII, 11], she frequented the church; so that he would often, when he saw me, burst forth into her praises, congratulating me that I had such a mother — little knowing what a son she had in me, who was in doubt as to all these things and did not imagine the way of life could be found out.

*Chapter III. As Ambrose was occupied with business and study, Augustine could seldom consult him concerning the Holy Scriptures.*

Nor did I now groan in my prayers that Thou wouldest help me; but my mind was wholly intent on knowledge and eager to dispute. And Ambrose himself I esteemed a happy man, as the world counted happiness, in that such great personages held him in honour; only his celibacy appeared to me a painful thing. But what hope he cherished, what struggles he had against the temptations that beset his very excellences, what solace in adversities, and what savoury joys Thy bread possessed for the hidden mouth of his heart when ruminating on it, I could neither conjecture nor had I experienced. Nor did he know my embarrassments nor the pit of my danger. For I could not request of him what I wished as I wished, in that I was debarred from hearing and speaking to him by crowds of busy people whose infirmities he devoted himself to. With whom when he was not engaged (which was but a little time), he either was refreshing his body with necessary sustenance or his mind with reading. But while reading, his eyes glanced over the pages and his heart searched out the sense but his voice and tongue were silent. Ofttimes, when we had come (for no one was forbidden to enter, nor was it his custom that the arrival of those who came should be announced to him), we saw him thus reading to himself and never otherwise; and, having long sat in silence (for who durst interrupt one so intent?), we were fain to depart, inferring that in the little time he secured for the recruiting of his mind, free from the clamour of other men's business, he was unwilling to be taken off. And perchance he was fearful lest, if the author he studied should express aught vaguely, some doubtful and attentive hearer should ask him to expound it or to discuss some of the more abstruse questions, as that, his time being thus occupied, he could not turn over as many volumes as he wished — although the preservation of his voice, which was very easily weakened, might be the truer reason for his reading to himself. But whatever was his motive in so doing doubtless in such a man was a good one.

*Chapter IV. He recognises the falsity of his own opinions, and commits to memory the saying of Ambrose.*

As, then, I knew not how this image of Thine should subsist, I should have knocked and propounded the doubt how it was to be believed, and not have insultingly opposed it as if it were believed. Anxiety, therefore, as to what to retain as certain did all the more sharply gnaw into my soul, the more shame I felt that, having been so long deluded and deceived by the promise of certainties, I had with puerile error and petulance prated of so many uncertainties as if they were certainties.  For that they were falsehoods became apparent to me afterwards.  However, I was certain that they were uncertain, and that I had formerly held them as certain when with a blind contentiousness I accused Thy Catholic Church, which though I had not yet discovered to teach truly, yet not to teach that of which I had so vehemently accused her.  In this manner was I confounded and converted, and I rejoiced, O my God, that the one Church, the body of Thine only Son (wherein the name of Christ had been set upon me when an infant), did not appreciate these infantile trifles, nor maintained, in her sound doctrine, any tenet that would confine Thee, the Creator of all, in space — though ever so great and wide, yet bounded on all sides by the restraints of a human form.

I rejoiced also that the old Scriptures of the law and the prophets were laid before me to be perused, not now with that eye to which they seemed most absurd before when I censured Thy holy ones for so thinking, whereas in truth they thought not so.  And with delight I heard Ambrose, in his sermons to the people, oftentimes most diligently recommend this text as a rule — "The letter killeth, but the Spirit giveth life" [II Cor. III, 6]; whilst, drawing aside the mystic veil, he spiritually laid open that which, accepted according to the "letter," seemed to teach perverse doctrines — teaching herein nothing that offended me, though he taught such things as I knew not as yet whether they were true.  For all this time I restrained my heart from assenting to anything, fearing to fall headlong; but by hanging in suspense I was the worse killed.  For my desire was to be as well assured of those things that I saw not as I was that seven and three are ten.  For I was not so insane as to believe that this could not be comprehended; but I desired to have other things as clear as this, whether corporeal things, which were not present to my senses, or spiritual whereof I knew not how to conceive except corporeally.  And by believing I might have been cured, that so the sight of my soul being cleared, it might in some way be directed towards Thy truth, which abideth always, and faileth in naught.  But as it happens that he who has tried a bad physician fears to trust himself with a good one, so was it with the health of my soul, which could not be healed but by believing, and, lest it should believe falsehoods, refused to be cured — resisting Thy hands, who hast prepared for us the medicaments of faith, and hast applied them to the maladies of the whole world, and hast bestowed upon them so great authority.

*Chapter V.  Faith is the basis of human life; man cannot discover that truth which Holy Scripture has disclosed.*

From this, however, being led to prefer the Catholic doctrine, I felt that it was with more moderation and honesty that it commanded things to be believed that were not demonstrated (whether it was that they could be demonstrated, but not to any one, or could not be demonstrated at all), than was the method of the Manichaeans, where our credulity was mocked by audacious promise of knowledge, and then so many most fabulous and absurd things were forced upon belief because they were not capable of demonstration. After that, O Lord, Thou by little and little with most gentle and most merciful hand drawing and calming my heart didst persuade me — taking into consideration what a multiplicity of things which I had never seen nor was present when they were enacted, like so many of the things in secular history and so many accounts of places and cities which I had not seen, so many of friends, so many of physicians, so many now of these men, now of those, which unless we should believe we should do nothing at all in this life; lastly with how unalterable an assurance I believed of what parents I was born, which it would have been impossible for me to know otherwise than by hearsay — taking into consideration all this, Thou persuadedst me that not they who believed Thy books (which with so great authority Thou hast established among nearly all nations) but those who believed them not were to be blamed, and that those men were not to be listened unto who should say to me, "How dost thou know that those Scriptures were imparted unto mankind by the Spirit of the one true and most true God?" For it was this same thing that was most of all to be believed, since no wranglings of blasphemous questions whereof I had read so many amongst the self-contradicting philosophers could once wring the belief from me that Thou art — whatsoever Thou wert, though what I knew not — or that the government of human affairs belongs to Thee.

Thus much I believed, at one time more strongly than another, yet did I ever believe both that Thou wert and hadst a care of us, although I was ignorant both what was to be thought of Thy substance and what way led or led back to Thee. Seeing, then, that we were too weak by unaided reason to find out the truth and for this cause needed the authority of the holy writings, I had now begun to believe that Thou wouldest by no means have given such excellency of authority to those Scriptures throughout all lands had it not been Thy will thereby to be believed in and thereby sought. For now those things which heretofore appeared incongruous to me in the Scripture and used to offend me, having heard divers of them expounded reasonably, I referred to the depth of the mysteries, and its authority seemed to me all the more venerable and worthy of religious belief in that, while it was visible for all to read it, it reserved the majesty of its secret within its profound significance, stooping to all in the great plainness of its language and lowliness of its style, yet exercising the application of such as are not light of heart; that it might receive all into its common bosom and through narrow passages waft over some few towards Thee, yet many more than if it did not stand upon such a height of authority, nor allured multitudes within its bosom by its holy humility. These things I meditated upon, and Thou wert with me; I sighed, and Thou heardest me; I vacillated, and Thou didst guide me; I roamed through the broad way of the world, and Thou didst not desert me.

### BOOK IX

*Chapter V.   At the recommendation of Ambrose, he reads the
prophecies of Isaiah, but does not understand them.*

The vintage vacation being ended, I gave the citizens of Milan
notice that they might provide their scholars with another seller
of words; because both of my election to serve Thee and my in-
ability, by reason of the difficulty of breathing and the pain in my
chest, to continue the professorship.   And by letters I notified to
Thy bishop, the holy man Ambrose, my former errors and present
resolutions, with a view to his advising me which of Thy books it
was best for me to read so that I might be readier and fitter for the
reception of such great grace.   He recommended Isaiah the Prophet,
I believe because he foreshows more clearly than others the Gospel
and the calling of the Gentiles.   But I, not understanding the first
portion of the book and imagining the whole to be like it, laid it
aside, intending to take it up hereafter, when better practised in
our Lord's words.

*Chapter VI.   He is baptized at Milan with Alypius and his son
Adeodatus.   The book "De Magistro."*

Alypius also was pleased to be born again with me in Thee, being
now clothed with the humility appropriate to Thy sacraments, and
being so brave a tamer of the body as with unusual fortitude to
tread the frozen soil of Italy with his naked feet.   We took into
our company the boy Adeodatus, born of me carnally, of my sin.
Well hadst Thou made him.   He was barely fifteen years, yet in
wit excelled many grave and learned men.   I confess unto Thee Thy
gifts, O Lord my God, Creator of all, and of exceeding power to
reform our deformities; for of me was there naught in that boy but
the sin.   For that we fostered him in Thy discipline, Thou in-
spiredst us, none other — Thy gifts I confess unto Thee.   There
is a book of ours, which is entitled *The Master*.   It is a dialogue
between him and me.   Thou knowest that all things there put into
the mouth of the person in argument with me were his thoughts
in his sixteenth year.   Many others more wonderful did I find in
him.   That talent was a source of awe to me.   And who but Thou
could be the worker of such marvels?   Quickly didst Thou remove
his life from the earth; and now I recall him to mind with a sense
of security, in that I fear nothing for his childhood or youth or
for his whole self.   We took him coeval with us in Thy grace, to
be educated in Thy discipline; and we were baptized, and solicitude
about our past life left us.   Nor was I satiated in those days with
the wondrous sweetness of considering the depth of Thy counsels
concerning the salvation of the human race.   How greatly did I
weep in Thy hymns and canticles, deeply moved by the voices of
Thy sweet-speaking Church!   The voices flowed into mine ears,

and the truth was poured forth into my heart, whence the agitation of my piety overflowed, and my tears ran over, and blessed was I therein.

### Chapter VII. Of the Church hymns instituted at Milan; of the Ambrosian persecution raised by Justina; and of the discovery of the bodies of two martyrs.

Not long had the Church of Milan begun to employ this kind of consolation and exhortation, the brethren singing together with great earnestness of voice and heart. For it was about a year or not much more since Justina, the mother of the boy-Emperor Valentinian, persecuted Thy servant Ambrose in the interest of her heresy, to which she had been seduced by the Arians. The pious people kept guard in the church, prepared to die with their bishop, Thy servant. There my mother, Thy handmaid, bearing a chief part of those cares and watchings, lived in prayer. We, still unmelted by the heat of Thy Spirit, were yet moved by the astonished and disturbed city. At this time it was instituted that, after the manner of the Eastern Church, hymns and psalms should be sung, lest the people should pine away in the tediousness of sorrow; which custom, retained from then till now, is imitated by many, yea, by almost all of Thy congregations throughout the rest of the world.

Then didst Thou by a vision make known to Thy renowned bishop the spot where lay the bodies of Gervasius and Protasius, the martyrs (whom Thou hadst in Thy secret storehouse preserved uncorrupted for so many years), whence Thou mightest at the fitting time produce them to repress the feminine but royal fury. For when they were revealed and dug up and with due honour transferred to the Ambrosian Basilica, not only they who were troubled with unclean spirits (the devils confessing themselves) were healed, but a certain man also who had been blind many years, a well-known citizen of that city, having asked and been told the reason of the people's tumultuous joy, rushed forth, asking his guide to lead him thither. Arrived there, he begged to be permitted to touch with his handkerchief the bier of Thy saints, whose death is precious in Thy sight [Ps. cxvi, 15]. When he had done this and put it to his eyes, they were forthwith opened. Thence did the fame spread; thence did Thy praises burn — shine; thence was the mind of that enemy, though not yet enlarged to the wholeness of believing, restrained from the fury of persecuting. Thanks be to Thee, O my God. Whence and whither hast Thou thus led my remembrance that I should confess these things also unto Thee — great, though I forgetful had passed them over? And yet then, when the "savour" of Thy "ointments" was so fragrant, did we not "run after Thee" [Cant. 1, 3, 4]. And so I did the more abundantly weep at the singing of Thy hymns, formerly panting for Thee and at last breathing in Thee, as far as the air can play in this house of grass.

*Chapter VIII.  Of the conversion of Evodius, and the death of his mother when returning with him to Africa.*

Thou, who makest men to dwell of one mind in a house [Ps. LXVIII, 6], didst associate with us Evodius also, a young man of our city, who, when serving as an agent for Public Affairs, was converted unto Thee and baptized prior to us; and relinquishing his secular service, prepared himself for Thine. We were together, and together were we about to dwell with a holy purpose. We sought for some place where we might be most useful in our service to Thee, and were going back together to Africa. And when we were at the Tiberine Ostia my mother died.

[tr. J. G. PILKINGTON]

# BOETHIUS

Philosophic accounts of man's world are usually based on a presumption of unity, duality, or trinity. As the Nicene Creed is the primary trinitarian text, and Augustine's *City of God* the center of western notions of dualism, Boethius' *Consolation of Philosophy* has been the most popular exposition of unitarian doctrine. It has especially appealed to men of action; among the numerous translators and paraphrasts in English are Alfred the Great, Chaucer, and Queen Elizabeth. The *Consolation* also belongs to the species of "prison-literature" — works written by prisoners as a relief from tedium and a consolation in despair, among them Sir Thomas More's *Utopia*, Cervantes' *Don Quixote*, Malory's *Morte d'Arthur*, Bunyan's *Grace Abounding* and the first part of *Pilgrim's Progress*, the first part of Thomas Paine's *The Age of Reason*, Sir Walter Raleigh's *History of the World*, and Voltaire's *Henriade*.

The terror of Boethius' life is apparently depicted with objectivity in the First Book of the *Consolation*. After the Roman state had fallen to its Gothic conquerors at the end of the fifth century, there emerged the strong king Theodoric, known in later northern legends as Dietrich von Bern, who ruled the Italian peninsula with enlightenment from his capital at Ravenna. He chose wise counselors and officials from among the native Roman aristocracy. Two of them, realizing that classical civilization was tending to disappear, devoted much of their lives to the salvation and transmission of ancient knowledge.

Magnus Aurelius Cassiodorus, senator and a chief minister to all the Ostrogothic kings of Italy, retired at the age of seventy when Belisarius defeated the Ostrogoths and ended their rule. He founded a monastery where for at least twenty-three years he stimulated teaching and the copying of manuscripts, which became the first elements in the medieval corpus of ancient writings.

Cassiodorus was better able to adapt himself to the caprices and the fears of the Gothic usurpers than was Anicius Manlius Severinus Boethius, the heir of one of the foremost patrician families, who became *princeps senatus* and Master of the Offices under Theodoric. He set for himself the major task of translating the whole body of Greek philosophy and science into Latin for the use of the western world, which was fast losing its knowledge of Greek. Though he completed translations of but a small portion of the writings of Plato, Aristotle, and their followers, these formed almost the exclusive knowledge of ancient philosophy until the thirteenth century. Like all usurpers, Theodoric became more sensitive about his position as he aged, and there came a day when he unjustly came to suspect Boethius of treason. Without a trial, the subservient senate passed sentence of confiscation and death. Boethius languished in prison for several months before execution. In that period he wrote the *Consolation*.

The work is composed in a form that had already achieved popularity through the *Satiricon* of Petronius, the *Alexander* of Julius Valerius, and the *Marriage of Business and Learning* of Martianus Capella. That is, it interspersed prose exposition with metrical passages designed to give relief to the mind and to stir the emotions. This form was employed by later medieval writers; see, for instance, *Aucassin and Nicolete,* which appears farther on in this book. In five books the allegorical figure Philosophy lifts Boethius from abject despondency to a noble optimism by means of a modified Socratic method of dialogue. The philosophy, though primarily Platonic, is of such practicality as might be expected from a man in Boethius' position. Though his isolation in prison precluded use of books, the *Consolation* clearly shows how steeped was its author's mind in the best of ancient learning. The work is a model of construction.

That no doctrine especially Christian enters into the work was a sufficient reason for many scholars to believe that it and five theological tracts ascribed to him could not have been written by the same man. However, despite its unitarian base there are no statements inconsonant with Christian orthodoxy and it is now generally agreed that he was an active Christian and the author of at least four of these expositions of orthodox trinitarianism. As their author, Boethius was glorified in the medieval Church as St. Severinus.

The selection below is the First Book, unabridged, of the five that make up the total work.

## THE CONSOLATION OF PHILOSOPHY

Boethius (A.D. 480?–524)

[From *The Consolation of Philosophy,* translated by W. V. Cooper; Temple Classics, J. M. Dent & Sons, Ltd., London, 1901. Reprinted by permission of the publisher.]

### BOOK I

[Met. I] "To pleasant songs my work was erstwhile given, and bright were all my labours then; but now in tears to sad refrains am I compelled to turn. Thus my maimed Muses guide my pen, and gloomy songs make no feigned tears bedew my face. Then could no fear so overcome to leave me companionless upon my way. They were the pride of my earlier bright-lived days: in my later gloomy days they are the comfort of my fate; for hastened by unhappiness has age come upon me without warning, and grief hath set within me the old age of her gloom. White hairs are scattered untimely on my head, and the skin hangs loosely from my worn-out limbs.

"Happy is that death which thrusts not itself upon men in their pleasant years, yet comes to them at the oft-repeated cry of their sorrow. Sad is it how deaths turns away from the unhappy with so deaf an ear, and will not close, cruel, the eyes that weep. Ill is it to trust to Fortune's fickle bounty, and while yet she smiled upon me, the hour of gloom had well-nigh overwhelmed my head. Now has the cloud put off its alluring face, wherefore without scruple my life drags out its wearying delays.

"Why, O my friends, did ye so often puff me up, telling me that I was fortunate? For he that is fallen low did never firmly stand."

[Prose I]  While I was pondering thus in silence, and using my pen to set down so tearful a complaint, there appeared standing over my head a woman's form, whose countenance was full of majesty, whose eyes shone as with fire and in power of insight surpassed the eyes of men, whose colour was full of life, whose strength was yet intact though she was so full of years that none would ever think that she was subject to such age as ours. One could but doubt her varying stature, for at one moment she repressed it to the common measure of a man, at another she seemed to touch with her crown the very heavens; and when she had raised higher her head, it pierced even the sky and baffled the sight of those who would look upon it. Her clothing was wrought of the finest thread by subtle workmanship brought to an indivisible piece. This had she woven with her own hands, as I afterwards did learn by her own shewing. Their beauty was somewhat dimmed by the dulness of long neglect, as is seen in the smoke-grimed masks of our ancestors. On the border below was inwoven the symbol $\pi$, on that above was to be read a $\theta$. And between the two letters there could be marked degrees, by which, as by the rungs of a ladder, ascent might be made from the lower principle to the higher. Yet the hands of rough men had torn this garment and snatched such morsels as they could therefrom. In her right hand she carried books, in her left was a sceptre brandished.

When she saw that the Muses of poetry were present by my couch giving words to my lamenting, she was stirred a while; her eyes flashed fiercely, and said she, "Who has suffered these seducing mummers to approach this sick man? Never do they support those in sorrow by any healing remedies, but rather do ever foster the sorrow by poisonous sweets. These are they who stifle the fruit-bearing harvest of reason with the barren briars of the passions; they free not the minds of men from disease, but accustom them thereto. I would think it less grievous if your allurements drew away from me some uninitiated man, as happens in the vulgar herd. In such an one my labours would be naught harmed, but this man has been nourished in the lore of Eleatics and Academics; and to him have ye reached? Away with you, Sirens, seductive unto destruction! leave him to my Muses to be cared for and to be healed."

Their band thus rated cast a saddened glance upon the ground, confessing their shame in blushes, and passed forth dismally over the threshold. For my part, my eyes were dimmed with tears, and I could not discern who was this woman of such commanding power.

I was amazed, and turning my eyes to the ground I began in silence to await what she should do. Then she approached nearer and sat down upon the end of my couch. She looked into my face heavy with grief and cast down by sorrow to the ground, and then she raised her complaint over the trouble of my mind in these words.

[Met. II] "Ah me! how blunted grows the mind when sunk below the o'erwhelming flood! Its own true light no longer burns within, and it would break forth to outer darknesses. How often care, when fanned by earthly winds, grows to a larger and unmeasured bane. This man has been free to the open heaven; his habit has it been to wander into the paths of the sky. His to watch the light of the bright sun, his to inquire into the brightness of the chilly moon. He, like a conqueror, held fast bound in its order every star that makes its wandering circle, turning its peculiar course. Nay, more, deeply has he searched into the springs of nature, whence came the roaring blasts that ruffle the ocean's bosom calm. What is the spirit that makes the firmament revolve; wherefore does the evening star sink into the western wave but to rise from the radiant East; what is the cause which so tempers the season of Spring that it decks the earth with rose-blossoms; whence comes it to pass that Autumn is prolific in the years of plenty and overflows with teeming vines? Deeply to search these causes was his wont, and to bring forth secrets deep in Nature hid.

"Now he lies there; extinct his reason's light, his neck in heavy chains thrust down, his countenance with grievous weight downcast. Ah! the brute earth is all he can behold.

[Prose II] "But now," said she, "is the time for the physician's art, rather than for complaining." Then fixing her eyes wholly on me, she said, "Are you the man who was nourished upon the milk of my learning, brought up with my food until you had won your way to the power of a manly soul? Surely I had given you such weapons as would keep you safe, and your strength unconquered; if you had not thrown them away. Do you know me? Why do you keep silence? Are you dumb from shame or from dull amazement? I would it were from shame, but I see that amazement has overwhelmed you."

When she saw that I was not only silent but utterly tongue-tied and dumb, she put her hand gently upon my breast, and said, "There is no danger: he is suffering from drowsiness, that disease which attacks so many minds which have been deceived. He has forgotten himself for a moment and will quickly remember, as soon as he recognises me. That he may do so, let me brush away from his eyes the darkening cloud of thoughts of matters perishable." So saying, she gathered her robe into a fold and dried my swimming eyes.

[Met. III] Then was dark night dispelled, the shadows fled away, and my eyes received returning power as before. 'Twas just as when the heavenly bodies are enveloped by the west wind's rush, and the sky stands thick with watery clouds; the sun is hidden and the stars are not yet come into the sky, and night descending from above o'erspreads the earth. But if the north wind smites this scene, launched forth from the Thracian cave, it unlocks the imprisoned daylight; the sun shines forth, and thus sparkling Phoebus smites with his rays our wondering eyes.

[Prose III] In such a manner were the clouds of grief scattered. Then I drew breath again and engaged my mind in taking knowledge of my physician's countenance. So when I turned my eyes towards her and fixed my gaze upon her, I recognised my nurse, Philosophy, in whose chambers I had spent my life from earliest manhood. And I asked her, "Wherefore have you, mistress of all virtues, come down from heaven above to visit my lonely place of banishment? Is it that you, as well as I, may be harried, the victim of false charges?" "Should I," said she, "desert you, my nursling? Should I not share and bear my part of the burden which has been laid upon you from spite against my name? Surely Philosophy never allowed herself to let the innocent go upon their journey unbefriended. Think you I would fear calumnies? that I would be terrified as though they were a new misfortune? Think you that this is the first time that wisdom has been harassed by dangers among men of shameless ways? In ancient days before the time of my child, Plato, have we not as well as nowadays fought many a mighty battle against the recklessness of folly? And though Plato did survive, did not his master, Socrates, win his victory of an unjust death, with me present at his side? When after him the followers of Epicurus, and in turn the Stoics, and then others did all try their utmost to seize his legacy, they dragged me, for all my cries and struggles, as though to share me as plunder; they tore my robe which I had woven with mine own hands, and snatched away the fragments thereof. And when they thought I had altogether yielded myself to them, they departed. And since among them were to be seen certain signs of my outward bearing, others ill-advised did think they wore my livery; thus were many of them undone by the errors of the herd of uninitiated. But if you have not heard of the exile of Anaxagoras, nor the poison drunk by Socrates, nor the torture of Zeno, which all were of foreign lands, yet you may know of Canius, Seneca, and Soranus, whose fame is neither small nor passing old. Naught else brought them to ruin but that, being built up in my ways, they appeared at variance with the desires of unscrupulous men. So it is no matter for your wonder if, in this sea of life, we are tossed about by storms from all sides; for to oppose evil men is the chief aim we set before ourselves. Though the band of such men is great in numbers, yet is it to be contemned; for it is guided by no leader, but is hurried along at random only by error running riot everywhere. If this band when warring against us presses too strongly upon us, our leader, Reason, gathers her forces into her citadel, while the enemy are busied in plundering useless baggage. As they seize the most worthless things, we laugh at them from above, untroubled by the whole band of mad marauders, and we are defended by that rampart to which riotous folly may not hope to attain.

[Met. IV] "He who has calmly reconciled his life to fate, and set proud death beneath his feet, can look fortune in the face, unbending both to good and bad: his countenance unconquered he can shew. The rage and threatenings of the sea will not move him though they stir from its depths the upheaving swell. Vesuvius's furnaces may never so often burst forth, and he may send rolling upwards smoke and fire; the lightning, whose wont it is to smite down lofty towers, may flash upon its way, but such men shall they never move. Why then stand they wretched and aghast when fierce tyrants rage in impotence? Fear naught, and hope naught; thus shall you have a weak man's rage disarmed. But whoso fears with trembling, or desires aught from them, he stands not firmly rooted, but dependent. Thus has he thrown away his shield. He can be rooted up, and he links for himself the very chain whereby he may be dragged.

[Prose IV] "Are such your experiences, and do they sink into your soul?" she asked. "Do you listen only as 'the dull ass to the lyre'? Why do you weep? Wherefore flow your tears? 'Speak, nor keep secret in thine heart.' If you expect a physician to help you, you must lay bare your wound."

Then did I rally my spirit till it was strong again, and answered, "Does the savage bitterness of my fortune still need recounting? does it not stand forth plainly enough of itself? Does not the very aspect of this place strike you? Is this the library which you had chosen for yourself as your sure resting-place in my house? Is this the room in which you would so often tarry with me expounding the philosophy of things human and divine? Was my condition like this, or my countenance, when I probed with your aid the secrets of nature, when you marked out with a wand the courses of the stars, when you shaped our habits and the rule of all our life by the pattern of the universe? Are these the rewards we reap by yielding ourselves to you? Nay, you yourself have established this saying by the mouth of Plato, that commonwealths would be blessed if they were guided by those who made wisdom their study, or if those who guided them would make wisdom their study. By the mouth of that same great man did you teach that this was the binding reason why a commonwealth should be governed by philosophers, namely that the helm of government should not be left to unscrupulous or criminal citizens lest they should bring corruption and ruin upon the good citizens. Since, then, I had learned from you in quiet and inaction of this view, I followed it further, for I desired to practise it in public government. You and God Himself, who has grafted you in the minds of philosophers, are my witnesses that never have I applied myself to any office of state except that I might work for the common welfare of all good men. Thence followed bitter quarrels with evil men which could not be appeased, and, for the sake of preserving justice, contempt of the enmity of those in power, for this is the result of a free and fearless conscience. How often have I withstood Conigastus to his face, whenever he has attacked a weak man's fortune! How often have I turned by force Trigulla, the overseer of the Emperor's household, from an unjust act that he had begun or even carried out! How many times have I put my own authority in danger by protecting those wretched people who were harried with unending false charges by the greed of barbarian Goths which ever went unpunished! Never, I say, has any man depraved me from justice to injustice. My heart has ached as bitterly as those of the sufferers when I have seen the fortunes of our subjects ruined both by the rapacity of persons and the taxes of the state. Again, in a time of severe famine, a grievous, intolerable sale by compulsion was decreed in Campania, and devastation threatened that province. Then I undertook for the sake of the common welfare a struggle against the commander of the imperial guard; though the king was aware of it, I fought against the enforcement of the sale, and fought successfully. Paulinus was a man who had been consul: the jackals of the court had in their own hopes and desires already swallowed up his possessions, but I snatched him from their very gaping jaws. I exposed myself to the hatred of the treacherous informer Cyprian, that I might prevent Albinus, also a former consul, being overwhelmed by the penalty of a trumped-up charge. Think you that I have raised up against myself bitter and great quarrels enough? But I ought to have been safer among those whom I helped; for, from my love of justice, I laid up for myself among the courtiers no resource to which I might turn for safety. Who, further, were the informers upon whose evidence I was banished? One was Basilius: he was formerly expelled from the royal service, and was driven by debt to inform against me. Again, Opilio and Gaudentius had been condemned to exile by the king for many unjust acts and crimes: this decree they would not obey, and they sought sanctuary in sacred buildings, but when the king was aware of it, he declared that if they departed not from Ravenna before a certain day, they should be driven forth branded upon their foreheads. What could be more stringent than this? Yet upon that very day information against me was laid by these same men and accepted. Why so? Did my character deserve this treatment? Or did my prearranged condemnation give credit and justification to my accusers? Did Fortune feel no shame for this? If not for innocence calumniated, at any rate for the baseness of the calumniators?

"Would you learn the sum of the charges against me? It was said that 'I had desired the safety of the Senate.' You would learn in what way. I was charged with 'having hindered an informer from producing papers by which the Senate could be accused of treason.' What think you, my mistress? Shall I deny it lest it shame you? Nay, I did desire the safety of the Senate, nor shall ever cease to desire it. Shall I confess it? Then there would have been no need to hinder an informer. Shall I call it a crime to have wished for the safety of that order? By its own decrees concerning myself it has established that this is a crime. Though want of foresight often deceives itself, it cannot alter the merits of facts, and, in obedience to the Senate's command, I cannot think it right to hide the truth or to assent to falsehood.

"However, I leave it to your judgment and that of philosophers to decide how the justice of this may be; but I have committed to writing for history the true course of events, that posterity may not be ignorant thereof. I think it unnecessary to speak of the forged letters through which I am accused of 'hoping for the freedom of Rome.' Their falsity would have been apparent if I had been free to question the evidence of the informers themselves, for their confessions have much force in all such business.

"But what avails it? No liberty is left to hope for. Would there were any! I would answer in the words of Canius, who was accused by Gaius Caesar, Germanicus's son, of being cognisant of a plot against himself: 'If I had known of it, you would not have.'

"And in this matter grief has not so blunted my powers that I should complain of wicked men making impious attacks upon virtue; but at this I do wonder, that they should hope to succeed. Evil desires are, it may be, due to our natural failings, but that the conceptions of any wicked mind should prevail against innocence while God watches over us, seems to me unnatural. Wherefore not without cause has one of your own followers asked, 'If God is, whence come evil things? If He is not, whence come good?'

"Again, let impious men, who thirst for the blood of the whole Senate and of all good citizens, be allowed to wish for the ruin of us too whom they recognise as champions of the Senate and all good citizens. But surely such as I have not deserved the same hatred from the members of the Senate too?

"Since you were always present to guide me in my words and my deeds, I think you remember what happened at Verona. When King Theodoric, desiring the common ruin of the Senate, was for extending to the whole order the charge of treason laid against Albinus, you remember how I laboured to defend the innocence of the order without any care for my own danger? You know that I declare this truthfully and with no boasting praise of self. For the secret value of a conscience, that approves its own action, is lessened somewhat each time that it receives the reward of fame by displaying its deeds. But you see what end has fallen upon my innocency. In the place of the rewards of honest virtue, I am suffering the punishments of an ill deed that was not mine. And did ever any direct confession of a crime find its judges so well agreed upon exercising harshness, that neither the liability of the human heart to err, nor the changeableness of the fortune of all mankind, could yield one dissentient voice? If it had been said that I had wished to burn down temples, to murder with sacrilegious sword their priests, that I had planned the massacre of all good citizens, even so I should have been present to plead guilty or to be convicted, before the sentence was executed. But here am I, nearly five hundred miles away, without the opportunity of defending myself, condemned to death and the confiscation of my property because of my too great zeal for the Senate. Ah! well have they deserved that none should ever be liable to be convicted on such a charge! Even those who laid information have seen the honour of this accusation, for, that they might blacken it with some criminal ingredient, they had need to lie, saying that I had violated my conscience by using unholy means to obtain offices corruptly. But you, by being planted within me, dispelled from the chamber of my soul all craving for that which perishes, and where your eyes were looking there could be no place for any such sacrilege. For you instilled into my ears, and thus into my daily thoughts, that saying of Pythagoras, 'Follow after God.' Nor was it seemly that I, whom you had built up to such excellence that you made me as a god, should seek the support of the basest wills of men. Yet, further, the innocent life within my home, my gathering of most honourable friends, my father-in-law Symmachus, a man esteemed no less in his public life than for his private conscientiousness, these all put far from me all suspicion of this crime. But — O the shame of it! — it is from you that they think they derive the warrant for such a charge, and we seem to them to be allied to ill-doing from this very fact that we are steeped in the principles of your teaching and trained in your manners of life. Thus it is not enough that my deep respect for you has profited me nothing, but you yourself have received wanton contumely from the hatred that had rather fallen on me. Yet besides this, is another load added to my heap of woes: the judgment of the world looks not to the deserts of the case, but to the evolution of chance, and holds that only this has been intended which good fortune may chance to foster; whence it comes that the good opinion of the world is the first to desert the unfortunate. It is wearisome to recall what were the tales by the people told, or how little their many various opinions agreed. This alone I would fain say: it is the last burden laid upon us by unkind fortune, that when any charge is invented to be fastened upon unhappy men, they are believed to have deserved all they have to bear. For kindness I have received persecutions; I have been driven from all my possessions, stripped of my honours, and stained for ever in my reputation. I think I see the intoxication of joy in the sin-steeped dens of criminals; I see the most abandoned of men intent upon new and evil schemes of spying; I see honest men lying crushed with the fear which smites them after the result of my perilous case; wicked men one and all encouraged to dare every crime without fear of punishment, nay, with hope of rewards for the accomplishment thereof. The innocent I see robbed not merely of their peace and safety, but even of all chance of defending themselves. So then I may cry aloud: —

[Met. V] "Founder of the star-studded universe, resting on Thine eternal throne whence Thou turnest the swiftly rolling sky, and bindest the stars to keep Thy law; at Thy word the moon now shines brightly with full face, ever turned to her brother's light, and so she dims the lesser lights; or now she is herself obscured, for nearer to the sun her beams shew her pale horns alone. Cool rises the evening star at night's first drawing nigh; the same is the morning star who casts off the harness that she bore before, and paling meets the rising sun. When winter's cold doth strip the trees, Thou settest a shorter span to day. And Thou, when summer comes to warm, dost change the short divisions of the night. Thy power doth order the seasons of the year, so that the western breeze of spring brings back the leaves which winter's north wind tore away; so that the dog-star's heat makes ripe the ears of corn whose seed Arcturus watched. Naught breaks that ancient law; naught leaves undone the work appointed to its place. Thus all things Thou dost rule with limits fixed. The lives of men alone dost Thou scorn to restrain, as a guardian, within bounds. For why does Fortune with her fickle hand deal out such changing lots? The hurtful penalty is due to crime, but falls upon the sinless head: depraved men rest at ease on thrones aloft, and by their unjust lot can spurn beneath their hurtful heel the necks of virtuous men. Beneath obscuring shadows lies bright virtue hid: the just man bears the unjust's infamy. They suffer not for forsworn oaths, they suffer not for crimes glozed over with their lies. But when their will is to put forth their strength, with triumph they subdue the mightiest kings whom peoples in their thousands fear. O Thou who dost weave the bonds of Nature's self, look down upon this pitiable earth! Mankind is no base part of this great work, and we are tossed on Fortune's wave. Restrain, our Guardian, the engulfing surge, and as Thou dost the unbounded heaven rule, with a like bond make true and firm these lands."

[Prose V] While I grieved thus in long-drawn pratings, Philosophy looked on with a calm countenance, not one whit moved by my complaints. Then said she, "When I saw you in grief and in tears I knew thereby that you were unhappy and in exile, but I knew not how distant was your exile until your speech declared it. But you have not been driven so far from your home; you have wandered thence yourself. Or if you would rather hold that you have been driven, you have been driven by yourself rather than by any other. No other could have done so to you. For if you recall your true native country, you know that it is not under the rule of the many-headed people, as was Athens of old, but there is one Lord, one King, who rejoices in the greater number of his subjects, not in their banishment. To be guided by his reins, to bow to his justice, is the highest liberty. Know you not that sacred and ancient law of your own state by which it is enacted that no man who would establish a dwelling-place for himself therein may lawfully be put forth? For there is no fear that any man should merit exile, if he be kept safe therein by its protecting walls. But any man that may no longer wish to dwell there does equally no longer deserve to be there. Wherefore it is your looks rather than the aspect of this place which disturb me. It is not the walls of your library, decked with ivory and glass, that I need, but rather the resting-place in your heart, wherein I have not stored books, but I have of old put that which gives value to books, a store of thoughts from books of mine. As to your services to the common weal, you have spoken truly, though but scantily, if you consider your manifold exertions. Of all wherewith you have been charged either truthfully or falsely, you have but recorded what is well known. As for the crimes and wicked lies of the informers, you have rightly thought fit to touch but shortly thereon, for they are better and more fruitfully made common in the mouth of the crowd that discusses all matters. You have loudly and strongly upbraided the unjust ingratitude of the Senate; you have grieved over the charges made against myself, and shed tears over the insult to my fair fame; your last outburst of wrath was against Fortune, when you complained that she paid no fair rewards according to deserts; finally, you have prayed with passionate Muse that the same peace and order that are seen in the heavens might also rule the earth. But you are overwhelmed by this variety of mutinous passions: grief, rage, and gloom tear your mind asunder; and so in this present mood stronger measures cannot yet come nigh to heal you. Let us therefore use gentler means, and since, just as matter in the body hardens into a swelling, so have these disquieting influences, let these means soften by kindly handling the unhealthy spot, until it will bear a sharper remedy.

[Met. VI] "When the sign of the crab doth scorch the field, fraught with the sun's most grievous rays, the husbandman that has freely intrusted his seed to the fruitless furrow, is cheated by the faithless harvest-goddess; and he must turn him to the oak tree's fruit.

"When the field is scarred by the bleak north winds, wouldst thou seek the wood's dark carpet to gather violets? If thou wilt enjoy the grapes, wouldst thou seek with clutching hand to prune the vines in spring? 'Tis in autumn Bacchus brings his gifts. Thus God marks out the times and fits to them peculiar works: He has set out a course of change, and lets no confusion come. If aught betake itself to headlong ways, and leaves its sure design, ill will the outcome be thereto.

[Prose VI] "First then," she continued, "will you let me find out and make trial of the state of your mind by a few small questions, that so I may understand what should be the method of your treatment?"

"Ask," said I, "what your judgment would have you ask, and I will answer you."

Then said she, "Think you that this universe is guided only at random and by mere chance? or think you there is any rule of reason constituted in it?"

"No, never would I think it could be so, nor believe that such sure motions could be made at random or by chance. I know that God, the founder of the universe, does overlook His work; nor ever may that day come which shall drive me to abandon this belief as untrue."

"So is it," she said, "and even so you cried just now, and only mourned that mankind alone has no part in this divine guardianship. You were fixed in your belief that all other things are ruled by reason. Yet, how strange! how much I wonder how it is that you can be so sick though you are set in such a health-giving state of mind! But let us look deeper into it; I cannot but think there is something lacking. Since you are not in doubt that the universe is ruled by God, tell me by what method you think that government is guided?"

"I scarcely know the meaning of your question; much less can I answer it."

"Was I wrong," said she, "to think that something was lacking, that there was some opening in your armour, some way by which this distracting disease has crept into your soul? But tell me, do you remember what is the aim and end of all things? what the object to which all nature tends?"

"I have heard indeed, but grief has blunted my memory."

"But do you not somehow know whence all things have their source?"

"Yes," I said; "that source is God."

"Is it possible that you, who know the beginning of all things, should not know their end? But such are the ways of these distractions, such is their power, that though they can move a man's position, they cannot pluck him from himself or wrench him from his roots. But this question would I have you answer: do you remember that you are a man?"

"How can I but remember that?"

"Can you then say what is a man?"

"Need you ask? I know that he is an animal, reasoning and mortal; that I know, and that I confess myself to be."

"Know you naught else that you are?" asked Philosophy.

"Naught," said I.

"Now," said she, "I know the cause, or the chief cause, of your sickness. You have forgotten what you are. Now therefore I have found out to the full the manner of your sickness, and how to attempt the restoring of your health. You are overwhelmed by this forgetfulness of yourself; hence you have been thus sorrowing that you are exiled and robbed of all your possessions. You do not know the aim and end of all things; hence you think that if men are worthless and wicked, they are powerful and fortunate. You have forgotten by what methods the universe is guided; hence you think that the chances of good and bad fortune are tossed about with no ruling hand. These things may lead not to disease only, but even to death as well. But let us thank the Giver of all health that your nature has not altogether left you. We have yet the chief spark for your health's fire, for you have a true knowledge of the hand that guides the universe: you do believe that its government is not subject to random chance, but to divine reason. Therefore have no fear. From this tiny spark the fire of life shall forthwith shine upon you. But it is not time to use severer remedies, and since we know that it is the way of all minds to clothe themselves ever in false opinions as they throw off the true, and these false ones breed a dark distraction which confuses the true insight, therefore will I try to lessen this darkness for a while with gentle applications of easy remedies, that so the shadows of deceiving passions may be dissipated, and you may have power to perceive the brightness of true light."

[Met. VII] "When the stars are hidden by black clouds, no light can they afford. When the boisterous south wind rolls along the sea and stirs the surge, the water, but now as clear as glass, bright as the fair sun's light, is dark, impenetrable to sight, with stirred and scattered sand. The stream, that wanders down the mountain's side, must often find a stumbling-block, a stone within its path torn from the hill's own rock. So too shalt thou: if thou wouldst see the truth in undimmed light, choose the straight road, the beaten path; away with passing joys! away with fear! put vain hopes to flight! and grant no place to grief! Where these distractions reign, the mind is clouded o'er, the soul is bound in chains.

[tr. W. V. COOPER]

# GREGORY THE GREAT

The sixth century witnessed the practical dissolution of the Roman Empire in the West. As Boethius prepared against the oncoming chaos by translating Greek philosophy, and Cassiodorus from his school at Vivarium taught monks to copy and to preserve manuscripts so that all knowledge would not perish, a third contemporary, Benedict of Nursia, founded a model monastery at Monte Cassino and not long thereafter wrote a *Rule* for monasteries that was destined to spread rapidly and to control the monastic establishments of all western Europe. The Romanesque period of the next six centuries may almost be known as the Benedictine period, for monasteries governed by his Rule were the centers of culture that acted not only as disseminators of the faith, hope, and charity so needed in a time of poverty and reorganization but as the revivers of education and culture in an age when schools and the arts had either fallen into ruin, as they had in the south, or had never existed, as in the northern lands of the Celts and the Teutons. Much of the development of monasticism was due to the wise and practical nature of Benedict's Rule, which united austerity with a human kindliness and firm government.

Beyond the Rule itself, nothing is known of St. Benedict except as stated in the *Life,* which forms Book II of the *Dialogues* of Pope Gregory the Great. Gregory, who came of good family, after the usual education for a civil career became *praetor urbanus* about A.D. 573; but when his father died and left him an ample inheritance, he used it to found seven monasteries, six in Sicily and one in his father's house in Rome. He advanced rapidly in the service of the Church and became Pope in 590 at a moment when the Lombards, the last and in many ways the fiercest of the migrant Teutons, were threatening the life of the city. Few men have been placed in so unenviable a position. The Emperor was far away in Constantinople and disinterested; his representative, the Exarch of Ravenna, was comparatively impotent. The Church, through gifts over more than two centuries, was the largest landowner in Italy and the hope of a populace weakened by starvation, plague, and war. Not only was Gregory's fourteen-year administration a model of its kind, but by his acts in forwarding monasticism, developing a school of music that was to influence not only the liturgy but the form of education throughout the West, and establishing a mission in England for converting the pagan English, he knit together the western Church which had previously been predominantly provincial.

In the course of this busy life he found time, despite painful ill-health, to write many works. His sermons were forceful, if not polished; his *Pastoral Care* became the manual for bishops; his *Moralia* directed the whole allegorizing tendency of western literature; and his *Letters,* numbering more than 800, settled many problems of ecclesiastical doctrine and rule. But it was his *Dialogues* that popularized the form of hagiology which was to become by steps not only the people's literature but also the romance which we now think of as characteristically medieval.

The *Dialogues,* published in four books in 594, represents Gregory himself as chief speaker at a moment of physical and spiritual weariness, being queried by his deacon Peter about the virtues and miracles (almost synonymous terms in this period) of the saints of Gregory's generation and before. Book II is devoted entirely to St. Benedict, the other books to a multitude of other saints. The tale is in the hagiological pattern popularized by Athanasius, Jerome, and others; its aim is exaltation and edification. Though it is hard to determine the relation of the historical St. Benedict to the hero of the *Dialogues,* there may be some elements of likeness.

The translation, which appeared in Paris in 1608 under the initials P.W., preserves in English an archaic flavor not unlike the archaisms that Gregory employed in the original. The book has been abridged.

# DIALOGUES

### Gregory the Great (A.D. 540–604)

[From *The Dialogues of Gregory,* translated by P. W., revised by Edmund G. Gardner; P. L. Warner, London, 1911. Reprinted by permission of the Medici Society, Ltd.]

#### BOOK II: BENEDICT OF NURSIA

There was a man of venerable life, blessed by grace and blessed in name, for he was called *Benedictus* or Bennet, who from his younger years carried always the mind of an old man; for his age was inferior to his virtue. All vain pleasure he contemned, and though he were in the world and might freely have enjoyed such commodities as it yieldeth, yet did he nothing esteem it nor the vanities thereof. He was born in the province of Nursia of honourable parentage and brought up at Rome in the study of humanity. But for as much as he saw many by reason of such learning to fall to dissolute and lewd life, he drew back his foot, which he had as it were now set forth into the world, lest, entering too far in acquaintance therewith, he likewise might have fallen into that dangerous and godless gulf. Wherefore, giving over his book and forsaking his father's house and wealth, with a resolute mind only to serve God, he sought for some place where he might attain to the desire of his holy purpose; and in this sort he departed, instructed with learned ignorance and furnished with unlearned wisdom. All the notable things and acts of his life I could not learn; but those few, which I mind now to report, I had by the relation of four of his disciples: to wit, of Constantinus, a most rare and reverent man, who was next Abbot after him; of Valentinianus, who many years had the charge of the Lateran Abbey; of Simplicius, who was the third General of his order; and lastly of Honoratus, who is now Abbot of that monastery in which he first began his holy life.

## CHAPTER I

### How he made a broken sieve whole and sound

Bennet having now given over the school with a resolute mind to lead his life in the wilderness, his nurse alone, who did tenderly love him, would not by any means give him over. Coming, therefore, to a place called Enside and remaining there in the church of St. Peter, in the company of other virtuous men which for charity lived in that place, it fell so out that his nurse borrowed of the neighbours a sieve to make clean wheat, which being left negligently upon the table, by chance it was broken in two pieces. Whereupon she fell pitifully a-weeping, because she had borrowed it. The devout and religious youth Bennet, seeing his nurse so lamenting, moved with compassion, took away with him both the pieces of the sieve and with tears fell to his prayers; and after he had done, rising up he found it so whole that the place could not be seen where before it was broken. And coming straight to his nurse and comforting her with good words, he delivered her the sieve safe and sound. Which miracle was known to all the inhabitants thereabout and so much admired that the townsmen for a perpetual memory did hang it up at the church door, to the end that not only men then living but also their posterity might understand how greatly God's grace did work with him upon his first renouncing of the world. The sieve continued there many years after, even to these very troubles of the Lombards, where it did hang over the church door.

But Bennet, desiring rather the miseries of the world than the praises of men, rather to be wearied with labour for God's sake than to be exalted with transitory commendation, fled privily from his nurse and went into a desert place called Sublacum, distant almost forty miles from Rome. In that place there was a fountain springing forth cool and clear water, the abundance whereof doth first in a broad place make a lake and afterward, running forward, cometh to be a river. As he was travelling to this place, a certain monk called Romanus met him and demanded whither he went; and understanding his purpose, he both kept it close, furthered him what he might, vested him with the habit of holy conversation, and as he could did minister and serve him.

The man of God, Bennet, coming to this foresaid place, lived there in a strait cave, where he continued three years unknown to all men except to Romanus, who lived not far off, under the rule of Abbot Theodacus, and very virtuously did steal certain hours, and likewise sometime a loaf given for his own provision, which he did carry to Bennet. And because from Romanus' cell to that cave there was not any way, by reason of an high rock which did hang over it, Romanus, from the top thereof, upon a long rope, did let down the loaf, upon which also with a band he tied a little bell, that by the ringing thereof the man of God might know when he came with his bread and so be ready to take it.  But the old enemy of mankind, envying at the charity of the one and the refection of the other, seeing a loaf upon a certain day let down, threw a stone and brake the bell; but yet, for all that, Romanus gave not over to serve him by all the possible means he could.

## CHAPTER II

### How he overcame a great temptation of the flesh

Upon a certain day when Bennet was alone, the tempter was at hand; for a little black bird, commonly called a merle or an ousel, began to fly about his face and that so near as the holy man, if he would, might have taken it with his hand.  But after he had blessed himself with the sign of the Cross, the bird flew away; and forthwith the holy man was assaulted with such a terrible temptation of the flesh as he never felt the like in all his life.  A certain woman there was which some time he had seen, the memory of which the wicked spirit put into his mind, and by the representation of her did so mightily inflame with concupiscence the soul of God's servant, which did so increase that, almost overcome with pleasure, he was of mind to have forsaken the wilderness.  But, suddenly assisted with God's grace, he came to himself and, seeing many thick briers and nettle-bushes to grow hard by, off he cast his apparel, and threw himself into the midst of them and there wallowed so long that, when he rose up, all his flesh was pitifully torn; and so by the wounds of his body he cured the wounds of his soul, in that he turned pleasure into pain and by the outward burning of extreme smart quenched that fire which, being nourished before with the fuel of carnal cogitations, did inwardly burn in his soul.  And by this means he overcame the sin because he made a change of the fire.  From which time forward, as himself did afterward report unto his disciples, he found all temptation of pleasure so subdued that he never felt any such thing.  Many after this began to abandon the world and to become his scholars; for being now freed from the vice of temptation, worthily and with great reason is he made a master of virtue.  For which cause in *Exodus* commandment is given by Moses that the Levites from five-and-twenty years and upward should serve but, after they came to fifty, that they should be ordained keepers of the holy vessels [Numbers VIII, 24–26].

PETER: Somewhat I understand of this testimony alleged; but yet I beseech you to tell me the meaning thereof more fully.

GREGORY: It is plain, Peter, that in youth the temptation of the flesh is hot; but after fifty years the heat of the body waxeth cold, and the souls of faithful people become holy vessels.  Wherefore necessary it is that God's elect servants, whiles they are yet in the

heat of temptation, should live in obedience, serve, and be wearied
with labour and pains. But when, by reason of age, the heat of
temptation is past, they become keepers of holy vessels; because they
then are made the doctors of men's souls.

PETER: I cannot deny but that your words have given me full
satisfaction. Wherefore, seeing you have now expounded the meaning of the former text alleged, prosecute, I pray, as you have begun,
the rest of the holy man's life.

CHAPTER III

### How Bennet, by the sign of the Holy Cross, brake a drinking-glass in pieces

GREGORY: When this great temptation was thus overcome, the
man of God, like unto a piece of ground well tilled and weeded, of
the seed of virtue brought forth plentiful store of fruit; and by reason
of the great report of his wonderful holy life, his name became very
famous. Not far from the place where he remained there was a
monastery, the Abbot whereof was dead. Whereupon the whole
convent came unto the venerable man Bennet, entreating him very
earnestly that he would vouchsafe to take upon him the charge and
government of their abbey. Long time he denied them, saying that
their manners were divers from his and therefore that they should
never agree together; yet at length, overcome with their entreaty,
he gave his consent. Having now taken upon him the charge of
the abbey, he took order that regular life should be observed so that
none of them could, as before they used, through unlawful acts
decline from the path of holy conversation either on the one side
or on the other. Which the monks perceiving, they fell into a great
rage, accusing themselves that ever they desired him to be their Abbot,
seeing their crooked conditions could not endure his virtuous kind
of government. And therefore when they saw that under him
they could not live in unlawful sort, and were loath to leave their
former conversation, and found it hard to be enforced with old
minds to meditate and think upon new things, and because the life
of virtuous men is always grievous to those that be of wicked conditions, some of them began to devise how they might rid him out
of the way. And therefore, taking counsel together, they agreed
to poison his wine. Which being done and the glass wherein that
wine was, according to the custom, offered to the Abbot to bless,
he, putting forth his hand, made the sign of the cross; and straightway the glass, that was holden far off, brake in pieces, as though the
sign of the Cross had been a stone thrown against it. Upon which
accident the man of God by and by perceived that the glass
had in it the drink of death, which could not endure the sign of
life; and therefore rising up, with a mild countenance and quiet
mind he called the monks together and spake thus unto them: "Almighty God have mercy upon you, and forgive you; why have you
used me in this manner? Did not I tell you beforehand that our

manner of living could never agree together? Go your ways and seek ye out some other father suitable to your own conditions, for I intend not now to stay any longer amongst you." When he had thus discharged himself, he returned back to the wilderness which so much he loved and dwelt alone with himself in the sight of his Creator, who beholdeth the hearts of all men.

PETER: I understand not very well what you mean when you say that he dwelt with himself.

GREGORY: If the holy man had longer, contrary to his own mind, continued his government over those monks, who had all conspired against him and were far unlike to him in life and conversation, perhaps he should have diminished his own devotion and somewhat withdrawn the eyes of his soul from the light of contemplation; and being wearied daily with correcting of their faults, he should have had the less care of himself, and so haply it might have fallen out that he should both have lost himself and yet not found them. For so often as by infectious motion we are carried too far from ourselves, we remain the same men that we were before, and yet be not with ourselves as we were before because we are wondering about other men's affairs, little considering and looking into the state of our own soul. For shall we say that he was with himself who went into a far country and after he had, as we read in the Gospel, prodigally spent that portion which he received of his father, was glad to serve a citizen, to keep his hogs, and would willingly have filled his hungry belly with the husks which they did eat? Who notwithstanding afterward, when he thought with himself of those goods which he had lost, it is written of him that, returning into himself, he said: "How many hired men in my father's house do abound with bread?" If then, before he were with himself, from whence did he return home unto himself? And therefore I said that this venerable man did dwell with himself, because carrying himself circumspectly and carefully in the sight of his Creator, always considering his own actions, always examining himself, never did he turn the eyes of his soul from himself to behold aught else whatsoever.

PETER: Your discourse doth very well content me. Yet I beseech you to answer me this question, whether he could in conscience give over those monks whose government he had now taken upon him?

GREGORY: In mine opinion, Peter, evil men may with good conscience be tolerated in that community where there be some good that may be holpen and reap commodity. But where there be none good at all that may receive spiritual profit, oftentimes all labour is lost that is bestowed in bringing of such to good order, especially if other occasions be offered of doing God presently better service elsewhere. For whose good, then, should the holy man have expected, seeing them all to persecute him with one consent? And (that which is not to be passed over with silence) those that be perfect carry always this mind, that when they perceive their labour to be fruitless in one place, to remove straight to another where more good may be done. And for this cause that notable preacher of the world, who was desirous to be dissolved and to be with Christ, *unto whom to live is Christ, and to die is gain* [Phil. 1, 21], and who not only desired himself to suffer persecution but did also animate and encourage others to suffer the same, yet being himself in persecution at Damascus, got a rope and a basket to pass over the wall and was privily let down. What then? Shall we say that Paul was afraid of death, when as himself said, that he desired it for Christ's sake? Not so. But when he perceived that in that place little good was to be done by great labour, he reserved himself to further labour, where more fruit and better success might be expected, and therefore the valiant soldier of Christ would not be kept within walls, but sought for a larger field where he might more freely labour for his master. And so, in like manner, you shall quickly perceive, if you mark well, that venerable Bennet forsook not so many in one place that were unwilling to be taught as he did in sundry other places raise up from the death of soul many more that were willing to be instructed.

PETER: It is so as you say and plain reason teacheth it and the example of St. Paul alleged doth confirm it. But I beseech you to return unto your former purpose and to prosecute the life of the holy man.

GREGORY: When as God's servant daily increased in virtue and became continually more famous for miracles, many were by him in the same place drawn to the service of almighty God, so that by Christ's assistance he built there twelve abbeys over which he appointed governors, and in each of them placed twelve monks; and a few he kept with himself, namely, such as he thought would more profit and be better instructed by his own presence. At that time also many noble and religious men of Rome came unto him and committed their children to be brought up under him for the service of God. Then also Evitius delivered him Maurus, and Tertullius the Senator brought Placidus, being their sons of great hope and towardness. Of which two, Maurus, growing to great virtue, began to be his master's co-adjutor; but Placidus as yet was but a boy of tender years.

CHAPTER IV

*How Bennet reformed a monk that would not stay at his prayers*

In one of the monasteries which he had built in those parts, a monk there was who could not continue at prayers; for when the other monks knelt down to serve God, his manner was to go forth and there with wandering mind to busy himself about some earthly and transitory things. And when he had been often by his abbot admonished of this fault without any amendment, at length he was sent to the man of God, who did likewise very much rebuke him for his folly. Yet notwithstanding, returning back again, he did scarce two days follow the holy man's admonition; for upon the third day he fell again to his old custom and would not abide within at the time of prayer. Word whereof being once more sent to the man of God by the father of the abbey whom he had there appointed, he returned him answer that he would come himself and reform what was amiss, which he did accordingly. And it fell so out that when the singing of psalms was ended and the hour come in which the monks betook themselves to prayer, the holy man perceived that the monk which used at that time to go forth was by a little black boy drawn out by the skirt of his garment; upon which sight he spake secretly to Pompeianus, father of the abbey, and also to Maurus, saying: "Do you not see who it is that draweth this monk from his prayers?" And they answered him that they did not. "Then let us pray," quoth he, "unto God, that you also may behold whom this monk doth follow." And after two days Maurus did see him, but Pompeianus could not. Upon another day, when the man of God had ended his devotions, he went out of the oratory, where he found the foresaid monk standing idle, whom for the blindness of his heart he strake with a little wand, and from that day forward he was so freed from all allurement of the little black boy that he remained quietly at his prayers as other of the monks did. For the old enemy was so terrified that he durst not any more suggest any such cogitations, as though by that blow not the monk but himself had been strooken.

CHAPTER VIII

*[Of the destruction of the Altar of Apollo]*

PETER: To what places, I pray you, after this did the holy man go, and whether did he afterward in them work any miracles or no?

GREGORY: The holy man, changing his place, did not for all that change his enemy. For afterward he endured so much the more grievous battles, by how much he had now the master of all wickedness fighting openly against him. For the town which is called Cassino standeth upon the side of an high mountain, which containeth as it were in the lap thereof the foresaid town and afterward so riseth in height the space of three miles that the top thereof seemeth to touch the very heavens. In this place there was an ancient chapel in which the foolish and simple country people, according to the custom of the old gentiles, worshipped the god Apollo. Round about it likewise upon all sides there were woods for the service of the devils, in which, even to that very time, the mad multitude of infidels did offer most wicked sacrifice. The man of God, coming thither, beat in pieces the idol, overthrew the altar, set fire on the woods, and in the temple of Apollo he built the oratory of St. Martin, and where the altar of the same Apollo was he made an oratory of St. John. And by his continual preaching he brought the people dwelling in those parts to embrace the faith of Christ. The old enemy of man-kind, not taking this in good part, did not now privily or in a dream but in open sight present himself to the eyes of that holy father, and with great outcries complained that he had offered him violence. The noise which he made the monks did hear, but himself they could not see; but, as the venerable father told them, he appeared visibly unto him most fell and cruel and as though, with his fiery mouth and flaming eyes, he would have torn him in pieces. What the devil said unto him, all the monks did hear; for first he would call him by his name, and because the man of God vouchsafed him not any answer, then would he fall a-reviling and railing at him: for when he cried out, calling him "Blessed Bennet," and yet found that he gave him no answer, straightways he would turn his tune and say: "Cursed Bennet and not blessed, what hast thou to do with me? And why dost thou thus persecute me?" Wherefore new battles of the old enemy against the servant of God are to be looked for, against whom willingly did he make war, but, against his will, did he give him occasion of many notable victories.

CHAPTER XI

*How Venerable Bennet revived a boy, crushed to death with the ruin of a wall*

Again, as the monks were making a certain wall somewhat higher because that was requisite, the man of God in the meantime was in his cell at his prayers. To whom the old enemy appeared in an in-sulting manner, telling him that he was now going to his monks that were a-working. Whereof the man of God in all haste gave them warning, wishing them to look unto themselves, because the devil was at that time coming amongst them. The message was scarce delivered when as the wicked spirit overthrew the new wall which they were a-building, and with the fall slew a little young child, a monk, who was the son of a certain courtier. At which pitiful chance all were passing sorry and exceedingly grieved, not so much for the loss of the wall as for the death of their brother; and in all haste they sent this heavy news to the venerable man Bennet, who commanded them to bring unto him the young boy, mangled and maimed as he was, which they did, but yet they could not carry him any otherwise than in a sack, for the stones of the wall had not only broken his limbs but also his very bones. Being in that manner brought unto the man of God, he bade them to lay him in his cell and in that place upon which he used to pray; and then, putting them all forth, he shut the door and fell more instantly to his prayers than he used at other times. And O strange miracle! for the very same hour he made him sound and as lively as ever he was before, and sent him again to his former work that he also might help the monks to make an end of that wall, of whose death the old serpent thought he should have insulted over Bennet and greatly triumphed.

CHAPTER XII

*How by revelation Venerable Bennet knew that his monks had*
*eaten out of the monastery*

Among other miracles which the man of God did, he began also
to be famous for the spirit of prophecy, as to foretell what was to
happen and to relate unto them that were present such things as
were done in absence. The order of his abbey was that when the
monks went abroad to deliver any message never to eat or drink
anything out of their cloister. And this being diligently observed
according to the prescription of their rule, upon a certain day some
of the monks went forth upon such business, and being enforced
about the dispatch thereof to tarry somewhat long abroad, it fell so
out that they stayed at the house of a religious woman, where they
did eat and refresh themselves. And being late before they came
back to the abbey, they went as the manner was and asked their
father's blessing. Of whom he demanded where they had eaten;
and they said nowhere. "Why do you," quoth he, "tell an untruth?
For did you not go into such a woman's house and eat such and such
kind of meat and drink so many cups?" When they heard him
recount so in particular both where they had stayed, what kind of
meat they had eaten, and how often they had drunk, and perceived
well that he knew all whatsoever they had done, they fell down
trembling at his feet and confessed that they had done wickedly. He
straightways pardoned them for that fault, persuading himself that
they would not any more in his absence presume to do any such
thing, seeing they now perceived that he was present with them in
spirit.

CHAPTER XIV

*How the dissimulation of King Totilas was discovered and*
*found out by Venerable Bennet*

GREGORY: In the time of the Goths, when Totilas their king understood that the holy man had the spirit of prophecy, as he was going
towards his monastery, he remained in a place somewhat far off,
and beforehand sent the father word of his coming; to whom answer
was returned that he might come at his pleasure. The king, as
he was a man wickedly disposed, thought he would try whether the
man of God were a prophet as it was reported or no. A certain man
of his guard he had called Riggo, upon whom he caused his own
shoes to be put and to be apparelled with his other princely robes,
commanding him to go as it were himself to the man of God; and
to give the better colour to this device, he sent three to attend upon
him, who especially were always about the king: to wit, Vultericus,
Rudericus, and Blindinus; charging them that in the presence of
the servant of God they should be next about him and behave themselves in such sort as though he had been king Totilas indeed, and
that diligently they should do unto him all other services to the end

that both by such dutiful kind of behaviour as also by his purple robes, he might verily be taken for the king himself. Riggo, furnished with that brave apparel and accompanied with many courtiers, came unto the abbey; at which time the man of God sat a little way off, and when Riggo was come so near that he might well understand what the man of God said, then, in the hearing of them all, he spake thus: "Put off, my good son, put off that apparel, for that which thou hast on is none of thine." Riggo, hearing this, fell straightways down to the ground and was very much afraid for presuming to go about to mock so worthy a man, and all his attendants and servitors fell down likewise to the earth, and after they were up again they durst not approach any nearer to his presence, but returned back to their king, telling him with fear how quickly they were discovered.

## CHAPTER XV

*How Venerable Bennet prophesied to King Totilas, and also to the Bishop of Camisina, such things as were afterward to fall out*

Then Totilas himself in person went unto the man of God; and seeing him sitting afar off, he durst not come near, but fell down to the ground. Whom the holy man (speaking to him twice or thrice) desired to rise up, and at length came unto him and with his own hands lifted him up from the earth, where he lay prostrate; and then, entering into talk, he reprehended him for his wicked deeds and in few words told him all that which should befall him, saying: "Much wickedness do you daily commit and many great sins have you done; now at length give over your sinful life. Into the city of Rome shall you enter and over the sea shall you pass; nine years shall you reign and in the tenth shall you leave this mortal life." The king, hearing these things, was wonderfully afraid, and desiring the holy man to commend him to God in his prayers, he departed; and from that time forward he was nothing so cruel as before he had been. Not long after, he went to Rome, sailed over into Sicily, and, in the tenth year of his reign, he lost his kingdom together with his life.

The Bishop also of Camisina used to visit the servant of God, whom the holy man dearly loved for his virtuous life. The Bishop, therefore, talking with him of king Totilas, of his taking of Rome, and the destruction of that city, said: "This city will be so spoiled and ruined by him that it will never be more inhabited." To whom the man of God answered: "Rome," quoth he, "shall not be utterly destroyed by strangers, but shall be so shaken with tempests, lightnings, whirlwinds, and earthquakes, that it will fall to decay of itself." The mysteries of which prophecy we now behold as clear as the day. For we see before our eyes in this very city, by a strange whirlwind the world shaken, houses ruined, and churches overthrown; and buildings rotten with old age we behold daily to fall down. True it is that Honoratus, by whose relation I had this, saith not that he received it from his own mouth but that he had it of other monks which did hear it themselves.

## CHAPTER XVI

### Of a certain clergyman, whom Venerable Bennet for a time delivered from a devil

At the same time a certain clergyman that served in the church of Aquinum was possessed, whom the venerable man Constantius, Bishop of the same city, sent unto many places of holy martyrs for help; but God's holy martyrs would not deliver him, to the end that the world might know what great grace was in the servant of God, Bennet. Wherefore at length he was brought unto him, who praying for help to Jesus Christ our Lord, did forthwith cast the old enemy out of the possessed man's body, giving him this charge: "Go your way, and hereafter abstain from eating of flesh and presume not to enter into holy orders, for whensover you shall attempt any such thing the devil again will have power over you." The man departed safe and sound, and because punishment fresh in memory useth to terrify the mind, he observed for a time what the man of God had given him in commandment. But after many years when all his seniors were dead and he saw his juniors preferred before him to holy orders, he neglected the words of the man of God, as though forgotten through length of time, and took upon him holy orders. Whereupon straightways the devil that before had left him entered again and never gave over to torment him until he had separated his soul from his body.

PETER: This holy man, as I perceive, did know the secret counsel of God; for he saw that this clergyman was delivered to the power of the devil, to the end he should not presume to enter into holy orders.

GREGORY: Why should he not know the secrets of God, who kept the commandments of God, when as the Scripture saith: "He that cleaveth unto our Lord is one spirit with him"? [I Cor. VI, 17.]

PETER: If he that cleaveth unto our Lord be one spirit with our Lord, what is the meaning of that which the Apostle saith: "Who knowth the sense of our Lord, or who hath been his counsellor?" [Rom. XI, 34]; for it seemeth very inconvenient to be ignorant of his sense, to whom being so united he is made one thing.

GREGORY: Holy men, in that they be one with our Lord, are not ignorant of his sense; for the same Apostle saith [I Cor. II, 11]: "For what man knoweth those things which belong to man, but the spirit of man which is in him? Even so, the things which belong to God, no man knoweth, but the spirit of God." And to show also that he knew such things as belong to God, he addeth straight after: "But we have not received the spirit of this world, but the spirit which is of God." And for this cause, again he saith: "That eye hath not seen, nor ear heard, nor it hath ascended into the heart of man, those things which God hath prepared for them that love him, but God hath revealed to us by his spirit" [II, 9–10].

PETER: If, then, the mysteries of God were revealed to the same Apostle by the spirit of God, why did he then, entreating of this question, set down these words beforehand, saying: "O the depth of the riches of the wisdom and knowledge of God: how incomprehensible be his judgments and his ways investigable"? [Rom. XI, 33.] And again, whiles I am thus speaking of this matter another question cometh to my mind; for the prophet David said to our Lord: "With my lips have I uttered all the judgments of thy mouth" [Ps. CXIX, 13]. Wherefore, seeing it is less to know than to utter, what is the reason that St. Paul affirmeth the judgments of God to be incomprehensible; and yet David saith that he did not only know them but also with his lips pronounce them?

GREGORY: To both these questions I have already briefly answered when I said that holy men, in that they be one with our Lord, are not ignorant of the sense of our Lord; for all such as do devoutly follow our Lord, be also by devotion one with our Lord. And yet for all this, in that they are laden with the burthen of their corruptible flesh, they be not with God. And so in that they be joined with him, they know the secret judgments of God, and in that they be separated from God, they know them not; for seeing they do not as yet perfectly penetrate his secret mysteries, they give testimony that his judgments be incomprehensible. But those that do with their soul adhere unto him and cleaving unto the sayings of the Holy Scripture or to secret revelations acknowledge what they receive, such persons both know these things and do utter them; for those judgments which God doth conceal they know not, and those which he doth utter they know. And therefore the prophet David, when he had said, "I have with my lips uttered all the judgments," he addeth immediately, "of thy mouth"; as though he should plainly say: Those judgments I may both know and utter, which I knew Thou didst speak, for those things which Thou dost not speak, without all question Thou dost conceal from our knowledge. Wherefore the saying of David and St. Paul agree together, for the judgments of God are incomprehensible, and yet those which Himself with His own mouth vouchsafeth to speak are uttered with men's tongues; because men may come to the knowledge of them, and being revealed, they may be uttered and by no means can be kept secret.

PETER: Now I see the answer to my question. But I pray you to proceed, if anything yet remaineth to be told of his virtue and miracles.

CHAPTER XVII

*How the Man of God Bennet did foretell the suppression of one of his own abbeys*

GREGORY: A certain noble man called Theoprobus was by the good counsel of holy Bennet converted, who, for his virtue and merit of life, was very intrinsical and familiar with him. This man upon a day, coming into his cell, found him weeping very bitterly. And having expected a good while and yet not seeing him to make an end (for the man of God used not in his prayers to weep but rather to be sad), he demanded the cause of that his so great heaviness; to whom he answered straightway, saying: "All this abbey which I have built and all such things as I have made ready for my brethren are by the judgment of almighty God delivered to the gentiles, to be spoiled and overthrown; and scarce could I obtain of God to have their lives spared that should then live in it." His words Theoprobus then heard, but we see them to be proved most true, who know that very abbey to be now suppressed by the Lombards. For not long since in the night time when the monks were asleep, they entered in and spoiled all things, but yet not one man could they retain there. And so almighty God fulfilled what he promised to his faithful servant; for though he gave them the house and all the goods, yet did he preserve their lives. In which thing I see that Bennet imitated St. Paul, whose ship [Acts xxvii, 22–44] though it lost all the goods, yet, for his comfort, he had the lives of all that were in his company bestowed upon him so that no one man was cast away.

CHAPTER XVIII

*How Blessed Bennet knew the hiding away of a flagon of wine*

Upon a certain time, Exhilaratus our monk, a lay-brother whom you know, was sent by his master to the monastery of the man of God to carry him two wooden bottles, commonly called flagons, full of wine; who in the way, as he was going, hid one of them in a bush for himself and presented the other to venerable Bennet, who took it very thankfully. When the man was going away, he gave him this warning: "Take heed, my son," quoth he, "that thou drinkest not of that flagon which thou hast hidden in the bush; but first be careful to bow it down, and thou shalt find what is within it." The poor man, thus pitifully confounded by the man of God, went his way, and coming back to the place where the flagon was hidden, and desirous to try the truth of what was told him, as he was bowing it down, a snake straightways leaped forth. Then Exhilaratus, perceiving what was gotten into the wine, began to be afraid of that wickedness which he had committed.

CHAPTER XXI

*[Of the appearance of the spirit of prophecy]*

PETER: Tell me, I pray you, whether this servant of God had always the spirit of prophecy when himself pleased or only at certain times?

GREGORY: The spirit of prophecy doth not always illuminate the minds of the prophets; because, as it is written of the Holy Ghost that *he breatheth where he will* [John iii, 8], so we are also to know that he doth breathe likewise for what cause and when he pleaseth. And hereof it cometh that when king David demanded of Nathan [I Chr. xvii, 2–4] whether he might build a temple for the honour of God, the prophet Nathan gave his consent; and yet afterward utterly forbade it. From hence likewise it proceedeth that, when Heliseus saw the woman weeping and knew not the cause, he said to his servant that did trouble her: "Let her alone, for her soul is in grief, and God hath concealed it from me and hath not told me" [II Kings IV, 27]. Which thing almighty God of great piety so disposeth; for giving at some times the spirit of prophecy and at other times withdrawing it, he doth both lift up the prophets' minds on high and yet doth preserve them in humility, that by the gift of the Spirit they may know what they are by God's grace, and at other times, destitute of the same Spirit, may understand what they are of themselves.

PETER: There is very great reason for what you say. But, I pray you, let me hear more of the venerable man Bennet, if there be anything else that cometh to your remembrance.

CHAPTER XXII

*How by vision Venerable Bennet disposed the building of the Abbey of Taracina*

GREGORY: At another time he was desired by a certain virtuous man to build an abbey for his monks upon his ground not far from the city of Taracina. The holy man was content and appointed an abbot and prior, with divers monks under them. And when they were departing, he promised that, upon such a day, he would come and shew them in what place the oratory should be made and where the refectory should stand and all the other necessary rooms. And so they, taking his blessing, went their way; and against the day appointed, which they greatly expected, they made all such things ready as were necessary to entertain him and those that should come in his company. But the very night before, the man of God in sleep appeared to the abbot and the prior, and particularly described unto them where each place and office was to be builded. And when they were both risen, they conferred together what either of them had seen in their sleep; but yet not giving full credit to that vision, they expected the man of God himself in person, according to his promise.

But when they saw that he came not, they returned back unto him very sorrowfully, saying: "We expected, father, that you should have come according to promise and told us where each place should have been built, which yet you did not." To whom he answered: "Why say you so, good brethren? Did not I come as I promised you?" And when they asked at what time it was: "Why," quoth he, "did not I appear to either of you in your sleep, and appointed how and where every place was to be builded? Go your way, and according to that platform which you then saw build up the abbey." At which word they much marvelled, and returning back they caused it to be builded in such sort as they had been taught of him by revelation.

PETER: Gladly would I learn by what means that could be done: to wit, that he should go so far to tell them that thing in their sleep, which they should both hear and know by vision.

GREGORY: Why do you, Peter, seek out and doubt in what manner this thing was done? For certain it is that the soul is of a more noble nature than the body. And by authority of Scripture we know that the prophet Abacuck was carried from Judea with that dinner which he had and was suddenly set in Chaldea [Apocryphal Old Testament: "Bel and the Dragon," 33 = Vulgate O.T.: "Daniel" xiv, 33]. By which meat the prophet Daniel was relieved, and presently after was brought back again to Judea. If, then, Abacuck could in a moment with his body go so far and carry provision for another man's dinner, what marvel is it if the holy father Bennet obtained grace to go in spirit and to inform the souls of his brethren that were asleep concerning such things as were necessary; and that as Abacuck about corporal meat went corporally, so Bennet should go spiritually about the dispatch of spiritual business?

PETER: I confess that your words have satisfied my doubtful mind. But I would know what manner of man he was in his ordinary talk and conversation.

CHAPTER XXIII

## *Of certain nuns absolved after their death*

GREGORY: His common talk, Peter, was usually full of virtue; for his heart conversed so above in heaven that no words could in vain proceed from his mouth. And if at any time he spake aught, yet not as one that determined what was best to be done, but only in a threatening manner, his speech in that case was so effectual and forcible, as though he had not doubtfully or uncertainly but assuredly pronounced and given sentence. For not far from his abbey there lived two nuns in a place by themselves, born of worshipful parentage, whom a religious good man did serve for the dispatch of their outward business. But as nobility of family doth in some breed ignobility of mind and maketh them in conversation to show less humility because they remember still what superiority they had above others, even so was it with these nuns; for they had not yet learned to temper their tongues and keep them under with the bridle of their habit. Often did they by their indiscreet speech provoke the foresaid religious man to anger; who having borne with them a long time, at length he complained to the man of God and told him with what reproachful words they entreated him. Whereupon he sent them by and by this message, saying: "Amend your tongues, otherwise I do excommunicate you"; which sentence of excommunication notwithstanding, he did not then presently pronounce against them but only threatened if they amended not themselves. But they, for all this, changed their conditions nothing at all. Both which not long after departed this life and were buried in the church. And when solemn mass was celebrated in the same church, and the Deacon according to custom said with loud voice, "If any there be that do not communicate, let them depart," the nurse which used to give unto our Lord an offering for them beheld them at that time to rise out of their graves and to depart the church. Having often times, at those words of the Deacon, seen them leave the church, and that they could not tarry within, she remembered what message the man of God sent them whiles they were yet alive. For he told them that he did deprive them of the communion unless they did amend their tongues and conditions. Then with great sorrow the whole matter was signified to the man of God, who straightways with his own hands gave an oblation, saying, "Go your ways, and cause this to be offered unto our Lord for them, and they shall not remain any longer excommunicate." Which oblation being offered for them. and the Deacon, as he used, crying out that such as did not communicate should depart, they were not seen any more to go out of the church. Whereby it was certain that, seeing they did not depart with them which did not communicate, that they had received the communion of our Lord by the hands of his servant.

PETER: It is very strange that you report; for how could he, though a venerable and most holy man, yet living in mortal body, loose those souls which stood now before the invisible judgment of God?

GREGORY: Was he not yet, Peter, mortal, that heard from our Saviour: "Whatsoever thou shalt bind upon earth, it shall be bound also in the heavens: and whatsoever thou shalt loose in earth, shall be loosed also in the heavens"? [Matt. XVI, 19.] Whose place of binding and loosing, those have at this time which by faith and virtuous life possess the place of holy government. And to bestow such power upon earthly men, the Creator of heaven and earth descended from heaven to earth, and that flesh might judge of spiritual things, God, who for man's sake was made flesh vouchsafed to bestow upon him; for from thence our weakness did rise up above itself, from whence the strength of God was weakened under itself.

PETER: For the virtue of his miracles, your words do yield a very good reason.

### CHAPTER XXVIII

*How a cruet of glass was thrown upon the stones, and not broken*

At such time as there was a great dearth in Campania, the man of God had given away all the wealth of the abbey to poor people so that in the cellar there was nothing left but a little oil in a glass. A certain sub-deacon called Agapitus came unto him, instantly craving that he would bestow a little oil upon him. Our Lord's servant, that was resolved to give away all upon earth that he might find all in heaven, commanded that oil to be given him; but the monk that kept the cellar heard what the father commanded, yet did he not perform it. Who, inquiring not long after whether he had given that which he willed, the monk told him that he had not, adding that if he had given it away, there was not any left for the convent. Then in an anger he commanded others to take that glass with the oil and to throw it out at the window, to the end that nothing might remain in the abbey contrary to obedience. The monks did so, and threw it out at a window, under which there was an huge downfall full of rough and craggy stones upon which the glass did light, but yet continued for all that so sound as though it had never been thrown out at all, for neither the glass was broken nor any of the oil shed. Then the man of God did command it to be taken up again, and, whole as it was, to be given unto him that desired it, and in the presence of the other brethren. He reprehended the disobedient monk both for his infidelity and also for his proud mind.

CHAPTER XXIX

### How an empty barrel was filled with oil

After which reprehension, with the rest of his brethren he fell to praying; and in the place where they were, there stood an empty barrel with a cover upon it. And as the holy man continued in his prayers, the oil within did so increase that the cover began to be lifted up and at length fell down, and the oil, that was now higher than the mouth of the barrel, began to run over upon the pavement. Which so soon as the servant of God, Bennet, beheld, forthwith he gave over his prayers, and the oil likewise ceased to overflow the barrel. Then he did more at large admonish that mistrusting and disobedient monk, that he would learn to have faith and humility, who upon so wholesome an admonition was ashamed, because the venerable father had by miracle shown the power of almighty God, as before he told him when he did first rebuke him. And so no cause there was why any should afterward doubt of his promise, seeing at one and the same time, for a small glass almost empty which he gave away, he bestowed upon them an whole barrel full of oil.

CHAPTER XXX

### How Bennet delivered a monk from a devil

PETER: I would gladly know whether he obtained always by prayer to work such notable miracles; or else sometimes did them only at his will and pleasure.

GREGORY: Such as be the devout servants of God, when necessity requireth, use to work miracles both manner of ways: so that sometime they effect wonderful things by their prayers, and sometime only by their power and authority. For St. John saith: "So many as received Him, He gave them power to be made the sons of God" [John I, 12]. They, then, that by power be the sons of God, what marvel is it if by power they be able to do wonderful things? And that both ways they work miracles, we learn of St. Peter, who by his prayers did raise up Tabitha, and by his sharp reprehension did sentence Ananias and Sapphira to death for their lying [Acts IX, 40–41; v, 1–11]. For we read not that in the death of them he prayed at all, but only rebuked them for that sin which they had committed. Certain therefore it is that sometimes they do these things by power and sometimes by prayer; for Ananias and Sapphira by a severe rebuke St. Peter deprived of life, and by prayer restored Tabitha to life.

CHAPTER XXXV

*How he saw the whole world represented before his eyes: and also the soul of Germanus, Bishop of Capua, ascending to heaven*

At another time Servandus, the Deacon and Abbot of that monastery which in times past was founded by the noble man Liberius in the country of Campania, used ordinarily to come and visit the man of God. And the reason why he came so often was because himself also was a man full of heavenly doctrine. And so they two had often together spiritual conference to the end that, albeit they could not perfectly feed upon the celestial food of heaven, yet by means of such sweet discourses they might at least with longing and fervent desire taste of those joys and divine delights. When it was time to go to rest, the venerable father Bennet reposed himself in the top of a tower, at the foot whereof Servandus the Deacon was lodged, so that one pair of stairs went to them both. Before the tower there was a certain large room in which both their disciples did lie. The man of God, Bennet, being diligent in watching, rose early up before the time of matins (his monks being yet at rest) and came to the window of his chamber, where he offered up his prayers to almighty God. Standing there, all on a sudden in the dead of the night as he looked forth he saw a light which banished away the darkness of the night and glittered with such brightness that the light which did shine in the midst of darkness was far more clear than the light of the day. Upon this sight a marvellous strange thing followed; for, as himself did afterward report, the whole world, gathered as it were together under one beam of the sun, was presented before his eyes. And whiles the venerable father stood attentively beholding the brightness of that glittering light, he saw the soul of Germanus, Bishop of Capua, in a fiery globe to be carried up by angels into heaven. Then, desirous to have some witness of this so notable a miracle, he called with a very loud voice Servandus the Deacon twice or thrice by his name, who, troubled at such an unusual crying out of the man of God, went up in all haste and looking forth saw not anything else but a little remnant of the light. But wondering at so great a miracle, the man of God told him all in order what he had seen and, sending by and by to the town of Cassino, he commanded the religious man Theoprobus to dispatch one that night to the city of Capua, to learn what was become of Germanus their Bishop. Which being done, the messenger found that reverent prelate departed this life, and enquiring curiously the time, he understood that he died at that very instant in which the man of God beheld him ascending up to heaven.

PETER: A strange thing and very much to be admired. But whereas you say that the whole world, as it were under one sunbeam, was presented before his eyes, as I must needs confess that in myself I never had experience of any such thing, so neither can I conceive by what means the whole world can be seen of any one man.

GREGORY: Assure yourself, Peter, of that which I speak: to wit, that all creatures be as it were nothing to that soul which beholdeth the Creator; for though it see but a glimpse of that light which is in the Creator, yet very small do all things seem that be created. For by means of that supernatural light, the capacity of the inward soul is enlarged and is in God so extended that it is far above the world. Yea and the soul of him that seeth in this manner is also above itself; for being rapt up in the light of God, it is inwardly in itself enlarged above itself, and when it is so exalted and looketh downward, then doth it comprehend how little all that is which before in former baseness it could not comprehend. The man of God, therefore, who saw the fiery globe, and the angels returning to heaven, out of all doubt could not see those things but in the light of God. What marvel, then, is it if he saw the world gathered together before him, who, rapt up in the light of his soul, was at that time out of the world? But albeit we say that the world was gathered together before his eyes, yet were not heaven and earth drawn into any lesser room than they be of themselves, but the soul of the beholder was more enlarged, which, rapt in God, might without difficulty see that which is under God, and therefore in that light which appeared to his outward eyes, the inward light which was in his soul ravished the mind of the beholder to supernal things, and shewed him how small all earthly things were.

PETER: I perceive now that it was to my more profit that I understood you not before — seeing, by reason of my slow capacity, you have delivered so notable an exposition. But now, because you have made me thoroughly to understand these things, I beseech you to continue on your former narration.

## CHAPTER XXXVI

### How Holy Bennet wrote a rule for his monks

GREGORY: Desirous I am, Peter, to tell you many things of this venerable father, but some of purpose I let pass, because I make haste to entreat also of the acts of other holy men. Yet I would not have you to be ignorant but that the man of God amongst so many miracles, for which he was so famous in the world, was also sufficiently learned in divinity; for he wrote a rule for his monks, both excellent for discretion and also eloquent for the style. Of whose life and conversation, if any be curious to know further, he may in the institution of that rule understand all his manner of life and discipline; for the holy man could not otherwise teach than himself lived.

CHAPTER XXXVII

*How Venerable Bennet did prophesy to his monks the time of his own death*

The same year in which he departed this life, he told the day of his holy death to his monks, some of which did live daily with him and some dwelt far off, willing those that were present to keep it secret and telling them that were absent by what token they should know that he was dead.   Six days before he left this world, he gave order to have his sepulchre opened, and forthwith falling into an ague, he began with burning heat to wax faint, and whenas the sickness daily increased, upon the sixth day he commanded his monks to carry him into the oratory, where he did arm himself with receiving the body and blood of our Saviour Christ.   And having his weak body holden up betwixt the hands of his disciples, he stood with his own lifted up to heaven.   And as he was in that manner praying, he gave up the ghost.   Upon which day two monks, one being in his cell and the other far distant, had concerning him one and the self-same vision.   For they saw all the way from the holy man's cell, towards the east even up to heaven, hung and adorned with tapestry and shining with an infinite number of lamps, at the top whereof a man, reverently attired, stood and demanded if they knew who passed that way; to whom they answered saying that they knew not.   Then he spake thus unto them: "This is the way," quoth he, "by which the beloved servant of God, Bennet, is ascended up to heaven."   And by this means, as his monks that were present knew of the death of the holy man, so likewise they which were absent, by the token which he foretold them, had intelligence of the same thing.   Buried he was in the oratory of St. John Baptist which himself built, when he overthrew the altar of Apollo; who also in that cave in which he first dwelled even to this very time worketh miracles, if the faith of them that pray requireth the same.

CHAPTER XXXVIII

*How a mad woman was cured in his cave*

For the thing which I mean now to rehearse fell out lately.   A certain woman, falling mad, lost the use of reason so far that she walked up and down, day and night, in mountains and valleys, in woods and fields, and rested only in that place where extreme weariness enforced her to stay.   Upon a day it so fell out that, albeit she wandered at random, yet she missed not the right way; for she came to the cave of the blessed man Bennet.   And not knowing anything, in she went and reposed herself there that night, and rising up in the morning she departed as sound in sense and well in her wits as though she had never been distracted in her whole life, and so continued always after, even to her dying day.

[tr. P. W., revised by EDMUND G. GARDNER]

# LITURGY, HYMNS, AND LYRICS

During the Christian persecutions of the apostolic age and later into the mid-fourth century, the services of the Church were largely based on oriental practice — the ritual of the Hebrew synagogue as modified by the Greeks, particularly those in Asia Minor. Congregational worship consisted of psalm singing, reading of Scripture, and instruction in the rites and dogmas of an alien religion. After Constantine had recognized Christianity as the religion of the Emperors and had tied together Church and State, the best minds of the West refined the service and spread the faith through poetry and prose. The result was a fusion of oriental and occidental forms of expression, a freeing of Latin from classical tradition, and the development of a Christian mythology that rapidly modified, where it did not supplant, the old. Most influential upon lyric poetry were the Psalms and the eastern hymnody that Ambrose and Hilary of Poitiers introduced in the late fourth century; the selection from Augustine's *Confessions* above describes how Ambrose introduced this into the liturgy at Milan. In this stir and fusion, the feeling for classical quantity was lost, and rhyme and accentual rhythms, which would have offended the ears of Augustan readers, began to find favor. Ambrose's hymns, for instance, can be scanned either by meter, as was classical poetry, or by accent, as was later Latin poetry. As the Christians rededicated pagan temples of Apollo to St. Sebastian and changed the pagan Lupercalia into St. Mary's Day, so they supplanted stories of Orpheus or Psyche by those of Hebrew patriarchs and Christian martyrs. Though a Claudian might cling to the dying paganism (Orosius remarked of him, "A great poet, indeed, but a most obstinate pagan."), his contemporaries, Prudentius, Ausonius, Paulinus, and many others, professed Christianity, and all but Ausonius dedicated themselves with intense zeal to spreading the Christian themes. Theirs was the last great poetical outburst before darkness began to fall upon Italy and Provence; fortunately it gave the benighted much good poetry to read.

The sixth century saw the culture of Rome topple. By the end of the century it was next to impossible to find a Roman poet who could write a syntactical sentence, much less write inspired verse. The last two memorable poets were Arator and Fortunatus. In the uproar of battle between Belisarius and Witiges, when the marble statues that crowned Hadrian's Tomb were hurled against the invaders below, Arator turned to religion and took orders. In the tradition of Juvencus, Prudentius, and Sedulius, he composed two books of epic poetry based on the Bible story. The citizens demanded a public reading, which Arator gave before the basilica of St. Peter in Chains in four separate sessions, not only because the poem was long but because the enthusiastic audience demanded many encores. Yet a modern critic says of it, "The *Historia Apostolica* is

79

entirely devoid of poetic merit.  The language is obscure, the treatment bald, the style vicious." It was the last recorded public reading in Rome — the end of a long tradition.

Fortunatus, though born in northern Italy, wandered through all the courts of France before he finally attached himself to the court of Queen Radegunde at Poitiers.  There he lived for many years writing both courtly and religious poetry; he died shortly after he was ordained Bishop of Poitiers.  His life and poetry in this period of decline and confusion remarkably anticipate in many ways both goliards and troubadours.  For two centuries after Fortunatus, the only poetry worth reading was written by the barbarians of the north.

## COMMEMORATION OF THE CHURCH IN HEAVEN

(Third and Fourth Prayers of the Canon of the Mass) [1]

### From the Apostolic Church

We pray in union with and honor the memory especially of the glorious ever Virgin Mary, Mother of our God and Lord Jesus Christ; as also of thy blessed apostles and martyrs, Peter and Paul, Andrew, James, John, Thomas, James, Philip, Bartholomew, Matthew, Simon and Thaddeus; of Linus, Cletus, Clement, Sixtus, Cornelius, Cyprian, Lawrence, Chrysogonus, John and Paul, Cosmas and Damian; and of all thy saints; by whose merits and prayers grant that we may in all things be defended by the aid of thy protection. Through the same Christ our Lord.  Amen.

This oblation, therefore, of our service and that of thy whole family, we beseech thee, O Lord, graciously to accept; and to dispose our days in thy peace, and to command us to be delivered from eternal damnation and to be numbered in the flock of thine elect. Through Christ our Lord.  Amen.

## THE NICENE CREED [2]

### (circ. 325)

I believe in one God, the Father almighty, Maker of heaven and earth, and of all things visible and invisible.  And in one Lord Jesus Christ, the only-begotten Son of God, born of the Father before all ages.  God of God; Light of Light; very God of very God; begotten, not made; of one substance with the Father, by whom all things

---

1. From *The Catholic Sunday Missal*, edited by Charles J. Callan, O.P., and John A. McHugh, O.P.; P. J. Kenedy & Sons, New York, 1935.  Reprinted by permission of the publisher.
2. Ibid.

were made. Who for us men, and for our salvation, came down
from heaven and was incarnate by the Holy Ghost of the Virgin
Mary; and was made man. He was crucified also for us, suffered
under Pontius Pilate, and was buried. The third day he rose again
according to the Scriptures; and ascended into heaven, and sitteth
at the right hand of the Father; and he shall come again with glory
to judge both the living and the dead; of whose kingdom there
shall be no end. And I believe in the Holy Ghost, the Lord and
Giver of life, who proceedeth from the Father and the Son: who
together with the Father and the Son is worshiped and glorified;
who spoke by the Prophets. And one, holy, catholic and apostolic
Church. I confess one baptism for the remission of sins. And I
look for the resurrection of the dead and the life of the world to
come. Amen.

## TE DEUM

### Nicetas of Remesiana (?) (A.D. 335–415?)

*Te Deum laudamus: te Dominum confitemur*
*Te aeternum Patrem, omnis terra veneratur.*

We praise thee, O God: we acknowledge thee to be the Lord.
All the earth doth worship thee: the Father everlasting.
To thee all Angels cry aloud: the Heavens, and all the Powers
    therein.
To thee Cherubin, and Seraphin: continually do cry,
Holy, Holy, Holy: Lord God of Sabaoth;
Heaven and earth are full of the Majesty: of thy Glory.
The glorious company of the Apostles: praise thee.
The goodly fellowship of the Prophets: praise thee.
The noble army of Martyrs: praise thee.
The holy Church throughout all the world: doth acknowledge thee;
The Father: of an infinite Majesty;
Thine honourable, true: and only Son;
Also the Holy Ghost: the Comforter.
Thou art the King of Glory: O Christ.
Thou art the everlasting Son: of the Father.
When thou tookest upon thee to deliver man: thou didst not abhor
    the Virgin's womb.
When thou hadst overcome the sharpness of death: thou didst open
    the Kingdom of Heaven to all believers.
Thou sittest at the right hand of God: in the Glory of the Father.
We believe that thou shalt come: to be our Judge.
We therefore pray thee, help thy servants: whom thou hast redeemed
    with thy precious blood.
Make them to be numbered with thy Saints: in glory everlasting.
O Lord, save thy people: and bless thine heritage.

Govern them: and lift them up for ever.
Day by day: we magnify thee;
And we worship thy Name: ever world without end.
Vouchsafe, O Lord: to keep us this day without sin.
O Lord, have mercy upon us: have mercy upon us.
O Lord, let thy mercy lighten upon us: as our trust is in thee.
O Lord, in thee have I trusted: let me never be confounded.

[from the Book of Common Prayer]


## HYMN

Ambrose of Milan (A.D. 340?–397)

*Aeterne rerum conditor,*
*Noctem diemque qui regis,*
*Et temporum das tempora,*
*Ut alleves fastidium;*

Framer of the earth and sky,
    Ruler of the day and night,
With a glad variety
    Tempering all, and making light;

Gleams upon our dark path flinging,
    Cutting short each night begun.
Hark! for chanticleer is singing,
    Hark! he chides the lingering sun.

And the morning star replies
    And lets loose the imprisoned day;
And the godless bandit flies
    From his haunt and from his prey.

Shrill it sounds; the storm relenting
    Soothes the weary seaman's ears;
Once it wrought a great repenting
    In that flood of Peter's tears.

Rouse we; let the blithesome cry
    Of that bird our hearts awaken,
Chide the slumberers as they lie,
    And arrest the sin o'ertaken.

Hope and health are in his strain
    To the fearful and the ailing;
Murder sheathes his blade profane;
    Faith revives when faith was failing.

Jesu, Master! when we sin
   Turn on us Thy healing face;
It will melt the offence within
   Into penitential grace.

Beam on our bewildered mind
   Till its dreamy shadows flee:
Stones cry out where Thou has shined,
   Jesu! musical with Thee.

To the Father and the Son
   And the Spirit, who in heaven
Ever witness, Three in One,
   Praise on earth be ever given.

            [tr. JOHN HENRY NEWMAN]


## Acrostic: *DE SAECULI*

### Commodian (*circ.* 250)

*Dat tuba caelo signum sublato leone*
*Et fiunt desubito tenebrae cum caeli fragore.*


Just after the lion is vanquished — the foreordained Antichrist, —
Under the vault of heaven the trumpet blares out its call.
Deepening shadows below are sundered by heavenly lightning;
God casts downward his eyes, as all the dominions tremble,
Mournfully waiting their doom.   And as the Savior addresses
Every creature below, His voice each hollow reëchoes:
"Now too long have I waited, silent, enduring your evil!"
Thousands cry out in anguish, too late they clamour together —

Damned, they shriek and implore — but no space is found for the
   wicked.
After the mother is burned, will she suckle traitorous offspring?
Yea, to the fiery flames the Master condemns the unrighteous.

            [tr. CHARLES W. JONES]


## Hymn: BURIAL OF THE DEAD

### Prudentius (A.D. 348–405?)

*Iam moesta quiesce querela,*
*Lacrymas suspendite, matres!*
*Nullus sua pignora plangat:*
*Mors haec reparatio vitae est.*

Now, O bitter grief be silent,
  Tears, ye mothers, banish hence!
Let no man lament his children:
  This is death, — life's recompense.

For what mean these rocky caverns,
  What these monuments so fair?
Save that this unto them trusted
  Is not dead but sleeping there.

For that body we see resting,
  Vacant and devoid of mind,
Only for a brief space waiteth,
  Better powers restored to find.

Swift will pass the coming ages,
  Friendly warmth these bones shall know
And these former habitations,
  Animate with life-blood, glow.

Then these bodies dull and moldering,
  Sleeping in the graves before,
Shall be borne on airy pinions,
  Joined unto their souls of yore.

Thus the seeds though dried and shriveled,
  Dead and buried, wake again,
And from 'neath the sod returning
  Think of former waving grain.

Now, O earth, receive, to cherish,
  In thy tender heart this dust!
Man's frail form to thee I render,
  And his goodly ashes trust.

This was once a spirit's dwelling,
  Fashioned by the breath of God;
Here from Christ, the mighty Leader,
  Ardent wisdom once abode.

Shelter thou this body laid here!
  Not unmindful, He shall trace
His own works who formed and framed them,
  Likenesses of His own face.

Soon shall come the times of justice,
  When shall God each hope transcend;
And laid open thou must render
  Back this form I to thee lend.

                              [tr. J. H. Van Buren]

Epilogue to *CATHEMERINON* [3]

Prudentius (A.D. 348-405?)

*Immolat deo patri*
*Pius, fidelis, innocens, pudicus*
*Dona conscientiae,*
*Quibus beata mens abundat intus.*

The pure and faithful saint, whose heart is whole,
  To God the Father makes his sacrifice
From out the treasures of a stainless soul,
  Glad gifts of innocence, beyond all price:
Another with free hand bestows his gold,
  Whereby his needy neighbour may be fed.
No wealth of holiness my heart doth hold,
  No store have I to buy my brothers bread:
So here I humbly dedicate to Thee
  The rolling trochee and iambus swift;
Thou wilt approve my simple minstrelsy,
  Thine ear will listen to Thy servant's gift.
The rich man's halls are nobly furnishèd;
  Therein no nook or corner empty seems;
Here stands the brazen laver burnishèd,
  And there the golden goblet brightly gleams;
Hard by some crock of clumsy earthen ware,
  Massive and ample lies a silver plate;
And rough-hewn cups of oak or elm are there
  With vases carved of ivory delicate.
Yet every vessel in its place is good,
  So be it for the Master's service meet;
The priceless salver and the bowl of wood
  Alike He needs to make His home complete.

                [tr. R. F. Davis]


From THE MOSELLE [4]

Ausonius (A.D. 310?-394?)

*Naviger, ut pelagus, devexas pronus in undas,*
*Ut fluvio, vitreoque lacus imitate profundo.*

3. From *The Hymns of Prudentius*, translated by R. M. Pope and R. F. Davis; Temple Classics, J. M. Dent & Sons, Ltd., London, 1905. Reprinted by permission of the publisher.
4. From *A History of Later Latin Literature*, by F. A. Wright and T. A. Sinclair; Routledge & Kegan Paul, Ltd., London, 1931. Reprinted by permission of the publisher.

Ships sail thee as on ocean's waves.
Thou hast a river's downward course,
A channel's fretful speed, thy stream
Is stainless as a fountain's source,
And as a lake profound and deep:
The charms we find combined in thee
Of channel, river, fountain-head,
Of glassy lake and tidal sea.

The golden sand in furrows lies
As o'er it sweeps thy rippling tide,
And water grasses in the depths
Of emerald sway from side to side.
The plants beneath their native waves
Endure the buffets of the stream,
And where red gravel stains the moss,
Bright pebbles through its covering gleam.

What colours then are on thy wave
When evening with its shades draws nigh,
And on Mosella's liquid stream,
The verdant hills reflected lie!
Upon thy rippling glass we see
The semblance of the distant vine
Whose tendrils with the bursting grapes
Beneath the surface intertwine.

[tr. F. A. WRIGHT]


## BUDDING ROSES

(Ausonius?)

*Ver erat et blando mordenti a fragore sensu*
  *Spirabat croceo mane revecta dies.*

'Twas spring, and dawn returning breathed new-born
From saffron skies the bracing chill of morn.
Before day's orient chargers went a breeze,
That whispered: Rise, the sweets of morning seize!
In watered gardens where the cross-paths ran,
Freshness and health I sought ere noon began:
I watched from bending grasses how the rime
In clusters hung, or gemmed the beds of thyme;
How the round beads, on herb and leaf outspread,
Rolled with the weight of dews from heaven's height shed;
Saw the rose-gardens in their Paestan bloom
Hoar 'neath the dawn-star rising through the gloom.

On every bush those separate splendours gleam,
Doomed to be quenched by day's first arrowy beam.
Here might one doubt: doth morn from roses steal
Their redness, or the rose with dawn anneal?
One hue, one dew, one morn makes both serene;
Of star and flower one Venus reigns the queen.
Perchance one scent have they; the star's o'erhead
Far, far exhales, the flower's at hand is shed.
Goddess of star, goddess of rose no less,
The Paphian flings o'er both her crimson dress.
Now had the moment passed wherein the brood
Of clustering buds seemed one twin sisterhood.
This flower, enlaced with leaves, shows naught but green;
That shoots a roseate streak from forth the screen:
One opes her pyramid and purple spire,
Emerging into plentitude of fire:
Another thrusts her verdant veil aside,
Counting her petals one by one with pride:
Expands her radiant cup of gorgeous hue,
And brings dense hidden veins of gold to view:
She who had burned erewhile, a flower of flame,
Now pales and droops her fainting head with shame: —
So that I mused how swift time steals all worth,
How roses age and wither with their birth;
Yea, while I speak, the flower with crimson crowned
Hath fallen and shed her glories on the ground.
So many births, forms, fates with changes fraught,
One day begins and one day brings to naught!
Grieve we that flowers should have so short a grace,
That Nature shows and steals her gifts apace?
Long as the day, so long the red rose lasts;
Eld following close on youth her beauty blasts:
That flower which Phosphor newly-born had known,
Hesper returning finds a wrinkled crone:
Yet well if, though some brief days past she die,
Her life be lengthened through posterity!
Pluck roses, girl, when flower, when youth is new,
Mindful the while that thus time flies for you.

[tr. JOHN ADDINGTON SYMONDS]


EPITAPH

Paulinus of Nola (A.D. 353–451)

*Tam modicum patribus tam dulci e pignore fructum
Defleo in exiguo temporis esse datum.*

For parent's fruit, so sweetly come,
  So shortly in the world, I weep;
He now is lost in blessed sleep.
  Not long he bore life's tedium.

But I take heart as I turn o'er
  God's everlasting goods of love
For innocents prepared above;
  He scarce at all earth's burden bore.

So now his labors are divine —
  No more with earth's contagion mixed —
His soul in God for ever fixed
  Beyond this fragile home of mine.

No crime his sacred soul shall blot
  In this dark valley filled with pain.
A purer home will he attain —
  To God he goes whom God begot.
                    [tr. CHARLES W. JONES]


OLD MAN OF VERONA [5]

Claudian (A.D. 365?–410?)

*Felix, qui propriis aevum transegit in arvis,*
  *Ipsa domus puerum quem vicet, ipsa senem.*

Happy the man whose hopes and fears
A few paternal acres bound,
Who lives in childhood and in age
  On his own ground.

The staff that helps him marks the sand
Where as a babe he used to lie,
And from his cottage porch he counts
  The years go by . . .

Unskilled in lawyer's arts he stays
A stranger to the neighbouring town,
And free from smoking chimneys calls
  The sky his own.

He reckons, not by consuls' names,
But by the crops the seasons bring,
He knows the autumn by its fruit,
  By flowers the spring . . .

5. Ibid.

He and the monarchs of the wood
Together in their age agree;
The acorn that he planted once
    He sees a tree.

But still his limbs are firm and hale,
And though he is a grandsire now
His children's children at his knee
    His strength allow.

Let others sail to distant lands
And seek for gold 'mid toil and strife,
They waste their days upon the road;
    He lives his life.
                      [tr. F. A. WRIGHT]

## From the APOSTOLIC HISTORY

### Arator (A.D. 544)

*Manet omne per aevum*
*Pignoris huius apex, et sideris obtinet instar,*
*Corpore quod Petrus sacravit, et angelus ore.*

Through ages long this honor'd pledge is fraught
With august import, beck'ning like a star,
By angel's word and Peter's hallow'd bones.
A solemn bond for you, these fetters, Rome,
Are lasting surety.  Enchained, you are
For ever free; for cannot chains of him,
Our guard who absolves all, all conquer? Walls
Inviolate by his hand and sanctified
By his triumphant death need never quail
Before barbarians.  He blocks War's path
Who flings apart the gates to starry heav'n.
                    [tr. CHARLES W. JONES]

## PROCESSIONAL FOR GOOD FRIDAY

### Fortunatus (A.D. 540–600?)

*Vexilla Regis prodeunt:*
*Fulget Crucis mysterium*
*Qua vita mortem pertulit*
*Et morte vitam protulit.*

Abroad the Regal Banners fly,
Now shines the Cross's mystery;
Upon it Life did death endure,
And yet by death did life procure.

Who, wounded with a direful spear,
Did, purposely to wash us clear
From stain of sin, pour out a flood
Of precious Water mixed with Blood.

That which the Prophet-King of old
Hath in mysterious verse foretold,
Is now accomplished, whilst we see
God ruling nations from a Tree.

O lovely and refulgent Tree,
Adorned with purpled majesty;
Culled from a worthy stock, to bear
Those limbs which sanctifièd were.

Blest Tree, whose happy branches bore
The wealth that did the world restore;
The beam that did that Body weigh
Which raised up hell's expected prey.

Hail, Cross, of hopes the most sublime!
Now in this mournful Passion time,
Improve religious souls in grace,
The sins of criminals efface.

Blest Trinity, salvation's spring,
May every soul Thy praises sing;
To those Thou grantest conquest by
The holy Cross, rewards apply.

[tr. W. K. BLOUNT]


## TO GOGO

### Fortunatus

*Nectar vina cibus vestis doctrına facultas —*
*Muneribus largis tu mihi, Gogo, sat es.*

With nectared food and wine, with scholarly discourse,
Choice and abundant, hast thou laden me;
Thou art Apicius and Tully now reborn,
With viands of the one, the other's repartee.

Grant pardon, Gogo!   I rest the beaded bowl
Lest paunch grow mutinous and gullet lose control.
Where the steer reclineth, cock and hen must flee,
For wings with horns would battle most unequally.

'Neath lethargic eyelids somnolent visions creep
As my muted verses serenade to sleep.

[tr. CHARLES W. JONES]


## TO QUEEN RADEGUNDE

### Fortunatus (A.D. 540–600?)

*O regina potens, aurum cui et purpura vile est,*
*Floribus ex parvis te veneratur amans.*

Sweet Sovereign Lady, Thou has spurned
      the gold and purple thine by queenly right.
Deign, an' it please thee, in their stead t'accept
      this nosegay by thy fond admirer sent:
A purer gold plays o'er the crocus' cup;
      Tyre's purple cannot match the violet's.
For God's sweet love this world's delights
      thou find'st no recompense;
The holy life to which thou'rt called
      the wealth I send does more befit.


Take then my offering of flowers —
      Fresh they will be when all
      this gaudy world's rewards have sunk to dust.
What joys the meads of heaven will hold
      from them thou may'st divine;
Of perfumes that will thee refresh,
      once thou hast left this woeful clime
      to be reborn in Paradise,
My fragrant sprays will be the merest shadow of a hint.
And when in that loved spot thou hast arrived,
May thy dear, soft, and merit-girded hand
      reach down for them and me, I pray.


Yet, though celestial blooms with all their charms
      await thy coming,
E'en now, these flowers of mine do yearn
      upon their native lea once more to greet thee;
There, though with odors rich and rare they'll strive
      with all their main to please thee,

To snuggle 'gainst thy passing foot
  they'll deck their flowery locks
  in even greater beauty.

[tr. HOWARD B. ADELMANN]

# II. IRISH LITERATURE

Before the expansion of the Roman Empire, Europe west of the Rhine and north of the Pyrenees including the British Isles was largely settled by people ethnologically similar called Celts. The invasions, first of the Romans and then of the Teutonic races, submerged these people culturally and eliminated their direct or traceable contributions to western literature except in those parts of the British Isles where the invaders did not reach, that is, primarily, Ireland. There the Church through its schools and parish work changed the fashion of native literature to conform at least superficially with the culture of Continental Europe, but did not seriously affect the original core. Though the manuscripts in which the literature now exists were written no earlier than the eleventh century (the raids of the Vikings no doubt destroyed many earlier ones), they preserve older poetry, and students of Gaelic (as the early Irish language is called) concede that many of the following pieces were little changed after the eighth or ninth centuries. Irish literature therefore shares with English the honor of being the earliest vernacular literature, but contrasts with it in both form and spirit.

Gaelic literature was no doubt largely created by the "men of music and playing and knowledge" described in *The Sons of Usnach* below. Most of it is *saga,* that is, tales written largely in prose but interspersed with verse to be sung as lyrics; it narrates actions of early, even prehistoric, heroes, of whom Cuchulainn, a kind of native King Arthur, to whose name isolated tales were attracted, is one of the earliest. In addition to the sagas there is a large and varied body of narrative and lyric verse. Scholars disagree in assigning dates to these verses, but all those reproduced below were composed before the twelfth century, the close of the Romanesque period. Many of the lyrics are found in Continental manuscripts, often written in the margin of a theological codex by a nostalgic Irish scribe, who had migrated and settled in a monastery in France, Germany, or Italy.

As early English poetry is marked by stolidity and intellectuality and on the whole by a certain fear of nature, the Irish is romantic in essence. Mystic islands, fair ladies, sylvan retreats, and intense and burning love are common themes. Loneliness, especially that of the hermit, is cultivated and often praised. There are many who maintain that Celtic poetry, especially Irish, instilled into the medieval stream of literature that attitude toward woman and interest in her processes of thought which we associate with the Gothic period, just as we find stronger evidence of mariolatry in early Irish literature than elsewhere.

A wide variation in the original meters and rhyme schemes developed from a common rhythm, that of the catalectic trochaic tetrameter of Latin poetry, in which the popular marching song of Caesar's soldiers was written:

*Caesar Gallias subegit, Nicomedes Caesarem,*
*Ecce Caesar nunc triumphat, qui subegit Gallias.*

This accentual verse helped to influence the medieval change away from metrical quantity to syllabic accent with rhyme. The translations of lyrics below vary in fidelity to the original form. Although specimen lines of the original lyrics have been included in the translations from other western tongues, they have been omitted in the lyrics of this section. Dates, too, have been omitted in all but one instance, for they are uncertain.

# THE VOYAGE OF BRAN

Professor Kuno Meyer, the editor and translator, says: "The Voyage of Bran was originally written down in the seventh century. From this original, some time in the tenth century, a copy was made, in which the language of the poetry, protected by the laws of metre and assonance, was left almost intact, while the prose was subjected to a process of partial modernization, which most affected the verbal forms. From this tenth century copy all our MSS. are derived."

Among a limited number of types of early Celtic sagas (the work of the *filid* or bards), a popular type is the *immrama,* or tales of voyaging, of which *Gulliver's Travels* is a late example based on the ancient tradition. One of the earliest cycles is that of Bran, whose story was constantly interwoven with and affected by the hagiological tales of St. Brendan, who died, according to the Annals of Ulster, in A.D. 577 or 583. The confusion was increased by Brendan's own voyaging, for he became a missionary to Scotland and England. The text given here is that of the secular saga. Like all such, it contains prose passages that link together the songs or lyrics of the bards.

Another equally popular voyage cycle of somewhat later origin is the *Imram of Maeldun,* which Tennyson modernized. Like the more famous southern legends of Odysseus, these sagas amalgamated a considerable amount of vision-literature and stories of visits to the underworld. Unsuccessful efforts have often been made to show that these stories describe explorations of America.

## THE VOYAGE OF BRAN
### (*Imram Brain*)

Anonymous   (10th cent.)

[From *The Voyage of Bran,* edited by Kuno Meyer; David
Nutt, London, 1895.]

'Twas fifty quatrains the woman from unknown lands sang on the floor of the house to Bran son of Febal, when the royal house was full of kings, who knew not whence the woman had come, since the ramparts were closed.

This is the beginning of the story. One day, in the neighbourhood of his stronghold, Bran went about alone, when he heard music behind him. As often as he looked back, 'twas still behind him the music was. At last he fell asleep at the music, such was its sweetness. When he awoke from his sleep, he saw close by him a branch of silver with white blossoms, nor was it easy to distinguish its bloom from that branch. Then Bran took the branch in his hand to his

95

royal house. When the hosts were in the royal house, they saw a
woman in strange raiment on the floor of the house. 'Twas then she
sang the fifty quatrains to Bran, while the host heard her, and all beheld the woman.

And she said:

A branch of the apple-tree from Emain
I bring, like those one knows;
Twigs of white silver are on it,
Crystal brows with blossoms.

There is a distant isle,
Around which sea-horses glisten:
A fair course against the white-swelling surge, —
Four feet uphold it.

A delight of the eyes, a glorious range,
Is the plain on which the hosts hold games:
Coracle contends against chariot
In southern Mag Findargat.

Feet of white bronze under it
Glittering through beautiful ages.
Lovely land throughout the world's age,
On which the many blossoms drop.

An ancient tree there is with blossoms,
On which birds call to the Hours.
'Tis in harmony it is their wont
To call together every Hour.

Splendours of every colour glisten
Throughout the gentle-voiced plains.
Joy is known, ranked around music,
In southern Mag Argatnél.

Unknown is wailing or treachery
In the familiar cultivated land,
There is nothing rough or harsh,
But sweet music striking on the ear.

Without grief, without sorrow, without death,
Without any sickness, without debility,
That is the sign of Emain —
Uncommon is an equal marvel.

A beauty of a wondrous land,
Whose aspects are lovely,
Whose view is a fair country,
Incomparable is its haze.

Then if Aircthech is seen,
On which dragonstones and crystals drop
The sea washes the wave against the land,
Hair of crystal drops from its mane.

Wealth, treasures of every hue,
Are in Ciuin, a beauty of freshness,
Listening to sweet music,
Drinking the best of wine.

Golden chariots in Mag Réin,
Rising with the tide to the sun,
Chariots of silver in Mag Mon,
And of bronze without blemish.

Yellow golden steeds are on the sward there,
Other steeds with crimson hue,
Others with wool upon their backs
Of the hue of heaven all-blue.

At sunrise there will come
A fair man illumining level lands;
He rides upon the fair sea-washed plain,
He stirs the ocean till it is blood.

A host will come across the clear sea,
To the land they show their rowing;
Then they row to the conspicuous stone,
From which arise a hundred strains.

It sings a strain unto the host
Through long ages, it is not sad,
Its music swells with choruses of hundreds —
They look for neither decay nor death.

Many-shaped Emne by the sea,
Whether it be near, whether it be far,
In which are many thousands of motley women,
Which the clear sea encircles.

If he has heard the voice of the music,
The chorus of the little birds from Imchiuin,
A small band of women will come from a height
To the plain of sport in which he is.

There will come happiness with health
To the land against which laughter peals,
Into Imchiuin at every season
Will come everlasting joy.

It is a day of lasting weather
That showers silver on the lands,
A pure-white cliff on the range of the sea,
Which from the sun receives its heat.

The host race along Mag Mon,
A beautiful game, not feeble,
In the variegated land over a mass of beauty
They look for neither decay nor death.

Listening to music at night,
And going into Ildathach,
A variegated land, splendour on a diadem of beauty,
Whence the white cloud glistens.

There are thrice fifty distant isles
In the ocean to the west of us;
Larger than Erin twice
Is each of them, or thrice.

A great birth will come after ages,
That will not be in a lofty place,
The son of a woman whose mate will not be known,
He will seize the rule of many thousands.

A rule without beginning, without end,
He has created the world so that it is perfect,
Whose are earth and sea,
Woe to him that shall be under His unwill!

'Tis He that made the heavens,
Happy he that has a white heart,
He will purify hosts under pure water,
'Tis He that will heal your sicknesses.

Not to all of you is my speech,
Though its great marvel has been made known:
Let Bran hear from the crowd of the world
What of wisdom has been told to him.

Do not fall on a bed of sloth,
Let not thy intoxication overcome thee,
Begin a voyage across the clear sea,
If perchance thou mayst reach the land of women.

Thereupon the woman went from them, while they knew not
whither she went.  And she took her branch with her.  The branch
sprang from Bran's hand into the hand of the woman, nor was
there strength in Bran's hand to hold the branch.

Then on the morrow Bran went upon the sea.  The number of

his men was three companies of nine. One of his foster-brothers and mates was set over each of the three companies of nine. When he had been at sea two days and two nights, he saw a man in a chariot coming towards him over the sea. That man also sang thirty other quatrains to him, and made himself known to him, and said that he was Manannan the son of Ler, and said that it was upon him to go to Ireland after long ages, and that a son would be born to him, even Mongan son of Fiachna — that was the name which would be upon him.

So he sang these thirty quatrains to him:

Bran deems it a marvellous beauty
In his coracle across the clear sea:
While to me in my chariot from afar
It is a flowery plain on which he rides about.

What is a clear sea
For the prowed skiff in which Bran is,
That is a happy plain with profusion of flowers
To me from the chariot of two wheels.

Bran sees
The number of waves beating across the clear sea:
I myself see in Mag Mon
Red-headed flowers without fault.

Sea-horses glisten in summer
As far as Bran has stretched his glance:
Rivers pour forth a stream of honey
In the land of Manannan son of Ler.

The sheen of the main, on which thou art,
The white hue of the sea, on which thou rowest about,
Yellow and azure are spread out,
It is land, and is not rough.

Speckled salmon leap from the womb
Of the white sea, on which thou lookest:
They are calves, they are coloured lambs
With friendliness, without mutual slaughter.

Though (but) one chariot-rider is seen
In Mag Mell of many flowers,
There are many steeds on its surface,
Though them thou seest not.

The size of the plain, the number of the host,
Colours glisten with pure glory,
A fair stream of silver, cloths of gold,
Afford a welcome with all abundance.

A beautiful game, most delightful,
They play (sitting) at the luxurious wine,
Men and gentle women under a bush,
Without sin, without crime.

Along the top of a wood has swum
Thy coracle across ridges,
There is a wood of beautiful fruit
Under the prow of thy little skiff.

A wood with blossom and fruit,
On which is the vine's veritable fragrance,
A wood without decay, without defect,
On which are leaves of golden hue.

We are from the beginning of creation
Without old age, without consummation of earth,
Hence we expect not that there should be frailty,
The sin has not come to us.

An evil day when the Serpent went
To the father to his city!
She has perverted the times in this world,
So that there came decay which was not original.

By greed and lust he has slain us,
Through which he has ruined his noble race:
The withered body has gone to the fold of torment,
And everlasting abode of torture.

It is a law of pride in this world
To believe in the creatures, to forget God,
Overthrow by diseases, and old age,
Destruction of the soul through deception.

A noble salvation will come
From the King who has created us,
A white law will come over seas,
Besides being God, He will be man.

This shape, he on whom thou lookest,
Will come to thy parts;
'Tis mine to journey to her house,
To the woman in Line-mag.

For it is Moninnan, the son of Ler.
From the chariot in the shape of a man,
Of his progeny will be a very short while
A fair man in a body of white clay.

Monann, the descendant of Ler, will be
A vigorous bed-fellow to Caintigern:
He shall be called to his son in the beautiful world,
Fiachna will acknowledge him as his son.

He will delight the company of every fairy-knoll,
He will be the darling of every goodly land,
He will make known secrets — a course of wisdom —
In the world, without being feared.

He will be in the shape of every beast,
Both on the azure sea and on land,
He will be a dragon before hosts at the onset,
He will be a wolf of every great forest.

He will be a stag with horns of silver
In the land where chariots are driven,
He will be a speckled salmon in a full pool,
He will be a seal, he will be a fair-white swan.

He will be throughout long ages
An hundred years in fair kingship,
He will cut down battalions, — a lasting grave —
He will redden fields, a wheel around the track.

It will be about kings with a champion
That he will be known as a valiant hero,
Into the strongholds of a land on a height
I shall send an appointed end from Islay.

High shall I place him with princes,
He will be overcome by a son of error;
Moninnan, the son of Ler,
Will be his father, his tutor.

He will be — his time will be short —
Fifty years in this world:
A dragon stone from the sea will kill him
In the fight at Senlabor.

He will ask a drink from Loch Ló,
While he looks at the stream of blood,
The white host will take him under a wheel of clouds
To the gathering where there is no sorrow.

Steadily then let Bran row,
Not far to the Land of Women,
Emne with many hues of hospitality
Thou wilt reach before the setting of the sun.

Thereupon Bran went from him.  And he saw an island.  He rows round about it, and a large host was gaping and laughing. They were all looking at Bran and his people, but would not stay to converse with them.  They continued to give forth gusts of laughter at them.  Bran sent one of his people on the island.  He ranged himself with the others, and was gaping at them like the other men of the island.  He kept rowing round about the island. Whenever his man came past Bran, his comrades would address him.  But he would not converse with them, but would only look at them and gape at them.  The name of this island is the Island of Joy.  Thereupon they left him there.

It was not long thereafter when they reached the Land of Women. They saw the leader of the women at the port.  Said the chief of the women: "Come hither on land, O Bran son of Febal!  Welcome is thy advent!"  Bran did not venture to go on shore.  The woman throws a ball of thread to Bran straight over his face.  Bran put his hand on the ball, which clave to his palm.  The thread of the ball was in the woman's hand, and she pulled the coracle towards the port.  Thereupon they went into a large house, in which was a bed for every couple, even thrice nine beds.  The food that was put on every dish vanished not from them.  It seemed a year to them that they were there, — it chanced to be many years.  No savour was wanting to them.

Home-sickness seized one of them, even Nechtan the son of Collbran.  His kindred kept praying Bran that he should go to Ireland with him.  The woman said to them their going would make them rue.  However, they went, and the woman said that none of them should touch the land, and that they should visit and take with them the man whom they had left in the Island of Joy.

Then they went until they arrived at a gathering at Srub Brain. The men asked of them who it was came over the sea.  Said Bran: "I am Bran the son of Febal," saith he.  However, the other saith: "We do not know such a one, though the Voyage of Bran is in our ancient stories."

The man leaps from them out of the coracle.  As soon as he touched the earth of Ireland, forthwith he was a heap of ashes, as though he had been in the earth for many hundred years.  'Twas then that Bran sang this quatrain:

> For Collbran's son great was the folly
> To lift his hand against age,
> Without any one casting a wave of pure water
> Over Nechtan, Collbran's son.

Thereupon, to the people of the gathering Bran told all his wanderings from the beginning until that time.  And he wrote these quatrains in Ogam, and then bade them farewell.  And from that hour his wanderings are not known.

[tr. KUNO MEYER]

# THE TRAGICAL DEATH OF THE
# SONS OF USNACH

This story of the Sons of Usnach exists in a large number of versions. The earliest manuscript containing the story is the twelfth-century "Book of Leinster." The translation below is based on the so-called Glenn Masáin manuscript of the fifteenth century, now in the Advocates' Library, Edinburgh. There is evidence that the story is at least as old as the ninth century and that the version here given was changed in few details after the eleventh; yet it is still told in remote districts of Ireland and Scotland.

It is clear that even before the introduction of Christianity in the fourth century, or the mission of St. Patrick in the fifth, the Irish cultivated poetry and storytelling in the courts, if such the lodges of petty chieftains may, with some stretch of meaning, be called. These petty rulers were willing, as were the feudal lords of France in a later day, to support bards primarily for their entertainment. The bards sang lays or lyrics, which passed from one to another, in a pattern based on accent and meter, assonance and even rhyme. They linked these sung passages together by prose narrative, a pattern not unlike the mingled prose and meter in the *Consolation of Philosophy* — partly for variety, partly to rest the voice, and partly to allow for impromptu expansion and contraction as the occasion merited.

Most of these so-called sagas dealt with ancient heroes, largely mythical but with possibly a kernel of historical reality, projected into a time before Christianity and even before Christ. Like the Arthurian legends, separate tales became attached to single groups of outstanding heroes. The two most popular of the Gaelic cycles are the tales of Cuchulainn, or the Red Branch, or the Ulster cycle, and the somewhat later tales of Finn and his son Oisin or Ossian, based largely in Munster. In the Ossianic revival of the eighteenth century, inspired largely by the writings of James MacPherson (1736-1796), these Irish stories were popularized throughout Europe and affected the content and form of romantic poetry not only in the British Isles but in Germany and France.

The two cycles contrast in the interests of the writers: The Cuchulainn cycle, whose hero has sometimes been compared with Achilles and whose heroine compares with Helen of Troy, Cassandra, and Deborah, is heroic and mythological; the stories deal with the wars of leaders of nations. The Finn stories introduce interests of the common people and deal largely with the life of hunters and farmers. A note of earthy humor, sometimes of the Til Eulenspiegel type, creeps in. In this, the two cycles contrast as do those of King Arthur and Robin Hood. Eleanor Hull tabulates 96 separate tales in the Cuchulainn cycle.

An example of the verse-structure of the songs is

*Tri dreaguin Dúna Monaidh,*
*na tri curaidh on Ccraoibh Ruaidh:*
*dá ndéis ni ba beo mise:*
*triur do bhrisedh gach aonruaig.*

Three dragons of Dún Monaid,
The three champions of the Red Branch:
After them I am not alive:
Three that used to break every onrush.

## THE TRAGICAL DEATH OF THE SONS OF USNACH

### Anonymous (12th cent.)

[From *The Cuchullin Saga,* edited by Eleanor Hull; David Nutt, London, 1898.]

A king renowned, exceeding mighty, became chief of the Province of Ulster. His name was Conchobar, son of Fachtna *fathach,* son of Capa, son of Ginga, son of Rury the Great from whom the Clan Rury are named. . . . And that valiant, victorious over-king went to enjoy a banquet and a feast, to the house of Fedlimid, son of Dall, Conchobar's own tale-teller. For thus was the feast of Emain Macha enjoyed at that time, to wit, three hundred threescore and five persons was the number of the knight's household that was computed in the house of each man of them. And while they were enjoying the banquet, Fedlimid's wife brought forth a daughter. Cathbad the Druid, who entered the assembly at that moment, uttered forebodings and prophecies about the girl, namely, that much evil and calamity would befall the province on her account. And when the warriors heard that, they desired to kill her on the spot.

But Conchobar said, "It shall not be so done; but I will bring her with me, and put her to fosterage, so that she may be my own one wife."

Cathbad, the Druid, named her Deirdre; and the king placed her in an enclosure apart, with a fosterer and a nurse to rear her. And none of the province durst go near her save her fosterer and her nurse and a female satirist called Levarcham, and Conchobar himself.

And thus she lived until she was ripe for marriage, and she outwent in beauty the women of her time.

Once on a snowy day it came to pass that her fosterer killed a calf for her dinner; and when the blood of the calf was poured upon the snow, a black raven swooped down to drink it. When Deirdre took heed of that, she said to Levarcham that she would desire a husband having the three colours which she beheld, namely, the colour of the raven on his hair, the colour of the calf's blood on his cheeks, and the colour of the snow on his skin.

"Even such a man is there in the household of Conchobar," saith Levarcham, "and he is called Naisi, son of Usnach, son of Conall Flatnailed, son of Rury the Great, of whose race came also Conchobar, as we said above."

"If that be so, O Levarcham," saith Deirdre, "I beseech thee to bring him to converse with me, no one knowing of it."

Levarcham disclosed that matter to Naisi. Then came Naisi secretly to meet Deirdre, and the girl declared to him the greatness of the love she had for him, and entreated him to take her away in flight from Conchobar. And Naisi consented, though he was slow to do so from dread of Conchobar.

Then Naisi and his two brothers, to wit, Ainle and Ardan, and a troop of thrice fifty warriors with them, journeyed to Scotland, where they found maintenance of quarterage from the king of Scotland, and there they remained until the king heard a description of the beauty of Deirdre, and sought her as a wife for himself.

Great wrath took hold on Naisi when he heard that, and he fared forth with his brothers out of Scotland to a sea-girt isle, fleeing with Deirdre after many battles had been fought between themselves and the followers of the king on every hand.

An exceeding beautiful and mighty feast was prepared by Conchobar, son of Fachtna *fathach* "the wise" and by the nobles of Ulster, in smooth-delightful Emain Macha. And the worthies of the province came unto that feast. Wine was dealt out to them until they were all glad, cheerful, and merry. Then arose the men of music and playing and knowledge, to recite before them their lays and songs and chants, to sound their melodious harps and sweet strings, and their bright, splendid timpans; to sing their poetic strains, their genealogies, and their branches of relationship.

These are the names of the poets who were present at the feast, namely, Cathbad the Generous Druid, son of Congal Flatnailed, son of Rury, and Genan Bright-cheek, son of Cathbad, and Genan Black-knee, son of Cathbad, and Sencha the Great, Fercertne the Poet, and many others.

And it was thus that they enjoyed the feast of Emain, to wit, a special night was set apart to each man of Conchobar's household. This is the number of Conchobar's household, even five and threescore and three hundred. They were sitting at feasting and enjoyment until Conchobar uplifted his loud king's voice on high, and this is what he said: "I would fain know, O warriors, have you ever seen a household that is braver than yourselves in Ireland or in Scotland or in the great world beside?" "Truly have we never seen a better," say they, "and we know not if there be such."

"If so," said Conchobar, "do you know of any great want that lies upon you?" "We know not, O high king," say they. "But I know, O warriors," saith he, "the great want that we have, to wit, that the three Lights of Valour of the Gael, the three sons of Usnach, Naisi and Ainle and Ardan, should be separated from us on account of any woman in the world. Naisi for valour and prowess has the making of an over-king of Ireland and sons of a king indeed are they; by the might of his own arm hath he gained for himself a district and a half of Scotland."

"Had we dared to utter that, O royal soldier, long since would we have said it. And, moreover, were these three alone in Ulster and none other with them, they would defend the province of Ulster against every other province in Ireland. For they are sons of a border-king; and heroes for bravery and lions for might and courage are they."

"If it be so," said Conchobar, "let messengers and envoys be sent for them into the fair regions of Alba, to Loch Etive, and to the strongholds of the sons of Usnach to solicit their return."

"Who will take that message?" said they all.

"I know," said Conchobar, "that it is Naisi's prohibition, to come into Ireland in peace, save with one of three, namely, Cuchulainn son of Sualtach, and Conall *cernach* son of Amargin, and Fergus mac Ross; and I will now discover unto which of these three I am dearest."

He took Conall into a place apart, and asked him, "What would be done, O royal soldier of the world, if thou wert sent for Usnach's sons, and they should be destroyed in spite of thy safeguard and thy honour — a thing I attempt not?"

Said Conall, "Not the death of one man only would result therefrom, but every Ulsterman who should do them harm, and upon whom I should lay my hand, he would not escape from me without death and destruction and slaughter being inflicted upon him."

"True it is, O Conall," saith the king. "Now I perceive that I am not dear to thee."

And he put Conall from him, and Cuchulainn came before him, and he questioned him in the same manner. "I pledge my word," said Cuchulainn, "that if you should ask that of me, and that they should be brought home to you to be slain, I would not take the greatest bribe of the globe from thee, though it be sought eastward as far as India itself, in lieu of thy own head to fall for that deed."
"That is true, O Cuchulainn, I understand that thou also hast but little love for me."

And he put Cuchalainn from him and Fergus was brought to him. And he asked the same thing of him. And Fergus said: "I promise not to attack thine own flesh or blood; yet there is not an Ulsterman whom I should catch doing them hurt, but he should have death and destruction at my hands."

"Thou it is who must go for the Children of Usnach, O royal soldier," said Conchobar. "Set forward tomorrow, for they would come with thee. And on thy return from the east betake thee to the fortress of Borrach son of Annte, and pledge thy word to me that whether they arrive in Ireland by night or day neither stop nor stay be allowed them, so that they may come that night to Emain Macha." Then they came in together, and Fergus told the others that he had undertaken the safe-conduct of the Children of Usnach. . . . And they bore away that night.

Then Conchobar addressed Borrach, son of Annte, and asked him, "Hast thou a feast prepared for me?" "I have," said Borrach; "but though I was able to prepare it for thee, I was not able to bring it to thee to Emain Macha." "If it be so," said Conchobar, "bestow it instead upon Fergus, for one of his prohibitions is to refuse a feast." And Borrach promised and they bore away that night in safety.

And, on the morrow, Fergus arose early, and took with him neither troops nor attendants, save his own two sons, Illann the Fair and Buinne the Ruthless Red, and Fuillend, the lad of the Iubrach, and the Iubrach. And they moved forward to the fastness of the sons of Usnach, and to Loch Etive in Alba.

Now thus were the sons of Usnach. Three spacious hunting-booths they had; and the booth in which they did their cooking, in that they ate not, and the booth in which they ate in that they slept not.

And when Fergus came into the harbour he sent forth a mighty cry, so that it was heard throughout the farthest part of the districts around them. And Naisi and Deirdre were seated together with Conchobar's draught-board between them, and they playing thereon. Naisi said: "I hear the cry of a man of Erin." Now, Deirdre had heard the cry, and knew that it was the cry of Fergus, but she concealed it from them. "It was not the cry of a man of Erin," said Deirdre, "but the cry of a man of Alba." Again Fergus sent forth a cry, and Naisi said: "I hear another cry, and it is the cry of a man of Erin." "Not so," said Deirdre, "let us play on. Not alike are the cry of a man of Erin and the cry of a man of Alba." Fergus sent forth a third cry, and the sons of Usnach knew that this of a certainty was the cry of Fergus. Naisi bade Ardan go and meet him. Then Deirdre told Naisi that she had known the first cry of Fergus. "Why didst thou conceal it, damsel?" said Naisi. "Because of a vision I saw last night," said Deirdre, "to wit, that three birds came to us out of Emain Macha; and in their bills three sips of honey; the sips of honey they left with us, but they took with them three sips of our blood." "How is thy rede of the vision, O damsel?" said Naisi. "It is this," said she: "Fergus hath come from our own native land with peace; for not sweeter is honey than a false message of peace; and the three sips of blood that have been taken from us, they are ye, who will go with him and will be beguiled."

And they were sorry that she had spoken so. "Let that pass," said Naisi. "Fergus is long in the port, go therefore, Ardan, and meet him, and bring him with thee." So Ardan went, and he gave him three kisses fervently, loyally, and brought them with him to the stronghold of the sons of Usnach, wherein were Naisi and Deirdre; and they, too, gave three kisses lovingly and fervently to Fergus and to his sons.  And they asked tidings of Erin, and of Ulster in special. "These are the best tidings that I have," said Fergus, "that Conchobar hath sent me for you, and that I have entered into covenant for your safeguard, for I am ever loving and loyal to you, and my word is on me to fulfil my covenant."

"It is not meet for you to go thither," said Deirdre, "for your own lordship in Alba is greater than Conchobar's lordship in Erin." "Better than everything is one's native land," saith Fergus; "for poor is every excellence and prosperity to him who sees not his native land."

"That is true," said Naisi; "for dearer is Erin to myself than Alba, though I should obtain a greater share of Alba's goods." "My word and my warranty are firm to you," said Fergus. "Verily, they are firm," said Naisi, "and we will go with thee." But Deirdre consented not to what they said, and she strove to hinder their going. But Fergus pledged his word that if all the men of Ireland should betray them, the protection of their shields and swords and helmets should avail them little, for he would overcome them all.

"We know it," said Naisi, "and we will go with you to Emain Macha."

They bore away that night till the bright dawn of early morning on the morrow.  And Naisi and Fergus arose and sat in the galley, and they passed over the sea and the mighty ocean until they arrived at the fortress of Borrach, son of Annte.  And Deirdre looked behind her at the coasts of Scotland, and she cried, "My love to thee, O land of the east!  It is sad for me to leave the sides of thy havens and thy bays, thy smooth-flowered, delightful, lovely plains, and thy bright green-sided hills.  Little need had we to leave thee!" And she sang this lay:

### DEIRDRE'S FAREWELL TO ALBA

A lovable land is yon eastern land,
Alba, with its marvels.
I would not have come hither out of it,
Had I not come with Naisi.

Lovable are Dún-fidga and Dún-finn,
Lovable the fortress over them;
Dear to the heart Inis Draigende,
And very dear is Dún Suibni.

Caill Cuan!
Unto which Ainle would wend, alas!
Short the time seemed to me,
With Naisi in the region of Alba.

Glenn Láid!
Often I slept there under the cliff;
Fish and venison and the fat of the badger
Was my portion in Glenn Láid.

Glenn Masáin!
Its garlic was tall, its branches white;
We slept a rocking sleep,
Over the grassy estuary of Masán.

Glenn Etive!
Where my first house I raised;
Beauteous its wood: — upon rising
A cattle-fold for the sun was Glenn Etive.

Glenn Dá-Rúad!
My love to every man who hath it as an heritage!
Sweet the cuckoos' note on bending bough.
On the peak over Glenn Dá-Rúad.

Beloved is Draigen,
Dear the white sand beneath its waves;
I would not have come from it, from the East,
Had I not come with my beloved.

After that they came to Borrach's stronghold; and Borrach gave three kisses to the sons of Usnach, and made welcome to Fergus and his sons. And Borrach said: "I have a feast for thee, O Fergus! and a prohibition of thine is to leave a feast before it shall be ended."

When Fergus heard that, he reddened with anger from sole to crown. "Ill done is it of you, O Borrach!" said Fergus, "to put me under prohibitions, for I am under promise to Conchobar to bring the sons of Usnach to Emain Macha on the very day that they land in Ireland."

"I lay you under prohibitions," saith Borrach, "even prohibitions that true heroes will not endure, that thou come to partake of the feast." And Fergus asked Naisi what he should do as to that. "Do," said Deirdre, "what is desired of thee, if thou dost prefer to forsake the sons of Usnach and to consume the feast. Howbeit, to forsake them is a good price to pay for a feast."

"I will not forsake them," said Fergus, "for I will send my two sons with them to Emain Macha, even Illann the Fair, and Buinne the Ruthless Red, and my own word of honour, moreover." "We give much thanks for that," said Naisi, "since no hands but our own have ever defended us in battle or in conflict." And Naisi turned in great wrath from the place, and Deirdre followed him, and Ainle and Ardan, and Fergus's two sons. But that plan was carried out in opposition to Deirdre's wishes.

Fergus remained sunk in gloom and sadness. But of one thing he felt certain: if the five great fifths of Erin should be on one spot, and all of one counsel together, they would not be able to destroy his safe-guard. As to the sons of Usnach, they passed onward by the shortest and clearest way that they could go.

And Deirdre said: "I would give you good counsel, though you would not carry out my advice."

"What counsel hast thou, O girl?" said Naisi.

"Let us go to-night to the island of Cuilenn between Erin and Alba, and let us remain there until Fergus has concluded his feast; so will the word of Fergus be fulfilled, and the days of your princedom will be prolonged."

"To us that is an evil counsel," said Illann the Fair and Buinne the Ruthless Red. "It is impossible for us to carry out that advice. For even were the might of your own good hands not with us, and the plighted faith of Fergus sworn to you, ye would not be betrayed."

"Now is woe come upon us by means of that plighted word of Fergus," said Deirdre, 'when he forsook us for a feast."

And she was in grief and in deep dejection because they had come into Erin relying on the faith of Fergus. And then she said:

DEIRDRE.   "Woe that I came at the word
Of Fergus, the rash son of Rôich;
I will utter only lamentation on account of it.
Alas and bitter is my heart!

My heart as a clot of sorrow
Is to-night under great shame.
My grief, O goodly sons!
Your last days have come."

NAISI.   "Say not, O vehement Deirdre,
O woman, that art fairer than the sun!
Fergus would not to the eastward have come
To us, for our destruction."

DEIRDRE.   "Alas, I am sad for you,
O delightful sons of Usnach!
To have come out of Alba of the red deer,
Lasting shall be the woe of it!"

After that they went forward to the White Cairn of the Watching, on Sliab Fuad, and Deirdre remained behind them in the glen, and sleep fell upon her there. And they did not at first perceive that, till Naisi, observing it, turned back to meet her at the moment when she awoke out of her sleep. "Wherefore didst thou stay there, O Queen?" said he. "I fell into a sleep," said Deirdre; "and a vision and a dream appeared to me there." "What was that dream?" "I beheld each of you," said Deirdre, "without a head, and Illann the Fair headless also, but Buinne the Ruthless Red with his own head upon him, and his assistance not with us." And she made the staves: "Sad is the vision that appeared to me —." Thence they went forward to Ard na Sailech, "the Height of the Willows," which is called Armagh to-day. Then said Deirdre, "Sad is my heart, O Naisi, for I perceive a cloud above your head, a cloud of blood; and I would give you counsel, O sons of Usnach!"

"What counsel hast thou?" said Naisi.

"To go to-night to Dún Delgan (Dundalk) where Cuchulainn dwells and to abide there until Fergus come, or else to go under the safeguard of Cuchulainn to Emain."

"Since we are not afraid we will not follow that advice," said Naisi. And the girl sang:

> "O Naisi, look at the cloud
> Which hangs above thee in the air!
> I see over green Emain
> A mighty cloud of crimson blood. . . ."

After these staves, they went forward by the shortest way till they beheld Emain Macha before them. "I will give you a sign," said Deirdre, "if Conchobar should intend to work treachery upon you." "What is that sign?" said Naisi. "If you are invited into the house wherein are Conchobar and the nobles of Ulster, the king intends no evil against you. But if ye are sent to the house of the Red Branch while Conchobar stays on in the house of Emain, then treachery and guile will be wrought upon you."

And they went forward in that wise to the door of the house of Emain and they struck a loud stroke of the hand-wood at the door and asked that it should be opened for them. The doorkeeper answered and demanded who was there. They told him that without were the three sons of Usnach and Fergus's two sons and Deirdre. This was told to the king and he called his servants and attendants and asked them how stood the house of the Red Branch as to food and drink. They said that if the five battalions of Ulster should be gathered there they would find sufficiency of food and drink. "If that be so," said Conchobar, "let the children of Usnach be taken into it." This was told to the sons of Usnach. Then said Deirdre, "Alas, Naisi, great hurt hath befallen you through neglect of my counsel. Let us even now go back?"

"We will not do so," said Illann the Fair, son of Fergus, "and we protest, O girl, that great is the timidity and cowardice thou dost suggest to us in saying that. We will go to the house of the Red Branch," saith he.

"Assuredly we will go," said Naisi. And they moved forward to the house of the Red Branch; and servants and attendants were sent to them, and they were supplied with noble sweet-tasted viands, and with sweet, intoxicating drinks, till every one of their servants and attendants was drunk and merry and loud-voiced. But they themselves partook not of food and drink from the weariness caused by their travel and journey; for they had neither stopped nor stayed from the time they left the fort of Borrach till they came to Emain Macha.

Then said Naisi: "Let the 'Fair-head' [a draught or chess-board] of Conchobar be brought to us, so that we may play upon it." The "Fair-head" was brought to them, and its men were placed upon it, and Naisi and Deirdre began to play.

At the same hour Conchobar said, "Which of you, O warriors, will bring me tidings whether her own form and shape remain on Deirdre; for if she is unchanged, there is not among the race of Adam a woman whose form is more beautiful than hers." "I myself will go thither," said Levarcham, "and I will bring tidings." Now Naisi was dearer to Levarcham than any other in the whole world, and often she had gone abroad to seek Naisi and to bear tidings to him and from him. Then she went forward to the place wherein were Naisi and Deirdre.

Thus were they, with the "Fair-head" of Conchobar between them, and they playing on it. And Levarcham gave the sons of Usnach and Deirdre kisses of loyalty, lovingly, fervently; and she wept showers of tears, so that her bosom and her breast were wet. And she spake and said, "It is not well for you, O beloved children, to have with you that which the king is most loath to lose and you in his power. For it is to see whether her own form and shape remain upon Deirdre that I am sent to visit you. Grievous to me is the deed that they will do to-night in Emain, the treachery and shame and breach of troth practised upon you, O darling friends. And till the world's end Emain will not be better for a single night than it is to-night." And she made this lay: —

> "Sad to my heart is the shame
> Which is done in Emain to-night;
> And owing to this deed henceforward
> It will be an Emain of contentions . . ."

Levarcham told the sons of Fergus to shut the doors and the windows of the house of the Red Branch. "If ye be attacked, victory and blessing be with you! Defend yourselves well and defend manfully your charge, and the charge of Fergus." After that she went forward gloomily, sadly, unhappily weeping quick-trickling showers of tears to the place where Conchobar was; and the king asked tidings of her. She said: "I have evil tidings for thee and I have tidings that are good." "Tell me them," said the king of Ulster.

"These are the good tidings that I have," said Levarcham: "The three whose form and make are best, whose motion and throwing of darts are best, whose action and valour and prowess are best in Erin and in Alba, and in the whole great world beside, have come to thee, and henceforth against the men of Erin thou wilt have but the driving of a flock of birds, since the sons of Usnach go with thee. That is the best tidings that I have. And the worst tidings that I have are these: that the woman whose form and make were the best in the world when she went from us out of Erin, her own form and features no longer remain upon her."

When Conchobar heard that, his jealousy and bitterness abated. And they drank a round or two after that, and the king asked again: "Who will go for me to discover whether her own form and fashion remain upon Deirdre?"

Thrice he asked the question before he had his answer.

Then said Conchobar to Tréndorn, "O Tréndorn, knowest thou who slew thy father and thy three brothers?"

"I know that it was Naisi, son of Usnach, who slew them."

"If so," said the king, "go and see whether her own shape and form remain on Deirdre."

And Tréndorn, moved forward, and came to the hostel, and found the doors and windows shut; and dread and great fear seized upon him, and he said, "There is no proper way to approach the sons of Usnach, for wrath is upon them." But he found a window that was left unclosed through forgetfulness in the hostel, and he began to watch Naisi and Deirdre through the window. Now Deirdre, who was the most quick-witted, saw him there, and she nudged Naisi, and Naisi followed her eye and caught sight of that man.

And thus was he, having a dead man of the men of the draught-board, he made thereof a fearful successful cast, so that it landed in the young man's eye, and his eye fell out on the young man's cheek, so that he returned to Conchobar having only one eye. And he told him tidings from beginning to end, and said, "The woman whose form and feature are loveliest in the world is there, and Naisi would be king of the world if she were left to him." When Conchobar heard that, he was filled with jealousy and envy, and he proclaimed to the troops that they should go forward and assault the house of the Red Branch. And Conchobar and the men of Ulster came round the hostel and uttered many mighty shouts without, and cast fire and fire-brands into the house. When the children of Usnach heard the shouts they asked who were about the Red Branch.

"Conchobar and the men of Ulster," say they.

"It is like that it is Fergus's safeguard you mean to break," said Illann the Fair.

"By my troth," said Conchobar, "you and the sons of Usnach are like to rue that you have my wife with you."

"That is true," said Deirdre, "and Fergus hath betrayed you, O Naisi." "By my troth!" said Buinne, "if he hath been treacherous we will not be so." And Buinne the Ruthless Red came forth and slew three fifties at that onset, and he quenched the fires and the torches, and confounded the troops with that shout of doom.

Conchobar asked, "Who causes this confusion to the troops?"

"I, Buinne the Ruthless Red, son of Fergus."

"Take a bribe from me," said Conchobar, "and desert the children of Usnach."

"What bribe?" said he.

"A cantred of land," said Conchobar, "and my privacy and counsel." "I accept," said Buinne, and he took those bribes; but through God's miracle that night the cantred became a desolate moorland, whence it is called the Moorland of Buinne's Portion.

And Deirdre heard that parley. "My conscience!" she said, "Buinne hath deserted you, O sons of Usnach, and the son is like his father."

"By my own word," said Illann the Fair, "I am not like to leave them so long as this hard sword is left in my hand." And Illann came forth and made three swift circuits of the house, and slew three hundred of the Ulstermen without, and re-entered the place where Naisi was playing draughts with Ainle the Rough. And Illann made a circuit round them and drank a drink, and carried a torch alight with him out upon the green and began cutting down the troops, so that they dared not close round the hostel. A generous youth was Illann the Fair, son of Fergus! Jewels and treasures he refused to none; he took no stipend from any king nor did he accept a cow save only from Fergus.

"Where is my own son, Fiacha?" said Conchobar. "I am here," said he.

"By my troth, on one and the same night thou and Illann the Fair were born. And he hath his father's arms; do thou take my arms with thee, even the Bright-rim and the Victorious, and the Gapped Spear, and my sword; and do thou with them valiantly."

Then the two youths approached each other; and Fiacha advanced straight to Illann, and Illann asked, "What is thy desire, O Fiacha?" "A combat and a conflict I wish to have with thee," he said.

"Thou doest not well," said Illann, "for the sons of Usnach are under my safeguard."

Then they attacked each other and they fought a combat war-like, heroic, bold, daring, rapid. And Illann got the better of Fiacha, and made him crouch beneath the shadow of his shield, and the shield roared at the greatness of the need wherein he lay. And the three chief waves of Erin answered to that roar, even the wave of Cleena, the wave of Tuag Inbir, and the wave of Rury.

Conall the Victorious, son of Amargin, was at the time in Dun-severick and he heard the thunder of the wave of Rury. "True it is," said Conall, "Conchobar is in danger, and we should do amiss not to go to him." And he took his arms and went forward to Emain, and found the fight on the lawn, Fiacha, son of Conchobar having been overthrown, and the shield roaring and crying, for none of the Ultonians dared to interfere to rescue him. And Conall came up to Illann from behind and thrust his blue-green spear "the Culghlas" through him, even through his heart.

"Who hath wounded me?" said Illann. "And whoever did it, by my hand of valour, he would have got battle opposite my face from me, though he hath pierced me at my back."

"I, Conall," saith he; "and who art thou?"

"I am Illann the Fair, son of Fergus, and ill is the deed that thou hast done, for the sons of Usnach are under my protection."

"Is it so indeed?" saith Conall. "True it is," said he.

"Ah, my sorrow," saith Conall; "by my word Conchobar shall not bear off his own son alive from me in vengeance for that deed." And with that he gave a stroke of a sword to Fiacha the Fair and shore his head from his body, and he left them.

Then came the weakness of death upon Illann and he flung his arms into the hostel, and he called on Naisi to do valiantly, for he himself was slain unwittingly by Conall the Victorious.

Then came the men of Ulster round the dwelling, and cast fires and fire-brands into it; and Ardan came forth and quenched the fires, and slew three hundred of the host outside. And the second third of the night went Ainle forth to protect the dwelling; and he slew an innumerable multitude of the Ultonians, so that they retired with loss from the hostel.

Then Conchobar began to hearten the host, and at length came Naisi forth for his third of the night, and it is not possible to number all who fell by his hand. Then the Ultonians gave the battle of the morning to Naisi, and with his single hand he inflicted on them a three hours' rout.

Then Deirdre arose to meet him, and she said, "Victorious is the conflict that thyself and thy two brothers have made, and do ye valiantly henceforward. Ill is the counsel that you took to trust in Conchobar and the Ultonians, and sad it is that you did not do as I counseled." Then the children of Usnach linked each other's shields together; and they put Deirdre between them, and set their faces against the host and they gave three bounds, actively, as birds, over the walls of Emain outwards and slew three hundred at that onrush.

Then Conchobar sought out Cathbad the Druid; and he said, "O Cathbad, stay the children of Usnach, and work enchantment upon them, for if they escape from the men of Ulster at this time, they will destroy this province for ever. And I pledge my word moreover, that I will not harm the children of Usnach provided they be of my accord."

Cathbad believed those sayings of Conchobar, and he went about to restrain the children of Usnach, and he cast spells about them, for he put a great-waved sea along the field before the children of Usnach. Two feet behind them pressed on the men of Ulster though they dared not approach them until their arms fell from their hands and before them was the great sea overwhelming them, and Naisi uplifting Deirdre on his shoulder lest she should be submerged.

Then the king cried out to kill the children of Usnach, but all the men of Ulster refused to do it. For there was not one man in Ulster who had not wages from Naisi.

There was a youth there with Conchobar whose name was Maine Red-hand, the son of the King of Norway. Now Naisi had slain his father and his two brothers, and he said that he himself was ready to behead the children of Usnach in vengeance for that deed. "If so," said Ardan, "let me be the first to die, since I am the youngest of my brothers that I may not see my brothers die."

"Not so," said Ainle, "let me be slain the first."

"It shall not be so," said Naisi; "behold the sword of Manannan mac Lir which he himself gave to me. It leaves no relic of stroke or blow behind. Let us three be struck by it at once, so that none of us may see his brother beheaded." Then these three noble ones stretched forth their necks on one block; and Maine gave them a sword-blow, and shore the three heads at one stroke from them on that spot.

And each of the Ultonians at that grievous sight gave forth three heavy cries of grief.

As to Deirdre, while each of them was attending to the other she came forward on the green of Emain fluttering hither and thither from one to another, till Cuchulainn happened to meet her. And he took her under his safeguard, and she told him tidings of the children of Usnach, from beginning to end, how they had been betrayed.

"That is sad news to me," said he; "and dost thou know who put them to death?" "Maine Red-hand, son of the King of Norway," she said. Then came Cuchulainn and Deirdre to where the children of Usnach lay, and Deirdre dishevelled her hair, and began to drink Naisi's blood, and the colour of burning embers came into her cheeks, and she uttered this lay:

"Great these deeds in Emain," etc.

Then Deirdre said, "Let me kiss my husband." And she kissed Naisi and drank his blood and she sang thus:

"Long the day without Usnach's children.
It was not mournful to be in their company:
Sons of a king, by whom sojourners were entertained,
Three lions from the Hill of the Cave.

Three dragons of Dún Monaid,
The three champions of the Red Branch:
After them I am not alive —
Three that used to break every onrush.

Three darlings of the women of Britain,
Three hawks of Slieve Gullion,
Sons of a king whom valour served,
To whom soldiers used to give homage.

Three heroes who were not good at homage,
Their fall is cause of sorrow —
Three sons of Cathbad's daughter,
Three props of the battalion of Cuailgne.

Three vigorous bears,
Three lions out of Lis Una,
Three heroes who loved their praise,
The three sons of the breast of the Ultonians.

Three who were fostered by Aifé,
To whom a district was under tribute —
Three columns of breach of battle,
Three fosterlings whom Scathach had.

Three who were reared by Boghmain,
At learning every feat:

Three renowned sons of Usnach.
It is mournful to be absent from them.

That I should remain after Naisi,
Let no one in the world suppose;
After Ardan and Ainle,
My time would not be long.

Ulster's over-king, my first husband,
I forsook for Naisi's love;
Short my life after them.
I will perform their funeral game.

After them I shall not be alive —
Three that would go into every conflict,
Three who liked to endure hardships,
Three heroes who refused not combats.

A curse on thee, O Wizard Cathbad,
That slewest Naisi through a woman!
Sad that there was none to help him
The one King that satisfies the world!

O man, that diggest the tomb
And puttest my darling from me,
Make not the grave too narrow;
I shall be beside the noble ones.

Much hardship would I take
Along with the three heroes;
I would endure without house, without fire:
It is not I would be gloomy.

Their three shields and their spears,
Were often a bed for me;
Put their three hard swords
Over the grave, O gillie!

Their three hounds, and their three hawks,
Will henceforth be without hunters —
The three who upheld every battle,
Three fosterlings of Conall the Victorious.

The three leashes of those three hounds
Have struck a sigh out of my heart;
With me was their keeping,
To see them is cause of wailing.

I was never alone
Save the day of making your grave,

Though often have I been
With you in a solitude.

My sight hath gone from me
At seeing Naisi's grave.
Shortly my soul will leave me,
And the folk of my lamentation remain not.

Through me guile was wrought upon them,
Three strong waves of the flood!
Sad that I was not in earth
Before Usnach's children were slain!

Sad my journey with Fergus,
To deceive me to the Red Branch:
With his soft sweet words
He ruined me at the same time.

I shunned the delightfulness of Ulster —
Many champions and friends.
Being after them alone,
My life will not be long.

After that, Deirdre flung herself upon Naisi in the tomb and gave
three kisses to Naisi, and died forthwith, and stones were laid over
their monumental heap; their Ogham names were inscribed, and
their dirge of lamentation sung. And Cuchulainn went onwards
to Dundalk sadly and mournfully.

Then Cathbad the Druid cursed Emain Macha, in vengeance for
that great evil. Cathbad said, moreover, that neither Conchobar
nor any of his race should possess that stead from henceforth to all
eternity. And this has been verified, for neither Conchobar nor
any of his race possessed Emain from that time to this.

[tr. ELEANOR HULL]

# LYRICS AND SHORT PIECES

## THE DEER'S CRY [1]

I arise to-day
Through a mighty strength, the invocation of the Trinity,
Through belief in the threeness,
Through confession of the oneness
Of the Creator of Creation.

I arise today
Through the strength of Christ's birth with His baptism,
Through the strength of His crucifixion with His burial,
Through the strength of His resurrection with His ascension,
Through the strength of His descent for the judgment of Doom.

I arise to-day
Through the strength of the love of Cherubim,
In obedience of angels,
In the service of archangels,
In hope of resurrection to meet with reward,
In prayers of patriarchs,
In predictions of prophets,
In preachings of apostles,
In faiths of confessors,
In innocence of holy virgins,
In deeds of righteous men.

I arise to-day
Through the strength of heaven:
Light of sun,
Radiance of moon,
Splendour of fire,
Speed of lightning,
Swiftness of wind,
Depth of sea,
Stability of earth,
Firmness of rock.

I arise to-day
Through God's strength to pilot me:
God's might to uphold me,
God's wisdom to guide me,
God's eyes to look before me,
God's ear to hear me,
God's word to speak for me,
God's hand to guard me,

1. From *Selections from Ancient Irish Poetry*, edited by Kuno Meyer; Constable & Co., Ltd., London, 1911. Reprinted by permission of the publisher.

God's way to lie before me,
God's shield to protect me,
God's host to save me
From snares of devils,
From temptations of vices,
From every one who shall wish me ill,
Afar and anear,
Alone and in a multitude.

I summon to-day all these powers between me and those evils,
Against every cruel merciless power that may oppose my body and
     soul,
Against incantations of false prophets,
Against black laws of pagandom,
Against false laws of heretics,
Against craft of idolatry,
Against spells of women and smiths and wizards,
Against every knowledge that corrupts man's body and soul.

Christ to shield me to-day
Against poison, against burning,
Against drowning, against wounding,
So that there may come to me abundance of reward.
Christ with me, Christ before me, Christ behind me,
Christ in me, Christ beneath me, Christ above me,
Christ on my right, Christ on my left,
Christ when I lie down, Christ when I sit down, Christ when I arise,
Christ in the heart of every man who thinks of me,
Christ in the mouth of every one who speaks of me,
Christ in every eye that sees me,
Christ in every ear that hears me.

I arise to-day
Through a mighty strength, the invocation of the Trinity,
Through belief in the threeness,
Through confession of the oneness
Of the Creator of Creation.

                              [tr. KUNO MEYER]


                    WINTER  SONG [2]

          Take my tidings!
          Stags contend;
          Snows descend —
                    Summer's end!

2. From *The Poem Book of the Gael*, edited by Eleanor Hull; Chatto & Windus,
London, 1913.  Reprinted by permission of the publisher.

A chill wind raging;
The sun low keeping,
Swift to set
O'er seas high sweeping.

Dull red the fern;
Shapes are shadows:
Wild geese mourn
O'er misty meadows.

Keen cold limes
Each weaker wing.
Icy times —
Such I sing!
                    Take my tidings!
        [tr. ALFRED PERCEVAL GRAVES]


## THE OPEN-AIR SCRIPTORIUM [3]

(9th cent.)

Over my head the forest wall
Rises; the ousel sings to me;
Above my booklet lined for words
The woodland birds shake out their glee.

There's the blithe cuckoo chanting clear
In mantle grey from bough to bough;
God keep me still!   For here I write
His gospel bright in great woods now.
                    [tr. ROBIN FLOWER]


## THE PHILOLOGIAN AND HIS CAT [4]

Pangur is proof the arts of cats
    And men are in alliance;
His mind is set on catching rats,
    And mine on snaring science.

I make my book, the world forgot,
    A kind of endless class-time;
My hobby Pangur envies not —
    He likes more childish pastime.

3. From *The Silver Branch,* edited by Sean O'Faolain; Jonathan Cape, London, 1938. Reprinted by permission of Barbara Flower.
4. From *The Romanesque Lyric,* by P. S. Allen and H. M. Jones; The University of North Carolina Press, Chapel Hill, 1928.   Reprinted by permission of the publisher.

When we're at home time quickly flies —
  Around us no one bustles;
Untiringly we exercise
  Our intellectual muscles.

Caught in his diplomatic net,
  A mouse jumps down his gullet;
And sometimes I can half-way get
  A problem when I mull it.

He watches with his shining eye
  The wall that guards his earnings;
As for my eyesight — well, I try
  To match my stare with learning's.

His joy is in his lightning leap;
  Me — I'm a mental wizard;
My claws are sunk in problems deep,
  His, in a mousie's gizzard.

As comrades we admit we shine,
  For each observes his station;
He practices his special line,
  And I, my avocation.

Our rivalry you'll find is nice,
  If in the scale you weigh us:
Each day Pangur goes hunting mice,
  I bring forth light from chaos.
              [tr. HOWARD MUMFORD JONES]


## THE SONG OF MANCHAN THE HERMIT [5]

### Abbot of Liath Manchan (d. A.D. 665)

I wish, O Son of the Living God, O Ancient Eternal King,
For a hidden hut in the wilderness, a simple secluded thing.

The all-blithe little lark in his place, chanting his lightsome lay;
The calm clear pool of the Spirit's grace, washing my sins away.

A wide, wild woodland on every side, its shades the nursery
Of glad-voiced songsters, who at day-dawn chant their sweet psalm
    for me.

   5. From *The Poem Book of the Gael*, edited by Eleanor Hull; Chatto & Windus,
London, 1913.  Reprinted by permission of the publisher.

A southern aspect to catch the sun, a brook across the floor,
A choice land, rich with gracious gifts, down-stretching from my
    door.

Few men and wise, these I would prize, men of content and power,
To raise Thy praise throughout the days at each canonical hour.

Four times three, three times four, fitted for every need,
To the King of the Sun praying each one, this were a grace, indeed.

Twelve in the church to chant the hours, kneeling there twain and
    twain;
And I before, near the chancel door, listening their low refrain.

A pleasant church with an altar-cloth, where Christ sits at the board,
And a shining candle shedding its ray on the white words of the
    Lord.

Brief meals between, when prayer is done, our modest needs supply;
No greed in our share of the simple fare, no boasting or ribaldry.

This is the husbandry I choose, laborious, simple, free,
The fragrant leek about my door, the hen and the humble bee.

Rough raiment of tweed, enough for my need, this will my King
    allow;
And I to be sitting praying to God under every leafy bough.

[tr. ELEANOR HULL]

## THE VIKING TERROR [6]

Fierce is the wind tonight,
It ploughs up the white hair of the sea.
I have no fear that the Viking hosts
Will come over the water to me.

[tr. F. N. ROBINSON]

## LAMENT OF LIADAIN FOR CURITHIR [7]

"Joyless
The bargain I have made!
The heart of him I loved I wrung.

6. From *A Thousand Years of Irish Poetry*, edited by Kathleen Hoagland; The
Devin-Adair Co., New York, 1947. Reprinted by permission of the publisher.
7. From *Liadain and Curithir*, translated by Kuno Meyer; David Nutt, London, 1902.

'Twas madness
Not to do his pleasure,
Were there not the fear of the King of Heaven.

To him the way he has wished
Was great gain,
To go past the pains of Hell into Paradise!

'Twas a trifle
That wrung Curithir's heart against me:
To him great was my greatness.

I am Liadain
Who loved Curithir:
It is true as they say.

A short while I was
In the company of Curithir:
Sweet was my intimacy with him.

The music of the forest
Would sing to me when with Curithir,
Together with the voice of the purple sea.

Would that
Nothing whatever of all I might do
Should wring the heart of Curithir against me!

Conceal it not!
He was the love my heart,
If I loved every other.

A roaring flame
Dissolved this heart of mine, —
However, for certain it will cease to beat."

[tr. KUNO MEYER]


## THE SONG OF CREDE, DAUGHTER OF GUARE [8]

These are the arrows that murder sleep
At every hour in the night's black deep;
Pangs of love through the long day ache,
All for the dead Dinertach's sake.

Great love of a hero from Roiny's plain
Has pierced me through with immortal pain,

8. From *The Poem Book of the Gael*, edited by Eleanor Hull; Chatto & Windus, London, 1913. Reprinted by permission of the publisher.

Blasted my beauty and left me to blanch
A riven bloom on a restless branch.

Never was song like Dinertach's speech
But holy strains that to Heaven's gate reach;
A front of flame without boast or pride,
Yet a firm, fond mate for a fair maid's side.

A growing girl — I was timid of tongue,
And never trysted with gallants young,
But since I have won into passionate age,
Fierce love-longings my heart engage.

I have every bounty that life could hold,
With Guare, arch-monarch of Aidne cold,
But fallen away from my haughty folk,
In Irluachair's field my heart lies broke.

There is chanting in glorious Aidne's meadow,
Under St. Colman's Church's shadow;
A hero flame sinks into the tomb —
Dinertach, alas my love and my doom!

Chaste Christ! that now at my life's last breath
I should tryst with Sorrow and mate with Death!
At every hour of the night's black deep,
These are the arrows that murder sleep.

[tr. ALFRED PERCEVAL GRAVES]


## A PRAYER TO THE VIRGIN [9]

Gentle Mary, noble maiden, give us help!
Shrine of our Lord's body, casket of the mysteries!

Queen of queens, pure holy maiden,
Pray for us that our wretched transgression be forgiven for Thy sake.

Merciful one, forgiving one, with the grace of the Holy Spirit,
Pray with us the true-judging King of the goodly ambrosial clan.

Branch of Jesse's tree in the beauteous hazel-wood,
Pray for me until I obtain forgiveness of my foul sins.

Mary, splendid diadem, Thou that hast saved our race,
Glorious noble torch, orchard of Kings!

9. From *Selections from Ancient Irish Poetry*, edited by Kuno Meyer; Constable &
Co., London, 1911. Reprinted by permission of the publisher.

Brilliant one, transplendent one, with the deed of pure chastity,
Fair golden illumined ark, holy daughter from Heaven!

Mother of righteousness, Thou that excellest all else.
Pray with me Thy first-born to save me on the day of Doom.

Noble rare star, tree under blossom,
Powerful choice lamp, sun that warmeth every one.

Ladder of the great track by which every saint ascends,
Mayest Thou be our safeguard towards the glorious Kingdom.

Fair fragrant seat chosen by the King,
The noble guest who was in Thy womb three times three months.

Glorious royal porch through which He was incarnated,
The splendid chosen sun, Jesus, Son of the living God.

For the sake of the fair babe that was conceived in Thy womb,
For the sake of the holy child that is High-King in every place,

For the sake of His cross that is higher than any cross,
For the sake of His burial when He was buried in a stone-tomb,

For the sake of His resurrection when He arose before every one,
For the sake of the holy household from every place to Doom,

Be Thou our safeguard in the Kingdom of the good Lord,
That we may meet with dear Jesus — that is our prayer — hail!

[tr. KUNO MEYER]


## ON THE FLIGHTINESS OF THOUGHT [10]

Shame to my thoughts, how they stray from me!
I fear great danger from it on the day of eternal Doom.

During the psalms they wander on a path that is not right:
They fash, they fret, they misbehave before the eyes of great God.

Through eager crowds, through companies of wanton women,
Through woods, through cities — swifter they are than the wind.

Now through paths of loveliness, anon of riotous shame!

Without a ferry or ever missing a step they go across every sea:
Swiftly they leap in one bound from earth to heaven.

They run a race of folly anear and afar:
After a course of giddiness they return to their home.

10. Ibid.

Though one should try to bind them or put shackles on their feet,
They are neither constant nor mindful to take a spell of rest.

Neither sword-edge nor crack of whip will keep them down strongly:
As slippery as an eel's tail they glide out of my grasp.

Neither lock nor firm-vaulted dungeon nor any fetter on earth,
Stronghold nor sea nor bleak fastness restrains them from their
course.

O beloved truly chaste Christ to whom every eye is clear,
May the grace of the seven-fold Spirit come to keep them, to check
them!

Rule this heart of mine, O dread God of the elements,
That Thou mayst be my love, that I may do Thy will.

That I may reach Christ with His chosen companions, that we may
be together!
*They* are neither fickle nor inconstant — not as I am.

[tr. KUNO MEYER]

# III. OLD ENGLISH LITERATURE

Between the middle of the fifth and the end of the sixth century, the greater part of Britain, including the rich lowlands, was overrun by migratory Teutonic groups variously named, but most commonly called Saxons (*Saxones*) or English (*Angli*). When at the beginning of the seventh century they were converted to Christianity by Irish missionaries working from the northwest and Roman missionaries working from the southeast, they established monastic schools and began a literature that during the two centuries following was the most flourishing in Europe. Not only did they compose in Latin on Christian and Mediterranean themes that they learned in the missions, but they composed English poetry on native themes which is, together with the Irish poetry, the earliest vernacular poetry of consequence in the West.

This was the start of English literature, from which the language and literature of all English-speaking peoples have evolved. During the period normally called Old English, i.e., before the Norman Conquest, neither the language nor the literary conventions were static. The very acceptance of the Latin alphabet carried with it an acceptance of many Mediterranean forms of expression. The early kings maintained close relations with Rome and intermarried with families of Frankish rulers. Before the end of the eighth century, the Danes and other Scandinavian peoples, variously called Norman and Viking, began to immigrate to England, where they conquered territory for themselves and mingled their very similar language with that of the English. Though the British and Irish Celts influenced the English less than might be expected, Celtic themes and modes of thought worked into Old English literature, in part because many Englishmen went to Ireland to study. The complete Normanization of important English courts and offices, including those of the Church, following the Conquest brought about so notable a change in language and cultural interests that all English writing in the vernacular after about the year 1200, now called Middle English, is sufficiently modern to fall outside the scope of this volume of translations.

Old English poetry has survived largely by chance; for not only were the Norman conquerors who took over the palaces and schools disdainful of the native language and literature, but English monasteries were secularized before historical interest was strong enough to stimulate individuals to preserve the old. Nearly all the remains of pre-Norman poetry are contained in four manuscripts. This chance survival does not assure us that the best has been preserved.

The earliest poet whose name and approximate period are known is Caedmon of Whitby, who, according to a famous tale in Bede's *Ecclesiastical History,* turned into English verse-paraphrase large portions of the Bible. The only extant poem assuredly his is the

129

hymn translated below. The other Old English poet of equal renown is Cynewulf, who lived probably at the end of the eighth century and composed tales of apostles and saints. Other poems in the four manuscripts consist of renditions of Teutonic and classical legends, martial and occasional verse, original lyrics, gnomes, and riddles. More extensive prose writings have been preserved, but they are less interesting to all save historians and linguistic specialists, since prose writers who wanted a wide audience and who wrote on themes of general interest usually chose Latin.

There have been periodic efforts to revive or to adapt Old English poetic forms. The most interesting and valuable attempts are those of mid-nineteenth century poets, especially Tennyson, who not only translated (*The Battle of Brunanburh,* below), and imitated (*Merlin and the Gleam*), but adapted the rhythms and assonances for particular effects, as in the first part of *Maud,* where he pictures his hero with some of the primitive melancholy of Old English verse.

# BEDE

The effect on Europe and western civilization of the flowering of English culture in the seventh century following the conversion to Christianity of the English and Saxons cannot be overestimated. As the whole continent lay exhausted, socially, politically, and economically, following the collapse of Rome and the inundations of the barbarians, a small and energetic group of new English Christians established, through Benedictine monasticism, schools and churches which acted as centers for a growing science and learning. Slowly but energetically they assembled books and other works of art from disrupted Roman centers and evolved a pattern of Christian education that was transferred to the Continent by missionaries and teachers in the eighth century. The two greatest of these were Boniface of Wessex, who became apostle to the Germans and who Christianized all of central Germany, and Alcuin, who left the famous school at York to lead Charlemagne's palace school and from there, under the authority of Charlemagne, to reform and to rehabilitate the monastic and diocesan schools throughout the Carolingian Empire, which then stretched from the Baltic Sea to Rome and from the Atlantic to the gates of the Byzantine Empire.

As thriving cultures usually have great authors to tell their story to the world, so did the English. Bede, a priest of the double monastery of Wearmouth and Jarrow, by the shores of the North Sea not far from the present Newcastle, was trained only in the local school, which absorbed the best not only from the Romans in the south but from the Irish (*Scotti*) who had extended their missions from Iona and Lindisfarne in the north. Though known to us now primarily as the "Father of English History" or "Father of English Literature," he was in his own time and for five centuries thereafter venerated throughout Europe as a writer and teacher but slightly inferior to the four great doctors of the Church. His sincere and imaginative *Ecclesiastical History of the English People* retains today the popularity it has enjoyed for twelve hundred years; Laistner lists 159 medieval codices containing the complete work and nearly as many more containing extracts. There have been eight editions of English translations since 1900. But he wrote many other works in both verse and prose — biographies, saints' lives, textbooks, scientific tracts, chronicles, scriptural commentaries, homilies, hymns, and letters. There are still in existence more than sixteen hundred medieval codices containing some one or more of his works.

The *Lives of the Abbots,* which is here translated in full from Bede's Latin, not only displays his pictorial power and pious honesty, which made the *History* famous, but also tells with an authenticity no modern history could equal how the English reversed the downward trend into ignorance and started Europe toward progressive intellectual and moral revival.

## LIVES OF THE ABBOTS OF WEARMOUTH AND JARROW

Bede (A.D. 673–735)

[From *Baedae Opera Historica*, VOL. II, edited by J. E. King; Loeb Classical Library; Harvard University Press, 1930. Reprinted by permission of the publisher.]

### BOOK I

Beginneth the life of the holy abbots of the monastery in Wearmouth and Jarrow, Benedict, Ceolfrid, Eosterwine, Sigfrid, and Hwaetbert set in order by Bede, priest and monk of the said monastery:

Biscop surnamed Benedict, a devout servant of Christ, being favoured of heavenly grace, built a monastery in honour of the most blessed Peter, chief of the apostles, by the mouth of the river Wear on the north side, Egfrid the venerable and right godly king of that nation aiding him with a grant of land; and amid innumerable travails of journeyings or sicknesses Biscop diligently ruled the said monastery for sixteen years with that same devotion wherewith he did build it. And that I may use the words of the blessed pope Gregory, where he extolleth the life of an abbot that had Biscop's surname: "He was a man of venerable life, Benedict in grace and in name, having the heart of a man of ripe age even from the time of his boyhood, for in the ways of his life he was beyond his years and gave not his heart to any pleasure." He was come of noble lineage among the English, but being no less noble of mind he was lifted up to be deserving of the company of angels for evermore. In brief, when he was thane to king Oswy and received of his hand a gift of land suitable to his degree, being at the time about 25 years of age, he disdained the perishable possession that he might obtain one that was eternal; he despised earthly warfare with its reward that decayeth, that in warfare for the true King he might be vouchsafed to have a kingdom without end in the heavenly city; he forsook home, kinsfolk and country for Christ's sake and the Gospel's, that he might receive an hundredfold and have everlasting life; he refused to be in the bonds of carnal wedlock, in order that in the glory of virginity he might follow the Lamb without spot in the kingdom of heaven; he would not beget mortal children by carnal generation, being foreordained of Christ to bring up for Him by spiritual instruction sons to be immortal in the heavenly life.

So, leaving his native land he went to Rome, and set himself also to visit and worship in the body the places where are the bodies of the blessed apostles, with love of which he had ever been kindled; and by and by having returned home he never ceased diligently to love, honour, and proclaim to all whom he might those rules of ecclesiastical life which he saw at Rome. At which time Alchfrid, son of the aforesaid king Oswy, being also himself minded to visit Rome for the purpose of worshipping at the churches of the blessed apostles, took Biscop for his companion in the same journey. But when his father recalled him from his purpose in the said journey and caused him to remain in his own country and kingdom, none the less Biscop, being a young man of virtuous nature, forthwith finished the journey which was begun, and hastened with great speed to return to Rome in the days of pope Vitalian of blessed memory, whom we named before; and on this, as also on the visit he made before, having enjoyed abundantly the delights of wholesome learning, he departed thence after a few months and came to the island of Lérins, where he joined the company of monks, received the tonsure, and having the mark of the vow of a monk he kept the rule of discipline with all due care; but after being for two years trained in the learning that belongeth to monastical conversation, he was once more overcome of the love he bore toward blessed Peter, the chief of the apostles, and determined once again to visit the city hallowed of his body.

And not long after, by the coming of a merchant vessel he had his wish. Now at that time Egbert, king of Kent, had sent from Britain a man named Wighard which had been chosen for the office of bishop, and had been well instructed in all ecclesiastical usage by the Roman scholars of the blessed pope Gregory in Kent; and Egbert desired to have him ordained bishop at Rome, so that having a prelate of his own nation and tongue, he and all the people under him might be the more perfectly instructed whether in the words or mysteries of the faith; insomuch as they would receive these things, not through an interpreter, but by the lips and hand withal of a man that was of their own kin and tribe. But when he came to Rome, this Wighard, with all his company that came with him, died of a disease that fell upon them, before he could receive pontifical rank. Whereupon the apostolical pope, unwilling that this godly embassy of the faithful should fail of its due fruit by reason of the death of the ambassadors, took counsel and chose one of his own men, whom he might send to Britain for archbishop, to wit Theodore, a man learned in secular no less than in ecclesiastical philosophy, and that in both languages, Greek that is and Latin, and he gave him for colleague and counsellor a man of no less stoutness of heart and wisdom, the abbot Hadrian: and because he saw that the venerable Benedict would be a prudent, diligent, devout and notable man, he entrusted unto him the bishop whom he had ordained, and all his company, bidding him give up the pilgrimage which he had undertaken for Christ's sake, and in regard of a higher advantage return to his countrymen, bringing the teacher of truth they had earnestly required, to the which teacher he might become interpreter as well as guide, both on the way thither and when he was teaching therein. Benedict did as he was bidden: they came to Kent, and were very gladly received. Theodore ascended the episcopal throne; Benedict took upon him the governance of the monastery of blessed Peter the apostle, whereof the aforementioned Hadrian was presently made abbot.

When Benedict had ruled that monastery for two years, he hastened to make his third journey to Rome; which he carried out with his accustomable success, and brought back many books of all subjects of divine learning, which had been either bought at a price or been given him freely of his friends. And when on his way home he was come to Vienne, he there recovered of the friends to whom he had entrusted them the books that he had bought. Whereupon having entered into Britain he was minded to go to Cenwalh, king of the West Saxons, of whose friendship he had before had benefit, and received help of his service. But at that same time, Cenwalh being cut off by untimely death, Benedict at length turned his steps to his own people and the land wherein he was born, and came to the court of Egfrid, king of the Transhumbrian region. Unto him he rehearsed all the things he had done since the time that he left home in his youth; he openly shewed the zeal for religion which was kindled in him; he discovered to him all the precepts of ecclesiastical and monastical usage which he had learned at Rome or anywhere about, displaying all the divine volumes and the precious relics of the blessed apostles or martyrs of Christ, which he had brought with him; and he found such grace and favour in the eyes of the king that he forthwith bestowed upon him, out of his own estate, seventy hides of land, and bade him build a monastery there in honour of the chief pastor of the Church. The which was built, as I also mentioned in the preface, at the mouth of the river Wear toward the north, in the 674th year from the Lord's incarnation, in the second Indiction, and in the fourth year of the rule of king Egfrid.

And when not more than a year had passed after the foundation of the monastery, Benedict crossed the ocean to France, where he required, procured, and brought away masons to build him a church of stone, after the Roman fashion which he always loved. And in this work, out of the affection he had for the blessed Peter in whose honour he wrought it, he shewed such zeal that within the course of one year from the time the foundations were laid, the roof was put on, and men might see the solemnities of mass celebrated therein. Further, when the work was drawing nigh to completion, he sent messengers to France, which should bring over makers of glass (a sort of craftsman till that time unknown in Britain) to glaze the windows of the church, its side-chapels and clerestory. And so it was done, and they came: and not only did they finish the work that was required of them, but also caused the English people thereby to understand and learn this manner of craft: the which without doubt was worthily meet for the fastening in of church lamps, and for the manifold employments to which vessels are put. Moreover, this devout buyer, because he could not find them at home, took care to fetch from oversea all manner of things, to wit sacred vessels and vestments that were suitable to the ministry of the altar and the church.

Further, to the intent he might obtain for his church from the boundaries of Rome those ornaments also and writings which could not be found even in France, this diligent steward made a fourth journey thither (after he had well ordered his monastery according to the rule), and when he had brought it to an end, he returned laden with a more abundant gain of spiritual merchandise than before. First, because he brought home a vast number of books of every kind; secondly, because he procured a plentiful grace of the relics of the blessed apostles and martyrs of Christ to be profitable to many English churches; thirdly, because he introduced into his monastery the order of chanting, singing, and ministering in church according to the manner of the Roman usage, having indeed asked and obtained of pope Agatho leave to bring to the English in Britain a Roman teacher for his monastery, to wit John, archchanter of the church of the blessed apostle Peter and abbot of the monastery of the blessed Martin. The which John coming thither, not only by the word of his lips delivered what he had learned at Rome to his scholars of ecclesiastical things, but also left good store of writings which are still preserved for the sake of his memory in the library of the said monastery. Fourthly, Benedict brought a worthy gift, namely, a letter of privilege from the venerable pope Agatho, which he obtained with the leave and consent of king Egfrid, and at his desire and request, whereby the monastery built by him was rendered wholly safe and secure continually from all assault from without. Fifthly, he brought home sacred pictures to adorn the church of the blessed apostle Peter built by him, namely, the similitude of the blessed mother of God and ever Virgin Mary, and also of the twelve apostles, with the which he might compass the central vault of the said church by means of a board running along from wall to wall; similitudes of the Gospel story for the adornment of the south wall of the church; similitudes of the visions in the Revelation of the blessed John for the ornament of the north wall in like manner, in order that all men which entered the church, even if they might not read, should either look (whatsover way they turned) upon the gracious countenance of Christ and His saints, though it were but in a picture, or might call to mind a more lively sense of the blessing of the Lord's incarnation, or having, as it were before their eyes, the peril of the last judgment might remember more closely to examine themselves.

So king Egfrid, being greatly delighted with the virtue, industry, and godliness of the venerable Benedict, and seeing that his former gift was well bestowed and bringing forth fruit, was minded to enlarge the grant of land that he had made him for the building of the monastery, by giving him yet another forty hides; and hither, a year after, Benedict sent about seventeen monks, setting Ceolfrid over them as abbot and priest; and with the advice or rather even by

the commandment of the said king Egfrid, he built the monastery of
the blessed apostle Paul; on this condition only, that there should be
unity of peace and agreement, and that friendship and kindness
should continually be preserved the same between the two places;
that just as, to make comparison, the body may not be severed from
the head whereby it breathes, and the head may not forget the body
without which it hath not life, so none should attempt by any means
to separate, the one from the other, these monasteries which were
joined together in the brotherly fellowship of the two chief apostles.
Now this Ceolfrid whom Benedict appointed abbot was from the
very beginning of the earlier monastery in all things his most zealous
helper, and he had gone with him to Rome at a convenient season,
both to receive needful instruction and to worship withal. At the
which time also he chose Eosterwine, priest of the monastery of the
blessed Peter, for abbot, and set him to be ruler over the said monastery: to the intent that the burden, which was too great for him to
bear alone, might be lightened when he was helped by the good
courage of a beloved fellow-soldier. Nor let any man think it
strange that one abbey should have two abbots at the same time.
The cause thereof was Benedict's often journeying in the service of
the monastery, his frequent departing and uncertain return across
the ocean. For history also relates that the most blessed apostle
Peter, of necessity laid upon him, appointed two bishops under him
in succession at Rome to rule the Church. And the great abbot
Benedict himself, as blessed Gregory telleth us of him, set twelve
abbots over his disciples, as he judged expedient; neither did he
thereby lessen brotherly love but rather enlarged it.

The man aforesaid then took over the charge of ruling the monastery in the ninth year from the time it was founded, and he continued
therein for four years until his death. He was of noble birth, but
did not, as is the manner of some, turn the ornament of noble birth
to an occasion for boasting and despising others, but, as becometh
a servant of God, to a means of greater nobility of soul. He was
indeed cousin of his abbot Benedict; but so high was the honourable
spirit of them both, so utterly did they look down upon worldly
honour as of nothing worth, that the one, when he entered into the
monastery, thought it not meet to seek any dignity for himself above
the rest in regard of family or noble birth, nor did the other think
it should be offered unto him; but of the good purpose of his heart
in eating of the same platter with the brethren his boast was to keep
the rule of discipline in all things as befitted his youth. And albeit
he had been thane to king Egfrid, he put away worldly cares once
for all, laid down his weapons, took up spiritual warfare only, and
continued humble and so wholly like the other brethren that he
was glad to winnow and thresh with them, to milk the ewes and cows,
and cheerfully and obediently to be employed in the bakehouse, the
garden, the kitchen, and all the business of the monastery. Moreover, after he had taken on him the governance and rank of abbot,
he continued to be of the same mind toward all as he had been be-

fore, according to the admonition of a wise man which said: "They have made thee ruler; be not lifted up, but be among them as one of the rest, gentle, courteous, and kindly to all." It is true that, when he found it convenient, he would check sinners by the discipline of the rule, but with the natural affection he was wont to shew he would rather diligently admonish them, that none should be willing to sin and cloud the fair light of the abbot's countenance with the shadow of their own disquietness. Often as he went abroad any whither to look to the business of the monastery, if he found the brethren at work, he would straightway join himself to their labour — either taking the plough handle to guide the furrow, or fashioning iron with the hammer, or shaking the winnowing-fan, or doing some other such thing. For he was a young man, both able for strength and gentle of speech; and beside of a cheerful spirit, a liberal giver, and of a comely presence. He ate of the same food as the rest of the brethren, and always in the same building with them; he slept in the selfsame common abode as he did before he was abbot, insomuch that even when smitten with sickness and already warned with sure tokens of his approaching death, he still lay for two days in the brethren's dormitory. For during the remaining five days, up to the hour of his departing, he bestowed himself in a more private dwelling; and coming out thence on a certain day and sitting in the open, he called unto him all the brethren, and according to the pitifulness of his nature he gave them the kiss of peace, as they wept and lamented for the departure of so good a father and shepherd. He died on the seventh day of March in the night, while all the brethren were employed in the praise of the early singing of psalms. He was twenty-four years of age when he entered into the monastery; he lived twelve years therein; he discharged the duties of the priesthood for seven years, four of which he spent in the governance of the monastery; and so, "leaving his earthly frame and limbs ready to die," he went to the kingdom of Heaven.

But now that thus much hath been given as foretaste touching the life of the venerable Eosterwine, let us return to the course of our story. No long time after Benedict had appointed him abbot over the monastery of the blessed apostle Peter, and Ceolfrid abbot over the monastery of blessed Paul, he hastened from Britain to Rome for the fifth time, and returned and enriched as always with a countless number of gifts of advantage to the churches, namely, a great store indeed of sacred books, yet with the wealth, as before, of no lesser a present of sacred pictures. For at this time also he brought with him paintings of the Lord's history, with the which he might compass about the whole church of the blessed Mother of God, built by him within the greater monastery; he also displayed, for the adorning of the monastery and church of the blessed apostle Paul, paintings shewing the agreement of the Old and New Testaments, most cunningly ordered: for example, a picture of Isaac carrying the wood on which he was to be slain, was joined (in the next space answerable above) to one of the Lord carrying the cross on

which He likewise was to suffer.  He also set together the Son of
Man lifted up on the cross with the serpent lifted up by Moses in
the wilderness.  Amongst other things he also brought home two
palls all of silk of exceeding goodly workmanship, with the which
he afterward purchased from king Aldfrid and his counsellors (for
Egfrid after his return he found had now been killed) three hides of
land south of the river Wear, near the mouth.

But in the midst of the gladness that he brought in his coming, he
found sorrowful tidings at home: to wit, that the venerable priest
Eosterwine (whom at the point to go away he had appointed abbot),
as well as no small number of the brethren committed to his charge,
had already departed this world of a pestilence which was everywhere
raging.  Yet was there comfort too, because he found that Sigfrid
the deacon, a man as meek as he was reverend, had been by and by
appointed in the room of Eosterwine out of the said monastery, being
chosen thereto both of the brethren as well as of his fellow-abbot
Ceolfrid.  He was a man well instructed in the knowledge of the
Scriptures, adorned with excellent virtues, endowed with a wonderful gift of abstinence, albeit he was grievously hampered in safe-
guarding the powers of his mind with bodily sickness, being sore
troubled to keep the innocency of his heart by reason of a noisome and
incurable malady of the lungs.

And not long after, Benedict also himself began to be distressed
with an attack of sickness.  For in order that the virtue of patience
might be added to give proof beside of their great zeal for religion,
the mercy of God caused them both to be cast into bed of a temporal
malady; to the end that after sickness had been conquered of death,
He might refresh them with the abiding rest of heavenly peace and
light.  For both Sigfrid, chastened (as I have said) with the long
trouble of his inward parts, drew to his end, and Benedict was so
weakened during three years with the ailment of a creeping palsy,
that he was utterly dead in all the lower part of his body, the upper
parts alone (without life in which a man may not remain alive)
being preserved for the exercise of the virtue of patience; and both
of them endeavoured in the midst of their pain to give continual
thanks to their Maker, and to be ever occupied with the praise of
God and the encouragement of their brethren.  Benedict set himself
to strengthen the brethren that ofttimes came unto him in the observance of the rule which he had given them: "For ye are not to
think," quoth he, "that of my own heart without direction I have
set forth the ordinances that I have appointed for you.  For all the
things I have found most excellent in seventeen monasteries, whereunto I came in the travel to and fro of my long and often journeyings,
I committed to memory and conveyed to you to keep and profit
therefrom."  The glorious library of a very great store of books
which he had brought with him from Rome (and which in regard
of instruction in the Church could not be spared) he commanded
to be diligently kept whole and complete and not marred by neglect
nor broken up and scattered.  Moreover, this charge he was con-

stantly wont to repeat to the said brethren, namely, that in the choice
of an abbot none of them should think that family kindred should
be sought for rather than uprightness of life and doctrine. "And I
tell you of a truth," quoth he, "that comparing the two evils, I deem
it far more tolerable that all this place where I have built the monastery should be made a wilderness for ever, if God so will, than that
my brother after the flesh, whom we know to be walking not in the
way of truth, should follow me in the governance thereof as abbot.
Therefore, my brethren, be ye always very careful never to choose
a father for the sake of his family, nor one from any place outside.
But in accordance with the rule of our sometime abbot, the great
Benedict, and in accordance with the decrees of our letter of privilege,
look ye out with common consent in the assembly of your congregation the man which, by reason of his good life and wise doctrine,
shall be shewn better fitted and more worthy than others for the
fulfilment of such a ministry, and whomsoever ye shall all with one
accord upon loving enquiry judge and choose to be the best: then
summon the bishop, and require him to confirm this man with the
accustomed blessing to be your abbot. "For they," he said, "which
beget carnal sons by carnal process must needs seek carnal and
earthly heirs for a carnal and earthly inheritance; but they which
beget spiritual sons by the spiritual seed of the word, must in all
things be spiritual in their doings. Let them then reckon him as
the eldest son among their spiritual children, who is thus endowed
with more abundant spiritual grace, just as earthly parents are wont
to acknowledge their firstborn son as the chief of their offspring,
and to consider him to be preferred before the rest, when they divide
their inheritance."

Nor must I forbear to tell how ofttimes the venerable abbot Benedict, in order to abate the weariness of the long nights when he could
not sleep by reason of his grievous malady, would call a reader and
have him read to him the story of Job's patience or some other passage of Scripture, whereby in his sickness he might be comforted and
be exalted with a more lively hope to things above out of the depth
wherein he was brought down. And because he could in no wise rise
to pray nor without difficulty give utterance or lift up his voice to
fulfill the course of the regular psalmody, this wise man, taught of his
love of religion, accustomed himself at the several hours of the daily
and nightly prayers to summon unto him some of the brethren which
should sing the appointed psalms antiphonally, that so he himself
singing with them so far as he might should by their aid fulfil what
he could not accomplish of himself.

But when the two abbots, worn out by long-continued sickness,
perceived that they were nigh unto death and would not be fit to rule
the monastery (for so sore lay their bodily sickness upon them, perfecting in them the power of Christ), that one day, when each desired
to see and speak with the other before departing this life, Sigfrid was
carried on a stretcher to the chamber where Benedict too was himself
laid upon his pallet, and their attendants placing them side by side,

their heads were set on the same pillow (a lamentable sight), and albeit their faces were close together they had not strength to bring them near to kiss each other; yet even this they brought to pass with the help of the brethren. Then Benedict, after wholesome counsel held with Sigfrid and all the brethren, summoned abbot Ceolfrid whom he had set over the monastery of the blessed apostle Paul, being his kinsman not in the bond of the flesh so much as in fellowship of virtue. And all the rest agreeing and deeming it most expedient, he appointed him father over both monasteries; for he judged it best in every way for the maintenance of the peace, unity, and agreement of the two places that they should continually have one father and governor — oftentimes recounting the example of the kingdom of Israel, which could not ever be driven from its boundaries by foreign nations and remained without hurt so long as it was ruled by one and the same leader from its own nation; but when afterward on account of its former sins the people became enemies to one another and were parted asunder with contention, it gradually perished and fell to ruin from its former stability. He likewise bade them unceasingly remember the Gospel precept, which says that "every kingdom divided against itself shall be brought to desolation."

BOOK II

So when after these things two months had gone by, in the first place Sigfrid the venerable abbot, beloved of God, was brought into the refreshment of eternal rest through the fire and water of temporal tribulation, and entered into his home in the kingdom of heaven, paying unto the Lord in sacrifices of continual praise the vows he had promised with often parting of clean lips; and when four more months were passed, Benedict, the conqueror over sin and glorious worker of righteousness, being conquered of bodily weakness came to his end. "The night falls chilly with winter blasts"; but for that holy man is soon to rise the day of everlasting happiness, peace and light. The brethren assemble at the church, and sleeplessly pass the dark hours in prayers and psalms: lightening the burden of their father's departure with the unceasing melody of praise to God. Others abide in the chamber, where Benedict, sick in body but strong in mind, was looking for his passage from death and his entry into life. All that night, as was the custom to be done other nights too, the Gospel is read aloud of a priest to comfort his pain; as the hour of his departure is at hand, the sacrament of the Lord's body and blood is given him for his voyage provision; and so this holy soul, searched and tried with the slow flames of profitable chastisement, leaveth the furnace of earth in the flesh, and flieth in deliverance to the glory of heavenly bliss. And to his departure in great triumph, which might not be let or hindered in any way of evil spirits, witness is borne also by the psalm which at that time was being sung for him. For the brethren, hurrying together to the church at nightfall, sang through the psalter, and had at that time reached the eighty-second psalm which has for its title "Lord, who shall be like unto Thee?" of the which psalm thus is the whole meaning, that the enemies of the name of Christ, whether they be carnal or ghostly, do strive to break up and destroy always the Church of Christ and always every faithful soul; but contrariwise they themselves shall be confounded and dismayed and perish everlastingly, their strength being weakened of the Lord, to Whom there is none like, Who only is the highest over all the earth. Whence it was rightly understood to be disposed from heaven that such psalm should be said in the hour when his soul was leaving his body, against whom, the Lord being his helper, no enemy might prevail. In the sixteenth year after he had founded the monastery, this confessor fell asleep in the Lord, on the twelfth day of January, and was buried in the church of the blessed apostle Peter; so that after death his body lay not far from the relics and the altar of him whom, whiles he was in the flesh, he ever loved, and who opened for him the door of entry into the kingdom of heaven. For sixteen years, as we have said, he ruled the monastery; the first eight of himself without appointment of a second abbot beside; the last eight with the venerable and holy Eosterwine, Sigfrid, and Ceolfrid to aid him with the title, authority, and office of abbot; the first during four years, the second during three years and the last during one.

And he that was third of these, namely Ceolfrid, a man diligent in all things, of quick understanding, not slothful in business, ripe in judgment and fervent in religious zeal, did first, as too we have said before, at the behest as well as with the help of Benedict, found, complete, and govern the monastery of the blessed apostle Paul for a space of seven years; and after for twenty-eight years did wisely govern over both monasteries, or, as we might say more truly, over the single monastery of the blessed apostles Peter and Paul situated in two different places. And all the notable works of righteousness begun by his predecessor, these Ceolfrid was as ready to endeavour to complete. For beside all other things needful for the monastery, which his long rule thereof taught him should be provided, he built many chapels; he multiplied the vessels of the church and altar, and all kinds of vestments; the library of either monastery, which abbot Benedict had been so instant to begin, was of him with no lesser diligence doubled, insomuch that he added three pandects of the new translation to the single copy of the old which he had brought from Rome; and one of these, when he went back in his old age to Rome, he carried with him amongst other things for a present, but two he bequeathed to the two monasteries. Moreover, in exchange for the manuscript, most excellent for workmanship, of the Cosmographers, which Benedict had bought at Rome, he procured from king Aldfrid, a man well learned in the Scriptures, eight hides of land beside the river Fresca for the possession of the monastery of the blessed apostle Paul; and this manner of procuring the land had been fixed by the estimation of Benedict, whilst he still lived, with the said king Aldfrid, but he died before he could complete it. But somewhat later under king Osred, Ceolfrid, paying a fit price in addition, exchanged this piece of land for twenty hides in the place which is called by the inhabitants At the Township Sambuce, because this land was seen to be nearer the said monastery. Having sent monks to Rome in the days of pope Sergius of blessed memory, Ceolfrid obtained from him a privilege for the protection of the monastery, like that which pope Agatho had granted to Benedict; and this being brought to Britain and made known before the synod was confirmed by the subscription of the bishops there present as well as by that of the noble king Aldfrid, in the manner in which, as is well known, the former privilege was publicly confirmed in a synod by the king and bishops of its time. It was in king Aldfrid's time that Witmer, an aged and devout servant of Christ, skilled in all secular learning as well as in knowledge of the Scriptures, giving himself to the monastery of the blessed apostle Peter (which Ceolfrid then ruled) made over to the same monastery ten hides of land for a continual possession, granted him for a possession by king Aldfrid and situate in the township called Dalton.

But Ceolfrid, after long discipline in observance of the rule which the father had providently given of the authority of men of former time for the profit of himself and his followers; after displaying a diligence which might not be equalled in prayer and chanting, wherein he ceased not to exercise himself daily; after shewing marvellous zeal in restraining the froward, and sobriety in comforting the weak; after practising an abstinence in food and drink and a poverty of dress rare among rulers, perceived that, being now old and full of days, he could no longer, on account of the hindrance of his great age, either by precept or example, require of them which were subject to him the due pattern of spiritual practice. After much pondering a long time in his heart, he judged it better to enjoin the brethren, in accordance with the decrees of their privilege and the rule of the holy abbot Benedict, to choose out of their number a fitter man to be their father, and determined himself to revisit the holy places of the blessed apostles at Rome, where in his youth he had been with Benedict: to the end that before his death he might both himself have for a season a respite from the cares of the world and freedom to remain privily with himself in peace apart, and that the brethren, having taken a younger man for abbot, might in accordance with the age of their new master keep with greater perfection the usages that belonged to the life of their rule.

Although at first all withstood him and knelt before him with sobs and tears and oft-repeated prayers, it was done as he willed. And so eager was he to set out that he hastened to begin his journey the third day after he had declared his secret purpose to the brethren. For he had fear, as indeed it came to pass, lest he should die before he might reach Rome and wished withal to avoid that his undertaking should be hindered by his friends or the principal men with all whom he was held in honour, and lest money should be given him by some whom he could not at once repay. For his constant habit was, if any man made him a gift, that he would recompense it either at once or after a meet interval with no less a favour. So, after mass had first been sung in the morning in the church of the blessed mother of God, the ever Virgin Mary, and in the church of blessed Peter, on the fourth day of June, being the fifth day of the week, all who were present having made their communion, he straightway prepared to go.  All assemble in the church of blessed Peter, and Ceolfrid, having himself lighted the incense and said the prayer at the altar, standing on the steps with the censer in his hands, giveth them all his peace.  From thence they go forth, the sound of weeping that all made being heard in the midst of the litanies, and enter the chapel of the blessed martyr Laurence, which stood opposite in the brethren's dormitory.  And bidding his last farewell, he warneth them to preserve mutual love and to correct offenders in accordance with the Gospel; he offereth to all who may have offended the grace of his forgiveness and good-will; he beseecheth all to pray for him and to be reconciled to him, if there were any whom he had rebuked with more harshness than he should.  They come to the shore; again he giveth the kiss of peace to all amidst their tears; he prayeth and goeth aboard the ship with his company.  The deacons of the church also embark, bearing lighted tapers and a golden cross.  He crosseth the river, adoreth the cross, mounteth his horse and departeth, leaving in his monasteries brethren to the number of about six hundred.

And as he departed with his company, the brethren return to the church, and with tears and prayers commend themselves and their belongings to God.  And after no long interval, having finished the psalms of the third hour, they all again assemble.  They consider what should be done; they determine with all speed to ask for a father from God with prayer and singing of psalms and fasting; they discover their determination to the monks of blessed Paul, which were their brethren, through some of them which were present as well as through some of their own company.  These also agree; both monasteries are of one mind; the hearts of all and the voices of all are lifted up unto the Lord.  At length on the third day, at the coming of Pentecost Sunday, all the monks of the monastery of blessed Peter met in council, and of the elders of the monastery of blessed Paul not a few.  All are of one mind and both have the same opinion.  And so Hwaetbert is chosen abbot, which had not only been taught from earliest childhood in that same monastery the rule of regular discipline, but was also very diligently practised in the arts of writing, chanting, reading, and teaching.  He too in the days of pope Sergius of blessed memory hastened to Rome, and after tarrying there no small time, learned, copied and brought home all things that he judged needful for himself.  Moreover he had also discharged the office of the priesthood for twelve years before.  Having therefore been chosen abbot by all the brethren of the two aforesaid monasteries, he straightway took with him some of the brethren and came to abbot Ceolfrid, who was waiting for a ship to take him across the ocean.  They inform him whom they had chosen abbot. He answereth, "Thanks be to God," confirmeth the election, and receiveth from Hwaetbert's hands a letter of recommendation to be delivered to the apostolical pope Gregory, some passages whereof we have also thought fit to set down in this work by way of record.

"To the most beloved lord in the Lord of all lords, the thrice blessed pope Gregory, Hwaetbert your humble servant, abbot of the monastery of Peter the most blessed chief of the apostles, which is in Saxony, continual health in the Lord.

"I, together with the holy brethren which in this place desire with me to bear Christ's most pleasant yoke to the end they may find rest for their souls, cease not to give thanks to the ordinance of the heavenly judgment, for that it hath vouchsafed to appoint you who are so glorious a vessel of election for the governance of the whole Church in our time, in order that by means of this light of truth and faith wherewith ye are filled He might shed abundantly the light of His love also on all which are of less account.  Now, most beloved father and lord in Christ, we commend to your holy grace the venerable grey hairs of our most beloved father, the abbot Ceolfrid, the nurse and guardian of our spiritual freedom and peace in monastical quietness.  And first of all we give thanks to the holy and undivided Trinity that, albeit he has himself departed from us to our exceeding grief amid sighing, lamentation, and shedding of tears, yet he hath attained the holy joys of the rest so long desired of him, seeing that even in the weariness of old age he hath devoutly again sought to come to those churches of the blessed apostles which he remembered with joy to have visited, seen, and worshipped in the time of his youth.  And after the long travail of more than forty years and the continual cares he had in ruling the monasteries over which he was made abbot, being as it were newly summoned for his unequalled love of virtue to the conversation of heavenly life, in his extreme old age and even now at the point to die, he is beginning again to be a pilgrim for Christ's sake, that so the burning fire of repentance may the more readily consume in the spiritual furnace the former thorns of worldly cares.  Next we further entreat your paternity carefully to perform for him the last office of compassion, which we have not been thought worthy to render, being well assured that, albeit his body is with you, yet we as well as you have in his Godfearing spirit (whether abiding in the body or set free from the bonds of the flesh) a mighty intercessor and advocate on behalf of our transgressions before the heavenly mercy." And hereon followeth the rest of the letter.

Now on Hwaetbert's return home, bishop Acca was summoned, of whom he was confirmed in the office of abbot with the accustomable benediction.  Among the privileges without number which with the wise exercise of his youthful diligence he recovered for the monastery, this was especially pleasant and grateful to all: he took up the bones of abbot Eosterwine, which had been laid in the porch of entry to the church of the blessed apostle Peter, and also the bones of his sometime master, abbot Sigfrid, which had been buried without the sanctuary toward the south, and placing both in one box (but divided by a middle partition) he laid them within the same church beside the body of the blessed father Benedict. Now this he did on Sigfrid's birthday, that is, on the twenty-second day of August, on which day it also happened by the wonderful providence of God that Witmer died, the venerable servant of Christ, of whom we have already spoken. And there where the aforesaid abbots were already buried, he who had been their follower was himself interred.

But Ceolfrid, the servant of Christ, as has been said before, was smitten of sickness as he was hastening to the churches of the blessed apostles and ended his last day before he arrived there. For, reaching Langres about the third hour of the day, he departed to the Lord the tenth hour of the self-same day. And on the morrow he was buried honourably in the church of the blessed Twin Martyrs, amidst the tears and lamentations not only of the Englishmen who to the number of more than eighty had been in his company but also of the inhabitants of that place, grieving that so reverend an old man had been hindered of his desire. Nor indeed was it easy for any man to restrain his tears when he saw some of Ceolfrid's companions go on the way they had begun without their father, and others change their purpose of desiring to come to Rome and rather return home where they might report his burial, while yet others, out of their undying love for their father, remained by the tomb of the dead man in the midst of a people whose language they did not understand.

Now at the time of his death he was seventy-four years of age, forty-seven of which he had spent in the priest's office, thirty-five in the discharge of an abbot's duties, or rather forty-three, because indeed from the first time in which Benedict began to build the monastery in honour of the most blessed chief of the apostles, Ceolfrid was not divided from his company and was his helper and fellow teacher of the regular and monastical life. And that no occasion either of age or sickness or travel should ever abate the practice of the strictness ordained of old, from the very day he set out to depart from his monastery until the day on which he died, namely, from the fourth day of June until the twenty-fifth day of September, for one hundred and fourteen days he had the psalter sung twice daily in due order, not reckoning the canonical hours of prayer; and even when he was grown so weak that he could no longer ride, but had to be carried in a horse-litter, after mass had been sung he daily made to God the offering of the saving Host, save only one day when he was on the ocean and the three days before his death.

Now he died on the twenty-fifth day of September in the 716th year of the incarnation of the Lord, on the sixth day of the week, after the ninth hour, in the fields belonging to the afore-named city; and he was buried on the morrow toward the south of the said city at the first milestone within the monastery of the Twins in the presence of a great host, not only of the English which had come with him, but also of the brethren of the said monastery and of the inhabitants of the city, which all sang psalms. Now these twin martyrs in whose monastery and church he was buried are Speusippis, Eleusippus, and

Meleusippus, which were delivered at one birth and born again in the same faith of the Church, together with their grandmother Leonilla; and they left behind them a memorial of their martyrdom worthy of the spot. And may they bestow even upon us unworthy and upon our father the pitiful help of their intercession and protection!

[tr. H. F. STEWART]

# BEOWULF

The most renowned Old English poem is the long narrative *Beowulf,* of 3182 lines, now existing in a single manuscript copied at the end of the tenth century. The language shows that the original was composed about the beginning of the eighth century by a poet who adapted and incorporated in his work songs and stories of Continental origin. In brief, the story deals with King Hrothgar, whose great hall, Heorot, has been ravaged by two primitive monsters who appear at night and slay his retainers. The spreading news reaches the land of the Geats, in southern Sweden, where Beowulf, the nephew of King Hygelac, resolves to pit his skill against the monsters. The poem falls into three major parts. In the first, Beowulf voyages to the land of the Danes, is entertained by Hrothgar, and at night fights singlehanded against Grendel, the first monster, who has come to the hall for his wonted carnage. Beowulf fatally wounds Grendel, who flees to the mere, leaving his severed claw in Beowulf's hands. The second part, given in full below, narrates the second struggle, with Grendel's dam, who comes to avenge his death. The third part tells how, after Beowulf has been feted and enriched by Hrothgar for ridding him of the two monsters, he returns to rule his own country. There, after a reign of fifty years, he must face a dragon who is ravaging his land. In a duel in keeping with Teutonic literary convention, Beowulf slays the dragon but receives a death-wound himself and dies while a single companion swears his vengeance on the retainers who deserted at time of need. The dragon's treasure is buried and Beowulf's remains are consumed on the great funeral pyre while the remaining Geats chant dirges and view the future with foreboding.

The verse pattern of *Beowulf* consists of lines broken into "staves" by a caesura. Each stave contains two strong accents and a variable number of unaccented syllables. The staves are bound by a recurring alliteration on the stressed syllables. According to J. C. Pope, this accent and alliteration fell together with the chord struck on the accompanying harp. The following lines, giving the first two sentences translated below, illustrate the verse pattern of the extant poetry written in English before the Norman Conquest and of a notable amount written before 1450.

> Sigonþa to slæpe.     Sum sare angeald
> æfen-ræste, swa him ful     oft gelamp,
> siþðan gold-sele     Grendel warode,
> unriht æfnde,     oþþæt ende becwom,
> swylt æfter synnum.

BEOWULF

Anonymous (8th cent.)

[From *Beowulf and the Finnesburh Fragment,* translated by C. G. Child; Houghton Mifflin Co., Boston, 1904. Reprinted by permission of the publisher.]

They sank then to sleep.  One paid sorely for his evening's rest, even as full often had befallen them after Grendel took the gold-hall for his own, did what was not right till the end came, death following upon his sins.  It became plain, and known far and wide of men, that an avenger still lived even yet after him, the loathly one, for a long time following upon that bitter warfare.  Grendel's mother kept thought of her sorrow, a she-one, a monster-wife, that was fated to dwell midst the water's terrors, in the cold streams, after Cain had slain by the sword his only brother, his kin by one father — outlawed he went away then with the mark of murder on him, to flee the joys of men, and dwelt in waste places.  Of him were born many demons ordained of fate; Grendel was one of them, an outcast filled with hatred, who found at Heorot a man watching, awaiting battle.  There the monster came to grips with him, but he was mindful of the strength of his might, the deep-seated gift God had given him, and trusted him for grace in the Almighty, for comfort and aid; hence he overcame the fiend, felled the demon of hell.  Then went he forth, that foe of mankind, abject and reft of joy, to look on the house of death.  And, still thereafter, his mother, greedy and dark of mood, was of mind to go a journey fraught with grief to avenge the death of her son, came therefore to Heorot, where the Ring-Danes slept in the hall.  Then when Grendel's mother made her way in, was there straightway there for the earls a turning backward to what had been before.  The terror was less even by so much as is woman's strength, the fierceness of a woman in fight, beside a weaponbearer's, when the sword bound with gold, wrought with the hammer, the blade blood-stained, sheareth with its tough edge the swine that standeth above the helmet.

Then in the hall from above the benches was the hard-edged sword taken down, many a broad shield lifted in the hand's grip; they whom the terror seized took no thought of helmet or broad burnie.  The monster was in haste, would thence away to save her life, for that she was discovered.  Quickly had she one of the athelings fast in her clutch, and went off to the fen.  He whom she slew at his rest was a strong shield-warrior, a warsman of enduring fame, of all the men in office of comrade the dearest to Hrothgar between the seas.  Beowulf was not there, for before then, after the treasure-giving, another resting-place had been fixed upon for the mighty Geat.  There was outcry in Heorot.  She had taken in its gore the hand of Grendel that so much had been made of. Sorrow was begun anew, was come again to their homes. The bargain was not good, seeing they must on either hand make purchase with the lives of friends.

Then was the old king, the hoar warrior, stricken in spirit when he knew his chief thane, the one dearest to him, to be lifeless and dead. Beowulf, the warrior crowned with victory, was quickly fetched to the bower. At daybreak, he, together with his earls, the high-born warrior himself with his followers, went where the wise king awaited if so be, after tidings thus grievous, the Almighty might ever will to work a change for him. The hero tried in battle went then with his fellowship over the floor — the timbered hall rang — to give words of greeting to the wise lord of the Ingwines, asked him, as courtesy bade, if his night had been peaceful.

Hrothgar, helm of the Scyldings, spake: "Ask not concerning that which gives joy. Sorrow is renewed among the Dane-folk. Dead is Æschere, Yrmenlaf's elder brother, my counsellor and adviser, the comrade who stood shoulder to shoulder with me when we kept guard of our heads in battle, when the footmen met together, and boar-helms clashed. Such an atheling, passing good, as Æschere was, should an earl be. The murderous demon, the wandering one, with her hand hath slain him in Heorot. I know not what path from here the fell one hath taken, glorying in her carrion food, glad of her fill. She hath avenged thine onslaught, that thou didst kill Grendel yesternight in pitiless wise by thy close grip, for that he long had minished and slain my people. Guilty of death, he fell in battle, and now hath a second come, a spoiler mighty for mischief; she is minded to avenge her kinsman, and hath carried her vengeance so far that it may seem torment of spirit hard to bear to many a thane that sorroweth in his soul for his treasure-giver. Now the hand lieth helpless that was earnest to thee of aught whatsoever that is worth the having.

"I have heard the dwellers in the land, my people, they that hold sway in their halls, say they have seen such twain as these, mighty prowlers along the borders of the homes of men, making the moors their own. One of these was, so far as they might most carefully judge, in form like a woman; the other misbegotten one trod in man's shape the path of exile, save that he was greater in size than any man. Him in days of old the earth-dwellers named Grendel; they knew not his father, or whether any lurking demons were ever born to him. They take as theirs a country hidden away, the wolf-fells and windy nesses, perilous fen-ways, where the flood of the mountain-stream goeth downward under the earth beneath the mists of the forelands. It is not far hence, measured in miles, where the mere standeth. Rime-covered thickets hang over it; a wood fast-rooted shadoweth the waters. There may a fearful marvel be seen each night, a fire in the flood. None liveth ever so wise of the children of men that knoweth the bottom. Though the rover of the heath, the stag, strong with his antlers, may seek, hunted from afar, that thick wood, he will yield up his spirit first, his life on its brink, ere he will hide away his head within it.  The place is not goodly. Thence riseth a coil of waters dark to the clouds, when the wind stirreth up foul weather till the air groweth thick and the heavens make outcry.

"Now, again, is help in thee alone.  That country thou know'st not yet, the fearsome place, where thou mayest find the much-sinning one.  Seek it if thou darest.  I shall requite thee for the strife with gifts for the keeping, with old-time treasures and twisted gold, as I did before, shouldst thou come thence away."

Beowulf spake, the son of Ecgtheow: "Sorrow not, man of wise mind!  It is better one should avenge his friend than mourn for him long.  Each of us must abide life's end in this world.  Let him that may, win fame ere death; that shall be best thereafter for a warrior, when life is no more.

"Arise, warden of the realm, let us go quickly to look upon the track of Grendel's fellow.  I promise thee he shall not flee to shelter, not in earth's bosom, or mountain forest, or ocean's bed, go where he will.  For this day have patience in thine every woe, as I ween thou wilt."

Then the old man sprang up and gave thanks to God, the mighty Lord, for that the hero had spoken.  A horse then, a steed with plaited mane, was bridled for Hrothgar.  The wise king went in state; with him fared forth a foot-band of shield-bearers.  The tracks were plain to see far along the forest-ways, the path she hath taken across the levels; straight went she over the murky moor, bare away, with his soul gone from him, the best of Hrothgar's kindred that with him governed the homestead.

Then over the steep stone-fells and narrow tracks, in close by-paths, an unknown way, by beetling cliffs and many a nicker's lair, went the son of athelings.  With a few wise-minded men, he went before to see the place, till he found suddenly the mountain trees, the joyless wood, leaning over the hoar rock.  The water stood beneath, blood-stained and troubled.  It was for all the Danes, for the friends of the Scyldings, a sorrow of soul to bear, grief to many a thane and every earl, when they came upon the head of Æschere on the sea-cliff.  The flood boiled, as the people gazed upon it, with blood and hot gore.

The horn at times sang its stirring lay of battle.  All the band sat them down.  They saw in the water many of the dragon-kind, strange sea-drakes making trial of the surge, likewise on the jutting rocks the nickers lying that oft at hour of dawn make foray grief-giving on the sail-road, and dragons and wild beasts beside.  In bitter wrath and swollen with fury, these hasted away; they heard the call, the war-horn singing.  The prince of the Geats severed the life from one with a bow, as it strove with the sea, so that the stout battle-shaft went home to its life.  Slower was it then in swimming the deep, seeing death had gripped it.  Then quickly was it hemmed in closely in the waves with boar-spears keen-barbed, assailed with shrewd thrusts, and drawn on the headland, the wondrous wave-lifter. The men gazed on the fearsome unfriendly thing.

Then Beowulf put on him his earl's armor: in no wise had he misgivings for his life. His war-burnie hand-woven, broad and cunningly adorned, that could well shield his body so battle-grip might not harm his breast or the foe's shrewd clasp his life, must needs make trial of the deeps. But his head the white helmet guarded, that must mingle with the sea-depths, seek the coil of the surges, well-dight as it was with treasure-work, bound with lordly chains, as the weapon-smith wrought it in far-off days, decked it with wonders, set it with swine-shapes, that thereafter brand nor battle blade might bite it. Not least of these great helps was that which Hrothgar's spokesman had loaned him in his need; the hafted sword was named Hrunting. It was one of the chiefest of old-time treasures. Its edge was iron, dyed with poison-twigs, hardened with blood; never in battle did it betray any that clasped it in hand, durst tread the ways of terror, the meeting-place of the foe. That was not the first time it should do a deed of prowess. Surely the son of Ecglaf in the might of his strength kept not thought of what he before spake, drunken with wine, when he lent that weapon to a warrior better with the sword than he. He durst not himself hazard his life beneath the waves, striving to do a warrior's duty: thereby he forfeited the honor, the acclaims of prowess. Not so was it with the other, after he had arrayed himself for the strife.

Beowulf spake, the son of Ecgtheow: "Keep thou now in mind, great son of Healfdene, wise prince, freehanded friend of men, now I am ready for my venture, that of which we already have spoken, that, should I for thy need be shorn of life, thou wouldst ever be to me, gone hence away, in the place of a father. Be thou a guardian to my thanes, my close comrades, if the strife take me. Likewise send the treasures thou gavest me, dear Hrothgar, to Hygelac; then may the lord of the Geats, the son of Hrethel, know by the gold and see, when he looketh on the treasure, that I found a giver of rings goodly in manly virtues, had joy of him whilst I might. And do thou let Hunferth, warrior famed afar, have his precious war-sword with its tough edge, handed down from old. I shall win fame for myself with Hrunting or death shall take me."

After these words the prince of the Weder-Geats hasted in his valor, would in no wise await an answer; the coil of the waters laid hold of the warrior. It was a day's while ere he might see the bottom-level. Soon she, that, ravenous for food, grim and greedy, had held for half a hundred winters the stretches of the flood, found that some one of men was there from above searching out the home of beings not man-like. She laid hold then upon him, seized him in her terrible claws. His hale body she hurt not thereby; his mail with-out shielded him round, so she might not, with her loathly fingers, reach through his war-coat, the linked battle-sark. The sea-wolf, when she came to the bottom, bare him then, the ring-giving prince, to her home, in such wise he might not, brave as he was, wield his weapons, though, because of it, many strange beings pressed him close in the deep, many a sea-beast with its fighting-tushes brake his battle-sark, harried their troubler.

Then the earl was aware he was in one knows not what fearsome hall, where no water might harm him aught, or the quick grip of the flood touch him, because of the roofed hall. He saw the light of fire, a flashing flare brightly shining. The worthy one looked then on the she-wolf of the sea bottom, the mighty water-wife. The full strength of onset he gave with his battle-axe, his hand held not back from the stroke, so that on her head the ring-decked blade sang out its greedy war-song. The foe found then that the battle-gleamer would not bite, or harm her life, for its edge betrayed the prince in his need. Erstwhile had it gone through many a close encounter, cloven oft the helm and battle-mail of the doomed; for the first time then did the dear treasure lay down its glory. Still was the kinsman of Hygelac, mindful of proud deeds, of one thought and in no wise lost courage. In wrath the warrior threw aside the chased sword, strong and steel-edged, set with jewels, that it lay on the earth; he trusted to his strength, to the might of his hand-grip. So must a man do when he thinketh to reach in battle enduring fame: he careth naught for his life.

Then the lord of the War-Geats — he shrank not at all from the strife — seized Grendel's mother by the shoulders. Strong in battle he hurled his life's foe, for that he was swollen with wrath, so she fell to the ground. Quickly she paid him back his dues to his hand in savage clinchings, and laid hold upon him. Spent in spirit, the fighter on foot, strongest of warriors, tripped so he fell. Then she threw herself on the stranger in her hall, and drew her dagger broad and bright-edged — she thought to avenge her son, her only child. His woven breast-mail lay on his shoulder; it shielded his life, withstood the in-thrust of point and blade. Then had the son of Ecgtheow, foremost fighter of the Geats, gone to his death beneath the broad deeps, had not his battle-burnie, the stout battle-mesh, given him help; and Holy God, the Wise Lord, Ruler of the Heavens, held sway over victory in battle, awarded it aright. Readily thereafter he found his feet.

He saw then among the war-gear a blade oft victorious, an old sword of the eotens, doughty of edge, one prized by warriors; it was the choicest of weapons, save that it was greater than any other man might bear out to the battle-play, good and brave to see, the work of giants. The warrior of the Scyldings seized it by its chain-bound hilt. Raging and battle fierce, he drew the ring-marked blade, and despairing of life smote so wrathfully that the hard edge gripped her by the neck, brake the bone-rings; the sword went clean through her fated body, and she fell to the ground.

The sword was bloody; the hero gloried in his deed. The fire flamed forth; light stood within there, even as when the candle of the sky shineth brightly from heaven. He looked about the dwelling, turned him then to the wall. The thane of Hygelac, wrathful and steadfast of thought, raised the hard weapon by the hilt. The edge was not useless to the warrior, for he was minded to requite Grendel speedily for the many onslaughts he had made on the West-Danes far oftener than a single time, when he slew Hygelac's hearth-comrades in their sleep, ate fifteen men as they slept of the Dane-folk, and bare off as many more, a loathly spoil. Beowulf, relentless warrior, so far paid Grendel with his dues for that, that he now saw him lying on his bed, battle-weary and lifeless, in such wise as the strife in Heorot had scathed him. The corse sprang far when it underwent a blow after death, a hard sword-stroke, and Beowulf cut off the head.

Soon the men of wise thought, who with Hrothgar looked on the water, saw that the swirl of the wave was all mingled with blood, that the flood was stained with it. The white-haired old men spake together of the goodly atheling, how they looked not he should come again, glorying in victory, to seek their mighty prince, for because of the blood, it seemed to many that the sea-wolf had slain him. Then came the ninth hour of the day. The brave Scyldings left the cliff; the gold-giving friend of men went him homeward. The strangers sat there, sick at heart, and stared on the mere. They wished and yet trusted not, to see their dear lord's self.

Then the war-brand, the sword, began, because of the monster's blood, to fall away in battle-icicles; a marvel was it how it all melted likest to ice, when the Father, that holdeth sway over times and seasons, freeth the bonds of the frost, unwindeth the flood's fetters. He is the true Lord.

The chief of the Weder-Geats took no more of the treasure-holdings in the dwelling, though he saw many there, but only the head, and with it the sword's hilt, brave with gold; the sword had already melted, its chased blade burned wholly, so hot was the blood, so poisonous the demon of the strange kind, that met her death there in the hall.

Soon was he swimming, that had borne erstwhile the battle-shock of the foe. He dove up through the water. The moil of the waves was all cleansed, the wide domains where the strange demon had yielded up her life's day and this world that passeth.

The safeguard of seafarers, the strong of heart, came swimming then to land; he joyed in his seaspoil, the mighty burden he had with him. Then went they to him, his chosen band of thanes; God they thanked, had joy of their lord, for that it was given them to see him safe. Speedily then the helmet and burnie of the unfaltering one were loosed. The pool, the water beneath the clouds, stained with the blood of slaughter, grew still.

Forth thence they fared by the foot-paths, joyful of heart. The men measured the earth-way, the well-known road, bold as kings. The head they bare from the sea-cliff with toil that was heavy for any of them, great of courage though they were; four it took to bear Grendel's head with labor on the shaft of death to the gold-hall, till to the hall came faring forthwith the fourteen Geats, picked men brave in battle. Their liege-lord together with them trod boldly in the midst of them the meadow-stretches.

Then the foremost of the thanes, the man brave of deed, exalted in glory, the warrior bold in strife, came in to greet Hrothgar. Grendel's head, grisly to behold, was borne into the hall, where the men were drinking before the earls and the lady as well. The men looked on that sight strange to see.

Beowulf spake, the son of Ecgtheow: "Lo, with joy we have brought thee, son of Healfdene, lord of the Scyldings, in token of glory, the sea-spoil thou here beholdest. Not easily came I forth with my life, hazarded with sore hardship the toils of war beneath the waters. Almost had the strife been ended, save that God shielded me. Naught might I achieve with Hrunting in the strife, good as that weapon is, but the Ruler of Men vouchsafed it me to see hanging on the wall an old sword, noble and mighty — most oft is He guide to the friendless — so that I drew the weapon. Then I slew in the struggle the guardians of the hall, for the chance was given me. The battle-blade then, the chased sword, was burned to naught, when the blood sprang forth, hottest of battle-gore; I bare away thence the hilt from my foes, avenged in fitting wise their evil deeds and the Danes' death-fall. I promise thee, therefore, thou mayest in Heorot sleep free from care with thy fellowship of warriors, and every thane of thy people likewise, young and old — that thou needest not, lord of the Scyldings, have dread of death-peril for them on this hand, for thine earls, as thou didst ere this." Then the golden hilt, the work of giants long ago, was given into the hand of the old prince, the white-haired battle-leader. After the overthrow of the devilish ones, it fell, the work of marvellous smiths, into the keeping of the Danes' lord; when the grim-hearted one, God's foe, with murder upon him, gave up the world, and his mother also, it fell in this wise into the keeping of the best of world-kings, between the seas, of those that in Scedenig parted gifts of gold.

Hrothgar spake, looked on the hilt, the old heirloom, on which was written the beginning of that far-off strife, when the flood, the streaming ocean, slew the giant kind — they had borne themselves lawlessly. The people were estranged from the Eternal Lord; the Wielder, therefore, gave them their requital through the whelming of the waters. So was it duly lined in rimed staves on the guard of gleaming gold, set down and told for them for whom that sword was wrought, choicest of blades, with twisted hilt and decked with dragon-shapes.

Then the wise one spake, the son of Healfdene; all were silent: "That, lo, may he say that worketh truth and right among the people (the old warden of the realm keepeth all in mind from of old) that this earl was born of a nobler race. Thy fame is exalted, my friend Beowulf, among every people throughout the wide ways. Wholly with quietness dost thou maintain it, thy might with wisdom of heart. I shall fulfil my troth to thee, that we spake of, ere now, together. Thou shalt be in every wise a comfort, long-established, to thy people, a help to the warriors.  Heremod was not so to the children of Ecgwela, the Honor-Scyldings.  He grew not up to do as they would have him, but to cause death-fall and deadly undoing for the Dane-folk.  In the swelling anger of his heart he slew his table-companions, they that stood at his shoulder, till he went alone, the mighty prince, from the joys of men.  Though the mighty God raised him up and set him forth in the joys of dominion and gifts of strength above other men, none the less there grew in his mind and soul a blood-greed.  He gave out rings to the Danes not at all as befitted his high estate, lived joyless, and so suffered stress for his vengeful doings, a fate long-enduring at the hands of his people.  Do thou learn by this.  Lay hold upon manly worth.  As one wise in years, I have framed thee this discourse.

"A marvel it is how mighty God in the greatness of His soul bestoweth wise judgment on mankind, land-holdings and earlship; He hath rule over all.  Whiles letteth He the heart's thought of a man of high race turn to having and holding, giveth him the joys of this world in his country, a fastness-city of men to keep, so contriveth for him that he ruleth parts of the earth, a wide realm, such that he may not know the bounds thereof.  He dwelleth in fatness; sickness nor age turn him aside no whit; preying sorrow darkeneth not his soul, nor doth strife show itself anywhere, nor warring hate, but all the world wendeth to his will.  He knoweth not the worse, till that within him a deal of overweening pride groweth and waxeth, while the warder sleepeth, shepherd of the soul.  Too fast is that sleep, bound round with troubles; very nigh is the slayer that in grievous wise shooteth with his bow.  Then is he smitten in the breast, with his helmet upon him, by a bitter shaft.

"He cannot guard him from the devious strange biddings of the Accursed Fiend.  That seemeth him too little which he hath long held.  Perverse of mind, he is greedy, giveth not at all out of pride the rings of plate-gold, and he forgetteth and taketh no heed of the fate to come, because of the deal of blessings God, the King of Glory, hath already given him.  Therefore, at the end, it happeneth that the fleeting body sinketh and falleth, marked for death.  Another taketh over the earl's former holdings, who dealeth out treasure without repining, and shall take no thought for fear.

"Guard thee from death-dealing malice, dear Beowulf, best of men, and choose the better, the eternal gain.  Give not thyself to over-pride, O warrior renowned.  Now is the flower of thy strength for one while; soon shall it be hereafter that sickness or the sword's edge, foe's clutch or flood's whelm, the sword's grip or the spear's flight, or grievous old age, shall part thee from thy strength, or the brightness of thine eyes shall fail and grow dark; straightway shall it be, princely one, that death shall overcome thee.

"Half a hundred years beneath the clouds I so ruled the Ring-Danes and warded them in war with spear and sword from many a people through this mid-earth, that I counted myself without a foe 'neath the stretch of the heaven.  Behold! a change came to my land, grief after joy, when Grendel, the old-time foe, became my invader; ceaselessly from that troubling I suffered exceeding sorrow of spirit. Thanks be to God, the Eternal Lord, that I have bided in life so long that I may look with mine eyes on this head, gory from the sword.

"Go now to thy mead-bench, honored warrior; taste of the joy of the feast; treasures full many shall be between us twain, when morn shall come."

The Geat was glad at heart and went therewith to find his place, as the wise one had bidden. Then anew, in fair wise, was the feast spread for them, mighty in valor, sitting in the hall. The helm of night darkened down dusky over the bandsmen. The press of warriors all arose; the white-haired prince, the old Scylding, desired to seek his bed. The Geat, the valiant shield-warrior, listed well, past the telling, to rest him. Soon the hall-thane, who took care with courteous observance for the hero's every need, such as in that day seafarers should have, led him forth, come from afar, worn with his venture. Then the great-hearted one took his rest.

The hall lifted itself broad and brave with gold. The guest slept within till the black raven, blithe of heart, heralded the joy of heaven. Then the bright sun came gliding over the plain. The warsmen hasted, the athelings were eager to fare again to their people. He who had come to them, the large of heart, would take ship far thence. The brave one bade the son of Ecglaf bear off Hrunting, bade him take his sword, his beloved blade, spake him thanks for its lending, said he accounted it a good war-friend, of might in battle, belied not in words the sword's edge. That was a man great of soul! And when the warriors were in forwardness for the journey, with their gear made ready, the atheling dear to the Danes, the hero brave in the fight, went to the high-seat, where the other was, and greeted Hrothgar.

Beowulf spake, the son of Ecgtheow: "We, seafaring ones, come from afar, wish now to say that we mean now to make our way to Hygelac. We have been well entreated here in all man could wish; thou has dealt well by us. If then on earth, O Lord of Men, I may earn more of thy heart's love by deeds of war than I yet have done, I shall straightway be ready. Should I learn over the stretches of the flood that thy neighbors burden thee with dread, as they that hate thee at times have done, I shall bring a thousand thanes, warriors, to thine help. I know of Hygelac, Lord of the Geat-folk, the people's herd, that though he be young he will uphold me in word and deed that I may do thee full honor and bear to thine aid the spear's shaft, the stay of his strength, when need of men shall be thine. If, furthermore, Hrethric, son of the king, take service at the court of the Geats, he shall find many friends there; far-off lands are better to seek by him that may trust in himself."

Hrothgar spake to him in answer: "Now hath the wise Lord sent these sayings into thy soul. Never heard I man so young in years counsel more wisely. Thou art strong in might and safe in thought, and wise in thy sayings. I account it likely that if it hap the spear, the fierce battlesword, sickness, or the steel, taketh away the son of Hrethel, thy prince, the people's herd, and thou hast thy life, that the Sea-Geats will have no man better to choose for king, for treasure-warden of the warriors, if thou art willing to rule the realm of thy kinsfolk. Thy brave spirit liketh me, passing well, ever the more, dear Beowulf. Thou hast so wrought that peace shall be between the Geat-folk and the Spear-Danes, and strife be at rest, the guileful onslaughts they have erstwhile undergone. Whilst I rule this wide realm, treasure shall be in common; greeting shall many a one send another by gifts across the gannet's bath; the ringed ship shall bring over the sea offerings and tokens of love. I know the peoples are fast wrought together both toward foe and toward friend, void of reproach in every wise as the way was of old."

Then, thereto, the son of Healfdene, shield of earls, gave him in the hall twelve treasures, bade him make his way with these gifts safe and sound to his dear people, and come again speedily. The king, then goodly of birth, Lord of the Scyldings, kissed the best of thanes and clasped him about the neck. The tears of the white-haired king fell; old and wise, two things he might look for, but of these the second more eagerly, that they might yet again see one another, mighty in counsel. The man was so dear to him, that he might not bear the tumult of his heart, for in his breast, fast in the bonds of thought, deep-hidden yearning for the dear warrior burned throughout his blood.

Beowulf, gold-proud warrior, trod thence over the grassy earth, rejoicing in his treasure. The sea-goer awaited her master, as she rode at anchor. Oft then, as they went, was the gift of Hrothgar spoken of with praise. That was a king in all things blameless, till old age, that hath scathed many a man, took from him the joys of might.

[tr. C. G. CHILD]

# LYRICS AND SELECTIONS

## CAEDMON'S HYMN [1]

### (7th cent.)

Now must we hymn the Master of heaven,
The might of the Maker, the deeds of the Father,
The thought of His heart.   He, Lord everlasting,
Established of old the source of all wonders:
Creator all-holy, He hung the bright heaven,
A roof high upreared, o'er the children of men;
The King of mankind then created for mortals
The world in its beauty, the earth spread beneath them,
He, Lord everlasting, omnipotent God.

[tr. ALBERT S. COOK]


## THE SEAFARER [2]

### Exeter Book (late 10th cent.)

What I know, I shall launch in this stave —
   Truth, from tired days.
The trailing hours, toilsome and grave,
   When the heart says: —
"All ships are keeps of care, islands of fear,
In the heavy bright water!"
           But night hid the clear
When we knocked past the cliffs —
Strait was the watch of old
Which found me at the stem in the pining cold,
My feet chained down with ice. — But burning care
Boiled round my heart. — And hunger often files
Its way in flesh. —
         O, when a man finds fair
Fortune on the isles,
He has then no thought for these rime-cold
Sliding seas of winter where I spend
This exile and tract of life! — Dead is my friend.
Icicles hang around me. — Hail is flung in the air! —

   Only the crawling of the wave
     I heard, and the ice-bound surges die.

1. From *Translations from Old English Poetry*, by A. S. Cook and C. B. Tinker; Ginn & Co., Boston, 1926.   Reprinted by permission of the Harvard University Press.
2. From *Anglo-Saxon Poetry*, by Gavin Bone; Clarendon Press, Oxford, 1943.   Reprinted by permission of the publisher.

Sometimes the swan would be so brave
  As, in her lonely way, to cry.

I made gay thoughts out of gannets' notes,
  I held the puffin-bird could smile:
The sea-mew was singing instead of the throats
  In the mead-hall, that beat up a ballad erewhile.

Storms struck the stone-cliffs as the tern
  With dewy feathers screamed above.
Over and over answered the erne
  With icy wings —
              No friend, no shelter of love
For the want in my heart! —
              So the burgher in lust
Who lives within great walls, engrossing joy,
  Happy and high with wine — drinks and does not trust
This talk of sailing —
              While I live, weary!

    It darkens.  From the North
    The curling snow steals forth.
    The frost is on the land.
    A smallish warning band
    Of hailstones falls in chain —
    The coldest kind of grain!
    And the thought knocks my heart
    To tempt those deep streams!
    Often in the day
    My wish tells me the way
    Over the sport of the waves
    To far lands!

O no man is proud yet in the earth,
  So gifted of heaven, so young or so hale,
So loved by his God, or so sure of his worth
  That he does not fear danger setting to sail!
He wonders how heaven will treat him.
  He hasn't the pleasure in gold
Nor the heart for a harp, nor the joy in a wife —
  All the pastimes of earth are grown old —
He can think about only the rolling and strife
  Of big waves beating the hold —
So his heart is fed with longing who wends to the blue and the cold!

  The boughs take blossom, towns are gay,
    The meadows green, and Spring's in train:
  All these things urge me on my way
    To seek the lonely floods again.
  O vainly does the cuckoo sing

(The keeper of the gate of Spring)
Who pines my ear with her boding tone!

(A thing to happier men unknown
What exiles feel, who tempt strange ways
With danger!)
              As my mind turns back the days,
It leaves the breast, the locker-up of woes,
To cross the whale's wet country — yearns and goes
Where men live happy — comes once more to me
Drooping and sad — till the slow bird of the sea
That wheels alone, and presses me from rest,
Chides my ship on, to cross a new sea-crest!

    The bliss of heaven is warm as a breath,
    But this dead life is cold to my clay.
    What Life thinks weal is brushed away
    Greedily, after a glance, by Death!

    Ere a man die, three things suffice
    To bring him to despair: —
    Age or disease or feud efface
    His keen life out of the air!

    The firmest track a man may leave
    Is in the thought of his land:
    Then let him bring the Devil to grieve
    By the dear works of his hand,
    That the children of men make a tale of him
    And he hold heaven fast! —

    But such deeds are fled, Caesar is dead,
    Kings look best in the past.
    Lordship is nothing to the old days
    When men lived in loyal fame.
    The flower is fallen, this is the stubble,
    Weak men walk in a world of trouble,
    What was noble runs lame!

The deeds that were glory halt out of our ways
Like each man in our province called Earth who grows old:
When age creeps upon him and powders his head,
The hoar-pate mourns that his friend is dead,
A son of the great — ready for the mould!

See then, the body, when the life is ta'en,
May not taste sweetness, may not sense a sore,
Or raise a hand, or reason with its brain!
And though a man should place a thing of worth
Early beside his brother in the grave,
It climbs not with that soul, but rots in earth . . .

Fear towards God is great, 'twas he who framed
The strong roots of the world, and the plains for men,
The leaning sky.  A fool who fears not is shamed,
Death comes in a moment and nooses him again.
But the humble man whose belief is sure
God will help to endure.

[tr. GAVIN BONE]


## THE RUINED CITY [3]

### Exeter Book (late 10th cent.)

Wondrously wrought and fair its wall of stone,
Shattered by Fate!  The castles rend asunder,
The work of giants moldereth away,
Its roofs are breaking and falling; its towers crumble
In ruin.  Plundered those walls with grated doors —
Their mortar white with frost.  Its battered ramparts
Are shorn away and ruined, all undermined
By eating age.  The mighty men that built it,
Departed hence, undone by death, are held
Fast in the earth's embrace.  Tight is the clutch
Of the grave, while overhead for living men
A hundred generations pass away.
    Long this red wall, now mossy gray, withstood,
While kingdom followed kingdom in the land,
Unshaken 'neath the storms of heaven — yet now
Its towering gate hath fallen. . . .
    Radiant the mead-halls in that city bright,
Yea, many were its baths.  High rose its wealth
Of hornèd pinnacles, while loud within
Was heard the joyous revelry of men —
Till mighty Fate came with her sudden change!
    Wide-wasting was the battle where they fell.
Plague-laden days upon the city came;
Death snatched away that mighty host of men. . . .
    There in the olden time full many a thane,
Shining with gold, all gloriously adorned,
Haughty in heart, rejoiced when hot with wine;
Upon him gleamed his armor, and he gazed
On gold and silver and all precious gems;
On riches and on wealth and treasured jewels,
A radiant city in a kingdom wide.
    There stood the courts of stone.  Hotly within,
The stream flowed with its mighty surge.  The wall

---

3. From *Translations from Old English Poetry*, by A. S. Cook and C. B. Tinker;
Ginn & Co., Boston, 1926.  Reprinted by permission of the Harvard University Press.

Surrounded all with its bright bosom; there
The baths stood, hot within its heart. . . .

[tr. CHAUNCEY B. TINKER]


## SATAN'S ADDRESS TO HIS FOLLOWERS [4]

### (from *Genesis*)

### Junius MS. (early 11th cent.)

Then said he: "Most unlike this narrow place
To that which once we knew, high in Heaven's realm,
Which my Lord gave me, though therein no more
For the Almighty we hold royalties.
Yet right hath He not done in striking us
Down to the fiery bottom of hot Hell,
Banished from Heaven's kingdom, with decree
That He will set in it the race of man.
Worst of my sorrows this, that, wrought of earth,
Adam shall sit in bliss on my strong throne,
Whilst we these pangs endure, this grief in Hell.
Woe! Woe! had I the power of my hands,
And for a season, for one winter's space,
Might be without; then with this host I —
But iron binds me round; this coil of chains
Rides me; I rule no more; close bonds of Hell
Hem me their prisoner. Above, below,
Here is vast fire, and never have I seen
More loathly landscape; never fade the flames,
Hot over Hell. Rings clasp me, smooth hard bands
Mar motion, stay my wandering — feet bound,
Hands fastened, and the ways of these Hell-gates
Accursed so that I cannot free my limbs;
Great lattice-bars, hard iron hammered hot,
Lie round me, wherewith God hath bound me down
Fast by the neck.
                    "So know I that He knew
My mind, and that the Lord of hosts perceived
That if between us two by Adam came
Evil towards that royalty of Heaven,
I having power of my hands —
But now we suffer throes in Hell, gloom, heat,
Grim, bottomless; us God Himself hath swept
Into these mists of darkness, wherefore sin
Can He not lay against us that we planned
Evil against Him in the land. Of light

4. From *English Writers*, by Henry Morley; Cassell & Co., Ltd., London, 1888. Reprinted by permission of the publisher.

He hath shorn us, cast us into utmost pain.
May we not then plan vengeance, pay Him back
With any hurt, since shorn by Him of light?
Now He hath set the bounds of a mid-earth
Where after His own image He hath wrought
Man, by whom He will people once again
Heaven's kingdom with pure souls.  Therefore intent
Must be our thought that, if we ever may,
On Adam and his offspring we may wreak
Revenge, and, if we can devise a way,
Pervert His will.  I trust no more the light
Which he thinks long to enjoy with angel-power.
Bliss we obtain no more, nor can attain
To weaken God's strong will; but let us now
Turn from the race of man that heavenly realm
Which may no more be ours, contrive that they
Forfeit His favor, undo what His word
Ordained; then wroth of mind He from His grace
Will cast them, then shall they too seek this Hell
And these grim depths.  Then may we for ourselves
Have them in this strong durance, sons of men
For servants.  Of the warfare let us now
Begin to take thought.  If of old I gave
To any thane, while we in that good realm
Sat happy and had power of our thrones,
Gifts of a prince, then at no dearer time
Could he reward my gift, if any now
Among my followers would be my friend,
That he might pass forth upward from these bounds,
Had power with him that, winged, he might fly,
Borne on the clouds, to where stand Adam and Eve
Wrought on earth's kingdom, girt with happiness,
While we are cast down into this deep dale.
Now these are worthier to the Lord, may own
The blessing rightly ours in Heaven's realm,
This the design apportioned to mankind.
Sore is my mind and rue is in my thought
That ever henceforth they should possess heaven.
If ever any of you in any way
May turn them from the teaching of God's word,
They shall be evil to Him, and if they
Break His commandment, then will He be wroth
Against them, then will be withdrawn from them
Their happiness, and punishment prepared,
Some grievous share of harm.  Think all of this,
How to deceive them.  In these fetters then
I can take rest, if they that kingdom lose.
He who shall do this hath prompt recompense
Henceforth for ever of what may be won

Of gain within these fires.  I let him sit
Beside myself."

                                    [tr. HENRY MORLEY]


## THE BATTLE OF BRUNANBURH

Old English Chronicle, A.D. 937

### I

Athelstan King,
Lord among Earls,
Bracelet-bestower and
Baron of Barons,
He with his brother,
Edmund Atheling,
Gaining a lifelong
Glory in battle,
Slew with the sword-edge
There by Brunanburh,
Brake the shield-wall,
Hewed the linden-wood,
Hacked the battle-shield,
Sons of Edward with hammered brands.

### II

Theirs was a greatness
Got from their grandsires —
Theirs that so often in
Strife with their enemies
Struck for their hoards and their hearths and their homes.

### III

Bowed the spoiler,
Bent the Scotsman,
Fell the ship-crews
Doomed to the death.
All the field with blood of the fighters
Flowed, from when first the great
Sun-star of morning-tide,
Lamp of the Lord God
Lord everlasting,
Glode over earth till the glorious creature
Sank to his setting.

### IV

There lay many a man
Marred by the javelin,

Men of the Northland
Shot over shield.
There was the Scotsman
Weary of war.

### v

We the West-Saxons,
Long as the daylight
Lasted, in companies
Troubled the track of the host that we hated.
Grimly with swords that were sharp from the grindstone,
Fiercely we hacked at the flyers before us.

### vi

Mighty the Mercian,
Hard was his hand-play,
Sparing not any of
Those that with Anlaf,
Warriors over the
Weltering waters
Borne in the bark's-bosom,
Drew to this island —
Doomed to the death.

### vii

Five young kings put asleep by the sword-stroke,
Seven strong Earls of the army of Anlaf
Fell on the war-field, numberless numbers,
Shipmen and Scotsmen.

### viii

Then the Norse leader,
Dire was his need of it,
Few were his following,
Fled to his war-ship;
Fleeted his vessel to sea with the king in it,
Saving his life on the fallow flood.

### ix

Also the crafty one,
Constantinus,
Crept to his North again,
Hoar-headed hero!

### x

Slender warrant had
*He* to be proud of
The welcome of war-knives —
He that was reft of his

Folk and his friends that had
Fallen in conflict,
Leaving his son too
Lost in the carnage,
Mangled to morsels,
A youngster in war!

### XI

Slender reason had
*He* to be glad of
The clash of the war-glaive —
Traitor and trickster
And spurner of treaties —
He nor had Anlaf
With armies so broken
A reason for bragging
That they had the better
In perils of battle
On places of slaughter —
The struggle of standards,
The rush of the javelins,
The crash of the charges,
The wielding of weapons —
The play that they played with
The children of Edward.

### XII

Then with their nailed prows
Parted the Norsemen, a
Blood-reddened relic of
Javelins over
The jarring breaker, the deep-sea billow,
Shaping their way toward Dyflen again
Shamed in their souls.

### XIII

Also the brethren,
King and Atheling,
Each in his glory,
Went to his own in his own West-Saxonland,
Glad of the war.

### XIV

Many a carcase they left to be carrion,
Many a livid one, many a sallow-skin —
Left for the white-tailed eagle to tear it, and
Left for the horny-nibbed raven to rend it, and
Gave to the garbaging war-hawk to gorge it, and
That gray beast, the wolf of the weald.

## XV

Never had huger
Slaughter of heroes
Slain by the sword-edge —
Such as old writers
Have writ of in histories —
Hapt in this isle, since
Up from the East hither
Saxon and Angle from
Over the broad billow
Broke into Britain with
Haughty war-workers who
Harried the Welshman, when
Earls that were lured by the
Hunger of glory gat
Hold of the land.

[tr. Alfred, Lord Tennyson]

# IV. ROMANESQUE LITERATURE

Culture and institutions cannot easily be broken into chronological units. They flow from generation to generation, constantly changing, yet always retaining much that is old. An era or an age does not suddenly start or suddenly stop. Nevertheless, we continue to use terms which imply that there are such units; we speak of the Classical Period, the Renaissance, the Age of Reason. Each has distinguishing or predominant elements. A cultural unit that can be distinguished quite as readily as these is that of western Europe during the five centuries from Gregory the Great to the First Crusade. The Roman Empire, which had established a second capital at Byzantium at the beginning of the fourth century, had by the seventh century concentrated in the Greek-speaking world, and the Latin west was largely left to shift for itself. In the seventh century, following the Hegira of Mohammed, the Moslems took over Africa and Spain and were only turned back from France by the victory of Charles Martel, the grandfather of Charlemagne, in 732 near Poitiers. The center of Christian culture was thus shifted to the north. The migrating Teutonic groups had settled in new homes, whether in France, Italy, Britain, or Germany; the only new migration of import after the seventh century was the great expansion of the Northmen. Old economic and political institutions had collapsed, and a pragmatic arrangement called feudalism, which combined agrarian production, military protection, and an ancient Teutonic concept of personal fealty, came into being. Through the missions started by Gregory I in England and from there spreading to Germany, the barbarians were Christianized and their whole religious life brought under the hegemony of the Bishop of Rome. The cultural vacuum created by the disappearance of pagan schools, art, and wealth was filled by the Benedictine monasteries, which were stable and placid islands established in a heaving sea. First for their own professional needs and then as a Christian public service they developed schools and cultivated the arts. The Church as, for a time, the only stable institution controlled the thoughts of the people, not through secular but through religious authority. It was not until near the close of this period, which we have called Romanesque, that ecclesiastical prelates became leading feudal barons as well. Since the Church was the center of culture and literacy was the exclusive possession of the clergy or of those who had been educated in ecclesiastical schools, Latin was the only language of literature. To be sure, some Teutons and Celts, like the Irish and English, wrote down poetry and some prose in the vernacular, but these works stand rather at one side of the general stream of medieval culture, affecting it but not flowing with it.

The main path of the arts and sciences can be rather definitely traced. What little remained of Mediterranean thought and letters was transplanted to England with the Gregorian mission, by such a process as Bede describes above (p. 135), where it met the Irish culture diffused from Irish missions in Scotland. From Britain it was transplanted by English and Irish missionairies and scholars: to Frisia by Willibrord, to central Germany by Boniface, to Burgundy, Swabia, and Lombardy by Columban, and to France by Alcuin — all of them monks as well as clergy. With the Carolingians we find the first revival of interest in schools for the laity; for Charlemagne developed a school at his palace at Aix-la-Chapelle (Aachen), where Alcuin taught. Some of his best students strengthened monastic and diocesan schools throughout the empire. Centers like Tours, Chartres, Laon, Cologne, Mainz, Fulda, Salzburg, St. Gall, Orleans, Limoges, Lyons, Bobbio, and Monte Cassino developed strong faculties and curricula and spread the love of learning. The Normans, who eagerly grasped any semblance of southern culture wherever they settled, encouraged cultivation of all the arts and sciences. By the end of the eleventh century, the Benedictines had taught the western peoples many arts of peace — agriculture, metalwork, music, and some basic science. The seven liberal arts — grammar, rhetoric, and dialectic, arithmetic, geometry, astronomy, and music — could be studied at accessible centers everywhere.

The groundwork was thus laid for a great era of expansion that would bring in a new age and allow the cultivation of fresh and revolutionary ideas. A change from Romanesque to Gothic architecture marks a fundamental change in society. The twelfth century is transitional — a transition artfully described by Henry Adams in his classic *Mont St. Michel and Chartres*. Barons gave way to nobles, as agrarian-military feudalism gave way to courtliness. The vernacular tongues supplanted Latin as the language of literature. The universities rose above the cathedral schools. Invocation of St. Michael was stilled by adoration of St. Mary. Money came in place of barter as trade expanded. Towns sprang up around feudal castles and a bourgeois class took on exclusive rights and privileges. New orders of friars, the Franciscan and Dominican brotherhoods, displaced the Benedictine monks in popularity. The isolated baronies consolidated into great duchies, and a kind of national self-consciousness began to emerge.

These changes brought to an end the kind of literature represented in this section, which, like the architecture of the period, is an adaptation of Roman forms to the stolid and barbarian ideas of the north. The Roman language was taken over as was the Roman arch; only occasionally does a narrative poet depart from the dactylic hexameter he painfully learned from the pages of Virgil. The images, the themes, and the syntax are simply conceived and earthbound. But the artists are laying strong foundations and here and there branching out into a cautious experiment. They are preparing the way for the Gothic period to come.

# THE DEEDS OF CHARLEMAGNE

From the misgovernment, anarchy, and misery depicted by Gregory of Tours in his *History of the Franks,* written in the seventh century, the nation of the Franks emerged under a strong series of Carolingian monarchs in the eighth and ninth centuries to rule practically all Europe, from the Netherlands to the Byzantine Empire. Charles Martel, Mayor of the Palace (*maior domo*), was followed by his son Pippin the Short, who in alliance with the Pope deposed the Merovingian king at a National Council, A.D. 751. When Pippin died, his kingdom went to his two sons, Charles and Carloman, who reigned jointly for three years until 771 when Carloman's death left Charles as sole ruler. From that time to his death in 814, Charles' activities were so widespread, his campaigns so successful, his reforms so sweeping, and his statecraft so efficient as to earn for him and his age lasting renown.

His reform of the Church and education fostered writing in many ways. He encouraged the copying down of ballads and sagas; he developed in his own palace school at Aachen (Aix-la-Chapelle) and elsewhere the study of neglected classics; he devoted himself to the study of rhetoric and science. Though on the whole the literary creations of his scholars were imitative and pedantic rather than inspired or original, his patronage did much to spread literacy, to encourage the arts, and to dispel the fear of pagan letters. He received his reward, for his reign and his exploits were accurately chronicled for posterity, especially by Einhard, one of Charles' ministers and courtiers, who also served his son Louis the Pious before forsaking the world for monastic life in A.D. 830. Einhard's *Life of Emperor Charles,* modeled in considerable part on Suetonius' *Life of Caesar,* has the pure style and trenchant expression of Bede's *Lives of the Abbots.*

But historical accuracy and factual synthesis are not the only qualities possible in biography. At the monastery of St. Gall, near the Lake of Constance in what was Swabia and is now Switzerland, another biography of Charlemagne was written about sixty years later which contrasts with Einhard's. Perhaps no other monastery had profited so much by the benefactions and reforms of the Carolingian monarchs. Founded in the early seventh century by the Irish Gall, a disciple of St. Columban, the monastery struggled in comparative obscurity until the gifts of the Carolingians brought it prosperity and the school reform brought renown for its library and teachers. In the ninth and tenth centuries it was possibly the most progressive educational center in Europe; the literature written by its masters is a key to the development, not only of romance, but to the liturgy, especially the sequence, and through it to medieval drama. There, in the year 883, a monk often identified as the great teacher and musician, Notker Balbulus, professedly at the request of Em-

peror Charles III, the great-grandson of Charlemagne, wrote the
*Deeds of Charles* (*Gesta Caroli*).

*Gesta* is itself descriptive — a term once appropriated by the writers
of saints' lives, hagiographers, as a term almost synonymous with
*virtues* or *heroic qualities* on the one hand and *miracles* on the other.
The work is very like hagiography in its structure, its content and
form of expression, and its purpose. It differs only in exalting a
secular ruler rather than a spiritual or religious teacher. It is a
series of anecdotes drawn from common gossip, written down as
a guide to ethics or a sort of book of manners — as the saints' lives
had been. The interest of the author in historical fact is subordinated
to his dual purpose of entertainment and guidance in the principles
of right action — in this instance primarily in right kingly action.
In short, it is a series of legends (*legenda*) designed to be read as
teaching (*doctrina*), as all legends written under ecclesiastical aus-
pices were. Here is a definite step in the secularization of monastic
literature and in the exaltation of a feudal lord into a chivalric hero.
The selections that follow constitute about a quarter of the work.


## THE DEEDS OF CHARLEMAGNE

### Notker of St. Gall (?) (A.D. 883)

[From *The Early Lives of Charlemagne,* translated by A. J.
Grant; Chatto & Windus, London, 1922. Reprinted by
permission of the publisher.]

After the omnipotent ruler of the world, who orders alike the fate
of kingdoms and the course of time, had broken the feet of iron and
clay in one noble statue, to wit the Romans, he raised by the hands
of the illustrious Charles the golden head of another, not less admirable, among the Franks. Now it happened, when he had begun
to reign alone in the western parts of the world, and the pursuit of
learning had been almost forgotten throughout all his realm, and
the worship of the true Godhead was faint and weak, that two
Scots came from Ireland to the coast of Gaul along with certain
traders of Britain. These Scotchmen were unrivalled for their
skill in sacred and secular learning; and day by day, when the
crowd gathered round them for traffic, they exhibited no wares for
sale, but cried out and said, "Ho, everyone that desires wisdom, let
him draw near and take it at our hands; for it is wisdom that we
have for sale."

Now they declared that they had wisdom for sale because they
said that the people cared not for what was given freely but only for
what was sold, hoping that thus they might be incited to purchase
wisdom along with other wares; and also perhaps hoping that by
this announcement they themselves might become a wonder and
a marvel to men, which indeed turned out to be the case. For so

long did they make their proclamation that in the end those who wondered at these men, or perhaps thought them insane, brought the matter to the ears of King Charles, who always loved and sought after wisdom. Wherefore he ordered them to come with all speed into his presence and asked them whether it were true, as fame reported of them, that they had brought wisdom with them. They answered, "We both possess it and are ready to give it, in the name of God, to those who seek it worthily." Again he asked them what price they asked for it; and they answered, "We ask no price, O king; but we ask only for a fit place for teaching and quick minds to teach; and besides food to eat and raiment to put on, for without these we cannot accomplish our pilgrimage."

This answer filled the king with a great joy, and first he kept both of them with him for a short time. But soon, when he must needs go to war, he made one of them named Clement reside in Gaul, and to him he sent many boys both of noble, middle, and humble birth, and he ordered as much food to be given them as they required, and he set aside for them buildings suitable for study. But he sent the second scholar into Italy and gave him the monastery of Saint Augustine near Pavia, that all who wished might gather there to learn from him.

But when Albinus (Alcuin), an Englishman, heard that that most religious Emperor Charles gladly entertained wise men, he entered into a ship and came to him. Now Albinus was skilled in all learning beyond all others of our times, for he was the disciple of that most learned priest Bede, who next to Saint Gregory was the most skilful interpreter of the scriptures. And Charles received Albinus kindly and kept him at his side to the end of his life, except when he marched with his armies to his vast wars. Nay, Charles would even call himself Albinus's disciple; and Albinus he would call his master. He appointed him to rule over the abbey of Saint Martin, near to the city of Tours, so that, when he himself was absent, Albinus might rest there and teach those who had recourse to him. And his teaching bore such fruit among his pupils that the modern Gauls or Franks came to equal the ancient Romans or Athenians.

Charles used to pick out all the best writers and readers from among the poor boys and transfer them to his chapel; for that was the name that the kings of the Franks gave to their private oratory, taking the word from the *cope* of St. Martin, which they always took with them in war for a defence against their enemies. Now one day it was announced to this most wary King Charles that a certain bishop was dead; and, when the king asked whether the dead bishop had made any bequests for the good of his soul, the messenger replied, "Sire, he has bequeathed no more than two pounds of silver." Thereupon one of his chaplains, sighing, and no longer able to keep the thoughts of his mind within his breast, spake in the hearing of the king these words: "That is a small provision for a long, a never-ending journey."

Then Charles, the mildest of men, deliberated a space, and said to the young man, "Do you think then, if you were to get the bishopric, you would care to make more provision for that same long journey?" These cautious words fell upon the chaplain as ripe grapes into the mouth of one who stands agape for them, and he threw himself at the feet of Charles and said, "Sire, the matter rests upon the will of God and your own power." Said the king, "Stand behind the curtain that hangs behind me, and mark what kind of help you would receive if you were raised to that honour."

Now, when the officers of the palace, who were always on the watch for deaths or accidents, heard that the bishop was dead, one and all of them, impatient of delay and jealous of each other, began to make suit for the bishopric through the friends of the emperor. But Charles still persisted unmoved in his design; he refused everyone, and said that he would not disappoint his young friend. At last Queen Hildigard sent some of the nobles of the realm, and at last came in person, to beg the bishopric for a certain clerk of her own. The emperor received her petition very graciously and said that he would not and could not deny her anything; but that he thought it shame to deceive his little chaplain. But still the queen, woman-like, thought that a woman's opinion and wish ought to outweigh the decrees of men; and so she concealed the passion that was rising in her heart. She sank her strong voice almost to a whisper, and with caressing gestures tried to soften the emperor's unspoken mind. "My sire and king," she said, "what does it matter if that boy does lose the bishopric? Nay, I beseech you, sweet sire, my glory and my refuge, give it to your faithful servant, my clerk." Then that young man, who had heard the petitions from behind the curtain close to the king's chair where he had been placed, embraced the king through the curtain and cried, "Sir king, stand fast and do not let anyone take from you the power that has been given you by God."

Then that strict lover of truth bade him come out and said, "I intend you to have the bishopric; but you must be very careful to spend more and make fuller provision for that same long and unreturning journey both for yourself and for me."

But I must not seem to forget or to neglect Alcuin; and will therefore make this true statement about his energy and his deserts: all his pupils without exception distinguished themselves by becoming either holy abbots or bishops. My master Grimald studied the liberal arts under him, first in Gaul and then in Italy. But those who are learned in these matters may charge me with falsehood for saying "all his pupils without exception"; when the fact is that there were in his schools two young men, sons of a miller in the service of the monastery of Saint Columban, who did not seem fit and proper persons for promotion to the command of bishoprics or monasteries; but even these men were, by the influence probably of their teacher, advanced one after the other to the office of minister in the monastery of Bobbio, in which they displayed the greatest energy.

So the most glorious Charles saw the study of letters flourishing throughout his whole realm, but still he was grieved to find that it did not reach the ripeness of the earlier fathers; and so, after super-human labours, he broke out one day with this expression of his sorrow: "Would that I had twelve clerks so learned in all wisdom and so perfectly trained as were Jerome and Augustine." Then the learned Alcuin, feeling himself ignorant indeed in comparison with these great names, rose to a height of daring that no man else attained to in the presence of the terrible Charles, and said, with deep indignation in his mind but none in his countenance, "The Maker of heaven and earth has not many like to those men and do you expect to have twelve?"

Here I must report something which the men of our time will find it difficult to believe; for I myself who write it could hardly believe it, so great is the difference between our method of chanting and the Roman, were it not that we must trust rather the accuracy of our fathers than the false suggestions of modern sloth. Well then, Charles, that never-wearied lover of the service of God, when he could congratulate himself that all possible progress had been made in the knowledge of letters, was grieved to observe how widely the different provinces — nay, not the provinces only but districts and cities — differed in the praise of God, that is to say in their method of chanting. He therefore asked of Pope Stephen of blessed memory — the same who, after Hilderich King of the Franks had been deposed and tonsured, had anointed Charles to be ruler of the kingdom after the ancestral custom of the people — he asked of Pope Stephen, I say, that he should provide him with twelve clerks deeply learned in divine song. The Pope yielded assent to his virtuous wish and his divinely inspired design and sent to him in Frankland from the apostolic see clerks skilled in divine song, and twelve in number, according to the number of the twelve apostles.

Now, when I said Frankland just above, I meant all the provinces north of the Alps; for as it is written, "In those days ten men shall take hold out of all the languages of the nations, shall even take hold of the skirt of him that is a Jew," so at that time, by reason of the glory of Charles, Gauls, Aquitanians, Æduans, Spaniards, Germans, and Bavarians thought that no small honour was paid to them if they were thought worthy to be called the servants of the Franks.

Now when the aforementioned clerks were departing from Rome, being, like all Greeks and Romans, torn with envy of the glory of the Franks, they took counsel among themselves, and determined so to vary their method of singing that his kingdom and dominion should never have cause to rejoice in unity and agreement. So when they came to Charles they were received most honourably and despatched to the chief places. And thereupon each in his allotted place began to chant as differently as possible, and to teach others to sing in like fashion and in as false a manner as they could invent. But as the most cunning Charles celebrated one year the feast of the

Birth and Coming of Christ at Trèves or Metz and most carefully and cleverly grasped and understood the style of the singing, and then the next year passed the same solemn season at Paris or Tours, but found that the singing was wholly different from what he had heard in the preceding year, as moreover he found that those whom he had sent into different places were also at variance with one another, he reported the whole matter to Pope Leo of holy memory, who had succeeded Stephen.

The Pope summoned the clerks back to Rome and condemned them to exile or perpetual imprisonment, and then said to Charles: "If I send you others they will be blinded with the same malice as their predecessors and will not fail to cheat you. But I think I can satisfy your wishes in this way. Send me two of the cleverest clerks that you have by you, in such a way that those who are with me may not know that they belong to you, and, with God's help, they shall attain to as perfect a knowledge of those things as you desire." So said, so done. Soon the Pope sent them back excellently trained to Charles. One of them he kept at his own court; the other upon the petition of his son Drogo, Bishop of Metz, he sent to that cathedral. And not only did his energy show itself powerful in that city, but it soon spread so widely throughout all Frankland, that now all in these regions who use the Latin tongue call the ecclesiastical chant Metensian; or, if they use the Teutonic or Teuthiscan tongue, they call it Mette; or if the Greek form is used it is called Mettisc. The most pious emperor also ordered Peter, the singer who had come to reside with him, to reside for a while in the monastery of St. Gall. There too Charles established the chanting as it is to-day, with an authentic song-book, and gave most careful instructions, being always a warm champion of Saint Gall, that the Roman method of singing should be both taught and learnt. He gave to the monastery also much money and many lands; he gave too relics contained in a reliquary made of solid gold and gems, which is called the Shrine of Charles.

There was a certain bishropric which lay full on Charles's path when he journeyed and which indeed he could hardly avoid; and the bishop of this place, always anxious to give satisfaction, put everything that he had at Charles's disposal. But once the emperor came quite unexpectedly and the bishop in great anxiety had to fly hither and thither like a swallow, and had not only the palaces and houses but also the courts and squares swept and cleaned; and then, tired and irritated, came to meet him. The most pious Charles noticed this, and after examining all the various details, he said to the bishop: "My kind host, you always have everything splendidly cleaned for my arrival." Then the bishop, as if divinely inspired, bowed his head and grasped the king's never-conquered right hand, and hiding his irritation, kissed it and said: "It is but right, my lord, that wherever you come, all things should be thoroughly cleansed." Then Charles, of all kings the wisest, understanding the state of affairs said to him: "If I empty I can also fill." And he added, "You may have that estate which lies close to your bishopric, and all your successors may have it until the end of time."

As we have shown how the most wise Charles exalted the humble, let us now show how he brought low the proud. There was a bishop who sought above measure vanities and the fame of men. The most cunning Charles heard of this and told a certain Jewish merchant, whose custom it was to go to the land of promise and bring from thence rare and wonderful things to the countries beyond the sea, to deceive or cheat this bishop in whatever way he could. So the Jew caught an ordinary household mouse and stuffed it with various spices, and then offered it for sale to the bishop, saying that he had brought this most precious never-before-seen animal from Judea. The bishop was delighted with what he thought a stroke of luck, and offered the Jew three pounds of silver for the precious ware. Then said the Jew, "A fine price indeed for so precious an article! I had rather throw it into the sea than let any many have it at so cheap and shameful a price." So the bishop, who had much wealth and never gave anything to the poor, offered him ten pounds of silver for the incomparable treasure. But the cunning rascal, with pretended indignation, replied: "The God of Abraham forbid that I should thus lose the fruit of my labour and journeying." Then our avaricious bishop, all eager for the prize, offered twenty pounds. But the Jew in high dudgeon wrapped up the mouse in the most costly silk and made as if he would depart. Then the bishop, as thoroughly taken in as he deserved to be, offered a full measure of silver for the priceless object. And so at last our trader yielded to his entreaties with much show of reluctance and, taking the money, went to the emperor and told him everything. A few days later the king called together all the bishops and chief men of the province to hold discourse with him; and, after many other matters had been considered, he ordered all that measure of silver to be brought and placed in the middle of the palace. Then thus he spoke and said: "Fathers and guardians, bishops of our Church, you ought to minister to the poor, or rather to Christ in them, and not to seek after vanities. But now you act quite contrary to this; and are vainglorious and avaricious beyond all other men." Then he added: "One of you has given a Jew all this silver for a painted mouse." Then the bishop, who had been so wickedly deceived, threw himself at Charles's feet and begged pardon for his sin. Charles upbraided him in suitable words and then allowed him to depart in confusion.

Now since envy always rages among the envious, so it is customary and regular with the Romans to oppose or rather to fight against all strong Popes, who are from time to time raised to the apostolic see. Whence it came to pass that certain of the Romans, themselves blinded with envy, charged the above-mentioned Pope Leo of holy memory with a deadly crime and tried to blind him.  But they were frightened and held back by some divine impulse, and after trying in vain to gouge out his eyes, they slashed them across the middle with knives.  The Pope had news of this carried secretly by his servants to Michael, Emperor of Constantinople; but he refused all assistance saying: "The Pope has an independent kingdom and one higher than mine; so he must act his own revenge upon his enemies." Thereupon the holy Leo invited the unconquered Charles to come to Rome — following in this the ordinance of God, that, as Charles was already in very deed ruler and emperor over many nations, so also by the authority of the apostolic see he might have now the name of Emperor, Caesar and Augustus.

Now Charles, being always ready to march and in warlike array, though he knew nothing at all of the cause of the summons, came at once with his attendants and vassals; himself the head of the world, he came to the city that had once been the head of the world.  And when the abandoned people heard of his sudden coming, at once, as sparrows hide themselves when they hear the voice of their master, so they fled and hid in various hiding-places, cellars and dens. Nowhere however under heaven could they escape from his energy and penetration; and soon they were captured and brought in chains to the Cathedral of St. Peter.  Then the undaunted Father Leo took the gospel of our Lord Jesus Christ and held it over his head, and then in the presence of Charles and his knights, in presence also of his persecutors, he swore in the following words: "So on the day of the great Judgment may I partake in the promises, as I am innocent of the charge that is falsely laid against me."  Then many of the prisoners asked to be allowed to swear upon the tomb of St. Peter that they also were innocent of the charge laid against them.  But the Pope knew their falseness and said to Charles: "Do not, I pray you, unconquered servant of God, give assent to their cunning; for well they know that Saint Peter is always ready to forgive.  But seek among the tombs of the martyrs the stone upon which is written the name of St. Pancras, that boy of thirteen years; and if they will swear to you in his name you may know that you have them fast." It was done as the Pope ordered.  And when many people drew near to take the oath upon this tomb, straightway some fell back dead and some were seized by the devil and went mad.  Then the terrible Charles said to his servants: "Take care that none of them escapes."  Then he condemned all who had been taken prisoner either to some kind of death or to perpetual imprisonment.

As Charles stayed in Rome for a few days, the bishop of the apostolic see called together all who would come from the neighbouring districts and then, in their presence and in the presence of all the knights of the unconquered Charles, he declared him to be Emperor and Defender of the Roman Church.  Now Charles had no guess of what was coming; and, though he could not refuse what seemed to have been divinely preordained for him, nevertheless he received his new title with no show of thankfulness.  For first he thought that the Greeks would be fired by greater envy than ever and would plan some harm against the kingdom of the Franks; or at least would take greater precautions against a possible sudden attack of Charles to subdue their kingdom and add it to his own empire. And further magnanimous Charles recalled how ambassadors from the King of Constantinople had come to him and had told him that their master wished to be his loyal friend; and that, if they became nearer neighbours, he had determined to treat him as his son and relieve the poverty of Charles from his resources; and how, upon hearing this, Charles was unable to contain any longer the fiery ardour of his heart and had exclaimed: "Oh, would that pool were not between us; for then we would either divide between us the wealth of the east, or we would hold it in common."

But the Lord, who is both the giver and the restorer of health, so showed his favour to the innocency of the blessed Leo that he restored his eyes to be brighter than they were before that wicked and cruel cutting; except only that, in token of his virtue, a bright scar (like a very fine thread) marked his eyelids.

When the most energetic Emperor Charles could rest awhile he sought not sluggish ease, but laboured in the service of God. He desired therefore to build upon his native soil a cathedral finer even than the works of the Romans, and soon his purpose was realised. For the building thereof he summoned architects and skilled workmen from all lands beyond the seas; and above all he placed a certain knavish abbot whose competence for the execution of such tasks he knew, though he knew not his character. When the august emperor had gone on a certain journey, this abbot allowed anyone to depart home who would pay sufficient money; and those who could not purchase their discharge or were not allowed to return by their masters, he burdened with unending labours, as the Egyptians once afflicted the people of God. By such knavish tricks he gathered together a great mass of gold and silver and silken robes; and, exhibiting in his chamber only the least precious articles, he concealed in boxes and chests all the richest treasures. Well, one day there was brought to him on a sudden the news that his house was on fire. He ran in great excitement and pushed his way through the bursting flames into the strong room where his boxes, stuffed with gold, were kept. He was not satisfied to take one away, but would only leave after he had loaded his servants with a box apiece. And as he was going out a huge beam, dislodged by the fire, fell on the top of him; and then his body was burnt by temporal and his soul by eternal flames. Thus did the judgment of God keep watch for the most religious Emperor Charles, when his attention was withdrawn by the business of his kingdom.

There was another workman, the most skilled of all in the working of brass and glass. Now this man (his name was Tancho and he was at one time a monk of St. Gall) made a fine bell and the emperor was delighted with its tone. Then said that most distinguished but most unfortunate worker in brass: "Lord Emperor, give orders that a great weight of copper be brought to me that I may refine it; and instead of tin give me as much silver as I shall need —a hundred pounds at least; and I will cast such a bell for you that this will seem dumb in comparison to it." Then Charles, the most liberal of monarchs, who "if riches abounded set not his heart upon them" readily gave the necessary orders, to the great delight of the knavish monk. He smelted and refined the brass; but he used, not silver, but the purest sort of tin. And soon he made a bell, much better than the one that the emperor had formerly admired, and, when he had tested it, he took it to the emperor, who admired its exquisite shape and ordered the clapper to be inserted and the bell to be hung in the bell-tower. That was soon done; and then the warden of the church, the attendants and even the boys of the place tried, one after the other, to make the bell sound. But all was in vain; and so at last the knavish maker of the bell came up, seized the rope, and pulled at the bell. When, lo and behold! down from on high came the brazen mass, fell on the very head of the cheating brass-founder, killed him on the spot, and passed straight through his carcass and crashed to the ground carrying his bowels with it. When the aforementioned weight of silver was found, the most righteous Charles ordered it to be distributed among the poorest servants of the palace.

Now it was a rule at that time that if the imperial mandate had gone out that any task was to be accomplished, whether it was the making of bridges or ships or causeways, or the cleansing or paving or filling up of muddy roads, the counts might execute the less important work by the agency of their deputies or servants; but for the greater enterprises, and especially such as were of an original kind, no duke or count, no bishop or abbot, could possibly get himself excused. The arches of the great bridge at Mainz bear witness to this; for all Europe, so to speak, laboured at this work in orderly cooperation, and then the knavery of a few rascals, who wanted to steal merchandise from the ships that passed underneath, destroyed it.

If any churches, within the royal domain, wanted decorating with carved ceilings or wall paintings, the neighbouring bishops and abbots had to take charge of the task; but if new churches had to be built, then all bishops, dukes and counts, all abbots and heads of royal churches, and all who were in occupation of any public office had to work at it with never-ceasing labour from its foundations to its roof. You may see the proof of the emperor's skill in the cathedral at Aix, which seems a work half human and half divine. You may see it in the mansions of the various dignitaries, which by Charles's device were built round his own palace in such a way that from the windows of his chamber he could see all who went out or came in and what they were doing, while they believed themselves free from observation. You may see it in all the houses of his nobles, which were lifted on high from the ground in such a fashion that beneath them the retainers of his nobles and the servants of those retainers and every class of man could be protected from rain or snow, from cold or heat, while at the same time they were not concealed from the eyes of the most vigilant Charles.

But I am a prisoner within my monastery walls and your ministers are free; and I will therefore leave to them the task of describing the cathedral, while I return to speak of how the judgment of God was made manifest in the building of it.

The most careful Charles ordered certain nobles of the neighbourhood to support with all their power the workmen whom he had set to their task, and to supply everything that they required for it. Those workmen who came from a distance he gave in charge to a certain Liutfrid, the steward of his palace, telling him to feed and clothe them and also most carefully to provide anything that was wanting for the building. The steward obeyed these commands for the short time that Charles remained in that place; but after his departure neglected them altogether, and by cruel tortures collected such a mass of money from the poor workmen that Dis and Pluto would require a camel to carry his ill-gotten gains to hell. Now this was found out in the following way.

The most glorious Charles used to go to lauds at night in a long and flowing cloak, which is now neither used nor known; then when the morning chant was over he would go back to his chamber and dress himself in his imperial robes. All the clerks used to come ready dressed to the nightly office, and then they would wait for the emperor's arrival and for the celebration of mass either in the church or in the porch, which then was called the outer court. Sometimes they would remain awake, or if anyone had need of sleep he would lean his head on his companion's breast. Now one poor clerk, who used often to go to Liutfrid's house to get his clothes (rags I ought to call them) washed and mended, was sleeping with his head on a friend's knees, when he saw in a vision a giant, taller than the adversary of Saint Anthony, come from the king's court and hurry over the bridge that spanned a little stream, to the house of the steward; and he led with him an enormous camel, burdened with baggage of inestimable value. He was, in his dream, struck with amazement and he asked the giant who he was and whither he wished to go. And the giant made answer: "I come from the house of the king and I go to the house of Liutfrid; and I shall place Liutfrid on these packages and I shall take him and them down with me to hell."

Thereupon the clerk woke up, in a fright lest Charles should find him sleeping. He lifted up his head and urged the others to wakefulness and cried: "Hear, I pray you, my dream. I seemed to see another Polyphemus, who walked on the earth and yet touched the stars, and passed through the Ionian Sea without wetting his sides. I saw him hasten from the royal court to the house of Liutfrid with a laden camel. And when I asked the cause of his journey, he said: 'I am going to put Liutfrid on the top of the load, and then take him to hell.' "

The story was hardly finished when there came from that house, which they all knew so well, a girl who fell at their feet and asked them to remember her friend Liutfrid in their prayers. And, when they asked the reason for her words, she said: "My lord, he went out but now in good health, and, as he stayed a long time, we went in search of him, and found him dead."

When the emperor heard of his sudden death, and was informed by the workmen and his servants of his grasping avarice, he ordered his treasures to be examined. They were found to be of priceless worth, and when the emperor, after God the greatest of judges, found by what wickedness they had been collected he gave this public judgment: "Nothing of that which was gained by fraud must go to the liberation of his soul from purgatory. Let his wealth be divided among the workmen of this our building and the poorer servants of our palace."

In the preface to this little work I said I would follow three authorities only. But as the chief of these, Werinbert, died seven days ago and to-day (the thirteenth of May) we, his bereaved sons and disciples, are going to pay solemn honour to his memory, here I will bring this book to an end, concerning the piety of Lord Charles and his care of the Church, which has been taken from the lips of this same clerk, Werinbert.

The next book which deals with the wars of the most fierce Charles is founded on the narrative of Werinbert's father, Adalbert. He followed his master Kerold in the Hunnish, Saxon, and Slavic wars, and when I was quite a child and he a very old man, I lived in his house and he used often to tell me the story of these events. I was most unwilling to listen and would often run away; but in the end by sheer force he made me hear.

### BOOK II

As I am going to found this narrative on the story told by a man of the world, who had little skill in letters, I think it will be well that I should first recount something of earlier history on the credit of written books. When Julian, whom God hated, was slain in the Persian war by a blow from heaven, not only did the transmarine provinces fall away from the Roman Empire, but also the neighbouring provinces of Pannonia, Noricum, Rhaetia, or in other words the Germans and the Franks or Gauls. Then too the kings of the Franks (or Gauls) began to decay in power because they had slain Saint Didier, Bishop of Vienna, and had expelled those most holy visitors, Columban and Gall. Whereupon the race of the Huns, who had already often ravaged Francia and Aquitania (that is to say the Gauls and the Spains), now poured out with all their forces, devastated the whole land like a wide-sweeping conflagration, and then carried off all their spoils to a very safe hiding-place. Now Adalbert, whom I have already mentioned, used to explain the nature of this hiding-place as follows: "The land of the Huns," he would say, "was surrounded by nine rings." I could not think of any rings except our ordinary wicker rings for sheepfolds; and so I asked: "What, in the name of wonder, do you mean, sire?" "Well," he said, "it was fortified by nine hedges." I could not think of any hedges except those that protect our cornfields, so again I asked and he answered: "One ring was as wide, that is, it contained as much within it, as all the country between Tours and Constance. It was fashioned with logs of oak and ash and yew and was twenty feet wide and the same in height. All the space within was filled with hard stones and binding clay; and the surface of these great ramparts was covered with sods and grass. Within the limits of the ring, shrubs were planted of such a kind that, when lopped and bent down, they still threw out twigs and leaves. Then between these ramparts hamlets and houses were so arranged that a man's voice could be made to reach from one to the other. And opposite to the houses, at intervals in those unconquerable walls, were constructed doors of no great size; and through these doors the inhabitants from far and near would pour out on marauding expeditions. The second ring was like the first and was distant twenty Teutonic miles (or forty Italian) from the third ring; and so on to the ninth, though of course the successive rings were each much narrower than the preceding one. But in all the circles the estates and houses were everywhere so arranged that the peal of the trumpet would carry the news of any event from one to the other."

For two hundred years and more the Huns had swept the wealth of the western states within these fortifications, and as the Goths and Vandals were disturbing the repose of the world at the same time the western world was almost turned into a desert. But the most unconquerable Charles so subdued them in eight years that he allowed scarcely any traces of them to remain. He withdrew his hand from the Bulgarians, because after the destruction of the Huns they did not seem likely to do any harm to the kingdom of the Franks. All the booty of the Huns, which he found in Pannonia, he divided most liberally among the bishoprics and the monasteries.

About the same time also envoys of the Persians were sent to him. They knew not where Frankland lay; but because of the fame of Rome, over which they knew that Charles had rule, they thought it a great thing when they were able to reach the coast of Italy. They explained the reason of their journey to the bishops of Campania and Tuscany, of Emilia and Liguria, of Burgundy and Gaul and to the abbots and counts of those regions. But by all they were either deceitfully handled or else actually driven off; so that a whole year had gone round before, weary and footsore with their long journey, they reached Aix at last and saw Charles, the most renowned of kings by reason of his virtues. They arrived in the last week of Lent, and, on their arrival being made known to the emperor, he postponed their presentation until Easter Eve. Then when that incomparable monarch was dressed with incomparable magnificence for the chief of festivals, he ordered the introduction of the envoys of that race that had once held the whole world in awe. But they were so terrified at the sight of the most magnificent Charles that one might think they had never seen king or emperor before. He received them however most kindly and granted them this privilege — that they might go wherever they had a mind to, even as one of his own children, and examine everything and ask what questions and make what inquiries they chose. They jumped with joy at this favour, and valued the privilege of clinging close to Charles, of gazing upon him, of admiring him, more than all the wealth of the east.

They went up into the ambulatory that runs around the nave of the cathedral and looked down upon the clergy and the nobles; then they returned to the emperor and by reason of the greatness of their joy, they could not refrain from laughing aloud; and they clapped their hands and said: "We have seen only men of clay before: here are men of gold." Then they went to the nobles, one by one, and gazed with wonder upon arms and clothes that were strange to them; and then came back to the emperor, whom they regarded with wonder still greater. They passed that night and the next Sunday continuously in church; and, upon the most holy day itself, they were invited by the most munificent Charles to a splendid banquet, along with the nobles of Frankland and Europe. There they were so struck with amazement at the strangeness of everything that they had hardly eaten anything at the end of the banquet.

> "But when the Morn, leaving Tithonus' bed,
> Illumined all the land with Phoebus' torch"

then Charles, who would never endure idleness and sloth, went out to the woods to hunt the bison and the urochs; and made preparations to take the Persian envoys with him. But when they saw the immense animals they were stricken with a mighty fear and turned and fled. The undaunted hero Charles, riding on a high-mettled charger, drew near to one of these animals and drawing his sword tried to cut through its neck. But he missed his aim, and the monstrous beast ripped the boot and let-thongs of the emperor, and, slightly wounding his calf with the tip of its horn, made him limp slightly. After that, furious at the failure of its stroke, it fled to the shelter of a valley, which was thickly covered with stones and trees.

Nearly all his servants wanted to take off their own hose to give to Charles, but he forbade it saying: "I mean to go in this fashion to Hildigard." Then Isambard, the son of Warin (the same Warin that persecuted your patron Saint Othmar), ran after the beast and, not daring to approach him more closely, threw his lance and pierced him to the heart between the shoulder and the wind-pipe,

and brought the beast yet warm to the emperor.  He seemed to pay
no attention to the incident; but gave the carcass to his companions
and went home.  But then he called the queen and showed her how
his leg-coverings were torn, and said: "What does the man deserve
who freed me from the enemy that did this to me?"  She made
answer: "He deserves the highest boon."  Then the emperor told
the whole story and produced the enormous horns of the beast in witness of his truth: so that the empress sighed and wept and beat her
breast.  But when she heard that it was Isambard who had saved him
from this terrible enemy, Isambard, who was in ill favour with the
emperor and who had been deprived of all his offices — she threw
herself at his feet and induced him to restore all that had been taken
from him; and a largess was given to him besides.

These same Persian envoys brought the emperor an elephant,
monkeys, balsam, nard, unguents of various kinds, spices, scents and
many kinds of drugs, in such profusion that it seemed as if the east
had been left bare that the west might be filled.  They came by-and-by
to stand on very familiar terms with the emperor; and one day, when
they were in a specially merry mood and a little heated with strong
beer, they spoke in jest as follows: "Sir Emperor, your power is indeed great; but much less than the report of it which is spread through
all the kingdoms of the east."  When he heard this he concealed his
deep displeasure and asked jestingly of them: "Why do you say that,
my children?  How did that idea get into your heads?"  Then they
went back to the beginning and told him everything that had happened to them in the lands beyond the sea; and they said: "We
Persians and the Medes, Armenians, Indians, Parthians, Elamites,
and all the inhabitants of the east fear you much more than our
own ruler Haroun.  And the Macedonians and all the Greeks (how
shall we express it?) they are beginning to fear your overwhelming greatness more than the waves of the Ionian Sea.  And the inhabitants of all the islands through which we passed were as ready
to obey you, and as much devoted to your service, as if they had
been reared in your palace and loaded with your favours.  But the
nobles of your own kingdom, it seems to us, care very little about
you except in your presence; for when we came as strangers to them
and begged them to show us some kindness for the love of you, to
whom we desired to make our way, they gave no heed to us and sent
us away empty-handed."  Then the emperor deposed all counts and
abbots through whose territories those envoys had come from all the
offices that they held and fined the bishops in a huge sum of money.
Then he ordered the envoys to be taken back to their own country
with all care and honour.

Soon after, the unwearied emperor sent to the emperor of the
Persians horses and mules from Spain and Frisian robes, white, grey,
red and blue, which in Persia, he was told, were rarely seen and highly
prized.  Dogs too he sent him of remarkable swiftness and fierceness, such as the King of Persia had desired, for the hunting and

catching of lions and tigers.  The King of Persia cast a careless eye
over the other presents, but asked the envoys what wild beasts or
animals these dogs were accustomed to fight with.  He was told that
they would pull down quickly anything they were set on to.  "Well,"
he said, "experience will test that."  Next day the shepherds were
heard crying loudly as they fled from a lion.  When the noise came
to the palace of the king, he said to the envoys: "Now, my friends
of Frankland, mount your horses and follow me."  Then they eagerly
followed after the king as though they had never known toil or
weariness.  When they came in sight of the lion, though he was
yet at a distance, the satrap of the satraps said to them: "Now set your
dogs on to the lion."  They obeyed and eagerly galloped forward;
the German dogs caught the Persian lion, and the envoys slew him
with swords of northern metal, which had already been tempered
in the blood of the Saxons.

At this sight Haroun, the bravest inheritor of that name, understood the superior might of Charles from very small indications, and
thus broke out in his praise: "Now I know that what I heard of my
brother Charles is true: how that by the frequent practice of hunting, and by the unwearied training of his body and mind, he has acquired the habit of subduing all that is beneath the heavens.  How
can I make worthy recompense for the honours which he has bestowed upon me?  If I give him the land which was promised to
Abraham and shown to Joshua, it is so far away that he could not
defend it from the barbarians; or if, like the high-souled king that
he is, he tried to defend it I fear that the provinces which lie upon the
frontiers of the Frankish kingdom would revolt from his empire.
But in this way I will try to show my gratitude for his generosity.  I
will give that land into his power; and I will rule over it as his representative.  Whenever he likes or whenever there is a good opportunity
he shall send me envoys; and he will find me a faithful manager of
the revenue of that province."

Thus was brought to pass what the poet spoke of as an impossi-
bility:

"The Parthian's eyes the Arar's stream shall greet
And Tigris' waves shall lave the German's feet";

for through the energy of the most vigorous Charles it was found
not merely possible but quite easy for his envoys to go and return,
and the messengers of Haroun, whether young or old, passed easily
from Parthia into Germany and returned from Germany to Parthia.
(And the poet's words are true, whatever interpretation the grammarians put on "the river Arar," whether they think it an affluent of
the Rhone or the Rhine; for they have fallen into confusion on this
point through their ignorance of the locality.)  I could call on Germany to bear witness to my words; for in the time of your glorious
father Lewis the land was compelled to pay a penny for every acre
of land held under the law towards the redemption of Christian cap-

tives in the Holy Land; and they made their wretched appeal in the name of the dominion anciently held over that land by your great-grandfather Charles and your grandfather Lewis.

But, after conquering the external foe, Charles was attacked at the hands of his own people in a remarkable but unavailing plot. For on his return from the Slavs into his own kingdom he was nearly captured and put to death by his son, whom a concubine had borne to him and who had been called by his mother by the ill-omened name of the most glorious Pippin. The plot was found out in the following manner. This son of Charles had been plotting the death of the emperor with a gathering of nobles, in the church of Saint Peter; and when their debate was over, fearful of every shadow, he ordered search to be made, to see whether anyone was hidden in the corners or under the altar. And behold they found, as they feared, a clerk hidden under the altar. They seized him and made him swear that he would not reveal their conspiracy. To save his life, he dared not refuse to take the oath which they dictated; but, when they were gone, he held his wicked oath of small account and at once hurried to the palace. With the greatest difficulty he passed through the seven bolted gates, and coming at length to the emperor's chamber knocked upon the door. The most vigilant Charles fell into a great astonishment, as to who it was that dared to disturb him at that time of night. He however ordered the women (who followed in his train to wait upon the queen and the princesses) to go out and see who was at the door and what he wanted. When they went out and found the wretched creature, they bolted the door in his face and then, bursting with laughter and stuffing their dresses into their mouths, they tried to hide themselves in the corners of the apartments. But that most wise emperor, whose notice nothing under heaven could escape, asked straitly of the women who it was and what he wanted. When he was told that it was a smoothfaced, silly, half-mad knave, dressed only in shirt and drawers, who demanded an audience without delay, Charles ordered him to be admitted. Then he fell at the emperor's feet and showed all that had happened. So all the conspirators, entirely unsuspicious of danger, were seized before the third hour of the day and most deservedly condemned to exile or some other form of punishment. Pippin himself, a dwarf and a hunchback, was cruelly scourged, tonsured, and sent for some time as a punishment to the monastery of Saint Gall; the poorest, it was judged, and the straitest in all the emperor's broad dominions.

A short time afterwards some of the Frankish nobles sought to do violence to their king. Charles was well aware of their intentions and yet did not wish to destroy them because, if only they were loyal, they might be a great protection to all Christian men. So he sent messengers to this Pippin and asked him his advice in the matter.

They found him in the monastery garden in the company of the elder brothers, for the younger ones were detained by their work. He was digging up nettles and other weeds with a hoe, that the useful herbs might grow more vigorously. When they had explained to him the reason of their coming he sighed deeply, from the very bottom of his heart, and said in reply: "If Charles thought my advice worth having he would not have treated me so harshly. I give him no advice. Go, tell him what you found me doing." They were afraid to go back to the dreaded emperor without a definite answer, and again and again asked him what message they should convey to their lord. Then at last he said in anger: "I will send him no message except — what I am doing! I am digging up the useless growths in order that the valuable herbs may be able to develop more freely."

So they went away sorrowfully thinking that they were bringing back a foolish answer. When the emperor asked them upon their arrival what answer they were bringing, they answered sorrowfully that after all their labour and long journeying they could get no definite information at all. Then that most wise king asked them carefully where they had found Pippin, what he was doing, and what answer he had given them; and they said: "We found him sitting on a rustic seat turning over the vegetable garden with a hoe. When we told him the cause of our journey we could extract no other reply than this, even by the greatest entreaties: 'I give no message except — what I am doing! I am digging up the useless growths in order that the valuable herbs may be able to develop more freely.'" When he heard this the emperor, not lacking in cunning and mighty in wisdom, rubbed his ears and blew out his nostrils and said: "My good vassals, you have brought back a very reasonable answer." So while the messengers were fearing that they might be in peril of their lives, Charles was able to divine the real meaning of the words.

He took all those plotters away from the land of the living; and so gave to his loyal subjects room to grow and spread, which had previously been occupied by those unprofitable servants. One of his enemies, who had chosen as his part of the spoil of the empire the highest hill in France and all that could be seen from it, was, by Charles's orders, hanged upon a high gallows on that very hill. But he bade his bastard son Pippin choose the manner of life that most pleased him. Upon this permission being given him, he chose a post in a monastery then most noble but now destroyed.

It happened too that on his wanderings Charles once came unexpectedly to a certain maritime city of Narbonensian Gaul. When he was dining quietly in the harbour of this town, it happened that some Norman scouts made a piratical raid. When the ships came in sight some thought them Jews, some African or British merchants, but the most wise Charles, by the build of the ships and their speed, knew them to be not merchants but enemies, and said to his companions: "These ships are not filled with merchandise, but crowded with our fiercest enemies." When they heard this, in eager rivalry they hurried in haste to the ships. But all was in vain, for when the Northmen heard that Charles, the Hammer, as they used to call him, was there, fearing lest their fleet should be beaten back or even smashed in pieces, they withdrew themselves by a marvellously rapid flight not only from the swords but even from the eyes of those who followed them. The most religious, just, and devout Charles had risen from the table and was standing at an eastern window. For a long time he poured down tears beyond price and none dared speak a word to him, but at last he explained his actions and his tears to his nobles in these words: "Do you know why I weep so bitterly, my true servants? I have no fear of those worthless rascals doing any harm to me; but I am sad at heart to think that even during my lifetime they have dared to touch this shore; and I am torn by a great sorrow because I foresee what evil things they will do to my descendants and their subjects."

May the protection of our Master Christ prevent the accomplishment of this prophecy; may your sword, tempered already in the blood of the Nordostrani, resist it! The sword of your brother Carloman will help, which now lies idle and rusted, not for want of spirit, but for want of funds, and because of the narrowness of the lands of your most faithful servant Arnulf. If your might wills it, if your might orders it, it will easily be made bright and sharp again. These and the little shoot of Bernard from the only branch that is left of the once prolific root of Lewis, to flourish under the wonderful growth of your protection. Let me insert here therefore in the history of your namesake Charles an incident in the life of your great-great-grandfather Pippin: which perhaps some future little Charles or Lewis may read and imitate.

When he found that the nobles of his army were accustomed in secret to speak contemptuously of him, he ordered one day a huge and ferocious bull to be brought out; and then a savage lion to be let loose upon him. The lion rushed with tremendous fury on the bull, seized him by the neck and cast him on the ground. Then the king said to those who stood round him: "Now, drag off the lion from the bull, or kill the one on the top of the other." They looked on one another, with a chill at their hearts, and could hardly utter these words amidst their sobs: "Lord, what man is there under heaven, who dare attempt it?" Then Pippin rose confidently from his throne, drew his sword, and at one blow cut through the neck of the lion and severed the head of the bull from his shoulders. Then he put back his sword into its sheath and sat again upon his throne and said: "Well, do you think I am fit to be your lord? Have you not heard what the little David did to the giant Goliath, or what the child Alexander did to his nobles?" They fell to the ground, as though a thunderbolt had struck them, and cried: "Who but a madman would deny your right to rule over all mankind?"

When after the death of the ever-victorious Pippin the Lombards were again attacking Rome, the unconquered Charles, though he was fully occupied with business to the north of the Alps, marched swiftly into Italy. He received the Lombards into his service after they had been humbled in a war that was almost bloodless, or (one might say) after they had surrendered of their own free will; and to prevent them from ever again revolting from the Frankish kingdom or doing any injury to the territories of Saint Peter, he married the daughter of Desiderius, chief of the Lombards.  But no long time afterwards, because she was an invalid and little likely to give issue to Charles, she was, by the counsel of the holiest of the clergy, put aside, even as though she were dead.  Whereupon her father in wrath bound his subjects to him by oath, and shutting himself up within the walls of Pavia, he prepared to give battle to the invincible Charles, who, when he had received certain news of the revolt, hurried to Italy with all speed.

Now it happened that some years before one of the first nobles, called Otker, had incurred the wrath of the most terrible emperor, and had fled for refuge to Desiderius.  When the near approach of the dreaded Charles was known, these two went up into a very high tower, from which they could see anyone approaching at a very great distance.  When therefore the baggage-wagons appeared, which moved more swiftly than those used by Darius or Julius, Desiderius said to Otker: "Is Charles in that vast army?"  And Otker answered: "Not yet."  Then when he saw the vast force of the nations gathered together from all parts of his empire, he said with confidence to Otker: "Surely Charles moves in pride among those forces."  But Otker answered: "Not yet, not yet."  Then Desiderius fell into great alarm and said, "What shall we do if a yet greater force comes with him?"  And Otker said, "You will see what he likes when he comes.  What will happen to us I cannot say."  And, behold, while they were thus talking, there came in sight Charles's personal attendants, who never rested from their labours; and Desiderius saw them and cried in amazement, "There is Charles."  And Otker answered: "Not yet, not yet."  Then they saw the bishops and the abbots and the clerks of his chapel with their attendants.  When he saw them he hated the light and longed for death, and sobbed and stammered, "Let us go down to hide ourselves in the earth from the face of an enemy so terrible."  And Otker answered trembling, for once, in happier days, he had had thorough and constant knowledge of the policy and preparations of the unconquerable Charles: "When you see an iron harvest bristling in the fields; and the Po and the Ticino pouring against the walls of the city like the waves of the sea, gleaming black with glint of iron, then know that Charles is at hand."  Hardly were these words finished when there came from the west a black cloud, which turned the bright day to horrid gloom.  But as the emperor drew nearer the gleam of the arms turned the darkness into day, a day darker than any night to that beleaguered garrison.  Then could be seen the iron Charles, helmeted with an iron helmet, his hands clad in iron gauntlets, his iron breast and broad shoulders protected with an iron breastplate.  An iron spear was raised on high in his left hand; his right always rested on his unconquered iron falchion.  The thighs, which with most men are uncovered that they may the more easily ride on horseback, were in his case clad with plates of iron.   I need make no special mention of his greaves, for the greaves of all the army were of iron.   His shield was all of iron; his charger was iron-coloured and iron-hearted.   All who went before him, all who marched by his side, all who followed after him and the whole equipment of the army imitated him as closely as possible.   The fields and open places were filled with iron; the rays of the sun were thrown back by the gleam of iron; a people harder than iron paid universal honour to the hardness of iron. The horror of the dungeon seemed less than the bright gleam of iron.   "Oh the iron!   Woe for the iron!" was the confused cry that rose from the citizens.   The strong walls shook at the sight of the iron; the resolution of young and old fell before the iron.   Now when the truthful Otker saw in one swift glance all this which I, with stammering tongue and the voice of a child, have been clumsily explaining with rambling words, he said to Desiderius: "There is the Charles that you so much desired to see": and when he had said this he fell to the ground half dead.

But as the inhabitants of the city, either through madness or because they entertained some hope of resistance, refused to let Charles enter on that day, the most inventive emperor said to his men: "Let us build to-day some memorial, so that we may not be charged with passing the day in idleness.   Let us make haste to build for ourselves a little house of prayer, where we may give due attention to the service of God, if they do not soon throw open the city to us."   No sooner had he said it than his men flew off in every direction, collected lime and stones, wood and paint, and brought them to the skilled workmen who always accompanied him.   And between the fourth hour of the day and the twelfth they built, with the help of the young nobles and the soldiers, such a cathedral so provided with walls and roofs, with fretted ceiling and frescoes, that none who saw it could believe that it had taken less than a year to build.   But, how on the next day some of the citizens wanted to throw open the gate, and some wanted to fight against him, even without hope of victory, or rather to fortify themselves against him; and how easily he conquered, took and occupied the city, without the shedding of blood, and merely by the exercise of skill; — all this I must leave others to tell, who follow your highness not for love, but in the hope of gain.

[tr. A. J. Grant]

# EKKEHARD I OF ST. GALL

*Walter of Aquitaine,* which may with some justice be called the first chivalric romance, though written in Latin rather than in the romance tongue, is not only a lively story well plotted and with consistent forward action, but in many ways of exceptional interest to all students of romance. It was long believed that *Walter* was written by Ekkehard I of St. Gall when, as a youth in his early twenties, he studied in a *schola externalis,* or secular school, attached to the monastery. At this time the monastic schools, patronized by royalty and therefore in part responsive to the demands of lay rulers, accepted the sons of the nobility for instruction in letters. The curriculum, taught by Benedictine masters, was that of the early choir-school, modified for its new clientele. The author of *Walter* combines a knowledge of Teutonic and Gallic ballads and folklore with the academic reading acquired. Strecker, the famous editor of *Walter* and other late Carolingian poetry, came to doubt the common attribution of this poem to Ekkehard and even to the school of St. Gall.

The poem illustrates the vulgarization of monastic literature. It shows how the materials taught in church schools, originally founded exclusively for the training of the clergy, were adapted to the entertainment of the nobility. The author takes the names of his characters from the vernacular literary tradition; hence we meet here Walter, who appears in the Old English fragment *Waldere,* Etzel, Hagen, and Gunther, who appear in the *Nibelungenlied,* and a certain number of types, such as the humorless Saxon, drawn from stock caricatures. Yet the diction and imagery are Mediterranean, drawn largely from Virgil and Prudentius. Whole lines — sometimes whole scenes — are lifted from Virgil's *Aeneid*. Strange as it seems, the scene of Walter's banquet orgy is stated partly in words of Prudentius as he described Christ's feeding of the five thousand. The journey of Walter and his virgin companion Hildegund across the upper Danube valley into the Vosges, probably through the Belfort Pass, was probably in part inspired by Jerome's *Life of St. Malchus.* (In the first of the medieval beast-epics, *Ecbasis Captivi,* contemporaneous with *Walter,* the unicorn reads *The Life of St. Malchus* to the assembled group in proper monastic fashion.) If, as is almost certain, the poem was written by a student, many of its lines were composed to impress the teacher with its author's mastery of his assignments. In such a fashion were the primitive tales of the north turned into literary form. The monastic schools, originating in revolt against secular literature, now aided its preservation and development.

Ekkehard, forsaking the secularity of his youth, was eventually ordained and became Dean of St. Gall. Though never again producing romantic literature, he became an important figure in the

Church of his day.  According to a later St. Gall historian, this
poem, which was locally circulated as school prize poems usually
are, became known to a wider audience only when the Bishop of
Mainz discovered it, had it revised to remove some schoolboy
solicisms, and "published" it through his scriptorium.


## WALTER OF AQUITAINE

### Ekkehard I of St. Gall (?) (A.D. 910?)

One third of earth, called Europe, Sirs, is home
For diverse races, diff'ring each from each
In manners, language, culture, name and faith.
One of these races, known in common speech
By name of Hun, a people strong in arms
As well as virtue, from the Pannonian plain
Uncircumscribed extended dominance
To ocean's tidal strand — for suppliants
Allies, a scourge to those who would rebel.
'Tis said they held their sway a thousand years.

There came a time when Attilla the King,
Grown zealous to renew their ancient feats
Of arms, commanded that their hordes migrate
To Frankish land, where Gibich held the throne —
A king but now made glad, as I shall tell,
In fathering a prince, Gunther by name.

Wide-spreading Fame the trembling kingly ears
Informed that hostile force outnumbering
The stars or sands had crossed the Danube flood.
The king, distrustful of his troops and arms,
Convoked a council to debate their moves.
As one they urged a pact whereby they'd pledge
To forfeit hostages and tribute pay,
If Attilla would join right hand in right —
This better than by single stroke to lose
Their lives and lands, their sons and wives as well.

A noble youth named Hagen, of the seed
Of Trojan heroes born, was now at court.
Because Prince Gunther, yet a babe, would lose
His tender life bereft of mother's care,
They charged that Hagen with the tribute should
At once be sent.  Then taking hoard and youth,
The envoys left, sought peace, and compact made.

At this same time in mighty Burgundy

Courageous Herric held the reins of power.
His only child, a daughter Hildegund,
Who matched nobility with filial grace,
Had long within the palace walls enjoyed
Her father's affluence, as rightful heir.

The wild Avars at length confirmed the truce
And at the Frankish marches stopped their horde.
But Attilla soon flicked his rapid reins
To haste the cohorts in their satrap's lead —
Drawn in long columns for the measured march,
As earth beneath the hooves of horses ground
And heaven quaked at shields resounding high.
An iron forest colored fields with red,
Like the resplendent sun at break of day
Whose rays the lambent sea incarnadine.
Once having crossed the Arar and the Rhone,
The host dispersed for looting and rapine.

Herric, it seems, at Chalons stayed, when lo!
A watchman on the guard cried out above,
"What is that cloud of dust that stirs the plain?
An enemy advances!   Close the gates!"
At once the Prince knew that the Franks had made
Their peace.   He to the marshalled elders spoke:
"If that stark race, to whom we can't compare,
Has left Pannonia, think you we have
The power sufficient to defend our homes?
Enough! We make a pact and tribute pay.
Without delay I'll trade my only child,
To free the land and seal the needed truce."

There go the legates, scabbards empty, to
Search out the foe and at their King's behest
Plead for an end to rapine.   Attilla
By wont receives them graciously and says:
"I pact prefer to sending troops to war.
E'en Huns want peaceful rule, but grudgingly
By sword exact full toll from rebels.   Tell
Your King to come and mutual pledge exchange."
Straightway the Prince with tribute gold confirmed
The pact, and to the foe released his child,
Now exiled — fairest and most precious jewel.

With one more pact confirmed and tribute set,
Westward stout Attilla defiled his troops.
   King Alpher then ruled Aquitania.
The story goes that he had princely heir
Named Walter, who in youthful vigor shone.

By mutual pledge 'twixt Herric and this King
They planned a union of their regal lines
Whene'er their offspring reached maturity.
   When Alpher learned Huns conquered his allies,
His heart leaped in an unaccustomed fear;
To stand with savage arms, all hope was lost.
"Why battle, say, if we must lose the fight?
Since Burgundy and France have showed the way,
No blame is meet to follow in their lead.
I'll send my legates, ordered to arrange
A pact, for hostage grant my dearest son,
And thus at once absolve the Hunnish debt."

But why delay?   His word fulfils the deed.
The Avar horde, weighed down with plundered wealth,
Escorts the hostage Hagen, Hildegund,
And now Prince Walter, as they homeward wend.
Pannonian confines and the castle reached,
King Attilla, with deep solicitude,
Nourished as if his own the exiled youths,
Committing to his Queen the maiden's charge.
Yea, more, at his command they ever bode
Within his view; he taught them manly arts,
With special stress on warlike tournament.
As one, they daily strengthened like the oak,
Combining guile with power, until ere long
They far outshone the martial Huns themselves.
Of all his cortege, Etzel ranked them first —
And rightly, since whene'er the army marched
To war, they gained transplendent victories:
Wherefore strong Etzel loved them both the more.
   Abounding in good works and industry
With the help of Highest God, the captive maid
The Queen regarded as a paragon,
So that in course she trusted all her wealth
Unstinted to the girl, who reigned with her —
The mistress of her fortune and her will.

Meanwhile King Gibich died, and in his stead
Gunther succeeded.  He at once dissolved
The hated Hunnish pact, and tribute barred.
The moment exiled Hagen was apprised,
He fled at night and hasted to his Lord,
While Walter, out campaigning for the Huns,
Won new successes, though a hostage still.

Queen consort Ospirn, noting the escape
Of Hagen, spoke as follows to her Lord:

"I pray Thy Majesty foreseest and fearst
That Walter, now thy empire's main support,
In whom thou vestest supereminence,
May, like his friend, escape thy vassalage
To follow, as I fear, in Hagen's lead.
Wherefore my mind is given to this plan:
When next he comst, address him in these words:
'In my campaigns, you've suffered mightily,
But with success.  Wherefore you know that we
Prize you above all others as our friend.
And lest we recompense brave deeds with words,
We charge you take the noblest Hunnish maid
To wife, with care her dowry is the best.
Indeed, we shall a castle grant, and land,
Lest anyone who gives his child should doubt.'
If thou speakst thus, thou'lt hold him in thy power."
This pleasing speech the King prepared to use.

The knight arrived.  The Prince made clear his wish
That Walter should be wed.  But even then
With plan maturing that brought later fruit,
He turned the urgent offer, answering thus:
"That thou so viewst the welfare of thy liege
Bespeaks thy grace.  Instinctively thou probst
Where my mind's indolence can follow not.
So understand thy humble servant's thought:
If, by the precepts of my Lord, I wed,
Then love of maid becomes my first of cares,
Whilst service to my King is mancipate.
Were I constrained to tend the rural fields
And fit a home — tasks meet for elder eyes —
I'd lose the skill required for ruling Huns;
For he who tastes love's pleasure, then
Intolerable finds his martial toil.
To be thy faithful subject is for me
The sweetest sweet.  Wherefore permit, I pray,
My life to carry on without love's bonds.
If late or at the midnight hour thou criest
Instant obedience, I stand prepared.
At war none could dissuade; nor child nor wife
Retard my actions, nor move me to flight.
Entreat I thee, Good Father, by my life
And by that still unconquered Hunnish race,
No more constraint to enter wedded life!"
  The King retracted, victim of those prayers,
Hoping that Walter would not choose to flee.
Anon the Satrap learned through channels sure
How certain peoples, recently subdued,
Now planned at once to rise against the Huns.

Then Walter girt himself for war.   At first
He mobilized his troops, then in array
Inspired their warrior hearts by stout harangue
To bear in mind the triumphs of the past,
Predicting tyrants would at last succumb
To vaunted worth, and foreign lands lie waste.

Without delay, as one the army moved.
    Embracing battle site with single glance,
He through the field deployed his numerous force.
    Each host advancing within cast of spear
There halted.   Then from every side the cry
Of battle smote the ears, the frenzied blare
Of trumpets, and the clang of hurtling spears.
Ash-tree and cornel mingled in that game,
As thunder-like the vibrant lances quaked.
Like blinding snow that in the winter storm
Blankets the earth, the savage arrows flew.
    Then with the long-arms cast, each phalanx charged
To single combat, with the short-arms bared.
Swords flashed from sheaths, targets revolved,
As battle lines commingled in the press
Of horses, impact bursting breast on breast.
On lifeless shields, unsaddled riders lay.
    Amid the fray raged Walter, mowing down
Obstruction with his arms, and cleared a path
Whereby the foe could glimpse confusion dire,
And so taste in advance impending death.
Wherever Walter moved, to left or right,
Opponents turned their backs, and, throwing down
Their bucklers, slackened rein and fled.
    The duke's example fired the Avars, who
With savage intrepidity pressed home
The slaughter grim.   Some fell and others fled,
Till Pannons wrested final victory,
And o'er the dead despoiling torrents streamed
Until the duke's curved horn a summons blew.
    With festal bough they wreathed his head and bound
His temples with the victor's laurel.   Then
Bchind him marched the standards and the men.
So with triumphant fillets in their hair
They neared the fatherland, each searching out
His home.   Meanwhile the leader hastes to court.

Now see the palace servants run about
With joy of aspect, as they hold the steed
While the illustrious hero quick dismounts.
Whenever things go well, they want to know.
He drops a word or two and hastens in,

For he is wearied and must seek repose
Within the castle.   There is Hildegund,
Whom he embraces and with kisses says,
"I am exhausted and must slake my thirst."
A bowl upon a precious salver she
Fills, and the hero offers.   He accepts
With sign of Cross, then takes her virgin hand.
She silent, standing close, drinks deep his gaze
While hero Walter drains the bowl to dregs;
For both knew and esteemed their settled troth.
    To his beloved he these words addressed:
"Long have we equally endured exile,
Well knowing that our parents firmly planned
Amongst them what our future life should be.
Have not our tacit lips some word of love?"
    Feeling her lover spoke as duty bade,
She said at length, though first her tongue was mute:
"Why dost thou speak that which thy feelings shun?
Thy mouth says one, thy heart another, word.
To lowly me must thou in shame be wed?"
    At this the perspicacious hero flinched:
"Banish the thought!   Let's set the meaning straight!
Know that from simulant mind I've nothing said,
Nor have I screened with words a wavering.
Nothing exists but us — we two for one!
Could I but know you shared one will with me —
Your hidden faith confided in my love —
The veil from secrets of my heart I'd rend."

With genuflexion low, the maid replied:
"Where'er though callst, my lord, I follow close;
Whate're thou willst, I haste me to obey."
Then he: "This long exile of ours I loathe,
And dream of fatherland so long bereft:
Wherefore I plan immediate secret flight,
Long ere this day I would have 'scaped except
I'd not leave wretched Hildegund behind."

Her maiden heart poured out her faith in words:
"Whate'er thy wish, that do I crave for mine;
My lord's commands, for good or ill, shall stand
Preeminent with me, graced by his love."
    Then Walter whispered in the maiden's ear:
"Now follow carefully my words.   The Queen
Has charged her treasure to your custody.
A helmet of the King and coat of mail
Take first, a cuirass of skilled workmanship;
Two small-sized chests thereafter fill with jewels —
Pannonian bracelets and such other gems —

Till you can scarce uplift them from the floor.
Four pairs of Grecian shoes for me, and like
Amount for you, will fill the vacant space.
Doubtless the chests will then be packed enough.
Next ask the smiths to forge some barbed hooks,
For on our way are fish and game enow,
And I must fisherman and fowler be.
All these you glean in secret by a week.
   Hear now my long premeditated plan
Of flight, which I in hopefulness unfold:
The seventh course of Phoebus from this day,
For King and Queen, their satraps, dukes, and serfs,
I'll have prepared a sumptuous feast and grand,
Where by my skill I'll bury all in drink
Until not one will sense what is afoot.
Meanwhile you take but little from the bowl
To quench your thirst, and delicately eat.
When they arise, speed to the needed tasks;
For as the stupor conquers those who drank,
We'll haste to seek our path to western lands."

The maiden his behests obeyed.   Now comes
The fated day of banquet.   Walter sees
The food upon enormous trenchers heap.
Dame Luxury, mid-table, sits enthroned
As through encircling tapestries the King
Parades.   Great-hearted Walter, bowing low,
Conducts him to the purple chair of state.
The vizier on each side the King commands
A duke to sit, and then the rest by rank.
By hundreds liegemen lie at tables close,
Perspiring freely as the liquor flows;
No empty plate is suffered unrefilled,
And savory maslin vapors drench the hall.
See byssine-covered, golden vessels with
A Bacchus inlaid on their covers rest
Enticingly at Walter's hand! He begs
In turn each one the fragrant potion drain.

Desire now lost to surfeit and the board
Bereft of viands, Walter nears the King
With wassail bowl: "I beg Thy Grace display
In this thy primacy, that all may joy."
Roused at the jovial word, the King receives
The proferred cup, in cunning art engraved
With olden tales, and drains it without breath
In challenge that the others match his draught.
   How fast the page-boys hasten to and fro,
Set down full beakers and remove the spent,

As all contend at bid of host and King!
   Then burning drunkenness o'erpowers the court,
And bib'lous throats spout fuddled eloquence.
Just watch intrepid heroes stagger off!
By midnight hour, the youth incited all
To inebriety, then quick withdrew
When every guest had fallen to the floor
About the hall, oppressed with drunken sleep.
And had he chose to set consuming flames
To walls, none would have lived to tell the tale.
   With fev'rish haste he called the loving maid
To set in play at once the ordained plan —
From stable chose himself the best of steeds,
Named Lion for his fearsome energy,
Who stood and proudly champed the foaming bit.
Then buckling taut the charger's trappings, he
Suspended from each flank the treasure chests
And dole of food, meet for the parlous course.
He thrust the slack reins in the maiden's hand
While donning hero's breastplate, capping it
With red-plumed helmet; girt on muscled calves
His golden greaves, and bound to his left hip
A double-bladed sword, and on his right
A second in Pannonian fashion fixt,
Its blade wound-dealing on one edge alone.
With right hand seizing lance, with left his shield,
Fearful he started through the hated wild.
   The damsel led the heavy-burdened steed
And carried in her hand a willow bough
With which a fisher could cast in a stream
A baited hook to snare a hungry fish;
For laden was the powerful man with arms,
Always alert for possible attack.
   Each night they hastened on the route, but when
Apollo's early rays carmined the earth,
They'd seek sequestered refuge in a glade,
And anxious, though in hiding, find repose.
A maiden's fear disquiets her pulsing breast —
At gentle whispers of the breeze she starts,
At spatting birds of crackling twigs turns pale.
Yet exile's hate and lust for home abide.
   They shun the hamlets and the new-tilled fields
And break a tortuous path in winding course
Through sinuous gorge and craggy mountain trail.

The urbane court, dissolved in sleep and wine,
In silence slumbered till the midday next.
But then they rose and signalled for their host
To thank him for the feast and make adieux.

When Attilla, his head betwixt both hands,
Came staggering from his chamber, and with moans
Called "Walter," seeking remedy for ills,
His ministers replied they could not find
The knight.   At this response the King presumed
That Walter was still held by sleep and would
Come to his quarters when he finally roused.
    But Ospirn later found that Hildegund
Was gone — her garments in disorder flung.
With loud lament, she clamored to her lord:
"Abhorrent banquet we consumed for him!
Foul wine, destroying all the Hunnish flower!
How many times I told thee, good My Lord!
The day has come which we cannot redeem.
This hour we see thy empire's column crack,
Since now its stoutest oak has been purloined.
Our Walter, light of Huns, has disappeared
And taken Hildegund, my dearest dear."

Then was the Prince consumed by savage rage,
And grieving heart supplanted former joy.
From tip to toe, he rent his kingly robe,
While, tempest-tost, his mind rocked to and fro.
Like breakers pulsed by winds of Aeolus,
The King swayed under stress of inward pain.
Delirious words echoed delirium,
Venting without all woe sustained within.
In wrath he granted right of speech to none.
Throughout the day rejecting food and drink,
At night he found no surcease from his woe;
For as black night obscured the tints of day,
He sank to couch, but shut not out the lights —
Now bolstered on his right side, now on left.
As though a sharpened barb transfixed his breast,
His head now pounded, now his body shook,
And frenzied at the post he'd sit erect.
Then tortured still, he'd rush into the court,
Then back to pillow, and then out again.
    So Attilla consumed his sleepless night,
While counts, who chanced upon him, hastily
As moonbeams in a friendly silence fled.

Scarce had the morning broke when to his chiefs
He said: "Will no one fleeing Walter fetch,
Chained like the worthless hound he proved himself?
For such an one, I'll fit him out with gold
Well-forged, and lade him standing here with coin
Until he scarce can struggle from the spot!"
    Not one in all the Empire — neither king

Nor duke nor count nor knight nor minister,
Much as he longed to show his virile strength
And carry off the laurel for his skill,
While stuffing money-bags with minted gold —
Who dared to tempt the fiery Walter's wrath
Or face the knight in combat with drawn sword;
For they his unexampled martial strength
Well knew, who'd seen his unscarred victories.
    The King could not induce a single man,
Whatever gold he offered for the feat.

Now as I said, the fleeing Walter rode
By night, and in the day sought woodland glades.
With art he lured, with art he caught the birds —
Ensnaring them with birdlime, traps, or sticks.
Whene'er he chanced upon a mazy stream,
His casting hook would draw therefrom some prize.
So did he toil to ward off famishment.
    Throughout the whole flight with the virgin maid
Continued hero Walter virtuous.

In this wise forty times the sun revolved
Since they had fled Pannonic castle walls,
Until that fated fortieth day they came
At vespertide to the wide-stretching flood —
That is, the Rhine — whose course bent toward the town
Of Worms, well known as kingly seat of power.
    For passage-money Walter gave some fish
He'd caught before, in anxious haste to cross.

When dawn of day dispersed the sable night,
The boatman rose and hied him into town
To the King's chef, the master cook of all,
To leave the fish received for passage fare.
The fish, all cooked and seasoned, then were served
To Gunther marveling, who saw and said:
"Fish of this breed ne'er have I seen in France,
Our fatherland; they must come from without.
Speak up at once: What churl conveyed them here?"
    The chef retold the boatman's narrative,
At which the Prince commanded he be brought
Into his presence, where he questioned him
In each detail, till he this story drew:
"Last night at eve I stood on Rhenish shore
And spied a trav'ler hasting toward my boat
Beclad in armor, as if battle-bound;
For, Noble King, all panoplied in bronze,
Afoot he carried shield and glinting spear.
A powerful man was he, for though he bore
A heavy load, his pace and step were brisk.

And heel to heel there followed close behind,
With beauty unbelievable, a damsel fair,
Who led by rein a peerless charger.  Strapped
Upon his back were chests of middle size
Which, as the palfrey quivered his high neck
Or tried in pride ebullient to prance,
Gave out a sound like chink of coin or jewels.
    They gave me for my pay this catch of fish."

Now Hagen, as he sat at council, heard,
And at the speech joy leaped within his breast:
"Rejoice for me, I beg — for now I know
That my companion Walter 'scaped the Huns!"
    At this Prince Gunther, haughty, cried aloud
That all his court obedient give ear:
"Rejoice for me, I order — that I live!
The treasure which King Gibich sent with him
He now returns to homeland and to me!"
    With this anathema, he kicked aside
The table, springing to command his steed
Be saddled fast, and that his best twelve knights
Should follow him, the choice of all his land
For arms and courage — Hagen at their head.
    Now he, with mind intent on ancient love,
Tried to divert the King from venture rash,
Without avail.  The King brooked no delay:
"No sloth, men!  Gird your fighting loins with steel;
Invest at once your frames in chained mail.
Should wealth like this slip through the bounds of France?"
    Then armed with spears at urgence of their King,
They sallied forth in lust to overtake
Thee, Walter, and despoil thee powerless,
Though Hagen ventured every guile to stay
Gunther from his mad purpose — all in vain.

Meanwhile the noble hero left the flood,
And entered mountain passes of the Vosges,
Extending far through forest, where the dens
Of beasts resounded from the hunting horns.
Adjacent mountains in a lone defile
Form at their base a cool, sequestered nook,
Not hollowed earth, but overhanging rock —
A fit retreat for knaves and robbers bold.
Within its shade grew green and tender herbs.
    The knight espied it: "Here," he said, "we go!
We'll make our camp and rest our weary frames."
For, from the time he fled the Avar land,
No other sleep he'd tasted than to doze
Upright on spear; scarce had he closed his eyes.

Then, throwing down, his battle gear, he said,
Pillowed in maiden's lap: "Keep thou the watch,
My Hildegund; and if thou seest dust-cloud
Arise, bestir me with a gentle shake,
E'en if thou sightst a powerful band of men,
Lest, dearest, from my sleep I sudden wake;
For in the pure air of this height thou canst
Explore the distant reaches at a glance."
　　This said, he closed his lustrous eyes, and long
In deepest slumber gained his needed rest.

As Gunther spies their footprints in the dust,
He pricks his hoovèd steed with savage spur
Delighted, and to listening ears exclaims:
"Speed up, men; now we'll overtake him soon!
He'll not escape to-day; his stolen gold
He'll lose!"　But dauntless Hagen in reply:
"I tell thee, Bravest King, he lacks a peer.
If thou hadst seen, as I so oft have done,
The furious Walter raging for new blood,
Thou wouldst not deem his spoiling easy game!
I oft have seen the Hunnish legions locked
Between two foes in battle, north and south.
There Walter, single-handed, fought supreme —
The bane of foe, the marvel of his friends.
Whoever stood against him plunged to Hell.
O King and Counts, believe me for I know
How strong his shield, what whirlwind is his lance!"
　　But still the King, engrossed by evil plan,
Would not be turned, and hurried toward the camp.

Then Hildegund descried from mountain top
The rising dust, sensed an attack, and warned
Her Walter, by a gentle touch, to wake.
He raised his head to glimpse the charging band,
Whilst she, above him, told what she espied.
Wiping away the sleep from sandy eyes,
With pain he girds his stiffened joints with steel
And torpidly takes up his shield and lance.
Then as he springs in air the steel resounds
While he prepares for bitter fight to come.
　　See how the woman shudders at the glint
Of metal.　"Are the Huns here?" whispers she.
To earth she falls, dissolved in flood of tears.
"I prithee, Sire, hew with thy sword this throat,
Lest she whom marriage-pact hath bound to thee
At other hands should suffer carnal stain!"
The knight exclaims: "Thy guiltless blood on me!
And how, perchance, could sword the faithless slay

If it had spared not its most faithful friend?
Banish thy want; unseat thy anxious mind.
He who led me through perils infinite
Will prove His power, I know, o'er present host."
   With this he raised her eyes to his and said:
"These are not Avars here, but Frankish scum —
Just local peasants, and — " in helmet spied
He Hagen, and at that he laughed aloud,
"And my old comrade Hagen in the lot!"

Therewith the hero placed himself before
The entrance, speaking to the maid behind:
"Fixt at this gate, I'll venture one proud word:
No man of France, returning to his wife,
Will boast he took that treasure unopposed!"
Scarce had he spoke when prostrate on the earth
He sought remission for his haughty speech.
Then he arose, to survey all with care:
"Of those I see, no one save Hagen do
I fear; for he was long acquainted with
My style of war, and is adroit himself.
If by God's grace I overcome him now,
Then, Hildegund, I shall be saved for thee."

[With Walter having chosen his ground so strategically, Gunther cannot easily deploy more than one or two knights against him. Of the twelve, the symbolic number of regal knightly retainers in medieval romance (compare *Song of Roland*), in a secularized ecclesiastical tradition arising from Christ and his twelve disciples, he sends eleven singly or in twos and Walter defeats them in a series of epic combats, which Hagen, standing aloof, refuses to join — enmeshed in the true feudal dilemma of a choice between vows of personal friendship and the vassal's fealty. The balance is tipped when Walter kills his young nephew, whom Hagen loved as a father. When all others have been killed he joins with Gunther in a dual attack on the wearied Walter. For hours they battle.]

No wait nor rest.  The bitter strife goes on —
Now one, now both, in turn attack the man.
The while he savagely pursues the one
The other flanks him and obstructs his lunge.
   As a Numidian bear, when in the hunt
At bay surrounded stands with lethal claws
And snarling, lowered head, crushes the dogs
Of Umbria who draw too near and makes
Them whine in pain, whilst wild Molossian hounds
Circle but dread to beard the cornered brute,
So fluxed the bitter conflict till the Nones —
Each steeped in three-fold care: the fear of death,
The pain of fighting, and the scorching sun.

Meanwhile there crept into the hero's mind
A thought which wordlessly his heart expressed:
"If Fortune cannot find a way, these men
Will trick me, as I tire, by some deceit."
   Straightway to Hagen, with raised voice, he spoke:
"O Hagedorn,* you're thorn-equipped to prick,
And by your feints you try to draw me in.
Down goes my guard now; close without ado.
Come!  Show that power I know is unsurpassed.
It irks me to endure this bootless toil."
He spoke and leaping hurled his pike at him,
Which overbore in flight the shield and pierced
Somewhat the cuirass, barely scratching skin;
For Hagen's mighty frame was stout encased.

And Walter, at the cast, then followed through,
Attacking savagely the King with sword
Unsheathed and, forcing back the cov'ring shield,
Levelled an almost superhuman blow
Which severed leg and knee clear to the thigh.
The King fell on his shield beneath his feet,
As vassal paled to see his stricken Lord.
Then Alpher's son raised high his bloody steel,
Burning to strike the felled a fatal blow;
But Hagen, blind to self and woe-begone,
Inclined his metal helm to ward it off.
The knight could not restrain his outstretched arm;
The helmet, forged with long and loving care,
Received the blow and kindled blazing sparks.
The sword, by helm astonied, broke to bits.
Alas!  Clanging, it glistened in the air and grass.

The warrior, as he saw the broken bits
Of sword, raged with a fiendish wrath
And, scorning hilt without the weight of blade,
Though precious for its peerless workmanship,
Cast it aside and spurned the sad remains.
While thus to throw he stretched his hand far out,
Like lightning fevered Hagen sliced it off.
In mid-cast dropped to earth the brave right hand,
So feared by many tyrants, tribes, and folk —
For victories uncounted wide-renowned.
   The stalwart man, not knowing how to yield
To evil luck, with sound mind fighting off
His fleshly woe, despaired not, nor lost face,
But slipped his severed forearm in his shield
And with the other hand drew his short-sword,
Which, you recall, was girt to his right side,

* English, *hawthorn;* Latin, *paliure.*

And straightway wrested vengeance from his foe;
For at a stroke he gouged out Hagen's eye,
Slashing from temple to his disjoined lips
And tearing out six molars from his mouth.

This damage done, the fight disintegrates.
His wounds and sheer exhaustion force each one
To drop his arms.  Who can escape unharmed
When two such noble heroes, equal matched
In strength and heart, dare stand the bolts of war?

Now at the end, each bears his lasting marks:
There Gunther's regal leg; there Walter's hand
Lies on the ground; there Hagen's twitching eye.
The timid maid then binds the wounds of all.
With that accomplished, Walter orders her:
"Now mix some wine, and serve stout Hagen first—
A prime athlete is he, and keeps the rules.
Then pour for me, for I endured the most.
And last let Gunther drink, for he is slack
Amongst stout hearts, and seems with hero's arms
Lukewarm and zestless at the trade of Mars."
   To all these sentiments nods Herric's child.
But at the offered wine the thirsty Frank,
"First give," says he, "to thy betrothed and lord,
The son of Alpher, maid.  I trow at arms
He's bravest, towering over me and all."

Now thorny Hagen and the Aquitaine,
Alert in mind, though tired in every joint
After the shifting battle's jolting blows,
Mid drinks begin to cap each other's jests.
Says Frank: "Henceforth you'll hunt the stags, my friend.
Their skins will furnish gauntlets endlessly.
But fill the right, I warn, with downy stuff
To gull the yokels with a scarecrow palm!
What say, sirrah!  You'll break an old folk way
To bind your trusty blade to your right thigh!
Then when desire to buss your wife provokes,
How awkward, man, to squeeze her with a left!
Why ring the changes?  What you need henceforth
Your left must gain."  And Walter answered back:
"You one-eyed Dutchman, what a wag you are!
While I hunt stags, eschew the flesh of boars!
From now on you'll call servants with a wink
And look askance whene'er you greet your peers.
For old times' sake, I venture this advice:
When you get home and settle by the fire,
Prepare a gruel of mush and milk in fat

And use it for a food and poultice both!"

These jests revived their friendship once again,
And then and there they lugged the suff'ring King
To place him on his horse, then went their ways:
The Franks to Worms, the Aquitaine to home.
   There was he met with thankfulness and praise
And publicly espoused to Hildegund.
   With parents dead and gone, he, dearly loved,
Ruled all his people wisely three decades.
   What wars thereafter and what triumphs won,
Alas, my blunted stylus fails to note.

Whoever reads, forgive a cricket's chirps.
Heed not its yet harsh voice, and tender years.
Though fledgling still, it sought to scale the heights.
Here, then, is Walter's tale.   May Jesus save!
                              [tr. CHARLES W. JONES]

# HROTSWITHA OF GANDERSHEIM

In the tenth century the English were battling the Scots and **Danes,**
as at Brunanburh (see above, p. 164), the French were trying to
confine the virile Normans to the Duchy of Normandy which they
founded about 911, and the Italians were sharing the rule of their
peninsula with Saracens, Greeks, and Germans. But Germany enjoyed what is probably the longest period of unified rule in all its
history. Otto I, the Great, elected Roman Emperor in 936, reigned
until 973 and was succeeded by his son and then grandson, who
died in 1002.

Hrotswitha, who was born about the time Otto I was crowned
Emperor at Aachen, celebrated his early deeds and also the founding
of her own monastery at Gandersheim, about forty miles south of
present Hannover, in two narrative poems that helped to popularize
the *leonine hexameter,** in which most Latin narratives of the succeeding century were written. She named as one of her two most
influential teachers at Gandersheim, Gerberga, a niece of Otto.
Though these and other poems are as enjoyable as most productions
of the period, her unique talent was reserved for later life, when she
composed six Christian imitations of Terence in rhymed prose. Her
reasons for this work are clearly set forth in the Preface to her plays,
translated below.

It may be doubted whether drama in either the classical or modern
sense was known in the period (see below, Drama, pp. 925–974).
Though works were constantly written in dialogue as catechism for
the schoolroom or as modified Platonic disquisition, the notion of
acting or staging dialogue parts was hardly in Hrotswitha's mind.
Nevertheless, she has a rare dramatic sense: her action is conveyed
through dialogue, her plot is limited to critical choices, and her
characters have distinguishing and individual touches that make them
breathe and move. Hence her plays have many times been publicly
presented with success during the past fifty years. All the plays have
women at the center of their action. *Gallicanus* is the story of a
pagan officer who demanded the hand of the Christian virgin Con-
stantia in marriage; he is converted and becomes a martyr for the
faith. *Dulcitius,* which contains the only comic scenes, shows how
three virgins checkmate a lustful Roman governor. In *Calimachus,*
a Christian wife and her passionate illicit suitor die in the manner
of Romeo and Juliet, but are restored to life through the prayers of
St. John the Apostle. *Sapientia,* allegorical rather than legendary,
describes a mother's grief at the loss of her virgin daughters, Fides,
Spes, and Caritas. What is usually regarded as Hrotswitha's most
successful work, *Abraham,* has the same theme as *Paphnutius* —
the conversion of a harlot by a monk disguised as a lover.

---

* In the Leonine line, the last word rhymes with the word before the mid-caesura:
*pectori maerenti ferret nimiumque dolenti.* See Bernard of Morval, below p. 265.

The Thaïs legend, which has been generally popular since Anatole France chose it as the subject of one of his greatest books and
since Massenet followed suit by turning it into a successful opera, is
a product of the hagiographers of the fourth and fifth centuries (see
above, pp. 14–15, *Life of St. Antony*).  It circulated widely in the
West through the collection known as the *Vitae Patrum,* or *Lives of
the Desert Fathers.*  Since the discovery in 1899 in Lower Egypt of
the tomb and body of a holy woman named Thaïs, there have been
renewed efforts to prove the legend factually true.  At all events,
Hrotswitha's dramatic sense quickened the rather lifeless hagiography,
and her play was Anatole France's primary inspiration.  The digression with which the play opens has been retained as a pleasant
exposition of early medieval education.


PREFACE TO THE PLAYS OF HROTSWITHA,
GERMAN RELIGIOUS AND VIRGIN OF THE
SAXON RACE

[From *The Plays of Roswitha,* translated by Christopher
St. John; Chatto & Windus, London, 1923.  Reprinted by
permission of the publisher.]

There are many Catholics, and we cannot entirely acquit ourselves
of the charge, who, attracted by the polished elegance of the style
of pagan writers, prefer their works to the Holy Scriptures.  There
are others who, although they are deeply attached to the sacred writings and have no liking for most pagan productions, make an exception in favour of the works of Terence, and, fascinated by the charm
of the manner, risk being corrupted by the wickedness of the matter.
Wherefore I, the strong voice * of Gandersheim, have not hesitated
to imitate in my writings a poet whose works are so widely read, my
object being to glorify, within the limits of my poor talent, the
laudable chastity of Christian virgins in that self-same form of
composition which has been used to describe the shameless acts of
licentious women.  One thing has all the same embarrassed me and
often brought a blush to my cheek.  It is that I have been compelled
through the nature of this work to apply my mind and my pen to
depicting the dreadful frenzy of those possessed by unlawful love,
and the insidious sweetness of passion — things which should not
even be named among us.  Yet if from modesty I had refrained from
treating these subjects I should not have been able to attain my
object — to glorify the innocent to the best of my ability.  For the
more seductive the blandishments of lovers the more wonderful the
divine succour and the greater the merit of those who resist, especially when it is fragile woman who is victorious and strong man
who is routed with confusion.

_____
* *clamor validus* is the Latin equivalent of Saxon Hrosvit.

I have no doubt that many will say that my poor work is much inferior to that of the author whom I have taken as my model, that it is on a much humbler scale, and indeed altogether different.

Well, I do not deny this. None can justly accuse me of wishing to place myself on a level with those who by the sublimity of their genius have so far outstripped me. No, I am not so arrogant as to compare myself even with the least among the scholars of the ancient world. I strive only, although my power is not equal to my desire, to use what talent I have for the glory of Him Who gave it to me. Nor is my self-love so great that I would, to avoid criticism, abstain from proclaiming wherever possible the virtue of Christ working in His saints. If this pious devotion gives satisfaction I shall rejoice; if it does not, either on account of my own worthlessness or of the faults of my unpolished style, I shall still be glad that I made the effort.

In the humbler works of my salad days I gathered up my poor researches in heroic strophes, but here I have sifted them into a series of dramatic scenes and avoided through omission the pernicious voluptuousness of pagan writers.

## PAPHNUTIUS

Hrotswitha of Gandersheim (A.D. 935? — after 973)

### SCENE I

DISCIPLES: Why do you look so gloomy, father Paphnutius? Why do you not smile at us as usual?

PAPHNUTIUS: When the heart is sad the face clouds over. It is only natural.

DISCIPLES: But why are you sad?

PAPHNUTIUS: I grieve over an injury to my Creator.

DISCIPLES: What injury?

PAPHNUTIUS: The injury His own creatures, made in His very image, inflict on Him.

DISCIPLES: Oh, father, your words fill us with fear! How can such things be?

PAPHNUTIUS: It is true that the impassible Majesty cannot be hurt by injuries. Nevertheless, speaking in metaphor, and as if God were weak with our weakness, what greater injury can we conceive than this — that while the greater world is obedient, and subject to His rule, the lesser world resists His guidance?

DISCIPLES: What do you mean by the lesser world?

PAPHNUTIUS: Man.

DISCIPLES: Man?

PAPHNUTIUS: Yes.

DISCIPLES: What man?

PAPHNUTIUS: Every man.

DISCIPLES: How can this be?

PAPHNUTIUS: It has pleased our Creator.

DISCIPLES: We do not understand.

PAPHNUTIUS: It is not plain to many.

DISCIPLES: Explain, father.

PAPHNUTIUS: Be attentive, then.

DISCIPLES: We are eager to learn.

PAPHNUTIUS: You know that the greater world is composed of four elements which are contraries, yet by the will of the Creator these contraries are adjusted in harmonious arrangement.  Now, man is composed of even more contrary parts.

DISCIPLES: What can be more contrary than the elements?

PAPHNUTIUS: The body and the soul.  The soul is not mortal like the body, nor the body spiritual as is the soul.

DISCIPLES: That is true.  But what did you mean, father, when you spoke of "harmonious arrangement"?

PAPHNUTIUS: I meant that as low and high sounds harmoniously united produce a certain music, so discordant elements rightly adjusted make one world.

DISCIPLES: It seems strange that discords can become concords.

PAPHNUTIUS: Consider.  No thing is composed of "likes" — neither can it be made up of elements which have no proportion among themselves, or which are entirely different in substance and nature.

DISCIPLES: What is music, master?

PAPHNUTIUS: One of the branches of the quadrivium of philosophy, my son.  Arithmetic, geometry, music and philosophy form the quadrivium.

DISCIPLES: I should like to know why they are given that name.

PAPHNUTIUS: Because just as paths branch out from the quadrivium, the place where four roads meet, so do these subjects lead like roads from one principle of philosophy.

DISCIPLES: We had best not question you about the other three, for our slow wits can scarcely follow what you have told us about the first.

PAPHNUTIUS: It is a difficult subject.

DISCIPLES: Still you might give us a general idea of the nature of music.

PAPHNUTIUS: It is hard to explain to hermits to whom it is an unknown science.

DISCIPLES: Is there more than one kind of music?

PAPHNUTIUS: There are three kinds, my son.  The first is celestial, the second human, the third is produced by instruments.

DISCIPLES: In what does the celestial consist?

PAPHNUTIUS: In the seven planets and the celestial globe.

DISCIPLES: But how?

PAPHNUTIUS: Exactly as in instruments.  You find the same number of intervals of the same length, and the same concords as in strings.

DISCIPLES: We do not understand what intervals are.

PAPHNUTIUS: The dimensions which are reckoned between planets or between notes.

DISCIPLES: And what are their lengths?

PAPHNUTIUS: The same as tones.

DISCIPLES: We are none the wiser.

PAPHNUTIUS: A tone is composed of two sounds, and bears the ratio of nine to eight.

DISCIPLES: As soon as we get over one difficulty, you place a greater one in our path!

PAPHNUTIUS: That is inevitable in a discussion of this kind.

DISCIPLES: Yet tell us something about concord, so that at least we may know the meaning of the word.

PAPHNUTIUS: Concord, harmony, or symphonia may be defined as a fitting disposition of modulation. It is composed sometimes of three, sometimes of four, sometimes of five sounds.

DISCIPLES: As you have given us these three distinctions, we should like to learn the name of each.

PAPHNUTIUS: The first is called a fourth, as consisting of four sounds, and it has the proportion of four to three. The second is called a fifth. It consists of five sounds and bears the ratio of one and a half. The third is known as the diapason; it is double and is perfected in eight sounds.

DISCIPLES: And do the spheres and planets produce sounds, since they are compared to notes?

PAPHNUTIUS: Undoubtedly they do.

DISCIPLE: Why is the music not heard?

DISCIPLES: Yes, why is it not heard?

PAPHNUTIUS: Many reasons are given. Some think is is not heard because it is so continuous that men have grown accustomed to it. Others say it is because of the density of the air. Some assert that so enormous a sound could not pass into the mortal ear. Others that the music of the spheres is so pleasant and sweet that if it were heard all men would come together, and, forgetting themselves and all their pursuits, would follow the sounds from east to west.

DISCIPLES: It is well that it is not heard.

PAPHNUTIUS: As our Creator foreknew.

DISCIPLES: We have heard enough of this kind of music. What of "human" music?

PAPHNUTIUS: What do you want to know about that?

DISCIPLES: How is it manifested?

PAPHNUTIUS: Not only, as I have already told you, in the combination of body and soul, and in the utterance of the voice, now high, now low, but even in the pulsation of the veins, and in the proportion of our members. Take the finger-joints. In them, if we measure, we find the same proportions as we have already found in concord; for music is said to be a fitting disposition not only of sounds, but of things with no resemblance to sounds.

DISCIPLES: Had we known the difficulty that such a hard point presents to the ignorant, we would not have asked you about your "lesser world." It is better to know nothing than to be bewildered.

PAPHNUTIUS: I do not agree. By trying to understand you have learned many things that you did not know before.

DISCIPLES: That is true.

DISCIPLE: True it may be, but I am weary of this disputation. We are all weary, because we cannot follow the reasoning of such a philosopher!

PAPHNUTIUS: Why do you laugh at me, children? I am no philospher, but an ignorant man.

DISCIPLES: Where did you get all this learning with which you have puzzled our heads?

PAPHNUTIUS: It is but a little drop from the full deep wells of learning — wells at which I, a chance passerby, have lapped, but never sat down to drain.

DISCIPLE: We are grateful for your patience with us; but I for one cannot forget the warning of the Apostle: "God hath chosen the foolish things of the world to confound the wise."

PAPHNUTIUS: Whether a fool or a wise man does wrong, he will be confounded.

DISCIPLES: True.

PAPHNUTIUS: Nor is God offended by Knowledge of the Knowable, only by undue pride on the part of the Knower.

DISCIPLES: That is well said.

PAPHNUTIUS: And I would ask you — unto whose praise can the knowledge of the arts be more worthily or more justly turned than to the praise of Him Who made things capable of being known, and gave us the capacity to know them?

DISCIPLES: Truly, to none.

PAPHNUTIUS: The more a man realizes the wonderful way in which God has set all things in number and measure and weight, the more ardent his love.

DISCIPLES: That is as it should be.

PAPHNUTIUS: But I am wrong to dwell on matters which give you so little pleasure.

DISCIPLES: Tell us the cause of your sadness. Relieve us of the burden of our curiosity.

PAPHNUTIUS: Perhaps you will not find the tale to your liking.

DISCIPLES: A man is often sadder for having his curiosity satisfied, yet he cannot overcome this tendency to be curious. It is part of our weakness.

PAPHNUTIUS: Brothers — there is a woman, a shameless woman, living in our neighbourhood.

DISCIPLES: A perilous thing for the people.

PAPHNUTIUS: Her beauty is wonderful; her impurity is — horrible.

DISCIPLES: What is her wretched name?

PAPHNUTIUS: Thais.

DISCIPLES: Thais! Thais, the harlot!

PAPHNUTIUS: Yes — she.

DISCIPLE: Everyone has heard of her and her wickedness.

PAPHNUTIUS: It is no wonder, for she is not satisfied to ruin herself with a small band of lovers. She seeks to allure all men through her marvellous beauty, and drag them down with her.

DISCIPLES: What a woeful thing!

PAPHNUTIUS: And it is not only fools and wastrels who squander their substance with her. Citizens of high standing and virtue lay precious things at her feet, and enrich her to their own undoing.

DISCIPLES: It is terrible to hear of such things.

PAPHNUTIUS: Flocks of lovers crowd to her doors.

DISCIPLES: And to their destruction!

PAPHNUTIUS: They are so crazed with desire that they quarrel and fight for admission to her house.

DISCIPLES: One vice brings another in its train.

PAPHNUTIUS: They come to blows. Heads are broken, faces bruised, noses smashed; at times they drive each other out with weapons, and the threshold of the vile place is dyed with blood!

DISCIPLES: Most horrible!

PAPHNUTIUS: This is the injury to the Creator for which I weep day and night. This is the cause of my sorrow.

DISCIPLES: We understand now. You have good reason to be distressed, and I doubt not that the citizens of the heavenly country share your grief.

PAPHNUTIUS: Oh, to rescue her from that wicked life! Why should I not try?

DISCIPLES: God forbid!

PAPHNUTIUS: Brother, our Lord Jesus went among sinners.

DISCIPLES: She would not receive a hermit.

PAPHNUTIUS: What if I were to go in the disguise of a lover?

DISCIPLE: If that thought is from God, God will give you strength to accomplish it.

PAPHNUTIUS: I will set out immediately. I shall need your best prayers. Pray that I may not be overcome by the wiles of the serpent. Pray that I may be able to show this soul the beauty of divine love.

DISCIPLE: May He Who laid low the Prince of Darkness give you the victory over the enemy of the human race.

## SCENE II

PAPHNUTIUS: I am bewildered in this town. I cannot find my way. Now I shut my eyes, and I am back in the desert. I can hear my children's voices praising God. Good children, I know you are praying for me! I fear to speak. I fear to ask my way. O God, come to my help! I see some young men in the market-place. They are coming this way. I will go up to them and ask where she is to be found.

THE YOUNG MEN: That stranger seems to want to speak to us.

YOUNG MAN: Let us go and find out.

PAPHNUTIUS: Your pardon, gentlemen. Am I speaking to citizens of this town?

YOUNG MAN: You are.  Can we do anything for you?

PAPHNUTIUS: My salutations!

YOUNG MAN: And ours, whether you are a native or a foreigner.

PAPHNUTIUS: I am a stranger.

YOUNG MAN: What brings you here?  Have you come for pleasure, business or learning?  This is a great city for learning.  Which is it?

PAPHNUTIUS: I cannot say.

YOUNG MAN: Why?

PAPHNUTIUS: That is my secret.

YOUNG MAN: It would be wiser to tell us your secret.  It will be difficult for you, a stranger, to do your business here without the advice of us citizens.

PAPHNUTIUS: But if I tell you, you may try to hinder me from carrying out my plans.

YOUNG MAN: You can trust us.  We are men of honour!

PAPHNUTIUS: I believe it.  I will trust in your loyalty and tell you my secret.

YOUNG MAN: We are not traitors.  No harm shall come to you.

PAPHNUTIUS: I am told that there lives in this town a woman who loves all who love her.  She is kind to all men; she'll not deny them anything.

YOUNG MAN: Stranger, you must tell us her name.  There are many women of that kind in our city.  Do you know her name?

PAPHNUTIUS: Yes, I know it.

YOUNG MAN: Who is she?

PAPHNUTIUS: Thais.

YOUNG MAN: Thais!  She is the flame of this land!  She sets all hearts on fire.

PAPHNUTIUS: They say she is beautiful.  The most exquisite woman of her kind in the world!

YOUNG MAN: They have not deceived you.

PAPHNUTIUS: For her sake I have made a long and difficult journey. I have come here only to see her.

YOUNG MAN: Well, what should prevent you?  You are young and handsome.

PAPHNUTIUS: Where does she live?

YOUNG MAN: Over there.  Her house is quite near this place.

PAPHNUTIUS: That house?

YOUNG MAN: Yes, to the left of the statue.

PAPHNUTIUS: I will go there.

YOUNG MAN: If you like, we will come with you.

PAPHNUTIUS: I thank you for the courtesy, but I would rather go alone.

YOUNG MAN: We understand.  Have you money in your purse, stranger?  Thais loves a handsome face, but she loves a full purse more.

PAPHNUTIUS: Gentlemen, I am rich.  I have a rare present to offer her.

YOUNG MAN: To our next meeting, then! Farewell. May Thais be kind!

PAPHNUTIUS: Farewell.

### SCENE III

PAPHNUTIUS: Thais! Thais!

THAIS: Who is there? I do not know that voice.

PAPHNUTIUS: Thais! Your lover speaks! Thais!

THAIS: Stranger, who are you?

PAPHNUTIUS: Arise, my love, my beautiful one, and come!

THAIS: Who are you?

PAPHNUTIUS: A man who loves you!

THAIS: And what do you want with me?

PAPHNUTIUS: I will show you.

THAIS: You would be my lover?

PAPHNUTIUS: I am your lover, Thais, flame of the world!

THAIS: Whoever loves me is well paid. He receives as much as he gives.

PAPHNUTIUS: Oh, Thais, Thais! If you knew what a long and troublesome journey I have come to speak to you — to see your face!

THAIS: Well? Have I refused to speak to you, or to show you my face?

PAPHNUTIUS: I cannot speak to you here. I must be with you alone. What I have to say is secret. The room must be secret too.

THAIS: How would you like a bedchamber, fragrant with perfumes, adorned as for a marriage? I have such a room. Look!

PAPHNUTIUS: Is there no room still more secret — a room that your lovers do not know? Some room where you and I might hide from all the world?

THAIS: Yes, there is a room like that in this house. No one even knows that it exists except myself, and God.

PAPHNUTIUS: God! What God?

THAIS: The true God.

PAPHNUTIUS: You believe that He exists?

THAIS: I am a Christian.

PAPHNUTIUS: And you believe that He knows what we do?

THAIS: I believe He knows everything.

PAPHNUTIUS: What do you think, then? That He is indifferent to the actions of the sinner, or that He reserves judgment?

THAIS: I suppose that the merits of each man are weighed in the balance, and that we shall be punished or rewarded according to our deeds.

PAPHNUTIUS: O Christ! How wondrous is Thy patience! How wondrous is Thy love! Even when those who believe in Thee sin deliberately, Thou dost delay their destruction!

THAIS: Why do you tremble? Why do you turn pale? Why do you weep?

PAPHNUTIUS: I shudder at your presumption. I weep for your

damnation. How, knowing what you know, can you destroy men in this manner and ruin so many souls, all precious and immortal?

THAIS: Your voice pierces my heart! Strange lover — you are cruel. Pity me!

PAPHNUTIUS: Let us pity rather those souls whom you have deprived of the sight of God — of the God Whom you confess! Oh, Thais, you have wilfully offended the divine Majesty. That condemns you.

THAIS: What do you mean? Why do you threaten me like this?

PAPHNUTIUS: Because the punishment of hell-fire awaits you if you remain in sin.

THAIS: Who are you, who rebuke me so sternly? Oh, you have shaken me to the depths of my terrified heart!

PAPHNUTIUS: I would that you could be shaken with fear to your very bowels! I would like to see your delicate body impregnated with terror in every vein, and every fibre, if that would keep you from yielding to the dangerous delights of the flesh.

THAIS: And what zest for pleasure do you think is left now in a heart suddenly awakened to a consciousness of guilt! Remorse has killed everything.

PAPHNUTIUS: I long to see the thorns of vice cut away, and the choked-up fountain of your tears flowing once more. Tears of repentance are precious in the sight of God.

THAIS: Oh, voice that promises mercy! Do you believe, can you hope that one so vile as I, soiled by thousands and thousands of impurities, can make reparation, can ever by any manner of penance obtain pardon?

PAPHNUTIUS: Thais, no sin is so great, no crime so black, that it cannot be expiated by tears and penitence, provided they are followed up by deeds.

THAIS: Show me, I beg you, my father, what I can do to be reconciled with Him I have offended.

PAPHNUTIUS: Despise the world. Leave your dissolute lovers.

THAIS: And afterwards? What then?

PAPHNUTIUS: You must retire to some solitary place, where you may learn to know yourself and realize the enormity of your sins.

THAIS: If you think this will save me, I will not delay a moment.

PAPHNUTIUS: I have no doubt it will.

THAIS: Yet give me a little time. I must collect the wealth that I have gained through the sins of my body — all the treasures I have kept too long.

PAPHNUTIUS: Do not give them a moment's thought. There will be no lack of people to find them and make use of them.

THAIS: I have another idea in my mind. I did not think of keeping this wealth or of giving it to my friends. Nor would I distribute it among the poor. The wages of sin are no material for good works.

PAPHNUTIUS: You are right. What then do you propose to do with your possessions?

THAIS: Give them to the flames! Burn them to ashes!

PAPHNUTIUS: For what reason?

THAIS: That they may no longer exist in the world.   Each one was acquired at the cost of an injury to the goodness and beauty of the Creator.   Let them burn.

PAPHNUTIUS: How you are changed!   Grace is on your lips!   Your eyes are calm, and impure passions no longer burn in them.   Oh, miracle!   Is this Thais who was once so greedy for gold?   Is this Thais, who seeks so humbly the feet of God?

THAIS: God give me grace to change still more.   My heart is changed, but this mortal substance — how shall it be changed?

PAPHNUTIUS: It is not difficult for the unchangeable substance to transform us.

THAIS: Now I am going to carry out my plan.   Fire shall destroy everything I have.

PAPHNUTIUS: Go in peace.   Then return to me here quickly.   Do not delay!   I trust your resolution, and yet —

THAIS: You need not be afraid.

PAPHNUTIUS: Thais, come back quickly!   God be with you!

### SCENE IV

THAIS: Come, my lovers!   Come all my evil lovers!   Hasten, my lovers!   Your Thais calls you!

LOVERS: That is the voice of Thais.   She calls us.   Let us make haste.   Let us make haste, for by delay we may offend her.

THAIS: Come, lovers!   Run!   Hasten!   What makes you so slow? Never has Thais been more impatient for your coming.   Come nearer.   I have something to tell you all.

LOVERS: Oh, Thais, what is the meaning of this pile of faggots? Why are you throwing all those beautiful and precious treasures on the pile?

THAIS: You cannot guess?   You do not know why I have built this fire?

LOVERS: We are amazed.   We wonder greatly what is the meaning of it and of your strange looks.

THAIS: You would like me to tell you, evil lovers?

LOVERS: We long to hear.

THAIS: Look, then!

LOVERS: Stop, Thais!   What are you doing?   Are you mad?

THAIS: I am not mad.   For the first time I am sane, and I rejoice!

LOVERS: To waste these pounds of gold, and all the other treasure! Oh, Thais, you have lost your senses!   These are beautiful things, precious things, and you burn them!

THAIS: All these things I have extorted from you as the price of shameful deeds.   I burn them to destroy all hope in you that I shall ever again turn to your love.   And now I leave you.

LOVERS: Wait, Thais.   Oh wait a little, and tell us what has changed you!

THAIS: I will not stay.   I will not tell you anything.   To talk with you has become loathsome.

LOVERS: What have we done to deserve this scorn and contempt?

Can you accuse us of being unfaithful? What wrong have we done? We have always sought to satisfy your desires. And now you show us this bitter hatred! Unjust woman, what have we done?

THAIS: Leave me, or let me leave you. Do not touch me. You can tear my garments, but you shall not touch me.

LOVERS: Cruel Thais, speak to us! Before you go, speak to us!

THAIS: I have sinned with you. But now is the end of sin, and all our wild pleasures are ended.

LOVERS: Thais, do not leave us! Thais, where are you going?

THAIS: Where none of you will ever see me again!

LOVERS: What monstrous thing is this? Thais, glory of our land, is changed! Thais, our delight, who loved riches and power and luxury — Thais, who gave herself up to pleasure day and night, has destroyed past remedy gold and gems that had no price! What monstrous thing is this? Thais, the very flower of love, insults her lovers and scorns their gifts. Thais, whose boast it was that whoever loved her should enjoy her love! What monstrous thing is this? Thais! Thais! this is a thing not to be believed.

### SCENE V

THAIS: Paphnutius, my father, I am ready now to obey you. Command what you will.

PAPHNUTIUS: Thais, I have been uneasy during your absence. I feared you had been caught in the world's snare. I feared you would not return.

THAIS: You need not have been afraid. The world does not tempt me now. My possessions are ashes. I have publicly renounced my lovers.

PAPHNUTIUS: Oh, happy guilt that has brought such happy penitence! Since you have renounced your earthly lovers, you can now be joined to your Heavenly Lover.

THAIS: It is for you to show me the way. Be a lantern to me, for all is obscure night.

PAPHNUTIUS: Trust me, daughter. Follow me.

THAIS: I can follow you with my feet. Would that I could follow you with my deeds!

### SCENE VI

THAIS: Oh, I am weary!

PAPHNUTIUS: Courage! Here is the monastery where a famous community of holy virgins live. I am anxious for you to pass the time of penance here if you will consent.

THAIS: I do not resist. I wish to obey you. I trust you.

PAPHNUTIUS: I will go in, and persuade the Abbess who is the head of the community to receive you.

THAIS: And what shall I do meanwhile? Do not leave me alone.

PAPHNUTIUS: You shall come with me. But look! The Abbess

has come out to meet us.  I wonder who can have told her so promptly of our arrival.

THAIS: Rumour, Father Paphnutius.  Rumour never delays.

### SCENE VII

PAPHNUTIUS: You come opportunely, illustrious Abbess.  I was just seeking you.

ABBESS: You are most welcome, venerated Father Paphnutius.  Blessed is your visit, beloved of the Most High.

PAPHNUTIUS: May the grace of Him Who is Father of all pour into your heart the beatitude of everlasting peace!

ABBESS: And what has brought your holiness to my humble dwelling?

PAPHNUTIUS: I need your help.

ABBESS: Speak but the word.  You will find me eager to do all in my power to carry out your wishes.

PAPHNUTIUS: Oh, Abbess, I have brought you a little wild gazelle who has been snatched half dead from the jaws of wolves.  Show it compassion, nurse it with all your tenderness, until it has shed its rough goatskin and put on the soft fleece of a lamb.

ABBESS: Explain yourself further.

PAPHNUTIUS: You see this woman.  From her youth she has led the life of a harlot.  She has given herself up to base pleasures —

ABBESS: What misery!

PAPHNUTIUS: She cannot offer the excuse that she was a pagan, to whom such pleasures bring no remorse of conscience.  She wore the baptismal robes of a child of God when she gave herself to the flames of profane love.  She was not tempted.  She chose this evil life.  She was ruined by her own will.

ABBESS: She is the more unfortunate.

PAPHNUTIUS: Yet such is the power of Christ, that at His word, of which my poor mouth was the instrument, she has fled from the surroundings which were her damnation.  Obedient as a child, she has followed me.  She has abandoned lust and ease and idle luxury.  She is resolved to live chastely.

ABBESS: Glory to the Author of the marvellous change!

PAPHNUTIUS: Amen.  But since the maladies of the soul, like those of the body, need physic for their cure, we must minister to this soul diseased by years of lust.  It must be removed from the foul breath of the world.  A narrow cell, solitude, silence — these must be her lot henceforth.  She must learn to know herself and her sins.

ABBESS: You are right.  Such a penance is necessary.

PAPHNUTIUS: Will you give orders for a little cell to be made ready as soon as possible?

ABBESS: Yes, my father.  It shall be done as quickly as we can.

PAPHNUTIUS: There must be no entrance, no opening of any kind, except a small window through which she can receive the food that will be brought her on certain days at certain fixed hours.  A pound of bread, and water according to her need.

ABBESS: Forgive me, dear father in God, but I fear she will not be able to endure such a rigorous life. The soul may be willing, but that fastidious mind, that delicate body used to luxury, how can we expect them to submit?

PAPHNUTIUS: Have no fear. We know that grave sin demands a grave remedy.

ABBESS: That is true, yet are we not told also to hasten slowly?

PAPHNUTIUS: Good mother, I am already weary of delay. What if her lovers should pursue her? What if she be drawn back into the abyss? I am impatient to see her enclosed.

ABBESS: Nothing stands in the way of your enclosing her now. The cell which you told us to prepare is ready.

PAPHNUTIUS: Then enter, Thais! This is just such a refuge as we spoke of on our journey. It is the very place for you. There is room and more than room here for you to weep over your sins.

THAIS: How small it is! How dark! How can a delicate woman live in such a place?

PAPHNUTIUS: You are not pleased with your new dwelling! You shudder at the thought of entering! Oh, Thais, have you not wandered long enough without restraint? Is it not right that you should now be confined in this narrow, solitary cell, where you will find true freedom?

THAIS: I have been so long accustomed to pleasure and distraction. My mind is still a slave to the senses.

PAPHNUTIUS: The more need to rein it, to discipline it, until it ceases to rebel.

THAIS: I do not rebel — but my weakness revolts against one thing here.

PAPHNUTIUS: Of what do you speak?

THAIS: I am ashamed to say.

PAPHNUTIUS: Speak, Thais! Be ashamed of nothing but your sins.

THAIS: Good father, what could be more repugnant than to have to attend to all the needs of the body in this one little room. . . . It will soon be uninhabitable.

PAPHNUTIUS: Fear the cruel punishments of the soul, and cease to dread transitory evils.

THAIS: My weakness makes me shudder.

PAPHNUTIUS: The sweetness of your guilty pleasures was far more bitter and foul.

THAIS: I know it is just. What grieves me most is that I shall not have one clean sweet spot in which to call upon the sweet name of God.

PAPHNUTIUS: Have a care, Thais, or your confidence may become presumption. Should polluted lips utter so easily the name of the unpolluted Godhead?

THAIS: Oh, how can I hope for pardon! Who will pity me — who save me! What shall I do if I am forbidden to invoke Him against Whom only I have sinned!   To whom should I pray if not to Him.

PAPHNUTIUS: You must indeed pray to Him, but with tears, not with words.  Let not a tinkling voice, but the mighty roar of a contrite heart sound in the ear of God.

THAIS: I desire His pardon.   Surely I may ask for it?

PAPHNUTIUS: Oh, Thais, the more perfectly you humble yourself, the more swiftly you will win it!   Let your heart be all prayer, but let your lips say only this: "O God Who made me, pity me!"

THAIS: O God, Who made me, pity me!   He alone can save me from defeat in this hard struggle!

PAPHNUTIUS: Fight manfully, and you will gain a glorious victory.

THAIS: It is your part to pray for me!   Pray I may earn the victor's palm.

PAPHNUTIUS: You need not remind me.

THAIS: Give me some hope!

PAPHNUTIUS: Courage!   The palm will soon be in this humble hand.   It is time for me to return to the desert.   I owe a duty to my dear disciples.   I know their hearts are torn by my absence.   Yes, I must go.   Venerable Abbess, I trust this captive to your charity and tenderness.   I beg you to take the best care of her.   Sustain her delicate body with necessaries.   Refresh her soul with the luxuries of divine knowledge.

ABBESS: Have no anxiety about her, for I will cherish her with a mother's love and tenderness.

PAPHNUTIUS: I go then.

ABBESS: In peace.

### SCENE VIII

DISCIPLES: Who knocks there?

PAPHNUTIUS: It is I — your father.

DISCIPLES: It is the voice of our father Paphnutius!

PAPHNUTIUS: Unbolt the door.

DISCIPLE: Good father, welcome.

ALL: Welcome, father!   Welcome!

PAPHNUTIUS: A blessing on you all!

DISCIPLE: You have given us great uneasiness by your long absence.

PAPHNUTIUS: It has been fruitful.

DISCIPLE: Your mission has succeeded?   Come, tell us what has happened to Thais.

PAPHNUTIUS: All that I wished.

DISCIPLE: She has abandoned her evil life?

PAPHNUTIUS: Yes.

DISCIPLE: Where is she living now?

PAPHNUTIUS: She weeps over her sins in a little cell.

DISCIPLES: Praise be to the Supreme Trinity!

PAPHNUTIUS: A little narrow cell, no wider than a grave.   Blessed be His Terrible Name now and for ever.

DISCIPLES: Amen.

### SCENE IX

PAPHNUTIUS: Three years of her penance are over, and I cannot tell whether her sorrow has found favour with God. For some reason He will not enlighten me. I know what I will do. I will go to my brother Antony and beg him to intercede for me. God will make the truth known to him.

### SCENE X

ANTONY: Who comes this way? By his dress it is some brother-dweller in the desert. My old eyes do not recognize you yet, friend. Come nearer.

PAPHNUTIUS: Brother Antony! Do you not know me?

ANTONY: This is joy indeed! What pleasures God sends us, when we resign ourselves to have none! I did not think to see my brother Paphnutius again in this world. Is it indeed you, brother?

PAPHNUTIUS: Yes, it is I.

ANTONY: You are welcome, very welcome. Your coming gives me great joy.

PAPHNUTIUS: I am no less rejoiced to see you.

ANTONY: But what is the cause? What has brought Paphnutius from his solitary retreat? He is not sick, I trust? He has not come to old Antony for healing?

PAPHNUTIUS: No, I am in good health.

ANTONY: That's well! I am glad of it.

PAPHNUTIUS: Brother Antony, it is three years since my peace was broken and disturbed by the persistent vision of a soul in peril. I heard a voice calling me night and day. But I stopped my ears — fearing my weakness. I thought "She calls me to ruin me." "No, no," the voice said. "I call you to save me."

ANTONY: A woman's voice!

PAPHNUTIUS: Before my vision it was well known to us all that in the great town on the edge of the desert there was a harlot called Thais, through whom many were destroyed body and soul.

ANTONY: It was she who called you!

PAPHNUTIUS: Brother Antony, it was God who called me. My disciples opposed me; nevertheless I went to the town to see Thais and wrestle with the demon.

ANTONY: A perilous enterprise.

PAPHNUTIUS: I went to her in the disguise of a lover, and began by flattering her with sweet words. Then I threw off the mask and brought terror to her soul with bitter reproaches and threats of God's punishment.

ANTONY: A prudent course. Hard words are necessary when natures have grown soft and can no longer distinguish between good and evil.

PAPHNUTIUS: I was disarmed by her docility. Truly, brother Antony, my heart melted like wax when she spurned her ill-gotten wealth and abandoned her lovers.

ANTONY: But you hid your tenderness?

PAPHNUTIUS: Yes, Brother Antony.

ANTONY: What followed?

PAPHNUTIUS: She chose to live in chastity. She consented to be enclosed in a narrow cell. She accepted her penance with sweetness and humility.

ANTONY: I am rejoiced by what you have told me! All the blood in my old veins exults and rejoices!

PAPHNUTIUS: That is because you are a saint.

ANTONY: Brother, you cannot mean that you are sad?

PAPHNUTIUS: I rejoice immeasurably in her conversion. Yet at times I am uneasy. I fear that the penance may have been too long and severe for a woman of such delicate frame.

ANTONY: That does you no wrong. Where true love is, loving compassion is not wanting.

PAPHNUTIUS: I came to beg yours for Thais. Of your charity give me your prayers. I beg you and your disciples to join with me in praying for a sign. Let us persevere in prayer until it is shown us from heaven that the penitent's tears have moved the divine mercy to indulgence.

ANTONY: Brother Paphnutius, I have never granted a request more gladly. Come, we will gather together my disciples.

PAPHNUTIUS: I know that God will listen to his good servant Antony.

### SCENE XI

ANTONY: Thanks be to God! The gospel's promise is fulfilled in us!

PAPHNUTIUS: What promise, blessed Antony?

ANTONY: Those who unite in prayer can obtain whatever they desire.

PAPHNUTIUS: What miracle has happened? What is it?

ANTONY: My disciple Paul has had a vision.

PAPHNUTIUS: What vision? Oh, call him!

ANTONY: He is here. Paul, my son, tell our brother, Paphnutius, the wonders you have seen.

PAUL: Father, I saw in my vision a splendid bed. It was adorned with white hangings and coverings, and a crown was laid on it, and round it were four radiant virgins. They stood there as if they were guarding the crown. There was a great brightness round the bed, and a multitude of angels. I, seeing this wonderful and joyful sight, cried out, "This glory must be for my master and father Antony!"

ANTONY: Son, did you not know Antony was unworthy of such honour?

PAUL: But a divine voice answered me, saying, "This glory is prepared, not, as you think, for Antony, but for the harlot, Thais!"

PAPHNUTIUS: O sweet Christ! How shall I praise Thee for so lovingly sending comfort to my sad heart?

ANTONY: He is worthy to be praised.

PAPHNUTIUS: Then farewell, Brother Antony. I must go at once to my captive.

ANTONY: You must indeed. It is time her valiant penance ended. You should assure her that her pardon is complete; you should fill her with hope, and speak to her only of the beatitude in store for her.

PAPHNUTIUS: Your blessing.

### SCENE XII

PAPHNUTIUS: Thais, my little daughter! Thais! Open the window and let me see you.

THAIS: Who speaks?

PAPHNUTIUS: Paphnutius.

THAIS: Why should you visit a poor sinner? Why should I be given this great joy and happiness?

PAPHNUTIUS: These years that I have been absent from you in the body have been weary to me too. I have thought of you night and day. I have yearned for your salvation.

THAIS: I never doubted that.

PAPHNUTIUS: Tell me how things are with you. How have you lived here? What have you been doing?

THAIS: Nothing worth the telling! I have nothing to offer God.

PAPHNUTIUS: The offering He loves best is a humble spirit.

THAIS: All I have done is to gather up the many sins on my conscience into a mighty bundle and keep them always in mind. All day I have sat gazing towards the East, saying only this one prayer: "O God Who made me, pity me!" If my bodily senses have always been conscious of the offensiveness of this place, my heart's eyes have never been blind to the dreadfulness of hell.

PAPHNUTIUS: Your great penitence has won a great forgiveness. Yet God has not pardoned you for your valiant expiation so much as for the love with which you have given yourself to Christ.

THAIS: Can that be true? Would that it were!

PAPHNUTIUS: Give me your hand. Let me bring you out of your cell to prove you are forgiven.

THAIS: No, father, leave me here. This place with all its uncleaness is best for me.

PAPHNUTIUS: The time has come for you to cast away your fear, and hope for life! God wishes your penance to end.

THAIS: Let the angels praise Him! He has not despised the love of a humble sinner.

PAPHNUTIUS: Thais, would you rejoice if now you were called upon to lay aside this body?

THAIS: Oh, father, my soul longs to escape from this earth.

PAPHNUTIUS: Thais, you have finished your course here. In fifteen days you will, by God's grace, pass straight to Paradise.

THAIS: To Paradise! I should be happy if I might be spared hell's torments and be mercifully cleansed in a gentle fire until my spirit is fit for the eternal happiness.

PAPHNUTIUS: Grace is the free gift of God and does not depend on our merits. If it did, it could not be called grace.

THAIS: For this let the choirs of heaven praise Him, and all the little twigs and fresh green leaves on earth, all animals, and the great waters. He is patient with us when we fall! He is generous in His gifts when we repent.

PAPHNUTIUS: He loves to be merciful. From all eternity He has preferred pardon to punishment.

### SCENE XIII

THAIS: Holy father, do not leave me. Be near to comfort me in this hour of my death.

PAPHNUTIUS: I will not leave you Thais, until your soul has taken flight to the stars, and I have buried your body.

THAIS: I feel the end is near. Brother, do not leave me!

PAPHNUTIUS: Now is the time to pray.

THAIS: O God Who made me, pity me! Grant that the soul which Thou didst breathe into me may now happily return to Thee. O God Who made me, pity me!

PAPHNUTIUS: Thais! Thais! Oh, loving humble spirit, pass to thy glory! . . . . Angels lead her into Paradise! . . . . O uncreated Beauty, existing in Truth without material form, grant that the divers parts of this human body now to be dissolved may return to their original elements! Grant that the soul, given from on high, may soar into light and joy, and that the body may be cherished peacefully in the soft lap of the earth until that day when, the ashes being brought together again, and the life-giving sap restored to the veins, this same Thais may rise again, a perfect human being as before, and take her place among the glorious white flock who shall be led into the joy of eternity! Grant this, O Thou Who alone art what Thou art — Who livest and reignest and art glorious in the Unity and perfect Trinity through infinite ages!

[tr. CHRISTOPHER ·ST. JOHN (CHRISTOBEL MARSHALL)]

# PETER ABELARD

As the twelfth century opened, western society, long stagnant, began to ferment and bubble. According to Henry Adams: "The First Crusade seems, in perspective, to have filled the whole vision in France at the time; but, in fact, France seethed with other emotions, and while the crusaders set out to scale heaven by force at Jerusalem, the monks, who remained at home, undertook to scale heaven by prayer and by absorption of body and soul in God; the Cistercian Order was founded in 1098, and was joined in 1112 [1113] by young Bernard, drawing with him or after him so many thousands of young men into the self-immolation of the monastery as carried dismay into the hearts of half the women of France. At the same time — that is, about 1098 or 1100 — Abelard came up to Paris from Brittany, with as much faith in logic as Bernard had in prayer or Godfrey of Bouillon in arms, and led an equal or even greater number of combatants to the conquest of heaven by force of pure reason. None showed doubt. Hundreds of thousands of young men wandered from their provinces, mostly to Palestine, largely to cloisters, but also in great numbers to Paris and the schools, while few ever returned."

Young Peter of Pallet, who called himself Abailard, found the cathedral school of Paris more popular than any school in the West had ever been. There, the pupils of Anselm of Bec and Roscellinus exalted dialectics over grammar and rhetoric as the highest study preparatory to theology. In debating the problem of universals they were ready to break into the opposing camps of Nominalism and Realism. Roscellinus had been condemned at a Council of Soissons in 1092 for his unqualified Nominalism; his pupil, William of Champeaux, rejected his master's view that universals are names only and taught his classes in Paris that they are, in the Platonic sense, Real. The acute Abelard, who soon turned teacher, easily slew William with his dialectical sword, without being forced to espouse the Nominalist extreme; but his flamboyant temper led him to apply dialectics directly to theology. The orthodox were soon enraged, and silencing Abelard became a preoccupation of the French Church. A statement attributed to him is crucial: *Nec quia Deus id dixerat creditur, sed quia hoc sic esse convincitur recipitur* (We do not believe a thing because God has said it, but because our reason convinces us that it is so). If dialectical reasoning could point the way to Heaven, there was no need for the Revelation of the Gospels, the Guidance of the Holy Spirit, or the Authority of the Church. The Church would be reduced to the level of a debating society.

Abelard did not teach in the cathedral school but established himself in the suburbs, eventually on the hill of Sainte-Geneviève on the Left Bank, where thousands trouped to listen and to question him in the dialectical Latin that has created the name Latin Quarter.

The University of Paris was taking shape, though not chartered as a center of secular learning for another half a century. Abelard gives one of the first and clearest pictures of its origin in the pages to follow.

His autobiography is unique in many ways. Medieval authors usually worked in a monastic anonymity. Since Augustine's *Confessions,* the only autobiography of note, Bede's, consisted of a single paragraph. It is remarkable, therefore, that Abelard, thinly disguising his work as a letter of justification and guidance to a friend, should write so clearly, trenchantly, and searchingly about himself and his actions in a controversy that was concerned with immaterial matters. This secular interest in the individual man, especially the author himself, marks a new age.

The love of Abelard and Héloïse has been a cornerstone of romantic literature and poetic imagery. As Abelard says, of songs he wrote to Héloïse, "the greater part are to this day repeated and sung in many parts." Those songs have either disappeared or have melted into anonymity among the Goliard songs of the *Carmina Burana,* examples of which are given below (pp. 913–919). But we read even now the strange and moving, often frightening, love letters exchanged by these illicit lovers.

The selections given below carry Abelard's story only to the time of his migration to Troyes, where his ardent students followed to live in caves and hayricks while they listened. But ecclesiastical pressure was strong, and Abelard finally accepted an invitation to become abbot of St. Gildas, a large and corrupt monastery in what Abelard, at least, called a wasteland of Brittany. Whether his "calamities" there were real or feigned and imagined (he maintained, in the literary convention of the hagiographers, that his monks tried to end his life on several occasions), he eventually escaped to his beloved Paris to teach once more. The autobiography, written at St. Gildas, may have been intended to pave the way for his act. At Paris his teaching incurred the wrath of Bernard of Clairvaux, now the most powerful ecclesiastical figure in the West. Abelard was condemned at a Council of Sens in 1140 before what is described as "a brilliant assembly of all the eminent ecclesiastics of France." Before Bernard's passion Abelard's dialectical tongue was strangely mute. Abelard, after recanting, retired to Cluny, where the kindly abbot Peter eventually effected a reconciliation between him and Bernard, and, when Abelard died, sent his body to Héloïse's convent for burial.

## MY STORY OF CALAMITY

Peter Abelard (A.D. 1079–1142)

[From *The Letters of Abelard and Heloise,* translated by
C. K. Scott Montcrieff; Alfred A. Knopf, Inc., New York,
1926. Reprinted by permission of the publisher and of
Professor Guy Chapman.]

Often examples serve better than words to excite or to mitigate
human passions. Wherefore, after certain comfort offered thee
in speech in thy presence, I have decided in absence to write by way
of comfort the experience of my own calamities, that in comparison
with mine thou mayest see thy trials to be none at all, or but slight
matters, and may be better able to endure them.

CHAPTER I

*Of the birthplace of Peter Abelard and of his parentage*

I then was born in a certain town which, situated at the entering
into Brittany, distant from the city of Nantes about eight miles, I
believe, in an easterly direction, is properly known as Palatium. As
by the nature of the soil or of my blood I am light of heart, so also
I grew up with an aptitude for the study of letters. A father, moreover, I had who was to no small extent imbued with letters before
he girded on himself the soldier's belt. Whence, at at later time,
he was seized with so great a love of letters that whatever sons he
had he was disposed to instruct in letters rather than in arms. And
so it befell us. I too, being the first-born, in so far as I was dearer
to him than the rest, so much the more diligently did he care for
my education. And I, when I advanced farther and had more
facility in the study of letters, so much the more ardently did I
adhere to it, and with such love of that study was I consumed that,
abandoning the pomp of military glory with the inheritance and the
privileges of a first-born son to my brother, I finally relinquished the
court of Mars that I might be educated in the lap of Minerva. And
inasmuch as I preferred the equipment of dialectic to all the teachings
of philosophy, I exchanged those weapons for these and to the
trophies of war preferred the conflicts of discussion. Thereafter, per-
ambulating divers provinces in search of discussion, wherever I had
heard the study of this art to flourish, I became an emulator of the
Peripatetics.

CHAPTER II

*Of the persecution of him by his master William. Of his mastership at Melun, at Corbeil, and in Paris. Of his retirement from the city of Paris to Melun, his return to Mont Sainte-Geneviève and to his own country*

I came at length to Paris, where this study had long been greatly flourishing, to William styled "of Champeau," my preceptor, a man at that time pre-eminent, rightly and by common repute, in this teaching, with whom I stayed for a while, welcomed by him at first but afterwards a grave burden to him, since I endeavoured to refute certain of his opinions and often ventured to reason with him, and at times shewed myself his superior in debate. Which things indeed those who among our fellow-scholars were esteemed the foremost suffered with all the more indignation in that I was junior to them in age and in length of study. Hence arose the beginnings of my calamities which have continued up to the present time, and the more widely my fame extended, the more the envy of others was kindled against me. At length it came to pass that, presuming upon my talents beyond the capacity of my years, I aspired, boy as I was, to the mastership of a school, and found myself a place in which to practise, namely Melun, at that time a town of note and a royal abode. My master afore-named suspected this plan and, seeking to remove my school as far as possible from his own, secretly employed all the means in his power to contrive that before I left his school he might take from me mine and the place that I had selected. But inasmuch as among the powerful in the land he numbered several there who were jealous of him, relying upon their help I succeeded in obtaining my desire and won the support of many for myself by the manifest display of his envy. And from this beginning of my school, so much did my name in the art of dialectic begin to be magnified that not only the repute of my fellow-scholars but that of the master himself began to decline and was gradually extinguished. Hence it came about that, presuming more largely upon myself, I made haste to transfer my school to the town of Corbeil, which is nearer to the city of Paris, so that there opportunity might furnish more frequent contests of disputation. Not long afterwards, however, being stricken with an infirmity by the immoderate burden of my studies, I was obliged to return home, and for some years, being banished, so to speak, from France, I was sought out more ardently by those to whom the teaching of dialectic appealed.

But a few years having gone by, when for some time I had recovered from my infirmity, that teacher of mine, William, Archdeacon of Paris, laying aside his former habit, transferred himself to the order of the regular clergy, with the intention, as was said, that being thought to be more religious he might be promoted to a higher grade in the prelacy, as shortly happened, he being made

Bishop of Chalons. Nor did this change of habit call him away either from the city of Paris or from his wonted study of philosophy; but in that same monastery to which for religion's sake he had repaired, he at once opened public classes in his accustomed manner. Then I, returning to him that from his lips I might learn rhetoric, among the other efforts of our disputations, contrived, by the clearest chain of argument, to make him alter, nay shatter, his former opinion with regard to universals. For he had been of this opinion touching the community of universals, that he maintained a thing as a whole to be essentially the same in each of its individuals, among which, forsooth, there was no difference in essence but only variety in the multitude of their accidents. He now so corrected this opinion that thereafter he proclaimed the thing to be the same not essentially, but indiscriminately. And inasmuch as this has always been the main question among dialecticians concerning universals, so much so that even Porphyry in his *Isagoga,* when he treats of universals, does not presume to define it, saying "For this is a most weighty business," after he had corrected and then perforce abandoned his opinion, into such neglect did his instruction fall that he was scarcely admitted to be a teacher of dialectic at all, as if in this opinion about universals consisted the sum total of that art. Hence did my teaching acquire so great strength and authority that they who formerly adhered most vehemently to our said master and attacked my doctrine most strongly now flocked to my school, and he who had succeeded to our master's chair in the school of Paris offered me his own place, that there among the rest he might submit himself to my teaching where formerly his master and mine had flourished.

And so after a few days, I reigning there in the study of dialectic, with what envy our master began to consume away, with what rage to boil, is not easily expressed. Nor long sustaining the heat of the affliction that had seized him, he cunningly attempted to remove me once again. And because in my conduct there was nothing whereon he could openly act, he laboured to remove the school from him who had yielded up his chair to me (charging him with the vilest accusations), and to substitute a certain other, one of my jealous rivals, in his place. Then I, returning to Melun, established my school there as before; and the more openly his jealousy pursued me, the more widely it enlarged my authority, according to the words of the poet:

> Envy seeketh the heights,
> The winds blow on the mountain-tops.

Not long after this, when it came to his knowledge that well-nigh all his disciples were in the utmost hesitation as to his religion, and were murmuring vehemently as to his conversion, in that evidently he had not retired from the city, he transferred himself and his conventicle of brethren, with his school, to a certain village at some

distance from the city. And immediately I returned from Melun
to Paris, hoping that thenceforth I should have peace from him.
But seeing that, as I have said, he had caused my place there to be
filled by one of my rivals, outside the city on the Mount of Saint
Geneviève I pitched the camp of our school, as though to beleaguer
him who had occupied my place. Hearing which, our master
straightway returning unashamed to the city, brought back such
pupils as he might still have, and the conventicle of brethren to their
former monastery, as though to deliver his soldier, whom he had
abandoned, from our siege. In truth, whereas he intended to advantage him, he greatly harmed him. He, forsooth, had until then
retained sundry disciples, principally for the lectures on Priscian in
which he was considered to excel. But after the master arrived he
lost them one and all, and so was compelled to cease from the
tenour of his school. And not long after this, as though despairing
for the future of any worldly fame, he too was converted to the
monastic life. Now after the return of our master to the city, the
conflicts of discussion which our scholars waged as well with him
as with his disciples, and the results which fortune in these wars
gave to my people, nay to myself in them, thou thyself hast long
known as matters of fact. But this saying of Ajax I may with more
modesty than he repeat and more boldly utter:

> Shouldst thou demand the issue of this fight,
> I was not vanquished by mine enemy.

As to which, were I silent, the facts themselves speak and its outcome indicates the whole matter. But while these things were
happening, my dearest mother Lucy obliged me to return home.
Who, to wit, after the conversion of Berenger, my father, to the
monastic profession, was preparing to do likewise. Which being
accomplished, I returned to France, principally that I might learn
divinity, when our afore-mentioned master William attained to the
Bishopric of Chalons. In this study, moreover, his own master,
Anselm of Laon, was of great and long-established authority.

### CHAPTER III

#### How he came to Laon to the master Anselm

I came therefore to this old man, who owed his name rather to long
familiarity than to his intelligence or his memory. To whom if any
came knocking upon his door in uncertainty as to some question, he
departed more uncertain still. Indeed, he was admirable in the eyes
of his hearers, but of no account in the sight of questioners. His
fluency of words was admirable but in sense they were contemptible
and devoid of reason. When he kindled a fire he filled his house
with smoke, rather than lighted it with the blaze. His tree, in full
life, was conspicuous from afar to all beholders, but by those who

stood near and diligently examined the same it was found to be barren.  To this tree therefore when I had come that I might gather fruit from it, I understood that it was the figtree which the Lord cursed, or that old oak to which Lucan compares Pompey, saying:

> There stands the shadow of a mighty name,
> Like to a tall oak in a fruitful field.

Having discovered this, not for many days did I lie idle in his shadow.  But as I gradually began to come to his lectures more rarely, certain among the more forward of his disciples took it amiss, as though I were shewing contempt for so great a master.  Thereafter him also secretly exciting against me with vile suggestions, they made me offensive in his sight.  But it fell upon a day that after certain controversies of opinion we scholars were disporting ourselves.  When, after a certain one had inquired of me with menacing intent what I thought as to the reading of the Holy Scriptures, I, who had as yet studied nothing save physics only, replied that it was indeed most salutary, the study of this lore in which the salvation of the soul is revealed, but that I marvelled greatly that, to them who were literate men, the Scriptures themselves or the glosses upon them should not be sufficient, so that they should require no other instruction.  Many of those present, laughing at me, asked whether I was able and presumed to approach this task.  I replied that I was ready to try it if they wished.  Then, shouting together and laughing all the more: "Certainly," they said, "we agree.  Let some one find, therefore, and bring to us here an expositor of some little read Scripture, and let us put what you promise to the proof."

And they all agreed upon the most obscure prophecy of Ezekiel.  And so, taking up the expositor, I at once invited them to attend my lecture on the morrow, who, pouring counsels into my unwilling ears, said that in so weighty a matter there was nothing to be gained by haste, but that seeing my inexperience I must give longer thought to the examination and strengthening of my exposition.  But I indignantly replied that it was not my custom to advance by practice but rather by intelligence; and added that either I abandoned the contest altogether or they, abiding by my judgment, must come to my lecture without delay.  And my first lecture indeed few attended, since that to all it seemed ridiculous that I, who hitherto had been almost wholly unacquainted with Holy Writ, should so hastily approach it.  To all, however, who did attend, that lecture was so pleasing that they extolled it with singular commendation, and compelled me to furnish further glosses in the style of my first lecture.  Which becoming known, those who had not been present began to flock eagerly to my second lecture and my third, and all alike were solicitous at the start of each to take down in writing the glosses which I had begun on the first day.

## CHAPTER IV

### *Of the persecution of him by his master Anselm*

Wherefore the old man aforesaid, being stirred by vehement envy, and having already been stimulated against me by the persuasion of divers persons, as I have before recounted, began no less to persecute me over the Holy Scriptures than our William had aforetime done over philosophy.   Now there were at the time in this old man's school two who appeared to predominate over the rest, namely Alberic of Rheims and Lotulph, a Lombard; who, the more they presumed upon themselves, were the more kindled against me.   And so, his mind greatly perturbed by their suggestions, as later it came to light, this old man boldly forbade me to continue further the work of interpretation which I had begun in his place of teaching.   Advancing this pretext forsooth, that if perchance I were to write anything in error in my work, being still untrained in that study, it might be imputed to him.   This coming to the ears of the scholars, they were moved with the utmost indignation against so manifest a calumny of envy, the like of which had never befallen any man yet.   Which, the more manifest it was, the more honourable was it to me, and so by persecution my fame increased.

## CHAPTER V

### *How, having returned to Paris, he completed the interpretations which he had begun to deliver at Laon*

So, after a few days, returning to Paris, the schools that had long before been intended for me and offered to me, from which I had at first been driven out, I held for some years in quiet, and there at the opening of my course I strove to complete those interpretations of Ezekiel which I had begun at Laon.   Which indeed were so acceptable to their readers that they believed me to be no less adept in the Holy Scriptures than they had seen me to be in philosophy. Whence in both kinds of study our school vehemently multiplying, what pecuniary gain and what reputation it brought me cannot have failed to reach yours ears.   But inasmuch as prosperity ever puffs up fools, and worldly tranquillity enervates the vigour of the mind, and easily loosens it by carnal allurements, when now I esteemed myself as reigning alone in the world as a philosopher, nor was afraid of any further disturbance, I began to give rein to my lust, who hitherto had lived in the greatest continence.   And the farther I advanced in philosophy or in the Holy Scriptures, the farther I receded by the impurity of my life from philosophers and divines.   For it is well known that philosophers, not to say divines, that is to say men intent on the exhortations of Holy Scripture, have excelled principally by the grace of continence.   When, therefore, I was labouring wholly in pride and lechery, the remedy for either malady was by divine grace conferred on me, albeit unwilling; and first for lechery, then for pride. For lechery, indeed, by depriving me of those parts with which I practised it; but for the pride which was born in me from my surpassing knowledge of letters, as is said by the Apostle: "Knowledge puffeth up" — by humiliating me by the burning of that book in which most I gloried. The story of both which things I wish you now to learn more accurately from a statement of the facts than by common hearsay, in the order in which they befell me. Since, therefore, I ever abhorred the uncleanness of harlots, and was withheld from the society of noble women by the assiduity of my studies, nor had ever held much conversation with those of the common sort, lewd fortune, as the saying is, caressing me, found a more convenient opportunity whereby she might the more easily dash me down from the pinnacle of this sublimity; so that in my overweening pride, and unmindful of the grace I had received, divine pity might recall me humbled to itself.

CHAPTER VI

### *How having fallen in love with Heloise he was thereby wounded as well in body as in mind*

Now there was in this city of Paris a certain young maiden by the name of Heloise, the niece of a certain canon who was called Fulbert, who, so great was his love for her, was all the more diligent in his zeal to instruct her, so far as was in his power, in the knowledge of letters. Who, while in face she was not inferior to other women, in the abundance of her learning was supreme. For inasmuch as this advantage, namely literary knowledge, is rare in women, so much the more did it commend the girl and had won her the greatest renown throughout the realm. Seeing in her, therefore, all those things which are wont to attract lovers, I thought it suitable to join her with myself in love, and believed that I could effect this most easily. For such renown had I then, and so excelled in grace of youth and form, that I feared no refusal from whatever woman I might deem worthy of my love. All the more easily did I believe that this girl would consent to me in that I knew her both to possess and to delight in the knowledge of letters; even in absence it would be possible for us to reach one another's presence by written intermediaries, and to express things more boldly in writing than in speech, and so ever to indulge in pleasing discussions.

So, being wholly inflamed with love for this girl, I sought an opportunity whereby I might make her familiar with me in intimate and daily conversation, and so the more easily lead her to consent. With which object in view, I came to terms with the aforesaid uncle of the girl, certain of his friends intervening, that he should take me into his house, which was hard by our school, at whatever price he might ask. Putting forward this pretext, that the management of our household gravely hindered my studies, and that the expense of it was too great a burden on me. Now he was avaricious, and most solicitous with regard to his niece that she should ever progress in the study of letters. For which two reasons I easily secured his consent and obtained what I desired, he being all agape for my money, and believing that his niece would gain something from my teaching. Whereupon earnestly beseeching me, he acceded to my wish farther than I might presume to hope and served the purpose of my love: committing her wholly to my mastership, that as often as I returned from my school, whether by day or night, I might devote my leisure to her instruction, and, if I found her idle, vehemently chastise her. In which matter, while marvelling greatly at his simplicity, I was no less stupefied within myself than if he had entrusted a tender lamb to a ravening wolf. For in giving her to me, not only to be taught but to be vehemently chastised, what else was he doing than giving every licence to my desires and providing an opportunity whereby, even if I did not wish, if I could not move her by blandishments I might the more easily bend her by threats and blows. But there were two things which kept him most of all from base suspicions, namely his love for his niece and the fame of my continence in the past.

What more need I say? First in one house we are united, then in one mind. So, under the pretext of discipline, we abandoned ourselves utterly to love, and those secret retreats which love demands, the study of our texts afforded us. And so, our books lying open before us, more words of love rose to our lips than of literature, kisses were more frequent than speech. Oftener went our hands to each other's bosom than to the pages; love turned our eyes more frequently to itself than it directed them to the study of the texts. That we might be the less suspected, blows were given at times, by love, not by anger, affection, not indignation, which surpassed all ointments in their sweetness. What more shall I say? No stage of love was omitted by us in our cupidity, and, if love could elaborate anything new, that we took in addition. The less experienced we were in these joys, the more ardently we persisted in them and the less satiety did they bring us. And the more this pleasure occupied me the less leisure could I find for my philosophy and to attend to my school. Most tedious was it for me to go to the school or to stay there; laborious likewise when I was keeping nightly vigils of love and daily of study. Which also so negligently and tepidly I now performed that I produced nothing from my mind but everything from memory; nor was I anything now save a reciter of things learned in the past, and if I found time to compose a few verses, they were amorous, and not secret hymns of philosophy. Of which songs the greater part are to this day, as thou knowest, repeated and sung in many parts, principally by those to whom a like manner of life appeals.

What was the sorrow, what the complaints, what the lamentations of my scholars when they became aware of this preoccupation, nay perturbation of my mind, it is not easy even to imagine. For few could fail to perceive a thing so manifest, and none, I believe, did fail save he to whose shame it principally reflected, namely the girl's uncle himself. Who indeed, when divers persons had at divers times suggested this to him, had been unable to believe it, both, as I have said above, on account of his unbounded affection for his niece and on account also of the well known continence of my previous life. For not readily do we suspect baseness in those whom we most love. Nor into vehement love can the base taint of suspicion find a way. Whence cometh the saying of Saint Jerome in his *Epistle to Sabinian* (the eight-and-fortieth): "We are always the last to learn of the evils of our own house, and remain ignorant of the vices of our children and wives when they are a song among the neighbours. But what one is the last to know one does at any rate come to know in time, and what all have learned it is not easy to keep hidden from one." And thus, several months having elapsed, it befell us also. Oh, what was the uncle's grief at this discovery!

What was the grief of the lovers themselves at their parting! What blushing and confusion for me! With what contrition for the girl's affliction was I afflicted! What floods of sorrow had she to bear at my shame! Neither complained of what had befallen himself, but each the other's misfortune. But this separation of our bodies was the greatest possible coupling of our minds, the denial of its satisfaction inflamed our love still further, the shame we had undergone made us more shameless, and the less we felt our shame the more expedient our action appeared. And so there occurred in us what the poets relate of Mars and Venus when they were taken. Not long after this, the girl found that she had conceived, and with the greatest exultation wrote to me on the matter at once, consulting me as to what I should decide to do; and so on a certain night, her uncle being absent, as we had planned together I took her by stealth from her uncle's house and carried her to my own country without delay. Where, in my sister's house, she stayed until such time as she was delivered of a man child, whom she named Astrolabe.

Her uncle, however, after her flight, being almost driven mad, with what grief he boiled, with what shame he was overwhelmed no one who had not beheld him could imagine. How he should act towards me, what snares he should lay for me he knew not. If he were to kill me, or to injure my body in any way, he feared greatly lest his beloved niece might be made to pay the penalty in my country. To seize my person and coerce me anywhere against my will was of no avail, seeing that I was constantly on my guard in this respect, because I had no doubt that he would speedily assault me if it were worth his while or if he dared. At length I, in some compassion for his exceeding anxiety and vehemently accusing myself of the fraud which my love had committed, as though of the basest treachery, went to supplicate the man, promising him also such further amends as he himself should prescribe. Nor, I asserted, did it appear remarkable to any who had experienced the force of love and retained a memory of the ruin to which even the greatest men, from the very beginning of the human race, had been brought down by women. And, that I might conciliate him beyond all that he could hope, I offered him the satisfaction of joining her whom I had corrupted to myself in marriage, provided that this were done in secret lest I incurred any detriment to my reputation. He assented, and with his own word and kiss, as well as with those of his household, sealed the concord that I had required of him, the more easily to betray me.

## CHAPTER VII

*The afore-mentioned girl's dissuasion of him from marriage. He takes her, however, to wife.*

Straightway I, returning to my country, brought back my mistress that I might make her my wife. She, however, did not at all approve this action, nay utterly deprecated it for two reasons, namely the danger as well as the disgrace to myself. She vowed that he could never be placated by any satisfaction in the matter, as the event proved. She asked me, also, what glory she was like to have from me when she made me inglorious and equally humiliated herself and me. What a penalty this world would be entitled to exact from her if she took from it so bright a lantern, what maledictions, what prejudice to the Church, what tears of philosophers would follow such a marriage. How indecorous, how lamentable it would be were I to dedicate myself, whom nature had created for all mankind, to a single woman, and subject myself to so base a condition. She vehemently detested this marriage, because it was in every respect a shame and a burden to me. She set before me at the same time my own disgrace and the difficulties of matrimony. Finally she observed both how dangerous it would be for me to bring her back, and how much dearer it would be to her, and more honourable to me, to be called mistress than wife, that affection alone might hold me, not any force of the nuptial bond fasten me to her; and that we ourselves, being parted for a time, would find the joy of meeting all the keener, the rarer our meetings were.

With these and similar arguments seeking to persuade or dissuade me, since she could not bend my obstinacy, nor bear to offend me, sighing vehemently and weeping, she brought her exhortation to an end in this manner. One thing, she said, remains to the last, that after the ruin of us both our suffering may be no less than the love before it. Nor in this speech, as the whole world was to know, was the spirit of prophecy lacking. And so, commending our infant son to my sister, we returned privily to Paris, and a few days later, having kept secret vigils of prayer by night in a certain church, there at the point of dawn, in the presence of her uncle and divers of our own and his friends, we were plighted together by the nuptial benediction.

Presently we withdrew privily apart, nor did we see each other afterwards save seldom and by stealth, concealing as far as possible what we had done. Her uncle, however, and his servants, seeking a solace for their ignominy began to divulge the marriage that had been celebrated, and to break the promise they had given me on that head. But she began to anathematise to the contrary, and to swear that their story was altogether false. Whereby he being vehemently moved began to visit her with frequent contumely.

On learning of this I removed her to a certain abbey of nuns near Paris, which is called Argenteuil, where she herself as a young girl had been bred up and schooled. The garments also of religion, which befitted the monastic profession, except the veil, I had fashioned for her and put them on her. Hearing which, the uncle and his kinsmen and associates were of the opinion that I had played a trick on them and had taken an easy way to rid myself of Heloise, making her a nun. Whereat vehemently indignant, and conspiring together against me, on a certain night while I slumbered and slept in an inner room of my lodging, having corrupted a servant of mine with money, they punished me with a most cruel and shameful vengeance, and one that the world received with the utmost amazement: amputating, to wit, those parts of my body wherewith I had committed that of which they complained. Who presently taking flight, two of them who could be caught were deprived of their eyes and genitals. One of whom the servant aforementioned, who while he remained with me in my service was by cupidity led to my betrayal.

CHAPTER VIII

*Of the injury to his body. He becomes a monk in the Monastery of Saint Denis: Heloise a nun at Argenteuil.*

Plunged in so wretched a contrition, it was the confusion of shame, I confess, rather than the devotion of conversion that drove me to the retirement of a monastic cloister. She, moreover, had already at my command willingly taken the veil and entered a convent. And so both the two of us at one time put on the sacred habit, I in the Abbey of Saint Denis and she in the Convent of Argenteuil aforesaid. Who indeed, I remember, when divers in compassion of her tried vainly to deter so young a woman from the yoke of the monastic rule, as from an intolerable burden, breaking out, as best she could amid her tears and sobs, into that famous complaint of Cornelia, answered:

> Great husband, undeserving of my bed!
> What right had I to bow so lofty a head?
> Why, impious female, did I marry thee,
> To cause thy hurt? Accept the penalty
> That of my own free will I'll undergo . . .

And with these words she hastened to the altar and straightway, before the Bishop, took the blessed veil from the altar and publicly bound herself to the monastic profession.

Meanwhile I had scarcely recovered from my injury when the clergy, pouring in upon me, began to make incessant demands both of our abbot and of myself, that what hitherto I had done from eagerness for wealth or praise I should study now to do for the love of God, considering that the talent which had been entrusted to me by God would be demanded of me by Him with usury, and that I who hitherto had aimed principally at the rich should henceforth devote myself to the education of the poor. And to this end chiefly, I should know that the hand of the Lord had touched me, namely that being naturally set free from carnal snares and withdrawn from the turmoil of secular life, I might devote myself to the study of letters. Nor should I become a philosopher of the world so much as of God.

Now this abbey of ours to which I had repaired was entirely abandoned to the secular life, and that of the lewdest. Whereof the abbot himself exceeded the rest of us no more in rank than in the dissoluteness and notorious infamy of his life. Their intolerable filthiness I frequently and vehemently, now in private now publicly attacking, made myself burdensome and odious beyond measure to them all. And so, greatly rejoicing at the daily importunities of my pupils, they sought an opportunity whereby they might remove me from their midst. And so my pupils long continuing to insist, and importuning the abbot also, and the brethren intervening, I withdrew to a certain cell, to devote myself as of old to my school. Thereto indeed so great a multitude of scholars poured in that neither was the place sufficient for their lodging nor the soil for their sustenance. There, as more became my profession, giving my attention principally to the Holy Scriptures, I did not altogether lay aside the teaching of the secular arts in which I was more fully versed, and which they demanded most of me; but made of them, as it were, a hook wherewith I might draw them, enticed by the philosophic savour, to the study of the true philosophy, as (the *Ecclesiastical History* reminds us) was the custom of the greatest of the Christian philosophers, Origen. Inasmuch, therefore, as the Lord appeared to have conferred on me no less of His grace in the Holy Scriptures than in profane letters, our school began to multiply exceedingly in both classes, and all the rest to be greatly attenuated. Whereby I aroused the envy and hatred of the other masters against myself. Who detracting me in every way possible, two of them in particular were always objecting to me in my absence that it was evidently contrary to the profession of a monk to be detained by the study of secular books, and that, without myself having had a master, I had presumed to aspire to a mastership in the Holy Scripture, seeking evidently thus to interdict me from every exercise of scholastic teaching, whereto they incessantly incited bishops, archbishops, abbots and whatever persons bearing a name in religion they might approach.

CHAPTER IX

*Of the book of his Theology, and of the persecution which he bore from his fellow-students. A Council is held against him.*

Now it so happened that I applied myself first to lecturing on the fundamentals of our faith by the analogy of human reason, and composed a certain tractate of theology, *Of Unity and the Holy Trinity,* for our scholars, who were asking for human and philosophical reasons, and demanded rather what could be understood than what could be stated, saying indeed that the utterance of words was superfluous which the intelligence did not follow, nor could anything be believed unless first it had been understood, and that it was ridiculous for anyone to preach to others what neither he himself nor they whom he taught could comprehend with their intellect, Our Lord Himself complaining that such were "blind leaders of the blind." Which tractate indeed, when numbers had seen and read it, began generally to please its readers, because it appeared to satisfy all alike upon these questions. And inasmuch as these questions appeared difficult beyond all others, the more their gravity was admitted, the more subtle my solution of them was considered to be, whereupon my rivals, vehemently incensed, assembled a Council against me, principally those two old plotters, namely Alberic and Lotulph, who now that their and my masters, to wit William and Anselm, were defunct, sought as it were to reign alone in their room and also to succeed them as if they had been their heirs. Since moreover both of them were conducting schools at Rheims, by repeated suggestions they moved their Archbishop Rodulph against me, that associating with himself Cono, Bishop of Palestrina, who then held the office of Legate in France, he should assemble a conventicle under the name of Council in the city of Soissons, and should invite me to appear there, bringing with me that famous work which I had written about the Holy Trinity. And so it came to pass. But before I came there, those two rivals of mine so defamed me among the clergy and the people, that almost the people stoned me and the few of my disciples who had come with me on the first day of our arrival; saying that I preached and had written that there were three Gods, as they themselves had been assured.

But on the last day of the Council, before they took their seats, the Legate and the Archbishop began to discuss at length with my rivals, and with divers persons, what should be decided about me and my book, the matter for which principally they had been called together. And as neither in my speech nor in the writings that were before them had they aught that they might charge against me, all being silent for a little space, or less open in their detraction of me, Geoffrey, Bishop of Chartres, who had precedence over the other bishops by the fame of his piety and the dignity of his see, thus began: "All of you, Sirs, that are here present know that this man's teaching, whatsoever it be, and his intellect have had many supporters and followers in whatsoever he has studied, that he has greatly diminished the fame as well of his own masters as of ours, and that, so to speak, his vine has spread its branches from sea to sea. If, as I do not think, ye condemn him by prejudice, even rightly, ye must know that ye will offend many, and there will not be wanting those who will wish to defend him; especially as in the writing here present we see nothing which may deserve any open calumny; and as is said by Jerome: 'Strength that is manifest ever excites jealousy, and the lightnings strike the highest mountain peaks.' Take heed lest ye confer more renown on him by violent action, and lest we earn more reproach for ourselves by the envy than for him by the justice of the charge. For a false rumour, as the aforesaid Doctor, in his Tenth Epistle, reminds us, is quickly stifled, and a man's later life pronounces judgment on his past. But if ye are disposed to act canonically against him, let his dogma or his writing be brought into our midst, and let him be questioned and allowed freely to reply, that convicted or confessing his error he be henceforward silent. Following at least those words of Saint Nicodemus, when, desirous of setting Our Lord Himself at liberty, he said: 'Doth our law judge any man before it hear him and know what he doeth?' "

Hearing which straightway my rivals interrupting him cried out: "O wise counsel, that we should contend against his verbosity whose arguments or sophisms the entire world could not withstand!" But of a surety it was far more difficult to contend with Christ Himself, and yet Nicodemus invited that He should be heard according to the sanction of the law. When therefore the bishop could not induce their minds to consent to what he had proposed, he tried by another way to restrain their envy; saying that for the discussion of so weighty a matter the few who were present could not suffice, and that this case needed a greater examination. His advice was, further, that to my abbey, that is the monastery of Saint Denis, my abbot, who was there present, should recall me; and that there, a greater number of more learned persons being called together, by a more diligent examination it should be decided what was to be done in the matter. The Legate assented to this last counsel, and so all the rest. Thereafter presently the Legate rose, that he might celebrate Mass before he entered the Council, and sent to me by the bishop the licence that had been granted, namely to return to my monastery, and there to await what should be determined.

Then my rivals, considering that they had achieved nothing if this business should be carried on outside their diocese, where forsooth they would not be able to sit in judgment, little trusting evidently in justice, persuaded the Archbishop that it was assuredly ignominious to himself if this case were to be transferred to another audience, and that it would be most dangerous if in that way I escaped. And straightway hastening to the Legate, they succeeded in altering his opinion and brought him reluctantly to the position that he should condemn the book without any inquiry, and at once burn it in the sight of all, and condemn me to perpetual enclosure in a strange

monastery.  For they said that for the condemnation of the book
this ought to be sufficient, that I had ventured publicly to read it,
though commended by the authority neither of the Roman Pontiff
nor of the Church, and had given it to be copied by many.  And this
would be of great benefit to the Christian faith, if by my example a
similar presumption were prevented in others.  And because the
Legate was less a scholar than he should have been he relied principally on the Archbishop's advice, as the Archbishop on theirs.
Which the Bishop of Chartres foreseeing straightway reported these
machinations to me, and vehemently exhorted me that I should
suffer them the more quietly, the more violently it was evident to
all that they were acting.  And that I must not doubt that this
violence of so manifest an envy would go greatly against them and
in my favour.  Nor should I be at all perturbed over my confinement
in a monastery, knowing that the Legate himself, who was doing
this under compulsion, after a few days, when he had removed
from the place, would set me wholly at liberty.  And so he gave me
what comfort he might, and to himself also, both of us in tears.

CHAPTER  X

*Of the burning of his book.  Of his persecution by the Abbot*
*and his brethren*

And so being summoned I went straightway before the Council, and
without any process of discussion they compelled me to cast my
aforesaid book upon the fire.

Then like a criminal and a convict I was handed over to the Abbot
of Saint Medard, who was present, and committed to his cloister as
though to a gaol.  And straightway the Council was dissolved.  Now
the Abbot and monks of that monastery, thinking that I was to remain longer with them received me with the greatest exultation and
using every diligence tried in vain to comfort me.  God, Who
judgest equity, with what gall then, with what bitterness of mind
did I, wretch that I was, challenge Thee, did I finally accuse Thee,
constantly repeating that plaint of Saint Anthony: "Good Jesus,
where wert Thou?"  But with what grief I boiled, with what blushing I was confounded, with what desperation perturbed, I then
could feel, I cannot now express.  I compared with what I had aforetime suffered in my body what I was now enduring, and of all
men reckoned myself the most unhappy.  That other I regarded as
a small betrayal in comparison with this outrage, and lamented far
more the detriment to my fame than that to my body, since to the
former I had come through my own fault, but to this so open a
violence, a sincere intent and love of our Faith had brought me which
had compelled me to write.  But when all those to whom the report
of it came vehemently protested that this had been cruelly and inconsiderately done, the several persons who had taken part in it,
repelling the blame from themselves, heaped it each on the others,
so much so that my rivals themselves denied that it had been done

by their counsel, and the Legate publicly deplored the jealousy of the French in this matter. Who being straightway moved to repentance, after some days, since at the time under compulsion he had given satisfaction to their jealousy, transferred me from the strange monastery to my own, where almost all the monks that had been there before were now, as I have already said, my enemies, for the vileness of their lives and their shameless conversation made suspect to them a man whose reproaches they could ill endure. And a few months having elapsed, fortune furnished them with an opportunity whereby they strove to undo me.

For it happened one day when I was lecturing that there came up a certain saying of Bede, when in expounding the Acts of the Apostles he asserts that Denys the Areopagite was Bishop of Corinth and not of Athens. Which seemed contrary to their taste, who boast that the famous Areopagite was their own Denys, whom his Acts profess to have been Bishop of Athens. Coming upon this I shewed it, as though jestingly, to certain of the brethren who were standing by. But they, greatly indignant, said that Bede was a most mendacious writer, and that they had a more truthful witness in Hilduin, their abbot, who to investigate this matter had travelled long in Greece, and, having acquainted himself with the facts, had in the Acts of that Saint, which he compiled, veraciously removed all doubt. Whereupon one of them challenged me with an importunate question: what seemed to me the truth in this controversy, namely between Bede and Hilduin? I replied that the authority of Bede, whose writings the entire body of the Latin churches consult, seemed to me the more acceptable. Whereat they, vehemently incensed, began to cry out, that now I had openly shewn that I had ever been the enemy of that our monastery, and that now I had greatly detracted from the whole realm, taking from it that honour wherein it singularly gloried when I denied that their Patron had been the Areopagite. I replied that neither had I denied this, nor was it any great matter whether he had been the Areopagite or had come from elsewhere, since he had won so bright a crown before God.

But they hastening straightway to the abbot told him what they had made me say. Who readily gave ear to them, rejoicing to find any occasion whereby he might oppress me, fearing me the more as he himself lived so much more vilely than the rest. Then, his chapter summoned and the brethren congregated, he threatened me severely and said that he would send me immediately before the King. And I offered myself to the discipline of the rule, if I had in any way offended, but in vain. Then, horrified at their villainy and having borne for so long such adverse fortune, utterly despairing as though the whole world had conspired against me, with the help of a certain consensus of the brethren who took pity on me, and of certain of my disciples, I stole out secretly by night and made for the neighbouring lands of Count Theobald, where formerly I had sojourned in a cell. He moreover was both somewhat acquainted with me and was full of compassion for my oppressions, whereof he had heard.

And so there I began to dwell in the town of Provins, to wit in a certain cell of monks of Troyes, whose prior had formerly been my bosom friend and loved me dearly.  Who, greatly rejoicing at my advent, cared for me with the utmost diligence.

[tr. C. K. Scott Moncrieff]

# ROMANESQUE LYRICS, HYMNS, AND SEQUENCES

The extant Latin lyrics written from the seventh to the twelfth centuries, here rather loosely called Romanesque, fill many volumes. Like all ponderous collections of lyric poetry, they seem dull and lifeless in the mass. Because the common people were creating and speaking new vernaculars, Latin became the language of scholars and reeked of archaism and pedantry. Because Latin was more often than not the secondary and acquired tongue of the poet, it lacked flexibility and variety. Because it was becoming the special property of the Church and religion, spiritual expression sounds ecclesiastical and secular comment sounds sacrilegious in it.

Yet in these centuries and in the Latin language the fundamentals of modern lyric expression were shaped. When the troubadours and other lyric writers composed in the vernacular in the twelfth and succeeding centuries, their images, their themes, their strophaic forms and meters were borrowed and developed from the Latin lyricists who preceded them. The common forms of accentual meter and end rhyme, the line patterns of fixed syllables, and even the rhetorical patterns of dawn-song, dance-song, complaint, martial song, drinking song, and the like may have been initiated by Latin writers.

The selections that follow, a few from the many lyrics that remain, illustrate the progress of musical verse from the time when the barbarians of the north acquired the strange Mediterranean tongue in monastic schools to the day when the Crusades opened up the West to trade and fresh ideas and agrarian feudalism declined before bourgeois urbanity. It will be noticed how, as with other forms of literature and art in the period, the Church takes the lead and binds all creative artists to it. Most of the authors were ecclesiastical teachers: Alcuin, who acted as a kind of minister of education for Charlemagne and became Abbot of Tours; Walafrid Strabo, Abbot of Reichenau, unique for his love and observation of nature, who died betimes at the age of forty; and Bernard of Clairvaux, through whose lips the Virgin became Queen of Heaven. But many anonymous songs were no doubt penned by students, drilled in the music and liturgy, who felt the urge to create. The collection now called the Cambridge Songs, preserved in a manuscript in the University Library, "is such as might have been compiled for some ecclesiastic, a man of learning and of catholic taste, such as were not lacking in this age . . . It is essentially a song-book" (Raby). Many of the poems are secular in subject, but even those imitate liturgical models in form and no doubt in melody.

One development, that of the sequence, calls for special comment, for its branches extend everywhere. Though the Ambrosian hymn was freely introduced into the Hours of Prayer (Office), no innovations were encouraged in the Mass. As the monasteries and cathedrals grew in affluence and choirs became professional, choir-masters, as a special enrichment of the service, prolonged the final *a* of the Alleluia following the Gradual into a *sequentia,* an extended melody without words. To this melody, quite possibly as an aid to the singers' memories, verses were attached as early as the eighth century. The combined words and music were known as *sequentiae cum prosa.* In this way the restrictive tradition of the Mass was broken, and the best creative minds were occupied during the next few centuries in the composition of sequences. The earliest known composer was Notker Balbulus (A.D. 840–912), scholar and musician of St. Gall, who composed an extant *Liber Hymnorum* containing the *Psallat Ecclesia,* a sequence of his own composition. Though written at first in rhythmical prose, these sequences eventually became regularly strophaic with complex rhyme, as can be seen below (p. 898).

## BOAT SONG [1]

### Columban (?) (A.D. 543–615)

*Heia, viri, nostrum reboans echo sonet heia!*
*Arbiter effusi late maris ore sereno*
*Placatum stravit pelagus posuitque procellam,*
*Edomitique vago sederunt pondere fluctus.*

Heia, fellows! Echo, resounding, sends back our heia!
Placid lies the wide-spread floor of the sea; the tempest,
Calmed by the serene face of ocean's arbiter, slumbers;
Under their sliding weight, conquered, the waves are quiet.

Heia, fellows! Echo, resounding, sends back our heia!
Beat with your equal oar-stroke, steadily shake the keelson!
Soon the smiling peace of sea and sky shall permit us,
Under our bellying sail, to run with the wind's swift motion.

Heia, fellows! Echo, resounding, sends back our heia!
So that our emulous prow may cut the waves like a dolphin,
Row till the timbers groan and the ship leap under your muscles —
Backward our whitened path flows in a lengthening furrow.

Heia, fellows! Echo, resounding, sends back our heia!
Over the waves play the Phorci: sing we, however, heia!
Stirred by our strokes the ocean foams; however, sing heia!
Voices unwearying, echo along the shore — sing heia!

[tr. HOWARD MUMFORD JONES]

1. From *The Romanesque Lyric,* by P. S. Allen and H. M. Jones; The University of North Carolina Press, Chapel Hill, 1928. Reprinted by permission of the publisher.

## THE CUCKOO [2]

### Alcuin (*circ.* 735–804)

*Heu, cuculus nobis fuerat cantare suetus,*
*Quae te nunc rapuit hora nefanda tuis?*

O cuckoo that sang to us and art fled,
    Where'er thou wanderest, on whatever shore
Thou lingerest now, all men bewail thee dead,
    They say our cuckoo will return no more.
Ah, let him come again, he must not die,
    Let him return with the returning spring,
And waken all the songs he used to sing.
    But will he come again?   I know not, I.

I fear the dark sea breaks above his head,
    Caught in the whirlpool, dead beneath the waves.
Sorrow for me, if that ill god of wine
    Hath drowned him deep where young things find their graves
But if he lives yet, surely he will come,
    Back to the kindly nest, from the fierce crows.
Cuckoo, what took you from the nesting place?
    But will he come again?   That no man knows.

If you love songs, cuckoo, then come again,
    Come again, come again, quick, pray you come.
Cuckoo, delay not, hasten thee home again,
    Daphnis who loveth thee longs for his own.
Now spring is here again, wake from thy sleeping,
    Alcuin the old man thinks long for thee.
Through the green meadows go the oxen grazing;
    Only the cuckoo is not.   Where is he?

Wail for the cuckoo, everywhere bewail him,
    Joyous he left us: shall he grieving come?
Let him come grieving, if he will but come again,
    Yea, we shall weep with him, moan for his moan.
Unless a rock begat thee, thou wilt weep with us.
    How canst thou not, thyself remembering?
Shall not the father weep the son he lost him,
    Brother for brother still be sorrowing?

Once were we three, with but one heart among us.
    Scarce are we two, now that the third is fled.
Fled is he, fled is he, but the grief remaineth;

2. From *Mediaeval Latin Lyrics,* translated by Helen Waddell; Constable & Co., London, 1934.   Reprinted by permission of the publisher.

Bitter the weeping, for so dear a head.
Send a song after him, send a song of sorrow,
   Songs bring the cuckoo home, or so they tell.
Yet be thou happy, wheresoe'er thou wanderest.
   Sometimes remember us.  Love, fare you well.

[tr. Helen Waddell]

## THE WANDERING SCHOLAR [3]

### Walafrid Strabo (A.D. 809–849)

*Musa, nostrum, plange, soror, dolorem,*
*Pande de nostro miserum recessum*
*Heu solo, quem continuo pudenda*
   *Pressit egestas.*

Sister, my Muse, weep thou for me I pray.
Wretched am I that ever went away
From my own land, and am continually
   Ashamed and poor.

Fool that I was, a scholar I would be,
For learning's sake I left my own country,
No luck have I and no man cares for me,
   Exiled and strange.

'Tis bitter frost and I am poorly happed,
I cannot warm my hands, my feet are chapped.
My very face shudders when I go out
   To brave the cold.

Even in the house it is cold as snow,
My frozen bed's no pleasure to me now,
I'm never warm enough in it to go
   To quiet sleep.

I think perhaps if I had any sense,
Even a little smattering pretence
Of wisdom, I could put up some defence,
   Warmed by my wits.

Alas, my father, if thou wert but here,
At whose behest thy scholar came so far,
I think there is no hurt that could come near
   His foolish heart.

Now start the sudden tears, remembering
How quiet it was there, the fostering

3. Ibid.

Of those low roofs that gave me sheltering
  At Reichenau.

O mother of thy sons, beloved, benign,
Thy saints have made thee holy, and the shrine
Of God's own Mother in thy midst doth shine,
  O happy isle.

What though deep waters round about thee are,
Most strong in love stand thy foundations sure,
And holy learning thou hast scattered far,
  O happy isle.

Still cries my heart that blessed place to see,
By day, by night, do I remember thee,
And all the kindness in thy heart for me,
  O happy isle.

Christ in His mercy give to me this grace,
That I may come back to that happy place,
And stand again and bless thee face to face,
  O mother isle.

Let me not die, O Christ, but live so long
To see again the land for which I yearn;
Back to her heart to win at last return,
  And praise Thee there.

                              [tr. HELEN WADDELL]


## SHARP BOREAS BLOWS [4]

Sedulius Scottus (fl. 848–874)

*Flamina nos Boreae miro canentia vultu*
*Perterrent subitis motibus atque minis.*

Into our startled faces blow the winds
Of Borea, whose sudden shift and flaw
And hoary burden scare us.  Earth itself,
Struck with unheard-of fury, shakes.  The sea
Murmurs amain, the strong rocks groan aloud,
Now while the north wind like an enemy
With thunderous and horrid-sounding voice
Ravages fields of air.  The clouded heavens
Grow thick with milk-white wool — a snowy stole
To cover up the withered world, whose hair

4. From *Medieval Latin Lyrics,* by P. S. Allen; The University of Chicago Press, Chicago, 1931.  Reprinted by permission of the publisher.

Of leaves falls swiftly from the wooded heights —
And there's no strength in reeds, nor in aught else.
The sun that shone with friendly brightness hides
His face and puts away his beams.   And us,
Learned grammarians and pious elders,
The swollen north wind — pitiable sight! —
Even us he ravages.   For flying storms
Which cut men with their beaks of cruelty
Spare unto none their honors.   Therefore thou,
O Hartgar who dost guard the weary, now receive
With charitable heart these Irish scholars —
Whereby through merit thou shalt climb to heaven
And all its temples, to celestial wisdom,
And to that Zion that shall never die.

[tr. HOWARD MUMFORD JONES]


## PIPPIN'S  VICTORY [5]

### Anonymous (9th cent.)

*Omnes gentes qui fecisti, tu Christe, Dei sobules,*
*Terras, fortes, rivos, montes et formasti hominem,*
*Avaresque convertisti ultimis temporibus.*

Now all the people Christ hath made are children of the Living
    Lord;
With hills and rocks, with field and stream the men He made are in
    accord;
And latterly to God He brought the Avarian race, a tribe abhorred.

They had wrought evil overmuch since first they sprang from out
    the void,
They burned both church and chapterhouse where monks were
    piously employed,
They smashed the earthen pots therein, and gold and silver they
    destroyed.

Their stealing vestments from the dead not even sacred tombs could
    stem;
The linen of the priests they tore, the levites' garments, hem from
    hem;
And from the nuns they stripped their clothes, the devil so persuading
    them.

King Pippin that is son of Christ, he moved against them foot and
    horse;

5. From *The Romanesque Lyric*, by P. S. Allen and H. M. Jones; The University
of North Carolina Press, Chapel Hill, 1928.  Reprinted by permission of the publisher.

The Lord He sent Saint Peter down, prince of the apostolic force,
To guide him on his marching there, and to direct the battle course.

Now Pippin our most Catholic king, the Lord with daring girt him
    round;
Beside the chalky Danube's flood he pitched his camp upon the
    ground
The enemy surrounded him — where'er he looked, a foe he found.

But Unguimeri our foeman shook and spake as boldly as he durst
Unto the queen Catina then, of all men's wives the most accursed,
And to her king, his liege, he said, "Do you, Cacanus, fear the worst!

"Your kingdom now hath seen its end, and longer you shall never
    reign;
God gave long since to Christian hands your governance of hill and
    plain —
Pippin shall now abolish you, that Catholic prince with all his train.

"King Pippin with his train draws nigh, he shall despoil you of
    your state —
Your people by that mighty host, they shall be slaughtered, small
    and great —
Your fortresses in plain and hill and forest he shall desolate.

"Go now and hasten, take with you presents and gifts magnificent;
Go now, adore that mighty lord, perhaps his anger will relent;
Bring cheerfully your gold and gems, he will not slay you in his tent."

When King Cacanus heard him speak, he stood completely terrified;
And with his Tarcan first-born then he sprang upon his mule to ride
And offer homage to our king and bring his costly gifts beside.

And to our king he said, "All hail, thou prince of princes, thou art
    lord;
Into thy hands I give my realm with field and forest, fall and ford;
And all the folk that dwell therein beneath the shadow of thy sword.

"My folk submit themselves to thee, now let thy clemency appear,
But spare our first-born, Lord," he said, "let not thine anger come
    so near,
We bow our heads beneath thy yoke — give not our nation to the
    spear!"

Now, faithful Christians that we be, let us deliver thanks to God —
He hath confirmed our governance of the Avarian stream and sod,
And over all the pagan tribes his mighty victories have trod.

And long live Pippin that great king, in fear and favor of our Lord,
And may he as a father reign until old age shall grant accord

Of sons that shall maintain in death and life the power of his sword!
Gloria aeterna patri, gloria sit filio!
[tr. HOWARD MUMFORD JONES]


## THE MONK OF ANGERS [6]

Anonymous (9th cent.)

*Andecavis abas esse dicitur,*
*Ille nomen primi tenet hominum;*
*Hunc fatentur vinum vellet bibere*
*Super omnes Andecavis homines.*
  *Eia eia eia laudes,*
  *Eia laudes dicamus Libero.*

Angers,    one hears,    has a monk of mighty thirst,
His name    the same    as Adam's was, of men the first;
Men think    his drink    runs to such vast quantities
No man    else can    run a score as large as his.

  Praise him, praise him, praise him, praise him!
  Sing we Bacchus' praises now!

They say    each day    he cries out for wine to drink;
Daylight    nor night    sees him pause or makes him shrink;
That sot    does not    cease until he staggers by,
Like a    tree that's
  wheeling    reeling    underneath a blowing sky.

  Praise him, praise him, praise him, praise him!
  Sing we Bacchus' praises now!

I swear    he'll bear    his carcase to eternity
So stained    and grained    with life-preserving wine is he;
He'll keep!    Don't steep    his body with embalmer's myrrh —
No spice    so nice    as alcohol, I do aver!

  Praise him, praise him, praise him, praise him!
  Sing we Bacchus' praises now!

He'll sup    no cup    politely like another man;
He passes    mere glasses    for a larger drinking can,
He'll ask    a cask    and, lifting it gigantically,
He'll drink    and swink,    surpassing mere mortality!

  Praise him, praise him, praise him, praise him!
  Sing we Bacchus' praises now!

6. Ibid.

Shed tears,      Angers,      if death should get him in his grip;
No other      such brother      in all your city's fellowship!
Who'll quaff      and laugh      and soak in wine as he has done?
Make eternal      his diurnal      deeds in stone or paint, my son!


Praise him, praise him, praise him, praise him!
Sing we Bacchus' praises now!

[tr. HOWARD MUMFORD JONES]


## HYMN FOR EASTER MORN

Anonymous (9th cent.?)

*Aurora lucis rutilat,*
*Coelum laudibus intonat,*
*Mundus exultans jubilat,*
*Gemens infernus ululat.*


Light's glittering morn bedecks the sky,
Heaven thunders forth its victor-cry;
The glad earth shouts its triumph high,
And groaning hell makes wild reply.

While He, the King of glorious might,
Treads down Death's strength in Death's despite,
And trampling hell by victor's right
Brings forth His sleeping saints to light.

Fast barred beneath the stone of late,
In watch and ward where soldiers wait,
Now, shining in triumphant state,
He rises victor from death's gate.

Hell's pains are loosed and tears are fled;
Captivity is captive led:
The angel, crowned with light, hath said:
"The Lord is risen from the dead."

The Apostles' hearts were full of pain
For their dear Lord so lately slain,
That Lord his servants' wicked train
With bitter scorn had dared arraign.

With gentle voice the Angel gave
The women tidings at the grave:
"Forthwith your Master shall ye see:
He goes before to Galilee."

And while with fear and joy they pressed
To tell these tidings to the rest,
Their Lord, their living Lord, they meet
And see his form and kiss his feet.

The eleven, when they hear, with speed
To Galilee forthwith proceed,
That there they may behold once more
The Lord's dear face, as oft before.

In this our bright and Paschal day
The sun shines out with purer ray,
When Christ, to earthly sight made plain,
The glad Apostles see again.

The wounds, the riven wounds He shows
In that His flesh with light that glows,
With public voice, both far and nigh,
The Lord's arising testify.

O Christ, the King who lov'st to bless,
Do thou our hearts and souls possess;
To Thee our praise that we may pay,
To whom our laud is due — for aye.

[tr. JOHN MASON NEALE]


ABBOT JOHN [7]

Cambridge Songs (*circ.* 1000)

*In vitis patrum veterum*
*Quiddem legi ridiculum,*
*Examplae tamen habile;*
*Quod vois dico rithmice.*

In records of the ancient dead
This quite amusing tale I read,
And as a lesson underlies it,
I've tried in rhyme to advertise it.

The Abbot John in size was small,
In virtues he outmeasured all;
To the brother of much greater age,
Who shared with him the hermitage,
One day he said: I would I were
Care-free as all the angels are,

---

7. From *Twenty-One Medieval Latin Poems*, by E. J. Martin; Scholartis Press, London, 1931. Reprinted by permission of Eric Partridge.

Relieved of food and clothing and
All that is won by toil of hand.
His brother answered: "Nay be wise,
Before you dare that enterprise,
Or you may find before you're done
Such schemes were better left alone."

"Yet he who never ventures in,
May never lose, but will not win,"
Was his reply.  With empty hands
He strode across the desert sands,
And seven days he had for fare
The grasses sparsely growing there.
Upon the eighth day hunger's grip
Sent him to th' old companionship.

Within his cell the brother sat,
The door was shut, the hour was late,
When to him came a feeble cry:
"My brother, open.  It is John.
At the old place in need I lie;
Of your good mercy do not shun
The victim of necessity."

From inside came the answer: "John
Is gone to be an angel.   On
The Door of Heaven he can gaze.
He cares no more for mortal ways."

John on the ground made shift to lie,
And passed a night of misery,
Unto the penance of his station
Adding to this supererogation.

Next day admission to the cell
He got, and got it hot as well.
He bore all meekly for his mind
To everything but crust was blind.
Only too grateful, as he said,
To have a roof above his head.
His arms might ache but never now
They ached too much to swing the hoe.

For chastened by privation's stress
He'd lost his former fickleness.
Angel he could not be, but he
Had learned a better man to be.

[tr. EDWARD JAMES MARTIN]

## THE VOICE OF THE TURTLE

Cambridge Songs (10th cent.)

*Vestiunt silve tenera meroven*
*Virgulta, suis onerata pomis,*
*Canunt de celsis seclibus palumbes*
    *Carmina cunctis.*

The woodlands now with tender green
Dress bare branches foretelling fruit;
High on their perches pigeons preen
    And link their song.

The dove moans and the thrush sings here,
The blackbirds recompose old tunes.
The sparrows keep their noisy cheer
    Deep in the elms.

Sunward the eagle; the lark is heard
Singing one ascending song, and then
With altered pitch both song and bird
    To earth descend.

The swallows dart in the gentle weather;
The bob-white whistles, the grackles call.
Birds everywhere celebrate summer together
    With varied song.

Yet not the birds, but bees afford
The pattern of sweet chastity
Like her who bearing Christ our Lord
    Was undefiled.

                    [tr. JOHN D. OGDEN]


## LOVE SONG [8]

(Anonymous (10th cent.)

*Iam, dulcis amica, venito,*
*Quam sicut cor meum diligo;*
*Intra in cubiculum meum,*
*Ornamentis cunctis onustum.*

8. From *The Romanesque Lyric*, by P. S. Allen and H. M. Jones; The University
of North Carolina Press, Chapel Hill, 1928. Reprinted by permission of the publisher.

Come, sweet friend, and be with me,
Darling of my heart, my treasure!
Come now into my chamber — see,
It is fresh-decked and fit for pleasure.

I have put cushions in the seats,
And hung bright cloths about the room,
Set fragrant herbs to mix their sweets
With flowers fresh-plucked and all in bloom.

There's a fair table set for dining
And laden down with dishes rare
And ruby wine in goblets shining —
Everything you ask is there.

And you shall hear soft symphonies
Blowing, and flute-music, too;
With a skilled boy a maiden vies
In singing songs to pleasure you.

He plucks the cithern with his quill,
Her lute accompanies the lass;
The servants bring tall cups they fill
With wine less ruddy than the glass.

But banquets please me not so much
As the dear converse coming after;
And freely to possess and touch
Is more than food and wine and laughter.

Come then, sweet sister, soul's elect,
Of all things dearest, most divine,
Your eyes, my soul's best part, reflect
Within their light, the light in mine.

I lived in sylvan solitudes,
And loved all solitary places;
I fled, among the secret woods,
Tumult, and men, and thronging faces.

But now, my dearest, stay no more,
Let us be studious of love!
I can not live without you, nor
Lack the sweet end and crown thereof.

You can not now postpone the employ
Which you must come to, spite of staying!
Quickly perfect our promised joy,
In me there is no more delaying!

                              [tr. HOWARD MUMFORD JONES]

## ALBA

Anonymous (10th cent.)

*Phoebi claro nondum orto iubare,*
*Fert Aurora lumen terris tenue:*
*Spiculator pigris clamat "surgite."*
  *L'alba part umet mar atra sol*
  *Poy pasa bigil mira clar tenebras.*

  Before the sun's clear orb is bright
  Dawn spreads her formless light on earth.
  The watcher calls the sleeper "Wake!"
Dawn brings the sun across the glistening sea;
Her vigil done, clear-eyed she fronts the dark.

  How like a hostile net it creeps
  To overwhelm the sluggards' beds
  Whose clamorous sentry calls to rise.
Dawn brings the sun across the glistening sea;
Her vigil done, clear-eyed she fronts the dark.

  The northwind quits the northland now,
  The Pole star softens its bright rays,
  The Wain swings eastward in its arc.
Dawn brings the sun across the glistening sea;
Her vigil done, clear-eyed she fronts the dark.
                                        [tr. JOHN D. OGDEN]


## THE PASCHAL SEQUENCE

Wipo(?) (d. 1050)

*Victimae Paschali*
*Laudes immolent Christiani.*

Christians now should sacrifice
In honor of the Paschal Lamb.

The Lamb has redeemed His sheep:
The guiltless Christ before His Father
Has mediated
For sinners.

Death and Life
Their strange conflict have resolved:

The dead Lord of Life
Reigns living.

"Tell us, Mary,
What hast thou seen on the way?"

"The sepulchre of the living Christ,
And the glory of the Resurrected One, I saw."

[Second Mary]  "Angelic witnesses,
The napkin and linen cloths."

[Third Mary]  "Christ, my hope, both risen:
He shall go before thee into Galilee."

[All]  "We know in truth that Christ
Hath risen from the dead.
Thou, victorious King,
Have mercy on us."

[tr. CHARLES W. JONES]


## LAMENT [9]

### Abelard (?)

*Hebet sidus laeti visus*
*Cordis nubilo,*
*Tepet oris mei risus*
*Carens jubilo;*
*Jure maereo,*
*Occultatur nam propinqua,*
*Cordis vigor floret in qua*
*Totus haereo.*

My clouded heart hath dulled my eyes —
They were stars before.
And on my lips my laughter lies
Joyfully no more.
Grieving I aver
She hath vanished, she my nearest;
Strength of heart was in my dearest,
And I cling to her!

All the band of maids that follow
Love, she hath outshone,
She that took from bright Apollo
His name for her own;

9. From *Medieval Latin Lyrics,* by P. S. Allen; The University of Chicago Press, Chicago, 1931. Reprinted by permission of the publisher.

And her face reflects
More than sunshine, and I burn for
Her I wish for, her I yearn for
This year and the next.

Now I mourn my time's diurnal
Solitariness!
Once I plundered (O nocturnal
Hours were apt for this!)
Kisses from her mouth:
'Tis a well of balsam flowing,
And her heart's a garden growing
Cassia from the south.

God! I waste away and know
Hope of solace not;
Flower o' youth, you dare not grow!
But if I could blot
Time that cuts and parts —
Could we meet again, ah surely
Plighted faith would bind securely
Our divided hearts!

[tr. HOWARD MUMFORD JONES]


ELEGY [10]

Abelard

*Vel confossus pariter*
*Morerer feliciter*
*Cum, quid amor faciat,*
*Maius hoc non habeat,*
*Et me post te vivere*
*Mori sit assidue,*
*Nec ad vitam anima*
*Satis sit dimidia.*

Low in thy grave with thee
  Happy to lie,
Since there's no greater thing left Love to do;
  And to live after thee
    Is but to die,
For with but half a soul what can Life do?

So share thy victory,
  Or else thy grave,

10. From *Mediaeval Latin Lyrics,* translated by Helen Waddell; Constable & Co., London, 1934. Reprinted by permission of the translator.

Either to rescue thee, or with thee lie:
  Ending that life for thee,
    That thou didst save,
So death that sundereth might bring more nigh.

Peace, O my stricken lute!
  Thy strings are sleeping.
Would that my heart could still
  Its bitter weeping!

                [tr. HELEN WADDELL]


## HYMN FOR THE CLOSE OF THE WEEK

### Abelard

*O quanta qualia sunt illa sabbata,*
*Quae semper celebrat superna curia!*
*Quae fessis requies, quae merces fortibus,*
*Cum erit omnia Deus in omnibus!*

O what their joy and their glory must be,
Those endless sabbaths the blessed ones see;
Crown for the valiant, to weary ones rest;
God shall be all and in all ever blest.

What are the Monarch, His court and His throne?
What are the peace and the joy that they own?
Tell us, ye blessed, that in it have share,
If what ye feel ye can fully declare.

Truly Jerusalem name we that shore,
Vision of peace, that brings joy evermore;
Wish and fulfilment can severed be ne'er,
Nor the thing prayed for come short of the prayer.

We, whom no trouble distraction can bring,
Safely the anthems of Sion shall sing;
While for Thy grace, Lord, their voices of praise
Thy blessed people shall evermore raise.

There dawns no sabbath; no sabbath is o'er;
Those sabbath-keepers have one and no more;
One and unending is that triumph-song
Which to the angels and us shall belong.

Now, in the meanwhile, with hearts raised on high
We for that country must yearn and must sigh;
Seeking Jerusalem, dear native land,
Through our long exile on Babylon's strand.

Low before Him with our praises we fall,
Of whom and in whom and through whom are all:
Of whom, the Father; and in whom the Son;
Through whom, the Spirit, with these ever one.

[tr. JOHN MASON NEALE]


### THE ROSY SEQUENCE

Bernard of Clairvaux (?) (A.D. 1090–1153)

*Dulcis Jesu memoria*
*Dans vera cordi gaudia:*
*Sed super mel et omnia*
*Eius dulcis praesentia.*

Jesu! — the very thought is sweet!
In that dear name all heart-joys meet;
But sweeter than the honey far
The glimpses of His Presence are.

No word is sung more sweet than this:
No name is heard more full of bliss:
No thought brings sweeter comfort nigh
Than Jesus, Son of God most high.

Jesu! the hope of souls forlorn!
How good to them for sin that mourn!
To them that seek Thee, oh how kind!
But what art Thou to them that find?

Jesu, Thou sweetness, pure and blest,
Truth's Fountain, light of souls distress'd,
Surpassing all that heart requires,
Exceeding all that soul desires!

No tongue of mortal can express,
No letters write its blessedness:
Alone who hath thee in his heart
Knows, love of Jesus! what thou art.

I seek for Jesus in repose,
When round my heart its chambers close;
Abroad, and when I shut the door,
I long for Jesus evermore.

With Mary, in the morning gloom,
I seek for Jesus at the tomb;
For Him, with love's most earnest cry,
I seek with heart, and not with eye. . . .

. . . O Jesu!   King of wondrous might!
O Victor, glorious from the fight!
Sweetness that may not be express'd,
And altogether loveliest!

Remain with us, O Lord, today!
In every heart Thy grace display;
That, now the shades of night are fled,
On Thee our spirits may be fed.

More glorious than the sun to see,
More fragrant than the balsam-tree,
My heart's desire, and boast, and mirth,
Jesu, salvation of the earth.

[tr. JOHN MASON NEALE]


## THE HEAVENLY CITY[11]

### (*De Contemptu Mundi*, lines 309–323, 335–346)

### Bernard of Morval (*circ.* 1135)

*Opprimit omne cor ille tuus decor, O Sion, O pax,*
*Urbs sine tempore, nulla potest fore laus tibi mendax;*
*O nova mansio, te pia concio, gens pia munit,*
*Provehit, excitat, auget, identitat, efficit, unit.*


No heart but faints under the sight of thy wonder, O Sion, our peace,
All praises excelling, before all time's telling, until time shall cease.
In thee God's own nation, God's own congregation a new home
     designs,
Increases, advances, upraises, enhances, in perfected lines.
God's right hand did mete thee and angels complete thee and order
     thy plan,
Foursquare without section in harmonic perfection of the decachord's
     span.
The prophets thy flowers; for gold on thy towers the patriarchs shine,
And saints earth-rejected, no longer neglected, are glories of thine.
White lilies are bedded about thee unwedded virginity's grace,
And blood-laden roses whose scarlet discloses the martyr's strong
     race.
Confessors adorn thee with faith unforsworn; Thee the One without
     guilt
Indwelleth, the Holiest whose blood for the lowliest of sinners was
     spilt.
He is thy president, he the great resident of thy King's hall,
Only-begotten He, Lion of mystery and Lamb withal . . .

11. From *Twenty-One Medieval Latin Poems*, by E. J. Martin; Scholartis Press, London, 1931.   Reprinted by permission of Eric Partridge.

. . . O land without passion or sorrow's obsession, O land without
   strife,
Magnificent towers, fair homeland of flowers, thou country of life.
Thy fame hath far sounded, a city deep founded in a country secure,
I seek thee, implore thee, yearn for thee, adore thee, with songs thee
   conjure.
I seek not by merit — for all I inherit myself is to die —
Nor dare I in silence to cover the vileness that by birth am I.
This life of my living is life of sin's weaving, a life of the dead
That guilt's domination with fell machination to destruction doth
   tread.
And yet in hope's way still I walk, night and day still in hope and
   in faith
I pray for the guerdon, the ever fresh pardon that lasts beyond death.
A holy creator whose love is far greater than I can betray
In foulness endured me, from foulness restored me and washed it
   away.

[tr. EDWARD JAMES MARTIN]

# V. ARTHURIAN LITERATURE

The body of stories about "the goodliest fellowship of famous knights whereof the world holds record" has been a mine for the imagery of modern poets richer than Ovid and as varied as the Old Testament. The stories burst like a deluge upon western Europe in the last half of the twelfth century, precipitated, it would seem, by the publication and instantaneous popularity of Geoffrey of Monmouth's *Histories of the Kings of Britain* in the year 1137. Very few evidences of Arthur and his knights now remain from an earlier period. Whether the popularity of twelfth-century stories destroyed older works is a question for scholarly debate.

There is no certain evidence for the existence of a historical King Arthur. The English migration from the Continent to the British Isles occurred around A.D. 500. By the year 600 they had taken practically all of present England from the British. The only contemporary account, an "Epistle" of the British monk Gildas, does not mention Arthur. But then, Gildas mentions little else contemporary — his concern being to lash his sinful compatriots with the flail of Biblical citation. The English kept no historical records at the time. Three hundred years later, a British chronicle usually called *Historia Brittonum,* or Nennius, after the name of one of its several editors, states that after Hengist died, Arthur, a *dux bellorum,* fought against the English with the British kings; it enumerates twelve victorious battles and states that at Badon Hill Arthur alone slew 960 of the enemy. Elsewhere the chronicle speaks of a stone in South Wales bearing the impress of the foot of Arthur's dog Cabal and explains the impress by a miraculous story that appears again in the post-Galfridian Welsh story of *Kulhwch and Olwen.* Obviously, by the ninth century Arthur had become the subject of legend among British storytellers.

No other Arthurian items appear in literature before the twelfth century. According to a contemporary chronicler, in the year 1113 a servant of certain French monks quarreled with a Cornishman about whether Arthur were still alive, "just as," says the chronicler, "the Bretons [in French Brittany] quarrel with the French over Arthur." A contemporary life of a Cornish saint tells of Arthur's reigning in Cornwall and hunting a dragon. In 1125, the famous and very conscientious historian William of Malmesbury spoke in scorn of the idle fables of the Britons which defame rather than glorify their hero Arthur. He added an account of the death of Arthur's nephew Gawain. In the first half of the century, on a portal of the Cathedral of Modena in Italy, masons represented in stone a siege of a castle by Arthur and his knights. There are other records that may have been created in this period, but their dates and often their meanings are disputed.

At all events, there is no extant precursor of Geoffrey for the full treatment of Arthur that extends through five of his twelve books of *Histories*. The aim and composition of that work are discussed below. Even for such readers as recognized Geoffrey's story as spurious history, King Arthur began to live as a mighty conqueror like Alexander, Julius Caesar, and Charlemagne — a different image from the fairy-tale king of Welsh legend. Writers like Wace and Làyamon worked this vein of historical fiction. Another group of writers adapted Arthur to the pattern of the "Breton lays"; the Continental Bretons and insular Cornish and Welsh were all of common Celtic stock and throughout the Middle Ages acknowledged kindred ties. Marie de France, who professed to tell her stories in the Breton manner, wrote comparatively short works of minstrelsy in which Arthur and his knights live in a world peopled by fairies and pixies not unlike the creations of Welsh imagination. Another group, inspired by the French poet Chrétien de Troyes, who was governed by troubadour fashions, adapted Arthur to the purposes of courtly poetry, with its emphasis on trials of love and derring-do. Chrétien's rambling and ununified tales may bore modern readers, but they inspired a host of adapters. Poets with a religious or mystical bent took from Chrétien and his predecessors the mythological Grail story and tied it to Christian history, with such a result as the mighty epic *Parzival* of Wolfram von Eschenbach. Others coined or repeated incidents in ballad form.

Some of the reasons why the Arthur stories proved so adaptable are clear enough. Authors were not bound to historical veracity, which hampered them in romancing about Caesar and Charlemagne, even though Geoffrey's *History* endowed Arthur with a convenient historicity. Again, he was king of a subject people, downtrodden for centuries, who showed no real signs of edging their way into a place in the sun; they could be conveniently internationalized and exalted without offending courtly sensibilities. Moreover, Geoffrey had presented his work to the Normans who, far from worrying about the British, welcomed their support against the English whom they were then uneasily subjugating. These Normans were the circulators of literature not only throughout the leisure class of England but over more than half of present France and into Italy and Sicily. Their monarchs, especially Henry II and his queen Eleanor of Aquitaine, dictated taste in literature and encouraged authors in one of the most prolific and fruitful literary periods in western culture. And last, Arthur and his knights, who arose from legends of proverbially musical people endowed with quixotic imagination, had been presented in the language of feudalism, the most powerful social system of the day, to a court where poetic clarity and vigor were common. Under those circumstances, the poetic imagination found in this rich quarry an infinite variety of materials.

# GEOFFREY OF MONMOUTH

Geoffrey of Monmouth, who presumably grew up in Wales, though he may have come of Norman Breton stock, received such orders in the Church as would allow a full literary education. For a considerable period he lived at Oxford, probably as Canon of St. George's Chapel in Oxford Castle, while he cultivated his literary talent. About 1135 he published a *Little Book of Merlin*, which he later incorporated as Book VII of his *Histories*, and dedicated it to the Bishop of Lincoln. Then, sometime between 1136 and 1138 he published his *Histories of the Kings of Britain*, with two dedications, one to King Stephen and one to Duke Robert of Gloucester. These time-serving dedications may have earned him desired preferment, for in 1140 he became an Archdeacon of Llandaff and in 1152, two years before his death, Bishop of St. Asaph, a see that he never visited. The recorded fact that he was ordained priest only eight days before he was appointed bishop may indicate his lack of concern about ecclesiastical duties.

The *Histories* tells, in twelve books, the story of the Britons from the time their eponymous progenitor Brutus, grandson of Ascanius, companion and successor Aeneas, left Italy to the time of Cadwallo, the last puissant king of the Britons. It follows the literary form of the chronicles of the preceding generation, especially cultivated by a numerous body of Anglo-Norman writers, usually monastic librarians. Following strict chronological progression *ab ovo,* either from Adam and Eve or from the foundation of a city, race, or state, these chronicles emphasized the relation of racial history to Biblical, ecclesiastical, and Roman imperial history. The narrations were largely factual, treating primarily the movements of kings and armies as well as the progress of ecclesiastical establishments and the rise and fall of ruling families. Chroniclers' sources were largely the brief annalistic entries on local calendars, the deeds and charters of state and Church, and the transcripts of acts of ecclesiastical councils. The chroniclers' imaginative reconstruction of previous ages was usually limited to the invention of rhetorical exhortations and addresses of political and military leaders, and the occasional insertion for variety and interest of a dialogue between historical characters. In the main, the chroniclers prided themselves upon their factual accuracy; they took little from oral legend and were skeptical of statements not traditionally accepted. For affairs within the range of their own observation or for past events where sound records were obtainable, such chroniclers as William of Malmesbury, Florence of Worcester, and Simeon of Durham are remarkably informative and reliable.

Geoffrey's *Histories* closely follows this literary form. It makes all the professions of historical accuracy common to medieval chroniclers. The narrative is succinct and restrained; the epistles, charters, and speeches that enliven and diversify it are in the conventional pattern. At a time when practically every city or people was trying to trace its foundations back to Trojan heroes, the *Histories'* story of Brutus was not unusual, and stories like those of Lear and Cymbeline have their own kind of verisimilitude. Yet Geoffrey's work is obviously fiction from beginning to end, though he clearly took pains to make his narrative agree with the popular histories of Eusebius, Jerome, and Bede at commonplace and memorable points. Though Geoffrey maintained that he no more than translated a Welsh history lent him by Walter, Archdeacon of Oxford, scholars debate whether any such antecedent history ever existed. That Geoffrey at least recorded many legends that were current among the British of Wales can be conceded; but which of these legends contain elements of fact will no doubt always remain a surmise.

At all events a political purpose is evident. The Britons, cuffed by the English for six hundred years, are pictured as the heroes of the West — making even the Rome of the Caesars quake. Only at moments of internal dissension can the British be withstood. This is the single theme of the narrative, no doubt the element that stirred English contemporaries, like William of Newburgh, to brand Geoffrey as a reporter of fables either from love of lying or to please the British. It is obvious that it would be of advantage to the British to build themselves up to the stature of allies of the conquering Normans in order to share in repressing the conquered English.

This "Matter of Britain," as the twelfth-century French poet Jean Bodel called it, has been consistently popular ever since. Through Wace, Layamon, Malory, and Holinshed, Geoffrey's Brut, Corineus, and Goemagot, Locrine, Sabrina, Lear, Gorboduc, Ferrex and Porrex, Cassibelaunus, Cymbeline, Maximian, Vortigern, Hengist, Horsa and Rowena, Merlin and Arthur became the material for poets, playwrights, and tellers of tales from that day to this, until they are more real in the minds of English readers than many whose names and deeds are recorded in factual history.

Milton in his youth, like a true son of England, dedicated himself to "singing of the Trojan craft traversing the narrow seas, and the ancient realm of Imogen, daughter of Pandras, and Brennus and Arviragus, the leaders, and old Belinus, and then the Armorican settlers beneath the dominion of the Britons, then Ierne pregnant of Arthur by fatal fraud, and the deceptive features and assumed arms of Gorlois; 'twas a wile of Merlin." (*Epitaphium Damonis*). These are Geoffrey's heroic tales.

The selections below form an abridgment of the first nine books — up to the time when Arthur was established as Conqueror of the West. The subsequent selections from Wace, who paraphrased Geoffrey, will sufficiently indicate the conclusion of Geoffrey's story of Arthur.

HISTORIES OF THE KINGS OF BRITAIN

Geoffrey of Monmouth (A.D. 1100?–1154)

[From *Geoffrey of Monmouth,* translated by Sebastian
Evans; Temple Classics, J. M. Dent & Sons, Ltd., London,
1904. Reprinted by permission of the publisher.]

(I, 3)    After the Trojan War, Aeneas, fleeing from the desolation
of the city, came with Ascanius by ship unto Italy.   There, for that
Aeneas was worshipfully received by King Latinus, Turnus, King
of the Rutulains, did wax envious and made war against him.   When
they met in battle, Aeneas had the upper hand, and after that Turnus
was slain, obtained the kingdom of Italy and Lavinia the daughter of
Latinus.   Later, when his own last day had come, Ascanius, now
king in his stead, founded Alba on Tiber, and begat a son whose
name was Silvius.   Silvius, unknown to his father, had fallen in
love with and privily taken to wife a certain niece of Lavinia, who
was now about to become a mother.   When this came to the knowledge of his father Ascanius, he commanded his wizards to discover
whether the damsel should be brought to bed of a boy or a girl.
When they had made sure of the matter by art of magic, they told him
that the child would be a boy that should slay his father and his
mother, and after much travel in many lands, should, albeit
an exile, be exalted unto the highest honours.   Nor were the wizards out in their forecast, for when the day came that she should
be delivered of a child, the mother bare a son, but herself died in
his birth.   Howbeit, the child was given in charge unto a nurse,
and was named Brute.   At last, after thrice five years had gone by,
the lad, bearing his father company out a-hunting, slew him by
striking him unwittingly with an arrow; for when the verderers
drave the deer in front of them, Brute, thinking to take aim at them,
smote his own father under the breast.   Upon the death of his father
he was driven out of Italy, his kinsfolk being wroth with him for
having wrought a deed so dreadful.   He went therefore as an exile
into Greece, and there fell in with the descendants of Helenus, the son
of Priam, who at that time were held in bondage under the power of
Pandrasus, King of the Greeks.   For Pyrrhus, the son of Achilles,
after the overthrow of Troy, had led away with him in fetters the
foresaid Helenus and a great number of others besides, whom he
commanded to be held in bondage by way of revenging upon them
his father's death.   And when Brute understood that they were of
the lineage of his former fellow-citizens, he sojourned amongst them.
Howbeit, in such wise did he achieve renown for his knighthood
and prowess that he was beloved by kings and dukes above all the
other youths of the country.   For among the wise he was as wise as he
was valiant among warriors, and whatsoever gold or silver or ornaments he won, he gave it all in largess to his comrades in battle.   His

fame was thus spread abroad among all nations, and the Trojans flocked unto him from all parts, beseeching him that he should be their king and deliver them from the slavery of the Greeks; the which they declared might easily be done, seeing that they had now so multiplied in the land as that without making count of little ones and women they were already reckoned to be seven thousand.

(4) Then Brute sent his letter addressed unto the King in these words: "To Pandrasus, King of the Greeks, Brute, Duke of them that are left of Troy, greeting: Whereas a nation sprung from the illustrious race of Dardanus deigned not to be treated in thy kingdom otherwise than as the purity of their nobility did demand, they have betaken them into the depths of the forests. For they held it better to live a life after the manner of wild beasts, to wit on flesh and herbs, with liberty, than to be cockered with dainties of every kind and remain any longer under the yoke of bondage unto thee. If this offendeth the loftiness of thy power, they are rather to be pardoned than held to blame, for of all that are in captivity it is the common aim and desire to recover their former dignity. Be thou, therefore, moved to mercy towards them, and deign to bestow upon them their lost liberty, allowing them to inhabit the forest glades that they have occupied to the end that thus they might flee beyond the reach of slavery. But if this thou wilt not, grant them at least that they may depart unto other nations of the world with thy good will."

(5) When Pandrasus, therefore, had learnt the drift of this letter, he was beyond measure amazed that they whom he had held in bondage should so abound in hardihood as to address any mandates of the kind unto him. He therefore summoned a council of his nobles, and decreed that an army should be levied in order to hunt them down. But whilst that he was searching the wildernesses wherein he supposed them to be, and the stronghold of Sparatinum, Brute issued forth with three thousand men, and suddenly attacked him when he was expecting nothing of the kind. For, hearing of his arrival, he had thrown himself into the said stronghold the night before, in order that he might make an unlooked-for onslaught upon them when they were unarmed and marching without order. The Trojans accordingly charged down upon them and attacked them stoutly, doing their best to overwhelm them with slaughter. The Greeks, moreover, suddenly taken aback, are scattered in all directions, and scamper off, the King at their head, to get across the river Akalon that runneth anigh. But in fording the stream they suffer sore jeopardy from the whirling currents of the flood. Whilst they are thus fleeing abroad, Brute overtaketh them, and smiteth down them that he overtaketh partly in the waters of the river and partly on the banks, and, hurrying hither and thither amongst them, rejoiceth greatly to inflict upon them a double death.

(10) Now Brute, when he had obtained possession of the royal tent, was careful to bind the King and to keep him safe. For he knew that he could attain the object at which he aimed more readily

by the King's life than by his death. But the company that were with him ceased not from the slaughter they made, which in the part of the camp they held had wrought a clearance that was nought less than extermination. When the night had thus been spent and the light of dawn revealed how mighty a loss had been inflicted on the people, Brute, in a very tempest of delight, now that the carnage was over, gave permission to his comrades to deal as they pleased with the spoils of the slain. Then he entereth the fortress with the King, and there awaiteth until he should have distributed the treasure. When this was all allotted, he again garrisoned the castle and gave orders for the burial of the dead. He then again collected his troops and returned rejoicing in his victory to the forest. The tidings filled the hearts of his men with no less joy, and the doughty Duke, after summoning the elders, made inquiry of them what they thought ought to be demanded of Pandrasus, for, now that he was placed in their power, he would grant any petition they might make to the utmost, provided he were allowed to go free. Some of them at once proposed one thing, and some another, according to their inclinations. Part exhorted him to ask for a portion of the kingdom for them to dwell therein; part for leave to go their way elsewhere and for whatever might be of use to them upon the journey. And seeing that after a long while they still hesitated, one amongst them, Mempricius by name, rose up and besought silence, when he spake thus in the hearing of the rest:—

"Wherefore, fathers, do ye hesitate about that which, in my opinion, is most expedient for your own welfare? There is but one thing to be asked for, to wit, leave to depart, if ye desire that yourselves and your children should have lasting peace. For if it be that ye grant Pandrasus his life on condition that ye obtain a part of Greece, and so be minded to sojourn in the midst of the Danai, never will ye enjoy an enduring peace so long as the brethren and sons and grandsons of them upon whom ye inflicted the slaughter of yesterday remain intermingled amongst ye or are your next neighbours without. For so long as they remember the slaying of their kinsfolk they will hold ye always in eternal hatred, and taking offence at every the merest trifle, will do their best to wreak vengeance upon ye. Nor will ye, seeing that your host is the smaller, have strength to resist the aggressions of so many indwellers of the land. For if any strife for the mastery should arise, their numbers will wax daily while your own will wane. Mine opinion, therefore, is that ye ask of him his eldest daughter, whom they call Ignoge, as a wife for our Duke, and along with her gold and silver, ships and corn, and whatsoever else may be needful for our voyage. And if so be that he will grant her, we will then with his leave go on our way to seek out other lands."

(11) When he had made an end of this speech, with more to the like effect, the whole assembly signified their assent, and counselled that Pandrasus be brought into their midst, and, save he should be favourable towards this their petition, should be condemned to a death as cruel as might be. No tarrying was there. He is brought

thither and set in a chair on high, where he is instructed, moreover, what tortures he will have to suffer in case he refuse to do according as he is commanded. Whereupon he made answer on this wise:

"Forasmuch as the gods are against me and have delivered me and my brother Anacletus into your hands, needs must I grant your petition, lest in case ye should meet with a denial we lose the life which ye have the power to give or to take away as ye may choose. For nought hold I better nor dearer than life, nor is it marvel that I should be willing to ransom it at the price of any outward goods and possessions. Wherefore, albeit against my will, I will obey your orders. Some comfort, nevertheless, seem I to have in this, that I shall give my daughter unto a youth of such prowess, whom the nobility that doth now burgeon within him no less than his renown which hath been made known to us, do declare to be a scion of the house of Priam and Anchises. For who but he could have delivered the exiles of Troy, the bondsmen of so many and such mighty princes, from their chains? Who but he could have urged them to successful resistance against the nation of the Greeks? Who but he with so few would have challenged to battle so mighty a host of armed warriors and at the first onset have led away their King in fetters? But sith that a youth so noble and of so mighty prowess hath been able to withstand me, I give him my daughter Ignoge. I give him, moreover, gold and silver, ships, corn, wine, and oil, and whatsoever ye shall deem needful for your journey. And if it be that ye turn aside from your present purpose, and be minded to abide with the Greeks, I yield ye the third part of my kingdom, wherein to dwell. But if otherwise, I will fulfil my first promises in deeds, and that ye may have the fuller assurance, with you will I remain as hostage until I shall have done all things whereunto I have pledged me."

The agreement thus confirmed, envoys are directed to gather ships together from all the shores of Greece. These, when they were assembled to the number of three hundred and twenty-four, are duly presented and laden with provision of all sorts. The daughter is married to Brute, and each man, according as his rank demanded, was presented with gold and silver. All his promises exactly fulfilled, the King is set free from prison; and at the same time the Trojans depart from his dominions with a prosperous wind. But Ignoge, standing on the lofty poop of the ship, falleth swooning again and again into the arms of Brute, and with sobbing and shedding of tears lamenteth to forsake her kinsfolk and her country; nor turneth she her eyes away from the shore, so long as the shore itself is in sight. Brute, the while, soothing her with gentle words, at one time foldeth her in a sweet embrace, or at another kisseth her as sweetly, nor doth he slacken his endeavour to comfort her until, weary with weeping, she falleth at last on sleep.

After ploughing the waves for a run of thirty days, they made the coast of Africa, still not knowing in which direction to steer their ships. Then came they to the Altars of the Phileni, and the place of the Salt-pans, steering from thence betwixt Ruscicada and the mountains Azarae, where they encountered sore peril from an attack by pirates. Natheless, they won the victory, and went on their way enriched by the spoil and plunder they had taken.

(12) From thence, passing the mouth of the river Malva, they arrived in Mauritania, where lack of food and drink compelled them to disembark, and dividing themselves into companies, they harried the whole region from end to end. When they had revictualled their ships, they made sail for the Columns of Hercules, where they saw many of the monsters of the deep called Sirens, which surrounded the ships and well-nigh overwhelmed them. Howbeit, they made shift to escape, and came to the Tyrrhene sea, where they found nigh the shore four generations born of the exiles from Troy, who had borne Antenor company in his flight. Their Duke was called Corineus, a sober-minded man and excellent in counsel, mighty in body, valiance, and hardiness, insomuch as that if it were he had to deal with a giant in single combat he would straightway overthrow him as though he were wrestling with a lad. Accordingly, when they knew the ancient stock whereof he was born, they took him into their company, as well as the people whereof he was chieftain, that in after-days were called Cornishmen after the name of their Duke. He it was that in all encounters was of more help to Brute than were any of the others.

Then came they to Aquitaine, and entering into the mouth of the Loire, cast anchor there. Here they abode seven days and explored the lie of the land. Goffarius Pictus then ruled in Aquitaine, and was King of the country, who, hearing the rumour of a foreign folk that had come with a great fleet and had landed within the frontier of his dominions, sent envoys to make inquiry whether they demanded peace or war? While the legates were on their way to the fleet, they met Corineus who had just landed with two hundred men to hunt for venison in the forest. Thereupon they accost him, and ask him by whose leave he hath thus trespassed into the King's forest to slay his deer? And when Corineus made them answer, that in such a matter no leave nor license whatever could be held as needful, one of their number, Imbert by name, rushed forward, and drawing his bow, aimed an arrow at him. Corineus avoided the arrow, and ran in upon Imbert as fast as he might, and with the bow that he carried all-to-brake his head in pieces. Thereupon the rest fled, just making shift to escape his hands, and reported the death of their fellow to Goffarius. The Duke of the Poitevins, taking the matter sorely to heart, forthwith assembled a mighty host to take vengeance upon them for the death of his messenger. Brute, hearing tidings of his coming, set guards over his ships, bidding the women and children remain on board while he himself along with the whole flower of his army marched forth to meet the enemy. When the engagement at last began, the fighting was fierce on both sides, and after they had spent a great part of the day in battling, Corineus thought it shame that the Aquitanians should hold their ground so stoutly, and the Trojans not be able to press forward to the victory. So taking heart afresh, he called his own men apart to the right of the battle and, forming them in rank, made a rapid charge upon the enemy, and when, with his men in close order, he had broken the front ranks, he never stinted striking down the enemy till he had cut his way right through the battalion, and forced them all to flee.

(15)  The Trojans are on their heels, hewing them down in pursuit, nor cease they to follow them up until the victory is their own. Brute, nevertheless, albeit he were right glad at heart to have achieved so signal a triumph, was sore grieved by anxiety on one account, for he saw that, whilst his own numbers were minished daily, those of the Gauls were daily multiplied. Wherefore, seeing it was doubtful whether he could any longer hold out against them, he chose rather to retire to his ships while the greater part of his army was still whole and the glory of the victory still fresh, and to set sail in quest of the island which the divine monition had prophesied should be his own. Nor was there any tarriance. With the assent of his men, he returned to his fleet, and after loading his ships with all the treasures and luxuries he had acquired, he re-embarked, and with a prosperous wind sought out the promised island, where he landed at last in safety at Totnes.

(16)  At that time the name of the island was Albion, and of none was it inhabited save only of a few giants. Natheless the pleasant aspect of the land, with the abundance of fish in the rivers and deer in the choice forests thereof did fill Brute and his companions with no small desire that they should dwell therein. Wherefore, after exploring certain districts of the land, they drove the giants they found to take refuge in the caverns of the mountains, and divided the country among them by lot according as the Duke made grant thereof. They began to till the fields, and to build them houses in such sort that after a brief space ye might have thought it had been inhabited from time immemorial. Then, at last, Brute calleth the island Britain, and his companions Britons, after his own name, for he was minded that his memory should be perpetuated in the derivation of the name. Whence afterward the country speech, which was aforetime called Trojan or crooked Greek, was called British.

But Corineus called that share of the kingdom which had fallen unto him by lot Cornwall, after the manner of his own name, and the people Cornishmen, therein following the Duke's example. For albeit that he might have had the choice of a province before all the others that had come thither, yet was he minded rather to have that share of the land which is now called Cornwall, whether from being, as it is, the cornu or horn of Britain, or from a corruption of the said name Corineus. For nought gave him greater pleasure than to wrestle with the giants, of whom was greater plenty there than in any of the provinces that had been shared amongst his comrades.

Among others was a certain hateful one by name Goemagot, twelve cubits in height, who was of such lustihood that when he had once uprooted it, he would wield an oak tree as lightly as it were a wand of hazel. On a certain day when Brute was holding high festival to the gods in the port whereat he had first landed, this one, along with a score of other giants, fell upon him and did passing cruel slaughter on the British. Howbeit, at the last, the Britons, collecting together from all quarters, prevailed against them and slew them all, save Goemagot only. Him Brute had commanded to be kept alive, as he was minded to see a wrestling bout betwixt him and Corineus, who was beyond measure keen to match himself against such monsters. So Corineus, overjoyed at the prospect, girt himself for the encounter, and flinging away his arms, challenged him to a bout at wrestling. At the start, on the one side stands Corineus, on the other the giant, each hugging the other tight in the shackles of their arms, both making the very air quake with their breathless gasping. It was not long before Goemagot, grasping Corineus with all his force, brake him three of his ribs, two on the right side and one on the left. Roused thereby to fury, Corineus gathered up all his strength, heaved him up on his shoulders and ran with his burden as fast as he could for the weight to the seashore nighest at hand. Mounting up to the top of a high cliff and disengaging himself, he hurled the deadly monster he had carried on his shoulder into the sea, where, falling on the sharp rocks, he was mangled all to pieces and dyed the waves with the blood, so that ever thereafter that place from the flinging down of the giant hath been known as Lamgoemagot, to wit, "Goemagot's Leap," and is called by that name unto this present day.

(17) After that he had seen his kingdom, Brute was minded to build him a chief city, and following out his intention, he went round the whole circuit of the land in search of a fitting site. When he came to the river Thames, he walked along the banks till he found the very spot best fitted to his purpose. He therefore founded his city there and called it New Troy, and by this name was it known for many ages thereafter, until at last, by corruption of the word, it came to be called Trinovantum. But afterward, Lud, the brother of Cassibelaunus, who fought with Julius Caesar, possessed him of the helm of the kingdom and surrounded the city with right noble walls as well as with towers builded with marvellous art, commanding that it should be called Kaerlud, that is, the City of Lud, after his own name. Whence afterward a contention arose betwixt him and his brother Nennius, who took it ill that he should be minded to do away the name of Troy in his own country. But since Gildas, the historian, hath treated of his contention at sufficient length, I have chosen the rather to pass it over, lest that which so great a writer hath already set forth in so eloquent a style, I should only seem to besmirch in mine own homelier manner of speech.

(18) Accordingly, when the aforesaid Duke founded the said city, he granted it as of right unto the citizens that should dwell therein, and gave them a law under which they should be peacefully entreated. At that time Eli the priest reigned in Judaea, and the Ark of the Covenant was taken by the Philistines. The sons of Hector reigned in Troy, having driven out the descendants of

Antenor. In Italy reigned Sylvius Aeneas, the son of Aeneas and uncle of Brute, he being the third of the Latin kings.

(II, 1)  Now Ignoge, the wife of Brute, bare unto him three sons of high renown, whose names were Locrine, Albanact and Camber. When their father departed this life in the twenty-fourth year after his arrival, they buried him within the city that he had builded, and divided the realm of Britain amongst themselves, each succeeding him in his share therein. Locrine, that was eldest born, had the midland part of the island, which in later days was called Loegria, after his name. Next, Camber had that part which lieth beyond the river Severn and is now called Wales, which afterward was for a long time called Cambria, after his name; whence unto this day do the folk of the country call them Cymry in the British tongue. But Albanact, the youngest, had the country which in these days in our tongue is called Scotland, and gave it the name of Albany, after his own. And after that these had of a long time reigned in peace and concord, Humber, the King of the Huns, landed in Albany, and engaging in battle with Albanact, slew him, and compelled the country folk to flee unto Locrine.

(2)  Locrine, accordingly, when he heard the rumour, besought his brother Camber to accompany him, called out the whole youth of the country, and went to meet the King of the Huns in the neighbourhood of the river Humber. When the armies met, he compelled Humber to flee, but when he had fled as far as the river, it chanced that he was drowned therein, and thus left his name to the stream. Locrine, therefore, after he had won the victory, distributed the spoil among his comrades, keeping nothing for himself save the gold and silver that he found in the enemy's ships. He also kept for himself three damsels of marvellous beauty, whereof one was the daughter of a certain King of Germany, whom the foresaid Humber had seized along with the two other damsels when he laid waste her father's country. Her name was Estrildis, and so fair was she that scarce might any be found to compare with her for beauty, for no polished ivory, nor newly-fallen snow, nor no lilies could surpass the whiteness of her flesh. Taken with love of her, Locrine would fain that she should share his bed, and that the marriage-torch should be lighted to celebrate their wedding. But when Corineus found out what he was minded to do he was wroth beyond measure, for that Locrine had pledged himself to marry Corineus' own daughter.

(3)  He came accordingly unto the King and, brandishing his battle-axe in his right hand, spake unto him on this wise: "Be these the wages, Locrine, that thou wouldst pay me for the wounds I have suffered in thy father's service when he was warring against unknown peoples, that you disdain my daughter and stoop to yoke you with a barbarian woman? If this indeed be so, thou dost it on peril of my vengeance, so long as any strength is left in this right hand, which hath quenched the delight of life in so many giants on the Tyrrhene shores." Shouting these words aloud again and yet again, he brandished the axe as if about to strike him, when the

friends of both flung themselves betwixt. And after that Corineus were somewhat appeased, they compelled Locrine to perform that which he had pledged him to do.

(4) Locrine accordingly married Corineus' daughter, Gwendolen by name; yet, natheless did he not forget the love he bare unto Estrildis. Wherefore, in the city of Trinovant, did he make fashion a chamber underground wherein he enclosed her, and caused her be right honourably served of the attendants of his household, for that he was minded to keep his love of her secret. For he was sore troubled by reason of his dread of Corineus, so that he durst not hold her openly, but, as hath been said already, kept her in hiding, and seven whole years did haunt her in secret, so that none knew thereof save only they that were the closest of his familiars. For, so often as he was minded to go unto her, he would feign that he made hidden sacrifice unto his gods, whereby he did lightly move others to believe the same, albeit in truth it were no such thing. In the meantime, Estrildis did become great with child, and brought forth a daughter of marvellous beauty, whom she called Sabrina. Gwendolen also became pregnant and bare a son, unto whom was given the name of Madden. This son was delivered into the charge of his grandfather Corineus, and had of him his teachings and nurture.

(5) Years later, after Corineus was dead, Locrine deserted Gwendolen and raised Estrildis to be Queen. Gwendolen thereupon, being beyond measure indignant, went into Cornwall and, gathering together all the youth of that kingdom, began to harass Locrine by leading forays into his land. At last, after both had mustered their armies, a battle was fought on the river Stour, and Locrine, smitten by an arrow, lost his life and all the joys thereof. Whereupon Gwendolen laid hold on the helm of state, maddened by the same revengeful fury as her father, insomuch as that she bade Estrildis and Sabrina her daughter be flung into the river that is now called Severn, issuing an edict throughout all Britain that the river should be called by the damsel's name. For she was minded that it should bear her name for ever, for that it was her own husband that begat her; whereby it cometh to pass that even unto this day the river in the British tongue is called Sabren, which by corruption in other speech is called Severn. . . .

(11) When Bladud was thus given over to the destinies, his son Lear was next raised to the kingdom, and ruled the country after manly fashion for three-score years. He it was that builded the city on the river Soar, that in the British is called Kaerleir, but in the Saxon, Leicester. Male issue was denied unto him, his only children being three daughters named Goneril, Regan, and Cordelia, whom all he did love with marvellous affection, but most of all the youngest born, to wit, Cordelia. And when that he began to be upon the verge of eld, he thought to divide his kingdom amongst them, and to marry them unto such husbands as were worthy to have them along with their share of the kingdom. But that he might know which of them was most worthy of the largest share, he went unto them to

make inquiry of each as to which of them did most love himself. When, accordingly, he asked of Goneril how much she loved him, she first called all the gods of heaven to witness that her father was dearer to her heart than the very soul that dwelt within her body. Unto whom saith her father: "For this, that thou hast set mine old age before thine own life, thee, my dearest daughter, will I marry unto whatsoever youth shall be thy choice, together with the third part of Britain." Next, Regan, that was second, fain to take ensample of her sister and to wheedle her father into doing her an equal kindness, made answer with a solemn oath that she could no otherwise express her thought than by saying that she loved him better than all the world beside. The credulous father thereupon promised to marry her with the same dignity as her elder sister, with another third part of the kingdom for her share. But the last, Cordelia, when she saw how her father had been cajoled by the flatteries of her sisters who had already spoken and desiring to make trial of him otherwise, went on to make answer unto him thus: "Father mine, is there a daughter anywhere that presumeth to love her father more than a father? None such, I trow, there is that durst confess as much, save she were trying to hide the truth in words of jest. For myself, I have ever loved thee as a father, nor never from that love will I be turned aside. Albeit that thou art bent on wringing more from me, yet hearken to the true measure of my love. Ask of me no more, but let this be mine answer: So much as thou hast, so much art thou worth, and so much do I love thee." Thereupon forthwith, her father, thinking that she had thus spoken out of the abundance of her heart, waxed mightily indignant, nor did he tarry to make known what his answer would be. "For that thou hast so despised thy father's old age that thou hast disdained to love me even as well as these thy sisters love me, I also will disdain thee, nor never in my realm shalt thou have share with thy sisters. Howbeit, sith that thou art my daughter, I say not but that I will marry thee upon terms of some kind unto some stranger that is of other land than mine, if so be that fortune shall offer such an one; only be sure of this, that never will I trouble me to marry thee with such honour as thy sisters, inasmuch as, whereas up to this time I have loved thee better than the others, it now seemeth that thou lovest me less than they."

Straightway thereupon, by counsel of the nobles of the realm, he giveth the twain sisters unto two Dukes, of Cornwall, to wit, and Albany, together with one moiety only of the island so long as he should live, but after his death he willed that they should have the whole of the kingdom of Britain. Now it so fell out about this time that Aganippus, King of the Franks, hearing report of Cordelia's beauty, forthwith despatched his envoys to the King, beseeching him that Cordelia might be entrusted to their charge as his bride whom he would marry with due rite of the wedding-torch. But her father, still persisting in his wrath, made answer that right willingly would he give her, but that needs must it be without land or fee, seeing that he had shared his kingdom along with all his gold and silver betwixt Cordelia's sisters Goneril and Regan. When this word was brought unto Aganippus, for that he was on fire with love of the damsel, he sent again unto King Lear saying that enow had he of gold and silver and other possessions, for that one-third part of Gaul was his, and that he was fain to marry the damsel only that he might have sons by her to inherit his land. So at last the bargain was struck, and Cordelia was sent to Gaul to be married unto Aganippus.

(12) Some long time after, when Lear began to wax more sluggish by reason of age, the foresaid Dukes, with whom and his two daughters he had divided Britain, rebelled against him and took away from him the realm and the kingly power which up to that time he had held right manfully and gloriously. Howbeit, concord was restored, and one of his sons-in-law, Maglaunus, Duke of Albany, agreed to maintain him with three-score knights, so that he should not be without some semblance of state. But after that he had sojourned with his son-in-law two years, his daughter Goneril began to wax indignant at the number of his knights, who flung gibes at her servants for that their rations were not more plentiful. Whereupon, after speaking to her husband, she ordered her father to be content with a service of thirty knights and to dismiss the other thirty that he had. The King, taking this in dudgeon, left Maglaunus, and betook him to Henvin, Duke of Cornwall, unto whom he had married his other daughter. Here, at first, he was received with honour, but a year had not passed before discord again arose betwixt those of the King's household and those of the Duke's, insomuch as that Regan, waxing indignant, ordered her father to dismiss all his company save five knights only to do him service. Her father, beyond measure aggrieved thereat, returned once more to his eldest daughter, thinking to move her to pity and to persuade her to maintain himself and his retinue. Howbeit, she had never renounced her first indignation, but swore by all the gods of Heaven that never should he take up his abode with her save he contented himself with the service of a single knight and were quit of all the rest. Moreover, she upbraided the old man for that, having nothing of his own to give away, he should be minded to go about with such a retinue; so that finding she would not give way to his wishes one single tittle, he at last obeyed and remained content with one knight only, leaving the rest to go their way. But when the remembrance of his former dignity came back unto him, bearing witness to the misery of the estate to which he was now reduced, he began to bethink him of going to his youngest daughter oversea. Howbeit, he sore misdoubted that she would do nought for him, seeing that he had held her, as I have said, in such scanty honour in the matter of her marriage. Natheless, disdaining any longer to endure so mean a life, he betook him across the Channel into Gaul. But when he found that two other princes were making the passage at the same time, and that he himself had been assigned but the third place, he brake forth into tears and sobbing, and cried aloud: "Ye destinies that do pursue your wonted way marked out by irrevocable decree, wherefore was it your will ever to uplift me to happiness so

fleeting?   For a keener grief it is to call to mind that lost happiness
than to suffer the presence of the unhappiness that cometh after.   For
the memory of the days when in the midst of hundreds of thousands
of warriors I went to batter down the walls of cities and to lay waste
the provinces of mine enemies is more grievous unto me than the
calamity that hath overtaken me in the meanness of mine estate, which
hath incited them that but now were grovelling under my feet to
desert my feebleness.   O angry fortune! will the day ever come
wherein I may requite the evil turn that hath thus driven forth the
length of my days and my poverty?   O Cordelia, my daughter, how
true were the words wherein thou didst make answer unto me, when
I did ask of thee how much thou didst love me!   For thou saidst,
'So much as thou hast, so much art thou worth, and so much do I love
thee.'   So long, therefore, as I had that which was mine own to give,
so long seemed I of worth unto them that were the lovers, not of myself but of my gifts.   They loved me at times, but better loved they
the presents I made unto them.   Now that the presents are no longer
forthcoming, they too have gone their ways.   But with what face, O
thou dearest of my children, shall I dare appear before thee?   I who,
wroth with thee for these thy words, was minded to marry thee less
honourably than thy sisters, who, after all the kindnesses I have
conferred upon them, have allowed me to become an outcast and
a beggar?"

Landing at last, his mind filled with these reflections and others
of a like kind, he came to Karitia, where his daughter lived, and
waiting without the city, sent a messenger to tell her into what
indigence he had fallen, and to beseech his daughter's compassion
inasmuch as he had neither food nor clothing.   On hearing the
tidings, Cordelia was much moved and wept bitterly.   When she
made inquiry how many armed men he had with him, the messengers told her that he had none save a single knight, who was
waiting with him without the city.   Then took she as much gold and
silver as was needful and gave it unto the messenger, bidding him
take her father to another city, where he should bathe him, clothe
him, and nurse him, feigning that he was a sick man.   She commanded also that he should have a retinue of forty knights well
appointed and armed, and that then he should duly announce his
arrival to Aganippus and herself.   The messenger accordingly forthwith attended King Lear into another city, and hid him there in
secret until that he had fully accomplished all that Cordelia had
borne him on hand to do.

(13)   As soon, therefore, as he was meetly arrayed in kingly
apparel and invested with the ensigns of royalty and a train of retainers, he sent word unto Aganippus and his daughter that he
had been driven out of the realm of Britain by his sons-in-law, and
had come unto them in order that by their assistance he might be
able to recover his kingdom.   They accordingly, with the great
counsellors and nobles, came forth to receive him with all honour,

and placed in his hands the power over the whole of Gaul until such time as they had restored him unto his former dignity.

(14)   In the meanwhile, Aganippus sent envoys throughout the whole of Gaul to summon every knight bearing arms therein to spare no pains in coming to help him to recover the kingdom of Britain for his father-in-law, King Lear.   When they had all made them ready, Lear led the assembled host together with Aganippus and his daughter into Britain, fought a battle with his sons-in-law, and won the victory, again bringing them all under his own dominion.   In the third year thereafter he died, and Aganippus died also, and Cordelia, now mistress of the helm of state in Britain, buried her father in a certain underground chamber which she had bidden be made under the river Soar at Leicester.   This underground chamber was founded in honour of the two-faced Janus, and there, when the yearly celebration of the day came round, did all the workmen of the city set hand unto such work as they were about to be busied upon throughout the year.

(16)   Afterwards succeeded Gorbodug.   Unto him were two sons born, whereof the one was called Ferrex and the other Porrex. But when their father began to verge upon eld, a contention arose betwixt the twain as to which should succeed him in the kingdom. Howbeit, Porrex, spurred on thereunto by a more grasping covetise, layeth snares for his brother with design of slaying him, whereupon Ferrex, when the matter was discovered unto him, betook him across the Channel into Gaul, and, having obtained the help of Suard, King of the Franks, returned and fought against his brother.   In this battle betwixt them, Ferrex was slain together with the entire host that accompanied him.   Thereupon their mother, who was named Widen, when she learnt the certainty of her son's death, was beyond measure troubled, and conceived a bitter hatred of the other, for she loved the one that was slain the better of the twain, and so hotly did her wrath blaze up by reason of his death, that she was minded to revenge it upon his brother.   She accordingly took possession of the tent wherein he was lying fast asleep, and setting upon him with her waiting-women hacked him all into little pieces.   Thenceforward the people was sore afflicted by civil war for a long space, and the kingdom was governed by five kings who harried the one another with mutual forays wherein was much blood spilt.

(IV, 1)   In the meantime it so fell out, as may be found in the Roman histories, that after he had conquered Gaul, Julius Caesar came to the coast of the Ruteni.   And when he had espied from thence the island of Britain, he asked of them that stood around what land it might be and who were they that dwelt therein?   Whilst that he was still looking out to seaward after he had learnt the name of the kingdom and of the people, "By Hercules," saith he, "we Romans and these Britons be of one ancestry, for we also do come of Trojan stock.   For after the destruction of Troy, Æneas was first father unto us, as unto them was Brute, whom Silvius, son of

Ascanius, son of Æneas, did beget. But, and if I mistake not, they be sore degenerate from us, and know not what warfare meaneth, seeing that they lie thus sundered from the world in the outer ocean. Lightly may they be compelled to give us tribute, and to offer perpetual obedience unto the dignity of Rome. Natheless, first of all let us send them word, bidding them pay us toll and tallage unvisited and untouched of the Roman people, and, like the rest of the nations, do homage to the Senate, lest haply, by shedding the blood of these our kinsmen, we should offend the ancient nobility of Priam, father of us all." Having sent this message in a letter to King Cassibelaunus, Cassibelaunus waxed indignant and sent him back an epistle in these words.

(2) "Cassibelaunus, King of the Britons, to Caius Julius Caesar: Marvellous, Caesar, is the covetousness of the Roman people, the which, insatiable of aught that is of gold or silver, cannot even let us alone that have our abode beyond the world and in peril of the ocean, but must needs presume to make a snatch at our revenues, which up to this time we have possessed in quiet. Nor is even this enow for them, save we also cast away our freedom for the sake of becoming subject unto them and enduring a perpetual bondage. An insult unto thyself, Caesar, is this which thou dost ask of us, seeing that the same noble blood that flowed in the veins of Æneas beateth in the heart of Briton and of Roman alike, and that those very same glorious links that unite us in a common kindred ought also no less closely to bind us in firm and abiding friendship. That friendship it was that thou shouldst have asked of us, not slavery. We know how to bestow our friendship freely; we know not how to bear the yoke of bondage. For such freedom have we been wont to enjoy, that bowing the neck unto slavery is a thing wholly unknown amongst us. Yea, should even the gods themselves think to snatch it from us, we would withstand them to the last gasp, and it should go hard but that we would hold to it in their despite. Be it therefore clearly understood, Caesar, that in case, as thou hast threatened, thou dost emprise the conquest of this island of Britain, thou shalt find us ready to fight both for our freedom and for our country."

(3) When he readeth this letter, Caius Julius Caesar fitteth out his fleet and only waiteth for a fair wind to adventure on the enterprise of carrying into effect the message he had sent to Cassibelaunus. As soon as the wished-for wind began to blow, he hoisted sail and came with a fair course into the mouth of the Thames with his army. They had already landed from the boats, when lo, Cassibelaunus with all his strength cometh to meet him. On reaching the town of Dorobellum he there held counsel with his barons how best to keep the enemy at a distance.

There were with him Belinus, his Commander-in-Chief of the army, by whose counsel the whole kingdom was governed; his two nephews, Androgeus to wit, Duke of Trinovantum, and Tenuantius, Duke of Cornwall. There were, moreover, three kings that were his vassals, Cridious King of Albany, Guerthaeth of Venedotia, and Britael of Demetia, who, as they had encouraged the rest to fight, and all were eager for the fray, gave counsel that they should forthwith march upon Caesar's camp, and before that he had taken any fortress or city, dash in upon him and drive him out, for that, so he once were within any of the garrisoned places of the country, it would be all the harder to dislodge him, as he would then know whither he and his men might repair for safety.

All having signified their assent, they accordingly marched to the coast where Julius had set up his camp and his tents, and there, both armies in battle-array, engage in combat hand-to-hand with the enemy, spear-thrust against spear-thrust and sword-stroke against sword-stroke. Forthwith on this side and on that the wounded fell smitten through the vitals, and the ground is flooded with the gore of the dying, as when a sudden south-wester drives back an ebbing tide. And in the thick of the melly, it so chanced that Nennius and Androgeus, who commanded the men of Kent and the citizens of Trinovantum, fell upon the bodyguard of the Emperor himself. When they came together, the Emperor's company was well-nigh scattered by the close ranks of the British assailants, and whilst they were confusedly battling together, blow on blow, good luck gave Nennius a chance of encountering Julius himself. Nennius accordingly ran in upon him, glad beyond measure that it should lie in his power to strike even one blow at a man so great. Caesar, when he saw him making a rush at him, received him on the shield he held before him, and smote him on the helmet with his naked sword as hard as his strength would allow. Then, lifting the sword again, he was fain to follow up the first by a second blow that should deal a deadly wound, but, Nennius, seeing his intention, lifted his shield between, and Caesar's blade, glancing off his helmet, stuck fast in the shield with so passing great force that when they could no longer maintain the combat for the press of the troops rushing in upon them, the Emperor had not strength to wrench it forth. Howbeit, Nennius, when he had laid hold on Caesar's sword on this wise, hurled away his own that he held and, tugging forth the other, falleth swiftly on the enemy. Whomsoever he smote therewith, he either smote off his head or wounded him so sore at the passing, as that no hope was there of his living thereafter. At last, whilst he was thus playing havoc with the enemy, Labienus the tribune came against him, but was slain by Nennius at the first onset. At last, when the day was far spent, the Britons pressed forward in close rank, and charging on undaunted time after time, by God's grace won the day, and Caesar with his wounded Romans retreated to the beach betwixt the camp and the ships. During the night he got together all that were left of his troops and betook him to his ships, glad enough to make the deep sea his camp of refuge. And when his comrades dissuaded him from continuing the campaign, he was content to abide by their counsel, and returned unto Gaul.

(4) Cassibelaunus, rejoicing in the victory he had achieved, gave thanks unto God, and calling together his comrades in success, bestowed exceeding abundant largesse upon each according to the merits of his prowess. On the other hand, his heart was wrung with sore grief for that his brother Nennius had been hurt mortally and was then lying in jeopardy of death. For Julius, in the combat aforesaid, had stricken him a wound beyond help of leechcraft, and within the fortnight after the battle he departed the light of this world by an untimely death, and was buried in the city of Trino-vantum nigh the north gate. At his funeral were kingly honours paid unto him, and they set by his side, in his coffin, the sword of Caesar that had stuck in his shield in the fight. And the name of that sword was Saffron Death, for that no man smitten thereby might escape on live.

(5) When Julius thus turned his back to the enemy and landed on the shores of Gaul, the Gauls made great effort to rebel and to cast off the dominion of Julius. For they made count that he had been so enfeebled as that they need no longer dread his power. For amongst them all was there but one same story, that the whole sea was seething over with the ships of Cassibelaunus, ready to pursue the flight of Julius himself. Whence the bolder spirits amongst the Gauls busied them in taking thought how best to drive him beyond their frontiers, which Julius getting wind of, he had no mind to take in hand a doubtful war against so fierce a people, but chose rather to open his treasuries and wait upon certain of the chief nobles, so as to bring back the receivers of his bounty to their allegiance. Unto the common folk he promiseth freedom; unto the disinherited the restoration of their losses, and even to the bondsman liberty. Thus he that aforetime had stripped them of all they possessed and roared at them with the fierceness of a lion, hath now become a gentle lamb, and humbly bleateth out what a pleasure it is unto him to be able to restore them everything; nor doth he stint his wheedling until such time as he hath recovered the power he had lost. In the meanwhile not a day passed but he chewed the cud over his flight and the victory of the Britons.

(6) After a space of two years he again maketh ready to cross the ocean-channel and revenge him upon Cassibelaunus, who on his part, as soon as he knew it, garrisoned his cities everywhere, repaired their ruined walls and stationed armed soldiers at all the ports. In the bed of the river Thames, moreover, whereby Caesar would have to sail unto the city of Trinovantum, he planted great stakes as thick as a man's thigh and shod with iron and lead below the level of the stream so as to crash into the bows of any of Caesar's ships that might come against them. Assembling, moreover, all the youth of the island, he constructed cantonments along the coast and waited for the enemy's arrival.

(7) Julius, meanwhile, after providing everything necessary for his expedition, embarked with a countless multitude of warriors on board, eager to wreak havoc upon the people who had defeated him,

and wreaked, no doubt, it would have been, so only he could have reached dry land without damage to his fleet — a feat, howbeit, that he failed to achieve. For whilst that he was making way up Thames towards the foresaid city, his ships ran upon the fixed stakes and suffered sore and sudden jeopardy. For by this disaster not only were his soldiers drowned to the number of many thousands, but his battered ships sank foundered by the inrush of the river. When Caesar found how matters were going, he made all haste to back sail and, setting all hands to work, to run inshore. They, moreover, who had made shift to escape the first peril by the skin of their teeth crawled up with him unto dry land.

Cassibelaunus, who stood on the bank all the time looking on, was glad enough of the peril of them that were drowned, but had little joy over the safety of the rest. He gave the signal to his fellow-soldiers, and charged down upon the Romans. But the Romans, albeit they had suffered this jeopardy in the river, so soon as they stood on dry land, withstood the charge of the Britons like men, and having hardihood for their wall of defence, made no small slaughter of their enemies, albeit that the slaughter they suffered was more grievous than that they inflicted, for the disaster at the river had sore thinned their companies, while the ranks of the Britons, multiplied every hour by fresh reinforcements, outnumbered them by three to one. No marvel, therefore, that the stronger triumphed over the weaker. Wherefore when Caesar saw that he was thoroughly routed, he fled with his minished numbers to his ships, and reached the shelter of the sea exactly as he wished, for a timely wind blew fair, and hoisting sail he made the coast of the Morini in safety. He then threw himself into a certain tower he had constructed at a place called Odnea before he went this time to Britain, for his mind misgave him as to the loyalty of the Gauls, and he feared they might rise against him a second time, as they did when, as the poet says, he first, "showed his back to the Britons." It was in view of this likelihood that he had builded this tower as a place of refuge, so that in case the people should raise an insurrection he might be able to withstand any rebellion.

(8) Cassibelaunus, after winning this second victory, was mightily elated, and issued an edict that all the barons of Britain and their wives should assemble in the city of Trinovantum to celebrate the solemnities due unto their country gods who had granted them the victory over so mighty an Emperor. They accordingly all came without tarrying and made sacrifice of divers kinds, and profuse slaying of cattle. Forty thousand kine did they offer, a hundred thousand sheep, and of all manner fowl a number not lightly to be reckoned, besides thirty thousand in all of every sort of forest deer. And when they had paid all due honour unto the gods, they feasted them on the remainder as was the wont on occasion of solemn sacrifices; and the day and the night they spent in playing games of divers kinds.

Now, while the sports were going on, it fell out that two noble youths whereof the one was nephew of the King and the other of Duke Androgeus, had tried conclusions man to man in a wrestling bout, and fell out as to which had had the upper hand. The name of the King's nephew was Hireglas, and of the other Evelin. And after many insults had been bandied about betwixt them, Evelin snatched up a sword and smote off the King's nephew's head, whereupon was a mighty ferment in the court, and the news of the murder forthwith flying abroad soon reached Cassibelaunus. Grievously troubled at his kinsman's fate, Cassibelaunus commanded Androgeus to bring his nephew into court before him, and that when so brought he should be ready to undergo such sentence as the barons might pronounce, so that Hireglas should not remain unavenged in case they should find that he had been unjustly slain. Howbeit, for that Androgeus had a suspicion as to the King's mind in the matter, he made answer that he himself had his own court, and that whatsoever claim any might have as against any of his men ought to be heard and decided therein. If, therefore, Cassibelaunus were resolved to have the law of Evelin, he ought by custom immemorial to have sought it in Androgeus's own court in the city of Trinovantum. Cassibelaunus, thereupon, finding that he could not obtain the satisfaction he meant to have taken, threatened Androgeus with a solemn oath that he would waste his duchy with sword and fire, save he agreed to allow his claim. Howbeit, Androgeus, waxing wroth, withheld obedience to his demand, and Cassibelaunus waxing wroth no less, made haste to ravage his dominions. Natheless, Androgeus, through his friends and kinsfolk about the court, besought the King to lay aside his wrath, but finding that he could in no wise allay his fury, began to take thought whether he might not make shift to devise some other means of withstanding him. At last, despairing utterly of compassing his purpose otherwise, he resolved to call in Caesar to his succour, and sent his letters unto him conceived in these words:

"To Caius Julius Caesar, Androgeus, Duke of Trinovantum, after aforetime wishing him death, now wisheth health. I do repent me of that I wrought against thee when thou didst battle with my King, for, had I eschewed such enterprise, thou wouldst have conquered Cassibelaunus, upon whom hath crept such pride of his triumph as that he is now bent on driving me beyond his frontiers — me, through whom he did achieve the triumph. This is the reward that he holdeth due unto my merits. I have saved him his inheritance, he now seeketh to disinherit me. I have restored him a second time his kingdom, he now desireth to reave me of mine own kingdom. For in fighting against thee all these benefits have I bestowed upon him. I call the gods of heaven to witness that never have I deserved his wrath, save I can be said to deserve it for refusing to deliver up unto him my nephew whom he doth earnestly desire to condemn to an unjust death . . . For which reason, praying thy mercy, I do beseech thy help that I may be restored, and by my means thou shalt be master of all Britain. In me hast thou no cause for misgiving, for here is no treason. The motives of men are swayed by events, and it may well be that some may become friends that have aforetime been at strife, and some there be that after flight may yet achieve the victory."

(9) When he had read this letter, Julius Caesar took counsel with his familiars and was advised by them not to go to Britain simply upon the Duke's verbal invitation, but to demand hostages in addition enough to ensure his good faith before starting on the expedition. Androgeus accordingly forthwith sent his son Scaeva along with thirty noble youths that were nigh kinsfolk of his own. When the hostages were delivered, Caesar was reassured, and recalling his troops, sailed with a stern wind to the haven of Rutupi. Cassibelaunus in the meanwhile had begun to besiege the city of Trinovantum and to sack the manor houses in the country round. Howbeit, as soon as he heard that Julius had landed, he raised the siege and hurried away to meet the Emperor. And, as he was marching into a valley near Dorobernia, he caught sight of the Roman army pitching their camp and the tents therein, for Androgeus had led them thither so as to fall upon them there by ambuscade. In a moment, the Romans, understanding that the Britons were upon them, armed them as swiftly as they might, and stationed their men in companies. On the other side, the Britons don their arms and advance together in squadrons. Howbeit, Androgeus with five thousand men in arms lay concealed in the forest nigh at hand ready to run to Caesar's assistance and make a stealthy and sudden onslaught upon Cassibelaunus and his comrades. As they came together in this order on the one side and the other, never a moment did they slack of flinging javelins that carried death into the enemies' ranks, and dealing wounds as deadly with blow on blow of their swords. The squadrons clash together, and mighty is the shedding of blood. On both sides the wounded drop like leaves of the trees in autumn. And while the battle is at the hottest, forth issueth Androgeus from the forest and falleth on the rear of Cassibelaunus's main army, whereupon depended the fate of the battle. Presently, his vanguard already in part cut down and disordered by the onset of the Romans, and his rear thus harassed by their own fellow-countrymen, he could stand his ground no longer; and his broken and scattered forces flee routed from the field. By the side of the valley rose a rocky hill with a thick hazel wood at the top, whereunto Cassibelaunus with his men fled for cover when they found themselves defeated on the level, and taking their stand in the wood, defended them like men and slew a number of the enemy that pursued them. For the Romans and the men of Androgeus were hard after them, cutting up the squadrons in their flight, and skirmishing heavily with them on the hillside without being able to force their way to the top. For the rocks on the hill and the steepness of the ridge afforded such good cover to the British that they could make sallies from the heights and still carry slaughter among the enemy. Caesar, therefore, beleaguered the hill all that night, for it was dark already,

and cut off every means of retreat, thinking to wring from the King by hunger what he could not force from him by arms.

O, but in those days was the British race worthy of all admiration, which had twice driven in flight before them him who had subjected the whole world beside unto himself, and even in defeat now withstood him whom no nation of the earth had been able to withstand, ready to die for their country and their freedom! To their praise it was that Lucan sang how Caesar

"Scared when he found the Britons that he sought for,
    Only displayed his craven back before them."

At the end of the second day, Cassibelaunus, who had all this time had nought to eat, began to fear that he must yield him captive to hunger and submit him to the prison of Caesar. He sent word accordingly to Androgeus to make peace for him with Julius, lest the dignity of the race whereof he was born should suffer by his being led into captivity. He sent word also that he had not deserved he should desire his death, albeit that he had harassed his country. And when the messengers had told him their errand, saith Androgeus:

"Not to be beloved is the prince that in war is gentle as a lamb, but in peace fierce as a lion. Gods of heaven and earth! My lord beseecheth me now that aforetime did command me: Doth he now desire to make peace with Caesar and to do him homage, of whom Caesar did first desire peace? Forsooth he might have known that he who drove an Emperor so mighty out of his kingdom could also bring him back. Why am I to be treated unfairly who could render my services either to him or to another? Led blindfolded of his own folly is he that doth exasperate with injuries and insults the fellow-soldiers unto whom he oweth his victories. For no victory is won by the commander alone, but by them that shed their blood for him in the battle. Natheless will I make his peace with him if I may, for the injury that he hath done me is enough revenged in this that he hath prayed my mercy."

(10) Thereupon Androgeus went straightway to Julius, and clasping his knees, spake unto him on this wise:

"Behold, already hast thou enough revenged thee upon Cassibelaunus. Have mercy now upon him! Naught more remaineth for him to do save only that he render homage unto thee and pay due tribute unto the dignity of Rome." And when Caesar answered him never a word, Androgeus spake again:

"This thing only, Caesar, have I promised unto thee, and nought more than this, that I would do mine utmost to make Cassibelaunus acknowledge him thy man and to subdue Britain unto thy sovereignty. Lo, now, Cassibelaunus is vanquished and Britain subdued unto thee by mine assistance. What more owe I unto thee? Maybe He that did create all things forbid that I should suffer lord of mine that prayeth me of mercy and hath done me right as touching the wrong he had done unto me, to be thrust into prison or chained in fetters. No light thing is it to slay Cassibelaunus while I am on live, nor shall I blush to render him all service that I may, save thou hearken unto my counsel."

Julius thereupon, his eagerness somewhat slackened by fear of Androgeus, accepted the allegiance of Cassibelaunus on condition of his paying tribute, the amount of the tribute he pledged himself to pay being three thousand pounds of silver. Thenceforward Julius and Cassibelaunus made friends together, and bestowed gifts of courtesy the one upon the other. Afterwards Caesar wintered in Britain, and with the return of spring crossed the Channel into Gaul. Some time later, after collecting an army of men of all nations, he marched to Rome against Pompey. . . .

(19) Lucius, being minded that his ending should surpass his beginning, he despatched his letters unto Pope Eleutherius beseeching that from him he might receive Christianity. For the miracles that were wrought by the young recruits of Christ's army in divers lands had lifted all clouds from his mind, and panting with love of the true faith, his pious petition was allowed to take effect, forasmuch as the blessed Pontiff, finding that his devotion was such, sent unto him two most religious doctors, Pagan and Duvian, who, preaching unto him the Incarnation of the Word of God, did wash him in holy baptism and converted him unto Christ. Straightway the peoples of all the nations around came running together to follow the King's example, and cleansed in the same holy laver, were made partakers of the kingdom of Heaven. The blessed doctors, therefore, when they had purged away the paganism of well-nigh the whole island, dedicated the temples that had been founded in honour of very many gods unto the One God and unto His saints, and filled them with divers companies of ordained religious. There were then in Britain eight-and-twenty flamens as well as three archflamens, unto whose power the other judges of public morals and officials of the temple were subject. These also, by precept of the Pope, did they snatch away from idolatry; and where there were flamens there did they set bishops, and archbishops where there were archflamens. The seats of the archflamens were in the three noblest cities, in London, to wit, and in York and in Caerleon, whereof the ancient walls and building still remaining on the Usk, in Glamorgan, do bear witness to the former dignity thereof. From these three was superstition purged away, and the eight-and-twenty bishops, with their several dioceses, were subordinated unto them. . . .

(V, 9) At last, worn out with eld, and desirous of making provision for his people at his death, Octavius inquired of his counsellors which of his family they would most gladly raise to be king after that he himself were departed. For he had but one single daughter, and was without heir male unto whom he might hand down the rule of the country. Some, accordingly, proposed that he should give his daughter to wife along with the kingdom unto some Roman noble, so as that thereby they should enjoy the firmer peace. But others gave their voice that Conan Meriadoc, his nephew, should be declared heir to the throne of the kingdom, and that his daughter should be given in marriage with dowry of gold and silver unto the prince of some other kingdom. Whilst that they were debating these matters amongst themselves, in came Caradoc, Duke of Cornwall, and gave it as his counsel that they should invite Maximian the Senator and give him the King's daughter and the kingdom, that so they might enjoy perpetual peace. For his father was a Welsh Briton, he being the son of Leoline. By his mother and by birth, howbeit, he was Roman, and by blood was he of royal pedigree on both sides. Caradoc held therefore that this marriage did promise an abiding peace, for that he knew Maximian, being at once of the family of the Emperors and also by origin a Briton, would have good right to the kingdom of Britain. But when the Duke of Cornwall had thus delivered his counsel, Conan, the King's nephew, waxed indignant, for his one endeavour was to make a snatch at the kingdom for himself, and aiming at this end only, stuck not to run counter to the whole court beside. But Caradoc, being in nowise minded to change his purpose, sent his son Maurice to Rome to sound Maximian on the matter. Maurice himself was a big man and a comely, as well as of great prowess and hardiment, and if any would gainsay aught that he laid down, he would prove the same in arms in single combat. When, therefore, he appeared in presence of Maximian, he was received in becoming wise, and honoured above the knights that were his fellows. At that time was there a mighty quarrel toward betwixt Maximian himself and the two Emperors Gratian and his brother Valentinian, for that he had been denied in the matter of one third part of the empire which he had demanded. When Maurice, therefore, saw that Maximian was being put upon by the twain Emperors, he spake unto him in these words:

"What cause hast thou, Maximian, to be afeard of Gratian, when the way lieth open unto thee to snatch the empire from him? Come with me into the island of Britain and thou shalt wear the crown of the kingdom. For King Octavius is sore borne down by eld and lethargy and desireth nought better than to find some man such as thyself unto whom he may give his kingdom and his daughter. For heir male hath he none, and counsel hath he sought of his barons unto whom he should give his daughter to wife, with the kingdom for dower. And, for that his barons would fain give obedient answer unto his address, his high court hath made resolve that the kingdom and the damsel should be granted unto thee, and unto me have they given commission that I should notify thee of the matter. If, therefore, thou wilt come with me into Britain, thou shalt achieve this adventure; the plenty of gold and silver that is in Britain shall be thine, and the multitude of hardy men of war that dwell therein. Thus wilt thou be enough strong to return unto Rome, and after that thou hast driven forth these Emperors, then mayst thou enjoy the empire thereof thyself. For even thus did Constantine thy kinsman before thee, and many another of our kings that hath ere now raised him unto the empire."

(10) Maximian, therefore, giving assent unto his words, came with him into Britain. On his way he sacked the cities of the Franks, and thereby purveyed him of heaps of gold and silver wherewith to pay the men of arms he mustered from every quarter. Soon afterward he put to sea and made for Hamo's Port with a fair wind. And when tidings thereof were brought unto the King, he was dismayed with sore amazement, weening that an enemy's army was upon him. Wherefore calling unto him Conan his nephew, he commanded him to summon every man in arms throughout the country and to march against the enemy. Conan accordingly assembled all the youth of the kingdom and came to Hamo's Port, where Maximian had pitched his tents. He, when he perceived how huge a multitude they were that had arrived, was in a grievous quandary, for what was there he could do? They that had come with him were a far smaller company — he dreaded the number and the courage of Conan's fighting men, and of peace had he no hope. Wherefore, calling unto him the elders of his host along with Maurice, he bade them say what they thought best to be done in such an overtake. Unto whom saith Maurice:

"Not for us, certes, is it to do battle with such an army of knights and warriors, nor came we hither for any such purpose as an invasion of Britain by force of arms. Behoveth us ask for peace and leave to abide in the land until such time as we know the King's mind. Let us say that we be envoys from the Emperors, and bear their mandates to Octavius, so as to humour these folk and wheedle them with politic words." So, all of them approving this scheme, he took with him twelve of the barons, hoary-headed and of sounder wit than the rest, all with boughs of olive in their right hands, and came to meet Duke Conan. When the Britons beheld these men of reverend age bearing the olive in token of peace, they uprose from their seats to do them honour, and made way for them to pass freely unto the Duke. Straightway, standing in the presence of Conan Meriadoc, when they had saluted him on behalf of the Emperors and the Senate, they said that Maximian had commission unto King Octavius to bear him the mandates of Gratian and Valentinian. Unto whom Conan: "Wherefore, then, is he followed by so large a company? This is not the guise wherein legates are wont to appear, but rather that of an invading army that is minded to do us a mischief." Then saith Maurice: "Unmeet had it been for a man of so high rank to come hither save in seemly state and with due escort of knights and men; and all the more for that as representing the Roman empire, and also by reason of deeds done by his forefathers, he may haply be hated of many kings. Were he to march through the land with a lesser company, like enow he might be slain by the enemies of the commonweal. In peace he cometh, and in peace he doth beseech, as in truth ought well to be believed from that which he hath done. For from the time that here we landed have we so behaved us as that we have done no wrong unto no man. All our charges have we paid like peaceful folk; we have bought fairly that which we needed, and nought have we taken from any man by force." And whilst that Conan was still wavering as to whether he would make choice of peace or war, Caradoc, Duke of Cornwall, accosted him, as also did other of the barons, and persuaded him not to enter upon a war after listening unto such a petition. Wherefore, albeit that he were fainer to fight, he laid down his arms and granted peace, himself escorting Maximian to the King in London, and setting forth unto him the whole matter in order as it had fallen out.

(11) Then Caradoc, Duke of Cornwall, taking him with his son Maurice, bade that the bystanders should withdraw them, and addressed the King in these words:

"Behold that which they, who do with truer affection observe their obedience and fealty towards thee, have so long time desired hath, by God's providence, now been brought unto a happy issue. For thou didst ordain that thy barons should give thee counsel as to what were best to do as concerning both thy daughter and thy kingdom, forasmuch as that in these days thine eld doth so sore let and hinder thee of governing thy people any longer. Some there were that counselled delivering up the crown unto Conan thy nephew and marrying thy daughter worthily elsewhere, as fearing the ruin of our countrymen should a prince of foreign tongue be set over them. Others would have granted the realm unto thy daughter so she were matched with some noble of our own speech who might succeed thee on thy departure. But the more part gave it as their counsel that some man of the blood of the Emperors should be sent for, unto whom might be given thy daughter and thy crown. For they promised that a firm and abiding peace would ensue therefrom, seeing that they would be protected by the power of Rome. Now, therefore, behold, God hath deigned that this youth should be wafted to thy shores, who is born not only of the blood of the Romans but of the blood royal of the Britons, and unto him, by my counsel, wilt thou not tarry to give thy daughter in wedlock. For, suppose thou shouldst deny him in this, what right canst thou confer upon any other as against him to the realm of Britain? For a kinsman is he of Constantine, and nephew of Coel our King, whose daughter Helena none can deny to have possessed the kingdom by right hereditary." And when Caradoc had thus made report of the counsel of the barons, Octavius agreed thereunto and by common consent forthwith gave the kingdom of Britain together with his daughter unto Maximian.

The which Conan Meriadoc beholding, he did wax indignant beyond all telling and betook him privily unto Albany where he busied him in raising an army to harass Maximian. When he had assembled his troops together he crossed the Humber river and ravaged the provinces both on the hither side thereof and on the further. When this was reported unto Maximian he assembled his whole strength, and hurrying forth to meet him defeated him in battle and returned home with victory. Natheless was Conan not

so enfeebled thereby that he could not again rally his men, and when
he had got them together he set him again to harrying the provinces.
Maximian accordingly returned and fought several battles with him,
wherein at one time he would come back victorious and at another
worsted. At last, after each had inflicted sore loss upon the other,
the friends of both did come betwixt and a reconciliation was brought
about.

(12) Five years later Maximian puffed up with pride and sur-
quedry by reason of the passing great store of gold and silver that
did daily flow in upon him, fitted out an exceeding mighty fleet and
assembled every single armed warrior in Britain. For the realm of
Britain was not enough for him, but he must needs seek also to
subjugate the Gauls. Crossing the Channel, he went first into the
kingdom of Armorica, that now is called Brittany, and made war
upon the Gaulish folk that did then inhabit therein. But the Gauls
under Duke Inbalt coming to meet him, did battle against him,
wherein the more part finding themselves in sore jeopardy did fettle
them to flee, for Duke Inbalt had fallen and fifteen thousand men-at-
arms that had come together from all parts of the kingdom. And
when Maximian had achieved so notable a slaughter, he was overjoyed beyond all measure, for well knew he that after the death of
so many fighting men he should soon subdue the country. He therefore called Conan unto him without the ranks, and saith unto him,
somewhat smiling the while: "Lo, we have won us one of the
fairest realms of Gaul, and herein, behold, lieth good hope that we
be able to win the rest. Hasten we, therefore, to take the cities and
strong places thereof, before the tidings of this jeopardy fly forth
unto further Gaul and call the rest of the peoples to arms. For,
so we can hold this kingdom, I misdoubt me not but we can subdue
the whole of Gaul unto our dominion. Nor let it irk thee to have
yielded the kingdom of Britain unto me, albeit that thou hadst hope
of possessing it thyself, for whatsoever thou hast lost therein will I
make good unto thee in this country; for in this kingdom will I
make thee King, and it shall be another Britain that we will re-
plenish with men of our own race after that we have driven out
them that do now abide therein. For the land is fruitful of corn
and the rivers of fish. The forests be passing fair, and the glades and
launds thereof right pleasant, insomuch as that in my judgment is
there nowhere to be found a land that is more delightful." And
therewithal did Conan bow his head before him and con him thanks,
promising that, so long as he should live, he would do him homage
and fealty as his loyal vassal.

(13) After this they called out their troops and marched upon
Rennes, taking it the same day. For when they heard how cruel
were the Britons and how they had slain their fellow-countrymen, the
citizens fled the swiftest they might, leaving behind them the women
and children. Others in the other cities and other towns did follow
their ensample, whereby was easy entrance made for the Britons,
who into whatsoever place they entered, slew all that therein was

of male kind, sparing only the women.  At last, when they had utterly done away every single male that dwelt in the whole of the provinces, they garrisoned the cities and towns with British warriors and established camps in divers places upon the headlands.  Accordingly, so soon as Maximian's cruelness was bruited abroad throughout the other provinces of Gaul, a mighty consternation fell upon every duke and every prince, so as none other hope had they save only in offering prayers and oblations to their gods.  From every country quarter they fled unto the cities and strongholds and whatsoever places seemed to offer a safe refuge.  Maximian, therefore, finding himself so mighty a terror unto them, took fresh hardihood and made haste to multiply his army by offer of swingeing bounties unto recruits.  For whomsoever he knew to be greedy of other men's goods, him did he enlist, and stinted not to stuff their wallets with gold or silver, or largesse of one kind or another.

(14)  Thereby did he gather such a host about him as he weened was enow for him to be able to subjugate the whole of Gaul.  Howbeit, he did put off practising further severities for a brief space, until the kingdom he had taken began to settle down and he should have replenished it with a British folk.  He accordingly issued an edict that a hundred thousand of the common folk in the island of Britain should be collected and should come to him, besides thirty thousand soldiers who should safeguard them that were to remain in the country from any incursion of the enemy.  And when all these things were accomplished and the Britons had arrived, he distributed them amongst all the nations of the kingdom of Amorica, and did thus create a second Britain the which he did bestow upon Conan Meriadoc.  But he himself with the rest of his fellow-soldiers went into further Gaul, and after divers most grievous battles did subdue the same, as well as the whole of Germany, having obtained the victory in every single battle.  Then, stablishing the throne of his empire at Trier, he did so furiously wreak his revenge upon the two Emperors Gratian and Valentinian, that he slew the one and put the other to flight from the city of Rome.

(15)  In the meanwhile the Gauls and Aquitanians did sore harass Conan and the Armorican Britons, and annoy them continually with repeated incursions, which Conan withstood, repaying slaughter with slaughter and right manfully defending the country committed unto him.  And when the victory had fallen unto him, he was minded to give wives unto his comrades-in-arms so that unto them might be born heirs that should possess that land in perpetuity.  And that they might make no mixture with the Gauls, he issued a decree that women should come from the island of Britain to be married unto them.  He therefore sent messengers into the island unto Dionotus, King of Cornwall, who had succeeded his brother Caradoc in the kingdom, that he should take charge of this business.  For he himself was noble and exceeding powerful, and unto him had Maximian entrusted the rule of the island while he himself was busied in the aforesaid emprises.  Now Dionotus had a daughter of

marvellous beauty whose name was Ursula, whom Conan did desire above all things beside.

(16) Dionotus accordingly, upon seeing Conan's messenger, being desirous of obeying his wishes, assembled together from the divers provinces the daughters of nobles to the number of eleven thousand, and of others born to the common people sixty thousand, and bade them all meet together within the city of London. He commanded further that ships should be brought thither from the various coasts wherein they might be sent oversea unto the husbands that awaited them. For albeit that in so vast a company many there were that were well-pleased with their lot, yet were there more unto whom it was displeasing, for that they loved their kinsfolk and their country with a greater affection. Nor, haply, were lacking some who preferring chastity to marriage would rather have lost their life even in some foreign nation than obtain wealth and a husband on this wise. For albeit that few were of the same mind, yet would wellnigh all have chosen somewhat different could they have had their own way in the matter. When the fleet was ready, the damsels go aboard and dropping down the river Thames make for the high seas. At last, just as they were tacking to make the shore of Armorica, a contrary wind sprang up in their teeth and very soon scattered all their company. The ships were all in sore jeopardy in the midst of the sea. The more part of them foundered, and those that did escape utter shipwreck were driven on to barbarous islands, where they were either slain or sold into bondage by the uncouth people, inasmuch as they had fallen among the detestable soldiery of Guanius and Melga, who by command of Gratian did ravage all the nations along the coast and Germany itself with dreadful slaughter. Guanius was King of the Huns and Melga of the Picts, whom Gratian had specially commissioned and sent into Germany to harass and slay them that favoured Maximian. Whilst these were roving along the seaboard plundering and murdering, they met the damsels as they were driven on to the shore in those parts. These Ambrones, beholding the beauty of the damsels, would fain have wantoned with them, but meeting denial, fell upon them and slaughtered by far the most part of them without mercy.

Then the detestable Dukes of the Picts and Huns, Guanius and Melga, who favoured the cause of Gratian and Valentinian, when they learnt that the island of Britain had been emptied of all its men-at-arms hurriedly steered thitherward, and taking them of the neighbour islands into their alliance made straight for Albany. Setting their men in marching order they accordingly invaded the kingdom wherein was neither ruler nor defender, and slaughtered the helpless common folk, for Maximian, as hath been said, had taken with him all the young fighting men that he could find and had left behind none but the unarmed and witless tillers of the soil. So when Guanius and Melga found that they could make no stand against them, they made no small slaughter amongst them, never ceasing to sack and ravage the cities and provinces as they had been so many sheepfolds. When, therefore, this so grievous calamity was reported unto Maximian, he sent Gratian the Burgess with two legions to their assistance, who as soon as they landed in the island gave battle to the enemy and drove them forth into Hibernia with sore slaughter. In the meanwhile Maximian was slain at Rome by the friends of Gratian, and the Britons whom he had brought with him were slain or scattered. They that made shift to escape betook them to their fellow-countrymen in Armorica that now was called the other Britain.

(VI, 1) Now Gratian the Burgess, when he heard of Maximian's being murdered, assumed the crown of the kingdom, and made himself King. Thenceforth such tyranny wrought he over the people, as that the common folk, banding them together, fell upon him and slew him. This news being bruited abroad among the other kingdoms, the enemies already spoken of returned from Hibernia, and bringing with them Scots, Norwegians, and Danes, did lay waste the realm from sea to sea with sword and fire. On account of this devastation and most cruel oppression, messengers are sent with letters to Rome, begging and entreating that in answer to this tearful petition an armed force may be sent to avenge them, and promising faithful subjection for ever, so only the Romans will drive their enemies away. A legion accordingly that had not suffered in their former disasters is placed under their command, and after disembarking from the ships wherein it was carried across the ocean, soon came to close quarters with the enemy. At last, after that a passing great multitude of them had been stricken down, the Romans drove them all out of the country and freed the wretched commonalty from this outrageous havoc.

(3) After this the Romans encourage the timid folk with brave counsel, and leave them patterns whereby to fashion their arms. They did likewise ordain that towers should be set at intervals overlooking the sea all along the ocean seaboard of the southern districts where they had their shipping, for that here was most peril to be dreaded from the barbarians. But easier is it to make a hawk of a haggard than presently to make a scholar of a ploughman, and he that poureth forth deep learning before them doth but scatter pearls before swine. For so soon as ever the Romans had bidden them farewell as they that never should return thither, behold the Dukes Guanius and Melga issue forth again from the ships wherein they had fled into Ireland, along with the rest of the companies of Scots and Picts, as well as of the Norwegians, Danes and others that they brought with them, and take possession of the whole of Albany as far as the wall. For knowing that the Romans had left the island, and had vowed never to return, they set to work to lay waste the island with more than their wonted assurance. And in face of all this, nought could the Britons find to do but to post their slow-witted yokels on the top of the wall, too clumsy to fight, and too addle-pated with the quaking of their midriffs to run away, who so stuck there day and night squatting on their silly

perches. Meanwhile the long hooked weapons of the enemy are never idle, wherewithal they dragged down the thrice-wretched clowns from the walls and dashed them to the ground. And well was it for them that were slain by this untimely death, for that by their speedy departure they avoided being snatched away by the same grievous and lingering torments as their brethren and their children.

O, the vengeance of God upon past sins! Such was the doom that befel through the wicked madness of Maximian that had drained the kingdom of so many gallant warriors, who, had they been present in so sore a strait, no people could have fallen upon them that they would not have forced to flee, as was well seen so long as they remained in the land. But enough hath been said.

Forsaking the cities and the high wall, again the country folk are put to flight, again are they scattered, even more hopelessly than they were wont; again are they pursued by the enemy, again are they overtaken by a yet bloodier slaughter, and the wretched common folk are torn to pieces by their foes as sheep are rent by the wolves. Yet once again therefore do the miserable remnant send letters, unto Agitius, the chief commander of the Roman forces, appealing unto him on this wise: "Unto Agitius, thrice consul, the groans of the Britons." Then, after some few words, the complaint proceedeth: "The sea driveth us upon the barbarians, the barbarians drive us back again unto the sea. Betwixt the twain we be thus but bandied from one death unto another, for either we be drowned or slain by the sword." Natheless, nought the more might they obtain the succour they sought. Sad and sorry return they home to tell their fellow-countrymen how ill their petition hath sped. . . .

(6) On the death of Constantine a dissension arose among the barons whom they should raise to the throne. Some were for Aurelius Ambrosius, others for Uther Pendragon, and others for others of the royal blood. At last, while they were still contending now for this one and now for that, Vortigern, Earl of the Gewissi, who was himself panting to snatch the crown at all hazards, went unto Constans the monk and spake unto him on this wise: "Behold, thy father is dead and neither of thy brethren can be made King by reason of their childish age, nor none other of thy family do I see whom the people can raise to be King. Now, therefore, if thou wilt be guided by my counsel, and wilt multiply my substance, I will bring the people into such a mind as that they shall choose thee for King, and albeit that thy religious order be against it, I will free thee from this habit of the cloister." When Constans heard him thus, he rejoiced with exceeding great joy, and promised with a solemn oath that he would do whatsoever he might will. So Vortigern took him and led him to London clad in royal array and made him King, albeit scarce with the assent of the people. At that time, Guethelin the Archbishop was dead, nor was there none other that durst presume to anoint him King, for that he had been monk and might not of right be so translated. Natheless, not for that did

he refuse the crown that Vortigern did set upon his head in lieu of a bishop.

(7) When Constans was thus raised to the throne, he committed unto Vortigern the whole ordinance of the kingdom, and gave him up utterly unto his counsel in such sort as that nought did he do without his bidding. And this did he out of sheer feebleness of wit, for that in the cloister nought had he learnt of the governance of a kingdom. The which when Vortigern understood, he began to take thought within himself by what means he might be made King in his stead, for of a long time this was that he had coveted above all other thing, and he now saw that this was a fitting time when his wish might lightly be carried into effect. For the whole realm had been committed unto his ordinance, and Constans, who was called King, was there as nought save the shadow of a prince. For nought of stern stuff had he in him, nor no will to do justice, insomuch as that of none was he dreaded, neither of his own people nor of the nations around. His brethren, moreover, the two children, to wit, Uther Pendragon and Aurelius Ambrosius, were not yet out of the cradle, and incapable of the rule of the kingdom. A further mischance, moreover, had befallen inasmuch as that all the elder barons of the realm were dead, and Vortigern alone, politic and prudent, seemed the only counsellor of any weight, for the rest were wellnigh all of them but mere lads and youths that had come into their honours as it might happen when their fathers and uncles had been slain in the battles that had been fought aforetime.

Vortigern, accordingly, finding all these things favourable, took thought by what contrivance he might most easily and craftily depose Constans the monk and step into his shoes with most renown. He therefore chose rather to put off his scheme for a time, until he had better stablished his power in the divers nations of the kingdom and accustomed them unto his rule. He began, therefore, by demanding that the King's treasures should be given into his custody, as well as the cities with their garrisons, saying that there was talk of the out-islanders intending an attack upon them. And when this demand was granted, he set everywhere familiars of his own to hold the cities in allegiance unto himself. Then, scheming in furtherance of the treason he designed, he went unto Constans, and told him that needs must he increase the number of his household that he might the more safely withstand the enemies that were coming against him.

Unto whom Constans: "Have I not committed all things unto thy disposition? Do, therefore, whatsoever thou wilt, so only that they abide in mine allegiance."

Whereupon Vortigern: "It hath been told me that the Picts are minded to lead the Danes and Norwegians against us so as that they may harry us to the uttermost. Wherefore I propose, and unto me seemeth it the safest counsel, that thou shouldst retain certain of the Picts in thy court that may serve as go-betweens to bring us witting from them that be without. For, an it be true that already they have begun to rebel, they will spy out the contrivances and crafty devices of their fellows in such sort as that lightly mayst thou escape them."

Herein behold the secret treachery of a secret enemy! For not in this wise did he counsel Constans as having regard unto his safety, but rather for that he knew the Picts to be a shifty folk and swift to every crime. When that they were drunken, therefore, or moved to wrath, they might full easily be egged on against the King, and so murder him out of hand. Whence, if aught of the kind should happen, the way would be open unto him of advancing himself unto the kingdom even as he had so often coveted to do.

Sending messengers, therefore, into Scotland, he invited a hundred Pictish soldiers from thence and received them into the King's retinue. And after that they were received, he showed them honour above all other, filling their pouches with all manner of bounties and their bellies with meats and drinks beyond measure, in such sort as that they held him to be a very king. Accordingly, they would wait upon him through the streets singing songs in his praise, saying: "Worthy is Vortigern of the empire! Worthy is he of the sceptre of Britain, whereof Constans is unworthy!" Upon this, Vortigern would bestow more and more largesse upon them that he might be yet more pleasing in their eyes.

But when he had won the hearts of them all, he made them drunken, saying that he was minded to retire from Britain that he might acquire more abundant treasure of his own, for that the scanty allowance he had could not possibly be enow to keep fifty soldiers in his pay. Then, in sorrowful-seeming wise he betook him privily unto his own lodging and left them drinking in the hall. Upon seeing this, the Picts, believing that what he said was true, were aggrieved beyond telling and began to mutter one with another, saying: "Wherefore suffer this monk to live? Why do we not rather slay him, so that Vortigern may possess the throne of the kingdom? For who but he ought to succeed him in the kingdom? For worthy is he of all dominion and honour, worthy is he of all sovereignty, that stinteth not to bestow such largesse upon us!"

(8) Thereupon they burst into the sleeping-chamber, and fall suddenly upon Constans, and smiting off his head, bare it to show to Vortigern, who when he beheld it burst into tears as one over-borne by sorrow, albeit that never aforetime was he so beside himself with joy. Calling together the citizens of London, for it was there that all this befel, he bade all the traitors be first set in fetters and then beheaded for presuming to perpetrate a crime so heinous. Some there were that deemed the treason had been devised by Vortigern, for that the Picts never durst have done the deed save with his knowledge and consent. Others again stuck not a moment to purge him of so black a crime. At last, the matter not being cleared up, they unto whom had been committed the nurture of the two brethren, Aurelius Ambrosius and Uther Pendragon, fled away with them into Little Britain, fearing lest they should be slain of Vortigern.

There King Budec received them and brought them up in due honour.

(9) Now Vortigern, when he saw that there was none his peer in the kingdom, set the crown thereof upon his own head and usurped precedence over all his fellow-princes. Howbeit, his treason at last being publicly known, the people of the neighbouring out-islands, whom the Picts had led with them into Albany, raised an insurrection against him. For the Picts, indignant that their comrades-in-arms had been thus put to death on account of Constans, were minded to revenge them upon Vortigern, who was thereby not only sore troubled in his mind, but suffered heavy loss amongst his fighting men in battle. On the other hand, he was still more sorely troubled in his mind by his dread of Aurelius Ambrosius and his brother Uther Pendragon, who, as hath been said, had fled into Little Britain for fear of him. For day after day was it noised in his ears that they were now grown men, and had builded a passing huge fleet, being minded to adventure a return unto the kingdom that of right was their own.

(10) In the meanwhile three brigantines, which we call "long-boats," arrived on the coasts of Kent full of armed warriors and captained by the two brethren, Horsus and Hengist. Vortigern was then at Dorobernia, which is now called Canterbury, his custom being to visit that city very often. When his messengers reported unto him that certain men unknown and big of stature had arrived, he took them into his peace, and bade them be brought unto him. Presently, when they came before him, he fixed his eyes upon the two brethren, for that they did surpass the others both in dignity and in comeliness. And, when he had passed the rest of the company under review, he made inquiry as to the country of their birth and the cause of their coming into his kingdom. Unto whom Hengist, for that he was of riper years and readier wit than the others, thus began to make answer on behalf of them all:

"Most noble of all the Kings, the Saxon land is our birthplace, one of the countries of Germany, and the reason of our coming is to offer our services unto thee or unto some other prince. For we have been banished from our country, and this for none other reason than for that the custom of our country did so demand. For such is the custom in our country that whensoever they that dwell therein do multiply too thick upon the ground, the princes of the divers provinces do meet together and bid the young men of the whole kingdom come before them. They do then cast lots and make choice of the likeliest and strongest to go forth and seek a livelihood in other lands, so as that their native country may be disburdened of its overgrown multitudes. Accordingly, owing to our country being thus overstocked with men, the princes came together, and casting lots, did make choice of these young men that here thou seest before thee, and bade them obey the custom that hath been ordained of time immemorial. They did appoint, moreover, us twain brethren, of whom I am named Hengist and this other Horsus, to be their captains, for that we were born of the family of the dukes. Wherefor, in obedience unto decrees ordained of yore, have we put to sea and under the guidance of Mercury have sought out this thy kingdom."

At the name of Mercury the King lifted up his countenance and asked of what manner religion they were. Unto whom Hengist:

"We do worship our country gods, Saturn, Jove and the rest of them that do govern the world, but most of all Mercury, whom in our tongue we do call Woden. Unto him have our forefathers dedicated the fourth day of the week that even unto this day hath borne the name of Wednesday after his name. Next unto him we do worship the goddess that is most powerful above all other goddesses, Frea by name, unto whom they dedicated the sixth day, which we call Friday after her name."

Saith Vortigern: "Right sore doth it grieve me of this your belief, the which may rather be called your unbelief, yet natheless, of your coming do I rejoice, for either God or some other hath brought ye hither to succour me in mine hour of need. For mine enemies do oppress me on every side, and so ye make common cause with me in the toils of fighting my battles, ye shall be worshipfully retained in my service within my realm, and right rich will I make ye in all manner of land and fee."

The barbarians forthwith agreed, and after the covenant had been duly confirmed, remained in the court. Presently thereupon, the Picts, issuing from Albany, mustered a huge army and began to ravage the northern parts of the island. As soon as ever Vortigern had witting thereof, he called his men together and marched forth to meet them on the further side Humber. When the men of the country came into close quarters with the enemy, both sides made a passing sharp onset; but little need had they of the country to do much of the fighting, for the Saxons that were there did battle in such gallant fashion as that the enemies that aforetime were ever wont to have the upper hand were put to flight, hot foot, without delay.

(11) Vortigern accordingly, when he had won the victory by their means, increased his bounties upon them and gave unto their duke, Hengist, many lands in the district of Lindsey for the maintenance of himself and his fellow-soldiers. Hengist therefore, as a politic man and a crafty, when that he found the King bare so great a friendship towards him, spake unto him on this wise:

"My lord, thy foemen do persecute thee on every side, and few be they of thine own folk that bear thee any love. They all do threaten thee and say that they will bring in hither thy brother Aurelius Ambrosius from the shores of Armorica, that, after deposing thee, they may raise him to be King. May it therefore please thee that we send unto our own country and invite warriors thence so that the number of our fighting men may be increased. Yet is there one thing further that I would beseech of the discretion of thy clemency, were it not that I misdoubt me I might suffer a denial thereof."

Upon this saith Vortigern: "Send therefore thine envoys unto Germany and invite whomsoever thou wilt, and, as for thyself, ask of me whatsoever thou wilt, and no denial thereof shalt thou suffer."

Thereupon Hengist bowed his head before him and gave him thanks, saying: "Thou hast enriched me of large dwelling-houses and lands, yet withal hast thou withheld such honour as may beseem a duke, seeing that my forefathers were dukes in mine own land. Wherefore, methinketh amongst so much beside, some city or castle might have been given unto me, whereby I might have been held of greater account by the barons of thy realm. The rank of an earl or a prince might have been granted unto one born of a family that hath held both these titles of nobility."

Saith Vortigern: "I am forbidden to grant any boon of this kind upon thee, for that ye be foreigner and heathen men, nor as yet have I learnt your manners and customs so as that I should make ye the equals of mine own folk; nor yet, were I to hold ye as mine own very countryfolk, could I set precedent of such a grant so the barons of the realm were against it."

Whereunto Hengist: "Grant," saith he, "unto thy servant but so much only as may be compassed round about by a single thong within the land that thou hast given me, that so I may build me a high place therein whereunto if need be I may betake me. For loyal liegemen unto thee I have been and shall be, and in thy fealty will I do all that it is within my mind to do."

Whereupon the King, moved by his words, did grant him his petition, and bade him send his envoys into Germany forthwith, so that the warriors he invited thence might hasten at once unto his succour. Straightway, as soon as he had despatched his envoys into Germany, Hengist took a bull's hide, and wrought the same into a single thong throughout. He then compassed round with his thong a stony place that he had right cunningly chosen, and within the space thus meted out did begin to build the castle that was afterwards called in British, Kaercorrei, but in Saxon, Thongceaster, the which in the Latin speech is called *Castrum corrigiae*.

(12) Meantime the envoys returned from Germany, bringing with them eighteen ships full of chosen warriors. They convoyed also the daughter of Hengist, Rowen by name, whose beauty was unparagoned of any. When they were arrived, Hengist invited King Vortigern into his house to look at the new building and the new warriors that had come into the land. The King accordingly came privily forthwith, and not only praised the work so swiftly wrought, but received the soldiers that had been invited into his retinue. And after that he had been entertained at a banquet royal, the damsel stepped forth of her chamber bearing a golden cup filled with wine, and coming next the King, bended her knee and spake, saying: "La-verd King, wacht heil!" But he, when he beheld the damsel's face, was all amazed at her beauty and his heart was enkindled of delight. Then he asked of his interpreter what it was that the damsel had said, whereupon the interpreter made answer: "She hath called thee 'Lord King,' and hath greeted thee by wishing thee health. But the

answer that thou shouldst make unto her is 'Drinc heil.'" Whereupon Vortigern made answer: "Drinc heil!" and bade the damsel drink. Then he took the cup from her hand and kissed her, and drank; and from that day unto this hath the custom held in Britain that he who drinketh at a feast saith unto another, "Wacht heil!" and he that receiveth the drink after him maketh answer, "Drinc heil!"

Howbeit, Vortigern, drunken with the divers kinds of liquor, Satan entering into his heart, did wax enamoured of the damsel, and demanded her of her father. Satan entering into his heart, I say, for that he, being a Christian, did desire to mate him with a heathen woman. Hengist, a crafty man and a prudent, herein discovering the inconstancy of the King's mind, forthwith held counsel with his brother Horsus and the rest of the aldermen that were with him what were best to be done as touching the King's petition. But they all were of one counsel, that the damsel should be given unto the King and that they should ask of him the province of Kent in return for her. So the matter was settled out of hand. The damsel was given unto Vortigern, and the province of Kent unto Hengist without the knowledge of Gorangon the Earl that of right was lord thereof. That very same night was the King wedded unto the heathen woman, with whom thenceforth was he beyond all measure well-pleased. Natheless, thereby full swiftly did he raise up enemies against him amongst the barons of the realm and amongst his own children. For aforetime had three sons been born unto him, whereof these were the names: Vortimer, Catigern, and Pascentius.

(13) At that time came St. Germanus, Bishop of Auxerre, and Lupus, Bishop of Troyes, to preach the word of God unto the Britons. For their Christianity had been corrupted, not only on account of the King having set a heathen folk in their midst, but on account of the Pelagian heresy, by the venom whereof they had long time been infected. Natheless, by the preaching of the blessed men the religion of the true faith was restored amongst them, the which they did daily make manifest by many miracles, for many miracles were wrought of God by them, as Gildas hath set forth in his tractate with abundant clearness and eloquence. Now when the damsel was given unto the King as hath been told, Hengist said unto him: "Behold, I am now thy father, and meet is it that I be thy counsellor; nor do thou slight my counsel, for by the valour of my folk shalt thou subdue all thine enemies unto thyself. Let us invite also hither my son Octa with his brother Ebissa, for gallant warriors they be; and give unto them the lands that lie in the northern parts of Britain nigh the wall betwixt Deira and Scotland, for there will they bear the brunt of the barbarians' assaults in such sort that thou upon the hither side of Humber shalt abide in peace. So Vortigern obeyed, and bade them invite whomsoever they would that might bring him any strength of succour. Envoys accordingly were sent, and Octa, Ebissa, and Cerdic came with three hundred ships all full of an armed host, all of whom did Vortigern receive kindly, bestowing upon them unstinted largesse. For by them he conquered all his enemies and won

every field that was fought. By little and little Hengist invited more and more ships and multiplied his numbers daily. So when the Britons saw what he was doing, they began to be adread of their treason and spake unto the King that he should banish them forth of his realm, for that Paynims ought not to communicate with Christians nor be thrust into their midst, for that this was forbidden by the Christian law; and, moreover, that so huge a multitude had already arrived as that they were a terror to the folk of the country, insomuch as that none could tell which were the Paynims and which Christians, for that the heathens had wedded their daughters and kinswomen. Upon these and the like grounds of objection they did urge the King to dismiss them from his retinue, lest at any time they should deal treacherously with him and overrun the folk of the country. But Vortigern did eschew giving heed unto their counsel, for he loved the Saxons above all other nations on account of his wife. Which when the Britons understood, they forthwith forsook Vortigern and with one accord raised up Vortimer his son to be their King, who accepting their counsel, at once began to drive out the barbarians everywhere, fighting against them and continually harassing them with fresh incursions and slaughter. Four pitched battles he fought with them; the first on the river Derwent, the second at the ford of Episford, where Horsus and Catigern, another son of Vortigern, met hand to hand, both falling in the encounter, each wounded to the death by the other. The third battle was on the seacoast, when the Saxons fled, sneaking away like women to their ships and taking refuge in the Isle of Thanet. But Vortimer there beleaguered them, and harassed them day after day by attacking them from his ships. And when they could no longer withstand the attack of the Britons, they sent King Vortigern who had been with them in all their battles to his son Vortimer to petition for leave to depart and to repair unto Germany in safety. And while a conference was being held upon the matter, they took the occasion to embark on board their brigantines, and returned into Germany leaving their women and children behind them.

(14) Vortimer thus having won the victory, at once began to restore their possessions unto the plundered countrymen, to treat them with affection and honour, and to repair the churches at the bidding of St. Germanus. But the devil did straightway wax envious of his goodness, and entering into the heart of his step-mother Rowen, did egg her on to compass his destruction. She, calling to her aid all the sleights of witchcraft, gave him by a certain familiar of his own, whom she had corrupted with bribes innumerable, a draught of poison. No sooner had the noble warrior drunk thereof than he was smitten with a sudden malady so grievous that hope of his life was none. Forthwith he bade all his soldiers come unto him, and making known unto them that death was already upon him, distributed amongst them his gold and silver and all the treasure that his forefathers had heaped together. He did comfort, moreover, them that were weeping and groaning around him, tell-

ing them that this way along which he was now about to journey
was none other than the way of all flesh. The brave young warriors, moreover, that wont to fight at his side in every battle, he did
exhort to fight for their country and to defend the same against all
attacks of their enemies. Moved by an impulse of exceeding hardihood, moreover, he commanded that a brazen pyramid should be
wrought for him, and set in the haven wherein the Saxons were wont
to land, and that after his death his body should be buried on the
top thereof, so as that when the barbarians beheld his image thereupon they should back sail and turn them home again to Germany.
For he said that not one of them durst come anigh so they did even
behold his image. O, the passing great hardihood of the man who
was thus desirous that even after death he might be dreaded by those
unto whom while living he had been a terror! Natheless, after his
death, the Britons did otherwise, for they buried his corpse in the
city of Trinovantum.

(15) After the death of his son, Vortigern was restored unto his
kingdom, and at the earnest instance of his wife sent his envoys to
Hengist in Germany, bidding him to come back again to Britain,
but privily and with but few men only, as he was afeard, in case he
came over otherwise, a quarrel might arise betwixt the barbarians and
the men of the country. Howbeit, Hengist, hearing of Vortimer's
death, raised an army of three hundred thousand armed men, and
fitting out a fleet returned unto Britain. But as soon as the arrival
of so huge a host was reported to Vortigern and the princes of the
realm, they took it in high dudgeon, and taking counsel together,
resolved to give them battle and drive them forth of their coasts.

Tidings of this resolve were at once sent to Hengist by messengers
from his daughter, and he forthwith bethought him what were best
to do by way of dealing a counter-stroke. After much brooding
over divers devices, the one that he made choice of in the end was
to betray the people of the kingdom by approaching them under
a show of peace. He accordingly sent messengers unto the King,
bidding them bear him on hand that he had not brought with him
so mighty an armament either with any purpose that they should
remain with him in the country, or in any way do violence unto
any that dwelt therein. The only reason he had brought them
with him was that he believed Vortimer to be still alive, and that
in case Vortimer had opposed his return he was minded to be able
to withstand him. Howbeit, now that he had no longer any doubt
as to Vortimer being dead, he committed himself and his people
unto Vortigern to dispose of as he should think best. So many of
their number as he might wish to retain with him in the kingdom
might stay, and so many as he might desire to dismiss he was quite
willing should return to Germany forthwith. And, in case Vortigern
were willing to accept these terms, he himself besought him to name
a day and place for them to meet, and they would then settle everything in accordance with his wishes.

When such a message was brought unto Vortigern, passing well-pleased was he, for he had no mind that Hengist should again depart. So at last he bade that the men of the country and the Saxons should meet together nigh the monastery of Ambruis on the Kalends of May, then just drawing on, that then and there the matter might be solemnly settled. Now Hengist, having a mind to put in use a new manner of treason, made ordinance unto his comrades that every single one of them should have a long knife hidden along the sole of his boot, and when the Britons were without any suspicion discussing the business of the meeting, he himself would give the signal, "Nemet oure saxas," whereupon each of them should be ready to fall boldly upon the Briton standing next him, and drawing forth his knife to cut his throat as swiftly as might be. Accordingly on the day appointed all met together in the city aforesaid, and began to talk together over the terms of peace, and when Hengist espied that the hour had come when his treachery might most meetly be carried into effect he shouted out, "Nemet oure saxas!" and forthwith laid hold on Vortigern and held him fast by his royal robe. The moment the Saxons heard the signal they drew forth their long knives and set upon the princes that stood around thinking of nought less at the instant, and cut the throats of about four hundred and sixty amongst the barons and earls, whose bodies the blessed Eldad did afterward bury and place in the ground after Christian fashion not far from Kaercaradoc, that is now called Salisbury, within the churchyard that lieth about the monastery of Abbot Ambrius, who of yore had been the founder thereof. For all of them had come unarmed, nor never deemed of aught save treating as touching the peace. Whence it came to pass that the others, which had come for nought but treachery, could lightly slay them as having done off their arms. Howbeit the Paynims wrought not their treason unavenged, for many of themselves were slain whilst that they were putting the others to death, the Britons snatching the stones and sticks that were on the ground and in self-defence doing no little execution upon their betrayers.

(16) Natheless, they were not minded to slay Vortigern, but bound him and threatened him with death, and demanded his cities and strong places as ransom for his life; he straightway granting all they had a mind to, so he were allowed to escape on live. And when he had confirmed this unto them by oath, they loosed him from his fetters, and marching first of all upon London, took that city, taking next York and Lincoln as well as Winchester, and ravaging the country at will, slaying the country folk as wolves do sheep forsaken of their shepherd. When therefore Vortigern beheld so terrible a devastation, he betook him privily into the parts of Wales, not knowing what to do against this accursed people.

(17) Howbeit, he at last took counsel of his wizards, and bade them tell him what he should do. They told him that he ought to build him a tower exceeding strong, as all his other castles he had lost. He sought accordingly in all manner of places to find one fit for such a purpose and came at last unto Mount Eryri, where,

assembling a great gang of masons from divers countries, he bade them build the tower. The stonemasons, accordingly, came together and began to lay the foundations thereof, but whatsoever they wrought one day was all swallowed up by the soil the next, in such sort as that they knew not whither their work had vanished unto. And when word was brought hereof unto Vortigern, he again held counsel with his wizards to tell him the reason thereof. So they told him that he must go search for a lad that had never a father, and when he had found him should slay him and sprinkle his blood over the mortar and the stones, for this, they said, would be good for making the foundation of the tower hold firm. Forthwith messengers are sent into all the provinces to look for such manner of man, and when they came into the city that was afterward called Carmarthen, they saw some lads playing before the gate and went to look on at the game. And being weary with travel, they sate them down in the ring and looked about them to see if they could find what they were in quest of. At last, when the day was far spent, a sudden quarrel sprang up betwixt a couple of youths whose names were Merlin and Dalbutius. And as they were wrangling together, saith Dalbutius unto Merlin: "What a fool must thou be to think thou art a match for me! Keep thy distance, prithee! Here am I, born of the blood royal on both sides of the house; and thou? None knoweth what thou art, for never a father hadst thou!" At that word the messengers lifted up their faces, and looking narrowly upon Merlin, asked the bystanders who he might be. They told them that none knew his father, but that his mother was daughter of the King of Demetia, and that she lived along with the nuns in St. Peter's Church in that same city.

(18) The messengers thereupon hurried off to the reeve of the city, and enjoined him in the King's name that Merlin and his mother should be sent unto the King. The reeve, accordingly, so soon as he knew the errand whereon they came, forthwith sent Merlin and his mother unto Vortigern for him to deal withal as he might list. And when they were brought into his presence, the King received the mother with all attention as knowing that she was of right noble birth, and afterward began to make inquiry as to who was the father of the lad. Unto whom she made answer: "As my soul liveth and thine, O my lord the King, none know I that was his father. One thing only I know, that on a time whenas I and the damsels that were about my person were in our chambers, one appeared unto me in the shape of a right comely youth and embracing me full straitly in his arms did kiss me, and after that he had abided with me some little time did as suddenly vanish away so that nought more did I see of him. Natheless, many a time and oft did he speak unto me when that I was sitting alone, albeit that never once did I catch sight of him. But after that he had thus haunted me of a long time I did conceive and bear a child. So much my lord King, is my true story, and so much leave I unto thee to interpret aright, for none other have I known that is father unto

this youth." Amazed at her words, the King commanded that Maugantius should be called unto him to declare whether such a thing might be as the lady had said. Maugantius was brought accordingly, and when he had heard the story from first to last, said unto Vortigern: "In the books of our wise men and in many histories have I found that many men have been born into the world on this wise. For, as Apuleius in writing as touching the god of Socrates doth make report, certain spirits there be betwixt the moon and the earth, the which we do call incubus daemons. These have a nature that doth partake both of men and angels, and whensoever they will they do take upon them the shape of men and do hold converse with mortal women. Haply one of these hath appeared unto this lady and is the father of the youth."

(19) And when Merlin had hearkened unto all this, he came unto the King and said: "Wherefore have I and my mother been called into thy presence?" Unto whom Vortigern: "My wizards have declared it unto me as their counsel that I should seek out one that had never a father, that when I shall have sprinkled his blood upon the foundation of the tower my work should stand firm." Then said Merlin: "Bid thy wizards come before me, and I will convict them of having devised a lie." The King, amazed at his words, straightway bade his wizards come and set them down before Merlin. Unto whom spake Merlin: "Know ye not what it is that doth hinder the foundation being laid of this tower? Ye have given counsel that the mortar thereof should be slacked of my blood, that so the tower should stand forthwith. Now tell me, what is it that lieth hid beneath the foundation, for somewhat is there that doth not allow it to stand?" But the wizards were adread and held their peace. Then saith Merlin, that is also called Ambrosius: "My lord the King, call thy workmen and bid delve the soil, and a pool shalt thou find beneath it that doth forbid thy tower to stand." And when this was done, straightway a pool was found under the earth, the which had made the soil unconstant. Then Ambrosius Merlin again came nigh unto the wizards and saith: "Tell me now, ye lying flatterers, what is it that is under the pool?" But they were all dumb and answered unto him never a word. And again spake he unto the King, saying: "Command, O King, that the pool be drained by conduits, and in the bottom thereof shalt thou behold two hollow stones and therein two dragons asleep." The King, believing his words for that he had spoken true as touching the pool, commanded also that the pool should be drained. And when he found that it was even as Merlin had said he marvelled greatly. All they that stood by were no less astonished at such wisdom being found in him, deeming that he was possessed of some spirit of God.

(VIII, 1) Vortigern himself, marvelling above all other, did applaud the young man's wit no less than the predictions themselves. For none had the then present age produced that had on any such wise opened his lips in his presence. Accordingly, being fain to learn what should be the ending of his own life, he besought the youth to tell him what he knew thereof. Unto this said Merlin:

"Flee thou from the fire of the sons of Constantine, if flee it thou mayst! Even now are they fitting forth their ships — even now are they leaving the coasts of Armorica behind and spreading their sails upon the deep. They will make for the island of Britain and invade the Saxon race. That accursed people will they subdue, but first will they shut up thyself in a tower and burn thee! Unto thine own bane didst thou betray their father and invite the Saxons into the island. Thou didst invite them as thy bodyguard; they have come over as thy headsmen. Two deaths await thee, nor is it clear which one of the twain thou mayst first escape. For upon the one side, the Saxons will lay waste thy kingdom and will seek to compass thy death. Upon the other, the two brethren Aurelius and Uther Pendragon will enter into thy land seeking to revenge their father's death upon thee. Seek out refuge if thou mayst. To-morrow will they make haven in Totnes. The faces of the Saxons shall be red with blood: Hengist shall be slain, and thereafter shall Aurelius Ambrosius be crowned King. He shall give peace unto the nations: he shall restore the churches, yet shall he die of poison. Unto him shall succeed his brother Uther Pendragon, whose days shall likewise be cut short by poison. At this so black betrayal shall thine own descendants be present, whom the Boar of Cornwall shall thereafter devour!"

Straightway, when the morrow dawned, came Aurelius Ambrosius with his brother unto land with ten thousand warriors in their company.

(2) He marcheth his army into Cambria and maketh toward the castle of Genoreu whither Vortigern had fled for refuge.

Forthwith they brought their engines of all kinds into play and strove their best to breach the walls, but when all else failed, they set the place on fire, and the fire, finding fuel, spread blazing up till it had burned up the tower and Vortigern therein.

(13) At that same time Pascentius, Vortigern's son, who had fled away to Germany, called out every knight in arms of that kingdom against Aurelius Ambrosius, being minded to avenge his father, and promised them exceeding plenty of gold and silver so he were able to subdue Britain unto himself with their assistance. And when he had bribed the whole youth of the country by his promises, he fitted out a passing great fleet, and, landing on the Northern parts of the island, began to lay them waste. And when message of this was brought unto the King, he assembled his host and marched forth to meet them, challenging his cruel foemen to do battle with him. They as willingly accepted the challenge, but coming into conflict with the Britons, were by the grace of God defeated and forced to take to flight.

(19) At last, when Uther had stablished his peace in the parts of the North, he went to London. And when the Easter festival drew nigh, he bade the barons of the realm assemble in that city

that he might celebrate so high holiday with honour by assuming the
crown thereon.   All obeyed accordingly, and repairing thither from
the several cities, assembled together on the eve of the festival.   The
King, accordingly, celebrated the ceremony as he had proposed, and
made merry along with his barons, all of whom did make great
cheer for that the King had received them in such joyful wise.   For
all the nobles that were there had come with their wives and daughters
as was meet on so glad a festival.   Among the rest, Gorlois, Duke
of Cornwall, was there, with his wife Igerne, that in beauty did
surpass all the other dames of the whole of Britain.   And when the
King espied her amidst the others, he did suddenly wax so fain of
her love that, paying no heed unto none of the others, he turned
all his attention only upon her.   Only unto her did he send dainty
tit-bits from his own dish; only unto her did he send the golden
cups with messages through his familiars.   Many a time did he
smile upon her and spake merrily unto her withal.   But when her
husband did perceive all this, straightway he waxed wroth and retired from the court without leave taken.   Nor was any that might
recall him thither, for that he feared to lose the one thing that he
loved better than all other.   Uther, waxing wroth hereat, commanded him to return and appear in his court that he might take
lawful satisfaction for the affront he had put upon him.   And when
Gorlois was not minded to obey the summons, the King was enraged
beyond all measure and sware with an oath that he would ravage
his demesnes so he hastened not to make him satisfaction.   Forthwith, the quarrel betwixt the two abiding unsettled, the King gathered a mighty army together and went his way into the province of
Cornwall and set fire to the cities and castles therein.   But Gorlois,
not daring to meet him in the field for that he had not so many armed
men, chose rather to garrison his own strong places until such time
as he obtained the succour he had besought from Ireland.   And,
for that he was more troubled upon his wife's account than upon his
own, he placed her in the Castle of Tintagel on the seacoast, as holding it to be the safer refuge.   Howbeit, he himself betook him into the
Castle of Dimilioc, being afeard that in case disaster should befall
him both might be caught in one trap.   And when message of this
was brought unto the King, he went unto the castle wherein Gorlois
had ensconced him, and beleagured him and cut off all access unto
him.   At length, at the end of a week, mindful of his love for
Igerne, he spake unto one of his familiars named Ulfin of Ricaradoc:
"I am consumed of love for Igerne, nor can I have no joy, nor do I
look to escape peril of my body save I may have possession of her.
Do thou therefore give me counsel in what wise I may fulfil my
desire, for, an I do not, of mine inward sorrow shall I die."   Unto
whom Ulfin: "And who shall give thee any counsel that may avail,
seeing that there is no force that may prevail whereby to come unto
her in the Castle of Tintagel?   For it is situate on the sea, and is
on every side encompassed thereby, nor none other entrance is there
save such as a narrow rock doth furnish, the which three armed

knights could hold against thee, albeit thou wert standing there with the whole realm of Britain beside thee. But, an if Merlin the prophet would take the matter in hand, I do verily believe that by his counsel thou mightest compass thy heart's desire."

The King, therefore, believing him, bade Merlin be called, for he, too, had come unto the leaguer. Merlin came forthwith accordingly, and when he stood in presence of the King, was bidden give counsel how the King's desire might be fulfilled. When he found how sore tribulation of mind the King was suffering, he was moved at beholding the effect of a love so exceeding great, and saith he: "The fulfilment of thy desire doth demand the practice of arts new and unheard of in this thy day. Yet know I how to give thee the semblance of Gorlois by my leechcrafts in such sort as that thou shalt seem in all things to be his very self. If, therefore, thou art minded to obey me, I will make thee like unto him utterly, and Ulfin will I make like unto Jordan of Tintagel his familiar. I also will take upon me another figure and will be with ye as a third, and in such wise we may go safely unto the castle and have access unto Igerne."

The King obeyed accordingly, and gave heed strictly unto that which Merlin enjoined him. At last, committing the siege into charge of his familiars, he did entrust himself unto the arts and medicaments of Merlin, and was transformed into the semblance of Gorlois. Ulfin was changed into Jordan, and Merlin into Bricel in such sort as that none could have told the one from the other. They then went their way toward Tintagel, and at dusk hour arrived at the castle. The porter, weening that the Duke had arrived, swiftly unmade the doors, and the three were admitted. For what other than Gorlois could it be, seeing that in all things it seemed as if Gorlois himself were there? So the King lay that night with Igerne, for as he had beguiled her by the false likeness he had taken upon him, so he beguiled her also by the feigned discourses wherewith he did full artfully entertain her. For he told her he had issued forth of the besieged city for naught save to see to the safety of her dear self and the castle wherein she lay, in such sort that she believed him every word, and had no thought to deny him in aught he might desire. And upon that same night was the most renowned Arthur conceived, that was not only famous in after years, but was well worthy of all the fame he did achieve by his surpassing prowess.

(IX, 1) After the death of Uther Pendragon, the barons of Britain did come together from the divers provinces unto the city of Silchester, and did bear on hand Dubricius, Archbishop of the City of Legions, that he should crown as king Arthur, the late King's son. For sore was need upon them, seeing that when the Saxons heard of Uther's death they had invited their fellow-countrymen from Germany and under their Duke Colgrin were bent upon exterminating the Britons. They had, moreover, entirely subdued all that part of the island which stretcheth from the river Humber as far as the sea of Caithness. Dubricius therefore, sorrowing over the calamities of the country, assembled the other prelates, and did invest Arthur with the crown of the realm. At that time Arthur was a youth of fifteen years, of a courage and generosity beyond compare, whereunto his inborn goodness did lend such grace as that he was beloved of well-nigh all the peoples in the land. After he had been invested with the ensigns of royalty, he abided by his ancient wont, and was so prodigal of his bounties as that he began to run short of wherewithal to distribute amongst the huge multitude of knights that made repair unto him. But he that hath within him a bountiful nature along with prowess, albeit that he be lacking for a time, natheless in no wise shall poverty be his bane for ever. Wherefore did Arthur, for that in him did valour keep company with largesse, make resolve to harry the Saxons, to the end that with their treasure he might make rich the retainers that were of his own household. And herein was he monished of his own lawful right, seeing that of right ought he to hold the sovereignty of the whole island in virtue of his claim hereditary.

(9) Lot, who in the days of Aurelius Ambrosius had married Arthur's own sister, who had borne unto him Gawain and Mordred, he did reinstate in the Dukedom of Lothian and of the other provinces thereby that had appertained unto him aforetime. At last, when he had re-established the state of the whole country in its ancient dignity, he took unto him a wife born of a noble Roman family, Guenevere, who, brought up and nurtured in the household of Duke Cador, did surpass in beauty all the other dames of the island.

(10) When the next summer came on he fitted out his fleet and sailed unto the island of Hibernia, that he desired to subdue unto himself. No sooner had he landed than Guillamur came to meet him with a host past numbering, purposing to do battle with him. But as soon as the fight began, his folk, naked and unarmed, fled whithersoever they might find a place of refuge. Guillamur was forthwith taken prisoner and compelled to surrender, and the rest of the princes of the country, smitten with dismay, likewise surrendered them after their King's ensample. All parts of Ireland thus subdued, he made with his fleet for Iceland, and there also defeated the people and subjugated the island. Next, for far and wide amongst the other islands it was rumoured that no country could stand against him, Doldavy, King of Gothland, and Gunfast, King of the Orkneys, came of their own accord and, promising a tribute, did homage unto him. At the end of winter he returned into Britain, and re-establishing his peace firmly throughout the realm, did abide therein for the next twelve years.

(11) At the end of this time he invited unto him all soever of most prowess from far-off kingdoms and began to multiply his household retinue, and to hold such courtly fashion in his household as begat rivalry amongst peoples at a distance, insomuch as the noblest in the land, fain to vie with him, would hold himself as nought, save in the cut of his clothes and the manner of his arms he followed the pattern of Arthur's knights. At last the fame of his

bounty and his prowess was upon every man's tongue, even unto the uttermost ends of the earth, and a fear fell upon the kings of realms oversea lest he might fall upon them in arms and they might lose the nations under their dominion. Grievously tormented of these devouring cares, they set them to repairing their cities and the towers of their cities, and builded them strongholds in places meet for defence, to the end that in case Arthur should lead an expedition against them they might find refuge therein should need be. And when this was notified unto Arthur, his heart was uplifted for that he was a terror unto them all, and he set his desire upon subduing the whole of Europe unto himself. Fitting forth his fleets accordingly, he made first of all for Norway, being minded to set the crown thereof upon the head of Lot, his sister's son. For Lot was grandson of Sichelm, King of Norway, who at that time had died leaving the kingdom unto him. But the Norwegians disdained to receive him, and had raised one Riculf to the kingly power, deeming that, so they garrisoned their cities, he would be able to withstand Arthur himself. At that time Gawain, the son of Lot, was a youth of twelve years, and had been sent by his uncle to be brought up as a page in the service of Pope Sulpicius, from whom he had received arms. Accordingly, when Arthur, as I had begun to tell, landed upon the coast of Norway, King Riculf met him with the whole people of the kingdom and did battle; but after much blood had been shed upon both sides, the Britons at last prevailed and, making an onset, slew Riculf with a number of his men. When they had won this victory they overran and set fire to the cities, scattering the country folk, nor did they cease to give full loose to their cruelty until they had submitted the whole of Norway as well as Denmark unto the dominion of Arthur. These countries thus conquered, as soon as Arthur had raised Lot to be King of Norway Arthur sailed for Gaul and, dividing his force into companies, began everywhere to lay the country waste.

After a space of nine years, when he had subdued all the parts of Gaul unto his dominion, Arthur again came unto Paris and there held his court. He there also summoned a convocation of the clergy and people, and did confirm the stablishment of the realm in peace and law. At that time, moreover, he made grant of Neustria, which is now called Normandy, unto Bedevere his butler, and the province of Anjou unto Kay his seneschal.

[tr. SEBASTIAN EVANS]

# WACE

Paraphrases and adaptations of Geoffrey's story began at once and continued. Between 1147 and 1151 the Norman Geoffrey Gaimar wrote in octosyllabic couplets what must have been an endless work, beginning with the Argonauts before the Trojan War and ending with the death of William Rufus. The portion that remains makes few regret that most of it was lost. More readable, and possibly the most influential of the Arthurian chronicles, was one based on the two Geoffreys by Master Wace, born in Jersey about 1100, student at Paris, clerk at Caen, and finally Canon at Bayeux. A number of poems and saints' lives that he wrote under the patronage of King Henry II remain, including his long but informative *Roman de Rou,* a versified chronicle of the Normans from the founding of the duchy by Rollo in the early tenth century. Here occurs the famous word-picture of the minstrel Taillifer singing to William the Conqueror of the deeds of Charlemagne, Roland, and Oliver, as the Normans rode into the Battle of Hastings. Wace suspended composition before the projected conclusion when he learned that the fickle King Henry had set the younger and more fashionable Benoit de Saint-More to the task. Tired and discouraged, Wace died shortly thereafter.

But in his heyday twenty years before, his *Roman de Brut,* which he called the *Geste des Bretons,* was better received. According to Layamon, Wace dedicated it to Henry's queen, Eleanor of Aquitaine. This, too, he wrote in octosyllabic couplets, thus forming a bridge between the monastic prose chronicle of Geoffrey and the romance of Chrétien and later writers. Here we first meet the image of the Round Table:

> *Por les nobles barons qu'il ot*
> *Dont cascuns mieldre estre quidot . . .*
> *Fist Artus la Roonde Table,*
> *Dont Breton dient mainte fable.*

Wace was no imitator; he clothed the skeleton story of Geoffrey with flesh. Though he held with fair accuracy to the "facts," his nimble imagination coined stirring speeches and vivid and picturesque details as he followed the mythical Arthur from point to point on his campaigns. He constantly substitutes direct for indirect discourse and talks to his reader through question and explanation as with a friend. No doubt, as he says below (p. 319), he had heard the minstrel sing his ballad and the storyteller tell his story so frequently that the truth stood hidden in the trappings of a tale.

The Arthurian tradition in English literature comes largely from Wace, for Layamon, who turned Wace's 15,000 Norman French lines into 32,000 lines of English alliterative verse, preserved all of Wace's story. The harsh ecclesiasticism of Geoffrey of Monmouth was transformed by the courtly grace and simplicity of Wace into the poetry of Malory and Spenser.

## THE GESTES OF ARTHUR

(From *Roman de Brut*)

Wace (A.D. 1155)

[From *Arthurian Chronicles;* Everyman Edition, J. M. Dent & Sons, Ltd., London, and E. P. Dutton & Co., Inc., New York, 1912. Reprinted by permission of the publishers.]

When Arthur had settled his realm in peace, righted all wrongs, and restored the kingdom to its ancient borders, he took to wife a certain fresh and noble maiden named Guenevere, making her his queen. This damsel was passing fair of face and courteous, very gracious of manner, and come of a noble Roman house. Cador had nourished this lady long and richly in his earldom of Cornwall. The maiden was the earl's near cousin, for by his mother he, too, was of Roman blood. Marvellously dainty was the maiden in person and vesture, right queenly of bearing, passing sweet and ready of tongue. Arthur cherished her dearly, for his love was wonderfully set upon the damsel; yet never had they a child together, nor betwixt them might get an heir.

As soon as winter was gone, and the warm days were come when it was good to wend upon the sea, Arthur made ready his ships to cross the straits to Ireland and conquer the land. Arthur made no long tarrying. He brought together the most lusty warriors of his realm, both poor and rich, all of the people who were most vigorous and apt in war. With these he passed into Ireland, and sent about the country seeking provand for his host. So the sergeants took seisin of cows and oxen, and brought to the camp in droves all that was desirable for meat.

Guillomer, the king of that realm, heard that Arthur had fastened this quarrel upon him. He hearkened to the cries and the tidings, the plaints and the burdens, raised by those villeins whose granges and fields were pillaged for the sustenance of his foes. Guillomer went forth to give battle to Arthur, but in an ill hour he drew to the field. His men were naked to their adversaries, having neither helmets nor coats of leather nor shields. They knew nothing of archery, and were ignorant of catapults and slings. The Britons were mighty bowmen. They shot their shafts thickly amongst their enemies, so that the Irish dared not show their bodies, and might find no shelter. The Irish could endure the arrows no longer. They fled from the fight, taking refuge where they were able. They hid in woods and thickets, in towns and in houses, seeking refuge from the stour. Right grievous was their discomfiture. Guillomer, their king, sought shelter within a forest, but his fate was upon him, and he might not conceal him from his foes. Arthur searched him out so diligently, following so hotly on his track, that at the last he was taken captive. Guillomer did very wisely. He paid fealty and homage to Arthur, and owned that of him he held his heritage. Moreover he put hostages within Arthur's power, for surety that he would render a yearly tribute to the king.

When Arthur had subdued Ireland, he went further and came even so far as Iceland. He brought the land in subjection to himself, so that the folk thereof owned themselves his men, and granted him the lordship. Now three princes, by name Gonfal, King of the Orkneys, Doldamer, King of Gothland, and Romarec, King of Finland, heard the rumour of these deeds. They sent spies to Iceland, and learned from their messengers that Arthur was making ready his host to pass the sea and despoil them of their realms. In all the world — said these messengers — there was no such champion, nor so crafty a captain in the ordering of war. These three kings feared mightily in case Arthur should descend upon them, and waste their land. Lest a worse thing should befall them, with no compulsion and of their own free wills, they set forth for Iceland and came humbly before the king. They gave of their substance rich gifts and offerings, and kneeling before Arthur did him fealty, putting their countries between his hands, and proclaiming themselves his men. They owned that of grace they held their inheritance; they swore to render tribute to his treasury, and gave hostages for assurance of their covenant. So they departed in peace to their own place. For his part Arthur came again to his ships. He returned to England, where he was welcomed of his people with marvellous joy.

Twelve years he abode in his realm in peace and content, since none was so bold as to do him a mischief, and he did mischief to none. Arthur held high state in a very splendid fashion. He ordained the courtesies of courts, and bore himself with so rich and noble a bearing, that neither the emperor's court at Rome, nor any other bragged of by man, was accounted as aught besides that of the king.

Arthur never heard speak of a knight in praise but he caused him to be numbered of his household. So that he might he took him to himself, for help in time of need. Because of these noble lords about his hall, of whom each knight pained himself to be the hardiest champion, and none would count him the least praiseworthy, Arthur made the Round Table, so reputed of the Britons. This Round Table was ordained of Arthur that when his fair fellowship sat to meat their chairs should be high alike, their service equal, and none before or after his comrade. Thus no man could boast that he was exalted above his fellow, for all alike were gathered round the board, and none was alien at the breaking of Arthur's bread. At this table sat Britons, Frenchmen, Normans, Angevins, Flemings, Burgundians, and Loherins. Knights had their place who held

land of the king, from the furthest marches of the west even unto
the Hill of St. Bernard.

A most discourteous lord would he be deemed who sojourned
not awhile in the king's hall; who came not with the countenance,
the harness, and the vesture that were the garb and usage of those
who served Arthur about his court. From all the lands there voyaged
to this court such knights as were in quest either of gain or worship.
Of these lords some drew near to hear tell of Arthur's courtesies,
others to marvel at the pride of his state; these to have speech with
the knights of his chivalry, and some to receive of his largess costly
gifts. For this Arthur in his day was loved right well of the poor
and honoured meetly by the rich. Only the kings of the world bore
him malice and envy, since they doubted and feared exceedingly
lest he should set his foot upon them every one, and spoil them of
their heritage.

I know not if you have heard tell the marvellous gestes and errant
deeds related so often of King Arthur. They have been noised
about this mighty realm for so great a space that the truth has turned
to fable and an idle song. Such rhymes are neither sheer bare lies
nor gospel truths. They should not be considered either an idiot's
tale or given by inspiration. The minstrel has sung his ballad, the
storyteller told over his story so frequently, little by little he has
decked and painted, till by reason of his embellishment the truth
stands hid in the trappings of a tale. Thus to make a delectable tune
to your ear, history goes masking as fable. Hear then how, because
of his valour, the counsel of his barons, and in the strength of that
mighty chivalry he had cherished and made splendid, Arthur purposed to cross the sea and conquer the land of France.

But first he deemed to sail to Norway, since he would make Lot, his
sister's lord, its king. Sichelin, the King of Norway, was newly dead,
leaving neither son nor daughter of his body. In the days of his
health, as alike when he fell on death, Sichelin had appointed Lot
to succeed him in his realm and fief. The crown was Lot's by right,
even as Sichelin proclaimed, since Lot was the king's nephew, and
there was no other heir. When the folk of Norway learned that
Sichelin had bequeathed his realm to Lot, they held his command and
ordinance in derision. They would have no alien for their lord,
nor suffer a stranger to meddle in their business, lest he should deem
them an ancient and feeble people, and give to outland folk what
was due to the dwellers in the realm. The Norwegians resolved
to make king one of their own house, that he might cherish them and
their children; and for this reason they chose from amongst them
a certain lord named Ridulph to be their king.

When Lot perceived that his right was despised save that he took
his heritage by force, he sought help of Arthur, his lord. Arthur
agreed to aid him in his quarrel, promising to render him his own,
and to avenge him bitterly on Ridulph. Arthur gathered together
many ships and a mighty host. He entered into Norway with this
great company, wasting the land, seizing on the manors, and spoiling

the towns. Ridulph was no trembler, and had no thought to leave the country to its fate. He assembled his people and prepared to give battle to the king. Since, however, his carles were not many and his friends but few, Ridulph was defeated in the fight and slain. The greater part of his fellowship perished with him, so that no large number remained. In this manner Lot the King of Lyones destroyed the Norwegians from the land. Having delivered Norway from itself, Arthur granted the kingdom to Lot, so only that he did Arthur homage as his lord.

Amongst the barons who rode in this adventure was Gawain, the hardy and famous knight, who had freshly come from St. Sulpicius the Apostle, whose soul may God give rest and glory. The knight wore harness bestowed on him by the Apostle, and wondrously was he praised. This Gawain was a courteous champion, circumspect in word and deed, having no pride nor blemish in him. He did more than his boast, and gave more largely than he promised. His father had sent him to Rome, that he might be schooled the more meetly. Gawain was dubbed knight in the same day as Wavain, and counted himself of Arthur's household. Mightily he strove to do his devoir in the field, for the fairer service and honour of his lord.

After Arthur had conquered Norway, and firmly established his justice in the land, he chose of his host those men who were the most valiant and ready in battle and assembled them by the sea. He brought to the same haven many ships and barges, together with such mariners as were needful for his purpose. When a quiet time was come, with a fortunate wind, Arthur crossed the sea into Denmark; for the realm was very greatly to his desire. Acil, the Danish king, considered the Britons and the folk from Norway. He considered Arthur, who had prevailed against so many kings. Acil knew and was persuaded that Arthur was mightier than he. He had no mind to suffer hurt himself, or to see his goodly heritage spoiled in a useless quarrel. What did it profit to waste wealth and honour alike, to behold slain friends and ruined towers? Acil wrought well and speedily. He sought peace, and ensued it. He gave costly gifts and made promises which were larger still, till by reason of his words, his prayers, and supplications, concord was established between Arthur and the king. Acil paid fealty and homage; he became Arthur's man, and owned that of Arthur's grace he held his fief. King Arthur rejoiced greatly at this adventure and of the conquest he had made. He desired honour the more greedily because of the worship he had gained. From out of Denmark he chose, by hundreds and by the thousands, the stoutest knights and archers he could find. These he joined to his host, purposing to lead this fair company into France.

Without any long tarrying the king acted on his purpose. Towns, cities, and castles fell before him, so that Flanders and the country about Boulogne were speedily in his power. Arthur was a prudent captain. He perceived no profit in wasting his own realm, burning his towns, and stealing from his very purse. His eyes were in every place, and much was forbidden by his commandment. No soldier might rob nor pill. If there was need of raiment, meat, or provand, then must he buy with good minted coin in the market. Nothing he dared to destroy or steal . . .

Guitard, the King of Poitiers, was a valiant captain, having good knights in his service. To uphold his realm and his rights Guitard fought many a hard battle. The luck went this way and that. Sometimes he was the hunter, sometimes the quarry: often he prevailed, and often, again, he lost. At the end Guitard was persuaded Arthur was the stronger lord and that only by submission could he keep his own. The land was utterly wasted and ravaged. Beyond the walls of town and castle there was nothing left to destroy; and of all the fair vineyards not a vine but was rooted from the ground. Guitard made overtures of peace and accorded himself with Hoel. He swore Arthur fealty and homage, so that the king came to love him very dearly. The other parcels of France Arthur conquered them every one by his own power.

When there was peace over all the country, so that none dared lift a spear against the king, Arthur sought such men as were grown old in his quarrels and desired greatly to return to their homes. To these feeble sergeants Arthur rendered their wages and gifts, and sent them rejoicing from whence they had come. The knights of his household and such lusty youths as were desirous of honour, having neither dame nor children to their hearths, Arthur held in his service for yet nine years.

During these nine years that Arthur abode in France, he wrought divers great wonders, reproving many haughty men and their tyrannies, and chastising many sinners after their deservings. Now it befell that when Easter was come, Arthur held high feast at Paris with his friends. On that day the king recompensed his servants for their losses, and gave to each after his deserts. He bestowed guerdon meetly on all, according to his zeal and the labour he had done. To Kay, the master seneschal of his house, a loyal and chivalrous knight, the king granted all Anjou and Angers. Bedevere, the king's cup-bearer and very privy counsellor, received that fief of Normandy which aforetime was called Neustria. These lords, Kay and Bedevere, were Arthur's faithful friends, knowing the inmost counsel of his mind. Boulogne was given to Holden; Le Mans to Borel, his cousin. On each and all, according to his gentleness of heart and diligence in his lord's service, Arthur bestowed honours and fees and granted largely of his lands.

After Arthur thus had feoffed his lords and given riches to his friends, in April, when winter was gone, he passed the sea to England, his own realm. Marvellous joy was shown of all good folk at the return of the king. Dames held those husbands close from whom they had been parted so long. Mothers kissed their sons, with happy tears upon their cheeks. Sons and daughters embraced their fathers.

Cousin clipped cousin, and neighbour that friend who once was his companion. The aunt made much of her sister's son. Ladies kissed long that lover who returned from France; yea, when the place was meet, clasped him yet more sweetly in their arms. Wondrous was the joy shown of all. In the lanes and crossways, in the highways and by-ways, you might see friends a many staying friend, to know how it fared with him, how the land was settled when it won, what adventures chanced to the seeker, what profit clave to him thereof, and why he remained so great a while beyond the sea. Then the soldier fought his battles once again. He told over his adventures, he spoke of his hard and weary combats, of the toils he had endured, and the perils from which he was delivered.

Arthur cherished tenderly his servants, granting largely, and promising richly, to the worthy. He took counsel with his barons, and devised that for the louder proclamation of his fame and wealth, he would hold a solemn feast at Pentecost, when summer was come, and that then in the presence of his earls and baronage he would be crowned king. Arthur commanded all his lords on their allegiance to meet him in Caerleon in Glamorgan.

He desired to be crowned king in Caerleon, because it was rich beyond other cities and marvellously pleasant and fair. Pilgrims told in those days that the mansions of Caerleon were more desirable than the palaces of Rome. This rich city, Caerleon, was builded on the Usk, a river which falls within the Severn. He who came to the city from a strange land might seek his haven by this fair water. On one side of the town flowed this clear river, whilst on the other spread a thick forest. Fish were very plentiful in the river, and of venison the burgesses had no lack. Passing fair and deep were the meadows about the city, so that the barns and granges were very rich. Within the walls rose two mighty churches, greatly praised. One of these famed churches was called in remembrance of Saint Julius the Martyr, and held a convent of holy nuns for the fairer service of God; the second church was dedicate to Saint Aaron, his companion. The bishop had his seat therein. Moreover, this church was furnished with many wealthy clergy and canons of seemly life. These clerks were students of astronomy, concerning themselves diligently with the courses of the stars. Often enough they prophesied to Arthur what the future would bring forth, and of the deeds that he would do. So goodly was the city, there was none more delectable in all the earth.

Now by reason of the lofty palaces, the fair woods and pastures, the ease and content, and all the delights of which you have heard, Arthur desired to hold his court at Caerleon, and to bid his barons to attend him every one. He commanded, therefore, to the feast, kings and earls, dukes and viscounts, knights and barons, bishops and abbots. Nor did Arthur bid Englishmen alone, but Frenchman and Burgundian, Auvergnat and Gascon, Norman and Poitivin, Angevin and Fleming, together with him of Brabant, Hainault, and Lorraine, the king bade to his dinner. Frisian and Teuton, Dane and Norwegian, Scot, Irish, and Icelander, him of Cathness and of Gothland, the lords of Galway and of the furthest islands of the Hebrides, Arthur summoned them all.

When these received the king's messages commanding them to his crowning, they hastened to observe the feast as they were bidden, every one. From Scotland came Aguisel the king, richly vested in his royal robes; there, too, was Urian, King of Murief, together with his son Yvain the courteous; Lot of Lyones also, to take a brave part in the revels, and with him that very frank and gentle knight Gawain, his son. There besides were Stater and Cadual, kings of South Wales and of North; Cador of Cornwall, right near to Arthur's heart; Morud, Earl of Gloucester; and Guerdon, Earl of Winchester. Anavalt came from Salisbury, and Rimarec from Canterbury. Earl Baldulph drew from Silchester, and Vigenin from Leicester. There, too, was Algal of Guivic, a baron much held in honour by the court. Other lords were there a many, in no wise of less reputation than their fellows. The son of Po that was hight Donander; Regian, son of Abauder; Ceilus, the son of Coil; that son of Chater named Chatellus; Griffin, the heir of Nagroil; Ron, the son of Neco; Margoil, Clefaut, Ringar, Angan, Rimar and Gorbonian, Kinlint, Neco and that Peredur, whom men deemed to be gotten by Eladur.

Besides these princes' there drew to Caerleon such knights as were of the king's house, and served him about his court. These were his chosen friends, who had their seats at the king's Round Table, but more of them I cannot tell. Many other lords were there of only less wealth and worship than those I have named. So numerous was this fair company that I have lost count of their numbers.

A noble array of prelates came also to Arthur's solemn feast. Abbots and mitred bishops walked in their order and degree. The three archbishops of the realm came in his honour, namely the Archbishop of London, his brother of York, and holy Dubricius, whose chair was in that self-same city. Very holy of life was this fair prelate. Very abundantly he laboured, being Archbishop of Caerleon and Legate of Rome. Many wonderful works were wrought by his hands. The sick were brought to him gladly, and by reason of his love and his prayers oftentimes they were healed of their hurt. In olden days this Dubricius abode in London, but now was Bishop in Wales, by reason of the evil times when kings regarded not God and the people forsook the churches of their fathers. These clergy assembled at Arthur's court for the king's feast together with so great a fellowship of barons that I know not even to rehearse you their names.

Yet these must be remembered, whomsoever I forget. Vilamus, King of Ireland, and Malinus, King of Iceland, and Doldamer, lord of that lean and meagre country known as the land of Goths. Acil, the King of the Danes; Lot, who was King of Norway, and Gonfal, jarl of the lawless Orkneys, from whence sail the pirates in their ships. From the parts beyond the seas came Ligier, holding the dukedom and honour of Burgundy; Holden, Earl of Flanders; and

Guerin, Earl of Chartres, having the twelve peers of France in his company, for the richer dignity and splendour of the state. Guitard was there, the Earl of Poitiers; Kay, whom the king had created Earl of Angers; and Bedevere of Neustria, that province which men now call Normandy. From Le Mans drew Earl Borel, and from Brittany Earl Hoel. Passing noble of visage was Hoel, and all those lords who came forth from France. They voyaged to Arthur's court in chased harness and silken raiment, riding on lusty horses with rich trappings and wearing jewels with many golden ornaments. There was not a prince from here even unto Spain, yea, to the very Rhine in the land of Germany, but hastened to Arthur's solemn feast, so only that he was bidden to that crowning. Of these some came to look on the face of the king, some to receive of his largess costly gifts, some to have speech with the lords of his council. Some desired to marvel over the abundance of Arthur's wealth, and others to hear tell of the great king's courtesies. This lord was drawn by the cords of love, this by compulsion of his suzerain's ban, this to learn by the witness of his eyes whether Arthur's power and prosperity exceeded that fame of which the whole world bragged.

When this proud company of kings, bishops, and princes was gathered together to observe Arthur's feast, the whole city was moved. The king's servants toiled diligently making ready for so great a concourse of guests. Soldiers ran to and fro busily seeking hostels for this fair assemblage. Houses were swept and garnished, spread with reeds, and furnished with hangings of rich arras. Halls and chambers were granted to their needs, together with stables for the horses and their provand. Those for whom hostelries might not be found abode in seemly lodgings, decently appointed to their degree. The city was full of stir and tumult. In every place you beheld squires leading horses and destriers by the bridle, setting saddles on hackneys and taking them off, buckling the harness and making the metal work shining and bright. Grooms went about their business. Never was such a cleansing of stables, such taking of horses to the meadows, such a currying and combing, shoeing and loosing of girths, washing and watering, such a bearing of straw and grass for the litter, and oats for the manger. Nor these alone, but in the courtyards and chambers of the hostels you might see the pages and chamberlains go swiftly about their tasks, in divers fashions. The varlets brushed and folded the habiliments and mantles of their lords. They looked to the stuff and the fastenings of their garments. You saw them hurry through the halls carrying furs and furred raiment, both the vair and the grey. Caerleon seemed rather a fair than a city, at Arthur's feast.

Now telleth the chronicle of this geste, that when the morning was come of the day of the high feast, a fair procession of archbishops, bishops, and abbots wended to the king's palace, to place the crown upon Arthur's head, and lead him within the church. Two of these archbishops brought him through the streets of the city, one walking on either side of his person. Each bishop sustained the king by his arm, and thus he was carried to his throne. Four kings went before Arthur and the clerks, bearing swords in their hands. Pommel, scabbard, and hilt of these four swords were of wrought gold. This was the office of these kings when Arthur held state at his court. The first of the princes was from Scotland, the second from South Wales, the third was of North Wales, and as to the last it was Cador of Cornwall who carried the fourth sword. All these fair princes were at one in their purpose, being altogether at unity, when Arthur was crowned king. To holy Dubricius it fell, as prelate of Caerleon and Roman legate, to celebrate the office and perform such rites as were seemly to be rendered in the church.

That the queen might not be overshadowed by her husband's state, the crown was set on her head in another fashion. For her part she had bidden to her court the great ladies of the country, and such dames as were the wives of her friends. Together with these had assembled the ladies of her kindred, such ladies as were most to her mind, and many fair and gentle maidens whom she desired to be about her person at the feast. The presence of this gay company of ladies made the feast yet more rich, when the queen was crowned in her chamber, and brought to that convent of holy nuns for the conclusion of the rite. The press was so great that the queen might hardly make her way through the streets of the city. Four dames preceded their lady, bearing four white doves in their hands. These dames were the wives of those lords who carried the golden swords before the king. A fair company of damsels followed after the queen, making marvellous joy and delight. This fair fellowship of ladies came from the noblest of the realm. Passing dainty were they to see, wearing rich mantles above their silken raiment. All men gazed gladly upon them, for their beauty was such that none was sweeter than her fellows. These dames and maidens went clothed in their softest garments. Their heads were tired in their fairest hennins, and they walked in their most holiday vesture. Never were seen so many rich kirtles of divers colours, such costly mantles, such precious jewels and rings. Never were seen such furs and such ornaments, both the vair and the grey. Never was known so gay and noble a procession of ladies, as this which hastened to the church lest it should be hindered from the rite.

Now within the church Mass was commenced with due pomp and observance. The noise of the organ filled the church, and the clerks sang tunably in the choir. Their voices swelled or failed, according as the chant mounted to the roof or died away in supplication. The knights passed from one church to the other. Now they would be at the convent of St. Julius, and again at the cathedral church of St. Aaron. This they did to compare the singing of the clerks, and to delight their eyes with the loveliness of the damsels. Although the knights passed frequently between churches, yet no man could answer for certain at which they remained the longer. They could not surfeit the heart by reason of the sweetness of the melody. Yea, had the song endured the whole day through, I doubt those knights would ever have grown weary or content.

When the office drew to its appointed end and the last words were chanted, the king put off his crown that he had carried to the church. He took another crown which sat more lightly on his head; and in such fashion did the queen. They laid aside their heavy robes and ornaments of state, and vested them in less tiring raiment. The king parted from St. Aaron's church and returned to his palace for meat. The queen, for her part, came again to her own house, carrying with her that fair fellowship of ladies, yet making marvellous joy. For the Britons held still to the custom brought by their sires from Troy, that when the feast was spread man ate with man alone, bringing no lady with him to the board. The ladies and damsels ate apart. No men were in their hall save only the servitors, who served them with every observance, for the feast was passing rich, as became a monarch's court. When Arthur was seated in his chair upon the daïs, the lords and princes sat around the board, according to the usage of the country, each in his order and degree. The king's seneschal, hight Sir Kay, served Arthur's table, clad in a fair dalmatic of vermeil silk. With Sir Kay were a thousand damoiseaux, clothed in ermine, who bore the dishes from the buttery. These pages moved briskly about the tables, carrying the meats in platters to the guests. Together with these were yet another thousand damoiseaux, gentle and goodly to see, clothed likewise in coats of ermine. These fair varlets poured the wine from golden beakers into cups and hanaps of fine gold. Not one of these pages but served in a vesture of ermine. Bedevere, the king's cupbearer, himself set Arthur's cup upon the board; and those called him master who saw that Arthur's servants lacked not drink.

The queen had so many servitors at her bidding that I may not tell you the count. She and all her company of ladies were waited on richly and reverently. Right worshipfully were they tended. These ladies had to their table many rich meats and wines and spiced drink of divers curious fashions. The dishes and vessels from which they ate were very precious and passing fair. I know not how to put before you the wealth and the splendour of Arthur's feast. Whether for goodly men or for chivalrous deeds, for wealth as for plenty, for courtesy as for honour, in Arthur's day England bore the flower from all the lands near by, yea, from every other realm whereof we know. The poorest peasant in his smock was a more courteous and valiant gentleman than was a belted knight beyond the sea. And as with the men, so, and no otherwise, was it with the women. There was never a knight whose praise was bruited abroad, but went in harness and raiment and plume of one and the self-same hue. The colour of surcoat and armour in the field was the colour of the gown he wore in hall. The dames and damsels would apparel them likewise in cloth of their own colour. No matter what the birth and riches of a knight might be, never, in all his days, could he gain fair lady to his friend till he had proved his chivalry and worth. That knight was accounted the most nobly born who bore himself the foremost in the press. Such a knight was indeed cherished of the ladies; for his friend was the more chaste as he was brave.

After the king had risen from the feast, he and his fellowship went without the city to take their delight amongst the fields. The lords sought their pleasure in divers places. Some amongst them jousted together, that their horses might be proven. Others fenced with the sword, or cast the stone, or flung pebbles from a sling. There were those who shot with the bow, like cunning archers, or threw darts at a mark. Every man strove with his fellow according to the game he loved. That knight who proved the victor in his sport and bore the prize from his companions was carried before the king in the sight of all the princes. Arthur gave him of his wealth so goodly a gift that he departed from the king's presence in great mirth and content. The ladies of the court climbed upon the walls, looking down on the games very gladly. She, whose friend was beneath her in the field, gave him the glance of her eye and her face so that he strove the more earnestly for her favour.

Now to the court had gathered many tumblers, harpers, and makers of music, for Arthur's feast. He who would hear songs sung to the music of the rote or would solace himself with the newest refrain of the minstrel might win to his wish. Here stood the viol player, chanting ballads and lays to their appointed tunes. Everywhere might be heard the voice of viols and harp and flutes. In every place rose the sound of lyre and drum and shepherd's pipe, bagpipe, psaltery, cymbals, monochord, and all manner of music. Here the tumbler tumbled on his carpet. There the mime and the dancing girl put forth their feats. Of Arthur's guests some hearkened to the teller of tales and fables. Others called for dice and tables, and played games of chance for a wager. Evil befalls to winner and loser alike from such sport as this. For the most part men played at chess or draughts. You might see them, two by two, bending over the board. When one player was beaten by his fellow, he borrowed moneys to pay his wager, giving pledges for the repayment of his debt. Dearly enough he paid for his loan, getting but eleven to the dozen. But the pledge was offered and taken, the money rendered, and the game continued with much swearing and cheating, much drinking and quarrelling, with strife and with anger. Often enough the loser was discontented, and rose murmuring against his fellow. Two by two the dicers sat at table, casting the dice. They threw in turn, each throwing higher than his fellow. You might hear them count, six, five, three, four, two, and one. They staked their raiment on the cast, so there were those who threw half naked. Fair hope had he who held the dice, after his fellow had cried his number. Then the quarrel rose suddenly from the silence. One called across the table to his companion, "You cheat, and throw not fairly. Grasp not the dice so tightly in your hand, but shake them forth upon the board. My count is yet before yours. If you still have pennies in your pouch bring them out, for I will meet you to your wish." Thus the dicers wrangled, and to many of Arthur's guests it chanced that he who sat to the board in furs, departed from the tables clothed in his skin.

When the fourth day of the week was come, on a certain Wednesday, the king made knights of his bachelors, granting them rents to support their stations. He recompensed those lords of his household who held of him their lands at suit and service. Such clerks as were diligent in their master's business he made abbots and bishops; and bestowed castles and towns on his counsellors and friends. To those stranger knights who for his love had crossed the sea in his quarrel, the king gave armour and destrier and golden ornaments, to their desire. Arthur divided amongst them freely of his wealth. He granted lordship and delights, greyhound and brachet, furred gown and raiment, beaker and hanap, sendal and signet, bliaut and mantle, lance and sword and quivers of sharp barbed arrows. He bestowed harness and buckler and weapons featly fashioned by the smith. He gave largesse of bears and of leopards, of palfreys and hackneys, of chargers with saddles thereon. He gave the helm as the hauberk, the gold as the silver, yea, he bestowed on his servants the very richest and most precious of his treasure. Never a man of these outland knights, so only he was worthy of Arthur's bounty, but the king granted him such gifts as he might brag of in his own realm. And as with the foreign lords, so to the kings and the princes, the knights and all his barons, Arthur gave largely many precious gifts.

Now as King Arthur was seated on a daïs with these princes and earls before him, there entered in his hall twelve ancient men, white and greyheaded, full richly arrayed in seemly raiment. These came within the palace two by two. With the one hand each clasped his companion, and in the other carried a fair branch of olive. The twelve elders passed at a slow pace down the hall, bearing themselves right worshipfully. They drew near to Arthur's throne and saluted the king very courteously. They were citizens of Rome, said the spokesman of these aged men, and were ambassadors from the Emperor, bringing with them letters to the king. Having spoken such words, one amongst them made ready his parchment, and delivered it in Arthur's hands. This was the sum of the writing sent by the Emperor of Rome.

"Lucius, the Emperor and lord of Rome, to King Arthur, his enemy, these, according to his deservings. I marvel very greatly, and disdain whilst yet I marvel, the pride and ill-will which have puffed you up to seek to do me evil. I have nothing but contempt and wonder for those who counsel you to resist the word of Rome, whilst yet one Roman draws his breath. You have acted lightly, and by reason of vanity have wrought mischief to us who are the front and avengers of the world. You resemble a blind man, whose eyes the leech prepares to open. You know not yet, but very soon you will have learned, the presumption of him who teaches law to the justice of Rome. It is not enough to say that you have acted after your kind, and sinned according to your nature. Know you not whom you are, and from what dust you have come, that you dare to dispute the tribute to Rome! Why do you steal our land and our truage? Why do you refuse to render Caesar that which is his own? Are you indeed so strong that we may not take our riches from your hand? Perchance you would show us a marvellous matter. Behold —you say—the lion fleeing from the lamb, the wolf trembling before the kid, and the leopard fearful of the hare. Be not deceived. Nature will not suffer such miracles to happen. Julius Caesar, our mighty ancestor—whom, maybe, you despise in your heart—conquered the land of Britain, taking tribute thereof, and this you have paid until now. From other islands also, neighbours of this, it was our custom to receive truage. These in your presumption you have taken by force, to your own most grievous hurt. Moreover, you have been so bold as to put yet greater shame and damage upon us, since Frollo, our tribune, is slain, and France and Britain, by fraud, you keep wrongfully in your power. Since, then, you have not feared Rome, neither regarded her honour, the senate summon you by these letters, and command you under pain of their displeasure, to appear before them at mid August, without fail or excuse. Come prepared to make restitution of that you have taken, whatever the cost; and to give satisfaction for all those things whereof you are accused. If so be you think to keep silence, and do naught of that you are bidden, I will cross the Mont St. Bernard with a mighty host, and pluck Britain and France from your hand. Do not deem that you can make head against me, neither hold France in my despite. Never will you dare to pass that sea, for my dearer pleasure; yea, were your courage indeed so great, yet never might you abide my coming. Be persuaded that in what place soever you await me, from thence I will make you skip. For this is my purpose, to bind you with bonds, and bring you to Rome, and deliver you, bound, to the judgment of the Senate."

When this letter was read in the hearing of those who were come to Arthur's solemnity, a great tumult arose, for they were angered beyond measure. Many of the Britons took God to witness that they would do such things and more also to those ambassadors who had dared deliver the message. They pressed about those twelve ancient men with many wild and mocking words. Arthur rose hastily to his feet, bidding the brawlers to keep silence. He cried that none should do the Romans a mischief, for they were an embassy, and carried the letters of their lord. Since they were but another's mouthpiece, he commanded that none should work them harm. After the noise was at an end and Arthur was assured that the elders were no longer in peril, he called his privy council and the lords of his household together in a certain stone keep that was named the Giant's Tower. The king would be advised by his barons—so ran the summons—what answer he should give to the messengers of Rome. Now as they mounted the stairs, earl and prince, pell-mell, together, Cador, who was a merry man, saw the king before him. "Fair king," said the earl gaily, "for a great while the thought has disturbed me that peace and soft living are rotting away the

British bone. Idleness is the stepdame of virtue, as our preachers have often told us. Soft living makes a sluggard of the hardiest knight, and steals away his strength. She cradles him with dreams of woman and is the mother of chambering and wantonness. Folded hands and idleness cause our young damoiseaux to waste their days over merry tales and dice, raiment to catch a lady's fancy and things that are worse. Rest and assurance of safety will in the end do Britain more harm than force or guile. May the Lord God be praised Who has jogged our elbow. To my mind He has persuaded these Romans to challenge our country that we may get us from sleep. If the Romans trust so greatly in their might that they do according to their letters, be assured the Briton has not yet lost his birthright of courage and hardness. I am a soldier, and have never loved a peace that lasts over long, since there are uglier things than war."

Gawain overheard these words. "Lord earl," said he, "by my faith be not fearful because of the young men. Peace is very grateful after war. The grass grows greener, and the harvest is more plenteous. Merry tales, and songs, and ladies' love are delectable to youth. By reason of the bright eyes and the worship of his friend, the bachelor becomes knight and learns chivalry."

Whilst the lords jested amongst themselves in this fashion, they climbed the tower, and were seated in the chamber. When Arthur marked that each was in his place, silent and attentive to the business, he considered for a little that he had to speak. Presently he lifted his head, and spoke such words as these. "Lords," said the king, "who are here with me, nay, rather my companions and friends, companions alike, whether the day be good or evil, by whose sustenance alone I have endured such divers quarrels, hearken well to me. In the days that are told, have we not shared victory and defeat together; partners, you with me, as I with you, in gain and in loss? Through you, and by reason of your help in time of trouble, have I won many battles. You have I carried over land and sea, far and near, to many strange realms. Ever have I found you loyal and true in business and counsel. Because of your prowess I hold the heritage of divers neighbouring princes in subjection. Lords, you have hearkened to the letters carried by the ambassadors of Rome and to the malice they threaten if we do not after their commandment. Very despiteful are they against us and purpose to work us bitter mischief. But if God be gracious to His people, we shall yet be delivered from their hand. Now these Romans are a strong nation, passing rich and of great power. It becomes us therefore to consider prudently what we shall say and do in answer to their message, looking always to the end. He who is assured of his mark gets there by the shortest road. When the arrows start to fly, the sergeant takes shelter behind his shield. Let us be cautious and careful like these. This Lucius seeks to do us a mischief. He is in his right, and it is ours to take such counsel that his mischief falls on his own head. To-day he demands tribute from Britain and other islands of the sea. To-morrow he purposes in his thought to receive truage of France. Consider first the case of Britain and how to answer wisely therein. Britain was conquered by Caesar of force. The Britons knew not how to keep them against his host, and perforce paid him their tribute. But force is no right. It is but pride puffed up and swollen beyond measure. They cannot hold of law what they have seized by violence and wrong. The land is ours by right, even if the Roman took it to himself by force. The Romans really reproach us for the shame and the damage, the loss and sorrow Caesar visited upon our fathers. They boast that they will avenge such losses as these by taking the land with the rent and making their little finger thicker than their father's loins. Let them beware. Hatred breeds hatred again, and things despiteful are done to those who despitefully use you. They come with threats, demanding truage and reproving us for the evil we have done them. Tribute they claim by the right of the strong, leaving sorrow and shame as our portion. But if the Romans claim to receive tribute of Britain because tribute was aforetime paid them from Britain, by the same reasoning we may establish that Rome should rather pay tribute to us. In olden days there lived two brothers, British born, namely, Belinus, King of the Britons, and Brennus, Duke of Burgundy, both wise and doughty lords. These stout champions arrived with their men before Rome and, shutting the city close, at the end gained it by storm. They took hostages of the citizens to pay them tribute; but since the burgesses did not observe their covenant, the brethren hanged the hostages, to the number of four-and-twenty, in the eyes of all their kinsfolk. When Belinus went to his own place, he commended Rome to the charge of Brennus, his brother. Now Constantine, the son of Helena, drew from Brennus and Belinus, and in his turn held Rome in his care. Maximian, King of Britain, after he had conquered France and Germany, passed the Mont St. Bernard into Lombardy and took Rome to his keeping. These mighty kings were my near kinsmen, and each was master of Rome. Thus you have heard, and see clearly, that not only am I King of Britain but by law Emperor of Rome also, so we maintain the rights of our fathers. The Romans have had truage of us, and my ancestors have taken seisin of them. They claim Britain, and I demand Rome. Let him have the fief and the rent who is mightier in the field. As to France and those other countries which have been removed from their hands, the Romans should not wish to possess that which they may not maintain. Either the land was not to their mind, or they had not the strength to hold it. Perchance the Romans have no rights in the matter, and it is by reason of covetousness rather than by love of law that they seek this quarrel. Let him keep the land who can, by the right of the most strong. For all these things the Emperor menaces us very grievously. I pray God that he may do us no harm. Our fiefs and goods he promises to take from us and lead us captive in bonds to Rome. We care not overmuch for this and are not greatly frighted at his words. If he seek us after his boast, please God, he will have no mind to threaten when he turns again to his own home. We accept his challenge and appeal to God's judgment, that all may be rendered to his keeping who is able to maintain it in his hand."

When Arthur the king had made an end of speaking in the ears of his barons, the word was with those who had hearkened to his counsel. Hoel followed after the king. "Sire," said he, "you have spoken much and right prudently; nor is there any who can add wisdom to your speech. Summon now your vassals and meinie, together with us who are of your household. Cross the sea straightway into France, and make the realm sure with no further tarrying. From thence we can pass Mont St. Bernard and overrun Lombardy. By moving swiftly we shall carry the war into the Emperor's own land. We shall fright him so greatly that he will have the less leisure to trouble Britain. Your movements, moreover, will be so unlooked for that the Romans will be altogether amazed and quickly confounded. Sire, it is the Lord's purpose to exalt you over all the kings of the earth. Hinder not the will of God by doubtfulness. He is able to put even Rome in your power, so only it be according to His thought. Remember the books of the Sibyl and of the prophecies therein. The Sibyl wrote that three kings should come forth from Britain, who of their might should conquer Rome. Of these three princes, two are dead. Belinus is dead, and Constantine is dead; but each in his day was the master of Rome. You are that third king destined to be stronger than the great city. In you the prophecy shall be fulfilled and the Sibyl's words accomplished. Why then scruple to take what God gives of His bounty? Rise up then, exalt yourself, exalt your servants, who would see the end of God's purpose. I tell you truly that nothing of blows or hurt, neither weariness nor prison nor death, counts aught with us in comparison with what is due to the king's honour. For my part, I will ride in your company so long as this business endures, with ten thousand armed horsemen at my back. Moreover, if your treasury has need of moneys for the quarrel, I will put my realm in pledge, and deliver the gold and the gain to your hand. Never a penny will I touch of my own, so long as the king has need."

Arthur and his baronage being of one mind together, the king wrote certain letters to Rome, and sealed them with his ring. These messages he committed to the embassy, honouring right worshipfully those reverend men. "Tell your countrymen," said the king, "that I am lord of Britain: that I hold France, and will continue to hold it, and purpose to defend it against the Roman power. Let them know of a surety that I journey to Rome presently at their bidding; only it will be not to carry them tribute, but rather to seek it at their hand."

The ambassadors, therefore, took their leave, and went again to Rome. There they told where and in what fashion they were welcomed of the king, and reported much concerning him. This Arthur — said these ancient men — is a lord amongst kings, generous

and brave, lettered and very wise. Not another king could furnish
the riches spent on his state, by reason of the attendance of his ministers and the glory of their apparel. It was useless to seek tribute from
Arthur, since in olden days Britain received tribute of Rome.

Now when the senate had heard the report of the messengers and
considered the letters wherewith they were charged, they were persuaded of ambassador and message alike that Arthur neither would
do homage nor pay them the tribute they demanded. The senate,
therefore, took counsel with the emperor, requiring him to summon
all the empire to his aid. They devised that with his host he should
pass through the mountains into Burgundy and, giving battle to
King Arthur, deprive him of kingdom and crown.

Lucius Tiberius moved very swiftly. He sent messages to kings,
earls, and dukes, bidding them as they loved honour to meet him on
a near day at Rome, in harness for the quest. At the emperor's
commandment came many mighty lords, whose names I find written
in the chronicles of those times. To meet Lucius came Epistrophius,
King of the Greeks; Ession, King of Boeotia; and Itarc, King of the
Turks, a passing strong and perilous knight. With these were
found Pandras, King of Egypt, and Hippolytus, King of Crete.
These were lords of very great worship, a hundred cities owning
their tyranny. Evander drew from Syria, and Teucer from Phrygia;
from Babylon came Micipsa, and from Spain, Aliphatma. From
Media came King Bocus, from Libya, Sertorius, from Bithynia,
Polydetes, and from Idumea, King Xerxes. Mustansar, the King of
Africa, came from his distant home, many a long days' journey.
With him were black men and Moors, bearing their king's rich
treasure. The senate gave of their number these patricians: Marcellus and Lucius Catellus, Cocta, Caius, and Metellus. Many other
lords gladly joined themselves to that company, whose names for all
my seeking I have not found. When the host was gathered together,
the count of the footmen was four hundred thousand armed men,
besides one hundred and eighty thousand riders on horses. This
mighty army, meetly ordered and furnished with weapons, set forth
on a day to give Arthur battle from Rome.

Arthur and his baronage departed from the court to make them
ready for battle. The king sent his messengers to and fro about
the land, calling and summoning each by his name, to hasten swiftly
with his power, so that he valued Arthur's love. Not a knight but
was bidden to ride on his allegiance, with all the men and horses that
he had. The lords of the isles, Ireland, Gothland, Iceland, Denmark, Norway and the Orkneys, promised for their part one hundred
and forty thousand men, armed and clad according to the fashion
of their country. Of these not a horseman but was a cunning rider;
not a footman but bore his accustomed weapon, battle-axe, javelin, or
spear. Normandy and Anjou, Auvergne and Poitou, Flanders and
Boulogne promised, without let, eighty thousand sergeants more,
each with his armour on his back. So much it was their right and
privilege to do, they said. The twelve peers of France, who were

of the fellowship of Guerin of Chartres, promised every one to ride at Arthur's need, each man with a hundred lances. This was their bounden service, said these peers. Hoel of Brittany promised ten thousand men; Aguisel of Scotland two thousand more. From Britain, his proper realm that we now call England, Arthur numbered forty thousand horsemen in hauberks of steel. As for the count of the footmen — arbalestriers, archers, and spearmen — it was beyond all measure, for the number of the host was as the grains of sand. When Arthur was certified of the greatness of his power, and of the harness of his men, he wrote letter to each of his captains, commanding him that on an appointed day he should come in ships to Barfleur in Normandy. The lords of his baronage, who had repaired from the court to their fiefs, hastened to make ready with those whom they should bring across the sea. In like manner Arthur pushed on with his business, that nothing should hinder or delay.

Arthur committed the care of his realm, and of Dame Guenevere his wife, to his nephew, Mordred, a marvellously hardy knight, whom Arthur loved passing well. Mordred was a man of high birth and of many noble virtues, but he was not true. He had set his heart on Guenevere, his kinswoman, but such a love brought little honour to the queen. Mordred had kept his love close, for easy enough it was to hide, since who would be so bold as to deem that he loved his uncle's dame? The lady on her side had given her love to a lord of whom much good was spoken; but Mordred was of her husband's kin! This made the shame more shameworthy. Ah, God, the deep wrong done in this season by Mordred and the queen.

Arthur, having put all the governance in Mordred's power, save only the crown, went his way to Southampton. His meinie was lodged about the city, whilst his vessels lay within the haven. The harbour was filled with the ships. They passed to and fro; they remained at anchorage; they were bound together by cables. The carpenter yet was busy upon them with his hammer. Here the shipmen raised the mast and bent the sail; there they thrust forth bridges to the land, and charged the stores upon the ship. The knights and the sergeants entered therein in their order, bearing pikes, and leading the fearful horses by the rein. You could watch them crying farewell and waving their hands to those remaining on the shore. When the last man had entered in the last ship the sailors raised the anchors and worked the galleys from the haven. Right diligently the mariners laboured, spreading the sails, and making fast the stays. They pulled stoutly upon the hoists and ropes, so that the ships ran swiftly out to sea. Then they made the ropes secure, each in its wonted place. The captain who was charged with the safety of the ship set his course carefully, whilst pilot and steersman heedfully observed his word. At his bidding they put the helm to port, to lee, as they might better fill their sails with the wind. As need arose the shipmen drew upon the cords and bowlines or let the canvas fall upon the deck, that the vessel might be the less beaten of the waves. Thus, loosing and making fast, letting go and bringing quickly to the deck, hauling and tugging at the ropes — so they proceeded on their way. When night was come, they steered their courses by the stars, furling the sails that the wind should not carry them from their path. Very fearful were the mariners of the dark, and went as slowly as they were able. Passing bold was he, that first courteous captain, who builded the first ship, and committing his body to the wind and waves, set forth to seek a land he might not see, and to find such haven as men had never known!

Now it came to pass that whilst the host voyaged in great content with a fair wind towards Barfleur, that Arthur slept, for he was passing heavy, and it was night. As the king slumbered he beheld a vision, and, lo, a bear flying high in air towards the east. Right huge and hideous of body was the bear, and marvellously horrible to see. Also the king saw a dragon flying over against him towards the west. The brightness of his eyes was such that the whole land and sea were filled with the radiance of his glory. When these two beasts came together, the dragon fell upon the bear, and the bear defended himself valiantly against his adversary. But the dragon put his enemy beneath him and, tumbling him to the earth, crushed him utterly in the dust. When Arthur had slept for awhile, his spirit came to him again, and he awoke and remembered his dream. The king called therefore for his wise clerks, and related to them and his household the vision that he had seen of the bear and of the dragon. Then certain of these clerks expounded to the king his dream and the interpretation thereof. The dragon that was beholden of the king signified himself. By the bear was shown forth a certain horrible giant, come from a far land, whom he should slay. The giant desired greatly that the adventure should end in another fashion; nevertheless all would be to the king's profit. But Arthur replied, "My interpretation of the dream is other than yours. To me it typifies rather the issue of the war between myself and emperor. But let the Creator's will be done."

After these words no more was spoken until the rising of the sun. Very early in the morning they came to haven at Barfleur in Normandy.

When the men of Ireland and those others for whom Arthur tarried had joined themselves to the host, the king set forth, a day's march every day, through Normandy. Without pause or rest he and his fellowship passed across France, tarrying neither at town nor castle, and came speedily into Burgundy. The king would get to Autun as swiftly as he might, for the Romans were spoiling the land, and Lucius their emperor, together with a great company, purposed to enter in the city. Now when Arthur drew to the ford leading across the waters of the Aube, his spies and certain peasants of those parts came near and warned him privily concerning the emperor, who lay but a little way thence, so that the king could seek him if he would. The Romans had sheltered them in tents and in lodges of branches. They were as the sand of the shore for multitude, so that the peasants marvelled that the earth could bring forth for the footmen and horses. Never might the king store and garner in that day; for where he reaped with one, Lucius the emperor would reap with four.

Arthur was in no wise dismayed at their words. He had gone through many and divers perils, and was a valiant knight, having faith and affiance in God. On a little hill near this river Aube, Arthur builded earthworks for his host, making the place exceeding strong. He closed the doors fast, and put therein a great company of knights and men-at-arms to hold it close. In this fortress he set his harness and stores, so that he could repair thither to his camp in time of need. When all was done Arthur summoned to his counsel two lords whom he esteemed for fair and ready speech. These two lords were of high peerage. Guerin of Chartres was one, and the other was that Boso, Earl of Oxford, right learned in the law. To these two barons Arthur added Gawain, who had dwelt in Rome for so long a space. This Arthur did by reason that Gawain was a good clerk, meetly schooled, and held in much praise and honour by his friends in Rome. These three lords the king purposed to send as an embassy to the emperor. They were to bear his message, bidding the Romans to turn again to their own land nor seek to enter France, for it pertained to the king. Should Lucius persist in his purpose, refusing to return whence he came, then let him give battle on the earliest day, to determine whether Arthur or he had the better right. This thing was certain. So long as Arthur had breath he would maintain his claim to France, despite the Roman power. He had gained it by the sword, and it was his by right of conquest. In ancient days Rome, in her turn, held it by the same law. Then let the God of battles decide whether Britain or Rome had the fairer right to France.

The messengers of the king apparelled themselves richly for their master's honour. They mounted on their fairest destriers, vested in hauberks of steel, with laced helmets and shields hung round their necks. They took their weapons in their hands and rode forth from the camp.

Now when certain knights and divers bold and reckless varlets saw the embassy make ready to seek the emperor, they came to Gawain and gave him freely of their counsel. These exhorted him that when he reached the court to which he fared, he should act in such fashion, right or wrong, that a war would begin which had threatened overlong. Yea, to use such speech that if no matter of dispute should be found at the meeting, there might yet be quarrel enough when they parted. The embassy accorded, therefore, that they would so do as to constrain the Romans to give battle.

Gawain and his comrades crossed a mountain and came through a wood upon a wide plain. At no great distance they beheld the tents and lodges of the host. When the Romans saw the three knights issue from the wood, they drew near to look upon their faces and to inquire of their business. They asked of them concerning whom they sought and if for peace they had come within the camp. But the three knights refused to answer, for good or evil, until they were led before the lord of Rome. The embassy got from their horses before the emperor's pavilion. They gave their bridles to the hands of the pages, but as to their swords concealed them beneath their mantles. The three knights showed neither salutation nor courtesy when they stood in the emperor's presence. They rehearsed over Arthur's message whilst Lucius hearkened attentively to their words. Each of the ambassadors said that which pleased him to be said and told over what he held proper to be told. The emperor listened to each and all without interruption. After he had considered at his leisure he purposed to reply.

"We come from Arthur, our lord," said Gawain, "and bear to thee his message. He is our king, and we are his liegemen, so it becomes us to speak only the words he has put in our mouth. By us, his ambassadors, he bids you refrain from setting a foot in France. He forbids you to intermeddle with the realm, for it is his, and he will defend his right with such power, that very certainly you may not snatch it from his hand. Arthur requires you to seek nothing that is his. If, however, you challenge his claim to France, then battle shall prove his title good, and by battle you shall be thrown back to your own land. Once upon a time the Romans conquered this realm by force and by force they maintained their right. Let battle decide again whether Rome or Britain has the power to keep. Come forth to-morrow with thy host, so that it may be proven whether you or we shall hold France. If you fear this thing, then go your way in peace, as indeed is best, for what else is there to do! The game is played, and Rome and you have lost."

Lucius the Emperor made answer that he did not purpose to return to his realm. France was his fief, and he would visit his own. If he might not pursue his road to-day, why, then to-morrow. But in heart and hope he deemed himself mighty enough to conquer France and to take all in his seisin.

The Romans hastened to get to their arms, for they were passing eager to fight. They arrayed and embattled the host, setting the sergeants in rank and company, and forming the columns in due order. The Romans were a mingled fellowship. Divers outland kings and many paynim and Saracens were mixed with the Christian folk; for all these people owned fealty to Rome and were in the service of the emperor. By thirties and forties, by fifties, by sixties, by hundreds and by legions, the captains apparelled the battle. In troops and in thousands the horsemen pricked to their appointed place. Multitudes of spearmen, multitudes of riders, were ranged in close order, and by hill and valley were despatched against Arthur's host. One mighty company, owning fealty to Rome and employed in the service of the emperor, descended within the valley. Another great company assaulted the Britons where they lay. Thereat broke forth a loud shrilling of clarions and sounding of trumpets, whilst the hosts drew together. As they approached, the archers shot so deftly, the spearmen launched their darts so briskly, that not a man dared to blink his eye or to show his face. The arrows flew like hail, and very quickly the melley became yet more contentious. There where the battle was set you might mark the lowered lance, the rent and piercéd buckler. The ash staves knapped with a shriek and flew in splinters about the field. When the spear was broken they turned to the sword, and plucked the brand from its sheath. Right marvellous was the melley, and wondrously hideous and grim. Never did men hew more mightily with the glaive. Not a man who failed at need; not a man of them all who flinched in the press; not one who took thought for his life. The sword smote upon the buckler as on an anvil. The earth shuddered beneath the weight of the fighting men, and the valley rang and clanged like a smithy with the tumult. Here a host rushed furiously against a legion which met it with unbroken front. There a great company of horsemen crashed with spears upon a company as valiant as itself. Horse and rider went down before the adversary, arrows flew and darts were hurled, lances were splintered and the sword shattered upon the covering shield. The strong prevailed against the weak, and the living brought sorrow to the dead. Horses ran madly about the field with voided saddles, broken girths, and streaming mane. The wounded pitied their grievous hurts, choosing death before life; but the prayer of their anguish was lost in the tumult of the cries.

Thus for a great while the two hosts contended mightily together, doing marvellous damage, one to the other. Neither Roman nor Briton could gain ground, so that no man knew who would triumph in the end. Bedevere and Kay considered the battle. They saw that the Romans held themselves closely. They were filled with anger at the malice of the Romans, and led their company to that place where the press was the most perilous. Ah, God, but Arthur had men for his seneschal and cupbearer! Knights of a truth were these who sat at his table! Kay and Bedevere smote like paladins with their brands of steel. Many fair deeds had they done, but none so fair as they did that day. They divided the forefront of the battle and, cleaving a passage with the sword, opened a road for their fellows. The Britons followed after, taking and rendering many strokes, so that divers were wounded and many slain. Blood ran in that place like water, and the dead they lay in heaps. Bedevere adventured deeper into the melley, giving himself neither pause nor rest. Kay came but a stride behind, beating down and laying low, that it was marvellous to see. The two companions halted for a breathing space, turning them about to encourage their men. Great was the praise and worship they had won, but they were yet desirous of honour. They were over-anxious for fame, and their courage led them to rashness. In their hope of destroying the Romans, they took no heed to their own safety. They trusted beyond measure in their strength, and in the strength of their company.

There was a certain pagan, named Bocus, King of the Medes. He was a rich lord in his land, and captain of a strong legion. Bocus hastened his men to the battle, for he was fearful of none, however perilous the knight. When the two hosts clashed together the contention was very courteous, and the melley passing well sustained. Pagan and Saracen were set to prove their manhood against Angevins and the folk of Beauce. King Bocus took a sword and discomfited the two paladins. May his body rot for his pains. He thrust Bedevere through the breast, so fiercely that the steel stood out beyond his back. Bedevere fell, for his heart was cloven. His soul went its way. May Jesus take it in His keeping! Kay lighted upon Bedevere lying dead. Since he loved him more than any living man, he was determined the pagans should not triumph over his body. He called around him as many men as he might, and did such deeds that the Medians fled before him, leaving the Britons on the field. Sertorius, King of Libya, beheld this adventure, and was passing wroth. He had with him a great company of pagans whom he had carried from his realm. Sertorius, hot with anger, drew near, and dealt much mischief to his adversaries. He wounded Kay to the death, and slew the best of his men. Mauled as he was with many grim strokes, Kay guarded his comrade's body. He set it amidst his men, and carried the burthen from the press, fighting as they went.

Hoel and Gawain, his cousin, were distraught with anger when they regarded the mischief dealt them by the Romans. To avenge their comrades, to wreak damage upon their adversaries, they entered amongst them as lions in the field. They smote down and did much havoc to their adversaries, cleaving a way with many terrible blows of their swords. The Romans defended their bodies to the death. If strokes they received, strokes they rendered again. They opposed themselves stoutly to those who were over against them, and were as heroes contending with champions. Gawain was a passing perilous knight. His force and manhood never failed, so that his strength was unabated and his hand unwearied in battle. He showed his prowess so grimly that the Romans quailed before him. Gawain sought the emperor in every place, because of his desire to prove his valour. He went to and fro, seeking so tirelessly and diligently that at the last he found. The captains looked on the other's face. The emperor knew again the knight, and Gawain remembered Lucius. The two hurtled together, but each was so mighty that he fell not from his horse. Lucius, the emperor, was a good knight, strong, and very valiant. He was skilled in all martial exercises and of much prowess. He rejoiced greatly to adventure himself against Gawain, whose praise was so often in the mouths of men. Should he return living from the battle, sweetly could he boast before the ladies of Rome. The paladins strove with lifted arm and raised buckler. Marvellous blows they dealt with the sword. They pained themselves greatly, doing all that craft might devise to bring the combat to an end. Neither of them flinched, nor gave back before the other. Pieces were hewn from the buckler and sparks flew from the brands. They joined together, smiting above and thrusting under, two perfect knights, two gentle paladins, so fierce and so terrible, that had they been left to themselves very quickly must one have come to a fair end.

The Roman legions recovered from the panic into which they had fallen. They ranged themselves beneath the golden eagle, and brought succour to the Emperor at the moment of his utmost need. The legions swept the Britons before them and won again the field from which they were driven. Arthur watched the fortunes of the day. He marked the discomfiture of his host and hearkened to the triumphant shouts of the legionaries. He could not, and dared not, wait longer. Arthur hastened with his chosen company to the battle. He rallied the rout, crying to the fleeing sergeants, "Whom seek you? Turn about, for it were better to be slain of the Romans than by your king. I am Arthur, your captain; and mortal man shall not drive me from the field. Follow me, for I will open a road; and beware lest the maidens of Britain hold you as recreant. Call to mind your ancient courage, by which you have overcome so many proud kings. For my part I will never go from this field alive, till I have avenged me on my adversaries."

Arthur did wondrously in the eyes of all the people. He struck many a Roman to the ground. Shield and hauberk and helmet he hewed asunder; heads, arms, and gauntlets were divided by his sword. Excalibur waxed red that day, for whom Arthur smote he slew. I cannot number the count of his blows, and every blow a death. For as the ravenous lion deals with his prey, so likewise did the fair king raven amongst his enemies. Not one he spared, he turned aside from none. That man he wounded required no surgeon for his hurt. All the press gave back before so stark a champion, till in his path stood neither great nor small.

The King of Libya — Sertorius to name — was a lord exceeding rich. Arthur struck the head from his shoulders. "In an ill hour you drew from the east to bear arms in this quarrel, and to furnish drink for Excalibur." But the dead man answered never a word. Polybetes, King of Bithynia, fought upon his feet. This was a pagan lord, and passing rich. Arthur found the paynim before him. He smote but one marvellous blow, and divided his head to the shoulders. Polybetes crashed to the earth. His soul rushed from his body, and his brains were spattered about the field. "Roman, speed to your doom," cried Arthur loudly, in the hearing of all.

When the Britons beheld Arthur's deeds, and hearkened to his high words, they took courage and charged upon the Romans. The Romans met them boldly with sword and spear, doing them many and great mischiefs. When Arthur saw that the battle was stayed, he increased in valour and did yet more dreadfully with Excalibur. He slew and cast down divers so that the ground was cumbered with the fallen. Lucius, the emperor, for his part, was not backward in the melley, and avenged himself grievously on the Britons. Emperor and king, for all their seeking, might not come together. This was heavy upon them, for each was a very courteous champion. The battle rolled this way and that since the contention was passing perilous. The Romans did well, nor might the Britons do better. A thousand men came swiftly to their deaths, for the two hosts arrayed themselves proudly one against the other and strove right scornfully. Not a judge on earth could declare which host should be vanquished, nor what man of them all would come victor and quick from the tourney.

Now Mordup, Earl of Gloucester, was constable of the bailly Arthur had hidden on a high place within a wood. Mordup remembered Arthur's counsel that should evil befall and the battle draw back to the wood, he must charge boldly on his adversaries. Mordup rode from his hiding with a company of six thousand six hundred and sixty-six riders, clad in gleaming helmets and coats of mail and carrying sharp lances and swords. These drew down the hillside, unnoticed of the Romans, and, coming out on their rear, charged hotly on the legion. The legion was altogether discomfited. Its ranks were pierced, its order was broken, with the loss of more than one thousand men. The Britons rode amongst the Romans, parting each from his fellow, trampling the fallen beneath the horses' hoofs, and slaying with the sword. The Romans could endure no longer, for the end of all was come. They broke from their companies and fled fearfully down the broad road, climbing one upon the other in their haste. There Lucius, the emperor, fell on death, being smitten in the body by a spear. I cannot tell who smote him down, nor of whose lance he was stricken. He was overtaken in the press, and amongst the dead he was found slain. Beneath the thickest of the battle he was discovered, dead, and the hurt within his breast was dealt him by a spear.

The Romans and their fellows from the east fled before the pursuers, but the Britons following after did them sore mischief. They waxed weary of slaying, so that they trod the Romans underfoot. Blood ran in runnels, and the slain they lay in heaps. Fair palfreys and destriers ran masterless about the field, for the rider was dead, and had neither joy nor delight in the sun. Arthur rejoiced and made merry over so noble a triumph, which had brought the pride of Rome to the dust. He gave thanks to the King of Glory, who alone had granted him the victory. Arthur commanded search to be made about the country for the bodies of the slain, whether they were friend or foe. Many he buried in the self-same place, but for the others he carried them to certain fair abbeys, and laid them together to rest. As for the body of Lucius the Emperor, Arthur bade it to be held in all honour and tended with every high observance. He sealed it in a bier and sent it worshipfully to Rome.  At the same time he wrote letters to the senate that no other truage would he pay them for Britain, which he guarded as his realm.  If truage they yet required, then truage they should receive coined in the very mint.  Kay, who was wounded to death in the battle, was carried to Chinon, the castle he had builded and called after his own name.  There he was interred in a holy hermitage, standing in a little grove near by the city.  Bedevere was brought to Bayeux in Normandy, a town of his lordship.  He was lain in the ground beyond the gate, looking over towards the south.

Arthur, for his part, sojourned all through the winter in Burgundy, giving peace and assurance to the land.  He purposed, when summer was come, to pass the mountains and get him to Rome.  He was hindered in his hope by Mordred, of whose shame and vileness you shall now hear.

This Mordred was the king's kin, his sister's very son, and had Britain in his charge.  Arthur had given the whole realm to his care, and committed all to his keeping.  Mordred did whatever was good in his own eyes and would have seized the land to his use.  He took homage and fealty from Arthur's men, demanding of every castle a hostage.  Not content with this great sin he wrought yet fouler villainy.  Against the Christian law he took to himself the wife of the king.  His uncle's queen, the dame of his lord, he took as wife, and made of her his spouse.

These tidings were carried to Arthur.  He was persuaded that Mordred observed no faith towards him, but had betrayed the queen, stolen his wife, and done him no fair service.  The king gave half his host to Hoel, committing Burgundy and France to his hand. He prayed him to keep the land shut from its foes till he came again in peace.  For himself he would return to Britain, to bring the kingdom back to its allegiance, and to avenge himself on Mordred, who had served his wife and honour so despitefully.  Britain, at any cost, must be regained, for if that were lost all the rest would quickly fall a prey.  Better to defer for a season the conquest of Rome than to be spoiled of his own realm.  In a little while he would come again, and then would go to Rome.  With these words Arthur set forth towards Wissant, making complaint of the falseness of Mordred, who had turned him away from his conquest; for the warships lay at Wissant ready for sea.

Mordred learned of Arthur's purpose.  He cared not though he came, for peace was not in his heart.  He sent letters to Cheldric of Saxony, praying him to sail to his aid.  The Saxon came with seven hundred galleys furnished with all manner of store and laden with fighting men.

Arthur saw to the harness of his men.  He got them on the ships, a multitude whom none could number, and set forth to Romney, where he purposed to cast anchor.  Arthur and his people had scarcely issued from the galleys when Mordred hastened against him with his own men and those folk from beyond the sea who had sworn to fight in his quarrel. The men in the boats strove to get them to shore whilst those on the land contended to thrust them deeper in the water. Arrows flew and spears were flung from one to the other, piercing heart and bowels and breast of those to whom they were addressed. The mariners pained themselves mightily to run their boats aground. They could neither defend themselves nor climb from the ships, so that those were swiftly slain who struggled to land. Often they staggered and fell, crying aloud; and in their rage they taunted those as traitors who hindered them from coming on shore. Ere the ships could be unladen in that port, Arthur suffered wondrous loss. Many a bold sergeant paid the price with his head. There, too, was Gawain his nephew slain, and Arthur made over him marvellous sorrow; for the knight was dearer to his heart than any other man. Aguisel was killed at Gawain's side; a mighty lord, and very helpful at need. Many others also were slain, for whom Arthur, the courteous prince, felt sore dolour.

So long as Mordred kept the shipmen from the sand, he wrought them much mischief. But when Arthur's sergeants won forth from the boats and arrayed them in the open country, Mordred's meinie might not endure against them. Mordred and his men had fared richly and lain softly overlong. They were sickly with peace. They knew not how to order the battle, neither to seek shelter nor to wield arms, as these things were known to Arthur's host, which was cradled and nourished in war. Arthur and his own ravened amongst them, smiting and slaying with the sword. They slew them by scores and by hundreds, killing many and taking captive many more. The slaughter was very grievous by reason of the greatness of the press. When daylight failed and night closed on the field, Arthur ceased from slaughter and called his war hounds off. Mordred's host continued their flight. They knew not how they went, nor whither; for there was none to lead them, and none took heed to his neighbour. Each thought of himself and was his own physician.

That queen who was Arthur's wife knew and heard tell of the war that was waged by Mordred in England. She learned also that Mordred had fled from before the king because he might not endure against him and durst not abide him in the field. The queen was lodged at York, in doubt and sadness. She called to mind her sin and remembered that for Mordred her name was a hissing. Her lord she had shamed and set her love on her husband's sister's son. Moreover, she had wedded Mordred in defiance of right, since she was wife already, and so must suffer reproach in earth and hell. Better were the dead than those who lived, in the eyes of Arthur's queen. Passing heavy was the lady in her thought. The queen fled to Caerleon. There she entered in a convent of nuns and took the veil. All her life's days were hidden in this abbey. Never again was this fair lady heard or seen; never again was she found or known of men. This she did by reason of her exceeding sorrow for her trespass and for the sin that she had wrought.

Mordred held Cornwall in his keeping, but for the rest the realm had returned to its allegiance. He compassed sea and land to gather soldiers to his banner. Saxon and Dane, the folk of Ireland and Norway, Saracen and pagan, each and all of them who hated Arthur and loathed his bondage, Mordred entreated to his aid. He promised everything they would, and gave what he could, like a man whom necessity drives hard.

Arthur was sick with wrath that he was not avenged of Mordred. He had neither peace nor rest whilst the traitor abode in his land. Arthur learned of Mordred's strength in Cornwall, and this was grievous to him. His spies brought tidings of the snares that Mordred spread, and the king waxed heavier thereat. Arthur sent after his men to the very Humber. He gathered to himself so mighty a host that it was as the sand for multitude. With this he sought Mordred where he knew he could be found. He purposed to slay and make an end of the traitor and his perjury alike. Mordred had no desire to shrink from battle. He preferred to stake all on the cast, yea, though the throw meant death — rather than be harried from place to place.

The battle was arrayed on the Camel, over against the entrance to Cornwall. A bitter hatred had drawn the hosts together, so that they strove to do each other sore mischief. Their malice was wondrous great and the murder passing grim. I cannot say who had the better part. I neither know who lost nor who gained that day. No man wists the name of overthrower or of overthrown. All are alike forgotten, the victor with him who died. Much people were slain on either side, so that the field was strewn with the dead and crimson with the blood of dying men. There perished the brave and comely youth that Arthur had nourished and gathered from so many and far lands. There also the knights of his Table Round, whose praise was bruited about the whole world. There, too, was Mordred slain in the press, together with the greater part of his folk; and in the self-same day were destroyed the flower of Arthur's host, the best and hardiest of his men.

So the chronicle speaks sooth, Arthur himself was wounded in his body to the death. He caused him to be borne to Avalon for the searching of his hurts. He is yet in Avalon, awaited of the Britons; for as they say and deem he will return from whence he went and live again.

Master Wace, the writer of this book, cannot add more to this matter of his end than was spoken by Merlin the prophet. Merlin said of Arthur — if I read aright — that his end should be hidden in doubtfulness. The prophet spoke truly. Men have ever doubted, and — as I am persuaded — will always doubt whether he liveth or is dead. Arthur bade that he should be carried to Avalon in this hope in the year 642 of the Incarnation. The sorer sorrow that he was a childless man. To Constantine, Cador's son, Earl of Cornwall, and his near kin, Arthur committed the realm, commanding him to hold it as king until he returned to his own.   The earl took the land to his keeping.   He held it as bidden, but nevertheless Arthur came never again.

[tr. Anonymous]

# MARIE DE FRANCE

According to contemporary testimony, in the twelfth century the Celts of Wales and Cornwall and the Celts of Brittany or Armorica still spoke languages so similar that they had little difficulty understanding each other. Moreover, they traveled back and forth; for the Cornish and Welsh, driven away from the natural roads to the Continent by the hated English, who settled in Kent, Sussex, and Hampshire, took the sea route from Wales and Cornwall to the Brittany peninsula. In the tenth century the Bretons fell under the rule of their new neighbors, the Normans. Since relations between them were congenial enough, stories were exchanged, as they were not between the insular Celts and their English conquerors. Little wonder, then, that Norman-French literature of the twelfth and thirteenth centuries is colored by Celtic images and often based on Celtic themes. How much of the Arthurian material may have come from the insular Celts and how much was invented by the Armorican Bretons will probably always remain a question of scholarly dispute. But none disputes that English writers derived most of that material by the circuitous path from France rather than directly from neighboring Wales and Cornwall.

In Chaucer's time, the "Breton lay" was a traditional term for a short romantic narrative with spritely trimmings:

> Thise olde gentil Britouns in hir dayes
> Of diverse aventures moden layes,
> Rymeyed in hir firste Briton tongue;
> Whiche layes with hir instrumentz they songe,
> Or elles redden hym for hir pleasaunce.

These lays, or songs, were chanted to the accompaniment of the Celtic rote, a kind of violin, or the harp.

The most characteristically Celtic of these Norman-French tales were composed by Marie de France. Nothing is known of her except her name, which suggests royalty. Even the dialect of her writings is in dispute: it is on the line between Norman-French and the French of Paris. Almost certainly the unknown king to whom she dedicated her lays was Henry II of England, and Fox ingeniously suggests that she was the Abbess of Shaftesbury who was an illegitimate half-sister of the king. She professes to have taken her material from Breton sources, and some borrowing has been demonstrated. Nevertheless, the corruptions of Breton words show that she knew little or nothing of the language. Her stories are French enough, but their plots and most of their images come from the Celts, who inspired the proverb that a Welshman has imagination enough for fifty poets without judgment enough for one. This Celtic imagination, extensively discussed in Matthew Arnold's *On the Study of Celtic Literature,* is found in its purest state in what is now known as the *Mabinogion,* a collection of medieval Welsh tales translated in 1838 by Lady Charlotte Guest. Though three of the tales that contain Arthurian material were undoubtedly inspired by French romance, two others, *Kulhwch and Olwen* and the *Dream of Rhonabwy,* seem to represent uncontaminated Welsh traditions from which Geoffrey of Monmouth drew. These tales have the same characteristics of the lays of Marie: the fairy-king quality of Arthur, the giants, pixies, gnomes, elves, pucks, dwarfs, goblins, fays, nymphs, werewolves, and supernatural animals of the spirit world, the use of magical formularies for advancing the action, the passionate love between humans and fairies, the wild but delicate fancies, the pictures of lakes and woods and still places, and, in contrast with Geoffrey and Wace, the avoidance of great numbers and campaigns.

## SIR LAUNFAL

Marie de France (*circ.* 1170)

[From *Guingamor, Launfal, Tyolet, The Were-Wolf,* by Jessie L. Weston; David Nutt, London, 1900.]

*This is the adventure of the rich and noble knight Sir Launfal, even as the Breton lay recounts it*

The valiant and courteous King Arthur was sojourning at Carduel, because of the Picts and the Scots who had greatly destroyed the land, for they were in the kingdom of Logres and often wrought mischief therein.

In Carduel, at Pentecost, the king held his summer court, and gave rich gifts to the counts, the barons, and all the knights of the Round Table. Never before in all the world were such gifts given. Honours and lands he shared forth to all, save to one alone, of those who served him.

This was Sir Launfal; of him and his the king thought not. And yet all men loved him, for worthy he was, free of hand, very valiant, and fair to look upon. Had any ill happened to this knight, his fellows would have been but ill-pleased.

Launfal was son to a king of high descent, but his heritage was far hence in a distant land; he was of the household of King Arthur, but all his money was spent, for the king gave him nothing, and nothing would Launfal ask from him. But now Sir Launfal was much perplexed, very sorrowful, and heavy of heart. Nor need ye wonder at it, for one who is a stranger and without counsel is but sorrowful in a foreign land when he knows not where to seek for aid.

This knight of whom I tell ye, who had served the king so well, one day mounted his horse and rode forth for diversion. He left the city behind him, and came all alone into a fair meadow through which ran a swift water. As he rode downwards to the stream, his horse shivered beneath him. Then the knight dismounted, and loosening the girth let the steed go free to feed at its will on the grass of the meadow. Then folding his mantle beneath his head he laid himself down; but his thoughts were troubled by his ill fortune, and as he lay on the grass he knew nothing that might pleasure him.

Suddenly, as he looked downward towards the bank of the river, he saw two maidens coming towards him; never before had he seen maidens so fair. They were richly clad in robes of purple grey, and their faces were wondrous beautiful. The elder bore in her hands a basin of gold finely wrought (indeed it is but truth I tell you); the other held a snow-white towel.

They came straight to where the knight was lying, and Launfal, who was well taught in courteous ways, sprang to his feet in their presence. Then they saluted him, and delivered to him their message. "Sir Launfal," said the elder, "my lady, who is most fair and courteous, has sent us to you, for she wills that you shall return with us. See, her pavilion is near at hand. We will lead you thither in all safety."

Then Launfal went with them, taking no thought for his steed, which was grazing beside him in the meadow. The maidens led him to the tent; rich it was and well placed. Not even the Queen Semiramis in the days of her greatest wealth and power and wisdom, nor the Emperor Octavian, could have equalled from their treasures the drapery alone.

Above the tent was an eagle of gold, its worth I know not how to tell you; neither can I tell that of the silken cords and shining lances which upheld the tent; there is no king under heaven who could purchase its equal, let him offer what he would for it.

Within this pavilion was a maiden, of beauty surpassing even that of the lily and the new-blown rose, when they flower in the fair summer-tide. She lay upon a rich couch, the covering of which was worth the price of a castle, her fair and gracious body clothed only in a simple vest. Her costly mantle of white ermine, covered with purple of Alexandria, had she cast from her for the heat, and face and throat and neck were whiter than flower of the thorn. Then the maiden called the knight to her, and he came near and seated himself beside the couch.

"Launfal," she said, "fair friend, for you have I come forth from my own land; even from Lains have I come to seek you. If you be of very truth valiant and courteous then neither emperor, count, nor king have known such joy as shall be yours, for I love you above all things."

Then Love smote him swiftly, and seized and kindled his heart, and he answered:

"Fair lady, if it so please you, and such joy may be my portion that you deign to love me, then be the thing folly or wisdom you can command nothing that I will not do to the utmost of my power. All your wishes will I fulfil. For you I will renounce folk and my land.

Nor will I ever ask to leave you, if that be what you most desire of me."

When the maiden heard him whom she could love well speak thus, she granted him all her heart and her love.

And now was Launfal in the way to good fortune. A gift the lady bestowed upon him: there should be nothing so costly but that it might be his if he so willed it. Let him give or spend as freely as he would he should always have enough for his need. Happy indeed was Launfal, for the more largely he spent the more gold and silver should he have.

"Friend," said the maiden, "of one thing must I now warn you, nay more, I command and pray you, reveal this your adventure to no man. The reason will I tell you; if this our love be known you would lose me for ever, never again might you look upon me, never again embrace me."

Then he answered that he would keep faithfully all that she should command him.

Thus were the two together even till the vesper-tide, and if his lady would have consented fain would Launful have remained longer.

"Friend," said she, "rise up, no longer may you linger here, you must go and I must remain. But one thing will I tell you: When you wish to speak with me (and I would that may ever be when a knight may meet his lady without shame and without reproach) I shall be ever there at your will, but no man save you shall see me or hear me speak."

When the knight heard that, he was joyful; and he kissed his lady and rose up and the maidens who led him to the tent brought him new and rich garments, and when he was clad in them there was no fairer knight under heaven. Then they brought him water for his hands, and a towel whereon to dry them, and laid food before him, and he supped with his lady. Courteously were they served, and great was the joy of Sir Launfal, for ever and again his love kissed him and he embraced her tenderly.

When they were risen from supper his horse was brought to him, saddled and bridled; right well had they tended it. Then the knight took leave of his lady, and mounted and rode towards the city; but often he looked behind him, for he marvelled greatly at all that had befallen him, and he rode ever thinking of his adventure, amazed and half-doubting, for he scarcely knew what the end thereof should be.

Then he entered his hostel and found all his men well clad, and he held great state but knew not whence the money came to him. In all the city there was no knight that had need of lodging but Launfal made him come unto him and gave him rich service. Launfal gave costly gifts; Launfal ransomed prisoners; Launfal clothed the minstrels; Launfal lavished wealth and honours; there was neither friend nor stranger to whom he gave not gifts. Great were his joy and gladness, for whether by day or by night he might full often look upon his lady, and all things were at his commandment.

Now in the self-same year, after the feast of St. John, thirty of the knights went forth to disport themselves in a meadow below the tower wherein the queen had her lodging. With them went Sir Gawain and his cousin, the gallant Iwein. Then said Gawain, the fair and courteous, who was loved of all: "Pardieu, my lords, we do ill in that we have not brought with us our companion, Sir Launfal, who is so free-handed and courteous, and son to so rich a king." Then they turned back to his hostelry, and by their prayers persuaded Launfal to come with them.

It so chanced that the queen leant forth from an open casement, and three of her chosen ladies with her. She looked upon Sir Launfal and knew him. Then she called one of her ladies, and bade her command the fairest and most graceful of her maidens to make ready and come forth with her to the meadow. Thirty or more she took with her, and descended the stairway of the tower. The knights were joyful at their coming, and hastened to meet them, and took them by the hand with all courtesy. But Sir Launfal went apart from the others, for the time seemed long to him ere he could see his lady, kiss her, and hold her in his arms. All other joys were but small to him if he had not that one delight of his heart.

When the queen saw him alone she went straight towards him, and seated herself beside him; then, calling him by his name, she opened her heart to him.

"Launfal," she said, "greatly have I honoured, cherished, and loved you. All my love is yours if you will have it, and if I thus grant you my favour, then ought you to be joyful indeed."

"Lady," said the knight, "let me be; I have small desire of your love. Long have I served King Arthur; I will not now deny my faith. Neither for you nor for your love will I betray my liege lord."

The queen was angry, and in her wrath she spoke scoffingly. "They but spake the truth," she said, "who told me that you knew not how to love. Coward and traitor, false knight, my lord has done ill to suffer you so long about him; he loses much by it, to my thinking."

When Sir Launfal heard that, he was wroth and answered her swiftly, and by misfortune he said that of which he afterwards repented sorely. "Lady," he said, "you have been ill-advised. I love and I am loved by one who deserves the prize of beauty above all whom I know. One thing I will tell you, hear and mark it well; one of her serving maidens, even the meanest among them, is worth more than you, my lady queen, in face and figure, in beauty, wisdom, and goodness."

. Then the queen rose up and went weeping to her chamber, shamed and angered that Launfal should have thus insulted her. She laid herself down on her bed as if sick; never, she said, would she arise off it till the king did justice on the plaint she would lay before him.

King Arthur came back from the woods after a fair day's hunting and sought the queen's chamber. When she saw him she cried out, and fell at his feet, beseeching his favour, and saying that Sir

Launfal had shamed her, for he had asked her love, and when she refused him had mocked and insulted her, for he had boasted of his
lady that she was so fair, so noble, and so proud that even the lowest
of her waiting women was worth more than the queen.

At this King Arthur fell into a rage, and swore a solemn oath that
unless the knight could defend himself well and fully in open court,
he should be hanged or burnt.

Forth from the chamber went the king and called three of his
barons to him, and bade them fetch Sir Launfal, who indeed was sad
and sorry enough. He had returned to his hostelry, but alas! he
learnt all too soon that he had lost his lady, since he had revealed
the secret of their love. He was all alone in his chamber, full of
anguish. Again and again he called upon his love, but it availed him
nothing. He wept and sighed, and once and again fell on the ground
in his despair. A hundred times he besought her to have mercy on
him, and to speak once more to her true knight. He cursed his heart
and his mouth that had betrayed him; 'twas a marvel he did not
slay himself. But neither cries nor blows nor lamentations sufficed to awaken her pity and make her show herself to his eyes.

Alas, what comfort might there be for the unhappy knight who had
thus made an enemy of his king? The barons came and bade him
follow them to court without delay, for the queen had accused him,
and the king, by their mouth, commanded his presence. Launfal
followed them, sorrowing greatly; had they slain him it would have
pleased him well. He stood before the king, mute and speechless,
his countenance changed for sorrow.

The king spoke in anger: "Vassal," he said, "you have greatly
wronged me; and evil excuse have you found to shame and injure
me and insult the queen. Foolish was your boast, and foolish must
be your lady to hold that her maid-servant is fairer than my queen."

Sir Launfal denied that he had dishonoured himself or insulted
his liege lord. Word by word he repeated what the queen had
said to him; but of the words he himself had spoken, and the
boast he had made concerning his love, he owned the truth; sorrowful enough he was, since by so doing he had lost her. And for this
speech he would make amends, as the court might require.

The king was sorely enraged against him, and conjured his knights
to say what might rightfully be done in such a case, and how Launfal
should be punished. And the knights did as he bade them, and
some spake fair, and some spake ill. Then they all took counsel
together and decreed that judgment should be given on a fixed
day; and that Sir Launfal should give pledges to his lord that he
would return to his hostelry and await the verdict. Otherwise, he
should be held a prisoner till the day came. The barons returned
to the king, and told him what they had agreed upon; and King
Arthur demanded pledges, but Launfal was alone, a stranger in a
strange land, without friend or kindred.

Then Sir Gawain came near, with all his companions, and said
to the king: "Take pledges of all ye hold of mine and these my friends,

fiefs or lands, each for himself." And when they had thus given pledges for him who had nothing of his own, he was free to go to his hostelry. The knights bore Sir Launfal company, chiding him as they went for his grief, and cursing the mad love that had brought him to this pass. Every day they visited him that they might see if he ate and drank, for they feared much that he would go mad for sorrow.

At the day they had named the barons were all assembled, the king was there, and the queen, and sureties delivered up Launfal. Very sorrowful they were for him. I think there were even three hundred of them who had done all in their power without being able to deliver him from peril. Of a great offence did they accuse him, and the king demanded that sentence should be given according to the accusation and the defence.

Then the barons went forth to consider their judgment, heavy at heart, many of them, for the gallant stranger who was in such stress among them. Others, indeed, were ready to sacrifice Launfal to the will of their seigneur.

Then spoke the Duke of Cornwall, for the right was his. Whoever might weep or rage, to him it pertained to have the first word, and he said:

"The king lays his plea against a vassal, Launfal ye call him, of felony and misdeed he accuses him in the matter of a love of which he boasted himself, thus making my lady, the queen, wrathful. None save the king, has aught against him; therefore do ye as I say, for he who would speak the truth must have respect unto no man, save only such honour as shall be due to his liege lord. Let Launfal be put upon his oath (the king will surely have naught against it) and if he can prove his words, and bring forward his lady, and that which he said and which so angered the queen be true, then he shall be pardoned; 'twas no villainy that he spake. But if he cannot bring proof of his word, then shall we make him to know that the king no longer desires his service and gives him dismissal from his court."

Then they sent messengers to the knight, and spake, and made clear to him that he must bring forth his lady that his word might be proved, and he held guiltless. But he told them that was beyond his power, never through her might succour come to him. Then the messengers returned to the judges, who saw there was no chance of aid, for the king pressed them hard, urged thereto by the queen, who was weary of awaiting their judgment.

But as they arose to seek the king they saw two maidens come riding on white palfreys. Very fair they were to look upon, clad in green sendal over their white skin. The knights beheld them gladly, and Gawain, with three others, hastened to Sir Launfal and told him what had chanced, and bade him look upon the maidens; and they prayed him eagerly to say whether one of the twain were his lady, but he answered them nay.

The two, so fair to look upon, had gone forward to the palace, and dismounted before the daïs whereon King Arthur was seated. If their beauty was great, so also was their speech courteous.

"King," they said, "command that chambers be assigned to us, fair with silken hangings, wherein our mistress can fitly lodge, for with you will she sojourn awhile."

They said no more, and the king called two knights, and bade them lead the maidens to the upper chambers.

Then the king demanded from his barons their judgment and their verdict, and said he was greatly wroth with them for their long delay.

"Sire," they answered, "we were stayed by the coming of the damsels. Our decision is not yet made, we go but now to take counsel together." Then they reassembled, sad and thoughtful, and great was the clamour and strife among them.

While they were yet in perplexity, they saw, descending the street, two maidens of noble aspect, clad in robes broidered with gold, and mounted on Spanish mules. Then all the knights were very joyful, and said each to the other: "Surely now shall Sir Launfal, the valiant and courteous, be safe."

Gawain and six companions went to seek the knight. "Sir," they said, "be of good courage, for the love of God speak to us. Hither come two damsels, most beautiful, and richly clad, one of them must of a truth be your lady!" But Launfal answered simply: "Never before to-day have I looked upon, or known, or loved them."

Meantime, the maidens had come to the palace and stood before the king. Many praised them for their beauty and bright colour, and some deemed them fairer even than the queen.

The elder was wise and courteous, and she delivered her message gracefully. "King," she said, "bid your folk give us chambers wherein we may lodge with our lady; she comes hither to speak with you."

Then the king commanded that they should be led to their companions who had come before them. Nor as yet was the judgment spoken. So when the maidens had left the hall, he commanded his barons to deliver their verdict, their judgment already tarried too long, and the queen waxed wrathful for their delay.

But even as they sought the king, through the city came riding a maiden, in all the world was none so fair. She rode a white palfrey, that bore her well and easily. Well shaped were its head and neck, no better trained steed was there in all the world. Costly were the trappings of that palfrey, under heaven was there no king rich enough to purchase the like, save that he sold or pledged his land.

And thus was the lady clad: her raiment was all of white, laced on either side. Slender was her shape, and her neck whiter than snow on the bough. Her eyes were blue, her skin fair. Straight was her nose, and lovely her mouth. Her eyebrows were brown, her forehead white, and her hair fair and curling. Her mantle was of purple, and the skirts were folded about her; on her hand she bare a hawk, and a hound followed behind her.

In all the burg there was no one, small nor great, young nor old, but was eager to look upon her as she passed. She came riding swiftly, and her beauty was no mere empty boast, but all men who looked upon her held her for a marvel, and not one of those who beheld her but felt his heart verily kindled with love.

Then those who loved Sir Launfal went to him, and told him of the maiden who came, if by the will of heaven she might deliver him. "Sir knight and comrade, hither comes one, no nutbrown maid is she, but the fairest of all fair women in this world." And Launfal heard, and sighed, for well he knew her. He raised his head and the blood flew to his cheek as he made swift answer: "Of a faith," he said, "*this* is my lady! Now let them slay me if they will and she has no mercy on me. I am whole if I do but see her."

The maiden reached the palace; fairer was she than any who had entered there. She dismounted before the king that all might behold her; she had let her mantle fall that they might the better see her beauty. King Arthur, in his courtesy, had risen to meet her, and all around him sprang to their feet and were eager to offer their service. When they had looked well upon her and praised her beauty, she spoke in these words, for no will had she to delay:

"King Arthur, I have loved one of your knights, behold him there, seigneur, Sir Launfal. He hath been accused at your court, but it is not my will that harm shall befall him. Concerning that which he said, know that the queen was in the wrong; never on any day did he pray her for her love. Of the boast that he hath made, if he may by me be acquitted, then shall your barons speak him free, as they have rightfully engaged to do."

The king granted that so it might be nor was there a single voice but declared that Launfal was guiltless of wrong, for their own eyes had acquitted him.

And the maiden departed; in vain did the king pray her to remain; and many there were who would fain have served her. Without the hall was there a great block of grey marble, from which the chief knights of the king's court were wont to mount their steeds; on this Launfal took his stand, and when the maiden rode forth from the palace he sprang swiftly upon the palfrey behind her. Thus, as the Bretons tell us, he departed with her for that most fair island, Avalon; thither the fairy maiden had carried her knight, and none hath heard man speak further of Sir Launfal. Nor know I more of his story.

[tr. JESSIE L. WESTON]

# GOTTFRIED VON STRASSBURG

The growth of the Tristan story from the name of a primitive chieftain in the Scotch Lothians to the most adept, cultured, and passionate narrative in medieval literature, as it came from the pen of Gottfried von Strassburg, is in itself a fascinating tale. Apparently, the renown of a Tristan who led a Celtic band in Caledonia traveled south to Wales and Cornwall as early as the ninth century. There, bards attached to it floating tales, as they were contemporaneously attached to the name of Arthur. Tristan became the central figure of an elopement story popular in pagan Irish literature involving a hero, his uncle and king, and the king's wife — found, for instance, in the story of Naisi, Conchobar, and Deirdre as told in *The Sons of Usnach,* above (pp. 104 ff.), and modified in Wace's tale of Arthur, Guenevere, and Mordred. The story of Tristan followed the path of Celtic tales to Brittany and seems to have been told at Eleanor's court at Poitou before she married Henry II of England. Like a rolling snowball, it gathered literary lore as it traveled, until finally, in poems of the late twelfth century, it contains literary devices and anecdotes from all the world: the ambiguous oath, the white and black sails, the giant and the youth, the fairy dog, the unhealable wound, the disguise as a leper, the separating sword, the human tribute, the love potion, and many others.

As Gaston Paris remarked, the story is essentially uncourtly: "Cet amour sauvage, indomptable et passionné n'a rien des conventions, des quintessences et des langueurs de l'amour chevaleresque." Nevertheless, it appealed to that center of courtly poetry, the Anglo-Norman court of Henry II and Eleanor. A certain Thomas was one of several who told the tale in the now conventional octosyllabic couplets of romance and added courtly trappings. From him Gottfried von Strassburg got his story, even though other German poets, notably Eilhart of Oberge, also retold it just before the twelfth century closed.

Gottfried's poem is assigned to the year 1210, the year that Wolfram finished his *Parzival.* That date marks the close of one of the greatest periods of German literature. With these two great writers must be counted the unknown author of the *Nibelungenlied,* the minnesinger Walther von der Vogelweide, and Hartmann von Aue, who wrote Arthurian stories derived from Chrétien but is more famous for his original story *Poor Henry (Der Arme Heinrich),* which a number of modern poets, Longfellow and Rossetti, for instance, have retold. Though imperial politics were confused and the great struggle between Pope and Emperor, which initiated the Guelf and Ghibelline parties (originally German Welf and Weiblingen) was in the making, poets were stirred with visions of a new way of life by what they had learned on the Crusades, in French courts, and through expanding trade with Byzantium and the East. The rising burgher class nowhere was more evident than at Strassburg. From a feudal stronghold, that town had suddenly burgeoned to 10,000 citizens in the year 1200, and was to become, by the fourteenth century, a city of 50,000. According to a contemporary chronicle it had eighty bankers in the year 1266. Gottfried is the best representative of this new burgher class. Though nothing is known of his life, there shines through his unfinished poem a worldly but gentle man, alternately puzzled, amused, and delighted at the conflict between primitive credulity and feudal courtesy that he found in Thomas' poem. His urbanity and sense of causality endow the capricious acts of his characters with motives that seem modern; his constant allusions echo the classics; his habitual understatement in telling an exaggerated story is piquant and charming; his smooth rhyme, rhythm, plot, and diction contrast with Wolfram's rough, almost unlettered verses:

> Ich han mir eine unmüezekeit
> Der werlt ze liebe vür geleit
> Und edelen herzen z'einer hage.
> Den herzen, den ich herze trage,
> Der werlde, in die nûn herze siht.

His poem was written at the moment when *minnesang* was at its height and has itself been called a *Hohelied der Minne* — a high song of love.

Gottfried's poem, in modern German translation, inspired Wagner's opera in 1859, which in turn excited Tennyson, Swinburne, Arthur Symons, Hardy, Masefield, Robinson and other recent poets. The part of the poem in translation below has been abridged.

## TRISTAN AND ISEULT

### Gottfried von Strassburg (A.D. 1210)

[From *The Story of Tristan and Iseult,* translated by Jessie L. Weston; David Nutt, London, 1899.]

[Child of the passionate love of Riwalin for Blanchefleur, sister of King Mark of Cornwall, Tristan, born in sorrow at his mother's death, is reared by Rual, a faithful retainer, as a paragon of courtly virtues before he is knighted by his uncle Mark. In ending the life of a giant Morolt, who has ravaged Cornwall, he receives a poisoned wound that can be healed only by the Irish queen Iseult. Disguised as a harper named Tantris he makes his way to the queen, who heals him and sets him to teaching her daughter, also Iseult, all his courtly arts. In time he returns to Cornwall.]

Now when Mark his uncle and all the folk of the land knew that Tristan had returned safe, and healed of his wound, there was great joy and gladness throughout the kingdom.

The king asked him how it had chanced, and he told him all the story from beginning to end, and they laughed and made great jest over his journey to Ireland, and his healing at the hand of his enemy, and said 'twas the most marvellous tale they had ever hearkened. And when they had laughed over it well they asked him of the Princess Iseult.

"Iseult," he said, "she is so fair a maiden that all we hear of beauty is but as an idle tale compared to her. No child nor maiden of woman born was ever so fair to look upon. Erewhile I read that Aurora's daughter, and her child fair Helen, were the fairest of all women, that in them was gathered all beauty, as in a flower. Such a tale do I believe no longer. Iseult has robbed me of all faith in it. The sun of beauty dawned not in Greece, it hath risen in our own day, and the hearts and eyes of all men turn to Ireland where the sun is born of the dawn — Iseult, daughter of Iseult. From Dublin doth it shine forth to gladden all men. Nor does her beauty lessen that of other women. Rather, through her fairness is all womankind honoured, and in her fame all women are crowned."

And all who heard Tristan speak felt their heart refreshed within them, even as the May dew refreshes the flowers.

So Tristan took up his life again, for it was as if new life had been granted to him, and he was as a man new born. But little by little envy crept into the hearts of the courtiers, and they waxed jealous of the honour and love in which Tristan was held, and a whisper went round among them that he was a sorcerer, and his victory over Morolt and his good luck in Ireland had been brought about by magic.

"Tell us," they said, "how did he escape from so fierce a foe as Morolt? How did he deceive Iseult, the wise queen, so that she tended him diligently with her own hand till his wounds were healed? A sorcerer is he who can thus blind the eyes of men, and bring to a good ending everything to which he sets his hand!"

So they took counsel together, and besieged Mark early and late with their prayers beseeching him to take to himself a wife, so that he might have an heir, whether son or daughter.

But Mark said: "God hath given us a valiant heir already; may he live long! Know ye that while Tristan is alive there shall be neither queen nor lady at this my court."

Then was their envy and hatred greater than before, so great that they could no longer hide it from Tristan, but often threatened him by word and gesture, till he feared for his life at their hands. And at last he spake to his uncle Mark, saying he would do well to give the lords their will, else sooner or later they would surely slay him by treachery.

But the king said: "Be silent, nephew Tristan, that will I never do. I ask no heir but thee; and as for thy life, have no fear of that. What is their ill-will to thee? Such is ever the lot of a brave man. For worth and envy, they are even as mother and child: the one must needs give birth to the other. Who is more hated than the lucky man? 'Tis a poor fortune that never saw envy! Go thy way, and know thou shalt never be free from envy: if thou wouldst have the bad love thee, then must thou sing their song, and deal their dealing, so will they cease to hate thee! Counsel me no more to that which may turn to thine own harm; in this will I follow neither them nor thee!"

"Lord and uncle," said Tristan, "give me leave to withdraw from court, for in sooth I see not how to shield myself from their ill-will, and rather than have a kingdom the holding of which shall cost me so much care and thought will I be landless!"

Then when Mark saw he was fully in earnest, he said: "Nephew, I had fain have kept faith with thee, but thou wilt not have it so. Now, whatever chances hereafter, shalt thou hold me guiltless. I am ready to do all thou wilt; say, what dost thou require of me?"

And Tristan said: "Call together thy council, who have aided thee hitherto. Ask them what they deem good for the present need and do after their advice."

So this was done, and the lords came together and took counsel among themselves, and said that the king should wed the Princess Iseult, for by the fame that had gone abroad of her wisdom and beauty they deemed her a fitting wife for their king. Then they chose a spokesman who should declare their wishes, and he said: "Sire, we have heard tell of the Lady Iseult of Ireland, how that she is a maiden in whom all womanly beauty finds its crown. Yea, thou thyself hast heard how she is perfect alike in soul and body. If it may so be that she become thy wife and our queen, we ask nothing better on earth."

And King Mark said: "How may that be, my lords? Even if I desired her as a wife, how might it be brought about? Ye know well how matters stand between the two countries: Gurmun hates me from his heart, and with good reason, for so do I hate him. How then may there be so close an alliance between us?"

"Lord," they said, "it doth often happen that when two lands are at strife peace is brought about through the children, and a great friendship groweth from a bitter enmity. Think the matter over, for it may well be that Ireland becometh thine. There are but the three there; the king and queen have no heir save Iseult, she is their only child."

Then Mark answered: "Of a sooth Tristan has made me think much of the maiden; since he praised her so she has often been in my mind, and 'tis true that the thought of her pleases me above all other maidens. I swear if I may not have her to wife I will have no other woman on earth!" Now, Mark said this not because he really desired Iseult, but because he thought there was little chance that the marriage should be brought about.

Then the councillors spake further: "My lord king, if it please thee that Sir Tristan here, who knows the court of Ireland well, serve as thy messenger, then the matter will surely be brought to a good end. He is wise and skilful in such matters, and, what is more, fortunate in all he takes in hand. He knows all tongues, and will bring to an end what should be ended."

"Ye counsel ill," said Mark; "ye are too jealous for Tristan's peril and hurt. He has been well-nigh dead once for ye and your children, and ye would now slay him again. Nay, men of Cornwall, go ye yourselves. I send my nephew no more!"

"Sire," said Tristan, "herein they do not speak amiss. 'Twere fitting that I should be more ready and willing to such a task than another man, and 'tis right that I should go. Uncle, bid me go, and none will do thine errand better than I. But do thou command that these lords, too, go with me, that together we may watch over thine interest and thine honour."

"Nay, since God hath sent thee home safely, thou comest no more into the land or the power of thy foes."

"Uncle, it must needs be so; and whether for good or for ill these lords must needs go with me and see if it be *my* blame that thy kingdom is without an heir! Bid them make ready, and I will myself be steersman and guide them to that happy Ireland, and to Dublin, whence shines forth the sun in which the joy of many a heart is hid. Who knows if the maiden be ours? And, sire, if thou dost win fair Iseult 'twill be little loss to thee if we all die on the quest."

When Mark's councillors heard how Tristan spake, never in their lives where they so sorrowful; but 'twas too late: the thing was and must be so. Tristan bade them choose twenty of the king's most valiant knights, and of the folk of the land and strangers he hired sixty, with twenty lords of the council, so that the whole company numbered one hundred; and they provisioned the ships well, and set sail over sea.

But the barons were ill pleased at the journey, and heavy at heart. Many a time they wished that they had said no word of Ireland and the Princess Iseult, for now their own lives were in danger, and they saw no way of escape. They had but the choice of two things: to carry the matter through either by daring or by cunning; and they liked neither. Nor could they think of any fitting ruse, but they said among themselves: "This Tristan hath wisdom and courage enough, and good luck too. If he will but put a curb on his blind rashness he may escape, and we with him. Yet is he so bold and so daring, he cares not a jot either for our lives or his own. Still, our best chance is in his good fortune; his wit must find a way out of this peril."

Now they drew near to the coast of Ireland, and one told them that the king abode in the harbour of Whiteford. So Tristan bade them cast anchor far enough from the haven to be out of bowshot; and the lords prayed him earnestly to tell them how he would set about his wooing, for their lives were in danger, and they would fain know what was in his mind.

And Tristan said: "Have a care that none of ye be seen by the landsfolk, save the serving-men and seamen only; they must remain on deck, but do ye abide in the cabin and keep hidden. I will shew myself, for I know their tongue; the citizens will send out and question us, and I must lie to them as I best can, for if ye be seen, then shall we have strife straightway, and none of us will get to land. And while I am absent on the morrow, for I think to ride forth early and see what may chance, Kurwenal, and another who knows the tongue, will keep guard over ye. But mark this: two days, or perchance three, shall I be absent; after that, if I come not, wait no longer, but flee away over seas and save yourselves, for I shall have paid for my wooing with my life. Then can ye counsel your lord to wed as ye may like — this is my thought and my purpose."

Now the marshal of the King of Ireland, under whose care both town and haven lay, came down in full armour, with a body of men, as the decree bade him, that he might ask of all new comers to the haven if they were from King Mark's land or no, and if they were, to put them to death. When Tristan saw them he put on such a hood as a man might wear on a journey, that his face might be the better hidden, and took a cup of red gold, worked in the English fashion, and entered a little boat, with Kurwenal to row him, and made for the shore, greeting them with courteous gestures.

When the folk saw the boat they all ran together, shouting: "To land! to land!"

Tristan put into the harbour, and said: "Good folk, what mean this roughness, and these threatening gestures? I know not what I have done amiss. If there be any one in authority here I pray that he will speak with me."

"Yea," said the marshal, "here am I, and I must needs know whence ye come and whither ye go?"

"Of a sooth," said Tristan, "an thou wilt bid this folk keep silence so that I may be heard, I will tell thee mine errand gladly." And when they were silent, he went on: "Sir, we are merchants, I and my fellows, and come from Normandy. Our wives and children are with us in the ship, and we go hither and thither, from land to land, buying such things as we have need of. Within this thirty days I and two other merchants set sail to go to Spain, and about an eight days agone a storm arose which separated us, and drave me northwards. I know not how the others have fared, whether they be living or dead; I had much ado to escape with my life. Yesterday at noon the wind fell, and I knew the look of the coast, so came hither to rest me. And at daybreak I made for Whiteford, for I know the town, and have been here aforetime with merchants. But if this folk will not be at peace with me I must perforce set sail again, though I have much need of rest."

Then the marshal bade his men return to land, and said to the stranger: "What will ye give the king if I protect your lives and goods in this land?"

"Sir, whatever our gains may be, I will give a mark of red gold for each day we sojourn in the land; and thou thyself shalt have this golden cup, if indeed thou art able to assure me of safety."

"Yea," said they all, "that can he, for he is the king's marshal."

Then he gave them the cup, and the marshal thought it a rich and precious gift, and bade him come ashore, and sware that he and his should be in peace and surety. And for that did they win rich payment in royal red gold; red gold for the king's tribute, red gold for the messenger's fee — and 'twas good too for Tristan, since it won him peace and favour.

Now, the story tells us that there was at that time in Ireland a monstrous dragon which devoured the people and wasted the land; so that the king at last had sworn a solemn oath that whoever slew the monster should have the Princess Iseult to wife; and because of the beauty of the maiden and fierceness of the dragon many a valiant knight had lost his life. The land was full of the tale, and it had come to Tristan's ears, and in the thought of this had he made his journey.

The next morning, ere it was light, he rose and armed himself secretly, and took his strongest spear, and mounted his steed and rode forth into the wilderness. He rode by many a rough path till the sun was high in the heavens, when he turned downwards into a valley, where, as the geste tells us, the dragon had its lair. Then he saw afar off four men galloping swiftly over the moor where there was no road. One of them was the queen's seneschal, who would fain have been the lover of the Princess Iseult, but she liked him not. Whenever knights rode forth bent on adventures the seneschal was ever with them, for nothing on earth save that men might say they had seen him ride forth, for never would he face the dragon, but would return swifter than he went.

Now, when Tristan saw the men in flight he knew the dragon must be near at hand, so he rode on steadily, and ere long he saw the monster coming towards him, breathing out smoke and flame from its open jaws. The knight laid his spear in rest, and set spurs to his steed, and rode so swiftly, and smote so strongly, that the spear went in at the open jaws, and pierced through the throat into the dragon's heart, and he himself came with such force against the dragon that his horse fell dead, and he could scarce free himself from the steed. But the evil beast fell upon the corpse and partly devoured it, till the wound from the spear pained it so sorely that it left the horse half eaten, and fled into a rocky ravine.

Tristan followed after the monster, which fled before him roaring for pain till the rocks rang again with the sound. It cast fire from its jaws and tare up the earth around, till the pain of the wound overcame it, and it crouched down under a wall of rock. Then Tristan drew forth his sword, thinking to slay the monster easily, but 'twas a hard strife, the hardest Tristan had ever fought, and in truth he thought it would be his death. For the dragon had as aids smoke and flame, teeth and claws sharper than a shearing knife; and the knight had much ado to find shelter behind the trees and bushes, for the fight was so fierce that the shield he held in his hand was burnt well-nigh to a coal. But the conflict did not endure over-long, for the spear in the vitals of the dragon began to pain him so that he lay on the ground, rolling over and over in agony. Then Tristan came near swiftly, and smote with his sword at the heart of the monster so that the blade went in right to the hilt; and the dragon gave forth a roar so grim and terrible that it was as if heaven and earth fell together, and the death-cry was heard far and wide through the land. Tristan himself was well-nigh terrified, but as he saw the beast was dead, he went near, and with much labour he forced the jaws open, and cut out the tongue, then he closed the jaws again, and put the tongue in his bosom. He turned him again to the wilderness, thinking to rest through the day, and come again to his people secretly in the shadows of night; but he was so overcome by the stress of the fight and the fiery breath of the dragon that he was well-nigh spent, and seeing a little lake near at hand into which a clear stream flowed from the rock, he went towards it, and as he came to the cool waters the weight of his armour and the venom of the dragon's tongue overpowered him, and he fell senseless by the stream.

But the seneschal, who would fain be the princess's lover, as he rode homeward, heard the death-cry of the dragon, and bethought him what it might mean; he said to himself: "The beast is either dead or sorely wounded; now is my chance if I work warily." So he stole away from his companions, and rode quietly down a hill to the valley, then he turned his bridle toward the place whence the sound came, and rode swiftly till he found the carcase of Tristan's horse, and there he halted, for his heart misgave him. Then as he heard and saw nothing he took courage and rode still fearful and trembling along the track made by the grass and broken underwood, and ere he knew he came right on the dragon lying dead. Over-come by terror at the sight, he turned his bridle so swiftly that horse and man alike stumbled and fell over a little hillock, and when he sprang to his feet he was so terrified he durst not wait to remount, but fled on foot. But as he found the dragon did not move he took heart, and stole back trembling; he led his horse to a fallen trunk and remounted, and then rode with caution nearer to the dragon to see whether it were alive or dead. And when he saw that the monster was in truth dead, he cried aloud: "Now by God's grace I have come hither in a happy hour!"

With that he laid his lance in rest and rode gaily toward the dragon, crying: "Now art thou mine, my Lady Iseult!" and smote with such force that the spear went through the dragon's jaws, and remained there. This he did out of pure cunning, for he thought: "If the knight who had slain the dragon be living he will not be able to deny that I have aided him." Then he turned, and sought all about to find the knight, for he thought if he were, as well might be, sorely wounded, then he could fight with him, and slay and bury him, and no man be aught the wiser. And when he found him not he said: "Well, let him go; whether he be living or dead I am the first here, and I have kinsmen and friends enow, so that if any man would take the credit of this deed he shall but lose by it." So he rode back to the dragon, and with his sword he gashed the carcase here and there. He had fain hewn off the head, but the neck was so thick he might not come at it. Then he took his spear, and brake it in two over the trunk of a tree, and stuck the pointed end in the monster's jaw, as if it had been broken in a joust.

Having thus as he deemed made all safe, he rode back to White-ford, and bade them go with a wagon and four horses to bring back the head of the dragon, and told every one what he had done, and the sore peril he had been in. "See, see," he cried, "what a man of brave heart and steadfast courage can do for the sake of the lady he loves. I marvelled, and marvel still, how I escaped the danger which beset me; had I been as soft as was another man I had never done it. I know not who he was, an adventurer, who for his cowardice, ere I came up, had met with an evil end. Both man and horse are dead and devoured; the horse still lies there half eaten. I have dared more for the love of a woman than ever a man before me!"

Then he called his friends together, and went again to the dragon, and bade them look again on the wonder, and bear testimony to what they saw. The head they cut off and brought again in the wagon, and he fixed a day for them to ride together with him to the court, and claim the fulfilment of the king's promise.

Now, the tale was speedily brought to court, and told in the women's chambers, and never were tidings more unwelcome! To that fair maid the Princess Iseult it was bitter as a death-blow; never had she seen a sadder day. But her mother spake: "Nay, sweet daughter, nay, let it not trouble thee so; we will see first whether this be truth or a lie. God forbid that the thing should be so! Weep not, my daughter; thy bright eyes should never be reddened for so small a grief!"

"Ah! mother," said the maiden, "insult not thy birth and thyself; ere I be that man's wife I will thrust a knife through my heart. Neither wife nor lady shall he have in Iseult, unless he have her dead."

"Nay, nay, fear not, sweet daughter; whatever the truth may be, thee has he lost, for if all the world were to swear it thou shouldst never wed the seneschal."

When the night fell the queen wove cunning spells, the virtue of which she knew well, for her daughter's sorrow, so that in a dream she saw all the truth and knew that the seneschal had dealt falsely; and as the day began to dawn she spake to Iseult: "Daughter, art thou waking?"

"Yea, mother mine."

"Then let thine heart be at peace: I have good tidings for thee. The seneschal slew not the dragon. 'Twas a stranger knight — I know not what brought him hither — who did the deed. Come, let us go thither quickly, and we will see for ourselves how the truth may be. Brangoene, rise up softly and bid the squire Paranise saddle our horses; we must ride forth, we four, I and my daughter, thou and he. Bid him bring the horses as quickly as may be to the little postern where the orchard opens on to the moorland."

When all was ready the little company mounted, and rode to the spot where they had heard that the dragon was slain, and there they found first the carcase of the horse, and beheld the trappings, and knew that never in Ireland had they seen the like; and they said to each other that whoever the man might be who rode the horse, 'twas he and no other who slew the dragon. Then they rode further and came on the monster as it lay, and it looked so grim and so ghastly in the dim morning light that the women grew pale with dread. The queen said to her daughter: "Now of one thing am I sure: our seneschal never dared face that monster! We may lay aside all care; and, daughter, whether the man be living or dead, methinks he is hidden somewhere near by; let us go and seek him. God grant we may find him, and with his aid overcome the dread that oppresses thine heart."

So they parted asunder and began to seek hither and thither, but 'twas the Princess Iseult who first found that which they sought, for she saw a helmet shining from afar, and called to her mother, saying: "Hasten hither, mother, for I see something gleaming there beyond: I know not what it may be, but methinks 'tis like a helmet."

"So think I," said her mother. "I ween we have found that which we sought."

With that they called the other two, and rode forward together. But when they came nearer and saw how the knight lay they deemed he was dead, and Iseult cried: "We are undone! the seneschal hath treacherously murdered him and borne him to this bog!"

They dismounted, and all four drew him out of the water to land; they did off his helmet and the steel cap beneath, and the wise queen saw that he yet lived, but that his life hung by a single hair.

"He is living," she said; "let us disarm him quickly. If he be not mortally wounded all may yet be well."

Then the three fair women bent over the knight and began to disarm him with their white hands, and behold, the dragon's tongue fell out from his breast. "What may that be, Brangoene, fair kinswoman, say?"

"Methinketh 'tis a tongue!"

"Thou speakest true, Brangoene, — a tongue it is, and I think me well 'twas once in the dragon's mouth! Sweet Iseult, daughter mine, of a truth we have come on a happy journey. 'Tis the venom of this tongue that has bereft him of his senses."

When they had disarmed the knight and found no wound upon him they were all joyful, and the queen took an antidote to the poison and poured it between his lips, and when she saw signs of life, "The man will recover," she said: "the venom of the tongue is yielding, he will speedily regain sight and speech." And in sooth, ere long Tristan opened his eyes and looked around him.

Then between them they helped Tristan on to a steed, and brought him secretly to the palace by the postern door, so that none knew of his coming, and made ready for him a couch and all he needed. Nor did they forget the dragon's tongue, nor his harness, but brought all with them.

Meanwhile the day had come that King Gurmun had set for re-deeming his pledge to the seneschal, and all the knights were gathered together for counsel, and the queen had also come thither, for the king trusted much to her wisdom. And before the council he spake with her in secret: "What counsel canst thou give, my wife? For 'twere bitter as death to give our daughter to the seneschal."

"Be at peace," said the queen; "that will we never do; I have well foreseen the matter."

"How, lady? Tell me quickly, that we may rejoice together."

"See thou, our seneschal never slew the dragon as he saith, but I know well who did, and when the time is ripe I will declare the matter. Go thou to thy lords, and say that when thou art well assured of the truth of the seneschal's word thou wilt be ready to keep thine oath. Then sit thou on thy judgment-seat, and bid thy knights to judge with thee, and let the seneschal bring his plea and say as he will, and when the time is ripe then will I come with Iseult, and will speak for thee, for her, and for myself. I will now seek her, and come again swiftly."

So the king went back to the palace and sat on the judgment-seat, with all the barons round him, and a great company of knights and nobles, for all were fain to know what should be the end of the matter. And when the queen and princess entered they said among themselves: " 'Twere good fortune for the seneschal who hath never had good fortune to win such a maid as this! All men might well envy him."

Then the seneschal came forth and stood before the king, and Gurmun arose, and said kindly: "Speak, what dost thou require of me?"

"Lord king," he answered, "I pray only that thine honour and thy plighted word be not broken. Thou didst swear that whosoever slew the dragon to him wouldst thou give thy daughter Iseult to wife, and this oath of thine hath slain many. But I recked little since I loved the maiden, and I risked my life more often and more valiantly than any man, till at length fortune befriended me, and I slew the monster. See there the head where it lies, I brought it for a token. Now fulfil thy pledge, for the king's word and the king's oath, they should be holy."

But the queen spake: "Seneschal, methinks thou knowest women so well thou hast become as one of them, for see, thou thyself lovest one who hateth thee, and desirest one who will naught of thee. If that be but the way of women, why do even as they? Deal thou rather as a man, and love the maiden who loveth thee, and desire her who desireth thee. We have heard over-much of thy love for Iseult; she loveth thee not, and that perchance she hath from me, for I loved thee never! And as for the king's oath, I tell thee thou didst never slay the dragon; another slew it; and if thou askest me, 'Who was he?' I answer that I know him, and will bring him hither at the fitting time."

"Lady, there is no man shall falsely deprive me of my right and my honour. If he lay claim to it, then must he stake life and limb upon it, hand to hand, before this court, ere I waive a tittle of my right."

" 'Tis well," spake the queen, "I will myself be his surety; the knight who slew the dragon will I bring hither on the second day from now."

Then the king and the council said: " 'Tis enough. Seneschal, go thou and take measures for the fight, and, my lady the queen, do thou see to thy champion." Then the king took pledges from either side, and they made fast the fight for the third day.

So the queen and the princess went back to Tristan, and when he saw them he knelt before them saying: "Peace, fair ladies. I pray ye grant me my life, since 'tis but for your honour and profit I have come hither."

The queen bade him rise, and each proffered him the kiss of peace, though Iseult the princess did it but unwillingly, and they sat down together.

"My queen," said Tristan, "wilt thou be my good friend, and aid me to persuade thy daughter, whom thou lovest, to take as husband a noble king, one well fitted to be her lord; fair, and free of hand; a valiant knight, of a royal race, and richer than her father?"

"Were I sure of the truth," said the queen, "I would even do my best."

"Yet it is so, lady, for since I was here aforetime I have spoken ever in praise and honour of thee and thy daughter to my uncle King Mark; and 'tis he who hath sent me hither, for we are both at one accord to pray that thy daughter become his wife and lady, and Queen of Cornwall and England."

"Yea, but if I counsel my husband to make peace with King Mark, shall I not do ill?"

"Nay, lady, he must needs know all the tale, only I prithee see that he be friends with me."

"Of that have no fear," said Queen Iseult.

Then the queen sent for the king, and prayed of him a boon, saying it lay near to her heart and to that of her daughter.

"Thou shalt have what thou desirest," said the king.

"Then, lord, I pray thee to pardon Tristan, who slew my brother Morolt; he is here in my keeping."

"Nay, that is more thy matter than mine. Morolt was *thy* brother. If thou hast pardoned Tristan, then so have I."

Now the day had come on which the single combat was to be fought, and a great folk had come together, for all wondered who should fight with the seneschal for the maiden Iseult; and each man asked his fellow: "Who may he be who claims to have slain the dragon?" And the question was passed from one to another, but none could give an answer. Meanwhile Tristan's comrades had come from the ship clad in their finest raiment, and he himself robed him as became his royal birth; and when the queen and Princess

Iseult saw him they said to themselves: "Truly this is a gallant knight; methinks our cause is in good hands." Seats were set for the barons in the halls, and the people gazed on them, and marvelled at their rich attire and their silence, for there was not one of them that knew the speech of the country.

Then a messenger came from the king to call the queen and the princess to the court, and she spake: "Rise, Iseult, and we will go. Sir Tristan, do thou abide here, and when I shall send for thee, come thou with Brangoene."

"Gladly, my lady queen."

So came Queen Iseult, leading with her her daughter, even as the dawn that brings with it the rising sun. With measured pace the maiden walked beside her mother, clad in a robe of brown samite, and a flowing mantle furred with ermine, which she held together with the fingers of her right hand. On her head was a circlet of gold set with jewels, and but for the gleaming stones one would scarce have known that the circlet was there, so golden were her shining locks.

So the fair women passed up the hall, greeting all as they came, the mother with word, the daughter with gesture. When they had taken their seat by the king the seneschal stood forth, and said: "My lord the king, I demand my right of battle. Where is the man who thinks to deprive me of mine honour? My friends and kinsmen are here, and my cause is so good that if this council do justice all must go well with me. Nor do I fear force, that be far from thee."

"Seneschal," said the queen, "if this combat may not be averted I scarce know what I may do. 'Twere well if thou wouldst leave thy claim on my daughter, and set her free; 'twould be to thy profit as well as to hers."

"Free?" said the seneschal, "yea, lady, thou wouldst fain throw up a game that is already won! But I should have put myself in much peril for little profit if I now gave up thy daughter. Lady, let there be an end of it — I will wed the princess, or do thou bring forth the man who slew the dragon."

"Seneschal, I hear what thou sayest, and I will prove my truth." She signed to her squire: "Bring hither the man."

All the nobles looked one on the other, and a murmur ran round the hall, question and answer — all asked who the man might be, but none could tell. But now Brangoene entered, tall and stately, leading by the hand Sir Tristan. He was richly clad in a robe of purple silk, all inwoven and embroidered with gold, that glittered as he moved, and on his head was a gold and jeweled circlet. His bearing was frank and fearless, and, as he drew nearer, all made way for him. But when the men of Cornwall saw him they sprang to their feet, and came forward, greeting him joyfully; and taking him and Brangoene by the hand, they led them up to the high daïs where sat the king and queen, and Tristan bowed low before them. Then as the folk clustered round, gazing at the strangers, the hostages from Cornwall saw that these were verily their kinsmen, and they made their way through the crowd, laughing and weeping, and greeted them gladly.

The king bade Tristan take his place beside him, and commanded silence to be made, and when all were still, he said: "Seneschal, what dost thou demand?"

"Sire, I slew the dragon."

The stranger rose and spake: "Sire, he slew it not."

"Sire, I did, and I will prove it here."

"What proof dost thou bring?" said Tristan.

"See his head, I brought it hither."

"My lord king," said Tristan, "since he brings the head as proof, bid them look within the jaws; if the tongue be there I withdraw my claim and renounce the combat."

Then they opened the jaws, and found nothing therein; and, as they marvelled, Tristan bade his squire stand forth with the tongue. "See, now, if this be the dragon's tongue or no." And all looked, and saw that it was in truth the tongue — all save the seneschal, who stood there and knew not what to say, nor whither to turn.

"Lords all," said Tristan, "mark this marvel. I slew the dragon, and cut this tongue from out the jaws, yet this man afterward smote it a second time to death!"

And all the lords said: "One thing is clear, he who came first and cut out the tongue was the man who slew the monster." And never a man said nay.

Then when the truth was clear, Tristan said: "My lord the king, I call thy covenant to mind; thy daughter falleth to me."

And the king said: "Sir Knight, thou hast redeemed thy pledge, I will fulfil mine."

But the seneschal cried: "Nay, he speaketh falsely! Sir King, I demand my right of combat ere I be robbed of mine honour."

"Why should he fight with thee, seneschal?" quoth the queen. "He has won what he would of my daughter. He were more foolish than a child did he fight with thee for nought."

"If he think I have done him wrong, lady," said Tristan, "I will fight with him; let him but go and make ready, and I will arm myself."

When the seneschal saw it would come to a combat he called his friends and kinsfolk aside to take counsel with them, but he found little comfort, for they thought the matter a shameful one, and they said: "Wherefore fight in an unrighteous cause? 'Twere but foolish to throw thy life after thy lost honour. Since the devil hath tempted thee to thine undoing, keep thy life at least."

"What would ye have me do?"

"Go thou, and say to the king that at thy friends' counsel thou dost withdraw thy challenge."

Then he did as they bade him. And the queen said mockingly: "Seneschal, never did I think to see thee give up a game that was already won." And throughout the palace, from the highest to the lowest, all made sport of the seneschal, till he scarce durst show his face for shame — so his falsehood brought him to an evil end.

Now when the matter was ended, King Gurmun made known to all his nobles the errand on which Tristan had come, and how he had granted his prayer, and solemnly in their presence he gave his daughter to Tristan's care, that he might lead her to Cornwall as bride to his uncle King Mark.

Then in the face of them all did Tristan take the princess by the hand, and he spake: "King, since this lady is now my queen and my liege lady, I pray thee to deliver to her all the hostages thou dost hold of Cornwall, for now they are become her subjects, and 'tis but fitting that they should journey with her to her kingdom."

And Gurmun was willing; so with much joy the hostages were released.

Then Tristan bade them prepare a ship, such as should please both Iseult and himself, and assemble together all the men of Cornwall who were in the land that they might set sail with him.

The while that Tristan and his folk made them ready for the journey did the wise Queen Iscult, with much thought and care, prepare a love potion of such power and magic that did any two drink thereof they must needs, without will of their own, love each other above all things from that day forward; death and life, sorrow and joy, were sealed within that little flask of crystal. Then the queen took the drink and spake softly to Brangoene: "Brangoene, my kinswoman, let not my words grieve thee: thou must go hence with my daughter, therefore hearken and heed what I say unto thee. Take thou this flask with the drink within it, and keep it in thy care. Treasure it above all thy treasures, see that none know of it; but when Iseult and King Mark be come together, then do thou pour out the drink as if it were wine, and see that the twain drink of it. Nor shalt thou share in it thyself, for 'tis a love potion, forget not that. I commend to thy care Iseult, my dearest daughter; my very life doth hang on her. She and I alike do I commend to thee on peril of thine eternal welfare — methinks I have said enough."

"My very true and dear lady," said Brangoene, "if this be the will of ye both, then will I gladly go with Iseult, and watch over her honour and her welfare as best I may."

Then Tristan and his folk departed with much joy for the haven of Whiteford, and for the love of Iseult, king and queen and all their household accompanied them thither. Weeping, her steadfast friends surrounded the princess; her father and mother filled the short space left to them with their lamentations; many eyes were red and tearful, and many hearts weighed down with sorrow for the loss of their life's delight, fair Iseult.

But the two Iseults, the sun and her rosy dawn, and the stately moon, fair Brangoene, when they three must part asunder, the one from the twain, then indeed was woe and wailing! Sad was the severance of such true companionship. Many a time and oft did the queen mother kiss them both.

Now they of Cornwall, and the men of Ireland the young queen's followers, were already aboard, and had taken their leave; Tristan was the last to enter the ship, leading by the hand the fair young Queen Iseult, the flower of Ireland. Sad and sorrowful she went with him. Then the two bent in greeting towards the land, and prayed God's blessing be on it and on its folk. They pushed off from the shore, and with a loud voice one and all sang: "So sail we forth in the name of God." Thus they departed from Ireland.

By Tristan's counsel they set apart a private cabin for the queen and her maidens, wherein none might join them, save only at times Tristan, who now and again would go thither to comfort the young queen as she sat and wept, for she bemoaned herself sorely that she must thus perforce part from her land where she knew all the folk, and from the friends who were dear to her, and journey with an unknown folk to a land she knew not. Then Tristan would comfort her as best could, and take her in his arms gently, even as a knight might his liege lady and the wife of his lord. But as often as he laid his arms around her, fair Iseult would bethink her of her uncle's death, and chide with him, saying: "Let be, sir; take thine arm away, thou art a weariful man; wherefore dost thou touch me?"

"Do I then vex thee so sore, fair lady?"

"Yea, forsooth, since I hate thee."

"But wherefore, sweetest lady?"

"Thou didst slay mine uncle."

"For that have I made my peace."

"May be, yet I love thee not, for ere I knew thee had I neither sorrow nor care; thou alone with thy craft and courage hast brought this sorrow upon me. What brought thee from Cornwall to Ireland to my hurt? They who brought me up from my childhood, from them hast thou reft me, and bearest me I know not whither! What price hath been paid for me I know not, nor what shall befall me."

"Nay, nay, fair Iseult, be at peace; wouldst thou not rather be a rich queen among strangers than poor and weak among thine own kin? Honour and wealth in a strange land, and shame in thy father's kingdom, they weigh not equal, I think me!"

"Yea, Sir Tristan," said the maiden, "but say what thou wilt, I would have the lower lot with love and pleasure, rather than displeasure and trouble with great riches."

"Thou sayest true," answered Tristan; "but where one may have riches and pleasure alike, the two good things pass better together than either of the twain alone. But say, were it come to that that thou must needs have taken the seneschal for thine husband, what then? I wot well that would have made thee glad! Hast no thanks for me that I came to thine aid, and freed thee from him?"

"Too late," quoth the maid. "I might well have thanked thee

then, when thou didst deliver me from him, but since then hast thou heaped such sorrow upon me that in sooth I had liever have wedded the seneschal than have sailed with thee! How worthless soever he may have been, had he dwelt but a short while with me then had he laid aside his evil ways, for this I know of a truth, that he loved me well."

Spake Tristan: "This tale seemeth me over-strange; 'twere great labour indeed for a man to act worthily against his nature. The world holds it for a lie that a worthless knight should do worthy deeds. Be content, fair lady; in a short while will I give thee for lord a king in whom thou shalt find henceforth virtue and honour, riches, joy, and fair living."

So they sailed onward with a favouring wind and a fair sea; but Iseult and her maidens were not wont to be exposed to the water and the wind, and ere long they were sorely in need of rest. Then Tristan bade them put to land for a little space, and as by good luck they came near a haven they ran the ship therein, and made it fast, and the more part of the folk went ashore to refresh themselves. But Iseult remained aboard, and Tristan went into the cabin to greet his liege lady, and sat him down beside her, and the twain spake of this thing and of that, till Tristan became thirsty and bade them bring whereof he might drink.

Now, beside the queen was there no one on board save little maidens, and one spied the flask where Brangoene had laid it, and said: "See, here is wine in this flask." But it was not wine that was therein, though like unto it, but bitter pain and enduring sorrow of heart, of which the twain at last lay dead. Yet the little maiden might know naught of this, so she took the flask from its hiding-place, and brought it to Tristan, and he gave forthwith of the drink to Iseult. She drank of it unwillingly enough, and after a space passed the cup to Tristan, and he too drank of it, and neither knew that it was other than wine. And even as it was done Brangoene entered, and saw well what had chanced.

For very terror she became white as death. Cold at heart, she took that vessel of ill chance, and bearing it forth flung it into the wild and stormy sea. "Woe is me," she said within herself, "that ever I was born into this world! Miserable that I am, I have lost mine honour and failed in my trust. Would to God I had never come on this journey. I must ever bemoan that death took me not ere I pledged myself to sail with Iseult on this evil voyage. Alas, Tristan and Iseult, for this drink shall be your death!"

Now, when the man and the maid, Tristan and Iseult, had drunk of the potion, Love, who never resteth but besetteth all hearts, crept softly into the hearts of the twain, and ere they were ware of it had she planted her banner of conquest therein, and brought them under her rule. They were one and undivided who but now were twain and at enmity. Gone was Iseult's hatred, no longer might there be strife between them, for Love, the great reconciler, had purified their hearts from all ill will, and so united them that each was clear as a mirror to the other. But one heart had they — her grief was his sadness, his sadness her grief. Both were one in love and sorrow, and yet both would hide it in shame and doubt. She felt shame of her love, and the like did he. She doubted of his love, and he of hers. For though both their hearts were blindly bent to one will, yet was the chance and the beginning heavy to them, and both alike would hide their desire.

When Tristan felt the pangs of love, then he bethought him straightway of his faith and honour, and would fain have set himself free. "Nay," he said to himself, "let such things be, Tristan; guard thee well, lest others perceive thy thoughts." So would he turn his heart, fighting against his own will, and desiring against his own desire. He would and would not, and, a prisoner, struggled in his fetters. There was a strife within him, for ever as he looked on Iseult, and love stirred his heart and soul, then did honour draw him back. Yet he must needs follow Love, for his liege lady was she, and in sooth she wounded him more sorely than did his honour and faith to his uncle, though they strove hard for the mastery. For Love looked smiling upon his heart, and led heart and eyes captive; and yet if he saw her not, then was he even more sorrowful. Much he vexed himself, marvelling how he might escape, and saying to his heart: "Turn thee here or there, let thy desire be other, love and long elsewhere." Yet ever the more he looked into his heart the more he found that therein was nought but Love — and Iseult.

Even so was it with the maiden: she was as a bird that is snared with lime. When she knew the snare of Love and saw that her heart was indeed taken therein, she strove with all her power to free herself, yet the more she struggled the faster was the hold Love laid upon her, and, unwilling, she must follow whither Love led. As with hands and feet she strove to free herself, so were hands and feet even more bound and fettered by the blinding sweetness of the man and his love, and never half a foot's length might she stir save that Love were with her. Never a thought might Iseult think save of Love and Tristan, yet she fain would hide it. Heart and eyes strove with each other; Love drew her heart towards him, and shame drove her eyes away. Thus Love and maiden shame strove together till Iseult wearied of the fruitless strife, and did as many have done before her — vanquished, she yielded herself body and soul to the man, and to Love.

Shyly she looked on him, and he on her, till heart and eyes had done their work. And Tristan, too, was vanquished, since Love would have it none otherwise. Knight and maiden sought each other as often as they might do so, and each found the other fairer day by day. For such is the way of Love, as it was of old, and is to-day, and shall be while the world endures, that lovers please each other more as love within them waxeth stronger, even as flowers and fruit are fairer in their fulness than in their beginning; and Love that beareth fruit waxeth fairer day by day till the fulness of time be come.

Love doth the loved one fairer make,
So love a stronger life doth take.
Love's eyes wax keener day by day,
Else would love fade and pass away.

So the ship sailed gaily onwards, even though Love had thus turned two hearts aside, for she who turneth honey to gall, sweet to sour, and dew to flame, had laid her burden on Tristan and Iseult, and as they looked on each other their colour changed from white to red and from red to white, even as it pleased Love to paint them. Each knew the mind of the other, yet was their speech of other things.

And that night Love, the physician, led Tristan to Iseult's side, and bound the twain together with such master skill and wondrous power that nevermore in all their lives might the bond betwixt them be loosed.

So they sailed on their journey, blissful in each other's love, yet fearful lest any should espy their secret; and sad at heart when they thought how fair Iseult must needs be the bride of one whom she loved not. When they saw the coast of Cornwall, and all on board were joyous that their voyage was well-nigh ended, Tristan and Iseult were heavy at heart, for if they might have had their will never again would they have looked on land, but sailed the seas together for evermore.

As they drew near to shore, Iseult bethought her of a ruse. She sought out Brangoene, and prayed her that she would, on the marriage night, take the place of the queen — for Brangoene was fair and a maiden, and Iseult had it in her heart to belong to none but her lover Tristan. So she spake on this wise to Brangoene, who kept silence a space, and then answered:

"Dear lady, thy mother, my liege lady and queen, committed thee to my care; 'twas my part on this ill-fated voyage to have kept thee from this very sorrow. Through my carelessness have sorrow and shame come upon thee, so may I not complain if I must needs share the shame with thee, 'tis but right that I should take my part therein. Ah God! how came I to be thus forgetful?"

"Dear cousin," said Iseult, "wherefore reproach thyself? I know not of what thou speakest."

"Lady, 'twas but the other day I cast a crystal flask into the sea."

" 'Tis true, but why should that so trouble thee?"

"Alas! that same flask, and the drink that was therein, 'twas the death of ye both!"

"How may that be? What is this wild tale?"

Then Brangoene told the twain the story, from beginning to end, even as it had chanced.

"Now in God's name," quoth Tristan, "were it death or life, the poison was sweet! I know not what may come of it, but such death it pleaseth me well! Shall fair Iseult indeed be my death, then would I die daily!"

And yet, however sweet love may be, a man must at whiles bethink him of his honour, and Tristan knew well that he owed both faith and honour to Mark, who had sent him to fetch his bride, and the twain fought hard with his love, and vexed heart and soul between them, yet was it of no avail, for since he had chosen Love, Honour and Faith alike must needs be put to the worse.

Then Tristan sent messengers in two boats to the land, to bear tidings of the coming of the fair Princess of Ireland; and Mark sent forth a thousand messengers through all the kingdom to bid his knights prepare a fitting welcome for their comrades and the strangers who came with them, and Mark himself received the twain even as a man welcomes that which he holds the dearest upon earth.

Then King Mark bade all his barons assemble at court within eighteen days, to witness his wedding with Iseult, and they came together, many a fair company of knights and ladies, all eager to behold fair Iseult, of whose beauty they had heard such tales. And when they had looked upon her, there was but one thought and one voice among them: "Iseult the fair is the marvel of all the world. 'Tis true what we have heard of her, she is even as the sun rejoiceth the hearts of men; never did any kingdom win so fair a maiden."

So King Mark and Iseult of Ireland were wedded, and the kingdoms of Cornwall and England were laid in her hands, with the pledge that if she bare no heir to Mark, then should Tristan inherit them, and so was homage done to her.

When night fell, then were matters wrought even as Iseult had planned. When the queen put out the lights in the bridal chamber, then Brangoene, in the royal robes, lay down beside the king; but when the king asked for wine, that men were wont to drink on the bridal night, Brangoene arose, and when Tristan bare the lights and the wine, 'twas Iseult sat beside the couch. But the drink that she and Mark should have shared had been drunk long since, and the flask lay in the depths of the sea.

Now King Mark and all his folk, and the people of the land, loved and honoured Queen Iseult, for the grace and the courtesy that they found in her, and no man but spake her praises; and none knew how the matter stood betwixt her and Tristan, or thought evil of them. With that there came a thought into the queen's mind, since none but Brangoene knew aught of the deceit that she had practised toward King Mark, might it not be for her safety that she should live no longer? Were she no longer there, there would be little fear of any man discovering aught against the queen's honour. And if it were so that Brangoene had any love or friendship for King Mark, might it not be that she would reveal his shame unto him? And in this did the queen make clearly manifest that men fear shame and mockery more than they fear God, for she sent for two squires, strangers of England, and made them swear an oath, on peril of their lives, to do her bidding without question. And when they had sworn she said: "Now mark well my mind: I will send a maiden with you, and ye three shall ride swiftly and secretly till ye be come to some wood, near or far, even as ye shall deem best, but apart from all dwelling-place of man. There shall ye smite off the maiden's head. And mark well all her words, and what she saith, that shall ye tell me, and bring me back her tongue. And be ye sure of this: if ye do my bidding well on the morrow will I make ye knights, and give ye lands and riches so long as ye shall live." And all this did they swear to do.

Then Iseult took Brangoene aside, and said: "Brangoene, look at me well; am I not pale? I know not what aileth me, but mine head doth pain me sorely. Thou must go forth and seek me herbs and roots, and we must take counsel, else I fear for my life."

The faithful Brangoene answered: "Lady, thine illness grieveth me sore; let us not delay. But say, where may I find that which may do thee good?"

"See, here are two squires, ride with them, they will guide thee aright."

"Gladly will I go, lady."

Thus the three rode forth together, and they came to a wood, where was great plenty of herbs, roots, and grass, and Brangoene dismounted from her steed. Then the squires led her deeper into the wild woodland, and when they were far from all haunts of men the two seized the faithful maiden and threw her on the ground, and drew forth their swords to slay her.

Brangoene was so terrified she lay still on the ground, trembling in every limb. Fearful, she looked up to them: "Sirs, of your pity, what will ye do to me?"

"Thou shalt die here!"

"Alas! wherefore? Tell me, I pray you."

And then one said: "What hast thou done to anger the queen? She bade us slay thee, and it must needs be so. Iseult, our lady and thine, she hath commanded thy death."

Brangoene folded her hands, and spake, weeping: "Nay, sirs, for God's sake, of your mercy delay a while, and let me live till I have answered ye; after that slay me if ye will. Know yourselves, and hereafter tell my lady the queen, that I have done nought to lose her favour, or that should bring her hurt, save perchance this one thing, and that I scarce believe it may be. When we twain sailed from Ireland we had each of us a garment white as snow, fairer and better than our other garments. When we were on the sea so great was the heat of the sun that the queen might not bear her robes, but did on this white robe, and ware that only, and she ware it till it was soiled and stained and its whiteness marred. But I had hid my garment within my coffer, and its white folds were all unsullied. And when my lady came hither, and took my lord the king for her husband, on the bridal night would she wear her white robe, but 'twas no longer so fair as she would have it, so prayed she the loan of mine. Yet at first I forgot my duty and refused it to her, but at the last did I do even as she prayed. If it be not this that hath angered her, then I know not what it may be. God knoweth never at any time did I transgress her will and her command. Now do what ye will with me.  Greet my lady from me as is fitting from a maiden to her mistress.  May God in His goodness preserve her in life and in honour, and may my death be forgiven her.  I commend my soul to God and my body to your will."

Then the squires looked pitifully the one on the other.  They had compassion on the maiden and her bitter weeping, and repented them much that they had sworn to slay her, for they could find no fault in her, nor anything that was worthy of death.  They took counsel together, and determined, happen what might to them, they would let her live.  So they bound the maiden to a tree, high up, that the wolves might not touch her before they could come to her again, and took one of their hounds and slew it, and cut out its tongue, and rode thence.

Then they told Queen Iseult how, with sorrow and pain, they had obeyed her commandment, and shewed her the tongue, and said it was that of the maiden.  And Iseult said: "Now tell me, what did the maid say to ye?"

Then they told her all from the beginning, even as Brangoene had told them, and forgat no word.

"Yea," quoth the queen, "said she no more?"

"Nay, lady."

Then Iseult cried: "Alas for these tidings!  Wretched murderers, what have ye done?  Ye shall hang, both of ye!"

"Lady," they said, "most gracious Queen Iseult, what dost thou say?  Didst thou not beseech us, and lay pressure upon us, that we should slay her?"

"I know not what ye say of prayers.  I gave my maiden into your care that ye should guard her on the road, that she might bring me back that which I desired.  Ye must restore her to me or your lives are forfeit.  Cowardly death-dealers, ye shall hang, both of ye, or be burnt on a pyre!"

"Nay," spake one of them, "lady, thy heart and thy mind, they are not pure and single.  Thy tongue is double indeed!  But rather than lose our lives we will give thee thy maiden again, whole and in good health."

Then Iseult spake, weeping bitterly: "Lie to me no more: doth Brangoene live, or is she dead?"

"She liveth, gracious Iseult."

"Ah! then bring her back to me, and I will keep the promise I sware to ye."

"Lady, it shall be done."

Iseult bade one squire remain with her, the other rode thence to the spot where he left Brangoene, and brought the maiden again to Iseult.  And when she came into the queen's presence Iseult clasped her in her arms, and kissed her lips and her cheek over and over again.  To the squires she gave for payment seventy marks of gold on the promise that they should keep the matter secret.

Now that Queen Iseult had tested Brangoene, and found that she was faithful and true, even to death, and that her courage was steadfast, even as gold tried in the furnace, the twain were henceforth so one in heart and mind that nought could befall the one but it touched the other as nearly. The court was full of Brangoene's praise. All loved her, and she bore ill will to no man. She was trusted alike by king and queen, nought was done in the counsel-chamber but Brangoene knew it. Also would she serve Iseult and her lover Tristan even as they might command her. But this was done so secretly that no man in the court had any suspicion. None dreamed what where the thoughts and words of Tristan and the queen.

And as the days passed on they learnt, even among the folk around them, to speak to each other by glances and hidden words, as is the way of lovers. And as they grew bolder even through their open speech there ran a meaning, known but to themselves, love working in their speech even as a gold thread running through silken tissue. None saw more in their words than was fitting betwixt near of kin, for all knew the love and confidence that were betwixt Tristan and King Mark.

In these days had Tristan a companion, a noble knight, who held his lands from the king, and was chief seneschal at court; he was named Marjodo. The same bare Tristan love and honour for the sake of the queen, whom he loved secretly, though no man was ware of it.

The two knights had their lodging in common, and were fain to be of each other's company. It was the seneschal's custom to have his couch spread by Tristan's at night, that they might speak freely to each other, and he be solaced by Tristan's fair speech.

One night it chanced that the two had spoken long together ere Marjodo fell asleep, and when at length he slept soundly the lover Tristan arose softly, and stole secretly on the track that led to much sorrow for him and the queen. He thought himself unmarked as he trod the path that had often led him gladly to Iseult's side; snow had fallen, and the moon shone clear, but Tristan had no care to conceal his steps.

When he came to the queen's chamber Brangoene took a chess-board, and leant it against the light so that the chamber was darkened, and then she laid her down to sleep; how it chanced I know not, but she left the door undone, whereof came sorrow and trouble.

Now, as the seneschal Marjodo lay and slept, he dreamed that a fierce boar came out of the forest and ran into the palace, foaming, and gnashing his tusks, and oversetting all in his way, so that no man durst withstand him. Thus he came even to the king's chamber, and burst open the door and tare the couch to pieces, tossing it hither and thither; and Mark's men beheld, but none dare lay hands upon him.

With that the seneschal awoke, and would fain tell Tristan his dream; so he called on him by name, and when he answered not he called again, and felt with his hands, and knew the bed to be empty. Then he bethought him that Tristan was gone forth on some secret errand, not that he had any thought of his love for the queen, but he was somewhat vexed that, such friends as they were, Tristan had not told him his secret. So he arose and did on his garments, and stole forth softly, and looked around, and saw the track made by Tristan in the snow.

He followed the path through a little orchard till he came to the door of the queen's chamber. There he stopped, trembling, for a strange doubt fell on him when he found the door undone. He stood awhile and gazed on Tristan's footprints, and thought now one thing, now another. One moment he deemed that Tristan had come hither for the love of one of the queen's maidens; and then again he deemed 'twas surely for love of the queen herself; so he wavered 'twixt one thought and another.

At last he went forward softly, and found neither taper nor moonlight; a taper was burning, yet he saw but little of it for the chess-board that was set over against it. Yet he went forward still, feeling with his hands against the wall till he came near the queen's couch, and heard the lovers as they spake softly to each other.

Then was Marjodo sorrowful at heart, for he had ever loved and honoured Queen Iseult, but now his love was overcome of anger. He hated and envied the twain, yet knew not what he might do in the matter. He bethought him of this and of that; he was so wrathful for the treachery that he fain had revealed it, but the thought of Tristan and the dread that his anger should do him a hurt restrained him. So he turned him about and went his way back and laid him down again as one who had been sorely wronged.

In a short space Tristan came back softly, and laid him to bed again. He spake no word, nor did Marjodo, which was little his custom. From his silence Tristan misdoubted him, and bethought him to keep a better watch over his speech and actions; but 'twas too late, his secret was his no longer.

Then Marjodo spake secretly to the king, and told him how a rumour went about the court touching Tristan and the queen, that was but ill pleasing to the folk, and he counselled the king to look into the matter, and do as should best beseem him, for 'twas a thing that touched his wedded honour. But he told him not the true story as he himself knew it.

The simple-hearted king, who was himself true and faithful, was much amazed and heard him unwillingly, for the guiding star of his joy in Iseult would he not suffer lightly to be belied. Yet in his heart was he ill at ease, and could not but watch them secretly to see if he might find aught unfitting in their speech and bearing; yet could he find nought, for Tristan had warned Iseult of the seneschal's suspicions.

Then the king bethought him of a ruse, and one evening when he was alone with the queen he spake on this wise: "Lady, I have a mind to go on a pilgrimage and may be long on the road; in whose care wilt thou that I leave thee?"

"My lord," answered Iseult, "wherefore ask me? In whose care shouldst thou leave thy folk and thy land save in that of thy nephew Tristan? He is valiant and wise, and can guard them well."

This saying misliked the king, and he watched even more closely, and spake to the seneschal of his suspicions; and Marjodo answered:

"Of a truth, sire, 'tis as I say. Thou canst thyself see that they may not hide the love they bear to each other. 'Tis a great folly thus to suffer them. Much as thou dost love thy wife and thy nephew, thou shouldst not for thine honour endure this shame."

The matter vexed Mark much, for he could not but doubt his nephew, yet might he find no ground for his doubt.

But Iseult was joyful, and told Brangoene, laughing and with much glee, of her lord's pilgrimage, and how he had asked her in whose care she would be left. Then Brangoene said: "My lady, lie not to me, but tell me truly, — whom didst thou choose?" And Iseult told her all, even as it had chanced.

"Ah, foolish child!" said Brangoene, "why didst thou say so? Of a truth 'twas but a ruse, and the counsel was the seneschal's — herewith he thought to take thee. If the king speak to thee again on the matter, do as I shall tell thee, and answer thus and thus." So she counselled the queen.

When now king and queen were alone, Mark took Iseult in his arms, and kissed her many times on her eyes and on her lips, and spake: "Sweetest, I love nought beside thee, and now that I needs must leave, God knoweth it lieth heavy on my heart."

Then the queen said sighing: "Alas and alas, my lord! I deemed thy speech was but in sport; now I see thou wert in very earnest." And she began to weep so bitterly that the simple king felt all his doubts vanish; he could have sworn that she spake from her heart (for in sooth women can weep without cause, and without meaning, so oft as it seemeth them good so to do).

Then, as Iseult still wept, Mark said: "Dearest, tell me what vexeth thee, why dost thou weep?"

"Well may I weep, and much cause have I to lament. I am but a woman, and have but one body and soul, and both have I so given over to thee and to thy love that I can care for none beside. And know for a truth that thou dost not love me as thou sayest, or thou couldst not have the heart to journey hence, and leave me all alone in a strange land; by this I know thou lovest me not, and I must needs be sorrowful."

"But wherefore, fair Iseult? Thou hast folk and land in thine own power, they are thine even as they are mine, thou art mistress, and what thou dost command, that shall be done. And while I am on my journey shalt thou be in the care of one who can guard thee well, my nephew Tristan: he is wise and of good counsel, and will do all he may for thine honour and happiness. I trust him well; thou art as dear to him as I may be, he will guard thee alike for thy sake and mine."

"Tristan!" said fair Iseult, "I were liever I were dead and buried than left in his care. He is but a flatterer who is ever at my side telling me how dear he holds me! Yet I know well wherefore he doeth so: he slew my uncle and doth fear my hatred! For that alone doth he ply me with flatteries, thinking to win my friendship, but it helpeth him little! 'Tis true, I have spoken to him oft with lying lips and friendly glances, and laid myself out to please him, but I did it for thy sake, and lest men should bring against me the reproach that women aye hate their husband's friend. Ofttimes have I deceived him with my friendly words, so that he would have sworn they came from my heart! Sir, leave me not in the care of thy nephew Tristan, no, not for a day, if I may persuade thee!"

Thus Iseult by her soft words soothed Mark's heart, and laid his doubts to rest; and he told the seneschal how that the queen had contented him. But Marjodo would not rest till he had persuaded the king to test Iseult once more.

So on an even, as they sat in their chamber, Mark said: "My lady queen, since I must journey hence I would fain see how a woman may rule a kingdom. All my friends and kinsmen who owe aught to me must needs treat thee with all honour, but any who have not found favour in thine eyes will I send out of the land, I will no longer love those whom thou lovest not. Otherwise live free and happy, and do as shall please thee. And since my nephew Tristan displeaseth thee, I will shortly send him hence, he shall return to Parmenie, and see to his own land; 'tis needful alike for him and the country."

"I thank thee, sire," said Iseult, "thou dost speak well and truly. Since I know now that thou art so swiftly displeased with those who trouble me, it seemeth to me that I should strive, in so far as I may, to honour those who are pleasing in thine eyes. 'Tis neither my mind nor my counsel that thou shouldst banish thy nephew from court; so were I dishonoured, for all the folk would say that I had counselled thee to do it, in revenge for the death of mine uncle, and that were shame to me and small honour to thee. Also bethink thee well, who shall guard thy two kingdoms? Shall they be safe in a woman's hand? I know none who may guard them so well as thy nephew Tristan, he is thy nearest of kin, and shall be best obeyed. Should he be banished, and war come upon us, as may chance any day, and we be put to the worse, then would men reproach me, saying: 'If Tristan had been here, then should we not have had such ill success'; and all will blame me, so shall I forfeit alike my honour and thine. Sir, bethink thee better; either let me go with thee, or bid Tristan guard the kingdom; however my heart may be towards him, 'tis better he guard us than another shame us."

Now the king saw truly that Iseult's heart was set on Tristan's honour, and he fell again into doubt and anger. Iseult also told Brangoene all that had passed, and it vexed the wise maiden that she had spoken thus, so she counselled her again as to what she should say. And when the king held her in his arms and kissed her, she said: "Sire, wast thou in very earnest when thou didst speak of sending Tristan hence for my sake? If it were true, then would

I be grateful to thee, and in sooth I know I should trust thee, yet my mind misgave me that thou saidst it but to try me? If I might know certainly that thou dost hate all who are my foes, then should I be assured of thy love for me. Of a truth had I thought thou wouldst hearken, I should ere now have made my request to thee to send thy nephew hence to his own land, for I misdoubt me much, should evil befall thee on thy journey, that he will take from me the kingdom; he has the power to do so. If then thou wert in earnest it might indeed be well to send him to his own land, or to take him with thee on thy journey; and bid the seneschal Marjodo guard me while thou art absent. Or if thou wilt but let me journey with thee, then mayest thou commit the land to whomsoever thou wilt."

So she caressed and flattered her lord till she had driven all doubts from his soul, and he held the queen for innocent, and the tale of her love for Tristan a dream, and Marjodo himself but a liar — yet had he spoken the truth.

So for a while Tristan and his lady Iseult led a happy life; their joy was full, their desire was granted them after much sorrow. But not for long might it endure, for do as they might Tristan and Iseult might not guard themselves so well but that the king should find fresh matter for suspicion. Again Mark knew not what to think: he suspected both, yet would suspect neither; he thought them true, yet deemed they lied to him; he would not have them guilty, yet would not speak them free of guilt. This was a heavy load on the heart of the doubter.

At last he bethought him he would call his lords together, and take counsel on the matter; so he summoned all those in whom he might trust, and laid all his trouble bare to them, telling them of the tale which went about the court, and which so nearly touched his honour, and how do what he might, he could not lay his doubts to rest. But now was the tale so spread abroad in the land that it seemed to him alike for his sake and the queen's 'twas time that her innocence should be made clear in the sight of all men. He besought their counsel as to how the matter be cleared up.

Then the lords, his friends bade him assemble a great council at London, in England, and there make known to all the bishops, who knew well the law of the church, the doubt and sorrow in which he found himself. The council was therefore summoned without delay to meet at London, after Pentecost, on the last days of May. Of priests and lay folk a great number came together by the king's command, and thereto came King Mark and Iseult his queen, heavy at heart, and in much fear and trembling: Iseult feared greatly lest she lose her life and her good fame, and Mark also feared lest his gladness and his honour be shamed through his wife Iseult.

Then Mark sat at the council, and laid bare to all the princes of his land how he was troubled and perplexed by this tale of scandal, and prayed them earnestly for God's sake that they would bethink them of some means by which the matter might be fairly judged, and, for good or for ill, an end put to it. And some said one thing and some another, till many men had spoken their minds.

Then there stood up one of the princes, who by his age and wisdom was well fitted to give good counsel: a man noble and ancient, grey-haired and wise, the Bishop of Thames. He leaned on his staff and spake: "My lord king, hear me. Thou hast called us princes of England together that we may aid thee by our counsel as thou hast need. Sire, I am one of these princes, and well advanced in age; I think I may well take upon me to speak my mind in the matter; if thou thinkest my counsel good thou canst follow it. My lady the queen and Sir Tristan are suspected by many of having betrayed thee, yet can nought be proved against them — so do I understand the matter. How then mayst thou pass judgment on thy nephew and thy wife, since none have found them offending? No man can accuse Tristan of it but he is ready with an answer to the charge; even so is it with the queen. Thou canst prove nought. But since the court holdeth them so strongly in suspicion, I counsel thee that thou forbid the queen thy bed and thy board till the day that she can shew herself free of offence against thee and against the land. The tale is spread abroad, and men speak of it daily, for alas! to such scandals, be they true or false, men's ears are ever wont to be open, and whatever evil be in the story, of that will they make the worst. But whether true or false the mischief and the scandal are so widespread they must needs injure thee and be held amiss by the court. Therefore I counsel thee to call the queen hither that all present may hear her answer to the charge, and see if she be ready to give open proof of her innocence."

This counsel seemed good to King Mark, and he bade them summon Queen Iseult, and she came to the council-chamber. When she was seated the grey-haired Bishop of Thames arose, and spake as the king bade him:

"Lady Iseult, gracious queen, be not wrathful at my speech; the king my master hath bid me speak, and I must needs obey him. God is my witness, I would fain say nought that could reflect on thine honour and on thy fair fame. My lady queen, thy lord and husband hath bid me speak to thee of a charge openly brought against thee. I know not, nor may he know, how it hath come about; he knoweth only that court and country alike couple thy name with that of the king's nephew, Sir Tristan. I pray God, my lady queen, that thou art innocent of this sin — yet doth the king doubt; the court is so full of the rumour. My lord himself hath found in thee nought but good; 'tis not his thought but the talk of the court that hath brought this suspicion upon thee. Therefore doth he call thee hither that his friends and councillors may hear thee, if perchance by their aid an end may be put to this slander. Now methinks it were well that thou shouldst make answer to the king in this matter, here in presence of us all."

Then Iseult, the quick-witted queen, seeing that it fell to her to speak, arose and answered: "My king, my lord bishop, lords of the land and all ye courtiers, ye shall all know well that I deny my lord's shame and mine, and I shall deny it both now and at all times. Ye lords all, I know well that this accusation hath been brought against me, it is now over a year, both at court and abroad; yet ye yourselves know that no man may be so fortunate that, however well he may live, evil shall never be spoken of him. Therefore I marvel not if such chance should also befall me. I may never be left in peace, I must ever be slandered and misjudged since I am here a stranger, and have neither friend nor kinsfolk in the land — there are but few here whom my shame may touch. Ye all and each, whether rich or poor, believe readily in my misdoing! If I knew now what I might do, or what counsel I might follow whereby I might prove mine innocence, and win again your favour and my lord's honour, I would readily agree to it. What would ye have me do? Whatever judgment may be passed upon me thereto will I readily submit, that your suspicions may be laid to rest, yet even more that mine honour and that of my lord may be maintained."

Then the king spake: "My lady queen, hereby shall the matter be set at rest. If I may pass judgment upon thee as thou hast prayed us to do, thus shalt thou give us certainty: submit to the ordeal by red-hot iron, as we here counsel thee!"

This the queen did; she sware to undergo the ordeal even as they should ordain, six weeks hence, in the town of Caerleon.

Thus the king and the lords departed from the council.

Iseult remained alone, sorrowful and sore dismayed at heart, for much she feared that her unfaithfulness must now be made manifest, and she knew not what to do. So with prayer and fasting she made supplication to Heaven to aid her. And a thought came to her mind. She wrote a letter to Tristan, bidding him be at Caerleon early on the morn of the day she must arrive there and await her on the shore. And this Tristan did, journeying thither in pilgrim's guise, his face stained and soiled, and his appearance changed.

Now, Mark and Iseult came thither by water, and as they drew to shore the queen saw Tristan and knew him. As the ship cast anchor in the stream Iseult commanded they should ask the pilgrim if he were strong enough to carry her to shore, for on that day she would have no knight to bear her.

Then all the folk cried: "Come hither, thou holy man, bear our lady the queen to land."

Tristan came at their call, and took the queen in his arms and bore her to the shore; and as he held her Iseult whispered in his ear that as he set foot on land he should fall with her. And this he did; as he stepped out of the water on to the shore the pilgrim sank down on the earth as if he could not help himself, so that the queen fell from his clasp and lay beside him on the ground.

Then the folk came swiftly with sticks and staves, and would do the pilgrim an harm. "Nay, nay, let be," cried Iseult, "the pilgrim could not help himself, he is sick and feeble, and fell against his will."

Then they all praised her much that she was not wrathful with the pilgrim, but Iseult spake, smiling a little: "Were it then so great a wonder if the pilgrim had thought to mock me?"  And as Mark stood near and harkened, she spake further: "Now I know not what shall befall me, for ye have all seen well that I may not swear that no man save the king ever held me in his arms or lay at my side!"

Thus they rode gaily, jesting the while of the palmer, till they came into Caerleon.  There were many nobles, priests, and knights, and of lesser folk a great crowd.  Bishops and prelates were there, ready to do their office and bless the ordeal.  They had all things in readiness, and the iron was brought forth.

The good Queen Iseult had given in charity her silks and her gold, her jewels and all she had, horses and raiment, praying that Heaven would look favourably on her, forgive her what she had done amiss, and preserve her honour.  Herewith she came to the Minster with good courage to face her ordeal.

She wore next her skin a rough garment of hair; above it a short gown of woollen stuff, a hand's breadth above her ankles; her sleeves were rolled up to her elbows, and her hands and feet bare.  Many hearts and many eyes beheld her with pity.

Herewith they brought forth the relics, and bade Iseult swear her innocence of this sin before God and the world.  Now had Iseult committed life and honour to Heaven, so hand and heart did she proffer reverently to the relics and the oath.

Now were there many there who would fain from ill will have had the queen's oath turned to her shame and downfall.  The envious seneschal, Marjodo, strove to harm her in every way he might; while there were many who honoured Iseult, and would fain see her come off scatheless; so there was great strife among them as to the manner of the queen's oath.

"My lord the king," spake Iseult, "whatever any may say, I must needs swear in such wise as shall content thee.  Say thyself what I shall speak or do.  All this talk is too much.  Hearken how I will swear to thee.  No man hath touched this my body, hath held me in his arms or lain beside me other than thou thyself, and this man whom I cannot deny, since ye all saw me in his arms — the poor pilgrim!  So help me God and all the saints, to the happy issue of this ordeal!  If this be not enough my lord, I will better mine oath as thou shalt bid me."

"Lady," said King Mark, "methinks 'tis enough.  Now take the iron in thine hand, and God help thee in thy need."

"Amen," said fair Iseult.  Then in God's name she seized the iron, and carried it, and it burnt her not.

And so, had men but known it, they might have seen that God at whiles doth let the wrong triumph, since He turned not this oath, which was true in the letter yet false in spirit, to the confusion of the queen, but ruled matters so that she came forth from the ordeal victorious, and was held in greater love and honour by Mark and his people than ever before; all his thoughts and all his heart were truly set upon her, and his doubts had passed away.

[Though thus tricked for the moment, Mark's suspicions continue, and the story is one of stratagem and deceit, until the day when Mark sees the two in each other's arms. They know that they have been discovered. Tristan sails for an exile's life in Brittany where he meets and marries another Iseult, Iseult of the White Hands. Here Gottfried's poem stops, ended by his death. The other Tristan tales variously conclude the story, but it is to be presumed that Gottfried intended to follow his source, Thomas, who adapted parts of the classical stories of Paris and Oenone and of Theseus. Tristan, again wounded with a poisoned sword, sends for Queen Iseult to heal him, with the stipulation that if she consents to return, the ship bearing her shall fly a white sail, but otherwise black. Iseult returns speedily but her ship is becalmed, and in order to catch the wind the black sail is hoisted above the white. Tristan, seeing it from shore, hurls himself to his death. Iseult, over his corpse, swallows poison and dies.]

[tr. JESSIE L. WESTON]

# WOLFRAM VON ESCHENBACH

Of the great German poets who lived at the end of the twelfth century, Wolfram was probably the least educated, though a petty noble. His rough spiritual vigor stands in colorful contrast with Gottfried's urbanity, as the latter was quick to note more than once. But to Gottfried's taunt about *findaere wilder maere* ("finders of wild tales"), Wolfram serenely replied, "Some praised *Parzival*, some contemned it and adorned their own tales the better." His *Parzival* captured the Grail story from its uneasy connection with Arthur's court and in an amplification of more than 25,000 lines made of it a psychological novel dealing sincerely with its hero's search, through bitter experiences, for peace of mind and true nobility.

Long before Wolfram wrote, the Grail story, which may in essence have been transmitted from the Orient through Moorish Spain and France, had united with a Celtic tale of Percival. In that tale Percival's widowed mother tried to protect him from the world by raising him in isolation. But as he came of age he discovered knight errantry and hastened to Arthur's court to win the accolade while his deserted mother died of grief. He typified a youth unfitted, not by nature but by training, to make his way in the world.

In Wolfram's story, he acquires the external knightly qualities in ill-considered adventures. Though he marries Condwiramurs, he leaves her to search for experience and understanding of what pain and sorrow are. The Percival story merges with the Grail story. In a great castle he finds, surrounded by his mourning court, a mighty king upon a stretcher, suffering from an incurable wound. His queen, a maiden pure and true, brings in the Grail, from which all riches flow. Though everything in this heroic court seems strange and unaccountable — with extremes of luxury and misery, joy and sorrow — Percival, partly from ineptitude and partly from bad instruction, refrains from asking questions. After a restless sleep he awakes in an empty castle. As he rides away he hears imprecations, he knows not why. He has missed his great opportunity, for if he had been stirred in his humanity to ask of Anfortas, the king, about his misery, the wound would have been cured and Percival would have acquired the Grail, the castle, and happiness. But now he must spend long weary years in requital for the opportunity lost. One by one his early feats of arms bring disaster on him; his decisions and actions had been unwise, though never consciously so. The bent of the tale is therefore ethical: error breeds pain, pain grief, and grief wisdom. In chagrin he renounces the God his mother had taught him to turn to. Yet as he wanders, some doubt enters his mind; perhaps the error was not of God's creation but his own. Eventually he finds his way to the hermit Trevrezent. Their colloquy, given below, is not only an exposition of the central situation but is the turning point of the whole poem. Percival, with newly acquired hope and faith, eventually finds his way back to Anfortas at Munsalvaesche and by the proper question and action brings happiness to all. He reigns as Grail king, and is followed by his son Lohengrin, the swan knight. Throughout the poem the adventures of Gawain, who acts as a kind of standard of the well-adjusted knight, are interwoven as a sub-plot.

The following family tree may make clear the relationship of the descendents of Titurel, as Trevrezent refers to them:

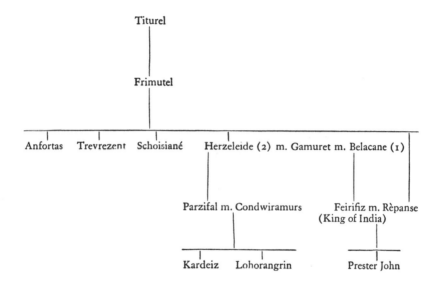

The reader will recognize distinct differences between this Grail legend of Wolfram, which, though he professes to scorn it, parallels an earlier poem of Chrétien de Troyes, and the version in early English poets, which is retold by Malory and Tennyson. The latter might be described as ascetic, the former humanistic. The notion of the Grail as Christ's chalice or any other specific symbol of Christianity is never suggested by Wolfram; he views this ill-defined source of good as a kind of oriental philosopher's stone or talisman. He conceives of the guardians of the Grail as a family of supermen set apart, though vaguely connected with the earthly house of Anjou on the one hand and the neutral angels on the other. This exaltation of Anjou may have come from the poem of Kiot, or Guyot, which Wolfram often refers to as his source. He applies to these guardians the name of Templars (*templeise*). The emphasis is religious only in the primitive fashion of early Greek and Hebrew poetry. It is universal in its sympathy for all races and creeds and even follies of men. Through symbols and specious adventures it propounds the human predicament — man's joy and woe and his everlasting struggle to rise above the errors of his own creation.

Miss Weston's translation, in anapestic hexameter, is remarkable in avoiding monotony in a poem twice the length of the *Aeneid* or *Paradise Lost*.   According to her, "The translator felt that the two points chiefly to be aimed at in an English version were that it should be faithful to the original text and easy to read.   The metre selected was chosen for several reasons, principally on account of the length of the poem, which seemed to render desirable a more flowing measure than the short lines of the original; and because by selecting this metre it was possible to retain the original form of *reim-paar*. As a general rule one line of the English version represents two of the German poem, but the difference of language has occasionally demanded expansion in order to do full justice to the poet's meaning.   Throughout, the translator's aim has been to be as literal as possible."

# PARZIVAL

## Wolfram von Eschenbach (A.D. 1210)

[From *Parzival*, translated by Jessie L. Weston; David Nutt, London, 1894.]

### BOOK IX, TREVREZENT

"Ope the portal!"  "To whom?   Who art thou?"  "In thine heart
    would I find a place!"
"Nay! if such be thy prayer, methinketh, too narrow shall be the
    space!"
"What of that?   If it do but hold me, none too close shall my presence
    be,
Nor shalt thou bewail my coming, such marvels I'll tell to thee!"
Is it thou, then, O Dame Adventure?   Ah! tell me of Parzival,
What doeth he now my hero? whom Kondrie, to find the Grail
Hath driven, with words sharp-pointed, and sore wept the maidens
    fair
That the path of his far wayfarings the knight from their side must
    bear.
So he passed from the court of King Arthur, where shall he abide
    to-day?
Ah! hasten the tale to tell us, where now shall his footsteps stray?
Say, if fame to himself he winneth, or be ever of joy bereft,
Shall his honour as fair and spotless as of old so to-day be left?
His renown is it broad as aforetime, or waxeth it small and thin?
Ah! tell us, nor stay the story, of the deeds that his hand shall win.

Hath he seen once again Monsalväsch, and Anfortas, the mournful
    king,
Whose heart was with sorrow laden?  Of thy pity swift comfort
    bring,
And say if his woe be ended — Speak, speak for we tidings pray
Of him whom alike we serve here, dwells Parzival there to-day?
Declare unto me his doings, how fares it with Gamuret's son,
And the child of fair Herzeleide, as the tale of his wanderings done?
Since he rode from the court of King Arthur has joy been his lot,
    or woe?
He hath striven, but rides he ever thro' the wide world nor rest doth
    know?
Or loveth he now, outwearied, to linger o'er-long at ease?
I were fain to know all his doings, so speak thou, as thou shalt please!
And this hath the venture told me — He hath ridden many a land,
And hath sailèd many a water; and ever, before his hand,
Were he man of the land or kinsman who would joust with him, he
    fell,
Nor abode his mighty onslaught, and all men of his praises tell.
And ever when in the balance the fame of his foe must lie,
'Twas outweighed by his fame, and his glory uprose to the stars on
    high,
And all other paled before it — In many a mighty strife
With sword and lance was he victor, and guarded full well his life.
And they would fame win from him, for such thinking they paid
    full dear —
The sword that Anfortas gave him, as ye once in this tale did hear,
Sprang asunder onewhile, yet 'twas welded afresh in the mystic spring
By Karnant, and much fame and honour the blade to its lord did
    bring!

So the son of Herzeleide rode onward, well taught was he
In all manly skill and courage, in mercy and purity;
And his mother had aye bequeathed him her faithful heart and true —
Yet ever his soul waxed sadder, and there sprang up thoughts anew
Of the might of the Maker of all things, Who hath made this earth
    of naught,
How He dealeth with all creation, and still on His power he thought
"How might it yet be if God sent me that which brought to an end
    my woe?
If ever a knight He favoured, if ever a knight might know
His payment for service done Him — if He thinketh His aid they
    earn
Who dauntless shall wield their weapons, and ne'er from a foeman
    turn,
Let Him aid me, who bear unstainèd shield and sword as befits a
    man,
If to-day be His Day of Redemption, let Him help me, if help He *can*."

Towards Fontaine-Sauvage the road led, and the chapel where once
he sware
The oath that should clear Jeschuté — A holy man dwelt there,
And Trevrezent men called him, and ever on Monday morn
Poor was his fare, and no richer it waxed as the week wore on.
Nor wine nor bread he tasted, no food that with blood was red,
Fish nor flesh, but his life so holy on the herb of the ground was fed.
And ever his thoughts, God-guided, were turning to Heaven's land,
And by fasting the wiles of the Devil he deemed he might best with-
stand.

And to Parzival the mystery of the Grail should he now reveal —
And he, who of this hath asked me, and since silence my lips must
seal
Was wroth with me as his foeman, his anger might naught avail,
Since I did but as Kiot bade me, for he would I should hide the tale,
And tell unto none the secret, till the venture so far were sped
That the hidden should be made open, and the marvel of men be read.

For Kiot of old, the master whom men spake of in days of yore,
Far off in Toledo's city, found in Arabic writ the lore
By men cast aside and forgotten, the tale of the wondrous Grail;
But first must he learn the letters, nor black art might there avail.
By the grace of baptismal waters, by the light of our Holy Faith,
He read the tale, else 'twere hidden; for never, the story saith,
Might heathen skill have shown us the virtue that hidden lies
In this mighty Grail, or its marvels have opened to Christian eyes.

'Twas a heathen, Flegetanis, who had won for his wisdom fame,
And saw many a wondrous vision (from Israel's race he came,
And the blood of the kings of old-time, of Solomon did he share),
He wrote in the days long vanished, ere we as a shield might bear
The cross of our Holy Baptism 'gainst the craft and the wiles of Hell,
And he was the first of earth's children the lore of the Grail to tell.
By his father's side a heathen, a calf he for God did hold,
How wrought the devil such folly, on a folk so wise, of old?
And the Highest Who knoweth all wonders, why stretched He not
forth His Hand
To the light of His truth to turn them? For who may His power
withstand!

And the heathen, Flegetanis, could read in the heavens high
How the stars roll on their courses, how they circle the silent sky,
And the time when their wandering endeth — and the life and the
lot of men
He read in the stars and strange secrets he saw, and he spake again
Low, with bated breath and fearful, of the thing that is called the
Grail,
In a cluster of stars was it written, the name, nor their lore shall fail.

And he quoth thus, "A host of angels this marvel to earth once bore,
But too pure for earth's sin and sorrow the heaven they sought once
    more,
And the sons of baptized men hold it, and guard it with humble
    heart,
And the best of mankind shall those knights be who have in such
    service part."

Then Kiot my master read this, the tale Flegetanis told,
And he sought for the name of the people, in Latin books of old,
Who of God were accounted worthy for this wondrous Grail to
    care,
Who were true and pure in their dealings and a lowly heart might
    bear.
And in Britain, and France, and Ireland thro' the chronicles he
    sought
Till at length, in the land of Anjou, the story to light was brought.
There, in true and faithful record, was it written of Mazadan,
And the heroes, the sons of his body, and further the story ran,
How Titurel, the grandsire, left his kingdom to Frimutel,
And at length to his son, Anfortas, the Grail and its heirdom fell:
That his sister was Herzeleide, and with Gamuret she wed
And bare him for son the hero whose wanderings ye now have read.
For he rideth upon a journey that shall lead him a road unknown,
Tho' the grey knight but now had wended his way from the fountain
    lone.

And he knew again the meadow, tho' now the snow lay white
On the ground that erst was blooming with flowers of springtide
    bright.
'Twas before the rocky hillside where his hand must wipe away
The stain from Jeschuté's honour, and her husband's wrath allay.
Yet still the road led onward, to Fontaine-Sauvage, the name
Of the goal that should end his journey and his hermit host he came.

Then out spake the holy hermit, "Alas, why doest thou so,
Sir Knight? at this Holy Season 'tis ill thus armed to go.
Dost thou bear perchance this harness thro' strife and danger dared?
Or hast thou unharmèd ridden, and in peace on thy way hast fared?
Other robe had beseemed thee better! List not to the voice of pride,
But draw thy rein here beside me, and with me for a space abide.
Not all too ill shalt thou fare here, thou canst warm thee beside my
    fire.
Dost thou seek here for knightly venture, and dost guerdon of love
    desire,
If the power of true Love constrain thee, then love Him who Love
    may claim!
As this day to His Love beareth witness, be His service to-day thine
    aim,

And serve for the love of fair women, if it please thee, another day;
But now get thee from off thy charger, and awhile from thy wander-
    ings stay."

The snow lay beneath our hero, no weakling was he, I ween,
Else the frost and cold of his harness o'er-much for his strength had
    been.
To a cavern the hermit led him where no breath of wind might blow,
And a fire of coals had warmed it, and burned with a ruddy glow.
And here might the guest refresh him by the fire and a taper's light
(Well strewn was the ground with fuel), then swiftly the gallant
    knight
Laid from off him his heavy armour, and warmed his limbs so cold,
And his skin in the light glowed ruddy, and his face might the host
    behold.
He might well be of wandering weary, for never a trodden way
Nor a roof save the stars of heaven had he known for many a day.
In the daylight the wood had he ridden, and his couch, it had been
    the ground:
'Twas well that he here a shelter, and a kindly host had found!

Then his host cast a robe around him, and he took him by his right
    hand,
And he led him into a cavern where his Missal did open stand.
And as fitted the Holy Season the Altar was stripped and bare;
And the shrine — Parzival must know it, 'twas the spot where he
    once did swear
With true hand, true oath and faithful, that ended Jeschuté's woe,
And turnèd her tears to laughter, and taught her fresh joy to know!

Quoth Parzival, "Well I know it this chapel and shrine!   Of yore,
As hither my wanderings led me, an oath on that shrine I swore;
And a spear, with fair colours blazoned, that did here by the altar
    stand
I bare hence, and in sooth, I think me, right well did it serve my
    hand!
Men say it much honour brought me, yet I wot not if it be so,
For in thoughts of my wife had I lost me, and naught of the thing
    I know.
Yet, unwitting, two jousts had I ridden, and two foemen I over-
    threw,
In those days all men gave me honour, nor sorrow nor shame I knew.
Now, alas! is my sorrow greater than ever to man befell!
Say, when did I bear the spear hence?   The days of my wanderings
    tell!"

"It was Taurian," quoth the hermit, "who his spear in my care did
    leave,

And much did he mourn its losing, and I with the knight must
grieve.
And four years and a half and three days shall have passed since we
lost the spear,
Sir Knight, an my word thou doubtest, behold! it is written here!"
Then he showed unto him in the Psalter how the time it had come
and gone,
And the weeks and the years he read him that silent and swift had
flown.
And he spake, "Now first do I learn them, the days that I aimless
stray,
And the weeks and the years that have vanished, since my joy hath
been reft away."
And he spake, "Now indeed me-seemeth that my bliss it was but a
dream,
For heavy the load of sorrow that so long hath my portion been!"

"And, Sir Host, I yet more would tell thee, where cloister or church
shall be
And men unto God give honour, there no eye hath looked on me,
And naught but strife have I sought me, tho' the time as thou sayst
be long,
For I against God bear hatred, and my wrath ever waxeth strong.
For my sorrow and shame hath He cherished, and He watched
them greater grow
Till too high they waxed, and my gladness, yet living, He buried
low!
And I think were God fain to help me other anchor my joy had
found
Than this, which so deep hath sunk it, and with sorrow hath closed
it round.
A man's heart is mine, and sore wounded, it acheth, and acheth still,
Yet once was it glad and joyous, and free from all thought of ill!
Ere sorrow her crown of sorrow, thorn-woven, with stern hand
pressed
On the honour my hand had won me o'er many a foeman's crest!
And I do well to lay it on Him, the burden of this my shame,
Who can help if He will, nor withholdeth the aid that men fain would
claim.
But *me* alone, hath He helped not, whate'er men of Him may speak,
But ever He turneth from me, and His wrath on my head doth
wreak!"

Then the hermit beheld him sighing, "Sir Knight, thou shalt put
away
Such madness, and trust God better, for His help will He never stay.
And His aid to us here be given, yea, alike unto me and thee.
But 'twere best thou shouldst sit beside me, and tell here thy tale to
me,

And make to me free confession — How first did this woe begin?
What foe shall have worked such folly that God should thine hatred
    win?
Yet first would I pray thee, courteous, to hearken the word I say,
For fain would I speak Him guiltless, ere yet thou thy plaint shall
    lay
'Gainst Him Who denieth never unto sinful man His aid,
But ever hath answered truly, who truly to Him hath prayed.

"From the lips of the whole world's Lover came a message of love
    and peace
(For He is a Light all-lightening, and never His faith doth cease),
And he to whom love He showeth, findeth aye in that Love his
    bliss,
Yet twofold I ween is the message, and His token some read amiss;
For the world may buy, as it pleaseth, God's Wrath or His Love so
    great.
Say, which of the twain wilt thou choose here, shall thy guerdon be
    Love or Hate?
For the sinner without repentance, he flieth God's faith and Face,
But he who his sin confesseth, doth find in His presence grace!

"From the shrine of his heart, who shall keep Him? Tho' hidden
    the thought within,
And secret, and thro' its darkness no sunbeam its way may win
(For thought is a secret chamber, fast locked, tho' no lock it bear),
Yet, tho' against man it be closèd, God's light ever shineth there.
He pierceth the wall of darkness, and silent and swift His spring,
As no sound betrayed His coming, as no footstep was heard to ring,
So silent His way He goeth — And swift as our thoughts have flown,
Ere God passed of our heart the threshold, our thoughts unto Him
    were known!
And the pure in heart He chooseth; he who doth an ill deed begin,
Since God knoweth the thoughts of all men, full sorely shall rue his
    sin.
And the man who by deeds God's favour doth forfeit, what shall
    he gain?
Tho' the world count him honour-worthy, his soul seeketh rest in
    vain.
And where wilt thou seek for shelter if *God* as thy foeman stand,
Who of wrath or of love giveth payment, as men serve Him, with
    equal hand?
Thou art lost if thy God be against thee — If thou wouldst His
    favour earn,
Then away from thy wrath and thy folly thy thoughts to His good-
    ness turn!"

Quoth Parzival, "Here I thank thee, from my heart, that such
    faithful rede

Thou hast given of Him who withholdeth from no man his right-
    ful meed,
But evil, as good, requiteth — Yet my youth hath been full of care,
And my faith hath but brought me sorrow, and ill to this day I fare!"

Then the hermit he looked on the Waleis, "If a secret be not thy grief,
Right willing thy woe I'll hearken, I may bring thee perchance re-
    lief;
Of some counsel may I bethink me such as yet to thyself dost fail!"
Quoth Parzival, "Of my sorrows the chiefest is for the Grail,
And then for my wife — none fairer e'er hung on a mother's breast,
For the twain is my heart yet yearning, with desire that ne'er findeth
    rest."

Quoth his host, "Well, Sir Knight, thou speakest, such sorrow is good
    to bear;
If thus for the wife of thy bosom thy heart knoweth grief and care,
And Death find thee a faithful husband, tho' Hell vex thee with
    torments dire
Yet thy pains shall be swiftly ended, God will draw thee from out
    Hell-fire.
But if for the Grail thou grievest, then much must I mourn thy woe,
O! foolish man, since fruitless thy labours, for thou shalt know
That none win the Grail save those only whose names are in Heaven
    known.
They who to the Grail do service, they are chosen of God alone;
And mine eyes have surely seen this, and sooth is the word I say!"
Quoth Parzival, "Thou hast been there?"  "Sir Knight," quoth the
    hermit, "Yea!"
But never a word spake our hero of the marvels himself had seen,
But he asked of his host the story, and what men by "The Grail"
    should mean?
Spake the hermit, "Full well do I know this, that many a knightly
    hand
Serveth the Grail at Monsalväsch, and from thence, throughout all
    the land,
On many a distant journey these gallant Templars fare,
Whether sorrow or joy befall them, for their sins they this penance
    bear!"

"And this brotherhood so gallant, dost thou know what to them shall
    give
Their life, and their strength and their valour — then know, by a
    stone they live,
And that stone is both pure and precious — Its name hast thou never
    heard?
Men call it *Lapis Exilis* — by its magic the wondrous bird,
The Phoenix, becometh ashes, and yet doth such virtue flow

From the stone, that afresh it riseth renewed from the ashes' glow,
And the plumes that erewhile it moulted spring forth yet more fair
  and bright —
And tho' faint be the man and feeble, yet the day that his failing
  sight
Beholdeth the stone, he dies not, nor can, till eight days be gone,
Nor his countenance wax less youthful — If one daily behold that
  stone
(If a man it shall be, or a maiden 'tis the same), for a hundred years,
If they look on its power, their hair groweth not grey, and their face
  appears
The same as when first they saw it, nor their flesh nor their bone
  shall fail
But young they abide for ever — And this stone all men call the
  Grail.
And its holiest power, and the highest shall I ween be renewed to-
  day,
For ever upon Good Friday a messenger takes her way.
From the height of the highest Heaven a Dove on her flight doth
  wing,
And a Host, so white and holy, she unto the stone doth bring.
And she layeth it down upon it; and white as the Host the Dove
That, her errand done, swift wingeth her way to the Heaven above.
Thus ever upon Good Friday doth it chance as I tell to thee:
And the stone from the Host receiveth all good that on earth may be
Of food or of drink, the earth beareth as the fulness of Paradise.
All wild things in wood or in water, and all that 'neath Heaven
  flies,
To that brotherhood are they given, a pledge of God's favour fair,
For His servants He ever feedeth and the Grail for their needs doth
  care!"

"Now hearken, the Grail's elect ones, say who doth their service
  claim?"
"On the Grail, in a mystic writing, appeareth each chosen name,
If a man it shall be, or a maiden, whom God calls to this journey blest.
And the message no man effaceth, till all know the high behest,
But when all shall the name have read there, as it came, doth the
  writing go:
As children the Grail doth call them, 'neath its shadow they wax and
  grow.
And blessèd shall be the mother whose child doth the summons hear,
Rich and poor alike rejoiceth when the messenger draweth near,
And the Grail son or daughter claimeth!   They are gathered from
  every land,
And ever from shame and sorrow are they sheltered, that holy band.
In Heaven is their rewarding, if so be that they needs must die,
Then bliss and desire's fulfilment are waiting them all on high!

"They who took no part in the conflict, when Lucifer would fight
With the Three-in-One, those angels were cast forth from Heaven's
    height.
To the earth they came at God's bidding, and that wondrous stone
    did tend,
Nor was it less pure for their service, yet their task found at last an
    end.
I know not if God forgave them, or if they yet deeper fell,
This one thing I know of a surety, what God doeth, He doeth well!
But ever since then to this service nor maiden nor knight shall fail,
For God calleth them all as shall please Him! — and so standeth
    it with the Grail!"

Quoth Parzival, "So, since knighthood may conquer, with spear and
    shield,
Both the fame of this life, and the blessing which Paradise shall yield,
Since my soul ever longed for knighthood, and I fought where'er
    strife might be,
And my right hand hath neared full often the guerdon of victory,
If God be the God of battles, if He know how a man should fight,
Let Him name me as one of His servants, of the Grail let Him make
    me knight!
They shall own that I fear no danger, nor from strife would I turn
    aside!"
But the hermit made answer gently, "First must thou beware of
    pride,
For lightly may youth mislead thee; and the grace of humility
Mayst thou lose, and the proud God doth punish, as full surely is
    known to me!"
And tears filled his eyes to o'erflowing, and his sad thoughts awhile
    did turn
To a story of old, and our hero he bade from its lesson learn.

And he quoth, "Sir Knight, at Monsalväsch a king reigned in days
    of yore,
His name all men know as Anfortas, and I weep for him evermore.
Yea, and thou too shalt mourn his sorrow, for bitter the woe, I ween,
And the torment of heart and body that his guerdon from pride
    hath been.
For his youth and his worldly riches they led him an evil road,
And he sought for Frau Minne's favour in paths where no peace
    abode.

"But the Grail all such ways forbiddeth, and both knight alike and
    squire
Who serve the Grail must guard them from the lust of untamed desire.
By meekness their pride must be conquered, if they look for a
    heavenly prize,

And the brotherhood holdeth hidden the Grail from all stranger
eyes:
By their warlike skill and prowess the folk from the lands around,
They keep afar, and none knoweth where the Grail and its Burg are
found
Save those whom the Grail shall summon within Monsalväsch'
wall —
Yet *one,* uncalled, rode thither and evil did then befall,
For foolish he was, and witless, and sin-laden from thence did fare,
Since he asked not his host of his sorrow and the woe that he saw
him bear.
No man would I blame, yet this man, I ween, for his sins must pay,
Since he asked not the longed-for question which all sorrow had
put away.
(Sore laden his host with suffering, earth knoweth no greater pain.)
And before him King Lähelein came there, and rode to the Lake
Brimbane.
Libbèals, the gallant hero, a joust there was fain to ride,
And Lähelein lifeless left him, on the grass by the water-side
(Prienlascours, methinks, was his birthplace), and his slayer then
led away
His charger, so men knew the evil thus wrought by his hand that day.

"And I think me, Sir Knight, thou art Lähelein? For thou gavest
unto my care
A steed that such token showeth as the steeds of the Grail Knights
bear!
For the white dove I see on its housing, from Monsalväsch it surely
came?
Such arms did Anfortas give them while joy yet was his and fame.
Their shields bare of old the token, Titurel gave it to his son
Frimutel, and such shield bare that hero when his death in a joust
he won.
For his wife did he love so dearly no woman was loved so well
By man, yet in truth and honour, — and the same men of thee shall
tell
If thou wakenest anew old customs, and thy wife from thine heart
dost love —
Hold thou fast to such fair example lest thy steps from the right path
rove!
And in sooth thou art wondrous like him who once o'er the Grail
did reign,
Say, what is thy race? whence art thou? and tell me I pray thy name!"

Each gazed for a space on the other, and thus quoth Parzival,
"Son am I to a king and hero who through knightly courage fell,
In a joust was he slain — Now I pray thee, Sir Hermit, of this thy
grace,
That thou, in thy prayers henceforward, wilt give to his name a place.

Know, Gamuret, did they call him, and he came from fair Anjou —
Sir Host I am not Lähelein; if ever such sin I knew
'Twas in my days of folly, yet in truth have I done the same,
Here I make of my guilt confession, and my sin unto thee I name,
For the prince who once fell a victim unto my sinful hand
Was he whom men called 'the Red Knight,' Prince Ither of Cumber-
     land.
On the greensward I lifeless stretched him, and as at my feet he lay,
Harness, and horse, and weapons, as my booty I bare away!"

Spake the host as his words were ended (the tale he ill pleased must
     hear),
"Ah! world, wherefore deal thus with us? since sorrow and grief
     and fear
Far more than delight dost thou give us!  Say, is this thy reward
     alone?
For ever the song that thou singest doth end in a mournful tone!"
And he spake, "O thou son of my sister, what rede may I give to
     thee?
Since the knight thou hast slain in thy folly, thy flesh and thy blood
     was he!
If thou, blood-guiltiness bearing, shalt dare before God to stand,
For one blood were ye twain, to God's justice thy life shall repay
     thine hand.
Say, for Ither of Gaheviess fallen, what payment dost think to give?
The crown he of knightly honour!  God gave him, while he might
     live,
All that decketh man's life; for all evil his true heart did truly mourn,
True balsam was he of the faithful, to honour and glory born.
And shame fled before his coming, and truth in his heart did dwell,
And for love of his lovely body many women shall hate thee well!
For well did they love his coming, and to serve them he aye was fain,
But their eyes that shone fair for his fairness he ne'er shall rejoice
     again!
Now, may God show His mercy to thee whose hand hath such evil
     wrought,
Herzeleide the queen, thy mother, thou too to her death hast
     brought — "
"Nay!  Nay!  not so, holy father!  What sayest thou?" quoth
     Parzival,
"Of what dost thou here accuse me?  Were I king o'er the wondrous
     Grail
Not all Its countless riches would repay me if this be sooth,
These words that thy lips have spoken!  And yet if I, in very truth,
Be son unto thy sister, then show that thou mean'st me well,
And say, without fear or falsehood, are these things true that thou
     dost tell?"

Then the hermit he spake in answer, "Ne'er learnt I to deceive,
Thy mother she died of sorrow in the day thou her side didst leave,

Such rewarding her love won for her!  Thou wast the beast that
    hung
On her breast, the wingèd dragon that forth from her body sprung,
That spread its wings and left her: in a dream was it all foretold
Ere yet the sorrowing mother the babe to her breast did hold!

"And two other sisters had I, Schoisiané she was one;
She bare a child — Woe is me, her death thro' this birth she won!
Duke Kiot of Katelangen was her husband, and since that day
All worldly joy and honour he putteth from him away.
Siguné, their little daughter, was left to thy mother's care:
And sorrow for Schoisiané in my heart do I ever bear!
So true was her heart and faithful, an ark 'gainst the flood of sin.
A maiden, my other sister, her pure life doth honour win,
For the Grail she ever tendeth — Rèpanse de Schoie, her name,
Tho' none from its place may move it whose heart showeth taint of
    shame,
In *her* hands is it light as a feather — And brother unto us twain
Is Anfortas, by right of heirship he king o'er the Grail doth reign;
And he knoweth not joy, but sorrow, yet one hope I ween is his,
That his pain shall at last be turnèd to delight and to endless bliss.
And wondrous the tale of his sorrow, as, nephew, I'll tell to thee,
And if true be thine heart and faithful his grief shall thy sorrow be!

"When he died, Frimutel, our father, they chose them his eldest son
As Lord of the Grail and its knighthood, thus Anfortas his king-
    dom won,
And of riches and crown was he worthy, and we were but children
    still —
When he came to the years of manhood, when love joyeth to work
    her will
On the heart, and his lips were fringèd with the down of early youth,
Frau Minne laid stress upon him who for torment hath little ruth.
But if love the Grail King seeketh other than he find writ,
'Tis a sin, and in sorrow and sighing full sore shall he pay for it!

"And my lord and brother chose him a lady for service fair,
Noble and true he deemed her, I say not what name she bare;
Well he fought in that lady's honour, and cowardice from him fled,
And his hand many a shield-rim shattered, by love's fire was he
    venture led.
So high stood his fame that no hero in knightly lands afar
Could he brook to be thought his equal, so mighty his deeds of war,
And his battle-cry was 'Amor,' yet it seemeth unto me
Not all too well such cry suiteth with a life of humility.

"One day as the king rode lonely, in search of some venture high
(Sore trouble it brought upon us,) with love's payment for victory,
For love's burden lay heavy on him, in a joust was he wounded sore

With a poisoned spear, so that healing may be wrought on him
    nevermore.
For thine uncle, the King Anfortas, he was smitten thro' the thigh
By a heathen who with him battled, for he jousted right skilfully.
He came from the land of Ethnisé, where forth from fair Paradise
Flow the streams of the River Tigris, and he thought him that heathen
    wise
He should win the Grail and should hold it — On his spear had he
    graven his name,
From afar sought he deeds of knighthood, over sea and land he came.
The fame of the Grail drew him thither, and evil for us his strife,
His hand joy hath driven from us and clouded with grief our life!

"But thine uncle had battled bravely and men praised his name that
    day —
With the spear-shaft yet fast in his body he wended his homeward
    way.
And weeping arose and wailing as he came once again to his own,
And dead on the field lay his foeman, nor did we for his death make
    moan!

"When the king came, all pale and bloodless, and feeble of strength
    and limb,
Then a leech stretched his hand to the spear-wound, and the iron
    he found fast within,
With the hilt, wrought of reed, and hollow, and the twain from the
    wound he drew.
Then I fell on my knees, and I vowed me to God, with a heart so
    true,
That henceforward the pride of knighthood, and its fame, would
    I know no more,
If but God would behold my brother and would succour his need
    so sore.
Then flesh, wine, and bread I foreswore there, and all food that by
    blood might live,
That lust might no longer move me my life I to God would give,
And I tell thee, O son of my sister, that the wailing arose anew
When my weapons I put from off me and ungirded my sword so
    true,
And they spake, 'Who shall guard our mysteries? who shall watch
    o'er the wondrous Grail?'
And tears fell from the eyes of the maidens, but their weeping might
    naught avail!

"To the Grail, then, they bare Anfortas, if its virtue might bring
    relief;
But, alas! when his eyes beheld it, yet heavier waxed his grief
As the life sprang afresh within him, and he knew that he might
    not die;

And he liveth, while here I hide me in this life of humility,
And the power of the Grail, and its glory, with their monarch have
    waxen weak.
For the venom, his wound that poisoned, tho' the leeches their books
    did seek
Yet found they nor help nor healing — Yea, all that their skill might
    learn
'Gainst the poison of Aspis, Elkontius, of Liseis and Ecidemon,
All spells 'gainst the worm empoisoned, 'gainst Jecis or Meàtris;
Or all that a wise man knoweth of roots or of herbs; I wis
Naught was there in all might help him; nor rede I a longer tale
Since *God* willeth not his healing what man's skill may aught avail?

"Then we sent to the mystic waters, in a far-off land they rise,
Pison, Gihon, Tigris, Euphrates, the rivers of Paradise,
And so near they flow that the perfumes which breathe from its
    scented air
Shall yet to their streams be wafted — If their waters perchance
    might bear
Some plant from the wondrous garden that might succour us in
    our woe,
But vain thought, and fruitless labour, fresh sorrow our heart did
    know!

"Nor here did we end our labour, for again for the bough we sought
Which the Sibyl unto Aeneas as a shield 'gainst Hell's dangers
    brought.
'Gainst the smoke and the fire of Phlegethon, and the rivers that
    flow in Hell
Would it guard, and for long we sought it, for we thought, if such
    chance befell
That the spear in Hell-fire was welded, and the poison from Hell
    did spring
That thus of our joy had robbed us, then this bough might salvation
    bring!

"But Hell, it knew naught of the poison! There liveth a wondrous
    bird
Who loveth too well her fledglings — Of the Pelican's love we heard,
How she teareth her breast and feedeth her young with the quicken-
    ing food
Of her own life-blood, and then dieth — So we took of that bird
    the blood,
Since we thought that her love might help us, and we laid it upon
    the sore
As best we could — Yet, I wot well, no virtue for us it bore!

"A strange beast, the Unicorn, liveth, and it doth in such honour
    keep
The heart of a spotless maiden that it oft at her knee will sleep.

And the heart of that beast we took us, and we took us the red-fire
stone
That lies 'neath its horn, if the king's wound might its healing virtue
own.
And we laid on the wound the carbuncle, and we put it the wound
within,
Yet still was the sore empoisoned nor aid from the stone might win!

"And sore with the king we sorrowed — Then a magic herb we
found,
(Men say, from the blood of a dragon it springeth from out the
ground),
With the stars, and the wind, and the heaven, close-bound, doth it
win its power,
Lest perchance, by the flight of the dragon, when the stars bring
the circling hour,
And the moon draweth near to her changing (for sorer then grows
the pain),
The herb might our grief have aided — Yet its magic we sought in
vain!

"Then the knights of the Grail knelt lowly, and for help to the
Grail they prayed,
And, behold! the mystic writing, and a promise it brought of aid;
For a knight should come to the castle, and so soon as he asked the
king
Of the woe that so sorely pained him his question should healing
bring.
But let them beware, man or maiden, or child, should they warn the
knight
Of his task, he no healing bringeth, greater waxeth the sorrow's
might.
And the writing it ran, "Ye shall mark this, forewarning shall bring
but ill,
And in the first night of his coming must the healer his task fulfil,
Or the question shall lose its virtue; but if at the chosen hour
He shall speak, his shall be the kingdom, and the evil hath lost its
power.
So the hand of the Highest sendeth to Anfortas the end of woe,
Yet King shall be no longer tho' healing and bliss he know.

"Thus we read in the Grail that our sorrow should come to an end that
day
That the knight should come who the meaning of the grief that
he saw should pray —
Then salve of Nard we took us, and Teriak, and the wound we
dressed,
And we burnt wood of Lignum Aloe for so might the king find rest.
Yet ever he suffereth sorely — Then fled I unto this place,

And my life little gladness knoweth till my brother hath gotten
grace.
And the knight, he hath come, and hath left us, and ill for us all
that day
(But now did I speak of his coming), sorrow-laden he rode away,
For he saw his host's woe and asked not, 'What aileth thee here, mine
host?'
Since his folly such words forbade him great bliss shall he there have
lost!"

Then awhile did they mourn together till the mid-day hour drew
near,
And the host spake, "We must be seeking for food; and thine horse,
I fear,
As yet shall be lacking fodder; nor know I how we shall feed
If not God in His goodness show us the herbs that shall serve our
need.
My kitchen but seldom smoketh! Forgive thou the lack to-day,
And abide here, so long as shall please thee, if they journey shall
brook delay.
Of plants and of herbs would I teach thee much lore, if so be the
grass
Were not hidden by snow — God grant us that this cold may be soon
o'erpast —
Now break we yew-boughs for thy charger, far better its fare hath
been
Erewhile 'neath the roof of Monsalväsch than shall here be its lot
I ween!
Yet never a host shall ye meet with who rider alike and steed
Would as gladly bid share of his substance as I, had I all ye need!"

Then the twain they went forth on their errand — Parzival for his
steed had care,
While the hermit for roots was seeking since no better might be
their fare;
And the host his rule forgat not, he ate naught, whate'er he found,
Till the ninth hour, but ever hung them, as he drew them from out
the ground,
On the nearest shrub, and there left them; many days he but ill
might fare
For God's honour, since oft he lost them, the shrubs which his roots
did bear.

Nor grudged they aught of their labour: then they knelt by the
streamlet's flow,
And the roots and the herbs they washed there, and no laughter
their lips might know.
Then their hands they washed, and the yew-boughs Parzival together bound

And bare them unto his charger ere the cavern again he found;
Then the twain by the fireside sat them, nor further might food be
     brought,
Nor on roast nor on boiled they fed them, nor found in their kitchen
     aught.
Yet so true was the love and the honour Parzival to the hermit bare
That he deemed he enough had eaten, and no better had been his fare
With Gurnemanz of Graharz, or e'en in Monsalväsch hall,
When the maidens passed fair before him and the Grail fed them
     each and all.

Then his kindly host quoth, "Nephew, despise not this food, for
     know
Lightly thou shalt not find one who shall favour and kindness show,
Of true heart, without fear of evil, as fain would I show to thee."
And Parzival quoth, "May God's favour henceforward ne'er light
     on me
If food ever better pleased me, or I ate with a better will
What a host ever set before me, such fare doth content me still."

Their hands they need not wash them for such food as before them lay,
'Twas no fish, that their eyes had harmèd as men oft are wont to say.
And were I or hawk or falcon I had lent me to the chase,
Nor stooped to the lure unwilling, nor fled from my master's face,
But an they no better fed me than at noontide they fed, these twain,
I had spread my wings right swiftly, nor come to their call again!
Why mock at this folk so faithful?  'Twas ever my way of old —
Yet ye know why, forsaking riches, they chose to them want and cold,
And the lack of all things joyful, such sorrow and grief of heart
They bare of true heart, God-fearing, nor had they in falsehood part;
And thus from the hand of the Highest they won payment for
     grief and woe,
And alike should the twain God's favour, as of old, so hereafter
     know.

Then up stood they again, and they gat them, Parzival and the holy
     man,
To the steed in its rocky stable, and full sadly the host began
As he spake to the noble charger, "Woe is me for thy scanty fare,
For the sake of the saddle upon thee and the token I see thee bear!"

When their care for the horse was ended, then sorrow sprang forth
     anew,
Quoth Parzival, "Host and uncle, my folly I needs must rue,
And fain would I tell the story if for shame I the word may speak;
Forgive me, I pray, of thy kindness, since in thee do I comfort seek,
For sorely, I ween, have I sinnèd; if thou canst no comfort find
No peace may be mine, but for ever the chains of remorse shall bind.

Of true heart shalt thou mourn my folly — He who to Monsalväsch
  rode,
He who saw Anfortas' sorrow, he who spake not the healing word,
'Twas I, child and heir of misfortune, 'twas I, Parzival, alone,
Ill have I wrought and I know not how I may for such ill atone!"

Spake the hermit, "Alas! my nephew, thou speakest the words of
  woe,
Vanished our joy, and sorrow henceforth must we grasp and know,
Since folly of bliss betrayed thee: senses five did God give to thee,
And methinks, in the hour of thy testing, their counsel should better
  be.
Why guarded they not thine honour, and thy love as a man to men,
In the hour that thou satst by Anfortas?  Of a truth hadst thou
  spoken then!

"Nor would I deny thee counsel; mourn not for thy fault too sore,
Thou shalt, in a fitting measure, bewail thee, and grief give o'er.
For strange are the ways, and fitful, of mankind, oft is youth too wise
And old age turneth back to folly, and darkened are wisdom's eyes,
And the fruit of a life lieth forfeit, while green youth doth wax old
  and fade —
Not in this wise true worth shall be rooted, and payment in praise be
  paid.
Thine youth would I see fresh blooming, and thine heart waxing
  strong and bold,
While thou winnest anew thine honour, nor dost homage from God
  withhold.
For thus might it chance unto thee to win for thyself such fame
As shall make amends for thy sorrow, and God thee, as His knight,
  shall claim!"

Then twice seven days he abode there, with the hermit his lot did
  share,
And the herb of the ground was his portion — yet he sought not for
  better fare,
Right gladly he bare such hardness that should bring to him food
  so sweet,
For as priest did his host absolve him, and as knight gave him counsel
  meet!

Quoth Parzival to the hermit, "Say who shall he be, who lay
Before the Grail? grey was he, yet his face it was as the day!"
Spake the host, "Titurel thou sawest, and he shall grandsire be
To thy mother, first king and ruler of the Grail and its knights was
  he.
But a sickness hath fallen on him, and he lieth, nor findeth cure,
Yet his face on the Grail yet looketh, by its power shall his life endure!

Nor his countenance changeth colour, and his counsel shall aye be
    wise —
In his youth he rode far and jousted, and won to him valour's prize.

"An thou wouldst that thy life be adornèd with true worth as thy
    crown of fame,
Then ne'er mayst thou hate a woman, but shall honour, as knight,
    her name,
For women and priests, thou knowest, unarmèd shall be their hand,
Yet the blessing of God watcheth o'er them, and as shield round
    the priest doth stand;
For the priest, he careth for thee, that thine end may be free from ill,
So treat thou no priest as a foeman, but serve him with right good will.
For naught on the earth thou seest that is like to his office high,
For he speaketh that word unto us which our peace and our life
    did buy;
And his hand hath been blest for the holding of the pledge on the
    altar laid,
To assure us of sin's forgiveness, and the price for our pardon paid.
And a priest who from sin doth guard him, and who to his Lord
    shall give
Pure heart and pure hand for His service, say, what man shall holier
    live?"

Now this day was their day of parting — Trevrezent to our hero
    spake,
"Leave thou here thy sins behind thee, God shall me for thy surety
    take,
And do thou as I have shown thee, be steadfast and true of heart!"
Think ye with what grief and sorrow the twain did asunder part.

                               [tr. JESSIE L. WESTON]

# VI. TEUTONIC LITERATURE

Medieval Teutonic literature comprises all the stories and songs composed north of the Rhine and Danube rivers and outside the British Isles. It is usually classified in three groups:

1. Southern or Gothic literature. There is only one Gothic book remaining — the Arian missionary Ulfilas' translation of the Gospels. The Visigoths and Ostrogoths, who at one time lived above the Danubian barrier to the Empire, were among the first Teutonic tribes to migrate into Italy. The Visigoths eventually settled in Spain, the Ostrogoths in north-central Italy.

2. Central, or Germanic literature. Germans living east of the Rhine River were described by Julius Caesar and Tacitus in classical times. Two important groups that migrated across the Rhine when the Empire collapsed were the Franks, in the north, and the Burgundians farther south. Two other groups important in medieval literature were the Swabians, located along the headwaters of the Danube, and the Saxons, who lived along the shore of the North Sea, south of the Danish peninsula. Many Saxons migrated to Britain; the rest remained to battle the Carolingians and were eventually moved by Charlemagne to what is now Saxony (capital, Leipzig). The Germanic dialects eventually settled into High German, the language of Helvetia, Swabia, Bavaria, Austria, Thuringia, and the other southern provinces and Low German, the language of Saxony, Frisia, and the flat northern provinces that bordered the Baltic Sea.

3. Northern, or Scandinavian literature. The Northmen, ancestors of modern Finns, Swedes, Norwegians, Danes, and Icelanders, since they lived farthest from the heart of empire, were last to feel the impact of Mediterranean civilization, but in the eighth century they began their migrations, and during the ninth, tenth, and eleventh centuries they pushed out in all directions in their piratical raids that preceded permanent settlement. Normans, Danes, and Vikings invaded Britain, Ireland, and Greenland, France, Spain, and Sicily, and Russia to Moscow, Kiev, and the Black Sea.

The tongues of these various groups and tribes were dialects of a common language, and their mythology folklore and saga have much in common. Tacitus tells of their songs, which commemorated heroes of the past, exalted to the state of demigods. The surviving literature seems to have been very considerably inspired by the Teutonic migrations, when Teutons were conquering the vaunted imperial forces, though the stories are interwoven with mythology of an earlier age. Minstrels wandered from one end of the Teutonic world to the other, so that we need not wonder, for instance, that Attila the Hun should appear not only in the Bavarian *Nibelungenlied,* but in Scandinavian literature as well. Charlemagne devoted serious official attention to these native songs and stories and instituted a plan for preserving them in writing. Perhaps to this plan we owe the preservation of the fragmentary *Song of Hildebrand* (*Hildebrandslied*), the oldest extant Teutonic heroic poem. There is other Germanic literature from the Carolingian period, notably the *Heliand,* a religious poem of nearly six thousand lines written in Old Saxon, and the *Gospel Book* of Otfrid, which was written in Frankish dialect between 863 and 871. But literature was not regularly composed in the German vernacular until the close of the tenth century, when Notker Labeo (not to be confused with the hymnologist Notker Balbulus) and his pupils at St. Gall translated freely and wrote texts and commentaries.

Native Teutonic poetry, like the Old English poetry, above (pp. 148 ff.), which was, of course, also Teutonic, was composed in an alliterative rhythmic pattern, but even the earliest extant examples show the influence of ecclesiastical Latin. Otfrid, for instance, rhymes the half-lines of his verse, and the *Ludwigslied,* a short poem celebrating the victory of Louis III over the Normans in 881, is not only rhymed but somewhat more regularly accentual. The *Nibelungenlied,* which seems archaic for its period, the end of the twelfth century, though based on the early Teutonic alliterative stress, is regularly rhymed. But the almost contemporary *Tristan* and *Parzival* are written in adapted romance verse form, as might be expected from their subjects.

# SNORRI STURLUSON

In the seventh and eighth centuries, commercial intercourse between the various Teutonic groups was fairly well developed. The dominant Franks, especially under Carolingian leadership, carried stories of the Nibelungs and Volsungs along with their wares to Norway and beyond; coins of Charlemagne are still being found in Scandinavia. Then, in the ninth and tenth centuries, the Northmen began to expand. In 872, Harold Haarfgar became sole ruler of Norway and the conquered nobles left the country to begin their career of piracy. Two years later they settled Iceland and developed a culture based on free society at home and wide travel abroad. The nobles cultivated oral literature based on the legends imported from Norway. Early in the eleventh century the whole Norwegian world was Christianized, and poems once transmitted orally were committed to writing.

Snorri Sturluson, whose life coincided with the period of chivalric romance on the Continent, inherited a culture three centuries old. He was one of the several *godar,* or chieftains, of the island who lived a life of intrigue and double-dealing in a time of changing political faith. Yet he found time to cultivate the arts and become a skillful antiquarian. It is now generally acknowledged that he is author of the *Heimskringla,* an account of Norwegian culture from its founding by the gods to the year 1184.

He planned the *Edda* as a handbook for poets, including not only the lore and history on which they could build their poems, but also rules for composition with illustrations drawn particularly from a class of poetry that he called Eddic. It must be remembered, in reading his book, that it is the product of a fully developed Christian culture, that these chieftains, however perverted their administration of justice, were wealthy and urbane, educated largely in France and Norway, and as courtly as the Scotch chieftains of a later day. In fact, the *Edda* corresponds with the writings of Walter Scott in many ways: though its author as antiquarian tries to reproduce past lore faithfully, he cannot always keep elements of current thought from intruding.

The meaning of the word Edda, found only in Sturluson's collection, is a subject of debate. The most convincing surmise is that of Magnússon — that it is the name of the town Oddi, where Sturluson lived for many years, and that the collection was known as The Book of Oddi. A collection of extant poems similar to those quoted by Sturluson has frequently been published under the title of *The Poetic Edda* or *Edda Saemundar.*

## THE PROSE EDDA

Snorri Sturluson (1179–1241)

[From *The Prose Edda by Snorri Sturluson,* translated by
A. B. Brodeur; The American-Scandinavian Foundation,
New York, 1916.   Reprinted by permission of the pub-
lisher.]

GODS AND HEROES

THE ÆSIR AND THE CHILDREN OF LOKI

Then said Gangleri: "Who are the Æsir, they in whom it behooves
men to believe?" Hárr answered: "The divine Æsir are twelve."
Then said Jafnhárr: "Not less holy are the Ásynjur, the goddesses,
and they are of no less authority." Then said Thridi: "Odin is
highest and eldest of the Æsir: he rules all things, and mighty as
are the other gods, they all serve him as children obey a father. Frigg
is his wife, and she knows all the fates of men, though she speaks no
prophecy, — as is said here, when Odin himself spake with him of
the Æsir whom men call Loki:

> Thou art mad now, Loki,     and reft of mind,—
>    Why, Loki, leav'st thou not off?
> Frigg, methinks,     is wise in all fates,
>    Though herself say them not!

Odin is called Allfather because he is father of all the gods. He is
also called Father of the Slain, because all those that fall in battle
are the sons of his adoption; for them he appoints Valhall and Vin-
gólf, and they are then called Champions. He is also called God of
the Hanged, God of Gods, God of Cargoes; and he has also been
named in many more ways, after he had come to King Geirrödr:

> We were called Grímr     and Gangleri,
>    Herjann, Hjálmberi;
> Thekkr, Thridi,     Thudr, Udr,
>    Helblindi, Hárr.

> Sadr, Svipall,     Sann-getall,
>    Herteitr, Hnikarr;
> Bileygr, Báleygr,     Bölverkr, Fjölnir,
>    Grímnir, Glapsvidr, Fjölsvidr.

> Sídhöttr, Sidskeggr,     Sigfödr, Hnikudr,
>    Alfödr, Atrídr, Farmatýr;
> Óski, Ómi,     Jafnhárr, Biflindi,
>    Göndlir, Hárbardr.

Svidurr, Svidrir,    Jálkr, Kjalarr, Vidurr,
    Thrór, Yggr, Thundr;
Vakr, Skilfingr,    Váfudr, Hroptatýr,
    Gautr, Veratýr."

Then said Gangleri: "Exceeding many names have ye given him; and by my faith, it must indeed be a goodly wit that knows all the lore and the examples of what chances have brought about each of these names." Then Hárr made answer: "It is truly a vast sum of knowledge to gather together and set forth fittingly. But it is briefest to tell thee that most of his names have been given him by reason of this chance: there being so many branches of tongues in the world, all peoples believed that it was needful for them to turn his name into their own tongue, by which they might the better invoke him and entreat him on their own behalf. But some occasions for these names arose in his wanderings; and that matter is recorded in tales. Nor canst thou ever be called a wise man if thou shalt not be able to tell of those great events."

Then said Gangleri: "What are the names of the other Æsir, or what is their office, or what deeds of renown have they done?" Hárr answered: "Thor is the foremost of them, he that is called Thor of the Æsir, or Öku-Thor; he is strongest of all the gods and men. He has his realm in the place called Thrúdvangar, and his hall is called Bilskirnir; in that hall are five hundred rooms and forty. That is the greatest house that men know of; it is thus said in *Grímnismál*:

Five hundred floors    and more than forty,
    So reckon I Bilskirnir with bending ways;
Of those houses    that I know of hall-roofed,
    My son's I know the most.

Thor has two he-goats, that are called Tooth-Gnasher and Tooth-Gritter, and a chariot wherein he drives, and the he-goats draw the chariot; therefore is he called Öku-Thor. He has also three things of great price: one is the hammer Mjöllnir, which the Rime-Giants and the Hill-Giants know, when it is raised on high; and that is no wonder, — it has bruised many a skull among their fathers or their kinsmen. He has a second costly thing, best of all: the girdle of might; and when he clasps it about him, then the godlike strength within him is increased by half. Yet a third thing he has in which there is much virtue, his iron gloves; he cannot do without them when he uses his hammer-shaft. But no one is so wise that he can tell all his mighty works; yet I can tell thee so much tidings of him that the hours would be spent before all that I know were told."

Then said Gangleri: "I would ask tidings of more Æsir." Hárr replied: "The second son of Odin is Baldr, and good things are to be said of him. He is best, and all praise him; he is so fair of feature, and so bright, that light shines from him. A certain herb is so white that it is likened to Baldr's brow; of all grasses it is whitest, and by it thou mayest judge his fairness, both in hair and in body. He is the wisest of the Æsir, and the fairest-spoken and most gracious; and that quality attends him, that none may gainsay his judgments. He dwells in the place called Breidablik, which is in heaven; in that place may nothing unclean be, even as is said here:

> Breidablik 't is called,    where Baldr has
> A hall made for himself:
> In that land    where I know lie
> Fewest baneful runes.

"The third among the Æsir is he that is called Njördr: he dwells in heaven, in the abode called Nóatún. He rules the course of the wind, and stills sea and fire; on him shall men call for voyages and for hunting. He is so prosperous and abounding in wealth, that he may give them great plenty of lands or of gear; and him shall men invoke for such things. Njördr is not of the race of the Æsir. He was reared in the land of the Vanir, but the Vanir delivered him as hostage to the gods, and took for hostage in exchange him that men call Hoenir; he became an atonement between the gods and the Vanir. Njördr has to wife the woman called Skadi, daughter of Thjazi the giant. Skadi would fain dwell in the abode which her father had had, which is on certain mountains, in the place called Thrymheimr; but Njördr would be near the sea. They made a compact on these terms: they should be nine nights in Thrymheimr, but the second nine at Nóatún. But when Njördr came down from the mountain back to Nóatún, he sang this lay:

> Loath were the hills to me,    I was not long in them,
> Nights only nine;
> To me the wailing of    wolves seemed ill,
> After the song of swans.

Then Skadi sang this:

> Sleep could I never    on the sea-beds,
> For the wailing of waterfowl;
> He wakens me,    who comes from the deep —
> The sea-mew every morn.

Then Skadi went up onto the mountain, and dwelt in Thrymheimr. And she goes for the more part on snowshoes and with a bow and arrow, and shoots beasts; she is called Snowshoe-Goddess or Lady of the Snowshoes. So it is said:

> Thrymheimr 't is called,    where Thjazi dwelt,
> He the hideous giant;
> But now Skadi abides,    pure bride of the gods,
> In her father's ancient freehold.

"Njördr in Nóatún begot afterward two children.  The son was called Freyr, and the daughter Freyja; they were fair of face and mighty.  Freyr is the most renowned of the Æsir; he rules over the rain and the shining of the sun, and therewithal the fruit of the earth; and it is good to call on him for fruitful seasons and peace. He governs the prosperity of men.  But Freyja is the most renowned of the goddesses; she has in heaven the dwelling called Fólkvangr, and wheresoever she rides to the strife, she has one-half of the kill, and Odin half, as is here said:

> Fólkvangr 't is called,　　where Freyja rules
> 　　　Degrees of seats in the hall;
> Half the kill　　she keepeth each day,
> 　　　And half Odin hath.

Her hall Sessrúmnir is great and fair.  When she goes forth, she drives her cats and sits in a chariot; she is most conformable to man's prayers, and from her name comes the name of honor, Frú, by which noblewomen are called.  Songs of love are well-pleasing to her; it is good to call on her for furtherance in love."

Then said Gangleri: "Great in power do these Æsir seem to me; nor is it a marvel that much authority attends you, who are said to possess understanding of the gods and know which one men should call on for what boon soever.  Or are the gods yet more?"  Hárr said: "Yet remains that one of the Æsir who is called Týr.  He is most daring and best in stoutness of heart, and he has much authority over victory in battle; it is good for men of valor to invoke him. It is a proverb that he is Týr-valiant who surpasses other men and does not waver.  He is wise, so that it is also said that he that is wisest is Týr-prudent.  This is one token of his daring: when the Æsir enticed Fenris-Wolf to take upon him the fetter Gleipnir, the wolf did not believe them, that they would loose him, until they laid Týr's hand into his mouth as a pledge.  But when the Æsir would not loose him, then he bit off the hand at the place now called 'the wolf's joint'; and Týr is one-handed and is not called a reconciler of men.

"One is called Bragi.  He is renowned for wisdom, and most of all for fluency of speech and skill with words.  He knows most of skaldship, and after him skaldship is called *bragr*, and from his name that one is called *bragr*-man or -woman, who possesses eloquence surpassing others, of women or men.  His wife is Idunn. She guards in her chest of ash those apples which the gods must taste whensoever they grow old; and then they all become young, and so it shall be even unto the Weird of the Gods."  Then said Gangleri: "A very great thing, methinks, the gods entrust to the watchfulness and good faith of Idunn."  Then said Hárr, laughing loudly: " 'Twas near being desperate once; I may be able to tell thee of it, but now thou shalt first hear more of the names of the Æsir.

"Heimdallr is the name of one: he is called the White God. He is great and holy; nine maids, all sisters, bore him for a son. He is also called Hallinskidi and Gullintanni; his teeth were of gold, and his horse is called Gold-top. He dwells in the place called Himinbjörg, hard by Bifröst: he is the warder of the gods, and sits there by Heaven's end to guard the bridge from the Hill-Giants. He needs less sleep than a bird; he sees equally well night and day a hundred leagues from him, and hears how grass grows on the earth or wool on sheep, and everything that has a louder sound. He has that trumpet which is called Gjallar-Horn, and its blast is heard throughout all worlds. Heimdallr's sword is called Head. It is said further:

> Himinbjörg 't is called,     where Heimdallr, they say,
>      Aye has his housing;
> There the gods' sentinel     drinks in his snug hall
>      Gladly good mead.

And furthermore, he himself says in *Heimdalar-galdr*:

> I am of nine     mothers the offspring,
> Of sisters nine     am I the son.

"One of the Æsir is named Hödr. He is blind. He is of sufficient strength, but the gods would desire that no occasion should rise of naming this god, for the work of his hands shall long be held in memory among the gods and men.

"Vídarr is the name of one, the silent god. He has a thick shoe. He is nearly as strong as Thor; in him the gods have great trust in all struggles.

"One is called Áli or Váli, son of Odin and Rindr. He is daring in fights, and a most fortunate marksman.

"Forseti is the name of the son of Baldr and Nanna daughter of Nep. He has that hall in heaven which is called Glitnir. All that come to him with such quarrels as arise out of law-suits, all these return thence reconciled. That is the best seat of judgment among gods and men; thus it is said here:

> A hall is called Glitnir,     with gold 'tis pillared,
>      And with silver thatched the same;
> There Forseti bides     the full day through,
>      And puts to sleep all suits.

"Also numbered among the Æsir is he whom some call the mischief-monger of the Æsir, and the first father of falsehoods, and blemish of all gods and men. He is named Loki or Loptr, son of Fárbauti the giant; his mother was Laufey or Nál; his brothers are

Býleistr and Helblindi. Loki is beautiful and comely to look upon, evil in spirit, very fickle in habit. He surpassed other men in that wisdom which is called 'sleight,' and had artifices for all occasions. He would ever bring the Æsir into great hardships, and then get them out with crafty counsel. His wife was called Sigyn, their son Nari or Narfi.

"Yet more children had Loki. Angrboda was the name of a certain giantess in Jötunheim, with whom Loki gat three children: one was Fenris-Wolf, the second Jörmungandr — that is the Midgard Serpent — the third is Hel. But when the gods learned that this kindred was nourished in Jötunheim, and when the gods perceived by prophecy that from this kindred great misfortune should befall them, and since it seemed to all that there was great prospect of ill (first from the mother's blood, and yet worse from the father's), then Allfather sent gods thither to take the children and bring them to him. When they came to him, straightway he cast the serpent into the deep sea, where he lies about all the land; and this serpent grew so greatly that he lies in the midst of the ocean encompassing all the land, and bites upon his own tail. Hel he cast into Niflheim, and gave to her power over nine worlds, to apportion all abodes among those that were sent to her: that is, men dead of sickness or of old age. She has great possessions there; her walls are exceeding high and her gates great. Her hall is called Sleet-Cold; her dish, Hunger; Famine is her knife; Idler, her thrall; Sloven, her maidservant; Pit of Stumbling, her threshhold, by which one enters; Disease, her bed; Gleaming Bale, her bed-hangings. She is half blue-black and half flesh-color (by which she is easily recognized), and very lowering and fierce.

The Wolf the Æsir brought up at home, and Týr alone dared go to him to give him meat. But when the gods saw how much he grew every day, and when all prophecies declared that he was fated to be their destruction, then the Æsir seized upon this way of escape: They made a very strong fetter, which they called Laedingr, and brought it before the Wolf, bidding him try his strength against the fetter. The Wolf thought that no overwhelming odds, and let them do with him as they would. The first time the Wolf lashed out against it, the fetter broke; so he was loosed out of Laedingr. After this, the Æsir made a second fetter, stronger by half, which they called Drómi, and bade the Wolf try that fetter, saying he would become very famous for strength, if such huge workmanship should not suffice to hold him. But the Wolf thought that this fetter was very strong; he considered also that strength had increased in him since the time he broke Laedingr; it came into his mind that he must expose himself to danger, if he would become famous. So he let the fetter be laid upon him. Now when the Æsir declared themselves ready, the Wolf shook himself, dashed the fetter against the earth and struggled fiercely with it, spurned against it, and broke the fetter, so that the fragments flew far. So he dashed himself out of Drómi.  Since then it passes as a proverb, 'to loose out of Laedingr,' or 'to dash out of Drómi,' when anything is exceeding hard.

"After that the Æsir feared that they should never be able to get the Wolf bound.  Then Allfather sent him who is called Skírnir, Freyr's messenger, down into the region of the Black Elves, to certain dwarves, and caused to be made the fetter named Gleipnir. It was made of six things: the noise a cat makes in foot-fall, the beard of a woman, the roots of a rock, the sinews of a bear, the breath of a fish, and the spittle of a bird.  And though thou understand not these matters already, yet now thou mayest speedily find certain proof herein that no lie is told thee: thou must have seen that a woman has no beard, and no sound comes from the leap of a cat, and there are no roots under a rock; and by my troth, all that I have told thee is equally true, though there be some things which thou canst not put to the test."

Then said Gangleri: "This certainly I can perceive to be true. These things which thou hast taken for proof, I can see; but how was the fetter fashioned?"  Hárr answered: "That I am well able to tell thee.  The fetter was soft and smooth as a silken ribbon, but as sure and strong as thou shalt now hear.  Then, when the fetter was brought to the Æsir, they thanked the messenger well for his errand. Then the Æsir went out upon the lake called Ámsvartnir, to the island called Lyngvi, and summoning the Wolf with them, they showed him the silken ribbon and bade him burst it, saying that it was somewhat stouter than appeared from its thickness.  And each passed it to the others, and tested it with the strength of their hands and it did not snap; yet they said the Wolf could break it.  Then the Wolf answered: 'Touching this matter of the ribbon, it seems to me that I shall get no glory of it, though I snap asunder so slender a band; but if it be made with cunning and wiles, then, though it seem little, that band shall never come upon my feet.'  Then the Æsir answered that he could easily snap apart a slight silken band, he who had before broken great fetters of iron, — 'but if thou shalt not be able to burst this band, then thou wilt not be able to frighten the gods; and then we shall unloose thee.'  The Wolf said: 'If ye bind me so that I shall not get free again, then ye will act in such a way that it will be late ere I receive help from you; I am unwilling that this band should be laid upon me.  Yet rather than that ye should impugn my courage, let some one of you lay his hand in my mouth, for a pledge that this is done in good faith.'  Each of the Æsir looked at his neighbor, and none was willing to part with his hand, until Týr stretched out his right hand and laid it in the Wolf's mouth.  But when the Wolf lashed out, the fetter became hardened; and the more he struggled against it, the tighter the band was.  Then all laughed except Týr: he lost his hand.

### THOR AND ÚTGARDA-LOKI

"Thereupon Thor left his goats behind, and began his journey eastward toward Jötunheim and clear to the sea; and then he went out over the sea, that deep one; but when he came to land, he went up, and Loki and Thjálfi and Röskva with him. Then, when they had walked a little while, there stood before them a great forest. They walked all that day till dark. Thjálfi was swiftest-footed of all men; he bore Thor's bag, but there was nothing good for food. As soon as it had become dark, they sought themselves shelter for the night, and found before them a certain hall, very great: there was a door in the end, of equal width with the hall, wherein they took up quarters for the night. But about midnight there came a great earthquake. The earth rocked under them exceedingly, and the house trembled. Then Thor rose up and called to his companions, and they explored farther, and found in the middle of the hall a side-chamber on the right hand, and they went in thither. Thor sat down in the doorway, but the others were farther in from him, and they were afraid; but Thor gripped his hammer-shaft and thought to defend himself. Then they heard a great humming sound, and a crashing.

"But when it drew near dawn, then Thor went out and saw a man lying a little way from him in the wood; and that man was not small. He slept and snored mightily. Then Thor thought he could perceive what kind of noise it was which they had heard during the night. He girded himself with his belt of strength, and his divine power waxed; and on the instant the man awoke and rose up swiftly. And then, it is said, the first time Thor's heart failed him, to strike him with the hammer. He asked him his name, and the man called himself Skrýmir, — 'but I have no need,' he said, 'to ask thee for thy name; I know that thou art Ása-Thor. But what? Hast thou dragged away my glove?' Then Skrýmir stretched out his hand and took up the glove; and at once Thor saw that it was that which he had taken for a hall during the night; and as for the side-chamber, it was the thumb of the glove. Skrýmir asked whether Thor would have his company, and Thor assented to this. Then Skrýmir took and unloosened his provision-wallet and made ready to eat his morning meal, and Thor and his fellows in another place. Skrýmir then proposed to them to lay their supply of food together, and Thor assented. Then Skrýmir bound all the food in one bag and laid it on his own back. He went before during the day, and stepped with very great strides; but late in the evening Skrýmir found them night-quarters under a certain great oak. Then Skrýmir said to Thor that he would lay him down to sleep, — 'and do ye take the provision-bag and make ready for your supper.'

"Thereupon Skrýmir slept and snored hard, and Thor took the provision-bag and set about to unloose it. Such things must be told as will seem incredible: he got no knot unloosened and no thong-end stirred, so as to be looser than before. When he saw that this work might not avail, then he became angered, gripped the hammer Mjöllnir in both hands, and strode with great strides to that place where Skrýmir lay, and smote him in the head. Skrýmir awoke, and asked whether a leaf had fallen upon his head; or whether they had eaten and were ready for bed? Thor replied that they were just then about to go to sleep; then they went under another oak. It must be told thee that there was then no fearless sleeping. At midnight Thor heard how Skrýmir snored and slept fast, so that it thundered in the woods. Then he stood up and went to him, shook his hammer eagerly and hard, and smote down upon the middle of his crown: he saw that the face of the hammer sank deep into his head. And at that moment Skrýmir awoke and said: 'What is it now? Did some acorn fall on my head? Or what is the news with thee, Thor?' But Thor went back speedily, and replied that he was then but new-wakened; said that it was then midnight, and there was yet time to sleep.

"Thor meditated that if he could get to strike him a third blow, never should the giant see himself again; he lay now and watched whether Skrýmir were sleeping soundly yet. A little before day, when he perceived that Skrýmir must have fallen asleep, he stood up at once and rushed over to him, brandished his hammer with all his strength, and smote upon that one of his temples which was turned up. But Skrýmir sat up and stroked his cheek, and said, 'Some birds must be sitting in the tree above me; I imagined, when I awoke, that some dirt from the twigs fell upon my head. Art thou awake, Thor? It will be time to arise and clothe us; but now ye have no long journey forward to the castle called Útgardr. I have heard how ye have whispered among yourselves that I am no little man in stature; but ye shall see taller men, if ye come into Útgardr. Now I will give you wholesome advice: do not conduct yourselves boastfully, for the henchmen of Útgarda-Loki will not well endure big words from such swaddling-babes. But if not so, then turn back, and I think it were better for you to do that; but if ye will go forward, then turn to the east. As for me, I hold my way north to these hills, which ye may now see.' Skrýmir took the provision-bag and cast it on his back, and turned from them across the forest; and it is not recorded that the Æsir bade him god-speed.

"Thor turned forward on his way, and his fellows, and went onward till mid-day. Then they saw a castle standing in a certain plain, and set their necks down on their backs before they could see up over it. They went to the castle; and there was a grating in front of castle-gate, and it was closed. Thor went up to the grating, and did not succeed in opening it; but when they struggled to make their way in, they crept between the bars and came in that way. They saw a great hall and went thither. The door was open. Then they went in, and saw there many men on two benches, and most of them were big enough. Thereupon they came before the King Útgarda-Loki and saluted him; but he looked at them in his own good time, and smiled scornfully over his teeth, and said: 'It is late to ask tidings of a long journey; or is it otherwise than I think: that this toddler is Óku-Thor? Yet thou mayest be greater than thou appearest to me. What manner of accomplishments are those, which thou and thy fellows think to be ready for? No one shall be here with us who knows not some kind of craft or cunning surpassing most men.'

"Then spoke the one who came last, who was called Loki: 'I know such a trick, which I am ready to try: that there is no one within here who shall eat his food more quickly than I.' Then Útgarda-Loki answered: 'That is a feat, if thou accomplish it; and this feat shall accordingly be put to the proof.' He called to the farther end of the bench, that he who was called Logi should come forth on the floor and try his prowess against Loki. Then a trough was taken and borne in upon the hall-floor and filled with flesh; Loki sat down at one end and Logi at the other, and each ate as fast as he could, and they met in the middle of the trough. By that time Loki had eaten all the meat from the bones, but Logi likewise had eaten all the meat, and the bones with it, and the trough too; and now it seemed to all as if Loki had lost the game.

"Then Útgarda-Loki asked what yonder young man could play at; and Thjálfi answered that he would undertake to run a race with whomsoever Útgarda-Loki would bring up. Then Útgarda-Loki said that that was a good accomplishment, and that there was great likelihood that he must be well endowed with fleetness if he were to perform that feat; yet he would speedily see to it that the matter should be tested. Then Útgarda-Loki arose and went out; and there was a good course to run on over a level plain. Then Útgarda-Loki called to him a certain lad, who was named Hugi, and bade him run a match against Thjálfi. Then they held the first heat; and Hugi was so much ahead that he turned back to meet Thjálfi at the end of the course. Then said Útgarda-Loki: 'Thou wilt need to lay thyself forward more, Thjálfi, if thou art to win the game; but it is none the less true that never have any men come hither who seemed to me fleeter of foot than this.' Then they began another heat; and when Hugi had reached the course's end, and was turning back, there was still a long bolt-shot to Thjálfi. Then spake Útgarda-Loki: 'Thjálfi appears to me to run this course well, but I do not believe of him now that he will win the game. But it will be made manifest presently, when they run the third heat.' Then they began the heat; but when Hugi had come to the end of the course and turned back, Thjálfi had not yet reached mid-course. Then all said that that game had been proven.

"Next, Útgarda-Loki asked Thor what feats there were which he might desire to show before them: such great tales as men have made of his mighty works. Then Thor answered that he would most willingly undertake to contend with any in drinking. Útgarda-Loki said that might well be; he went into the hall and called his serving-boy, and bade him bring the sconce-horn which the henchmen were wont to drink off. Straightway the serving-lad came forward with the horn and put it into Thor's hand. Then said Útgarda-Loki: 'It is held that this horn is well drained if it is drunk off in one drink, but some drink it off in two; but no one is so poor a man at drinking that it fails to drain off in three.' Thor looked upon the horn, and it did not seem big to him; and yet it was somewhat long. Still he was very thirsty. He took and drank, and swallowed enormously, and thought that he should not need to bend oftener to the horn. But when his breath failed, and he raised his head from the horn and looked to see how it had gone with the drinking, it seemed to him that there was very little space by which the drink was lower now in the horn than before. Then said Útgarda-Loki: 'It is well drunk, and not too much; I should not have believed, if it had been told me, that Ása-Thor could not drink a greater draught. But I know that thou wilt wish to drink it off in another draught.' Thor answered nothing. He set the horn to his mouth, thinking now that he should drink a greater drink, and struggled with the draught until his breath gave out; and yet he saw that the tip of the horn would not come up so much as he liked. When he took the horn from his mouth and looked into it, it seemed to him then as if it had decreased less than the former time; but now there was a clearly apparent lowering in the horn. Then said Útgarda-Loki: 'How now, Thor? Thou wilt not shrink from one more drink than may be well for thee? If thou now drink the third draught from the horn, it seems to me as if this must be esteemed the greatest; but thou canst not be called so great a man here among us as the Æsir call thee, if thou give not a better account of thyself in the other games than it seems to me may come of this.' Then Thor became angry, set the horn to his mouth, and drank with all his might, and struggled with the drink as much as he could; and when he looked into the horn, at least some space had been made. Then he gave up the horn and would drink no more.

"Then said Útgarda-Loki: 'Now it is evident that thy prowess is not so great as we thought it to be; but wilt thou try thy hand at more games? It may readily be seen that thou gettest no advantage hereof.' Thor answered: 'I will make trial of yet other games; but it would have seemed wonderful to me, when I was at home with the Æsir, if such drinks had been called so little. But what game will ye now offer me?' Then said Útgarda-Loki: 'Young lads here are wont to do this (which is thought of small consequence): lift my cat up from the earth; but I should not have been able to speak of such a thing to Ása-Thor if I had not seen that thou hast far less in thee than I had thought.' Thereupon there leaped forth on the hall-floor a gray cat, and a very big one; and Thor went to it and took it with his hand down under the middle of the belly and lifted up. But the cat bent into an arch just as Thor stretched up his hands; and when Thor reached up as high a he could at the very utmost, then the cat lifted up one foot, and Thor got this game no further advanced. Then said Útgarda-Loki: 'This game went even as I had forseen; the cat is very great, whereas Thor is low and little beside the huge men who are here with us."

"Then said Thor: 'Little as ye call me, let any one come up now and wrestle with me; now I am angry.' Then Útgarda-Loki answered, looking about him on the benches, and spake: 'I see no such man here within, who would not hold it a disgrace to wrestle with thee;' and yet he said: 'Let us see first; let the old woman my nurse be called hither, Elli, and let Thor wrestle with her if he will. She has thrown such men as have seemed to me no less strong than Thor.' Straightway there came into the hall an old woman, stricken in years. Then Útgarda-Loki said that she should grapple with Ása-Thor. There is no need to make a long matter of it: that struggle went in such wise that the harder Thor strove in gripping, the faster she stood; then the old woman essayed a hold, and then Thor became totty on his feet, and their tuggings were very hard. Yet it was not long before Thor fell to his knee, on one foot. Then Útgarda-Loki went up and bade them cease the wrestling, saying that Thor should not need to challenge more men of his body-guard to wrestling. By then it had passed toward night; Útgarda-Loki showed Thor and his companions to a seat, and they tarried there the night long in good cheer.

"But at morning, as soon as it dawned, Thor and his companions arose, clothed themselves, and were ready to go away. Then came there Útgarda-Loki and caused a table to be set for them; there was no lack of good cheer, meat and drink. So soon as they had eaten, he went out from the castle with them; and at parting Útgarda-Loki spoke to Thor and asked how he thought his journey had ended, or whether he had met any man mightier than himself. Thor answered that he could not say that he had not got much shame in their dealings together. 'But yet I know that ye will call me a man of little might, and I am ill-content with that.' Then said Útgarda-Loki: 'Now I will tell thee the truth, now that thou art come out of the castle; and if I live and am able to prevail, then thou shalt never again come into it. And this I know, by my troth! that thou shouldst never have come into it, if I had known before that thou haddest so much strength in thee, and that thou shouldst so nearly have had us in great peril. But I made ready against thee eye-illusions; and I came upon you the first time in the wood, and when thou wouldst have unloosed the provision-bag, I had bound it with iron, and thou didst not find where to undo it. But next thou didst smite me three blows with the hammer; and the first was least, and was yet so great that it would have sufficed to slay me, if it had come upon me. Where thou sawest near my hall a saddle-backed mountain, cut at the top into three square dales, and one the deepest, those were the marks of thy hammer. I brought the saddle-back before the blow, but thou didst not see that. So it was also with the games, in which ye did contend against my henchmen: that was the first, which Loki did; he was very hungry and ate zealously, but he who was called Logi was "wild-fire," and he burned the trough no less swiftly than the meat. But when Thjálfi ran the race with him called Hugi, that was my "thought," and it was not to be expected of Thjálfi that he should match swiftness with it.

" 'Moreover, when thou didst drink from the horn, and it seemed to thee to go slowly, then, by my faith, that was a wonder which I should not have believed possible: the other end of the horn was out in the sea, but thou didst not perceive it. But now, when thou comest to the sea, thou shalt be able to mark what a diminishing thou hast drunk in the sea: this is henceforth called "ebb-tides."'

"And again he said: 'It seemed to me not less noteworthy when thou didst lift up the cat; and to tell thee truly, then all were afraid who saw how thou didst lift one foot clear of the earth. That cat was not as it appeared to thee: it was the Midgard Serpent, which lies about all the land, and scarcely does its length suffice to encompass the earth with head and tail. So high didst thou stretch up thine arms that it was then but a little way more to heaven. It was also a great marvel concerning the wrestling-match, when thou didst withstand so long, and didst not fall more than on one knee, wrestling with Elli; since none such has ever been and none shall be, if he become so old as to abide "Old Age," that she shall not cause him to fall. And now it is truth to tell that we must part; and it will be better on both sides that ye never come again to seek me. Another time I will defend my castle with similar wiles or with others, so that ye shall get no power over me.'

"When Thor had heard these sayings, he clutched his hammer and brandished it aloft; but when he was about to launch it forward, then he saw Útgarda-Loki nowhere. Then he turned back to the castle, purposing to crush it to pieces; and he saw there a wide and fair plain, but no castle. So he turned back and went his way, till he was come back again to Thrúdvangar. But it is a true tale that then he resolved to seek if he might bring about a meeting between himself and the Midgard Serpent, which afterward came to pass. Now I think no one knows how to tell thee more truly concerning this journey of Thor's."

### THE DEATH OF BALDR

Then spake Gangleri: "Have any more matters of note befallen among the Æsir? A very great deed of valor did Thor achieve on that journey." Hárr made answer: "Now shall be told of those tidings which seemed of more consequence to the Æsir. The beginning of the story is this, that Baldr the Good dreamed great and perilous dreams touching his life. When he told these dreams to the Æsir, then they took counsel together; and this was their decision, to ask safety for Baldr from all kinds of dangers. And Frigg took oaths to this purport, that fire and water should spare Baldr, likewise iron and metal of all kinds, stones, earth, trees, sicknesses, beasts, birds, venom, serpents. And when that was done and made known, then it was a diversion of Baldr's and the Æsir, that he should stand up in the Thing, and all the others should some shoot at him, some hew at him, some beat him with stones. But whatsoever was done hurt him not at all, and that seemed to them all a very worshipful thing.

"But when Loki Laufeyarson saw this, it pleased him ill that Baldr took no hurt. He went to Fensalir to Frigg, and made himself into the likeness of a woman. Then Frigg asked if that woman knew what the Æsir did at the Thing. She said that all were shooting at Baldr, and moreover, that he took no hurt. Then said Frigg: 'Neither weapons nor trees may hurt Baldr: I have taken oaths of them all.' Then the woman asked: 'Have all things taken oaths to spare Baldr?' And Frigg answered: 'There grows a tree-sprout alone westward of Valhall; it is called the Mistletoe. I thought it too young to ask the oath of.' Then straightway the woman turned away; but Loki took Mistletoe and pulled it up and went to the Thing.

"Hödr stood outside the ring of men, because he was blind. Then spake Loki to him: 'Why dost thou not shoot at Baldr?' He answered: 'Because I see not where Baldr is; and for this also, that I am weaponless.' Then said Loki: 'Do thou also after the manner of other men, and show Baldr honor as the other men do. I will direct thee where he stands; shoot at him with this wand.' Hödr took Mistletoe and shot at Baldr, being guided by Loki. The shaft flew through Baldr, and he fell dead to the earth; and that was the greatest mischance that has ever befallen among gods and men.

"Then, when Baldr was fallen, words failed all the Æsir, and their hands likewise to lay hold of him; each looked at the other, and all were of one mind as to him who had wrought the work, but none might take vengeance, so great a sanctuary was in that place. But when the Æsir tried to speak, then it befell first that weeping broke out, so that none might speak to the others with words concerning his grief. But Odin bore that misfortune by so much the worst, as he had most perception of how great harm and loss for the Æsir were in the death of Baldr.

"Now when the gods had come to themselves, Frigg spake, and asked who there might be among the Æsir who would fain have for his own all her love and favor: let him ride the road to Hel, and seek if he may find Baldr, and offer Hel a ransom if she will let Baldr come home to Ásgard. And he is named Hermódr the Bold, Odin's son, who undertook that embassy. Then Sleipnir was taken, Odin's steed, and led forward; and Hermódr mounted on that horse and galloped off.

"The Æsir took the body of Baldr and brought it to the sea. Hringhorni is the name of Baldr's ship. It was greatest of all ships. The gods would have launched it and made Baldr's pyre thereon, but the ship stirred not forward. Then word was sent to Jötunheim after that giantess who is called Hyrrokkin. When she had come, riding a wolf and having a viper for bridle, then she leaped off the steed. And Odin called to four berserks to tend the steed; but they were not able to hold it until they had felled it. Then Hyrrokkin went to the prow of the boat and thrust it out at the first push, so that fire burst from the rollers, and all lands trembled. Thor became angry and clutched his hammer, and would straightway have broken her head, had not the gods prayed for peace for her.

"Then was the body of Baldr borne out on shipboard; and when his wife Nanna, the daughter of Nep, saw that, straightway her heart burst with grief, and she died; she was borne to the pyre, and fire was kindled. Then Thor stood by and hallowed the pyre with Mjöllnir.

"Now this is to be told concerning Hermódr, that he rode nine nights through dark dales and deep, so that he saw not before he was come to the river Gjöll and rode unto the Gjöll-Bridge; which bridge is thatched with glittering gold. Módgudr is the maiden called who guards the bridge; she asked him his name and race, saying that the day before there had ridden over the bridge five companies of dead men; 'but the bridge thunders no less under thee alone, and thou hast not the color of dead men. Why ridest thou hither on Hel-way?' He answered: 'I am appointed to ride to Hel to seek out Baldr. Hast thou perchance seen Baldr on Hel-way?' She said that Baldr had ridden there over Gjöll's Bridge, — 'but down and north lieth Hel-way.'

"Then Hermódr rode on till he came to Hel-gate; he dismounted from his steed and made his girths fast, mounted and pricked him with his spurs; and the steed leaped so hard over the gate that he came nowise near to it. Then Hermódr rode home to the hall and dismounted from his steed, went into the hall, and saw sitting there in the high-seat Baldr, his brother; and Hermódr tarried there overnight. At morn Hermódr prayed Hel that Baldr might ride home with him, and told her how great weeping was among the Æsir. But Hel said that in this wise it should be put to the test, whether Baldr were so all-beloved as had been said: 'If all things in the world, quick and dead, weep for him, then he shall go back to the Æsir; but he shall remain with Hel if any gainsay it or will not weep.' Then Hermódr arose; but Baldr led him out of the hall, and took the ring Draupnir and sent it to Odin for a remembrance. And Nanna sent Frigg a linen smock, and yet more gifts, and to Fulla a golden finger-ring.

"Then Hermódr rode his way back, and came into Ásgard, and told all those tidings which he had seen and heard. Thereupon the Æsir sent over all the world messengers to pray that Baldr be wept out of Hel; and all men did this, and quick things, and the earth, and stones, and trees, and all metals, — even as thou must have seen that these things weep when they come out of frost and into the heat. Then, when the messengers went home, having well wrought their errand, they found, in a certain cave, where a giantess sat: she called herself Thökk. They prayed her to weep Baldr out of Hel; she answered:

> Thökk will weep    waterless tears
>     For Baldr's bale-fare;
> Living or dead,    I loved not the churl's son;
>     Let Hel hold to that she hath!

And men deem that she who was there was Loki Laufeyarson, who hath wrought most ill among the Æsir."

### THE WEIRD OF THE GODS

Then said Gangleri: "What tidings are to be told concerning the Weird of the Gods? Never before have I heard aught of this." Hárr answered: "Great tidings are to be told of it, and much. The first is this, that there shall come that winter which is called the Awful Winter. In that time snow shall drive from all quarters; frosts shall be great then, and winds sharp; there shall be no virtue in the sun. Those winters shall proceed three in succession, and no summer between; but first shall come three other winters, such that over all the world there shall be mighty battles. In that time brothers shall slay each other for greed's sake, and none shall spare father or son in manslaughter and in incest; so it says in *Völuspá:*

> Brothers shall strive       and slaughter each other;
> Own sisters' children       shall sin together;
> Ill days among men,         many a whoredom:
> An axe-age, a sword-age,       shields shall be cloven
> A wind-age, a wolf-age,       ere the world totters.

Then shall happen what seems great tidings: the Wolf shall swallow the sun; and this shall seem to men a great harm. Then the other wolf shall seize the moon, and he also shall work great ruin; the stars shall vanish from the heavens. Then shall come to pass these tidings also: all the earth shall tremble so, and the crags, that trees shall be torn up from the earth, and the crags fall to ruin; and all fetters and bonds shall be broken and rent. Then shall Fenris-Wolf get loose; then the sea shall gush forth upon the land, because the Midgard Serpent stirs in giant wrath and advances up onto the land. Then that too shall happen, that Naglfar shall be loosened, the ship which is so named. (It is made of dead men's nails; wherefore a warning is desirable, that if a man die with unshorn nails, that man adds much material to the ship Naglfar, which gods and men were fain to have finished late.) Yet in this sea-flood Naglfar shall float. Hrymr is the name of the giant who steers Naglfar. Fenris-Wolf shall advance with gapping mouth, and his lower jaw shall be against the earth, but the upper against heaven, — he would gape yet more if there were room for it; fires blaze from his eyes and nostrils. The Midgard Serpent shall blow venom so that he shall sprinkle all the air and water; and he is very terrible, and shall be on one side of the Wolf. In this din shall the heaven be cloven, and the Sons of Múspell ride thence: Surtr shall ride first, and both before him and after him burning fire. His sword is exceeding good: from it radiance shines brighter than from the sun. When they ride over Bifröst, then the bridge shall break, as has been told before. The Sons of Múspell shall go forth to that field which is called Vígrídr; thither shall come Fenris-Wolf also and the Midgard Serpent; then Loki and Hrymr shall come there also, and with him all the Rime-Giants. All the champions of Hel follow Loki; and the Sons of Múspell shall have a company by themselves, and it shall be very bright. The field Vígrídr is a hundred leagues wide each way.

"When these tidings come to pass, then shall Heimdallr rise up and blow mightily in the Gjallar-Horn, and awaken all the gods; and they shall hold council together.  Then Odin shall ride to Mímir's Well and take counsel of Mímir for himself and his host.  Then the Ash of Yggdrasill shall tremble, and nothing then shall be without fear in heaven or in earth.  Then shall the Æsir put on their war-weeds, and all the Champions, and advance to the field: Odin rides first with the gold helmet and a fair birnie, and his spear, which is called Gungnir.  He shall go forth against Fenris-Wolf, and Thor stands forward on his other side, and can be of no avail to him, because he shall have his hands full to fight against the Midgard Serpent.  Freyr shall contend with Surtr, and a hard encounter shall there be between them before Freyr falls; it is to be his death that he lacks that good sword of his, which he gave to Skírnir.  Then shall the dog Garmr be loosed, which is bound before Gnípa's Cave. He is the greatest monster; he shall do battle with Týr, and each become the other's slayer.  Thor shall put to death the Midgard Serpent, and shall stride away nine paces from that spot; then shall he fall dead to the earth, because of the venom which the Snake has blown at him.  The Wolf shall swallow Odin; that shall be his ending.  But straight thereafter shall Vídarr stride forth and set one foot upon the lower jaw of the Wolf; on that foot he has the shoe, materials for which have been gathering throughout all time.  (They are the scraps of leather which men cut out of their shoes at toe or heel; therefore he who desires in his heart to come to the Æsir's help should cast those scraps away.)  With one hand he shall seize the Wolf's upper jaw and tear his gullet asunder; and that is the death of the Wolf.  Loki shall have battle with Heimdallr, and each be the slayer of the other.  Then straightwày shall Surtr cast fire over the earth and burn all the world; so is said in *Völuspá:*

> High blows Heimdallr,    the horn is aloft;
> Odin communes    with Mímir's head;
> Trembles Yggdrasill's    towering Ash;
> The old tree wails    when the Ettin is loosed.

> What of the Æsir?    What of the Elf-folk?
> All Jötunheim echoes,    the Æsir are at council;
> The dwarves are groaning    before their stone doors,
> Wise in rock-walls;    wit ye yet, or what?

> Hrymr sails from the east,    the sea floods onward;
> The monstrous Beast    twists in mighty wrath;
> The Snake beats the waves,    the Eagle is screaming;
> The gold-neb tears corpses,    Naglfar is loosed.

> From the east sails the keel;    come now Múspell's folk
> Over the sea-waves,    and Loki steereth;
> There are the warlocks    all with the Wolf, —
> With them is the brother    of Býleistr faring.

Surtr fares from southward    with switch-eating flame;
On his sword shimmers    the sun of the war-gods;
The rocks are falling,    and fiends are reeling,
Heroes tread Hel-way,    heaven is cloven.

Then to the Goddess    a second grief cometh,
When Odin fares    to fight with the Wolf,
And Beli's slayer,    the bright god, with Surtr;
There must fall    Frigg's beloved.

Odin's son goeth    to strife with the Wolf, —
Vídarr, speeding    to meet the slaughter-beast;
The sword in his hand    to the heart he thrusteth
Of the fiend's offspring;    avenged is his Father.

Now goeth Hlödyn's    glorious son
Not in flight from the Serpent,    of fear unheeding;
All the earth's offspring    must empty the homesteads,
When furiously smiteth    Midgard's defender.

The sun shall be darkened,    earth sinks in the sea, —
Glide from the heaven    the glittering stars;
Smoke-reek rages    and reddening fire:
The high heat licks    against heaven itself.

Then said Gangleri: "What shall come to pass afterward, when all the world is burned, and dead are all the gods and all the champions and all mankind? Have ye not said before, that every man shall live in some world throughout all ages?" Then Thridi answered: "In that time the good abodes shall be many, and many the ill; then it shall be best to be in Gimlé in Heaven. Moreover, there is plenteous abundance of good drink, for them that esteem that a pleasure, in the hall which is called Brimir: it stands in Ókólnir. That too is a good hall which stands in Nida Fells, made of red gold; its name is Sindri. In these halls shall dwell good men and pure in heart.

"On Nástrand is a great hall and evil, and its doors face to the north: it is all woven of serpent-backs like a wattle-house; and all the snake-heads turn into the house and blow venom, so that along the hall run rivers of venom; and they who have broken oaths, and murderers, wade those rivers, even as it says here:

I know a hall standing    far from the sun,
In Nástrand: the doors    to northward are turned;
Venom-drops fall    down from the roof-holes;
That hall is bordered    with backs of serpents.

Then spake Gangleri: "Shall any of the gods live then, or shall there be then any earth or heaven?" Hárr answered: "In that time the earth shall emerge out of the sea, and shall then be green and fair; then shall the fruits of it be brought forth unsown. Vídarr and Váli shall be living, inasmuch as neither sea nor the fire of Surtr shall have harmed them; and they shall dwell at Ida-Plain, where Ásgard was before. And then the sons of Thor, Módi and Magni, shall come

there, and they shall have Mjöllnir there.   After that Baldr shall come
thither, and Hödr, from Hel; then all shall sit down together and hold
speech with one another, and call to mind their secret wisdom, and
speak of those happenings which have been before: of the Midgard
Serpent and of Fenris-Wolf.   Then they shall find in the grass those
golden chess-pieces which the Æsir had had; thus it is said:

> In the deities' shrines        shall dwell Vídarr and Váli,
>     When the Fire of Surtr is slackened;
> Módi and Magni        shall have Mjöllnir
>     At the ceasing of Thor's strife.

In the place called Hoddmímir's Holt there shall lie hidden during
the Fire of Surtr two of mankind, who are called Líf and Lífthrasir,
and for food they shall have the morning-dews.   From these folk
shall come so numerous an offspring that all the world shall be peopled, even as is said here:

> Líf and Lífthrasir,        these shall lurk hidden
>     In the Holt of Hoddmímir;
> The morning dews        their meat shall be;
>     Thence are gendered the generations.

And it may seem wonderful to thee, that the sun shall have borne a
daughter not less fair than herself; and the daughter shall then tread
in the steps of her mother, as is said here:

> The Elfin-beam        shall bear a daughter,
>     Ere Fenris drags her forth;
> That maid shall go, when the great gods die,
>     To ride her mother's road.

But now, if thou art able to ask yet further, then indeed I know not
whence answer shall come to thee, for I never heard any man tell
forth at greater length the course of the world; and now avail thyself
of that which thou hast heard."

### THE NIFLUNG HOARD

"For what reason is gold called Otter's Wergild?   It is related that
when certain of the Æsir, Odin and Loki and Hoenir, went forth to
explore the earth, they came to a certain river, and proceeded along
the river to a water-fall.   And beside the fall was an otter, which
had taken a salmon from the fall and was eating, blinking his eyes
the while.   Then Loki took up a stone and cast it at the otter, and
struck its head.   And Loki boasted in his catch, that he had got otter
and salmon with one blow.   Then they took up the salmon and the
otter and bore them along with them, and coming to the buildings of
a certain farm, they went in.   Now the husbandman who dwelt there
was named Hreidmarr: he was a man of much substance, and very
skilled in black magic.   The Æsir asked him for a night's lodging,
saying that they had sufficient food with them, and showed him their
catch.   But when Hreidmarr saw the otter, straightway he called to

him his sons, Fáfnir and Reginn, and told them that the otter their brother was slain, and who had done that deed.

"Now father and sons went up to the Æsir, seized them, bound them, and told them about the otter, how he was Hreidmarr's son. The Æsir offered a ransom for their lives, as much wealth as Hreidmarr himself desired to appoint; and a covenant was made between them on those terms and confirmed with oaths. Then the otter was flayed, and Hreidmarr, taking the otter-skin, bade them fill the skin with red gold and also cover it altogether; and that should be the condition of the covenant between them. Thereupon Odin sent Loki into the Land of the Black Elves, and he came to the dwarf who is called Andvari, who was as a fish in the water. Loki caught him in his hands and required of him in ransom of his life all the gold that he had in his rock; and when they came within the rock, the dwarf brought forth all the gold he had, and it was very much wealth. Then the dwarf quickly swept under his hand one little gold ring, but Loki saw it and commanded him to give over the ring. The dwarf prayed him not to take the ring from him, saying that from this ring he could multiply wealth for himself if he might keep it. Loki answered that he should not have one penny left, and took the ring from him and went out; but the dwarf declared that that ring should be the ruin of every one who should come into possession of it. Loki replied that this seemed well enough to him, and that this condition should hold good provided that he himself brought it to the ears of them that should receive the ring and the curse. He went his way and came to Hreidmarr's dwelling, and showed the gold to Odin; but when Odin saw the ring, it seemed fair to him, and he took it away from the treasure, and paid the gold to Hreidmarr. Then Hreidmarr filled the otter-skin as much as he could, and set it up when it was full. Next Odin went up, having the skin to cover with gold, and he bade Hreidmarr look whether the skin were yet altogether hidden. But Hreidmarr looked at it searchingly, and saw one of the hairs of the snout, and commanded that this be covered, else their covenant should be at an end. Then Odin drew out the ring and covered the hair, saying that they were now delivered from their debt for the slaying of the otter. But when Odin had taken his spear and Loki his shoes and they had no longer any need to be afraid, then Loki declared that the curse which Andvari had uttered should be fulfilled: that this ring and this gold should be the destruction of him who received it. And that was fulfilled afterward. Now it has been told wherefore gold is called Otter's Wergild, or Forced Payment of the Æsir, or Metal of Strife.

"What more is to be said of the gold? Hreidmarr took the gold for his son's wergild, but Fáfnir and Reginn claimed some part of their brother's blood-money for themselves. Hreidmarr would not grant them one penny of the gold. This was the wicked purpose of those brethren: they slew their father for the gold. Then Reginn demanded that Fáfnir share the gold with him, half for half. Fáfnir answered that there was little chance of his sharing it with his brother, seeing that he had slain his father for its sake; and he bade Reginn go hence, else he should fare even as Hreidmarr. Fáfnir had taken the helmet which Hreidmarr had possessed, and set it upon his head (this helmet was called the Helm of Terror, of which all living creatures that see it are afraid), and the sword called Hrotti. Reginn had that sword which was named Refill. So he fled away, and Fáfnir went up to Gnita Heath, and made himself a lair, and turned himself into a serpent, and laid him down upon the gold.

"Then Reginn went to King Hjálprekr at Thjód, and there he became his smith; and he took into his fostering Sigurdr, son of Sigmundr, Völsungr's son, and of Hjördís, daughter of Eylimi. Sigurdr was most illustrious of all Host-Kings in race, in prowess, and in mind. Reginn declared to him where Fáfnir lay on the gold, and incited him to seek the gold. Then Reginn fashioned the sword Gramr, which was so sharp that Sigurdr, bringing it down into running water, cut asunder a flock of wool which drifted down-stream onto the sword's edge. Next Sigurdr clove Reginn's anvil down to the stock with the sword. After that they went, Sigurdr and Reginn, to Gnita Heath, and there Sigurdr dug a pit in Fáfnir's way and laid himself in ambush therein. And when Fáfnir glided toward the water and came above the pit, Sigurdr straightway thrust his sword through him, and that was his end.

"Then Reginn came forward saying that Sigurdr had slain his brother, and demanded as a condition of reconciliation that he take Fáfnir's heart and roast it with fire; and Reginn laid him down and drank the blood of Fáfnir, and settled himself to sleep. But when Sigurdr was roasting the heart, and thought that it must be quite roasted, he touched it with his finger to see how hard it was; and then the juice ran out from the heart onto his finger, so that he was burned and put his finger to his mouth. As soon as the heart's blood came upon his tongue, straightway he knew the speech of birds, and he understood what the nuthatches were saying which were sitting in the trees. Then one spake:

There sits Sigurdr
Blood-besprinkled,
Fáfnir's heart
With flame he roasteth:
Wise seemed to me
The Spoiler of Rings
If the gleaming
Life-fibre he ate.

There lies Reginn — sang another —
Rede he ponders,
Would betray the youth
Who trusteth in him:
In his wrath he plots
Wrong accusation;
The smith of bale
Would avenge his brother.

Then Sigurdr went over to Reginn and slew him, and thence to his horse, which was named Grani, and rode till he came to Fáfnir's lair. He took up the gold, trussed it up in his saddle-bags, laid it upon Grani's back, mounted up himself, and then rode his ways. Now the tale is told why gold is called Lair or Abode of Fáfnir, or Metal of Gnita Heath, or Grani's Burden.

"Then Sigurdr rode on till he found a house on the mountain, wherein a woman in helm and birnie lay sleeping. He drew his sword and cut the birnie from her. She awoke then, and gave her name as Hildr; she is called Brynhildr, and was a Valkyr. Sigurdr rode away and came to the king who was named Gjúki, whose wife was Grímhildr; their children were Gunnarr, Högni, Gudrún, Gudný; Gotthormr was Gjúki's stepson. Sigurdr tarried there a long time, and then he obtained the hand of Gudrún, daughter of Gjúki, and Gunnarr and Högni swore oaths of blood brotherhood with Sigurdr. Thereafter Sigurdr and the sons of Gjúki went unto Atli, Budli's son, to sue for the hand of Brynhildr his sister in marriage to Gunnarr. Brynhildr abode on Hinda-Fell, and about her hall there was a flaring fire; and she had made a solemn vow to take none but that man who should dare to ride through the flaring fire.

"Then Sigurdr and the sons of Gjúki (who were also called Niflungs) rode up onto the mountain, and Gunnarr should have ridden through the flaring fire: but he had the horse named Goti, and that horse dared not leap into the fire. So they exchanged shapes, Sigurdr and Gunnarr, and names likewise; for Grani would go under no man but Sigurdr. Then Sigurdr leapt onto Grani and rode through the flaring fire. That eve he was wedded with Brynhildr. But when they came to bed, he drew the Sword Gramr from its sheath and laid it between them. In the morning when he arose and clothed himself, he gave Brynhildr as linen-fee the same gold ring which Loki had taken from Andvari, and took another ring from her hand for remembrance. Then Sigurdr mounted his horse and rode to his fellows, and he and Gunnarr changed shapes again and went home to Gjúki with Brynhildr. Sigurdr and Gudrún had two children, Sigmundr and Svanhildr.

"It befell on a time that Brynhildr and Gudrún went to the water to wash their hair. And when they came to the river, Brynhildr waded out from the bank well into the river, saying that she would not touch to her head the water which ran out of the hair of Gudrún, since herself had the more valorous husband. Then Gudrún went into the river after her and said that it was her right to wash her hair higher upstream, for the reason that she had to husband such a man as neither Gunnarr nor any other in the world matched in valor, seeing that he had slain Fáfnir and Reginn and succeeded to the heritage of both. And Brynhildr made answer: 'It was a matter of greater worth that Gunnarr rode through the flaring fire and Sigurdr durst not.' Then Gudrún laughed, and said: 'Dost thou think that Gunnarr rode through the flaring fire? Now I think that he who went into the bride-bed with thee was the same that gave me this gold ring; and the gold ring which thou bearest on thine hand and didst receive for linen-fee is called Andvari's Yield, and I believe that it was not Gunnarr who got the ring on Gnita Heath.' Then Brynhildr was silent, and went home.

"After that she egged on Gunnarr and Högni to slay Sigurdr; but because they were Sigurdr's sworn blood-brothers, they stirred up Gotthormr their brother to slay him. He thrust his sword through Sigurdr as he slept; but when Sigurdr felt the wound, he hurled his sword Gramr after Gotthormr, so that it cut the man asunder at the middle. There fell Sigurdr and Sigmundr, his son of three winters, whom they slew. Then Brynhildr stabbed herself with a sword, and she was burned with Sigurdr; but Gunnarr and Högni took Fáfnir's heritage and Andvari's Yield, and ruled the lands thereafter.

"King Atli, Budli's son, and brother of Brynhildr, then wedded Gudrún, whom Sigurdr had had to wife; and they had children. King Atli invited to him Gunnarr and Högni, and they came at his invitation. Yet before they departed from their land, they hid the gold, Fáfnir's heritage, in the Rhine, and that gold has never since been found. Now King Atli had a host in readiness, and fought with Gunnarr and Högni; and they were made captive. King Atli bade the heart be cut out of Högni alive, and that was his end. Gunnar he caused to be cast into a den of serpents. But a harp was brought secretly to Gunnarr, and he struck it with his toes, his hands being bound; he played the harp so that all the serpents fell asleep, saving only one adder, which glided over to him and gnawed into the cartilage of his breastbone so far that her head sank within the wound, and she clove to his liver till he died. Gunnar and Högni were called Niflungs and Gjúkings, for which reason gold is called Treasure, or Heritage, of the Niflungs.

[tr. ARTHUR GILCHRIST BRODEUR]

# THE NIBELUNGENLIED

The story of the Franks, Burgundians, Goths, and Huns, as it existed in medieval legend, has been represented twice before in this volume — in *Walter of Aquitaine* and in the *Prose Edda*. There is a glimpse of Dietrich von Bern in Boethius' *Consolation* and of Hildebrand in the *Song of Hildebrand*. From such sources and many more did a poet in the age of chivalric literature compose what may not unfairly be described as the only medieval epic that resembles the classical. Who wrote the poem no doubt will never be known; the language is the Austrian dialect of High German, and students fix the date of composition between 1190 and 1205. Its author had the means of attracting a considerable audience quickly, for the poem was, for instance, already referred to in the sixth book of Wolfram's *Parzival*. The number of manuscripts, larger than that of any other poem of this high period of German poetry, indicates its deserved popularity. Though modern interest has largely been aroused for comparatively extraneous reasons — the folklore, the pan-Germanism, the relation to primitive Teutonic analogues, the historical and quasi-historical references, and the like — a reader will find greatest enjoyment in the *Nibelungenlied* if he forgets these matters and concentrates, as he would in reading the *Iliad,* on the poem's heroic theme and view of the world.

Unlike most epics the *Nibelungenlied* avoids the common rhetorical flourishes. The diction is simple, almost elementary. The images, though vivid, are commonplace. Metaphors occur so seldom that they startle the reader when they appear. The author, though he constantly intrudes with choral echoes and comments, is an impartial, almost phlegmatic observer of the tragedy he narrates. He takes all sides and sympathizes with winner and loser alike. The plot, at least at first sight, seems to ramble and to break completely in the middle, as the *Aeneid* does. But though the author exercises little care in detail, he has a firm grasp of the development of his story. The two distinguishing qualities of this epic are its panoramic view of history and its depiction of human choice.

How much the panoramic view can be attributed to the author and how much to the nature of the material that lay ready at hand we cannot say. Those who have long studied analogues are inclined in the end to attribute it to the selective genius of the author. At all events, the reader is caught up in the sweep of history, delineated in legendary form, from the misty, almost magical, and certainly prehistoric past, represented by episodes in the life of Siegfried and by Brunhild, through the economy of petty monarchs like Sieglind and Siegmund, to the fixed agrarian-military economy of the Burgundian court, and its dissolution under the impact of the totalitarianism represented by Etzel or Attila. It is as if the poet, who was perhaps himself a crusader under Frederick Barbarosa and saw the topless towers of Byzantium, were telling his readers how in this new age of trade, commerce, and gold, centralized government and strong monarchs who rule impassively must supplant the feudal baronry. Etzel, in sharp contrast with Gunther, is regal, not baronial. At first, he seems hardly aware and certainly little concerned with the squabbles about him. He has the calm of inexhaustible power.

But so fierce is the struggle for survival of the Burgundians that at one moment, at least, even the omnipotent Etzel is brought to his knees. Perhaps the poet laments the coming of this new day, to be in part exemplified by Philip Augustus and Emperor Frederick II; his poem ends with a line expressing extreme pessimism: "At the last all joy turneth to sorrow." It is no accident of history that in the year 1204, when the *Nibelungenlied* was fresh to its audience, England lost its feudal duchies of Normandy, Maine, and Anjou and the old stronghold of Norman feudalism was brought under the French crown.

This emergence of civilization through progressive steps is depicted in terms of characters and their choices. Brunhild and Siegfried, who represent an early stage of society, properly disappear from the poem. Like all the other major characters, they fulfil Aristotle's requirements that they be good, true to type, true to life, and self-consistent. Each has his tragic flaw. Brunhild, who reminds us of the Girl of the Golden West, the prospector's daughter, rich but bulgy, has the frontier girl's excessive reverence for caste and unreasoning fear that she will not be given her due. Siegfried, who is hero through and through, has the hero's tragic flaw that brings about his downfall — pride, combined, as in Samson and Adam, with uxoriousness. Other characters have their own truth and consistency — the rather bumbling Gunther, solemn Gernot and youthful Giselher his brothers, the minstrel Folker and even the epicurean Rumolt, who, as we should expect, is cook. The tragic figure of Rudeger, torn, like the Hagen of *Walther,* between two oaths of loyalty, is uneclipsed in literature.

But it is Kriemhild and Hagen who unify the story, and their epic struggle is symbolic as well as realistic. The initial evil choice was made when Kriemhild was betrothed to Siegfried, the possessor of great primitive wealth. The fondled sister of three loving brothers is apt to be both spoiled and materialistic, and Kriemhild is both. Even to the end, her answer to all problems is gold; she buys loyalty with gold in the court of Etzel as she tried to in the feudal state. Hagen, the perfect feudal vassal, is her natural enemy, for feudalism thrived in a world without trade and commerce, when the true nexus between man and man, according to Carlyle, was the feudal oath. Hagen properly sees Kriemhild and her gold as the overpowering threat to his society, and in the end Kriemhild does overcome it — not without the most awful blood-bath of all epic poetry. If Hagen looks to us a villain, it is only that we do not know his times and their morals. From the day when he exclaims, in fear of a weakening of feudal primogeniture, "Shall our kings rear bastards!" to the day when he is maneuvered by a trick into agreeing to leave the base of defense, he illustrates the canons of perfect vassalage. Once on the road to Etzel's castle and bereft of his code of life, he becomes crazed, as any leader does who has lost his principles of choice; and some of his actions on the road are inhuman. A reader is constantly reminded of Macbeth, even to a witch's scene. In Bechlaren, once more in an ordered feudalism that he had deserted, he temporarily recovers his sanity; nevertheless in Hunland he conducts himself with an iron courage but with wanton savagery.

The strophaic pattern, though similar to the verses of Otfrid's *Gospel Book* of the ninth century, is unique. Each strophe consists of four lines, rhymed *a a b b*; each line is broken by a single strong caesura. The first half-line consists of three primary stresses with a secondary stress on the final syllable; the second half-line has three primary stresses. The fourth line of the strophe has an extra stress that marks the end of the strophe. The stressed syllables are not usually alliterative, as in earlier Teutonic poetry. The first strophe of the poem is:

Uns íst in álten máerèn     wúnders víl geséit
Von héleden lóbebáerèn,     von grózer árebéit,
Von fröúde und hóchgezítèn,     von wéinen únd von klágen,
Von küéner récken strítèn     muget ír mu wúnder hoéren ságen.

The text that follows is a drastically abridged version of the complete poem.

## THE NIBELUNGENLIED

### Anonymous (*circ.* 1200)

[From *The Fall of the Nibelungs*, translated by Margaret Armour; J. M. Dent & Sons, Ltd., London, and E. P. Dutton & Co., Inc., New York, 1897. Reprinted by permission of the publishers.]

(1) In old tales they tell us many wonders of heroes and of high courage, of glad feasting, of wine and of mourning; and herein ye shall read of the marvellous deeds and of the strife of brave men.

There grew up in Burgundy a noble maiden; in no land was a fairer. Kriemhild was her name. Well favoured was the damsel, and by reason of her died many warriors. Doughty knights in plenty wooed her, as was meet, for of her body she was exceeding comely, and her virtues were an adornment to all women.

Three kings noble and rich guarded her, Gunther and Gernot, warriors of fame, and Giselher the youth, a chosen knight. The damsel was their sister, and the care of her fell on them. These lords were courteous and of high lineage, bold and very strong, each of them the pick of knights. The name of their country was Burgundy, and they did great deeds, after, in Etzel's land. At Worms, by the Rhine, they dwelled in might with many a proud lord for vassal.

Their mother was a rich queen and hight Uta, and the name of their father was Dankrat, who, when his life was ended, left them his lands. A strong man was he in his time, and one that in his youth won great worship.

Now it so fell that Kriemhild, the pure maid, dreamed a dream that she fondled a wild falcon, and eagles wrested it from her; the which to see grieved her more than any ill that had happened to her heretofore.

This dream she told to Uta, her mother, who interpreted it on this wise. "The falcon that thou sawest is a noble man; yet if God keep him not, he is a lost man to thee."

"What speakest thou to me of a man, mother mine? Without their love would I still abide, that I may remain fair till my death, nor suffer dole from any man's love."

Said her mother then, "Be not so sure; for wouldst thou ever on this earth have heart's gladness, it cometh from the love of a man. And a fair wife wilt thou be, if God but lead hither to thee a true and trusty knight."

"Say not so, mother mine," answered the maiden, "for on many a woman and oft hath it been proven that the meed of love is sorrow. From both I will keep me, that evil betide not."

Long in such wise abode the high, pure maiden, nor thought to love any. Nevertheless, at the last, she wedded a brave man; that was the falcon she dreamed of erstwhile, as her mother foretold it. Yea, bitter was her vengeance on her kinsmen that slew him, and by reason of his death died many a mother's son.

(2) There grew up in the Netherland a rich king's child, whose father hight Siegmund and his mother Sieglind, in a castle high and famous called Xanten, down by the Rhine's side. Goodly was this knight, by my troth, his body without blemish, a strong and valiant man of great worship; abroad, through the whole earth, went his fame. The hero hight Siegfried, and he rode boldly into many lands. Ha! in Burgundy, I trow, he found warriors to his liking. Or he was a man grown he had done marvels with his hand, as is said and sung, albeit now there is no time for more word thereof.

(3) Little recked Siegfried of heart's dole till that the news reached him of a fair maid of Burgundy, than whom none could wish a fairer; by reason of her, joy befell him, and sorrow.

Her beauty was rumoured far and wide, and the fame of her virtues, joined thereto, brought many strangers into Gunther's land. Yet, though many wooed her, Kriemhild was firm-minded to wed none. The man that was to win her was yet a stranger.

Thereupon Siegmund's son yearned to her with true love.

Weighed with him all other suitors were as wind, for he was meet to be chosen of fair women; and, or long, Kriemhild the high maiden was bold Sir Siegfried's bride.

The tidings came to Siegmund's ear.  His knight told him Siegfried's intent, and it irked him that his son should woo the royal maiden.  To Sieglind, the king's wife, they told it also, and she feared for his life, for she knew Gunther and his men.

They would have turned him from his quest.

Spake bold Siegfried then, "Dearest father mine, either I will think no more on women at all, or I will woo where my heart's desire is." And for all they could say, he changed not his purpose.

Then said the king, "If thou wilt not yield in this, i' faith, I approve thy choice, and will further thee therein as I best can.  Nevertheless, Gunther hath many mighty men, were it none other than Hagen, an arrogant and overweening knight.  I fear both thou and I must rue that thou goest after this king's daughter."

Siegfried answered, "I will not ride with an army of warriors to the Rhine; it would shame me so to win the maiden by force.  I would win her with mine own hand.  One of twelve I will forth to Gunther's land, and to this shalt thou help me, my father Siegmund."

They gave to his knights cloaks of fur, some grey and some striped.

Now the time was come to ride forth, and all the folk, men and women, made dole, lest they should return never more.

The knights were downcast, and the maidens wept.  Their hearts told them, I ween, that by reason of this day's doings, many a dear one would lie dead.  Needs made they dole, for they were sorrowful.

On the seventh morning after this, the fearless band drew toward Worms on the Rhine.

They told the king that a valiant knight, fair equipped and apparelled, that knew none in Burgundy, was come thither.  And the king marvelled where these proud knights in shining harness, with their shields new and massy, might hie from.  It irked him that none knew it.

Ortwin of Metz, a goodly man of high courage, spake to the king then, "Since we know naught thereof, bid to thee Hagen mine uncle, and show them to him.  For he hath knowledge of the mighty men of all lands; and what he knoweth he will tell us."

The king summoned Hagen with his vassals, and he drew nigh with proud step, and asked the king his will.

"Strange knights are come to my court that none knoweth.  If thou hast ever seen them afore, tell me thereof truly."

"That will I," spake Hagen, and went to the window, and looked down on the strangers below.  The show of them and their equipment pleased him, but he had not seen them afore in Burgundy.  And he said, "From wheresoever they be come, they must be princes, or princes' envoys.  Their horses are good, and wonderly rich their vesture.  From whatso quarter they hie, they be seemly men.  But for this I vouch, that, though I never saw Siegfried, yonder knight that goeth so proud is, of a surety, none but he.  New adventures he bring-

eth hither.   By this hero's hand fell the brave Nibelungs, Shilbung
and Nibelung, the high princes.   Wonders hath he wrought by his
prowess.   I have heard tell that on a day when he rode alone, he came
to a mountain, and chanced on a company of brave men that guarded
the Nibelung's hoard, whereof he knew naught.   The Nibelung men
had, at that moment, made an end of bringing it forth from a hole
in the hill, and oddly enow, they were about to share it.   Siegfried
saw them and marvelled thereat.   He drew so close that they were
ware of him and he of them.   Whereupon one said, 'Here cometh
Siegfried, the hero of the Netherland!'   Strange adventure met he
amidst of them.   Shilbung and Nibelung welcomed him, and with
one accord the princely youths asked him to divide the treasure
atween them, and begged this so eagerly that he could not say them
nay.   The tale goeth that he saw there more precious stones than an
hundred double waggons had sufficed to carry, and of the red Nibelung gold yet more.   This must bold Siegfried divide.   In guerdon
therefor they gave him the sword of the Nibelungs, and were
ill paid by Siegfried for the service.   He strove vainly to end the
task, whereat they were wroth.   And when he could not bear it
through, the kings, with their men, fell upon him.   But with their
father's sword that hight Balmung, he wrested from both hoard
and land.   The princes had twelve champions — stark giants, yet
little it bested them.   Siegfried slew them wrathfully with his hand,
and, with Balmung, vanquished seven hundred knights; and many
youths there, afraid of the man and his sword, did homage for
castles and land.   He smote the two kings dead.   Then he, himself,
came in scathe by Albric, that would have avenged the death of his
masters then and there, till that he felt Siegfried's exceeding might.
When the dwarf could not overcome him, they ran like lions to the
mountain, where Siegfried won from Albric the cloud-cloak that
hight *Tarnkappe*.   Then was Siegfried, the terrible man, master of
the hoard.   They that had dared the combat lay slain; and he bade
carry the treasure back whence the Nibelungs had brought it forth;
and he made Albric the keeper thereof, after that he had sworn an
oath to serve him as his man, and to do all that he commanded
him.

"These are his deeds," said Hagen; "bolder knight there never
was.   Yet more I might tell of him.   With his hand he slew a dragon,
and bathed him in its blood, that his skin is as horn, and no weapon
can cut him, as hath been proven on him ofttimes.

"Let us welcome the young lord, that we come not in his hate.   So
fair is he of his body that one may not look unfriendly thereon;
with his strength he hath done great deeds."

"Thou art welcome," said Uta's son; "thou and thy comrades that
are with thee.   We will serve thee gladly, I and my kinsmen."

They let pour for them Gunther's wine, and the host of the land,
even Gunther the king, said, "All that is ours, and whatsoever thou

mayest with honour desire, is thine to share with us, body and goods."

The king and his men busied them with sports, and in each undertaking Siegfried still approved him the best. Whether they threw the stone or shot with the shaft, none came near him by reason of his great strength. Held the doughty warriors tourney before the women, then looked these all with favour on the knight of the Netherland. But, as for him, he thought only on his high love. The fair women of the court demanded who the proud stranger was. "He is so goodly," they said, "and so rich his apparel."

And there answered them folk enow, "It is the king of the Netherland." Whatsoever sport they followed, he was ready. In his heart he bare the beautiful maiden that as yet he had not seen: the which spake in secret kind words also of him. When the youths tilted in the courtyard, Kriemhild, the high princess, looked down at them from her window; nor, at that time, desired she better pastime. Neither had he asked better, had he known that his heart's dear one gazed upon him.

When the rich kings rode abroad, it behoved the knights to go with them, wherefore Siegfried also rode forth, the which irked the damsel sore; and likewise, for love of her, he was heavy enow of his cheer.

So a year (I say sooth) he abode by these princes, nor in all that time had once seen his dear one, that afterward brought him much gladness and dole.

(5) On Whitsun morning there drew toward the hightide a goodly company of brave men, fairly clad: five thousand or more, and they made merry far and wide, and strove with one another in friendly combat.

Now Gunther knew well how, truly and from his heart, the hero of the Netherland loved his sister whom he had not yet seen, and whose beauty the people praised before that of all other maidens.

And he said, "Now counsel me, my kinsmen and my lieges, how we may order this hightide, that none may blame us in aught; for only unto such deeds as are good, pertaineth lasting fame."

Then answered Ortwin, the knight, to the king, "If thou wilt win for thyself glory from the hightide, let now the maidens that dwell with honour in our midst appear before us. For what shall pleasure or glad a man more than to behold beautiful damsels and fair women? Bid thy sister come forth and show herself to thy guests."

And this word pleased the knights.

"That will I gladly do," said the king; and they that heard him rejoiced. He sent a messenger to Queen Uta, and besought her that she would come to the court with her daughter and her womenfolk.

And these took from the presses rich apparel, and what lay therein in wrapping-cloths; they took also brooches, and their silken girdles worked with gold, and attired themselves in haste. Many a noble maiden adorned herself with care, and the youths longed exceedingly to find favour in their eyes, and had not taken a rich king's land in lieu thereof. And they that knew not one another before looked each upon each right gladly.

The rich king commanded an hundred men of his household, his kinsmen and hers, to escort his sister, their swords in their hand. Uta, with an hundred and more of her women, gorgeously attired, came forth from the female apartments, and many noble damsels followed after her daughter. The knights pressed in upon them, thinking thereby to behold the beautiful maiden.

And lo! the fair one appeared, like the dawn from out the dark clouds. And he that had borne her so long in his heart was no more aweary, for the beloved one, his sweet lady, stood before him in her beauty. Bright jewels sparkled on her garments, and bright was the rose-red of her hue, and all they that saw her proclaimed her peerless among maidens.

As the moon excelleth in light the stars shining clear from the clouds, so stood she, fair before the other women, and the hearts of the warriors were uplifted. The chamberlains made way for her through them that pressed in to behold her. And Siegfried joyed, and sorrowed likewise, for he said in his heart, "How should I woo such as thee? Surely it was a vain dream; yet I were liefer dead than a stranger to thee."

Thinking thus he waxed oft white and red; yea, graceful and proud stood the son Sieglind, goodliest of heroes to behold, as he were drawn on parchment by the skill of a cunning master. And the knights fell back as the escort commanded, and made way for the high-hearted women, and gazed on them with glad eyes. Many a dame of high degree was there.

She greeted him mild and maidenly, and her colour was kindled when she saw before her the high-minded man, and she said, "Welcome, Sir Siegfried, noble knight and good." His courage rose at her words, and graceful, as beseemed a knight, he bowed himself before her and thanked her. And love that is mighty constrained them, and they yearned with their eyes in secret. I know not whether, from his great love, the youth pressed her white hand, but two love-desirous hearts, I trow, had else done amiss.

Nevermore, in summer or in May, bore Siegfried in his heart such high joy, as when he went by the side of her whom he coveted for his dear one. And many a knight thought, "Had it been my hap to walk with her, as I have seen him do, or to lie by her side, certes, I had suffered it gladly! Yet never, truly, hath warrior served better to win a queen." From what land soever the guests came, they were ware only of these two. And she was bidden kiss the hero. He had never had like joy before in this world.

(6) A fresh rumour spread beyond the Rhine. It was reported that many maidens dwelt there; and Gunther was minded to woo one of them, whereat his knights and his liegeman were well pleased.

There was a queen high throned across the sea, that had not her like, beyond measure fair and of mickle strength, and her love was for that knight only that could pass her at the spear. She hurled the stone and leapt after it to the mark. Any that desired the noble damsel's love must first win boldly in these three games. If he failed but in one, he lost his head.

On a day that the king sat with his men, and they cast to and fro whom their prince might best take to wife for his own comfort and the good of his land, the lord of Rhineland said, "I will hence across the sea to Brunhild, let what will betide. For her sake I will peril my body, for I lose it if I win her not to wife."

"Do not so," said Siegfried. "Cruel is the queen, and he that would woo her playeth too high a stake. Make not this journey."

But King Gunther answered, "Never yet was woman born so stark and bold, that, with this single hand, I could not vanquish her in strife."

"Then I counsel thee," said Hagen, "to ask Siegfried to share with thee this hard emprise. It were well, since he knoweth so much of Brunhild."

So the king spake, "Wilt thou help me, most noble Siegfried, to woo the damsel? Grant me this, and if I win the royal maiden for my dear one, I will adventure honour and life for thy sake."

Siegfried, the son of Siegmund, made answer, "Give me thy sister Kriemhild, the high princess, and I will do it. Other meed I ask not."

Said Gunther, "I swear it, Siegfried, on thy hand. If Brunhild come hither, I will give thee my sister to wife; and mayest thou live joyfully with her to thy life's end."

The noble warriors sware an oath; and travail enow they endured, or they led back the fair one to the Rhine; yea, ofttimes they were straightened sore.

I have heard tell of wild dwarfs: how that they dwell in hollow mountains, and wear wonderful cloaks called *Tarnkappes*. And whoso hath this on his body cometh not in scathe by blows or spear-thrusts; nor is he seen of any man so long as he weareth it, but may spy and hearken at his will. His strength also waxeth thereby; so runneth the tale.

Siegfried took the *Tarnkappe* with him that he had wrested from Albric the dwarf. And these high and noble knights made ready for the journey. When stark Siegfried did on the *Tarnkappe,* he was strong with the strength of twelve men, and with these cunning devices he won the royal maiden; for the cloak of cloud was fashioned on such wise, that whoso wore it did what him listed, none seeing; and he won Brunhild thereby, that after brought him dole.

Kriemhild said, "Dear brother, thou didst better to stay here and woo other women without risk to thy body. It were easy to find, nigh at hand, a wife of as high lineage."

I ween her heart told her the dole that was to come.

She spake further, "Sir Siegfried, to thy care and good faith I commend my dear brother, that no evil betide him in Brunhild's land." The knight gave his hand thereon, and promised it. He said, "Fear not, lady; if I live, I will bring him back safe to the Rhine. I swear it by mine own body."

And the fair maiden thanked him.

They say that by the twelfth morning the wind had blown them afar to Isenstein in Brunhild's land, the which none had seen before that, save Siegfried. When King Gunther beheld so many towers and broad marches, he cried out, "Now say, friend Siegfried; knowest thou whose are these castles and these fair lands? By my troth, I have never in my life seen castles so many and so goodly as stand there before us. A mighty man he must be that hath builded them."

Whereto Siegfried made answer, "Yea, I know well. They are all Brunhild's — towers and lands, and the castle of Isenstein. I say sooth; and many fair women shall ye behold this day. Now I counsel you, O knights, for so it seemeth good to me, that ye be all of one mind and one word; we must stand warily before Brunhild the queen. And when we see the fair one amidst of her folk, be sure ye tell all the same story: that Gunther is my lord and I his liegeman. So shall he win to his desire. Yet this I do less for love of thee than for the fair maid, thy sister, that is to me as my soul and mine own body, and for whom I gladly serve, that I may win her to wife."

They promised with one accord, and none gainsayed him through pride, the which stood them in good stead when the king came to stand before Brunhild.

(7) They left the vessel unguarded on the beach, and rode up to the castle. There they saw eighty and six towers, three great palaces, and a stately hall of costly marble, green like grass, wherein the queen sat with her courtiers.

Brunhild's men unlocked the castle gate and threw it wide, and ran toward them, and welcomed the guests to their queen's land. They bade hold the horses, and take the shields from their hands. And the chamberlain said, "Do off your swords now, and your bright armour." "Not so," answered Hagen of Trony; "we will bear these ourselves."

But Siegfried told them the custom of the court. "It is the law here that no guest shall bear arms. Wherefore ye did well to give them up."

Gunther's man obeyed, much loth. They bade pour out the wine for the guests, and see that they were well lodged. Willing knights in princely attire ran to and fro to serve them, spying with many glances at the strangers.

They brought word to Brunhild that unknown warriors in rich apparel were come thither, sailing on the sea, and the beautiful maiden questioned them. "Tell me," said the queen, "who these strangers be that stand yonder so proudly, and for whose sake they be come." And one of the courtiers made answer. "In sooth, Lady, albeit I never set eyes on them, one among them much resembleth

Siegfried, and him I counsel thee to welcome. The second of the
company hath so lofty a mien that, if his power be equal thereto,
he might well be a great king and a ruler of wide lands, for he
standeth right proudly before the others. The third, O Queen, is
grim, yet a goodly man withal. His glance is swift and dark; he
is fierce-tempered, I ween. The youngest pleaseth me well. Maidenly and modest he standeth, yet it went hard, methinketh, with any
that angered him. For all that he seemeth gentle, and is fashioned
daintily, if his wrath were once kindled, many a woman might
weep, for he is a bold and virtuous knight, and right worshipful."

The queen said, "Bring me my robe. If stark Siegfried be come
into my land to woo me, he shall pay for it with his life. I fear
him not so greatly that I should yield me to be his wife."

Then Brunhild attired her in haste. An hundred or more of her
damsels went with her, richly adorned, whom the guests beheld
gladly. Brunhild's knights of Issland gave them escort, to the
number of five hundred or thereabout, their swords in their hands,
the which irked the bold strangers. They stood up from their
seats; and the queen spake courteously to them when she saw Siegfried, "Thou art welcome, Siegfried, to this land. To what end art
thou come? I prithee tell me."

"I thank thee, O Brunhild, fair daughter of a king, that thou
greetest me before this worshipful knight. Thou showest Siegfried
too much honour, for he is my lord, and the king of Rhineland."

She answered, "If he be thy lord, and thou be his man, let him
withstand me at the games. If he have the mastery, then am I his
wife, but let him fail in one of them, and ye be all dead men."

Then said Hagen of Trony, "Lady, show us the games that thou
proposest. It will go hard with Gunther or he yield thee the mastery,
for he troweth well to win so fair a maiden."

"He must put the stone, and leap after it, and throw the spear
with me. Ye may easily forfeit honour and life; wherefore be not
so confident, but bethink you well."

Then bold Siegfried went to the king, and bade him fear naught,
but speak freely to the queen. "For," said he, "I will aid thee with
cunning devices."

And King Gunther said, "Command me, great queen, and were it
more yet, I would risk it for thy sake. I will lose my head, or win
thee to wife."

When the queen heard this word, she bade haste to the sports,
as was meet, and let them bring her harness, a golden buckler and
a goodly shield. She did on a surcoat of silk from Libya, that had
never been pierced in combat, cunningly fashioned and embroidered,
and shining with precious stones. Her pride greatly angered the
knights, and Dankwart and Hagen were downcast, for they feared
for their lord, and thought, "Ill-starred was this journey."

Meanwhile, Siegfried, the cunning man, went, when none spied
him, to the ship, where he found the *Tarnkappe,* and he did it on
swiftly, that none knew. Then he hasted back to the crowd of

knights, where the queen gave order for the sports, and, by his magic, he stole in among them, that no man was ware of him. The ring was marked out in the presence of armed knights to the number of seven hundred. These were the umpires, that should tell truly who won in the sports.

Then came Brunhild. She stood armed, as she had meant to do battle with all the kings of all the world. The silk was covered with gold spangles that showed her white skin. Her attendants brought her, for the strife, a shield of ruddy gold with iron studs, mickle and broad. The maid's thong was an embroidered band, whereon lay stones green like grass, that sparkled among the gold. The knight must, certes, be bold that won such a lady. They say the shield the maiden bore was three spans thick under the folds, rich with steel and gold, that four of her chamberlains scarce could carry it.

When stark Hagen saw them drag the shield forward, the hero of Trony was wroth, and cried, "How now, King Gunther? We be dead men, for thou wooest the Devil's wife!"

Yet more must ye hear of her vesture. Her coat of mail was covered with silk from Azagouc, costly and rich, and the stones thereof sparkled on the queen's body. They brought her the spear, heavy and big and sharp, that she was wont to throw. Stark and huge it was, mickle and broad, and made grim wounds with its edges. And hear, now, the marvel of its heaviness. Three weights and a half of iron were welded for it. Three of Brunhild's lords scarce carried it. A woeful man was King Gunther, and he thought, "Lo! now, not the Devil in Hell could escape her. Were I in Burgundy with my life, she might wait long enough for my wooing." He stood dismayed. Then they brought him his armour, and he did it on.

Brunhild's great strength appeared. They brought her a stone into the circle, heavy and huge, round also, and broad. Twelve strong knights scarce sufficed thereto. And this she threw when she had hurled the spear. Whereat the Burgundians were sore troubled, and Hagen cried, "Who is this that Gunther wooeth? Would she were the Devil's bride in Hell!"

Then she turned back the sleeves from her white arms, and seized the shield, and brandished the spear above her head, and the contest began. Gunther was sore dismayed. If Siegfried had not helped him, certes he had lost his life; but Siegfried went up to him secretly, and touched his hand. Gunther fell in fear by reason of his magic, and he thought, "Who touched me?" He looked round and saw no man. But Siegfried said, "It is I, Siegfried, thy friend. Fear naught from the queen. Give me the shield from thy hands, and let me carry it, and give heed to what I say. Make thou the gestures, and I will do the work." And Gunther was glad when he knew him. "Guard well the secret of my magic, for all our sakes, lest the queen slay thee. See how boldly she challengeth thee."

Thereupon the royal maiden hurled her spear against the mickle and broad shield of Sieglind's child, that sparks flew from it, as before a wind. The stark spear pierced through the shield, and struck fire from the coat of mail below. And the mighty man fell, and had perished but for the *Tarnkappe*. The blood gushed from Siegfried's mouth. But he sprang up swiftly, and took the spear that she had shot through his buckler, and threw it back again with great force. He thought, "I will not slay so fair a maiden," and he turned the spear, and hurled it with the haft loud against her harness. From her mail, also, the sparks flew as on the wind, for Siegmund's child threw mightily; and her strength failed before the blow. King Gunther, I ween, had never done it alone.

Brunhild sprang to her feet again, and cried, "I thank thee, Gunther, for that blow." For she thought he had done it with his own strength, nor guessed that a far mightier man had felled her.

Then, greatly wroth, she hasted and lifted the stone on high; she flung it far from her, and leaped after it with loud-ringing armour. The stone landed twenty and four paces off; but the maid sprang further. Then Siegfried went swiftly where the stone lay. Gunther lifted it, but it was the man they saw not that threw it. Siegfried was mighty, bold and big. He hurled the stone further, and he leaped further; moreover, through his magic, he had strength enow to bear King Gunther with him. The spring was made, the stone lay on the ground, and none was seen there but Gunther, the knight. Fair Brunhild was red with anger.

So Siegfried saved Gunther from death.

Then Brunhild said aloud to her folk, when she saw the hero at the far end of the ring unhurt, "Come hither at once, my kinsmen and my lieges. Ye are subject henceforth to King Gunther."

The bold men laid the weapons from their hands at the feet of great Gunther of Burgundy. For they deemed he had won the game by his own strength.

He greeted them fair, for he was a courteous man, and he took the beautiful maiden by the hand. She gave him power in her kingdom, whereat bold Hagen rejoiced.

(8) She chose from among her knights two thousand men to follow her to the Rhine, and the thousand Nibelung warriors. Then she made ready for the journey, and rode down to the shore. She took with her six and eighty women, and an hundred fair damsels, and they tarried not longer, but set out. They that were left behind wept sore! Graciously and sweetly the lady quitted her land. She kissed her nearest of kin that stood round. With loving farewells they reached the sea. To the land of her fathers the maiden returned nevermore.

(10) On the far bank of the Rhine appeared a mighty host — the king with his guests — and they drew nigh to the strand, where damsels, led by the bridle, stood ready with welcome.

Gunther, with his friends, went down from the ships; he led Brunhild by the hand; garments and precious stones shone bright and sparkled. And Kriemhild went eagerly toward them and

greeted Brunhild and her following. They drew back their head-
bands with white fingers, and kissed one another through love.
Then Kriemhild the maid spake courteously, "Thou are right welcome in this land, to me and to my mother, and to our friends."
And they courtsied and embraced. Never, I ween, was any greeted
fairer than the bride by Uta and her daughter, for they ceased not
to kiss her sweet mouth.

When Brunhild's women were all gotten to land, the knights led
them before the queen, where welcome was not stinted them and
where many a red mouth was kissed. The rich kings' daughters
stood long side by side, and the warriors gazed on them. What
these had heard tell they saw with their eyes, that none surpassed
those two women in beauty, neither was any blemish found in them.
They that esteem women for the comeliness of the body and what
the eye beholdeth, extolled King Gunther's wife, but the wise that
look deeper said, "Praised shall Kriemhild be before Brunhild."
And the bright-attired women drew together where the silken
canopies were spread, and the goodly tents, in the field before
Worms.

The chairs were set, for the king was ready to go to table with his
guests, and beautiful Brunhild stood by him and wore her crown
in Gunther's land. Certes, she was proud enough.

Many were the seats, they say, and the tables goodly and broad
and laden with food. Little, I trow, was lacking! And many a
noble guest sat there with the king. Gunther's chamberlains carried round water in golden ewers. If any tell you of a prince's table
better served, believe it not.

Or Gunther took the water, Siegfried, as was meet, minded him
of his oath that he had sworn or ever he saw Brunhild in Issland.

He said, "Forget not the vow thou swarest with thy hand that, if
Brunhild came into Burgundy, thou wouldst give me thy sister.
Where is thine oath now? Mickle toil was mine on the journey."

The king answered his guest, "Thou hast done well to remind
me. I go not back from the oath of my hand. What I can do therein
I will do."

They bade Kriemhild to the court before the king. She went up
to the hall with her maidens, but Giselher sprang down the stair and
cried, "Send back these maidens. My sister goeth alone to the king."

They brought Kriemhild before Gunther, where he stood amidst
of knights from many lands. And they bade her stand in the
middle of the hall. Brunhild, by this time, was come to the table,
and knew naught of what was toward. Then said Dankrat's son
to his kinsmen, "Help me now, that my sister take Siegfried to her
husband."

And they answered with one accord, "That may she do with
honour."

Gunther said, "Dear sister, I prithee of thy goodness, loose me
from mine oath. I promised thee to a knight; and truly thou wilt do
my will, if thou take him to husband."

The maiden answered, "Dear brother mine, thou needest not to entreat. Command and I will obey. Him that thou givest me to husband I will gladly wed."

Siegfried grew red for love and joy, and vowed his service to Kriemhild. And they bade them stand together in a circle, and asked her if she would take the knight.

On maidenly wise she was shamefast at the first, yet so great was Siegfried's good fortune and his grace that she refused not his hand; and the king of the Netherland, from his side also, plighted his troth to Kriemhild.

When their word was given, Siegfried took his queen in his arms straightway, and kissed her before the warriors.

The circle brake up when this was ended, and Siegfried took the seat of honour with Kriemhild. The vassals served before them, and his Nibelung knights stood nigh.

The king and Brunhild were seated and Brunhild saw Kriemhild sitting by Siegfried, the which irked her sore; she fell to weeping, and the hot tears ran down her bright cheeks.

Whereupon the host said, "What aileth thee sweet Lady, that the light of thine eyes is dim? Rejoice shouldst thou rather, for my land and rich castles and true liegeman are all subject to thee."

"I have cause to weep," said the maiden. "I grieve from my heart for thy sister, that she sitteth there by thy vassal. I must ever weep to see her so shamed."

But King Gunther answered, "I prithee, silence! Another time I will tell thee why I gave my sister to Siegfried. May she live happily with the knight."

But she said, "I must grieve for her beauty and her birth. If I knew whither I might flee, I would not suffer thee by me, till that thou hadst told me how Siegfried hath gotten Kriemhild."

Gunther answered then, "Hearken, and I will tell thee. Know that he hath lands and castles even as I, and is a rich king; wherefore I give him my beautiful sister gladly to wife." Yet, for all the king could say to her, she was downcast.

The knights rose from the table, and the tourney waxed so fierce that the castle rang with the noise. But the king wearied amidst of his guests. He thought, "It were softer alone with my wife." And his heart dwelled on the mickle joy her love must bring him, and he looked at her sweetly.

Then they stopped the tourney, that the king might retire with his wife.

At the foot of the stair that led forth from the hall, Kriemhild and Brunhild came face to face. They were not foes yet. Their attendants followed them, and longer they tarried not. The chamberlains brought candles, and the knights of the two kings parted in two companies, and many followed Siegfried.

Then came the heroes where they were to lie, and each thought to win his wife's favour, whereat their hearts melted.

With Siegfried all went well. He caressed the maiden lovingly, and she was as his life. He had not given her alone for a thousand other women.

Of them I will tell no further. Hear now how it fared with Gunther. Better had been his case with any but Brunhild.

The folk had departed, dames and knights. The door was made fast. He thought to win her love, but it was long yet or she became his wife. He lay down in a white garment and thought, "Now have I my heart's desire." The king's hand hid the light. He went to Brunhild and embraced her with his arm. He was greatly glad. He would have caressed her sweetly if she had let him. But she was so wroth that he was dismayed. He thought to find joy, but found deep hate.

She said, "Noble knight, let me alone, for it shall not be as thou desirest. Mark well that I will have naught to do with thee, till that thou hast answered me concerning Kriemhild."

Then Gunther began to be angry with her, and fought with her, and tore her raiment. And the royal maiden seized a girdle, a strong embroidered silk cord that she wore round her waist, and did hurt enow to the knight. She bound his hands and his feet, and carried him to a nail, and hung him on the wall. She forbade him to touch her because he disturbed her sleep. He almost perished from her strength.

Then he that should have been master began to pray, "Now loose my bands, most noble queen. I promise never to touch thee, or even to come nigh thee."

She asked not how he fared while she lay soft. There must he hang the long night through till the day, when the bright morning shone through the window. If he had ever had strength, he had little in his body now.

"Tell me, Sir Gunther," said the beautiful maiden, "doth it not irk thee that thy chamberlains find thee bound by the hand of a woman."

The noble knight answered, "It were the worse for thee. Also little were my honour therein. Of thy charity allow me to lie down. Seeing thou hatest my love, I will not so much as touch thy garment with my hand."

Then she loosed his bands, and let him go, and he laid him down, but so far from her that he ruffled not her beautiful gown. Even that she had gladly foregone.

Thereupon their attendants came and brought them new apparel, as much as they could wear, that had been made ready against the wedding morn. But, amidst of them that rejoiced, the king was heavy of his cheer beneath his crown that day.

According to the good custom of the land, Gunther and Brunhild tarried not longer, but went to the minster to hear mass. Thither also went Siegfried and there was great press of people.

He and Siegfried were unlike of their moods. The hero guessed what ailed him, and went to him and asked him, "Tell me how it hath fared with thee."

Then said the host to his guest, "Shame and hurt have I suffered from my wife in my house. When I would have caressed her, she bound me tight, and took me to a nail, and hung me up on the wall. There I dangled in fear the night through till the day, or she loosed me. How soft she lay there! I tell thee this in secret."

And stark Siegfried said, "I grieve for thee. I will tell thee a remedy if thou keep it from her. I will so contrive it that this night she will defy thee no longer." The word was welcome to Gunther after his pain.

"Now see my hands, how they are swollen. She overmastered me, as I had been a child, that the blood spurted all over me from my nails. I thought not to come off with my life."

Said Siegfried, "It will yet be well. Unequal was our fortune last night. Thy sister Kriemhild is dearer to me than mine own body. This day must Brunhild be thy wife. I will come to-night to thy room secretly in my *Tarnkappe,* that none may guess the trick. Send the chamberlains to their beds. I will put out the lights in the hands of the pages, and by this sign thou shalt know that I am nigh. I will win thy wife for thee or perish."

"If only thou winnest her not for thy self. She is my dear wife. Otherwise I rejoice. Do to her what thou wilt. If thou tookest her life, I would bear it. She is a terrible woman."

"I vow to thee on mine honour that I will have naught to do with her. Thy dear sister is more to me than any I have ever seen." And Gunther believed Siegfried's word.

Fair Kriemhild and also Brunhild were led to their chambers. Ha! what bold knights went before the queens!

Joyful and without hate Siegfried the knight sat sweetly beside his beautiful wife. With her white hand she caressed his, till, she knew now how, he vanished from before her eyes. When she played with him and saw him no longer, she said to her maidens, "I marvel much where the king is gone. Who took his hands out of mine?" And so the matter dropped.

He had gone where he found the chamberlains with the lights, which he began to put out. By this sign Gunther perceived that it was Siegfried. He knew well what he wanted, and he sent away the women and maidens. When that was done, the king himself locked the door, and shot two strong bolts before it. He hid the light quickly behind the bed curtain, and the struggle that had to come began between stark Siegfried and the beautiful maiden. King Gunther was both glad and sorry.

Siegfried lay down by the queen, but she said "Stop, Gunther, lest thou suffer as afore. Thou mayest again receive a hurt at my hand."

Siegfried concealed his voice and spake not. Gunther heard well all that passed, albeit he saw nothing. There was little ease for the twain. Siegfried feigned that he was Gunther and put his arm round the valiant maiden. She threw him on to a bench, that his head rang loud against a foot-stool.

The bold man sprang up undaunted, but evil befell him. Such

defence from a woman I ween the world will never see more. Because he would not let her be, Brunhild rose up.

"It is unseemly of thee," said the brave maiden. "Thou wilt tear my beautiful gown. Thou art churlish and must suffer for it. Thou shalt see!"

She caught the good knight in her arms, and would have bound him as she had done to the king, that she might have peace. Grimly she avenged her torn raiment.

What availed him then his strength and his prowess? She proved to him the mastery of her body, and carried him by force, since there was no other way, and squeezed him hard against a press that stood by the bed.

"Alack!" thought the knight, "if I lose my life by the hand of a woman, all wives evermore will make light of their husbands, that, without this, would not dare."

The king heard it well. He feared for the man. Then Siegfried was ashamed and waxed furious. He grappled fiercely with her, and, in terror of his life, strove to overcome Brunhild. When she squeezed him down, he got up again in spite of her, by dint of his anger and his mickle strength. He came in great scathe. In the chamber there was smiting with many blows. King Gunther, likewise, stood in peril. He danced to and fro quickly before them. So mightily they strove, it was a wonder they came off with their lives. The trouble of the king was twofold, yet most he feared Siegfried's death. For she had almost killed the knight. Had he dared, he had gone to his help.

The strife endured long atwixt them. Then Siegfried got hold of Brunhild. Albeit she fought valiantly, her defence was grown weak. It seemed long to the king, that stood there, till Siegfried had won. She squeezed his hands till, by her strength, the blood spurted out from his nails. Then he brake the strong will that she had shown at the first. The king heard it all, but he spake no word. Siegfried pressed her down till she cried aloud, for his might hurt her greatly. She clutched at her side, where she found her girdle, and sought to tie his hands. But he gripped her till the joints of her body cracked. So the strife was ended.

She said, "Noble king, let me live. I will make good to thee what I have done, and strive no more; truly I have found thee to be my master."

Siegfried rose up then and left her, as though he would throw off his clothes. He drew from her hand a gold ring, without that she was ware of it. He took her girdle also, a good silken band. I know not if he did it from pride. He gave them to his wife, and suffered for it after.

The king and the fair maiden were left together, and, for that she was grown weak, she hid her anger, for it availed her nothing. So they abode there till the bright day.

Meanwhile Siegfried went back to his sweet love, that received him kindly. He turned the questions aside that she asked him, and hid from her for long what he had brought with him, till at the last, when they were gotten home to the Netherland, he gave her the jewel; the which brought him and many knights to their graves.

Much merrier was Gunther of his cheer the next morning than before. Throughout his lands many a noble knight rejoiced, and the guests that he had bidden to the hightide were well feasted and served.

(14) One day, before vespers, there arose in the court of the castle a mighty din of knights that tilted for pastime, and the folk ran to see them.

The queens sat together there, thinking each on a doughty warrior. Then said fair Kriemhild, "I have a husband of such might that all these lands might well be his."

But Brunhild answered, "How so? If there lived none other save thou and he, our kingdom might haply be his, but while Gunther is alive it could never be."

But Kriemhild said, "See him there. How he surpasseth the other knights, as the bright moon the stars! My heart is uplifted with cause."

Whereupon Brunhild answered, "Howso valiant thy husband, comely and fair, thy brother Gunther excelleth him, for know that he is the first among kings."

But Kriemhild said, "My praise was not idle; for worshipful is my husband in many things. Trow it, Brunhild. He is, at the least, thy husband's equal."

"Mistake me not in thine anger, Kriemhild. Neither is my word idle; for they both said, when I saw them first, and the king vanquished me in the sports, and on knightly wise won my love, that Siegfried was his man. Wherefore I hold him for a vassal, since I heard him say it."

Then Kriemhild cried, "Evil were my lot if that were true. How had my brothers given me to a vassal to wife? Prithee, of thy courtesy, cease from such discourse."

"That will I not," answered Brunhild. "Thereby should I lose many knights that, with him, owe us homage."

Whereat fair Kriemhild waxed very wroth. "Lose them thou must, then, for any service he will do thee. He is nobler even than Gunther, my noble brother. Wherefore, spare me thy foolish words. I wonder, since he is thy vassal, and thou art so much mightier than we, that for so long time he hath failed to pay tribute. Of a truth thine arrogancy irketh me."

"Thou vauntest thyself too high," cried the queen; "I would see now whether thy body be holden in like honour with mine."

Both the women were angry.

Kriemhild answered, "That shalt thou see straightway. Since thou hast called Siegfried thy vassal, the knights of both kings shall see this day whether I dare enter the minster before thee, the queen. For I would have thee know that I am noble and free, and that my husband is of more worship than thine. Nor will I be chidden by thee. To-day thou shalt see thy vassals go at court before the Burgundian knights, and me more honoured than any queen that ever wore a crown."

Fierce was the wrath of the women.

"If thou art no vassal," said Brunhild, "thou and thy women shall walk separate from my train when we go to the minster."

And Kriemhild answered, "Be it so."

"Now adorn ye, my maidens," said Siegfried's wife, "that I be not shamed. If ye have rich apparel, show it this day. She shall take back what her mouth hath spoken."

She needed not to bid twice; they sought out their richest vesture, and dames and damsels were soon arrayed.

Then the wife of the royal host went forth with her attendants. Fair to heart's desire were clad Kriemhild and the forty and three maidens that she had brought with her to the Rhine. Bright shone the stuffs, woven in Araby, whereof their robes were fashioned. And they came to the minster, where Siegfried's knights waited for them.

The folk marvelled much to see the queens apart, and going not together as afore. Many a warrior was to rue it.

Gunther's wife stood before the minster, and the knights dallied in converse with the women, till that Kriemhild came up with her company. All that noble maidens had ever worn was but as a wind to what these had on. So rich was Kriemhild that thirty king's wives together had not been as gorgeous as she was. None could deny, though they had wished it, that the apparel Kriemhild's maidens wore that day was the richest they had ever seen. Kriemhild did this on purpose to anger Brunhild.

So they met before the minster. And Brunhild, with deadly spite, cried out to Kriemhild to stand still. "Before the queen shall no vassal go."

Out then spake Kriemhild, for she was wroth. "Better hadst thou held thy peace. Thou hast shamed thine own body. How should the leman of a vassal become a king's wife?"

"Whom namest thou leman?" cried the queen.

"Even thee," answered Kriemhild. "For it was Siegfried my husband, and not my brother, that won thee first. Where were thy senses? It was surely ill done to favour a vassal so. Reproaches from thee are much amiss."

"Verily," cried Brunhild, "Gunther shall hear of it."

"What is that to me? Thine arrogancy hath deceived thee. Thou hast called me thy vassal. Know now of a truth it hath irked me, and I am thine enemy evermore."

Then Brunhild began to weep, and Kriemhild tarried not longer, but went with her attendants into the minster before the king's wife. There was deadly hate, and bright eyes grew wet and dim.

Whether they prayed or sang, the service seemed too long to Brunhild, for her heart and her mind were troubled, the which many a bold and good man paid for afterward.

Brunhild stopped before the minster with her women, for she thought, "Kriemhild, the foul-mouthed woman, shall tell me further whereof she so loud accuseth me. If he hath boasted of this thing, he shall answer for it with his life."

Then Kriemhild with her knights came forth, and Brunhild began, "Stop! thou hast called me a wanton and shalt prove it, for know that thy words irk me sore."

Said Kriemhild, "Let me pass. With this gold that I have on my hand I can prove it. Siegfried brought it when he came from thee."

It was a heavy day for Brunhild. She said, "That gold so precious was stolen from me, and hath been hidden these many years. Now I know who hath taken it." Both the women were furious.

"I am no thief," cried Kriemhild. "Hadst thou prized thine honour thou hadst held thy peace, for, with this girdle round my waist, I can prove my word, and that Siegfried was verily thy leman." She wore a girdle of silk of Nineveh, goodly enow, and worked with precious stones.

When Brunhild saw it she started to weep. And soon Gunther knew it, and all his men, for the queen cried, "Bring hither the King of Rhineland; I would tell him how his sister hath mocked me, and sayeth openly that I be Siegfried's leman."

The king came with his warriors, and, when he saw that his dear one wept, he spake kindly, "What aileth thee, dear wife?"

She answered, "Shamed must I stand, for thy sister would part me from mine honour? I make my plaint to thee. She proclaimeth aloud that Siegfried hath had me to his leman."

Gunther answered, "Evilly hath she done."

"She weareth here a girdle that I have long lost, and my red gold. Woe is me that ever I was born! If thou clearest me not from this shame, I will never love thee more."

Said Gunther, "Bid him hither, that he confess whether he hath boasted of this, or no."

They summoned Siegfried, who, when he saw their anger and knew not the cause, spake quickly, "Why weep these women? Tell me straight; and wherefore am I summoned?"

Whereto Gunther answered, "Right vexed am I. Brunhild, my wife, telleth me here that thou hast boasted thou wert her leman. Kriemhild declareth this. Hast thou done it, O knight?"

Siegfried answered, "Not I. If she hath said so, I will rest not till she repent it. I swear with a high oath in the presence of all thy knights, that I said not this one thing."

The king of the Rhine made answer, "So be it. If thou swear the oath here, I will acquit thee of the falsehood." Then the Burgundians stood round in a ring, and Siegfried swore it with his hand; whereupon the great king said, "Verily, I hold thee guiltless, nor lay to thy charge the word my sister imputeth to thee."

Said Siegfried further, "If she rejoiceth to have troubled thy fair wife, I am grieved beyond measure." The knights glanced at each other.

"Women must be taught to bridle their tongues. Forbid proud speech to thy wife: I will do the like to mine. Such bitterness and pride are a shame."

Angry words have divided many women. Brunhild made such dole, that Gunther's men had pity on her. And Hagen of Trony went to her and asked what ailed her, for he found her weeping. She told him the tale, and he sware straightway that Kriemhild's husband should pay for it, or never would Hagen be glad again.

While they talked together, Ortwin and Gernot came up, and the warriors counselled Siegfried's death. But when Giselher, Uta's fair child, drew nigh and heard them, he spake out with true heart, "Alack, good knights, what would ye do? How hath Siegfried deserved such hate that he should lose his life? A woman is lightly angered."

"Shall we rear bastards?" cried Hagen. "That were small honour to good knights. I will avenge on him the boast that he hath made, or I will die."

But the king himself said, "Good, and not evil, hath he done to us. Let him live. Wherefore should I hate the knight? He hath ever been true to me."

"Not so," said Hagen. "Assure thee on that score. For I will contrive secretly that he pay for Brunhild's weeping. Hagen is his foe evermore."

(15) Then went Hagen of Trony to Kriemhild.

"Well for me," said Kriemhild, "that ever I won to husband a man that standeth so true by his friends, as doth Siegfried by my kinsmen. Right proud am I. Bethink thee now, Hagen, dear friend, how that in all things I am at thy service, and have ever willed thee well. Requite me through my husband, that I love, and avenge not on him what I did to Brunhild. Already it repenteth me sore. My body hath smarted for it, that ever I troubled her with my words. Siegfried, the good knight, hath seen to that."

Whereto Hagen answered, "Ye will shortly be at one again. But Kriemhild, prithee tell me wherein I can serve thee with Siegfried, thy husband, and I will do it, for I love none better."

"I should fear naught for his life in battle, but that he is fool-hardy, and of too proud a courage. Save for that, he were safe enow."

Then said Hagen, "Lady, if thou fearest hurt for him in battle, tell me now by what device I may hinder it, and I will guard him afoot and on horse."

She answered, "Thou art my cousin, and I thine. To thy faith I commend my dear husband, that thou mayst watch and keep him."

Then she told him what she had better have left unsaid.

"My husband is stark and bold. When that he slew the dragon on the mountain, he bathed him in its blood; wherefore no weapon can pierce him. Nevertheless, when he rideth in battle, and spears fly from the hands of heroes, I tremble lest I lose him. Alack! for Siegfried's sake how oft have I been heavy of my cheer! And now, dear cousin, I will trust thee with the secret, and tell thee, that thou mayst prove thy faith, where my husband may be wounded. For that I know thee honourable, I do this. When the hot blood flowed from the wound of the dragon, and Siegfried bathed therein, there fell atween his shoulders the broad leaf of a lime tree. There one might stab him, and thence is my care and dole."

Then answered Hagen of Trony, "Sew, with thine own hand, a small sign upon his outer garment, that I may know where to defend him when we stand in battle."

She did it to profit the knight, and worked his doom thereby. She said, "I will sew secretly, with fine silk, a little cross upon his garment, and there, O knight, shalt thou guard to me my husband when ye ride in the thick of the strife, and he withstandeth his foemen in the fierce onset."

"That will I do, dear lady," answered Hagen.

Kriemhild thought to serve Siegfried; so was the hero betrayed.

Then Hagen took his leave and went forth glad; and his king bade him say what he had learned.

"Let us go hunting; for I have learned the secret, and have him in my hand. Wilt thou contrive this?"

"That will I," said the king.

The next morning Siegfried rode to the king, that thanked him.

"I hold thee trustiest of all my friends. Seeing we be quit of war, let us ride a hunting to the Odenwald after the bear and the boar, as I have often done."

Hagen, the false man, had counselled this.

"Let it be told to my guests straightway that I will ride early. Whoso would hunt with me, let him be ready betimes. But if any would tarry behind for pastime with the women, he shall do it, and please me thereby."

Siegfried answered on courtly wise, "I will hunt with thee gladly, and will ride to the forest, if thou lend me a huntsman and some brachs."

(16) But or he set out, and when the hunting-gear was laid ready on the sumpters that they were to take across the Rhine, he went to Kriemhild, and that was right doleful of her cheer. He kissed his lady on the mouth. "God grant I may see thee safe and well again, and thou me. Bide here merry among thy kinsfolk, for I must forth."

Then she thought on the secret she had betrayed to Hagen, but durst not tell him. The queen wept sore that ever she was born, and made measureless dole.

She said, "Go not hunting. Last night I dreamed an evil dream: how that two wild boars chased thee over the heath; and the flowers were red with blood. Have pity on my tears, for I fear some treachery. There be haply some offended, that pursue us with deadly hate. Go not, dear lord; in good faith I counsel it."

But he answered, "Dear love, I go but for a few days. I know not any that beareth me hate. Thy kinsmen will me well, nor have I deserved otherwise at their hand."

"Nay, Siegfried, I fear some mischance. Last night I dreamed an evil dream: how that two mountains fell on thee, and I saw thee no more. If thou goest, thou wilt grieve me bitterly."

But he caught his dear one in his arms and kissed her close; then he took leave of her and rode off.

She never saw him alive again.

Siegfried's horse bare him smoothly, and the others pricked fast behind. The noise roused a grim bear, whereat the knight cried to them that came after him, "Now for sport! Slip the dog, for I see a bear that shall with us to the tryst-fire. He cannot escape us, if he ran ever so fast."

They slipped the limehound; off rushed the bear. Siegfried thought to run him down, but he came to a ravine and could not get to him; then the bear deemed him safe. But the proud knight sprang from his horse, and pursued him. The beast had no shelter. It could not escape from him, and was caught by his hand, and, or it could wound him, he had bound it, that it could neither scratch nor bite. Then he tied it to his saddle, and, when he had mounted up himself, he brought it to the tryst-fire for pastime.

When he had alighted, he loosed the band from the paws and from the mouth of the bear that he had bound to his saddle.

So soon as they saw the bear, the dogs began to bark. The animal tried to win back to the wood, and all the folk fell in great fear. Affrighted by the noise, it ran through the kitchen. Nimbly started the scullions from their place by the fire. Pots were upset and the brands strewed over all. Alack! the good meats that tumbled into the ashes!

Then up sprang the princes and their men. The bear began to growl, and the king gave order to slip the hounds that were on leash. I' faith, it had been a merry day if it had ended so.

Hastily, with their bows and spears, the warriors, swift of foot, chased the bear, but there were so many dogs that none durst shoot among them, and the forest rang with the din. Then the bear fled before the dogs, and none could keep pace with him save Kriemhild's husband, that ran up to him and pierced him dead with his sword, and carried the carcase back with him to the fire. They that saw it said he was a mighty man.

Then they bade the sportsmen to the table, and they sat down a goodly company enow, on a fair meadow. Ha! what dishes, meet for heroes, were set before them. But the cup-bearers were tardy, that should have brought the wine. Save for that, knights were never better served. If there had not been false-hearted men among them, they had been without reproach. The doomed man had no suspicion that might have warned him, for his own heart was pure of all deceit. Many that his death profited not at all had to pay for it bitterly.

Then said Sir Siegfried, "I marvel, since they bring us so much from the kitchen, that they bring not the wine. If good hunters be entreated so, I will hunt no more. Certes, I have deserved better at your hands."

Whereto the king at the table answered falsely, "What lacketh to-day we will make good another time. The blame is Hagen's, that would have us perish of thirst."

Then said Hagen of Trony, "Dear master, methought we were to hunt to-day at Spessart, and I sent the wine thither. For the present we must go thirsty; another time I will take better care."

But Siegfried cried, "Small thank to him. Seven sumpters with meat and spiced wines should he have sent here at the least, or, if that might not be, we should have gone nigher to the Rhine."

Hagen of Trony answered, "I know of a cool spring close at hand. Be not wroth with me, but take my counsel, and go thither." The which was done, to the hurt of many warriors. Siegfried was sore athirst and bade push back the table, that he might go to the spring at the foot of the mountain. Falsely had the knights contrived it. The wild beasts that Siegfried's hand had slain they let pile on a waggon and take home, and all they that saw it praised him.

Foully did Hagen break faith with Siegfried. He said, when they were starting for the broad lime tree, "I hear from all sides that none can keep pace with Kriemhild's husband when he runneth. Let us see now."

Bold Siegfried of the Netherland answered, "Thou mayst easily prove it, if thou wilt run with me to the brook for a wager. The praise shall be to him that winneth there first."

"Let us see then," said Hagen the knight.

And stark Siegfried answered, "If I lose, I will lay me at thy feet in the grass."

A glad man was King Gunther when he heard that!

Said Siegfried further, "Nay, I will undertake more. I will carry on me all that I wear — spear, shield, and hunting gear." Whereupon he girded on his sword and his quiver in haste. Then the others did off their clothes, till they stood in their white shirts, and they ran through the clover like two wild panthers; but bold Siegfried was seen there the first. Before all men he won the prize in everything. He loosed his sword straightway, and laid down his quiver. His good spear he leaned against the lime tree; then the noble guest stood and waited, for his courtesy was great. He laid down his shield by the stream. Albeit he was sore athirst, he drank not till that the king had finished, who gave him evil thanks.

The stream was cool, pure, and good. Gunther bent down to the water, and rose again when he had drunk. Siegfried had gladly done the like, but he suffered for his courtesy. Hagen carried his bow and his sword out of his reach, and sprang back and gripped the spear. Then he spied for the secret mark on his vesture; and while Siegfried drank from the stream, Hagen stabbed him where the cross was, that his heart's blood spurted out on the traitor's clothes. Never since hath knight done so wickedly. He left the spear sticking deep in his heart, and fled in grimmer haste than ever he had done from any man on this earth afore.

When stark Siegfried felt the deep wound, he sprang up maddened from the water, for the long boar spear stuck out from his heart. He thought to find bow or sword; if he had, Hagen had got his due. But the sore-wounded man saw no sword, and had nothing save his shield. He picked it up from the water's edge and ran at Hagen. King Gunther's man could not escape him. For all that he was wounded to the death, he smote mightily that the shield well-nigh brake, and the precious stones flew out. The noble guest had fain taken vengeance.

Hagen fell beneath his stroke. The meadow rang loud with the noise of the blow. If he had had his sword to hand, Hagen had been a dead man. But the anguish of his wound constrained him. His colour was wan; he could not stand upright; and the strength of his body failed him, for he bare death's mark on his white cheek. Fair women enow made dole for him.

Then Kriemhild's husband fell among the flowers. The blood flowed fast from his wound, and in his great anguish he began to upbraid them that had falsely contrived his death. "False cowards!" cried the dying knight. "What availeth all my service to you, since ye have slain me? I was true to you, and pay the price for it. Ye have done ill by your friends. Cursed by this deed are your sons yet unborn. Ye have avenged your spite on my body all too bitterly. For your crime ye shall be shunned by good knights."

All the warriors ran where he lay stabbed. To many among them it was a woeful day. They that were true mourned for him, the which the hero had well deserved of all men.

The King of Burgundy also wept for his death, but the dying man said, "He needeth not to weep for the evil, by whom the evil cometh. Better had he left it undone, for mickle is his blame."

Then said grim Hagen, "I know not what ye rue. All is ended for us — care and trouble. Few are they now that will withstand us. Glad am I that, through me, his might is fallen."

"Lightly mayst thou boast now," said Siegfried; "if I had known thy murderous hate, it had been an easy thing to guard my body from thee. My bitterest dole is for Kriemhild, my wife. God pity me that ever I had a son. For all men will reproach him that he hath murderers to his kinsmen. I would grieve for that, had I the time."

He said to the king, "Never in this world was so foul a murder as thou hast done on me. In thy sore need I saved thy life and thine honour. Dear have I paid for that I did well by thee." With a groan the wounded man said further, "Yet if thou canst show truth to any on this earth, O King, show it to my dear wife, that I commend to thee. Let it advantage her to be thy sister. By all princely honour stand by her. Long must my father and my knights wait for my coming. Never hath woman won such woe through a dear one."

He writhed in his bitter anguish, and spake painfully, "Ye shall rue this foul deed in the days to come. Know this of a truth, that in slaying me ye have slain yourselves."

The flowers were all wet with blood. He strove with death, but not for long, for the weapon of death cut too deep. And the bold knight and good spake no more.

When the warriors saw that the hero was dead, they laid him on a shield of ruddy gold, and took counsel how they should conceal that Hagen had done it. Many of them said, "Evil hath befallen us. Ye shall all hide it, and hold to one tale — when Kriemhild's husband was riding alone in the forest, robbers slew him."

But Hagen of Trony said, "I will take him back to Burgundy. If she that hath troubled Brunhild know it, I care not. It concerneth me little if she weep."

Of that very brook where Siegfried was slain ye shall hear the truth from me. In the Odenwald is a village that hight Odenheim, and there the stream runneth still; beyond doubt it is the same.

(17) They tarried there that night, and then crossed the Rhine. Heroes never went to so woeful a hunt. For one thing that they slew, many women wept, and many a good knight's body paid for it. Of overweening pride ye shall hear now, and grim vengeance.

Hagen bade them bear dead Siegfried of the Nibelung land before the chamber where Kriemhild was, and charged them to lay him secretly outside the door, that she might find him there when she went forth to mass or it was day, the which she was wont to do.

The minster bell was rung as the custom was. Fair Kriemhild waked her maidens, and bade them bring her a light and her vesture.

Then a chamberlain came and found Siegfried. He saw him red with blood, and his garment all wet, but he knew not yet that he was his king. He carried the light into the room in his hand, and from him Kriemhild heard evil tidings.

When she would have gone with her women to the minster, the chamberlain said, "Lady, stop! A murdered knight lieth on the threshold."

"Woe is me!" cried Kriemhild. "What meanest thou by such news?"

Or she knew for certain that it was her husband, she began to think on Hagen's question, how he might guard him. From that moment her dole began; for, with his death, she took leave of all joy. She sank on the floor speechless; they saw the miserable woman lying there. Kriemhild's woe was great beyond measure, and after her swoon she cried out, that all the chamber rang.

Then said her attendants, "What if it be a stranger?"

But the blood burst from her mouth by reason of her heart's anguish, and she said, "Nay, it is Siegfried, my dear husband. Brunhild hath counselled it, and Hagen hath done it."

Gunther said, "Dear sister, woe is me for this grief of thine, and that this great misadventure hath befallen us.  We must ever mourn Siegfried's death."

"Ye do wrongly," said the wailing queen.  "If it grieved thee, it had never happed.  I was clean forgotten by thee when thou didst part me from my dear husband.  Would to God thou hadst done it to me instead!"

But they held to their lie, and Kriemhild went on, "Let him that is guiltless prove it.  Let him go up to the bier before all the folk, and soon we shall know the truth."

It is a great marvel, and ofttimes seen even now, how that, when the murderer standeth by the dead, the wounds bleed again.  And so it fell then, and Hagen's guilt was plain to all.

The wounds burst open and bled as they had done afore; and they that had wept already wept now much more.  King Gunther said, "Hear the truth.  He was slain by robbers.  Hagen did it not."

"These robbers," she answered, "I know well.  God grant that his kinsmen's hands may avenge it.  By you, Gunther and Hagen, was it done."

(19)  When noble Kriemhild was widowed, Count Eckewart stayed by her in Burgundy with his men, as honour bade him, and served his mistress with goodwill till his death.

At Worms, by the minster, they gave her a room, wide and high, rich and spacious, where she sat joyless with her attendants.  To church she went often and gladly.  Since her dear one was buried, how seldom she failed there!  She went thither sorrowfully every day, and prayed to great God for his soul.  Faithfully and without stint the knight was mourned.

Soon after, they contrived that Kriemhild won the great hoard from the land of the Nibelungs, and brought it to the Rhine.  It was her marriage-morning gift, and rightly hers.  Giselher and Gernot went for it.  Kriemhild sent eighty hundred men to fetch it from where it lay hid, and where Albric with his nearest kinsmen guarded it.

When they saw the men of the Rhine come for the treasure, bold Albric spake to his friends, "We dare not refuse her the treasure, for it is the noble queen's wedding gift.  Yet we had never parted with it, if we had not lost with Siegfried the good *Tarnkappe*.  At all times it was worn by fair Kriemhild's husband.  A woeful thing hath it proved for Siegfried that he took from us the *Tarnkappe,* and won all this land to his service."

Then the chamberlain went and got the keys.  Kriemhild's men and some of her kinsmen stood before the mountain.  They carried the hoard to the sea, on to the ships, and bare it across the waves from the mountain to the Rhine.

Now hear the marvels of this treasure.  Twelve waggons scarce carried it thence in four days and four nights, albeit each of them made the journey three times.  It was all precious stones and gold, and had the whole world been bought therewith, there had not been one coin the less.   Certes, Hagen did not covet it without cause.

The wishing-rod lay among it, the which, if any discovered it, made him master over every man in all the world.

Many of Albric's kinsmen went with Gernot.   When Gernot and Giselher the youth got possession of the hoard, there came into their power lands, and castles, also, and many a good warrior, that served them through fear of their might.

When the hoard came into Gunther's land, and the queen got it in her keeping, chambers and towers were filled full therewith.   One never heard tell of so marvelous a treasure.   But if it had been a thousand times more, but to have Siegfried alive again, Kriemhild had gladly stood bare by his side.   Never had hero truer wife.

Now that she had the hoard, it brought into the land many stranger knights; for the lady's hand gave more freely than any had ever seen. She was kind and good; that must one say of her.

To poor and rich she began to give, till Hagen said that if she lived but a while longer, she would win so many knights to her service that it must go hard with the others.

But King Gunther said, "It is her own.   It concerneth me not how she useth it.   Scarcely did I win her pardon.   And now I ask not who she divideth her jewels and her red gold."

But Hagen said to the king, "A wise man would leave such a treasure to no woman.   By reason of her largess, a day will come that the bold Burgundians may rue."

Then King Gunther said, "I sware an oath to her that I would do her no more hurt, nor will I do it.   She is my sister."

But Hagen said, "Let me be the guilty one."

And so they brake their oath and took from the widow her rich hoard.   Hagen got hold of all the keys.

Gernot was wroth when he heard thereof, and Giselher said, "Hagen hath greatly wronged Kriemhild.   I should have withstood him.   Were he not my kinsman, he should answer for it with his life."

Then Siegfried's wife began to weep anew.

And Gernot said, "Sooner than be troubled with this gold, let us sink it in the Rhine.   Then it were no man's."

She went wailing to Giselher, and said, "Dear brother, forsake me not, but be my kind and good steward."

He answered her, "I will, when we win home again.   For the present we ride on a journey."

The king and his kinsmen left the land.   He took the best he had with him.   Only Hagen tarried behind through the hate he bare Kriemhild, and that he might work her ill.

Or the great king came back, Hagen had seized all the treasure and sunk it in the Rhine at Lochheim.   He thought to profit thereby, but did not.

Or Hagen hid the treasure, they had sworn a mighty oath that it should remain a secret so long as they lived.   Neither could they take it themselves nor give it to another.

(20)   It was in the days when Queen Helca died, and King Etzel wooed other women, that his friends commended to him a proud widow in the land of Burgundy, that hight Queen Kriemhild.

Seeing fair Helca was dead, they said, "If thou wouldst win a noble wife, the highest and the best that ever a king won, take this woman. Stark Siegfried was her husband."

The great king answered, "How could that be, since I am a heathen, and have not received baptism?   The woman is a Christian — she will not consent.   It were a wonder, truly, if it came to pass."

But the good knights said, "What if she do it gladly, for thy high name's sake, and thy great possessions?   One can ask her at the least; she were a fitting and comely mate for thee."

Then the noble king answered, "Which among ye knoweth the folk by the Rhine, and their land?"

Said good Rudeger of Bechlaren, "From a child I have known the high and noble kings, Gunther and Gernot, good knights both. The third hight Giselher; each of these doeth whatso goeth best with honour and virtue.   The like did their fathers."

He said, "Then woo her, Rudeger, in my name and for my sake. And come I ever to wed Kriemhild, I will reward thee as I best can. Thereto, thou wilt have done my will faithfully.   From my store I will bid them give thee what thou requirest of horses and apparel, that thou and thy fellows may live merrily.   They shall give thee therefrom without stint for thine embassy."

Within twelve days they came to the Rhine.   The news was not slow to spread.   They told the king and his men that stranger guests had arrived.   Then the king began to ask that, if any knew them, he might declare it.   They perceived that their sumpters were heavy laden, and saw that they were rich; and they gave them lodging in the wide city straightway.

When the strangers arrived, the folk spied at them curiously.   They wondered whence they had journeyed to the Rhine.

The king asked Hagen who the knights were, and the hero of Trony answered, "So far as I know, for it is long since I saw the knights, they ride like the men of Rudeger, a bold warrior from the land of the Huns."

Then said the faithful envoy, "My great lord commendeth his true service to thee at the Rhine, and to all the friends thou hast. This he doth with true heart.   The noble king biddeth thee mourn for his loss.   His people are joyless, for my mistress, great Helca, my lord's wife is dead; whereby many high-born maidens, children of great princes, that she hath reared, are orphaned.   By reason thereof the land is full of sorrow, for these, alack! have none now to care for them.   The king also ceaseth not to make dole."

Then said Gernot of Burgundy, "The world may well rue beautiful Helca's death, for the sake of her many virtues."

Hagen and many another knight said the same.

But Rudeger, the noble envoy, went on: "If thou allow it, O king,

I will tell thee further what my dear master hath charged me with. Dolefully hath he lived since Helca's death. And it hath been told him that Kriemhild is without a husband, for that Siegfried is dead. If that be so, and thou grant it, she shall wear the crown before Etzel's knights. This hath my lord bidden me say."

Then the great king spake courteously, "If she be willing, she followeth my desire therein. In three days I will let thee know. If she say not nay to Etzel, wherefore should I?"

Meanwhile they gave the guests good lodging. On such wise were they entreated that Rudeger was fain to confess he had friends among Gunther's men. Hagen served him gladly, the which Rudeger had done to Hagen aforetime.

So Rudeger tarried there till the third day. The king did prudently, and called a counsel, to ask his friends whether it seemed good to them that Kriemhild should take King Etzel to husband.

And they all counselled it save Hagen, that said to Gunther, the bold knight, "If thou be wise, thou wilt see to it that she do it not, even if she desire it."

"Why should I hinder it?" said Gunther. "If any good fall to the queen, I may well grant it. She is my sister. If it be to her honour, we ourselves should seek the alliance."

But Hagen answered, "Say not so. Didst thou know Etzel as I do, thou wouldst see that thou, first of all, must suffer if she wedded him as thou counsellest."

"How so?" answered Gunther. "Were she his wife, I need not come so nigh him that I must feel his hate."

But Hagen said, "I will never approve it."

They summoned Gernot and Giselher, and asked whether it seemed good to them that Kriemhild should take the great king. And none save Hagen was against it.

Gernot and Giselher, the proud knights and good, and Gunther, the great king, agreed in the end, that they would allow it gladly, if Kriemhild were so minded.

They brought Rudeger to Kriemhild. And the knight asked the queen gently to let him bear the message she sent to Etzel. He won nothing from her but denial, for never could she love another man.

Then said the Margrave, "That were ill done. Wherefore ruin so fair a body? Still mayest thou with honour become a good man's wife." Yet all their entreaty availed not, till that Rudeger said secretly to the queen that he would make good to her any hurt that might befall her. At that, her grief abated somewhat.

He said to the queen, "Weep no more. If thou hadst none among the Huns save me, by faithful kinsmen, and my men, sore must he pay for it that did thee wrong."

Much milder was the lady's mood, and she said, "Swear me an oath that, should any do aught against me, thou wilt be the first to avenge it."

The Margrave answered, "I will swear."

So Rudeger swore with all his men alway to serve her truly, and to deny her nothing in Etzel's land that her honour called for, and he confirmed it with his hand.

Then thought the faithful woman, "Since I, a forlorn woman, can win so many friends, I will let the folk say what they please. Haply I may yet avenge my dear husband's death. Etzel hath so many knights, that, were they mine to command, I could do what I would. Thereto, he is so wealthy that I shall have wherewith to bestow gifts. Cruel Hagen hath taken my treasure from me."

She said to Rudeger, "Had I not heard he was a heathen, I would go gladly at his bidding, and take him to husband."

The Margrave answered, "Say no more of that, Lady. He is not quite a heathen, be assured, for my dear master hath been christened; albeit he hath turned again. Haply he will think better of it shouldst thou wed him. He hath so many Christian knights that no ill could betide thee. And thou mightst easily win back the good prince, heart and soul, to God."

Her brothers said, "Promise it, sister, and give over grieving."

They begged it so long that at the last the sorrowful woman promised, before the warriors, to become Etzel's wife.

She said, "Poor queen that I am, I will follow you! I will go to the Huns, if I find friends to lead me thither." Fair Kriemhild gave her hand on it before the knights.

(22) Etzel's household, that Helca had aforetime ruled, passed many a happy day with Kriemhild. Noble maidens stood waiting, that since Helca's death had suffered heart's dole. Kriemhild found there seven kings' daughters that were an adornment to Etzel's whole land. The charge of the damsels was with Herrat, Helca's sister's daughter, famed for virtue, and the betrothed of Dietrich, a noble king's child, the daughter of Nentwine; the which afterward had much worship. Glad of her cheer was she at the coming of the guests, and many a goodly thing was made ready. What tongue might tell how merrily King Etzel dwelled there? Never under any queen fared the Huns better.

When the king rode up with his wife from the strand, Kriemhild was told the name of them that led forward the maidens, that she might greet them the more fitly. Ha! how mightily she ruled in Helca's stead! She had true servants in plenty. The queen gave gold and vesture, silver and precious stones. All that she had brought with her from over the Rhine to the Huns, she divided among them. All the king's kinsmen and liegemen vowed their service to her, and were subject to her, so that Helca herself had never ruled so mightily as Kriemhild, that they had all to serve till her death.

So famous was the court and the country, that each found there, at all times, the pastime he desired; so kind was the king and so good the queen.

(23) So in high honour (I say sooth), they dwelled together till the seventh year. Meanwhile Kriemhild had borne a son. Nothing

could have rejoiced Etzel more. She set her heart on it that he should receive Christian baptism. He was named Ortlieb, and glad was all Etzel's land.

When now she saw that none withstood her (the which a king's knights will sometimes do to their prince's wife), and that twelve kings stood ever before her, she thought on the grievous wrongs that had befallen her in her home. She remembered also the honour that was hers among the Nibelungs, and that Hagen's hand had robbed her of by Siegfried's death, and she pondered how she might work him woe.

One night, when she lay by the king, and he held her in his arms, as was his wont, for she was to him as his life, the royal woman thought on her foes, and said to him, "My dearest lord, I would fain beg a boon of thee. I would have thee show, if I have deserved it at thy hand, that my kinsmen have found favour in thy sight."

The great king answered with true heart, "That will I readily prove to thee. All that profiteth and doth honour to the knights rejoiceth me, for through no woman's love have I won better friends."

Then said the queen, "Thou knowest well that I have noble kinsmen. It irketh me that they visit me so seldom. The folk here deem me kinless."

Whereto King Etzel answered, "If it seem good to thee, dearest wife, I will send my minstrels as envoys to thy friends in Burgundy."

He bade summon the good fiddlers straightway, that hasted to where he sat by the queen, and he told them both to go as envoys to Burgundy.

Then said the great king, "I will tell ye what ye shall do. I send to my friends love and every good wish, and pray them to ride hither to my land. I know few other guests so dear. And if Kriemhild's kinsmen be minded to do my will, bid them fail not to come, for love of me, to my hightide, for my heart yearneth toward the brethren of my wife."

Whereto Schwemmel, the proud minstrel, answered, "When shall thy hightide fall, that we may tell thy friends yonder?"

King Etzel said, "Next midsummer."

"Thy command shall be obeyed," answered Werbel.

The queen bade summon the envoys secretly to her chamber, and spake with them. Little good came thereof. She said to the two envoys, "Ye shall deserve great reward if ye do my bidding well, and deliver the message wherewith I charge you, at home, in my land. I will make you rich in goods, and give you sumptuous apparel. See that ye say not to any of my friends at Worms, by the Rhine, that ye have ever seen me sad of my cheer, and commend my service to the heroes bold and good. Beg them to grant the king's prayer and end all my sorrow. The Huns deem me without kin. Were I a knight, I would go to them myself. Say to Gernot, my noble brother, that none is better minded to him in the world than I.

Bid him bring here our best friends, that we win honour. And tell Giselher to remember that never, through his fault, did ill betide me; for which reason mine eyes are fain to behold him. Evermore I would serve him. Tell my mother, also, what worship is mine. And if Hagen of Trony tarry behind who shall lead them through the land? From a child up he hath known the roads hither to the Huns."

The envoys guessed not why she could not leave Hagen of Trony at the Rhine. They knew it afterward to their cost, for, through him, many a knight was brought face to face with grim death.

Letters and greetings were given to them. They rode forth rich in goods, that they might live merrily by the way. They took leave of Etzel and his fair wife. Their bodies were adorned with goodly vesture.

(24) Within twelve days Werbel and Schwemmel reached Worms on the Rhine. And the kings and their men were told the news, that foreign envoys were come.

The gracious prince greeted them, and said, "Ye are both welcome, Etzel's minstrels, ye and your followers. Wherefore hath the mighty Etzel sent you into Burgundy?"

They bowed before him, and Werbel answered, "First of all, we are sent to the king, to invite you to ride into Etzel's land, and Sir Gernot with you. Mighty Etzel commanded me to say to you all that, even if ye desire not to see your sister, he would fain learn what wrong he hath done you, that ye are such strangers to him and his court. Had ye never known the queen, he deserveth no less of you than that ye come to see him. If ye consent to this, ye shall please him well."

And Gunther answered, "A sennight from now I will let thee know what I and my friends have determined on. Go meanwhile to thy lodging and rest."

The Huns went to their lodging. Meanwhile, the great king had sent for his friends, and noble Gunther asked his men how the message pleased them. And many of them began to say that he might well ride into Etzel's land. The best among them counselled him thereto — all save Hagen. Him it irked exceedingly. He said to the king apart, "Ye strike at your own life. Surely ye know what we have done. Evermore we stand in danger from Kriemhild. I smote her husband dead with my hand. How dare we ride into Etzel's land?"

But the great king answered, "My sister forgot her anger. With a loving kiss she forgave us for all we had done to her or she rode away. Hath she aught against any, it is against thee alone, Hagen."

"Be not deceived," said Hagen, "by the words of the Hunnish envoys. If thou goest to see Kriemhild, thou mayst lose thine honour and thy life. The wife of King Etzel hath a long memory."

Then Gernot spake out before the assembly, "Because thou fearest death with reason among the Huns, it were ill done on our part to keep away from our sister."

And Sir Giselher said to the knight, "Since thou knowest thyself guilty, friend Hagen, stay thou at home, and guard thyself well, and let them that dare, journey with us to the Huns."

Then the knight of Trony fell in a passion. "None that ye take with you will be readier to ride to the court than I. And well I will prove it, since ye will not be turned."

But knight Rumolt, the cook, said, "Strangers and friends ye can entertain at home, at your pleasure. For here is abundance. Hagen, I trow, hath never held you back afore. If ye will not follow him in this, be counselled by Rumolt (for your true and loving servant am I) and tarry here as I would have ye do, and leave King Etzel yonder by Kriemhild. Where in the wide world could ye be better? Here ye are safe from your enemies. Ye can adorn your bodies with goodly vesture, drink the best wine, and woo fair women. Thereto, ye are given meats, the best on earth that ever king ate. The land is prosperous. Ye may give up Etzel's hightide with honour, and live merrily at home with your friends. Even had ye nothing else to feast on here, I could always give you your fill of one dish — cutlets fried in oil. This is Rumolt's advice, my masters, since there is danger among the Huns."

And there were many that would not go, and said, "God guard you among the Huns."

The king was wroth when he saw they desired to take their ease at home. "We will go none the less. The prudent are safe in the midst of danger."

Hagen answered, "Be not wroth at my word. Whatever betide, I counsel thee in good faith to ride strongly armed to the Huns. Since thou wilt not be turned, summon the best men thou canst find, or knowest of, among thy vassals, and from among them I will choose a thousand good knights, that thou come not in scathe by Kriemhild's anger."

Kriemhild's envoys were bidden to Gunther's presence. When they appeared, Gernot said, "The king will obey Etzel's wish. We go gladly to his hightide to see our sister. She may count on us."

Gunther asked, "Can ye tell us when the hightide falleth, or when we must set forth?"

And Schwemmel answered, "Next midsummer, without fail."

The king gave them leave, for the first time, to visit Brunhild, but Folker, to please her, said them nay.

(25) Hagen counselled them now to the journey, but he rued it later. He had withstood them, but that Gernot had mocked him. He minded him on Siegfried, Kriemhild's husband, and said, "It is for that, that Hagen durst not go."

But Hagen said, "I hold not back from fear. If ye will have it so, heroes, go forward. I am ready to ride with you to Etzel's land." Soon many a helmet and shield were pierced by him.

The Christian faith was still weak in those days. Nevertheless they had a chaplain with them to say mass. He returned alive, escaped from much peril. The rest tarried dead among the Huns.

Gunther's men shaped their course toward the Main, up through East Frankland. Hagen led them, that knew the way well. Their marshal was Dankwart, the knight of Burgundy. As they rode from East Frankland to Schwanfeld, the princes and their kinsmen, knights of worship, were known by their stately mien.

On the twelfth morning the king reached the Danube. Hagen of Trony rode in front of the rest. He was the helper and comforter of the Nibelungs. The bold knight alighted there on the bank, and tied his horse to a tree. The river was swoln, there was no boat, and the knights were troubled how to win across. The water was too wide. Many a bold knight sprang to the ground.

"Mischief might easily befall thee here, King of Rhineland," said Hagen; "thou canst see for thyself that the river is swoln, and the current very strong. I fear me we shall lose here to-day not a few good knights."

Then he sought the ferrymen up and down. He heard the splash of water and began to listen. It came from mermaidens that bathed their bodies in a clear brook to cool them.

Hagen spied them, and stole up secretly. When they were ware of him, they fled. Well pleased were they to escape him. The hero took their garments, but did them no further annoy.

Then one of the mermaids (she hight Hadburg) said, "We will tell thee, noble Hagen, if thou give us our clothes again, how ye shall all fare on this journey among the Huns."

They swayed like birds in the water before him. He deemed them wise and worthy of belief, so that he trusted the more what they told him. They informed him concerning all he asked them. Hadburg said, "Ye may ride safely into Etzel's land; I pledge my faith thereon, that never yet heroes journeyed to any court to win more worship. I say sooth."

Hagen's heart was uplifted at her word; he gave them back their clothes and stayed no longer. When they had put on their wonderful raiment, they told him the truth about the journey.

The other mermaid, that hight Sieglind, said, "Be warned, Hagen, son of Aldrian. My aunt hath lied to thee because of her clothes. If ye go to the Huns, ye are ill-advised. Turn while there is time, for ye bold knights have been bidden that ye may die in Etzel's land. Who rideth thither hath death at his hand."

But Hagen said, "Your deceit is vain. How should we all tarry there, dead, through the hate of one woman?"

Then they began to foretell it plainer, and Hadburg said also, "Ye are doomed. Not one of you shall escape, save the king's chaplain: this we know for a truth. He, only, shall return alive into Gunther's land."

Grimly wroth spake bold Hagen then. "It were a pleasant thing to tell my masters that we must all perish among the Huns! Show us a way across the water, thou wisest of womankind."

She answered, "Since thou wilt not be turned from the journey, up yonder by the river standeth an inn. Within it is a boatman; there is none beside."

He betook him thither to ask further. But the mermaiden cried after the wrothful knight, "Stay, Sir Hagen. Thou art too hasty. Hearken first concerning the way. The lord of this march hight Elsy. The name of his brother is Gelfrat, a prince in Bavaria. It might go hard with thee if thou wentest through his march. Look well to thyself, and proceed warily with the boatman. He is so grim of his mood that he will kill thee, if thou speak him not fair. If thou wouldst have him ferry thee across, give him hire. He guardeth this land, and is Gelfrat's friend. If he come not straightway, cry across the river to him that thou art Amelrich; he was a good knight, that a feud drove from this land. The boatman will come when he heareth that name."

Proud Hagen thanked the women for their warning and their counsel, and said no more. He went up the river's bank, till he came to an inn that stood on the far side. He began to shout across the water, "Boatman, row me over, and I will give thee, for thy meed, an armlet of red gold. I must across."

The boatman was so rich that he needed not to serve for hire, and seldom took reward from any. His men also were overweening, and Hagen was left standing on the bank of the river.

Thereupon he shouted so loud that all the shore rang with it. He was a stark man. "Row across for Amelrich. I am Elsy's liegeman, that, for a feud, fled the country." He swung the armlet aloft on his sword — it was of red gold, bright and shining — that they might ferry him over to Gelfrat's march. At this the haughty boatman himself took the oar, for he was greedy and covetous of gain, the which bringeth oft to a bad end. He thought to win Hagen's red gold, but won, in lieu thereof, a grim death by his sword.

He rowed over to the shore with mighty strokes. When he found not him that had been named, he fell in a fury; he saw Hagen, and spake wrothfully to the hero, "Thy name may be Amelrich, but, or I greatly err, thy face is none of his. By one father and one mother he was my brother. Since thou hast deceived me, thou canst stay where thou art."

"Nay, for the love of God," said Hagen. "I am a stranger knight that have the charge of other warriors. Take thy fee and row me over, for I am a friend."

But the boatman answered, "I will not. My dear masters have foemen, wherefore I must bring no stranger across. If thou lovest thy life, step out on to the shore again."

"Nay now," said Hagen, "I am sore bested. Take, as a keepsake, this goodly gold, and ferry us over with our thousand horses and our many men."

But the grim boatman answered, "Never!" He seized an oar, mickle and broad, and smote Hagen (soon he rued it), that he staggered and fell on his knees. Seldom had he of Trony encountered so grim a ferryman. Further, to anger the bold stranger, he brake a boat-pole over his head, for he was a strong man. But he did it to his own hurt.

Grimly wroth, Hagen drew a weapon from the sheath, and cut off his head, and threw it on the ground. The Burgundians were soon ware of the tidings.

In the same moment that he slew the ferryman, the boat was caught by the current, which irked him no little, for he was weary or he could bring her head round, albeit Gunther's man rowed stoutly. With swift strokes he sought to turn it, till the oar brake in his hand. He strove to reach the knights on the strand, but had no other oar. Ha! how nimbly he bound it together with the thong of his shield, a narrow broidered band, and rowed to a wood down the river.

There he found his masters waiting on the beach. Many a valiant knight ran to meet him, and greeted him joyfully. But when they saw the boat full of blood from the grim wound he had given the ferryman, they began to question him.

When Gunther saw the hot blood heaving in the boat, he said quickly, "Tell me what thou hast done with the ferryman. I ween he hath fallen by thy strength."

But he answered with a lie, "I found the boat by a waste meadow, and loosed it. I have seen no ferryman this day, nor hath any suffered hurt at my hand."

Then said Sir Gernot of Burgundy, "I am heavy of my cheer because of the dear friends that must die or night, for boatmen we have none. Sorrowfully I stand, nor know how we shall win over."

But Hagen cried, "Lay down your burdens on the grass, ye squires. I was the best boatman by the Rhine, and safe, I trow, I shall bring you into Gelfrat's land."

That they might cross the quicker, they drave in the horses. These swam so well that none were drowned, albeit a few, grown weary, were borne down some length by the tide. Then they carried their gold and harness on board, since they must needs make the passage. Hagen was the helmsman, and steered many a gallant knight to the unknown land. First he took over a thousand, and thereto his own band of warriors. Then followed more: nine thousand squires. The knight of Trony was not idle that day. The ship was huge, strongly built and wide enow. Five hundred of their folk and more, with their meats and weapons, it carried easily at a time. Many a good warrior that day pulled sturdily at the oar.

When he had brought them safe across the water, the bold knight and good thought on the strange prophecy of the wild mermaids. Through this the king's chaplain came nigh to lose his life. He found the priest beside the sacred vessels, leaning with his hand upon the holy relics. This helped him not. When Hagen saw him, it went hard with the poor servant of God. He threw him out of the ship on the instant. Many cried, "Stop, Hagen, stop!" Giselher, the youth, was very wroth, but Hagen ceased not, till he had done him a hurt.

Then stark Gernot of Burgundy said, "What profiteth thee the chaplain's death, Hagen? Had another done this, he had paid dear for it. What hast thou against the priest?"

The chaplain swam with all his might. He had gotten on board again had any helped him. But none could do it, for stark Hagen pushed him fiercely under. None approved his deed.

When the poor man saw that they would not aid him, he turned and made for the shore. He was in sore peril. But, albeit he could not swim, the hand of God upbore him, that he won safe to the dry land again. There he stood, and shook his clothes.

By this sign Hagen knew there was no escape from what the wild women of the sea had foretold. He thought, "These knights be all dead men."

When they had unloaded the ship, and brought all across that belonged to the three kings, Hagen brake it in pieces and threw these on the water. Much the bold knights marvelled thereat.

"Wherefore dost thou so, brother?" said Dankwart. "How shall we get over when we ride home from the Huns to the Rhine?"

Hagen told him, after, that that would never be, but for the meantime he said, "I did it a-purpose. If we have any coward with us on this journey, that would forsake us in our need, he shall die a shameful death in these waves."

(26) Then they rode into Rudeger's country. When Rudeger had heard the news, he was glad.

(27) The Margrave went to find his wife and daughter, and told them the good news that he had heard, how that their queen's brethren were coming to the house.

"Dear love," said Rudeger, "receive the high and noble kings well when they come here with their followers. Hagen, Gunther's man, thou shalt also greet fair. There is one with them that hight Dankwart; another hight Folker, a man of much worship. These six thou shalt kiss — thou and my daughter. Entreat the warriors courteously."

The women promised it, nothing loath. They took goodly apparel from their chests, wherein to meet the knights. The fair women made haste enow. Their cheeks needed little false colour. They wore fillets of bright gold on their heads, fashioned like rich wreaths, that the wind might not ruffle their beautiful hair. They were dainty and fresh.

The noble Margravine came out before the castle with her beautiful daughter. Lovely women and fair maids not a few stood beside her, adorned with bracelets and fine apparel. Precious stones sparked bright on their rich vesture. Goodly was their raiment.

The guests rode up and sprang to the ground.  Ha! courteous men all were they of Burgundy!  Six and thirty maidens and many women beside, fair to heart's desire, came forth to meet them, with bold men in plenty.  The noble women welcomed them sweetly. The Margravine kissed the kings all three.  Her daughter did the like.  Hagen stood by.  Him also her father bade her kiss.  She looked up at him, and he was so grim that she had gladly let it be. Yet must she do as the host bade her.  Her colour came and went, white and red.  She kissed Dankwart, too, and, after him, the fiddler. By reason of his body's strength he won this greeting.  Then the young Margravine took Giselher, the youth of Burgundy, by the hand. Her mother did the same to Gunther, and they went in merrily with the heroes.

The host led Gernot into a wide hall.  There knights and ladies sat down, and good wine was poured out for the guests.  Never were warriors better entreated.

Rudeger's daughter was looked at with loving eyes, she was so fair; and many a good knight loved her in his heart.  And well they might, for she was an high-hearted maiden.  But their thoughts were vain: it could not be.

Women and knights were parted then, as was the custom, and went into separate rooms.  The table was made ready in the great hall, and willing service was done to the strangers.

To show love to the guests, the Margravine went to table with them.  She left her daughter with the damsels, as was seemly, albeit it irked the guests to see her no longer.

When they had all drunk and eaten, they brought the fair ones into the hall again, and there was no lack of sweet words.  Folker, a knight bold and good, spake plenty of them.  This same fiddler said openly, "Great Margrave, God hath done well by thee, for he hath given thee a right beautiful wife, and happy days.  Were I a king," said the minstrel, "and wore a crown, I would choose thy sweet daughter for my queen.  She would be the choice of my heart, for she is fair to look upon, and thereto, noble and good."

The Margrave answered, "How should a king covet my dear daughter?  My wife and I are both strangers here, and have naught to give.  What availeth then her beauty?"

But said Gernot, the courteous man, "Might I choose where I would, such a wife were my heart's desire."

Then said Hagen graciously, "It is time Giselher wedded.  Of such high lineage is the noble Margravine, that we would gladly serve her, I and his men, if she wore the crown in Burgundy."

The word pleased both Rudeger and Gotelind greatly.  Their hearts were uplifted.  So it was agreed among the heroes that noble Giselher should take her to wife; the which a king might well do without shame.

If a thing be right, who can withstand it?  They bade the maiden before them, and they swore to give her to him, whereupon he vowed to cherish her.  They gave her castles and lands for her share.  The

king and Gernot sware with the hand that it should be even as they
had promised.

Then said the Margrave, "Since I have no castles, I can only prove
me your true friend evermore. I will give my daughter as much
silver and gold as an hundred sumpters may carry, that ye warriors
may, with honour, be content."

Then the twain were put in a circle, as the custom was. Many a
young knight stood opposite in merry mood, and thought in his
heart as young folk will. They asked the lovely maiden if she would
have the hero. She was half sorry, yet her heart inclined to the
goodly man. She was shamefast at the question, as many a maid
hath been.

Rudeger her father counselled her to say "yes," and to take him
gladly. Giselher, the youth, was not slow to clasp her to him with
his white hands. Yet how little while she had him!

Then said the Margrave, "Great and noble kings, I will give you
my child to take with you, for this were fittest, when ye ride home
again into your land." And it was so agreed.

The din of tourney was bidden cease. The damsels were sent
to their chambers, and the guests to sleep and to take their rest till
the day. Then meats were made ready, for their host saw well to
their comfort.

When they had eaten, they would have set out again for the country of the Huns, but Rudeger said, "Go not, I pray you. Tarry here
yet a while, for I had never dearer guests."

Dankwart answered, "It may not be. Where couldst thou find
the meat, the bread and the wine, for so many knights?"

But when the host heard him, he said, "Speak not of that. Deny
me not, my dear lords. I can give you and all them that are with
you, meat for fourteen days. Little hath King Etzel ever taken of
my substance."

Albeit they made excuse, they had to tarry till the fourth morning.
He gave both horses and apparel so freely that the fame of it spread
abroad.

But longer than this it could not last, for they must needs forth.
Rudeger was not sparing of his goods. If any craved for aught, none
denied him. Each got his desire.

The attendants brought the saddled horses to the door. There
many stranger knights joined them, shield in hand, to ride with them
to Etzel's court. To each of the noble guests Rudeger offered a gift,
or he left the hall. He had wherewithal to live in honour and give
freely. Upon Giselher he had bestowed his fair daughter. He gave
to Gernot a goodly weapon enow, that he wielded well afterward in
strife. The Margrave's wife grudged him not the gift, yet Rudeger,
or long, was slain thereby.

To Gunther, the valiant knight, he gave a coat of mail, that did
the rich king honour, albeit he seldom took gifts. He bowed before Rudeger and thanked him.

Gotelind offered Hagen a fair gift, as was fitting, since the king had taken one, that he might not fare to the hightide without a keep-sake from her, but he refused.

"Naught that I ever saw would I so fain bear away with me as yonder shield on the wall. I would gladly carry it into Etzel's land."

When the Margravine heard Hagen's word, it minded her on her sorrow, and she fell to weeping. She thought sadly on the death of Nudung, that Wittich had slain; and her heart was heavy.

She said to the knight, "I will give thee the shield. Would to God he yet lived that once bore it! He died in battle. I must ever weep when I think on him, for my woman's heart is sore."

The noble Margravine rose from her seat, and took down the shield with her white hands and carried it to Hagen, that used it as a hero should. A covering of bright stuff lay over its device. The light never shone on better shield. It was so rich with precious stones that had any wanted to buy it it had cost him at the least a thousand marks.

The knight bade his attendants bear it away. Then came his brother Dankwart, to whom the Margrave's daughter gave richly broidered apparel, that afterward he wore merrily among the Huns.

None had touched any of these things but for love of the host that offered them so kindly. Yet, or long, they bare him such hate that they slew him.

Bold Folker then stepped forth with knightly bearing and stood before Gotelind with his viol. He played a sweet tune and sang her his song. Then he took his leave and left Bechlaren. But first the Margravine bade them bring a drawer nearer. Of loving gifts now hear the tale. She took therefrom twelve armlets, and drew them over his hand, saying, "These shalt thou take with thee and wear for my sake at Etzel's court. When thou comest again, I will hear how thou hast served me at the hightide." Well he did her behest.

The host said to the guest, "That ye may journey the safer, I will myself escort you, and see that none fall on you by the way." And forthwith they loaded his sumpter. He stood ready for the road with five hundred men, mounted and equipped. These he led merrily to the hightide. Not one of them came back alive to Bech-laren.

The swift envoys pressed down through Austria, and soon the folk knew, far and near, that the heroes were on their way from Worms beyond the Rhine. It was welcome news to the king's vassals. The envoys spurred forward with the tidings that the Nibelungs were come to the Huns.

"Receive them well, Kriemhild, my wife. Thy brethren are come to show thee great honour."

Kriemhild stood at a window and looked out as a friend might for friends. Many drew thither from her father's land. The king was joyful when he heard the news.

"Glad am I," said Kriemhild, "my kinsmen come with many new shields and shining bucklers. I will ever be his friend that taketh my gold and remembereth my wrong."

She thought in her heart, "Now for the reckoning! If I can contrive it, it will go hard at this hightide with him that killed all my happiness. Fain would I work his doom. I care not what may come of it: my vengeance shall fall on the hateful body of him that stole my joy from me. He shall pay dear for my sorrow."

(28) King Etzel saw them, and asked, "I would know who yonder knight is that Dietrich welcometh so lovingly. He beareth him proudly. Howso is his father hight, he is, certes, a goodly warrior."

One of Kriemhild's men answered the king, "He was born at Trony. The name of his father was Aldrian. Albeit now he goeth gently, he is a grim man. I will prove to thee yet that I lie not."

"How shall I find him so grim?" He knew nothing, as yet, of all that the queen contrived against her kinsmen: by reason whereof not one of them escaped alive from the Huns.

"I know Hagen well. He was my vassal. Praise and mickle honour he won here by me. I made him a knight, and gave him my gold. For that he proved him faithful, I was ever kind to him. Wherefore I may well know all about him. I brought two noble children captive to this land — him and Walter of Spain. Here they grew to manhood. Hagen I sent home again. Walter fled with Hildegund."

So he mused on the good old days, and what had happed long ago, for he had seen Hagen, that did him stark service in his youth. Yet now that he was old, he lost by him many a dear friend.

(29) The Huns gaped at the proud heroes as they had been wild beasts, and Etzel's wife saw them through a window and was troubled anew. She thought on her old wrong and began to weep. Etzel's men marvelled much what had grieved her so sore. She said, "Good knights, it is Hagen that hath done it."

Then said they to the queen, "How came it to pass? A moment ago we saw thee of good cheer. There is no man so bold, had he done thee a hurt and thou badest us avenge thee, but he should answer for it with his life."

"Him that avenged my wrong I would thank evermore. All that he asked I would give him. I fall at your feet; only avenge me on Hagen, that he lose his life."

Thereupon sixty bold men armed them swiftly, and would have gone out with one accord to slay Hagen, the bold knight, and the fiddler, for Kriemhild's sake.

But when the queen saw so small a number, she spake wrothfully to the heroes, "Think not to withstand Hagen with so few. Stark and bold as is Hagen of Trony, much starker is he that sitteth by him, Folker the fiddler by name, a wicked man. Ye shall not so lightly overcome them."

(30) They led the guests to a spacious hall, where they found beds, big and costly, standing ready. Gladly had the queen worked

their doom. Coverlets of bright stuffs from Arras were there, and testers of silk of Araby, the goodliest that could be, broidered and shining with gold. The bed-clothes were of ermine and black sable, for them to rest under, the night through, till the day. In such state never king lay before with his men.

"Woe is me for our lodging!" said Giselher the youth, "and for my friends that came hither with us. My sister sent us fair words, but I fear we must all soon lie dead through her."

"Grieve not," said Hagen the knight. "I will myself keep watch, and will guard thee well, I trow, till the day. Fear naught till then. After that, each shall look to himself."

They bowed to him and thanked him. They went to their beds, and, or long, the valiant men were lying soft. Then bold Hagen began to arm him.

Folker the fiddler said, "If thou scorn not my help, Hagen, I would keep watch with thee till the morning."

The hero thanked Folker, "God in Heaven quit you, dear Folker. In all my troubles and my straits I desire thee only and no other. I will do as much for thee, if death hinder it not."

They both did on their shining harness. Each took his shield in his hand, and went out before the door to keep watch over the strangers. They did it faithfully.

Brave Folker leaned his good shield against the wall, and went back and took his fiddle, and did fair and seemly service to his friends. He sat down under the lintel upon the stone. There never was a bolder minstrel. When the sweet tones sounded from his strings, the proud homeless ones all thanked him. He struck so loud that the house echoed. Great were his skill and strength both. Then he played sweeter and softer, till he had lulled many a careworn man to sleep. When Folker found they were all asleep, he took his shield in his hand again, and went out and stood before the door, to guard his friends from Kriemhild's men.

About the middle of the night, or sooner, bold Folker saw a helmet in the distance, shining in the dark. Kriemhild's vassals were fain to do them a hurt. Or she sent them forth, she said, "For God's sake, if ye win at them, slay none save the one man, false Hagen; let the others live."

Then spake the fiddler, "Friend Hagen, we must bear this matter through together. I see armed folk before the house. I ween they come against us."

"Hold thy peace," answered Hagen. "Let them come nigher. Or they are ware of us, there will be helmets cloven by the swords in our two hands. They shall be sent back to Kriemhild in sorry plight."

One of the Hunnish knights saw that the door was guarded, and said hastily, "We cannot carry this thing through. I see the fiddler standing guard. He hath on his head a shining helmet, bright and goodly, with no dint therein, and stark thereto. The rings of his harness glow like fire. Hagen standeth by him. The strangers are well watched."

They turned without more ado. When Folker saw this, he spake angrily to his comrade, "Let me go out to these knights. I would ask Kriemhild's men a question."

"Nay, as thou lovest me," said Hagen. "If thou wentest to them, thou wouldst fall in such strait by their swords that I must help thee, though all my kinsmen perished thereby. If both the twain of us fell to fighting, two or three of them might easily spring into the house, and do such hurt to the sleepers as we could never mourn enow."

But Folker said, "Let us tell them that we have seen them, that they deny not their treachery." Then Folker called out to them, "Why go ye there armed, valiant knights? Is it murder ye are after, ye men of Kriemhild? Take me and my comrade to help you."

None answered him. Right wroth was he.

"Shame on you, cowards! Would ye have slain us sleeping? Seldom afore hath so foul a deed been done on good knights."

The queen was heavy of her cheer when they told her that her messengers had failed. She began to contrive it otherwise, for grim was her mood, and by reason thereof many a good knight and bold soon perished.

(31) "My harness is grown so cold," said Folker, "that I ween the night is far spent. I feel, by the air, that it will soon be day."

Then they waked the knights that still slept.

The bright morning shone in on the warriors in the hall, and Hagen began to ask them if they would go to the minster to hear mass. The bells were ringing according to Christian custom.

The folk sang out of tune: it was not mickle wonder, when Christian and heathen sang together. Gunther's men were minded to go to church, and rose from their beds. They did on their fine apparel — never knights brought goodlier weed into any king's land. But Hagen was wroth, and said, "Ye did better to wear other raiment. Ye know how it standeth with us here. Instead of roses, bear weapons in your hands, and instead of jewelled caps, bright helmets. Of wicked Kriemhild's mood we are well aware. I tell you there will be fighting this day. For your silken tunics wear your hauberks, and good broad shields for rich mantles, that, if any fall on you, ye may be ready. My masters dear, my kinsmen, and my men, go to the church and bewail your sorrow and your need before great God, for know, of a surety, that death draweth nigh. Forget not wherein ye have sinned, and stand humbly before your Maker. Be warned, most noble knights. If God in heaven help you not, ye will hear mass no more."

So the kings and their men went to the minster. Hagen bade them pause in the churchyard, that they might not be parted. He said, "None knoweth yet what the Huns may attempt on us. Lay your shields at your feet, my friends, and if any give you hostile greeting, answer him with deep wounds and deadly. That is Hagen's counsel, that ye may be found ready, as beseemeth you."

Folker and Hagen went and stood before the great minster. They did this that the queen might be forced to push past them. Right grim was their mood.

Then came the king and his beautiful wife. Her body was adorned with rich apparel, and the knights in her train were featly clad. The dust rose high before the queen's attendants.

When the rich king saw the princes and their followers armed, he said hastily, "Why go my friends armed? By my troth it would grieve me if any had done aught to them. I will make it good to them on any wise they ask it. Hath any troubled their hearts, he shall feel my displeasure. Whatso they demand of me I will do."

Hagen answered, "None hath wrought us annoy. It is the custom of my masters to go armed at all hightides for full three days. If any did us a mischief, Etzel should hear thereof."

Right well Kriemhild heard Hagen's word. She looked at him from under her eyelids with bitter hate. Yet she told not the custom of her land, albeit she knew it well from aforetime. Howso grim and deadly the queen's anger was, none had told Etzel how it stood, else he had hindered what afterward befell. They scorned, through pride, to tell their wrong.

The queen advanced with a great crowd of folk, but the twain moved not two hands' breadth, whereat the Huns were wroth, for they had to press past the heroes. This pleased not Etzel's chamberlains, and they had gladly quarrelled with them, had they dared before the king. There was much jostling, and nothing more.

When mass was over, many a Hun sprang to horse.

The host went with his guests into the palace, and bade the anger cease. They set the table, and brought water. The knights of the Rhine had stark foemen enow. Though it irked Etzel, many armed knights pressed in after the kings, when they went to table, by reason of their hate. They waited a chance to avenge their kinsman.

"Ye be too unmannerly," said the host, "to sit down armed to eat. Whoso among you toucheth my guests shall pay for it with his head. I have spoken, O Huns."

It was long or the knights were all seated. Bitter was Kriemhild's wrath. She said, "Prince of Bern, I seek thy counsel and thy kind help in my sore need."

But Hildebrand, the good knight, answered, "Who slayeth the Nibelungs shall do it without me; I care not what price thou offerest. None shall essay it but he shall rue it, for never yet have these doughty knights been vanquished."

"I ask the death of none save Hagen, that hath wronged me. He slew Siegfried, my dear husband. He that chose him from among the others for vengeance should have my gold without stint. I were inly grieved did any suffer save Hagen."

But Hildebrand answered, "How could one slay him alone? Thou canst see for thyself, that if he be set upon, they will all to battle, and poor and rich alike must perish."

Said Dietrich also, courteously, "Great queen, say no more. Thy kinsmen have done naught to me that I should defy them to the death. It is little to thine honour that thou wouldst compass the doom of thy kinsmen. They came hither under safe conduct, and not by the hand of Dietrich shall Siegfried be avenged."

When she found no treachery in the knight of Bern, she tempted Bloedel with the promise of a goodly estate that had been Nudung's. Dankwart slew him after, that he clean forgot the gift.

She said, "Help me, Sir Bloedel. In this house are the foes that slew Siegfried, my dear husband. If any avenge me, I will ever serve him."

Bloedel, that sat by her, answered, "I dare not show thy kinsmen such hate, so long as my brother showeth them favour. The king would not forgive me if I defied them."

"Nay now, Sir Bloedel, I will stand by thee, and give thee silver and gold for meed, and, thereto, a beautiful woman, the widow of Nudung, that thou mayest have her to thy dear one. I will give thee all, land and castles, and thou shalt live joyfully with her on the march that was Nudung's. In good sooth I will do what I promise."

When Bloedel heard the fee, and because the woman pleased him for her fairness, he resolved to win her by battle. So came he to lose his life.

He said to the queen, "Go back into the hall. Or any is ware thereof, I will raise a great tumult. Hagen shall pay for what he hath done. I will bring thee King Gunther's man bound."

"Now arm ye, my men," cried Bloedel, "and let us fall on the foemen in their lodging. King Etzel's wife giveth me no peace, and at her bidding we must risk our lives."

When the queen had left Bloedel to begin the strife, she went in to table with King Etzel and his men. She had woven an evil snare against the guests.

I will tell you now how they went into the hall. Crowned kings went before her; many high princes and knights of worship attended the queen. Etzel assigned to all the guests their places, the highest and the best in the hall. Christians and heathens had their different meats, whereof they ate to the full; for so the wise king ordered it. The yeomen feasted in their own quarters, where sewers served them, that had been charged with the care of their food. But revel and merriment were soon turned to weeping.

Kriemhild's old wrong lay buried in her heart, and when the strife could not be kindled otherwise, she bade them bring Etzel's son to table. Did ever any woman so fearful a thing for vengeance?

Four of Etzel's men went straightway and brought in Ortlieb, the young king, to the princes' table, where Hagen also sat. Through his murderous hate the child perished.

When Etzel saw his son, he spake kindly to his wife's brethren, "See now, my friends, that is my only son, and your sister's child.

Some day he will serve you well. If he take after his kin, he will be a valiant man, rich and right noble, stark and comely. If I live, I will give him the lordship of twelve countries. Fair service ye may yet have from young Ortlieb's hand. Wherefore I pray ye, my dear friends, that, when ye ride back to the Rhine, ye take with you your sister's son, and do well by the child. Rear him in honour till he be a man, and when he is full grown, if any harry your land, he will help you to avenge it." Kriemhild, the wife of Etzel, heard all that the king said.

Hagen answered, "If he grow to be a man, he may well help these knights. But he hath a weakly look. Methinketh I shall seldom go to Ortlieb's court."

The king eyed Hagen sternly, for his word irked him. Albeit he answered not again, he was troubled, and heavy of his cheer. Hagen was no friend to merriment.

The king and his liegemen misliked sore what Hagen had said of the child, and were wroth that they must bear it. They knew not yet what the warrior was to do after. Not a few that heard it, and that bare him hate, had gladly fallen upon him: the king also, had not honour forbidden him. Ill had Hagen sped. Yet soon he did worse: he slew his child before his eyes.

(32) Bloedel's knights all stood ready. With a thousand hauberks they went where Dankwart sat at table with the yeomen. Grim was soon the hate between the heroes.

When Sir Bloedel strode up to the table, Dankwart the marshal greeted him fair. "Welcome to this house, Sir Bloedel. What news dost thou bring?"

"Greet me not," said Bloedel. "My coming meaneth thy death, because of Hagen, thy brother, that slew Siegfried. Thou and many another knight shall pay for it."

"Nay now, Sir Bloedel," said Dankwart. "So might we well rue this hightide. I was a little child when Siegfried lost his life. I know not what King Etzel's wife hath against me."

"I can tell thee nothing, save that thy kinsmen, Gunther and Hagen, did it. Now stand on your defense, ye homeless ones. Ye must die, for your lives are forfeit to Kriemhild."

"Dost thou persist?" said Dankwart. "Then it irketh me that I asked it. I had better have spared my words."

The good knight and bold sprang up from the table, and drew a sharp weapon that was mickle and long, and smote Bloedel a swift blow therewith, that his head, in its helmet, fell at their feet.

"That be thy wedding-gift to Nudung's bride, that thou thoughtest to win!" he cried. "Let them mate her to-morrow with another man; if he ask the dowry, he can have the like." A faithful Hun had told him that morning, secretly, that the queen plotted their doom.

When Bloedel's men saw their master lying slain, they endured it no longer, but fell with drawn swords in grim wrath on the youths.

The homeless youths made grim defence. They drave the armed

men from the house.   Yet five hundred and more lay therein dead.
They were red and wet with blood.

He fought his way through his foemen like a wild boar in the forest
through the hounds — bolder he could not have been.   His path
was ever wet anew with hot blood.   When did single knight withstand foemen better?   Proudly Hagen's brother went to court.

(33)   Bold Dankwart strode in through the door, and bade Etzel's
followers void the way; all his harness was covered with blood.   It
was at the time they were carrying Ortlieb to and fro from table
to table among the princes, and through the terrible news the child
perished.

Dankwart cried aloud to one of the knights, "Thou sittest here
too long, brother Hagen.   To thee, and God in Heaven, I bewail our
wrong.   Knights and squires lie dead in our hall."

Hagen called back to him, "Who hath done it?"

"Sir Bloedel and his men.   He paid for it bitterly, I can tell thee.
I smote off his head with my hands."

"He hath paid too little," said Hagen, "since it can be said of him
that he hath died by the hand of a hero.   His womenfolk have the
less cause to weep.   Now tell me, dear brother; wherefore art thou
so red?   I ween thy wounds are deep.   If he be anywhere near that
hath done it, and the devil help him not, he is a dead man."

"Unwounded I stand.   My harness is wet with the blood of other
men, whereof I have to-day slain so many, that I cannot swear to the
number."

Hagen said, "Brother Dankwart, keep the door, and let not a single
Hun out; I will speak with the knights as our wrong constraineth
me.   Guiltless, our followers lie dead."

"To such great kings will I gladly be chamberlain," said the bold
man; "I will guard the stairs faithfully."

Kriemhild's men were sore dismayed.

"I marvel much," said Hagen, "what the Hunnish knights whisper
in each other's ears.   I ween they could well spare him that standeth
at the door, and hath brought this court news to the Burgundians.   I
have long heard Kriemhild say that she could not bear her heart's
dole.   Now drink we to Love, and taste the king's wine.   The young
prince of the Huns shall be the first."

With that, Hagen slew the child Ortlieb, that the blood gushed
down on his hand from his sword, and the head flew up into the
queen's lap.   Then a slaughter grim and great arose among the
knights.   He slew the child's guardian with a sword stroke from
both his hands, that the head fell down before the table.   It was
sorry pay he gave the tutor.   He saw a minstrel sitting at Etzel's
table, and sprang at him in wrath, and lopped off his right hand on his
viol: "Take that for the message thou broughtest to the Burgundians."

"Woe is me for my hand!" cried Werbel.   "Sir Hagen of Trony,
what have I done to thee?   I rode with true heart to thy master's
land.   How shall I make my music now?"

Little recked Hagen if he never fiddled more. He quenched on Etzel's knights, in the house there, his grim lust for blood, and smote to death not a few.

Swift Folker sprang from the table; his fiddle-bow rang loud. Harsh were the tunes of Gunther's minstrel. Ha! many a foe he made among the Huns!

The three kings, too, rose hastily. They would have parted them or more harm was done. But they could not, for Folker and Hagen were beside themselves with rage.

When the King of Rhineland could not stint the strife, he, also, smote many a deep wound through the shining harness of his foemen. Well he showed his hardihood.

Then stark Gernot came into the battle, and slew many Huns with the sharp sword that Rudeger had given him. He brought many of Etzel's knights to their graves therewith.

Uta's youngest son sprang into the fray, and pierced the helmets of Etzel's knights valiantly with his weapon. Bold Giselher's hand did wonderly.

But howso valiant all the others were, the kings and their men, Folker stood up bolder than any against the foes. He was a hero; he wounded many, that they fell down in their blood.

Etzel's liegemen warded them well, but the guests hewed their way with their bright swords up and down the hall. From all sides came the sound of wailing. They that were without would gladly have won in to their friends, but could not; and they that were within would have won out, but Dankwart let none of them up the stair or down.

The host and his wife fell in great fear. Many a dear friend was slain before their eyes. Etzel himself scarce escaped from his foemen. He sat there affrighted. What did it profit him that he was a king?

Proud Kriemhild cried to Dietrich, "Help me, noble knight, by the princely charity of an Amelung king, to come hence alive. If Hagen reach me, death standeth by my side."

"How can I help thee, noble queen? I cannot help myself. Gunther's men are so grimly wroth that I can win grace for none."

"Nay now, good Sir Dietrich, show thy mercy, and help me hence or I die. Save me and the king from this great peril."

"I will try. Albeit, for long, I have not seen good knights in such a fury. The blood gusheth from the helmets at their sword-strokes."

The chosen knight shouted with a loud voice that rang out like the blast of a buffalo horn, so that all the castle echoed with its strength, for stark and of mickle might was Dietrich.

King Gunther heard his cry above the din of strife, and hearkened. He said, "The voice of Dietrich hath reached me. I ween our knights have slain some of his men. I see him on the table, beckoning with his hand. Friends and kinsmen of Burgundy, hold, that we may learn what we have done to Dietrich's hurt."

When King Gunther had begged and prayed them, they lowered

their swords. Thereby Gunther showed his might, that they smote no blow. Then he asked the Prince of Bern what he wanted. He said, "Most noble Dietrich, what hurt have my friends done thee? I will make it good. Sore grieved were I, had any done thee scathe."

But Sir Dietrich answered, "Naught hath been done against me. With thy safe-conduct let me quit this hall, and the bitter strife, with my men. For this I will ever serve thee."

"Why ask this grace?" said Wolfhart. "The fiddler hath not barred the door so fast that we cannot set it wide, and go forth."

"Hold thy peace," cried Dietrich. "Thou hast played the devil."

Then Gunther answered, "I give thee leave. Lead forth few or many, so they be not my foemen. These shall tarry within, for great wrong have I suffered from the Huns."

When the knight of Bern heard that, he put one arm round the queen, for she was greatly affrighted, and with the other he led out Etzel. Six hundred good knights followed Dietrich.

Then said noble Rudeger, the Margrave, "If any more of them that love and would serve thee may win from this hall, let us hear it; that peace may endure, as is seemly, betwixt faithful friends."

Straightway Giselher answered his father-in-law. "Peace and love be betwixt us. Thou and thy liegemen have been ever true to us, wherefore depart with thy friends, fearing nothing."

When Sir Rudeger left the hall, five hundred or more went out with him. The Burgundian knights did honourably therein, but King Gunther suffered scathe for it after.

One of the Huns would have saved himself when he saw King Etzel go out with Dietrich, but the fiddler smote him such a blow that his head fell down at Etzel's feet.

All that they would let go were gone. Then arose a mighty din. The guests avenged them bitterly. Ha! many a helmet did Folker break!

Of the Huns that had been in the hall, not one was left alive. The tumult fell, for there was none to fight, and the bold warriors laid down their swords.

(34) The knights sat down through weariness. Folker and Hagen went out before the hall. There the overweening men leaned on their shields and spake together.

Then said Giselher of Burgundy, "Rest not yet, dear friends. Ye must carry the dead out of the house. We shall be set upon again; trow my word. These cannot lie longer among our feet. Or the Huns overcome us, we will hew many wounds; to the which I am nothing loth."

"Well for me that I have such a lord," answered Hagen. "This counsel suiteth well such a knight as our young master hath approved him this day. Ye Burgundians have cause to rejoice."

They did as he commanded, and bare the seven thousand dead bodies to the door, and threw them out. They fell down at the foot of the stair. Then arose a great wail from their kinsmen. Some of them were so little wounded that, with softer nursing, they had come to. Now, from the fall, these died also. Their friends wept and made bitter dole.

Then said bold Folker the fiddler, "Now I perceive they spake the truth that told me the Huns were cowards. They weep like women, when they might tend these wounded bodies."

A Margrave that was there deemed he meant this truly. He saw one of his kinsmen lying in his blood, and put his arms round him to bear him away. Him the minstrel shot dead.

(35) When the Thuringians and Danes saw their masters slain, they rushed yet fiercer against the house, and grisly was the strife or they won to the door. Many a helmet and buckler were hewn in pieces.

"Give way," cried Folker, "and let them in. They shall not have their will, but, in lieu thereof, shall perish. They will earn the queen's gift with their death."

The proud warriors thronged into the hall, but many an one bowed his head, slain by swift blows. Well fought bold Gernot; the like did Giselher.

A thousand and four came in. Keen and bright flashed the swords; but all the knights died. Great wonders might be told of the Burgundians.

When the tumult fell, there was silence. Over all the blood of the dead men trickled through the crannies into the gutters below. They of the Rhine had done this by their prowess.

Then the Burgundians sat and rested, and laid down their weapons and their shields.

(36) Before nightfall the king and queen had prevailed on the men of Hungary to dare the combat anew. Twenty thousand or more stood before them ready for battle. These hasted to fall on the strangers.

The day was done; they were in sore straits. They deemed a quick death had been better than long anguish. The proud knights would fain have had a truce. They asked that the king might be brought to them.

The heroes, red with blood, and blackened with the soil of their harness, stepped out of the hall with the three kings. They knew not whom to bewail their bitter woe to.

Both Etzel and Kriemhild came.

Then said young Giselher, "Fairest sister mine, right evil I deem it that thou badest me across the Rhine to this bitter woe. How have I deserved death from the Huns? I was ever true to thee, nor did thee any hurt. I rode hither, dearest sister, for that I trusted to thy love. Needs must thou show mercy."

"I will show no mercy, for I got none. Bitter wrong did Hagen of Trony to me in my home yonder, and here he hath slain my child. They that came with him must pay for it. Yet, if ye will deliver

Hagen captive, I will grant your prayer, and let you live; for ye are my brothers, and the children of one mother. I will prevail upon my knights here to grant a truce."

"God in heaven forbid!" cried Gernot. "Though we were a thousand, liefer would we all die by thy kinsmen, then give one single man for our ransom. That we will never do."

"We must perish then," said Giselher; "but we will fall as good knights. We are still here; would any fight with us? I will never do falsely by my friend."

Cried bold Dankwart too (he had done ill to hold his peace), "My brother Hagen standeth not alone. They that have denied us quarter may rue it yet. By my troth, ye will find it to your cost."

Then said the queen, "Ye heroes undismayed, go forward to the steps and avenge our wrong. I will thank you forever, and with cause. I will requite Hagen's insolence to the full. Let not one of them forth at any point, and I will let kindle the hall at its four sides. So will my heart's dole be avenged."

Etzel's knights were not loth. With darts and with blows they drave back into the house them that stood without. Loud was the din; but the princes and their men were not parted, nor failed they in faith to one another.

Etzel's wife bade the hall be kindled, and they tormented the bodies of the heroes with fire. The wind blew, and the house was soon all aflame. Folk never suffered worse, I ween. There were many that cried, "Woe is me for this pain! Liefer had we died in battle. God pity us, for we are all lost. The queen taketh bitter vengeance."

One among them wailed, "We perish by the smoke and the fire. Grim is our torment. The stark heat maketh me so athirst, that I die."

Said Hagen of Trony, "Ye noble knights and good, let any that are athirst drink the blood. In this heat it is better than wine, and there is naught sweeter here."

Then went one where he found a dead body. He knelt by the wounds, and did off his helmet, and began to drink the streaming blood. Albeit he was little used thereto, he deemed it right good. "God quit thee, Sir Hagen!" said the weary man, "I have learned a good drink. Never did I taste better wine. If I live, I will thank thee."

When the others heard his praise, many more of them drank the blood, and their bodies were strengthened, for the which many a noble woman paid through her dear ones.

The fire-flakes fell down on them in the hall, but they warded them off with their shields. Both the smoke and the fire tormented them. Never before suffered heroes such sore pain.

Then said Hagen of Trony, "Stand fast by the wall. Let not the brands fall on your helmets. Trample them with your feet deeper in the blood. A woeful hightide is the queen's."

The night ended at last. The bold gleeman, and Hagen, his comrade, stood before the house and leaned upon their shields. They waited for further hurt from Etzel's knights. It advantaged the strangers much that the roof was vaulted. By reason thereof more were left alive.

Etzel deemed the guests were all dead of their travail and the stress of the fire. But six hundred bold men yet lived. Never king had better knights. They that kept ward over the strangers had seen that some were left, albeit the princes and their men had suffered loss and dole. They saw many that walked up and down in the house.

They told Kriemhild that many were left alive, but the queen answered, "It cannot be. None could live in that fire. I trow they all lie dead."

The kings and their men had still gladly asked for mercy, had there been any to show it. But there was none in the whole country of the Huns. Wherefore they avenged their death with willing hand.

They were greeted early in the morning with a fierce onslaught, and came in great scathe. Stark spears were hurled at them. Well the knights within stood on their defence.

Etzel's men were the bolder, that they might win Kriemhild's fee. Thereto, they obeyed the king gladly; but soon they looked on death.

One might tell marvels of her gifts and promises. She bade them bear forth red gold upon shields, and gave thereof to all that desired it, or would take it. So great treasure was never given against foemen.

Twelve hundred warriors strove once and again to win entrance. The guests cooled their hardihood with wounds. None could part the strife. The blood flowed from death-deep wounds. Many were slain. Each bewailed some friend. All Etzel's worthy knights perished. Their kinsmen sorrowed bitterly.

(37) The strangers did valiantly that morning. Gotelind's husband came into the courtyard and saw the heavy loss on both sides, whereat the true man wept inly.

"Woe is me," said the knight, "that ever I was born, since none can stop this strife! Fain would I have them at one again, but the king holdeth back, for he seeth alway more done to his hurt."

Good Rudeger sent to Dietrich, that they might seek to move the great king. But the knight of Bern sent back answer, "Who can hinder it? King Etzel letteth none intercede."

A knight of the Huns, that had oft seen Rudeger standing with wet eyes, said to the queen, "Look how he standeth yonder, that Etzel hath raised above all others, and that hath land and folk at his service. Why hath Rudeger so many castles from the king? He hath struck no blow in this battle. I ween he careth little for our scathe, so long as he has enow for himself. They say he is bolder than any other. Ill hath he shown it in our need."

The faithful man, when he heard that word, looked angrily at the knight. He thought, "Thou shalt pay for this. Thou callest me a coward. Thou hast told thy tale too loud at court."

He clenched his fist, and ran at him, and smote the Hun so fiercely that he fell down at his feet, dead. Whereat Etzel's grief waxed anew.

"Away with thee, false babbler!" cried Rudeger. "I had trouble and sorrow enow. What was it to thee that I fought not? Good cause have I also to hate the strangers, and had done what I could against them, but that I brought them hither. I was their escort into my master's land, and may not lift my wretched hand against them."

Then said Etzel, the great king, to the Margrave, "How hast thou helped us, most noble Rudeger? We had dead men enow in the land, and needed no more. Evilly hast thou done."

But the knight answered, "He angered me, and twitted me with the honour and the wealth thou hath bestowed on me so plenteously. It hath cost the liar dear."

Then came the queen, that had seen the Hun perish by Rudeger's wrath. She mourned for him with wet eyes, and said to Rudeger, "What have we ever done to thee that thou shouldst add to our sorrow? Thou hast oft times promised, noble Rudeger, that thou wouldst risk, for our sake, both honour and life, and I have heard many warriors praise thee for thy valour. Hast thou forgotten the oath thou swearest to me with thy hand, good knight, when thou didst woo me for King Etzel — how that thou wouldst serve me till my life's end, or till thine? Never was my need greater than now."

"It is true, noble lady. I promised to risk for thee honour and life, but I sware not to lose my soul. I brought the princes to this hightide."

She said, "Remember, Rudeger, thy faith, and thine oath to avenge all my hurt and my woe."

The Margrave answered, "I have never said thee nay."

Etzel began to entreat likewise. They fell at his feet. Sore troubled was the good Margrave. Full of grief, he cried, "Woe is me that ever I saw this hour, for God hath forsaken me. All my duty to heaven, mine honour, my good faith, my knightliness, I must forego. God above have pity, and let me die! Whether I do this thing, or do it not, I sin. And if I take the part of neither, all the world will blame me. Let Him that made me guide me."

Then the bold man said to the king, "Take back what thou hast given me — castles and land. Leave me nothing at all. I will go forth afoot into exile. I will take my wife and my daughter by the hand, and I will quit thy country empty, rather than I will die dishonoured. I took thy red gold to my hurt."

King Etzel answered, "Who will help me then? Land and folk I gave to thee, Rudeger, that thou mightest avenge me on my foes. Thou shalt rule with Etzel as a great king."

But Rudeger said, "How can I do it? I bade them to my house and home; I set meat and drink before them, and gave them my gifts. Shall I also smite them dead? The folk may deem me a coward. But I have always served them well. Should I fight with them now, it were ill done. Deep must I rue past friendship. I gave my daughter to Giselher. None better in this world had she found, of so great lineage and honour, and faith, and wealth. Never saw I young king so virtuous."

But Kriemhild answered, "Most noble Rudeger, take pity on us both. Bethink thee that never host had guests like these."

Then said the Margrave, "What thou and my master have given me I must pay for, this day, with my life. I shall die, and that quickly. Well I know that, or nightfall, my lands and castles will return to your keeping. To your grace I commend my wife and my child, and the homeless ones that are at Bechlaren."

"God reward thee, Rudeger," cried the king. He and the queen were both glad. "Thy folk shall be well seen to; but thou thyself, I trow, will come off scatheless."

So he put his soul and body on the hazard. Etzel's wife began to weep. He said, "I must keep my vow to thee. Woe is me for my friends, that I must fall upon in mine own despite!".

They saw him turn heavily from the king. To his knights that stood close by, he said, "Arm ye, my men all. For I must fight the Burgundians, to my sorrow."

The heroes called for their harness, and the attendants brought helm and buckler. Soon the proud strangers heard the sad news.

Rudeger stood armed with five hundred men, and twelve knights that went with him, to win worship in the fray. They knew not that death was so near.

Rudeger went forth with his helmet on; his men carried sharp swords, and, thereto, broad shields and bright. The fiddler saw this, and was dismayed. But when Giselher beheld his father-in-law with his helmet on, he weened that he meant them well. The noble king was right glad. "Well for me that I have such friends," cried Giselher, "as these we won by the way! For my wife's sake he will save us. By my faith, I am glad to be wed."

"Thy trust is vain," said the fiddler. "When ever did ye see so many knights come in peace, with helmets laced on, and with swords? Rudeger cometh to serve for his castles and his lands."

Or the fiddler had made an end of speaking, Rudeger, the noble man, stood before the house. He laid his good shield before his feet. He must needs deny greeting to his friends.

Then the Margrave shouted into the hall, "Stand on your defence, ye bold Nibelungs. I would have helped you, but must slay you. Once we were friends, but I cannot keep my faith."

The sore-tried men were dismayed at this word. Their comfort was gone, for he that they loved was come against them. From their foemen they had suffered enow.

"God in Heaven forbid," said Gunther the knight, "that thou shouldst be false to the friendship and the faith wherein we trusted. It cannot be."

"I cannot help it," said Rudeger. "I must fight with you, for I have vowed it. As ye love your lives, bold warriors, ward you well. King Etzel's wife will have it so."

Then said the youngest of fair Uta's sons, "How canst thou do this thing, Sir Rudeger? All that came hither with me are thy friends. A vile deed is this. Thou makest thy daughter too soon a widow. If thou and thy knights defy us, ill am I apayed, that I trusted thee before all other men, when I won thy daughter for my wife."

"Forget not thy troth, noble king, if God send thee hence," answered Rudeger. "Let not the maiden suffer for my sin. By thine own princely virtue, withdraw not thy favour from her."

"Fain would I promise it," said Giselher the youth. "Yet if my high-born kinsmen perish here by thy hand, my love for thee and thy daughter must perish also."

"Then God have mercy!" cried the brave man; whereat he lifted his shield, and would have fallen upon the guests in Kriemhild's hall.

But Hagen called out to him from the stairhead, "Tarry awhile, noble Rudeger. Let me and my masters speak with thee yet awhile in our need. What shall it profit Etzel if we knights die in a strange land? I am in evil case," said Hagen. "The shield that Gotelind gave me to carry, the Huns have hewn from my hand. In good faith I bore it hither. Would to God I had such a shield as thou hast, noble Rudeger! A better I would not ask for in the battle."

"I would gladly give thee my shield, durst I offer it before Kriemhild. Yet take it, Hagen, and wear it. Ha! mightst thou but win with it to Burgundy!"

When they saw him give the shield so readily, there were eyes enow red with hot tears. It was the last gift that Rudeger of Bechlaren ever gave.

Then the Margrave's men ran at their foemen, and followed their master like good knights. They carried sharp weapons, wherewith they clove many a helmet and buckler. The weary ones answered the men of Bechlaren with swift blows that pierced deep and straight through their harness to their life's blood. They did wonderly in the battle.

Gernot cried out to the Margrave, "Noble Rudeger, thou leavest none of my men alive. It irketh me sore; I will bear it no longer. I will turn thy gift against thee, for thou hast taken many friends from me. Come hither, thou bold man. What thou gavest me I will earn to the uttermost."

Or the Margrave had fought his way to him, bright bucklers grew dim with blood. Then, greedy of fame, the men ran at each other, and began to ward off the deadly wounds. But their swords were so sharp that nothing could withstand them. Rudeger the knight smote Gernot through his flint-hard helmet, that the blood brake out. Soon the good warrior was avenged. He swung Rudeger's gift on high, and, albeit he was wounded to the death, he smote him through his good shield and his helmet, that Gotelind's husband died. So rich a gift was never worse requited. So they fell in the strife — Gernot and Rudeger — slain by each other's hand.

(38) So loud they wept on all sides, that palace and towers echoed with the sound. One of Dietrich's men of Bern heard it, and hasted with the news.

The prince of Amelung bade them inquire further. He sat down at a window sore troubled, and bade Hildebrand go to the guests, and ask them what had happened.

Master Hildebrand, bold in strife, took with him neither shield nor sword, and would have gone to them on peaceful wise. But his sister's child chid him. Grim Wolfhart cried, "Why goest thou naked? If they revile thee, thou wilt have the worst of the quarrel, and return shamed. If thou goest armed, none will withstand thee."

The old man armed him as the youth had counselled. Or he had ended, all Dietrich's knights stood in their harness, sword in hand.

Hildebrand laid his shield at his feet, and said to Gunther's men, "Alack! ye good knights! What have ye done to Rudeger? Dietrich, my master, sent me hither to ask if any here slew the good Margrave, as they tell us. We could ill endure such loss."

Hagen of Trony answered, "The news is true. Glad were I had the messenger lied to thee, for Rudeger's sake, and that he lived still. Both men and women must evermore bewail him."

Hildebrand could ask no more for grief. He said, "Grant now, ye warriors, that for which my master sent me. Give us dead Rudeger from out the hall, with whom all our joy hath perished, and let us requite him for all the kindness he hath shown to us and many another. Like him we are homeless. Why tarry ye? Let us bear him hence, and serve him dead, as we had gladly served him living."

But Folker answered, "Ye shall get him from none here. Come and take him out of the house, where he lieth with his death-wounds in the blood. So shall ye serve Rudeger truly."

Then Dietrich's men rushed in from all sides. They smote till the links of their foemen's mail whistled asunder, and their broken sword-points flew on high. They struck hot-flowing streams from the helmets.

When Hagen of Trony saw Folker dead, he grieved more bitterly than he had done yet, all the hightide, for kinsmen or vassal. Alack! how grimly he began to avenge him!

"Old Hildebrand shall not go scatheless, for his hand hath slain my friend, the best comrade I ever had."

Hagen thought on the fiddler that old Hildebrand had slain, and he said to the knight, "Thou shalt pay for my teen. Thou hast robbed us of many a good warrior." He smote Hildebrand, that Balmung, the sword he had taken from Siegfried when he slew him, rang loud. But the old man stood boldly on his defence. He brought his sharp-edged sword down on Hagen, but could not wound him. Then Hagen pierced him through his good harness.

When Master Hildebrand felt the wound, he feared more scathe from Hagen, so he threw his shield over his back and fled.

Now, of all the knights, none were left alive save two, Gunther and Hagen.

Old Hildebrand, covered with blood, ran with the news to Dietrich, that he saw sitting sadly where he had left him. Soon the prince had more cause for woe. When he saw Hildebrand in his bloody harness, he asked fearfully for his tale. "Now tell me, Master Hildebrand, why thou art so wet with thy life's blood? Who did it? I ween thou hast fought with the guests in the hall, albeit I so sternly forbade it. Thou hast better have forborne."

Hildebrand answered his master, "Hagen did it. He gave me this wound in the hall when I turned to flee from him. I scarce escaped the devil with my life."

Said the prince of Bern, "Thou art rightly served. Thou heardest me vow friendship to the knights, and thou hast broken the peace I gave them. Were it not that I shame me to slay thee, thy life were forfeit."

"Be not so wroth, my lord Dietrich. Enough woe hath befallen me and mine. We would have borne away Rudeger's body, but Gunther's men denied it."

"Woe is me for this wrong! Is Rudeger then dead? That is the bitterest of my dole. Noble Gotelind is my cousin's child. Alack! The poor orphans of Bechlaren!" With ruth and sorrow he wept for Rudeger. "Woe is me for the true comrade I have lost. I must mourn Etzel's liegeman forever. Canst thou tell me, Master Hildebrand, who slew him?"

Hildebrand answered, "It was stark Gernot, but the hero fell by Rudeger's hand."

Said Dietrich, "Bid my men arm them, for I will thither straightway. Send me my shining harness. I, myself, will question the knights of Burgundy."

But Master Hildebrand answered, "Who is there to call? Thy sole living liegeman standeth here. I am the only one. The rest are dead."

Dietrich trembled at the news, and was passing doleful, for never in this world had he known such woe. He cried, "Are all my men slain? then God hath forgotten poor Dietrich! I was a great king, rich and proud. Yet how could they all die, these valiant heroes, by foemen so battle-weary and sore beset? Death had spared them, but that I am doomed to sorrow. Since this hard fate is needs mine, tell me if any of the guests be left alive."

Hildebrand answered, "None save Hagen, and Gunther, the king. God knoweth I say sooth."

(39) Dietrich came where both the knights stood outside the house, leaning against the wall. Good Dietrich laid down his shield,

and, moved with deep woe, he said, "There is nothing for it. Of thy knightliness, atone to me for the wrong thou hast done me, and I will avenge it no further. Yield thee captive, thee and thy man, and I will defend thee to the uttermost against the wrath of the Huns. Thou wilt find me faithful and true."

"God in Heaven forbid," cried Hagen, "that two knights, armed as we are for battle, should yield them to thee! I would hold it a great shame, and ill done."

"Deny me not," said Dietrich. "Ye have made me heavy-hearted enow, O Gunther and Hagen; and it is no more than just, that ye make it good. I swear to you, and give you my hand thereon, that I will ride back with you to your own country. I will bring you safely thither, or die with you, and forget my great wrong for your sakes."

"Ask us no more," said Hagen. "It were a shameful tale to tell of us, that two such bold men yielded them captive. I see none save Hildebrand by thy side."

When Dietrich heard grim Hagen's mind, he caught up his shield, and sprang up the steps. The Nibelung sword rang loud on his mail. Sir Dietrich knew well that the bold man was fierce. The prince of Bern warded off the strokes. He needed not to learn that Hagen was a valiant knight. Thereto, he feared stark Balmung. But ever and anon he struck out warily, till he had overcome Hagen in the strife. He gave him a wound that was deep and wide. Then thought Sir Dietrich, "Thy long travail hath made thee weak. I had little honour in thy death. Liefer will I take thee captive." Not lightly did he prevail. He threw down his shield. He was stark and bold, and he caught Hagen of Trony in his arms. So the valiant man was vanquished. King Gunther grieved sore.

Dietrich bound Hagen, and led him to the queen, and delivered into her hand the boldest knight that ever bare a sword. After her bitter dole, she was glad enow. She bowed before the knight for joy. "Blest be thou in soul and body. Thou hast made good to me all my woe. I will thank thee till my dying day."

Then said Dietrich, "Let him live, noble queen. His service may yet atone to thee for what he hath done to thy hurt. Take not vengeance on him for that he is bound."

She bade them lead Hagen to a dungeon. There he lay locked up, and none saw him.

Then King Gunther called aloud, "Where is the hero of Bern? He hath done me a grievous wrong."

Sir Dietrich went to meet him. Gunther was a man of might. He tarried not, but ran toward him from the hall. Loud was the din of their swords.

Howso famed Dietrich was from aforetime, Gunther was so wroth and so fell, and so bitterly his foeman, by reason of the wrong he had endured, that it was a marvel Sir Dietrich came off alive. They were stark and mighty men both. Palace and towers echoed with their blows, as their swift swords hewed their good helmets. A high-hearted king was Gunther.

But the knight of Bern overcame him, as he had done Hagen. His blood gushed from his harness by reason of the good sword that Dietrich carried. Yet Gunther had defended him well, for all he was so weary.

The knight was bound by Dietrich's hand, albeit a king should never wear such bonds. Dietrich deemed, if he left Gunther and his man free, they would kill all they met.

He took him by the hand, and led him before Kriemhild. Her sorrow was lighter when she saw him. She said, "Thou art welcome, King Gunther."

He answered, "I would thank thee, dear sister, if thy greeting were in love. But I know thy fierce mind, and that thou mockest me and Hagen."

Then said the prince of Bern, "Most high queen, there were never nobler captives than these I have delivered here into thy hands. Let the homeless knights live for my sake."

She promised him she would do it gladly, and good Dietrich went forth weeping. Yet soon Etzel's wife took grim vengeance, by reason whereof both the valiant men perished. She kept them in dungeons, apart, that neither saw the other again, till she bore her brother's head to Hagen. Certes, Kriemhild's vengeance was bitter.

The queen went to Hagen, and spake angrily to the knight. "Give me back what thou hast taken from me, and ye may both win back alive to Burgundy."

But grim Hagen answered, "Thy words are wasted, noble queen. I have sworn to show the hoard to none. While one of my masters liveth, none other shall have it."

"I will end the matter," said the queen. Then she bade them slay her brother, and they smote off his head. She carried it by the hair to the knight of Trony. He was grieved enow.

When the sorrowful man saw his master's head, he cried to Kriemhild, "Thou hast wrought all thy will. It hath fallen out as I deemed it must. The noble King of Burgundy is dead, and Giselher the youth, and eke Gernot. None knoweth of the treasure now save God and me. Thou shalt never see it, devil that thou art."

She said, "I come off ill in the reckoning. I will keep Siegfried's sword at the least. My true love wore it when I saw him last. My bitterest heart's dole was for him."

She drew it from the sheath. He could not hinder it. She purposed to slay the knight. She lifted it high with both hands, and smote off his head.

King Etzel saw it, and sorrowed. "Alack!" cried the king, "The best warrior that ever rode to battle, or bore a shield, hath fallen by the hand of a woman! Albeit I was his foeman, I must grieve."

Then said Master Hildebrand, "His death shall not profit her.

I care not what come of it. Though I came in scathe by him myself, I will avenge the death of the bold knight of Trony."

Hildebrand sprang fiercely at Kriemhild, and slew her with his sword. She suffered sore by his anger. Her loud cry helped her not.

Dead bodies lay stretched over all. The queen was hewn in pieces. Etzel and Dietrich began to weep. They wailed piteously for kinsmen and vassals. Mickle valour lay there slain. The folk were doleful and dreary.

The end of the king's hightide was woe, even as, at the last all joy turneth so sorrow.

I know not what fell after. Christian and heathen, wife, man, and maid, were seen weeping and mourning for their friends.

I WILL TELL YOU NO MORE. LET THE DEAD LIE. HOWEVER IT FARED AFTER WITH THE HUNS, MY TALE IS ENDED. THIS IS THE FALL OF THE NIBELUNGS.

[tr. MARGARET ARMOUR]

# GERMAN LYRICS

Although the earliest extant Teutonic lyric poetry, in the modern sense of the word, was written in the second half of the twelfth century, there is evidence enough of early narrative poetry, composed to be sung to musical accompaniment. The *Lay of Hildebrand* (*Hildebrandslied*) is the first and best example. A part of the poem was copied on the covers of a theological manuscript by two monks of Fulda in the second decade of the eighth century and with other precious treasures from that home of Boniface, the apostle to the Germans, was lovingly preserved for over eleven centuries until the recent war. A letter received just as this preface was written reports as unaccountably lost that manuscript, which no doubt Walafrid Strabo read and which was the only extant example of the *barbara et antiquissima carmina* that Charlemagne ordered preserved. Other extant verse of the early period is interesting only to the antiquarian, with the possible exception of the laudatory *Ludwigslied;* but there is evidence enough that love songs, drinking songs, dance songs, jests, and riddles now lost were composed in abundance. Charlemagne, though he loved popular literature, had to pass a law against nuns' circulating vulgar poetry (*ut nullatenus ibi uuinoleodos scribere vel mittere praesumant*).

Only when the secular nobles became literate and wealthy and settled enough to create their own books were lyrics preserved. By that time the age of chivalry had arrived and love and knight errantry were the two popular themes. The German lyric we know is *minnesang,* that is, love song. The earliest were either didactic verses called *sprüche,* or *trûtlieder,* addressed to *mîn trût,* a term of affection for a loved one. Somewhat after 1160 Kurenburg and Dietmar von Aist composed songs that seem purely native, in contrast with the songs of a generation later that borrowed conventions from Provence. Toward the close of the century many active poets lived near the upper reaches of the Rhine and the Rhone, where Teuton and troubadour met and exchanged themes.

Though troubadour poetry is thought to be older and was more aggressively circulated, the same social conditions controlled compositions in both languages. Heinrich von Morungen, *qui visitavit Indiam,* like crusaders of all countries, was stirred to poetry and cultivated the international vogue of courtly love. Like many another minnesinger, he was a noble knight, presumably of small estate, capable of accepting patronage in return for poetry in the conventional forms: the *kriuzliet* (crusading song), *klageliet* (lament), *lobeliet* (praise), *hügeliet* (song of joy), *tanzliet* (dance song), *tageliet* (dawn song), *wechsel* (change of speakers), *rüegliet* (taunting song), *leich* (secular adaptation of the sequence), and others. These parallel the Provençal and Latin lyrics printed below (pp. 668 ff., and 910 ff.). External nature, though a constant theme, is thoroughly con-

497

ventionalized; it is a symbol, or a series of symbols.  Albrecht von
Johansdorf, who was a secular minister for the bishop of Passau, is
exceptional in being more natural and yet saying less about nature.

By the common consent of his contemporaries and of posterity, the
greatest minnesinger was Walther von der Vogelweide.  Gottfried
von Strassburg called him a leader of a choir of nightingales.
Walther, born in the South Tyrol, spent nine congenial years in the
Viennese court when the minnesinger Reinmar von Hagenau held
sway and was, during his long life, patronized by both rivals for
the Empire, Philip of Swabia (*Weiblingen*) and Otho (*Welf*),
and by the great Emperor Frederick II, who gave him a small fief
near Würzburg as pension for his declining years.  As an ardent
supporter of the Emperor, he violently opposed the politics of Pope
Innocent III.  He is the first known political poet in German Literature.  In the romantic castle of Wartburg, ruled by one of the
greatest patrons of poetry, Landgrave Hermann of Thuringia, he
met the author of *Parzival*, himself a minnesinger.  Four of the
eight songs of Wolfram that survive are *tagelieder*.  As the *minnesang* began to wane in the mid-thirteenth century, eventually to
be taken over by the Renaissance *meistersingers*, the poets sought
novelty to atone for worn-out convention, primarily by cultivating
the *Volkslied*.  Niedhart von Reuental, the best of the generation
following Walther, relished the revels of the villagers, though he
condescended to them as an aristocrat.  The result is an introduction of a sardonic, cynical, or intellectualized note that was coming
into vogue everywhere, as the *Romance of the Rose*, below, indicates.
In the main, the later poets were high nobles: Wenceslaus II, King
of Bohemia, Otto, Margrave of Brandenburg, John, Duke of Brabant,
and Henry, Duke of Breslau, to name a few.

The courts that produced the chivalric lyrics throughout Europe
were weakening before the impact of trade and the growth of the
merchant class, with their new tastes and manners.  During the
next centuries the best literature is bourgeois literature, with its interest in high politics and nationalism, in "good business" and trickery, and in the puritanical phases of religion.  Folklore, not
previously interesting to the literate, now became a source for poetry,
and the fable and ballad that close the section are characteristic of
the times.  Ulrich Boner's *Edelstein* became, somewhat more than
a century after composition, the first book printed in the German
language (A.D. 1461).  *The Battle of Sempach,* composed by Halbsuter of Lucerne according to the concluding strophe of one version
(transcribed below), commemorates the great victory of the Swiss
over Hapsburg Leopold in their struggle for independence.

## THE SONG OF HILDEBRAND [1]

(Old High German, *circ.* 800 A.D.)

*Ik gihôrta ðat seggen,*
*ðat sih urhêttun      aenon muotîn,*
*Hiltibrant enti Haðubrant      untar heriun tuêm.*

I heard this tale      [of hap and harm],
That two warriors wielded      their weapons amain,
Hildebrand and Hadubrand,      between two hosts.
The father and son      fastened their armor,
Buckled their harness,      belted their swords on
Over coat of mail      as to combat they rode.
Hildebrand spake then,      the hoary-hair'd warrior,
More wise in life's wisdom:      he warily asked,
And few were his words,      who his father was
In the folk of the foemen.      "[Thy friends would I know,
And kindly tell me]      what kin thou dost claim.
If thou namest but one,      I shall know then the others:
The kin of this kingdom      are couth to me all."
Hadubrand answer'd,      Hildebrand's son:
"This lore I learned      from long ago,
From the wise and old      who were of yore,
That Hildebrand hight my father:      my name is Hadubrand.
Off to the east he wander'd,      the anger of Ottokar fleeing,
Marching away with Dietrich,      and many a man went with him.
He left in the land      a little one lorn,
A babe at the breast      in the bower of the bride,
Bereft of his rights:      thus he rode to the east.
But later Dietrich      lost my father
And lived henceforth      a lonely man.
For the foe of Ottokar,      so fierce and keen,
Was the dearest of thanes      to Dietrich his lord.
He was fain to fight      where the fray was thick:
Known was his bravery      among bold warriors.
I can not believe      that he lives longer."
"I swear by the God      who sways the heavens
That the bonds of blood      forbid our strife."
Then he unclaspt from his arm      the clinging gold,
Which was wrought of coin      that the king had given,
The lord of the Huns:      "With love I give it."
But Hadubrand answer'd,      Hildebrand's son:
"With the tip of the spear      one takes the gift
From the sharpened edge      of the foeman's shaft.
Thou thinkest, old Hun,      thy thoughts are deep,

1. From *The Hildebrandslied,* by Francis A. Wood; The University of Chicago Press, Chicago, 1914. Reprinted by permission of the publisher.

Thou speakest alluring words     with the spear it would like thee
     to wound me.
With untruth art thou come to old age     for trickery clings to thee
     ever.
It was said to me     by seafarers
Coming west over the wave     that war slew him.
Dead is Hildebrand,     Heribrand's son."
"Great Weirdwielder,     woe worth the day!
For sixty winters     and summers I wander'd,
Battling with foemen     where blows keen fell.
From the scarpèd wall     unscathed I came.
Now the son of my loins     with the sword will hew me;
He will deal me death     or I dash him to earth.
But now canst thou strike,     if strong be thine arm,
Canst win the harness     from so hoary a man,
And strip the spoils     from the stricken foe."
Hadubrand answer'd,     Hildebrand's son:
"Full well I hold,     from thy harness rich,
That thou comest hither     from a kindly lord,
In whose kingdom thou wast not     a wandering wretch."
"The heart of a coward     would the Hun now have
Who would shrink from a foe     so fain to fight,
To struggle together.     Let each now strive
To see whether today     he must bite the dust
Or may bear from the field     the byrnies of both."
Then first they hurled     the hurtling spears
In sharpest showers     that shook the shields.
Then they clasht with their brands,     the battle-boards bursting
And hewed with might     the white linden
Till they shivered the shields     with shattering strokes,
As they wielded their weapons. . . .

                              [tr. FRANCIS A. WOOD]


## QUATRAINS [2]


### Dietmar von Aist (Austria? circ. 1175)


*Uf der linden obene     dâ sanc ein kleinez vogellîn.*
*Vor dem walde wart ez lut:     dô huop sich aber daz herze mîn.*


On the linden overhead     a bird was carolling its lay.
From the wood its music pealed,     whereat my heart was borne
     away
To seek a place where once it dwelled.     I saw the roses blooming
     where
They call into my mind the thoughts     that link me to a lady fair.

     2. From *Essays on the Mediaeval German Love Lyric*, by Margaret F. Richey; B. H.
Blackwell, Ltd., Oxford, 1943.  Reprinted by permission of the publisher.

"Methinks a thousand years are fled     since in my lover's arms I lay.
Without or cause or fault of mine     he leaves me friendless many
    a day
Since the time when last I saw     the flowers and heard the sweet
    birds' song,
Short, alas, my joy has been,     and my heart-sorrow all too long."

            [tr. MARGARET F. RICHEY]


## WECHSEL [3]

### Heinrich von Morungen (*circ.* 1200)

*Owê, sol aber mir ienmer mê*
*Gelûhten dur die naht . . .*

Alas! shall ever I see again,
Gleaming athwart the night,
Whiter than driven snow,
Her body bright?
Thus were my eyes deceived,
For I believed
It was the moon's clear ray
That shone.
Suddenly day
Broke, and the night was gone.

"Alas! and will he ever again
Be here when the dawn turns grey,
So that we need not rue
The approach of day —
As when he made lament
The last night he spent
Lying by the side of me.
Anon
Day suddenly
Broke, and the night was gone."

Alas! she kissed me in my sleep
Times beyond all telling.
Her cheek was wet with tears
From her eyes welling.
Gently I bade her cease,
And she, at peace,
Her arms about me, lay
Held fast.
Suddenly day
Broke, and the night was past.

3. Ibid.

"Alas! how often has he stayed
His wondering gaze on me!
My white arms he unbared
So lovingly.
It was a deep surprise
That his rapt eyes
He could not draw away.
At last,
Too soon, the day
Broke, and the night was past.

[tr. Margaret F. Richey]


## KRIUZLIET [4]

Albrecht von Johansdorf (*circ.* 1200)

*Die hinnen varn, die sagen durch Got*
*Daz Iersalêm der reinen stat und ouch dem laude*
*Helf noch nie noeter wart.*

They who fare hence may in God's name aver
That Jerusalem the fair city and the holy land
Never needed help more truly.
Fools make mock at that lament, and stir
Up laughter, saying: "Without them, could not the Lord's right
    hand
Alone deal vengeance throughly?
Let them remember now that He for us in anguish died:
There was no need for Him to be thus crucified,
But that His pity bowed itself to save us.

He who cares nothing for the Cross and Grave in their sore plight,
Shall stand ungraced and naked in His sight!

In what, think ye, can such a man believe,
Or who shall come at last to help him in his dying day,
Who to God's cause his help denies?
So far as I can for my part perceive,
Unless, indeed, it be a lawful hindrance bars his way,
I think he sinneth otherwise.
Now what avails to speak of Cross and Grave? the heathen horde
Think they can silence us with one contemptuous word,
That God's Mother was no Maiden holy.

He whose heart burns not at that impious defiance,
Where and with whom, alas, seeks he alliance?

4. Ibid.

With me, at least, my cares have this way wrought,
That I would gladly purge my will of all low weaknesses,
Whereof my heart has not been quit
Ere now.  For often in the night a thought
Assails me: if I stay behind, how shall I make redress,
That God so deign to pardon it?
Even so, I do not know of many sins whereto I cleave,
Save one, but this is all too dear for me to leave,
I could renounce all sins but that alone:

I love a woman more than all the world deep in my soul.
Lord God, direct that to a blessed goal!

[tr. MARGARET F. RICHEY]


## KLAGELIET [5]

Walther von der Vogelweide (fl. 1198–1228)

*Owê wir meuzigen liute, wie sîn wir versezzen . . .*

Alas, we idle people, we have sat down unheeding
Between two joys on the sad and lowly ground!
We had forgotten how to toil and strive, nought needing,
While liberal Summer all our wishes crowned.
To flower and fleeting leaf our lives were bound:
Bird-song ensnared us with a dream of mirth.
O well for him whose joys outlast the earth!

Alas for the tune which the cricket gaily taught us,
When we should have made provision against the winter's chill!
Had we struggled with the ant, what high honour this had brought
    us:
Of peace and calm aplenty we should now possess our fill.
This was ever the world's distempered will:
Fools have always mocked and spurned the wise.
These shall be judged according to their lies.

Alas, what honour from the German land is driven!
Clear wit and manly prowess, gold and silver gain,
He who has these, and lags with guilt unshriven,
Shall he not look for Heaven's reward in vain?
Angels there, fair ladies here his worth disdain.
Stripped, arraigned in the eyes of God and Man,
Let him face the double sentence, if he can!

Alas, there comes a wind, know that and mark it surely,
Whereof we hear the baleful tidings told and sung.

5. Ibid.

This shall pass through all kingdoms of the earth in fury.
Palmers and pilgrims lament with sorrowing tongue.
Trees, towers in headlong ruin to the ground are flung,
Heads blown from off the strongest of the brave.
Now let us flee for refuge to God's grave!

[tr. Margaret F. Richey]


TRÄUMERI

Walther von der Vogelweide

*Dô der sumer komen was,*
*Und die bluomen dur daz gras*
*Wünneclîchen sprungen,*
*Aedâ die vogele sungen . . .*


'Twas summer, — through the opening grass
  The joyous flowers upsprang,
The birds in all their diff'rent tribes
  Loud in the woodlands sang:
Then forth I went, and wander'd far
  The wide green meadow o'er;
Where cool and clear the fountain play'd,
  There stray'd I in that hour.

Roaming on, the nightingale
  Sang sweetly in my ear;
And by the greenwood's shady side,
  A dream came to me there;
Fast by the fountain, where bright flowers
  Of sparkling hue we see,
Close shelter'd from the summer heat,
  That vision came to me.

All care was banish'd, and repose
  Came o'er my wearied breast;
And kingdoms seem'd to wait on me,
  For I was with the blest.

Yet, while it seem'd as if away
  My spirit soar'd on high,
And in the boundless joys of heaven
  Was wrapt in ecstasy,
E'en then, my body revel'd still
  In earth's festivity;
And surely never was a dream
  So sweet as this to me.

Thus I dream'd on, and might have dwelt
    Still on that rapturous dream,
When, hark! a raven's luckless note
    (Sooth, 'twas a direful scream,)
Broke up the vision of delight,
    Instant my joy was past:
O, had a stone but met my hand,
    That hour had been his last. . . .

                      [tr. EDGAR TAYLOR]


## TO HERMANN, LANDGRAVE OF THURINGIA [6]

### Walther von der Vogelweide

*Der in den ôren siech von ungesühte sî,*
*Daz ist mîn rât, der lâ den hof ze Düringen frî.*


Whose ears are sore, I rede him to keep free
From the Thuringian court with its wild glee:
If he go there, his wits will gather wool.
I am tired of elbowing the crowd about:
By night and day one troop goes in, another out;
That any hear at all is wonderful.
The Landgrave in this delights:
To spend his substance with proud knights,
And everyone a champion in the land.
So generous is he, though men should ask
For good wine a thousand pounds the cask,
Never would a knight's glass empty stand.

                      [tr. JETHRO BITHELL]


## ON POPE INNOCENT III [7]

### Walther von der Vogelweide

*Der stuol ze Rôme ist allerêrst berihtet rehte,*
*Als hie vor bî einem zouberaere Gêrbrehte.*


A necromancer holds the Roman chair —
In the black art Pope Gerbert's heir.
But Gerbert gave none but himself to Hell:
This one will give all Christendom as well.
Why cry not all, out of their sorrow deep,

---

6. From *The Minnesingers,* by Jethro Bithell; Longmans, London, 1909.  Reprinted
by permission of the translator.
   7. Ibid.

To Heaven, and ask how long the Lord will sleep?
Priest foil His works, and to His words false witness bear;
His treasurer steals the hoard of grace given in his care;
His peace-maker plunders here and murders there;
His shepherd has become a wolf among His sheep.

[tr. JETHRO BITHELL]


## ON THE POPE'S CRUSADE BOX [8]

### Walther von der Vogelweide

*Sagt an, hêr Stoc, hât iuch der bâbest her gesendet,*
*Daz ir in rîchet und uns Tiutschen ermet unde pfendet?*

Sir Savings-Box, hath the Pope sent you with his sermons
To enrich himself and beggar all the Germans?
Soon as the heaps of money he shall hold
A fine trick he will play — his trick of old:
He will say the Empire's in a parlous state —
And with our money will again be satiate.
Ah! little of the silver will reach the Holy Land:
Rich treasure seldom gives away priest's hand.
Sir Box, to rob us right and left is your command,
And to cozen all the fools that take the bait.

[tr. JETHRO BITHELL]


## MILLENNIUM [9]

### Walther von der Vogelweide

*Nu wachet! uns gêt zuo der tac,*
*Gein dem wol angest haben mac*
*Ein ieglich kristen, iuden unde heiden.*

Awake! The day is coming now
That brings the sweat of anguish to the brow
Of Christians, Jews, and Pagans all!
Many a token in the sky
And on the earth shows it is nigh:
Foretold in Holy Writ withal.
The sun no longer shows
His face; and treason sows
His secret seeds that no man can detect;
Fathers by their children are undone;

8. Ibid.
9. Ibid.

The brother would the brother cheat;
And the cowled monk is a deceit,
Who should the way to Heaven direct;
Might is right, and justice there is none.
Arise! we slept, nor of the peril recked.

[tr. JETHRO BITHELL]

## TAGELIET [10]

### Wolfram von Eschenbach (Bavaria, *circ.* 1165–1220)

*Den morgenblic bî wahtaers sange erkôs*
*Ein frowe dâ si tougen*
*An ir werden friundes arme lac.*


Morn, and the watchman's song that hailed it, broke
The slumbers of a lady where she lay
Secretly in her noble friend's embrace.
The joy that filled them both was driven away.
Her bright eyes dimmed; her face
Grew wan again.  She spoke:
"O Day, both wild and tame rejoice in thee,
And see thee gladly, save I alone.  What shall become of me?
My friend can stay no longer here.  Thy light
Hunts him away from me, out of my sight!"

Day thrust its brightness through the window-pane.
They, locked together, strove to keep Day out
And could not, whence they grew aware of dread.
She, his beloved, casting her arms about
Her loved one, caught him close to her again.
Her eyes drenched both their cheeks.  She said:
"One body and two hearts are we.
Nought is, can mar or separate our mated fealty.
From that great love of ours my heart lies waste,
Save when thou comest to me, and I to thee make haste."

Thus did the sorrowing man take swift farewell:
Their fair smooth skins drew closer, closer yet.
This the sun saw and shined upon: a kiss
From a sweet lady's mouth, with eyes all wet.
How they lay twined in the intricacies
Of blended lips, breasts, arms and thighs, whose art can tell?
If a shield-painter could have limned them there,
Where they lay clasped, no other picture could have been as fair.

10. From *Essays on the Mediaeval German Love Lyric*, by Margaret F. Richey: B. H.
Blackwell, Oxford, 1943.  Reprinted by permission of the publisher.

Yet was this last love-bliss of theirs pierced through
With grief.  Their faithful love was all too true.

[tr. MARGARET F. RICHEY]


TANZLIET [11]

Neithart von Reuental (Bavaria, 13th cent.)

*Ûf dem berge und in dem tal
Hebt sich aber der vogele schal;
Hiwer als ê
Grüener klê.*

On the hill and in the dale
Sings again the nightingale;
Clover green
Now is seen:
Out, old winter, thy pain is keen!
    The trees that erstwhile stood all gray
Show on blooming summer spray
Birds that sing
To the spring;
May takes toll of everything.
    An old wife wrestled well with death,
Both day and night she fought for breath.
Then like a sheep
She did leap,
And knocked the young ones in a heap.

[tr. BAYARD QUINCY MORGAN]


DEBATE

Heinrich von Pressela (Duke of Breslau, 1266–1299)

*Ich klage dir, meie! ich klage dir sumer wunne!
Ich klage dir, liehti heide breit!
Ich klage dir, ouge brehender klê!*

Poet.   To thee, O *May*, I must complain,
        O *summer*, I complain to thee,
    And thee, thou flower-bespangled *plain*,
        And *meadow*, dazzling bright to see!

11. From *Nature in Middle High German Lyrics*, by Bayard Quincy Morgan; published as "Hesperia," *Schriften zur Germanischen Philologie*, No. 4; The Johns Hopkins University Press, Baltimore, 1912.  Reprinted by permission of the publisher.

To thee, O *greenwood*, thee, O *sun*,
  And thee, too, *Love!* my song shall be
Of all the pain my lady's scorn
  Relentlessly inflicts on me.
Yet, would ye all with one consent
Lend me your aid, she might repent:
Then for king heaven's sake hear, and give me back content!

*May, &c.*   "What is the wrong? stand forth and tell us what;
      Unless just cause be shown, we hear thee not."

*Poet.*   She lets my fancy feed on bliss;
      But when, believing in her love,
        I seek her passion's strength to prove,
      She lets me perish, merciless:
      Ah! woe is me, that e'er I knew
      Her from whose love such misery doth ensue!

*May.*   "I, *May*, will strait my flowers command;
      My roses bright, and lilies white,
    No more for her their charms expand."

*Summer.*   "And I, bright *summer*, will restrain
        The birds' sweet throats; their tuneful notes
    No more shall charm her ear again."

*Plain.*   "When on the *plain* she doth appear,
      My flow'rets gay shall fade away;
    Thus crost, perchance to thee she'll turn again her ear."

*Mead.*   "And I, the *mead*, will help thee too;
      Gazing on me, her fate shall be,
    That my bright charms shall blind her view."

*Wood.*   "And I, the *greenwood*, break my bowers
      When the fair maid flies to my shade,
    Till she to thee her smile restores."

*Sun.*   "I *sun*, will pierce her frozen heart,
      Till from the blaze of my bright rays,
    Vainly she flies: — then learns a gentler part."

*Love.*   "I, *Love*, will banish instantly
      Whatever dear and sweet I bear,
    Till she in pity turn to thee."

*Poet.*   Alas! must *all* her joys thus flee?
      Nay, rather I would joyless die,
    How great soe'er my pain may be.

*Love.* "Seek'st thou revenge?" saith *Love,* "then at my nod
     The paths of joy shall close, so lately trod."

*Poet.* Nay then!  Oh leave her not thus shorn of bliss;
     Leave me to die forlorn, so hers be happiness.
                                        [tr. EDGAR TAYLOR]


## WOMAN'S CRAFT [12]

### Heinrich von Meissen (Frauenlob, d. 1318)

*Adam dén êrsten menschen den betrouc ein wîp*

A woman cheated Adam, first of men;
Samson was fooled, and fooled again
By a woman, till he lost his eyes;
Fell by a woman David; and his son,
King Solomon the wise,
Was by a woman spoiled of Paradise;
Absalom's beauty saved him not from one;
And Alexander, maugre empery of the world, was thus
Cozened; and Virgilius
Came by a perjured woman in distress;
And Holofernes lay a corse,
Head dissevered from the streaming torse;
Troy, town and land, smoked for a woman's loveliness;
Achilles wild became,
And the wild Asahel grew tame;
King Arthur's shame
Sullied his knighthood only from a dame;
And Percival is such another name.
Since Love was ever used to such a game,
Now that to me does hap the same,
I burnt and frozen how should I expect redress?
                                        [tr. JETHRO BITHELL]


## THE FROG AND THE STEER

### (From *Edelstein*)

### Ulrich Boner (Berne, 14th cent.)

*Ein vrösch mit sinem sune kan
Eis mâls gesprungen ûf den plan,
Da er ein grôzen ochsen sach.*

12. From *The Minnesingers,* by Jethro Bithell; Longmans, London, 1909.  Reprinted
by permission of the translator.

A frog with frogling by his side
Came hopping through the plain, one tide:
There he an ox at grass did spy;
Much angered was the frog thereby;
He said: "Lord God, what was my sin,
Thou madest me so small and thin?
Likewise I have no handsome feature,
And all dishonored is my nature,
To other creatures far and near,
For instance, this same grazing steer."
The frog would fain with bullock cope,
'Gan brisk outblow himself in hope.
Then spake his frogling: "Father o' me,
It boots not, let thy blowing be;
Thy nature hath forbid this battle,
Thou canst not vie with the black-cattle."
Nathless let be the frog would not,
Such prideful notion had he got;
Again to blow right sore 'gan he,
And said: "Like ox could I but be
In size, within this world there were
No frog so glad, to thee I swear."
The son spake: "Father, me is woe
Thou shouldst torment thy body so;
I fear thou art to lose thy life;
Come, follow me, and leave this strife:
Good father, take advice of me,
And let thy boastful blowing be."
Frog said: "Thou need'st not beck and nod,
I will not do 't, so help me God!
Big as this ox is, I must turn,
Mine honor now it doth concern."
He blew himself, and burst in twain:
Such of that blowing was his gain.

The like hath oft been seen of such
Who grasp at honor overmuch;
They must with none at all be doing,
But sink full soon and come to ruin.
He, that, with wind of pride accursed,
Much puffs himself, will surely burst;
He men miswishes and misjudges,
Inferiors scorns, superiors grudges,
Of all his equals is a hater,
Much grieved he is at any better:
Wherefore it were a sentence wise,
Were his whole body set with eyes,
Who envy hath, to see so well
What lucky hap each man befell,

That so he filled were with fury,
And burst asunder in a hurry;
And so full soon betide him this
Which to the frog betided is.

[tr. THOMAS CARLYLE]

## THE BATTLE OF SEMPACH (A.D. 1386)

Halbsuter (Lucerne, 14th cent.)

*Halbsuter unvergessen*
*Also ist er genant,*
*Zuo Lucern ist er gesessen,*
*Und war gar wol erkant,*
*He, er was ein Biderman:*
*Dis Lied hat er gemachet,*
*Als er ab der Schlacht is kan.*

'Twas when among our linden-trees
  The bees had housed in swarms
(And gray-haired peasants say that these
  Betoken foreign arms), —

Then looked we down to Willisow,
  The land was all in flame;
We knew the Archduke Leopold
  With all his army came.

The Austrian nobles made their vow,
  So hot their heart and bold,
"On Switzer carles we'll trample now,
  And slay both young and old."

With clarion loud, and banner proud,
  From Zurich on the lake,
In martial pomp and fair array,
  Their onward march they make.

"Now list, ye lowland nobles all, —
  Ye seek the mountain strand,
Nor wot ye what shall be your lot
  In such a dangerous land.

"I rede ye, shrive ye of your sins,
  Before ye farther go;
A skirmish in Helvetian hills
  May send your souls to woe."

"But where now shall we find a priest
  Our shrift that he may hear?"
"The Switzer priest has ta'en the field,
  He deals a penance drear.

"Right heavily upon your head
  He'll lay his hand of steel;
And with his trusty partisan
  Your absolution deal."

'T was on a Monday morning then,
  The corn was steeped in dew,
And merry maids had sickles ta'en
  When the host to Sempach drew.

The stalwart men of fair Lucerne
  Together have they joined;
The pith and core of manhood stern,
  Was none cast looks behind.

It was the lord of Hare-castle,
  And to the Duke he said,
"Yon little band of brethren true
  Will meet us undismayed."

"O Hare-castle, thou heart of hare!"
  Fierce Oxenstern replied.
"Shalt see, then, how the game will fare,"
  The taunted knight replied.

There was lacing then of helmets bright,
  And closing ranks amain;
The peaks they hewed from their boot-points
  Might well-nigh load a wain.

And thus they to each other said,
  "Yon handful down to hew
Will be no boastful tale to tell,
  The peasants are so few."

The gallant Swiss Confederates there
  They prayed to God aloud,
And he displayed his rainbow fair
  Against a swarthy cloud.

Then heart and pulse throbbed more and more
  With courage firm and high,
And down the good Confederates bore
  On the Austrian chivalry.

The Austrian Lion 'gan to growl,
  And toss his mane and tail;
And ball, and shaft, and crossbow bolt
  Went whistling forth like hail.

Lance, pike, and halbert mingled there,
  The game was nothing sweet;
The boughs of many a stately tree
  Lay shivered at their feet.

The Austrian men-at-arms stood fast,
  So close their spears they laid;
It chafed the gallant Winkelreid,
  Who to his comrades said, —

"I have a virtuous wife at home,
  A wife and infant son;
I leave them to my country's care, —
  This field shall soon be won.

"These nobles lay their spears right thick,
  And keep full firm array;
Yet shall my charge their order break,
  And make my brethren way."

He rushed against the Austrian band,
  In desperate career,
And with his body, breast, and hand,
  Bore down each hostile spear.

Four lances splintered on his crest,
  Six shivered in his side;
Still on the serried files he pressed, —
  He broke their ranks, and died.

This patriot's self-devoted deed
  First tamed the Lion's mood,
And the four forest cantons freed
  From thraldom by his blood.

Right where his charge had made a lane,
  His valiant comrades burst,
With sword, and axe, and partisan,
  And hack, and stab, and thrust.

The daunted Lion 'gan to whine,
  And granted ground amain;
The Mountain Bull he bent his brows,
  And gored his sides again.

Then lost was banner, spear and shield,
  At Sempach, in the flight;
The cloister vaults at Konigsfield
  Hold many an Austrian knight.

It was the Archduke Leopold,
  So lordly would he ride,
But he came against the Switzer churls,
  And they slew him in his pride.

The heifer said unto the bull,
  "And shall I not complain?
There came a foreign nobleman
  To milk me on the plain.

"One thrust of thine outrageous horn
  Has galled the knight so sore,
That to the churchyard he is borne,
  To range our glens no more."

An Austrian noble left the stour,
  And fast the flight 'gan take;
And he arrived in luckless hour
  At Sempach on the lake.

He and his squire a fisher called
  (His name was Hans von Rot),
"For love, or meed, or charity,
  Receive us in thy boat!"

Their anxious call the fisher heard,
  And, glad the meed to win,
His shallop to the shore he steered,
  And took the fliers in.

And while against the tide and wind
  Hans stoutly rowed his way,
The noble to his follower signed
  He should the boatman slay.

The fisher's back was to them turned,
  The squire his dagger drew,
Hans saw his shadow in the lake,
  The boat he overthrew.

He whelmed the boat, and, as they strove
  He stunned them with his oar:
"Now drink ye deep, my gentle Sirs,
  You'll ne'er stab boatman more.

"Two gilded fishes in the lake
  This morning have I caught;
Their silver scales may much avail,
  Their carrion flesh is naught."

It was a messenger of woe
  Has sought the Austrian land:
"Ah, gracious lady! evil news!
  My lord lies on the strand.

"At Sempach, on the battle-field,
  His bloody corpse lies there."
"Ah, gracious God!" the lady cried,
  "What tidings of despair!"

Now would you know the minstrel wight
  Who sings of strife so stern?
Albert the Souter is he hight,
  A burgher of Lucerne.

A merry man was he, I wot,
  The night he made the lay,
Returning from the bloody spot,
  Where God had judged the day.

[tr. Sir Walter Scott]

# VII. ROMANCE LITERATURE

Any living language changes from century to century. Romance language is not otherwise than living Latin many centuries removed from the classical Latin we know. While, in the sixth to ninth centuries, literacy was an attribute almost exclusively the clergy's, the language of writing changed but slowly because it was tied to the Scriptures and to the liturgy. But oral Latin, the language of business and mundane affairs, changed the faster for being no longer anchored by writing. The language of literature and the language of speech were no longer one. Speech followed provincial lines, so that shortly it broke into many dialectical variations of three main groups — what Dante below (p. 745) and others distinguished as the languages of *oc* (Spain and Provence), *oil* (France), and *si* (Italy), according to the word of assent in each.

These vulgar tongues were enriched and developed by the barbarians who settled in the Roman provinces: the Goths in Spain and northern Italy, the Burgundians on the Saone, and the Franks on the Seine and Meuse. What Gaston Paris says of the Franks may be more generally applied: "Their tongue, which they did not hesitate to exchange for vulgar Latin, nevertheless gave to that language a tremendous number of words, and very much more important words than had been given by Celtic — not only substantives, which always attach themselves to the objects they designate, but adjectives and verbs, signs of the most intimate kind of relationships."

As early as the seventh century the Church asked its clergy to compose sermons in the vernacular, or non-ecclesiastical, tongue; but authors hesitated to put into a dialect what might be more widely read and appreciated in Latin. Hence it was not until the beginning of the tenth century, when education spread to secular lords, that very much was written in the newer languages. The Strassburg Oaths, exchanged by Charles the Bald and Louis II in 842, were written down in Teutonic and *lingua Romana,* the precursor of modern French. *La Cantilène de Sainte Eulalie* is ascribed to the last years of the ninth century. But not until the beginning of the twelfth century is vernacular literature important.

The relationship between ecclesiastical and secular literature in this early period is not clear. Nearly every one of the vernacular works has its parallel in contemporary or preceding Latin literature. How much the secular writers learned from the clergy who schooled them and how much the writings of the Church expressed lay thought cannot be settled. If *Walter of Aquitaine* was written in a monastic school by a church scholar, whether its author be Ekkehard or another, then the Church appears to have initiated chivalric romance, and the forerunners of Charlemagne and Arthur were St. Anthony and St. George. As early as the sixth century the future bishop Fortunatus was writing Provençal Latin verses that contained in embryo the popular themes of troubadours, and in succeeding centuries church writers developed strophe, accent, and rhyme which the secular writers freely borrowed. The development of the sequence in the Mass was followed, step by step, first by Latin parodies and imitations composed by wandering scholars, and then by *canzone* and *leich* of the vernaculars. Yet did romance literature suddenly burgeon in the twelfth century, branching from the liturgy and patristic lore, or had there long been a vernacular literature that has not survived because the nobility was not stable enough to preserve it? The incidence of the crusader and vernacular literature is no doubt important. Not only did travel bring exchange of ideas among a laity previously isolated from each other, but the long periods of idle waiting in camps gave time for storytelling and cultivation of the arts.

Literature thrived in Provence and France before it did in Spain and Italy. Spain was only beginning to flex its muscles against the Moorish overlords in the twelfth century. Italy was partitioned among Greeks, Saracens, Normans, Germans, and the Pope. In Provence, isolation determined the form of literature: though the dukes constantly shifted boundaries and allegiance, distant sovereigns ruled loosely, for the hills and woods protected the natives. The wealth developed from uninterrupted tillage meant leisure for the local count, who lived in new stone bastions like Carcassonne. But isolation breeds peculiarity in art, as prison literature often shows — an excessive interest in attributes of form, a narrow range in ideas, a subjective and personalized view of life. Though the *chansons de gestes* were cultivated and there are some stories — *Aucassin and Nicolete,* for instance — Provençal literature lacks universal appeal. It is the lyrics, particularly the love lyrics, that survive; for they grow like tropical plants in such surroundings. In the main, the fortune of Provence was to inspire great art in others; for politics determined that Provençal literature should spread north, east, and south, as it was wiped out by religious wars at home. English, French, German, and Italian literature sprang to life under the goad of troubadour poetry. Chivalric and courtly literature would probably never have existed, and Gottfried, Dante, Chaucer, and Villon would have written quite differently, had it not been for the Provençal lyricists.

This provinciality contrasts with the comparative urbanity of France. Paris was, from the twelfth to the fourteenth centuries, the crossroads of the world, and the new university growing out of the cathedral school dominated the intellectual life of Europe. French manners, French dress, and French thoughts were aped everywhere, at least until the cities of Tuscany and Lombardy in the times of Dante and Giotto began to vie with Paris. The feudal courts were centers of international affairs and adjusted themselves to the new world of trade and commerce. The artisans of Flanders and Artois created a demand for their metalwork and textiles everywhere. The

Normans were ubiquitous and curious — whatever they found and thought good they assimilated. Champagne, which cradled the reforming Cistercians and taught the world through Bernard of Clairvaux the cult of the Virgin Mary, also spread through Chrétien the new romance and the cult of Countess Marie. The Church had extolled Virgil and called him The Poet; he was saved from paganism by his Messianic Eclogue. But the poet of the new vernacular was Ovid, who knew how to tell of *ars amatoria* and the escapades of demigods. Romance, which was thoroughly French, wherever it was written, bloomed and faded quickly. The century between 1150 and 1250 witnessed its rise and fall. Thereafter France retained some pre-eminence in literature, though it found its later metier in rational, cynical, didactic works, as if its great effort at idealism had exhausted its powers for flight.

Italy cannot be said to have had a literature worth reading until the Emperor Frederick II established his renowned court at Naples. "A man pestiferous and accursed, a schismatic, heretic, and epicurean, who corrupted the whole earth," according to the Franciscan Salimbene, he welcomed all novelty and encouraged all thought however heterodox. To his court came Greek, Saracen, Teuton, and Spaniard. Michael the Scot, with a reputation for wizardry and an ability to translate Hebrew and Arabic science and philosophy, was co-worker with the poet Henry of Avranches, the mathematician Leonardo of Pisa, the Jewish philosopher Jacob Anatoli, to mention but a few. Frederick welcomed troubadour and minnesinger, and himself wrote verses. After his death in 1250, the art and science concentrated in Naples spread throughout Europe; his successor as King of Naples, Charles of Anjou, was in an anomalous position common to feudalism — for Naples and Sicily he was vassal of the Pope, for Provence of the Emperor, and for Anjou of the King of France. Little wonder that ideas were exchanged. The newly regularized communes of northern Italy, Florence, Pisa, Bologna, Ravenna, Milan, and Venice, enriched by the trade of the East, which poured through to France, Germany, and England, profited most. Dante, who drew into his all-embracing mind the lyric measures of the courtly poets, the new concept of the world of the explorers, the urbanity of the bourgeoisie, the philosophy of the universities, the idealism of the Franciscans, and the universality of the Church, was not, as Carlyle would have it, "the voice of ten silent centuries" — that any reader of this volume knows; but he does represent the apex of medieval literature. It was part of his greatness as a poet that he chose to write, not in Latin, but in the romance tongue, the language of the people.

# THE SONG OF ROLAND

The oldest extant French poetry of any scope is the *Song of Roland*. It is also the best of its class of literature, the *chanson de geste*. The manuscript containing the present work was written about 1130, before Geoffrey composed his *Histories,* but there is general agreement that it was originally formed before the eleventh century came to a close — in the days of popularity of the pilgrim road to Compostella when forces were gathering for the First Crusade. In fact, on the testimony of both William of Malmesbury (A.D. 1120) and Wace, some story like this one was sung by the Norman warriors as they went into battle at Hastings, inspired by William the Conqueror's jongleur, Taillefer:

| | |
|---|---|
| Taillefer qui muet bien chantont | Taillefer who was famed for song, |
| Sor un cheval qui tost alout | Mounted on a charger strong, |
| Devant le duc alout chantant | Rode on before the Duke, and sang |
| De Karlemaigne e de Rollant | Of Roland and of Charlemagne, |
| E d'Oliver e des vassals | Oliver and the vassals all |
| Qui morurent en Rencevals. | Who fell in fight at Roncevals. |
| (Wace, *Roman de Rou*) | (tr. Henry Adams) |

There are extant more than eighty *chansons de geste,* that is, French narrative poems treating a subject of French or Provençal history usually connected in fact or imagination with Charlemagne, written in stanzas of varying length (from 1800 to 18,000 lines) but nearly all composed of strophes or *laisses* of ten-syllabled lines, each ending with the same rhyme or assonance. The twelfth century was the high period of composition, though some were composed in the thirteenth century. All purport to tell factual history, usually of Charlemagne's crusades against the "paynim" Saracens.

Needless to say, the amount of true history in the *chansons* is infinitesimal. They tell not of the eighth century but of their own times. How the stories grew, we cannot know, but we can compare with *Roland* the historical record of Einhard: "As the army moved along, drawn out into a thin column because of the narrow passes, the Gascons, having lain in ambush on a mountain top (for the spot is especially favorable for ambush because the dense forests hide the view), attacked the last part of the baggage train and those who had been detailed to guard it, and hurled them into the ravine below. In the struggle they killed every one and, stealing the baggage, dispersed from the spot under the benificent cover of night with all speed . . . In this battle Eggihard the king's steward, Anselm the Count Palatine, and Hrouland the Prefect of the March of Brittany were slain along with many others. Nor could this deed be avenged at the time, because the enemy scattered so quickly that no clew to their whereabouts could be discovered." (*Vita Karoli,* ix). Two other virtually contemporary records yield no additional information. A comparatively obscure skirmish in the Pyrenees became, in three centuries, a great battle between Christian and Mohammedan worlds.

The poem consists of 4001 lines and falls into three episodes: (1) Ganelon's treachery, (2) the battle at Roncevals, (3) Charlemagne's revenge. The third part, satisfying though it may have been to French sensibilities, is an excrescence and is not represented in the selections below. Parts one and two are a moving whole, detailing at once the results of pride and feudal loyalty. We have already seen the central problem of feudalism developed in two languages — in *Walter of Aquitaine* and *The Lay of the Nibelungs*. We can imagine that all truly moving secular literature of the tenth and eleventh centuries must have treated the problem. In the tenth century the author of *Walter* could not settle his problem. In the eleventh century, the *Song of Roland* seems, despite our love of Oliver and exasperation with Roland, to say that honor and vassalage are measured in terms of greatest sacrifice, not greatest reason. In the twelfth century, the poet of the *Nibelungenlied* counts the age of vassalage as waning.

During the 1930's a beautiful edition and commentary on all the Roland material was prepared in eleven volumes by Raoul Mortier.

## THE SONG OF ROLAND

### Anonymous (12th cent.)

#### PART I

##### GANELON'S TREACHERY

Charles the King, our great Emperor, has been for seven long years in Spain; he has conquered all the high land down to the sea; not a castle holds out against him, not a wall or city is left unshattered, save Saragossa, which stands high on a mountain. King Marsila holds it, who loves not God, but serves Mahound, and worships Apollon; ill hap must in sooth befall him.

King Marsila abides in Saragossa. And on a day he passes into the shade of his orchard; there he sits on a terrace of blue marble, and around him his men are gathered to the number of twenty thousand. He speaks to his dukes and his counts, saying: "Hear, lords, what evil overwhelms us; Charles the Emperor of fair France has come into this land to confound us. I have no host to do battle against him, nor any folk to discomfort his. Counsel me, lords, as wise men and save me from death and shame." But not a man has any word in answer, save Blancandrin of the castle of Val-Fonde.

Blancandrin was among the wisest of the paynims, a good knight of much prowess, discreet and valiant in the service of his lord. He saith to the King: "Be not out of all comfort. Send to Charles the proud, the terrible, proffer of faithful service and goodly friendship; give him bears and lions and dogs, seven hundred camels and a thousand falcons past the moulting time, four hundred mules laden with gold and silver, that he may send before him fifty full wains. And therewith shall he richly reward his followers. Long has he waged war in this land; it is meet he return again to Aix in France. And do thou pledge they word to follow him at the feast of Saint Michael, to receive the faith of the Christians, and to become his man in all honour and loyalty. If he would have hostages, send them to him, or ten or twenty, to make good the compact. We will send him the sons of our wives; yea, though it be to death, I will send mine own. Better it were that they lose their lives than that we be spoiled of lands and lordship, and be brought to beg our bread.

"By this my right hand," saith Blancandrin, "and by the beard that the wind blows about my breast, ye shall see the Frankish host straightway scatter abroad, and the Franks return again to their land of France. When each is in his own home, and Charles is in his chapel at Aix, he will hold high festival on the day of Saint Michael. The day will come, and the term appointed will pass, but of us he will have no word nor tidings. The King is proud and cruel of heart, he will let smite off the heads of our hostages, but better it is that they lose their lives than that we be spoiled of bright Spain, the fair, or suffer so great dole and sorrow." And the paynims cry: "Let it be as he saith."

So King Marsila hath ended his council; he then called Clarin de Balaguer, Estramarin, and Endropin, his fellow, and Priamon, and Garlan the Bearded, Machiner, and Maheu his uncle, Joïmer, and Malbien from oversea, and Blancandrin; ten of the fiercest he hath called, to make known his will unto them. "Lords, barons," he saith, "go ye to Charlemagne, who is at the siege of the city of Cordova, bearing olive branches in your hands in token of peace and submission. If by your wit ye can make me a covenant with Charles, I will give you great store of gold and silver, and lands and fiefs as much as ye may desire." "Nay," say the paynims, "of these things we have and to spare."

King Marsila has ended his council. And again he saith to his men: "Go ye forth, lords, and bear in your hands branches of olive; bid Charles the King that he have mercy on me for the love of his God; say before this first month ends, I will follow him with a thousand of my true liege people, to receive the Christian faith and become his man in all love and truth. If he would have hostages, they shall be given him." Then said Blancandrin: "We will make thee a fair covenant."

And King Marsila let bring the ten white mules the which had been sent him by the King of Suatilie; their bridles are of gold and their saddles wrought of silver. They who are to do the king's message set forth, bearing in their hands branches of olive. Anon thereafter they come before Charles, who holds France as his domain; alack, he cannot but be beguiled by them.

The Emperor is joyous and glad at heart; he has taken Cordova and overthrown its walls; and with his mangonels he has beaten down its towers.  Great was the plunder which fell to his knights in gold and silver and goodly armour.  Not a heathen is left in the city; all are either slain or brought to Christianity.  The Emperor is in a wide orchard, and with him are Roland, and Oliver, Samson the Duke, and Anseïs the Proud, Geoffrey of Anjou, the King's standard bearer, and thereto are Gerin, and Gerier, and with them is many another man of France to the number of fifteen thousand. Upon the grass are spread cloths of white silk whereon the knights may sit; and some of these play at tables for their delight, but the old and wise play at chess, and the young lords practise the sword-play.  Under a pine, beside an eglantine, stands a throne made all of beaten gold; there sits the King who rules sweet France; white is his beard and his head is hoary, his body is well fashioned and his countenance noble; those who seek him have no need to ask which is the King.  And the messengers lighted down from their mules and saluted him in all love and friendship.

Blancandrin was the first to speak, and said to the King: "Greeting in the name of God the Glorious whom ye adore.  Thus saith to you King Marsila the valiant: much has he enquired into the faith which brings salvation; and now he would fain give you good store of his substance, bears and lions, and greyhounds in leash, seven hundred camels and a thousand falcons past the moulting time, four hundred mules laden with gold and silver, that ye may carry away fifty full wains of treasure; so many bezants of fine gold shall there be that well may ye reward your men of arms therewith.  Long have you tarried in this land, it is meet that ye return again to Aix in France; there my lord will follow you, he gives you his word (and will receive the faith that you hold; with joined hands he will become your man, and will hold from you the kingdom of Spain)." At these words the Emperor stretches his two hands towards heaven, and then bows his head and begins to think.

The Emperor sat with bowed head, for he was in no wise hasty of his words, but was ever wont to speak at his leisure.  When again he raised his head, proud was his face, and he said to the messengers: "Fairly have ye spoken.  Yet King Marsila is much mine enemy. By what token may I set my trust in the words that ye have said?" "By hostages," the Saracen made answer, "of which you shall have or ten or fifteen or twenty.  Though it be to death I will send mine own son, and you shall have others, methinks, of yet gentler birth. When you are in your kingly palace at the high feast of Saint Michael of the Peril, my lord will come to you, he gives you his word, and there in the springs that God made flow for you, he would be baptized a Christian."  "Yea, even yet he may be saved," Charles made answer.

Fair was the evening and bright the sun. Charles has let stable the ten mules, and in a wide orchard has let pitch a tent wherein the ten messengers are lodged. Ten sergeants make them right good cheer; and there they abide the night through, till the clear dawn. The Emperor has risen early, and heard mass and matins; and now he sits under a pine tree, and calls his barons into council, for he would act in all matters by the advice of those of France.

The Emperor sits under the pine tree and summons his barons to council. Thither came Ogier, and Archbishop Turpin, Richard the Old, with Henry his nephew, and the brave Count Acelin of Gascony, Tedbalt of Rheims and Milon his cousin, and thereto Gerin and Gerier, and with them came Count Roland, and Oliver the brave, the gentle; of the Franks of France there are more than a thousand, and with the rest came Ganelon who did the treason. And now begins the council that wrought so great woe.

"Lords, barons," then saith Charles the Emperor, "King Marsila has sent me messengers: he would give me great store of his havings, bears and lions and leashed greyhounds, seven hundred camels and a thousand moulted falcons, four hundred mules laden with gold of Arabia, more than enough to fill fifty wains; but thereto he charges me that I go back to France, giving his word to come to me at my abiding place at Aix, and there to receive our most holy faith, and to hold his marches of me; but I know not what may be in his heart." "We must bethink ourselves," say the Franks in answer.

Now when the Emperor had ceased from speaking, Count Roland, who is in no wise in accord with his words, stands forth and nay-says him. He saith to the King: "It were ill done to set thy trust in Marsila. It is seven full years since we came into Spain, and for you I have conquered Noples and Commibles, and I have taken Valtierra and the land of Pina, and Balaguer and Tudela and Sezilie. Now King Marsila was ever a traitor; aforetime he sent fifteen of his paynims, each bearing an olive branch, and they came unto you with a like tale. Then ye advised with your Franks, who counselled you folly; and you sent two of your counts, Basan and Basil, into the paynims, and thereafter, below Haltilie, their heads were smitten off. Wherefore I counsel carry on the war even as ye have begun it; lead your assembled host unto Saragossa, lay siege to it, even though it be for all the days of your life, and revenge us for those whom the felons slew aforetime."

The Emperor sat with bent head; he stroked his beard and tugged at his moustache, nor answered he his nephew for either good or ill. The Franks are silent, all save Ganelon. He rises and comes before Charles, and speaks right haughtily, saying to the King: "It were ill done to hearken to a braggart — either me or any other — save that his counsel be to thine own profit. When King Marsila lets tell thee he will do homage to thee as thy vassal, and will hold all Spain in fief of thee, and thereafter will receive the faith that we hold, he who counsels thee that thou reject this proffer, recks little, lord, of what death we die. The counsel of pride should not prevail. Let us leave folly and hold with the wise."

Thereafter Naymes stood forth — no better vassal was there in all the court — and thus bespoke the King: "Thou hast heard the answer of Ganelon the Count, and wise it is, an it be but heeded. King Marsila is spent with war, thou hast taken his castles, and with thy mangonels hast beaten down his walls, thou hast burned his cities and vanquished his men; when now that he entreats thy mercy, it were sin to press him further, the more that he would give thee surety by hostages. This great war should have an end." "The Duke hath spoken wisely," cry the Franks.

"Lords, barons, what messenger shall we send to King Marsila at Saragossa?" And Duke Naymes made answer: "By thy leave I will go; give me now the glove and the staff." But the King answered him: "Nay, thou art a man of good counsel, and thou shalt not at this time go thus far from me. Sit thou again in thy place since none hath summoned thee."

"Lords, barons, what messenger shall we send to the Saracen that holds Saragossa?" And Roland made answer: "Right glad were I to go." "Nay certes, not you," saith Count Oliver, "for you are fierce and haughty of temper and I fear lest you embroil yourself; I will myself go, if the King so wills it." "Peace," the King answered, "nor you nor he shall go thither; and by my beard which thou seest whiten, not one of the Twelve Peers shall be chosen." The Franks answer not, and lo, all are silent.

Turpin of Rheims then stood forth from the rest and bespoke the King, saying: "Let be thy Franks. Seven years hast thou been in this land, and much travail and woe hath been theirs. Give me, lord, the staff and the glove, and I will go to the Saracen of Spain, and learn what manner of man he is." But wrathfully the King made answer: "Sit thou again in thy place upon the white silk and speak not, save as I command thee.

"Ye knights of France," then said Charles the Emperor, "now choose me a baron of my marches who shall do my message to King Marsila." Then saith Roland: "Let it be Ganelon my stepfather." "Yea," say the Franks, "well will he do your errand; if ye pass him by ye will send none so wise."

Then said the King: "Ganelon, come thou hither, and receive the glove and the staff. Thou hast heard thou art chosen of the Franks." "Sir," Ganelon answered him, "it is Roland who has done this thing. Never again shall I hold him in my love all the days of my life, nor yet Oliver in that he is his comrade, nor the Twelve Peers in that they hold him dear, and here in thy sight, lord, I defy them." "Thy wrath is over great," then saith the King, "and certes, go thou must in that I command thee." "Go I may, but without surety. None was there for Basil and Basan his brother.

"Well I know I needs must go unto Saragossa, but for him who

goes thither there is no return.  And more than that, thy sister is
my wife, and I have a son, never was there a fairer, and if he lives
he will be a man of good prowess.  To him I leave my lands and
honours; guard him well, for never again shall I see him with these
eyes."  "Thou art too tender of heart," Charles answered him,
"since I command thee, needs must thou go."

And Count Ganelon was in sore wrath thereat; he lets slip from
about his neck his great cloak of sables, and stands forth in his tunic
of silk.  Gray blue are his eyes and proud his face, well fashioned
is he of body and broad of chest.  So comely he is, all his peers turn
to look upon him.  And he speaks to Roland, saying: "Thou fool,
why art thou in so great wrath?  It is known of all that I am thy
stepfather, and thou hast named me to go unto Marsila.  If God
grants me to return again I shall bring woe upon thee so great it
shall endure all the days of thy life."  "Thou speakest pride and
folly," Roland answered him, "and all men know I reck naught of
threats.  But a man of counsel should bear this message, and if
the King wills it, I am ready to go in thy stead."

"Nay," Ganelon made answer, "in my stead thou shalt not go.
Thou art not my man, nor am I thy over-lord.  Charles has commanded me that I do his errand, and I will go unto Marsila in
Saragossa.  But mayhap I shall do there some folly to ease me of
my great wrath."  At these words Roland falls a-laughing.

When Ganelon sees that Roland bemocks him, so great anger is
his he is near to bursting with wrath, and he wellnigh goes out of
his senses.  He saith to the Count: "Little love have I for thee in
that thou hast brought false judgment upon me.  O just King, lo,
I stand before thee, ready to do thy commandment."

The Emperor holds out to him his right glove, but fain had Count
Ganelon been elsewhere, and when he should have taken it, he lets
it fall to earth.  And the Franks cry: "God, what may this betide?
Great woe shall come upon us from this embassage."  "Lords," saith
Ganelon, "ye shall have tidings thereof.

"And O King," he said again, "I pray thy leave; since go I must,
I would not delay."  "Go in Jesus' name and in mine," the King
made answer.  With his right hand he shrove and blessed him, and
then he gave him the staff and the letter.

Now Ganelon the Count gets him to his lodging and begins to
don his armour, the goodliest he can find; he has fastened spurs of
gold upon his feet, and at his side he has girt Murglais his sword;
and when he mounted Tachebrun his steed, Guinemer his uncle
it was, held his stirrup.  Many a knight ye may see weep, and they
say to him: "Woe worth the day, baron!  Long hast thou been in
the King's court; and ever hast thou been accounted a man of
worship.  He who judged thee to go will be nowise shielded or saved
by Charles; Count Roland ought never to have had the thought, for
ye twain are near of kin."  And they say further: "Lord, we pray
thee take us with thee."  But Ganelon answers: "No, so help me
God!  Better it were that I die alone than that so many good knights

take their end. Ye will return again into sweet France, lords; greet ye my wife for me, and likewise Pinabel my friend and peer, and aid ye Baldwin my son, whom ye know, and make him your over-lord." Therewith he set forth and rode on his way.

As Ganelon fares forth under the high olives he overtakes the Saracen messengers. Anon Blancandrin falls back to ride beside him. Cunningly they speak one to another. "A marvel of a man is this Charles," saith Blancandrin. "He has conquered Apulia and all Calabria; he has crossed the salt sea into England and has won tribute therefrom for the profit of Saint Peter; but what would he of us in our marches?" Quoth Ganelon: "Such is his will; and no man avails to withstand him."

"The Franks are goodly men," then saith Blancandrin, "but your dukes and counts do much hurt to their liege lord in so advising him; they will bring loss and discomfiture to him and to others." But Ganelon answers him saying: "In sooth, I know no man save only Roland who shall be brought to shame thereby. On a day, as the Emperor was seated under the shade of the trees, his nephew came to him, clad in his hauberk — for he was come from the taking of spoils below Carcassonne — and in his hand he held a scarlet apple: 'Take it, fair sir,' saith Roland to his uncle, 'for even so I give over to thee the crowns of all the kings of the earth.' Of a surety, his great pride must undo him, for each day he runs in hazard of death; and if he be but slain we shall have quiet on the earth."

Then saith Blancandrin: "Fell and cruel is this Roland who would make all peoples yield them, and claim all lands for his. But by means of what folk does he think to win thus much?" "By the folk of France," Ganelon answers, "for he is so beloved by them that they will never fail him; many a gift he gives them of gold and silver, mules and war horses, silk and armour. And the Emperor likewise has all his desire; for him Roland will conquer all the lands from here even unto the East."

So Ganelon and Blancandrin rode on till each had pledged other to do what he might to compass the death of Roland. So they rode by highways and bypaths till they alighted under a yew tree in Saragossa. Hard by, under the shade of a pine tree, stood a throne covered over with silk of Alexandria; there sat the King who held all Spain, and around him were his Saracens to the number of twenty thousand; yet not one opened his lips or spoke a word, so eager were they for tidings; and now behold you, Blancandrin and Ganelon.

So Blancandrin came before Marsila; he held Count Ganelon by the hand, and he spoke to the King, saying: "Greeting in the name of Mahound and Apollon whose blessed law we hold. We did thy message to Charles, who lifted up both his hands towards heaven, and praised his God, nor made he other answer. But here he sends thee one of his barons, who is of France, and a mighty man, and from him thou shalt hear if thou art to have peace or war." Saith Marsila: "Now speak, for we listen."

Count Ganelon had well bethought himself, and begins to speak with much cunning, as one who is skilful in words, saying to the King: "Greeting in the name of God the Glorious whom we should adore. Thus saith to thee Charles the mighty: if thou wilt receive Christianity he will give thee the half of Spain in fee; the second half he will give unto Roland, in whom thou shalt find a haughty compeer. If thou wilt not accept this covenant, he will lay siege to Saragossa, and thou shalt be taken and bound by force, and brought unto the King's seat at Aix, and thou shalt be adjudged to end thy days, and there thou shalt die a vile and shameful death." At these words King Marsila was sore troubled; in his hand he held a javelin tipped with gold, and with it he would have struck Ganelon had his men not withheld him.

King Marsila hath waxed red with wrath, and hath shaken the shaft of his javelin. When Ganelon saw this, he laid a hand on his sword, and drew it forth from the sheath the length of two fingers, and spoke to it, saying: "Most fair and bright thou art; so long as I wear thee at this King's court, the Emperor of France will never say I should die here alone in a strange land, before the bravest have paid thee dear." But the paynims cry: "Let us stay this quarrel."

And the best of the Saracens so besought him, that Marsila again took his place on the throne. He breaks the seal and casts away the wax, he looks at the letter and sees the sum of it. "Charles who holds France in his power bids me bethink me of his sorrow and wrath: that is to say of Basan, and Basil, his brother, whose heads I did let smite off in the hills below Haltilie. If I would ransom the life of my body I must send him the Caliph my uncle, otherwise he will not hold me in his love." Thereafter spoke Marsila's son, and said to the King: "Ganelon hath uttered folly. Such words hath he said to thee it is unmeet that he live; give him over to me, and I will do justice upon him." When Ganelon hears him he brandishes his sword, and sets his back against the trunk of a pine tree.

Now for council the King hath passed into his orchard, and gathered his chief men about him. Thither came Blancandrin the hoary-headed, and Jurfaleu, his son and heir, and the Caliph, Marsila's uncle and faithful liegeman. Then saith Blancandrin: "Call hither the Frank. He has pledged me his faith to our welfare." "Do thou bring him," saith the King. And Blancandrin took Ganelon by the right hand, and brought him into the orchard before the King. And there they plotted the foul treason.

"Fair Sir Ganelon," saith the King, "I was guilty of some folly toward thee when I would have struck thee in my wrath. I give thee as a pledge these skins of sable, the border whereof is worth more than five hundred pounds. Before tomorrow at evening a fair amend shall be thine." "I will not refuse it," Ganelon answered him, "and may it please God give thee good thanks."

Then quoth Marsila: "Ganelon, in good faith I have it in my heart to love thee well. Tell me now of Charlemagne. Methinks he is of great age and has outlived his time, for I deem him more than two hundred years old. Through many lands has he journeyed, and many a blow has he taken on his embossed shield, and many a mighty king has he brought low; when will he yield him in the strife?" "Nay, not such is Charles," Ganelon answered him: "Whosoever looks on the Emperor, or knows him, must account him a man of much prowess. I know not how to praise and glorify him to the full sum of his honour and bounty. Who can reckon his worth? And God has gifted him with such valour that rather had he die than give up his lordship.

"That will never be," saith Ganelon, "so long as his nephew is a living man, he hath not his fellow for courage under the cope of heaven; and Oliver his comrade is of good prowess, and likewise the Twelve Peers whom Charles holds right dear; they, together with twenty thousand knights, make up the vanguard; and Charles is safe and unafraid."

"Fair Sir Ganelon," thus saith King Marsila, "a fairer folk than mine ye shall not see. I have upon four hundred thousand knights; with them I may well do battle against Charles and his Franks." "Nay, not at this time," Ganelon answers him, "or great will be the slaughter of thy paynims. Leave thou folly and seek after wisdom; give such store of thy substance into the Emperor that there will be no Frank that does not marvel thereat. Send him thereto twenty hostages, and the King will return again into fair France. But his rearguard he will leave behind him, and in it, of a surety, will be Count Roland, his nephew, and Oliver the valiant, the courteous; and both counts shall be slain, if thou wilt put thy trust in me. And the great pride of Charles shall come to its fall, and thenceforth he will have no desire to wage more war upon thee."

"Fair Sir Ganelon," then saith King Marsila, "how may I slay this Roland?" Quoth Ganelon: "Even that will I tell thee. The King will be at the main pass of Cizre, and he will have set his rearguard behind him; in it will be the mighty Count Roland, his nephew, and Oliver, in whom he sets his trust, and in their company will be twenty thousand Franks. But do thou send against them one hundred thousand of thy paynims, and do them battle a first time, that the men of France may be smitten and sore hurt. Now mayhap, in this first stour, thine own may be slain with great slaughter, but do thou set upon the Franks a second time, with like array, that Roland may in no wise escape. And for thy part thou wilt have done a noble deed of arms, and thou shalt be untroubled by war all the days of thy life.

"Whosoever may compass the death of Roland in that place will thereby smite off the right arm of Charles; his great armies will have an end, never again shall he call together such hosts, and the Great Land shall have peace." When Marsila heard this saying he kissed Ganelon upon the neck; then he began to open his treasures.

Quoth Marsila: "What need of more words? No counsel is good

in which a man may not set his trust. Now do thou therefore swear me straight the treason." "Let it be as thou wilt," said Ganelon; and he swore the treason upon the relics in his sword Murglais, and therewith became a traitor.

Hard by was a throne wrought of ivory, and to it Marsila let bring a book wherein was writ the law of Mahound and Tervagant, and upon it the Saracen of Spain swore that if he found Roland in the rearguard, he would set upon him with all his folk, and if that he might, forthwith slay him. "Blessed be our covenant," quoth Ganelon.

Then the King calls Malduit his treasurer, saying: "Hast thou made ready the gifts for Charles?" "Yea, lord," he answers, "all is ready, — seven hundred camels laden with gold and silver, and twenty hostages, the noblest under heaven."

Marsila lays a hand on Ganelon's shoulder and speaks to him, saying: "A goodly baron and wise thou art, but by that faith thou deemest most holy, have a heed that thou turn not thy heart from us; and I will give the great store of my substance, ten mules laden with the finest gold of Arabia; and each year thou shalt have a like gift. Now take thou the keys of this great city, and convey thou to Charles the rich gifts, but thereafter have a care the rearguard be adjudged to Roland. And so be it I may come upon him in pass or defile, I will do him battle to the death." "Methinks I tarry too long," saith Ganelon in answer; and therewith he mounts his horse and rides on his way.

Meantime the Emperor has turned back towards his own land, and has come to the city of Valtierra, which aforetime Count Roland had taken, and so destroyed that thenceforward for the space of a hundred years it was waste and desolate. There the King awaits tiding of Ganelon, and the tribute of the great land of Spain. And now on a morning, at dawn, with the first light, comes Ganelon into the camp.

The Emperor had risen early and heard mass and matins; and now he is on the green grass before his tent, and with him is Roland, and Oliver the valiant, Naymes the Duke and many another. Thither comes Ganelon, the felon, the traitor, and with cunning and falsehood speaks to the King, saying: "Blessed be thou of God! I bring thee hereby the keys of Saragossa, and great store of gifts, and twenty hostages — guard thou them well. But King Marsila bids thee blame him not that the Caliph be not among them; with mine own eyes I saw him and four hundred men of arms, clad in hauberks, with helms on head, and girt with swords whose hilts were inlaid with gold, embark together upon the sea. They were fleeing from Christianity which they would not receive or hold. But before they had sailed four leagues, storm and tempest fell upon them, and even there they were drowned. Never shall ye see them more. Had the Caliph been alive I had brought him hither. As for the paynim King, in very truth, lord, this month shall not pass but he will come to thee in thy kingdom of France, and will receive the faith that thou holdest, and will join his hands in thine and become thy man, and will hold of thee his kingdom of Spain." Then saith the King: "Thanks be to God therefor. Well hast thou done, and great shall be thy reward." Thereafter he let sound a thousand trumpets throughout the host, and the Franks break up their camp, and load their sumpters, and set forth together towards fair France.

Charles the Great has laid waste all Spain, he has taken its castles and sacked its cities. But now the war is ended, so saith the King, and he rides on towards fair France. Count Roland has set the King's standard on the crest of a hill against the sky; and the Franks pitch their tents in all the country round about. Meantime the paynims ride on through the valleys, clad in their hauberks and two-fold harness, helms on head, and girt with their swords, shields on shoulder, and lances in hand. They made stay in a wood, on the top of the mountains, and there four hundred thousand await the dawn. God, what sorrow the Franks know it not!

The day fades and night darkens; and Charles, the great Emperor, sleeps. He dreamed that he was come to the great pass of Cizre, and it seemed to him that he held the oaken shaft of his lance in his hand, but Ganelon the Count snatched it from him, brandished and broke it, that its pieces flew towards heaven. But still Charles sleeps and does not waken.

Thereafter he dreamed another dream; that he was before his chapel at Aix and a bear bit him in his arm right cruelly; and anon, from towards Ardennes, he saw come a leopard which fiercely assaulted him; but even then, from within the hall a greyhound sprang out, and ran leaping to Charles; first he snapped off the right ear of the bear, then wrathfully he set upon the leopard; and the Franks cried that it was a great battle. Yet none knew which of the twain should conquer. But Charles still sleeps and doth not waken.

Night passes and the clear dawn shines forth; proudly the Emperor gets to horse, and lets sound the trumpets aloud throughout the host. "Lords, barons," then saith Charles, "nigh at hand is the pass and the strait defiles, now choose ye who shall be in the rearguard." And Ganelon answered: "Let it be Roland, my stepson, thou hast no baron so brave as he." Now when the King hears him, he looks at him haughtily, saying: "Thou art a very devil; and a mortal anger has entered into thee. And who shall go before me in the vanguard?" And Ganelon answered: "Let it be Ogier of Denmark, no baron hast thou more apt thereto."

When Count Roland hears that he is chosen, he speaks out in knightly wise, saying: "Sir kinsman, I should hold thee right dear in that thou hast adjudged the rearguard to me; and by my faith, Charles the King shall lose naught thereby, neither palfrey nor warhorse, nor any he-mule or she-mule whereon man may ride, nay, not so much as a pack-horse or sumpter, an it be not first well paid for by the sword." "Yea, thou speakest truly," saith Ganelon, "that I know well."

And Count Roland turns to Charles, saying: "Give me now the bow that you bear in your hand; verily, you shall have no need to chide me that I let it fall, as did Ganelon your right glove when you gave him the herald's staff." But still the Emperor sits with bent head; he plucks at his beard and strokes his moustache, and he may not help but weep.

Thereafter Naymes came before him, a better vassal was not in all the court, and he spoke to the King, saying: "Well hast thou heard, Count Roland is all in wrath; but the rearguard is adjudged to him, and thou hast no baron who would dare supplant him therein. Give him therefore the bow that you hold, and take heed that he hath good aid." The King holds out the bow and Roland receives it.

And the Emperor speaks to Roland, saying: "Fair sir nephew, know for sooth that I will give over unto thee the half of my army, keep them with thee that they may be thy safeguard." "Nay, not so will I," saith the Count. "May God confound me if I belie my house. I will keep with me twenty thousand Franks of good valour; and do thou cross the mountains in all surety, for so long as I live thou needst fear no man."

Count Roland has mounted his horse; and Oliver his comrade came to stand over against him, and thither came Gerier, and Oton, and Berengier, and thereto came Samson, and Anseïs the Proud, Ivon and Ivory whom the King holds full dear; and after them came Gerard the Old of Rousillon, and thereto Engelier the Gascon. Then said the Archbishop: "By my head, I too will go." "And I with thee," quoth Count Gualter, "I am Roland's man and to follow him is my devoir." Then among them they choose out twenty thousand knights.

Thereafter Count Roland calls Gualter del Hum, saying: "Take thou one thousand Franks of our land of France, and hold the hills and defiles that the Emperor may lose none of his own." "It is my part to do this for thee," saith Gualter. And with a thousand Franks of France he ranges through the hills and passes, nor will he leave the heights for any ill tidings before seven hundred swords have been drawn. Now the same day King Almaris of the kingdom of Belferne shall do him and his men fierce battle.

High are the hills and dark the valleys, brown are the rocks and dread the defiles. That same day the main host of the Franks pass with toil and travail, and fifteen leagues away men might hear the noise of their march. But when that they draw near to the Great Land, and see Gascony, their lord's domain, they call to mind their own fiefs and havings, their young maidens and gentle wives, till there is not one that does not weep for pity. More than all the rest is Charles heavy of heart, in that he has left his nephew in the passes of Spain; pity takes him, and he cannot help but weep.

The Twelve Peers abide in Spain, and in their fellowship are twenty thousand Franks who know not fear or any dread of death. But the Emperor as he draws near to France, hides his face in his mantle. Beside him rides Duke Naymes and he speaks to the King, saying: "Why makest thou such sorrow?" "Ye do ill to ask it,"

Charles answers him; "such grief is mine I cannot help but make lament. I fear lest through Ganelon France shall be destroyed. This past night, by means of an angel, a dream came to me, and it seemed to me that Ganelon shattered to bits the lance I held in my hand; and he it was who adjudged the rearguard to Roland. And now him I have left behind in a strange land. God, if I lose him never shall I find his fellow."

Charles the Great cannot help but weep; and a hundred thousand Franks are full of pity for him, and a marvellous fear for Roland. Ganelon the felon has done this treason; and rich are the gifts he has received therefor from the paynim king, gold and silver, silks and ciclatons, mules and horses, and camels and lions.

Meantime King Marsila calls together the barons of Spain, counts, and viscounts, dukes, and almaçurs, and emirs, and sons of counts; four hundred thousand has he gathered together in three days. He lets sound his tabours throughout Saragossa; and on the topmost tower the paynims raise an image of Mahound, and there is not a man but offers prayers to it and worships it. Thereafter they ride through the land of Cerdagne, over hill and through dale, each seeking to outdo other, till they see the gonfanons of the men of France, the rearguard of the Twelve Peers; they will not fail to do them battle.

The paynims arm themselves with Saracen hauberks, of which the more part are of threefold thickness; they lace on helms of right good Saracen work, and gird on swords of Viennese steel; fair are their shields, and their lances are of Valencia, tipped with gonfanons white and blue and scarlet. They leave behind them the mules and palfries, and mounting their war-horses, ride forth in close ranks. Fair was the day and bright the sun, and all their harness glistens in the light. And for the more joy they let sound a thousand trumpets; so great is the noise thereof that the Franks hear it. Then saith Oliver: "Sir comrade, methinks we shall have ado with the Saracens." "Now God grant it be as thou sayest," Roland answers him, "for to make stand here for our King is to do as good men ought to do. Verily for his liege a man well ought to suffer pain and woe, and endure both great heat and great cold, and should hold him ready to lose both hide and hair in his lord's service. Now let each have a care that he strikes good blows and great, that no man may mis-say us in his songs. These misbelieving men are in the wrong, and right is with the Christians, and for my part I will give ye no ill example."

PART II

THE BATTLE AT RONCEVALS

Then Oliver goes up into a high mountain, and looks away to the right, all down a grassy valley, and sees the host of the heathen coming on, and he called to Roland, his comrade, saying: "From the side of Spain I see a great light coming, thousands of white hauberks and thousands of gleaming helms. They will fall upon our Franks with great wrath. Ganelon the felon has done this treason, and he it was adjudged us to the rearguard, before the Emperor." "Peace Oliver," saith Count Roland, "he is my mother's husband, speak thou no ill of him."

Oliver has fared up the mountain, and from the summit thereof he sees all the kingdom of Spain and the great host of the Saracens. Wondrous is the shine of helmets studded with gold, of shields and broidered hauberks, of lances and gonfanons. The battles are without number, and no man may give count thereof, so great is the multitude. Oliver was all astonied at the sight; he got him down the hill as best he might, and came to the Franks, and gave them his tidings.

"I have seen the paynims," said Oliver; "never was so great a multitude seen of living men. Those of the vanguard are upon a hundred thousand, all armed with shields and helmets, and clad in white hauberks; right straight are the shafts of their lances, and bright the points thereof. Such a battle we shall have as was never before seen of man. Ye lords of France, may God give you might! and stand ye firm that we be not overcome." "Foul fall him who flees!" then say the Franks. "For no peril of death will we fail thee."

"Great is the host of the heathen," saith Oliver, "and few is our fellowship. Roland, fair comrade, I pray thee sound thy horn of ivory that Charles may hear it and return again with all his host." "That were but folly," quoth Roland, "and thereby would I lose all fame in sweet France. Rather will I strike good blows and great with Durendal, that the blade thereof shall be blooded even unto the hilt. Woe worth the paynims that they came into the passes! I pledge thee my faith short life shall be theirs."

"Roland, comrade, blow now thy horn of ivory, and Charles shall hear it, and bring hither his army again, and the King and his barons shall succour us." But Roland answers him, saying: "Now God forfend that through me my kinsman be brought to shame, or aught of dishonour befall fair France. But first I will lay on with Durendal, the good sword that is girded here at my side, and thou shalt see the blade thereof all reddened. Woe worth the paynims when they gathered their hosts! I pledge me they shall all be given over to death."

"Roland, comrade, blow thy horn of ivory, that Charles may hear it as he passes the mountains, and I pledge me the Franks will return hither again." But Roland saith: "Now God forfend it be said of any living man that I sounded my horn for dread of paynims. Nay, that reproach shall never fall upon my kindred. But when I am in the stour I will smite seven hundred blows, or mayhap a thousand, and thou shalt see the blade of Durendal all crimson. The Franks are goodly men, and they will lay on right valiantly, nor shall those of Spain have any surety from death."

Saith Oliver, "I see no shame herein. I have seen the Saracens of

Spain, they cover the hills and the valleys, the heaths and the plains. Great are the hosts of this hostile folk, and ours is but a little fellowship." And Roland makes answer: "My desire is the greater thereby. May God and His most holy angels forfend that France should lose aught of worship through me. Liefer had I die than bring dishonour upon me. The Emperor loves us for dealing stout blows."

Roland is brave, and Oliver is wise, and both are good men of their hands; once armed and a-horseback, rather would they die than flee the battle. Hardy are the Counts and high their speech. The felon paynims ride on in great wrath. Saith Oliver: "Roland, prithee look. They are close upon us, but Charles is afar off. Thou wouldst not deign to sound thy horn of ivory; but were the King here we should suffer no hurt. Look up towards the passes of Aspre and thou shalt see the woeful rearguard; they who are of it will do no more service henceforth." But Roland answers him: "Speak not so cowardly. Cursed be the heart that turns coward in the breast! Hold we the field, and ours be the buffets and the slaughter."

When Roland sees that the battle is close upon them he waxes fiercer than lion or leopard. He calls to the Franks, and he saith to Oliver: "Comrade, friend, say not so. When the Emperor left us his Franks he set apart such a twenty thousand of men that, certes, among them is no coward. For his liege lord a man ought to suffer all hardship, and endure great heat and great cold, and give both his blood and his body. Lay on with thy lance, and I will smite with Durendal, my good sword that the King gave me. If I die here, may he to whom it shall fall, say, 'This was the sword of goodly vassal.'"

Nigh at hand is Archbishop Turpin; he now spurs his horse to the crest of a knoll, and speaks to the Franks, and this is his sermon: "Lords, barons, Charles left us here, and it is a man's devoir to die for his King. Now help ye to uphold Christianity. Certes, ye shall have a battle, for here before you are the Saracens. Confess your sins and pray God's mercy, and that your souls may be saved I will absolve you. If ye are slain ye will be held martyrs, and ye shall have seats in the higher Paradise." The Franks light off their horses and kneel down, and the Archbishop blesses them, and for a penance bids them that they lay on with their swords.

The Franks get upon their feet, freed and absolved from sin; and the Archbishop blesses them in the name of God. Then they mounted their swift horses, and armed themselves after the manner of knights, and made them ready for battle. Count Roland calls to Oliver, saying: "Sir comrade, rightly thou saidst Ganelon hath betrayed us all, and hath received gold and silver and goods therefor; but the Emperor will well revenge us. King Marsila hath bought and sold us, but he shall pay for it with the sword."

Roland rides through the passes of Spain on Veillantif, his good horse and swift. He is clad in his harness, right well it becomes him, and as he rides he brandishes his spear, turning its point towards heaven; and to its top is bound a gonfanon of pure white, whereof the golden fringes fall down even unto his hands. Well fashioned is his body, and his face fair and laughing. Close behind him rides his comrade; and all the Franks claim him as their champion. Full haughtily he looks on the Saracens, but gently and mildly on the Franks, and he speaks to them courteously, saying: "Lords, barons, ride on softly. The paynims come seeking destruction, and this day we shall have plunder so goodly and great that no King of France hath ever taken any of so great price." At these words the two hosts come together.

Saith Oliver: "I have no mind for more words. Thou wouldst not deign to sound thy horn of ivory, and no help shalt thou get from Charles. Naught he knows of our case, nor is the wrong his, the baron. They who are beyond the mountains are no wise to blame. Now ride on with what might ye may. Lords, barons, hold ye the field! And in God's name I pray you bethink you both how to deal good blows and how to take them. And let us not forget the device of our King." At these words all the Franks cried out together, and whosoever may have heard that cry of Montjoy must call to mind valour and worth. Then they rode forward, God! how proudly, spurring their horses for the more speed, and fell a-smiting — how else should they do? But no whit adread were the Saracens. And lo you, Franks and paynims come together in battle.

The nephew of Marsila, who was called Ælroth, rides before all his host, and foul are his words to our Franks: "Ye Frankish felons, today ye shall do battle with us. He who should have been your surety has betrayed you; mad is the King who left you behind in the passes. Today shall fair France lose her fame, and the right arm of Charles shall be smitten off from his body." When Roland hears this, God! how great is his wrath. He spurs as fast as his horse may run, and with all the might he hath he smites Ælroth, and breaks his shield, and rends apart his hauberk, that he cleaves his breast and breaks the bone, and severs the spine from the back; with his lance he drives out the soul from the body, for so fierce is the blow Ælroth wavers, and with all the force of his lance Roland hurls him from his horse dead, his neck broken in two parts. Yet Roland still chides him, saying: "Out coward! Charles is not mad, nor loves he treason. He did well and knightly to leave us in the passes. Today shall France lose naught of her fame. Franks, lay on! Ours is the first blow. Right is with us, and these swine are in the wrong."

Among the paynims is a duke, Falsaron by name, who was brother to King Marsila, and held the land of Dathan and Abiram; there is no more shameless felon on all the earth. So wide is his forehead that the space between his eyes measures a full half foot. When he sees his nephew slain, he is full of dole, and he drives through the press as swift as he may, and cries aloud the paynim war-cry. Great is his hatred of the Franks. "Today shall fair France lose her fame!" Oliver hears him and is passing wroth; with his golden spurs he pricks on his horse and rides upon him like a true baron. He breaks the shield, tears asunder the hauberk, and drives his lance into the body up to the flaps of his pennon, and with the might of his blow hurls him dead from the saddle. He looks to earth where lies the felon, and speaks him haughtily: "Coward, naught care I for thy threats. Lay on Franks, certes, we shall overcome them." And he cries out Montjoy, the war-cry of Charles.

A King there is, Corsablis by name; he is of Barbary, a far-off land, and he spoke to the Saracens, saying: "We shall win a fair day on these Franks, for few is their fellowship. And such as be here shall prove themselves of small avail, nor shall one be saved alive for Charles. The day has come whereon they must die." Archbishop Turpin hears him right well, and to no man under heaven has he ever borne such hate. With his spurs of fine gold he pricks on his horse, and rides upon the King with great might, cleaves his shield and rends his hauberk, and thrusts his great lance into his body, and so drives home the blow that sorely the King wavers, and with all the force of his lance Turpin hurls him dead into the path. He looks on the ground where he sees the glutton lie, nor doth he withhold him from speech, but saith: "Coward and heathen, thou hast lied! Charles, my liege lord, is ever our surety, and our Franks have no mind to flee; and we shall have a care that thy comrades go not far hence; yea, and a second death must ye suffer. Lay on ye Franks, let no man forget himself! This first blow is ours, thanks be to God." And he cries out Montjoy, to hold field.

And Gerin smites Malprimis de Brigal, that his good shield no whit avails him, he shatters the jewelled boss thereof, and half of it falls to earth; he pierces the hauberk to the flesh, and drives his good lance into the body. The paynim falls down in a heap, and his soul is carried away by Satan.

And Gerier, the comrade of Gerin, smites the Emir, and shatters his shield and unmails his hauberk, and thrusts his good lance into his heart; so great is the blow his lance drives through the body and with all the force of his shaft he throws him to the ground dead. "Ours is a goodly battle," quoth Oliver.

Samson the Duke rides upon the Almaçur, and breaks his shield all flowered and set with gold, nor doth his good hauberk give him any surety, but Samson pierces him through heart and liver and lungs, and fells him dead, whether any one grieves for him or no. Saith the Archbishop: "That was knightly stricken."

And Anseïs urges on his horse and encounters with Turgis of Tortosa, cleaves his shield below the golden boss, rends asunder his twofold hauberk, and sets the point of his good lance in his body and thrusts so well that the iron passes sheer through him, that the might of the blow hurls him to the ground dead. "That was the buffet of a man of good prowess," saith Roland.

And Engelier, the Gascon of Bordeaux, spurs his horse, slackens his rein, and encounters with Escremis of Valtierra, breaks and carves the shield from his shoulder, rends apart the ventail of his hauberk, and smites him in his breast between his two collar bones, and with the might of the blow hurls him from the saddle, saying: "Ye are all given over to destruction."

And Oton smites the paynim Esturgant upon the leathern front of his shield, marring all the blue and white thereof, breaks through the sides of his hauberk, and drives his good spear and sharp into his body, and casts him from his swift horse, dead. "Naught may save thee," saith Oliver thereat.

And Berengier rides on Estramaris, shatters his shield, rends asunder his hauberk, and drives his stout lance into his body, and smites him dead amid a thousand Saracens. Of the Twelve [Saracen] Peers ten are now slain and but two are still living men, to wit, Chernuble and Count Margaris.

Margaris is a right valiant knight, strong and goodly, swift and keen; he spurs his horse and rides on Oliver, breaks his shield below the boss of pure gold, that the lance passed along his side, but by God's help, it did not pierce the body; the shaft grazes him but doth not overthrow him, and Margaris drives on, in that he has no hindrance, and sounds his horn to call his men about him.

Now the battle waxes passing great on both parties. Count Roland spares himself no whit, but smites with his lance as long as the shaft holds, but by fifteen blows it is broken and lost; thereupon he draws out Durendal his good sword, all naked, spurs his horse and rides on Chernuble, breaks his helm whereon the carbuncles blaze, cleaves his mail-coif and the hair of his head that the sword cuts through eyes and face, and the white hauberk of fine mail, and all the body to the fork of the legs, sheer into the saddle of beaten gold, nor did the sword stint till it had entered the horse and cleft the backbone, never staying for joint, that man and horse fell dead upon the thick grass. Thereupon Roland cried: "Coward, woe worth the day thou camest hither! no help shalt thou get from Mahound; nor by such swine as thou shall today's battle be achieved."

Count Roland rides through the press; in his hand he hath Durendal, right good for hacking and hewing, and doth great damage upon the Saracens. Lo, how he hurls one dead upon another, and the bright blood flows out on the field. All reddened are his hauberk and his arms, and the neck and shoulders of his good horse. Nor doth Oliver hold back from the battle; the Twelve Peers do not shame themselves, and all the Franks smite and slay, that the paynims perish or fall swooning. Then saith the Archbishop, "Our barons do passing well," and he cries out Montjoy, the war-cry of Charles.

Oliver drives through the stour; his lance is broken and naught is left him but the truncheon; yet he smites the paynim Malsaron that his shield patterned with gold and flowers is broken, and his two eyes fly out from his head, and his brains fall at his feet; among seven hundred of his fellows Oliver smites him dead. Then he slew Turgin and Esturgus, and thereby broke his lance that it splintered even unto the pommel. Thereat Roland saith: "Comrade what dost thou? I have no mind for a staff in so great battle, rather a man hath need of iron and steel. Where is thy sword Halteclere?" "I may not draw it," Oliver answered him. "So keen am I to smite."

But now the lord Oliver hath drawn his good sword, even as his comrade had besought him, and hath shown it to him in knightly wise; and therewith he smites the paynim Justin de Val Ferrée that he severs his head in twain, cuts through his broidered hauberk and his body, through his good saddle set with gold, and severs the backbone of his steed, that man and horse fall dead on the field before him. Then said Roland: "Now I hold you as my brother, and 'tis for such buffets the Emperor loves us." And on all sides they cry out Montjoy.

Count Gerin rides his horse Sorel, and Gerier, his comrade, rides Passecerf; both slacken rein, and spurring mightly set upon the paynim Timosel; one smites him on the shield, and the other on the hauberk, that both their lances break in his body; and he falls dead in the field. I wot not, nor have I ever heard man say, which of the twain was the more swift. Then Esperveris, son of Borel, died at the hand of Engelier of Bordeaux. And the Archbishop slew Siglorel, that enchanter who of old had passed down into Hell, led thither by the spells of Jupiter. "Of him we are well rid," quoth Turpin. And Roland answered him: "Yea, the coward is overthrown. Oliver, my brother, such buffets please me right well."

Meantime the battle waxes passing hard, and both Franks and paynims deal such blows that it is wonder to see; here they smite, and there make what defence they may; and many a lance is broken and reddened, and there is great rending of pennons and ensigns. Many a good Frank loses his youth, and will never again see wife or mother, or the men of France who await him in the passes. Charles the Great weeps for them, and makes great sorrow; but what avails it? No help shall they get therefrom. An ill turn Ganelon did them the day he sold his own kindred in Saragossa. Thereafter he lost both life and limb therefor; in the council at Aix, he was condemned to hang, and with him upon thirty of his kindred to whom death left no hope.

Dread and sore is the battle. Roland and Oliver lay on valiantly and the Archbishop deals more than a thousand buffets, nor are the Twelve Peers backward, and all the Franks smite as a man. The paynims are slain by hundreds and thousands; whosoever does not flee has no surety from death, but will he, nill he, must take his end. But the Franks lose their goodliest arms; never again shall they see father or kindred, or Charles their liege lord who abides for them in the passes.

Meantime, in France, a wondrous tempest broke forth, a mighty storm of wind and lightning, with rain and hail out of all measure, and bolts of thunder that fell ever and again; and verily therewith came a quaking of the earth that ran through all the land from Saint Michael of the Peril, even unto Xanten, and from Besançon to the port of Guitsand; and there was not a dwelling whose walls were not rent asunder. And at noon fell a shadow of great darkness, nor was there any light save as the heavens opened. They that saw these things were sore afraid, and many a one said: "This is the day of judgment and the end of the world is at hand." But they were deceived, and knew not whereof they spoke; it was the great mourning for the death of Roland.

Meantime the Franks smote manfully and with good courage, and the paynims were slain by thousands and by multitudes; of a hundred thousand not two may survive. Then said the Archbishop: "Our Franks are of good prowess, no man under heaven hath better. It is written in the annals of France that valiant they are for our Emperor." And the Franks fare through the field seeking their fellows, and weeping from dole and pity for their kin, in all love and kindness. But even now King Marsila is upon them with his great host.

Marsila comes on down the valley with the mighty host that he has assembled; full twenty battles the King has arrayed. There is a great shining of helmets, set with gold and precious stones, and of shields and of broidered hauberks. Trumpets to the number of seven thousand sound the onset, and the din thereof runs far and wide. Then saith Roland: "Oliver, comrade and brother, Ganelon the felon has sworn our death. The treason is manifest, and great vengeance shall the Emperor take therefor. The battle will be sore and great, such a one as was never before fought of man. I will smite with Durendal my sword, and do thou, comrade, lay on with Halteclere. Through many lands have we carried them, and with them have we conquered many a battle, no ill song must be sung of them."

When the Franks see how great is the multitude of the paynims, that on all sides they cover the field, they call upon Roland and Oliver and the Twelve Peers, that they be their defence. Then the Archbishop tells them his mind, saying: "Lords, barons, put from you all cowardly thoughts; and in God's name I pray you give not back. Better it were that we die in battle than that men of worship should speak foully of us in their songs. Certain it is we shall straightway take our end, nor shall we from today be living men; yet there is a thing I can promise ye, blessed paradise shall be opened to you, and ye shall take your place among the innocent." At his words, the Franks take heart, and every man cries out Montjoy.

Among the paynims is a Saracen of Saragossa, lord he is of half the city, and Climborin he hight; never will he flee from any living man. He it was who swore fellowship with Count Ganelon, kissed him in all friendship upon the lips, and gave him his helm and his carbuncle. And he hath sworn to bring the Great Land to shame, and to strip the Emperor of his crown. He rides his horse whom he calls Barbamusche, that is swifter than falcon or swallow; and slackening his rein, he spurs mightily, and rides upon Engelier of Gascony that neither shield nor byrnie may save him, but he drives the head of his lance into his body, thrusting so manfully that the point thereof passes through to the other side, and with all the might of his lance hurls him in the field dead. Thereafter he cries: "These folk are good to slay!" But the Franks say: "Alack, that so good a knight should take his end."

And Count Roland speaks to Oliver, saying: "Sir comrade, now is Engelier slain, nor have we any knight of more valour." And the Count answers him, saying: "Now God grant me to avenge him." He pricks on his horse with spurs of pure gold, and he grasps Halteclere — already is the blade thereof reddened — and with all his strength he smites the paynim; he drives the blow home that the Saracen falls; and the devils carry away his soul. Then Oliver slew Duke Alphaïen, and cut off the head of Escababi, and unhorsed seven Arabs, — never again shall they do battle. Then said Roland: "Wroth is my comrade, and now at my side he wins great worship; for such blows Charles holds us the more dear." And he cried aloud: "To battle, knights, to battle!"

Hard by is the paynim Valdabrun, that had stood godfather to King Marsila; on the sea he is lord of four hundred dromonds, and well honoured of all shipmen. He it was who aforetime took Jerusalem by treason, violated the temple of Solomon, and slew the patriarch before the baptismal fonts. And he had sworn fellowship with Ganelon, and had given him a sword and a thousand mangons. He rides a horse called Gramimond, swifter than any falcon; he spurs him well with his sharp spurs, and rides upon Samson the mighty Duke, breaks his shield, and rends his hauberk, and drives the flaps of his gonfanon into his body, and with all the force of his lance hurls him from the saddle dead. "Lay on, paynims, for hardily we shall overthrow them!" But the Franks cry: "God, woe worth the good baron!"

When Roland sees that Samson is dead, ye may guess he is sore stricken. He spurs his horse and lets him run as fast as he may, in his hand he holds Durendal, of greater worth than is pure gold, and with all the might he hath, he smites the paynim on the helm set with gold and gems, and cuts through head and hauberk and body, and through the good saddle set with gold and jewels, deep into the back of the horse, and slays both him and his rider, whosoever has dole or joy thereof. Cry the paynims: "That was a woeful blow for us." Then quoth Roland: "No love have I for any one of ye, for yours is the pride and the iniquity."

Among the paynims is an African, Malquiant, son of King Malcud; his armour is all of the beaten gold, and brighter than all the rest it shines to heaven. His horse, which he calls Salt-Perdut, is so swift that he has not his fellow in any four-footed beast. And now Malquiant rode on Anseïs, and smote him full on the shield that its scarlet and blue were hewn away, and he rent the sides of his hauberk, and drave his lance into his body, both point and shaft. Dead is the Count and done are his life days. Thereat cry the Franks: "Alack for thee, good baron!"

Through the press rides Turpin the Archbishop — never did another priest say mass who did with his own strength so great deeds of arms — and he saith to the paynim: "Now may God bring all evil

upon thee! for thou hast slain one for whom my heart is sore stricken."
Then he set his good horse at a gallop, and smote Malquiant on his
shield of Toledo, that he fell dead upon the green grass.

Hard by is the paynim Grandonie, son of Capuel, King of Cap-
padocia; he rides a horse called Marmorie, swifter than any bird that
flies; he now slackens rein, and spurring well, thrusts mightily upon
Gerin, breaks his crimson shield that it falls from his shoulder, and
rends all asunder his hauberk, and thereafter drives all his blue gonfanon into his body that he falls dead beside a great rock. Then he
slays Gerier, Gerin's comrade, and Berengier, and Guyon of Saint-
Antonie; and thereafter he smote Austor, the mighty Duke that held
Valence and the land along the Rhône, and felled him dead that the
paynims had great joy thereof. But the Franks cry: "How many
of ours are stricken!"

Roland holds his ruddied sword in his hand; he has heard the
Franks make lament, and so great is his sorrow that his heart is nigh
to bursting, and he saith to the paynims: "Now may God bring all
evil upon thee! Methinks thou shalt pay me dear for him thou hast
slain." And he spurs his horse, which springs forward eagerly; and
let whoso will pay the price, the two knights join battle.

Grandonie was a man of good prowess, of much valour and hardiness, and amid the way he encounters with Roland, and albeit before
that time he had never set eyes upon him, he none the less knew him
of a certainty by his look and countenance; and he could not but be
sore adread at the sight, and fain would he have fled, but he could not.
The Count smites him mightily that he rends all his helm down to
the nasal, cleaves through nose and mouth and teeth, through the
hauberk of fine mail, and all the body, splits the silver sides from off
the golden saddle, and cuts deep into the back of the horse, that both
he and his rider are slain beyond help. Thereat those of Spain
make great lament, but the Franks cry: "That was well stricken of
our captain!"

Wondrous and fierce is the battle; the Franks lay on in their wrath
and their might, that hands and sides and bones fall to earth, and garments are rent off to the very flesh, and the blood runs down to the
green grass. The paynims cry: "We may not longer endure. May
the curse of Mahound fall upon the Great Land, for its folk have not
their fellows for hardiness." And there was not a man but cried
out: "Marsila! haste, O King, for we are in sore need of thy help."

Wondrous and great is the battle. And still the Franks smite with
their burnished lances. There is great dolour of folk, and many a
man is slain and maimed and bleeding, and one lies on another, or on
his back, or face down. The Saracens may not longer endure, but
howsoever unwillingly they must give back. And eagerly the Franks
pursue after them.

Marsila sees the slaughter of his people, and lets sound his horns
and bussynes, and gets to horse with all his vassal host. In the foremost front rides the Saracen Abisme, the falsest knight of his fellowship, all compact of evil and villainy. He believes not in God the

son of Mary; and he is black as melted pitch. Dearer than all the gold of Galicia he loves treachery and murder, nor did any man ever see him laugh or take disport. But he is a good man of arms, and bold to rashness, wherefor he is well beloved of the felon King Marsila, and to him it is given to bear the Dragon, around which the paynims gather. The Archbishop hath small love for Abisme, and so soon as he sees him he is all desirous to smite him, and quietly, within himself, he saith: "This Saracen seems a misbelieving felon, I had liefer die than not set upon him to slay him; never shall I love coward or cowardice."

Whereupon the Archbishop begins the battle. He rides the horse that he won from Grossaille, a King whom he slew in Denmark; the good steed is swift and keen, featly fashioned of foot, and flat of leg; short in the thigh and large of croupe, long of flank and high of back; his tail is white and yellow his mane, his head is the colour of the fawn, and small are his ears; of all four-footed beasts none may outstrip him. The Archbishop spurs mightily, and will not fail to meet with Abisme and smite him on his shield, a very marvel, set with gems, — topaz and amethysts, and precious crystals, and blazing carbuncles; the gift it was of Galafré the Amiral, who had received it of a devil in Val-Metas. Now Turpin smites it and spares it not, that after his buffet it has not the worth of a doit. And he pierces Abisme through the body, and hurls him dead in the open field. And the Franks say: "That was a good deed of arms; in the hands of our Archbishop safe is the crosier."

And Count Roland speaks to Oliver, saying: "Sir Comrade, what say ye, is not the Archbishop a right good knight, that there is no better under heaven? For well he knows how to smite with lance and spear." "Now let us aid him," the Count makes answer. And at these words the Franks go into battle again; great are the blows and grievous the slaughter, and great is the dolour of the Christians.

Would ye had seen Roland and Oliver hack and hew with their swords, and the Archbishop smite with his lance. We can reckon those that fell by their hands for the number thereof is written in charter and record; the Geste says more than four thousand. In four encounters all went well with the Franks, but the fifth was sore and grievous to them, for in this all their knights were slain save only sixty, spared by God's mercy. Before they die they will sell their lives dear.

When Count Roland is ware of the great slaughter of his men, he turns to Oliver, saying: "Sir comrade, as God may save thee, see how many a good man of arms lies on the ground; we may well have pity on sweet France, the fair, that must now be desolate of such barons. Ah, King and friend, would thou wert here! Oliver, my brother, what shall we do? How shall we send him tidings?" "Nay, I know not how to seek him," saith Oliver; "but liefer had I die than bring dishonour upon me."

Then saith Roland: "I will sound my horn of ivory, and Charles, as he passes the mountains, will hear it; and I pledge thee my faith the Franks will return again." Then saith Oliver: "Therein would be great shame for thee, and dishonour for all thy kindred, a reproach that would last all the days of their life. Thou wouldst not sound it when I bid thee, and now thou shalt not by my counsel. And if thou dost sound it, it will not be hardily, for now both thy arms are stained with blood." "Yea," the Count answers him, "I have dealt some goodly blows."

Then saith Roland: "Sore is our battle, I will blow a blast, and Charles the King will hear it." "That would not be knightly," saith Oliver; "When I bid thee, comrade, thou didst disdain it. Had the King been here, we had not suffered this damage; but they who are afar off are free from all reproach. By this my beard, an I see again my sister, Aude the Fair, never shalt thou lie in her arms."

Then saith Roland: "Wherefore art thou wroth with me?" And Oliver answers him, saying: "Comrade, thou thyself art to blame. Wise courage is not madness, and measure is better than rashness. Through thy folly these Franks have come to their death; nevermore shall Charles the King have service at our hands. Hadst thou taken my counsel, my liege lord had been here, and this battle had been ended, and King Marsila had been or taken or slain. Woe worth thy prowess, Roland! Henceforth Charles shall get no help of thee; never till God's Judgment Day shall there be such another man; but thou must die, and France shall be shamed thereby. And this day our loyal fellowship shall have an end; before this evening grievously shall we be parted."

The Archbishop, hearing them dispute together, spurs his horse with his spurs of pure gold, and comes unto them, and rebukes them, saying: "Sir Roland, and thou, Sir Oliver, in God's name I pray ye, let be this strife. Little help shall we now have of thy horn; and yet it were better to sound it; if the King come, he will revenge us, and the paynims shall not go hence rejoicing. Our Franks will light off their horses, and find us dead and maimed, and they will lay us on biers, on the backs of sumpters, and will weep for us with dole and pity; and they will bury us in the courts of churches, that our bones may not be eaten by wolves and swine and dogs." "Sir, thou speakest well and truly," quoth Roland.

And therewith he sets his ivory horn to his lips, grasps it well and blows it with all the might he hath. High are the hills, and the sound echoes far, and for thirty full leagues they hear it resound. Charles and all his host hear it, and the King saith: "Our men are at battle." But Count Ganelon denies it, saying: "Had any other said so, we had deemed it great falsehood."

With dolour and pain, and in sore torment, Count Roland blows his horn of ivory, that the bright blood springs out of his mouth, and the temples of his brain are broken. Mighty is the blast of the horn, and Charles, passing the mountains, hears it, and Naymes hears it, and all the Franks listen and hear. Then saith the King: "I hear the horn of Roland; never would he sound it, an he were not at battle."

But Ganelon answers him, saying: "Battle is there none; thou art old and white and hoary, and thy words are those of a child. Well thou knowest the great pride of Roland; — a marvel it is that God hath suffered it thus long. Aforetime he took Noples against thy commandment, and when the Saracens came out of the city and set upon Roland the good knight, he slew them with Durendal his sword; thereafter with water he washed away the blood which stained the meadow, that none might know of what he had done. And for a single hare he will blow his horn all day long; and now he but boasts among his fellows, for there is no folk on earth would dare do him battle. I prithee ride on. Why tarry we? The Great Land still lies far before us."

Count Roland's mouth has burst out a-bleeding, and the temples of his brain are broken. In dolour and pain he sounds his horn of ivory; but Charles hears it and the Franks hear it. Saith the King: "Long drawn is the blast of that horn." "Yea," Naymes answers, "for in sore need is the baron who blows it. Certes, our men are at battle; and he who now dissembles hath betrayed Roland. Take your arms and cry your war-cry, and succour the men of your house. Dost thou not hear Roland's call?"

The Emperor has commanded that his trumpets be sounded, and now the Franks light down from their horses and arm themselves with hauberks and helms and swords adorned with gold; fair are their shields, and goodly and great their lances, and their gonfanons are scarlet and white and blue. Then all the barons of the host get them to horse, and spur through the passes; and each saith to other: "An we may but see Roland a living man, we will strike good blows at his side." But what avails it? for they have abode too long.

Clear is the evening as was the day, and all their armour glistens in the sun, and there is great shining of hauberks, and helms, and shields painted with flowers, and lances, and gilded gonfanons. The Emperor rides on in wrath, and the Franks are full of care and foreboding; and not a man but weeps full sore and hath great fear for Roland. Then the King let take Count Ganelon, and gave him over to the cooks of his household; and he called Besgon their chief, saying: "Guard him well, as beseems a felon who hath betrayed my house." Besgon took him, and set a watch about him of a hundred of his fellows of the kitchen, both best and worst. They plucked out the hairs of Ganelon's beard and moustache, and each one dealt him four blows with his fist, and hardily they beat him with rods and staves; then they put about his neck a chain and bound him even as they would a bear, and in derision they set him upon a sumpter. So they guard him till they return him unto Charles.

High are the hills and great and dark, deep the valleys, and swift the waters. To answer Roland's horn all the trumpets are sounded, both rear and van. The Emperor rides on in wrath, and the Franks are full of care and foreboding; there is not a man but weepeth and maketh sore lament, praying to God that he spare Roland until they come unto the field, that at his side they may deal good blows. But what avails it? They have tarried too long, and may not come in time.

Charles the King rides on in great wrath, and over his hauberk is spread his white beard. And all the barons of France spur mightily, not one but is full of wrath and grief that he is not with Roland the captain who is at battle with the Saracens of Spain. If he be wounded, what hope that one soul be left alive? God, what a sixty he still hath in his fellowship; no king or captain ever had better.

Roland looks abroad over hill and heath and sees the great multitude of the Frankish dead, and he weeps for them as beseems a gentle knight, saying: "Lords and barons now may God have mercy upon you, and grant Paradise to all your souls, that ye may rest among the blessed flowers. Man never saw better men of arms than ye were. Long and well, year in and year out, have ye served me, and many wide lands have ye won for the glory of Charles. Was it to such an end that he nourished you? O France, fair land, today art thou made desolate by rude slaughter. Ye Frankish barons, I see ye die through me, yet can I do naught to save or defend you. May God, who knows no lie, aid you! Oliver, brother, I must not fail thee; yet I shall die of grief, and I be not slain by the sword. Sir comrade, let us get us into battle."

So Count Roland falls a-smiting again. He holds Durendal in his hand, and lays on right valiantly, that he cleaves in twain Faldron de Pui, and slays four and twenty of the most worshipful of the paynims. Never shall ye see man more desirous to revenge himself. And even as the hart flies before the hounds, so flee the heathen from before Roland. "Thou dost rightly," then said the Archbishop; "such valour well beseems a knight who bears arms and sits a good horse; in battle such a one should be fell and mighty, or he is not worth four deniers, and it behooves him to turn monk and get him into a monastery to pray the livelong day for our sins." And Roland answered him, saying: "Smite and spare not." And at these words the Franks go into battle again; but great is the slaughter of the Christians.

That man who knows he shall get no mercy defends him savagely in battle. Wherefore the Franks are fierce as lions. Marsila like a true baron sits his horse Gaignon; he spurs him well and rides on Bevon — lord he was of Beaune and Dijon — and breaks his shield, and rends his hauberk, that without other hurt he smites him dead to ground. And thereafter he slew Ivon and Ivory, and with them Gerard the Old of Roussillon. Now nigh at hand is Count Roland, and he saith to the paynim: "May the Lord God bring thee to mishap! And because thou hast wrongfully slain my comrades thou shalt thyself get a buffet before we twain dispart, and this day thou shalt learn the name of my sword." And therewith he rides upon him like a true baron, and smites off his right hand, and thereafter he takes off the head of Jurfaleu the Fair, the son of King Marsila. Thereat the paynims cry: "Now help us, Mahound! O ye, our gods, revenge us upon Charles! He has sent out against us into our marches men so fierce that though they die they will not give back." And one saith to another: "Let us fly." At these words a hundred thousand turn and flee, and let whosoever will, call them, they will not return again.

King Marsila has lost his right hand; and now he throws his shield to earth, and pricks on his horse with his sharp spurs, and with slackened rein, flees away towards Spain. Upon twenty thousand Saracens follow after him, nor is there one among them who is not maimed or hurt of body, and they say one to another: "The nephew of Charles has won the field."

But alack, what avails it? For though Marsila be fled, his uncle the Caliph yet abides, he who ruled Aferne, Carthage, Garmalie, and Ethiopia, a cursed land; under his lordship he has the black folk, great are their noses and large their ears, and they are with him to the number of fifty thousand. And now they come up in pride and wrath, and cry aloud the war-cry of the paynims. Then saith Roland: "Now must we needs be slain, and well I know we have but a little space to live; but cursed be he who doth not sell himself right dear. Lay on, lords, with your burnished swords, and debate both life and death; let not sweet France be brought to shame through us. When Charles, my liege lord, shall come into this field, he will see such slaughter of the Saracens, that he shall find fifteen of them dead over against each man of ours, and he will not fail to bless us."

When Roland sees the cursed folk whose skin is blacker than any ink, and who have naught of white about them save their teeth, he saith: "Now I know in very sooth that we shall die this day. Lay on, lords, and yet again I bid thee, smite." "Now foul fall him who lags behind," quoth Oliver. And at this word the Franks haste into the fray.

Now when the paynims see how few are the Franks, they have great pride and joy thereof; and one saith to another: "Certes, the Emperor is in the wrong." The Caliph bestrides a sorrel horse, he pricks him on with his spurs of gold, and smites Oliver from behind, amid the back, that he drives the mails of his white hauberk into his body, and his lance passes out through his breast: "Now hast thou got a good buffet," quoth the Caliph. "On an ill day Charles the Great left thee in the passes; much wrong hath he done us, yet he shall not boast thereof, for on thee alone have I well revenged us."

Oliver feels that he is wounded unto death; in his hand he holds Halteclere, bright was its blade, and with it he smites the Caliph on his golden pointed helmet, that its flowers and gems fall to earth, and he cleaves the head even unto the teeth, and with the force of the blow smote him dead to earth, and said: "Foul fall thee, paynim! Say not that I am come to my death through Charles; and neither to thy wife, nor any other dame, shalt thou ever boast in the land from which thou art come, that thou has taken from me so much as one farthing's worth, or hast done any hurt to me or to others." And thereafter he called to Roland for succour.

Oliver feels that he is wounded unto death; never will he have his fill of vengeance. In the thick of the press he smites valiantly, cleaving lances and embossed shields, and feet and hands and flanks and shoulders. Whosoever saw him thus dismember the Saracens, and hurl one dead upon another, must call to mind true valiance; nor did he forget the war-cry of Charles, but loud and clear he cries out Montjoy! And he calls to Roland, his friend and peer: "Sir comrade, come stand thou beside me. In great dolour shall we twain soon be disparted."

Roland looks Oliver in the face, pale it is and livid and all discoloured; the bright blood flows down from amid his body and falls in streams to the ground. "God," saith the Count, "now I know not what to do. Sir comrade, woe worth thy valour! Never shall the world see again a man of thy might. Alas, fair France, today art thou stripped of goodly vassals, and fallen and undone. The Emperor will suffer great loss thereby." And so speaking he swoons upon his horse.

Lo, Roland has swooned as he sits his horse, and Oliver is wounded unto death, so much has he bled that his sight is darkened, and he can no longer distinguish any living man whether far off or near at hand; and now, as he meets his comrade, he smites him upon the helm set with gold and gems, and cleaves it down to the nasal, but does not come unto the head. At the blow Roland looks up at him, and asks him full softly and gently: "Comrade, dost thou this wittingly? I am Roland who so loves thee. Never yet hast thou mistrusted me." Then saith Oliver: "Now I hear thee speak, but I cannot see thee; may the Lord God guard thee. I have struck thee, but I pray thy pardon." "Thou hast done me no hurt," Roland answers him; "I pardon thee before God, as here and now." So speaking each leans forward towards other, and lo, in such friendship they are disparted.

Oliver feels the anguish of death come upon him; his two eyes turn in his head; and his hearing goes from him, and all sight. He lights down from his horse and lies upon the ground, and again and again he confesses his sins; he holds out his clasped hands toward heaven and prays God that He grant him Paradise, and he blesses Charles and sweet France, and Roland, his comrade, above all men. Then his heart fails him, and his head sinks upon his breast, and he lies stretched at all his length upon the ground. Dead is the Count and gone from hence. Roland weeps for him and is sore troubled; never on the earth shall ye see a man so sorrowful.

When Count Roland sees his friend lie prone and dead, facing the East, gently he begins to lament him: "Sir comrade, woe worth thy hardiness! We twain have held together for years and days, never didst thou me wrong or I thee. Since thou art dead, alack that I yet live." So speaking, the Count swoons as he sits Veillantif his horse, but his golden spurs hold him firm, and let him go where he will, he cannot fall.

So soon as Roland comes to his senses, and is restored from his swoon, he is ware of the great slaughter about him. Slain are the Franks, he has lost them all save only Gualter del Hum and the Archbishop. Gualter has come down from the mountains where he fought hardily with those of Spain; the paynims conquered, and his men are slain, and howsoever unwillingly, he must perforce flee down into the valley and call upon Roland for succour. "O gentle Count, brave captain, where art thou? for where thou art I have no fear. It is I, Gualter, who conquered Maëlgut, I the nephew of Droön the old, the hoary, I whom thou wert wont to love for my hardihood. Now my shield is pierced, and the shaft of my lance is broken, and my hauberk rent and unmailed; I have the wounds of eight lances in my body, and I must die, but dear have I sold myself." So he saith, and Roland hears him, and spurs his horse and rides towards him.

Count Roland is a full noble warrior, and a right good knight is Gualter del Hum, the Archbishop is of good valour and well tried; not one would leave aught to his fellows, and together, in the thick of the press, they smite the paynims. A thousand Saracens get them to foot, and there are still forty thousand on horseback, yet in sooth they dare not come nigh unto the three, but they hurl upon them lances and spears, arrows and darts and sharp javelins. In the first storm they slew Gualter, and sundered the shield of Turpin of Rheims, broke his helmet and wounded him in his head, and rent and tore his hauberk that he was pierced in the body by four spears; and his horse was slain under him. The Archbishop falls; great is the pity thereof.

But so soon as Turpin of Rheims finds himself beaten down to earth with the wounds of four lances in his body, he right speedily gets him afoot again; he looks toward Roland, and hastes to him, and saith: "I am nowise vanquished; no good vassal yields him so long as he is a living man." And he draws Almace, his sword of brown steel, and in the thick of the press he deals well more than a thousand buffets. Afterwards Charles bore witness that Turpin spared himself no whit, for around him they found four hundred dead, some wounded, some cut in twain amid the body, and some whose heads had been smitten off; so saith the Geste and he who was on the field, the valiant Saint Gilles, for whom God wrought miracles; he it was who wrote the annals of the monastery of Laon. And he who knows not this, knows naught of the matter.

Count Roland fights right nobly, but all his body is a-sweat and burning hot, and in his head he hath great pain and torment, for when he sounded his horn he rent his temples. But he would fain know that Charles were coming, and he takes his horn of ivory, and feebly he sounds it. The Emperor stops to listen: "Lords," he saith, "now has great woe come upon us, this day shall we lose Roland my nephew, I wot from the blast of his horn that he is nigh to death. Let him who would reach the field ride fast. Now sound ye all the trumpets of the host." Then they blew sixty thousand, so loud that the mountains resound and the valleys give answer. The paynims hear them and have no will to laugh, but one saith to another: "We shall have ado with Charles anon."

Say the paynims: "The Emperor is returning, we hear the trumpets of France; if Charles come hither, we shall suffer sore loss. Yet if Roland live, our war will begin again, and we shall lose Spain our land." Then four hundred armed in their helmets, and of the best of those on the field, gather together, and on Roland they make onset fierce and sore. Now is the Count hard bestead.

When Count Roland sees them draw near he waxes hardy and fierce and terrible; never will he yield as long as he is a living man. He sits his horse Veillantif, and spurs him well with his spurs of fine gold, and rides into the stour upon them all; and at his side is Archbishop Turpin. And the Saracens say one to another: "Now save yourselves, friends. We have heard the trumpets of France; Charles the mighty King is returning."

Count Roland never loved the cowardly, or the proud, or the wicked, or any knight who was not a good vassal, and now he calls to Archbishop Turpin, saying: "Lord, thou art on foot and I am a-horseback, for thy love I would make halt, and together we will take the good and the ill; I will not leave thee for any living man; the blows of Almace and of Durendal shall give back this assault to the paynims." Then saith the Archbishop: "A traitor is he who doth not smite; Charles is returning, and well will he revenge us."

"In an evil hour," say the paynims, "were we born; woeful is the day that has dawned for us! We have lost our lords and our peers. Charles the valiant cometh hither again with his great host, we hear the clear trumpets of those of France, and great is the noise of their cry of Montjoy. Count Roland is of such might he cannot be vanquished by any mortal man. Let us hurl our missiles upon him, and then leave him." Even so they did; and cast upon him many a dart and javelin, and spears and lances and feathered arrows. They broke and rent the shield of Roland, tore open and unmailed his hauberk, but did not pierce his body: but Veillantif was wounded in thirty places, and fell from under the Count, dead. Then the paynims flee, and leave him; Count Roland is left alone and on foot.

The paynims flee in anger and wrath, and in all haste they fare toward Spain. Count Roland did not pursue after them, for he has lost his horse Veillantif, and whether he will or no, is left on foot. He went to the help of Archbishop Turpin, and unlaced his golden helm from his head, and took off his white hauberk of fine mail, and he tore his tunic into strips and with the pieces bound his great wounds. Then he gathers him in his arms, and lays him down full softly upon the green grass, and gently he beseeches him: "O gracious baron, I pray thy leave. Our comrades whom we so loved are slain, and it is not meet to leave them thus. I would go seek and find them, and range them before thee." "Go and return again," quoth the Archbishop. "Thank God, this field is thine and mine."

Roland turns away and fares on alone through the field; he searches the valleys and the hills; and there he found Ivon and Ivory, and

Gerin, and Gerier his comrade, and he found Engelier the Gascon, and Berengier, and Oton, and he found Anseïs and Samson, and Gerard the Old of Rousillon. One by one he hath taken up the barons, and hath come with them unto the Archbishop, and places them in rank before him. The Archbishop cannot help but weep; he raises his hand and gives them benediction, and thereafter saith: "Alas for ye, lords! May God the Glorious receive your souls, and bring them into Paradise among the blessed flowers. And now my own death torments me sore; never again shall I see the great Emperor."

Again Roland turned away to search the field; and when he found Oliver his comrade, he gathered him close against his breast, and as best he might returned again unto the Archbishop, and laid his comrade upon a shield beside the others; and the Archbishop absolved and blessed him. Then their sorrow and pity broke forth again, and Roland saith: "Oliver, fair comrade, thou wert son of the great Duke Reinier, who held the Marches of Rivier and Genoa; for the breaking of lances or the piercing of shields; for vanquishing and affrighting the proud, for upholding and counselling the good, never in any land was there a better knight."

When Roland sees the peers, and Oliver whom he so loved, lying dead, pity takes him and he begins to weep; and his face is all discoloured; so great is his grief he cannot stand upright, but will he, nill he, falls to the ground in a swoon. Saith the Archbishop: "Alack for thee, good baron."

When the Archbishop sees Roland swoon, he has such dole as he has never known before. He stretches out his hand and takes the horn of ivory, for in Roncevals there is a swift streamlet and he would go to it to bring of its water to Roland. Slowly and falteringly he sets forth, but so weak he is he cannot walk, his strength has gone from him, too much blood has he lost, and before a man might cross an acre his heart faileth, and he falls forward upon his face, and the anguish of death comes upon him.

When Count Roland recovers from his swoon he gets upon his feet with great torment; he looks up and he looks down, and beyond his comrades, on the green grass, he sees that goodly baron, the Archbishop, appointed of God in His stead. Turpin saith his *mea culpa,* and looks up, and stretches out his two hands towards heaven, and prays God that he grant him Paradise. And so he dies, the warrior of Charles. Long had he waged strong war against the paynims, both by his might battling and his goodly sermons. May God grant him his holy benison.

Count Roland sees the Archbishop upon the ground; his bowels have fallen out of his body, and his brains are oozing out of his forehead; Roland takes his fair, white hands and crosses them upon his breast between his two collar bones; and lifting up his voice, he mourns for him, after the manner of his people: "Ah gentle man, knight of high parentage, now I commend thee to the heavenly Glory; never will there be a man who shall serve Him more willingly; never since the days of the apostles hath there been such a prophet to up-hold the law, and win the hearts of men; may thy soul suffer no dole or torment, but may the doors of Paradise be opened to thee."

Now Roland feels that death is near him, and his brains flow out at his ears; he prays to the Lord God for his peers that He will re-ceive them, and he prays to the Angel Gabriel for himself. That he may be free from all reproach, he takes his horn of ivory in the one hand, and Durendal, his sword, in the other, and farther than a cross-bow can cast an arrow, through a cornfield he goeth on towards Spain. At the crest of a hill, beneath two fair trees, are four stairs of marble; there he falls down on the green grass in a swoon, for death is close upon him.

High are the hills and very tall are the trees; the four stones are of shining marble; and there Count Roland swoons upon the green grass. Meantime a Saracen is watching him; he has stained his face and body with blood, and feigning death, he lies still among his fel-lows; but now he springs to his feet and hastens forward. Fair he was, and strong, and of good courage; and in his pride he breaks out into mighty wrath, and seizes upon Roland, both him and his arms, and he cries: "Now is the nephew of Charles overthrown. This his sword will I carry into Arabia." But at his touch the Count re-covered his senses.

Roland feels that his sword hath been taken from him, he opens his eyes, and saith: "Certes, thou art not one of our men." He holds his horn of ivory which he never lets out of his grasp, and he smites the Saracen upon the helm which was studded with gold and gems, and he breaks steel and head and bones that his two eyes start out, and he falls down dead at his feet. Then saith Roland: "Coward, what made thee so bold to lay hands upon me, whether right or wrong? No man shall hear it but shall hold thee a fool. Now is my horn of ivory broken in the bell, and its gold and its crystals have fallen."

Now Roland feels that his sight is gone from him. With much striving he gets upon his feet; the colour has gone from his face; be-fore him lies a brown stone, and in his sorrow and wrath he smites ten blows upon it. The sword grates upon the rock, but neither breaks nor splinters; and the Count saith: "Holy Mary, help me now! Ah Durendal, alas for your goodness! Now am I near to death, and have no more need of you. Many a fight in the field have I won with you, many a wide land have I conquered with you, lands now ruled by Charles with the white beard. May the man who would flee before another, never possess you. For many a day have you been held by a right good lord, never will there be such another in France the free."

Roland smote upon the block of hard stone, and the steel grates, but neither breaks nor splinters. And when he sees that he can in nowise break it, he laments, saying: "O Durendal, how fair and bright thou art, in the sunlight how thou flashest and shinest! Charles was once in the valley of Moriane, when God commanded him by one of his angels that he should give thee to a chieftain Count; then the great and noble King girded thee upon me; and with thee I won for him Anjou and Bretagne, and I conquered Poitou and Maine for him, and for him I conquered Normandy the free, and Provence, and Aquitaine; and Lombardy, and all of Romagna; and I conquered for him Bavaria, and Flanders, and Bulgaria, and all of Poland; Constantinople which now pays him fealty, and Saxony, where he may work his will. And I conquered for him Wales, and Scotland, and Ireland, and England which he holds as his demesne. Many lands and countries have I won with thee, lands which Charles of the white beard rules. And now am I heavy of heart because of this my sword; rather would I die than that it should fall into the hands of the paynims. Lord God our Father, let not this shame fall upon France."

And again Roland smote upon the brown stone and beyond all telling shattered it; the sword grates, but springs back again into the air and is neither dinted nor broken. And when the Count sees he may in no wise break it, he laments, saying: "O Durendal, how fair and holy a thing thou art! In thy golden hilt is many a relic, — a tooth of Saint Peter, and some of the blood of Saint Basil, and hairs from the head of my lord, Saint Denis, and a bit of the raiment of the Virgin Mary. It is not meet that thou fall into the hands of the paynims, only Christians should wield thee. May no coward ever possess thee! Many wide lands have I conquered with thee, lands which Charles of the white beard rules; and thereby is the Emperor great and mighty."

Now Roland feels that death has come upon him, and that it creeps down from his head to his heart. In all haste he fares under a pine tree, and hath cast himself down upon his face on the green grass. Under him he laid his sword and his horn of ivory; and he turned his face towards the paynim folk, for he would that Charles and all his men should say that the gentle Count had died a conqueror. Speedily and full often he confesses his sins, and in atonement he offers his glove to God.

Roland lies on a high peak looking towards Spain; he feels that his time is spent, and with one hand he beats upon his breast: "O God, I have sinned; forgive me through thy might the wrongs, both great and small, which I have done from the day I was born even to this day on which I was smitten." With his right hand he holds out his glove to God; and lo, the angels of heaven come down to him.

Count Roland lay under the pine tree; he has turned his face towards Spain, and he begins to call many things to remembrance, — all the lands he had won by his valour, and sweet France, and the men of his lineage, and Charles, his liege lord, who had brought him up in his household; and he cannot help but weep. But he would not wholly forget himself, and again he confesses his sins and begs forgiveness of God: "Our Father, Who art Truth, Who raised up Lazarus from the dead, and Who defended Daniel from the lions, save Thou my soul from the perils to which it is brought through the sins I wrought in my life days." With his right hand he offers his glove to God, and Saint Gabriel has taken it from his hand. Then his head sinks on his arm, and with clasped hands he hath gone to his end. And God sent him His cherubim, and Saint Michael of the Seas, and with them went Saint Gabriel, and they carried the soul of the Count into Paradise.

[tr. Isabel Butler]

# THE CID

The Cid became a legendary hero for Spain as Arthur did for Britain, Siegfried for Germany, Charlemagne for France, and George Washington for America. After the thirteenth century his exploits were circulated in ballad and story, and every Spanish town pointed to some token of his presence. But the legendary heroes of every country differ. Unlike Arthur and Siegfried, the Cid was a historical reality. More like Robin Hood than like Charlemagne and Arthur, he belonged to the common people and lacked the chivalric qualities of the typical romantic hero. Unlike Siegfried, his deeds were exploits of cunning, not physical invincibility. Fortunately, one of the best medieval poems was written about him no more than a century after he died in A.D. 1099, when some memory of the living man remained to control the romantic imagination. *The Poem of the Cid,* as it is now called, lies at the very beginning of Spanish literature; it is the first complete poem of any length in that language.

*The Cid* is written in the loose accentual and assonantal structure that characterizes the *Song of Roland,* which it resembles in many ways. The basic line consists of fifteen syllables arranged in octameter catalectic with strong caesural pause after the eighth syllable, as follows:

De los/ sos oi/os tan/ fuer/te — mi/entre/ loran/do
Torna/va la/ cabe/ca e/ esta/ba — los/ catan/do.

There are many rhythmical irregularities in the 3735 lines. Though the original is entirely in verse structure, the translator has confined his use of meter and rhyme to the essentially poetic portions of the tale.

The poem falls into two parts. It opens with Ruy or Rodrigo Diaz of Bivar, called the Cid ( == Arabic, "My Lord"), or Campeador, who has fallen under the displeasure of King Alfonso and is bankrupt, homeless, and outlawed. By a trick he borrows money enough to place his family in a convent and to launch from the mountains a campaign of piracy and conquest, aided by his faithful retainers, especially Alvar Fanez, his cousin, and Pero Bermuez, whom the Cid calls Pero Mudo, "Dumb Peter." Success attends his every venture. In turn he conquers the Moors, the Spaniards, and the Provençal French. When Valencia capitulates, he makes it his capital, though continuing to swear fidelity to his king, Alfonso, who finally pardons him with the betrothal of the Cid's daughters to the Infantes of Carrion (Ferrando and Diego Gonzales), who represent the House of Leon, rivaling that of Castile. The Cid, with some foreboding, consents to the marriage only on the condition that his king commands it. The second part, from which the following selections are taken, opens with the Cid at the height of his power, lord of Valencia and father-in-law of two presumably loyal nobles who live with him.

## THE CID

### Anonymous Spanish (12th cent.)

My Cid was in Valencia, with his vassals and his sons-in-law the Infantes of Carrion. Stretched upon a couch, the Campeador was sleeping, when, wot ye, a mishap befel them. The lion broke loose and escaped from the cage, and in sore fear were they in the midst of the court. They of the Campeador wrapped their mantles upon their arms, and gathered round the couch, and stood over their lord. But Ferran Gonzalez seeing no place of safety, neither open chamber nor tower, crept beneath the couch, so great was his fear, and Diego Gonzalez fled through the door, crying, "I shall never see Carrion more," and in his terror threw himself across a wine-press beam, with his mantle and robe all besmeared. Thereupon he who was born in a good hour awoke, and seeing the couch surrounded by his good barons, he said: "What means this, comrades? what would ye?" "Honoured lord," said they, "it is the lion gives us dread." Then my Cid rose to his feet, and drew his mantle on his neck, and advanced on the lion. And the lion, when he saw him, was abashed and bent his head before my Cid, and Don Roderick grasped him by the mane, and dragging him put him in the cage: a marvel to all that were by. And returning to the palace through the court, he asked for his sons-in-law, but found them not. Despite of calling, there came no answer. And when they were found, they came back so pale, that laughter — you never saw the like — ran round the court. My Cid the Campeador bade it cease, but the Infantes of Carrion held themselves grievously insulted.

While matters stood so, a thing befel which gave them sore trouble. The army of Morocco and King Bucar, if you have heard tell of him, came and beleaguered Valencia with fifty thousand pitched tents. My Cid and all his barons were glad. Thanks to God, it was more spoil for them. But, look you, the Infantes of Carrion were troubled at heart to see so many tents of the Moors, for which they had no relish. "We look for booty," said they, "and not loss. Now we shall have to go forth to battle, and it is certain we shall never see Carrion again, and the Campeador's daughters will be left widows." Muño Gustioz heard their discourse, and carried the news to my Cid. "See how your sons-in-law are afeared; how courageous they are: at the prospect of battle they are longing for Carrion. Go give them heart, and God speed you." And my Cid Don Roderick went out smiling. "God be with you, sons-in-law," said he. "Battle is my desire, Carrion is yours. In your arms ye have my daughters, bright as the sun. Rest in Valencia at your will. I know how to deal with the Moors, and with God's grace I will endeavour to overthrow them."

[A break, owing to the abstraction of a leaf from the Bivar Codex, occurs at this point. The defect in the narrative is partially supplied farther on by the speech of Pero Bermuez at the Cortes of Toledo. We may assume that the brothers, or at least Ferrando, stung by the imputation of cowardice, make some demonstration of zeal, which leads to the encounter described by Pero.]

"May the time come when I may deserve as much of both of you."
They went back together, and as Don Pero agreed, the honour was
bestowed upon Ferrando. My Cid and his vassals rejoiced. "Please
God," said he, "both my sons-in-law will yet bear themselves stoutly
in battle," and so say his followers all.

Loud from among the Moorish tents the call to battle comes,
And some there are, unused to war, awed by the rolling drums.
Ferrando and Diego most: of troubled mind are they;
Not of their will they find themselves before the Moors that day.
"Pero Bermuez," said the Cid, "my nephews stanch and true,
Ferrando and Diego do I give in charge to you;
Be yours the task in this day's fight my sons-in-law to shield,
For, by God's grace, to-day we sweep the Moors from off the field."
"Nay," said Bermuez, "Cid, for all the love I bear to thee,
The safety of thy sons-in-law no charge of mine shall be.
Let him who will the office fill; my place is at the front,
Among the comrades of my choice to bear the battle's brunt;
As it is thine upon the rear, against surprise to guard,
And ready stand to give support where'er the fight goes hard."
Came Alvar Fanez: "Loyal Cid Campeador," he cried,
"This battle surely God ordains — He will be on our side;
Now give the order of attack as seems to thee the best,
And, trust me, every man of us will do his chief's behest."
But lo! all armed from head to heel the Bishop Jerome shows;
He ever brings good fortune to my Cid where'er he goes.
"Mass have I said, and now I come to join you in the fray;
To strike a blow against the Moor in battle if I may,
And in the field win honour for my order and my hand.
It is for this that I am here, far from my native land.
Unto Valencia did I come to cast my lot with you,
All for the longing that I had to slay a Moor or two.
And so, in warlike guise I come, with blazoned shield, and lance,
That I may flesh my blade to-day, if God but give the chance.
Then send me to the front to do the bidding of my heart:
Grant me this favour that I ask, or else, my Cid, we part."
"Good!" said my Cid. "Go, flesh thy blade; there stand thy Moorish
    foes.
Now shall we see how gallantly our fighting Abbot goes."
He said; and straight the Bishop's spurs are in his charger's flanks,
And with a will he flings himself against the Moorish ranks.
By his good fortune, and the aid of God, that loved him well,

Two of the foe before his point at the first onset fell.
His lance he broke, he drew his sword — God! how the good steel
    played!
Two with the lance he slew, now five go down beneath his blade.
But many are the Moors, and round about him fast they close,
And on his hauberk, and his shield, they rain a shower of blows.
He in the good hour born beheld Don Jerome sorely pressed;
He braced his buckler on his arm, he laid his lance in rest,
And aiming where beset by Moors the Bishop stood at bay,
Touched Babieca with the spur and plunged into the fray;
And flung to earth unhorsed were seven, and lying dead were four,
Where breaking through the Moorish ranks came the Campeador.
God, it so pleased, that this should be the finish of the fight;
Before the lances of my Cid the fray became a flight;
And then to see the tent-ropes burst, the tent-poles prostrate flung!
As the Cid's horsemen crashing came the Moorish tents among.
Forth from the camp King Bucar's Moors they drove upon the plain,
And charging on the rout, they rode and cut them down amain;
Here severed fell the mail-clad arm, there lay the steel-capped head,
And here the charger, riderless, ran trampling on the dead.
Behind King Bucar, as he fled, my Cid came spurring on;
"Now, turn thee, Bucar, turn!" he cried; "here is the Bearded One;
Here is that Cid you came to seek, King from beyond the main,
Let there be peace and amity to-day between us twain."
Said Bucar, "Nay; thy naked sword, thy rushing steed, I see;
If these mean amity, then God confound such amity.
Thy hand and mine shall never join unless in yonder deep,
If the good steed that I bestride his footing can but keep."
Swift was the steed, but swifter borne on Babieca's stride,
Three fathoms from the sea my Cid rode at King Bucar's side;
Aloft his blade a moment played, then on the helmet's crown,
Shearing the steel-cap dight with gems, Colada he brought down.
Down to the belt, through helm and mail, he cleft the Moor in twain.
And so he slew King Bucar, who came from beyond the main.
This was the battle, this the day, when he the great sword won,
Worth a full thousand marks of gold — the famous Brand, Tizon.

And as my Cid came back from the slaughter, he lifted up his eyes
and saw Diego and Ferrando coming, and he rejoiced, smiling
brightly. "Welcome, sons-in-law," said he; "my sons are ye both.
I know now that ye delight in battle. Good news of you will go to
Carrion, how we have vanquished King Bucar." Then came
Minaya Alvar Fanez, from the elbow down dripping with blood, for
twenty Moors and more had he slain; his shield upon his neck all
dinted. Little recked he of the lance-thrusts; those who had given
them had not profited by them. "To God be thanks," said he, "and
to you, Cid, born in a good hour. You have slain Bucar, we have
won the field, and your sons-in-law have fleshed their swords in battle with the Moors." Said my Cid: "I too am glad. Now that they

are brave, henceforth will they be esteemed." With good intent he said it, but they took it ill. They withdrew apart: verily they were brothers. "Let us," said they, "have no regard for what they say. Let us depart for Carrion; we delay too long here. Great and rich is the wealth we have gained. While we live we cannot spend it. Let us demand our wives of the Cid, that we take them to the lands of Carrion, to show them our heritage. Let us remove them from Valencia and from the power of the Campeador, and afterwards on the road we will do our will, so that they reproach us no more with the affair of the lion. We will flout the daughters of the Campeador. With this wealth we shall be rich for ever; we shall be able to wed the daughters of kings or emperors, for by birth we are Counts of Carrion." With this design they returned, and said Ferran Gonzalez: "God be with you, Cid Campeador. May it please Doña Ximena, and you, and Minaya Alvar Fanez, and all present: give us our wives, that we take them to our lands of Carrion and establish them in the towns we give them for portions and honours, so that your daughters may see what we possess and what will be the possessions of the sons we beget." Said the Campeador, "I will give you my daughters and somewhat of my wealth;" for the Cid cared not to be thus slighted. "Ye give them towns and lands for portions in the lands of Carrion, and I as a marriage portion give them three thousand marks of silver, and to you I give mules and palfreys and horses strong and swift, and raiment of cloth and robes, and two swords, Colada and Tizon: well you know I won them in knightly fashion. My sons are ye, since I give you my daughters, and in them ye take from me the core of my heart. Let them of Galicia, and Castile, and Leon know how I have sent my sons-in-law home with wealth." Thus did they go forth from Valencia the Bright, and held their way across the Huerta. Cheerful went my Cid and all his company; but he who girt the sword in a good hour saw in the omens that these marriages would not be without some mishap, but it was vain to repent of having made them. And he said: "Feliz Muñoz, thou art my nephew and the cousin of my daughters. I charge thee go with them even unto Carrion, and see the heritage given to them, and return with the tidings. Take ye your way by Molina, and salute my friend Abengalvon the Moor, that he receive my sons-in-law with honour, and for love of me escort them as far as Medina." The parting was as that of the nail from the flesh, and then he of the good hour returned to Valencia.

And the Infantes of Carrion took their way by Santa Maria de Albarracin and came to Molina, to the Moor Abengalvon, who received them with great joy, and on the morrow rode forth with them with two hundred cavaliers, to escort them through the forest of Luzon and Arbuxuelo, till they reached the Salon. But the brothers, seeing the wealth the Moor carried, plotted treachery together: "If we could slay the Moor Abengalvon, we might possess ourselves of his wealth, and hold it as surely as our possessions of Carrion; and the Cid Campeador could never have satisfaction of us." But a Moor versed in Latin overheard the plot, and said to Abengalvon: "Have a care, my lord. The Infantes of Carrion plot thy death." And Abengalvon was very wroth, and with his two hundred men he presented himself, arms in hand, before the Infantes. "Say, Infantes of Carrion, what have I done to you? Without guile am I serving you, and ye plot my death. Were it not for my Cid of Bivar, I would serve you so that the world should ring with it. I would restore his daughters to the loyal Campeador, and ye should never set foot in Carrion. Here I leave you as villains and traitors. Under your favour, Ladies Elvira and Sol, I will depart. God the Lord of the earth give the Campeador joy of this marriage."

So saying the Moor returned across the Salon towards Molina, and the Infantes moved forward and crossed the Sierra of Miedes, and leaving Griza on the left and San Estéban on the right, but far beyond, they entered the oak wood of Corpes, — a tall forest, where branches lifted themselves to the clouds, and fierce beasts roamed around. They found a glade with a clear fountain, and they caused the tents to be pitched, and there they passed the night with their wives in their arms, making a show of love, which they ill proved at sunrise. Then they ordered the mules to be loaded and their servants to go forward, and when they four were left alone, then did the Infantes do a cruel wrong. "Here," said they, "in this wild forest, do we cast you off, and the Cid Campeador shall know that this is our vengeance for the affair of the lion." Then plucking off mantles and pelisses, the cruel traitors strip them to their smocks and undercoats, and seize the hard strong saddle-girths. Seeing this, said Doña Sol, "For God's sake we entreat you, as ye have trenchant swords in your hands, rather cut off our heads, and let us be martyrs. If we are beaten, ye will be reviled of Moors and Christians, and called to answer it in Council or in Cortes." But all their entreaties availed them nothing, for straightway the Infantes began to lash them with the saddle-girths and sharp spurs, tearing their linen and their flesh till the bright blood ran down their clothing. "Ah!" thought the ladies in their hearts, "if it were God's will, what fortune it would be if the Campeador should now appear." Then, weary of striking and striving which could give the hardest blows, the Infantes left Elvira and Sol for dead, a prey to the beasts and birds of the forest. O for the Cid Campeador to come upon them that hour! Then the Infantes went on their way rejoicing through the wood. "Now are we avenged of our marriages," said they. "Thus is the dishonour of the lion avenged."

But I must tell you of Feliz Muñoz, the nephew of the Cid. They bade him go forward, and against his will he went. His heart smote him as he followed the road, and he drew aside from the others, and hid himself in a thicket to watch whether his cousins came, and what the Infantes did. He saw them pass and heard their talk: had they seen him, look you, he had not escaped death. But they spurred onwards, and he turned back and found his cousins in a swoon, and sprang from his horse, crying, "Cousins! cousins! for the love of God, waken while it is yet day, that the savage beasts of the forest devour us not." Coming to themselves, Doña Elvira and Doña Sol opened their eyes and saw Feliz Muñoz, and in sore pain said Doña Sol: "If our father the Campeador deserve aught of you, for God's sake give us water." And with his hat (new and fresh was it when he brought it out of Valencia) he fetched water and gave it to his cousins, and urging them and encouraging them, he set them upon his horse, and they took their way through the oak wood of Corpes, and by nightfall they issued forth from the wood and reached the waters of Duero. He left them at the Tower of Doña Urraca, and came to San Estéban, where he found Diego Tellez, kinsman of Alvar Fanez. He, when he heard it, was grieved to the heart; and he took beasts and proper raiment, and fetched Doña Elvira and Doña Sol and lodged them in San Estéban, showing them all the honour he could. They of San Estéban are ever courteous, and it grieved them to the heart when they knew of the matter, and they comforted the daughters of the Cid and tended them till they were restored.

These tidings came to Valencia, and when they were told to my Cid, he thought and pondered a full hour; and he raised his hand and grasped his beard, saying, "Christ be thanked, since the Infantes of Carrion have done me such honour. By this beard that none hath reaped, the Infantes of Carrion shall not profit by this, and well shall I marry my daughters." And he ordered Minaya and Pero Bermuez and Martin Antolinez to go with two hundred cavaliers to bring back his daughters to Valencia.

When Doña Elvira and Doña Sol saw Minaya, "We are as thankful to see you," said they, "as if we had seen the Creator; and give ye thanks unto Him that we are alive. When we are on our journey, we will tell you all our grievance." And said Pero Bermuez, "Be of good cheer, since ye are alive and well and without other hurt. Ye have lost a good marriage, but ye can win a better, and may we see the day when we shall be able to avenge you." And the next day they set forth, they of San Estéban attending them with loving kindness as far as the river-side. And Minaya and the ladies passed through Alcoceba to the right of San Estéban de Gormaz and halted at the King's ford at the Casa de Berlanga, and the next day they reached Medina, and the next Molina. The Moor Abengalvon was glad, and went forth to receive them, and made them a rich supper for the love of the Cid.

Thence they went to Valencia, and he in the good hour born went forth to meet them, and he embraced them and kissed them. "Welcome, my daughters," said he. "God keep you from evil. I accepted this marriage, for I dared not gainsay it. God grant that I see you better married hereafter, and that I have my revenge of my sons-in-law of Carrion."

Then he took counsel with his followers, and he said to Muño Gustioz, "Carry the tidings to Castile, to King Alfonso, of this dishonour the Infantes have done me. It will cut the good king to the heart, for he and not I gave my daughters in marriage, and if any dishonour falls on us, great or small it falls on my lord. Let him summon me the Infantes of Carrion to council, assembly, or cortes, that I have justice of them, for heavy is the grievance on my heart."

And Muño Gustioz set forth, travelling day and night, and found the king at Sahagun. And the king was silent and meditated a good hour. "Sooth to tell," said he, "it grieves me to the heart, for it was I married his daughters to the Infantes of Carrion. I did it for his advantage, but to-day I wish the match had not been made. It is his right that I should aid him; so my heralds shall go through all my kingdom to summon my court to Toledo. And I shall summon the Infantes of Carrion, that they do justice to my Cid the Campeador, so that he have no grievance if I can prevent it. Tell the Campeador to come to me to Toledo at the end of seven weeks. For the love of him do I summon this court."

Then without delay Alfonso of Castile sent letters to Leon and Santiago, to the Portuguese and Galicians, and to them of Carrion, and to the barons of Castile, that the honoured king would hold a court in Toledo at the end of seven weeks, and that he who came not to the court should not be esteemed his vassal. It weighed heavily upon the Infantes of Carrion, for they feared my Cid the Campeador would come; and they entreated the king to excuse them this court. "That will I not do," said the king, "so help me God. My Cid the Campeador will come, and you have to render him justice, for he has a grievance against you. He who will not come to my court, let him quit my kingdom, for I relish him not." Then the Infantes saw there was no help for it, and they took counsel with their kinsmen; and the Count Don García, the enemy of my Cid, who always sought to do him harm, was among them.

When the appointed day came, among the first went the good King Don Alfonso, and the Count Don Anrrich, and the Count Don Remond, the father of the good Emperor, and the Count Don Vella, and the Count Don Beltran, and many other prudent men of the kingdom. With the Infantes were the Count Don García, and Assur Gonzalez, and Gonzalo Asurez, and a great band, which they brought to the court, thinking to overawe my Cid. On the fifth day came my Cid (he had sent Alvar Fanez before him), and when he saw the good King Alfonso, he lighted down to humble himself and honour his lord. Said the king, "By San Esidro, I will have none of that. Mount, Cid! With heart and soul I salute you. What grieves you, pains me to the heart."

That night my Cid did not cross the Tagus, but lodged in San Servan, for he wished to watch and pray in that sanctuary and commune with Minaya and his trusty men. When morning came he said to Minaya, "Let a hundred of my good men get ready, with vests under the hauberks bright as the sun, and over the hauberks ermines and furs, the girdles bound tight, so that the arms show not, and sweet trenchant swords under the mantles. In this wise will I go the court to demand my rights and plead my plea, and, if the Infantes of Carrion try treachery, with a hundred such I shall have no fear." He himself put on breeches of fine cloth, and bravely wrought shoes, and a linen shirt white as the sun, with loops of gold and silver at the wrists, for so he would have it. And over that, and under the surcoat, a tunic embroidered with gold, and next a robe of red fur with border of gold, which the Campeador always wore; and over his hair a coif of rich scarlet worked with gold, for the hair of the good Campeador was not cut. Long was the beard he bore, and he bound it with a cord, so doing because he would fain preserve it; and over all he threw a mantle of great price. Then mounting quickly, he issued forth from San Servan, and thus arrayed did my Cid go to the court.

When they saw him enter, the good King Don Alfonso and the Count Don Anrrich and the Count Don Remond, and all the others rose to their feet. But the Crespo de Grañon would not rise, nor they of the party of the Infantes of Carrion. My Cid seated himself upon a couch, and the hundred who guarded him placed themselves around him; and all that were in the court were gazing at my Cid and at the long beard he bore bound in a cord. In his port he looked a true baron, but for shame the Infantes of Carrion could not look upon him.

Then the king rose to his feet. "But two Cortes have I held since I have been king, one in Burgos, the other in Carrion. This third have I summoned to Toledo this day for the love of my Cid, him that was born in a good hour, that he have justice of the Infantes, who, as we all know, have done him a wrong. Let the Count Don Anrrich and the Count Don Remond and the other counts that are not of the party be judges in this matter; and give ye your minds to it, to search out the right, for wrong I will not have. Let us have peace on each side. I swear by San Esidro, he who disturbs my court shall quit my kingdom and forfeit my love, and he who shall prove his right, on his side am I. Now let the Cid make his demand, and we will hear what answer the Infantes make."

My Cid kissed the king's hand and rose to his feet. "Much do I thank you, my lord and king, that in love of me you have summoned this court. This do I demand of the Infantes of Carrion. It is not I that am dishonoured because they deserted my daughters, for it was you, O king, who married them, and you will know what to do to-day. But when they carried away my daughters from Valencia the Great, I, of the love I bore them, gave them two swords that I won in knightly fashion, Colada and Tizon, that with them they might do honour to themselves and service to you. When they deserted my daughters in the oak-wood of Corpes, they meant to have nought of mine. Let them restore my swords, since they are no longer my sons-in-law." And the judges agreed it was just.

Then said the Count Don García, "We must speak about this"; and going aside with their kinsmen, the Infantes said, "Still does the Cid bear love to us, since he urges not against us the dishonour of his daughters. Easily shall we reconcile ourselves with the king. Let us give him his swords, since this is the end of the dispute. When he has them, he will quit the court." And returning to the court they said, "So please ye, King Alfonso, we cannot deny that he gave us two swords, and as he desires them, we give them up in your presence." And they drew forth the swords Colada and Tizon and placed them in the hands of the king. And he drew the swords and dazzled all the court; of gold were the pummels and guards. And all that were in the court marvelled. The Cid, receiving the swords, held them in his hands, gazing on them. They could not change them, for he knew them well. And his whole body was glad, and from his heart he smiled, and grasping his beard, the beard that none had reaped, "Thus," said he, "are Doña Elvira and Doña Sol being avenged." Then he called his nephew, and stretching forth his arm, gave him the sword Tizon. "Take it," he said, "and it will have a better master." And to Martin Antolinez, the worthy Burgalese, he gave the sword Colada. "Take Colada," he said: "I won it from a brave master, the Count Don Remont Berengel of Barcelona; therefore do I give it to you, that you take good care of it. I know if you have the chance with it, you will win honour and glory."

Then he rose to his feet. "Thanks be to God and you, my lord the king, I am satisfied in my swords, but I have another grievance against the Infantes of Carrion. When they carried away my daughters from Valencia, I gave them three thousand marks in gold and silver. Let them restore my treasure, since they are no longer my sons-in-law."

Then made anwer the Infantes, "We gave him back his swords, that he should make no further demand, and that the dispute should end here. This, if it please the king, is our answer." But said the king, "Ye must satisfy the Cid in his demand." With that the Infantes retired apart, perplexed in mind, for the sum was great and they had spent all. "The conqueror of Valencia bears hard on us," said they, "in this eagerness to seize our possessions. We must pay out of our heritage in the lands of Carrion." Said the judges, "If this please the Cid we will not refuse it, but our judgement is that ye make restitution here in the court." Said Ferran Gonzalez, "We have no money." The Count Don Remond made answer, "Ye have spent the gold and silver; then our award before King Alfonso is that ye pay him in kind, and that the Campeador accept it." Then the Infantes saw there was no help, and you might see them bring many a swift steed and stout mule and trained palfrey, and good sword with its furniture. My Cid received them on the appraising of the court, and the Infantes paid him, borrowing of others, for their own means sufficed not. Ill did they come, and scoffed at, look you, out of this debate. My Cid received the appraisements, and his men took charge of them; but when this was done, they turned to another matter.

"So please your Grace! once more upon your clemency I call;
A grievance yet remains untold, the greatest grief of all.
And let the court give ear, and weigh the wrong that hath been done.
I hold myself dishonoured by the Lords of Carrion.

Redress by combat they must yield; none other will I take.
How now, Infantes! what excuse, what answer do ye make?
Why have ye laid my heartstrings bare? In jest or earnest, say,
Have I offended you? and I will make amends to-day.
My daughters in your hands I placed the day that forth ye went,
And rich in wealth and honours from Valencia were ye sent.
Why did ye carry with you brides ye loved not, treacherous curs?
Why tear their flesh in Corpes wood with saddle-girths and spurs,
And leave them to the beasts of prey? Villains throughout were ye!
What answer ye can make to this 'tis for the court to see."
The Count García was the first that rose to make reply.
"So please ye, gracious king, of all the Kings of Spain most high;
Strange is the guise in which my Cid before you hath appeared;
To grace your summoned court he comes, with that long straggling
    beard;
With awe struck dumb, methinks, are some; some look as though
    they feared.
The noble Lords of Carrion of princely race are born;
To take the daughters of my Cid for lemans they should scorn;
Much more for brides of equal birth: in casting them aside —
We care not for his blustering talk — we hold them justified."
Upstood the Champion, stroked his beard, and grasped it in his hands:
"Thanks be to God above," he cried, "who heaven and earth com-
    mands,
A long and lordly growth it is, my pleasure and my pride;
In this my beard García, say, what find you to deride?
Its nurture since it graced my chin hath ever been my care;
No son of woman born hath dared to lay a finger there;
No son of Christian or of Moor hath ever plucked a hair.
Remember Cabra, Count! of thine the same thou canst not say:
On both thy castle and thy beard I laid my hand that day.
Nay! not a groom was there but he his handful plucked away.
Look, where my hand hath been, my lords, all ragged yet it grows!"
With noisy protest breaking in Ferran Gonzalez rose:
"Cid, let there be an end of this; your gifts you have again,
And now no pretext for dispute between us doth remain.
Princes of Carrion are we, with fitting brides we mate;
Daughters of emperors or kings, not squires of low estate:
We brook not such alliances, and yours we rightly spurned."
My Cid, Ruy Diaz, at the word, quick to Bermuez turned.
"Now is the time, Dumb Peter, speak, O man that sittest mute!
My daughters' and thy cousins' name and fame are in dispute:
To me they speak, to thee they look to answer every word.
If I am left to answer now, thou canst not draw thy sword."
Tongue-tied Bermuez stood, awhile he strove for words in vain,
But, look you, when he once began he made his meaning plain.
"Cid, first I have a word for you: you always are the same,
In Cortes ever jibing me, 'Dumb Peter' is the name:
It never was a gift of mine, and that long since you knew;

But have you found me fail in aught that fell to me to do?
You lie, Ferrando; lie in all you say upon that score.
The honour was to you, not him, the Cid Campeador;
For I know something of your worth, and somewhat I can tell:
That day beneath Valencia wall — you recollect it well —
You prayed the Cid to place you in the forefront of the fray;
You spied a Moor, and valiantly you went that Moor to slay;
And then you turned and fled — for his approach you would not
    stay;
Right soon he would have taught you 'twas a sorry game to play,
Had I not been in battle there to take your place that day.
I slew him at the first onfall; I gave his steed to you;
To no man have I told the tale from that hour hitherto.
Before my Cid and all his men you got yourself a name,
How you in single combat slew a Moor — a deed of fame;
And all believed in your exploit; they wist not of your shame.
You are a craven at the core; tall, handsome, as you stand:
How dare you talk as now you talk, you tongue without a hand?
Again, Ferrando, call to mind — another tale for you —
That matter of the lion; it was at Valencia too.
My Cid lay sleeping when you saw the unchained lion near;
What did you do, Ferrando, then, in your agony of fear?
Low did you crouch behind the couch whereon the Champion lay:
You did, Ferrando, and by that we rate your worth to-day.
We gathered round to guard our lord, Valencia's conqueror.
He rose, and to the lion went, the brave Campeador;
The lion fawned before his feet and let him grasp its mane;
He thrust it back into the cage, he turned to us again.
His trusty vassals to a man he saw around him there:
Where were his sons-in-law? he asked, and none could tell him where.
Now take thou my defiance as a traitor, trothless knight —
Upon this plea before our King Alfonso will I fight;
The daughters of my lord are wronged, their wrong is mine to right.
That ye those ladies did desert, the baser are ye then;
For what are they? — weak women, and what are ye? — strong men.
On every count I deem their cause to be the holier,
And I will make thee own it when we meet in battle here.
Traitor thou shalt confess thyself, so help me God on high,
And all that I have said to-day my sword shall verify."
    Thus far these two.  Diego rose, and spoke as ye shall hear:
"Counts by our birth are we, of stain our lineage is clear.
In this alliance with my Cid there was no parity.
If we his daughters cast aside, no cause for shame we see.
And little need we care if they in mourning pass their lives,
Enduring the reproach that clings to scorned rejected wives.
In leaving them we but upheld our honour and our right,
And ready to the death am I, maintaining this, to fight."
Here Martin Antolinez sprang upon his feet: "False hound!
Will you not silent keep that mouth where truth was never found?

For you to boast! the lion scare have you forgotten too?
How through the open door you rushed, across the courtyard flew;
How sprawling in your terror on the wine-press beam you lay?
Ay! never more, I trow, you wore the mantle of that day.
There is no choice; the issue now the sword alone can try;
The daughters of my Cid ye spurned; that must ye justify.
On every count I here declare their cause the cause of right,
And thou shalt own thy treachery the day we join in fight."
He ceased, and striding up the hall Assur González passed;
His cheek was flushed with wine, for he had stayed to break his fast;
Ungirt his robe, and trailing low his ermine mantle hung;
Rude was his bearing to the Court, and reckless was his tongue.
"What a to-do is here, my lords! was the like ever seen?
What talk is this about my Cid — him of Bivar I mean?
To Riodouirna let him go to take his millers' rent,
And keep his mills agoing there, as once he was content.
He, forsooth, mate his daughters with the Counts of Carrion!"
Upstarted Muño Gustioz: "False, foul-mouthed knave, have done!
Thou glutton, wont to break thy fast without a thought of prayer,
Whose heart is plotting mischief when thy lips are speaking fair;
Whose plighted word to friend, or lord hath ever proved a lie;
False always to thy fellow-man, falser to God on high.
No share in thy good will I seek; one only boon I pray,
The chance to make thee own thyself the villain that I say."
Then spoke the king: "Enough of words: ye have my leave to fight,
The challenged and the challengers; and God defend the right."

[After procastination by the Infantes and Assur, the Cid's three champions engage them in a trial of combat and emerge victorious.]

Valencia the Great was glad, rejoiced at heart to see
The honoured champions of her lord return in victory.
And Ruy Diaz grasped his beard: "Thanks be to God," said he,
"Of part or lot in Carrion now are my daughters free;
Now may I give them without shame whoe'er the suitors be."
And favoured by the king himself, Alfonso of Leon,
Prosperous was the wooing of Navarre and Aragon.
The bridals of Elvira and of Sol in splendour passed;
Stately the former nuptials were, but statelier far the last.
And he that in a good hour was born, behold how he hath sped!
His daughters now to higher rank and greater honour wed:
Sought by Navarre and Aragon for queens his daughters twain;
And monarchs of his blood to-day upon the thrones of Spain.
And so his honour in the land grows greater day by day.
Upon the feast of Pentecost from life he passed away.
For him and all of us the Grace of Christ let us implore.
And here ye have the story of my Cid Campeador.
                                        [tr. JOHN ORMSBY]

# AUCASSIN AND NICOLETE

The *chantefable* of Aucassin and Nicolete is unique in extant romantic literature because of its form — part verse, part prose; but it is unique, too, in subtlety of authorship, which has set it apart from the many stories of its day in which young and passionate love triumphs over obstacles. The tale seems not to have been popular, for it exists in a single manuscript, whereas the analogous and probably slightly earlier story of Floire and Blanchefleur not only survives in many, but was almost immediately rendered into practically every language of the West. Both stories probably originated in Arabic; at all events, Aucassin is an Arabic name (*Alkacim*). Perhaps it made its way from Moorish Spain into Provence, where it took on its locale. We may imagine a Provençal jongleur entertaining the Count of Arles or Montaubon with a tale that had additional interest after the Crusades. But the present text is written in a northern dialect, of Picardy or Hainault. Scholars vary in calculating the date: Gaston Paris thought it as early as 1130, Jeanroy about 1180, and Cohen in the thirteenth century. The author describes himself as *un vieil caitif,* which may mean a captive, or only a wretched man. His remarks about the Saracens make it seem very doubtful that he had ever been a prisoner among them, as some readers like to imagine.

There is an artful simplicity about the story. It is a tale of courtesy that includes the conflict between love and filial duty, the tears of separation, and a pastoral idyl with lovers reunited. There are snarling villains and peasant buffoons, and here and there a touch of life, as when Nicolete picks up her skirts to protect them from the damp night grass. The single-minded interest of the lovers was as unworldly then as now, but the old jongleur seems to smile at the excess of his story, even to the introduction of lions into Provence, and holds his audience spellbound at the progress of the tale. Love alone will set broken bones, by God's will who loveth lovers. The story really ends with Aucassin and Nicolete reunited in silhouette on the shore as the dawning sun breaks over the sea:

> *Passent les vaus et les mons*
> *Et les viles et les bors*
> *A la mer vinrent au jor,*
> *Si descendent u sablon*
> *Les le rivage.*

The story has been conducted like an orchestra recital, with crescendo and diminuendo in harmony. But now the jongleur may stop for his deserved applause. As an encore he recites a grossly humorous piece about the country of Torelore that readers inevitably compare with Rabelais. Then, having properly varied his program, he responds to applause once more with a sweet melody of lovers reunited, sending his listeners away with the properly romantic feeling that in this best of worlds all will end well.

The version given below is unabridged.

## THE SONG-STORY OF AUCASSIN AND NICOLETE

### Anonymous (*circ.* A.D. 1200)

[From *Aucassin and Nicolete*, translated by Andrew Lang; David Nutt, London, 1887.]

'Tis of Aucassin and Nicolete.

> Who would list to the good lay
> Gladness of the captive grey?
> 'Tis how two young lovers met,
> Aucassin and Nicolete,
> Of the pains the lover bore
> And the sorrows he outwore,
> For the goodness and the grace,
> Of his love, so fair of face.
>
> Sweet the song, the story sweet,
> There is no man hearkens it,
> No man living 'neath the sun,
> So outwearied, so foredone,
> Sick and woful, worn and sad,
> But is healèd, but is glad
> 'Tis so sweet.

So say they, speak they, tell they the Tale:

How the Count Bougars de Valence made war on Count Garin de Biaucaire, war so great, and so marvellous, and so mortal that never a day dawned but alway he was there, by the gates and walls, and barriers of the town with a hundred knights, and ten thousand men at arms, horsemen and footmen: so burned he the Count's land, and spoiled his country, and slew his men. Now the Count Garin de Biaucaire was old and frail, and his good days were gone over. No heir had he, neither son nor daughter, save one young man only; such an one as I shall tell you. Aucassin was the name of the damoiseau: fair was he, goodly, and great, and featly fashioned of his body and limbs. His hair was yellow, in little curls, his eyes blue and laughing, his face beautiful and shapely, his nose high and well set, and so richly seen was he in all things good, that in him was none evil at all. But so suddenly overtaken was he of Love, who is a great master, that he would not, of his will, be dubbed knight, nor take arms, nor follow tourneys, nor do whatsoever him beseemed. Therefore his father and mother said to him:

"Son, go take thine arms, mount thy horse, and hold thy land, and help thy men, for if they see thee among them, more stoutly will they keep in battle their lives, and lands, and thine, and mine."

"Father," said Aucassin, "I marvel that you will be speaking. Never may God give me aught of my desire if I be made knight, or mount my horse, or face stour and battle wherein knights smite and are smitten again, unless thou give me Nicolete, my true love, that I love so well."

"Son," said the father, "this may not be. Let Nicolete go. A slave girl she is, out of a strange land, and the captain of this town bought her of the Saracens, and carried her hither, and hath reared her and let christen the maid, and took her for his daughter in God, and one day will find a young man for her, to win her bread honourably. Herein hast thou naught to make or mend, but if a wife thou wilt have, I will give thee the daughter of a King, or a Count. There is no man so rich in France, but if thou desire his daughter, thou shalt have her."

"Faith! my father," said Aucassin, "tell me where is the place so high in all the world, that Nicolete, my sweet lady and love, would not grace it well? If she were Empress of Constantinople or of Germany, or Queen of France or England, it were little enough for her; so gentle is she and courteous, and debonaire, and compact of all good qualities."

Here singeth one:

Aucassin was of Biaucaire
Of a goodly castle there,
But from Nicolete the fair
None might win his heart away
Though his father, many a day,
And his mother said him nay,
"Ha! fond child, what wouldest thou?
Nicolete is glad enow!
Was from Carthage cast away,
Paynims sold her on a day!
Wouldst thou win a lady fair
Choose a maid of high degree
Such an one is meet for thee."
"Nay of these I have no care,
Nicolète is debonaire,
Her body sweet and the face of her
Take my heart as in a snare,
Loyal love is but her share
        That is so sweet."

Then speak they, say they, tell they the Tale:
When the Count Garin de Biaucaire knew that he would avail not

to withdraw Aucassin his son from the love of Nicolete, he went to the Captain of the city, who was his man, and spake to him, saying:

"Sir Count, away with Nicolete thy daughter in God; cursed be the land whence she was brought into this country, for by reason of her do I lose Aucassin, that will neither be dubbed knight, nor do aught of the things that fall to him to be done. And wit ye well," he said, "that if I might have her at my will, I would burn her in a fire, and yourself might well be sore adread."

"Sir," said the Captain, "this is grievous to me that he comes and goes and hath speech with her. I had bought the maiden at mine own charges, and nourished her, and baptized, and made her my daughter in God. Yea, I would have given her to a young man that should win her bread honourably. With this had Aucassin thy son naught to make or mend. But, sith it is thy will and thy pleasure, I will send her into that land and that country where never will he see her with his eyes."

"Have a heed to thyself," said the Count Garin, "thence might great evil come on thee."

So parted they each from other. Now the Captain was a right rich man: so had he a rich palace with a garden in face of it; in an upper chamber thereof he let place Nicolete, with one old woman to keep her company, and in that chamber put bread and meat and wine and such things as were needful. Then he let seal the door, that none might come in or go forth, save that there was one window, over against the garden, and strait enough, where through came to them a little air.

Here singeth one:

Nicolete as ye heard tell
Prisoned is within a cell
That is painted wondrously
With colours of a far countrie,
And the window of marble wrought,
There the maiden stood in thought,
With straight brows and yellow hair
Never saw ye fairer fair!
On the wood she gazed below,
And she saw the roses blow,
Heard the birds sing loud and low,
Therefore spoke she wofully:
"Ah me, wherefore do I lie
Here in prison wrongfully:
Aucassin, my love, my knight,
Am I not thy heart's delight,
Thou that lovest me aright!
'Tis for thee that I must dwell
In the vaulted chamber cell,

Hard beset and all alone!
By our Lady Mary's Son
Here no longer will I wonn,
    If I may flee!"


Then speak they, say they, tell they the Tale:

Nicolete was in prison, as ye have heard soothly, in the chamber. And the noise and bruit of it went through all the country and all the land, how that Nicolete was lost. Some said she had fled the country, and some that the Count Garin de Biaucaire had let slay her. Whosoever had joy thereof, Aucassin had none, so he went to the Captain of the town and spoke to him saying:

"Sir Captain, what hast thou made of Nicolete, my sweet lady and love, the thing that best I love in all the world? Hast thou carried her off or ravished her away from me? Know well that if I die of it, the price shall be demanded of thee, and that will be well done, for it shall be even as if thou hadst slain me with thy two hands, for thou hast taken from me the thing that in this world I loved the best."

"Fair Sir," said the Captain, "let these things be. Nicolete is a captive that I did bring from a strange country. Yea, I bought her at my own charges of the Saracens, and I bred her up and baptized her, and made her my daughter in God. And I have cherished her, and one of these days I would have given her a young man, to win her bread honourably. With this hast thou naught to make, but do thou take the daughter of a King or a Count. Nay more, what wouldst thou deem thee to have gained, hadst thou made her thy leman, and taken her to thy bed? Plentiful lack of comfort hadst thou got thereby, for in Hell would thy soul have lain while the world endures, and into Paradise wouldst thou have entered never."

"In Paradise what have I to win? Therein I seek not to enter, but only to have Nicolete, my sweet lady that I love so well. For into Paradise go none but such folk as I shall tell thee now: Thither go these same old priests, and halt old men and maimed, who all day and night cower continually before the altars, and in the crypts; and such folk as wear old amices and old clouted frocks, and naked folk and shoeless, and covered with sores, perishing of hunger and thirst, and of cold, and of little ease. These be they that go into Paradise, with them have I naught to make. But into Hell would I fain go; for into Hell fare the goodly clerks, and goodly knights that fall in tourneys and great wars, and stout men at arms, and all men noble. With these would I liefly go. And thither pass the sweet ladies and courteous that have two lovers, or three, and their lords also thereto. Thither goes the gold, and the silver, and cloth of vair, and cloth of gris, and harpers, and makers, and the prince of this world. With these I would gladly go, let me but have with me Nicolete, my sweetest lady."

"Certes," quoth the Captain, "in vain wilt thou speak thereof, for never shalt thou see her; and if thou hadst word with her, and thy father knew it, he would let burn in a fire both her and me, and thyself might well be sore adread."

"That is even what irketh me," quoth Aucassin. So he went from the Captain sorrowing.

Here singeth one:

Aucassin did so depart
Much in dole and heavy at heart
For his love so bright and dear,
None might bring him any cheer,
None might give good words to hear,
To the palace doth he fare
Climbeth up the palace-stair,
Passeth to a chamber there,
Thus great sorrow doth he bear,
For his lady and love so fair.

"Nicolete how fair art thou,
Sweet thy foot-fall, sweet thine eyes,
Sweet the mirth of thy replies,
Sweet thy laughter, sweet thy face,
Sweet thy lips and sweet thy brow,
And the touch of thine embrace,
All for thee I sorrow now,
Captive in an evil place,
Whence I ne'er may go my ways
    Sister, sweet friend!"

So say they, speak they, tell they the Tale:

While Aucassin was in the chamber sorrowing for Nicolete his love, even then the Count Bougars de Valence, that had his war to wage, forgat it no whit, but had called up his horsemen and his footmen, so made he for the castle to storm it. And the cry of battle arose, and the din, and knights and men at arms busked them, and ran to walls and gates to hold the keep. And the towns-folk mounted to the battlements, and cast down bolts and pikes. Then while the assault was great, and even at its height, the Count Garin de Biaucaire came into the chamber where Aucassin was making lament, sorrowing for Nicolete, his sweet lady that he loved so well.

"Ha! son," quoth he, "how caitiff art thou, and cowardly, that canst see men assail thy goodliest castle and strongest. Know thou that if thou lose it, thou losest all. Son, go to, take arms, and mount thy horse, and defend thy land, and help thy men, and fare into the stour. Thou needst not smite nor be smitten. If they do but see thee among them, better will they guard their substance, and their lives, and thy land and mine. And thou art so great, and hardy of thy hands, that well mightst thou do this thing, and to do it is thy devoir."

"Father," said Aucassin, "what is this thou sayest now? God grant me never aught of my desire, if I be dubbed knight, or mount steed, or go into the stour where knights do smite and are smitten, if thou givest me not Nicolete, my sweet lady, whom I love so well."

"Son," quoth his father, "this may never be: rather would I be quite disinherited and lose all that is mine, than that thou shouldst have her to thy wife, or to love *par amours*."

So he turned him about. But when Aucassin saw him going he called to him again, saying,

"Father, go to now, I will make with thee fair covenant."

"What covenant, fair son?"

"I will take up arms, and go into the stour, on this covenant, that, if God bring me back sound and safe, thou wilt let me see Nicolete my sweet lady, even so long that I may have of her two words or three, and one kiss."

"That will I grant," said his father.

At this was Aucassin glad.

Here one singeth:

Of the kiss heard Aucassin
That returning he shall win.
None so glad would he have been
Of a myriad marks of gold
Of a hundred thousand told.
Called for raiment brave of steel,
Then they clad him, head to heel,
Twyfold hauberk doth he don,
Firmly braced the helmet on.
Girt the sword with hilt of gold,
Horse doth mount, and lance doth wield,
Looks to stirrups and to shield,
Wondrous brave he rode to field.
Dreaming of his lady dear
Setteth spurs to the destrere,
Rideth forward without fear,
Through the gate and forth away
  To the fray.

So speak they, say they, tell they the Tale:

Aucassin was armed and mounted as ye have heard tell. God! how goodly sat the shield on his shoulder, the helm on his head, and the baldric on his left haunch! And the damoiseau was tall, fair, featly fashioned, and hardy of his hands, and the horse whereon he rode swift and keen, and straight had he spurred him forth of the gate. Now believe ye not that his mind was on kine, nor cattle of the booty, nor thought he how he might strike a knight, nor be stricken again: nor no such thing. Nay, no memory had Aucassin of aught of these; rather he so dreamed of Nicolete, his sweet lady, that he dropped his reins, forgetting all there was to do, and his horse that had felt the spur, bore him into the press and hurled among the foe, and they laid hands on him all about, and took him captive, and seized away his spear and shield, and straightway they led him off a prisoner, and were even now discoursing of what death he should die.

And when Aucassin heard them,

"Ha! God," said he, "sweet Saviour. Be these my deadly enemies that have taken me, and will soon cut off my head? And once my head is off, no more shall I speak with Nicolete, my sweet lady, that I love so well. Natheless have I here a good sword, and sit a good horse unwearied. If now I keep not my head for her sake, God help her never, if she love me more!"

The damoiseau was tall and strong, and the horse whereon he sat was right eager. And he laid hand to sword, and fell a-smiting to right and left, and smote through helm and nasal, and arm and clenched hand, making a murder about him, like a wild boar when hounds fall on him in the forest, even till he struck down ten knights, and seven he hurt, and straightway he hurled out of the press, and rode back again at full speed, sword in hand. The Count Bougars de Valence heard say they were about hanging Aucassin, his enemy, so he came into that place, and Aucassin was ware of him, and gat his sword into his hand, and lashed at his helm with such a stroke that he drave it down on his head, and he being stunned, fell grovelling. And Aucassin laid hands on him, and caught him by the nasal of his helmet, and gave him to his father.

"Father," quoth Aucassin, "lo here is your mortal foe, who hath so warred on you with all malengin. Full twenty years did this war endure, and might not be ended by man."

"Fair son," said his father, "thy feats of youth shouldst thou do, and not seek after folly."

"Father," saith Aucassin, "sermon me no sermons, but fulfil my covenant."

"Ha! what covenant, fair son?"

"What, father, hast thou forgotten it? By mine own head, whosoever forgets, will I not forget it, so much it hath me at heart. Didst thou not covenant with me when I took up arms, and went into the stour, that if God brought me back safe and sound, thou wouldst let me see Nicolete, my sweet lady, even so long that I may have of her two words or three, and one kiss? So didst thou covenant, and my mind is that thou keep thy word."

"I!" quoth the father, "God forsake me when I keep this covenant! Nay, if she were here, I would let burn her in the fire, and thyself shouldst be sore adread."

"Is this thy last word?" quoth Aucassin.

"So help me God," quoth his father, "yea!"

"Certes," quoth Aucassin, "this is a sorry thing meseems, when a man of thine age lies!"

"Count of Valence," quoth Aucassin, "I took thee?"

"In sooth, Sir, didst thou," saith the Count.

"Give me thy hand," saith Aucassin.

"Sir, with good will."

So he set his hand in the other's.

"Now givest thou me thy word," saith Aucassin, "that never whiles thou art living man wilt thou avail to do my father dishonour, or harm him in body, or in goods, but do it thou wilt?"

"Sir, in God's name," saith he, "mock me not, but put me to my ransom; ye cannot ask of me gold nor silver, horses nor palfreys, vair nor gris, hawks nor hounds, but I will give you them."

"What?" quoth Aucassin. "Ha, knowest thou not it was I that took thee?"

"Yea, sir," quoth the Count Bougars.

"God help me never, but I will make thy head fly from thy shoulders, if thou makest not troth," said Aucassin.

"In God's name," said he, "I make what promise thou wilt."

So they did the oath, and Aucassin let mount him on a horse, and took another and so led him back till he was all in safety.

Here one singeth:

When the Count Garin doth know
That his child would ne'er forego
Love of her that loved him so,
Nicolete, the bright of brow,
In a dungeon deep below
Childe Aucassin did he throw.
Even there the Childe must dwell
In a dun-walled marble cell.
There he waileth in his woe
Crying thus as ye shall know.

"Nicolete, thou lily white,
My sweet lady, bright of brow,
Sweeter than the grape art thou,
Sweeter than sack posset good
In a cup of maple wood!
Was it not but yesterday
That a palmer came this way,
Out of Limousin came he,
And at ease he might not be,
For a passion him possessed
That upon his bed he lay,
Lay, and tossed, and knew not rest
In his pain discomforted.
But thou camest by the bed,
Where he tossed amid his pain,
Holding high thy sweeping train,
And thy kirtle of ermine,
And thy smock of linen fine,

Then these fair white limbs of thine,
Did he look on, and it fell
That the palmer straight was well,
Straight was hale — and comforted,
And he rose up from his bed,
And went back to his own place,
Sound and strong, and full of face!
My sweet lady, lily white,
Sweet thy footfall, sweet thine eyes,
And the mirth of thy replies.
Sweet thy laughter, sweet thy face,
Sweet thy lips and sweet thy brow,
And the touch of thine embrace.
Who but both in thee delight?
I for love of thee am bound
In this dungeon underground,
All for loving thee must lie
Here where loud on thee I cry,
Here for loving thee must die
For thee, my love."

Then say they, speak they, tell they the Tale:

Aucassin was cast into prison as ye have heard tell, and Nicolete, of her part, was in the chamber. Now it was summer time, the month of May, when days are warm, and long, and clear, and the night still and serene. Nicolete lay one night on her bed, and saw the moon shine clear through a window, yea, and heard the nightingale sing in the garden, so she minded her of Aucassin her lover whom she loved so well. Then fell she to thoughts of Count Garin de Biaucaire, that hated her to the death; therefore deemed she that there she would no longer abide, for that, if she were told of, and the Count knew whereas she lay, an ill death would he make her die. Now she knew that the old woman slept who held her company. Then she arose, and clad her in a mantle of silk she had by her, very goodly, and took napkins, and sheets of the bed, and knotted one to the other, and made therewith a cord as long as she might, so knitted it to a pillar in the window, and let herself slip down into the garden, then caught up her raiment in both hands, behind and before, and kilted up her kirtle, because of the dew that she saw lying deep on the grass, and so went her way down through the garden.

Her locks were yellow and curled, her eyes blue and smiling, her face featly fashioned, the nose high and fairly set, the lips more red than cherry or rose in time of summer, her teeth white and small; her breasts so firm that they bore up the folds of her bodice as they had been two apples; so slim she was in the waist that your two hands might have clipped her, and the daisy flowers that brake beneath her as she went tip-toe, and that bent above her instep, seemed black against her feet, so white was the maiden. She came to the postern gate, and unbarred it, and went out through the streets of

Biaucaire, keeping always on the shadowy side, for the moon was shining right clear, and so wandered she till she came to the tower where her lover lay. The tower was flanked with buttresses, and she cowered under one of them, wrapped in her mantle. Then thrust she her head through a crevice of the tower that was old and worn, and so heard she Aucassin wailing within and making dole and lament for the sweet lady he loved so well. And when she had listened to him she began to say:

Here one singeth:

Nicolete the bright of brow
On a pillar leanest thou,
All Aucassin's wail dost hear
For his love that is so dear,
Then thou spakest, shrill and clear,
"Gentle knight withouten fear
Little good befalleth thee,
Little help of sigh or tear,
Ne'er shalt thou have joy of me.
Never shalt thou win me; still
Am I held in evil will
Of thy father and thy kin,
Therefore must I cross the sea,
And another land must win."
Then she cut her curls of gold,
Cast them in the dungeon hold,
Aucassin doth clasp them there,
Kissed the curls that were so fair,
Them doth in his bosom bear,
Then he wept, even as of old,
All for his love!

Then say they, speak they, tell they the Tale:

When Aucassin heard Nicolete say that she would pass into a far country, he was all in wrath.

"Fair sweet friend," quoth he, "thou shalt not go, for then wouldst thou be my death. And the first man that saw thee and had the might withal, would take thee straightway into his bed to be his leman. And once thou camest into a man's bed, and that bed not mine, wit ye well that I would not tarry till I had found a knife to pierce my heart and slay myself. Nay, verily, wait so long I would not: but would hurl myself on it so soon as I could find a wall, or a black stone, thereon would I dash my head so mightily, that the eyes would start, and my brain burst. Rather would I die even such a death, than know thou hadst lain in a man's bed, and that bed not mine."

"Aucassin," she said, "I trow thou lovest me not as much as thou sayest, but I love thee more than thou lovest me."

"Ah, fair sweet friend," said Aucassin, "it may not be that thou shouldst love me even as I love thee. Woman may not love man as man loves woman, for a woman's love lies in the glance of her eye, and the bud of her breast, and her foot's tip-toe, but the love of man is in his heart planted, whence it can never issue forth and pass away."

Now while Aucassin and Nicolete held this parley together, the town's guards came down a street, with swords drawn beneath their cloaks, for the Count Garin had charged them that if they could take her they should slay her. But the sentinel that was on the tower saw them coming, and heard them speaking of Nicolete as they went, and threatening to slay her.

"God!" quoth he, "this were great pity to slay so fair a maid! Right great charity it were if I could say aught to her, and they perceive it not, and she should be on her guard against them, for if they slay her, then were Aucassin, my damoiseau, dead, and that were great pity."

Here one singeth:

Valiant was the sentinel,
Courteous, kind, and practised well,
So a song did sing and tell
Of the peril that befell.
"Maiden fair that lingerest here,
Gentle maid of merry cheer,
Hair of gold, and eyes as clear
As the water in a mere,
Thou, meseems, hast spoken word
To thy lover and thy lord,
That would die for thee, his dear;
Now beware the ill accord,
Of the cloaked men of the sword,
These have sworn and keep their word,
They will put thee to the sword
  Save thou take heed!"

Then speak they, say they, tell they the Tale:

"Ha!" quoth Nicolete, "be the soul of thy father and the soul of thy mother in the rest of Paradise, so fairly and so courteously hast thou spoken me! Please God, I will be right ware of them, God keep me out of their hands."

So she shrank under her mantle into the shadow of the pillar till they had passed by, and then took she farewell of Aucassin, and so fared till she came unto the castle wall. Now that wall was wasted and broken, and some deal mended, so she clomb thereon till she came between wall and fosse, and so looked down, and saw that the fosse was deep and steep, whereat she was sore adread.

"Ah God," saith she, "sweet Saviour! If I let myself fall hence, I shall break my neck, and if here I abide, to-morrow they will take me and burn me in a fire. Yet liefer would I perish here than that to-morrow the folk should stare on me for a gazing-stock."

Then she crossed herself, and so let herself slip into the fosse, and when she had come to the bottom, her fair feet, and fair hands that had not custom thereof, were bruised and frayed, and the blood springing from a dozen places, yet felt she no pain nor hurt, by reason of the great dread wherein she went. But if she were in cumber to win there, in worse was she to win out. But she deemed that there to abide was of none avail, and she found a pike sharpened, that they of the city had thrown out to keep the hold. Therewith made she one stepping place after another, till, with much travail, she climbed the wall. Now the forest lay within two crossbow shots, and the forest was of thirty leagues this way and that. Therein also were wild beasts, and beasts serpentine, and she feared that if she entered there they would slay her. But anon she deemed that if men found her there they would hale her back into the town to burn her.

Here one singeth:

Nicolete, the fair of face,
Climbed upon the coping stone,
There made she lament and moan
Calling on our Lord alone
For his mercy and his grace.

"Father, king of Majesty,
Listen, for I nothing know
Where to flee or whither go.
If within the wood I fare,
Lo, the wolves will slay me there.
Boars and lions terrible,
Many in the wild wood dwell,
But if I abide the day,
Surely worse will come of it,
Surely will the fire be lit
That shall burn my body away,
Jesus, lord of Majesty,
Better seemeth it to me,
That within the wood I fare,
Though the wolves devour me there
Than within the town to go,
        Ne'er be it so!"

Then speak they, say they, tell they the Tale:

Nicolete made great moan, as ye have heard; then commended she herself to God, and anon fared till she came unto the forest. But to go deep in it she dared not, by reason of the wild beasts, and beasts serpentine. Anon crept she into a little thicket, where sleep came upon her, and she slept till prime next day, when the shepherds issued forth from the town and drove their bestial flock between wood and water. Anon came they all into one place by a fair fountain which was on the fringe of the forest, thereby spread they a mantle, and thereon set bread. So while they were eating, Nicolete wakened, with the sound of the singing birds, and the shepherds, and she went unto them, saying, "Fair boys, our Lord keep you!"

"God bless thee," quoth he that had more words to his tongue than the rest.

"Fair boys," quoth she, "know ye Aucassin, the son of Count Garin de Biaucaire?"

"Yea, well we know him."

"So may God help you, fair boys," quoth she, "tell him there is a beast in this forest, and bid him come chase it, and if he can take it, he would not give one limb thereof for a hundred marks of gold, nay, nor for five hundred, nor for any ransom."

Then looked they on her, and saw her so fair that they were all astonied.

"Will I tell him thereof?" quoth he that had more words to his tongue than the rest; "foul fall him who speaks of the thing or tells him the tidings. These are but visions ye tell of, for there is no beast so great in this forest, stag, nor lion, nor boar, that one of his limbs is worth more than two deniers, or three at the most, and ye speak of such great ransom. Foul fall him that believes your word, and him that telleth Aucassin. Ye be a Fairy, and we have none liking for your company, nay, hold on your road."

"Nay, fair boys," quoth she, "nay, ye will do my bidding. For this beast is so mighty of medicine that thereby will Aucassin be healed of his torment. And lo! I have five sols in my purse, take them, and tell him: for within three days must he come hunting it hither, and if within three days he find it not, never will he be healed of his torment."

"My faith," quoth he, "the money will we take, and if he come hither we will tell him, but seek him we will not."

"In God's name," quoth she; and so took farewell of the shepherds, and went her way.

Here singeth one:

Nicolete the bright of brow
From the shepherds doth she pass
All below the blossomed bough
Where an ancient way there was,
Overgrown and choked with grass,
Till she found the cross-roads where
Seven paths do all way fare,
Then she deemeth she will try,
Should her lover pass thereby,
If he love her loyally.
So she gathered white lilies,
Oak-leaf, that in green wood is,

Leaves of many a branch I wis,
Therewith built a lodge of green,
Goodlier was never seen,
Swore by God who may not lie
"If my love the lodge should spy,
He will rest awhile thereby
If he love me loyally."
Thus his faith she deemed to try,
"Or I love him not, not I,
Nor he loves me!"

Then speak they, say they, tell they the Tale:

Nicolete built her lodge of boughs, as ye have heard, right fair and feteously, and wove it well, within and without, of flowers and leaves.  So lay she hard by the lodge in a deep coppice to know what Aucassin will do.  And the cry and the bruit went abroad through all the country and all the land, that Nicolete was lost.  Some told that she had fled, and some that the Count Garin had let slay her.  Whosoever had joy thereof, no joy had Aucassin.  And the Count Garin, his father, had taken him out of prison, and had sent for the knights of that land, and the ladies, and let make a right great feast, for the comforting of Aucassin his son.  Now at the high time of the feast, was Aucassin leaning from a gallery, all woful and discomforted.  Whatsoever men might devise of mirth, Aucassin had no joy thereof, nor no desire, for he saw not her that he loved.  Then a knight looked on him, and came to him, and said:

"Aucassin, of that sickness of thine have I been sick, and good counsel will I give thee, if thou wilt hearken to me — "

"Sir," said Aucassin, "gramercy, good counsel would I fain hear."

"Mount thy horse," quoth he, "and go take thy pastime in yonder forest; there wilt thou see the good flowers and grass, and hear the sweet birds sing.  Perchance thou shalt hear some word, whereby thou shalt be the better."

"Sir," quoth Aucassin, "gramercy, that will I do."

He passed out of the hall, and went down the stairs, and came to the stable where his horse was.  He let saddle and bridle him, and mounted, and rode forth from the castle, and wandered till he came to the forest, so rode till he came to the fountain and found the shepherds at point of noon.  And they had a mantle stretched on the grass, and were eating bread, and making great joy.

Here one singeth:

There were gathered shepherds all,
Martin, Esmeric, and Hal,
Aubrey, Robin, great and small.
Saith the one, "Good fellows all,
God keep Aucassin the fair,
And the maid with yellow hair,

Bright of brow and eyes of vair.
She that gave us gold to ware.
Cakes therewith to buy ye know,
Goodly knives and sheaths also.
Flutes to play, and pipes to blow,
　　May God him heal!"

Here speak they, say they, tell they the Tale:

When Aucassin heard the shepherds, anon he bethought him of Nicolete, his sweet lady he loved so well, and he deemed that she had passed thereby; then set he spurs to his horse, and so came to the shepherds.

"Fair boys, God be with you."

"God bless you," quoth he that had more words to his tongue than the rest.

"Fair boys," quoth Aucassin, "say the song again that anon ye sang."

"Say it we will not," quoth he that had more words to his tongue than the rest, "foul fall him who will sing it again for you, fair sir!"

"Fair boys," quoth Aucassin, "know ye me not?"

"Yea, we know well that you are Aucassin, our damoiseau, natheless we be not your men, but the Count's."

"Fair boys, yet sing it again, I pray you."

"Hearken! by the Holy Heart," quoth he, "wherefore should I sing for you, if it likes me not?   Lo, there is no such rich man in this country, saving the body of Garin the Count, that dare drive forth my oxen, or my cows, or my sheep, if he finds them in his fields, or his corn, lest he lose his eyes for it, and wherefore should I sing for you, if it likes me not?"

"God be your aid, fair boys, sing it ye will, and take ye these ten sols I have here in a purse."

"Sir, the money will we take, but never a note will I sing, for I have given my oath, but I will tell thee a plain tale, if thou wilt."

"By God," saith Aucassin, "I love a plain tale better than naught."

"Sir, we were in this place, a little time agone, between prime and tierce, and were eating our bread by this fountain even as now we do, and a maid came past, the fairest thing in the world, whereby we deemed that she should be a fay, and all the wood shone round about her.   Anon she gave us of that she had, whereby we made covenant with her, that if ye came hither we would bid you hunt in this forest, wherein is such a beast that, an ye might take him, ye would not give one limb of him for five hundred marks of silver, nor for no ransom; for this beast is so mighty of medicine, that, an ye could take him, ye should be healed of your torment, and within three days must ye take him, and if ye take him not then, never will ye look on him.   So chase ye the beast, an ye will, or an ye will let be, for my promise have I kept with her."

"Fair boys," quoth Aucassin, "ye have said enough.   God grant me to find this quarry."

Here one singeth:

Aucassin when he had heard,
Sore within his heart was stirred,
Left the shepherds on that word,
Far into the forest spurred
Rode into the wood; and fleet
Fled his horse through paths of it,
Three words spake he of his sweet,
"Nicolete the fair, the dear,
'Tis for thee I follow here
Track of boar, nor slot of deer,
But thy sweet body and eyes so clear,
All thy mirth and merry cheer,
That my very heart have slain,
So please God to me maintain
I shall see my love again,
          Sweet sister, friend!"

Then speak they, say they, tell they the Tale:

Aucassin fared through the forest from path to path after Nicolete, and his horse bare him furiously. Think ye not that the thorns him spared, nor the briars, nay, not so, but tare his raiment, that scarce a knot might be tied with the soundest part thereof, and the blood sprang from his arms, and flanks, and legs, in forty places, or thirty, so that behind the Childe men might follow on the track of his blood in the grass. But so much he went in thoughts of Nicolete, his lady sweet, that he felt no pain nor torment, and all the day hurled through the forest in this fashion nor heard no word of her. And when he saw Vespers draw nigh, he began to weep for that he found her not. All down an old road, and grassgrown he fared, when anon, looking along the way before him, he saw such an one as I shall tell you. Tall was he, and great of growth, laidly and marvellous to look upon: his head huge, and black as charcoal, and more than the breadth of a hand between his two eyes, and great cheeks, and a big nose and broad, big nostrils and ugly, and thick lips redder than a collop, and great teeth yellow and ugly, and he was shod with hosen and shoon of bull's hide bound with cords of bark over the knee, and all about him a great cloak twy-fold, and he leaned on a grievous cudgel, and Aucassin came unto him, and was afraid when he beheld him.

"Fair brother, God aid thee."

"God bless you," quoth he.

"As God he helpeth thee, what makest thou here?"

"What is that to thee?"

"Nay, naught, naught," saith Aucassin, "I ask but out of courtesy."

"But for whom weepest thou," quoth he, "and makest such heavy lament? Certes, were I as rich a man as thou, the whole world should not make me weep."

"Ha! know ye me?" saith Aucassin.

"Yea, I know well that ye be Aucassin, the son of the Count, and if ye tell me for why ye weep, then will I tell you what I make here."

"Certes," quoth Aucassin, "I will tell you right gladly. Hither came I this morning to hunt in this forest; and with me a white hound, the fairest in the world; him have I lost, and for him I weep."

"By the Heart our Lord bare in his breast!" quoth he. "Are ye weeping for a stinking hound? Foul fall him that holds thee high henceforth! For there is no such rich man in the land, but if thy father asked it of him, he would give thee ten, or fifteen, or twenty, and be the gladder for it. But I have cause to weep and make dole."

"Wherefore so, brother?"

"Sir, I will tell thee. I was hireling to a rich vilain, and drove his plough; four oxen had he. But three days since came on me great misadventure, whereby I lost the best of mine oxen, Roger, the best of my team. Him go I seeking, and have neither eaten nor drunken these three days, nor may I go to the town, lest they cast me into prison, seeing that I have not wherewithal to pay. Out of all the wealth of the world have I no more than ye see on my body. A poor mother bare me, that had no more but one wretched bed; this have they taken from under her, and she lies in the very straw. This ails me more than mine own case, for wealth comes and goes; if now I have lost, another tide will I gain, and will pay for mine ox whenas I may; never for that will I weep. But you weep for a stinking hound. Foul fall whoso thinks well of thee!"

"Certes thou art a good comforter, brother, blessed be thou! And of what price was thine ox?"

"Sir, they ask me twenty sols for him, whereof I cannot abate one doit."

"Nay, then," quoth Aucassin, "take these twenty sols I have in my purse, and pay for thine ox."

"Sir," saith he, "gramercy. And God give thee to find that thou seekest."

So they parted each from other, and Aucassin rode on. The night was fair and still, and so long he went that he came to the lodge of boughs, that Nicolete had builded and woven within and without, over and under, with flowers, and it was the fairest lodge that might be seen. When Aucassin was ware of it, he stopped suddenly, and the light of the moon fell therein.

"God!" quoth Aucassin, "here was Nicolete, my sweet lady, and this lodge builded she with her fair hands. For the sweetness of it, and for love of her, will I alight, and rest here this night long."

He drew forth his foot from the stirrup to alight, and the steed was great and tall. He dreamed so much on Nicolete, his right sweet lady, that he slipped on a stone, and drave his shoulder out of its place. Then knew he that he was hurt sore; natheless he bore him with what force he might, and fastened with the other hand the mare's son to a thorn. Then turned he on his side, and crept backwise into the lodge of boughs. And he looked through a gap in the lodge and saw the stars in heaven, and one that was brighter than the rest; so began he to say:

Here one singeth:

"Star, that I from far behold,
Star, the Moon calls to her fold,
Nicolete with thee doth dwell,
My sweet love with locks of gold,
God would have her dwell afar,
Dwell with him for evening star,
Would to God, whate'er befell,
Would that with her I might dwell.
I would clip her close and strait,
Nay, were I of much estate,
Some king's son desirable,
Worthy she to be my mate,
Me to kiss and clip me well,
    Sister, sweet friend!"

So speak they, say they, tell they the Tale:
When Nicolete heard Aucassin, right so came she unto him, for she was not far away. She passed within the lodge, and threw her arms about his neck, and clipped and kissed him.

"Fair sweet friend, welcome be thou."

"And thou, fair sweet love, be thou welcome."

So either kissed and clipped the other, and fair joy was them between.

"Ha! sweet love," quoth Aucassin, "but now was I sore hurt, and my shoulder wried, but I take no force of it, nor have no hurt therefrom since I have thee."

Right so felt she his shoulder and found it was wried from its place. And she so handled it with her white hands, and so wrought in her surgery, that by God's will who loveth lovers, it went back into its place. Then took she flowers, and fresh grass, and leaves green, and bound these herbs on the hurt with a strip of her smock, and he was all healed.

"Aucassin," saith she, "fair sweet love, take counsel what thou wilt do. If thy father let search this forest to-morrow, and men find me here, they will slay me, come to thee what will."

"Certes, fair sweet love, therefore should I sorrow heavily, but, an if I may, never shall they take thee."

Anon gat he on his horse, and his lady before him, kissing and clipping her, and so rode they at adventure.

Here one singeth:

Aucassin the frank, the fair,
Aucassin of the yellow hair,
Gentle knight, and true lover,
From the forest doth he fare,
Holds his love before him there,

Kissing cheek, and chin, and eyes,
But she spake in sober wise,
"Aucassin, true love and fair,
To what land do we repair?"
"Sweet my love, I take no care,
Thou art with me everywhere!"
So they pass the woods and downs,
Pass the villages and towns,
Hills and dales and open land,
Came at dawn to the sea sand,
Lighted down upon the strand,
          Beside the sea.

Then say they, speak they, tell they the Tale:

Aucassin lighted down and his love, as ye have heard sing. He
held his horse by the bridle, and his lady by the hands; so went they
along the sea shore, and on the sea they saw a ship, and he called
unto the sailors, and they came to him. Then held he such speech
with them, that he and his lady were brought aboard that ship, and
when they were on the high sea, behold a mighty wind and tyrannous
arose, marvellous and great, and drave them from land to land, till
they came unto a strange country, and won the haven of the castle
of Torelore. Then asked they what this land might be, and men
told them that it was the country of the King of Torelore. Then he
asked what manner of man was he, and was there war afoot, and
men said,

"Yea, and mighty!"

Therewith took he farewell of the merchants, and they commended him to God. Anon Aucassin mounted his horse, with his
sword girt, and his lady before him, and rode at adventure till he was
come to the castle. Then asked he where the King was, and they
said that he was in childbed.

"Then where is his wife?"

And they told him she was with the host, and had led with her all
the force of that country.

Now when Aucassin heard that saying, he made great marvel, and
came into the castle, and lighted down, he and his lady, and his
lady held his horse. Right so went he up into the castle, with his
sword girt, and fared hither and thither till he came to the chamber
where the King was lying.

          Here one singeth:

Aucassin the courteous knight
To the chamber went forthright,
To the bed with linen dight
Even where the King was laid.
There he stood by him and said:
"Fool, what mak'st thou here abed?"

Quoth the King: "I am brought to bed
Of a fair son, and anon
When my month is over and gone,
And my healing fairly done,
To the Minster will I fare
And will do my churching there,
As my father did repair.
Then will sally forth to war,
Then will drive my foes afar
　　From my countrie!"

Then speak they, say they, tell they the Tale:

When Aucassin heard the King speak on this wise, he took all the sheets that covered him, and threw them all abroad about the chamber. Then saw he behind him a cudgel, and caught it into his hand, and turned, and took the King, and beat him till he was well-nigh dead.

"Ha! fair sir," quoth the King, "what would you with me? Art thou beside thyself, that beatest me in mine own house?"

"By God's heart," quoth Aucassin, "thou ill son of an ill wench, I will slay thee if thou swear not that never shall any man in all thy land lie in of child henceforth for ever."

So he did that oath, and when he had done it,

"Sir," said Aucassin, "bring me now where thy wife is with the host."

"Sir, with good will," quoth the King.

He mounted his horse, and Aucassin gat on his own, and Nicolete abode in the Queen's chamber. Anon rode Aucassin and the King even till they came to that place where the Queen was, and lo! men were warring with baked apples, and with eggs, and with fresh cheeses, and Aucassin began to look on them, and made great marvel.

Here one singeth:

Aucassin his horse doth stay,
From the saddle watched the fray,
All the stour and fierce array;
Right fresh cheeses carried they,
Apples baked, and mushrooms grey,
Whoso splasheth most the ford
He is master called and lord.
Aucassin doth gaze awhile,
Then began to laugh and smile
And made game.

Then speak they, say they, tell they the Tale:

When Aucassin beheld these marvels, he came to the King, and said, "Sir, be these thine enemies?"

"Yea, Sir," quoth the King.

"And will ye that I should avenge you of them?"

"Yea," quoth he, "with all my heart."

Then Aucassin put hand to sword, and hurled among them, and began to smite to the right hand and the left, and slew many of them. And when the King saw that he slew them, he caught at his bridle and said,

"Ha! fair sir, slay them not in such wise."

"How," quoth Aucassin, "will ye not that I should avenge you of them?"

"Sir," quoth the King, "overmuch already hast thou avenged me. It is nowise our custom to slay each other."

Anon turned they and fled. Then the King and Aucassin betook them again to the castle of Torelore, and the folk of that land counselled the King to put Aucassin forth, and keep Nicolete for his son's wife, for that she seemed a lady high of lineage. And Nicolete heard them, and had no joy of it, so began to say:

*Here singeth one:*

Thus she spake the bright of brow:
"Lord of Torelore and King,
Thy folk deem me a light thing,
When my love doth me embrace,
Fair he finds me, in good case,
Then am I in such derray,
Neither harp, nor lyre, nor lay,
Dance nor game, nor rebeck play
      Were so sweet."

Then speak they, say they, tell they the Tale:

Aucassin dwelt in the castle of Torelore, in great ease and great delight, for that he had with him Nicolete his sweet love, whom he loved so well. Now while he was in such pleasure and such delight, came a troop of Saracens by sea, and laid siege to the castle and took it by main strength. Anon took they the substance that was therein and carried off the men and maidens captives. They seized Nicolete and Aucassin, and bound Aucassin hand and foot, and cast him into one ship, and Nicolete into another. Then rose there a mighty wind over sea, and scattered the ships. Now that ship wherein was Aucassin, went wandering on the sea, till it came to the castle of Biaucaire, and the folk of the country ran together to wreck her, and there found they Aucassin, and they knew him again. So when they of Biaucaire saw their damoiseau, they make great joy of him, for Aucassin had dwelt full three years in the castle of Torelore, and his father and mother were dead. So the people took him to the castle of Biaucaire, and there were they all his men. And he held the land in peace.

*Here singeth one:*

Lo ye, Aucassin hath gone
To Biaucaire that is his own,

Dwelleth there in joy and ease
And the kingdom is at peace.
Swears he by the Majesty
Of our Lord that is most high,
Rather would he they should die
All his kin and parentry,
So that Nicolete were nigh.
"Ah sweet love, and fair of brow,
I know not where to seek thee now,
God made never that countrie,
Not by land, and not by sea,
Where I would not search for thee,
       If that might be!"


Then speak they, say they, tell they the Tale:

Now leave we Aucassin, and speak we of Nicolete. The ship wherein she was cast pertained to the King of Carthage, and he was her father, and she had twelve brothers, all princes or kings. When they beheld Nicolete, how fair she was, they did her great worship, and made much joy of her, and many times asked her who she was, for surely seemed she a lady of noble line and high parentry. But she might not tell them of her lineage, for she was but a child when men stole her away. So sailed they till they won the City of Carthage, and when Nicolete saw the walls of the castle, and the country-side, she knew that there had she been nourished and thence stolen away, being but a child. Yet was she not so young a child but that well she knew she had been daughter of the King of Carthage; and of her nurture in that city.


### Here singeth one:

Nicolete the good and true
To the land hath come anew,
Sees the palaces and walls,
And the houses and the halls!
Then she spake and said, "Alas!
That of birth so great I was,
Cousin of the Amiral
And the very child of him
Carthage counts King of Paynim,
Wild folk hold me here withal;
Nay Aucassin, love of thee
Gentle knight, and true, and free,
Burns and wastes the heart of me.
Ah God grant it of his grace,
That thou hold me, and embrace,
That thou kiss me on the face
       Love and lord!"

Then speak they, say they, tell they the Tale:

When the King of Carthage heard Nicolete speak in this wise, he cast his arms about her neck.

"Fair sweet love," saith he, "tell me who thou art, and be not adread of me."

"Sir," said she, "I am daughter to the King of Carthage, and was taken, being then a little child, it is now fifteen years gone."

When all they of the court heard her speak thus, they knew well that she spake sooth: so made they great joy of her, and led her to the castle in great honour, as the King's daughter. And they would have given her to her lord a King of Paynim, but she had no mind to marry. There dwelt she three days or four. And she considered by what means she might seek for Aucassin. Then she got her a viol, and learned to play on it, till they would have married her on a day to a great King of Paynim, and she stole forth by night, and came to the seaport, and dwelt with a poor woman thereby. Then took she a certain herb, and therewith smeared her head and her face, till she was all brown and stained. And she let make coat, and mantle, and smock, and hose, and attired herself as if she had been a harper. So took she the viol and went to a mariner, and so wrought on him that he took her aboard his vessel. Then hoisted they sail, and fared on the high seas even till they came to the land of Provence. And Nicolete went forth and took the viol, and went playing through all that country, even till she came to the castle of Biaucaire, where Aucassin lay.

Here singeth one:

At Biaucaire below the tower
Sat Aucassin, on an hour,
Heard the bird, and watched the flower,
With his barons him beside,
Then came on him in that tide,
The sweet influence of love
And the memory thereof;
Thought of Nicolete the fair,
And the dainty face of her
He had loved so many years,
Then was he in dule and tears!
Even then came Nicolete.
On the stair a foot she set,
And she drew the viol bow
Through the strings and chanted so:
"Listen, lords and knights, to me,
Lords of high or low degree,
To my story list will ye
All of Aucassin and her
That was Nicolete the fair;
And their love was long to tell
Deep woods through he sought her well,

Paynims took them on a day
In Torelore and bound they lay.
Of Aucassin nought know we,
But fair Nicolete the free
Now in Carthage doth she dwell,
There her father loves her well,
Who is king of that countrie.
Her a husband hath he found,
Paynim lord that serves Mahound!
Ne'er with him the maid will go,
For she loves a damoiseau,
Aucassin, that ye may know,
Swears to God that never mo
With a lover will she go
Save with him she loveth so
    In long desire."

So speak they, say they, tell they the Tale:

When Aucassin heard Nicolete speak in this wise, he was right joyful, and drew her on one side, and spoke, saying:

"Sweet fair friend, know ye nothing of this Nicolete, of whom ye have thus sung?"

"Yea, Sir, I know her for the noblest creature, and the most gentle, and the best that ever was born on ground. She is daughter to the King of Carthage that took her there where Aucassin was taken, and brought her into the city of Carthage, till he knew that verily she was his own daughter, whereon he made right great mirth. Anon wished he to give her for her lord one of the greatest kings of all Spain, but she would rather let herself be hanged or burned, than take any lord, how great soever."

"Ha! fair sweet friend," quoth the Count Aucassin, "if thou wilt go into that land again, and bid her come and speak to me, I will give thee of my substance, more than thou wouldst dare to ask or take. And know ye, that for the sake of her, I have no will to take a wife, howsoever high her lineage. So wait I for her, and never will I have a wife, but her only. And if I knew where to find her, no need would I have to seek her."

"Sir," quoth she, "if ye promise me that, I will go in quest of her for your sake, and for hers, that I love much."

So he sware to her, and anon let give her twenty livres, and she departed from him, and he wept for the sweetness of Nicolete. And when she saw him weeping, she said:

"Sir, trouble not thyself so much withal. For in a little while shall I have brought her into this city, and ye shall see her."

When Aucassin heard that, he was right glad thereof. And she departed from him, and went into the city to the house of the Captain's wife, for the Captain her father in God was dead. So she dwelt there, and told all her tale; and the Captain's wife knew her, and knew well that she was Nicolete that she herself had nourished.

Then she let wash and bathe her, and there rested she eight full days. Then took she an herb that was named Eyebright and anointed herself therewith, and was as fair as ever she had been all the days of her life. Then she clothed herself in rich robes of silk whereof the lady had great store, and then sat herself in the chamber on a silken coverlet, and called the lady and bade her go and bring Aucassin her love, and did even so. And when she came to the Palace she found Aucassin weeping, and making lament for Nicolete his love, for that she delayed so long. And the lady spake unto him and said:

"Aucassin, sorrow no more, but come thou on with me, and I will shew thee the thing in the world that thou lovest best; even Nicolete thy dear love, who from far lands hath come to seek of thee." And Aucassin was right glad.

Here singeth one:

When Aucassin heareth now
That his lady bright of brow
Dwelleth in his own countrie,
Never man was glad as he.
To her castle doth he hie
With the lady speedily,
Passeth to the chamber high,
Findeth Nicolete thereby.
Of her true love found again
Never maid was half so fain.
Straight she leaped upon her feet:
When his love he saw at last,
Arms about her did he cast,
Kissed her often, kissed her sweet,
Kissed her lips and brows and eyes.
Thus all night do they devise,
Even till the morning white.
Then Aucassin wedded her,
Made her Lady of Biaucaire.
Many years abode they there,
Many years in shade or sun,
In great gladness and delight.
Ne'er hath Aucassin regret
Nor his lady Nicolete.
Now my story all is done,
 Said and sung!

[tr. Andrew Lang]

# OUR LADY'S TUMBLER

Nothing in the history of popular religion has eclipsed the medieval cult of the Virgin Mary. Though the western Church always accorded her special veneration, we find that her name appeared infrequently except in the literature of the Irish, where women occupied a place in society which the Benedictines seemed loth to acknowledge. In the period of agrarian feudalism other saints, Michael in particular, sprang to the tongues of the laity. But following the First Crusade, as an integral part of the development of towns, courtliness, and the bourgeoisie, and stimulated by the rapid spread of French culture, St. Mary, the Virgin, Stella Maris, drew to herself all adoration. Hardly a new Gothic cathedral in the centuries of most frenzied building, the twelfth and thirteenth, that was not dedicated to her: Notre Dame de Chartres, de Paris, d'Amiens, de Rouen. Every stone church had a Lady Chapel, often more lavish than the nave. There were more battle cries of Notre Dame than even of Montjoie. The new universities adopted her, and Albert the Great, teacher of St. Thomas, proved that she possessed perfect mastery of the seven arts. The merchants and traders, quailing before the sublime but frightening justice of Godhead, found a human intercessor in the Mother of God. The peasantry saw in her the maid of stable and manger and felt that her humility would respond to theirs. As Hope and Charity, she belonged to no class, but showed the way to Heaven for all, however sinful.

In 1098, an English monk, Stephen Harding, revolted by the worldliness that he found in one monastery after another, persuaded eighteen brothers and the abbot of the monastery of Moleme to forsake their comfortable living to found a new settlement at Citeaux, where the Rule of St. Benedict would be applied with rigor. The order did not flourish; one by one the brothers died or returned to the easier life. Then in 1113 in a moment of greatest discouragement, there came to Abbot Stephen a young zealot, Bernard, who brought with him thirty others whom he had converted, including all his blood brothers except one who was yet too young for orders. The son of pious parents, Bernard was to become the most dynamic, the most powerful, prelate of his age. Harding's austerity was divine food for the youth who felt a direct call from God. Two years later, with a traditional twelve disciples, he established a cell at Clairvaux in what had been called The Valley of Wormwood. This reforming zeal caught fire in a world moved by thoughts of evil. There is no accurate count of the hundreds of monastic communities that became priories of Citeaux throughout all Britain, Germany, Spain, and Italy as well as France; but they disseminated Bernard's doctrine everywhere, and at the heart of that doctrine lay veneration of the Queen of Heaven. According to Sparrow-Simpson: "St. Bernard represents Mary, if not with theological accuracy, at least with dignity

and grace, as deciding by one word the destinies of mankind. All
the human race is prostrate at her feet. The angel [of the Annuncia-
tion] waits for her reply. 'Behold, there is offered to thee,' St.
Bernard exclaims, 'the price of our redemption; if thou consentest,
we are free. Upon thy lips depends the consolation of the sorrowful,
the freedom of the enslaved, the rescue of the lost, the salvation of
all the sons of Adam, of all thy race.'"

Though the most renowned collection of legends of the Virgin is
one in verse of 30,000 lines composed by Gaultier de Coincy, a monk
of St. Medard, near Soissons, between 1214 and 1233, it is proper that
our representative of this class of popular literature should be an
anonymous work particularly told of Bernard's abbey at Clairvaux,
though probably written in Picardy and originating in some oriental
tale brought home by the crusaders. The original has been abridged.

## OUR LADY'S TUMBLER

### Anonymous French (13th cent.)

[From *Of the Tumbler of Our Lady and Other Miracles,*
by Alice Kemp-Welch; Chatto & Windus, London, 1903.
Reprinted by permission of the publisher.]

In the "Lives of the Fathers," the matter of which is of profit, a
story is told, than which I do not say that none more pleasing has
been heard, but this one is not so without worth that it may not well
be told. Now will I tell and rehearse unto you of that which happened to a minstrel.

So much had he journeyed to and fro in so many places, and so
prodigal had he been, that he became a monk of a holy Order, for
that he was weary of the world. Therefore he entered this holy
profession at Clairvaux.

And when that this tumbler, who was so graceful, and fair, and
comely, and well formed, became a monk, he knew not how to perform any office that fell to be done there. Of a truth, he had lived
only to tumble, to turn somersaults, to spring, and to dance. To leap
and to jump, this he knew, but naught else, and truly no other learning had he, neither the "Paternoster," nor the "Canticles," nor the
"Credo," nor the "Ave Maria," nor aught that could make for his
salvation. He was sore affrighted in their midst, for he knew not
what to say, or what to do of all that fell to be done there. And because of this, he was very sad and pensive. And everywhere he saw
the monks and the novices each one serving God in such office as he
held. He saw the priests at the altars, for such was their office, the
deacons at the Gospels, and the subdeacons at the epistles. And at
the proper time, the acolytes straightway rang the bell at the vigils.
One recited a verse, and another a lesson, and the young priests were

at the psalter, and the novices at the misereres, and the least experienced were at the paternosters, for in suchwise was their work ordered. And he looked everywhere throughout the offices and the cloisters, and saw hidden in the corners here four, here three, here two, here one. And he observed each one as closely as he was able. One made lamentation, another wept, and another groaned and sighed. And much did he marvel what ailed them.

And at length he said, "Holy Mary, what ails these folk that they deport themselves thus, and make show in this manner of such grief? Much disquieted must they be, it seems to me, when they all with one accord make such great dolour!" And then he said, "Ah, miserable being! By the Holy Mary, what have I said? I trow that they pray God's grace. But, unhappy being that I am, what do I here, when that he who, in his calling, serves God with all his might, is thus enslaved? Never shall I render any service here, for naught can I do or say. Very hapless was I when that I became a monk, for I know not how even to pray aright. I look hither and thither, and naught do I, save to waste time and to eat bread to no purpose. If in this I am found out, I shall be utterly undone. I am a lusty villain, and if I do naught here but eat, I shall be turned out into the fields. Very miserable am I in this high office!"

Then he wept to allay his grief, and truly did he desire to be dead. "Holy Mother Mary," said he, "beseech your sovereign Father of His grace to guide me, and to bestow upon me such wisdom that I may be able to serve both Him and you in suchwise as to be worthy of the food which I eat here, for well know I that now I do wrong."

And when he had thus made lament, he went prying about the Church until that he entered a crypt, and he crouched down nigh unto an altar, and hid himself there as best he could. And above the altar was the image of Our Lady, the Holy Mary. And in nowise did it surprise him that he felt in safety there, and he perceived not that it was God, who well knows how to guide His own, who had led him there.

And when he had heard the bell ring for the Mass, he rushed forth from the crypt all trembling. "Ah!" said he, "I am like unto a traitor! Even now each one is saying his response, and here am I a tethered ox, and I do naught here but browse, and waste food in vain. Shall I therefore neither speak nor act? By the Mother of God, this will I do, and never shall I be blamed for it. I will do that which I have learnt, and thus, after mine own manner, will I serve the Mother of God in her Church. The others do service with song, and I will do service with tumbling."

And he took off his habit, and then stripped himself, and laid his garments beside the altar, but so that his body should not be uncovered, he kept on a tunic, the which was very clinging and close fitting. Little better was it than a shift; nevertheless was his body wholly covered. And thus was he fitly clad and equipped, and he girded his tunic, and duly prepared him, and he turned him to the image, and gazed on it very humbly. "Lady," said he, "to your keeping I commend my body and my soul. Gentle Queen and Lady, despise not that which I am acquainted with, for, without ado, I will essay me to serve you in good faith, if so be that God will aid me."

Then he began to turn somersaults, now high, now low, first forwards, then backwards, and then he fell on his knees before the image, and bowed his head. "Ah, very gentle Queen!" said he, "of your pity, and of your generosity, despise not my service." Then he tumbled, and leaped, and turned gaily the somersault of Metz. And he bowed to the image, and worshipped it, for he paid homage to it as much as he was able. And anon he turned the French somersault, and then the somersault of Champagne, and after that, those of Spain and of Brittany, and then that of Lorraine. And he laboured to the utmost of his power.

And after that, he did the Roman somersault, and then he put his hand before his face, and turned him with great grace, and looked very humbly at the image of the Mother of God. "Lady," said he, "I do homage to you with my heart, and my body, and my feet, and my hands, for naught beside this do I understand. Now would I be your gleeman. Yonder they are singing, but I am come here to divert you. Lady, you who can protect me, for God's sake do not despise me." Then he beat his breast, and sighed, and mourned very grievously that he knew not how to do service in other manner. And then he turned a somersault backwards. "Lady," said he, "so help me God, never before have I done this. Lady! How that one would have his utmost desire, who could dwell with you in your right glorious mansion! For God's sake, Lady, receive me there. I do this for your sake, and in nowise for mine own." Then he again turned the somersault of Metz, and tumbled and capered full many a time.

And when he heard the monks celebrating, he began to exert himself, and so long as the Mass dured, he ceased not to dance, and to jump, and to leap, until that he was on the point to faint, and he could not stand up, and thus he fell to the ground, and dropped from sheer fatigue. And like as the grease issues from the spitted meat, so the sweat issued from him all over, from head to foot. "Lady," said he, "no more can I do now, but of a surety I shall come back again."

And he was quite overcome of heat. And he took up his clothing, and when that he was dressed, he took his leave, and he bowed to the image, and went his way. "Farewell, very gentle friend," said he. "For God's sake, grieve not at all, for if that I am able, and it is permitted unto me, I will come back, for each hour would I serve you to the utmost of my power, so gracious are you."

And longwhiles he led this life, and, at each hour precisely he repaired to the image, to render service and homage. Certes, so greatly did it please him, and with such right good will did he do this, that never a day was he so tired that he could not do his very utmost to delight the Mother of God, and never did he desire to do other service.

Well known was it that he went each day into the crypt, but no one, save God, knew what he did there, nor would he, for all the riches of the whole world, that any, save the supreme God alone, should know of his doings.

Think you now that God would have prized his service if that he had not loved Him? By no means, however much he tumbled. But He prized it because of his love. Much labour and fatigue, many fasts and vigils, many tears and sighs and groans and prayers, much diligence in discipline, both at Mass and at matins, the bestowal of all that you have and the payment of whatsoever you owe, if you love not God with all your heart, all these are wholly thrown away in such manner, understand well, that they avail naught for true salvation. Of a truth, without love and without pity, before God all counts for naught. God asks not for gold or for silver, but only for true love in the hearts of men, and this one loved God truly. And because of this, God prized his service.

Longwhiles did the good man live thus, but for how long time he so lived contented, I cannot tell unto you, but in the course of time sore trouble came to him, for one of the monks, who in his heart greatly blamed him that he came not to matins, kept watch on him. And he much marvelled what happened, and said that never would he desist until that he knew who he was, and for what he was worth, and in what manner he earned his bread. And so closely did the monk pursue him, and follow him, and keep watch on him, that he distinctly saw him perform his service in a simple manner, even as I have told it unto you. "By my faith," said he, "he has a good time of it, and much greater diversion, it seemeth to me, than we have all together. Whiles that the others are at prayer, and at work in the house, this one dances with as much vigour as if he had an hundred silver marks. Right well does he perform his service, and in this manner he pays for us that which is his due. A goodly proceeding, this, forsooth! We sing for him, and he tumbles for us! We pray for him, and he plays for us! If we weep, he soothes us! I would that all the convent could see him at this very moment just as I do, even if I had to fast for it till dusk! Not one would there be, me-thinks, who would be able to restrain his laughter if that he wit-nessed the tumbling of this fellow, who thus kills himself, and who so excites him by tumbling, that he has no pity on himself. God counts it unto him for penance, for he does it without evil intent, and, certes, I hold it not to be ill, for, as I believe, he does it, according to his lights, in good faith, for he wishes not to be idle."

And the monk saw how that he laboured without ceasing all the day long. And he laughed much, and made merry over the matter, but it caused him sorrow as well as merriment. And he went to the abbot, and rehearsed unto him, from beginning to end, all that he had learnt, even as you have heard it.

And the abbot arose, and said to the monk, "On your vow of obedience, I command that you keep silence, and noise this not abroad, and that you so well observe this command, that you speak not of this matter save to me alone, and we will both go thither, and we shall see if this can be, and we will beseech the heavenly King, and His very gentle and dear Mother, who is so precious, and of so great renown, that she, of her sweetness, will go pray of her Son, her Father, and her Lord, that if it so pleases Him, He will this day suffer me to witness this service in such sort that God may be the more loved on account of this, and that, if thus it pleases Him, the good man may not be found worthy of blame for it."

And then they went thither quite quietly, and without delay they hid themselves in a covert nook nigh unto the altar, so that he saw them not. And the abbot, watching there, observed all the service of the novice, and the divers somersaults the which he turned, and how that he capered, and danced, and bowed before the image, and jumped, and leaped, until that he was nigh fainting. And so greatly was he overcome of fatigue, that he fell heavily to the ground, and so exhausted was he, that he sweated all over from his efforts, so that the sweat ran all down the middle of the crypt. But in a little, the Mother of God, whom he served all without guile, came to his succour, and well knew she how to aid him.

And anon the abbot looked, and he saw descend from the vaulting so glorious a lady, that never had he seen one so fair or so richly crowned, and never had another so beautiful been created. Her vesture was all wrought with gold and precious stones, and with her were the angels and the archangels from the heavens above, who came around the tumbler, and solaced and sustained him. And when that they were ranged around him, he was wholly comforted, and they made ready to tend him, for they desired to make recompense unto him for the services the which he had rendered unto their Lady, who is so precious a gem. And the sweet and noble Queen took a white cloth, and with it she very gently fanned her minstrel before the altar. And the noble and gracious Lady fanned his neck and body and face to cool him, and greatly did she concern herself to aid him, and gave herself up to the care of him; but of this the good man took no heed, for he neither perceived, nor did he know, that he was in such fair company.

And the holy angels who remained with him, paid him much honour, but the Lady no longer sojourned there, and she made the sign of the cross as she turned away, and the holy angels, who greatly rejoiced to keep watch over their companion, took charge over him, and they did but await the hour when God would take him from this life, and they might bear away his soul.

And full four times did the abbot and the monk witness, without hindrance, how that each hour he went there, and how that the Mother of God came there to aid and succour her liegeman, for well knows she how to protect her own. And the abbot had much joy of it, for very desirous had he been to know the truth concerning it. Now had God verily shown unto him that the services the which this poor man rendered were pleasing unto Him. And the monk was quite bewildered by it, and from anguish he glowed like fire. "Your mercy, Sire!" said he to the abbot, "this is a holy man whom I see here. If that I have said aught concerning him that is evil, it is right that my body should make amends for it. Therefore ordain me a penance, for without doubt he is altogether an upright man. Verily have we seen all, and no longer can we be mistaken."

And the abbot said, "You speak truly. God has indeed made us to know that He loves him with a very great love. And now I straightway give command unto you that, in virtue of obedience, and so that you fall not under condemnation, you speak to no one of that which you have seen, save to God or to me."

"Sire," said he, "to this do I assent."

And at these words they departed, and no longer did they stay in the crypt, and the good man did not remain, but when that he had done all his service, he clothed himself again in his garments, and went to divert himself in the monastery.

And thus passed the time, until that, a little while after, it came to pass that the abbot sent for him who was so good. And when he heard that he was sent for, and that it was the abbot who made enquiry for him, so greatly was he troubled, that he knew not what he should say. "Alas," said he, "I am found out. Never a day passes without distress, or without toil or disgrace, for my service counts for naught. Methinks it is not pleasing unto God. Gentle Lady, Holy Mary, how troubled is my mind! I know not, Lady, from whom to get counsel, so come now to mine aid. And at the first word, anon will they say, 'Away with you!' Woe is me! How shall I be able to make answer when I know not one single word with the which to make explanation? But what avails this? It behoves me to go."

And weeping, so that his face was all wet, he came before the abbot, and he knelt before him in tears. "Sire," said he, "for God's sake, have mercy! Would you drive me hence? Tell me all your behests, and all your bidding will I do."

Then said the abbot, "This would I know, and I would that you answer me truly. Longwhiles have you been here, both winter and summer, and I would know by what services, and in what manner, you earn your bread."

"Alas," said he, "well knew I that all would become known, and that when all my doings were known, no longer would any one have to do with me. Sire," said he, "now will I depart hence. Miserable am I, and miserable shall I be, for I never do aught that is right."

Then the abbot made answer, "Never have I said this, but I pray and demand of you, and further I command you, that, in virtue of obedience, you wholly reveal unto me your thoughts, and tell unto me in what manner you serve us in our monastery."

"Sire," said he, "this will be my death! This command will kill me."

Then he straightway unfolded unto him, howsoever grievous it was, his whole life, from beginning to end, in such sort that he left naught unsaid, just as I have told it unto you. And with clasped hands, and weeping, he told and rehearsed unto him everything, and, sighing, he kissed his feet.

And the holy abbot turned to him, and, all weeping, raised him up. And he kissed both his eyes. "Brother," said he, "be silent now, for truly do I promise unto you that you shall be at peace with us. God grant that we may have your fellowship so long as we are deserving of it. Good friends shall we be. Fair, gentle brother, pray for me and I will pray in return for you. And so I beseech and command of you, my sweet friend, that you forthwith render this service openly, just as you have done it, and still better even, if that you know how."

"Sire," said he, "are you in good earnest?"

"Yea, truly," said the abbot, "and I charge you, on pain of penance, that you no longer doubt it."

Then was the good man so very joyous, so the story relates, that he scarce knew what he did. But despite himself, he was constrained to rest, for he had become all pale. And when that he was come to himself again, he was so overcome of joy, that he was seized with a sickness, of the which in a short space he died. But very cheerfully did he perform his service without ceasing, morning and evening, by night and by day, so that not an hour did he miss, until that he fell ill. Then verily such great sickness laid hold upon him, that he could not move from his bed. But that which distressed him the most, since never did he make complaint of his sufferings, was that he could not pay for his sustenance, for the which he was much troubled in mind, and moreover he feared that his penance would be in vain, for that he did not busy himself with such service as was his wont, and very deserving of blame did he seem unto himself to be.

And the good man, who was so filled with anguish, besought of God that He would receive him before that more shame came unto him. For so much grieved was he that his doings were become known, that he could not endure it. And he was constrained to lie down forthwith.

And greatly did the holy abbot hold him in honour, and he and his monks went each hour to chant beside his bed, and such great delight had he in that which was sung to him of God, that in nowise did he long for Poitou, so much did it pleasure him to learn that all would be pardoned unto him. And he made a good confession and repentance, but nevertheless he was fearful. And, as I have told unto you, at last it came to pass that he died.

And the abbot was there, and all his monks, and the novices and good folk, who kept watch over him very humbly, and quite clearly did they see a right wondrous miracle. Of a truth they saw how that, at his death, the angels, and the Mother of God, and the archangels, were ranged around him. And there, also, were the very evil and cruel and violent devils, for to possess them of his soul, and no fancy is this. But to no purpose had they so long lain in wait for him, and striven so earnestly for him and pursued him, for now no power had they over his soul. And forthwith his soul quitted his body, but in nowise was it lost, for the Mother of God received it. And the holy angels who were there, sang for joy, and then they departed, and bare it to heaven, and this was seen of all the monks, and of all the others who were there.

Now they wholly knew and perceived that God willed it that the love of His good servant should no longer be hid, and that all should know and perceive his goodness, and they had great joy and great wonderment of it, and much honour did they pay to his body, and they carried it into the Church, and heartily did they celebrate the service of God. And they buried him with honour in the choir of the mother-church.

With great honour did they bury him, and then, like some saintly body, they kept watch over him. And anon, without concealing aught, the abbot told unto them all his doings, and his whole life, and all that he had seen in the crypt, even as you have heard it. And eagerly did the monks listen unto him. "Certes," said they, "well may it be believed. It cannot be misdoubted, for the truth bears witness to it. Fully is the matter proven, and certain is it that he has done his penance." And greatly did they rejoice together there.

Thus died the minstrel. Cheerfully did he tumble, and cheerfully did he serve, for the which he merited great honour, and none was there to compare unto him.

And the holy Fathers have related unto us that it thus befel this minstrel. Now let us pray God, without ceasing, that He may grant unto us so worthily to serve Him, that we may be deserving of His love. The story of the Tumbler is set forth.

[tr. ALICE KEMP-WELCH]

# FABLIAUX

The urban middle class in the growing towns of the twelfth and thirteenth centuries affected the general taste in literature; but it also cultivated forms of storytelling of its own. To that class may be attributed the exceptional popularity of Aesop's fables and kindred stories of beasts with human attributes. These stories told of cunning and double-dealing and the triumph of wit over stupidity; they delighted the merchant class, who liked caricatures and conventional moral tags. A cycle of stories in both prose and verse about Renard the Fox grew enormously in England, Flanders, France, and Germany. Chaucer's Nun's Priest's Tale of Chanticleer and Pertelote was taken from this class.

Equally popular were moral tales called *fabliaux,* many of which were imported from the East and reclothed to western styling. Perhaps the traders who brought exotic goods for the expanding western market bartered stories as well, in traveling-salesman fashion. Taste for this sort of tale, often gross, sometimes satirical, and usually intended to be hilarious, if not humorous, may have been cultivated by popular preachers, who had long used the anecdote or *exemplum* as a means of enlivening their sermons and enforcing their doctrine. Chaucer's tales of the Summoner and Friar represent the ecclesiastical *exemplum,* those of the Miller and Reeve the *fabliaux.* Such stories are perennial. The penitentials of the eighth century enjoined the clergy to restrain the popular taste for *fabulae inanes, fabulae ignobilium, verba stultiloquia.* Marie de France is supposed to have translated a collection of such works, written in Latin in the tenth century. As they appear in the romance tongue, they are dressed up in octosyllabic rhymed couplets, designed to aid the memory and to provide quotable aphorisms. In the fourteenth century the *fabliaux* waned before the popular favor accorded the prose *novella.*

## THE LAY OF THE LITTLE BIRD

Anonymous French (*circ.* A.D. 1200)

In days of yore, at least a century since,
There lived a carle as wealthy as a prince:
His name I wot not; but his wide domain
Was rich with stream and forest, mead and plain;
To crown the whole, one manor he possessed
In choice delight so passing all the rest,
No castle burgh or city might compare
With the quaint beauties of that mansion rare.
The sooth to say, I fear my words may seem
Like some strange fabling, or fantastic dream,

603

If, unadvised, the portraiture I trace,
And each brave pleasure of that peerless place;
Foreknow ye, then, by necromantic might
Was raised this paradise of all delight.
A good knight owned it first; he, bowed with age,
Died, and his son possessed the heritage;
But the lewd stripling, all to riot bent, —
His chattels quickly wasted and forespent, —
Was driven to see this patrimony sold
To the base carle of whom I lately told:
Ye wot right well there only needs be sought
One spendthrift heir, to bring great wealth to naught.
A lofty tower and strong, the building stood
'Midst a vast plain surrounded by a flood;
And hence one pebble-pavèd channel strayed,
That compassed in a clustering orchard's shade:
'T was a choice, a charming plat; abundant round,
Flowers, roses, odorous spices clothed the ground;
Unnumbered kinds; and all profusely showered
Such aromatic balsam, as they flowered,
Their fragrance might have stayed man's parting breath,
And chased the hovering agony of death.
The sward one level held; and close above,
Tall, shapely trees their leafy mantles wove,
All equal growth, and low their branches came,
Thickset with goodliest fruits of every name.
In midst, to cheer the ravished gazer's view,
A gushing fount its water upward threw,
Thence slowly on with crystal current passed,
And crept into the distant flood at last;
But nigh its source a pine's umbrageous head
Stretched far and wide, in deathless verdure spread.
Met with broad shade the summer's sultry gleam,
And through the livelong year shut out the beam.
    Such was the scene; — yet still the place was blessed
With one rare pleasure passing all the rest:
A wondrous bird, of energies divine,
Had fixed his dwelling in the tufted pine;
There still he sat, and there with amorous lay
Waked the dim morn and closed the parting day:
Matched with these strains of linkèd sweetness wrought,
The violin and full-toned harp were naught;
Of power they were with new-born joy to move
The cheerless heart of long-desponding love;
Of power so strange, that, should they cease to sound,
And the blithe songster flee the mystic ground,
That goodly orchard's scene, the pine-tree's shade,
Trees, flowers, and fount, would all like vapor fade.

"Listen, listen to my lay!"
  Thus the merry notes did chime,
"All who mighty love obey,
  Sadly wasting in your prime,
Clerk and laic, grave and gay!
  Yet do ye, before the rest,
Gentle maidens, mark me tell!
  Store my lesson in your breast:
Trust me, it shall profit well:
  Hear and heed me, and be blessed!"

So sang the bird of old; but when he spied
The carle draw near, with altered tone he cried, —
"Back, river, to thy source! and thee, tall tower,
Thee, castle strong, may gaping earth devour!
Bend down your heads, ye gaudy flowers, and fade!
And withered be each fruit-tree's mantling shade!
Beneath these beauteous branches once were seen
Brave gentle knights disporting on the green,
And lovely dames; and oft these flowers among
Stayed the blithe bands, and joyed to hear my song;
Nor would they hence retire, nor quit the grove,
Till many a vow were passed of mutual love:
These more would cherish, those would more deserve
Cost, courtesy, and arms, and nothing swerve.
O, bitter change! for master now we see
A traitor villain carle of low degree;
Foul gluttony employs his livelong day,
Nor heeds nor hears he my melodious lay."
So spake the bird; and as he ceased to sing,
Indignantly he clapped his downy wing,
And straight was gone; — but no abasement stirred
In the clown's breast at his reproachful word:
Bent was his wit alone by quaint device
To snare, and sell him for a passing price.
So well he wrought, so craftily he spread
In the thick foliage green his slender thread,
That, when at eve the little songster sought
His wonted spray, his heedless foot was caught.
"How have I harmed you?" straight he 'gan to cry,
"And wherefore would you do me thus to die?"
"Nay, fear not," quoth the clown, "for death or wrong;
I only seek to profit by thy song;
I'll get thee a fine cage, nor shalt thou lack
Good store of kernels and of seeds to crack; —
But sing thou shalt; for if thou play'st the mute,
I'll spit thee, bird, and pick thy bones to boot."
"Ah, woe is me!" the little thrall replied,

"Who thinks of song, in prison doomed to bide?
And, were I cooked, my bulk might scarce afford
One scanty mouthful to my hungry lord."
    What may I more relate?   The captive wight
Assayed to melt the villain all he might;
And fairly promised, were he once set free,
In gratitude to teach him secrets three:
Three secrets, all so marvellous and rare,
His race knew naught that might with these compare.
The carle pricked up his ears amain; he loosed
The songster thrall, by love of gain seduced.
Up to the summit of the pine-tree's shade
Sped the blithe bird, and there at ease he stayed,
And tricked his plumes full leisurely, I trow,
Till the carle claimed his promise from below.
"Right gladly," quoth the bird; "now grow thee wise:
All human prudence few brief lines comprise:
First, then, lest haply in the event it fail,
*Yield not a ready faith to every tale.*"
"Is this your secret?" cried the stupid oaf,
"Keep for yourself that lesson which you quote;
I need it not." "Howbe, 't is not amiss
To prick thy memory with advice like this;
But late, meseems, thou hadst forgot the lore;
Now may'st thou hold it fast for evermore.
Mark next my second rule, and sadly know,
*What's lost, 't is wise with patience to forego.*"
    The carle, though rude of wit, now chafed amain;
He felt the mockery of the songster's strain.
"Peace," quoth the bird; "my third is far the best;
Store thou the precious treasure in thy breast:
*What good thou hast, ne'er lightly from thee cast.*"
He spoke, and twittering fled away full fast.
Straight, sunk in earth, the gushing fountain dries;
Down fall the fruits; the withered pine-tree dies;
Fades all the beauteous plat, so cool, so green,
Into thin air, and never more is seen.
    Such was the meed of avarice: — bitter cost!
The carle, who all would gather, all has lost.

                                        [tr. G. L. WAY]

## THE DIVIDED HORSECLOTH

### Anonymous French (13th cent.)

[From *Aucassin and Nicolete and Other Mediaeval Romances,* translated by Eugene Mason; J. M. Dent & Sons, Ltd., London, 1910. Reprinted by permission of the publisher.]

Each owes it to his fellows to tell as best he may, or, better still, to write with fair enticing words, such deeds and adventures as are good and profitable for us to know.  For as men come and go about their business in the world, many things are told them which it is seemly to keep in remembrance.  Therefore, it becomes those who say and relate, diligently and with fair intent to keep such matters in thought and study, even as did our fathers before us.  Theirs is the school to which we all should pass, and he who would prove an apt scholar and live beyond his day must not be idle at his task.  But the world dims our fine gold: the minstrel is slothful, and singers forget to sing, because of the pain and travail which go to the finding of their songs.  So without waiting for any tomorrow, I will bring before you a certain adventure which chanced, even as it was told to me.

Some seven years ago it befell that a rich burgess of Abbeville departed from the town, together with his wife, his only son, and all his wealth, his goods and plenishing.  This he did like a prudent man, since he found himself at enmity with men who were stronger and of more substance than he.  So, fearing lest a worse thing should bechance him, from Abbeville he went up to Paris.  There he sought a shop and dwelling and, paying his service, made himself a vassal and burgess of the King.  The merchant was diligent and courteous, his wife smiling and gracious, and their son was not given over to folly, but went soberly, even as his parents taught him. Much were they praised of their neighbours, and those who lived in the same street often set foot in their dwelling.  For very greatly are those loved and esteemed by their fellows who are courteous in speech and address.  He who has fair words in his mouth receives again sweet words in his ear, and foul words and foul deeds bring naught but bitterness and railing.  Thus was it with this prudent merchant.  For more than seven years he went about his business, buying and selling, concerning himself with matters of which he had full knowledge, putting by of his earnings a little every day, like a wise and worthy citizen.  So this wealthy merchant lived a happy blameless life, till, by the will of God, his wife was taken from him, who had been his companion for some thirty years.  Now these parents had but one only child, a son, even as I have told you before.  Very grievously did he mourn the death of her who cherished him so softly, and lamented his mother with many tears, till he came nigh to swoon. Then, to put a little comfort in his heart, his father said to him —

"Fair son, thy mother is dead, and we will pray to God that He grant her mercy in that day. But dry now thine eyes and thy face, for tears can profit thee nothing. By that road we all must go; neither can any man pass Death upon the way, nor return to bring us any word. Fair son, for thee there is goodly comfort. Thou art a young bachelor, and it is time to take thee a wife. I am full of years and, so I may find thee a fair marriage in an honourable house, I will endow thee with my substance. I will now seek a bride for thee of birth and breeding — one of family and descent, one come of ancient race, with relations and friends a gracious company, a wife from honest folk and from an honest home. There, where it is good and profitable to be, I will set thee gladly, nor of wealth and moneys shalt thou find a lack."

Now in that place were three brethren, knights of high lineage, cousins to mighty lords of peerage, bearing rich and honourable blazons on their shields. But these knights had no heritage, since they had pawned all that they owned of woods and houses and lands, the better to take their pleasure at the tourney. Passing heavy and tormented were these brethren because in no wise might they redeem their pledge. The eldest of these brothers had a daughter, but the mother of the maid was dead. Now this damsel owned in Paris a certain fair house, over against the mansion of the wealthy merchant. The house was not of her father's heritage, but came to her from her mother, who had put the maid in ward to guardians, so that the house was free from pledge. She received in rent therefrom the sum of twenty Paris pounds every year, and her dues were paid her right willingly. So the merchant, esteeming her a lady of family and estate, demanded her hand in marriage of her father and of all her friends. The knight inquired in his turn of the means and substance of the merchant, who answered very frankly —

"In merchandise and in moneys I have near upon fifteen hundred pounds. Should I tell you that I had more, I should lie, and speak not the truth. I have besides one hundred Paris pounds, which I have gained in honest dealings. Of all this I will give my son the half."

"Fair sir," made answer the knight, "in no wise can this be agreed to. Had you become a Templar, or a White or a Black monk, you would have granted the whole of your wealth either to the Temple or your Abbey. By my faith, we cannot consent to so grudging an offer, certes, sir merchant, no."

"Tell me then what you would have me do."

"Very willingly, fair, dear sir. We would that you grant to your son the sum and total of your substance, so that he be seised of all your wealth, and this in such fashion that neither you, nor any in your name, may claim return of any part thereof. If you consent to this the marriage can be made, but otherwise he shall never wed our child and niece."

The merchant turned this over for a while, now looking upon his son, now deep in thought.  But very badly he was served of all his thought and pondering. For at the last he made reply to him and said —

"Lord, it shall even be done according to your will.  This is our covenant and bargain, that so your daughter is given to my son I will grant him all that I have of worth.  I take this company as witness that here I strip myself of everything I own, so that naught is mine, but all is his, of what I once was seised and possessed."

Thus before the witnesses he divested himself utterly of all his wealth and became naked as a peeled wand in the eyes of the world, for this merchant now had neither purse nor penny nor wherewithal to break his fast, save it were given him by his son.  So when the words were spoken and the merchant altogether spoiled, then the knight took his daughter by the hand and handfasted her with the bachelor and she became his wife.

For two years after this marriage the husband and the dame lived a quiet and peaceful life.  Then a fair son was born to the bachelor, and the lady cherished and guarded him fondly. With them dwelt the merchant in the same lodging, but very soon he perceived that he had given himself a mortal blow in despoiling himself of his substance to live on the charity of others.  But perforce he remained of their household for more than twelve years, until the lad had grown up tall and began to take notice, and to remember that which often he heard of the making of his father's marriage. And well he promised himself that it should never go from mind.

The merchant was full of years.  He leaned upon his staff and went bent with age, as one who searches for his lost youth.  His son was weary of his presence and would gladly have paid for the spinning of his shroud. The dame, who was proud and disdainful, held him in utter despite, for greatly he was against her heart.  Never was she silent, but always was she saying to her lord —

"Husband, for love of me, send your father upon his business.  I lose all appetite just for the sight of him about the house."

"Wife," answered he, "this shall be done according to your wish."

So because of his wife's anger and importunity, he sought out his father straightway, and said —

"Father, father, get you gone from here.  I tell you that you must do the best you can, for we may no longer concern ourselves with you and your lodging.  For twelve years and more we have given you food and raiment in our house.  Now all is done, so rise and depart forthwith, and fend for yourself, as fend you must."

When the father heard these words he wept bitterly, and often he cursed the day and the hour in which he found he had lived too long.

"Ah, fair, sweet son, what is this thou sayest to me!  For the love of God turn me not from thy door.  I lie so close that thou canst not want my room.  I require of thee neither seat in the chimney corner, nor soft bed of feathers, no, nor carpet on the floor; but only the attic,

where I may bide on a little straw. Throw me not from thy
house because I eat of thy bread, but feed me without grudging for
the short while I have to live. In the eyes of God this charity will
cover all thy sins better than if thou went in haircloth next the flesh."

"Fair father," replied the bachelor, "preach me no preachings, but
get you forth at once, for reason that my wife would have you gone."

"Fair son, where then shall I go, who am esteemed of nothing
worth?"

"Get you gone to the town, for amongst ten thousand others very
easily you may light on good fortune. Very unlucky you will be if
there you cannot find a way to live. Seek your fortune bravely. Perchance some of your friends and acquaintance will receive you into
their houses."

"Son, how then shall men take me to their lodging, when you turn
me from the house which I have given you? Why should the
stranger welcome that guest whom the son chases from his door?
Why should I be received gladly by him to whom I have given naught,
when I am evilly entreated of the rich man for whose sake I go
naked?"

"Father," said he, "right or wrong, I take the blame upon my own
head; but go you must because it is according to my will."

Then the father grieved so bitterly that for a little his very heart
would have broken. Weak as he was, he raised himself to his feet
and went forth from the house weeping.

"Son," said he, "I commend thee to God; but since thou wilt that
I go, for the love of Him give me at least a portion of packing cloth
to shelter me against the wind. I am asking no great matter;
nothing but a little cloth to wrap about me, because I am but lightly
clad, and fear to die for reason of the cold."

Then he who shrank from any grace of charity made reply —

"Father, I have no cloth, so neither can I bestow, nor have it taken
from me."

"Fair, sweet son, my heart trembles within me, so greatly do I
dread the cold. Give me, then, the cloth you spread upon your horse,
so that I come to no evil."

So he, seeing that he might not rid himself of his father save by
the granting of a gift, and being desirous above all that he should
part, bade his son to fetch this horsecloth. When the lad heard his
father's call he sprang to him, saying —

"Father, what is your pleasure?"

"Fair son," said he, "get you to the stable, and if you find it open
give my father the covering that is upon my horse. Give him the
best cloth in the stable, so that he may make himself a mantle or a
habit, or any other sort of cloak that pleases him."

Then the lad, who was thoughtful beyond his years, made answer —

"Grandsire, come now with me."

So the merchant went with him to the stable, exceedingly heavy
and wrathful. The lad chose the best horsecloth he might find in the
stable, the newest, the largest, and the most fair; this he folded in

two, and drawing forth his knife, divided the cloth in two portions. Then he bestowed on his grandfather one half of the sundered horsecloth.

"Fair child," said the man, "what have you done? Why have you cut the cloth that your father has given me? Very cruelly have you treated me, for you were bidden to give me the horsecloth whole. I shall return and complain to my son thereof."

"Go where you will," replied the boy, "for certainly you shall have nothing more from me."

The merchant went forth from the stable.

"Son," said he, "chastise now thy child, since he counts thy word as nothing but an idle tale, and fears not to disobey thy commandment. Dost thou not see that he keeps one half of the horsecloth?"

"Plague take thee!" cried the father; "give him all the cloth."

"Certes," replied the boy, "that will I never do, for how then shall you be paid? Rather will I keep the half until I am grown a man, and then give it to you. For just as you have chased him from your house, so I will put you from my door. Even as he has bestowed on you all his wealth, so, in my turn, will I require of you all your substance. Naught from me shall you carry away, save that only which you have granted to him. If you leave him to die in his misery, I wait my day, and surely will leave you to perish in yours."

The father listened to these words, and at the end sighed heavily. He repented him of the evil that he purposed, and from the parable that his child had spoken took heed and warning. Turning himself about towards the merchant, he said —

"Father, return to my house. Sin and the Enemy thought to have caught me in the snare, but, please God, I have escaped from the fowler. You are master and lord, and I render all that I have received into your hands. If my wife cannot live with you in quiet, then you shall be served and cherished elsewhere. Chimney corner, and carpet, pillow and bed of feathers, at your ease you shall have pleasure in them all. I take St. Martin to witness that never will I drink stoup of wine, never carve morsel from dish, but that yours shall be the richer portion. Henceforth you shall live softly in the ceiled chamber, near by a blazing fire, clad warmly in your furred robe, even as I. And all this is not of charity, but of your right, for, fair sweet father, if I am rich it is because of your substance."

Thus the brave witness and the open remonstrance of a child freed his father from the bad thoughts that he harboured. And deeply should this adventure be considered of those who are about to marry their children. Let them not strip themselves so bare as to have nothing left. For he who gives all and depends upon the charity of others prepares a rod for his own back.

[tr. Eugene Mason]

# THE ROMANCE OF THE ROSE

In the twelfth century, the most popular work of literature was Geoffrey of Monmouth's *Histories;* a century later it was *The Romance of the Rose.* There still exist more than two hundred manuscripts of the work — half the number of Geoffrey manuscripts, but nearly four times those of Chaucer. The most widely read poem of what has somewhat hyperbolically been called "the greatest of centuries" warrants the scrutiny of historians. It was written in the Paris of St. Louis and St. Thomas Aquinas. But the common reader, too, will be amply repaid, despite the work's frequent rambling and verbosity. It is a storehouse of Ovidian lore of romantic and courtly love; it is filled with good stories well told, classical vignettes firmly planted in a French countryside, happily-phrased epigrams, maxims, and adages, and, especially in the latter part, humor that may well have taught Chaucer much of his art.

The poem, written entirely in octosyllabic rhymed couplets, is the work of two authors. About 1225 Guillaume de Lorris wrote somewhat more than four thousand lines, apparently leaving his project incomplete. It was his purpose to present, in the form of allegory, the fortunes of a lover; characters like Hope, Fond-thought, and Evil-tongue support the action. The author seems thoroughly orthodox and conventional in his use of the spring season, nature-worship, the dream-frame, personification of virtues and vices, allegory of the lady as a rose, and exposition of romantic love. Yet his tender emotion and idealism inspire the conventional with high poetry.

A number of times he maintains that his work is novel: *"La matiere en est bone et nueve,"* and he is justified. Though dream stories, love romances, allegories, tales of courtesy, and roses were stock patterns, no one before had told of a dream except in superlatives, of love as a subtle relation between two human beings, of courtesy as a classless and universal virtue, and of allegory as a representation of the psychology of man. Jeanroy calls Guillaume a true stylist: simple without platitude, brilliant but not esoteric, easygoing without prolixity, and capable of describing all facets of a thought with nicety and precision. His lines are almost the finale of the passing romantic age.

Fifty years later Jean de Meun, called Clopinel (the Halt), added more than eighteen thousand lines. The two poets, equally versatile, contrast even more than do their generations. Jean's inquiring, speculative mind almost turns the poem into a satire on the theme of love — so much so that Chaucer, in the Prologue to his *Legend of Good Women,* portrays the God of Love as bitter:

> For in pleyn text, with-outen nede of glose,
> Thou hast translated the Romance of the Rose,
> That is an heresye ageyns my lawe,
> And makest wyse folk fro me withdrawe.

Reason, but a minor actor for Guillaume, becomes Jean's foremost agent.   Idealization is played down or disappears, to be supplanted by rationalization; a jealous husband and a deceiving woman, a hypocritical churchman and a peculating official, become memorable characters.   The author's long digressions make the work an encyclopedia of the manners and beliefs of the times.   Jean, of bourgeois birth and university training, was an early humanist in popular demand; among his other compositions are translations of such diverse works as Vegetius' *Military Affairs,* the Letters of Abelard and Héloïse, and Gerald of Wales' *Marvels of Ireland.*   No doubt the color lent by contrast between the poets added much to the popularity of the poem.

The two selections below represent the two authors.   The first, lines 1603–1954 from Guillaume, depicts the Lover, who has dreamily stumbled upon Narcissus' pool, becoming the victim of Cupid's shafts.   The second, lines 15,891–16,148, from Jean, is a part of the poet's introduction to Nature's Confession, which forms an extensive and unique summary of the popular science of the day.   The translation of F. S. Ellis, which has become a kind of modern classic, has been altered, with the assistance of Professor Marshall Stearns, to eliminate unnecessary archaism and, in some places, to conform more closely to the original text.

## THE ROMANCE OF THE ROSE
### *(Roman de la Rose)*

[From *The Romance of the Rose,* translated by F. S. Ellis; Temple Classics, J. M. Dent and Sons, Ltd., London, 1903. Reprinted by permission of the publisher.]

### I

#### THE ROSE AND THE GOD OF LOVE
#### Guillaume de Lorris (*circ.* 1225)

Beside the spring a while I stayed,
Admiring how the crystals made
Mirrors for all the lovely things
That filled the garden.   Memory brings
The thought that I too long had let
Its charm bemuse me, vain regret!
I feel that magic glass deceived
My soul, but had I then perceived
What sorrow to its sight was wed,
I would have whirled about and fled
As man pursued by plague will flee.
And yet misfortune captured me.

From all things mirrored there I chose
A rose bush, charged with many a rose,
Surrounded by a thick grown hedge,
And doubt not if I held in pledge
Paris and Pavia faithfully,
My heart would surely then agree
To render up the two, so I
Might gaze on it unceasingly.
And when I felt this passion seize
My heart, which often gives unease
To wisest men, my longing drew
Me towards the rose-bush.  Then there flew
Through all my soul its flavour sweet,
Which set my heart and pulse abeat
Like fire.  And were it not for fear
That I might pay a price too dear,
I surely should have dared to seize
A rosebud.  Nothing else could please
My senses equally, but dread
Restrained my hand lest, angered
At that, the guardian of the place
Might thrust me out straightway apace.

Thousands of roses!  Deeply hued,
No one in this wide world has viewed
Such rich profusion; some as yet
Mere buds, which therefore had not met
The rude winds' kiss, while others were
Half opened, and such beauty rare
Displayed as no man would despise
Who once upon them cast his eyes;
For roses which are fully blown
Will soon begin to let fall down
Their petals, while the tender new
Fresh buds, as yet untouched by dew,
Will keep their beauty while the sun
His course through three full days will run.
What ardent longing in my breast
These buds inspired!  He who possessed
The power to pick but one, right glad
Must be that such a prize he had.
And if I could secure the crown
Of it, I would give up renown
And fortune fair.  Amongst them all
My rapturous eyes on one did fall,
Whose perfect loveliness outvied
All those beside it.  Then I spied
With joy its lovely petals, which
Kind Nature's hand had dyed with rich

Deep crimson hue.   Its perfect leaves
Were formed of two quadruple sheaves,
Which side by side stood firm and fair,
With stalk grown strong enough to bear
The full-grown bloom which was not bent
Or wilted, but most sweetly spent
It's fragrance on the air around,
And wrapped my senses in profound
Yet soft delight.   And when I caught
Its odor, I was wholly fraught
With strong desire that now I might
Snatch for my own that sweet delight.
But thorns and thistles grew so thick
Around the rose-bush, set to prick
And wound the profane hand that dared
Approach and grasp it, that I spared
To risk the rash attempt, afraid
My love with wounds would be repaid.

The God of Love, whose bow was bent
With deadly aim, where'er I went
Pursued my steps, and took his stand
Beneath a fig-tree, close at hand
To where, with arm aloft, I sought
To pluck the Rose whose beauty brought
Me hither; then he took a shaft
And placing it with bowman's craft,
Drew the string taut against his ear
With mighty arm, for he that gear
Knows how to handle; straightway flew
The shaft from it, which surely knew
Its fatal target; through my heart
Quick pierced the golden-headed dart,
And on my forehead ice-cold sweat
Burst forth, nor can I soon forget
How through my cloak I felt the breath
Of mortal fear, as one near death.
Pierced by the fatal shaft I fell
Flat on the ground.   How can I tell
What sudden faintness seemed to seize
My heart, as I then felt my knees
Give way, and when I from the swoon
Awoke, I felt as does the moon
In glare of day.   And then I thought
To see blood flow, but when I sought
The wounded spot, 'twas clear and dry.
At once both hands I did apply,
And strove, with sighs and groans, to draw
The arrow from the cruel flaw:

Alas for me, although the bole
I drew from out that fatal hole,
The iron barb, which was named Beauty,
Remained fast-fixed, as was its duty,
Past power to move it, yet no drop
Of crimson blood welled to the top.

Ah! then what anguish and distress,
What grief twice told, what heaviness,
I suffered: lost to speech I stood
Distrustful where or how I could
Some cure discover, or what herb
To seek that might be sure to curb
My painful wound.
                        The rosebud still
My heart desired: that wish did fill
My whole true being; and the gain
Of that dear treasure all my pain
Would ease away, and give to me
New life, from grief to sorrow free.
For just to see it and inhale
Its fragrance made the somber vale
Of life seem brighter, and though death
Drew near, I strove to smell its breath.
But then again beheld that Love
Another arrow raised above
My trembling body.
                        Innocence
This second shaft was called, nor less
Of strength it had than Beauty; oft
Have men and maidens felt its soft
But potent stroke.   All suddenly
The God, without once warning me,
This golden arrow raised and sped,
With mighty force against my head
Its cruel point, which through the eye
Piercèd my soul; and if I die
I fear no man of woman born
Can ever from my breast that thorn
Pull out, for though one might release
The shaft, yet have I lost my lease
On peace of mind; and even so
At once desire began to grow
Fiercer within me than before
To win the rosebud.   More and more
It then increased, as more I felt
Love's second shaft, until to melt
Did seem my soul.   Oh sweeter far
That Rose to me, than violets are

When spring awakes; it drew me on
Though it were wiser if I'd gone
Away in swift and hasty flight;
One often finds that folly's might
Subdues the reason, so I bent
My steps towards the Rose whose scent
Subdued my will.
                                A careful watch
Meanwhile the archer kept to snatch
Advantage of me as I strove
To reach the fragrant flower, whose love
Entranced my soul.
                                Now third there flew
The shaft called Courtesy, which through
My heart pierced once again.  In swoon
Like death I fell to Love's harpoon,
Stretched out beneath the somber shade
An olive tree's broad branches made.
   The wound this time was wide and deep.
When I awoke from fainting sleep,
And strove with all my strength and craft
To pull the weapon out, the haft
Was all of it I surely gained;
Fast fixed the jagged point remained.
   Then sitting on the grass upright
My painful anguish as I might
Ignore, I saw that woe must be
My lot, for this last wound to me
Brought new desire to win the Rose.
And yet again the archer chose
Another shaft of beauty rare,
Gold wrought with feathered plumage fair:
Well might I then bewail my fate,
For scalded man does water hate,
Whether it cold or lukewarm be.
A powerful force, Necessity!
Though I see arrows thickly hail
Like stones and boulders thrown pell-mell,
I'd pluck that bud!
                                Almighty Love,
Whose influence reigns far above
All else, to me such courage gave
As dared his worst assault to brave.
Wounded and weak I gained my feet
And staggered on, prepared to meet
The archer, towards that rose-grown bush,
But found strong spines and thistles push
A barrier up against me.  Vain
All efforts seemed the prize to gain.

Yet near the hedge I stood, and might
Freely enjoy the lovely sight
Of roses sweet, prepared to scorn
The pain of decimating thorn,
If only I might smell the air
With fragrance laden, and the fair
Sweet rosebuds gaze upon, upset
By no repulse.  I did forget
All pain and suffering, lost in joy
Naught could diminish or destroy;
As long as I might remain near
The Rose, then gone was all my fear,
Healed were my wounds, what more could I
Desire, than thus to live and die?

While I remained thus resting there
The God of Love came (for his care
Seemèd to me my heart to rack)
As though his aim was to attack
Me once again.  With full intent
His bright and handsome bow he bent,
Driving a shaft beneath my breast,
Which found my heart, its final rest.
Companionship, this dart was called.
It is, all know who are enthralled,
Potent in curing maid or dame
Of foolish coyness, pride, or shame.
It suddenly within me wrought
Renewed distress, and to me brought
Three fainting spells.  When I awoke,
More cruelly my deep sadness broke
Upon me, and all hope had fled
Of cure or balm.  And then I said:
More welcome death were, than to lead
A life so vile, where troubles breed
New troubles still, for Cupid now
Will make of me I do allow
A martyr; had I but the wit
To flee, I would escape from it!
  Meanwhile the God against me aimed
Another arrow, which was named
Fair-Seeming.  Dangerous it is,
Yet he who feels its force on his
True heart will bless the pain.  Its point
Is keen and pierces thigh and joint
Like steel-made razor.  But the head
With ointment is by Cupid spread
To dull the pain, for he asks not
The death of those whom he has got

Within his toils, but less torment
Delights to give them; thus is sent
To all his vassals fragrant balm,
Made by his hands, their hurts to calm.
Lovers in him great comfort find;
Sores does he heal and all wounds bind.
This arrow love against me drew,
Tearing my heart, but like a dew
Of sweet effect its ointment spread
Through all my frame.   From heel to head,
My senses cleared, and gave me back
That strength which all my limbs did lack.
And by that precious ointment death
Was cheated — Love revived my breath.

   I had enough true strength to draw
The arrow forth, but like a claw
The point held fast, so all the five
Fair shafts did Cupid thus contrive
To lodge within me, so to prove
No force or time could them remove.
And though the ointment helped me much
The pains I still endured were such,
That of my countenance the hue
Was altered, and right well I knew
That this last shaft both marred and made;
For anguish tipped its pointed blade.
Meanwhile the ointment, soft and pure,
Made my wounds easy to endure.
At the same time it hurt and healed,
Brought forth new pains, and old ones sealed.
With bounding step the God of Love
Hastened toward me, and stood above
My prostrate form, then gaily cried:
"Vassal!   In vain have you denied
Yourself my prisoner; no dread
Or gloom need haunt you, cheer instead.
The readier you do my will,
The quicker I shall be to fill
Your heart with joy.   But mad were you
To fear him whom you ought to view
As kindly friend.   It's yours to seek
From him benevolence; all too weak
Are you for struggle.   Learn of me
That pride and foolish vanity
Will serve you not.   If you submit
To me, then you'll be glad of it."
   I answered: "Sir, to you I give
Myself as long as I shall live:

Before God, I will never fight
Against you, Lord; yours is the right.
You can do with me as you will.
I'm in your hands.  For good or ill
My strength's as nothing, without you.
Your vassal grants the homage due.
My life is yours to waste or save.
I cheerfully remain your slave,
For you alone have power to give
Me joy or sorrow while I live.
If your strong hand, which has of late
Betrayed my soul to cruellest fate,
Refuses now my woes to cure,
Or shackles me, you may be sure
I shall not murmur nor complain
For your decrees I've no disdain.
For if through you my heart is whole
I've placed myself in your control,
But trust in time you'll manifest
That grace which hope plants in my breast."
This said, I dropped upon my knee,
To kiss his royal foot; but he,
His hand in mine, said: "Well content
Am I with you; such words are sent
Out from a loyal heart, and you
For that fair speech shall win your due
Of honor.  Homage just to me
Is yours to do, and I grant free
This boon — my very mouth to kiss;
No favor thus permitted is
To peasants, churls, or such as be
Mere youths; it is a warranty
Of Love's sweet mercy, and alone
Permitted those whose hearts are known
As courteous, honest, good and true;
Ready and waiting service due.
My bondage weighty is, but I
Reward good servants plentifully.
You well may feel right fine and proud
To be Love's vassal, and allowed
His livery from this day to wear.
Love does the noble banner bear
Of Courtesy, and always shows
Himself as sweet and kind to those
Who love him, and upon them take
His lordship.  He will surely make
From out their hearts soon disappear
All base desire, all servile fear."

## II

### NATURE

#### Jean de Meun (*circ.* 1275)

And while, as this great oath they took,
The barons roared till heaven shook,
Nature, who is the fond ally
Of all live things beneath the sky,
Into her workshop entered straight,
Where she works both soon and late,
To forge such species as may be
Used for the continuity
Of life; all things she fashions so
That never shall a species know
The power of Death, but as one dies
Immediately others rise
To fill its place. In vain does Death
With hurrying footsteps waste his breath —
So closely Nature follows him,
That if a few are by his grim
And massive club destroyed who are
His due (for some of them no bar
To him oppose, but readily
Give welcome wheresoe'er they be,
Wasting themselves in common course,
While others through their waste gain force)
When he perhaps does fondly think
That one and all his cup must drink,
He is deceivèd: as one dies
Another opens new-born eyes.
While this he seizes on the right
That on the left escapes his blight.
If Death perhaps the father kill,
Mother and son, or daughter, still
Remain. Though cheered by their escape,
They in their day are wrapped in crepe.
They too must fall beneath Death's power,
No man can stay the fateful hour;
Nor medicine, nor vow, nor prayer.
Nephews and nieces quickly fare
Afar, with hurrying feet, upbuoyed
With hope they may dread death avoid.
One to the dance does him betake,
Another seeks the church to make
His refuge, and a third the school,

A fourth will undertake the rule
Of merchants, or of arts, which he
Perhaps has studied formerly.
And some will vanquish care with fine
Expensive meats and rare old wine,
While others with a wish to fly
From death or changeless destiny,
You may on prancing steeds behold,
Their stirrups bright with glistening gold;
Thinking that thus they may escape
More rapidly Death's grisly shape.
Another on frail planks will set
His hope, and trust thereby to get
O'er sea, if so the stars avail
To guide his boat and help him sail
Away from Death.   Another tries
By base hypocrisy and lies
And show of prayer to give the slip
To Death, when Death his foot would trip;
Though truly must all men be known
By actions which are all their own,
And thus it is that all men try
Vainly the grip of Death to fly.

But he, with fearful blackened face,
To all these fugitives gives chase,
Until he treads upon their heels,
And each in turn his weapon feels
At ten years, twenty, or two score,
Or maybe double that or more;
For some to four score years and ten
Escape, or five score, but all men
His foot will overtake at last.
And though it seem as if he passed
Some few, he turns himself again
To strike them down.   Futile and vain
Is medicine at last; each one
He catches when his course is run.
Even the great physicians he
Seizes however skilled they be:
Hippocrates and Galen too,
Though wise, were forced to pay Death's due;
Constantine, Razis, Avicene,
Are vassals now in his demesne.
For far though men may run, Death will
With tireless foot run further still,
Thus he, whom nothing satisfies
Just like a greedy glutton tries
To swallow all, and therefore he

Pursues them over land and sea.
And yet no matter how he strives,
All living things he never drives
At once within his net, nor shapes
His snares so well that none escapes.
For if but only one remain,
That one will soon give birth again;
And this we by the Phoenix know,
Which, though but one, again does grow
Unfailingly.
              On all the earth
One Phoenix only comes to birth
In five-and-twenty score of years;
And when the fabulous creature nears
Its end, it builds a funeral pyre
Of spices sweet, then sets afire
Itself and burns again to dust,
In the way it seems it must
Perish, but then it does arise
And from the ashes to the skies
Once more arises.  This is done
By God's command.  As soon as one
Is dead, at once Dame Nature straight
To fill its place does one create
Unceasingly, for otherwise
Everything in this world dies.
Think that on land or sky or sea
No Phoenix in this world would be!
But as it is, though many died,
Nature has many more supplied.
And thus likewise does everything
That dies through Nature once more spring
To life anew.  Beneath the moon
Whatever fails shall late or soon
Revive, if only one remain
From which new life the race may gain,
For Nature, pitiful and good,
Abhors and hates Death's envious mood,
Who ruthlessly would mar and break
The fairest thing her skill does make;
And seeing naught can fairer be,
Her own form ever thus stamps she
On all her works, as men who mint
New coins, and stamp with their imprint,
And form and color give to each.

This is the goal Art strives to reach
In copying Nature's models, though
Such perfect work no man can show.

Art, falling on his knees before
Dame Nature humbly does implore,
Beseech, and earnestly require
In humble form, that she inspire
His heart, if but in small degree,
How he may copy carefully
Her handiwork, and reproduce
Its form, for ornament or use,
Acknowledging his best works are
Inferior to hers by far.
Anxious to imitate her ways,
Our human Art may closely gaze
On Nature's workings, as an ape
Will counterfeit man's acts and shape.

Yet Art to no avail may try
With Nature's mastery to vie.
To nothing that man's hand makes live
Can he her heavenly nature give.
For Art, although he nothing shirk
To imitate great Nature's work,
And set his hand to every kind
Of thing he may around him find,
Of whatsoever sort it be,
Painting and carving curiously
(And none of all the arts men leave
Untried; they paint, dye, carve, and weave)
Armed warriors on their coursers light
Adorned and clad in colors bright,
Purple and yellow, green and blue,
And many another varied hue:
Fair birds that sing in branches green,
And fish in crystal waters seen,
And all the savage beasts that roam
In forest haunts, their native home;
And flowers and herbs in sunny glades,
Which merry youths and pretty maids
Go forth in pleasant days of spring
To gather in their wandering:
Tame birds, and beasts all unafraid,
Games, dances underneath the shade,
And noble dames in dresses fair,
In metal, wax, or wood with care
Portrayed, as they in life might stand,
And lovers clasping hand in hand.
Never on panel, cloth, or wall,
Can subtlest Art, in spite of all
Make Nature's figures live and move,
Or speak, or feel joy, grief, or love.

Or if of alchemy Art learn
So much that he can metals turn
To varied colors, ne'er can he
Work them so that they changèd be,
Unless he by his skill may lead
Them back to that whence they proceed;
Nor working deftly till he die
Can pierce the subtle mystery
Of Nature. If he would attain
The knowledge to transmute again
Metals to primary estate,
Needful it is to calculate
Their qualities of tempering
If he would his elixir bring
To good result, and thus produce
Pure metal for his later use.
But those who know it best agree
How great an art is alchemy,
And who will thus devote his mind
In study, wondrous things shall find;
For as in every species we
Find parts which taken separately
Are isolated, yet compose
One body when these join with those,
And this with that does ever change
Throughout all Nature's varying range,
And in such fashion it revolves
Till that one into this resolves
Its nature, and they reappear
In different guise from what they were
Before the change.
                    Now see we not
What different form the fern has got
When it's by fire to ash reduced,
And in this way clear glass produced
By depuration as we learn?
And yet we know glass is not fern,
And none would say that fern is glass.
And when we watch the lightning pass
Which thunder brings, why do we see
Stones from the clouds fall presently
Which are not formed of stone at all?
To learn about this we must call
On learned men, for they alone
Can say why vapors turn to stone,
And how it is things wide apart
Are changed by Nature's or man's art.
And so may men change metals who
Know with their matter what to do.

Drawing the dross apart from gold
Till nothing base the metals hold,
And brought together then shall be
Pure metals by affinity.
In short, books of philosophy
Teach us the truth of alchemy —
How different sorts of metals form
Down in the earth, where it is warm,
From sulphur and quicksilver, too —
A reader knows just what to do;
For whosoever there has found
The means these spirits to compound,
And cause them so to mix and lie
That they no more apart can fly,
But in one mass with welding sure
Together come, purged clear and pure,
And force the sulphur to lie dead,
Colored at will, or white or red,
That man shall have, who works just so,
All metals in his power, I know.
And thus of mercury, fine gold
They make who perfect knowledge hold
Of alchemy, and color add
And weight, with things that may be had
At little cost, and precious stones
Men make from gold, whose worth atones
For all the labor.          And likewise
Men may with subtle art devise
How to pure silver may be turned
All baser metals, when they've learned
By means of drugs, strong, clear, and fine,
To prosecute this art divine.
But this alone is for the ken
Of learned and right worthy men,
Who labor hard nor seek to shirk
The perfecting of Nature's work.
Frauds and imposters strive in vain —
To them her marvels sealed remain.

[tr. F. S. Ellis, revised]

# MARCO POLO

Great books are only occasionally an accident of circumstances, but the book of Ser Marco Polo is one. Had he not been captured in battle and thrown into a Genoese prison, had he not there in prison met the literate and inquiring Rustician of Pisa, a kind of professional author who, for example, edited and translated prose romances of the Round Table, and had not Rustician been able to write down in French the tale as Marco Polo told it to him, the book that has stirred travelers' imaginations more than any other in the western world would never have existed. In the year 1298, when Dante was first venturing into Florentine politics, Joinville was recording the history of St. Louis, Edward I was defeating the pestiferous Scots, and Albert, the son of Rudolf of Hapsburg, was crowned Emperor, Marco was able to recall with unique impersonality and precision of detail his travel to Cathay and his life there, which covered twenty-four years, from 1271 to 1295. The book evidently circulated freely. But few believed the tale, for, according to a contemporary, when Marco was on his deathbed (1324 or 1325) friends begged him to tone down what they apparently thought were fabulous stories; to them he rejoined that he had not told half of what he had seen. His nickname *Milioni* suggests that his stories reminded readers of The Thousand and One Nights. Not until the second half of the nineteenth century were western travelers really in a position to judge the truth of the book; though they acknowledge Marco's many inaccuracies of observation and memory and concede that the book is primitive in its depiction of distance and locale, they praise its brilliance, its essential reliability, and its storyteller's art.

Marco Polo lived in an age of swiftly expanding horizons. The Orient east of the Ganges had been practically unknown to the ancient western world, though early Christians, notably St. Thomas the Apostle, had established themselves in India. With the decline in the West and the expansion of heretic Mohammedanism, all knowledge of the East disappeared except the scanty and inaccurate lore of Pliny. But by the beginning of the thirteenth century three factors combined to make travel and exploration possible once more: the Crusades and the Latin Kingdom of Jerusalem created a base in Asia and an entry to the unknown world. The incredible expansion of the Mongols under Genghis Khan created a single rule from the borders of Byzantium to the China Sea. And the emergence of the West from poverty created a demand for exotic goods, which encouraged traders to risk long journeys and their attendant perils. Before the close of the twelfth century, apparently, the magnet was in use among sailors, but land routes remained the regular avenue of trade until the mid-fourteenth century. It was Polo's book, strangely enough, that seems to have stimulated the imagination of many seamen. The famous Catalan Map, which showed the maritime explorations down the coast of Africa, relies on Polo for notions of the East; Prince Henry the Navigator evidently read the work with profit; and there still exists Columbus' copy of the Latin version, with notes in his own hand.

Marco Polo, the son of a noble Venetian trader, Nicolò Polo, was born in 1254. His father and uncle Maffeo left before or during 1260 for the East and returned in 1269 with a letter to the Pope from Kublai Khan, asking for one hundred Christian missionaries for China. Two years later, they set out again for the East, with two of the one hundred asked for, and these deserted at Lajazzo. But this time they took with them Nicolò's son Marco, now seventeen years old. It took them four years to reach Peking, where they remained in the Khan's service for seventeen years. Apparently Marco became an especially trusted legate. They started back in 1292 and arrived in Venice, affluent but forgotten, in 1295.

The Polos' first journey is the first on record of medieval travel to Cathay, though many others, especially Franciscans, were to follow shortly. Marco Polo's account of Japan is the first on record; no doubt he was the first Occidental to land there. Other travels took him to Sumatra and Java. On the journey out, the caravan traveled north of the Himalayas through the fabled home of Prester John; the journey home was made by Burma, India, and Madagascar. The two selections that follow give some account of the two great Khans, Genghis and his grandson Kublai.

## THE BOOK OF WONDERS
### (*Livre des Diversités*)

Marco Polo (1254–1324?) and Rusticien de Pise

[From *The Book of Sir Marco Polo*, edited by Sir Henry Yule; John Murray, London, 1875.]

#### CHINGHIS KAAN (GENGHIS KHAN)

Originally the Tartars dwelt in the north on the borders of Chorcha. Their country was one of great plains; and there were no towns or villages in it, but excellent pasturelands, with great rivers and many sheets of water; in fact it was a very fine and extensive region. But there was no sovereign in the land. They did, however, pay tax and tribute to a great prince who was called in their tongue Unc Can, the same that we call Prester John, him in fact about whose great dominion all the world talks. The tribute he had of them was one beast out of every ten, and also a tithe of all their other gear.

Now it came to pass that the Tartars multiplied exceedingly. And when Prester John saw how great a people they had become, he began to fear that he should have trouble from them. So he made a scheme to distribute them over sundry countries, and sent one of his barons to carry this out. When the Tartars became aware of this they took it much amiss, and with one consent they left their country and went off across a desert to a distant region towards the north, where Prester John could not get at them to annoy them. Thus they revolted from his authority and paid him tribute no longer. And so things continued for a time.

Now it came to pass in the year of Christ's incarnation 1187 that the Tartars made them a King whose name was Chinghis Kaan. He was a man of great worth, and of great ability, eloquence, and valour. And as soon as the news that he had been chosen King was spread abroad through those countries, all the Tartars in the world came to him and owned him for their Lord. And right well did he maintain the sovereignty they had given him. What shall I say? The Tartars gathered to him in astonishing multitude, and when he saw such numbers he made a great furniture of spears and arrows and such other arms as they used, and set about the conquest of all those regions till he had conquered eight provinces.

When he conquered a province he did no harm to the people or their property, but merely established some of his own men in the country along with a proportion of theirs, whilst he led the remainder to the conquest of other provinces. And when those whom he had conquered became aware how well and safely he protected them against all others, and how they suffered no ill at his hands, and saw what a noble prince he was, then they joined him heart and soul and became his devoted followers. And when he had thus gathered such a multitude that they seemed to cover the earth, he began to think of conquering a great part of the world.

Now in the year of Christ 1200 he sent an embassy to Prester John, and desired to have his daughter to wife. But when Prester John heard that Chinghis Kaan demanded his daughter in marriage he waxed very wroth, and said to the envoys, "What impudence is this, to ask my daughter to wife! Wist he not well that he was my liegeman and serf? Get ye back to him and tell him that I had liever set my daughter in the fire than give her in marriage to him, and that he deserves death at my hand, rebel and traitor that he is!" So he bade the envoys begone at once, and never come into his presence again. The envoys, on receiving this reply, departed straightway, and made haste to their master, and related all that Prester John had ordered them to say, keeping nothing back.

When Chinghis Kaan heard the brutal message that Prester John had sent him, such rage seized him that his heart came nigh to bursting within him, for he was a man of a very lofty spirit. At last he spoke, and that so loud that all who were present could hear him: "Never more might he be prince if he took not revenge for the brutal message of Prester John, and such revenge that insult never in this world was so dearly paid for. And before long, Prester John should know whether he were his serf or no!"

So then he mustered all his forces, and levied such a host as never before was seen or heard of, sending word to Prester John to be on his defence. And when Prester John had sure tidings that Chinghis was really coming against him with such a multitude, he still professed to treat it as a jest and a trifle, for, quoth he, "these be no soldiers." Natheless he marshalled his forces and mustered his people, and made great preparations, in order that if Chinghis did come, he might take him and put him to death. In fact he marshalled such an host of many different nations that it was a world's wonder.

And so both sides gat them ready to battle. And why should I make a long story of it? Chinghis Kaan with all his host arrived at a vast and beautiful plain which was called Tanduc, belonging to Prester John, and there he pitched his camp; and so great was the multitude of his people that it was impossible to number them. And when he got tidings that Prester John was coming, he rejoiced greatly, for the place afforded a fine and ample battle-ground, so he was right glad to tarry for him there, and greatly longed for his arrival.

Now the story goes that when Prester John became aware that Chinghis with his host was marching against him, he went forth to meet him with all his forces, and advanced until he reached the same plain of Tanduc, and pitched his camp over against that of Chinghis Kaan at a distance of twenty miles. And then both armies remained at rest for two days that they might be fresher and heartier for battle.

So when the two great hosts were pitched on the plains of Tanduc as you have heard, Chinghis Kaan one day summoned before him his astrologers, both Christians and Saracens, and desired them to let him know which of the two hosts would gain the battle, his own or Prester John's. The Saracens tried to ascertain, but were unable to give a true answer; the Christians however did give a true answer, and showed manifestly beforehand how the event should be. For they got a cane and split it lengthwise, and laid one half on this side and one half on that, allowing no one to touch the pieces. And one piece of cane they called Chinghis Kaan, and the other piece they called Prester John. And they said to Chinghis: "Now mark! and you will see the event of the battle, and who shall have the best of it; for whose cane soever shall get above the other, to him shall victory be." He replied that he would fain see it, and bade them begin. Then the Christian astrologers read a Psalm out of the Psalter, and went through other incantations. And lo! whilst all were beholding, the cane that bore the name of Chinghis Kaan, without being touched by anybody, advanced to the other that bore the name of Prester John, and got on the top of it. When the Prince saw that, he was greatly delighted, and seeing how in this matter he found the Christians to tell the truth, he always treated them with great respect, and held them for men of truth for ever after.

And after both sides had rested well those two days, they armed for the fight and engaged in desperate combat; and it was the greatest battle that ever was seen. The numbers that were slain on both sides were very great, but in the end Chinghis Kaan obtained the victory. And in the battle Prester John was slain. And from that time forward, day by day, his kingdom passed into the hands of Chinghis Kaan till the whole was conquered.

I may tell you that Chinghis Kaan reigned six years after this battle and engaged continually in conquest, taking many a province and city and stronghold. But at the end of those six years he went against a certain castle that was called Caaju, and there he was shot with an arrow in the knee, so that he died of his wound. A great pity it was, for he was a valiant man and a wise.

### CUBLAY KAAN (KUBLAI KHAN)

Now am I come to that part of our Book in which I shall tell you of the great and wonderful magnificence of the Great Kaan now reigning, by name Cublay Kaan; Kaan being a title which signifyeth "The Great Lord of Lords," or Emperor. And of a surety he hath good right to such a title, for all men know for a certain truth that he is the most potent man, as regards forces and lands and treasure, that existeth in the world, or ever hath existed from the time of our first father Adam until this day. All this I will make clear to you for truth, in this book of ours, so that every one shall be fain to acknowledge that he is the greatest Lord that is now in the world, or ever hath been. And now ye shall hear how and wherefore.

Now this Cublay Kaan is of the right imperial lineage, being descended from Chinghis Kaan, the first sovereign of all the Tartars. And he is the sixth Lord in that succession, as I have already told you in this book. He came to the throne in the year of Christ 1256, and the Empire fell to him because of his ability and valour and great worth, as was right and reason. His brothers, indeed, and other kinsmen disputed his claim, but his it remained, both because maintained by his great valour, and because it was in law and right his, as being directly sprung of the imperial line.

Up to the year of Christ now running, to wit 1298, he hath reigned two and forty years, and his age is about eighty-five, so that he must have been about forty-three years of age when he first came to the throne. Before that time he had often been to the wars, and had shown himself a gallant soldier and an excellent captain. But after coming to the throne he never went to the wars in person save once.

The personal appearance of the Great Kaan, Lord of Lords, whose name is Cublay, is such as I shall now tell you. He is of a good stature, neither tall nor short, but of a middle height. He has a becoming amount of flesh, and is very shapely in all his limbs. His complexion is white and red, the eyes black and fine, the nose well formed and well set on. He has four wives, whom he retains permanently as his legitimate consorts; and the eldest of his sons by those four wives ought by rights to be emperor; — I mean when his father dies. Those four ladies are called empresses, but each is distinguished also by her proper name. And each of them has a special court of her own, very grand and ample, no one of them having fewer than 300 fair and charming damsels. They have also many pages and eunuchs, and a number of other attendants of both sexes; so that each of these ladies has not less than 10,000 persons attached to her court.

When the Emperor desires the society of one of these four consorts, he will sometimes send for the lady to his apartment and sometimes visit her at her own. He has also a great number of concubines, and I will tell you how he obtains them.

You must know that there is a tribe of Tartars called Ungrat, who are noted for their beauty. Now every year an hundred of the most beautiful maidens of this tribe are sent to the Great Kaan, who commits them to the charge of certain elderly ladies dwelling in his palace. And these old ladies make the girls sleep with them, in order to ascertain if they have sweet breath and do not snore, and are sound in all their limbs. Then such of them as are of approved beauty, and are good and sound in all respects, are appointed to attend on the Emperor by turns. Thus six of these damsels take their turn for three days and nights, and wait on him when he is in his chamber and when he is in his bed, to serve him in any way, and to be entirely at his orders. At the end of the three days and nights they are relieved by other six. And so throughout the year, there are reliefs of maidens by six and six, changing every three days and nights.

The Emperor hath, by those four wives of his, twenty-two male children; the eldest of whom was called Chinkin for the love of the good Chinghis Kaan, the first Lord of the Tartars. And this Chinkin, as the Eldest Son of the Kaan, was to have reigned after his father's death; but, as it came to pass, he died. He left a son behind him, however, whose name is Temur, and he is to be the Great Kaan and Emperor after the death of his Grandfather, as is but right; he being the child of the Great Kaan's eldest son. And this Temur is an able and brave man, as he hath already proven on many occasions.

The Great Kaan hath also twenty-five other sons by his concubines; and these are good and valiant soldiers, and each of them is a great chief. I tell you moreover that of his children by his four lawful wives there are seven who are kings of vast realms or provinces, and govern them well; being all able and gallant men, as might be expected. For the Great Kaan their sire is, I tell you, the wisest and most accomplished man, the greatest Captain, the best to govern men and rule an Empire, as well as the most valiant, that ever has existed among all the tribes of Tartars.

You must know that for three months of the year, to wit December, January, and February, the Great Kaan resides in the capital city of Cathay, which is called Cambaluc and which is at the north-eastern extremity of the country. In that city stands his great palace, and now I will tell you what it is like.

It is enclosed all round by a great wall forming a square, each side of which is a mile in length; that is to say, the whole compass thereof is four miles. This you may depend on; it is also very thick, and a good ten paces in height, whitewashed and loop-holed all around. At each angle of the wall there is a very fine and rich palace in which the war-harness of the Emperor is kept, such as bows and quivers, saddles and bridles, and bowstrings, and everything needful for an army. Also midway between every two of these corner palaces there is another of the like; so that taking the whole compass of the enclosure you find eight vast palaces stored with the Great Lord's harness of war. And you must understand that each palace is assigned to only one kind of article; thus one is stored with bows, a second with saddles, a third with bridles, and so on in succession right round.

The great wall has five gates on its southern face, the middle one being the great gate which is never opened on any occasion except when the Great Kaan himself goes forth or enters. Close on either side of this great gate is a smaller one by which all other people pass; and then towards each angle is another great gate, also open to people in general; so that on that side there are five gates in all.

Inside of this wall there is a second, enclosing a space that is somewhat greater in length than in breadth. This enclosure also has eight palaces corresponding to those of the outer wall, and stored like them with the Lord's harness of war. This wall also hath five gates on the southern face, corresponding to those in the outer wall, and hath one gate on each of the other faces as the outer wall hath also. In the middle of the second enclosure is the Lord's Great Palace, and I will tell you what it is like.

You must know that it is the greatest palace that ever was. Towards the north it is in contact with the outer wall, whilst towards the south there is a vacant space which the Barons and the soldiers are constantly traversing. The palace itself hath no upper story, but is all on the ground floor, only the basement is raised some ten palms above the surrounding soil and this elevation is retained by a wall of marble raised to the level of the pavement, two paces in width and projecting beyond the base of the palace so as to form a kind of terrace-walk, by which people can pass round the building, and which is exposed to view, whilst on the outer edge of the wall there is a very fine pillared balustrade; and up to this the people are allowed to come. The roof is very lofty, and the walls of the palace are all covered with gold and silver. They are also adorned with representations of dragons sculptured and gilt, beasts and birds, knights and idols, and sundry other subjects. And on the ceiling too you see nothing but gold and silver and painting. On each of the four sides there is a great marble staircase leading to the top of the marble wall, and forming the approach to the palace.

The hall of the palace is so large that it could easily dine 6000 people; and it is quite a marvel to see how many rooms there are besides. The building is altogether so vast, so rich, and so beautiful, that no man on earth could design anything superior to it. The outside of the roof also is all coloured with vermilion and yellow and green and blue and other hues, which are fixed with a varnish so fine and exquisite that they shine like crystal, and lend a resplendent lustre to the palace as seen for a great way round. This roof is made, too, with such strength and solidity that it is fit to last for ever.

On the interior side of the palace are large buildings with halls and chambers, where the Emperor's private property is placed, such as his treasures of gold, silver, gems, pearls, and gold plate, and in which reside the ladies and concubines. There he occupies himself at his own convenience, and no one else has access.

Between the two walls of the enclosure which I have described, there are fine parks and beautiful trees bearing a variety of fruits. There are beasts also of sundry kinds, such as white stags and fallow deer, gazelles and roebucks, and fine squirrels of various sorts, with numbers also of the animal that gives the musk, and all manner of other beautiful creatures, insomuch that the whole place is full of them, and no spot remains void except where there is traffic of people going and coming. The parks are covered with abundant grass; and the roads through them being all paved and raised two cubits above the surface, they never become muddy, nor does the rain lodge on them, but flows off into the meadows, quickening the soil and producing that abundance of herbage.

From that corner of the enclosure which is towards the north-west there extends a fine lake, containing foison of fish of different kinds which the Emperor hath caused to be put in there, so that whenever he desires any he can have them at his pleasure. A river enters this lake and issues from it, but there is a grating of iron or brass put up so that the fish cannot escape in that way.

Moreover on the north side of the palace, about a bow-shot off, there is a hill which has been made by art from the earth dug out of the lake; it is a good hundred paces in height and a mile in compass. This hill is entirely covered with trees that never lose their leaves, but remain ever green. And I assure you that wherever a beautiful tree may exist, and the Emperor gets news of it, he sends for it and has it transported bodily with all its roots and the earth attached to them, and planted on that hill of his. No matter how big the tree may be, he gets it carried by his elephants; and in this way he has got together the most beautiful collection of trees in all the world. And he has also caused the whole hill to be covered with the ore of azure, which is very green. And thus not only are the trees all green, but the hill itself is all green likewise; and there is nothing to be seen on it that is not green; and hence it is called the Green Mount; and in good sooth 'tis named well.

On the top of the hill again there is a fine big palace which is all green inside and out; and thus the hill and the trees and the palace form together a charming spectacle; and it is marvellous to see their uniformity of colour! Everybody who sees them is delighted. And the Great Kaan has caused this beautiful prospect to be formed for the comfort and solace and delectation of his heart.

You must know that beside the palace that we have been describing, i.e. the Great Palace, the Emperor has caused another to be built just like his own in every respect, and this he hath done for his son when he shall reign and be Emperor after him. Hence it is made just in the same fashion and of the same size, so that everything can be carried on in the same manner after his own death. It stands on the other side of the lake from the Great Kaan's palace, and there is a bridge crossing the water from one to the other. The Prince in question holds now a Seal of Empire, but not with such complete authority as the Great Kaan, who remains supreme as long as he lives.

Now I am going to tell you of the Chief City of Cathay, in which these palaces stand; and why it was built, and how.

Now there was on that spot in old times a great and noble city called Cambaluc, which is as much as to say in our tongue "The City of the Emperor." But the Great Kaan was informed by his astrologers that this city would prove rebellious, and raise great disorders against his imperial authority. So he caused the present city to be built close beside the old one, with only a river between them. And he caused the people of the old city to be removed to the new town that he had founded; and this is called Taidu. However, he allowed a portion of the people which he did not suspect to remain in the old city, because the new one could not hold the whole of them, big as it is.

As regards the size of this new city you must know that it has a compass of twenty-four miles, for each side of it hath a length of six miles, and it is four-square. And it is all walled round with walls of earth which have a thickness of full ten paces at bottom, and a height of more than ten paces; but they are not so thick at top, for they diminish in thickness as they rise, so that at top they are only about three paces thick. And they are provided throughout with loop-holed battlements, which are all whitewashed.

There are twelve gates, and over each gate there is a great and handsome palace, so that there are on each side of the square three gates and five palaces; for, I ought to mention, there is at each angle also a great and handsome palace. In those palaces are vast halls, in which are kept the arms of the city garrison.

The streets are so straight and wide that you can see right along them from end to end and from one gate to the other. And up and down the city there are beautiful palaces, and many great and fine hostelries, and fine houses in great numbers. All the plots of ground on which the houses of the city are built are four-square, and laid out with straight line — all the plots being occupied by great and spacious palaces, with courts and gardens of proportionate size. All these plots were assigned to different heads of families. Each square plot is encompassed by handsome streets for traffic; and thus the whole city is arranged in squares just like a chess-board, and disposed in a manner so perfect and masterly that it is impossible to give a description that should do it justice.

Moreover, in the middle of the city there is a great clock — that is to say, a bell — which is struck at night. And after it has struck three times no one must go out in the city, unless it be for the needs of a woman in labour, or of the sick. And those who go about on such errands are bound to carry lanterns with them. Moreover, the established guard at each gate of the city is one thousand armed men; not that you are to imagine this guard is kept up for fear of any attack, but only as a guard of honour for the sovereign, who resides there, and to prevent thieves from doing mischief in the town.

You must know that the Great Kaan, to maintain his state, hath a guard of twelve thousand horsemen, who are styled Keshican, which is as much as to say "Knights devoted to their Lord." Not that he keeps these for fear of any man whatever, but merely because of his own exalted dignity. These twelve thousand men have four captains, each of whom is in command of three thousand, and each body of three thousand takes a turn of three days and nights to guard the palace, where they also take their meals. After the expiration of three days and nights they are relieved by another three thousand, who mount guard for the same space of time, and then another body takes its turn, so that there are always three thousand on guard. Thus it goes until the whole twelve thousand who are styled, as I said, Keshican, have been on duty; and then the tour begins again, and so runs on from year's end to year's end.

And when the Great Kaan sits at table on any great court occasion, it is in this fashion. His table is elevated a good deal above the others, and he sits at the north end of the hall, looking towards the south, with his chief wife beside him on the left. On his right sit his sons and his nephews, and other kinsmen of the Blood Imperial, but lower, so that their heads are on a level with the Emperor's feet. And then the other barons sit at other tables lower still. So also with the women; for all the wives of the Lord's sons, and of his nephews and other kinsmen, sit at the lower table to his right, and below them again the ladies of the other barons and knights, each in the place assigned by the Lord's orders. The tables are so disposed that the Emperor can see the whole of them from end to end, many as they are. Further, you are not to suppose that everybody sits at table; on the contrary, the greater part of the soldiers and their officers sit at their meal in the hall on the carpets. Outside the hall will be found more than forty thousand people; for there is a great concourse of folk bringing presents to the Lord, or come from foreign countries with curiosities.

In a certain part of the hall near where the Great Kaan holds his table, there is set a large and very beautiful piece of workmanship in the form of a square coffer, or buffet, about three paces each way, exquisitely wrought with figures of animals, finely carved and gilt. The middle is hollow, and in it stands a great vessel of pure gold, holding as much as an ordinary butt; and at each corner of the great vessel is one of smaller size of the capacity of a firkin, and from the former the wine or beverage flavoured with fine and costly spices is drawn off into the latter. And on the buffet aforesaid are set all the Lord's drinking vessels, among which are certain pitchers of the finest gold, which are called verniques, and are big enough to hold drink for eight or ten persons. And one of these is put between every two persons, besides a couple of golden cups with handles, so that every man helps himself from the pitcher that stands between him and his neighbour. And the ladies are supplied in the same way. The value of these pitchers and cups is something immense; in fact, the Great Kaan has such a quantity of this kind of plate, and of gold and silver in other shapes as no one ever before saw or heard tell of or could believe.

There are certain barons specially deputed to see that foreigners, who do not know the customs of the Court, are provided with places suited to their rank; and these barons are continually moving to and fro in the hall, looking to the wants of the guests at table, and causing the servants to supply them promptly with wine, milk, meat, or whatever they lack. At every door of the hall (or, indeed, wherever the Emperor may be) there stand a couple of big men like giants, one on each side, armed with staves. Their business is to see that no one steps upon the threshold in entering, and if this does happen, they strip the offender of his clothes, and he must pay a forfeit to have them back again; or in lieu of taking his clothes, they give him a certain number of blows. If they are foreigners ignorant of the order, then there are barons appointed to introduce them, and explain it to them. They think, in fact, that it brings bad luck if any one touches the threshold. Howbeit, they are not expected to stick at this in going forth again, for at that time some are like to be the worse for liquor and incapable of looking to their steps.

And you must know that those who wait upon the Great Kaan with his dishes and his drink are some of the great barons. They have the mouth and nose muffled with fine napkins of silk and gold, so that no breath nor odour from their persons should taint the dish or the goblet presented to the Lord. And when the Emperor is going to drink, all the musical instruments, of which he has vast store of every kind, begin to play. And when he takes the cup all the barons and the rest of the company drop on their knees and make the deepest obeisance before him, and then the Emperor doth drink. But each time that he does so the whole ceremony is repeated.

I will say nought about the dishes, as you may easily conceive that there is a great plenty of every possible kind. But you should know that in every case where a baron or knight dines at those tables, their wives also dine there with the other ladies. And when all have dined and the tables have been removed, then come in a great number of players and jugglers, adepts at all sorts of wonderful feats, and perform before the Emperor and the rest of the company, creating great diversion and mirth, so that everybody is full of laughter and enjoyment. And when the performance is over, the company breaks up and everyone goes to his quarters.

You must know that the Tartars keep high festival yearly on their birthdays. And the Great Kaan was born on the 28th day of the

September moon, so on that day is held the greatest feast of the year at the Kaan's Court, always excepting that which he holds on New Year's day.

Now, on his birthday, the Great Kaan dresses in the best of his robes, all wrought with beaten gold; and full twelve thousand barons and knights on that day come forth dressed in robes of the same colour, and precisely like those of the Great Kaan, except that they are not so costly; but still they are all of the same colour as his, and are also of silk and gold. Every man so clothed has also a girdle of gold; and this as well as the dress is given him by the sovereign. And I will aver that there are some of these suits decked with so many pearls and precious stones that a single suit shall be worth full ten thousand golden bezants.

And of such raiment there are several sets. For you must know that the Great Kaan, thirteen times in the year, presents to his barons and knights such suits of raiment as I am speaking of. And on each occasion they wear the same colour that he does, a different colour being assigned to each festival. Hence you may see what a huge business it is, and that there is no prince in the world but he alone who could keep up such customs as these.

On his birthday also, all the Tartars in the world, and all the countries and governments that owe allegiance to the Kaan, offer him great presents according to their several ability, and as prescription or orders have fixed the amount. And many other persons also come with great presents to the Kaan, in order to beg for some employment from him. And the Great Kaan has chosen twelve barons on whom is laid the charge of assigning to each of these supplicants a suitable answer.

On this day likewise all the Idolaters, all the Saracens, and all the Christians and other descriptions of people make great and solemn devotions, with much chaunting and lighting of lamps and burning of incense, each to the God whom he doth worship, praying that He would save the Emperor, and grant him long life and health and happiness.

And thus, as I have related, is celebrated the joyous feast of the Kaan's birthday.

The three months of December, January, and February, during which the Emperor resides at his capital city, are assigned for hunting and fowling, to the extent of some forty days' journey round the city; and it is ordained that the larger game taken be sent to the Court. To be more particular: of all the larger beasts of the chase, such as boars, roebucks, bucks, stags, lions, bears, &c., the greater part of what is taken has to be sent, and feathered game likewise. The animals are gutted and despatched to the Court on carts. This is done by all the people within twenty or thirty days' journey, and the quantity so despatched is immense. Those at a greater distance cannot send the game, but they have to send the skins after tanning them, and these are employed in the making of equipments for the Emperor's army.

The Emperor hath numbers of leopards trained to the chase, and hath also a great many lynxes taught in like manner to catch game, and which afford excellent sport. He hath also several great lions, bigger than those of Babylonia, beasts whose skins are coloured in the most beautiful way, being striped all along the sides with black, red, and white. These are trained to catch boars and wild cattle, bears, wild asses, stags, and other great or fierce beasts. And 'tis a rare sight, I can tell you, to see those lions giving chase to such beasts as I have mentioned! When they are to be so employed the lions are taken out in a covered cart, and every lion has a little doggie with him. They are obliged to approach the game against the wind, otherwise the animals would scent the approach of the lion and be off.

There are also a great number of eagles, all broken to catch wolves, foxes, deer, and wild-goats, and they do catch them in great numbers. But those especially that are trained to wolf-catching are very large and powerful birds, and no wolf is able to get away from them.

After he has stopped at his capital city those three months that I mentioned, to wit, December, January, February, he starts off on the 1st day of March, and travels southward towards the Ocean Sea, a journey of two days. He takes with him full ten thousand falconers, and some five hundred gerfalcons besides peregrines, sakers, and other hawks in great numbers; and goshawks also to fly at the water-fowl. But do not suppose that he keeps all these together by him; they are distributed about, hither and thither, one hundred together, or two hundred at the utmost, as he thinks proper. But they are always fowling as they advance, and the most part of the quarry taken is carried to the Emperor. And let me tell you when he goes thus a-fowling with his gerfalcons and other hawks, he is attended by full ten thousand men who are disposed in couples; and these are called Toscaol, which is as much as to say, "Watchers." And the name describes their business. They are posted from spot to spot, always in couples, and thus they cover a great deal of ground! Every man of them is provided with a whistle and hood, so as to be able to call in a hawk and hold it in hand. And when the Emperor makes a cast, there is no need that he follow it up, for those men I speak of keep so good a lookout that they never lose sight of the birds, and if these have need of help they are ready to render it.

All the Emperor's hawks, and those of the barons as well, have a little label attached to the leg to mark them, on which is written the names of the owner and the keeper of the bird. And in this way the hawk, when caught, is at once identified and handed over to its owner. But if not, the bird is carried to a certain baron who is styled the Bularguchi, which is as much as to say "The Keeper of Lost Property." And I tell you that whatever may be found without a known owner, whether it be a horse, or a sword, or a hawk, or what not, it is carried to that baron straightway, and he takes charge of it. And if the finder neglects to carry his trover to the baron, the latter punishes him. Likewise the loser of any article goes to the baron, and if the thing be in his hands it is immediately given up to the owner. Moreover, the said baron always pitches on the highest spot of the camp, with his banner displayed, in order that those who have lost or found anything may have no difficulty in finding their way to him. Thus nothing can be lost but it shall be incontinently found and restored.

And so the Emperor follows this road that I have mentioned, leading along in the vicinity of the Ocean Sea, which is within two days' journey of his capital city Cambaluc, and as he goes there is many a fine sight to be seen, and plenty of the very best entertainment in hawking; in fact, there is no sport in the world to equal it!

The Emperor himself is carried upon four elephants in a fine chamber made of timber, lined inside with plates of beaten gold, and outside with lions' skins, for he always travels in this way on his fowling expeditions because he is troubled with gout. He always keeps beside him a dozen of his choicest gerfalcons, and is attended by several of his barons who ride on horseback alongside. And sometimes, as they may be going along, and the Emperor from his chamber is holding discourse with the barons, one of the latter shall exclaim: "Sire! Look out for cranes!" Then the Emperor instantly has the top of his chamber thrown open, and having marked the cranes he casts one of his gerfalcons, whichever he pleases; and often the quarry is struck within his view, so that he has the most exquisite sport and diversion, there as he sits in his chamber or lies on his bed; and all the barons with him get the enjoyment of it likewise! So it is not without reason I tell you that I do not believe there ever existed in the world or ever will exist, a man with such sport and enjoyment as he has, or with such rare opportunities.

And when he has travelled till he reaches a place called Cachar Modun, there he finds his tents pitched, with the tents of his sons, and his barons, and those of his ladies and theirs, so that there shall be full ten thousand tents in all, and all fine and rich ones. And I will tell you how his own quarters are disposed. The tent in which he holds his courts is large enough to give cover easily to a thousand souls. It is pitched with its door to the south, and the barons and knights remain in waiting in it, whilst the Lord abides in another close to it on the west side. When he wishes to speak with any one he causes the person to be summoned to that other tent. Immediately behind the great tent there is a fine large chamber where the Lord sleeps; and there are also many other tents and chambers, but they are not in contact with the Great Tent as these are. The two audience-tents and the sleeping-chamber are constructed in this way. Each of the audience-tents has three poles, which are of spice-wood, and are most artfully covered with lions' skins, striped with black and white and red, so that they do not suffer from any weather. All three apartments are also covered outside with similar skins of striped lions, a substance that lasts for ever. And inside they are all lined with ermine and sable, these two being the finest and most costly furs in existence. For a robe of sable, large enough to line a mantle, is worth two thousand bezants of gold, or one thousand at least, and this kind of skin is called by the Tartars "the king of furs." The beast itself is about the size of a marten. These two furs of which I speak are applied and inlaid so exquisitely, that it is really something worth seeing. All the tent-ropes are of silk. And in short I may say that those tents, to wit the two audience-halls and the sleeping-chamber, are so costly that it is not every king could pay for them.

Round about these tents are others, also fine ones and beautifully pitched, in which are the Emperor's ladies, and the ladies of the other princes and officers. And then there are the tents for the hawks and their keepers, so that altogether the number of tents there on the plain is something wonderful. To see the many people that are thronging to and fro on every side and every day there, you would take the camp for a good big city. For you must reckon the leeches, and the astrologers, and the falconers, and all the other attendants on so great a company, and add that everybody there has his whole family with him, for such is their custom.

The Lord remains encamped there until the spring, and all that time he does nothing but go hawking round about among the cane-brakes along the lakes and rivers that abound in that region, and across fine plains on which are plenty of cranes and swans, and all sorts of other fowl. The other gentry of the camp also are never done with hunting and hawking, and every day they bring home great store of venison and feathered game of all sorts. Indeed, without having witnessed it, you would never believe what quantities of game are taken, and what marvellous sport and diversion they all have whilst they are in camp there.

There is another thing I should mention; to wit, that for twenty days' journey round the spot nobody is allowed, be he who he may, to keep hawks or hounds, though anywhere else whosoever list may keep them. And furthermore throughout all the Emperor's territories, nobody however audacious dares to hunt any of these four animals, to wit, hare, stag, buck, and roe, from the month of March to the month of October. Anybody who should do so would rue it bitterly. But those people are so obedient to their Lord's commands that even if a man were to find one of those animals asleep by the roadside he would not touch it for the world! And thus the game multiplies at such a rate that the whole country swarms with it, and the Emperor gets as much as he could desire. Beyond the term I have mentioned, however, to wit that from March to October, everybody may take these animals as he list.

You must know that the City of Cambaluc hath such a multitude of houses, and such a vast population inside the walls and outside, that it seems quite past all possibility. There is a suburb outside each of the gates, which are twelve in number; and these suburbs are so great that they contain more people than the city itself, for the suburb of one gate spreads in width till it meets the suburb of the next, whilst they extend in length some three or four miles. In those suburbs lodge the foreign merchants and travellers, of whom there are always great numbers who have come to bring presents to the Emperor, or to sell articles at Court, or because the city affords so good a mart to attract traders. There are in each of the suburbs, to a distance of a mile from the city, numerous fine hostelries for the lodgment of merchants from different parts of the world, and a special hostelry is assigned to each description of people, as if we should say there is one for the Lombards, another for the Germans, and a third for the Frenchmen. And thus there are as many good houses outside of the city as inside, without counting those that belong to the great lords and barons, which are very numerous.

You must know that it is forbidden to bury any dead body inside the city. If the body be that of an Idolater it is carried out beyond the city and suburbs to a remote place assigned for the purpose, to be burnt. And if it be of one belonging to a religion the custom of which is to bury, such as the Christian, the Saracen, or what not, it is also carried out beyond the suburbs to a distant place assigned for the purpose. And thus the city is preserved in a better and more healthy state.

Moreover, no public woman resides inside the city, but all such abide outside in the suburbs. And 'tis wonderful what a vast number of these there are for the foreigners; it is a certain fact that there are more than twenty thousand of them living by prostitution. And that so many can live in this way will show you how vast is the population.

Guards patrol the city every night in parties of thirty or forty, looking out for any persons who may be abroad at unseasonable hours, i.e. after the great bell hath stricken thrice. If they find any such person he is immediately taken to prison, and examined next morning by the proper officers. If these find him guilty of any misdemeanour they order him a proportionate beating with the stick. Under this punishment people sometimes die; but they adopt it in order to eschew bloodshed; for their Bacsis say that it is an evil thing to shed man's blood.

To this city also are brought articles of greater cost and rarity and in greater abundance of all kinds than to any other city in the world. For people of every description and from every region bring things (including all the costly wares of India, as well as the fine and precious goods of Cathay itself with its provinces), some for the sovereign, some for the court, some for the city which is so great, some for the crowds of barons and knights, some for the great hosts of the Emperor which are quartered round about; and thus between court and city the quantity brought in is endless.

As a sample, I tell you, no day in the year passes that there do not enter the city a thousand cart-loads of silk alone, from which are made quantities of cloth of silk and gold, and of other goods. And this is not to be wondered at; for in all the countries round about there is no flax, so that everything has to be made of silk. It is true, indeed, that in some parts of the country there is cotton and hemp, but not sufficient for their wants. This, however, is not of much consequence, because silk is so abundant and cheap, and is a more valuable substance than either flax or cotton.

Round about this great city of Cambaluc there are some two

hundred other cities at various distances, from which traders come to sell their goods and buy others for their lords; and all find means to make their sales and purchases, so that the traffic of the city is passing great.

Now that I have told you in detail of the splendour of this city of the Emperor's, I shall proceed to tell you of the Mint which he hath in the same city, in the which he hath his money coined and struck, as I shall relate to you. And in doing so I shall make manifest to you how it is that the Great Lord may well be able to accomplish even much more than I have told you, or am going to tell you, in this book. For, tell it how I might, you never would be satisfied that I was keeping within truth and reason!

The Emperor's Mint then is in this same City of Cambaluc, and the way it is wrought is such that you might say he hath the secret of alchemy in perfection, and you would be right! For he makes his money after this fashion.

He makes them take of the bark of a certain tree, in fact of the mulberry tree, the leaves of which are the food of the silkworms, — these trees being so numerous that whole districts are full of them. What they take is a certain fine white bast or skin which lies between the wood of the tree and the thick outer bark, and this they make into something resembling sheets of paper, but black. When these sheets have been prepared they are cut up into pieces of different sizes. The smallest of these sizes is worth a half tornesel; the next, a little larger, one tornesel; one, a little larger still, is worth half a silver groat of Venice; another a whole groat; others yet two groats, five groats, and ten groats. There is also a kind worth one bezant of gold, and others of three bezants, and so up to ten. All these pieces of paper are issued with as much solemnity and authority as if they were of pure gold or silver; and on every piece a variety of officials, whose duty it is, have to write their names, and to put their seals. And when all is prepared duly, the chief officer deputed by the Kaan smears the Seal entrusted to him with vermilion, and impresses it on the paper, so that the form of the Seal remains printed upon it in red; the money is then authentic. Any one forging it would be punished with death. And the Kaan causes every year to be made such a vast quantity of this money, which costs him nothing, that it must equal in amount all the treasure in the world.

With these pieces of paper, made as I have described, he causes all payments on his own account to be made; and he makes them to pass current universally over all his kingdoms and provinces and territories, and whithersoever his power and sovereignty extends. And nobody, however important he may think himself, dares to refuse them on pain of death. And indeed everybody takes them readily, for wheresoever a person may go throughout the Great Kaan's dominions he shall find these pieces of paper current, and shall be able to transact all sales and purchases of goods by means of them just as well as if they were coins of pure gold. And all the while they are so light that ten bezants' worth does not weigh one golden bezant.

Furthermore all merchants arriving from India or other countries, and bringing with them gold or silver or gems and pearls, are prohibited from selling to anyone but the Emperor.  He has twelve experts chosen for this business, men of shrewdness and experience in such affairs; these appraise the articles, and the Emperor then pays a liberal price for them in those pieces of paper.  The merchants accept his price readily, for in the first place they would not get so good an one from anybody else, and secondly they are paid without any delay.  And with this paper-money they can buy what they like anywhere over the Empire, whilst it is also vastly lighter to carry about on their journeys.  And it is a truth that the merchants will several times in the year bring wares to the amount of 400,000 bezants, and the Grand Sire pays for all in that paper.  So he buys such a quantity of those precious things every year that his treasure is endless, whilst all the time the money he pays away costs him nothing at all.  Moreover several times in the year proclamation is made through the city that any one who may have gold or silver or gems or pearls, by taking them to the Mint shall get a handsome price for them.  And the owners are glad to do this, because they would find no other purchaser to give so large a price.  Thus the quantity they bring in is marvellous, though those who do not choose to do so may let it alone.  Still, in this way, nearly all the valuables in the country come into the Kaan's possession.

When any of those pieces of paper are spoilt — not that they are so very flimsy neither — the owner carries them to the Mint, and by paying three per cent on the value he gets new pieces in exchange.  And if any baron, or any one else soever, hath need of gold or silver or gems or pearls in order to make plate or girdles or the like, he goes to the Mint and buys as much as he list, paying in this paper-money.

Now you must know that from this City of Cambaluc proceed many roads and highways leading to a variety of provinces, one to one province, another to another; and each road receives the name of the province to which it leads; and it is a very sensible plan.  And the messengers of the Emperor in travelling from Cambaluc, be the road whichsoever they will, find at every twenty-five miles of the journey at station which they call Yamb, or, as we should say, the "Horse-Post-House."  And at each of those stations used by the messengers there is a large and handsome building for them to put up at, in which they find all the rooms furnished with fine beds and all other necessary articles in rich silk, and where they are provided with everything they can want.  If even a king were to arrive at one of these, he would find himself well lodged.

At some of these stations, moreover, there shall be posted some four hundred horses standing ready for the use of the messengers; at others there shall be two hundred, according to the requirements, and to what the Emperor has established in each case.  At every twenty-five miles, as I said, or anyhow at every thirty miles, you find one of these stations, on all the principal highways leading to the different provincial governments; and the same is the case throughout all the chief provinces subject to the Great Kaan. Even when the messengers have to pass through a roadless tract where neither house nor hostel exists, still there the station-houses have been established just the same, excepting that the intervals are somewhat greater, and the day's journey is fixed at thirty-five to forty-five miles, instead of twenty-five to thirty. But they are provided with horses and all the other necessaries just like those we have described, so that the Emperor's messengers, come they from what region they may, find everything ready for them.

And in sooth this is a thing done on the greatest scale of magnificence that ever was seen. Never had emperor, king, or lord, such wealth as this manifests! For it is a fact that on all these posts taken together there are more than 300,000 horses kept up, specially for the use of the messengers. And the great buildings that I have mentioned are more than 10,000 in number, all richly furnished as I told you. The thing is on a scale so wonderful and costly that it is hard to bring oneself to describe it.

But now I will tell you another thing that I had forgotten, but which ought to be told whilst I am on this subject. You must know that by the Great Kaan's orders there has been established between those post-houses, at every interval of three miles, a little fort with some forty houses round about it, in which dwell the people who act as the Emperor's foot-runners. Every one of those runners wears a great wide belt, set all over with bells, so that as they run the three miles from post to post their bells are heard jingling a long way off. And thus on reaching the post the runner finds another man similarly equipt, and all ready to take his place, who instantly takes over whatsoever he has in charge, and with it receives a slip of paper from the clerk who is always at hand for the purpose; and so the new man sets off and runs his three miles. At the next station he finds his relief ready in like manner; and so the post proceeds, with a change at every three miles. And in this way the Emperor, who has an immense number of these runners, receives despatches with news from places ten days' journey off in one day and night; or, if need be, news from a hundred days off in ten days and nights; and that is no small matter! In fact in the fruit season many a time fruit shall be gathered one morning in Cambaluc, and the evening of the next day it shall reach the Great Kaan at Chandu, a distance of ten days' journey. The clerk at each of the posts notes the time of each courier's arrival and departure; and there are often other officers whose business it is to make monthly visitations of all the posts, and to punish those runners who have been slack in their work. The Emperor exempts these men from all tribute, and pays them besides.

Moreover, there are also at those stations other men equipt similarly with girdles hung with bells, who are employed for expresses when there is a call for great haste in sending despatches to any governor of a province, or to give news when any baron has revolted, or in other such emergencies, and these men travel a good two hundred or two hundred and fifty miles in the day, and as much in the night.

I'll tell you how it stands. They take a horse from those at the station which are standing ready saddled, all fresh and in wind, and mount and go at full speed, as hard as they can ride in fact. And when those at the next post hear the bells they get ready another horse and a man equipt in the same way, and he takes over the letter or whatever it be, and is off full-speed to the third station, where again a fresh horse is found all ready, and so the despatch speeds along from post to post, always at full gallop with regular change of horses. And the speed at which they go is marvellous. By night, however, they cannot go so fast as by day, because they have to be accompanied by footmen with torches, who could not keep up with them at full speed.

Those men are highly prized; and they could never do it did they not bind hard the stomach, chest, and head with strong bands. And each of them carries with him a gerfalcon tablet, in sign that he is bound on an urgent express; so that if perchance his horse break down, or he meet with other mishap, whomsoever he may fall in with on the road, he is empowered to make him dismount and give up his horse. Nobody dares refuse in such a case; so that the courier hath always a good fresh nag to carry him.

Now all these numbers of post-horses cost the Emperor nothing at all; and I will tell you the how and the why. Every city, or village, or hamlet that stands near one of those post-stations has a fixed demand made on it for as many horses as it can supply, and these it must furnish to the post. And in this way are provided all the posts of the cities, as well as the towns and villages round about them; only in uninhabited tracts the horses are furnished at the expense of the Emperor himself.

It is a fact that all over the country of Cathay there is a kind of black stones existing in beds in the mountains, which they dig out and burn like firewood. If you supply the fire with them at night, and see that they are well kindled, you will find them still alight in the morning; and they make such capital fuel that no other is used throughout the country. It is true that they have plenty of wood also, but they do not burn it, because those stones burn better and cost less.

Moreover with that vast number of people, and the number of hot-baths that they maintain — for every one has such a bath at least three times a week, and in winter if possible every day, whilst every nobleman and man of wealth has a private bath for his own use — the wood would not suffice for the purpose.

You must know that when the Emperor sees that corn is cheap and abundant, he buys up large quantities, and has it stored in all his provinces in great granaries, where it is so well looked after that it will keep for three or four years.

And this applies, let me tell you, to all kinds of corn, whether wheat, barley, millet, rice, panic, or what not, and when there is any scarcity of a particular kind of corn he causes that to be issued. And if the price of the corn is at one bezant the measure, he lets them have it at a bezant for four measures, or at whatever price will produce general cheapness; and every one can have food in this way. And by this providence of the Emperor's, his people can never suffer from dearth. He does the same over his whole Empire; causing these supplies to be stored everywhere according to calculation of the wants and necessities of the people.

[tr. Sir Henry Yule]

# JEAN FROISSART

During the early Middle Ages monastic chroniclers wrote nearly all the history that was recorded. As the monasteries lost their zeal and initiative, historiography passed first to the bishops and their staffs, as with the author of the philosophical chronicle *The Two Cities* (Bishop Otto of Freising, 12th cent.) and then to the friars. Nobility who wished to exalt their family lines or who took pride in their conquests encouraged these writers of church histories; for example, the Norman Conquest was followed by a plethora of Anglo-Norman chronicles written by churchmen who glorified the deeds of the lay lords.

Secular historiography began with the Crusades and the rise of trade. Of numerous fine accounts of campaigns in the East, the judicious, honest, and admirably informed memoirs of an active campaigner, Geoffrey de Villehardouin (A.D. 1212) stand out. Jean, Sire de Joinville, Senechal de Campagne, looking back over eighty years of active life, wrote memoirs of his companion in arms, Louis IX, King of France, that resulted in the canonization of his subject by the Church and in the hearts of the populace. The ubiquitous friars soon forgot St. Francis' injunctions against books and wrote down the history they gleaned in their wanderings; the chronicler Salimbene had an all-seeing eye, and he recorded what he saw in Italy and France, but always with a view to exaltation of his order and the Pope against the pretensions of the Ghibellines and their "devil" leader, Frederick II. These authors may have been highly observant, truthful, and even entertaining. But they wrote history for a pur-pose, as Augustine and Orosius long ago wrote history to defend the Church against the charges of pagans.

Froissart wrote history to entertain his readers, without political or moral purpose. To be sure, in his pages his patrons were always models of virtue, and he always glorified the party or state to which he owed his keep. But he was a journalist, a reporter, much like the ancient Herodotus, who captured the look of things, the external show, in entertaining and often exciting prose. He relies on word of mouth, not documentary evidence. He records the purple pag-eantry, not the suffering of the populace. He accepts the bountiful life without complaint. The conception of the Middle Ages that dominated the minds of nineteenth century romanticists was dictated more by Froissart than by any other writer; he was the favorite of Walter Scott, whose novels retold Froissart for all Europe, and the recent popular movie version of *Henry V* is, at least in its battle scenes, more Froissart than Shakespeare.

Jean Froissart was born near Valenciennes, in the heart of Flemish manufacture, about 1338, just when the Hundred Years' War was precipitated by Edward III's alliance with the Flemings. In 1361, bundling a sheaf of poetry and romance that he had written under his arm, he made his way to Westminster, where Queen Philippa, who came from his own province of Hainaut, gave him a place in court and urged him to write history. There he especially cultivated the French prisoners from the Battle of Poitiers (1356) who were being held as hostages. In 1365 he was in Scotland, in 1367 in Guienne and then in Italy, where he met Petrarch. When Queen Philippa died (1369) he returned to Hainaut. The Queen's friends and relatives — Robert of Namur, Guy of Blois, Wenceslas of Brabant, and Aubert, Duke of Hainaut — continued the patronage of his historical writing. In 1373, he was named curate of Estines — a post that gave him leisure for composition. The early part of the chronicles, from 1325 to 1356, he adapted largely from his fellow-townsman, Jean le Bel. Thereafter, his observations are almost entirely his own. After fifteen years, his restless curiosity led him again to travel, and he made his way south through Provence, stopping at Orthez with the renowned Gaston Phoebus, Count of Foix, and at Avignon, where the humanists were breaking ground. He was back in Paris about 1390. In 1395 he returned to England, to the court of Richard II. Thereafter, trace of his movements is lost, but since the fourth book of his *Chronicles* halts abruptly, it is believed that he died at Chimay in Hainaut about 1410. His colorful life, which ended in complete obscurity, spans years almost identical with Chaucer's.

Such biographical details, probably unimportant in a writer of another type, show not only how the secular lords now patronized literature, but how the world was breaking open to travel and an international society. Of the two selections that follow, the second has been abridged.

## CHRONICLES OF ENGLAND, FRANCE, AND SPAIN

### Jean Froissart (A.D. 1337?–1410?)

#### THE BATTLE OF CRECY

Two battalions of the marshals came, on a Friday in the afternoon, to where the King was; and they fixed their quarters, all three together, near Crecy in Ponthieu.

The King of England, who had been informed that the King of France was following him in order to give him battle, said to his people: "Let us post ourselves here; for we will not go farther before we have seen our enemies. I have good reason to wait for them on this spot as I am now upon the lawful inheritance of my lady-mother, which was given her as her marriage-portion; and I am resolved to defend it against my adversary, Philippe de Valois."

On account of his not having more than an eighth part of the forces which the King of France had, his marshals fixed up the most advantageous situation; and the army went and took possession of it. He then sent his scouts toward Abbeville, to learn if the King of France meant to take the field this Friday, but they returned and said they saw no appearance of it; upon which, he dismissed his men to their quarters with orders to be in readiness betimes in the morning and to assemble in the same place.

The King of France remained all Friday in Abbeville, waiting for more troops. He sent his marshals, the Lord of St. Venant and Lord Charles of Montmorency, out of Abbeville to examine the country and get some certain intelligence of the English. They returned about vespers with information that the English were encamped on the plain.

That night the King of France entertained at supper in Abbeville all the princes and chief lords. There was much conversation relative to war; and the King intreated them, after supper, that they would always remain in friendship with each other, that they would be friends without jealousy and courteous without pride. The King was still expecting the Earl of Savoy, who ought to have been there with a thousand lances, as he had been well paid for them at Troyes in Champaign, three months in advance.

The King of England, as I have mentioned before, encamped this Friday in the plain, for he found the country abounding in provisions; but, if they should have failed, he had plenty in the carriages which attended on him. The army set about furbishing and repairing their armour; and the King gave a supper that evening to the earls and barons of his army, where they made good cheer. On their taking leave, the King remained alone with the lords of his bedchamber: he retired into his oratory and, falling on his knees before the altar, prayed to God that, if he should combat his enemies on the morrow, he might come off with honor. About midnight he went to his bed; and, rising early the next day, he and the Prince of Wales heard mass and communicated. The greater part of his army did the same, confessed, and made proper preparations.

After mass, the King ordered his men to arm themselves and assemble on the ground he had before fixed on. He had inclosed a large park near a wood on the rear of his army, in which he placed all his baggage-waggons and horses; and this park had but one entrance. His men at arms and archers remained on foot.

The King afterwards ordered, through his constable and his two marshals, that the army should be divided into three battalions. In the first, he placed the young Prince of Wales, and with him the Earls of Warwick and Oxford, Sir Godfrey de Harcourt, the Lord Reginald Cobham, Lord Thomas Holland, Lord Stafford, Lord Mauley, the Lord Delaware, Sir John Chandos, Lord Bartholomew Burgherst, Lord Robert Neville, Lord Thomas Clifford, the Lord Bourchier, the Lord Latimer, and many other knights and squires whom I cannot name. There might be, in this first division, about eight hundred men at arms, two thousand archers, and a thousand Welchmen. They advanced in regular order to their ground, each lord under his banner and pennon and in the centre of his men.

In the second battalion were the Earl of Northampton, the Earl of

Arundel, the Lords Roos, Willoughby, Baffet, Saint-Albans, Sir Lewis Tufton, Lord Multon, the Lord Lascels, and many others amounting in the whole to about eight hundred men at arms and twelve hundred archers.

The third battalion was commanded by the King, and was composed of about seven hundred men at arms and two thousand archers.

The King then mounted a small palfry, having a white wand in his hand, and attended by his two marshals on each side of him. He rode a foot's pace through all the ranks, encouraging and intreating the army that they would guard his honor and defend his right. He spoke this so sweetly and with such a cheerful countenance that all who had been dispirited were directly comforted by seeing and hearing him.

When he had thus visited all the battalions, it was near ten o'clock; he retired to his own division and ordered them all to eat heartily and drink a glass after. They ate and drank at their ease; and, having packed up pots, barrels, &c. in the carts, they returned to their battalions, according to the marshals' orders, and seated themselves on the ground, placing their helmets and bows before them, that they might be the fresher when their enemies should arrive.

That same Saturday the King of France rose betimes and heard mass in the monastery of St. Peter's in Abbeville, where he was lodged. Having ordered his army to do the same, he left that town after sunrise. When he had marched about two leagues from Abbeville and was approaching the enemy, he was advised to form his army in order of battle and to let those on foot march forward, that they might not be trampled on by the horses. The king, upon this, sent off four knights, the Lord Moyne of Bastleberg, the Lord of Noyers, the Lord of Beaujeu, and the Lord of Aubigny, who rode so near to the English that they could clearly distinguish their position. The English plainly perceived they were come to reconnoitre them; however, they took no notice of it, but suffered them to return unmolested. When the King of France saw them coming back, he halted his army; and the knights, pushing through the crowds, came near the king, who said to them, "My lords, what news?" They looked at each other, without opening their mouths: for neither chose to speak first. At last, the king addressed himself to the Lord Moyne, who was attached to the King of Bohemia and had performed very many gallant deeds so that he was esteemed one of the most valiant knights in Christendom. The Lord Moyne said, "Sir, I will speak, since it pleases you to order me, but under the correction of my companions. We have advanced far enough to reconnoitre your enemies. Know, then, that they are drawn up in three battalions and are waiting for you. I would advise for my part (submitting, however, to better counsel) that you halt your army here and quarter them for the night; for before the rear shall come up and the army be properly drawn out it will be very late, your men will be tired and in disorder, whilst they will find your enemies fresh and properly arrayed. On the morrow, you may draw up your army more at your ease, and may reconnoitre at leisure on what part it will be most advantageous to begin the attack; for, be assured, they will wait for you."

The King commanded that it should be so done; and the two marshals rode, one towards the front, and the other to the rear, crying out, "Halt banners, in the name of God and St. Denis." Those that were in the front halted; but those behind said they would not halt until they were as forward as the front. When the front perceived the rear pressing on, they pushed forward; and neither the King nor the marshals could stop them, but they marched on without any order until they came in sight of their enemies. As soon as the foremost rank saw them they fell back at once in great disorder, which alarmed those in the rear, who thought they had been fighting. There was then space and room enough for them to have passed forward, had they been willing so to do; some did so, but others remained shy.

All the roads between Abbeville and Crecy were covered with common people, who, when they were come within three leagues of their enemies, drew their swords, bawling out, "Kill, kill"; and with them were many great lords that were eager to make shew of their courage. There is no man, unless he had been present, that can imagine or describe truly the confusion of that day; especially the bad management and disorder of the French, whose troops were out of number. What I know, and shall relate in this book, I have learnt chiefly from the English, who had well observed the confusion they were in, and from those attached to Sir John of Hainault, who was always near the person of the King of France.

The English, who were drawn up in three divisions and seated on the ground, on seeing their enemies advance, rose undauntedly up and fell into their ranks. That of the Prince was the first to do so, whose archers were formed in the manner of a portcullis, or harrow, and the men at arms in the rear.

The Earls of Northhampton and Arundel, who commanded the second division, had posted themselves in good order on his wing to assist and succour the Prince if necessary.

You must know that these kings, dukes, earls, barons and lords of France did not advance in any regular order, but one after the other or any way most pleasing to themselves. As soon as the King of France came in sight of the English his blood began to boil and he cried out to his marshals, "Order the Genoese forward, and begin the battle, in the name of God and St. Denis."

There were about fifteen thousand Genoese crossbowmen; but they were quite fatigued, having marched on foot that day six leagues, completely armed and with their cross-bows. They told the constable they were not in a fit condition to do any great things that day in battle. The Earl of Alençon, hearing this, said, "This is what one gets by employing such scoundrels, who fall off when there is any need for them."

During this time a heavy rain fell, accompanied by thunder and a very terrible eclipse of the sun; and before this rain a great flight of crows hovered in the air over all those battalions, making a loud noise. Shortly afterwards it cleared up, and the sun shone very bright; but the Frenchmen had it in their faces, and the English in their backs.

When the Genoese were somewhat in order, and approached the English, they set up a loud shout in order to frighten them; but they remained quite still and did not seem to attend to it. They then set up a second shout and advanced a little forward; but the English never moved. They hooted a third time, advancing with their cross-bows presented, and began to shoot. The English archers then advanced one step forward, and shot their arrows with such force and quickness that it seemed as if it snowed.

When the Genoese felt these arrows, which pierced their arms, heads, and through their armour, some of them cut the strings of their cross-bows, others flung them on the ground, and all turned about and retreated, quite discomfited. The French had a large body of men at arms on horseback, richly dressed, to support the Genoese.

The King of France, seeing them thus fall back, cried out, "Kill me those scoundrels; for they stop up our road, without any reason." You would then have seen the above-mentioned men at arms lay about them, killing all they could of these runaways.

The English continued shooting as vigorously and quickly as before; some of their arrows fell among the horsemen, who were sumptuously equipped, and, killing and wounding many, made them caper and fall among the Genoese, so that they were in such confusion they could never rally again. In the English army there were some Cornish and Welshmen on foot who had armed themselves with large knives; these, advancing through the ranks of the men at arms and archers, who made way for them, came upon the French when they were in this danger and, falling upon earls, barons, knights and squires, slew many, at which the King of England was afterwards much exasperated.

The valiant King of Bohemia was slain there. He was called Charles of Luxembourg; for he was the son of the gallant King and Emperor, Henry of Luxembourg. Having heard the order of the battle, he inquired where his son, the Lord Charles, was. His attendants answered that they did not know, but believed he was fighting. The King said to them, "Gentlemen, you are all my people, my friends and brethren at arms this day; therefore, as I am blind, I request of you to lead me so far into the engagement that I may strike one stroke with my sword." The knights replied, they would directly lead him forward; and, in order that they might not lose him in the crowd, they fastened all the reins of their horses together, and put the King at their head, that he might gratify his wish, and advanced towards the enemy.

The Lord Charles of Bohemia, who already signed his name as King of Germany and bore the arms, had come in good order to the engagement; but when he perceived that it was likely to turn out against the French he departed, and I do not well know what road he took.

The King, his father, had rode in among the enemy and made good use of his sword; for he and his companions had fought most gallantly. They had advanced so far that they were all slain; and on the morrow they were found on the ground, with their horses all tied together.

The Earl of Alençon advanced in regular order upon the English to fight with them, as did the Earl of Flanders in another part. These two lords with their detachments, coasting, as it were, the archers, came to the Prince's battalion, where they fought valiantly for a length of time. The King of France was eager to march to the place where he saw their banners displayed, but there was a hedge of archers before him.

He had that day made a present of a handsome black horse to Sir John of Hainault, who had mounted on it a knight of his called Sir John de Fusselles, that bore his banner: which horse ran off with him and forced his way through the English army and, when about to return, stumbled and fell into a ditch and severely wounded him. He would have been dead if his page had not followed him round the battalions and found him unable to rise. He had not, however, any other hindrance than from his horse; for the English did not quit the ranks that day to make prisoners. The page alighted and raised him up; but he did not return the way he came, as he would have found it difficult from the crowd.

This battle, which was fought on the Saturday between La Broyes and Crecy, was very murderous and cruel; and many gallant deeds of arms were performed that were never known.

Towards evening many knights and squires of the French had lost their masters; they wandered up and down the plain, attacking the English in small parties. They were soon destroyed, for the English had determined that day to give no quarter or hear of ransom from any one.

Early in the day some French, Germans, and Savoyards had broken through the archers of the Prince's battalion and had engaged with the men at arms; upon which the second battalion came to his aid. And it was time, for otherwise he would have been hard pressed. The first division, seeing the danger they were in, sent a knight in great haste to the King of England, who was posted upon an eminence near a windmill. On the knight's arrival, he said, "Sir, the Earl of Warwick, the Lord Stafford, the Lord Reginald Cobham, and the others who are about your son are vigorously attacked by the French; and they intreat that you would come to their assistance with your battalion, for, if their numbers should increase, they fear he will have too much to do."

The King replied: "Is my son dead, unhorsed, or so badly wounded that he cannot support himself?" "Nothing of the sort, thank God," rejoined the knight; "but he is in so hot an engagement that he has great need of your help." The King answered, "Now, Sir Thomas, return back to those that sent you and tell them from me not to send again for me this day or expect that I shall come, let what will happen, as long as my son has life; and say that I command them to let the boy win his spurs; for I am determined, if it please God, that all the glory and honor of this day shall be given to him and to those into whose care I have intrusted him."

The knight returned to his lords and related the King's answer, which mightily encouraged them, and made them repent they had ever sent such a message.

It is a certain fact that Sir Godfrey de Harcourt, who was in the Prince's battalion, having been told by some of the English that they had seen the banner of his brother engaged in the battle against him, was exceedingly anxious to save him; but he was too late, for he was left dead on the field, and so was the Earl of Aumarle, his nephew.

On the other hand, the Earls of Alençon and of Flanders were fighting lustily under their banners and with their own people; but they could not resist the force of the English and were there slain, as well as many other knights and squires that were attending on or accompanying them.

The Earl of Blois, nephew to the King of France, and the Duke of Lorraine, his brother-in-law, with their troops, made a gallant defence; but they were surrounded by a troop of English and Welch and slain in spite of their prowess. The Earl of St. Pol and the Earl of Auxerre were also killed, as well as many others.

Late after vespers the King of France had not more about him than sixty men, every one included. Sir John of Hainault, who was of the number, had once remounted the King; for his horse had been killed under him by an arrow. He said to the King, "Sir, retreat whilst you have an opportunity, and do not expose yourself so simply; if you have lost this battle, another time you will be the conqueror." After he had said this, he took the bridle of the King's horse and led him off by force; for he had before intreated of him to retire.

The King rode on until he came to the castle of La Broyes, where he found the gates shut, for it was very dark. The King ordered the governor of it to be summoned. He came upon the battlements and asked who it was that called at such an hour? The King answered, "Open, open, governor; it is the fortune of France." The governor, hearing the King's voice, immediately descended, opened the gate, and let down the bridge. The King and his company entered the castle; but he had only with him five barons, Sir John of Hainault, the Lord Charles of Montmorency, the Lord of Beaujeu, the Lord of Aubigny, and the Lord of Montfort.

The King would not bury himself in such a place as that, but, having taken some refreshments, set out again with his attendants about midnight and rode on under the direction of guides who were well acquainted with the country until, about daybreak, he came to Amiens, where he halted.

This Saturday the English never quitted their ranks in pursuit of any one, but remained on the field, guarding their position and defending themselves against all who attacked them. The battle was ended at the hour of vespers.

When on this Saturday night the English heard no more hooting or shouting nor any more crying out to particular lords or their banners, they looked upon the field as their own and their enemies as beaten.

They made great fires and lighted torches because of the obscurity of the night. King Edward then came down from his post, who all that day had not put on his helmet and with his whole battalion advanced to the Prince of Wales, whom he embraced in his arms and kissed, and said, "Sweet son, God give you good perseverance; you are my son, for most loyally have you acquitted yourself this day. You are worthy to be a sovereign." The Prince bowed down very low and humbled himself, giving all honour to the King his father.

The English during the night made frequent thanksgivings to the Lord for the happy issue of the day, and without rioting; for the King had forbidden all riot or noise.

On the Sunday morning there was so great a fog that one could scarcely see the distance of half an acre. The King ordered a detachment from the army, under the command of the two marshals, consisting of about five hundred lances and two thousand archers, to make an excursion and see if there were any bodies of French collected together.

The quota of troops from Rouen and Beauvais had this Sunday morning left Abbeville and St. Ricquier in Ponthieu to join the French army, and were ignorant of the defeat of the preceding evening; they met this detachment and, thinking they must be French, hastened to join them.

As soon as the English found who they were they fell upon them, and there was a sharp engagement; but the French soon turned their backs and fled in great disorder. There were slain in this flight in the open fields, under hedges and bushes, upwards of seven thousand; and had it been clear weather, not one soul would have escaped.

A little time afterwards, this same party fell in with the Archbishop of Rouen and the great Prior of France, who were also ignorant of the discomfiture of the French; for they had been informed that the King was not to fight before Sunday. Here began a fresh battle; for those two lords were well attended by good men at arms. However, they could not withstand the English, but were almost all slain, with the two chiefs who commanded them, very few escaping.

In the course of the morning, the English found many Frenchmen who had lost their road on the Saturday and had lain in the open fields, not knowing what was become of the King or their own leaders. The English put to the sword all they met; and it has been assured to me for fact that of foot soldiers sent from the cities, towns and municipalities, there were slain this Sunday morning four times as many as in the battle of the Saturday.

This detachment, which had been sent to look after the French, returned as the King was coming from mass and related to him all that they had seen and met with. After he had been assured by them that there was not any appearance of the French collecting another army, he sent to have the numbers and condition of the dead examined.

He ordered on this business, Lord Reginald Cobham, Lord Stafford, and three heralds to examine their arms, and two secretaries to write down all the names. They took much pains to examine all the dead and were the whole day in the field of battle, not returning but just as the King was sitting down to supper. They made to him a very circumstantial report of all they had observed and said they had found eighty banners, the bodies of eleven princes, twelve hundred knights, and about thirty thousand common men.

The English halted there that day, and on the Monday morning prepared to march off. The King ordered the bodies of the principal knights to be taken from the ground and carried to the monastery of Montenay, which was hard by, there to be interred in consecrated ground. He had it proclaimed in the neighborhood that he should grant a truce for three days in order that the dead might be buried. He then marched on.

### FROISSART JOURNEYS TO FOIX

I have been a considerable time without speaking of the affairs of distant countries. Those nearer home were at the moment so fresh in my memory and so much more agreeable that I have delayed mentioning others. Such valiant men, however, as were desirous of advancing themselves, whether in Castille, Portugal, Gascony, Rouergue, Quercy, Limousin, or in Bigorre, did not remain idle, but employed themselves underhand against each other in the wish to perform deeds of arms that might surprise and conquer towns, castles, or fortresses. And for this reason I, Sir John Froissart, having undertaken to indite and chronicle this history at the request and pleasure of the high and renowned prince, Guy de Châtillon, Count of Blois, Lord of Avesnes, Beauvois, Estonnehonne, de la Geude, my good and sovereign master and lord, considered in myself that grand deeds of arms would not fall out for a long space of time in the marches of Picardy and the country of Flanders, since there was peace in those parts; and it was very tiresome to me to be idle, for I well know that when the time shall come when I shall be dead and rotten this grand and noble history will be in much fashion, and all noble and valiant persons will take pleasure in it and gain from it augmentation of profit. And moreover, since I had, God be thanked, sense and memory and a good collection of all past things with a clear understanding to conceive all the facts of which I should be informed touching my principal matters, and since I was of an age and constitution of body and fit to encounter difficulties, I determined not to delay pursuing my subject. And in order to know the truth of distant transactions, without sending upon the enquiry any other in place of myself, I took an opportunity of visiting that high and redoubted Prince Gaston Phoebus Count de Foix and de Béarn; for I well knew that if I were so fortunate as to be admitted into his household and to remain there in quiet, I could not choose a situation more proper to learn the truth of every event, as numbers of foreign knights and squires assembled there from all countries, attracted by his high birth and gentility.  It fell out just as I had imagined.

I told this my intention to my very renowned lord, the Count de Blois, and also the journey I wished to undertake, who gave me letters of recommendation to the Count de Foix.  I began my journey, inquiring on all sides for news, and through the grace of God continued it, without peril or hurt, until I arrived at the Count's residence, at Orthez in Béarn, on St. Catherine's day in the year of grace 1388.

The Count de Foix as soon as he saw me gave me a hearty welcome, adding with a smile and in good French that he was well acquainted with me, though he had never seen me before, but he had frequently heard me spoken of.  He retained me in his household and, by means of the letters which I had brought, gave me full liberty to act as I pleased as long as I should wish to remain with him.  I there learnt the greater part of those events which had happened in the kingdoms of Castille, Portugal, Navarre, Arragon, even in England, in the Bourbonnois, and every thing concerning the whole of Gascony.  He himself, when I put any question to him, answered it most readily, saying that the history I was employed on would in times to come be more sought after than any other; "because," added he, "my fair Sir, more gallant deeds of arms have been performed within these last fifty years, and more wonderful things have happened, than for three hundred years before."

Between the county of Foix and Béarn lies the county of Bigorre, which belongs to France, and is bounded on one side by the Toulousain and the other by Comminges and Béarn.  In this country of Bigorre is situated the strong castle of Lourde, which has always been regarded as English since the country was given up to the King of England and the Prince, as part of the ransom for King John of France, according to the treaty of peace made at Bretigny near Chartres and afterwards ratified at Calais, as it has already been mentioned in the former part of this history.

When the Prince of Wales left England to take possession of the duchy of Aquitaine (which the King his father had given to him to hold as a fief and inheritance under him, in which were two archbishoprics and twenty-two bishoprics), accompanied by the Princess of Wales, they resided at Bourdeaux about a year.  They were entreated by John Count d'Armagnac to come to the handsome city of Tarbes, in the county of Bigorre, to see and visit that part of the country, which the Prince had never yet done.

The Count d'Armagnac imagined that the Count de Foix would pay his respects to the Prince and Princess during the time they were in Bigorre; and, as he was indebted to him two hundred and fifty thousand francs for his ransom, he thought he would try to prevail on them to request the Count de Foix to release him from a part, if not the whole of it. The Count d'Armagnac managed so well that the Prince and Princess of Wales came with their court, which at that time was very numerous and splendid, into Bigorre, and fixed their residence at Tarbes.

Tarbes is a handsome town, situated in a champaign country among rich vineyards; there is a town, a city, and a castle, all separated from each other and inclosed with gates, walls, and towers. The beautiful river Lisse, which rises in the mountains of Béarn and Catalonia and is as clear as rock-water, runs through and divides the town. Five leagues from thence is situated the town of Morlans, in the county of Foix, at the entrance into Béarn and under a mountain. Six leagues distant from Tarbes is the town of Pau, which belongs also to the Count de Foix. During the time the Prince and Princess were at Tarbes, the Count was in his town of Pau, erecting a handsome castle adjoining the outskirts of the town and on the river Gave.

As soon as he was informed of the arrival of the Prince and Princess at Tarbes, he made his preparations and visited them in great state, accompanied by upwards of six hundred horse and sixty knights. They were much pleased at his visit and entertained him handsomely as he was well deserving of it, and the Princess paid him the most engaging attentions. The Count d'Armagnac and the Lord d'Albreth were present, and the Prince was entreated to request the Count de Foix to release the Count from all or part of what he was indebted to him for his ransom.

The Prince being a prudent as well as a valiant man, having considered a while, said he would not do so, and added: "Count d'Armagnac, you were made prisoner by fair deeds of arms and in open battle; you put our cousin the Count de Foix, his person and his men, to the hazard of the fight; and, if fortune has been favourable to him and adverse to you, he ought not to fare the worse for it. Neither my lord and father nor myself would have thanked you if you had entreated us to give back what we had honourably and fortunately won at the battle of Poitiers, for which we return thanks to the Lord God."

The Count d'Armagnac, on hearing this, was quite thunderstruck; and, notwithstanding he had failed in his expectations, he made a similar request to the Princess, who cheerfully entreated the Count de Foix to grant her a boon. "Madame," replied the Count, "I am but a small gentleman, and an insignificant bachelor; therefore, I cannot make large gifts. But, if the boon you request do not exceed sixty thousand francs, I grant it." The Princess was anxious to gain the whole, but the Count, being a wary man, paid much attention to all his personal affairs; besides, he suspected this boon regarded the ransom of the Count d'Armagnac. He therefore continued, "Madam, for a poor knight like me, who am building towns and castles, the gift I offer you ought to suffice."

When the Princess found she could not gain more, she said, "Count de Foix, I request and entreat you would forgive the Count d'Armagnac." "Madame," answered the Count, "I ought to comply with your request. I have said that if the boon you solicited did not exceed sixty thousand francs, I would grant it. The Count d'Armagnac owes me two hundred and fifty thousand, and at your entreaty I give you sixty thousand of them." Thus ended the matter; and the Count d'Armagnac, by the Princess's entreaty, gained sixty thousand francs. The Count de Foix, shortly afterwards, returned to his own country.

At the time I undertook my journey to visit the Count de Foix, reflecting on the diversity of countries I had never seen, I set out from Carcassone, leaving the road to Toulouse on the right hand, and came to Monteroral, then to Tonges, then to Belle, then to the first town in the county of Foix; from thence to Maisieres, to the castle of Sauredun, then to the handsome city of Pamiers, which belongs to the Count de Foix, where I halted, to wait for company that were going to Béarn, where the Count resided.

I remained in the city of Pamiers three days. It is a very delightful place, seated among fine vineyards and surrounded by a clear and broad river called the Liege. Accidentally, a knight attached to the Count de Foix, called Sir Espaign du Lyon, came thither on his return from Avignon. He was a prudent and valiant knight, handsome in person, and about fifty years of age. I introduced myself to his company, as he had a great desire to know what was doing in France. We were six days on the road travelling to Orthez. As we journeyed, the knight, after saying his orisons, conversed the greater part of the day with me, asking for news; and when I put any questions to him, he very willingly answered them. On our departure from Pamiers we crossed the mountain of Cesse, which is difficult of ascent, and passed near the town and castle of Ortingas, which belongs to the King of France, but did not enter it. We went to dine at a castle of the Count de Foix, half a league further, called Carlat, seated on a high mountain.

After dinner the knight said: "Let us ride gently; we have but two leagues of this country (which are equal to three of France) to our lodging." "Willingly," answered I. "Now," said the knight, "we have this day passed the castle of Ortingas, the garrison of which did great mischief to all this part of the country. Peter d'Anchin has possession of it. He took it by surprise, and has gained sixty thousand francs from France."

"How did he get so much?" said I. "I will tell you," replied the knight. "On the feast of Our Lady, the middle of August, a fair is holden, where all the country assemble, and there is much merchandise brought thither during that time. Peter d'Anchin and his companions of the garrison of Lourde had long wanted to gain this town and castle, but could not devise the means. They had, however, in the beginning of May, sent two of their men of very simple outward appearance to seek for service in the town; they soon found masters, who were so well satisfied with them that they went in and out of the town whenever they pleased, without any one having the smallest suspicion of them.

"When mid-August arrived, the town was filled with foreign merchants from Foix, Béarn and France, and, you know, when merchants meet after any considerable absence, they are accustomed to drink plentifully together to renew their acquaintance, so that the houses of the masters of these two servants were quite filled, where they drank largely, and their landlords with them. At midnight Peter d'Anchin and his company advanced towards Ortingas and hid themselves and horses in the wood through which we passed. He sent six varlets with two ladders to the town, who, having crossed the ditches where they had been told was the shallowest place, fixed their ladders against the walls. The two pretended servants, who were in waiting, assisted them (whilst their masters were seated at table) to mount the walls. They were no sooner up than one of the servants conducted their companions towards the gate where only two men guarded the keys. He then said to them, 'Do you remain here, and not stir until you shall hear me whistle; then sally forth and slay the guards. I am well acquainted with the keys, having more than seven times guarded the gate with my master.'

"As he had planned so did they execute, and hid themselves well. He then advanced to the gate and, having listened, found the watch drinking; he called to them by their names, for he was well acquainted with them, and said, 'Open the door. I bring you the best wine you ever tasted, which my master sends you that you may watch the better.' Those who knew the varlet imagined he was speaking truth and opened the door of the guard-room; upon this, he whistled, and his companions sallied forth and pushed between the door so that they could not shut it again. The guards were thus caught cunningly and so quietly slain that no one knew any thing of it. They then took the keys and went to the gate, which they opened, and let down the draw-bridge so gently it was not heard. This done, they sounded a horn with one blast only, which those in ambuscade hearing, they mounted their horses and came full gallop over the bridge into the town, where they took all its inhabitants either at table or in their beds.

"Thus was Ortingas taken by Peter d'Anchin of Bigorre and his companions in Lourde."

I then asked the knight, "But how did they gain the castle?" "I will tell you," said Sir Espaign du Lyon. "At the time the town was taken, by ill luck the governor was absent, supping with some merchants from Carcassone, so that he was made prisoner; and on the morrow Peter d'Anchin had him brought before the castle, wherein were his wife and children, whom he frightened by declaring he would order the governor's head to be struck off, if they did not enter into a treaty to deliver up the castle. It was concluded that if his lady would surrender, the governor should be given up to her, with permission to march unmolested away with every thing that belonged to them. The lady, who found herself in such a critical situation through love to him who could not now defend her, in order to recover her husband and to avoid greater dangers, surrendered the castle. Then the governor, his wife and children set out with all that belonged to them and went to Pamiers. By this means, Peter d'Anchin captured the town and castle of Ortingas; and when they entered the place, he and his companions gained thirty thousand francs, as well in merchandise which they found there as in good French prisoners. All those who were from the county of Foix or Béarn received their liberty, with their goods untouched.

"Peter d'Anchin held Ortingas for full five years; and he and his garrison made frequent excursions as far as the gates of Carcassone, which is sixteen long leagues distant, greatly ruining the country, as well by the ransoms of towns which compounded as by the pillage they made.

"During the time Peter d'Anchin garrisoned Ortingas, some of his companions made a sally, being desirous of gain, and came to a castle a good league off called Le Paillier, of which Raymond du Paillier, a French knight, was the lord. They this time accomplished their enterprise, having before attempted it in vain; and by means of a scalado they took the castle, the knight and his lady in bed. They kept possession of it, allowing the lady and the children to depart, but detained the knight four months in his own castle until he had paid four thousand francs for his ransom. In short, after they had sufficiently harrassed the country, they sold these two castles, Ortingas and Le Paillier, for eight thousand francs, and then retired to Lourde, their principal garrison. Such feats of arms and adventures were these companions daily practicing.

"It happened likewise at this time that a very able man at arms, one of the garrison of Lourde, a Gascon, called le Mengeant de Sainte Basile, set out from Lourde with twenty-nine others and rode towards the Toulousain and the Albigeois, seeking adventures. His wishes were to surprise the castle of Penne in the Albigeois, which he was nearly doing, but failed. When he found he was disappointed, he rode up to the gate, where he skirmished, and several gallant deeds were done.

"At this same hour, the castellan of Toulouse, Sir Hugh de Froidville, had also made an excursion with sixty lances, and by accident arrived at Penne whilst this skirmish was going forward. He and his men instantly dismounted and advanced to the barriers. Le Mengeant would have made off; but as that was impossible, he fought valiantly hand to hand with the knight. He behaved gallantly and wounded his adversary in two or three places, but at last was made prisoner, for he was not the strongest; and of his men few escaped being killed or taken. Le Mengeant was carried to Toulouse; and the seneschal had great difficulty to save him from the populace, who wanted to put him to death when they saw him in the hands of their own officer, so much was he hated at Toulouse.

"Fortunately for him, the Duke of Berry chanced to come to that city, and he had such good friends that the Duke gave him his liberty in consideration of a thousand francs being paid the seneschal for his ransom. Le Mengeant, on gaining his liberty, returned to Lourde, where he ceased not from his usual enterprises. One time he set out with others, without arms, disguised as an abbot attended by four monks; for he and his companions had shaven the crowns of their heads, and no one would have imagined who saw them but that they were real monks, for they had every appearance in dress and look. In this manner he came to Montpelier, and alighted at the hôtel of the Angel, saying he was an abbot from Upper Gascony going to Paris on business. He made acquaintance with a rich man of Montpelier, called Sir Beranger, who was likewise bound for Paris on his affairs. On the abbot telling him he would carry him thither free from all expense, he was delighted that the journey would cost him nothing, and set out with le Mengeant attended only by a servant. They had not left Montpelier three leagues when le Mengeant made him his prisoner, and conducted him through crooked and bye roads to his garrison of Lourde, whence he afterwards ransomed him for five thousand francs."

"Holy Mary!" cried I, "this le Mengeant must have been a clever fellow." "Aye, that he was indeed," replied he; "and he died in his armour at a place we shall pass in three days, called Larre in Bigorre, below a town called Archinach." "I will remind you of it," said I, "when we shall arrive at the spot."

Thus rode we on to Montesquieu, a good inclosed town belonging to the Count de Foix, which the Armagnacs and Labrissiens took by surprise, but held it only three days. In the morning we left Montesquieu and rode towards Palaminich, another inclosed town, situated on the Garonne, and belonging to the Count de Foix. When we were close to it and thought of entering it by the bridge over the Garonne, we found it impossible; for the preceding day it had rained so heavily in the mountains of Catalonia and Arragon that a river called the Saluz, which rises among them and falls into the Garonne with great rapidity, was so much swelled as to carry away one of the arches of the bridge, which was of wood. We were therefore forced to return to Montesquieu to dinner and remain there the whole day.

On the morrow, the knight was advised to cross the Garonne, opposite the town of Casseres in a boat. We therefore rode thither, and by our exertions the horses passed, and we ourselves afterwards with some difficulty and danger; for the boat was so small that only two horses and their men could cross at a time with those who managed the boat. When we had crossed, we made for Casseres, where we stayed the whole day. While our servants were preparing the supper, Sir Espaign du Lyon said, "Sir John, let us go and see the town." "Come then," replied I. We walked through the town to a gate which opens towards Palaminich, and, having passed it, went near the ditches. The knight, pointing to the walls, said, "Do you observe that part of the walls?" "Yes, sir; why do you ask?" "I will tell you: because it is newer than the rest." "That is true," answered I. "I will relate to you how this happened ten years ago. You have heard of the wars between the Count d'Armagnac and the Count de Foix, which took place in the county of Béarn, that appertains to the Count de Foix. The Count d'Armagnac over-ran it, though at present he is quiet on account of the truces made between them. I must say, the Armagnacs and Labrissiens gained nothing, but had often great losses.

"On the night of the feast of St. Nicholas, in the winter of the year of 1362, the Count de Foix made prisoners, near to Montmarsen, the Count d'Armagnac and his nephew the Lord d'Albreth, and many nobles with them, whom he carried to Orthez and confined them in the tower of the castle; by which capture he received ten times told one hundred thousand francs.

"It happened afterwards that the Count d'Armagnac, father of the present, called Sir John d'Armagnac, set on foot an armament with which he came and took Casseres by scalado. They were full two hundred men at arms, who seemed resolved to keep the place by force. News was brought to the Count de Foix at Pau, that the Armagnacs and Labrissiens had taken his town of Casseres. He, who was a prudent and valiant knight and prepared for all events, called to him two bastard brothers whom he had among his knights, Sir Arnault Guillaume and Sir Peter de Béarn, and ordered them to march instantly to Casseres, telling them he would send men from all parts and in three days would be there in person. 'Be careful, therefore,' added he, 'that none get out of the town without being fought with, as you will have strength enough; and on your arrival at Casseres, make the country people bring you plenty of large pieces of wood, which you will fix strongly round the gates, and completely bar them up; for I am resolved that those now in the town shall be so shut up in it, that they never pass through the gates. I will make them take another road.'

"The two knights obeyed his orders, and marched to Palaminich, accompanied and followed by all the men at arms in Béarn. They encamped before the town of Casseres; but those within paid no attention to them, nor observed that they were so completely shut in they could not pass through the gates. On the third day the Count de Foix came with five hundred men at arms, and on his arrival had the town encompassed with fortifications of wood, as well as by his army, that no sally might be made from it in the night. In this state, without making any attack, he blockaded them until their provisions began to fail; for though they had wine in plenty they had nothing to eat and could not escape by fording the river, which was then too deep. They therefore thought it better to surrender themselves as prisoners than shamefully perish with hunger.

"The Count de Foix listened to their offers. He had them informed that as they could not pass through any of the town-gates, he would make a hole in the wall through which the garrison, one by one, must pass without arms in their common dress. They were forced to accept these terms, otherwise the business was at an end. And if the Count de Foix had not been thus appeased, all within were dead men. He had a hole made in the wall, which was not too large, through which they came out one by one. The Count was there, with his forces drawn up in battle-array; and as they came out of the town they were brought before him, and sent to different castles and towns as prisoners. He took there his cousin, Sir John d'Armagnac, Sir Bernard d'Albreth, Sir Manaut de Barbasan, Sir Raymond de Benach, Sir Benedict de la Corneille, and about twenty of the most respectable, whom he carried with him to Orthez, and received from them, before they gained their liberty, one hundred thousand francs twice told. For this, my fair sir, was this wall broken down, as a passage for those of Armagnac and Albreth. Afterwards it was rebuilt and repaired." When he had finished his history we returned to our lodgings and found the supper ready.

On the morrow we mounted our horses and, riding up the side of the Garonne, passed through Palaminich and entered the lands of the Counts de Comminges and d'Armagnac. On the opposite side, fronting us, was the Garonne, and the territories of the Count de Foix. As we rode on, the knight pointed out to me a town, which appeared tolerably strong, called Marteras le Toussac, which belongs to the Count de Comminges, and on the other side of the river two castles of the Count de Foix, seated on a mountain, called Montaural and Monclare. As we were riding among these towns and castles, in a beautiful meadow by the side of the Garonne, the knight said: "Sir John, I have witnessed here many excellent skirmishes and combats between the Armagnacs and the Foixiens; for there was neither town nor castle that was not well garrisoned with men at arms, who engaged with and pursued each other. Do you see yonder those ruins? They are the remains of a fort which the Armagnacs raised against these two castles and which they filled with men at arms, who did much damage to the lands of the Count de Foix, on the other side of the river; but I will tell you how they paid for it.

"The Count de Foix one night sent his brother, Sir Peter de Béarn, with two hundred lances and four hundred peasants, laden with faggots, and as much wood as they could cut from the hedges, which they piled around this fort and set on fire, so that the fort was burnt with all in it; for none received quarter. And since that time no one has dared to rebuild it."

With such conversation did we daily travel, travelling towards the source of the river Garonne, on each side of which were handsome castles and forts. All on the left hand belonged to the Count de Foix, and on the other to the Count d'Armagnac.

[tr. THOMAS JOHNES]

# LYRICS AND SELECTIONS

The romance lyric begins with Duke William IX of Aquitaine and Count William VII of Poitou. The two titles were borne by the same man at the end of the eleventh century. William ruled by cunning and military might, establishing a hegemony over all Provence and losing, it is said, 300,000 men on the First Crusade. He relaxed by cultivating the social graces at his court. What his sources were for the forms and subjects of the lyrics which he composed is a matter for debate. He may well have drawn ideas from popular rustic songs, the repertoire of the jongleurs, and Latin lyrics. At all events, his are the first we know of what shortly became a flood of vernacular songs. Nearly twenty-five hundred Provençal lyrics written in the twelfth and early thirteenth centuries still exist. The composers of these songs, usually members of the noble class, are called *troubadours*. The paid performers who circulated their compositions from court to court are called *jongleurs*.

The isolation and polity of Provence no doubt determined the limited range of the poetry. Only three subjects were regarded as worthy: *salus* (war), *venus* (love), and *virtus* (honor). Of these, the second was most popular. Its common theme was the troubadour's love for a married *dame*. The forms, like those of the minnesingers, were standardized: *chanson* (long poem in five or six strophes of twenty or more lines, all lines of each strophe ending with the same rhyme), *alba* (dawn-song), *planh* (lament), *tenso* (dialogue), *sirventes* (political satire), and the like. The audience expected originality within these conventional patterns. A kind of rule developed that no troubadour could use (except in a *sirventes*) a strophaic form ever employed before. It is very doubtful whether any modern lyric poet can invent a strophe written with accent and end-rhyme in which he has not been anticipated by a troubadour. The intricacy of the patterns often became an end in itself, and in the mid-twelfth century such writers as Arnaut Daniel, Rambaut d'Orange, and Guiraut de Borneil cultivated the *trobar clus,* or obscure style, which "veiled poverty of thought under splendors of form." Scores for instrumental accompaniment survive for many of the songs.

The troubadour lyrics stimulated vernacular poetry in all countries. Provence fell to the English crown when Eleanor of Aquitaine, the granddaughter of our Count William, married Henry II. Bernart de Ventadorn followed the queen to the English court. Her sons, who lived much of their lives in Provence, were troubadours. A daughter by her previous marriage to the king of France settled in Troyes as Marie de Champagne and gathered troubadours to her court. They taught Chrétien their art, and it infected his romances. Marie's half-brother Richard the Lion-hearted composed his prison-song for her. Eleanor's famous granddaughter, Blanche of Castile, mother of

King Louis IX of France (St. Louis), adroitly ruled France in the early thirteenth century; the poetical homage paid to her by Count Theobald of Champagne caused a state scandal.

The Albigensian holy wars at the beginning of the thirteenth century so pauperized Provence that it could no longer support the effete art. Once rich courts, where a Bernart de Ventadorn could rise from peasant poverty to fame, disappeared.

Navarre, Aragon, and Castile, in Spain, which were Provençal in language and taste, cultivated the lyric. From Spain, the art spread to Sicily and Naples, which were ruled by Spanish nobility. Other troubadours crossed the Rhone to the East; from Savoy the songs moved across the lower Alps to Lombardy and Tuscany. Here the Sordello of Dante and Browning composed similar verses. When Charles of Anjou attained hegemony in Italy, he and his courtiers composed vernacular poetry. The minnesingers of Germany took ideas from Provence, as we have seen. Even the teachings of St. Francis contain troubadour images and turns of phrase.

The Italian lyric followed its Provençal model until the mid-thirteenth century, when Guido Guinicelli of Bologna began to compose in what Dante called the "sweet new style (*dolce stil nuovo*)." He adjusted the feudal ideas to urban life and exalted the themes; what was physical became spiritual and what was local and obscure became universal under his pen. Dante and his circle recognized Guido as their master. The Italian lyric of the period ranges from coarse and lusty ribaldry to the most exalted spiritual expressions in any language.

In France, there apparently was an indigenous lyric, composed in both town and country castle, before the troubadour age, though none of this poetry has survived. The early *pastourelles,* dances, and drinking songs are at once more natural and more universal than anything composed in Provence. As we might expect, the earliest of them are vulgar in more than language; poets freed from the restraint of ecclesiastical Latin could easily abuse their freedom. These French poets also concentrated on the theme of illicit love, either on the plane of the nobles of the castles, as in the *chanson de malmariée, chanson d'istoire,* and *chanson de toile,* or else in the pastoral songs of Robin and Marian and other traditional rustics, which appealed to the chatelains of the rural districts.

During the crusades, especially the Third Crusade, poets of all languages mingled and exchanged ideas. Thereafter, composition of verse became more professional than it had been, and the poems are not so often anonymous or of questionable authorship. From the middle of the thirteenth century to the fifteenth century, when Villon stands pre-eminent as one equally medieval and modern, French lyric poetry was largely written by courtiers patronized by the nobility, or else by the nobles themselves. In the main, these courtly poets, who lived in the center of an expanding world, have none of the concern with external form that characterized their predecessors. Some of their verse is strangely moving; all of it is worldly.

## A SONG OF NOTHING

William, Count of Poitou (A.D. 1071–1127)

*Farai un vers de dreyt nien:*
*Non er de me ni d'autra gen,*
*Non er d'amor ni de joven,*
  *Ni de ren au,*
*Qu' enans fo trobatz en durmen*
  *Sobre chevau.*

I'll make some verses just for fun
Not about me nor any one,
Nor deeds that noble knights have done
    Nor love's ado: —
I made them riding in the sun
  (My horse helped, too.)

When I was born I cannot say;
I am not sad, I am not gay,
I am not stiff nor dégagé;
    What can I do?
Long since enchanted by a fay
    Star-touched I grew.

Dreaming for living I mistake
  Unless I'm told when I'm awake.
  My heart is sad and nigh to break
    With bitter rue —
  And I don't care three crumbs of cake
    Or even two.

I have a lady, who or where
I cannot tell you, but I swear
She treats me neither ill nor fair
    But I'm not blue
Just so the Normans stay up there
    Out of Poitou.

I have not seen yet I adore
This distant love; she sets no store
By what I think and furthermore
    ('Tis sad but true)
Others there are, some three or four,
  I'm faithful to.

So ill I am that death I fear;
I nothing know but what I hear;
I hope there is a doctor here,

No matter who.
If he can cure me I'll pay dear,
　If not, he's through.

I've made the verse; if you'll allow
I think I'll send it off right now
To one who'll pass it on somehow
　Up in Anjou;
He'd tell me what it means, I vow,
　If he but knew.

[tr. THOMAS G. BERGIN]

## ALBA [1]

### Anonymous Provençal (12th cent.)

*En un vergier sotz folha d'albespi*
*Tenc la dompna son amic costa si,*
*Tro la gaita crida que l'alba vi.*
*Oi deus, oi deus, de l'alba! tan tost ve.*

In orchard where the leaves of hawthorn hide,
The lady holds a lover to her side,
Until the watcher in the dawning cried.
*Ah God, ah God, the dawn! it comes how soon.*

"Ah, would to God that never night must end,
Nor this my lover far from me should wend,
Nor watcher day nor dawning ever send!
*Ah God, ah God, the dawn! it comes how soon.*

Come let us kiss, dear lover, you and I,
Within the meads where pretty song-birds fly;
We will do all despite the jealous eye:
*Ah God, ah God, the dawn! it comes how soon.*

Sweet lover come, renew our lovemaking
Within the garden where the light birds sing,
Until the watcher sound the severing.
*Ah God, ah God, the dawn! it comes how soon.*

Through the soft breezes that are blown from there,
From my own lover, courteous, noble and fair,
From his breath have I drunk a draught most rare.
*Ah God, ah God, the dawn! it comes how soon."*

Gracious the lady is, and debonaire,
For her beauty a many look at her,

1. From *Early Mediaeval French Lyrics*, edited by C. C. Abbott; Constable & Co., London, 1932. Reprinted by permission of The Oxford University Press.

And in her heart is loyal love astir.
*Ah God, ah God, the dawn! it comes how soon.*

[tr. CLAUDE COLLEER ABBOTT]


## CANSO [2]

Bernart de Ventadorn (12th cent.)

*Tant ai mo cor ple de joya,*
*tot me desnatura.*

Such delight has come to me,
Reason it o'erpowers,
Frost and snowflakes seem to be
Red and yellow flowers,
For my joy grows mightily
With the wind and showers,
And my verse and melody
With fresh beauty dowers
With love and with delight
My heart is flooded quite,
Winter seems like summer bright,
Snowdrifts leafy bowers.

Now, though all around me freezes,
I, in light attire,
Can defy the bitter breezes,
Warmed by true love's fire.
Overbearing pride displeases
Her whom I desire,
Humbleness in love more pleases
Me, since I aspire
To win love and delight
From her whose eyes' glad light
Is more precious in my sight
Than the wealth of Tyre.

Though her presence I must leave,
Far from her be hiding,
In her friendship I believe
Still with faith confiding.
If I see her, or receive
Of her any tiding,
On that day I shall achieve
Happiness abiding.
She is my heart's delight,

2. From *Trobador Poets*, by Barbara Smythe; Chatto & Windus, London, 1929. Reprinted by permission of the publisher.

My soul to her takes flight,
I myself, unhappy wight,
Far in France am biding.

All my joy despair submerges,
Then, good hope returning
To my heart it bravely urges
Me to fear no spurning.
As a ship on ocean surge is
Ever tost and turning,
So my heart's great joy now merges
Into sorrow burning.
Now fled is my delight
— E'en Tristan, the true knight,
For Isolde and the night
Longed with less of yearning

Would that I the form could take
Of a bird, then, flying
Through the night, my way I'd make
There where she is lying!
Lady, see, for pity's sake,
Your true love is dying,
And my heart is like to break
With my tears and sighing.
Oh, Queen of all delight,
I yield me to your might;
Prithee now my love requite,
Make no more denying!

All my hopes and thoughts unbroken
Never from her part,
When I hear her praises spoken
Then by true love's dart
In my soul is joy awoken,
Grief must needs depart,
And my happy face is token
Of my joyous heart.
I weep for sheer delight,
No grief my joy can blight
Nor my heart with sorrow smite,
Pain has lost its smart.

This song which I indite,
Go sing my love aright,
Let her know my piteous plight
Through my verse's art.

[tr. BARBARA SMYTHE]

## SIRVENTES [3]

### Bertran de Born (fl. 1180–1194)

*D'un sirventes no'm chal far lonhor guanda,*
*Tal talan ai que'l diga e que l'espanda,*
*Quar n'ai razo tan novela e tan granda*
*De'l jove rei qu'a fenit sa demanda*
*So frair Richart, puois sos pairs lo comanda;*
  *Tan es forzatz!*
*Puois n' Aenrics terra no te ni manda,*
  *Sia reis de'ls malvatz.*

*Explanation.* — At the time when the Young King had made
peace with his brother Richard, and had given up the claim which
he made on his land, as King Henry their father wished, his father
gave him a certain allowance of money for food and necessaries; and
he did not hold or possess any land, nor did any man come to him for
support or help in war, and Sir Bertran de Born and all the other
barons who had supported him against Sir Richard were much
grieved. And the Young King went off to Normandy to fight in
tournaments and to amuse himself, and he left all these barons at
war with Sir Richard. And Sir Richard besieged burgs and castles,
and took lands, and pulled down and burned and set fire; and the
Young King was tilting and sleeping and amusing himself; wherefore Sir Bertran made this sirventes.*

I care not to delay longer over making a sirventes, such desire have
  I to say and to spread it; for I have such a new and such a great
  reason in the Young King, who has given up his claim on his
  brother Richard, since his father wishes it, so bullied is he!
  Since Sir Henry does not hold or command land, let him be
  King of the dastards!

For he acts like a dastard since he lives thus just on a paid and
  promised allowance. A crowned King who takes a pension
  from others is not much like Arnaut, the Marquis of Bellanda,
  or the noble Guilhelm who conquered Tor Mirmanda, so brave
  was he! Since he has lied to them in Poitou and reduced them
  to beggary, he will never be so much loved.

Never by sleeping will the King of the English gain Cumberland,
  nor will he conquer Ireland, or hold Anjou or Montsoreau or
  Candé, nor will he have the watch-tower of Poitou, nor will he be
  called Duke of the Norman country, nor will he be Count Pala-

3. Ibid.
* This explanation was written by a later anonymous Provençal commentator.

tine of Bordeaux here, or lord of the Gascons beyond Landes or of Basatz.

I want to give advice in the tune of Lady Alamanda to Sir Richard, though he does not ask for it; he need never treat his men well for fear of his brother, by no means does he do it; but he besieges and pillages them, he takes their castles and pulls down and burns on every side. And let the King tilt up there with the people of Garlande, and the other (King), his brother-in-law.

I would that Count Jaufre, who holds Bresilianda, had been the first-born.

For he is courteous, and would that kingdom and duchies were in his command.

[tr. Barbara Smythe]


## STROPHES FROM A CANSO (*trobar clus*) [4]

### Arnaut Daniel (fl. 1180–1200)

| | |
|---|---|
| *L'aura amara* | Breeze that's bitter |
| *Fa'ls bruoills brancutz* | makes boughs their leaves |
| *Clazir* | to shed |
| *Que'l doussa espeissa ab fuoills,* | which in the spring were green. |
| *E'ls letz* | And sweet |
| *Becs* | beaks |
| *Dels auzels ramencs* | of the birds above |
| *Ten balps e mutz* | of song bereaves, |
| *Pars* | paired |
| *E non-pars;* | and not paired. |
| *Per qu'eu m'esfortz* | Why have I e'er |
| *De far e dir* | or done or said |
| *Plazers* | pleasure |
| *A mains, per liei* | to all? For her |
| *Que m'a virat bas d'aut,* | who's set me — once high — low. |
| *Don tem morir* | I'll soon be dead |
| *Si'ls afans no m'asoma.* | of this, unless she save me. |
| | |
| *Tant fo clara* | Though to quit her |
| *Ma prima lutz* | my heart sore grieves, |
| *D'eslir* | yet dread |
| *Lieis don cre'l cors los huoills* | I of her eyes the sheen |
| *Non pretz.* | to meet. |
| *Necs* | Weak's |
| *Mans dos agovencs;* | any other's love; |
| *D'autra s'es dutz* | cold it me leaves |
| *Rars* | scared |
| *Mos preiars:* | not, but spared. |
| *Pero deportz* | Her words I care |

4. Ibid.

| | |
|---|---|
| *M'es ad auzir* | to hear instead, |
| *Volers,* | treasure |
| *Bos motz ses grei* | more, I aver |
| *De liei, don tant m'azaut.* | for I do love her so. |
| *Qu'al sieu servir* | From foot to head |
| *Sui del pe tro c'al coma.* | into her power I gave me. |

[tr. Barbara Smythe]

## SESTINA [5]

### Arnaut Daniel

*Lo ferm voler qu'el cor m'intra*
*No'm pot jes becs escoissendre ni ongla*
*De lausengier, qui pert per mal dir s'arma;*
*E car non l'aus batr'ab ram ni ab verga,*
*Sivals a frau, lai on non aurai oncle,*
*Jauzirai joi, en vergier o dinz cambra.*

Longing that my heart doth enter
Cannot uprooted be by beak or nail
Of slanderer, who by lies ruins his soul.
Since I dare not beat him with twig or rod,
At least in secret, where I have no uncle,
I will have joy in orchard or in room.

And when I recall the room
Where to my grief I know no man can enter,
To me are all more than brother or uncle;
In every limb I quake, even to the nail,
Just as a child does when it sees the rod,
So fear I she regards too much her soul.

There in body, not in soul,
I'd be, had she concealed me in her room!
For more it hurts my soul than blows of rod
That where she is her servant cannot enter.
I shall be to her even as flesh and nail,
And warning will not heed from friend or uncle.

Not the sister of my uncle
Loved I so much or more, upon my soul!
For close as is the finger to the nail,
If she so pleased, would I be to her room,
And love, which now within my heart doth enter,
Can bend me as a strong man a weak rod.

5. Ibid.

Since first flourished the dry rod,
Or nephew from Sir Adam sprang, or uncle,
Such faithful love as in my heart doth enter
Ne'er was, I think, in body or in soul.
Where'er she be, outdoors or in her room,
I part no more from her than length of nail.

I am held as with a nail
Fastened to her as bark is to the rod;
To me of joy she's palace, tower and room;
I do not love so much brother or uncle,
And double joy in Heaven 'twill give my soul
If ever man for true love there doth enter.

Now Arnaut sends his song of nail and uncle
By leave of her whose rod doth rule his soul,
To Desirat, in whose room worth doth enter.

[tr. BARBARA SMYTHE]


## ALBIGENSIAN DEFIANCE

Tomier e'en Palazi (early 13th cent.)

*De chantar farai*
*Una esdemessa,*
*Que temps ven e vai,*
*E reman promessa,*
*E de grant esmai*
*Fai Deus tost defessa.*
*Segur estem, seignors,*
*E ferm de ric socors.*

I'll make a song shall utter forth
    My full and free complaint,
To see the heavy hours pass on,
    And witness to the feint
Of coward souls, whose vows were made
In falsehood, and are yet unpaid.
        Yet, noble sirs, we will not fear,
        Strong in the hope of succours near.

    Yes! full and ample help for us
        Shall come — so trusts my heart;
    God fights for us, and these our foes,
        The French, must soon depart:
For on the souls that fear not God,
Soon, soon shall fall the vengeful rod.

Then, noble sirs, we will not fear,
　　Strong in the hope of succours near.

And hither they believe to come
　　(The treacherous, base crusaders!) —
But, e'en as quickly as they come,
　　We'll chase those fierce invaders:
Without a shelter they shall fly
Before our valiant chivalry.
　　Then, noble sirs, we will not fear,
　　　Strong in the hope of succours near.

And e'en if Frederic, on the throne
　　Of powerful Germany,
Submit the cruel ravages
　　Of Louis' hosts to see,
Yet, in the breast of England's king,
Wrath deep and vengeful shall upspring.
　　Then, noble sirs, we will not fear,
　　　Strong in the hope of succours near.

Not much those meek and holy men —
　　The traitorous bishops — mourn,
Though from our hands the sepulchre
　　Of our dear Lord be torn;
More tender far their anxious care
For the rich plunder of Belcaire.
　　But, noble sirs, we will not fear,
　　　Strong in the hope of succours near.

And look at our proud cardinal,
　　Whose hours in peace are past;
Look at his splendid dwelling-place
　　(Pray Heaven it may not last!) —
He heeds not, while he lives in state,
What ills on Damietta wait.
　　But, noble sirs, we will not fear,
　　　Strong in the hope of succours near.

I cannot think that Avignon
　　Will lose its holy zeal, —
In this our cause so ardently
　　Its citizens can feel.
Then shame to him who will not bear
In this our glorious cause his share!
　　And, noble sirs, we will not fear,
　　　Strong in the hope of succours near.
                                [tr. Edgar Taylor]

## THE SONG OF THE CREATURES

### St. Francis of Assisi (A.D. 1182–1226)

*Altissimu, onnipotente, bon signore, tue so' le laude la gloria e
l'onore et onne benedizione a te solu, altissimu, se konfanno e nullu
homo ene dignu te mentovare.*

O most high, almighty, good Lord God, to Thee belong praise, glory,
    honor and all blessing!
Praised be my Lord God with all His creatures, and especially our
    brother the sun, who brings us the day and who brings us the
    light; fair is he and shines with very great splendor; O Lord, he
    signifies to us Thee!
Praised be my Lord for our sister the moon, and for the stars, the
    which He has set clear and lovely in heaven.
Praised be my Lord for our brother the wind, and for air and cloud,
    calms and all weather by which Thou upholdest life in all crea-
    tures. —
Praised be my Lord for all those who pardon one another, for His
    love's sake, and who endure weakness and tribulation; blessèd
    are they who peaceably shall endure. For thou, O Most Highest,
    shalt give them a crown!
Praised be my Lord for our sister, the death of the body, from which
    no man escapeth. Woe to him who dieth in mortal sin!
    Blessèd are they who are found walking by Thy most holy will,
    for the second death shall have no power to do them harm.
Praise ye and bless the Lord, and give thanks unto Him and serve
    Him with great humility.

                      [tr. MATTHEW ARNOLD]

## CANZONE

### Emperor Frederick II (A.D. 1194–1250)

*Di duol mi convien cantare,
Com' altr' uom per allegranza . . .*

For grief I am about to sing,
  Even as another would for joy;
  Mine eyes which the hot tears destroy
Are scarce enough for sorrowing:
To speak of such a grievous thing
  Also my tongue I must employ,
Saying: Woe's me, who am full of woes!

Not while I live shall my sighs cease
For her in whom my heart found peace:
I am become like unto those
That cannot sleep for weariness,
Now I have lost my crimson rose.

And yet I will not call her lost;
　　She is not gone out of the earth;
　　She is but girded with a girth
Of hate, that clips her in like frost.
Thus says she every hour almost: —
　　"When I was born, 'twas an ill birth!
O that I never had been born,
　　If I am still to fall asleep
　　Weeping, and when I wake to weep;
If he whom I most loathe and scorn
　　Is still to have me his, and keep
Smiling about me night and morn!

　　"O that I never had been born
　　A woman! a poor, helpless fool,
　　Who can but stoop beneath the rule
Of him she needs must loathe and scorn!
If ever I feel less forlorn,
　　I stand all day in fear and dule,
Lest he discern it, and with rough
　　Speech mock at me, or with his smile
　　So hard you scarce could call it guile:
No man is there to say, 'Enough.'
　　O, but if God waits a long while,
Death cannot always stand aloof!

　　"Thou, God the Lord, dost know all this:
　　Give me a little comfort then.
　　Him who is worst among bad men
Smite thou for me.  Those limbs of his
Once hidden where the sharp worm is,
　　Perhaps I might see hope again.
Yet for a certain period
　　Would I seem like as one that saith
Strange things for grief, and murmureth
With smitten palms and hair abroad:
　　Still whispering under my held breath,
'Shall I not praise Thy name, O God?'

　　"Thou, God the Lord, dost know all this:
　　It is a very weary thing
　　Thus to be always trembling:
And till the breath of his life cease,

The hate in him will but increase,
  And with his hate my suffering.
Each morn I hear his voice bid them
  That watch me, to be faithful spies
  Lest I go forth and see the skies;
Each night, to each, he saith the same; —
  And in my soul and in mine eyes
There is a burning heat like flame."

Thus grieves she now; but she shall wear
  This love of mine, whereof I spoke,
  About her body for a cloak,
And for a garland in her hair,
Even yet: because I mean to prove,
Not to speak only, this my love.
                    [tr. DANTE GABRIEL ROSSETTI]


Canzone: THE GENTLE HEART

Guido Guinicelli (A.D. 1240?-1274?)

*Al cor gentil ripara sempre Amore*
*Come, a la silva, augello, in la verdura.*

Within the gentle heart Love shelters him,
  As birds within the green shade of the grove.
Before the gentle heart, in Nature's scheme,
  Love was not, nor the gentle heart ere Love.
    For with the sun, at once,
So sprang the light immediately; nor was
    Its birth before the sun's.
And Love hath his effect in gentleness
    Of very self; even as
Within the middle fire the heat's excess.

The fire of Love comes to the gentle heart
  Like as its virtue to a precious stone;
To which no star its influence can impart
  Till it is made a pure thing by the sun:
    For when the sun hath smit
From out its essence that which there was vile,
    The star endoweth it.
And so the heart created by God's breath
    Pure, true, and clean from guile,
A woman, like a star, enamoureth.

In gentle heart Love for like reason is
  For which the lamp's high flame is fanned and bow'd:

Clear, piercing bright, it shines for its own bliss;
  Nor would it burn there else, it is so proud.
    For evil natures meet
With Love as it were water met with fire,
    As cold abhorring heat.
Through gentle heart Love doth a track divine, —
    Like knowing like; the same
As diamond runs through iron in the mine.


The sun strikes full upon the mud all day:
  It remains vile, nor the sun's worth is less.
"By race I am gentle," the proud man doth say:
  He is the mud, the sun is gentleness.
    Let no man predicate
That aught the name of gentleness should have,
    Even in a king's estate,
Except the heart there be a gentle man's.
    The star-beam lights the wave, —
Heaven holds the star and the star's radiance.


God, in the understanding of high Heaven,
  Burns more than in our sight the living sun:
There to behold His Face unveiled is given;
  And Heaven, whose will is homage paid to One,
    Fulfils the things which live
In God, from the beginning excellent.
    So should my lady give
That truth which in her eyes is glorified,
    On which her heart is bent,
To me whose service waiteth at her side.


My lady, God shall ask, "What daredst thou?"
  (When my soul stands with all her acts review'd:)
"Thou passedst Heaven, into My sight, as now,
  To make Me of vain love similitude.
    To Me doth praise belong,
And to the Queen of all the realm of grace
    Who slayeth fraud and wrong."
Then may I plead: "As though from Thee he came,
    Love wore an angel's face:
Lord, if I loved her, count it not my shame."
                    [tr. Dante Gabriel Rossetti]

## Sonnet: TO THE GUELF FACTION

Folgore da San Geminiano (A.D. 1250?–1315?)

*Guelfi, per fare scudi de le reni*
*Avete fatti i conigli leoni*
*E per ferir si forte di speroni*
*Tenendo volti verso casa i freni.*

Because ye made your backs your shields, it came
   To pass, ye Guelfs, that these your enemies
From hares grew lions: and because your eyes
Turned homeward, and your spurs e'en did the same,
Full many an one who still might win the game
   In fevered tracts of exile pines and dies.
   Ye blew your bubbles as the falcon flies,
And the wind broke them up and scattered them.
This counsel, therefore.  Shape your high resolves
   In good king Robert's humour, and afresh
     Accept your shames, forgive, and go your way.
     And so her peace is made with Pisa!  Yea,
   What cares she for the miserable flesh
That in the wilderness has fed the wolves?
              [tr. DANTE GABRIEL ROSSETTI]

## Sonnet: BECCHINA IN A RAGE

Cecco Angiolieri da Siena (A.D. 1251–1305?)

*Quando veggio Becchina corrucciata,*
*Se io avesse allor cuor di leone,*
*Si tremarei com' un picciol garzone*
*Quando 'l maestro gli vuol dar palmata.*

When I behold Becchina in a rage,
   Just like a little lad I trembling stand
   Whose master tells him to hold out his hand;
Had I a lion's heart, the sight would wage
Such war against it, that in that sad stage
   I'd wish my birth might never have been plann'd,
   And curse the day and hour that I was bann'd
With such a plague for my life's heritage.
Yet even if I should sell me to the Fiend,
   I must so manage matters in some way
   That for her rage I may not care a fig;
Or else from death I cannot long be screen'd.
   So I'll not blink the fact, but plainly say
   It's time I got my valour to grow big.
              [tr. DANTE GABRIEL ROSSETTI]

## Sonnet: WHY HE IS UNHANGED

Cecco Angiolieri da Siena

Whoever without money is in love
  Had better build a gallows and go hang;
  He dies not once, but oftener feels the pang
Than he who was cast down from Heaven above.
And certes, for my sins, it's plain enough,
  If Love's alive on earth, that he's myself,
  Who would not be so cursed with want of pelf
If others paid my proper dues thereof.
Then why am I not hanged by my own hands?
  I answer: for this empty narrow chink
  Of hope; — that I've a father old and rich,
And that if once he dies I'll get his lands;
  And die he must, when the sea's dry, I think.
  Meanwhile God keeps him whole and me i' the ditch.

                    [tr. DANTE GABRIEL ROSSETTI]

## CHANSON DE MALMARIÉE [6]

Anonymous (12th cent.)

*En un vergier lez une fontenele,*
*Dont clere est l'onde et blanche la gravele,*
*Siet fille a roi, sa main a sa maxele:*
*En sospirant son douz ami rapele.*
  *"Ae cuens Guis amis!*
  *La vostre amors me tout solaz et ris.*

Within an orchard by a fountain spring,
The water limpid, white the gravelling,
With hand on cheek, the daughter of a king
Sits sighing, her sweet love remembering.
  *"Ah, Count Guy, my friend!*
  *Your love brings all my joy and peace to end.*

Count Guy, my friend, how cursed a thing is fate!
My father gave me for an old man's mate.
Who shut me in this house, locked fast the gate;
I cannot walk abroad, early or late!
  *Ah, Count Guy, my friend!*
  *Your love brings all my joy and peace to end."*

6. From *Early Mediaeval French Lyrics*, edited by C. C. Abbott; Constable & Co.,
1932.  Reprinted by permission of The Oxford University Press.

Her jealous husband heard the plaint she spelt,
Enters the orchard, 'gan unloose his belt;
Beat her till she was blue with many a welt:
Near to her death between his feet she knelt.
      *Ah, Count Guy, my friend!*
      *Your love brings all my joy and peace to end.*

When he had used her in this shameful way
Her man had fear of it, his knavish play.
For spite of all he owned her father's sway.
She is a king's daughter, whate'er he say.
      *Ah, Count Guy, my friend!*
      *Your love brings all my joy and peace to end.*

When fair Yoland was risen from her swoon
Then upon God she called to grant this boon:
"O dear my Lord, Thou who didst maken me,
Grant me, O Lord, forgotten not to be,
Ere evening send back my love to me."
      *Ah, Count Guy, my friend!*
      *Your love brings all my joy and peace to end.*

And our dear Lord, He listened what she said:
Now with her lover she is comforted,
They sit with leafy branches overhead,
And there full many a lover's tear is shed.
      *Ah, Count Guy, my friend!*
      *Your love brings all my joy and peace to end.*
                        [tr. CLAUDE COLLEER ABBOTT]


### PASTOURELLE MOTET [7]

Anonymous (*circ.* A.D. 1200)

*C'est la jus c'on dist an la praielle,*
*Marion et Robeson.*

Over there in the meadow
Rejoice and sing
Marion and Robin
With the fresh green spring.
She calls to him, "Sweetheart,
Come hither to me,
Robin, Robin, Robin,
Look how lovely I be!"
                        [tr. CLAUDE COLLEER ABBOTT]

7. Ibid.

## DRINKING SONG [8]

Anonymous (*circ.* A.D. 1200)

*Bon vin doit l'en a li tirer,*
*Et le mauvès en sus bouter;*
*Puis doivent compagnons chanter:*
   *Cis chans veult boire!*

Who has good wine should flagon it out
And thrust the bad where the fungus sprout;
Then must merry companions shout:
   *This song wants drink!*

When I see wine into the clear glass slip
How I long to be matched with it;
My heart sings gay at the thought of it:
   *This song wants drink!*

I thirst for a sup; come circle the cup:
   *This song wants drink!*
               [tr. CLAUDE COLLEER ABBOTT]


## PLANH

(from *Le roman du castelain de Couci*)

Anonymous French (13th cent.)

Still will I sing to soothe my heart,
   Deprest, alas! and full of care,
Not even yet shall hope depart —
   Not even yet will I despair.
Though none from that wild shore return
   Where he abides I love so well,
Whose absence I for ever mourn,
   Whose voice to me was music's spell;
God! when the battle cry resounds,
   Thy succour to the Pilgrim show,
Whom fatal treachery surrounds —
   For faithless is the Pagan foe!

No time my sorrow can assuage,
   Till I behold him once again;
He roams in weary pilgrimage,
   And I await in ceaseless pain:

8. Ibid.

And though my lineage urge me long
  With threats another's bride to be,
In vain they seek to do him wrong —
  All idle seem their frowns to me.
Noble he is, and I am fair;
  Ah, Heaven! all mercy since thou art,
Why doom two hearts to this despair,
  Why bid us thus so rudely part!

One tender solace yet I find —
  His vows are mine, my treasured store!
And when I feel the gentle wind
  That blows from yonder distant shore,
I turn me to the balmy gale,
  Its whisp'ring breath my fancy charms,
I list his tender voice to hail,
  He seems to clasp me in his arms!

He left me! ah, what vain regret!
  I may not follow where he flies! —
The scarf he gave, when last we met,
  A cherish'd relic still I prize:
I fold it to my throbbing heart,
  And many a vanish'd scene recall;
For quiet to my soul distrest,
  For joy, for solace — this is all!
God, when the battle cry resounds,
  Thy succour to the Pilgrim show,
Whom fatal treachery surrounds,
  For faithless is the Pagan foe!

                    [tr. LOUISA S. COSTELLO]


CRUSADER'S FAREWELL

Thibaud, King of Navarre (A.D. 1201–1253)

*Dame, ensi est qu'il m'en convient aler,*
*Et departir de la doce contrée,*
*Ou tant ai mauz soffers et endurez;*
*Quant je vos lais, droiz est, que je m'en hée:*
*Dex! porquoi fu la terre d'outremer,*
*Qui tant amans aura fait desevrer,*
*Dont puis ne fu l'amour reconforté,*
*Ne ne porent lor joie remembrer?*

Lady, the fates command, and I must go, —
  Leaving the pleasant land so dear to me:
Here my heart suffer'd many a heavy woe;

But what is left to love, thus leaving thee?
Alas! that cruel land beyond the sea!
  Why thus dividing many a faithful heart,
Never again from pain and sorrow free,
  Never again to meet, when thus they part?

I see not, when thy presence bright I leave,
  How wealth, or joy, or peace can be my lot;
Ne'er yet my spirit found such cause to grieve
  As now in leaving thee: and if thy thought
Of me in absence should be sorrow-fraught,
  Oft will my heart repentant turn to thee,
Dwelling, in fruitless wishes, on this spot,
  And all the gracious words here said to me.

O gracious God! to thee I bend my knee,
  For thy sake yielding all I love and prize;
And O how mighty must that influence be,
  That steals me thus from all my cherish'd joys!
Here, ready, then, myself surrendering,
  Prepared to serve thee, I submit; and ne'er
To one so faithful could I service bring,
  So kind a master, so beloved and dear.

And strong my ties — my grief unspeakable!
  Grief, all my choicest treasures to resign;
Yet stronger still the affections that impel
  My heart toward Him, the God whose love is mine. —
That holy love, how beautiful! how strong!
  Even wisdom's favourite sons take refuge there;
'Tis the redeeming gem that shines among
  Men's darkest thoughts — for ever bright and fair.

                          [tr. EDGAR TAYLOR]


## THE FOUNTAIN OF YOUTH

### (from *The Land of Cokaigne*)

Anonymous French (13th cent.)

Well I wot 't is often told,
Wisdom dwells but with the old;
Yet do I, of greener age,
Boast and bear the name of sage.
Briefly, sense was ne'er conferred
By the measure of the beard.
    List, — for now my tale begins, —

How, to rid me of my sins,
Once I journeyed far from home
To the gate of holy Rome:
There the Pope, for my offence,
Bade me straight, in penance, thence
Wandering onward, to attain
The wondrous land that hight Cokaigne.
Sooth to say, it was a place
Blessed with Heaven's especial grace;
For every road and every street
Smoked with food for man to eat:
Pilgrims there might halt at will,
There might sit and feast their fill,
In goodly bowers that lined the way,
Free for all, and naught to pay.
Through that blissful realm divine
Rolled a sparkling flood of wine;
Clear the sky, and soft the air,
For eternal spring was there;
And all around, the groves among,
Countless dance and ceaseless song.

\*  \*  \*  \*  \*

But the chiefest, choicest treasure,
In that land of peerless pleasure,
Was a well, to saine the sooth,
Cleped the living well of youth.
There, had numb and feeble age
Crossed you in your pilgrimage,
In those wondrous waters pure
Laved awhile you found a cure;
Lustihead and youth appears
Numbering now but twenty years.
Woe is me, who rue the hour!
Once I owned both will and power
To have gained this precious gift;
But, alas! of little thrift,
From a kind, o'erflowing heart,
To my fellows to impart
Youth, and joy, and all the lot
Of this rare, enchanted spot,
Forth I fared, and now in vain
Seek to find the place again.
Sore regret I now endure, —
Sore regret beyond a cure.
List, and learn from what is passed,
Having bliss, to hold it fast.

[tr. G. L. WAY]

## RONDEL

### Christine de Pisan (A.D. 1362?-1431)

*Je ne sçay comment je dure;*
*Car mon dolent cuer font d'yre,*
*Et plaindre n'oze, ne dire*
*Ma doulereuse aventure,*
*Ma dolente vie obscure,*
*Riens, fors la mort, ne desire;*
*Je ne sçay comment je dure.*

I know not how my life I bear!
   For sad regrets my hours employ,
Yet may I not betray a tear,
   Nor tell what woes my heart destroy;
My weary soul a prey to care,
I know not how my life I bear!

And must I still these pangs conceal!
   And feign the joys that others feel;
Still vainly tune my lute to sing,
   And smile while sighs my bosom wring;
Seem all delight amidst despair! —
I know not how my life I bear!
               [tr. Louisa S. Costello]

## PLAINT

### Alain Chartier (*circ.* 1390-1430)

*Ou dixieme an de mon dolent exil*
*Apres maint deuil et maint mortel peril*
*Et les dangiers quay jusquicy passez*
*Dont jai souffert graces a dieu assez.*

Ten seasons of a hapless exile's life,
With ceaseless woes and frequent perils rife,
Opprest with suffering past, and present care,
Of which Heaven will'd that I should have my share,
Brief time had I to dwell on history's page,
Or with heroic deeds my mind engage:
To trace the rapid steps of chiefs, whose fame
Has given to glorious France her deathless name,
Who ruled with sov'reign right sublime and sage,
And left unstain'd the noble heritage

To sons, who saw, beneath their wise command,
Encreased the power and glory of the land;
Their manners kept, their precepts made their guide,
And follow'd where they led with filial pride;
Beloved and honour'd through their wide domain,
And fear'd, where foreign shores the waves restrain;
Just in each act, in friendship never slow,
Stern to the bad, and haughty to the foe.
Ardent in honour, in adventure warm,
All good protecting, and chastising harm:
Reigning with justice, and with mercy blest,
Sway, strength, and conquest on their mighty crest.

'Twas thus they lived, 'twas thus the land was sway'd,
By truth and equity unequall'd made,
And leaving, after countless victories past,
Their country peace and glorious fame at last.

Oh! great and envied lot! ordain'd by Heaven,
And for their virtues to our fathers given,
Whose lives pass'd on, ere Death undreaded came,
Calm and secure in the repose of fame.
But we — ah, wretches! — we, whose stars malign
Did at our birth in evil spells combine,
And cast us forth to view our country's fall,
Our wrongs a mockery and reproach to all!
And those once noble, just, revered, and high,
Now slaves, confounded in their misery.
Ah, wretched exiles! shunn'd, despised, forlorn
Who ev'ry ill of fate have tried, and borne:
Who, day by day, lament our blasted fame,
And hunted, helpless, lost, grow old in shame!
Deserted! outcast! and is this our due,
For following right, and keeping truth in view?

Alas! what bitter thoughts, what vain regret,
Our ever-wakeful hearts would fain forget!
Those vanish'd hours no sorrow can restore,
Our land another's, and our friends no more!
We dare not towards the future turn our eyes,
So little hope our dismal lot supplies,
While we behold fair France contemn'd, o'erthrown,
And in her low estate deplore our own.

And how should I, though youth my lays inspire,
To joyous numbers rouse my slumb'ring lyre?
Ah! in its strain far other accents flow —
No joy can issue from the soul of woe!

Grief, dread, and doubt, and adverse fortunes still
Besiege my thoughts, and turn their course to ill;
Till fainting genius, fancy, wit, decline,
And all is changed that once I deem'd was mine.
Sorrow has made me, with his touch, so cold,
In early years unnaturally old:
Subdues my powers, contemns my thirst of praise,
And dictates all my melancholy lays!

[tr. Louisa S. Costello]


## THE CHILD ASLEEP

Clotilde de Surville (b. 1405)

*O cher enfantelet, vray pourtraiet de ton pere,*
*Dors sur le seyn que ta bouche a presse!*
*Dors, petiot; cloz, amy, sur le seyn de ta mere,*
*Tien doulx oeillet par le somme oppresse!*

Sweet babe! true portrait of thy father's face!
  Sleep on the bosom that thy lips have pressed!
Sleep, little one; and closely, gently place
  Thy drowsy eyelid on thy mother's breast.

Upon that tender eye, my little friend,
  Soft sleep shall come, that cometh not to me!
I watch to see thee, nourish thee, defend;
  'T is sweet to watch for thee, — alone for thee!

His arms fall down; sleep sits upon his brow;
  His eye is closed; he sleeps, nor dreams of harm.
Wore not his cheek the apple's ruddy glow,
  Would you not say he slept on Death's cold arm?

Awake, my boy!  I tremble with affright!
  Awake, and chase this fatal thought!  Unclose
Thine eye but for one moment on the light!
  Even at the price of thine, give me repose!

Sweet error! he but slept, I breathe again;
  Come, gentle dreams, the hour of sleep beguile!
Oh, when shall he, for whom I sigh in vain,
  Beside me watch to see thy waking smile?

[tr. Henry W. Longfellow]

## QUATRAIN [9]

Which Villon wrote when he had been sentenced to die.

François Villon (A.D. 1431 – after 1463)

*Je suis Françoys, dont il me poise,*
*Né de Paris emprès Pontoise,*
*Et de la corde d'une toise*
*Sçaura mon col que mon cul poise.*

I am François, luckless jay,
Born at Paris, Ponthoise way,
My neck, looped up beneath the tree,
Will learn how heavy buttocks be.

[tr. LEWIS WHARTON]

## BALLADE OF VILLON IN PRISON

*Aiez pitie, aiez pitie de moy,*
*A tout le moins, si vous plaist, mes amis!*

Have pity, friends, have pity now, I pray,
    If it so please you, at the least, on me!
I lie in fosse, not under holm or may
    In this duresse, wherein, alas! I dree
    Ill fate, as God did thereanent decree.
Lasses and lovers, younglings manifold,
Dancers and mountebanks, alert and bold,
    Nimble as squirrel from a crossbow shot,
Singers, that troll as clear as bells of gold, —
    *Will you all leave poor Villon here to rot?*

Clerks, that go caroling the livelong day,
    Scant-pursed, but glad and frank and full of glee;
Wandering at will along the broad highway,
    Hare-brained, perchance, but wit-whole too, perdie:
    Lo! now, I die, whilst that you absent be,
Song-singers, when poor Villon's days are told,
You will sing psalms for him and candles hold;
    Here light nor air nor levin enters not,
Where ramparts thick are round about him rolled.
    *Will you all leave poor Villon here to rot?*

Consider but his piteous array,
    High and fair lords, of suit and service free,

9. From *The Poems of François Villon*, translated by Lewis Wharton; J. M. Dent & Sons, Ltd., London, 1935. Reprinted by permission of the publisher.

That nor to king nor kaiser homage pay,
   But straight from God in heaven hold your fee!
   Come fast or feast, all days alike fasts he,
Whence are his teeth like rakes' teeth to behold:
No table hath he but the sheer black mould
   After dry bread (not manchets), pot on pot
They empty down his throat of water cold:
   *Will you all leave poor Villon here to rot?*

Princes and lords aforesaid, young and old,
Get me the King his letters sealed and scrolled
   And draw me from this dungeon: for, God wot,
Even swine, when one squeaks in the butcher's fold,
Flock around their fellow and do squeak and scold.
   *Will you all leave poor Villon here to rot?*

                                        [tr. JOHN PAYNE]

## BALLADE OF THE GIBBET [10]

An epitaph in the form of a ballad that François Villon
wrote of himself and his company, they expecting
shortly to be hanged

   *Freres humains qui apres nous vivez,*
   *N'ayez les cuers contre nous endurcis,*
   *Car, se pitie de nous povres avez,*
   *Dieu on aura plus tost de vous mercis.*

Brothers and men that shall after us be,
   Let not your hearts be hard to us:
For pitying this our misery
   Ye shall find God the more piteous.
   Look on us six that are hanging thus,
And for the flesh that so much we cherished
How it is eaten of birds and perished,
   And ashes and dust fill our bones' place,
Mock not at us that so feeble be,
   But pray God pardon us out of His grace.

Listen, we pray you, and look not in scorn,
   Though justly, in sooth, we are cast to die;
Ye wot no man so wise is born
   That keeps his wisdom constantly.
   Be ye then merciful, and cry
To Mary's Son that is piteous,
That His mercy take no stain from us,
   Saving us out of the fiery place.

10. From *Ballads and Lyrics*, by Andrew Lang; Longmans, London, 1907. Reprinted by permission of the publisher.

We are but dead, let no soul deny
  To pray God succour us of His grace.

The rain out of heaven has washed us clean,
  The sun has scorched us black and bare,
Ravens and rooks have pecked at our eyne,
    And feathered their nests with our beards
      and hair.
    Round are we tossed, and here and there,
This way and that, at the wild wind's will,
Never a moment my body is still;
    Birds they are busy about my face
Live not as we, nor fare as we fare;
    Pray God pardon us out of His grace.

### L'ENVOY

Prince Jesus, Master of all, to thee
We pray Hell gain no mastery,
    That we come never anear that place;
And ye men, make no mockery,
    Pray God pardon us out of His grace.

[tr. ANDREW LANG]

## BALLADE OF DEAD LADIES

### Villon

Tell me now in what hidden way is
  Lady Flora the lovely Roman?
Where's Hipparchia, and where is Thaïs,
    Neither of them the fairer woman?
    Where is Echo, beheld of no man,
Only heard on river and mere, —
    She whose beauty was more than human? . . .
But where are the snows of yester-year?

Where's Heloise, the learned nun,
  For whose sake Abeillard, I ween,
Lost manhood and put priesthood on?
    (From Love he won such dule and teen!)
    And where, I pray you, is the Queen
Who willed that Buridan should steer
    Sewed in a sack's mouth down the Seine? . . .
But where are the snows of yester-year?

White Queen Blanche, like a queen of lilies,
  With a voice like any mermaiden, —
Bertha Broadfoot, Beatrice, Alice,

And Ermengarde the lady of Maine, —
And that good Joan whom Englishmen
At Rouen doomed and burned her there, —
Mother of God, where are they then? . . .
But where are the snows of yester-year?

Nay, never ask this week, fair lord,
Where they are gone, nor yet this year,
Except with this for an overword, —
But where are the snows of yester-year?

[tr. DANTE GABRIEL ROSSETTI]

## BALLADE OF THE WOMEN OF PARIS

### Villon

Albeit the Venice girls get praise
For their sweet speech and tender air,
And though the old women have wise ways
Of chaffering for amorous ware,
Yet at my peril dare I swear,
Search Rome, where God's grace mainly tarries,
Florence and Savoy, everywhere,
There's no good girl's lip out of Paris.

The Naples women, as folk prattle,
Are sweetly spoken and subtle enough:
German girls are good at tattle,
And Prussians make their boast thereof;
Take Egypt for the next remove,
Or that waste land the Tartar harries,
Spain or Greece, for the matter of love,
There's no good girl's lip out of Paris.

Breton and Swiss know nought of the matter,
Gascony girls or girls of Toulouse;
Two fishwives here with a half-hour's chatter
Would shut them up by threes and twos;
Calais, Lorraine, and all their crews,
(Names enow the mad song marries)
England and Picardy, search them and choose,
There's no good girl's lip out of Paris.

Prince, give praise to our French ladies
For the sweet sound their speaking carries;
'Twixt Rome and Cadiz many a maid is,
But no good girl's lip out of Paris.

[tr. A. C. SWINBURNE]

# POPULAR BALLADS

Though, throughout this book, the selections have been dated and arranged in order of time and the author has been named wherever possible, the nature of the popular ballad prevents consistency in this section. When the ballad, which was designed for oral transmission, is written down, and time and place are assigned, it ceases to be a ballad. Even the translations given below, since they were made by men of letters of the nineteenth century, take from the ballad its essential nature. Yet any presentation of medieval literature would be incomplete without a representation, however deceptive, of this form, which was equally popular among all western people. Suffice it to quote Professor William J. Entwhistle: " . . . the European ballad is the result of a social condition which is defined, for each nation, within precise limits. It opens after the great migrations and crusades have subsided, and medieval man has settled down to cultivate his own acre; and it closes when reading draws away the ballad-monger's best patronage. Such conditions are, in the west of Europe, definitely medieval in time; in the east, they are medieval in spirit and partly in time." (*European Balladry,* p. 91)

## THE BRIDGE OF DEATH [1]

Anonymous French Ballad (date uncertain)

"The dance is on the Bridge of Death
   And who will dance with me?"
"There's never a man of living men
   Will dare to dance with thee."

Now Margaret's gone within her bower
   Put ashes in her hair,
And sackcloth on her bonny breast,
   And on her shoulders bare.

There came a knock to her bower door,
   And blithe she let him in;
It was her brother from the wars,
   The dearest of her kin.

"Set gold within your hair, Margaret,
   Set gold within your hair,
And gold upon your girdle band,
   And on your breast so fair.

1. From *Ballads and Lyrics,* by Andrew Lang; Longmans, London, 1907. Reprinted by permission of the publisher.

"For we are bidden to dance to-night,
  We may not bide away;
This one good night, this one fair night,
  Before the red new day."

"Nay, no gold for my head, brother,
  Nay, no gold for my hair;
It is the ashes and dust of earth
  That you and I must wear.

"No gold work for my girdle band,
  No gold work on my feet;
But ashes of the fire, my love,
  But dust that the serpents eat."

They danced across the Bridge of Death,
  Above the black water,
And the marriage-bell was tolled in hell
  For the souls of him and her.

[tr. ANDREW LANG]


## THE THREE CAPTAINS [2]

Anonymous French Ballad (date uncertain)

All beneath the white-rose tree
Walks a lady fair to see,
  She is as white as the snows,
She is as fair as the day:
  From her father's garden close
Three knights have ta'en her away.

He has ta'en her by the hand,
  The youngest of the three —
"Mount and ride, my bonnie bride,
  On my white horse with me."

And ever they rode, and better rode,
  Till they came to Senlis town,
The hostess she looked hard at them
  As they were lighting down.

"And are ye here by force," she said,
  "Or are ye here for play?"
"From out my father's garden close
  Three knights me stole away.

2. Ibid.

"And fain would I win back," she said,
  "The weary way I come;
And fain would see my father dear,
  And fain go maiden home."

"Oh, weep not, lady fair," said she,
  "You shall win back," she said,
"For you shall take this draught from me;
  Will make you lie for dead."

"Come in and sup, fair lady," they said,
  "Come busk ye and be bright;
It is with three bold captains
  That ye must be this night."

When they had eaten well and drunk,
  She fell down like one slain:
"Now, out and alas! for my bonny may
  Shall live no more again."

"Within her father's garden stead
  There are three white lilies;
With her body to the lily bed,
  With her soul to Paradise."

They bore her to her father's house,
  They bore her all the three,
They laid her in her father's close,
  Beneath the white-rose tree.

She had not lain a day, a day,
  A day but barely three,
When the may awakes, "Oh, open, father,
  Oh, open the door for me.

" 'Tis I have lain for dead, father,
  Have lain the long days three,
That I might maiden come again
  To my mother and to thee."
                              [tr. ANDREW LANG]


THE ADMIRAL GUARINOS
(as taken down by Cervantes)

Spanish Ballad (date uncertain)

The day of Roncesvalles was a dismal day for you,
Ye men of France! for there the lance of King Charles was broke
  in two:

Ye well may curse that rueful field; for many a noble peer,
In fray or fight, the dust did bite, beneath Bernardo's spear.

There captured was Guarinos, King Charles's admiral;
Seven Moorish kings surrounded him, and seized him for their
    thrall:
Seven times, when all the chase was o'er, for Guarinos lots they cast;
Seven times Marlotes won the throw, and the knight was his at last.

Much joy had then Marlotes, and his captive much did prize;
Above all the wealth of Araby, he was precious in his eyes.
Within his tent at evening he made the best of cheer,
And thus, the banquet done, he spake unto his prisoner: —

"Now, for the sake of Alla, Lord Admiral Guarinos,
Be thou a Moslem, and much love shall ever rest between us:
Two daughters have I; — all the day thy handmaid one shall be;
The other — and the fairer far — by night shall cherish thee.

"The one shall be thy waiting-maid, thy weary feet to lave,
To scatter perfumes on thy head, and fetch thee garments brave;
The other — she the pretty — shall deck her bridal bower,
And my field and my city they both shall be her dower.

"If more thou wishest, more I'll give; speak boldly what thy thought
    is."
Thus earnestly and kindly to Guarinos said Marlotes.
But not a moment did he take to ponder or to pause;
Thus clear and quick the answer of the Christian captain was: —

"Now, God forbid, Marlotes, — and Mary, his dear Mother, —
That I should leave the faith of Christ and bind me to another!
For women, — I've one wife in France, and I'll wed no more in
    Spain:
I change not faith, I break not vow, for courtesy or gain."

Wroth waxed King Marlotes, when thus he heard him say,
And all for ire commanded he should be led away, —
Away unto the dungeon-keep, beneath its vaults to lie,
With fetters bound in darkness deep, far off from sun and sky.

With iron bands they bound his hands: that sore, unworthy plight
Might well express his helplessness, doomed never more to fight.
Again, from cincture down to knee, long bolts of iron he bore,
Which signified the knight should ride on charger never more.

Three times alone, in all the year, it is the captive's doom
To see God's daylight bright and clear, instead of dungeon-gloom;
Three times alone they bring him out, like Samson long ago,
Before the Moorish rabble-rout to be a sport and show.

On three high feasts they bring him forth, a spectacle to be, —
The feast of Pasque, and the great day of the Nativity,
And on that morn, more solemn yet, when maidens strip the bowers,
And gladden mosque and minaret with the firstlings of the flowers.

Days come and go of gloom and show: seven years are come and
    gone;
And now doth fall the festival of the holy Baptist John;
Christian and Moslem tilts and jousts, to give it homage due,
And rushes on the paths to spread they force the sulky Jew.

Marlotes, in his joy and pride, a target high doth rear, —
Below the Moorish knights must ride and pierce it with the spear;
But 't is so high up in the sky, albeit much they strain,
No Moorish lance so far may fly, Marlotes' prize to gain.

Wroth waxed King Marlotes, when he beheld them fail;
The whisker trembled on his lip, — his cheek for ire was pale;
And heralds proclamation made, with trumpets, through the town, —
"Nor child shall suck, nor man shall eat, till the mark be tumbled
    down."

The cry of proclamation, and the trumpet's haughty sound,
Did send an echo to the vault where the admiral was bound:
"Now help me, God!" the captive cries; "what means this din so
    loud?
O Queen of Heaven, be vengeance given on these thy haters proud!

"O, is it that some pagan gay doth Marlotes' daughter wed,
And that they bear my scorned fair in triumph to his bed?
Or is it that the day is come, — one of the hateful three, —
When they, with trumpet, fife, and drum, make heathen game of
    me?"

These words the jailor chanced to hear, and thus to him he said:
"These tabours, Lord, and trumpets clear, conduct no bride to bed;
Nor has the feast come round again, when he that has the right
Commands thee forth, thou foe of Spain, to glad the people's sight!

"This is the joyful morning of John the Baptist's day,
When Moor and Christian feasts at home, each in his nation's way;
But now our king commands that none his banquet shall begin,
Until some knight, by strength or sleight, the spearsman's prize do
    win."

Then out and spake Guarinos: "O, soon each man should feed,
Were I but mounted once again on my own gallant steed!
O, were I mounted as of old, and harnessed cap-a-pie,
Full soon Marlotes' prize I'd hold, whate'er its price may be!

"Give me my horse, mine old gray horse, — so be he is not dead, —
All gallantly caparisoned, with plate on breast and head;
And give the lance I brought from France; and if I win it not,
My life shall be the forfeiture, — I'll yield it on the spot."

The jailor wondered at his words: thus to the knight said he:
"Seven weary years of chains and gloom have little humbled thee;
There's never a man in Spain, I trow, the like so well might bear;
And if thou wilt, I with thy vow will to the king repair."

The jailer put his mantle on, and came unto the king;
He found him sitting on the throne, within his listed ring:
Close to his ear he planted him, and the story did begin,
How bold Guarinos vaunted him the spearman's prize to win:

That, were he mounted but once more on his own gallant gray,
And armed with the lance he bore on Roncesvalles' day,
What never Moorish knight could pierce, he would pierce it at a
    blow,
Or give with joy his life-blood fierce at Marlotes' feet to flow.

Much marvelling, then said the king: "Bring Sir Guarinos forth,
And in the grange go seek ye for his gray steed of worth;
His arms are rusty on the wall; — seven years have gone, I judge,
Since that strong horse has bent his force to be a carrion drudge.

"Now this will be a sight indeed, to see the enfeebled lord
Essay to mount that ragged steed and draw that rusty sword;
And for the vaunting of his phrase he well deserves to die:
So, jailer, gird his harness on, and bring your champion nigh."

They have girded on his shirt of mail, his cuisses well they've clasped,
And they've barred the helm on his visage pale, and his hand the
    lance hath grasped;
And they have caught the old gray horse, the horse he loved of yore,
And he stands pawing at the gate, caparisoned once more.

When the knight came out, the Moors did shout, and loudly laughed
    the king,
For the horse he pranced and capered and furiously did fling:
But Guarinos whispered in his ear, and looked into his face;
Then stood the old charger like a lamb, with a calm and gentle grace.

O, lightly did Guarinos vault into the saddle-tree,
And, slowly riding down, made halt before Marlotes' knee:
Again the heathen laughed aloud: "All hail, Sir knight!" quoth he;
"Now do thy best, thou champion proud! thy blood I look to see!"

With that, Guarinos, lance in rest, against the scoffer rode,
Pierced at one thrust his envious breast, and down his turban trode.

Now ride, now ride, Guarinos, — nor lance nor rowel spare, —
Slay, slay, and gallop for thy life: the land of France lies *there!*

[tr. J. G. LOCKHART]

## THE CONQUEST OF ALHAMA

Moorish Ballad (date uncertain)

The Moorish king rides up and down,
Through Granada's royal town;
From Elvira's gates to those
Of Bivarambla on he goes.
    Woe is me, Alhama!

Letters to the monarch tell
How Alhama's city fell:
In the fire the scroll he threw
And the messenger he slew.
    Woe is me, Alhama!

He quits his mule, and mounts his horse,
And through the street directs his course;
Through the street of Zacatin
To the Alhambra spurring in.
    Woe is me, Alhama!

When the Alhambra walls he gain'd
On the moment he ordain'd
That the trumpet straight should sound
With the silver clarion round.
    Woe is me, Alhama!

And when the hollow drums of war
Beat the loud alarm afar,
That the Moors of town and plain
Might answer to the martial strain.
    Woe is me, Alhama!

Then the Moors, by this aware,
That bloody Mars recall'd them there,
One by one, and two by two,
To a mighty squadron grew.
    Woe is me, Alhama!

Out then spake an aged Moor
In these words the king before,
"Wherefore call on us, O King?
What may mean this gathering?"
    Woe is me, Alhama!

"Friends! ye have, alas! to know
Of a most disastrous blow;
That the Christians, stern and bold,
Have obtain'd Alhama's hold."
    Woe is me, Alhama!

Out then spake old Alfaqui,
With his beard so white to see,
"Good King! thou art justly served,
Good King! this thou hast deserved.
    Woe is me, Alhama!

"By thee were slain, in evil hour,
The Abencerrage, Granada's flower;
And strangers were received by thee
Of Cordova the Chivalry.
    Woe is me, Alhama!

"And for this, O King! is sent
On thee a double chastisement:
Thee and thine, thy crown and realm,
One last wreck shall overwhelm.
    Woe is me, Alhama!

"He who hold no laws in awe,
He must perish by the law;
And Granada must be won,
And thyself with her undone."
    Woe is me, Alhama!

Fire flash'd from out the old Moor's eyes;
The Monarch's wrath began to rise,
Because he answer'd, and because
He spake exceeding well of laws.
    Woe is me, Alhama!

"There is no law to say such things
As may disgust the ear of kings:" —
Thus, snorting with his choler, said
The Moorish King and doom'd him dead.
    Woe is me, Alhama!

Moor Alfaqui!  Moor Alfaqui!
Though thy beard so hoary be,
The King hath sent to have thee seized,
For Alhama's loss displeased.
    Woe is me, Alhama!

And to fix thy head upon
High Alhambra's loftiest stone;
That this for thee should be the law,
And others tremble when they saw.
　　　Woe is me, Alhama!

"Cavalier! and man of worth!
Let these words of mine go forth!
Let the Moorish Monarch know,
That to him I nothing owe.
　　　Woe is me, Alhama!

"But on my soul Alhama weighs,
And on my inmost spirit preys;
And if the King his land hath lost,
Yet others may have lost the most.
　　　Woe is me, Alhama!

"Sires have lost their children, — wives,
Their lords, — and valiant men, their lives!
One what best his love might claim
Hath lost, — another, wealth or fame.
　　　Woe is me, Alhama!

"I lost a damsel in that hour,
Of all the land the loveliest flower;
Doubloons a hundred I would pay,
And think her ransom cheap that day."
　　　Woe is me, Alhama!

And as these things the old Moor said,
They sever'd from the trunk his head;
And to the Alhambra's wall with speed
'T was carried, as the King decreed.
　　　Woe is me, Alhama!

And men and infants therein weep
Their loss, so heavy and so deep;
Granada's ladies, all she rears
Within her walls, burst into tears.
　　　Woe is me, Alhama!

And from the windows o'er the walls
The sable web of mourning falls;
The King weeps as a woman o'er
His loss, — for it is much and sore.
　　　Woe is me, Alhama!
　　　　　　　　[tr. GEORGE GORDON, LORD BYRON]

# VIII.  DANTE

Dante Alighieri was born at Florence in May 1265, the year of the battle at Benevento when Charles of Anjou defeated the King of Naples and Sicily, Manfred, the natural son of Emperor Frederick II (26 Feb. 1265/6).  Manfred's defeat initiated the decline of the Empire, in which the Ghibellines and Dante centered their hopes for peace and order in the West.  Concurrently, the Guelfs, who depended for their support primarily upon the Pope and the new bourgeoisie, rose to power, and with them the Capetian dynasty of France.

Dante's father was a Guelf notary of good, perhaps noble, ancestry. He died when Dante was eighteen, leaving a modest estate to the family, which included a half brother and two half sisters.  Apparently Dante's formal education was sketchy.  Though he acquired some learning by studying popular works like Brunetto Latini's *Tresor* and turned his hand to poetry and probably to painting and sketching, there is no evidence of systematic study until after the death of Beatrice in June 1290.  Then, he says in his *Banquet,* he turned to Boethius and Cicero, "and though at first it was hard for me to understand their meaning, I succeeded so far as my knowledge of Latin and my powers of understanding allowed me."  This is a strange record for one who is generally regarded as the most erudite poet in the West.

In fact, Dante seems to have been as little disciplined in books as the other young blades of the teeming, overcrowded city.  In the battle of Campaldino, 11 June 1289, when Florence won a great victory over Arezzo, "he fought vigorously," according to Bruni, a fifteenth-century biographer, "on horseback in the front rank, where he was exposed to the gravest danger."  Two records of borrowing in behalf of his family during this period suggest lack of affluence, but not poverty.  In 1295 or 1296, he enrolled in the Guild of Physicians and Apothecaries in order to qualify to hold public office.  That Guild, one of the most powerful, included authors and artists, since apothecaries sold books, paints, and paintings.

According to Dante's statement in the *New Life,* below, he first met Beatrice when both were nine years old.  She was the daughter of Folco Portinari, a wealthy and respected Florentine.  Their next meeting, as far as is known, was nine years later, an occasion that inspired Dante's first poem, the sonnet *A ciascun' alma presa e gentil core.*  This sonnet he sent to the leading Tuscan poets; among the replies is a sonnet by Guido Cavalcanti, who from that event became Dante's "first friend."  The sonnet is translated below (p. 869).  A fresco by Giotto on a wall of the Bargello includes in the throng of leading citizens of Florence the Dante of this period.  Before 1288, Beatrice married Simone de' Bardi of the great Florentine banking house that was eventually ruined in 1345 by the default by King Edward III of England on a loan of nearly a million gold florins. Not long after her death, Dante published his *New Life,* in which he narrates the course of his love for her.

After Beatrice died and before 1298, Dante married Gemma Donati, daughter of an ancient and honorable Guelf family. Their children were born before 1302: Pietro, who became a lawyer and author of a commentary on the *Comedy;* Jacopo, who entered the Church and eventually became a canon at Verona and likewise commented on the *Comedy;* and Beatrice, who became a nun at Ravenna, and on whom Boccaccio, in 1350, bestowed a gift of ten gold florins in behalf of the Capitani of Or San Michele of Florence. Whether Antonia, of whom there is mention, was a fourth child or the name for Beatrice before she took orders is a matter of dispute. The three children, at any rate, eventually followed their father into exile and lived with him at Ravenna.

The year 1300, as the *Comedy* makes abundantly evident, marked the turning point in Dante's life. After serving at least once as ambassador, he was elected one of six priors of Florence for two months, 15 June to 15 August. Bruni quotes a lost letter of Dante that reads, "All my woes and all my misfortunes had their origin and commencement with my unlucky election to the priorate."

Florence had been rapidly gaining wealth and power under Guelf rule. According to the contemporary Florentine historian Villani: "At this time our city of Florence was in the greatest and happiest state it had ever been in since it was rebuilt, or even before, as well in size and power as in the number of her people, for there were more than thirty thousand citizens in her city, and more than seventy thousand fit to bear arms in the districts belonging to her territory; and by reason of the nobility of her brave knights and of her free people, as well as of her great riches, she was mistress of almost the whole of Tuscany."

But in that year a feud broke out between the noble but comparatively poor Donati (the Blacks) and the rich but parvenu Cerchi (the Whites), and the town was rent by disorder and civil strife. The priors, Dante among them, decided to banish the leaders of both parties (including the White Guido Cavalcanti, who contracted malaria in exile and died that year). During the next year, Pope Boniface VIII intervened by sending Charles of Valois as papal representative to restore order. His known sympathy for the Blacks impelled the White faction to send an embassy, including Dante, to the Pope in October 1301, in an effort to head off Charles. But Charles entered Florence on All Saints' Day, while the embassy was at Rome, and immediately established the Black hegemony, treacherously allowing the leader, Corso Donati, to return from exile. On 27 January 1301/2, the Podestà pronounced sentence against the absent Dante and four other Whites for barratry and conspiracy. The first sentence, consisting of a heavy fine, exile for two years, and permanent disqualification for public office, was changed on 10

March to confiscation of all property and burning alive, should Dante and his fellow-adjudged come within the power of the Florentine state. Dante never again set foot within the boundaries of Florence.

Villani, himself a Black, who witnessed the events, says in his chronicle: "Dante was one of the chief magistrates of our city, and was of the White party, and a Guelf withal; and on that account, *without any other fault,* with the said White party he was driven out and banished from Florence."

Knowledge of Dante's movements in exile is limited. After living for some time with his fellow-exiles, Dante parted from them in disgust. In *Paradise,* his ancestor Cacciaguida warns him that his greatest sorrow will be the wickedness and folly of that company of expatriates with whom his lot will be cast. Very shortly he settled with the famous della Scala (Scaliger) family in Verona. In 1306, he acted as agent for the Malaspini of Lunigiana. Boccaccio and Villani both testify that in this period Dante studied at Paris.

When, in 1310, Henry of Luxemburg, as Emperor Henry VII, initiated plans for consolidating the states of northern Italy within the Empire, Dante's hopes and aspirations rose. He addressed an open letter to the people of Italy in Henry's favor, a sulphurous blast against the citizens of Florence for preparing to resist him, and an exhortation to Henry himself. In 1312, the Emperor beseiged Florence, but had to withdraw. His death, 24 August 1313, near Siena, shattered the last of Dante's hopes of return, for he had been expressly excluded from a Florentine edict of amnesty, 2 September 1311, probably because of his activities in Henry's behalf. On 6 November 1315, the death sentence was extended to his sons.

In 1317 or 1318, at the invitation of Guido Novello da Polenta, the now-famous poet went to Ravenna, where he lived out his life. The laurel wreath offered by Bologna he refused, since it could not be awarded in his native city. In 1321, Guido sent him as a member of an embassy to the Doge of Venice. On the overland journey back he contracted malaria and died 14 September. His body was interred in the Franciscan chapel at Ravenna, where it has remained, despite all efforts of the Florentines, officially initiated in 1396, to recover the bones of him whom they would have burned had they caught him alive.

Tributes to Dante's unique genius began before his death; among those who wrote elegies were his poet-friends Cino da Pistoia and Giovanni Quirini. Villani recorded the event, remarking: "This man was a great scholar in almost every branch of learning, although he was a layman. He was a great poet and philosopher, and a perfect rhetorician in both prose and verse, and in public debate he was a very noble speaker; in rime he was supreme, with the most polished and beautiful style that ever had been in our language up to his time and since. . . . This Dante, on account of his great learning, was somewhat haughty and reserved and scornful, and, after the manner of a philosopher, little gracious, not adapting himself to the conversation of the unlearned." Fifty years after Dante's death, Florence established a professorship for the exposition of his poetry. Its first incumbent was Boccaccio, the second of the triumvirate of world-famous Tuscan fourteenth-century poets, Petrarch being the third. Boccaccio had already, twenty-five years after Dante's death, traveled in homage to Ravenna and talked with those who knew Dante alive. Dante is no doubt the world's most translated poet, appealing to oriental and occidental taste alike. Paget Toynbee has gathered together fourteen hundred closely packed pages of references to Dante in English literature before 1844, a date that marks only the beginning of intense interest in Dante among English-speaking people. The epithets include "extravagant, absurd, disgusting," "Methodist parson in Bedlam," and "bawdy historiographer," as well as "wonderful original," "father of modern poetry," "accurate and profound observer of human nature," "sublime genius," "great and holy," and "prince of poets."

In addition to the works represented in the following pages, Dante composed many other *canzoni* and short lyrics, the *Banquet* (*Convivio*) — an unfinished outline of popular philosophy composed before 1311 — a number of Latin letters, two remarkable eclogues, and, probably, a tract (*Quaestio de Aqua et Terra*) on geological science.

# THE NEW LIFE
## (*La Vita Nuova*)

After the death of Beatrice Portinari in 1290, Dante gathered together the poems she had inspired, strung them on a thread of prose narrative and analysis, and sent them in dedication to his poet-friend, Guido Cavalcanti. According to Charles Eliot Norton, "The narrative of the *New Life* is quaint, embroidered with conceits, deficient in artistic completeness, but it has the simplicity of youth, the charm of sincerity, the freedom of personal confidence; and so long as there are lovers in the world, and so long as lovers are poets, this first and tenderest love-story of modern literature will be read with appreciation and responsive sympathy."

The external form of alternating prose and verse was known to Dante in the book that he was probably studying hardest at the moment, Boethius' *Consolation*. But this form as well as the content of the whole is more directly in the tradition of the Provençal troubadours, whose poems were linked by *razos, or prose biographies*, which detailed the events inspiring the composition. The story of *Aucassin and Nicolete* above is a variant of the form. The divisions and analyses of each poem were an adaptation of the method of Albertus Magnus and St. Thomas Aquinas in expounding the work of Aristotle. The earthy and often coarse theme of love of the troubadours, transplanted first to the Neapolitan court of Frederick II and then to northern Italy, was exalted and idealized by the writers in the "sweet new style" (*dolce stil nuovo*), of whom Dante counted Guido Guinicelli of Bologna the first and Cavalcanti his greatest contemporary. Though the *New Life* is formally close to the Provençal tradition and the story of Dante's love for Beatrice conforms to courtly pattern in the remoteness of the principals and the various screening devices and calculated deceptions, it is at once simpler and more direct in its expression, with none of the tortuous verse-patterns and diction, and more elevated and ennobled in its concept of love as divine as God Himself. In fact, so ethereal is Dante's portrait of Beatrice that many have maintained that she represents no physical woman but only an abstract ideal. Readers who so limit Dante's words lose much of the charm of the work, but there can be no question that already Dante was turning his hand to exposition of meaning beyond the physical world. Even the title is ambiguous, indicating as it does not only the experiences of youth or early life but also the rededication of life through ennobling love (see p. 734).

We meet in the *New Life* Dante's concern for symbolism in form and numbers. The thirty-one poems consist of twenty-five sonnets (two irregular), five *canzoni* (two imperfect), and one ballata, symmetrically arranged about the three principal *canzoni*. The theme of the number 9, itself thrice-holy as being the square of trinity, informs all the historical events. In conformity with the divinely perfected 7, there are seven visions narrated. The closing resolution to speak no more of Beatrice until the poet can utter of her what has never yet been said of any woman anticipates the *Comedy*.

The classic translation of Dante Gabriel Rossetti, given below, has been abridged, especially in the omission of all but the first few scholastic "divisions" of the poems.


# THE NEW LIFE

## Dante

In that part of the book of my memory before the which is little that can be read, there is a rubric, saying, *Incipit Vita Nova*. Under such rubric I find written many things; and among them the words which I purpose to copy into this little book; if not all of them, at the least their substance.

Nine times already since my birth had the heaven of light returned to the selfsame point almost, as concerns its own revolution, when first the glorious Lady of my mind was made manifest to mine eyes; even she who was called Beatrice by many who knew not wherefore.[1] She had already been in this life for so long as that, within her time, the starry heaven had moved towards the Eastern quarter one of the twelve parts of a degree; so that she appeared to me at the beginning of her ninth year almost, and I saw her almost at the end of my ninth year. Her dress, on that day, was of a most noble colour, a subdued and goodly crimson, girdled and adorned in such sort as best suited with her very tender age. At that moment, I say most truly that the spirit of life, which hath its dwelling in the secretest chamber of the heart, began to tremble so violently that the least pulses of my body shook therewith; and in trembling it said these words: *Ecce deus fortior me, qui veniens dominabitur mihi.*[2] At that moment the animate spirit, which dwelleth in the lofty chamber whither all the senses carry their perceptions, was filled with wonder, and speaking more especially unto the spirits of the eyes, said these words: *Apparuit jam beatitudo vestra.*[3] At that moment the natural spirit, which dwelleth there where our nourishment is administered, began to weep, and in weeping said these words: *Heu miser! quia frequenter impeditus ero deinceps.*[4]

1. Boccaccio says that this first meeting took place at a May Feast, given in the year 1274 by Folco Portinari, father of Beatrice, principal citizen of Florence. Dante accompanied his father, Alighiero Alighieri.
2. "Here is a deity stronger than I; who, coming, shall rule over me."
3. "Your beatitude hath now been made manifest unto you."
4. "Alas! how often shall I be disturbed from this time forth!"

I say that, from that time forward, Love quite governed my soul; which was immediately espoused to him, and with so safe and undisputed a lordship (by virtue of strong imagination), that I had nothing left for it but to do all his bidding continually. He oftentimes commanded me to seek if I might see this youngest of the Angels: wherefore I in my boyhood often went in search of her, and found her so noble and praiseworthy that certainly of her might have been said those words of the poet Homer, "She seemed not to be the daughter of a mortal man, but of God." And albeit her image, that was with me always, was an exultation of Love to subdue me, it was yet of so perfect a quality that it never allowed me to be over-ruled by Love without the faithful counsel of reason, whensoever such counsel was useful to be heard. But seeing that were I to dwell overmuch on the passions and doings of such early youth, my words might be counted something fabulous, I will therefore put them aside; and passing many things that may be conceived by the pattern of these, I will come to such as are writ in my memory with a better distinctness.

After the lapse of so many days that nine years exactly were completed since the above-written appearance of this most gracious being, on the last of those days it happened that the same wonderful lady appeared to me dressed all in pure white, between two gentle ladies elder than she. And passing through a street, she turned her eyes thither where I stood sorely abashed: and by her unspeakable courtesy, which is now guerdoned in the Great Cycle, she saluted me with so virtuous a bearing that I seemed then and there to behold the very limits of blessedness. The hour of her most sweet salutation was certainly the ninth of that day; and because it was the first time that any words from her reached mine ears, I came into such sweetness that I parted thence as one intoxicated. And betaking me to the loneliness of mine own room, I fell to thinking of this most courteous lady; thinking of whom I was overtaken by a pleasant slumber, wherein a marvellous vision was presented to me: for there appeared to be in my room a mist of the colour of fire, within the which I discerned the figure of a lord of terrible aspect to such as should gaze upon him, but who seemed therewithal to rejoice inwardly that it was a marvel to see. Speaking he said many things, among the which I could understand but few; and of these, this: *Ego dominus tuus.*[5] In his arms it seemed to me that a person was sleeping, covered only with a blood-coloured cloth; upon whom looking very attentively, I knew that it was the lady of the salutation who had deigned the day before to salute me. And he who held her held also in his hand a thing that was burning in flames; and he said to me, *Vide cor tuum.*[6] But when he had remained with me a little while, I thought that he set himself to awaken her that slept; after the which he made her to eat that thing which flamed in his hand; and she ate as one fearing. Then, having waited again a space,

5. "I am thy master."
6. "Behold thy heart."

all his joy was turned into most bitter weeping; and as he wept he
gathered the lady into his arms, and it seemed to me that he went
with her up towards heaven; whereby such a great anguish came
upon me that my light slumber could not endure through it, but
was suddenly broken.   And immediately having considered, I knew
that the hour wherein this vision had been made manifest to me
was the fourth hour (which is to say, the first of the nine last hours)
of the night.

Then, musing on what I had seen, I proposed to relate the same
to many poets who were famous in that day: and for that I had
myself in some sort the art of discoursing with rhyme, I resolved
on making a sonnet, in the which, having saluted all such as are subject
unto Love, and entreated them to expound my vision, I should write
unto them those things which I had seen in my sleep.   And the
sonnet I made was this:

> To every heart which the sweet pain doth move,
>   And unto which these words may now be brought
>   For true interpretation and kind thought,
> Be greeting in our Lord's name which is Love.
> Of those long hours wherein the stars, above,
>   Wake and keep watch, the third was almost nought
>   When Love was shown me with such terrors fraught
> As may not carelessly be spoken of.
> He seem'd like one who is full of joy, and had
>   My heart within his hand, and on his arm
>     My lady, with a mantle round her, slept;
> Whom (having waken'd her) anon he made
>   To eat that heart; she ate, as fearing harm.
>     Then he went out; and as he went, he wept.

*This sonnet is divided into two parts. In the first part I give
greeting, and ask an answer: in the second, I signify what thing
has to be answered to. The second part commences here "Of
those long hours."*

To this sonnet I received many answers, conveying many different opinions; of which, one was sent by him whom I now call the
first among my friends; and it began thus: "Unto my thinking
thou beheld'st all worth." [7]   And indeed, it was when he learned
that I was he who had sent those rhymes to him, that our friendship
commenced.   But the true meaning of that vision was not then
perceived by any one, though it be now evident to the least skilful.

Now it fell on a day, that this most gracious creature was sitting
where words were to be heard of the Queen of Glory; and I was in
a place whence mine eyes could behold their beatitude.   And betwixt her and me, in a direct line, there sat another lady of a pleasant

7. See sonnet of Guido Cavalcanti, p. 869.

favour; who looked round at me many times, marvelling at my continued gaze which seemed to have *her* for its object. And many perceived that she thus looked, so that departing thence, I heard it whispered after me, "Look you to what a pass *such a lady* hath brought him;" and in saying this they named her who had been midway between the most gentle Beatrice, and mine eyes. Therefore I was reassured, and knew that for that day my secret had not become manifest. Then immediately it came into my mind that I might make use of this lady as a screen to the truth. And so well did I play my part that the most of those who had hitherto watched and wondered at me, now imagined they had found me out. By her means I kept my secret concealed till some years were gone over; and for my better security, I even made divers rhymes in her honour; whereof I shall here write only as much as concerneth the most gentle Beatrice, which is but a very little. Moreover, about the same time, while this lady was a screen for so much love on my part, I took the resolution to set down the name of this most gracious creature accompanied with many other women's names, and especially with hers whom I spake of. And to this end I put together the names of sixty of the most beautiful ladies in that city where God had placed mine own lady; and these names I introduced in an epistle in the form of a *sirvent,* which it is not my intention to transcribe here. Neither should I have said anything of this matter, did I not wish to take note of a certain strange thing, to wit: that having written the list, I found my lady's name would not stand otherwise than ninth in order among the names of these ladies.

Now it so chanced with her by whose means I had thus long time concealed my desire, that it behoved her to leave the city I speak of, and to journey afar. Wherefore I, being sorely perplexed at the loss of so excellent a defence, had more trouble than even I could before have supposed. And thinking that if I spoke not somewhat mournfully of her departure, my former counterfeiting would be the more quickly perceived, I determined that I would make a grievous sonnet thereof; the which I will write here, because it hath certain words in it whereof my lady was the immediate cause, as will be plain to him that understands. And the sonnet was this:

> All ye that pass along Love's trodden way,
> Pause ye awhile and say
>   If there be any grief like unto mine:
> I pray you that you hearken a short space
> Patiently, if my case
>   Be not a piteous marvel and a sign.
>
> Love (never, certes, for my worthless part,
> But of his own great heart)
>   Vouchsafed to me a life so calm and sweet
> That oft I heard folk question as I went

What such great gladness meant:—
    They spoke of it behind me in the street.

But now that fearless bearing is all gone
    Which with Love's hoarded wealth was given me;
        Till I am grown to be
So poor that I have dread to think thereon.

And thus it is that I, being like as one
    Who is ashamed and hides his poverty,
        Without seem full of glee,
And let my heart within travail and moan.

*This poem has two principal parts; for, in the first, I mean to call the Faithful of Love in those words of Jeremias the Prophet,[8] "O vos omnes qui transitis per viam, attendite et videte si est dolor sicut dolor meus," and to pray them to stay and hear me. In the second I tell where Love had placed me, with a meaning other than that which the last part of the poem shows, and I say what I have lost. The second part begins here: "Love (never, certes)."*

A certain while after the departure of that lady, it pleased the Master of the Angels to call into His glory a damsel, young and of a gentle presence, who had been very lovely in the city I speak of: and I saw her body lying without its soul among many ladies, who held a pitiful weeping. Whereupon, remembering that I had seen her in the company of excellent Beatrice, I could not hinder myself from a few tears; and weeping, I conceived to say somewhat of her death, in guerdon of having seen her somewhile with my lady; which thing I spake of in the latter end of the verses that I writ in this matter, as he will discern who understands. And I wrote two sonnets, which are these:

### I

Weep, Lover, sith Love's very self doth weep,
    And sith the cause for weeping is so great;
    When now so many dames, of such estate
In worth, show with their eyes a grief so deep:
For Death the churl has laid his leaden sleep
    Upon a damsel who was fair of late,
    Defacing all our earth should celebrate,—
Yea all save virtue, which the soul doth keep.
Now hearken how much Love did honour her.
    I myself saw him in his proper form
        Bending above the motionless sweet dead,
And often gazing into Heaven; for there
    The soul now sits which when her life was warm
        Dwelt with the joyful beauty that is fled.

8. Lamentations 1:12.

*This first sonnet is divided into three parts. In the first, I call and beseech the Faithful of Love to weep; and I say that their Lord weeps, and that they, hearing the reason why he weeps, shall be more minded to listen to me. In the second, I relate this reason. In the third, I speak of honour done by Love to this Lady. The second part begins here: "When now so many dames;" the third here: "Now hearken."*

## II

Death, alway cruel, Pity's foe in chief,
Mother who brought forth grief,
   Merciless judgment and without appeal!
   Since thou alone hast made my heart to feel
   This sadness and unweal,
My tongue upbraideth thee without relief.

And now (for I must rid thy name of ruth)
Behoves me speak the truth
   Touching thy cruelty and wickedness:
   Not that they be not known; but ne'ertheless
   I would give hate more stress
With them that feed on love in very sooth.

Out of this world thou hast driven courtesy,
   And virtue, dearly prized in womanhood;
   And out of youth's gay mood
The lovely lightness is quite gone through thee.

Whom now I mourn, no man shall learn from me
   Save by the measures of these praises given.
   Whoso deserves not Heaven
May never hope to have her company.

*This poem is divided into four parts. In the first I address Death by certain proper names of hers. In the second, speaking to her, I tell the reason why I am moved to denounce her. In the third, I rail against her. In the fourth, I turn to speak to a person undefined, although defined in my own conception. The second part commences here, "Since thou alone;" the third here, "And now (for I must);" the fourth here, "Whoso deserves not."*

I began to be harassed with many and divers thoughts, by each of which I was sorely tempted; and in especial, there were four among them that left me no rest. The first was this: "Certainly the lordship of Love is good; seeing that it diverts the mind from all mean things." The second was this: "Certainly the lordship of Love is evil; seeing that the more homage his servants pay to him, the more grievous and painful are the torments wherewith he torments them." The third was this: "The name of Love is so sweet in the hearing that it would not seem possible for its effects to be other than sweet; seeing that the name must needs be like unto the thing named: as it is written: *Nomina sunt consequentia rerum.*[9] And the fourth was this: "The lady whom Love hath chosen out to govern thee is not as other ladies, whose hearts are easily moved."

And by each one of these thoughts I was so sorely assailed that I was like unto him who doubteth which path to take, and wishing to go, goeth not. And if I bethought myself to seek out some point at which all these paths might be found to meet, I discerned but one way, and that irked me; to wit, to call upon Pity, and to commend myself unto her. And it was then that, feeling a desire to write somewhat thereof in rhyme, I wrote this sonnet:

All my thoughts always speak to me of Love,
   Yet have between themselves such difference
   That while one bids me bow with mind and sense,
A second saith, "Go to: look thou above;"
The third one, hoping, yields me joy enough;
   And with the last come tears, I scarce know whence:
   All of them craving pity in sore suspense,
Trembling with fears that the heart knoweth of.
And thus, being all unsure which path to take,
   Wishing to speak I know not what to say,
   And lose myself in amorous wanderings:
Until (my peace with all of them to make),
   Unto mine enemy I needs must pray,
   My lady Pity, for the help she brings.

*This sonnet may be divided into four parts. In the first, I say and propound that all my thoughts are concerning Love. In the second, I say that they are diverse, and I relate their diversity. In the third, I say wherein they all seem to agree. In the fourth, I say that, wishing to speak of Love, I know not from which of these thoughts to take my argument; and that if I would take it from all, I shall have to call upon mine enemy, my Lady Pity. "Lady" I say as in a scornful mode of speech. The second begins here, "Yet have between themselves;" the third, "All of them craving;" the fourth, "And thus."*

After this battling with many thoughts, it chanced on a day that my most gracious lady was with a gathering of ladies in a certain place; to the which I was conducted by a friend of mine; he thinking to do me a great pleasure by showing me the beauty of so many women. Then I, hardly knowing whereunto he conducted me, but trusting in him (who yet was leading his friend to the last verge of life), made question: "To what end are we come among these ladies?" and he answered: "To the end that they may be worthily served." And they were assembled around a gentlewoman who

9. "Names are the consequents of things."

was given in marriage on that day; the custom of the city being that these should bear her company when she sat down for the first time at table in the house of her husband. Therefore I, as was my friend's pleasure, resolved to stay with him and do honour to those ladies.

But as soon as I had thus resolved, I began to feel a faintness and a throbbing at my left side, which soon took possession of my whole body. Whereupon I remember that I covertly leaned my back unto a painting that ran round the walls of that house; and being fearful lest my trembling should be discerned of them, I lifted mine eyes to look on those ladies, and then first perceived among them the excellent Beatrice. And when I perceived her, all my senses were overpowered by the great lordship that Love obtained, finding himself so near unto that most gracious being, until nothing but the spirits of sight remained to me; and even these remained driven out of their own instruments because Love entered in that honoured place of theirs, that so he might the better behold her. And although I was other than at first, I grieved for the spirits so expelled which kept up a sore lament, saying: "If he had not in this wise thrust us forth, we also should behold the marvel of this lady." By this, many of her friends, having discerned my confusion, began to wonder; and together with herself, kept whispering of me and mocking me. Whereupon my friend, who knew not what to conceive, took me by the hands, and drawing me forth from among them, required to know what ailed me. Then, having first held me at quiet for a space until my perceptions were come back to me, I made answer to my friend: "Of a surety I have now set my feet on that point of life, beyond the which he must not pass who would return."

Afterwards, leaving him, I went back to the room where I had wept before; and again weeping and ashamed, said: "If this lady but knew of my condition, I do not think that she would thus mock at me; nay, I am sure that she must needs feel some pity." And in my weeping I bethought me to write certain words in the which, speaking to her, I should signify the occasion of my disfigurement, telling her also how I knew that she had no knowledge thereof: which, if it were known, I was certain must move others to pity. And then, because I hoped that peradventure it might come into her hearing, I wrote this sonnet:

> Even as the others mock, thou mockest me;
>     Not dreaming, noble lady, whence it is
>     That I am taken with strange semblances,
> Seeing thy face which is so fair to see:
> For else, compassion would not suffer thee
>     To grieve my heart with such harsh scoffs as these.
>     Lo! Love, when thou art present, sits at ease,
> And bears his mastership so mightily,
> That all my troubled senses he thrusts out,
>     Sorely tormenting some, and slaying some,

Till none but he is left and has free range
To gaze on thee.   This makes my face to change
Into another's; while I stand all dumb,
And hear my senses clamour in their rout.

*This sonnet I divide not into parts, because a division is only
made to open the meaning of the thing divided: and this, as it is
sufficiently manifest through the reasons given, has no need of
division.   True it is that, amid the words whereby is shown the
occasion of this sonnet, dubious words are to be found; namely, when
I say that Love kills all my spirits, but that the visual remain in life,
only outside of their own instruments.   And this difficulty it is impossible for any to solve who is not in equal guise liege unto Love;
and, to those who are so, that is manifest which would clear up the
dubious words.   And therefore it were not well for me to expound
this difficulty, inasmuch as my speaking would be either fruitless
or else superfluous.*

A while after this strange disfigurement, I became possessed with
a strong conception which left me but very seldom, and then to
return quickly.   And it was this: "Seeing that thou comest into
such scorn by the companionship of this lady, wherefore seekest
thou to behold her?   If she should ask thee this thing, what answer
couldst thou make unto her? yea, even though thou wert master of
all thy faculties, and in no way hindered from answering."   Unto
the which, another very humble thought said in reply: "If I were
master of all my faculties, and in no way hindered from answering,
I would tell her that no sooner do I image to myself her marvellous
beauty than I am possessed with the desire to behold her, the which
is of so great strength that it kills and destroys in my memory all
those things which might oppose it; and it is therefore that the
great anguish I have endured thereby is yet not enough to restrain
me from seeking to behold her."   And then, because of these
thoughts, I resolved to write somewhat, wherein, having pleaded
mine excuse, I should tell her of what I felt in her presence.   Whereupon I wrote this sonnet:—

The thoughts are broken in my memory,
    Thou lovely Joy, whene'er I see thy face;
    When thou art near me, Love fills up the space,
Often repeating, "If death irk thee, fly."
My face shows my heart's colour, verily,
    Which, fainting, seeks for any leaning-place;
    Till, in the drunken terror of disgrace,
The very stones seem to be shrieking, "Die!"
It were a grievous sin, if one should not
    Strive then to comfort my bewilder'd mind
        (Though merely with a simple pitying),
For the great anguish which thy scorn has wrought

In the dead sight o' the eyes grown nearly blind,
Which look for death as for a blessed thing.[10]

Through the sore change in mine aspect, the secret of my heart
was now understood of many. Which thing being thus, there
came a day when certain ladies to whom it was well known (they
having been with me at divers times in my trouble) were met together for the pleasure of gentle company. And as I was going that
way by chance (but I think rather by the will of Fortune), I heard
one of them call unto me, and she that called was a lady of very
sweet speech. And when I had come close up with them, and
perceived that they had not among them mine excellent lady, I
was reassured; and saluted them, asking of their pleasure. The
ladies were many; divers of whom were laughing one to another,
while divers gazed at me as though I should speak anon. But when
I still spake not, one of them, who before had been talking with
another, addressed me by my name, saying, "To what end lovest
thou this lady, seeing that thou canst not support her presence?
Now tell us this thing, that we may know it: for certainly the end
of such a love must be worthy of knowledge." And when she had
spoken these words, not she only, but all they that were with her,
began to observe me, waiting for my reply. Whereupon, I said
thus unto them: "Ladies, the end and aim of my Love was but the
salutation of that lady of whom I conceive that ye are speaking;
wherein alone I found that beatitude which is the goal of desire.
And now that it hath pleased her to deny me this, Love, my Master,
of his great goodness, hath placed all my beatitude there where
my hope will not fail me." Then those ladies began to talk closely
together; and as I have seen snow fall among the rain, so was their
talk mingled with sighs. But after a little, that lady who had been
the first to address me, addressed me again in these words: "We
pray thee that thou wilt tell us wherein abideth this thy beatitude."
And answering, I said but thus much: "In those words that do
praise my lady." To the which she rejoined, "If thy speech were
true, those words that thou didst write concerning thy condition
would have been written with another intent."

Then I, being almost put to shame because of her answer, went
out from among them; and as I walked, I said within myself: "Seeing
that there is so much beatitude in those words which do praise my
lady, wherefore hath my speech of her been different?" And then
I resolved that thenceforward I would choose for the theme of my
writings only the praise of this most gracious being. But when
I had thought exceedingly, it seemed to me that I had taken to myself a theme which was much too lofty, so that I dared not begin;
and I remained during several days in the desire of speaking, and
the fear of beginning. After which it happened, as I passed one

10. Dante's "divisions," which he gives for almost every lyric, are
omitted here and for many subsequent lyrics.

day along a path which lay beside a stream of very clear water, that
there came upon me a great desire to say somewhat in rhyme; but
when I began thinking how I should say it, methought that to
speak of her were unseemly, unless I spoke to other ladies in the
second person; which is to say, not to *any* other ladies; but only to
such as are so called because they are gentle, let alone for mere
womanhood.  Whereupon I declare that my tongue spake as though
by its own impulse, and said, "Ladies that have intelligence in love."
These words I laid up in my mind with great gladness, conceiving
to take them as my commencement.  Wherefore, having returned
to the city I spake of, and considered thereof during certain days, I
began a poem with this beginning:

Ladies that have intelligence in love,
   Of mine own lady I would speak with you;
   Not that I hope to count her praises through,
      But telling what I may, to ease my mind.
And I declare that when I speak thereof
   Love sheds such perfect sweetness over me
   That if my courage fail'd not, certainly
      To him my listeners must be all resign'd.
      Wherefore I will not speak in such large kind
That mine own speech should foil me, which were base;
But only will discourse of her high grace
   In these poor words, the best that I can find,
With you alone, dear dames and damozels:
'Twere ill to speak thereof with any else.

An Angel of his blessed knowledge, saith
   To God: "Lord, in the world that Thou hast made,
   A miracle in action is display'd
      By reason of a soul whose splendours fare
Even hither: and since Heaven requireth
   Nought saving her, for her it prayeth Thee,
   Thy Saints crying aloud continually."
      Yet Pity still defends our earthly share
      In that sweet soul; God answering thus the prayer:
"My well-beloved, suffer that in peace
Your hope remain, while so My pleasure is,
   There where one dwells who dreads the loss of her;
And who in Hell unto the doom'd shall say,
'I have look'd on that for which God's chosen pray.'"

My lady is desired in the high Heaven:
   Wherefore, it now behoveth me to tell,
   Saying: Let any maid that would be well
      Esteem'd keep with her: for as she goes by,
Into foul hearts a deathly chill is driven

By Love, that makes ill thought to perish there;
  While any who endures to gaze on her
    Must either be made noble, or else die.
    When one deserving to be raised so high
Is found, 'tis then her power attains its proof,
Making his heart strong for his soul's behoof
  With the full strength of meek humility.
Also this virtue owns she, by God's will:
Who speaks with her can never come to ill.

Love saith concerning her: "How chanceth it
  That flesh, which is of dust, should be thus pure?"
    Then, gazing always, he makes oath: "For sure,
    This is a creature of God till now unknown."
She hath that paleness of the pearl that's fit
  In a fair woman, so much and not more;
  She is as high as Nature's skill can soar;
    Beauty is tried by her comparison.
    Whatever her sweet eyes are turn'd upon,
Spirits of love do issue thence in flame,
Which through their eyes who then may look on them
  Pierce to the heart's deep chamber every one.
And in her smile Love's image you may see;
Whence none can gaze upon her steadfastly.

Dear Song, I know thou wilt hold gentle speech
  With many ladies, when I send thee forth:
  Wherefore (being mindful that thou hadst thy birth
    From Love, and art a modest, simple child),
Whomso thou meetest, say thou this to each:
  "Give me good speed! To her I wend along
  In whose much strength my weakness is made strong."
    And if, i' the end, thou wouldst not be beguiled
    Of all thy labour, seek not the defiled
And common sort; but rather choose to be
Where man and woman dwell in courtesy.
  So to the road thou shalt be reconciled,
And find the lady, and with the lady, Love.
Commend thou me to each, as doth behove.

When this song was a little gone abroad, a certain one of my friends, hearing the same, was pleased to question me, that I should tell him what thing love is; it may be, conceiving from the words thus heard a hope of me beyond my desert. Wherefore I, thinking that after such discourse it were well to say somewhat of the nature of Love, and also in accordance with my friend's desire, proposed to myself to write certain words in the which I should treat of this argument. And the sonnet I then made is this:

Love and the gentle heart are one same thing,
   Even as the wise man [11] in his ditty saith.
   Each, of itself, would be such life in death
As rational soul bereft of reasoning.
'Tis Nature makes them when she loves: a king
   Love is, whose palace where he sojourneth
   Is called the Heart; there draws he quiet breath
At first, with brief or longer slumbering.
Then beauty seen in virtuous womankind
   Will make the eyes desire, and through the heart
   Send the desiring of the eyes again;
Where often it abides so long enshrined
   That Love at length out of his sleep will start.
And women feel the same for worthy men.

Having treated of love in the foregoing, it appeared to me that
I should also say something in praise of my lady, wherein it might be
set forth how love manifested itself when produced by her; and
how not only she could awaken it where it slept, but where it was
not she could marvelously create it. To which end I wrote another
sonnet; and it is this:

My lady carries love within her eyes;
   All that she looks on is made pleasanter;
   Upon her path men turn to gaze at her;
He whom she greeteth feels his heart to rise,
And droops his troubled visage, full of sighs,
   And of his evil heart is then aware:
   Hate loves, and Pride becomes a worshipper.
O women, help to praise her in somewise.
Humbleness, and the hope that hopeth well,
   By speech of hers into the mind are brought,
   And who beholds is blessed oftenwhiles.
   The look she hath when she a little smiles
Cannot be said, nor holden in the thought;
'Tis such a new and gracious miracle.

Not many days after this (it being the will of the most High God,
who also from Himself put not away death), the father of wonderful
Beatrice, going out of this life, passed certainly into glory. Thereby
it happened, as of very sooth it might not be otherwise, that this
lady was made full of the bitterness of grief: seeing that such a
parting is very grievous unto those friends who are left, and that
no other friendship is like to that between a good parent and a
good child; and furthermore considering that this lady was good
in the supreme degree, and her father (as by many it hath been
truly averred) of exceeding goodness. And because it is the usage
of that city that men meet with men in such a grief, and women

11. Guido Guinicelli.

with women, certain ladies of her companionship gathered themselves unto Beatrice, where she kept alone in her weeping. And as they passed in and out, I could hear them speak concerning her, how she wept. At length two of them went by me, who said: "Certainly she grieveth in such sort that one might die for pity, beholding her." Then, feeling the tears upon my face, I put up my hands to hide them; and had it not been that I hoped to hear more concerning her (seeing that where I sat, her friends passed continually in and out), I should assuredly have gone thence to be alone, when I felt the tears come. But as I still sat in that place, certain ladies again passed near me, who were saying among themselves: "Which of us shall be joyful any more, who have listened to this lady in her piteous sorrow?" And there were others who said as they went by me: "He that sitteth here could not weep more if he had beheld her as we have beheld her;" and again: "He is so altered that he seemeth not as himself." And still as the ladies passed to and fro, I could hear them speak after this fashion of her and of me.

Wherefore afterwards, having considered and perceiving that there was herein matter for poesy, I resolved that I would write certain rhymes in the which should be contained all that those ladies had said. And because I would willingly have spoken to them if it had not been for discreetness, I made in my rhymes as though I had spoken and they had answered me. And thereof I wrote two sonnets; in the first of which I addressed them as I would fain have done; and in the second related their answer, using the speech that I had heard from them, as though it had been spoken unto myself. And the sonnets are these: —

I

You that thus wear a modest countenance
  With lids weigh'd down by the heart's heaviness,
  Whence come you, that among you every face
Appears the same, for its pale troubled glance?
Have you beheld my lady's face, perchance,
  Bow'd with the grief that Love makes full of grace?
Say now, "This thing is thus;" as my heart says,
Marking your grave and sorrowful advance.
And if indeed you come from where she sighs
  And mourns, may it please you (for his heart's relief)
  To tell how it fares with her unto him
Who knows that you have wept, seeing your eyes,
  And is so grieved with looking on your grief
  That his heart trembles and his sight grows dim.

II

Canst thou indeed be he that still would sing
  Of our dear lady unto none but us?
  For though thy voice confirms that it is thus,

Thy visage might another witness bring.
And wherefore is thy grief so sore a thing
    That grieving thou mak'st others dolorous?
    Hast thou too seen her weep, that thou from us
Canst not conceal thine inward sorrowing?
Nay, leave our woe to us: let us alone:
    'Twere sin if one should strive to soothe our woe,
        For in her weeping we have heard her speak:
Also her look's so full of her heart's moan
    That they who should behold her, looking so,
        Must fall aswoon, feeling all life grow weak.

A few days after this, my body became afflicted with a painful infirmity, whereby I suffered bitter anguish for many days, which at last brought me unto such weakness that I could no longer move. And I remember that on the ninth day, being overcome with intolerable pain, a thought came into my mind concerning my lady: but when it had a little nourished this thought, my mind returned to its brooding over mine enfeebled body. And then perceiving how frail a thing life is, even though health keep with it, the matter seemed to me so pitiful that I could not choose but weep; and weeping I said within myself: "Certainly it must sometime come to pass that the very gentle Beatrice will die." Then, feeling bewildered, I closed mine eyes; and my brain began to be in travail as the brain of one frantic, and to have such imaginations as here follow.

And at the first, it seemed to me that I saw certain faces of women with their hair loosened, which called out to me, "Thou shalt surely die;" after which, other terrible and unknown appearances said unto me, "Thou art dead." At length, as my phantasy held on in its wanderings, I came to be I knew not where, and to behold a throng of dishevelled ladies wonderfully sad, who kept going hither and thither weeping. Then the sun went out, so that the stars showed themselves and they were of such a colour that I knew they must be weeping; and it seemed to me that the birds fell dead out of the sky, and that there were great earthquakes. With that, while I wondered in my trance, and was filled with a grievous fear, I conceived that a certain friend came unto me and said: "Hast thou not heard? She that was thine excellent lady hath been taken out of life." Then I began to weep very piteously; and not only in mine imagination, but with mine eyes, which were wet with tears. And I seemed to look towards Heaven, and to behold a multitude of angels who were returning upwards, having before them an exceedingly white cloud; and these angels were singing together gloriously, and the words of their song were these: *Osanna in excelsis.* And there was no more that I heard. Then my heart that was so full of love said unto me: "It is true that our lady lieth dead." And it seemed to me that I went to look upon the body wherein that blessed and most noble spirit had had its abiding place.

And so strong was this idle imagining that it made me to behold
my lady in death, whose head certain ladies seemed to be covering
with a white veil; and who was so humble of her aspect that it
was as though she had said, "I have attained to look on the beginning
of peace." And therewithal I came unto such humility by the
sight of her that I cried out upon Death, saying: "Now come unto
me, and be not bitter against me any longer; surely, there where
thou hast been, thou hast learned gentleness. Wherefore come now
unto me who do greatly desire thee. Seest thou not that I wear thy
colour already?" And when I had seen all those offices performed
that are fitting to be done unto the dead, it seemed to me that I
went back unto mine own chamber, and looked up towards heaven.
And so strong was my phantasy, that I wept again in very truth, and
said with my true voice: "O excellent soul! how blessed is he that
now looketh upon thee!"

And as I said these words, with a painful anguish of sobbing and
another prayer unto Death, a young and gentle lady, who had been
standing beside me where I lay, conceiving that I wept and cried out
because of the pain of mine infirmity, was taken with trembling and
began to shed tears. Whereby other ladies, who were about the
room, becoming aware of my discomfort by reason of the moan
that she made (who indeed was of my very near kindred), led her
away from where I was, and then set themselves to awaken me,
thinking that I dreamed, and saying: "Sleep no longer, and be not
disquieted."

Then, by their words, this strong imagination was brought suddenly
to an end, at the moment that I was about to say, "O Beatrice! peace
be with thee." And already I had said, "O Beatrice!" when, being
aroused, I opened mine eyes, and knew that it had been a deception.
But albeit I had indeed uttered her name, yet my voice was so broken
with sobs, that it was not understood by these ladies; so that in spite
of the sore shame that I felt, I turned towards them by Love's
counseling. And when they beheld me, they began to say, "He
seemeth as one dead," and to whisper among themselves, "Let us
strive if we may not comfort him." Whereupon they spake to me
many soothing words, and questioned me moreover touching the
cause of my fear. Then I, being somewhat reassured, and having
perceived that it was a mere phantasy, said unto them, "This thing
it was that made me afeard;" and told them of all I had seen, from
the beginning even unto the end, but without once speaking the
name of my lady. Also, after I had recovered from my sickness, I
bethought me to write these things in rhyme; deeming it a lovely
thing to be known. Whereof I wrote this poem:

> A very pitiful lady, very young,
>     Exceeding rich in human sympathies,
>         Stood by, what time I clamour'd upon Death;
> And at the wild words wandering on my tongue
>     And at the piteous look within mine eyes

She was affrighted, that sobs choked her breath.
So by her weeping where I lay beneath,
Some other gentle ladies came to know
My state, and made her go:
  Afterward, bending themselves over me,
  One said, "Awaken thee!"
And one, "What thing thy sleep disquieteth?"
With that, my soul woke up from its eclipse,
The while my lady's name rose to my lips:

But utter'd in a voice so sob-broken,
  So feeble with the agony of tears,
    That I alone might hear it in my heart;
And though that look was on my visage then
  Which he who is ashamed so plainly wears,
    Love made that I through shame held not apart,
    But gazed upon them.   And my hue was such
That they look'd at each other and thought of death;
Saying under their breath
  Most tenderly, "Oh, let us comfort him:"
  Then unto me: "What dream
    Was thine, that it hath shaken thee so much?"
And when I was a little comforted,
"This, ladies, was the dream I dreamt," I said.

"I was a-thinking how life fails with us
  Suddenly after such a little while;
    When Love sobb'd in my heart, which is his home.
Whereby my spirit wax'd so dolorous
  That in myself I said, with sick recoil:
    'Yea, to my lady too this Death must come.'
    And therewithal such a bewilderment
Possess'd me, that I shut mine eyes for peace;
And in my brain did cease
  Order of thought, and every healthful thing.
  Afterwards, wandering
    Amid a swarm of doubts that came and went,
Some certain women's faces hurried by,
And shriek'd to me, 'Thou too shalt die, shalt die!'

"Then saw I many broken hinted sights
  In the uncertain state I stepp'd into.
    Meseem'd to be I know not in what place,
Where ladies through the street, like mournful lights,
  Ran with loose hair, and eyes that frighten'd you
    By their own terror, and a pale amaze:
    The while, little by little, as I thought,
The sun ceased, and the stars began to gather,

And each wept at the other;
  And birds dropp'd in mid-flight out of the sky;
  And earth shook suddenly;
    And I was 'ware of one, hoarse and tired out,
Who ask'd of me: 'Hast thou not heard it said? . . .
Thy lady, she that was so fair, is dead.'

"Then lifting up mine eyes, as the tears came,
  I saw the Angels, like a rain of manna,
    In a long flight flying back Heavenward;
Having a little cloud in front of them,
  After the which they went and said, 'Hosanna!'
    And if they had said more, you should have heard.
    Then Love spoke thus: 'Now all shall be made clear:
Come and behold our lady where she lies.'
These idle phantasies
  Then carried me to see my lady dead:
  And standing at her head
    Her ladies put a white veil over her;
And with her was such very humbleness
That she appeared to say, 'I am at peace.'

"And I became so humble in my grief,
  Seeing in her such deep humility,
    That I said: 'Death, I hold thee passing good
Henceforth, and a most gentle sweet relief,
  Since my dear love has chosen to dwell with thee:
    Pity, not hate, is thine, well understood.
      Lo! I do so desire to see thy face
That I am like as one who nears the tomb;
My soul entreats thee, Come.'
  Then I departed, having made my moan;
  And when I was alone
    I said, and cast my eyes to the High Place:
'Blessed is he, fair soul, who meets thy glance!'
. . . Just then you woke me, of your complaisaunce."

A short while after, I saw coming towards me a certain lady who
was very famous for her beauty, and of whom that friend whom
I have already called the first among my friends had long been
enamoured. This lady's right name was Joan; but because of her
comeliness (or at least it was so imagined) she was called of many
Primavera (Spring), and went by that name among them. Then
looking again, I perceived that the most noble Beatrice followed
after her. And when both these ladies had passed by me, it seemed
to me that Love spake again in my heart, saying: "She that came
first was called Spring, only because of that which was to happen
on this day. And it was I myself who caused that name to be

given her; seeing that as the Spring cometh first in the year, so should she come first on this day,[12] when Beatrice was to show herself after the vision of her servant.  And even if thou go about to consider her right name, it is also as one should say, 'She shall come first;' inasmuch as her name, Joan, is taken from that John who went before the True Light, saying, *'Ego vox clamantis in deserto: Parate viam Domini'."* [13]  And also it seemed to me that he added other words, to wit: "He who should inquire delicately touching this matter, could not but call Beatrice by mine own name, which is to say, Love; beholding her so like unto me."

Than I, having thought of this, imagined to write it with rhymes and send it unto my chief friend; but setting aside certain words which seemed proper to be set aside, because I believed that his heart still regarded the beauty of her that was called Spring.  And I wrote this sonnet:

> I felt a spirit of love begin to stir
>     Within my heart, long time unfelt till then;
>     And saw Love coming towards me, fair and fain
> (That I scarce knew him for his joyful cheer),
> Saying, "Be now indeed my worshipper!"
>     And in his speech he laugh'd and laugh'd again.
>     Then, while it was his pleasure to remain,
> I chanced to look the way he had drawn near,
> And saw the Ladies Joan and Beatrice
>     Approach me, this the other following,
>         One and a second marvel instantly.
> And even as now my memory speaketh this,
>     Love spake it then: "The first is christen'd Spring;
>         The second Love, she is so like to me."

It might be here objected unto me (and even by one worthy of controversy), that I have spoken of Love as though it were a thing outward and visible: not only a spiritual essence, but as a bodily substance also.  The which thing, in absolute truth, is a fallacy; Love not being of itself a substance, but an accident of substance. Yet that I speak of Love as though it were a thing tangible and even human, appears by three things which I say thereof.  And firstly, I say that I perceived Love coming towards me; whereby, seeing that *to come* bespeaks locomotion, and seeing also how philosophy teacheth us that none but a corporeal substance hath locomotion, it seemeth that I speak of Love as of a corporeal substance.  And secondly, I say that Love smiled; and thirdly, that Love spake; faculties (and especially the risible faculty) which appear proper unto man: whereby it further seemeth that I speak of

12. There is a play in the original upon the words *Primavera* (Spring) and *prima verrà* (she shall come first).

13. "I am the voice of one crying in the wilderness: 'Prepare ye the way of the Lord' " (Matt. 3:3; Mark 1:3; Luke 3:4; John 1:23).

Love as of a man. Now that this matter may be explained (as is fitting), it must first be remembered that anciently they who wrote poems of Love wrote not in the vulgar tongue, but rather certain poets in the Latin tongue. I mean, among us, although perchance the same may have been among others, and although likewise, as among the Greeks, they were not writers of spoken language, but men of letters treated of these things. And indeed it is not a great number of years since poetry began to be made in the vulgar tongue; the writing of rhymes in spoken language corresponding to the writing in metre of Latin verse, by a certain analogy. And I say that it is but a little while, because if we examine the language of *oco* and the language of *si* [14] we shall not find in those tongues any written thing of an earlier date than the last hundred and fifty years. Also the reason why certain of a very mean sort obtained at the first some fame as poets is, that before them no man had written verses in the language of *si*: and of these, the first was moved to the writing of such verses by the wish to make himself understood of a certain lady, unto whom Latin poetry was difficult. This thing is against such as rhyme concerning other matters than love; that mode of speech having been first used for the expression of love alone. Wherefore, seeing that poets have a licence allowed them that is not allowed unto the writers of prose, and seeing also that they who write in rhyme are simply poets in the vulgar tongue, it becomes fitting and reasonable that a larger licence should be given to these than to other modern writers; and that any metaphor or rhetorical similitude which is permitted unto poets should also be counted not unseemly in the rhymers of the vulgar tongue. Thus, if we perceive that the former have caused inanimate things to speak as though have sense and reason, and to discourse one with another; yea, and not only actual things, but such also as have no real existence (seeing that they have made things which are not, to speak; and oftentimes written of those which are merely accidents as though they were substances and things human), it should therefore be permitted to the latter to do the like; which is to say, not inconsiderately, but with such sufficient motive as may afterwards be set forth in prose.

That the Latin poets have done thus, appears through Virgil, where he saith that Juno (to wit, a goddess hostile to the Trojans) spake unto Aeolus, master of the Winds; as it is written in the first book of the Aeneid, *Aeolus, for to thee, etc*; and that this master of the Winds made reply: *Thy task, O queen, to weigh what thou desirest, etc*. And through the same poet, the inanimate thing speaketh unto the animate, in the third book of the Aeneid, where it is written: *Ye hardy Trojans, etc*. With Lucan, the animate thing speaketh to the inanimate, as thus: *Yet much, O Rome, thou owest to civil arms*. In Horace, man is made to speak his own intelligence as unto another person (and not only hath Horace done this but

14. I.e., the language of Provence (Languedoc) and Tuscany.

herein he followeth the excellent Homer), as thus in his Poetics: *Tell me, Muse, of the man, etc.* Through Ovid, Love speaketh as a human creature, in the beginning of his discourse *De Remediis Amoris*; as thus: *Wars, I perceive, wars are in store for me.* By which ensamples this thing shall be made manifest unto such as may be offended at any part of this my book. And lest some of the common sort should be moved to jeering hereat, I will here add, that neither did these ancient poets speak thus without consideration, nor should they who are makers of rhyme in our day write after the same fashion, having no reason in what they write; for it were a shameful thing if one should rhyme under the semblance of metaphor or rhetorical similitude, and afterwards, being questioned thereof, should be unable to rid his words of such semblance, unto their right understanding. Of whom (to wit, of such as rhyme thus foolishly), myself and the first among my friends do know many.

I, wishing to resume the endless tale of her praises, resolved to write somewhat wherein I might dwell on her surpassing influence. And it was then that I wrote this sonnet:

> My lady looks so gentle and so pure
>   When yielding salutation by the way,
>   That the tongue trembles and has nought to say,
> And the eyes, which fain would see, may not endure.
> And still, amid the praise she hears secure,
>   She walks with humbleness for her array;
>   Seeming a creature sent from Heaven to stay
> On earth, and show a miracle made sure.
> She is so pleasant in the eyes of men
>   That through the sight the inmost heart doth gain
>     A sweetness which needs proof to know it by:
> And from between her lips there seems to move
>   A soothing spirit that it full of love,
>     Saying for ever to the soul, "O sigh!"

I wrote the sonnet here following; wherein is signified the power which her virtue had upon other ladies:

> For certain he hath seen all perfectness
>   Who among other ladies hath seen mine:
>   They that go with her humbly should combine
> To thank their God for such peculiar grace.
> So perfect is the beauty of her face
>   That it begets in no wise any sign
>   Of envy, but draws round her a clear line
> Of love, and blessed faith, and gentleness.
> Merely the sight of her makes all things bow:
>   Not she herself alone is holier
>     Than all; but hers, through her, are raised above.

From all her acts such lovely graces flow
That truly one may never think of her
Without a passion of exceeding love.

Thereafter on a day, I began to consider that which I had said
of my lady: to wit, in these two sonnets aforegone: and becoming
aware that I had not spoken of her immediate effect on me at that
especial time, it seemed to me that I had spoken defectively. Whereupon I resolved to write somewhat of the manner wherein I was
then subject to her influence, and of what her influence then was.
And conceiving that I should not be able to say these things in the
small compass of a sonnet, I began therefore a poem with this
beginning:

Love hath so long possess'd me for his own
    And made his lordship so familiar
That he, who at first irk'd me, is now grown
    Unto my heart as its best secrets are.
    And thus, when he in such sore wise doth mar
My life that all its strength seems gone from it,
Mine inmost being then feels throughly quit
    Of anguish, and all evil keeps afar.
Love also gathers to such power in me
    That my sighs speak, each one a grievous thing,
    Always soliciting
My lady's salutation piteously.
Whenever she beholds me, it is so,
Who is more sweet than any words can show.

\* \* \* \* \*
\* \* \* \* \*

*Quomodo sedet sola civitas plena populo! facta est quasi vidua
domina gentium.*[15]

I was still occupied with this poem (having composed thereof
only the above-written stanza), when the Lord God of justice called
my most gracious lady unto Himself, that she might be glorious
under the banner of that blessed Queen Mary, whose name had
always a deep reverence in the words of holy Beatrice. And because
haply it might be found good that I should say somewhat concerning
her departure, I will herein declare what are the reasons which make
that I shall not do so.

And the reasons are three. The first is, that such matter belongeth not of right to the present argument, if one consider the
opening of this little book. The second is, that even though the

15. "How doth the city sit solitary, that was full of people! how is she
become as a widow, she that was great among the nations!" (Lamentations 1:1).

present argument required it, my pen doth not suffice to write in a fit manner of this thing.   And the third is, that were it both possible and of absolute necessity, it would still be unseemly for me to speak thereof, seeing that thereby it must behove me to speak also mine own praises: a thing that in whosoever doeth it is worthy of blame. For the which reasons, I will leave this matter to be treated of by some other than myself.

Nevertheless, as the number nine, which number hath often had mention in what hath gone before (and not, as it might appear, without reason), seems also to have borne a part in the manner of her death, it is therefore right that I should say somewhat thereof.  And for this cause, having first said what was the part it bore herein, I will afterwards point out a reason which made that this number was so closely allied unto my lady.

I say, then, that according to the division of time in Italy, her most noble spirit departed from among us in the first hour of the ninth day of the month; and according to the division of time in Syria, in the ninth month of the year: seeing that Tismim, which with us is October, is there the first month.   Also she was taken from among us in that year of our reckoning (to wit, of the years of our Lord) in which the perfect number was nine times multiplied within that century wherein she was born into the world: which is to say, the thirteenth century of Christians.[16]

And touching the reason why this number was so closely allied unto her, it may peradventure be this.   According to Ptolemy (and also to the Christian verity), the revolving heavens are nine; and according to the common opinion among astrologers, these nine heavens together have influence over the earth.   Wherefore it would appear that this number was thus allied unto her for the purpose of signifying that, at her birth, all these nine heavens were at perfect unity with each other as to their influence.   This is one reason that may be brought: but more narrowly considering, and according to the infallible truth, this number was her own self: that is to say, by similitude.   As thus.   The number three is the root of the number nine; seeing that without the interposition of any other number, being multiplied merely by itself, it produceth nine, as we manifestly perceive that three times three are nine.   Thus, three being of itself the efficient of nine, and the Great Efficient of Miracles being of Himself Three Persons (to wit: the Father, the Son, and the Holy Spirit), which, being Three, are also One: — this lady was accompanied by the number nine to the end that men might clearly perceive her to be a nine, that is, a miracle, whose only root is the Holy Trinity.   It may be that a more subtile person would find for this thing a reason of greater subtilty: but such is the reason that I find, and that liketh me best.

After this most gracious creature had gone out from among us, the whole city came to be as it were widowed and despoiled of all dignity.

16. Beatrice Portinari will thus be found to have died during the first hour of the ninth day of June 1290.

Then I, left mourning in this desolate city, wrote unto the principal persons thereof, in an epistle, concerning its condition; taking for my commencement those words of Jeremias: *Quomodo sedet sola civitas! etc.* And I make mention of this, that none may marvel wherefore I set down these words before, in beginning to treat of her death. Also if any should blame me, in that I do not transcribe that epistle whereof I have spoken, I will make it mine excuse that I began this little book with the intent that it should be written altogether in the vulgar tongue; wherefore, seeing that the epistle I speak of is in Latin, it belongeth not to mine undertaking: more especially as I know that my chief friend, for whom I write this book, wished also that the whole of it should be in the vulgar tongue.

When mine eyes had wept for some while, until they were so weary with weeping that I could not longer through them give ease to my sorrow, I bethought me that a few mournful words might stand me instead of tears. And therefore I proposed to make a poem, that weeping I might speak therein of her for whom so much sorrow had destroyed my spirit; and I then began "The eyes that weep."

The eyes that weep for pity of the heart
 Have wept so long that their grief languisheth
  And they have no more tears to weep withal:
And now, if I would ease me of a part
 Of what, little by little, leads to death,
  It must be done by speech, or not at all.
  And because often, thinking, I recall
How it was pleasant, ere she went afar,
 To talk of her with you, kind damozels,
  I talk with no one else,
But only with such hearts as women's are.
 And I will say, — still sobbing as speech fails, —
That she hath gone to Heaven suddenly,
And hath left Love below, to mourn with me.

Beatrice is gone up into high Heaven,
 The kingdom where the angels are at peace;
  And lives with them; and to her friends is dead.
Not by the frost of winter was she driven
 Away, like others; nor by summer-heats;
  But through a perfect gentleness, instead.
  For from the lamp of her meek lowlihead
Such an exceeding glory went up hence
 That it woke wonder in the Eternal Sire,
  Until a sweet desire
Enter'd Him for that lovely excellence,
 So that He bade her to Himself aspire:
Counting this weary and most evil place
Unworthy of a thing so full of grace.

Wonderfully out of the beautiful form
   Soar'd her clear spirit, waxing glad the while;
     And is in its first home, there where it is.
Who speak thereof, and feels not the tears warm
   Upon his face, must have become so vile
     As to be dead to all sweet sympathies.
     Out upon him! an abject wretch like this
May not imagine anything of her, —
   He needs no bitter tears for his relief.
   But sighing comes, and grief,
And the desire to find no comforter
   (Save only Death, who makes all sorrow brief),
To him who for a while turns in his thought
How she hath been among us, and is not.

With sighs my bosom always laboureth
   On thinking, as I do continually,
     Of her for whom my heart now breaks apace;
And very often when I think of death,
   Such a great inward longing comes to me
     That it will change the colour of my face;
     And, if the idea settles in its place,
All my limbs shake as with an ague-fit;
   Till, starting up in wild bewilderment,
   I do become so shent
That I go forth, lest folk misdoubt of it.
   Afterward, calling with a sore lament
On Beatrice, I ask, "Canst thou be dead?"
And calling on her, I am comforted.

Grief with its tears, and anguish with its sighs,
   Come to me now whene'er I am alone;
     So that I think the sight of me gives pain.
And what my life hath been, that living dies,
   Since for my lady the New Birth's begun,
     I have not any language to explain.
     And so dear ladies, though my heart were fain,
I scarce could tell indeed how I am thus.
   All joy is with my bitter life at war;
   Yea, I am fallen so far
That all men seem to say, "Go out from us,"
   Eyeing my cold white lips, how dead they are.
But she, though I be bow'd unto the dust,
Watches me; and will guerdon me, I trust.

Weep, piteous Song of mine, upon thy way,
   To the dames going, and the damozels,
   For whom, and for none else,
Thy sisters have made music many a day.

Thou, that art very sad and not as they,
  Go dwell thou with them as a mourner dwells.

On that day which fulfilled the year since my lady had been made
of the citizens of eternal life, remembering me of her as I sat alone,
I betook myself to draw the resemblance of an angel upon certain
tablets.  And while I did thus, chancing to turn my head, I perceived
that some were standing beside me to whom I should have given
courteous welcome, and that they were observing what I did: also I
learned afterwards that they had been there a while before I perceived
them.  Perceiving whom, I arose for salutation, and said: "Another
was with me."

Afterwards, when they had left me, I set myself again to mine
occupation, to wit, to the drawing figures of angels: in doing which,
I conceived to write of this matter in rhyme, as for her anniversary,
and to address my rhymes unto those who had just left me.  It was
then that I wrote the sonnet which saith, "That lady."

That lady of all gentle memories
  Had lighted on my soul; — whose new abode
  Lies now, as it was well ordain'd of God,
Among the poor in heart, where Mary is.
Love, knowing that dear image to be his,
  Woke up within the sick heart sorrow-bow'd,
  Unto the sighs which are its weary load,
Saying, "Go forth."  And they went forth, I wis;
Forth went they from my breast that throbb'd and ached;
  With such a pang as oftentimes will bathe
  Mine eyes with tears when I am left alone.
And still those sighs which drew the heaviest breath
Came whispering thus: "O noble intellect!
  It is a year to-day that thou art gone."


### Second Commencement

That lady of all gentle memories
  Had lighted on my soul; — for whose sake flow'd
  The tears of Love; in whom the power abode
Which led you to observe while I did this.
Love, knowing that dear image to be his, etc.


Then, having sat for some space sorely in thought because of the
time that was now past, I was so filled with dolorous imaginings that
it became outwardly manifest in mine altered countenance.  Whereupon, feeling this and being in dread lest any should have seen me,
I lifted mine eyes to look; and then perceived a young and very beautiful lady, who was gazing upon me from a window with a gaze full
of pity, so that the very sum of pity appeared gathered together in
her.  And seeing that unhappy persons, when they beget compas-

sion in others, are then most moved unto weeping, as though they also felt pity for themselves, it came to pass that mine eyes began to be inclined unto tears. Wherefore, becoming fearful lest I should make manifest mine abject condition, I rose up, and went where I could not be seen of that lady; saying afterwards within myself: "Certainly with her also must abide most noble Love."

It happened after this that whensoever I was seen of this lady she became pale and of a piteous countenance, as though it had been with love; whereby she remembered me many times of my own most noble lady, who was wont to be of a like paleness. And I know that often, when I could not weep nor in any way give ease unto mine anguish, I went to look upon this lady, who seemed to bring the tears into my eyes by the mere sight of her.

At length, by the constant sight of this lady, mine eyes began to be gladdened overmuch with her company; through which thing many times I had much unrest, and rebuked myself as a base person; also, many times I cursed the unsteadfastness of mine eyes, and said to them inwardly: "Was not your grievous condition of weeping wont one while to make others weep? And will ye now forget this thing because a lady looketh upon you? Who so looketh merely in compassion of the grief ye then showed for your own blessed lady. But whatso ye can, that do ye, accursed eyes! many a time will I make you remember it! for never, till death dry you up, should ye make an end of your weeping." And when I had spoken thus unto mine eyes, I was taken again with extreme and grievous sighing. And to the end that this inward strife which I had undergone might not be hidden from all saving the miserable wretch who endured it, I proposed to write a sonnet, and to comprehend in it this horrible condition. And I wrote this which begins, "The very bitter weeping."

"The very bitter weeping that ye made
    So long a time together, eyes of mine,
    Was wont to make the tears of pity shine
In other eyes full oft, as I have said.
But now this thing were scarce rememberèd
    If I, on my part, foully would combine
    With you, and not recall each ancient sign
Of grief, and her for whom your tears were shed.
It is your fickleness that doth betray
    My mind to fears, and makes me tremble thus
    What while a lady greets me with her eyes.
Except by death, we must not any way
    Forget our lady who is gone from us."
    So far doth my heart utter, and then sighs.

The sight of this lady brought me into so unwonted a condition that I often thought of her as of one too dear unto me; and I began to consider her thus: "This lady is young, beautiful, gentle, and wise: perchance it was Love himself who set her in my path, that so my life might find peace." And there were times when I thought yet more fondly, until my heart consented unto its reasoning. But when it had so consented, my thought would often turn around upon me, as moved by reason, and cause me to say within myself: "What hope is this which would console me after so base a fashion, and which hath taken the place of all other imagining?" Also there was another voice within me that said: "And wilt thou, having suffered so much tribulation through Love, not escape while yet thou mayest from so much bitterness? Thou must surely know that this thought carries with it the desire of Love, and drew its life from the gentle eyes of that lady who vouchsafed thee so much pity." Wherefore I, having striven sorely and very often with myself, bethought me to say somewhat thereof in rhyme. And seeing that in the battle of doubts, the victory most often remained with such as inclined towards the lady of whom I speak, it seemed to me that I should address this sonnet unto her: in the first line whereof, I call that thought which spake of her a gentle thought, only because it spoke of one who was gentle; being of itself most vile.

A gentle thought there is will often start,
　Within my secret self, to speech of thee;
　Also of Love it speaks so tenderly
That much in me consents and takes its part.
"And what is this," the soul saith to the heart,
　"That cometh thus to comfort thee and me,
　And thence where it would dwell, thus potently
Can drive all other thoughts by its strange art?"
And the heart answers: "Be no more at strife
　'Twixt doubt and doubt: this is Love's messenger
　　And speaketh but his words, from him received;
And all the strength it owns and all the life
　It draweth from the gentle eyes of her
　　Who, looking on our grief, hath often grieved."

But against this adversary of reason, there rose up in me on a certain day, about the ninth hour, a strong visible phantasy, wherein I seemed to behold the most gracious Beatrice, habited in that crimson raiment which she had worn when I had first beheld her; also she appeared to me of the same tender age as then. Whereupon I fell into a deep thought of her; and my memory ran back according to the order of time, unto all those matters in the which she had borne a part. And my heart began painfully to repent of the desire by which it had so basely let itself be possessed during so many days, contrary to the constancy of reason.

And then, this evil desire being quite gone from me, all my thoughts turned again unto their excellent Beatrice. And I say most truly that from that hour I thought constantly of her with the whole humbled and ashamed heart; the which became often manifest in sighs, that had among them the name of that most gracious creature, and how she departed from us.   Also it would come to pass very often, through the bitter anguish of some one thought, that I forgot both it, and myself, and where I was.   By this increase of sighs, my weeping, which before had been somewhat lessened, increased in like manner; so that mine eyes seemed to long only for tears and to cherish them, and came at last to be circled about with red as though they had suffered martyrdom; neither were they able to look again upon the beauty of any face that might again bring them to shame and evil.   From which things it will appear that they were fitly guerdoned for their unsteadfastness.   Wherefore I (wishing that mine abandonment of all such evil desires and vain temptations should be certified and made manifest, beyond all doubts which might have been suggested by the rhymes aforewritten) proposed to write a sonnet, wherein I should express this purport.   And I then wrote, "Woe's me!"

Woe's me! by dint of all these sighs that come
    Forth of my heart, its endless grief to prove,
    Mine eyes are conquer'd, so that even to move
Their lids for greeting is grown troublesome.
They wept so long that now they are grief's home
    And count their tears all laughter far above:
    They wept till they are circled now by Love
With a red circle in sign of martyrdom.
These musings, and the sighs they bring from me,
    Are grown at last so constant and so sore
        That Love swoons in my spirit with faint breath;
Hearing in those sad sounds continually
    The most sweet name that my dead lady bore,
        With many grievous words touching her death.

About this time, it happened that a great number of persons undertook a pilgrimage, to the end that they might behold that blessed portraiture bequeathed unto us by our Lord Jesus Christ as the image of His beautiful countenance [17] (upon which countenance my dear lady now looketh continually).   And certain among these pilgrims, who seemed very thoughtful, passed by a path which is well-nigh in the midst of the city where my most gracious lady was born, and abode, and at last died.

Then I, beholding them, said within myself: "These pilgrims seem to be come from very far; and I think they cannot have heard speak of this lady, or know anything concerning her.   Their thoughts are not of her, but of other things; it may be, of their friends who are far distant, and whom we, in our turn, know not."   And I went on to say: "I know that if they were of a country near unto us, they would in some wise seem disturbed, passing through this city which is so full of grief."   And I said also: "If I could speak with them a space, I am certain that I should make them weep before they went forth

17. See below, *Paradise,* Canto XXXI.

of this city; for those things that they would hear from me must needs beget weeping in any."

And when the last of them had gone by me, I bethought me to write a sonnet, showing forth mine inward speech; and that it might seem the more pitiful, I made as though I had spoken it indeed unto them. And I wrote this sonnet, which beginneth: "Ye pilgrim-folk." I made use of the word *pilgrim* for its general signification; for "pilgrim" may be understood in two senses, one general, and one special. General, so far as any man may be called a pilgrim who leaveth the place of his birth; whereas, more narrowly speaking, he only is a pilgrim who goeth towards or frowards the House of St. James. For there are three separate denominations proper unto those who undertake journeys to the glory of God. They are called Palmers who go beyond the sea, eastward, whence often they bring palm-branches. And Pilgrims, as I have said, are they who journey unto the holy House of Gallicia; seeing that no other apostle was buried so far from his birthplace as was the blessed Saint James. And there is a third sort who are called Romers; in that they go whither these whom I have called pilgrims went: which is to say, unto Rome.

> Ye pilgrim-folk, advancing pensively
>     As if in thought of distant things, I pray,
>     Is your own land indeed so far away
> As by your aspect it would seem to be, —
> That nothing of our grief comes over ye
>     Though passing through the mournful town midway;
>     Like unto men that understand to-day
> Nothing at all of her great misery?
> Yet if ye will but stay, whom I accost,
>     And listen to my words a little space,
>         At going ye shall mourn with a loud voice.
> It is her Beatrice that she hath lost;
>     Of whom the least word spoken holds such grace
>         That men weep hearing it, and have no choice.

A while after these things, two gentle ladies sent unto me, praying that I would bestow upon them certain of these my rhymes. And I (taking into account their worthiness and consideration) resolved that I would write also a new thing, and send it them together with those others, to the end that their wishes might be more honourably fulfilled. Therefore I made a sonnet, which narrates my condition, and which I caused to be conveyed to them, accompanied with the one preceding, and with that other which begins, "Stay now with me and listen to my sighs." And the new sonnet is, "Beyond the sphere."

> Beyond the sphere which spreads to widest space
>     Now soars the sigh that my heart sends above:
>     A new perception born of grieving Love

Guideth it upward the untrodden ways.
When it hath reach'd unto the end, and stays,
   It sees a lady round whom splendours move
   In homage; till, by the great light thereof
Abash'd, the pilgrim spirit stands at gaze.
It sees her such, that when it tells me this
   Which it hath seen, I understand it not,
     It hath a speech so subtile and so fine.
And yet I know its voice within my thought
   Often remembereth me of Beatrice:
     So that I understand it, ladies mine.

After writing this sonnet, it was given unto me to behold a very wonderful vision; wherein I saw things which determined me that I would say nothing further of this most blessed one, until such time as I could discourse more worthily concerning her. And to this end I labour all I can; as she well knoweth. Wherefore if it be His pleasure through whom is the life of all things, that my life continue with me a few years, it is my hope that I shall yet write concerning her what hath not before been written of any woman. After the which, may it seem good unto Him who is the Master of Grace, that my spirit should go hence to behold the glory of its lady: to wit, of that blessed Beatrice who now gazeth continually on His countenance *qui est per omnia saecula benedictus.*[18] *Laus Deo.*

[tr. DANTE GABRIEL ROSSETTI]

18. "Who is blessed throughout all ages."

# THE ILLUSTRIOUS VERNACULAR
## (*De Vulgari Eloquentia*)

The medieval period produced few theoretical treatises on art. The several "Rhetorics" and "Poetics" were usually academic paraphrases of ancient models to be used in the schoolroom, though there were several texts on the *dictamen,* or art of letter writing, which were not so traditional. Dante showed his modernity and heralded the Renaissance by composing his *Illustrious Vernacular,* which is not only without precedent in its presentation of theories about language and composition, but is several centuries in advance of its time in its author's theory of change in language. The *Illustrious Vernacular,* like the *Banquet,* is a theoretical tract in Latin, left incomplete; both works were probably written in exile before Henry VII invaded Italy and abandoned in their present incomplete form when Dante threw his energies into supporting Henry's cause. This work represents, then, a transitional stage between the *New Life* and the *Comedy.*

The *Illustrious Vernacular,* as statements within it show, was planned to extend to at least four books, but breaks off abruptly in the course of the second. The reader needs to bear in mind that the literary language of western Europe, and especially of Italy, was Latin. By composing in the vernacular poetry with pretensions to lasting and universal acclaim, as opposed to the popular lyrics of court poets, Dante broke with fixed tradition and taste. He set for himself the difficult, almost insoluble, problem of presenting universal concepts in idioms that had never yet been used for more than local or provincial exchange of thought. His tract is therefore no scientific description of extant literature, but an inventive search for the future. Though modern readers may tend to compare Dante's problem with that of Wordsworth, as set forth in his Preface to his *Lyrical Ballads,* it is probably less deceptive to compare Dante with Jerome, who more than nine hundred years earlier struggled to find in colloquial Latin of the fourth century diction and syntax capable of bearing the new ideas of Christianity imported from the East.

Though the *Illustrious Vernacular* was known to Villani and Boccaccio, it did not circulate widely during the Renaissance. It was first published anonymously in an Italian translation in 1529; not until fifty years later was the Latin text made available. If the critics of the Renaissance had accorded the work the attention it has received since the Romantic Revival, no doubt many of their notions of the static nature of literature would have been modified. The abridgment that follows represents approximately one quarter of the whole.

## THE ILLUSTRIOUS VERNACULAR

[From *The Latin Works of Dante;* Temple Classics, J. M.
Dent & Sons, Ltd., London, 1904.   Reprinted by permission of the publisher.]

### BOOK I

(1)   Since we do not find that any one before us has treated of the
science of the vernacular language, while in fact we see that this
language is highly necessary for all, inasmuch as not only men, but
even women and children, strive, in so far as nature allows them,
to acquire it; and since it is our wish to enlighten to some little extent the discernment of those who walk through the streets like
blind men, generally fancying that those things which are really in
front of them are behind them, we will endeavour, the Word aiding
us from heaven, to be of service to the vernacular speech; not only
drawing the water of our own wit for such a drink, but mixing with
it the best of what we have taken or compiled from others, so that
we may thence be able to give draughts of the sweetest hydromel. But
because the business of every science is not to prove but to explain
its subject, in order that men may know what this is with which the
science is concerned, we say (to come quickly to the point) that
what we call the vernacular speech is that to which children are
accustomed by those who are about them when they first begin to
distinguish words; or to put it more shortly, we say that *the vernacular speech is that which we acquire without any rule, by imitating
our nurses.*   There further springs from this another secondary
speech, which the Romans called grammar.   And this secondary
speech the Greeks also have, as well as others, but not all.   Few, however, acquire the use of this speech, because we can only be guided
and instructed in it by the expenditure of much time, and by assiduous study.   Of these two kinds of speech also, the vernacular is
the nobler, as well because it was the first employed by the human
race, as because the whole world makes use of it, though it has been
divided into forms differing in pronunciation and vocabulary.   It is
also the nobler as being natural to us, whereas the other is rather of
an artificial kind; and it is of this our nobler speech that we intend
to treat.

(8)   On account of the confusion of tongues [at Babel] we have no
slight reason for thinking that men were at that time first scattered
through all the climes of the world, and the habitable regions and
corners of those climes.   And as the original root of the human race
was planted in the regions of the East, and our race also spread out
from there on both sides by a manifold diffusion of shoots, and finally
reached the boundaries of the West, it was then perhaps that rational

throats first drank of the rivers of the whole of Europe, or at least of some of them.   But whether these men then first arrived as strangers, or whether they came back to Europe as natives, they brought a three-fold language with them, and of those who brought it some allotted to themselves the southern, others the northern part of Europe, while the third body, whom we now call Greeks, seized partly on Europe and partly on Asia.

Afterwards, from one and the same idiom received at the avenging confusion, various vernaculars drew their origin, as we shall show farther on.   For one idiom alone prevailed in all the country which from the mouths of the Danube, or marshes of Mæotis to the western boundary of England, is bounded by the frontiers of Italy and France by the ocean; though afterwards through the Sclavonians, Hungarians, Teutons, Saxons, English, and many other nations it was drawn off into various vernaculars, this alone remaining to almost all of them as a sign of their common origin, that nearly all the above-named answer in affirmation *iò*.

Starting from this idiom, that is to say eastward from the Hungarian frontier, another language prevailed over all the territory in that direction comprised in Europe, and even extended beyond.   But a third idiom prevailed in all that part of Europe which remains from the other two, though it now appears in a threefold form.   For of those who speak it, some say in affirmation *oc*, others *oïl*, and others *sì*, namely the Spaniards, the French, and the Italians.   Now the proof that the vernaculars of these nations proceed from one and the same idiom is obvious, because we see that they call many things by the same names, as *Deum, celum, amorem, mare, terram, vivit, moritur, amat,* and almost all other things.   Now these of them who say *oc* inhabit the western part of the South of Europe, beginning from the frontier of the Genoese; while those who say *sì* inhabit the country east of the said frontier, namely that which extends as far as that promontory of Italy where the Gulf of the Adriatic Sea begins, and Sicily.   But those who say *oïl* lie in some sort to the north of these last; for they have the Germans on their east and north; on the west they are enclosed by the English sea, and bounded by the mountains of Aragon; they are also shut off on the south by the inhabitants of Provence, and the precipices of the Apennines.

(9)   Let us now inquire why it is that this language has varied into three chief forms, and why each of these variations varies in itself; why, for instance, the speech of the right side of Italy varies from that of the left (for the Paduans speak in one way and the Pisans in another); and also why those who live nearer together still vary in their speech, as the Milanese and Veronese, the Romans and the Florentines, and even those who have the same national designation, as the Neapolitans and the people of Gaeta, those of Ravenna and those of Faenza, and what is stranger still, the inhabitants of the same city, like the Bolognese of the Borgo S. Felice and the Bolognese

of the Strada Maggiore.   One and the same reason will explain why all these differences and varieties of speech occur.

We say, therefore, that no effect as such goes beyond its cause, because nothing can bring about that which itself is not.   Since therefore every language of ours, except that created by God with the first man, has been restored at our pleasure after the confusion, which was nothing else but forgetfulness of the former language, *and since man is a most unstable and changeable animal, no human language can be lasting and continuous, but must needs vary like other properties of ours, as for instance our manners and our dress, according to distance of time and place.*   And so far am I from thinking that there is room for doubt as to the truth of our remark that speech varies "according to difference of time," that we are of opinion that this is rather to be held as certain.   For, if we consider our other actions, we seem to differ much more from our fellow-countrymen in very distant times than from our contemporaries very remote in place. Wherefore we boldly affirm that if the ancient Pavians were to rise from the dead they would talk in a language varying or differing from that of the modern Pavians.   Nor should what we are saying appear more wonderful than to observe that a young man is grown up whom we have not seen growing.   For the motion of those things which move gradually is not considered by us at all; and the longer the time required for perceiving the variation of a thing, the more stable we suppose that thing to be.   Let us not therefore be surprised if the opinions of men who are but little removed from the brutes suppose that the citizens of the same town have always carried on their intercourse with an unchangeable speech, because the change in the speech of the same town comes about gradually, not without a very long succession of time, whilst the life of man is in its nature extremely short.

If, therefore, the speech of the same people varies (as has been said) successively in course of time, and cannot in any wise stand still, the speech of people living apart and removed from one another must needs vary in different ways; just as manners and dress vary in different ways, since they are not rendered stable either by nature or by intercourse, but arise according to men's inclinations and local fitness.   Hence were set in motion the inventors of the art of grammar, which is nothing else but a kind of unchangeable identity of speech in different times and places.   This having been settled by the common consent of many peoples, seems exposed to the arbitrary will of none in particular, and consequently cannot be variable.   They therefore invented grammar in order that we might not, on account of the variation of speech fluctuating at the will of individuals, either fail altogether in attaining, or at least attain but a partial knowledge of the opinions and exploits of the ancients, or of those whom difference of place causes to differ from us.

(10)   Our language being now spoken under three forms (as has been said above), we feel, when comparing it with itself, according

to the three forms that it has assumed, such great hesitation and timidity in placing its different forms in the balances, that we dare not, in our comparison, give the preference to any one of them, except in so far as we find that the founders of grammar have taken *sic* as the adverb of affirmation, which seems to confer a kind of precedence on the Italians, who say *sì*. For each of the three divisions of our language defends its pretensions by copious evidence. That of *oïl*, then, alleges on its behalf that because of its being an easier and pleasanter vernacular language, whatever has been translated into or composed in vernacular prose belongs to it, namely, the compilations of the exploits of the Trojans and Romans, the exquisite legends of King Arthur, and very many other works of history and learning. Another, namely that of *oc*, claims that eloquent speakers of the vernacular first employed it for poetry, as being a more finished and sweeter language, for instance Peter of Auvergne and other ancient writers. The third also, which is the language of the Italians, claims pre-eminence on the strength of two privileges: first, that the sweetest and most subtle poets who have written in the vernacular are its intimate friends and belong to its household, like Cino of Pistoia and his friend; second, that it seems to lean more on grammar, which is common: and this appears a very weighty argument to those who examine the matter in a rational way.

We, however, decline to give judgment in this case, and confining our treatise to the vernacular Italian, let us endeavour to enumerate the variations it has received into itself, and also to compare these with one another. In the first place, if we would calculate the primary, secondary, and subordinate variations of the vulgar tongue of Italy, we should find that in this tiny corner of the world the varieties of speech not only come up to a thousand but even exceed that figure.

[Dante then specifically examines each major provincial dialect and finds each unsatisfactory in one or more respects.]

(16) Now the supreme standards of those activities which are generically Italian are not peculiar to any one town in Italy, but are common to all; and among these can now be discerned that vernacular language which we were hunting for above, whose fragrance is in every town, but whose lair is in none. It may, however, be more perceptible in one than in another, just as the simplest of substances, which is God, is more perceptible in a man than in a brute, in an animal than in a plant, in a plant than in a mineral, in a mineral than in an element, in fire than in earth. And the simplest quantity, which is unity, is more perceptible in an odd than in an even number; and the simplest colour, which is white, is more perceptible in orange than in green.

Having therefore found what we were searching for, we declare the *illustrious, cardinal, courtly,* and *curial* vernacular language in Italy to be that which belongs to all the towns in Italy but does not appear to belong to any one of them, and by which all the municipal dialects of the Italians are measured, weighed, and compared.

(17)  We must now set forth why it is that we call this language we have found by the epithets illustrious, cardinal, courtly, and curial; and by doing this we disclose the nature of the language itself more clearly.  First, then, let us lay bare what we mean by the epithet illustrious, and why we call the language illustrious.  Now we understand by this term "illustrious" something which shines forth, illuminating and illuminated.  And in this way we call men illustrious either because, being illuminated by power, they illuminate others by justice and charity; or else because, having been excellently trained, they in turn give excellent training, like Seneca and Numa Pompilius.  And the vernacular of which we are speaking has both been exalted by training and power, and also exalts its followers by honour and glory.

Now it appears to have been exalted by training, inasmuch as from amid so many rude Italian words, involved constructions, faulty expressions, and rustic accents we see that it has been chosen out in such a degree of excellence, clearness, completeness, and polish as is displayed by Cino of Pistoia and his friend in their canzoni.

And that it has been exalted by power is plain; for what is of greater power than that which can sway the hearts of men, so as to make an unwilling man willing, and a willing man unwilling, just as this language has done and is doing?

Now that it exalts by honour is evident.  Do not they of its household surpass in renown kings, marquises, counts, and all other magnates?  This has no need at all of proof.

But how glorious it makes its familiar friends we ourselves know, who for the sweetness of this glory cast our exile behind our back.  Wherefore we ought deservedly to proclaim this language illustrious.

(18)  Nor is it without reason that we adorn this illustrious vernacular language with a second epithet, that is, that we call it cardinal: for as the whole door follows its hinge, so that whither the hinge turns the door also may turn, whether it be moved inward or outward, in like manner also the whole herd of municipal dialects turns and returns, moves and pauses according as this illustrious language does, which really seems to be the father of the family.  Does it not daily root out the thorny bushes from the Italian wood?  Does it not daily insert grafts or plant young trees?  What else have its foresters to do but to take away and bring in, as has been said?  Wherefore it surely deserves to be adorned with so great a name as this.

Now the reason why we call it "courtly" is that if we Italians had a court it would be spoken at court.  For if a court is a common home of all the realm and an august ruler of all parts of the realm, it is fitting that whatever is of such a character as to be common to all parts without being peculiar to any, should frequent this court and dwell there; nor is any other abode worthy of so great an inmate.

Such in fact seems to be that vernacular language of which we are speaking; and hence it is that those who frequent all royal palaces always speak the illustrious vernacular. Hence also it is that our illustrious language wanders about like a wayfarer, and is welcomed in humble shelters, seeing we have no court.

This language is also deservedly to be styled "curial", because "curiality" is nothing else but the justly balanced rule of things which have to be done; and because the scales required for this kind of balancing are only wont to be found in the most excellent courts of justice, it follows that whatever in our actions has been well balanced is called curial. Wherefore since this illustrious language has been weighed in the balances of the most excellent court of justice of the Italians, it deserves to be called curial. But it seems mere trifling to say that it has been weighed in the balances of the most excellent court of justice of the Italians, because we have no Imperial court of Justice. To this the answer is easy. For though there is no court of justice of Italy in the sense of a single supreme court, like the court of the king of Germany, still the members of such a court are not wanting. And just as the members of the German court are united under one prince, so the members of ours have been united by the gracious light of Reason. Wherefore, though we have no prince, it would be false to assert that the Italians have no such court of justice, because we have a court, though in the body it is scattered.

(19)  Now we declare that this vernacular language, which we have shown to be illustrious, cardinal, courtly, and curial, is that which is called the Italian vernacular. For just as a vernacular can be found peculiar to Cremona, so can one be found peculiar to Lombardy; and just as one can be found peculiar to Lombardy, so can one be found peculiar to the whole of the left side of Italy. And just as all these can be found, so also can that which belongs to the whole of Italy. And just as the first is called Cremonese, the second Lombard, and the third semi-Italian, so that which belongs to the whole of Italy is called the Italian vernacular language. For this has been used by the illustrious writers who have written poetry in the vernacular throughout Italy, as Sicilians, Apulians, Tuscans, natives of Romagna, and men of both the Marches. And because our intention is, as we promised in the beginning of this work, to give instruction concerning the vernacular speech, we will begin with this illustrious Italian as being the most excellent, and treat in the books immediately following of those whom we think worthy to use it; and for what, and how, and also where, when, and to whom, it ought to be used. And after making all this clear, we will make it our business to throw light on the lower vernaculars, gradually coming down to that which belongs to a single family.

### BOOK II

(1)  Urging on once more the nimbleness of our wit, which is returning to the pen of useful work, we declare in the first place

that the illustrious Italian vernacular is equally fit for use in prose and in verse. But because prose writers rather get this language from poets, and because poetry seems to remain a pattern to prose writers, and not the converse, which things appear to confer a certain supremacy, let us first disentangle this language as to its use in metre, treating of it in the order we set forth at the end of the first book.

Let us then first inquire whether all those who write verse in the vernacular should use this illustrious language; and so far as a superficial consideration of the matter goes, it would seem that they should, because every one who writes verse ought to adorn his verse as far as he is able. Wherefore, since nothing affords so great an adornment as the illustrious vernacular does, it would seem that every writer of verse ought to employ it.

And since language is as necessary an instrument of our thought as a horse is of a knight, and since the best horses are suited to the best knights, as has been said, the best language will be suited to the best thoughts. But the best thoughts cannot exist except where knowledge and genius are found; therefore the best language is only suitable in those in whom knowledge and genius are found; and so the best language is not suited to all who write verse, since a great many write without knowledge and genius; and consequently neither is the best vernacular suited to all who write verse. Wherefore, if it is not suited to all, all ought not to use it, because no one ought to act in an unsuitable manner. And as to the statement that every one ought to adorn his verse as far as he can, we declare that it is true. But we should not describe an ox with trappings or a swine with a belt as adorned; nay rather, we laugh at them as disfigured, for adornment is the addition of some suitable thing.

(2) After having proved that not all those who write verse, but only those of the highest excellence, ought to use the illustrious vernacular, we must in the next place establish whether every subject ought to be handled in it or not; and if not, we must set out by themselves those subjects that are worthy of it.

It must be observed that, as man has been endowed with a threefold life, namely, vegetable, animal, and rational, he journeys along a threefold road; for in so far as he is vegetable he seeks for what is useful, wherein he is of like nature with plants; in so far as he is animal he seeks for that which is pleasurable, wherein he is of like nature with the brutes; in so far as he is rational he seeks for what is right — and in this he stands alone, or is a partaker of the nature of the angels. It is by these three kinds of life that we appear to carry out whatever we do; and because in each one of them some things are greater, some greatest, within the range of their kind, it follows that those which are greatest appear the ones which ought to be treated of supremely, and consequently, in the greatest vernacular.

But we must discuss what things are greatest; and first in respect of what is useful. Now in this matter, if we carefully consider the object of all those who are in search of what is useful, we shall find that it is nothing else but *safety*.  Secondly, in respect of what is pleasurable; and here we say that that is most pleasurable which gives pleasure by the most exquisite object of appetite, and this is *love*. Thirdly, in respect of what is right; and here no one doubts that *virtue* has the first place.  Wherefore these three things, namely, safety, love, and virtue, appear to be those capital matters which ought to be treated of supremely, I mean the things which are most important in respect of them, as prowess in arms, the fire of love, and the direction of the will.  And if we duly consider, we shall find that the illustrious writers have written poetry in the vulgar tongue on these subjects exclusively; namely, Bertran de Born on Arms, Arnaut Daniel on Love, Giraut de Borneil on Righteousness, Cino of Pistoia on Love, his friend on Righteousness.  I do not find, however, that any Italian has as yet written poetry on the subject of Arms.

Having then arrived at this point, we know what are the proper subjects to be sung in the highest vernacular language.

(3)  But now let us endeavour carefully to examine how those matters which are worthy of so excellent a vernacular language are to be restricted.  As we wish, then, to set forth the form by which these matters are worthy to be bound, we say that it must first be borne in mind that those who have written poetry in the vernacular have uttered their poems in many different forms, some in that of canzoni, some in that of ballate, some in that of sonnets, some in other illegitimate and irregular forms, as will be shown farther on. Now we consider that of these forms that of canzoni is the most excellent; and therefore, if the most excellent things are worthy of the most excellent, as has been proved above, those subjects which are worthy of the most excellent vernacular are worthy of the most excellent form, and consequently ought to be handled in canzoni.

(4)  Having then laboured by a process of disentangling to show what persons and things are worthy of the courtly vernacular, as well as the form of verse which we deem worthy of such honour that it alone is fitted for the highest vernacular, before going off to other topics, let us explain the form of the canzone, which many appear to adopt rather at haphazard than with art; and let us unlock the workshop of the art of that form which has hitherto been adopted in a casual way, omitting the form of ballate and sonnets, because we intend to explain this in the fourth book of this work, when we shall treat of the middle vernacular language.

Reviewing, therefore, what has been said, we remember that we have frequently called those who write verse in the vernacular poets; and this we have doubtless ventured to say with good reason, because they are in fact poets, if we take a right view of poetry, which is nothing else but a rhetorical composition set to music.  But these poets differ from the great poets, that is, the regular ones, for the language of the great poets was regulated by art, whereas these, as has been said, write at haphazard.  It therefore happens that the more closely we copy the great poets, the more correct is the poetry we write; whence it behoves us, by devoting some trouble to the work of teaching, to emulate their poetic teaching.

Before all things therefore we say that each one ought to adjust the weight of the subject to his own shoulders, so that their strength may not be too heavily taxed, and he be forced to tumble into the mud. This is the advice our master Horace gives us when he says in the beginning of his *Art of Poetry,* "Ye who write take up a subject suited to your strength."

Next we ought to possess a discernment as to those things which suggest themselves to us as fit to be uttered, so as to decide whether they ought to be sung in the way of *tragedy, comedy,* or *elegy.* By tragedy we bring in the higher style, by comedy the lower style, by elegy we understand the style of the wretched. If our subject appears fit to be sung in the tragic style, we must then assume the illustrious vernacular language, and consequently we must bind up a canzone. If, however, it appears fit to be sung in the comic style, sometimes the middle and sometimes the lowly vernacular should be used; and the discernment to be exercised in this case we reserve for treatment in the fourth book. But if our subject appears fit to be sung in the elegiac style, we must adopt the lowly vernacular alone.

But let us omit the other styles and now, as is fitting, let us treat of the tragic style. We appear then to make use of the tragic style when the stateliness of the lines as well as the loftiness of the construction and the excellence of the words agree with the weight of the subject. And because, if we remember rightly, it has already been proved that the highest things are worthy of the highest, and because the style which we call tragic appears to be the highest style, those things which we have distinguished as being worthy of the highest song are to be sung in that style alone, namely, Safety, Love, and Virtue, and those other things, our conceptions of which arise from these; provided that they be not degraded by any accident.

Let every one therefore beware and discern what we say; and when he purposes to sing of these three subjects simply, or of those things which directly and simply follow after them, let him first drink of Helicon, and then, after adjusting the strings, boldly take up his plectrum and begin to ply it. But it is in the exercise of the needful caution and discernment that the real difficulty lies; for this can never be attained to without strenuous efforts of genius, constant practice in the art, and the habit of the sciences. And it is those so equipped whom the poet in the sixth book of the Æneid describes as beloved of God, raised by glowing virtue to the sky, and sons of the Gods, though he is speaking figuratively. And therefore let those who, innocent of art and science, and trusting to genius alone, rush forward to sing of the highest subjects in the highest style, confess their folly and cease from such presumption; and if in their natural sluggishness they are but geese, let them abstain from imitating the eagle soaring to the stars.

(5)  We seem to have said enough, or at least as much as our work requires, about the weight of the subjects.  Wherefore let us hasten on to the stateliness of the lines, in respect of which it is to be observed that our predecessors made use of different lines in their canzoni, as the moderns also do; but we do not find that any one has hitherto used a line of more than eleven or less than three syllables.  And though the Italian poets have used the lines of three and of eleven syllables and all the intermediate ones, those of five, seven, and eleven syllables are more frequently used than the others, and next to them, that of three syllables in preference to the others.  But of all these the line of eleven syllables seems the stateliest, as well by reason of the length of time it occupies as of its capacity in regard to subject, construction, and words.  And the beauty of all these things is more multiplied in this line than in the others, as is plainly apparent; for wherever things that weigh are multiplied so also is weight.

We say also that the line of seven syllables follows next after that which is greatest in celebrity.  After this we place the line of five, and then that of three syllables.  But the line of nine syllables, because it appeared to consist of the line of three taken three times, was either never held in honour or fell into disuse on account of its being disliked.  As for the lines of an even number of syllables, we use them but rarely, because of their rudeness; for they retain the nature of their numbers, which are subject to the odd numbers as matter to form.  And so, summing up what has been said, the line of eleven syllables appears to be the stateliest line, and this is what we were in search of.

(7)  The next division of our progress now demands that an explanation be given as to those words which are of such grandeur as to be worthy of being admitted into that style to which we have awarded the first place.  We declare therefore to begin with that the exercise of discernment as to words involves by no means the smallest labour of our reason, since we see that a great many sorts of them can be found.  For some words are childish, some feminine, and some manly; and of these last some are sylvan, others urban; and of those we call urban we feel that some are combed-out and glossy, some shaggy and rumpled.  Now among these urban words the combed-out and the shaggy are those which we call grand; whilst we call the glossy and the rumpled those whose sound tends to superfluity, just as among great works some are works of magnanimity, others of smoke; and as to these last, although when superficially looked at there may be thought to be a kind of ascent, to sound reason no ascent, but rather a headlong fall down giddy precipices will be manifest, because the marked-out path of virtue is departed from.  Therefore look carefully, Reader, consider how much it behoves thee to use the sieve in selecting noble words; for if thou hast regard to the illustrious vulgar tongue which (as has been said above) poets ought to use when writing in the tragic style in the vernacular (and

these are the persons whom we intend to fashion), thou wilt take care that the noblest words alone are left in thy sieve. And among the number of these thou wilt not be able in any wise to place childish words, because of their simplicity, as *mamma* and *babbo, mate* and *pate*; nor feminine words, because of their softness, as *dolciada* and *placevole*; nor sylvan words because of their roughness, as *greggia* and *cetra*; nor the glossy nor the rumpled urban words, as *femina* and *corpo*. Therefore thou wilt see that only the combed-out and the shaggy urban words will be left to thee, which are the noblest, and members of the illustrious vulgar tongue. Now we call those words combed-out which have three, or as nearly as possible three syllables; which are without aspirate, without acute or circumflex accent, without the double letters z or x, without double liquids, or a liquid placed immediately after a mute, and which, having been planed (so to say), leave the speaker with a certain sweetness, like *amore, donna, disio, vertute, donare, letitia, salute, securitate, defesa.*

We call shaggy all words besides these which appear either necessary or ornamental to the illustrious vulgar tongue. We call necessary those which we cannot avoid, as certain monosyllables like *sì, no, me, te, se, a, e, i, o, u,* the interjections, and many more. We describe as ornamental all polysyllables which when mixed with combed-out words produce a fair harmony of structure, though they may have the roughness of aspirate, accent, double letters, liquids, and length; as *terra, honore, speranza, gravitate, alleviato, impossibilità, impossibilitate, benaventuratissimo, inanimatissimamente, disaventuratissimamente, sovramagnificentissimamente,* which last has eleven syllables. A word might yet be found with more syllables still; but as it would exceed the capacity of all our lines it does not appear to fall into the present discussion; such is that word *honorificabilitudinitate,* which runs in the vernacular to twelve syllables, and in grammar to thirteen, in two oblique cases.

In what way shaggy words of this kind are to be harmonised in the lines with combed-out words, we leave to be taught farther on, and what has been said here on the pre-eminent nature of the words to be used may suffice for every one of inborn discernment.

[tr. A. G. FERRERS HOWELL]

# SINGLE GOVERNMENT
## (De Monarchia)

Those unfamiliar with medieval literature cannot conceive how the concept of Eternal Rome and the Roman Empire captured and held the medieval imagination. Jerome's pessimism at the Sack of Rome changed in favor of Augustine's optimistic view that God had ordained the Roman Empire and the *pax Romana* as a part of the Christian plan of regeneration and that the *imperium*, or governance of men's civil relations as a working out of God's plan, was as lasting as the earth itself. When Charlemagne was crowned Emperor in St. Peter's at Rome on Christmas Day in the year 800, men were willing to overlook the illegality and ensuing political instability because they were inspired by the concept of a ruler acting as vicar of God in temporal affairs as the Pope acted in spiritual. Pope Gregory VIII coined a simile of "two lights in the firmament of the Church militant," the Pope as the sun and the Emperor as the moon. The simile was a two-edged sword that pricked the Emperors when they came in conflict with the Pope. "And as moonlight is to the sunlight," says Bryce, "so was the Empire to the Papacy. The rays of the one were borrowed, feeble, often interrupted; the other shone with an unquenchable brilliance all her own." Dante felt the force of the simile in defending the Empire, but could only counter with his unpersuasive comparison of Pope and Emperor with two suns; according to Dante, God ordained that power shall flow from Christ equally to Peter and to Caesar.

Unfortunately for Dante, the imperial idea never became the stable reality that the Papacy became. From the time that the Saxon Otto I was crowned Emperor in 962 until Frederick II died in 1250, the German rulers had successively been crowned "King of the Romans ever Augustus" and had maintained an uneasy hegemony over the Italian peninsula; but France had never conceded the principle of Empire, and as trade and commerce began to undermine the agrarian feudalism on which it depended, the power of the more adaptable Capetian dynasty began to assert itself in Italian affairs. The fate of the Empire was decided the year Dante was born, at Benevento, but Dante never realized it. Partly in hate of a Papacy in league with French royalty in such abuses as had brought about his exile and partly in an intellectual conviction that only a strong emperor could bring peace to northern Italy, Dante fought his life through as advocate for the Ghibelline cause, though he was reared a Guelf.

*Single Government*, then, is as backward-looking as the *Illustrious Vernacular* looks forward. Yet it is to this day one of the most popular of Dante's works outside the *Comedy* and is universally read and enjoyed for its pervasive sincerity, fervor, and idealism. The date of its composition is disputed, but Boccaccio's statement that it was inspired by the excursion into Italy of Emperor Henry VII (A.D. 1311–1313) seems credible.  The selections below comprise about one quarter of the whole.

## SINGLE GOVERNMENT

[From *The Latin Works of Dante;* Temple Classics, J. M. Dent & Sons, Ltd., London, 1904.  Reprinted by permission of the publisher.]

### BOOK I

(1)  It would seem that all men on whom the Higher Nature has stamped the love of truth must make it their chief concern, like as they have been enriched by the toil of those who have gone before, so themselves in like manner to toil in advance for those that shall be hereafter, that posterity may have of them whereby to be enriched.

For he who, himself imbued with public teachings, yet cares not to contribute aught to the public good, may be well assured that he has fallen far from duty; for he is not "a tree by the streams of waters, bearing his fruit in due season," but rather a devouring whirlpool, ever sucking in, and never pouring back what it has swallowed.  Wherefore, often pondering these things with myself, lest I should one day be convicted of the charge of the buried talent, I long not only to burgeon, but also to bear fruit for the public advantage, and to set forth truths unattempted by others.  For what fruit would he bear who should demonstrate once more some theorem of Euclid; who should strive to expound anew felicity, which Aristotle has already expounded; who should undertake again the apology of old age, which Cicero has pleaded?  Naught at all, but rather would such wearisome superfluity provoke disgust.

And inasmuch as amongst other unexplored and important truths the knowledge of the temporal monarchy is most important and least explored, and (for that it stands in no direct relation to gain) has been attempted by none; therefore am I minded to extract it from its recesses, on the one hand that I may keep vigil for the good of the world, and on the other that I may be the first to win for my glory the palm of so great a prize.  A hard task in truth do I attempt, and beyond my strength, trusting not so much in my proper power as in the light of that giver who giveth to all liberally and upbraideth not.

(2)  First, therefore, we have to consider what the temporal monarchy means; in type to wit, and after intention.  The temporal monarchy, then, which is called empire is "a unique princedom extending over all persons in time," or, "in and over those things which

are measured by time." And there rise three main inquiries concerning the same: for in the first place we may inquire and examine whether it is needful for the well-being of the world; in the second, whether the Roman people rightfully assumed to itself the function of monarchy; and in the third, whether the authority of the monarchy depends immediately upon God, or upon some other minister or vicar of God.

(3) So now we must consider what is the goal of human civilisation as a whole, which, when we see, more than half our work will be done, according to the Philosopher *Ad Nicomachum*. There is one end for which she produces the individual man, another for which the domestic group, another for which the district, another for which the city-state, and another for which the kingdom; and lastly, there is an ultimate goal for which the eternal God, by his art, which is nature, brings into being the human race in its universality. And it is this last for which we are now seeking as the first principle to direct our inquiry.

What this function is will be obvious if the specific potentiality of mankind generally be made clear. I say, then, that no capacity which is shared by many beings, differing in species, is the specific capacity of any one of them. For since that which is specific constitutes a species, it would follow that one essence would be specifically assigned to several species, which is impossible. The specific capacity, then, which differentiates man is not merely being, taken without qualification, for this he shares with the elements; either compound being, for this we find in the minerals; nor animated being, for this is in plants; nor apprehension, for this is shared by the brutes; but apprehension by means of the potential intellect, which mode of being is not competent to any other save man, either above him or below.

It is plain, then, that the specific potentiality of humanity as such is a potentiality or capacity of intellect.

Moreover, the intellectual faculty of which I am speaking deals not only with universal forms or species, but also, by a kind of extension, with particular ones. Whence it is commonly said that the speculative intellect by extension becomes the practical intellect, the end of which is doing and making. And I draw this distinction because there are things to be done which are regulated by political wisdom, and things to be made, which are regulated by art. But they are all alike handmaids of speculation, as the supreme function for which the Prime Excellence brought the human race into being. And now we have already reached a point at which that saying of the *Politics* begins to be luminous: "The intellectually vigorous have natural sway over others."

(4) And since it is with the whole as it is with the part, and it is the fact that in sedentary quietness the individual man is perfected in knowledge and in wisdom, it is evident that in the quiet or tran-

quility of peace the human race is most freely and favourably disposed towards the work proper to it (which is almost divine, even as it is said "Thou hast made him a little lower than the angels"). Whence it is manifest that universal peace is the best of all those things which are ordained for our blessedness. And that is why there rang out to the shepherds from on high, not riches, not pleasures, not honours, not length of life, not health, not strength, not beauty, but peace. For the celestial soldiery proclaims, "Glory to God in the highest; and, on earth, peace to men of good will." Hence, also, "Peace be with you" was the salutation of him who was the salvation of man. For it was meet that the supreme saviour should utter the supreme salutation.

(5) And now, to resume what we said at the outset, three main questions are raised and discussed about the temporal monarchy, more commonly called the empire; concerning which, as already declared, we purpose to make inquiry, in the order indicated above, under the first principle now laid down. Let us therefore first discuss whether a temporal monarchy is needful for the well-being of the world.

Now against its being needful there is no force either of argument or of authority, whereas most powerful and most patent arguments establish that it is. Of which let the first be drawn from the authority of the philosopher in his *Politics*. For there his venerable authority asserts that when more things than one are ordained for a single purpose, needs must one of them guide or rule, and the others be guided or ruled. And to this not only the glorious name of the author, but inductive argument also forces assent.

Now it is admitted that the whole human race is ordained for a single end, as was set forth before. Therefore there must be one guiding or ruling power. And this is what we mean by monarch or emperor. Thus it appears that for the well-being of the world there must be a monarchy or empire.

(8) And everything is well and best disposed which is disposed after the intention of the prime agent, which is God. And this is self-evident to all who deny not that the divine excellence attains the height of perfection. It is of the intention of God that every created thing should present the divine likeness in so far as its proper nature is capable of receiving it. Wherefore it is said, "Let us make man after our image and likeness." And although "after our image" may not be said of things lower than man, yet "after our likeness" may be said of all things soever, since the whole universe is nought else than a certain footprint of the divine excellence. Therefore the human race is well and best disposed when, to the measure of its power, it is likened to God.

But the human race is then most one when it is all united in one, which can not be save when it is subject in its totality to one prince, as is self-evident. Therefore, it is when subject to one prince that the human race is most likened to God, and consequently most conforms to the divine intention.

(10) Wheresoever contention may arise there must needs be judgment, else there were an imperfection without its proper perfector; which is impossible, since God and nature fails not in things necessary. Now between any two princes, one of whom is in no way subject to the other, contention may arise, either through their own fault or that of their subjects, as is self-evident. Wherefore there must needs be judgment between such. And since the one may not take cognisance of what concerns the other, the one not being subject to the other (for a peer has no rule over his peer), there must needs be a third of wider jurisdiction who, within the compass of his right, has princedom over both. Therefore monarchy is necessary for the world. And this reasoning was perceived by the Philosopher when he said, "Things love not to be ill-disposed; but a multiplicity of princedoms is ill; therefore, one prince."

(11) Moreover, the world is best disposed when justice is most potent therein; whence Virgil, in praise of that age which was visibly rising in his own day, sang in his Bucolics: —

*Iam redit et Virgo, redeunt Saturnia regna.*

By "Virgin" he meant Justice, who was also called Astraea. By "Saturnian kingdoms" he meant the best ages, which were also called the golden.

Justice is most potent under a monarch only; therefore for the best disposition of the world it is needful that there should be a monarchy or empire.

We must note that greed is the chief opponent of justice, as Aristotle indicates in the fifth *Ad Nicomachum*. If greed be absolutely removed, nothing is left to oppose justice; whence it is the opinion of the Philosopher that such things as can be determined by law should in no case be left to the judge. And this for fear of greed, which readily turns the minds of men aside. Now where there is nought that can be desired, there it is impossible for greed to be; for when their objects are destroyed the passions cannot persist. But the monarch has nought that he can desire, for his jurisdiction is bounded by the ocean alone, which is not the case with other princes, since their principalities are bounded by others; as for instance the King of the Castile's by the King of Aragon's. Whence it follows that the monarch may be the purest subject of justice amongst mortals.

Moreover, just as greed, though it be never so little, clouds to some extent the disposition of justice, so does charity or right love sharpen and brighten it. In whomsoever therefore right love has the greatest power of inhering, in him justice may take the most commanding place. The monarch is such; therefore when he exists justice is most powerful, or at any rate may be so. Now, that right love has the action I have said may be shown thus. Greed, scorning the intrinsic significance of man, seeks other things; but charity, scorning all other things, seeks God and man, and consequently the good of man. And since, amongst the other blessings of man, living in peace is the chief (as was said above), and justice is the chiefest and mightiest accomplisher of this, therefore charity will chiefly give vigour to justice; and the stronger she is, the more.

And that right love should inhere in the monarch most of all men is shown thus. Everything lovable is the more loved the closer it is to the lover. But men are closer to the monarch than to other princes; therefore they are most loved by him, or at least they ought to be. The first proposition is manifest if the nature of patients and agents be considered. The second proposition is demonstrated thus. Men only come into contact with other princes partwise, but with the monarch in their totality. And again, men come into contact with other princes through the monarch, and not conversely; and thus, charge of all men primarily and immediately inheres in the monarch, and in other princes only through the monarch, inasmuch as their charge is derived from that supreme charge.

(12) And the human race when most free is best disposed. This will be clear if the principle of freedom be understood. Wherefore be it known that the first principle of our freedom is freedom of choice, which many have on their lips but few in their understanding.

I say that judgment is the link between apprehension and appetite. For first a thing is apprehended, then when apprehended it is judged to be good or bad, and finally he who has so judged it pursues or shuns it. If, then, the judgment altogether sets the appetite in motion, and is in no measure anticipated by it, it is free. But if the judgment is moved by the appetite, which to some extent anticipates it, it cannot be free, for it does not move of itself, but is drawn captive by another. And hence it is that brutes cannot have free judgment because their judgments are always anticipated by appetite. And hence too it may be seen that the intellectual substances whose wills are immutable, and separated souls departing from this life in grace, do not lose their freedom of choice because of the immutability of their wills, but retain it in its most perfect and potent form.

When we see this we may further understand that this freedom (or this principle of all our freedom) is the greatest gift conferred by God on human nature; for through it we have our felicity here as men, through it we have our felicity elsewhere as deities. It is only when a monarch is reigning that the human race exists for its own sake, and not for the sake of something else. For it is only then that perverted forms of government are made straight, to wit democracies, oligarchies, and tyrannies, which force the human race into slavery (as is obvious to whosoever runs through them all), and that government is conducted by kings, aristocrats (whom they call optimates), and zealots for the people's liberty. And such right governments purpose freedom, to wit that men should exist for their own sakes. For the citizens are not there for the sake of the consuls, nor the nation for the sake of the king, but conversely the consuls for the sake of the citizens, the king for the sake of the nation. For just as the body politic is not established for the benefit of the laws, but the laws for the benefit of the body politic, so too they who live under the law are not ordained for the benefit of the legislator, but rather he for theirs, as saith the Philosopher again in what has been left by him on the present matter. Hence it is clear that, albeit the consul or king be masters of the rest as regards the way, yet as regards the end they are their servants; and the monarch most of all, for he must assuredly be regarded as the servant of all. Hence it may begin to appear at this point how the monarch is conditioned in laying down the laws by the end set before him.

Therefore the human race is best disposed when under a monarchy. Whence it follows that for the well-being of the world the existence of a monarchy is necessary.

(14) Doubtless, we should note that when we say the human race can be ruled by one supreme prince we are not to be so understood, as that every petty decision of each municipality (since even the bye-laws sometimes leave us in the lurch and themselves need direction, as is clear from the Philosopher in the fifth *Ad Nicomachum,* in his commendation of *epyekia*) could issue from him immediately. For nations, kingdoms, and cities have their special conditions which ought to be regulated by different laws. For a law is a rule to direct life. And naturally the Scythians who live outside the seventh clima, and experience great inequality of days and nights, and are oppressed by an almost intolerable chill of frost, must needs be regulated in a different way from the Garamantes who live under the equinoctial circle and always have the light of day equal in length to the darkness of night, and because of the excessive heat of the air cannot endure to be covered with a superfluity of garments. But it must be thus understood, that the human race in those things which are common, and are inherent in all, should be ruled by him, and guided by his common rule to peace. And this rule or law, the particular princes ought to receive from him, as the practical intellect receives the major proposition from the speculative intellect, and adds under it the particular proposition which is properly its own, and so proceeds to the particular practical conclusion. And not only is this possible to one; but it must of necessity flow from one, that all confusion concerning universal principles may be removed. And thus Moses writes in the Law that he himself did; for joining to himself the chiefs of the tribes of the sons of Israel, he relegated to them the inferior judgments, reserving to himself alone the higher and more general; which more general judgments the chieftains made use of throughout their tribes according as they were applicable to each of them.

(15) All concord depends on unity in wills. The human race when best disposed is a concord. For as a single man when best disposed both as to mind and body is a concord, and so also a house, a city, and a kingdom, so likewise is the whole human race. Therefore the human race when best disposed depends upon a unity in wills. But this unity cannot be unless there is one will dominating and ruling all the rest to oneness; inasmuch as the wills of mortals, because of the seductive delights of youth, have need of a directive principle, as the philosopher teaches in the last *Ad Nicomachum*. Nor can that one will exist unless there be a single prince of all, whose will may be the mistress and ruler of all others.

(16) All the reasons set forth above are confirmed by a memorable experience; namely, of that state of mortal things which the Son of God, when about to become man for man's salvation, either awaited, or, when He would, produced. For if we go through all the states and periods of man, even from the fall of our first parents, which was the point at which we turned aside on our wanderings, we shall find that the world was never quiet on every side except under divus Augustus, the monarch, when there was a perfect monarchy. And that in truth the human race was then blessed in the tranquillity of universal peace is witnessed by all the historians, witnessed by illustrious poets. To this the scribe of the gentleness of Christ has likewise deigned to bear witness; and finally Paul has called that most happy state the "fulness of time." Verily the time and all temporal things were full, for no ministry to our felicity was then vacant of its minister.

But what the state of the world has been since that seamless garment first suffered rending by the nail of covetousness we may read — would that we might not also see! O race of men in what storms and losses, in what shipwrecks must thou needs be tossed, so long as, transformed into a beast of many heads, thou strivest after many things! Thou art sick in either intellect, sick in affection. Thou dost not minister to the higher intellect by reasonings that cannot be gainsaid, nor to the lower by the aspect of experience, nor even to thy affection by the sweetness of divine persuasion, when there sounds to thee through the trumpet of the Holy Spirit, "Behold how good and how pleasant it is for brethren to dwell together in unity."

### BOOK II

(1) Time was that I, too, marvelled that the Roman people had been raised to supremacy on the terrestrial globe, with none to resist. For it was my thought, as I looked upon the surface only, that they had gained it by no right but merely by force of arms. But now that I have pierced with the eyes of my mind to the marrow of it, and have seen by most convincing signs that it was divine Providence which effected this, my wonder has vanished.

Now the truth concerning this question may be shown not only by the light of human reason but also by the ray of divine authority.

And when these two unite in one, needs must heaven and earth consent together. Wherefore leaning upon the confidence afore noted and trusting to the testimony of reason and authority, I proceed to the solution of the second question.

(2) Be it known then that like as art exists in three grades — in the mind of the artificer, in the instrument, and in the material informed by art — so too we may regard nature in three grades. For nature is in the mind of the first mover, which is God, and further in the heaven as in the instrument by means of which the likeness of the eternal excellence is spread over fluctuating matter. And as when the artificer is perfect and the instrument is in perfect order, any flaw that may occur in the form of art must be imputed to the material alone, so, since God realises the supreme perfection, and his instrument, the heaven, falls no way short of its due perfection, it remains that whatsoever flaw there is in things below is a flaw on the part of the material submitted to the action of God and the heaven, and is beside the intention both of God as the active principle of nature, and of the heaven; and that whatsoever good there is in things below, since it cannot come from the matter itself, which only exists as potentiality, must come primarily from the artificer, God, and secondarily from heaven, which is the instrument of that divine art which men commonly call nature.

Hence it is clear that right, since it is a good, exists primarily in the mind of God. And since everything that is in the mind of God is God (according to that word "What was made was life in him"), and since God supremely wills Himself, it follows that right is willed by God, inasmuch as it is in Him. And since in God the will and what is willed are identical, it follows further that the divine will is right itself, and hence it follows again that right as manifested in things is nought else than the similitude of the divine will. Whence it comes to pass that whatever is not consonant with the divine will cannot be right, and whatever is consonant with the divine will is right. Wherefore to ask whether anything takes place by right, though the words differ, is yet nought else than to inquire whether it takes place according to what God wills. Let this, then, be our underlying principle: that whatever God wills in the society of men is to be regarded as true and pure right.

(3) It was meet for the noblest people to be set above all others. The Roman people was the noblest. Therefore it was meet for it to be set above all others. The assumed is proved by reason: since honour is a reward of virtue and promotion is honour, promotion is a reward of virtue. But it is clear that men are ennobled by merit of virtue, their own to wit, or that of their forebears. For nobility is "virtue and ancient wealth" according to the Philosopher in the *Politics*.

Our divine poet Virgil, throughout the Æneid testifies, for an everlasting memorial, that the glorious king Æneas was the father of the Roman people. And Titus Livius, the choice scribe of the feats of the Romans, bears witness with him, in the first part of his volume, which takes its start from the capture of Troy.

But as concerns his hereditary nobility, we find that each several portion of the tripartite world had ennobled him both with ancestors and with consorts.

For Asia had ennobled him with his more immediate ancestors as Assaracus and the others who ruled over Phrygia, a region of Asia. Europe again ennobled him with his most ancient ancestor, to wit, Dardanus. Africa again ennobled him with his most ancient ancestress, Electra to wit, born of King Atlas of great name.

And in like manner I find that he was ennobled by wedlock. For his first wife, Creusa, daughter of King Priam, was of Asia, as may be gathered above from what has there been said. And that she was his wife our poet bears witness in the third, where Andromache questions the father, Æneas, about his son, Ascanius. His second wife was Dido, queen and mother of the Carthaginians in Africa. The third was Lavinia, the mother both of the Albans and Romans, daughter and heir alike of King Latinus, if the testimony of our poet be true in the last.

Who is not satisfied that the father of the Roman people, and therefore that people itself, was the noblest under heaven? or who will fail to note the divine predestination in that twofold concourse of blood from every several portion of the world upon a single man?

(4) Moreover, that which is helped to its own perfection by the support of miracles is willed by God and consequently comes to pass by right. And that this is true is evident; for as Thomas says in his third *Contra Gentiles,* "A miracle is that which takes place through divine agency, beside the order commonly instituted in things." Whence he himself proves that it is competent to God alone to work miracles.

But that God did show forth miracles to perfect the Roman Empire is proved by the witness of illustrious authors. For when Numa Pompilius, the second king of the Romans, was sacrificing, after the manner of the Gentiles, Livy, in his first part, testifies that a shield fell down from heaven into the city chosen of God.

And when the Gauls, who had already captured the rest of the city, trusting to the darkness of the night, were secretly creeping up to the Capitol, which alone remained to avert the final extinction of the Roman name, Livy and many illustrious writers bear concordant witness that a goose, never seen there before, chanted the approach of the Gauls, and waked the guards to defend the Capitol.

And when the nobleness of Rome, under pressure of Hannibal, had fallen so low that for the final obliteration of the affairs of Rome nought was lacking save that the Poeni should trample on the very city, Livy, in the *Punic War,* tells, amongst other gestes, that a sudden and intolerable hailstorm so dismayed them that the victors might not follow up their victory.

And was not Cloelia's passage miraculous, when, as Porsenna was besieging the city, she, a woman and a captive, broke her chains, supported by the wondrous aid of God, and swam across the Tiber, as almost all the scribes of the affairs of Rome record to her glory?

Thus was it altogether fitting that he should do who from eternity provided for all things in symmetrical beauty; that he who, when visible, was about to do miracles as testimony to things invisible, should, when invisible, do the like in testimony of things visible.

(5) Again, whosoever purposes the good of the commonwealth, purposes the goal of right.

Now that the Roman people, in subjecting the terrestrial globe to itself, did contemplate the aforesaid good, their deeds declare; for in those deeds, banishing all greed, which is ever hostile to the common weal, and loving universal peace, with liberty, that people, holy, compassionate, and glorious, is seen to have taken no thought for its own advantage so long as it might look to the weal of the human race.

Did not that great Cincinnatus leave us a holy example of freely laying down office at the proper term, when, having been taken from the plough and made dictator (as Livy tells), after his victory and after his triumph he restored the sceptre of command to the consuls and returned, of his own free will, to sweat at the plough-tail after his oxen?

(7) The Roman people was ordained by nature to command. Which is thus made clear: Just as he would fall short of the perfection of art who should consider the final form alone, but should take no heed for the means by which to attain to the form, so would nature if she contemplated only the universal form of the divine similitude in the universe, and neglected the means thereto. But nature lacks no perfection, since she is the work of the divine intelligence. Therefore she contemplates all the means by which the final goal of her intention is approached.

We see that not only individual men, but peoples, are some of them apt by nature to rule and others to be subject and to serve, as the Philosopher sets forth in what he has written *de Politicis*. And for such as these last, even as he says, it is not only expedient to be ruled, but also just, even though they be forced thereto.

And if these things are so, it is not to be doubted that nature ordained in the world a place and a people for universal command; else she would have been lacking to herself, which is impossible. Now what this place and what this people were is sufficiently manifest from what has been said above and what will be said below, to wit, Rome and her citizens or people. The which our poet too has touched upon right subtly in the sixth, introducing Anchises admonishing Æneas, the father of the Romans, thus: —

Others shall beat out the breathing bronze more softly, I do well believe it! And shall draw living features from the marble; shall plead causes better, and trace with the rod the movements of the sky, and tell of the rising stars.   Roman! do thou be mindful how to sway the peoples with command.   These be thy arts; to lay upon them the custom of peace, to spare the subject and fight down the proud.

And the disposition of the place he subtly touches on in the fourth, when he introduces love discoursing to Mercury concerning Æneas, after this fashion: —

"Not such did his fairest mother promise us that he should be — twice rescuing him therefore from Grecian arms, — but that he should be the man to rule o'er Italy, pregnant with empires, and snorting war."

Wherefore it has been sufficiently urged that the Roman people was ordained by nature for command.   Therefore the Roman people, in subjecting the world to itself, attained to empire by right.

(8)   That judgment of God is hidden, to which human reason can attain neither by the law of nature nor by the law of Scripture, but sometimes by special grace, which may come to pass in divers ways, sometimes by simple revelation, sometimes by revelation through the intervention of some ordeal: by simple revelation in two ways, either by the spontaneous act of God, or at the instance of prayer.   By the spontaneous act of God in two ways, either expressly or by a sign.   Expressly, as the judgment against Saul was revealed to Samuel.   By a sign, as God's judgment concerning the deliverance of the sons of Israel was revealed to Pharaoh by signs. At the instance of prayer, as he knew who said in the second *Paralipomenon*, "When we know not what we should do, this only have we left, to turn our eyes to thee."

By the intervention of ordeal in two ways: either by lot or by contest, *certamen*.   For the word "to contend," *certare*, is derived from "making certain," *certum*.   The judgment of God is sometimes revealed to man by lot, as appears in the substitution of Matthias, in the Acts of the Apostles.   By contest the judgment of God is revealed in two ways, either by clash of strength, as when a pair of champions contend (which kind are called combatants), or by the strife of rivals, each of whom strains to get first to some mark, as happens in the contests of athletes running for a prize.

(9)   That people, then, which prevailed when all were contending for the empire of the world, prevailed by divine judgment.   For since the settlement of the universal contention must engage God's care more deeply than the settlement of a particular contention, there is no doubt but that success amongst the athletes contending for empire of the world must have followed the judgment of God. Now it was the Roman people which prevailed when all were striving for empire; which will be manifest if we consider the athletes, and consider also the prize or goal.

For the first amongst mortals who panted after this prize was Ninus, King of the Assyrians; and though, together with the partner of his bed, Semiramis, he strove in arms for the empire of the world, through the course of ninety years and more (as Orosius reports), and subdued all Asia to himself, yet were not the western parts of the world ever subject to them.

Secondly, Vesoges, King of Egypt, aspired to this prize; and although he harried south and north in Asia (as Orosius records), yet never did he secure the half part of the world.

Next, Cyrus, King of the Persians, attempted the same; who having destroyed Babylon and transferred the empire thereof to the Persians, ere he had made trial of western regions, laid down his life and his project together at the hands of Tamiris, queen of the Scythians.

But after these, Xerxes, son of Darius, and King of the Persians, invaded the world with so great multitude of nations, and with so great might that he spanned with a bridge the passage of the sea that parts Asia from Europe betwixt Sestos and Abydos; yet finally miserably repelled from his attempt, he failed to attain the prize.

Besides these, and after them, Alexander, the Macedonian King, drawing nearest of all to the palm of monarchy, forewarned the Romans by his ambassadors to surrender to him; but or ever their answer came, as Livy tells us, he collapsed in mid-course, in Egypt.

But that Rome attained the palm of so great a prize is proved by many testimonies. Luke, the scribe of Christ, who speaketh all things true, upheld in that part of his discourse: "There went out an edict from Caesar Augustus that the universal world should be enrolled." In which words we may clearly learn that the universal jurisdiction of the world then pertained to the Romans.

From all which things it is manifest that when all were contending for empire of the world the Roman people prevailed. Therefore it was by divine judgment that it so prevailed; and therefore it obtained such empire by the divine judgment, which is to say that it obtained it by right.

(10) Moreover, what is acquired by ordeal is acquired by right. For wheresoever human judgment is at fault, either because it is involved in the darkness of ignorance or because there is no presiding judge, then, lest justice should go to lea, we must have recourse to him who so loved her as himself to meet her claim with his own blood, in death. Which clash, since it was first tried in the single combat of one to one, we call *duellum*.

But we must ever take heed that like as, when it is a question of war, all means should first be tried in the way of award, and only in the last resort should the way of battle be tried (as Tully and Vegetius agree in saying, the one in *Re Militari,* the other in *Officiis*), and like as in medical treatment, everything else should be tried before steel and fire, and they only in the last resort; so when every other way of finding judgment in a dispute has been exhausted, we are to recur in the last instance to this remedy, forced by a kind of compulsion of justice.

There are, then, two formal characteristics of the ordeal; one that has just now been spoken of; the other that was touched upon above, to wit that the contenders or champions should enter the palaestra, not in hate or love, but in sole zeal for justice, with common consent.

If the wonted point be urged concerning the inequality of men's strength, let the objection be refuted by the victory which David won over Goliath. And if the Gentiles should seek another instance let them refute it by the victory of Hercules over Antaeus. For it were a foolish thing indeed to hold that the strength which God sustains is weaker than a chance champion.

(11) But the Roman people acquired empire by single combat, as is proved by witnesses worthy of faith. And the exposition of this will not only make the present matter plain, but will also show that at every turning-point, from the early times of the Roman Empire, the issue was determined by single combat.

For at the first when the matter of contention was about the abode of father Æneas, who was the first father of this people, Turnus the King of the Rutuli being his opponent, a single combat was finally accepted by the common consent of the two kings as a means of inquiring into the divine will, as is sung in the last of the Æneid.

And when two peoples had sprung up in Italy from the same Trojan root, the Romans to wit and the Albans, and long contention had been between them for the ensign of the eagle and the household gods of the Trojans and the honour of principality, finally, by common consent of those concerned, to solve the debate, three brothers Horatii on the one side and as many brothers Curiatii on the other, fought in the sight of kings and people, who gazed in suspense on either side.

Then with the observance of every right of war, they fought for empire with neighbouring peoples, with the Sabines and with the Samnites, under the form of ordeal, albeit with a multiplicity of combatants, as Livy tells.

But when the strifes among the Italians were settled, and the contest for divine judgment had not yet been fought out with the Greeks and the Carthaginians, both the one and the other of whom pretended to empire, then Fabricius on the Roman side and Pyrrhus on the Greek contended for the glory of empire with a multitude of soldiery; and it fell to Rome. Again, when Scipio for the Italians and Hannibal for the Africans waged war under form of ordeal, the Africans fell before the Italians as Livy and the other writers of Roman affairs bear witness.

Who, then, is so dull of mind as not by this time to see that by right of ordeal the glorious people gained for itself the crown of the whole world? Truly might a Roman have said what the apostle saith to Timothy, "There is laid up for me a crown of righteousness"; laid up, to wit, in the eternal Providence of God.

And now it has been shown that the Roman people acquired empire by single combat. Therefore it acquired it by right, which is the main proposition of the present book.

Hitherto this proposition has been established by arguments which find their chief support in the principles of reason; but from this point forward it must be demonstrated once again from the principles of Christian faith.

(12) I say, then, that if the Roman empire was not of right, then Christ, by his birth, presupposed a wrong. The consequent is false, therefore the contradictory of the antecedent is true, for contradictories may be deduced from each other in the counter sense.

The sequence I thus demonstrate: Whosoever observes an edict by choice, urges its justice by so doing; and since deeds are more persuasive than words (as the Philosopher holds in the last *Ad Nicomachum*), he urges it more potently than if he approved it in word. But Christ, as Luke, his scribe, bears witness, chose to be born of a virgin mother under edict of the Roman authority, in order that the Son of God, made man, might be enrolled as a man in that unique register of the human race.

Christ, then, gave assurance by deed that the edict of Augustus, who exercised the authority of the Romans, was just; and since jurisdiction is implied in the just issuing of an edict, it follows that he who sanctioned the edict as just also sanctioned the jurisdiction whence it emanated, which jurisdiction, however, was unjust unless it was of right.

(13) Again, if the Roman empire was not of right, the sin of Adam was not punished in Christ. But this is false, therefore the contradictory of that from which it follows is true.

And to establish this congruity be it known that punishment does not simply mean penalty inflicted on him who worked the wrong, but penalty so inflicted by one who has penal jurisdiction. Wherefore unless the penalty be inflicted by a qualified judge it should not be looked upon as a punishment, but rather as itself a wrong.

If, then, Christ had not suffered under a qualified judge, that suffering would not have been a punishment. And the judge would not have been qualified had he not had jurisdiction over the whole human race; since it was the whole human race that was to be punished in that flesh of Christ, who, as the prophet saith, was bearing or sustaining our griefs. And Tiberius Caesar, whose vicar Pilate was, would not have had such jurisdiction unless the Roman empire had been of right.

So let them cease to reproach the Roman empire who feign themselves to be sons of the church, when they see that the Bridegroom, Christ, thus confirmed it at either limit of his warfare. And now, I take it, it has been sufficiently shown that the Roman people acquired to itself the empire of the world by right.

Oh blessed people! Oh glorious thou, Ausonia! had he who enfeebled thy empire either ne'er been born, or ne'er been misled by his own pious purpose!

### BOOK III

(1)  In the beginning of this work it was proposed to inquire into three questions in such fashion as their subject-matter would allow. And in the foregoing books I believe the task has been sufficiently accomplished with respect to the first two of them.

The present question, then, concerning which we are to make inquiry, lies between two great lights, to wit the Roman pontiff and the Roman prince; and we are to ask whether the authority of the Roman monarch, who is monarch of the world by right, as proved in the second book, is immediately dependent upon God; or rather on some vicar or minister of God, by whom I understand the successor of Peter, who in very truth bears the keys of the kingdom of heaven.

(4)  Now those for whom the whole disputation that follows will be conducted assert that the authority of the empire depends upon the authority of the church, as the inferior artisan is dependent on the architect; and thereto they are moved by sundry adverse arguments which they draw from sacred scripture, and from certain things done alike by the supreme pontiff and by the emperor himself; though they strive also to gain some support from reason.

For they say firstly, following the scripture of Genesis, that God made two great luminaries, a greater luminary and a lesser luminary, that the one might rule over the day and the other the night.  And these they have been accustomed to understand as spoken allegorically of those two regimens, to wit the spiritual and the temporal.  Thence they argue that like as the moon, which is the lesser luminary, has no light save as she receives it from the sun, so neither has the temporal regimen any authority save as it receives it from the spiritual regimen.

But it may be shown in two ways that this interpretation of the passage can by no means be defended.  First, since such regimens are certain accidents of man himself, God would seem to have followed a perverse order in producing the accidents before their proper subject, and to say this of God is absurd.  For those two luminaries were produced on the fourth day, and man on the sixth day, as may be seen in the text.

Moreover, since those regimens exist to direct men to certain ends (as will be shown below), if man had remained in the state of innocence in which he was made by God he would have had no need of such directive regimens.  Such regimens, then, are remedial against the infirmity of sin.  Now since on the fourth day not only was man not sinful but man was not at all, to produce remedies would have been superfluous, which is counter to the divine excellence. For a physician were foolish to prepare a plaster to apply to the future abscess of one as yet not born.  It must not be said, then, that on the fourth day God made these two regimens; and consequently Moses cannot have meant what they make out that he did.

But even if we allow this false statement we may disarm it by the method of distinction. And this is a gentler way of proceeding with an adversary, for it does not show that he is uttering an absolute falsehood, as the method by destruction does. I say, then, that although the moon has no abundant light save as she receives it from the sun, it does not therefore follow that the moon herself is derived from the sun. Wherefore be it known that the existence of the moon is one thing, her virtue another, and her operation yet a third. As to her existence the moon is in no way dependent on the sun, neither is she with respect to her virtue, and not absolutely with respect to her operation; for her motion is derived from her proper mover, and her influence from her proper rays. For she has a certain light from herself as is manifest in her eclipse. But with respect to her better and more virtuous operation she does receive something from the sun, to wit, abundance of light by the receipt of which she operates with more virtue.

(5) They also draw an argument from the text of Moses, saying that from the loins of Jacob flowed the type of these two regimens, to wit, Levi and Judah, the one of whom was the father of the priesthood, and the other of the temporal regimen. Then they argue from them thus: "As Levi was related to Judah so is the church related to the empire. Levi preceded Judah in birth, as is evident in the text, therefore the church precedes the empire in authority."

This is easily indeed refuted; for the assertion that Levi and Judah, the sons of Jacob, represent those regimens I might refute as before by denying it; but let it be granted; yet when they infer in their argument that as Levi was first in birth so the church is first in authority, I say, as before, that the predicate of the conclusion is one and the major term is another; for authority is one thing and nativity another, both in subject and sense. Therefore there is an error in form. And it runs like this: "A preceded B in C; D is in the same relation to E that A is in to B; therefore D preceded E in F," whereas F and C are different.

And if, by way of rejoinder, they should say that F follows from C, that is to say authority from seniority, and that the consequent may be substituted in an inference for the antecedent (as animal for man), I reply that it is false; for there are many seniors by birth who not only do not precede those younger than themselves in authority but are preceded by them; as is evident when bishops are younger in years than their arch-presbyters. And thus the objection is seen to err in alleging as a cause what is not a cause.

8) They also allege from the text of the same that word of Christ to Peter, "And whatsoever thou hast bound on earth shall be bound in heaven also, and whatsoever thou hast loosed on earth shall be loosed in heaven also." And they gather from this text of Matthew, and likewise from the text of John, that the same was said to all the

apostles. Whence they argue that, by concession of God, the successor of Peter can both bind and loose everything; and hence they infer that he can loose the laws and decrees of the empire, and bind laws and decrees for the temporal regimen; from which what they assert would really follow.

We must proceed against this by distinction, applied to the major of the syllogism they employ. For their syllogism runs: "Peter had power to loose and bind all things. Peter's successor has whatsoever Peter had. Therefore Peter's successor has power to loose and bind all things." Whence they infer that he has power to loose and bind the authority and decrees of the empire.

I grant the minor, but the major only with a distinction. And therefore I say that this sign of universality "all," which is implied in "whatsoever," never distributes beyond the scope of the term distributed. For if I say "every animal runs," the distribution of "every" covers all that is included under the genus "animal." But if I say "every man runs," then the universal qualification only distributes over what is covered by this term "man." And when I say "every grammarian" the distribution is still further contracted.

Wherefore we must always consider what it is which the universal qualification has to distribute, and when we do so we shall easily see how far the distribution extends, on considering the nature and scope of the distributed term. Wherefore when it is said "Whatsoever thou hast bound," if this "whatsoever" were to be taken absolutely their contention would be true, and he would not only be able to do what they assert, but to loose a wife from her husband and bind her to another while the first still lived, which he by no means can. He would also be able to absolve me while I am not penitent, which even God himself could not do.

Since this, then, is so, it is manifest that the distribution in question is not to be taken absolutely, but relatively to something. And to what it is relative is sufficiently evident when we consider what it was that was being granted to him, in connection with which that distributive qualification was added. For Christ says to Peter, "I will give thee the keys of the kingdom of heaven," that is, "I will make thee doorkeeper of the kingdom of heaven." Then he adds, "And whatsoever," that is "everything which," that is "everything which has reference to that office" thou shalt have power to loose and bind. And thus the sign of universality which is implied in "whatsoever" is restricted in its distribution by the office of the keys of the kingdom of heaven. And taken thus the proposition under discussion is true; but absolutely it clearly is not so. And therefore I say that although Peter's successor can loose and bind within the requirements of the office committed to Peter, yet it does not follow from that that he can loose or bind the decrees of the empire, or the laws (as was their contention), unless it could be further proved that this concerns the office of the keys; and the contrary of this will be shown below.

(10)  It is further urged by some that the Emperor Constantine, when cleansed of his leprosy at the intercession of Sylvester, who was then supreme pontiff, granted the seat of empire, to wit Rome, to the church, together with many other dignities of the empire. Whence they argue that no one can assume those dignities thenceforth except he receive them from the church, whose they say they are.  And from this it would certainly follow that the one authority is dependent on the other, as they would have it.

I say that it has no force, because Constantine had no power to alienate the imperial dignity, nor had the church power to receive it.

It were counter to human right should the empire destroy itself. Therefore the empire may not destroy itself.  Since, then, to rend the empire were to destroy it (inasmuch as the empire consists in the unity of universal monarchy), it is manifest that he who wields the authority of the empire may not rend the empire.  And that it is counter to human right to destroy the empire is manifest from what has gone before.

Moreover, every jurisdiction is prior to its judge, for the judge is appointed to the jurisdiction, and not conversely.  But the empire is a jurisdiction embracing every temporal jurisdiction in its scope; therefore it is prior to its judge, who is the emperor, because the emperor is appointed to it, and not conversely.  Whence it is clear that the emperor, as emperor, cannot change it since it is the source of his being what he is.  Now I say thus: Either he was emperor when he is said to have made the grant to the church, or he was not.  And if not, it is obvious that he had no power of making grants with respect to the empire.  If he was, then, since such a grant was to the prejudice of his jurisdiction, he, as emperor, had no power to make it.

Further, if one emperor had power to tear never so little a piece from the jurisdiction of the empire, so on the same showing had another also.  And since the temporal jurisdiction is finite, and any finite thing can be used up by finite subtractions, it would follow that the prime jurisdiction might be reduced to nothing, which is contrary to reason.

And again, in order for a grant to be legitimate there must be the due disposition not only of him who grants but of him to whom the grant is made.  For it seems that the acts of the agents inhere in a suitably disposed patient.  But the church was entirely undisposed for receiving temporal things, in virtue of express prohibitive command, as we learn from Matthew, thus: "Possess not gold nor silver, nor money in your girdles, nor purse for your journey," and the rest. For, although we find in Luke a relaxation of the precept with respect to certain things, yet nowhere have I been able to find that permission was given to the church, after that prohibition, to possess gold and silver.  Wherefore if the church had no power to receive, then even if Constantine, as far as he was concerned, had power to give, still the action was impossible because the patient had not the due disposition.

(11)   They further say that pope Hadrian summoned Charles the Great to his aid and the church's, because of the wrongs wrought by the Lombards in the time of Desiderius, their king; and that Charles received from him the dignity of the empire, notwithstanding that Michael was the ruling emperor at Constantinople.   Wherefore they say that all who have been emperors of the Romans after him are themselves advocates of the church, and by the church must be called to office.   And from this, too, that dependence which they wish to prove would follow.

And to invalidate this, I say that their contention amounts to nothing; for the usurpation of a right does not create a right.   Else in the same way it might be shown that the authority of the Church depends upon the emperor, since the emperor Otho restored pope Leo, and deposed Benedict and carried him off into exile in Saxony.

(12)   But their argument from reason is this.   All men are of one kind; therefore they must be reduced to the unit, as measure of them all.   And since the supreme pontiff and the emperor are men, if that conclusion is true they must be reduced to the unit man; and since the pope must not be reduced to any other, it remains that the emperor, together with all others, must be reduced to him, as the measure and norm.

They fall into a fallacy *secundum accidens*.   To demonstrate which, be it known that it is one thing to be a man and another thing to be pope.   And in like manner it is one thing to be a man and another to be emperor; just as it is one thing to be a man and another to be a father and master; for a man is such in virtue of a substantial form from which he acquires his species and genus, and by which he is brought under the predicament of substance.   But a father is such in virtue of an accidental form, or relation, from which indeed he acquires a species and genus, in a sense, but is brought under the class *ad aliquid,* or relativity.   Otherwise, since no accidental form exists in itself, apart from the foundation of the substance that underlies it, everything would be reduced to the predicament of substance; and this is false.

Wherefore I maintain that the standard to which they must be reduced as men is one, and that to which they must be reduced as pope and emperor another.   For as men they have to be referred to the best man, whoever that may be; who is the standard and idea of all others, so to speak; that is, to him who is most supremely one in his own kind, as may be gathered from the last *Ad Nicomachum*.

(13)   Having set forth and refuted the errors on which they chiefly rely who say that the authority of the Roman prince depends on the Roman pontiff, we must return to the demonstration of the truth as to this third matter which was laid down for discussion from the beginning.   And this truth will be sufficiently unfolded if I show, under the principle of inquiry which we have laid down, that the said authority depends immediately upon the summit of all being,

which is God.  And this will be shown if we either disprove the church's authority over it (since no other is even alleged), or prove by direct demonstration that it depends immediately on God.

Now that the authority of the church is not the cause of the imperial authority is thus proved.  If, while one thing does not exist or is not exercising its virtue, another thing has its full virtue, the first thing is not the cause of that virtue.  But when the church did not exist, or was not exercising its virtue, the empire had its full virtue.

The major proposition of this demonstration is explained by the terms; the second, Christ and the church confirm, Christ by his birth and death as set forth above, the church when Paul in the Acts of the Apostles says to Festus, "I stand at the judgment seat of Caesar where I must be judged"; and also when the angel of God says to Paul a little after, "Fear not, Paul.  It behoves thee to stand before Caesar."  And below Paul says again to the Jews in Italy, "Now when the Jews opposed I was compelled to appeal to Caesar, not as having aught of which to accuse my nation, but that I might snatch my soul from death."

And if Constantine had not possessed authority over the patronage of the church, what he deputed to her from the empire he could not have deputed of right, and thus the church would be wrongfully enjoying that grant, since God will have offerings without spot, according to that of Leviticus, "Every offering which ye shall bring to the Lord shall be without leaven."

(15)  Again, that which is against the nature of anything is not in the number of its virtues, since the virtues of each thing follow its nature, for the attainment of its end.  But virtue to authorise rule over our mortality is contrary to the nature of the church.  Therefore it is not of the number of her virtues.

To prove the minor be it known that the nature of the church is the form of the church.  For though nature is predicated of material and of form, yet it is more properly predicated of form as is shown in the *De Naturali Auditu*.  But the form of the church is no other than the life of Christ, embraced both in his words and in his deeds.  For his life was the idea and exemplar of the church militant, especially of pastors, and most of all of the supreme pastor, whose it is to feed the lambs and sheep.  Whence he himself in John, when bequeathing the form of his life, says, "I have given you an example that as I have done to you should ye also do."  And specifically to Peter when he had committed to him the office of pastor, as we learn from the same source, he said, "Peter, follow thou me."  But Christ in the presence of Pilate renounced any such regimen as that in question.  "My kingdom," said he, "is not of this world.  If my kingdom were of this world, my servants would fight that I should not be given over to the Jews.  But now my kingdom is not hence."

Whence we gather that the power of authorising this kingdom is counter to the nature of the church.

(16)  It has been shown that the authority of the empire is not caused by the authority of the supreme pontiff, yet it has not been altogether proved that it depends immediately on God, save by consequential inference; for the consequential inference is that if it does not depend on the vicar of God it depends on God.   And, therefore, for the perfect establishment of the proposition, we must prove by direct demonstration that the emperor or monarch of the world is in immediate relation to the Prince of the universe, who is God.

Now to understand this be it known that man alone of beings holds a mid-place between corruptible and incorruptible; wherefore he is rightly likened by the philosophers to the horizon which is between two hemispheres.  For man, if considered after either essential part, to wit soul and body, is corruptible if considered only after the one, to wit the body, but if after the other, to wit the soul, he is incorruptible.  Wherefore the Philosopher says well of the soul (in that it is incorruptible), in the second *De Anima,* "And it alone is capable of being separated from the corruptible as perpetual."

If man, then, is a kind of mean between corruptible and incorruptible things, since every mean savors of the nature of the extremes, it is necessary that man should savour of either nature.  And since every nature is ordained to a certain end it follows that there must be a twofold end of man, so that like as he alone amongst all beings partakes of corruptibility and incorruptibility, so he alone amongst all beings should be ordained for two final goals, of which the one should be his goal as a corruptible being, and the other as an incorruptible.

That unutterable providence, then, has set two ends before man to be contemplated by him: the blessedness, to wit, of this life, which consists in the exercise of his proper power and is figured by the terrestrial paradise, and the blessedness of eternal life, which consists in the fruition of the divine aspect, to which his proper power may not ascend unless assisted by the divine light.  And this blessedness is given to be understood by the celestial paradise.

Now to these two as to diverse ends it behoves him to come by diverse means.  For to the first we attain by the teachings of philosophy, following them by acting in accordance with the moral and intellectual virtues.  To the second by spiritual teachings, which transcend human reason, as we follow them by acting according to the theological virtues: faith, hope, to wit, and charity.  Now albeit these ends and means are made plain to us, the one by human reason (which the philosophers have wholly brought to our knowledge), the other by the Holy Spirit (which hath revealed the truth that is beyond our nature, but yet needful to us, by means of the prophets and sacred writers and by Jesus Christ the Son of God co-eternal with the said Spirit, and by his disciples), yet would human greed cast them behind were not men, like horses going astray in their brutishness, held in the way by bit and rein.

Wherefore man had need of a twofold directive power according to his twofold end, to wit, the supreme pontiff, to lead the human race, in accordance with things revealed, to eternal life; and the emperor, to direct the human race to temporal felicity in accordance with the teachings of philosophy. And since none, or few (and they with extremest difficulty) could reach this port, were not the waves of seductive greed assuaged and the human race left free to rest in the tranquility of peace, this is that mark on which he who has charge of the world and is called the Roman prince should chiefly fix his mind, to wit, that on this threshing floor of mortality life should be lived in freedom and in peace. And since the disposition of this world follows the disposition that inheres in the circulation of the heavens, in order to accomplish this end, namely, that the charters which conduce to liberty and peace should be applied by the ruler in question with due reference to time and place, it is needful that they should be dispensed by him who looks upon the whole disposition of the heavens presently. And that is he only who so preordained that disposition that by it he in his providence might weave all things together, each in its due order.

But if this be so, God alone chooses, he alone confirms, since he hath no superior. Whence we may further gather that neither they who now are, nor such others of any kind as have ever been called the electors, should so be called; but rather should they be reckoned the heralds of divine Providence. Whence it comes to pass that they to whom is granted the honour of making the proclamation are subject from time to time to dissent; because either all or some of them are clouded by the mists of greed, and discern not the face of the divine dispensation.

Thus, then, it is plain that the authority of the temporal monarch descends upon him without any mean from the Fountain of universal authority. Which Fountain, one in the citadel of Its simplicity, flows into manifold channels out of the abundance of Its excellence.

And now already methinks I have sufficiently reached the mark I set before myself. For the truth of that question has been searched out in which was asked whether the office of monarch were necessary to the well-being of the world, and of that in which was asked whether the Roman people acquired empire for itself by right, and also of that last question in which was asked whether the monarch's authority depended from God, or immediately from some other. The truth concerning which last question is not to be received in such narrow sense as that the Roman prince is subordinate in naught to the Roman pontiff; inasmuch as mortal felicity is in a certain sense ordained with reference to immortal felicity. Let Caesar, therefore, observe that reverence to Peter which a first-born son should observe to a father, so that illuminated by the light of paternal grace he may with greater power irradiate the world, over which he is set by him alone who is ruler of all things spiritual and temporal.

[tr. PHILIP H. WICKSTEED]

# THE COMEDY
## (*Commedia*)

According to Dante in his letter to Can Grande (*Epistola X*), to whom *Paradise* is dedicated, the *Comedy* is, in its literal sense, the state of souls after death, but in an allegorical sense "man as, by freedom of will, through merit and demerit, he is subject to rewarding or punishing Justice." The poem is therefore based on the popular medieval notion that man's temporal world, the microcosm, is a faithful reflection of God's eternal world, the macrocosm. What happens as an event in this finite, physical world typifies God's eternity. Conversely, what souls may suffer *in secula seculorum,* they suffer while they live, and they are to the poetic eye walking embodiments of that rewarding Justice which knows no error.

Dante's poetic method of depicting this philosophical belief is more common to the plastic arts than to poetry. The *Comedy,* whatever the author's devices for variation, is a series of set scenes that suggest rather than narrate action. Dante, the protagonist, wanders through Hell, Purgatory, and Paradise under the guidance first of Virgil, symbolizing intelligence without revelation, then Statius, the slothful Christian, then Beatrice, who symbolizes illuminating grace, and finally Bernard, the mystic, and Mary, the intercessor, until at last he comes to the beatific vision of Unity, wherein the scattered leaves of the universe are bound in one volume by that Love which moves the sun and all the stars. In Dante's footsteps we, the readers, pace the gallery of the universe, seeing with his eyes portraits of worthies and unworthies, circle on circle, ledge on ledge, and sphere on sphere.

Dante explains his title, *Comedy,* as follows: "Tragedy at the beginning is admirable and placid, but at the end or issue is foul and horrible . . . whereas comedy begins with sundry adverse conditions, but ends happily. . . . Tragedy and comedy differ likewise in their style of language; for that of tragedy is high-flown and sublime, while that of comedy is unstudied and lowly. . . . The style [of the *Comedy*] is unstudied and lowly, as being in the vulgar tongue, in which even women-folk hold their talk."

Dante deliberately encouraged his readers to interpret his words in more than one sense. *Polysemous* interpretation of the Scriptures was a method that the early Fathers, notably Cassian and Gregory the Great, derived from Hebrew expositors. Theoretically, if the word is divinely inspired, it will be in all ways true, however the reader may choose to view it. Though a dangerous principle of reading and interpretation in general application, it may fairly be applied to the *Comedy,* providing the reader always obeys Dante's admonition to understand the literal meaning first. He may then from one statement derive not only literal but allegorical, moral, political, or typical meaning as well.

The symbolism evident in elementary form in the *New Life,* Dante here worked out in great detail. Number patterns appear in the external form of 100 cantos ($1 + 33 + 33 + 33$) and the *terza rima*. Each of the *cantiche* is formed by taking the divine number 7, adding two unlike elements to bring it to the thrice-holy 9, and then adding a totally unlike one to achieve the perfect number 10. So, for instance, in *Paradise,* Dante travels through the seven spheres of the seven planets, then the spheres of the fixed stars and the *primum mobile,* and then into the all-enveloping Empyrean. This arrangement is faithfully reflected in the microcosmic Purgatory, and distorted and perverted in Hell only in the way a badly formed mirror distorts a reflection. Symbolism is equally contained in the time references, the geographical references, the references to light and sound. Dante's age, 35 years, and the year, 1300, are important historically and symbolically. Dante was lost in the Dark Wood on Maundy Thursday and was full of sleep as were Christ's disciples at Gethsemane; he met the Roman authority on Friday, as Christ came before Pilate; and he descended into Hell on Friday night as Christ was believed to have done. He rose again before the dawn on the Easter of Resurrection, and his vision, or journey, consumed the seven days used to create the universe. In geography Dante is equally precise: Satan fell from Heaven at the antipodes to Jerusalem, the exact center of the inhabited earth and the spot where Christ redeemed mankind; the earth drew away from him in horror, forming a pit under all the inhabited earth and raising at the antipodes the Mount of Purgatory, with Eden at its summit, thereby simultaneously creating at the same spot the means for man's fall and for his return to innocence. As God is all Light, source of warmth, melody, and love, a triune power without mass or weight, permeating and pervading all his creatures, so is Satan at the nadir a three-headed monster of gross flesh whose disorderly struggles in gloom and ice serve only to confirm his impotence.

Visions of the afterlife were possibly the most popular form of medieval literature. The apocryphal gospels, deriving their inspiration from the East and from the apocalyptic books of the Bible, moved the early ascetics and monks to narrate countless visions. Dante was well acquainted with the *Vision of Paul,* printed above (p. 4). But though he refers to it more than once and to the commonplace stories of Christ's harrowing of Hell, he wished his reader to think equally of Virgil, who in the sixth book of the *Aeneid* depicted, in imitation of Homer, his hero descending to Avernus. These analogies, Paul and Aeneas, typify Dante's two consuming interests: the Church and the Roman state.

The other sources for Dante's poem were equally popular: Boethius' *Consolation*; Lucan and Ovid; the *Celestial Hierarchy* believed to have been written by Dionysius, convert of Paul and first bishop of Athens and Paris; the Thomistic expositions of Aristotle; the liturgy, especially the Ambrosian hymns and Victorine sequences; Gregory's *Morals on Job*; Orosius' *Universal History*; the mystical tracts of Bernard of Clairvaux; and the Franciscan literature, es-

pecially the writings of Bonaventure.   The more carefully one examines Dante's sources, the more one is convinced that the poet's erudi-
tion came from no more extensive reading than might be expected
of any educated layman of that day.   It is in degree of intensity of
cultivation, inventive imagination, and powers of synthesis that Dante
is without peer in any age.

Many amateurs of the twentieth century are prone to feel that the
remarkable unity of concept and informing idea in the *Comedy* was
inherited by Dante full-blown — that he did no more than describe
a unity and order that his age believed in and that all Europe aspired
to as an article of faith.   But for those who have read widely in the
literature of Dante's period, this view is fallacious: never, even in our
own day, were conditions more chaotic.   The established social order
was falling apart, as agrarian and chivalric feudalism yielded to fast-
growing towns and trade, which created new-rich and new-poor.
The whole continent was wracked by civil and national wars.   The
one symbol of Eternal Rome, after the recent fall of the Empire,
was the Papacy; yet it had just been transplanted to the provincial
French town of Avignon.   England and France were gathering
forces for the Hundred Years' War.   Heresy, drowned in blood in
Provence, reared hydra heads in every province without even the
Papacy's being quite sure what heresy was.   Those of the trade of
Marco Polo were bringing back tales of Japan and Java that dwarfed
the West as tales of galaxies now dwarf the solar system.   The new
universities were discarding Plato for Aristotle, Pliny for Roger Bacon,
and Roman fractions for Arabic decimals; and the poets, Dante especially, were discarding a language that had stood for a millennium
in the form used by Virgil, Horace, and Ovid.   No, if greatness depends upon conceptual unity, then Dante is great not because of his
times, but in spite of them.   If more recent poets have not achieved
his synthesis, it is evidence of how singular he is.

According to Boccaccio, Dante composed seven cantos of *Hell* before
he went into exile, and the last cantos of *Paradise* were published only
after his death.   The *Comedy,* then, was the fruit of intermittent
effort over twenty years.   As there are few complete medieval cathedrals, so are there few complete long narratives.   The medieval
artist, whether Abbé Suger, Thomas Aquinas, or Chaucer, planned beyond his powers.   But the *Comedy* is complete, without even the
unfinished lines that mark the *Aeneid* of Dante's master, Virgil.   Its
immediate popularity has been sustained for these six centuries without diminution; today, the Dante collections at Cornell and Harvard
Universities each contain thousands of volumes.

For the selection below, consisting of thirty-three cantos, or one-
third of the whole, I have chosen from the many admirable translations available that of Charles Eliot Norton because it is literally
most faithful to Dante's words and makes no pretense, in the employment of meter, rhyme, or archaism, of suggesting the tone of
the original, which has not yet been satisfactorily duplicated in English.   Although throughout this volume the texts are not annotated,

I have included here a few of Norton's notes, revised and in a few instances amplified. The *Comedy*, unlike any other work represented in the volume, apparently needed amplification even for contemporaries, and the actions of Dante's sons in adding "dull patchwork" to their father's text seems a reasonable justification.

## HELL

[From *The Divine Comedy of Dante Alighieri*, by Charles Eliot Norton; Houghton Mifflin Co., Boston, 1902. Reprinted by permission of the publisher.]

### CANTO I

*Dante, astray in a wood, reaches the foot of a hill which he begins to ascend; he is hindered by three beasts; he turns back and is met by Virgil, who proposes to guide him into the eternal world.*

Midway upon the journey of our life I found myself in a dark wood, where the right way was lost.[1]   Ah! how hard a thing it is to tell what this wild and rough and difficult wood was, which in thought renews my fear!  So bitter is it that death is little more. But in order to treat of the good that I found in it, I will tell of the other things that I saw there.

I cannot well report how I entered it, so full was I of slumber at that moment when I abandoned the true way.  But after I had reached the foot of a hill, where that valley ended which had pierced my heart with fear, I looked upward, and saw its shoulders clothed already with the rays of the planet which leads man aright along every path.  Then was the fear a little quieted which had lasted in the lake of my heart through the night that I had passed so piteously. And even as one who with spent breath, issued forth from the sea upon the shore, turns to the perilous water and gazes, so did my mind, which still was flying, turn back to look again upon the pass which never left person alive.

After I had rested a little my weary body, I again took my way along the desert slope, so that the firm foot was always the lower. And lo! almost at the beginning of the steep a she-leopard,[2] light and very nimble, which was covered with a spotted coat.  And she did not withdraw from before my face, nay, hindered so my road that I often turned to go back.

The time was the beginning of the morning, and the Sun was mounting up with those stars that were with him when the Love Divine first set in motion those beautiful things;[3] so that the hour

1. The action begins on the night before Good Friday, A.D. 1300. Dante was thirty-five years old.

2. The type of pleasures of sense.

3. It was a common belief that the spring was the season of the Creation and that on March 25, the vernal equinox, the Sun was created and placed in Aries, to begin his course.

of the time and the sweet season were occasion to me of good hope
concerning that wild beast with the dappled skin; but not so that the
sight which appeared to me of a lion [4] did not give me fear. He
appeared to be coming against me, with his head high and with
ravening hunger, so that it appeared that the air was affrighted at
him; and a she-wolf,[5] which in her leanness seemed laden with all
cravings, and ere now had made many folk to live forlorn, — she
brought on me so much heaviness, with the fear that came from the
sight of her, that I lost hope of the height. And such as is he who
gains willingly, and the time arrives which makes him lose, so that
in all his thoughts he laments and is sad, such did the beast without
peace make me, which, coming on against me, was pushing me back,
little by little, thither where the Sun is silent.

While I was falling back to the low place, one who appeared faint-
voiced through long silence presented himself before my eyes. When
I saw him in the great desert, "Have pity on me!" I cried to him,
"whatso thou be, whether shade or real man." He answered me:
"Not man; man once I was, and my parents were Lombards, and
both Mantuans by country. I was born *sub Julio,* though late,[6]
and I lived at Rome under the good Augustus, at the time of the
false and lying gods. I was a poet, and sang of that just son of
Anchises who came from Troy, after proud Ilion had been burned.
But thou, why dost thou return to such great annoy? Why dost
thou not ascend the delectable mountain which is the source and
cause of all joy?" "Art thou then that Virgil and that fount which
pours forth so broad a stream of speech?" replied I with bashful
front to him: "O honor and light of the other poets! may the long
study avail me and the great love, which have made me search thy
volume! Thou art my master and my author; thou alone art he
from whom I took the fair style that has done me honour. Behold
the beast because of which I turned; help me against her, famous
sage, for she makes my veins and pulses tremble." "It behoves thee
to hold another course," he replied, when he saw me weeping, "if
thou wouldst escape from this savage place; for this beast, because of
which thou criest out, lets not any one pass along her way, but so
hinders him that she kills him; and she has a nature so malign and
evil that she never sates her greedy will, and after food has more
hunger than before. Many are the animals with which she wives,
and there shall be more yet, until the hound shall come that will make
her die of grief. He shall not feed on land or pelf, but wisdom and
love and valor, and his birthplace shall be between Feltro and Feltro.
Of that low Italy shall he be the salvation, for which the virgin
Camilla died, and Euryalus, Turnus and Nisus of their wounds. He

4. Pride.
5. Avarice. Cf. Jeremiah 5:6. These three beasts correspond with
the triple division of sins into those of incontinence, of violence, and of
fraud which Virgil makes in the eleventh canto, according to which
the sinners in Hell are divided into three main classes.
6. Virgil was twenty-five years old at the time of Caesar's death, 44 B.C.

shall hunt her through every town till he shall have put her back again in Hell, there whence envy first sent her forth. Wherefore I think and deem it for thy best that thou follow me, and I will be thy guide, and will lead thee hence through the eternal place where thou shalt hear the despairing shrieks, shalt see the ancient spirits woeful who each proclaim the second death.[7] And then thou shalt see those who are contented in the fire, because they hope to come, whenever it may be, to the blessed folk; to whom if thou wouldst then ascend, there shall be a soul more worthy than I for that. With her I will leave thee at my departure; for that Emperor who reigns there above wills not, because I was rebellious [8] to His law, that through me any one should come into His city. In all parts He governs and there He reigns; there is His city and His lofty seat. O happy the man whom thereto He elects!" And I to him: "Poet, I beseech thee by that God whom thou didst not know, in order that I may escape this ill and worse, that thou lead me thither where thou now hast said, so that I may see the gate of St. Peter,[9] and those whom thou reportest so afflicted."

Then he moved on, and I held behind him.

CANTO II

*Dante, doubtful of his own powers, is discouraged at the outset. — Virgil cheers him by telling him that he has been sent to his aid by a blessed Spirit from Heaven, who revealed herself as Beatrice. — Dante casts off fear, and the poets proceed.*

The day was going, and the dusky air was taking the living things that are on earth from their fatigues, and I alone was preparing to sustain the war alike of the journey and of the woe, which my memory that errs not shall retrace.

O Muses, O lofty genius, now assist me! O memory that didst inscribe that which I saw, here shall thy nobility appear!

I began: —

"Poet, who guidest me, consider my power, if it be sufficient, before thou trust me to the deep pass. Thou sayest [1] that the parent of Silvius while still corruptible went to the immortal world and was there in the body; and truly if the Adversary of every ill was courteous to him, it seems not unmeet to the man of understanding, thinking on the high effect that should proceed from him, and on the who and the what; for in the empyrean heaven he was chosen for father of revered Rome and of her empire; both which (would one say truth) were ordained for the holy place where the successor of the greater Peter has his seat. Through this going, whereof thou givest him vaunt, he learned things which were the cause of his victory

7. Cf. Revelation 20:10, 14.
8. Cf. *Hell,* Canto iv.
9. *Purgatory,* Canto ix.
1. *Aeneid* vi.

and of the papal mantle.    Afterward the Chosen Vessel [2] went thither
to bring thence comfort to that faith which is the beginning of the
way of salvation.    But I, why go I thither? or who concedes it?    I
am not Aeneas, I am not Paul; neither I nor others believe me worthy
of this; wherefore if I yield myself to go, I fear lest the going may be
mad.    Thou art wise, thou understandest better than I speak."

And as is he who unwills what he willed, and by reason of new
thoughts changes his purpose, so that he withdraws wholly from
what he had begun, such I became on that dark hillside: because in
my thought I abandoned the enterprise which had been so hasty
in its beginning.

"If I have rightly understood thy speech," replied that shade of
the magnanimous one, "thy soul is hurt by cowardice, which oftentimes encumbers a man so that it turns him back from honorable
enterprise, as false seeing does a beast when it shies.    In order that
thou loose thee from this fear I will tell thee why I came, and what
I heard at the first moment that I grieved for thee.    I was among
those who are suspended, and a Lady blessed and beautiful called
me, such that I besought her to command.    Her eyes were more
shining than the star, and she began to say to me sweet and clear,
with angelic voice, in her speech: 'O courteous Mantuan soul! of
whom the fame yet lasts in the world, and shall last so long as motion
continues, my friend, and not of fortune, is so hindered on his road
upon the desert hillside that he has turned for fear, and I am afraid,
through that which I have heard of him in heaven, lest he be already
so astray that I may have risen late to his succor.    Now do thou
move, and with thy ornate speech and with whatever is needful
for his deliverance, assist him so that I may be consoled thereby.    I
am Beatrice who make thee go.    I come from a place whither I desire to return.    Love moved me, that makes me speak.    When I
shall be before my Lord, I will often praise thee to Him.'    Then she
was silent, and thereon I began: 'O Lady of Virtue! through whom
alone the human race excels all contained within that heaven which
has the smallest circles,[3] thy command so pleases me that to obey
it, were it already done, were slow to me.    There is no need for thee
further to open to me thy will; but tell me the reason why thou
dost not beware of descending down here into this centre, from the
ample place [4] whither thou burnest to return.'    'Since thou wishest
to know so inwardly, I will tell thee briefly,' she replied to me, 'wherefore I fear not to come here within.    One need be afraid only of
those things that have power to do one harm, of others not, for they
are not fearful.    I am made by God, thanks be to Him, such that
your misery touches me not, nor does the flame of this burning assail
me.    A gentle Lady [5] is in heaven who feels compassion for this

2. St. Paul (Acts 9:15, and 2 Corinthians 12:1–4.  See *The Vision of
Paul,* above).
   3. The heaven of the moon.
   4. I.e., from the Empyrean to Limbo.
   5. The Virgin Mary, never spoken of by name in Hell.

hindrance whereto I send thee, so that she breaks stern judgment there above. She summoned Lucia [6] in her request, and said, "Thy faithful one now has need of thee, and I commend him to thee." Lucia, the foe of every cruel one, moved and came to the place where I was seated with the ancient Rachel.[7] She said, "Beatrice, true praise of God, why dost thou not succor him who so loved thee that for thee he came forth from the vulgar throng? Dost thou not hear the pity of his plaint? Dost thou not see the death that combats him on the stream where the sea has no vaunt?" Never were persons in the world swift to do their good, or to fly their harm, as I, after these words were uttered, came down here from my blessed seat, putting my trust in thy upright speech, which honors thee and them who have heard it.' After she had said this to me, weeping she turned her lucent eyes, whereby she made me more quick to come. And I came to thee thus as she willed. I withdrew thee from before that wild beast which took from thee the short way on the beautiful mountain. What is it then? Why, why dost thou hold back? why dost thou harbor such cowardice in thy heart? why hast thou not daring and assurance, since three such blessed Ladies care for thee in the court of Heaven, and my speech pledges thee such good?"

As the flowerets, bent and closed by the chill of night, when the sun brightens them erect themselves all open on their stem, so I became with my drooping courage, and such good daring ran to my heart that I began like a person enfreed: "O compassionate she who succored me, and courteous thou who didst speedily obey the true words that she addressed to thee! Thou by thy words hast so disposed my heart with desire of going, that I have returned to my first intent. Now go, for one sole will is in us both: thou leader, thou lord, and thou master." Thus I said to him; and when he moved on, I entered along the deep and savage road.

## CANTO III

*The gate of Hell. — Virgil leads Dante in. — The punishment of those who had lived without infamy and without praise. — Acheron, and the sinners on its bank. — Charon. — Earthquake. — Dante swoons.*

"Through me is the way into the woeful city; through me is the way into the eternal woe; through me is the way among the lost people. Justice moved my lofty maker: the divine Power, the supreme Wisdom and the primal Love made me. Before me were no things created, save eternal, and I eternal last. Leave every hope, ye who enter!"

These words of obscure color I saw written at the top of a gate; whereat I: "Master, their meaning is dire to me."

6. Illuminating Grace.
7. The type of contemplative life.

And he to me, like a person well advised: "Here it behoves to leave every fear; it behoves that all cowardice should here be dead. We have come to the place where I have told thee that thou shalt see the woeful people, who have lost the good of the understanding."

And when he had put his hand on mine with a cheerful look, wherefrom I took courage, he brought me within to the secret things. Here sighs, laments, and deep wailings were resounding through the starless air; wherefore at first I wept thereat. Strange tongues, horrible utterances, words of woe, accents of anger, voices high and faint, and sounds of hands with them, were making a tumult which whirls always in that air forever dark, like the sand when the whirlwind breathes.

And I, who had my head girt with horror, said: "Master, what is that which I hear? and what folk is it that seems so overcome with its woe?"

And he to me: "The wretched souls of those who lived without infamy and without praise maintain this miserable mode. They are mingled with that caitiff choir of the angels, who were not rebels, nor were faithful to God, but were for themselves. The heavens chased them out in order to be not less beautiful, nor does the deep Hell receive them, for the damned would have some boast of them."

And I: "Master, what is so grievous to them, that makes them lament so bitterly?"

He answered: "I will tell thee very briefly. These have not hope of death; and their blind life is so debased, that they are envious of every other lot. Fame of them the world permits not to be; mercy and justice disdain them. Let us not speak of them, but do thou look and pass on."

And I, who was gazing, saw a banner, which, whirling, ran so swiftly that it seemed to me disdainful of any pause, and behind it came so long a train of folk, that I should never have believed death had undone so many. After I had recognized some among them, I saw and knew the shade of him who made, through cowardice, the great refusal.[1] At once I understood and was certain, that this was the sect of the caitiffs displeasing to God and to his enemies. These wretches, who never were alive, were naked, and much stung by gad-flies and by wasps that were there; these streaked their faces with blood, which, mingled with tears, was gathered at their feet by loathsome worms.

And when I gave myself to looking onward, I saw people on the bank of a great river; wherefore I said: "Master, now grant to me that I may know who these are, and what rule makes them appear so ready to pass over, as I discern through the faint light." And he to me: "The things will be clear to thee, when we shall stay our steps on the sad shore of Acheron." Then with eyes ashamed and

---

1. Dante purposely refrains from naming anyone in this group and thereby immortalizing him. This soul is often identified with Pope Celestine V. Compare the Laodiceans in Revelations, and Kipling's *Tomlinson*.

downcast, fearing lest my speech might be troublesome to him, far as to the river I refrained from speaking.

And behold! coming toward us in a boat, an old man, white with ancient hair, crying: "Woe to you, wicked souls! hope not ever to see the Heavens! I come to carry you to the other bank, into the eternal darkness, into heat and into frost. And thou who art there, living soul, depart from these that are dead." But when he saw that I did not depart, he said: "By another way, by other ports thou shalt come to the shore, not here, for passage; a lighter bark must carry thee." [2]

And my Leader to him: "Charon, vex not thyself; it is thus willed there where is power for that which is willed; and ask no more." Thereon were quiet the fleecy jaws of the ferryman of the livid marsh, who round about his eyes had wheels of flame.

But those souls, who were weary and naked, changed color and gnashed their teeth, soon as they heard his cruel words. They blasphemed God and their parents, the human race, the place, the time and the seed of their sowing and of their birth. Then, all of them bitterly weeping, drew together to the evil bank, which awaits every man who fears not God. Charon the demon, with eyes of glowing coal, beckoning to them, collects them all; he beats with his oar whoever lingers.

As in autumn the leaves depart one after the other, until the bough sees all its spoils upon the earth, in like wise the evil seed of Adam throw themselves from that shore one by one, at signals, as the bird at his recall. Thus they go over the dusky wave, and before they have landed on the farther side, already on this a new throng is assembled.

"My son," said the courteous Master, "those who die in the wrath of God, all come together here from every land; and they are eager to pass over the stream, for the divine justice spurs them so that fear is turned to desire. A good soul never passes this way; and therefore if Charon fret at thee, well mayest thou now know what his speech signifies."

This ended, the gloomy plain trembled so mightily that the memory of the terror even now bathes me with sweat. The tearful land gave forth a wind that flashed a crimson light which vanquished all sensation in me, and I fell as a man whom slumber seizes.

2. I.e., the boat to Purgatory. Charon recognizes that Dante is not among the damned. Personages of heathen mythology were held by the Church to have been demons who had a real existence; they were adopted into the Christian mythology, and hence appear with entire propriety as characters in Hell.

CANTO IV

*The further side of Acheron. — Virgil leads Dante into Limbo,*
*the First Circle of Hell, containing the spirits of those who lived*
*virtuously but without faith in Christ. — Greeting of Virgil by his*
*fellow poets. — They enter a castle, where are the shades of an-*
*cient worthies. — After seeing them Virgil and Dante depart.*

A heavy thunder broke the deep sleep in my head, so that I started
up like a person who is waked by force, and, risen erect, I moved my
rested eye round about, and looked fixedly to distinguish the place
where I was.   True it is, that I found myself on the brink of the
woeful valley of the abyss which collects a thunder of infinite wailings.   It was so dark, deep, and cloudy, that, though I fixed my
sight on the depth, I did not discern anything there.

"Now let us descend here below into the blind world," began the
Poet all deadly pale, "I will be first, and thou shalt be second."

And I, who had observed his color, said: "How shall I come, if
thou fearest, who art wont to be the comfort to my doubting?"   And
he to me: "The anguish of the folk who are here below paints on
my face that pity which thou takest for fear.   Let us go on, for
the long way urges us."

Thus he placed himself,[1] and thus he made me enter into the first
circle that girds the abyss.   Here, as one listened, there was no lamentation but that of sighs which made the eternal air to tremble;
this came of the woe without torments felt by the crowds, which were
many and great, of infants and of women and of men.

The good Master to me: "Thou dost not ask what spirits are these
that thou seest.   Now I would have thee know, before thou goest
farther, that these did not sin; and though they have merits it suffices
not, because they did not have baptism, which is part of the faith
that thou believest; and if they were before Christianity, they did
not duly worship God: and of such as these am I myself.   For such
defects, and not for other guilt, are we lost, and only so far harmed
that without hope we live in desire."

Great woe seized me at my heart when I heard him, because I
knew that people of much worth were suspended in that limbo.
"Tell me, my Master, tell me, Lord," I began, with wish to be assured of that faith which vanquishes every error, "did ever any one
who afterwards was blessed go forth from here, either by his own
or by another's merit?"   And he, who understood my covert speech,
answered: "I was new in this state [2] when I saw a Mighty One come
hither crowned with sign of victory.[3]   He drew out hence the shade
of the first parent, of Abel his son, and that of Noah, of Moses the
law-giver and obedient, Abraham the patriarch, and David the King,
Israel with his father and with his offspring, and with Rachel, for

1. In the lead, in front of Dante.
2. Virgil died in 19 B.C.
3. Christ's Harrowing of Hell.

whom he did so much, and many others; and He made them blessed. And I would have thee know that before these, human spirits were not saved."

We ceased not going on because he spoke, but all the while were passing through the wood, the wood, I mean, of crowded spirits; nor yet had our way been long from the place of my slumber, when I saw a fire, which overcame a hemisphere of darkness. We were still a little distant from it, yet not so far but that I could in part discern that honorable folk possessed that place. "O thou who honorest both science and art, who are these, who have such honor that it separates them from the manner of the others?" And he to me: "The honorable renown of them which sounds above in thy life wins grace in heaven which thus advances them." At this a voice was heard by me: "Honor the loftiest Poet! his shade returns which had departed." When the voice had stopped and was quiet, I saw four great shades coming to us; they had a semblance neither sad nor glad. The good Master began to say: "Look at him with that sword in hand who comes before the three, even as lord; he is Homer, the sovereign poet; the next who comes is Horace, the satirist; Ovid is the third, and the last is Lucan. Since each shares with me the name which the single voice sounded, they do me honor, and in that do well."

Thus I saw assembled the fair school of that Lord of the loftiest song who soars above the others like an eagle. After they had discoursed somewhat together, they turned to me with sign of salutation; and my Master smiled thereat. And far more of honor yet they did me, for they made me of their band, so that I was the sixth amid so much wisdom. Thus we went on as far as the light, speaking things concerning which silence is becoming, even as was speech there where I was.

We came to the foot of a noble castle,[4] seven times circled by high walls,[5] defended round about by a fair streamlet. This we passed as if hard ground; through seven gates [6] I entered with these sages; we came to a meadow of fresh verdure. People were there with slow and grave eyes, of great authority in their looks; they spoke seldom, and with soft voices. Thereon we withdrew ourselves upon one side, into an open, luminous, and high place, so that they all could be seen. There before me upon the green enamel were shown to me the great spirits, whom for having seen I inwardly exalt myself.

I saw Electra with many companions, among whom I recognized Hector and Aeneas, Caesar in armor, with his gerfalcon eyes; I saw Camilla and Penthesilea, on the other side I saw the King Latinus, who was sitting with Lavinia his daughter. I saw that Brutus who drove out Tarquin; Lucretia, Julia, Marcia, and Cornelia; and alone, apart, I saw the Saladin. When I raised my brows a little more, I

4. Philosophy.
5. The virtues.
6. The liberal arts.

saw the Master of those who know,[7] seated amid the philosophic family; all regard him, all do him honor. Here I saw Socrates and Plato, who in front of the others stand nearest to him; Democritus, who ascribes the world to chance; Diogenes, Anaxagoras, and Thales, Empedocles, Heraclitus, and Zeno; and I saw the good collector of the qualities, Dioscorides, I mean, and I saw Orpheus, Tully, and Linus, and moral Seneca, Euclid the geometer, and Ptolemy, Hippocrates, Avicenna, and Galen, and Averrhoës, who made the great comment. I cannot report of all in full, because the long theme so drives me that many times the speech comes short of the fact.

The company of six is reduced to two. By another way the wise guide leads me out from the quiet into the air that trembles, and I come into a region where is nothing that can give light.

CANTO V

*The Second Circle, that of Carnal Sinners. — Minos. — Shades renowned of old. — Francesca da Rimini.*

Thus I descended from the first circle down into the second, which girdles less space, and so much more woe that it goads to wailing. There stands Minos horribly, and snarls; he examines the transgressions at the entrance; he judges, and he sends according as he entwines himself. I mean, that when the ill born soul comes there before him, it confesses itself wholly, and that discerner of the sins sees what place of Hell is for it; he girds himself with his tail so many times as the grades he wills that it be sent down. Always many of them stand before him; they go, in turn, each to the judgment; they speak and hear, and then are whirled below.

"O thou that comest to the woeful inn," said Minos to me, when he saw me, leaving the act of so great an office, "beware how thou enterest, and to whom thou trustest thyself; let not the amplitude of the entrance deceive thee." And my Leader to him: "Wherefore dost thou too cry out? Hinder not his fated going; thus is it willed there where is power for that which is willed; and ask no more."

Now the notes of woe begin to make themselves heard by me; now I am come where much wailing smites me. I had come into a place mute of all light, that bellows as the sea does in a tempest, if it be combated by contrary winds. The infernal hurricane which never rests carries along the spirits with its rapine; whirling and smiting it molests them. When they arrive before its rush, here are the shrieks, the complaint, and the lamentation; here they blaspheme the divine power. I understood that to such torment are condemned the carnal sinners who subject the reason to the appetite. And as their wings bear along the starlings in the cold season in a large and full troop, so did that blast the evil spirits; hither, thither, down, up it carries them; no hope ever comforts them, neither of repose, nor of less pain.

7. Aristotle.

And as the cranes go singing their lays, making in air a long line of themselves, so I saw come, uttering wails, shades borne along by the aforesaid strife. Wherefore I said: "Master, who are these folk whom the black air so castigates?" "The first of those of whom thou wishest to have knowledge," said he to me then, "was empress of many tongues. She was so abandoned to the vice of luxury that lust she made licit in her law, to take away the blame into which she had been brought. She is Semiramis, of whom it is read that she succeeded Ninus and had been his wife; she held the land which the Sultan rules. That other is she [1] who, for love, slew herself, and broke faith to the ashes of Sichaeus; next is Cleopatra, the luxurious. See Helen, for whom so long a time of ill revolved; and see the great Achilles, who fought to the end with love. See Paris, Tristan, — " and more than a thousand shades whom love had parted from our life he showed me, and, pointing to them, named to me.

After I had heard my Teacher name the dames of eld and the cavaliers, pity overcame me, and I was well nigh bewildered. I began: "Poet, willingly would I speak with those two that go together, and seem to be so light upon the wind." [2] And he to me: "Thou shalt see when they are nearer to us, and do thou then pray them by that love which leads them, and they will come." Soon as the wind sways them toward us, I lifted my voice: "O wearied souls, come to speak with us, if Another [3] deny it not."

As doves, called by desire, with wings open and steady, come through the air borne by their will to their sweet nest, these issued from the troop where Dido is, coming to us through the malign air, so strong was the compassionate cry.

"O living creature, gracious and benign, that goest through the black air visiting us who stained the world blood-red, if the King of the universe were a friend we would pray Him for thy peace, since thou hast pity on our perverse ill. Of what it pleases thee to hear, and what to speak, we will hear and we will speak to you, while the wind, as now, is hushed for us. The city where I was born sits upon the seashore, where the Po, with his followers, descends to have peace. Love, which quickly lays hold on gentle heart, seized this one for the fair person that was taken from me, and the mode still hurts me. Love, which absolves no loved one from loving, seized me for the pleasing of him so strongly that, as thou seest, it does not even now abandon me. Love brought us to one death. Caina awaits him who quenched our life." These words were borne to us from them.

Soon as I had heard those injured souls I bowed my face, and held it down so long until the Poet said to me: "What art thou thinking?"

1. Dido.

2. Francesca da Rimini, daughter of Guido Vecchio da Polenta, lord of Ravenna; and her lover, Paolo, the brother of her husband, the son of Malatesta da Verrucchio, lord of Rimini. Their death, at the hands of her husband, took place about 1285.

3. The name of God is never spoken by the spirits in Hell, save once, in blasphemous defiance, by Vanni Fucci; nor by Dante in addressing them.

When I replied, I began: "Alas! how many sweet thoughts, how great desire, led these unto the woeful pass." Then I turned me again to them, and spoke, and began: "Francesca, thy torments make me sad and piteous to weeping. But tell me, at the time of the sweet sighs, by what and how did love concede to thee to know thy dubious desires?" And she to me: "There is no greater woe than the remembering in misery the happy time, and that thy Teacher knows.[4] But if thou hast so great desire to know the first root of our love, I will do like one who weeps and tells.

"We were reading one day, for delight, of Lancelot, how love constrained him. We were alone and without any suspicion. Many times that reading urged our eyes, and took the color from our faces, but only one point was it that overcame us. When we read of the longed-for smile being kissed by such a lover, this one, who never shall be divided from me, kissed my mouth all trembling. Gallehaut was the book, and he who wrote it.[5] That day we read no farther in it."

While the one spirit said this, the other was so weeping that through pity I swooned as if I had been dying, and fell as a dead body falls.

### CANTO VI

*The Third Circle, that of the Gluttonous. — Cerberus. — Ciacco.*

### CANTO VII

*The Fourth Circle, that of the Avaricious and the Prodigal. — Pluto. — Fortune. The Styx. — The Fifth Circle, that of the Wrathful.*

### CANTO VIII

*The Fifth Circle. — Phlegyas and his boat. — Passage of the Styx. — Filippo Argenti. — The City of Dis. — The demons refuse entrance to the poets.*

### CANTO IX

*The City of Dis. — Erichtho. — The Three Furies. — The Heavenly Messenger. — The Sixth Circle: that of the Heresiarchs.*

### CANTO X

*The Sixth Circle: Heresiarchs. — Farinata degli Uberti. — Cavalcante Cavalcanti. — Frederick II.*

Now, along a solitary path between the wall of the city and the torments, my Master goes on, and I behind his shoulders.

"O virtue supreme," I began, "that through the impious circles

4. Thy Teacher who lives sorrowfully in Limbo without hope, but with memory of the life lighted by the Sun.

5. In the romance, it was Gallehaut that prevailed on Guenever to give a kiss to Lancelot.

dost turn me according to thy pleasure, speak to me and satisfy my desires. The folk that are lying in the sepulchres, might they be seen? all the lids are now lifted, and no one keeps guard." And he to me: "All will be locked in when they shall return here from Jehoshaphat with the bodies which they have left on earth.[1] Upon this side Epicurus with all his followers, who make the soul mortal with the body, have their burial place. Therefore as to the request that thou makest of me, thou shalt soon be satisfied here within; and also as to the desire of which thou art silent to me."[2] And I: "Good Leader, I hold not my heart hidden from thee except in order to speak little; and not only now hast thou disposed me to this."

"O Tuscan, who goest thy way alive through the city of fire, speaking thus modestly, may it please thee to stop in this place. Thy mode of speech makes manifest that thou art native of that noble fatherland to which perchance I was too molestful." Suddenly this sound issued from one of the coffers, wherefore in fear I drew a little nearer to my Leader. And he said to me: "Turn thee: what art thou doing? See there Farinata who has risen erect; all from the girdle upwards wilt thou see him."[3]

I had already fixed my face on his, and he was straightening himself up with breast and front as though he had Hell in great scorn. And the bold and ready hands of my Leader pushed me among the sepulchres to him, saying: "Let thy words be clear."

When I was at the foot of his tomb, he looked at me a little, and then, as though disdainful, asked me, "Who were thy ancestors?" I, who was desirous to obey, concealed it not from him, but disclosed it all to him; whereon he raised up his brows a little, then said:"They were fiercely adverse to me and to my forefathers and to my party, so that at two times I scattered them."[4] "If they were driven out, they returned from every side," replied I to him, "both the one and the other time, but yours have not learned well that art."[5]

Then there arose to sight alongside of this one, a shade uncovered far as to the chin: I think that it had risen on its knees. It looked round about me, as if it had desire to see if another were with me, but when its expectancy was quite spent, weeping it said: "If through this blind prison thou goest by reason of loftiness of genius, where is my son? and why is he not with thee?" And I to him: "I come not of myself; he who waits yonder is leading me through here, whom perchance your Guido had in disdain."[6]

1. Joel 3:12.
2. Probably the wish to see Farinata, concerning whom Dante had already asked.
3. Farinata degli Uberti was the head of the Ghibelline party in Tuscany for many years. He died not far from the time of Dante's birth.
4. Dante's ancestors were Guelfs; Farinata had dispersed the Guelfs in 1248 and 1260.
5. The Guelfs had returned to Florence in 1251 and 1266 and, regaining power, had finally expelled the Ghibellines permanently.
6. Guido Cavalcanti, Dante's first friend and Farinata's son-in-law. See below, p. 869. Guido died a few months after Dante's vision.

His words and the mode of the punishment had already read to me the name of this one; wherefore my answer was so full.

Suddenly straightening up, he cried: "How didst thou say, 'he had'? lives he not still? does not the sweet light strike his eyes?" When he became aware of some delay that I made before answering, he fell again supine, and appeared no more outside.

But that other magnanimous one, at whose instance I had stayed, changed not aspect, nor moved his neck, nor bent his side. "And if," he said, continuing his first discourse, "they have ill learned that art, it torments me more than this bed. But the face of the Lady who rules here [7] will not be rekindled fifty times ere thou shalt know how much that art weighs. And, so mayest thou return to the sweet world, tell me wherefore is that people so pitiless against my party in its every law?" Thereon I to him: "The rout and the great carnage which colored the Arbia red cause such prayer to be made in our temple." After he had, sighing, shaken his head, "In that I was not alone," he said, "nor surely without cause would I have moved with the others; but I was alone there,[8] where it was agreed by every one to destroy Florence, he who defended her with open face." "Ah! so may your seed ever have repose," I prayed to him, "loose for me that knot, which has here entangled my judgment. It seems, if I hear rightly, that ye see in advance that which time is bringing with it, and as to the present have another way." [9] "We see," he said, "like him who has bad light, the things that are far from us, so much the supreme Ruler still shines on us; when they draw near, or are, our intelligence is wholly vain, and if another report not to us, we know nothing of your human state; wherefore thou canst comprehend that our knowledge will be utterly dead from that moment when the gate of the future shall be closed." Then, as compunctious for my fault, I said: "Now, then, you will tell to that fallen one that his son is still conjoined with the living, and if just now I was dumb to answer, make him know that I was so because I was already thinking in the error which you have solved for me."

And now my Master was recalling me, wherefore more hastily I prayed the spirit that he would tell me who was with him. He said to me: "Here I lie with more than a thousand; here within is the second Frederick [10] and the Cardinal,[11] and of the others I am silent."

7. Proserpine, identified with the mystical Hecate, and hence with the Moon.

8. At Empoli, in 1260, after the terrible rout of the Florentine Guelfs at Montaperti on the Arbia.

9. That is, are ignorant of the present. Farinata foretells future events, but Cavalcante shows himself ignorant of present conditions.

10. The famous Frederick II, *"stupor mundi,"* Emperor from 1212 to 1250.

11. Ottaviano degli Ubaldini, a fierce Ghibelline, who was reported as saying, "If there be a soul I have lost it for the Ghibellines." He died in 1273.

Thereon he hid himself; and I turned my steps toward the ancient Poet, reflecting on that speech which seemed hostile to me. He moved on, and then, thus going, he said to me: "Why art thou so disturbed?" And I satisfied him as to his question. "Let thy memory preserve that which thou hast heard against thyself," that Sage bade me, "and now give heed here — " and he raised his finger: "When thou shalt be in presence of the sweet radiance of her whose beautiful eye sees everything, from her thou shalt learn the journey of thy life." Then to the left he turned his step.

We left the wall, and went toward the middle by a path that strikes into a valley which even up there was making its stench displeasing.

CANTO XI

*The Sixth Circle: Heretics. — Tomb of Pope Anastasius. — Discourse of Virgil on the divisions of the lower Hell.*

Upon the edge of a high bank which great rocks broken in a circle made, we came above a more cruel pen. And here, because of the horrible excess of the stench which the deep abyss throws out, we drew aside behind the lid of a great tomb, whereon I saw an inscription which said: "I hold Pope Anastasius, whom Photinus drew from the right way."

"It behoves that our descent be slow, so that the sense may first accustom itself a little to the dismal blast, and then it will be of no concern." Thus the Master, and I said to him: "Some compensation do thou find that the time pass not lost." And he: "Behold, I am thinking of that. My son, within these rocks," he began then to say, "are three lesser circles from grade to grade, like those which thou art leaving. All are full of accursed spirits; but, in order that hereafter the sight alone may suffice thee, hear how and wherefore they are in bonds.

"Of every wickedness that acquires hate in heaven injury is the end, and every such end afflicts others either by force or by fraud. But because fraud is an evil peculiar to man, it more displeases God; and therefore the fraudulent are the lower, and woe assails them more.

"The first circle [1] is wholly of the violent: but because violence is done to three persons it is divided and constructed in three rounds. To God, to one's self, to one's neighbor may violence be done; I say to them and to their belongings, as thou shalt hear with plain discourse. By violence, death and grievous wounds are inflicted on one's neighbor; and on his substance ruins, burnings, and harmful extortions. Wherefore the first round torments homicides, and every one who smites wrongfully, all despoilers and plunderers, in various troops.

"Man may lay violent hands upon himself and on his goods; and, therefore, in the second round it behoves that he repent without

1. The first circle below.

avail who deprives himself of your world, gambles away and dissipates his property, and laments there where he ought to be joyous.

"Violence may be done to the Deity, by denying and blaspheming Him in the heart, and by contemning nature and His bounty: and therefore the smallest round seals with its signet both Sodom and Cahors [2] and him who, contemning God, speaks from his heart.

"The fraud, by which every conscience is stung, man may practice on one that confides in him, or on one that has no stock of confidence. This latter mode seems to destroy only the bond of love which nature makes; wherefore in the second circle nest hypocrisy, flatteries, and he who bewitches, falsity, robbery, and simony, panders, barrators, and such like filth.

"By the other mode that love is forgotten which nature makes and that which is thereafter added, whereby special confidence is created. Hence, in the smallest circle, where is the point of the universe, upon which Dis sits, whoso betrays is consumed forever."

And I: "Master, full clearly thy discourse proceeds, and full well divides this pit, and the people that possess it; but, tell me, they of the fat marsh, and they whom the wind drives, and they whom the rain beats, and they who encounter with such rough tongues, why are they not punished within the ruddy city [3] if God be wroth with them? and if he be not so, why are they in such plight?"

And he said to me: "Why does thy wit so wander beyond its wont? or thy mind, where else is it gazing? Dost thou not remember those words with which thy Ethics treats in full of the three dispositions that Heaven abides not: incontinence, wickedness, and mad bestiality; and how incontinence less offends God, and incurs less blame? [4] If thou consider well this doctrine, and bring to mind who are those that up above suffer punishment outside, thou wilt see clearly why they are divided from these felons, and why less wroth the divine vengeance hammers them."

"O Sun that healest every troubled vision, thou dost content me so, when thou solvest, that doubt, not less than knowledge, pleases me; yet turn thee a little back," said I, "to where thou sayest that usury offends the Divine Goodness, and loose the knot."

"Philosophy," he said to me, "points out to him who understands it, not only in one part alone, how Nature takes her course from the Divine Intellect and from Its art. And if thou note thy Physics [5] well thou wilt find, after not many pages, that your art follows her so far as it can, as the disciple does the master, so that your art is as it were grandchild of God. From these two, if thou bring to mind Genesis at its beginning, [6] it behoves mankind to gain their life and to advance. But because the usurer holds another way, he

2. Cahors, a town in southern France, on the river Lot, noted in the Middle Ages for usury.
3. In this lower Hell, within the walls of the city of Dis.
4. Aristotle *Ethics* vii. 1.
5. Aristotle *Physics* ii. 2.
6. "In the sweat of thy face shalt thou eat bread." Genesis 3:19.

contemns Nature in herself, and in her follower, since upon other thing he sets his hope. But follow me now, for to go on pleases me; for the Fishes are quivering on the horizon, and the Wain lies quite over Caurus,[7] and far onwards is the descent of the steep."

CANTO XII

*The Seventh Circle, first round: those who do violence to others. — The Minotaur. — The Centaurs. — Chiron. — Nessus. — The River of boiling blood, and the sinners in it.*

CANTO XIII

*The Seventh Circle, second round: those who have done violence to themselves and to their goods. — The Wood of Self-murderers. — The Harpies. — Pier delle Vigne. — Lano of Siena and others.*

CANTO XIV

*The Seventh Circle, third round: those who have done violence to God. — The Burning Sand. — Capaneus. — Figure of the Old Man in Crete. — The Rivers of Hell.*

CANTO XV

*Third round of the Seventh Circle: of those who have done violence to Nature. — Brunetto Latini. — Prophecies of misfortune to Dante.*

CANTO XVI

*The Seventh Circle, third round: those who have done violence to Nature. — Guido Guerra, Tegghiaio Aldobrandi and Jacopo Rusticucci. — The roar of Phlegethon as it pours downward. — The cord thrown into the abyss.*

CANTO XVII

*Third round of the Seventh Circle: of those who have done violence to Art. — Geryon. — The Usurers. — Descent to the Eighth Circle.*

CANTO XVIII

*Eighth Circle: the fraudulent; the first pouch: panders and seducers. — Venedico Caccianimico. — Jason. — Second Valley: false flatterers. — Alessio Interminei. — Thaïs.*

7. The sign of the Fishes precedes that of the Ram, and, as the Sun was in the latter sign, the time indicated is about 4, or from 4 to 5 A.M.

Rejoice, Florence, since thou art so great that thou beatest thy wings over sea and land, and thy name is spread through Hell! Among the thieves I found five such, thy citizens, whereat shame comes to me, and thou dost not mount unto great honor thereby. But, if near the morning one dreams of the truth, thou shalt feel within short time what Prato, as well as others, craves for thee. And if already it were, it would not be too soon. So were it! since surely it must be; for it will weigh the more on me as the more I age.

We departed thence, and, up along the stairs which the bourns had before made for our descent, my Leader remounted and drew me. And pursuing the solitary way among the fragments and the rocks of the craggy bridge, the foot sped not without the hand. I sorrowed then, and now I sorrow again when I direct my mind to what I saw; and I curb my genius more than I am wont, that it may not run unless virtue guide it; so that if a good star, or better thing, have given me the good, I may not grudge it to myself.[1]

As many as the fireflies which, in the season when he that brightens the world keeps his face least hidden from us, the rustic, who is resting on the hillside what time the fly yields to the gnat, sees down in the valley, perhaps there where he makes his vintage and ploughs, — with so many flames all the eighth pit was gleaming, as I perceived so soon as I was there where the bottom became apparent. And as he[2] who was avenged by the bears saw the chariot of Elijah at its departure, when the horses rose erect to heaven, — for he could not so follow it with his eyes as to see aught save the flame alone, like a little cloud, mounting upward, — thus each of those flames was moving through the gulley of the ditch, for not one shows its theft, and every flame steals away a sinner.

I was standing on the bridge, risen up to look, so that, if I had not taken hold of a rock, I should have fallen below without being pushed. And my Leader, who saw me thus intent, said: "Within these fires are the spirits; each is swathed by that wherewith he is burnt." "My Master," I replied, "through hearing thee am I more certain, but already I deemed that it was so, and already I wished to say to thee: Who is in that fire which comes so divided at its top that it seems to rise from the pyre on which Eteocles was put with his brother?"[3] He answered me: "Therewithin Ulysses and Diomed are tormented, and thus they go together in their punishment, as in their wrath. And within their flame they groan for the ambush of the horse which made the gate whence the noble seed of the Romans issued forth; within it they lament the artifice whereby the dead Deidamia[4] still mourns for Achilles, and there they bear the penalty for the Palladium."[5] "If they have power to speak within those sparks,"

1. Dante is coming to men distinguished for their natural gifts who, by misuse of them, brought eternal condemnation on themselves. It turns his thought on the risks attending the use of his own genius.

2. Elisha. 2 Kings 2:9–24.

3. So great was the mutual hate of the brothers Eteocles and Polynices that, when their bodies were burned on the same funeral pile, the flames divided in two (Statius *Thebaid* xii. 431).

4. Thetis committed her son Achilles, disguised as a maiden, to Deidamia that he might not go to the siege of Troy. Deidamia, who became the mother of a son by Achilles, killed herself, when, by the craft of Ulysses, accompanied by Diomed, Achilles was discovered and persuaded to go to Troy. (Statius *Achilleis.*)

5. The Palladium was the image of Athena, on which the safety of

said I, "Master, much I pray thee, and repray, that my prayer avail
a thousand, that thou make not to me denial of waiting till the
horned flame come hither: thou seest that with desire I bend me
toward it."    And he to me: "Thy prayer is worthy of much praise,
and therefore I accept it; but mind that thy tongue restrain itself.
Leave speech to me, for I have conceived that which thou wishest;
for, because they were Greeks, they would perhaps be disdainful of
thy words."

When the flame had come there where it seemed to my Leader time
and place, I heard him speak to it in this form: "O ye, who are
two within one fire, if I deserved of you while I lived, if I deserved
of you much or little, when in the world I wrote my lofty verses,
move not, but let one of you tell, whither, being lost, he went away
to die."    The greater horn of the ancient flame began to wag, murmuring, even as a flame that the wind wearies.    Then waving its
tip to and fro, as if it were the tongue that spoke, it cast forth a
voice, and said: —

"When I departed from Circe, who had detained me more than a
year there near to Gaeta, before Aeneas had so named it,[6] neither
fondness for my son, nor piety for my old father, nor the due love
which should have made Penelope glad, could overcome within
me the ardor which I had to become experienced of the world,
and of the vices of men, and of their virtue.    But I put forth on the
deep, open sea, with one vessel only, and with that little company
by which I had not been deserted.    I saw one shore and the other
as far as Spain, as far as Morocco and the island of Sardinia, and the
others which that sea bathes round about.    I and my companions
were old and slow when we came to that narrow strait where
Hercules set up his bounds, to the end that man should not put out
beyond.    On the right hand I left Seville, on the other I had already
left Ceuta.    'O brothers,' I said, 'who through a hundred thousand
perils have reached the West, to this so brief vigil of your senses
which remains wish not to deny the experience, following the sun, of
the world that has no people.    Consider your origin; ye were not
made to live as brutes, but to pursue virtue and knowledge.'    With
this little speech I made my companions so keen for the voyage
that hardly afterwards could I have held them back.    And turning
our stern to the morning, with our oars we made wings for the mad
flight, always gaining on the left hand side.    The night saw now
all the stars of the other pole, and ours so low that it rose not forth
from the ocean floor.    The light beneath the moon had been five
times rekindled and as many quenched since we had entered on the
passage of the deep, when there appeared to us a mountain dark in
the distance, and it seemed to me so high as I had never seen one.[7]

---

Troy depended, and which was stolen by the two heroes (*Aeneid* ii.
163–70).

  6. *Aeneid* vii. 1–4.

  7. The Mount of Purgatory.

We rejoiced, and soon it turned to lamentation, for from the new land a whirlwind rose and struck the fore part of the vessel. Three times it made her whirl with all the waters, the fourth it made her stern lift up and the prow go down, as pleased Another, till the sea had closed over us."

If I had rhymes both harsh and raucous, such as would befit the dismal hole on which all the other rocks thrust, I would press out more fully the juice of my conception; but since I have them not, not without fear I bring myself to speak; for to describe the bottom of the whole universe is no enterprise to take up in jest, nor for a tongue that cries mamma and papa.[1] But may those Dames aid my verse, who aided Amphion to enclose Thebes,[2] so that the speech may not be diverse from the fact.

1. The undisciplined vernacular.
2. The Muses endowed the lyre of Amphion with such power that its sound charmed the rocks to move from Mount Cithaeron and build themselves up for the walls of Thebes.

O ye, beyond all others, miscreated rabble, that are in the place whereof to speak is hard, better had ye here [3] been sheep or goats!

When we were down in the dark pit beneath the feet of the giant, far lower, and I was still gazing at the high wall, I heard say to me: "Take heed how thou steppest; go so that thou trample not with thy soles the heads of thy wretched weary brothers." Whereat I turned and saw before me, and under my feet, a lake which by reason of frost had semblance of glass and not of water.

The Danube in Austria never made in winter so thick a veil for its current, nor the Don yonder under the cold sky, as there was here: for if Tambernich [4] had fallen on it, or Pietrapana,[5] it would not have given a creak even at the edge. And as the frog lies to croak with muzzle out of the water, what time the peasant woman often dreams of gleaning, so, livid up to where shame appears, were the woeful shades within the ice, setting their teeth to the note of the stork. Every one held his face turned downward: from the mouth the cold, and from the eyes the sad heart provides testimony of itself among them.

When I had looked round awhile, I turned to my feet, and saw two so close that they had the hair of their heads mixed together. "Tell me, ye who thus press tight your breasts," said I, "who are ye?" And they bent their necks, and after they had raised their faces to me, their eyes, which before were moist only within, gushed up through the lids, and the frost bound the tears between them, and locked them up again; clamp never girt board to board so strongly: and thereupon they, like two he-goats, butted one another, such anger overcame them.

And one who had lost both his ears by the cold, with his face still downward, said to me: "Why dost thou so mirror thyself on us? If thou wouldst know who are these two, the valley whence the Bizenzio descends belonged to their father Albert, and to them.[6] They issued from one body; and thou mayst search all Caina, and thou wilt not find shade more worthy to be fixed in ice; not he whose breast and shadow were broken by one self-same blow by the hand of Arthur; [7] not Focaccia; [8] not this one who so encumbers me with his head that I see no further, and who was named Sassol Mas-

3. On earth.
4. A mountain, the locality of which is unknown.
5. One of the Tuscan Apennines.
6. Counts Napoleone and Alessandro degli Alberti, one Ghibelline, the other Guelf. They quarrelled over their inheritance, and each seeking treacherously to kill the other, they were both slain. The Bizenzio falls into the Arno some ten miles west below Florence.
7. Sir Mordred. Arthur smote Sir Mordred with such a thrust of his spear that, on the withdrawal of the lance, a ray of light passed through the wound.
8. Focaccia de' Cancellieri of Pistoia, who, enraged by a trifling offense committed by his cousin, cut off the boy's hand, and then treacherously killed the boy's father. From this crime sprang the feud of the Black and the White factions, which, from Pistoia, was introduced into Florence.

cheroni; [9] if thou art a Tuscan, thou now knowest well who he was. And that thou mayst not put me to more speech, know that I was Camicion de' Pazzi,[10] and I await Carlino [11] to exculpate me."

Then I saw a thousand faces made currish by the cold: whence a shudder comes to me, and will always come, at frozen pools.

And while we were going toward the centre to which all gravity collects, and I was trembling in the eternal chill, whether it was will, or destiny, or fortune I know not, but walking among the heads, I struck my foot hard in the face of one. Wailing he railed at me: "Why dost thou kick me? If thou dost not come to increase the vengeance of Mont' Aperti, why dost thou molest me?" And I: "My Master, now wait here for me, so that by means of this one I may free me from a doubt, then thou shalt make as much haste for me as thou wilt." The Leader stopped; and I said to that shade [12] who was still bitterly blaspheming: "Who art thou that thus chidest another?" "Now who art thou, that goest through the Antenora," [13] he answered, "smiting the cheeks of others, so that if thou wert alive, it would be too much?" "I am alive, and it may be dear to thee," was my reply, "if thou demandest fame, that I set thy name among my other notes." And he to me: "For the contrary have I desire; take thyself hence, and give me no more trouble, for ill thou knowest to flatter on this swamp." Then I took him by the hair of the nape, and said: "It shall needs be that thou name thyself, or that not a hair remain upon thee here." Whereon he to me, "Though thou strip me of hair, I will not tell thee who I am, nor show it to thee, though thou fall a thousand times upon my head."

I had already twisted his hair in my hand, and had pulled out more than one tuft, he barking, with his eyes kept close down, when another cried out: "What ails thee, Bocca? Is it not enough for thee to make a noise with thy jaws, but thou must bark too? What devil is at thee?" "Now," said I, "I do not want thee to speak, accursed traitor, for to thy shame will I carry true news of thee." "Begone," he answered, "and tell what thou wilt; but be not silent, if thou go forth from here within, about him who now had his tongue so ready. He is lamenting here the silver of the French: I saw, thou canst say, him of Duera,[14] there where the sinners stand cold.

9. He murdered his nephew for an inheritance.

10. He betrayed and killed his kinsman Ubertino.

11. In 1302 the castle of Piantravigne was held by a body of the recently exiled "Whites" of Florence. The castle was besieged by the "Blacks," and Carlino for a bribe opened its gates to them. Many of the chief exiles were slain, others were held for ransom.

12. Bocca degli Abati, the most infamous of Florentine traitors, in the heat of the battle of Mont' Aperti, in 1260, cut off the hand of the standard-bearer of the cavalry, so that the standard fell, and the Guelfs of Florence, disheartened thereby, were put to rout with frightful slaughter.

13. The second division of the ninth circle. According to tradition Antenor betrayed Troy.

14. Buoso da Duera, of Cremona, in command of a part of the Ghibel-

Shouldst thou be asked who else was there, thou hast at thy side him of the Beccheria [15] whose gorge Florence cut. Gianni de' Soldanier [16] I think is farther on with Ganelon, and Tribaldello [17] who opened Faenza when it was sleeping."

We had now departed from him, when I saw two frozen in one hole, so that the head of one was a hood for the other. And as bread is devoured for hunger, so the upper one set his teeth upon the other where the brain joins with the nape. Not otherwise Tydeus gnawed for despite the temples of Menalippus,[18] than this one was doing to the skull and the other parts. "O thou that by so bestial a sign showest hatred against him whom thou art eating, tell me the wherefore," said I, "with this compact, that if thou with reason complainest of him, I knowing who ye are, and his sin, may yet make thee quits with him in the world above, if that with which I speak be not dried up."

CANTO XXXIII

*Ninth circle: traitors. Second ring: Antenora. — Count Ugolino. — Third ring: Ptolomea. — Brother Alberigo. — Branca d' Oria.*

From his savage repast that sinner raised his mouth, wiping it with the hair of the head that he had spoiled behind: then he began: "Thou wishest that I should renew a desperate grief which oppresses my heart already only in thinking, ere I speak of it. But, if my words are to be seed that may bear fruit of infamy for the traitor whom I gnaw, thou shalt see me speak and weep together. I know not who thou art, nor by what mode thou art come down here, but Florentine thou seemest to me truly when I hear thee. Thou hast to know that I was Count Ugolino and this one the Archbishop Ruggieri.[1] Now I will tell thee why I am such a neighbor.

---

line forces in Lombardy, assembled to oppose the troops of Charles of Anjou in 1265. Bribed, he let them pass unmolested.

15. Tesauro de' Beccheria, Abbot of Vallombrosa and Papal Legate, beheaded by the Florentines in 1258 because of his treacherous dealings with the exiled Ghibellines.

16. A Ghibelline of Florence, who, after the defeat of Manfred in 1266, plotted against his own party.

17. In 1280.

18. Tydeus, one of the Seven Kings against Thebes, mortally wounded by Menalippus, slew his adversary, and then gnawed his cut-off head (Statius *Thebaid* viii. 740–63).

1. Ugolino della Gherardesca, Count of Donoratico, many years the most powerful citizen of Pisa, in 1285 was elected Podestà of Pisa and permitted his ambitious grandson, Nino dei Visconti, the "noble Judge Nino" whom Dante greets in Purgatory, to share in the rule of the city. Discord soon broke out between the old and the young man. The Ghibellines' chief, the Archbishop Ruggieri degli Ubaldini, pretending friendship with Count Ugolino, joined forces with him to expel his

That, by the effect of his evil thoughts, I, trusting to him, was taken and then put to death, there is no need to tell; but what thou canst not have heard, that is, how cruel my death was, thou shalt hear, and shalt know if he has wronged me.

"A narrow slit in the mew, which from me has the title of Hunger, and in the which others must yet be shut up, had already shown me through its opening many moons, when I had the bad dream which rent for me the veil of the future.

"This one appeared to me master and lord, chasing the wolf and his whelps upon the mountain [2] because of which the Pisans cannot see Lucca. With lean, eager, and trained hounds, he had put before him at the front Gualandi with Sismondi and with Lanfranchi.[3] After short course, the father and his sons seemed to me weary, and it seemed to me I saw their flanks ripped by the sharp fangs.

"When I awoke before the morrow, I heard my sons, who were with me, wailing in their sleep, and asking for bread. Truly thou art cruel if already thou dost not grieve, at thought of that which my heart was foreboding: and if thou dost not weep, at what art thou wont to weep? They were now awake, and the hour was drawing near at which food used to be brought to us, and because of his dream each one was apprehensive. And I heard the door below of the horrible tower being nailed up; whereat I looked on the faces of my sons without saying a word. I did not weep, I was so turned to stone within. They were weeping; and my poor little Anselm said, 'Thou lookest so, father, what ails thee?' I shed no tear for that; nor did I answer all that day, nor the night after, until the next sun came forth upon the world. When a little ray made its way into the woeful prison, and I discerned by their four faces my own very aspect, I bit both my hands for woe; and they, thinking I did it through desire of eating, of a sudden raised themselves up, and said: 'Father, it will be far less pain to us if thou eat of us; thou didst clothe us with this wretched flesh, and do thou strip it off.' I quieted me then, not to make them more sad: that day and the next we all stayed dumb. Ah, thou hard earth! why didst thou not open? After we had come to the fourth day, Gaddo threw himself stretched out at my feet, saying: 'My father, why dost thou not help me?' Here he died; and, even as thou seest me, I saw the three fall one by one between the fifth day and the sixth; then I betook me, already blind, to groping over each, and for two days

---

grandson with his followers. The strength of the Guelfs in the city being thus weakened, the Archbishop turned against the Count and defeated the Guelfs; the Count and two of his sons and two of his grandsons were taken prisoner, and were shut up in the tower of the Gualandi alle Sette Vie in July 1288. In the succeeding March the keys of the tower were thrown into the Arno, and the prisoners were starved to death.

2. Monte San Giuliano; Lucca is about fourteen miles northeast of Pisa.

3. Three of the chief Ghibelline families of Pisa.

I called them after they were dead: then fasting was more powerful than woe."

When he had said this, with his eyes twisted, he seized again the wretched skull with his teeth, that were strong as a dog's upon the bone.

Ah Pisa! reproach of the people of the fair country where the *sì* doth sound,[4] since thy neighbors are slow to punish thee, let Caprara and Gorgona [5] move and make a hedge for Arno at its mouth, so that it may drown every person in thee: for even if Count Ugolino had repute of having betrayed thee in thy strongholds, thou oughtest not to have set his sons on such a cross. Their young age, thou modern Thebes, made Uguccione and Il Brigata [6] innocent, and the other two that my song names above.

We passed onward to where the ice roughly enswathes another folk, not turned downward but all reversed.[7] The very weeping allows not weeping there, and the grief, which finds a barrier on the eyes, turns inward to increase the anguish; for the first tears form a block, and like a visor of crystal fill all the cup beneath the eyebrow.

And although, as in a callus, all feeling, because of the cold, had ceased to abide in my face, it now seemed to me I felt some wind, wherefore I: "My Master, who moves this? Is not every vapor [8] quenched here below?" Whereon he to me, "Speedily shalt thou be where thine eye, beholding the cause that rains down the blast, shall make answer to thee of this."

And one of the wretches of the cold crust cried out to us: "O souls so cruel that the last station has been given to you, lift from my eyes the hard veils, so that, before the weeping recongeal, I may vent a little the woe which swells my heart." Wherefore I to him: "If thou wishest that I succor thee, tell me who thou art, and if I relieve thee not, may I have to go to the bottom of the ice." [9] He replied then: "I am friar Alberigo; [10] I am he of the fruits of the bad garden,

4. Italy, whose language Dante calls *il volgare di sì,* the common tongue in which *sì* is the word for yes.

5. Two little islands not far from the mouth of the Arno, on whose banks Pisa lies.

6. Uguccione was a son, and Il Brigata a grandson of Count Ugolino; they were in fact grown men.

7. With faces upturned, so that the tears freeze in their eyes.

8. Wind being supposed to be caused by the action of the sun on the vapors of the atmosphere.

9. Misleading words, with their double meaning.

10. Alberigo de' Manfredi, of Faenza, having received a blow from his younger brother Manfred, pretended to forgive it, and invited him and his son to a feast. Toward the end of the meal he gave a preconcerted signal by calling out: "Bring the fruit," upon which his emissaries rushed in and killed the two guests. The "bad fruit of Brother Alberigo" became a proverb.

who here get back a date for a fig." [11]  "Oh!" said I to him, "art thou then dead already?"  And he to me, "How my body may fare in the world above I have no knowledge.  Such vantage hath this Ptolomea [12] that oftentimes the soul falls down here before Atropos has given motion to it. [13]  And that thou mayst the more willingly scrape the glassy tears from my face, know that soon as the soul betrays, as I did, its body is taken from it by a demon, who thereafter governs it until its time be all revolved.  It falls headlong into such cistern as this, and perhaps the body of the shade that is wintering here behind me still appears above.  Thou shouldst know him if thou comest down but now; he is Ser Branca d' Oria, [14] and many years have passed since he was thus shut up."  "I believe," said I to him, "that thou art deceiving me; for Branca d' Oria is not yet dead, and he eats, and drinks, and sleeps, and puts on clothes."  "In the ditch of the Malebranche above," he said, "there where the sticky pitch is boiling, Michel Zanche [15] had not yet arrived, when this one left a devil in his stead in his own body, and in that of one of his next kin, who committed the treachery together with him.  But now stretch hither thy hand; open my eyes for me."  And I did not open them for him, and to be churlish to him was courtesy. [16]

Ah Genoese! men strange to all morality and full of all corruption, why are ye not scattered from the world?  For with the worst spirit of Romagna [17] I found one of you, such that for his deeds he is already in soul bathed in Cocytus, and in body he appears still alive on earth.

11. A fig is the cheapest of Tuscan fruits; the imported date is more costly.

12. The third ring of ice, named for Ptolemy, Captain of Jericho, who, having invited them to a banquet, treacherously slew his father-in-law, the high-priest Simon, and his two sons (1 Maccabees 16:11–16).

13. That is, before Atropos has cut the thread of its life on earth.

14. Murderer, in or about 1290, of his father-in-law, Michel Zanche, Governor of Logodoro, in Sardinia.  The date of the death of Branca d' Oria is not known.

15. In the fifth *bolgia* (Canto xxii).

16. "Courtesy and propriety of behavior (*onestade*) are one and the same thing" (*Convito* ii. 11, 69).  Pity or compassion may be rightly felt, according to St. Thomas Aquinas, for sinners still on earth, for they may yet repent and turn from sin.  But in the future life there is no repentance.  The punishment of the sinner is the evidence of the justice of God; there can be no pity for him; charity cannot wish the damned to be less wretched, for this would be to call in question the Divine justice (*S. T. Suppl.* xciv. 2).

17. That is, with Friar Alberigo.

## CANTO XXXIV

*Ninth Circle: traitors. Fourth ring: Judecca.—Lucifer.—*
*Judas, Brutus and Cassius.—Centre of the universe.—Passage*
*from Hell.—Ascent to the surface of the Southern Hemisphere.*

"*Vexilla regis prodeunt inferni*[1] toward us; therefore look forward," said my Master; "see if thou discern him."   As when a thick fog breathes, or when our hemisphere darkens to night, a mill which the wind is turning seems from afar, such a structure it seemed to me that I then saw.

Then, because of the wind, I drew me behind my Leader; for no other shelter was there.   I was now (and with fear I put it into verse), there[2] where the shades were wholly covered, and showed through like a straw in glass.   Some are lying down; some are upright, this one with his head, and that with his soles uppermost; another, like a bow, bends his face to his feet.

When we had gone so far forward that it pleased my Master to show me the creature which had the fair semblance, he took himself from before me and made me stop, saying: "Lo Dis! and lo the place where it is needful that thou arm thyself with fortitude!"   How frozen and faint I then became, ask it not, Reader, for I do not write it, because all speech would be little.   I did not die, and did not remain alive: think now for thyself, if thou hast a grain of wit, what I became, deprived of one and the other.

The emperor of the woeful realm issued forth from the ice from the middle of his breast; and I compare better with a giant, than the giants do with his arms.   See now how great must be that whole which is conformed to such a part.   If he was as fair as he now is foul, and lifted up his brows against his Maker, well should all tribulation proceed from him.   Oh how great a marvel it seemed to me, when I saw three faces on his head! one in front, and that was crimson; the others were two, which were adjoined to this above the very middle of each shoulder, and they were joined up to the place of the crest; and the right seemed between white and yellow, the left was such in appearance as those who come from there whence the Nile descends.[3]   Beneath each came forth two great wings, of size befitting so great a bird; sails of the sea I never saw such.   They had no feathers, but their fashion was of a bat; and he was flapping them so that three winds were proceeding from him, whereby Cocytus was all congealed.   With six eyes he was weeping, and over three

1. "The banners of the King of Hell advance."   An allusion to the hymn *Vexilla Regis prodeunt,* given above, p. 89.
2. In the fourth, innermost ring of ice of the ninth circle — the Judecca.
3. The three faces exhibit the devilish counterpart of the attributes of the three persons of the Godhead, Impotence, Ignorance, and Hate as opposed to Power, Wisdom, and Love; Impotence scarlet with rage, Ignorance black with its own darkness, Hate pale yellow with jealousy and envy.

chins were trickling the tears and bloody drivel. At each mouth he was crushing a sinner with his teeth, in manner of a heckle, so that he thus was making three of them woeful. To the one in front the biting was nothing to the clawing, whereby sometimes his back remained all stripped of the skin.

"That soul up there which has the greatest punishment," said the Master, "is Judas Iscariot, who has his head within, and plies his legs outside. Of the other two who have their heads downwards, he who hangs from the black muzzle is Brutus; see how he writhes and says not a word; and the other is Cassius, who seems so large-limbed.[4] But the night is rising again; and now we must depart, for we have seen the whole."

As was his pleasure, I clasped his neck, and he took advantage of time and place, and when the wings were wide opened he caught hold on the shaggy flanks; down from shag to shag he then descended between the matted hair and the frozen crusts. When we were where the thigh turns just on the thick of the haunch, my Leader, with effort and stress of breath, turned his head to where he had had his shanks,[5] and grappled to the hair like one who mounts, so that I believed we were returning again to hell.

"Cling fast hold," said the Master, panting like one weary, "for by such stairs must we depart from so great evil." Then he came forth through the cleft of a rock, and placed me upon its edge to sit; then stretched toward me his cautious step.

I raised my eyes, and thought to see Lucifer as I had left him, and I saw him holding his legs upward; and if I then became perplexed, let the dull folk suppose it, who see not what that point is which I had passed.

"Rise up on foot," said the Master; "the way is long and the road is difficult, and already the sun returns to mid-tierce."

It was no hallway of a palace where we were, but a natural dungeon which had a bad floor, and lack of light. "Before I tear myself from the Abyss," said I when I had risen up, "my Master, talk a little with me to draw me out of error. Where is the ice? and this one, how is he fixed thus upside down? and how in such short while has the sun made transit from evening to morning?" And he to me: "Thou imaginest that thou still art on the other side of the centre, where I laid hold on the hair of the wicked Worm that pierces the world. On that side thou wast so long as I descended; when I turned, thou didst pass the point to which from every part all weighty things are drawn;[6] and thou art now arrived beneath the hemisphere which is opposite so that which the great dry land covers, and beneath whose zenith the Man was slain who was born and lived without sin: thou

---

4. Christ, betrayed by Judas, was the head of the Church, the supreme spiritual authority. Caesar, betrayed by Brutus and Cassius, was regarded by Dante as the founder of the Empire, the supreme authority in temporal affairs.

5. *Conversion,* in the literal sense.

6. "The center of gravity."

hast thy feet upon a little circle which forms the other face of the Judecca. Here it is morning when it is evening there; and this one who made a ladder for us with his hair is still fixed even as he was before. On this side he fell down from heaven, and the earth, which before was spread out on this side, through fear of him made of the sea a veil, and came to our hemisphere; and perhaps to fly from him that land which appears on this side left here this vacant space and ran back upward."

A place is there below, stretching as far from Beelzebub as his tomb extends, which is not known by sight, but by the sound of a rivulet which descends here along the hollow of a rock that it has gnawed with its winding and gently sloping course.[7] My Leader and I entered by that hidden road, to return into the bright world; and without care to have any repose, we mounted up, he first and I second, so far that through a round opening I saw some of the beautiful things which Heaven bears, and thence we issued forth again to see the stars.

## PURGATORY

### CANTO I

*The new theme. — Invocation of the Muses. — Dawn of Easter on the shore of Purgatory. — The Four Stars. — Cato. — The cleansing of Dante from the stains of Hell.*

To run over better waters the little vessel of my genius now hoists her sails, as she leaves behind her a sea so cruel; and I will sing of that second realm where the human spirit is purified, and becomes worthy to ascend to heaven.

But here let dead poesy rise again, O holy Muses, since I am yours, and here let Calliope somewhat mount up, accompanying my song with that sound of which the wretched Picae felt the stroke such that they despaired of pardon.[1]

A sweet color of oriental sapphire, which was gathering in the serene aspect of the mid sky, pure even to the first circle,[2] renewed delight to my eyes, soon as I issued forth from the dead air which had afflicted my eyes and my breast. The fair planet which incites to love was making all the Orient to smile, veiling the Fishes that were in her train.[3] I turned me to the right hand, and gave heed to

7. It is the streamlet of sin from Purgatory, which finds its way back to Satan.

1. The nine daughters of Pieros, King of Emathia, who, contending in song with the Muses, were for their presumption changed to magpies.

2. The horizon.

3. At the spring equinox Venus is in the sign of the Pisces, which immediately precedes that of Aries, in which is the Sun. The time indicated is therefore an hour or more before sunrise on Easter morning, April 10.

the other pole, and saw four stars, never seen save by the first people.[4] The heavens appeared to rejoice in their flamelets. O widowed northern region, since thou art deprived of beholding these!

When I had withdrawn from regarding them, turning me a little to the other pole, there whence the Wain had already disappeared, I saw close to me an old man alone, in aspect worthy of so much reverence that no son owes more to his father. He wore his beard long and mingled with white hair, like his locks, of which a double list fell upon his breast. The rays of the four holy stars so adorned his face with light, that I saw him, as though the sun had been in front.

"Who are ye that, counter to the blind stream, have fled from the eternal prison?" said he, moving those venerable plumes. "Who has guided you? Or who was a lamp to you, issuing forth from the deep night which ever makes the infernal valley black? Are the laws of the abyss thus broken? or is a new design changed in heaven that, being damned, ye come to my rocks?"

My Leader then took hold of me, and with words, and with hands, and with signs, controlled to reverence my knees and brow. Then he answered him: "Of myself I came not; a Lady descended from Heaven, by reason of whose prayers I succored this man with my company. But since it is thy will that more of our condition be unfolded to thee, how it truly is, mine cannot be that this be denied to thee. This man has not yet seen his last evening, but through his folly was so near thereto that there was very little time to turn. Even as I have said, I was sent to him to rescue him, and there was no other way than this, along which I have set myself. I have shown to him all the guilty people; and now I intend to show him those spirits that purge themselves under thy ward. How I have brought him, it would be long to tell thee; from on high descends power which aids me to lead him to see thee and to hear thee. Now may it please thee to look graciously upon his coming. He goes seeking liberty,[5] which is so dear, as he knows who for it renounces life. This thou knowest; for death for its sake was not bitter to thee in Utica, where thou didst leave the vesture which on the great day shall be so bright.[6] The eternal edicts are not violated by us, for this one is alive, and Minos does not bind me; but I am of the circle where are the chaste eyes of thy Marcia, who in her look still prays thee, O holy breast, that for thine own still hold her. For her love, then, incline thyself to us; allow us to go on through thy seven realms: I will report this grace from thee to her, if thou deignest to be mentioned there below."

"Marcia so pleased my eyes while I was on earth," said he then, "that whatsoever grace she wished from me, I did; now that she

4. The four stars are the symbols of the cardinal virtues — prudence, temperance, fortitude, and justice — the virtues of active life.

5. See last sentence, Canto XXVII.

6. That is, Cato, though a heathen, is at the Last Judgment to be among the blessed.

dwells on the other side of the evil stream, she can move me no more, by that law which was made when thence I issued forth. But if a Lady of Heaven move and direct thee, as thou sayest, there is no need of flatteries; it may well suffice thee that thou ask me for her sake. Go then, and see thou gird this one with a smooth rush, and that thou wash his face so that thou cleanse it from all stain, for it were not befitting to go with eye dimmed by any cloud before the first minister that is of those of Paradise. This little island, round about at its very base, down there yonder where the wave beats it, bears rushes upon its soft ooze. No plant of other kind, that puts forth leaf or grows hard, can there have life, because it yields not to the shocks. Thereafter let not your return be this way; the Sun, which now is rising, will show you how to take the mountain by easier ascent."

On this he disappeared, and I rose up, without speaking, and drew me quite close to my Leader, and bent my eyes on him. He began: "Son, follow my steps; let us turn back, for from here this plain slopes to its low bounds."

The dawn was vanquishing the matin hour, which was flying before it, so that from afar I discerned the trembling of the sea. We went along over the solitary plain like a man who turns to the road which he has lost and, till he find it, seems to himself to go in vain. When we were where the dew contends with the sun, and, through being in a place where there is shade, is little dispersed, my Master softly placed both his hands outspread upon the grass; whereon I, who was aware of his intent, stretched toward him my tearful cheeks. Then he wholly uncovered on me that color which hell had concealed.

We came, then, to the desert shore which never saw man navigate its waters who afterwards had experience of return. Here he girt me, even as pleased the other. O marvel! that such as he culled the humble plant, such it instantly sprang up again there whence he had plucked it.

### CANTO V

*Ante-Purgatory. — Spirits who had delayed repentance, and met with death by violence, but died repentant. — Jacopo del Cassero. — Buonconte da Montefeltro. — Pia de' Tolomei.*

I had now parted from those shades, and was following the footsteps of my Leader, when behind me one, pointing his finger, cried out: "Look how the ray seems not to shine on the left hand of that lower one, and he seems to bear himself as if alive." I turned my eyes at the sound of these words, and I saw them watching, for marvel, only me, only me, and the light which was broken.

"Why is thy mind so caught," said the Master, "that thou slackenest thy going? What matters to thee that which is whispered here? Come on after me, and let the people talk. Stand like a firm tower that never wags its top for blowing of the winds: for always the man in whom thought on thought wells up removes from himself his mark, because one weakens the force of the other." What could I answer, save: "I come"? I said it, overspread somewhat with the color, which, at times, makes a man worthy of pardon.

And therewhile, across upon the mountain-side, a little in front of us, were coming people singing *"Miserere,"* [1] verse by verse. When they observed that I gave no place for passage of the rays through my body, they changed their song into a long and hoarse Oh! and two of them, in form of messengers, ran to meet us, and asked of us: "Make us acquainted with your condition." And my Master: "Ye can go back, and report to those who sent you, that the body of this one is true flesh. If, as I suppose, they stopped because of seeing his shadow, enough is answered them: let them do him honor and it may profit them." [2]

Never did I see enkindled vapors [3] at early night so swiftly cleave the clear sky, or the clouds of August at set of sun, that these did not return up in less time; and, arrived there, they with the others wheeled round toward us, like a troop that runs without curb. "These folk that press to us are many, and they come to pray thee," said the Poet; "yet do thou still go on, and in going listen." "O soul," they came crying, "that with those limbs with which thou wast born art on thy way to be glad, a little stay thy step. Look if thou hast ever seen any one of us, so that thou mayst carry news of him to earth. Pray, why dost thou go on? Pray, why dost thou not stop? We all of old were slain by violence, and sinners up to the last hour; then light from Heaven made us mindful, so that both penitent and pardoning we issued forth from life at peace with God, who fills our hearts with the desire of seeing Him." And I: "Although I gaze upon your faces, I recognize no one; but if aught that I can do be

1. Psalm 50 (Vulgate); 51 (English).
2. Since Dante may secure for them the prayers of the good on his return home.
3. Shooting stars.

pleasing to you, spirits well-born, speak ye and I will do it by that peace which makes me, following the feet of such a guide, seek it from world to world." And one began: "Each of us trusts in thy good service, without thy swearing it, provided that want of power cut not off the will; wherefore I, who speak alone before the others, pray thee, if ever thou see that land which lies between Romagna and the land of Charles,[4] that thou be courteous to me with thy prayers in Fano, so that supplication may be well made in my behalf, that I may be able to purge away my grave offenses. Of that place was I; but the deep wounds, wherefrom issued the blood in which I had my seat,[5] were dealt me in the bosom of the Antenori,[6] there where I thought to be most secure; he of Este had it done, who held me in wrath far beyond what justice willed. But if, when I was overtaken at Oriaco, I had fled toward La Mira, I should still be yonder where men breathe. I ran to the marsh, and the reeds and the mire hampered me so that I fell, and there I saw a lake made by my veins upon the ground."

Then said another: "Ah! so may that desire be fulfilled which draws thee to the high mountain, with good piety do thou help mine. I was of Montefeltro, and am Buonconte. Joan,[7] or any other, has no care for me, wherefore I go among these with downcast front." And I to him: "What violence, or what chance caused thee to stray so far from Campaldino,[8] that thy burial place was never known?" "Oh!" replied he, "at foot of the Casentino crosses a stream, named the Archiano, which rises in the Apennine above the Hermitage. Where its name becomes vain I arrived, pierced in the throat, flying on foot, and bloodying the plain. Here I lost my sight, and I ended my speech with the name of Mary, and here I fell, and my flesh remained alone. I will tell the truth, and do thou repeat it among the living. The Angel of God took me, and he of Hell cried out, 'O thou from Heaven, why dost thou rob me?[9] Thou bearest away for thyself the eternal part of him for one little tear which takes him from me; but of the rest I will make other disposal.' Thou knowest well how in the air that moist vapor is collected which turns to water soon as it rises where the cold condenses it. He joined that evil will, which seeks only evil, with intelligence, and moved the

4. The March of Ancona. Jacopo del Cassero, who speaks, was a valiant member of the leading Guelf family in Fano. On his way to take the place of Podestà of Milan, in 1298, he was assassinated by the minions of Azzo VIII of Este, whose enmity he had incurred.

5. (Levit. 17:14.) *"Anima enim omnis carnis in sanguine est."*

6. Territory of Padua, reputed to have been founded by Antenor.

7. His wife.

8. The battle of Campaldino was fought on the 11th of June, 1289, between the Florentine Guelfs and the Ghibellines of Arezzo. Buonconte was the captain of the Aretines.

9. St. Francis and one of the black Cherubim had had a similar contention, with an opposite result, over the soul of Buonconte's father (*Hell*, Canto xxvii).

mist and the wind by the power that his nature gave. Then, when the day was spent, he covered the valley with cloud from Pratomagno to the great chain,[10] and made the sky above so dense that the pregnant air was turned to water. The rain fell, and what of it the earth did not endure came to the gullies, and as it gathered in great streams it rushed so swiftly towards the royal river that nothing held it back. The robust Archiano found my frozen body near its mouth, and pushed it into the Arno, and loosed on my breast the cross which I made of myself when the pain overcame me. It rolled me along its banks, and along its bottom, then with its spoil it covered and girt me."

"Pray, when thou shalt have returned unto the world, and rested from the long journey," the third spirit followed on the second, "remember me, who am Pia.[11] Siena made me, Maremma unmade me; he knows it, who, before wedding, had enringed me with his gem."

CANTO VI

*Ante-Purgatory. — More spirits who had deferred repentance till they were overtaken by a violent death. — Efficacy of prayer. — Sordello. — Apostrophe to Italy.*

When the game of hazard is broken up, he who loses remains sorrowful, repeating the throws, and saddened, learns; with the other all the folk go along; one goes before, and one plucks him from behind, and one at his side brings himself to mind: he does not stop, and listens to one and the other; the man to whom he reaches forth his hand presses on him no longer, and thus from the throng he defends himself. Such was I in that dense crowd, turning my face to them this way and that; and, promising, I loosed myself from it.

Here was the Aretine,[1] who from the fierce arms of Ghin di Tacco had his death; and the other who was drowned when running in pursuit. Here Frederigo Novello[2] was praying with hands outstretched, and he of Pisa, who made the good Marzucco show

10. Pratomagno forms the western boundary of the Casentino, the upper valley of the Arno; "the great chain" is the main ridge of the Apennines on the opposite side.

11. This sad Pia is supposed to have belonged to the Sienese family of the Tolomei, and to have been the wife of Nello or Paganello de' Pannocchieschi, who was reported to have had her put to death in his stronghold of Pietra in the Tuscan Maremma. Her fate seems the more pitiable that she does not pray Dante to seek for her the prayers of any living person.

1. Messer Benincasa da Laterina, a learned judge, condemned to death two relatives of Ghin di Tacco, the most famous highwayman of the day. Some time after, when Messer Benincasa was sitting as papal auditor in Rome, Ghino entered the city with a band of his followers, made his way to the tribunal, slew Benincasa, and escaped unharmed.

2. Slain in 1291.

himself strong.[3]   I saw Count Orso; [4] and the soul divided from its body by spite and envy, as it said, and not for fault committed, Pierre de la Brosse,[5] I mean; and here let the Lady of Brabant have foresight, while she is on earth, so that for this she be not of the worse flock.

When I was free from each and all those shades who prayed only that someone else should pray, so that their becoming holy may be speeded, I began: "It seems to me, O Light of mine, that thou deniest expressly, in a certain text, that orison can bend decree of Heaven, and these folk pray only for this, — shall then their hope be vain? or is thy saying not rightly clear to me?" [6]

And he to me: "My writing is plain, and the hope of these is not fallacious, if it be well regarded with sound mind; for top of judgment vails not itself because a fire of love may, in one instant, fulfil that which he who is here installed must satisfy.   And there where I affirmed this proposition, defect was not amended by a prayer, because the prayer was disjoined from God.[7]   However, in regard to matter of doubt so deep decide thou not, unless she tell it thee, who shall be a light between the truth and the understanding.   I know not if thou understandest; I speak of Beatrice: thou shalt see her above, smiling and happy, upon the summit of this mountain."

And I: "My Lord, let us go on with greater speed, for now I am not weary as a while ago; and see how the hill now casts its shadow." "We will go forward with this day," he answered, "as much farther as is now possible for us; but the fact is otherwise than thou supposest.   Before thou canst be there-above thou wilt see him return, who is now hidden by the hill-side so that thou dost not make his rays to break.   But see there a soul which, stationed all alone, is looking toward us; it will point out to us the speediest way."   We came to it.   O Lombard soul, how lofty and disdainful didst thou hold thyself; and in the movement of thine eyes grave and slow! It said not anything to us, but let us go on, only eyeing us in manner of a lion when he is couching.   Still Virgil drew near to it, praying that it would show to us the best ascent; and it made no answer to his request, but of our country and life enquired of us.   And the sweet Leader began: "Mantua" — and the shade, all in itself recluse, rose toward him from the place where first it was, saying: "O Mantuan, I am Sordello of thy city." [8]   And they embraced each other.

3. Identification doubtful.

4. Murdered by his cousin, the son of Count Alessandro (*Hell,* Canto xxxii, n. 6).

5. Chamberlain of Philip the Bold of France.   It was believed that he had incurred the hatred of the queen, Mary of Brabant, the second wife of Philip, and that his death was brought about by her.   She lived till 1321, so that Dante's warning may have reached her ears.

6. *Aeneid* vi. 376.

7. The prayer of Palinurus was not heard because it was that of one not in the grace of God.

8. Thirteenth-century troubadour.

Ah, servile Italy! hostel of grief! ship without pilot in great tempest! not lady of provinces, but a brothel! that noble soul was so ready, only at the sweet name of his native town, to give glad welcome here unto his fellow-citizen; and now in thee thy living men exist not without war, and of those whom one wall and one moat shut in one gnaws the other. Search, wretched one, around its shores, thy seaboard, and then look within thy bosom, if any part of thee enjoys peace! What avails it that for thee Justinian readjusted thy bridle, if the saddle be empty? [9] Without this, the shame would be less. Ah folk, that oughtest to be devout and let Caesar sit in the saddle, if thou rightly understandest what God notes for thee! [10] Look how fell this wild beast has become, through not being corrected by the spurs, since thou didst put thy hand upon the rein. O German Albert, who abandonest her that has become untamed and savage, and oughtest to bestride her saddle-bows, may a just judgment from the stars fall upon thy blood, and may it be so strange and manifest, that thy successor may have fear thereat! [11] For thou and thy father, held back up there [12] by greed, have suffered the garden of the empire to become desert. Come thou to see the Montecchi and Cappelletti,[13] the Monaldi and Filippeschi,[14] thou man without care, those already wretched, and these in dread. Come, cruel one, come, and see the distress of thy nobility, and cure their hurts; and thou shalt see Santafiora [15] how safe he is. Come to see thy Rome, that weeps, widowed and alone, and cries day and night: "My Caesar, wherefore dost thou not keep me company?" Come to see how the people love one another; and, if no pity for us move thee, come to be shamed for thine own renown! And if it be lawful for me, O Supreme Jove, who wast on earth crucified for us, are Thy just eyes turned aside elsewhere? Or is it preparation, which in the abyss of Thy counsel Thou are making, for some good utterly cut off from our perception? For the cities of Italy are all full of tyrants, and every churl that comes playing the partisan becomes a Marcellus.[16]

My Florence! surely thou mayst be content with this digression, which does not touch thee, thanks to thy people that takes such heed.

9. What avails a reform of the law if there be no emperor to enforce it?

10. Matthew 22:21.

11. Albert of Hapsburg was elected King of the Romans in 1298, but, like his father, never went to Italy to be crowned. He was murdered by his nephew, John, called the Parricide, in 1308, at Königsfelden. It is plain that Dante wrote after the murder. Albert's successor was Henry VII of Luxemburg, who was crowned at Rome in 1312, and died at Buonconvento in 1313. His death ended the hopes of Dante.

12. In your German states.

13. The Montagues and Capulets of Verona.

14. Enemies in Orvieto.

15. The Counts of Santafiora were once the most powerful Ghibelline nobles in the Sienese territory. Their power had declined, and the district was full of lawlessness and misery.

16. Bitter opponent of Caesar.

Many have justice at heart, but shoot slowly, through not coming to the bow without deliberation; but thy people has it on the edge of its lips. Many reject the common burden, but thy people eagerly responds without being called, and cries, "I load myself." Now make thee glad, for thou has truly wherefore: thou rich, thou at peace, thou wise! If I speak the truth, the fact does not hide it. Athens and Lacedaemon, that made the ancient laws and were so civilized, made in regard to living well but little sign, compared with thee that makest such fine-spun provisions, that what thou spinnest in October reaches not to mid-November. How often in the time that thou rememberest hast thou changed law, money, office, and custom, and renewed thy members! And if thou mind thee well and see the light, thou wilt see thyself resembling that sick woman, who cannot find repose upon the feathers, but with her tossing seeks to ease her pain.

## CANTO VII

*Virgil makes himself known to Sordello. — Sordello leads the Poets to the Valley of the Princes who have been negligent of salvation. — He points them out by name.*

## CANTO VIII

*Valley of the Princes. — Two Guardian Angels. — Nino Visconti. — The Serpent. — Corrado Malaspina.*

## CANTO IX

*Slumber and Dream of Dante. — The Eagle. — Lucia. — The Gate of Purgatory. — The Angelic Gatekeeper. — Seven P's inscribed on Dante's Forehead. — Entrance to the First Ledge.*

The concubine of old Tithonus [1] was now gleaming white on the balcony of the east, forth from the arms of her sweet friend; her forehead was bright with gems set in the shape of the cold animal that strikes people with its tail. [2] And in the place where we were the night had taken two of the steps with which she ascends, and the third was already bending its wings downward, when I, who had somewhat of Adam with me, overcome by sleep, reclined upon the grass, there where all five of us [3] were already seated.

At the hour near the morning when the little swallow begins her sad lays, [4] perhaps in memory of her former woes, and when our mind, more a wanderer from the flesh, and less captive to the thought,

1. The lunar aurora.
2. The constellation Scorpion.
3. Dante, Virgil, Sordello, Nino, and Corrado.
4. The allusion is to the tragic story of Progne and Philomela, transformed the one into a swallow, the other into a nightingale (Ovid's *Metamorphoses*, Bk. VI).

is in its visions almost divine, in dream I seemed to see an eagle with feathers of gold poised in the sky, with wings spread, and intent to stoop. And I seemed to be there [5] where his own people were abandoned by Ganymede, when he was rapt to the supreme consistory. In myself I thought, perhaps this bird strikes only here through wont, and perhaps from other place disdains to carry anyone upward in its feet. Then it seemed to me that, having wheeled a little, it descended terrible as a thunderbolt, and snatched me upwards far as the fire. There it seemed that it and I burned, and the imagined fire so scorched that of necessity my sleep was broken.

Not otherwise Achilles shook himself, — turning around his awakened eyes, and not knowing where he was, when his mother stole him away, sleeping in her arms, from Chiron to Scyros, thither whence afterwards the Greeks withdrew him, — than I started, as from my face sleep fled away; and I became pale, as does a man who, frightened, turns to ice. At my side was my Comforter alone, and the sun was now more than two hours high, and my face was turned toward the sea. "Have no fear," said my Lord; "be reassured, for we are at a good point, restrain not, but put forth all thy strength. Thou art now arrived at Purgatory; see there the cliff that closes it round; see the entrance there where it appears divided. Short while ago, in the dawn that precedes the day, when thy soul was sleeping within thee upon the flowers wherewith the place down yonder is adorned, came a lady, and said: 'I am Lucia; [6] let me take this one who is sleeping; thus will I assist him along his way.' Sordello remained and the other noble forms; she took thee up, and as the day grew bright, she came upward, and I along her footprints. Here she laid thee down, and first her beautiful eyes showed me that open entrance; then she and slumber went away together." Like a man who in perplexity is reassured, and who changes his fear into confidence after the truth is disclosed to him, so did I change; and when my Leader saw me free from disquiet, up along the cliff he moved on, and I behind, toward the height.

Reader, thou seest well how I exalt my theme, and therefore marvel not if I support it with more art.

We drew near to it, and reached a place such that there, where at first there seemed to me to be a rift, like a cleft which divides a wall, I saw a gate, and three steps beneath for going to it, of divers colors, and a gatekeeper who as yet said not a word. And as I opened my eye upon him more and more, I saw him sitting on the upper step, such in his face that I endured it not. And he had in his hand a naked sword, which so reflected the rays toward us that I often raised my sight in vain. "Tell it from there, what would ye?" he began to say: "Where is the guide? Beware lest the coming up be harmful to you." [7] "A lady from Heaven versed in these things," replied my Master to him, "only just now said to us: 'Go thither, here is the

5. On Mount Ida.
6. As in the second canto of *Hell,* the symbol of assisting grace.
7. The angel recognizes that Dante and Virgil are not souls coming

gate.'" "And may she speed your steps in good," began again the courteous gatekeeper, "come forward then unto our stairs."

Thither we came to the first great stair; it was of white marble so polished and smooth that I mirrored myself in it as I appear. The second, of deeper hue than perse, was of a rough and scorched stone, cracked lengthwise and athwart. The third, which uppermost lies massy, seemed to me of porphyry as flaming red as blood that spirts forth from a vein. Upon this the Angel of God held both his feet, sitting upon the threshold, which seemed to me stone of adamant.[8] Up over the three steps my Leader drew me with good will, saying: "Beg humbly that he undo the lock." Devoutly I threw myself at the holy feet; I besought for mercy's sake that he would open for me; but first upon my breast I struck three times. Seven P's he inscribed upon my forehead with the point of his sword,[9] and: "See that thou wash these wounds when thou art within," he said.

Ashes or earth dug out dry would be of one color with his vestment, and from beneath that he drew two keys. One was of gold and the other was of silver: first with the white and then with the yellow he so did to the gate, that I was content.[10] "Whenever one of these keys fails, so that it turns not rightly in the lock," said he to us, "this narrow entrance does not open. The one is more precious; but the other requires exceeding much of art and wit before it unlocks, because it is that which disentangles the knot. From Peter I hold them; and he told me to err rather in opening than in keeping shut, if but the people prostrate themselves at my feet." Then he pushed the valve of the sacred gate, saying: "Enter, but I give you warning that whoso looks backward returns outside." [11] And when the pivots of that sacred portal, which are of metal, sonorous and strong, were turned within their hinges, Tarpeia roared not so loud nor showed herself so harsh, when the good Metellus was taken from her, whereby she afterwards remained lean.[12]

---

to undergo the penalties of Purgatory. His question corresponds with Cato's, "Who has guided you?" The inner meaning of his warning may be that the teaching of the reason is not sufficient so to convince Man of his sin as to make him fit for justification; cooperating grace must be added; and unless the penitence be proportioned to the sin the penitent may lose rather than gain in grace.

8. The stairs symbolize contrition, confession, and works of penitence.

9. The seven P's stand for the seven so-called mortal sins, *Peccati:* pride, envy, anger, sloth (*accidia*), avarice, gluttony, and lust. After justification these dispositions, which already have been overcome, must be utterly removed from the soul.

10. Note that Dante depicts St. Peter's keys here at the entrance to Purgatory. They symbolize judgment and discernment.

11. Luke 9:62.

12. When Caesar forced the doors of the temple of Saturn on the Tarpeian rock, in order to lay hands on the sacred treasure of Rome, he was unsuccessfully resisted by the tribune Metellus. Lucan tells of the clamor of the rock when Marcellus was dragged away, and of the impoverishment of the treasury.

I turned away attentive to the first tone, and it seemed to me I heard *"Te Deum laudamus"* [13] in a voice mingled with the sweet sound. That which I heard gave me just such an impression as we are wont to receive when people stand singing with an organ, and the words now are, now are not heard.

CANTO X

*Purgatory proper. — First Ledge: the Proud. — Examples of Humility sculptured on the rock.*

When we were within the threshold of the gate, which the evil love of souls disuses, because it makes the crooked way seem straight, I heard by its resounding that it was closed again. And, if I had turned my eyes to it, what excuse would have been befitting for the fault?

We were ascending through a cloven rock, which was moving to one side and to the other, even as the wave which retreats and approaches. "Here must be used a little art," began my Leader, "in keeping close, now on this hand, now on that, to the side which recedes." And this made our steps so scant that the waning disk of the moon had regained its bed to go to rest, before we were out from that needle's eye. But when we were free and open above, where the mountain gathers itself back, I weary, and both uncertain of our way, we stopped upon a level more solitary than roads through deserts. From its edge, where it borders the void, to the foot of the high bank which ever rises, a human body three times told would measure; and as far as my eye could stretch its wings, now on the left and now on the right side, such did this cornice seem to me. Our feet had not yet moved upon it, when I perceived the circling bank, which, being perpendicular, allowed no ascent, to be of white marble and adorned with such carvings that not only Polycletus but Nature herself would have been shamed there.

The Angel who came to earth with the announcement of the peace, many years wept for, which opened Heaven from its long interdict, appeared before us, carved here so truly in a sweet attitude, that he did not seem an image that is silent. One would have sworn that he was saying "Ave"; for she was imaged there who turned the key to open the exalted love. And on her action she had these words impressed, *"Ecce ancilla Dei!"* [1] as exactly as a shape is sealed in wax.

"Keep not thy mind only on one place," said the sweet Master, who had me on that side where people have their heart. Whereupon I moved my eyes and saw, beyond Mary, upon that side where he was who was moving me, another story imposed upon the rock; wherefore I passed Virgil, and drew near so that it might be set before my eyes. There in the very marble were carved the cart and

13. Above, p. 81.
1. "Behold the handmaid of the Lord!" Luke 1:38.

the oxen drawing the holy ark, by reason of which men fear an office not given in charge.[2]  In front appeared people; and all of
them, divided in seven choirs, of two of my senses made the one say:
"No," the other: "Yes, they are singing."  In like manner, by the
smoke of the incense that was imaged there, my eyes and nose
were made in *Yes* and *No* discordant.  There, preceding the blessed
vessel, dancing, girt up, was the humble Psalmist, and more and less
than king was he on that occasion.  Opposite, portrayed at a window
of a great palace, Michal was looking on, even as a lady scornful
and troubled.[3]

I moved my feet from the place where I was standing, in order
to look from near at another story which, beyond Michal, was gleaming white to me.  Here was storied the high glory of the Roman
prince, whose worth incited Gregory to his great victory:[4]  I speak of
Trajan the emperor; and a poor widow was at his bridle in attitude
of weeping and grief.  Round about him it seemed trampled
and thronged with knights, and above him the eagles in the gold
were moving in appearance in the wind.  The wretched woman
among all these seemed to be saying: "Lord, do me vengeance for
my son who is slain, whereat I am broken-hearted."  And he to
answer her: "Now wait till I return"; and she: "My Lord," — like
one in whom grief is urgent, — "if thou return not?"  And he: "He
who shall be where I am will do it for thee."  And she: "What will
the good deed of another be to thee, if thou art unmindful of thine
own?"  Whereon he: "Now comfort thee; for it behoves that I
discharge my duty ere I go; justice so wills, and pity holds me back."
He who never beheld a new thing produced that visible speech,
novel to us, because it is not found on earth.

While I was delighting myself with looking at the images of
such great humilities, and for their Maker's sake dear to see: "Behold," murmured the Poet, "on this side many people, but they
make few steps; they will put us on the way to the lofty stairs."
My eyes which were intent on gazing, were not slow in turning
toward him in order to see novelties, whereof they are fain.

I would not, indeed, Reader, that thou be diverted from thy good
purpose, through hearing how God wills that the debt be paid.  Heed
not the form of the suffering; think on what follows; think that,
at the worst, beyond the Great Judgment it cannot go!

I began: "Master, that which I see moving toward us does not
seem to me to be persons, but what I know not, I am so at loss in
looking."  And he to me: "The heavy condition of their torment
bows them to earth, so that my own eyes at first had contention with
it.  But look fixedly there, and disentangle with thy sight that which

2.  2 Samuel 6:4–7.
3.  2 Samuel 6:12–16.
4.  It was believed that Pope Gregory the Great interceded for Trajan,
praying that he might be delivered from Hell; "then God because of these
prayers drew that soul from pain and put it into glory."  Trajan appears
in *Paradise,* Canto xx.

is coming beneath those stones; already thou canst discern how each is stricken."

O proud Christians, wretched and weary, who, diseased in vision of the mind, have confidence in backward steps, are ye not aware that we are worms born to form the angelic butterfly, which flies unto judgment without defence? Wherefore does your mind float up aloft, since ye are as it were defective insects even as a worm in which formation fails?

As to support ceiling or roof, by way of corbel, a figure is something seen joining its knees to its breast, which out of the unreal gives birth to a real distress in him who sees it, thus fashioned did I see these, when I gave good heed. True it is, that they were more or less bowed down, according as they had more or less upon their backs; and he who had most patience in his looks, weeping, appeared to say: "I can no more."

CANTO XI

*First Ledge: the Proud. — Prayer. — Omberto Aldobrandeschi. — Oderisi d' Agubbio. — Provenzan Salvani.*

CANTO XII

*First Ledge: the Proud. — Instances of the punishment of Pride graven on the pavement. — Meeting with an Angel who removes one of the P's. — Ascent to the Second Ledge.*

With even pace, like oxen that go yoked, I went on with that burdened soul so long as the sweet Pedagogue allowed it; but when he said: "Leave him, and pass on, for here it is well for every one to urge his bark, both with the sail and with the oars, as much as he can," I straitened up my body again, as is required for walking, although my thoughts remained both stooping and abased.

I had moved on, and was following willingly the steps of my Master, and both were now showing how light we were, when he said to me: "Turn thine eyes downward; it will be well for thee, in order to cheer the way, to look upon the bed of thy footsteps." As above the buried, so that there may be memory of them, their tombs on the ground bear engraved what they were before, — whence often is weeping for them there, through the pricking of remembrance, which only to the pious gives the spur, — so I saw figured there, but of better semblance in respect of the workmanship, all that for pathway juts out from the mountain.

I saw, on one side, him who was created more noble than any other creature, falling down as lightning from heaven.

I saw Briareus,[1] on the other side, transfixed by the celestial bolt, lying heavy upon the earth in mortal chill.

1. Examples from classic and biblical mythology alternate. Briareus, one of the giants who fought against the gods.

I saw Thymbraeus,[2] I saw Pallas and Mars, still armed, around their father, gazing at the scattered limbs of the giants.

I saw Nimrod at the foot of his great toil, as if bewildered, and looking round upon the people that had been proud with him in Shinar.

O Niobe! with what grieving eyes did I see thee portrayed upon the road between thy seven and seven children slain!

O Saul! how on thine own sword didst thou here appear dead on Gilboa, which thereafter felt not rain or dew! [3]

O foolish Arachne,[4] so did I see thee, already half spider, wretched on the shreds of the work which to thy harm by thee was made!

O Rehoboam! here thine image seems not now to threaten, but a chariot bears it away full of terror before anyone pursues it.[5]

The hard pavement showed also how costly to his mother Alcmaeon made the ill-fated ornament appear.[6]

It showed how his sons threw themselves upon Sennacherib within the temple, and how, he dead, they left him there.[7]

It showed the ruin and the cruel butchery that Tomyris wrought, when she said to Cyrus, "For blood thou hast thirsted, and with blood I fill thee." [8]

It showed how the Assyrians fled in rout after Holofernes was killed, and also the remnants of the victim.[9]

I saw Troy in ashes, and in caverns: O Ilion, how cast down and abject did the image which is there discerned show thee!

What Master has there been of pencil or of style that could draw the shadows and the lines which there would make every subtile genius wonder? Dead seemed the dead, and the living alive. He who saw the truth saw not better than I all that I trod on, while I went bent down. — Now be ye proud, and go your way with haughty look, ye sons of Eve, and bend not down your face so that ye may see your evil path!

More of the mountain had now been circled by us, and of the sun's course far more spent, than my mind, not disengaged, was aware,

2. Apollo.
3. 1 Samuel 31:4; 2 Samuel 1:21.
4. Changed to a spider by Athena, whom she had challenged to a trial of skill at the loom.
5. 1 Kings 12:18.
6. Amphiaraüs, the soothsayer, foreseeing his own death if he went to the Theban war, hid himself to avoid being forced to go. His wife, Eriphyle, bribed by an ill-fated golden necklace made by Vulcan, betrayed his hiding place, and was killed by her son Alcmaeon, for thus bringing about his father's death.
7. 2 Kings 19:37.
8. Tomyris, Queen of the Massagetae, having defeated and slain Cyrus, filled a skin full of human blood and plunged his head in it.
9. "Behold Holofernes lieth upon the ground without a head. . . . And fear and trembling fell upon them, so that . . . rushing out all together, they fled into every way of the plain, and of the hill country." Judith 14:18; 15:2.

when he, who always went attentive in advance, began: "Lift up thy head; there is no longer time for going thus abstracted. See yonder an Angel, who is making ready to come toward us: see how the sixth hand-maiden is returning from the service of the day.[10] With reverence adorn thine acts and thy face so that it may please him to direct us upward. Think that this day never dawns again."

I was well used to his admonition never to lose time, so that on that theme he could not speak to me obscurely.

The beautiful creature came toward us, clothed in white, and in his face such as seems the tremulous morning star. His arms he opened, and then he opened his wings; he said: "Come: here at hand are the steps, and easily henceforth does one ascend. Very few come to these tidings. O human race, born to fly upward, wherefore at a little wind dost thou so fall?"

He led us to where the rock was cleft; here he struck his wings across my forehead,[11] then promised me secure progress.

As on the right hand, to ascend the mountain,[12] where the church sits which above Rubaconte dominates the well-guided city, the bold flight of the ascent is broken by the stairs, which were made in an age when the record and the stave were secure,[13] so the bank which falls here very steeply from the next round is made easier; but on this side and that the high rock grazes. As we turned our persons thither, voices sang *"Beati pauperes spiritu"* [14] in such wise that speech could not tell it. Ah, how different are these passes from those of Hell! for here one enters with songs, and there below with fierce lamentations.

Already we were mounting up over the holy stairs, and it seemed to me I was far more light than I had seemed before upon the plain. Whereon I: "Master, say, what heavy thing has been lifted from me, so that almost no fatigue is felt by me as I go on?" He answered: "When the P's which, almost extinct, still remain on thy forehead, shall be, as one is, quite erased, thy feet will be so conquered by good-will, that not only they will not feel fatigue but it will be delight to them to be urged upward." Then I did like those who are going with something on their head unknown to them, unless the signs of others make them suspect; wherefore the hand

10. The sixth hour of the day.

11. Removing the first P that the Angel of the Gate had incised on Dante's brow.

12. The hill of San Miniato, above the upper bridge at Florence.

13. In 1299 one Messer Niccola Acciaiuoli, in order to conceal a fraudulent transaction, had a leaf torn out from the public notarial record; and about the same time an officer in charge of the revenue from salt measured the salt he received with an honest measure, but sold with a measure diminished by the removal of a stave.

14. "Blessed are the poor in spirit." Almost extinct, because as St. Thomas Aquinas says, "Pride is said to be the beginning of every sin, not because every single sin has its immediate source in pride, but because every kind of sin is born of pride."

assists to ascertain, and seeks and finds, and performs that office which cannot be accomplished by the sight; and with the fingers of my right hand outspread, I found six only of those letters which he of the keys had incised upon my temples: looking at which my Leader smiled.

CANTO XXI

*Fifth Ledge: the Avaricious. — Statius. — Cause of the trembling of the Mountain. — Statius does honor to Virgil.*

CANTO XXII

*Ascent to the Sixth Ledge. — Discourse of Statius and Virgil. — Entrance to the Ledge: the Gluttonous. — The Mystic Tree. Examples of Temperance.*

CANTO XXIII

*Sixth Ledge: the Gluttonous. — Forese Donati. — Nella. — Rebuke of the women of Florence.*

CANTO XXIV

*Sixth Ledge: the Gluttonous. — Forese Donati. — Piccarda Donati. — Bonagiunta of Lucca. — Pope Martin IV. — Ubaldin dalla Pila. — Bonifazio. — Messer Marchese. — Prophecy of Bonagiunta concerning Gentucca, and of Forese concerning Corso de' Donati. — Second Mystic Tree. — The Angel of the Pass.*

CANTO XXV

*Ascent to the Seventh Ledge. — Discourse of Statius on generation, the infusion of the Soul into the body, and the corporeal semblance of Souls after death. — The Seventh Ledge: the Lustful. — The mode of their Purification.*

CANTO XXVI

*Seventh Ledge: the Lustful. — Sinners in the fire, going in opposite directions. — Guido Guinicelli. — Arnaut Daniel.*

CANTO XXVII

*Seventh Ledge: the Lustful. — Passage through the Flames. — Stairway in the rock. — Night upon the stairs. — Dream of Dante. — Morning. — Ascent to the Earthly Paradise. — Last Words of Virgil.*

As when he darts forth his first rays there where his Maker shed His blood (Ebro falling under the lofty Scales, and the waves in the Ganges scorched by noon) so the sun was now standing; [1] and thus the day was departing, when the glad Angel of God appeared to us. Outside the flame he was standing on the bank, and was singing:

1. It was near sunrise at Jerusalem, and consequently near sunset in Purgatory, midnight in Spain, and midday at the Ganges.

*Beati mundo corde,*[2] in a voice far more living than ours.  Then:
"No one goes farther, ye holy souls, if first the fire sting not: enter
into it, and to the song beyond be ye not deaf," he said to us, as we
drew near to him: whereat I became such, when I heard him, as is
he who is put in the pit.  I stretched forward above my clasped hands,
looking at the fire, and vividly imagining human bodies I had once
seen burnt.  My good Escort turned toward me, and Virgil said to
me: "My son, here may be torment, but not death.  Bethink thee!
bethink thee! . . . lo, if I even upon Geryon guided thee safe, what
shall I do now that I am nearer God?  Believe for certain that if
within the belly of this flame thou shouldst stand full a thousand
years it could not make thee bald of a single hair.  And if perchance
thou believest that I am deceiving thee, draw towards it, and make
trial for thyself with thine own hands upon the hem of thy garments.
Put aside now, put aside every fear, turn hitherward, and come on
secure."

And I still motionless and against conscience!

When he saw me still stand motionless and obdurate, he said, disturbed a little: "Now see, son, between Beatrice and thee is this
wall."

As at the name of Thisbe, Pyramus, at point of death, opened his
eyelids and looked at her, what time the mulberry became dark
red, so, my obduracy becoming softened, I turned to my wise Leader,
hearing the name that in my memory is ever welling up.  Whereat
he nodded his head, and said: "How? do we want to stay on this
side?" then he smiled as one does at a child who is conquered by an
apple.

Then within the fire he set himself in front of me, praying Statius,
that he would come behind, who previously, for a long way, had
divided us.  When I was within, I would have thrown myself into
boiling glass to cool me, so without measure was the burning there.
My sweet Father, to encourage me, went talking only of Beatrice,
saying: "I seem already to see her eyes."

A voice which was singing on the other side was guiding us, and
we, attentive ever to it, came forth where the ascent began.  *"Venite,
benedicti patris mei,"*[3] sounded within a light that was there such
that it overcame me, and I could not look on it.  "The sun is going,"
it added, "and the evening comes; tarry not, but hasten your steps
so long as the west grows not dark."

The way mounted straight, through the rock, in such direction
that in front of me I cut off the rays of the sun which was already
low.  And of few stairs had we made essay ere, by the vanishing of
my shadow, both I and my Sages perceived the setting of the sun
behind us.  And before the horizon in all its immeasurable regions
had become of one aspect, and night had all her dispensations, each
of us make his bed of a stair; for the nature of the mountain took
from us the power, more than the delight, of ascending.

2. "Blessed are the pure in heart."
3. "Come, ye blessed of my Father."  Matthew 25:34.

As goats, that have been swift and wanton on the peaks ere they were fed, become tranquil while they ruminate, hushed in the shade so long as the sun is hot, watched by the shepherd, who on his staff is leaning and, leaning, tends them; and as the herdsman, who lodges out of doors, passes the night beside his quiet flock, watching that the wild beast may not scatter it: such were we all three then, I like a goat, and they like shepherds, hemmed in on this side and on that by the high rock. Little of the outside could there be seen, but in that little I saw the stars both brighter and larger than their wont. Thus ruminating, and thus gazing upon them, sleep overcame me, sleep which oft before the deed be done knows news thereof.

At the hour, I think, when from the east Cytherea, who with fire of love seems always burning, first beamed upon the mountain, I seemed in dream to see a lady, young and beautiful, going through a meadow gathering flowers, and singing she was saying: "Let him know, whoso asks my name, that I am Leah, and I go moving my fair hands around to make me a garland. To please me at the mirror I here adorn me, but my sister Rachel never departs from her looking-glass, and sits all day. She is as fain to look at her fair eyes as I to adorn me with my hands. Her, seeing, and me, doing satisfies." [4]

And now before the splendors which precede the sun, and rise the more grateful unto pilgrims as in returning they lodge less far away, the shadows were fleeing on every side, and my sleep with them; whereupon I rose, seeing the great Masters already risen. "That sweet fruit which the care of mortals goes seeking upon so many branches, to-day shall set at peace thy hungerings." These words did Virgil use toward me, and never were there gifts which for pleasure were equal to these. Such great wish upon wish came to me to be above, that at every step thereafter I felt my wings growing for the flight.

When beneath us all the stairway had been run over, and we were on the topmost step, Virgil fixed his eyes on me, and said: "The temporal fire and the eternal thou hast seen, Son, and art come to a place where of myself I discern no farther. I have brought thee here with understanding and with art; thine own pleasure take thou henceforward for guide: forth art thou from the steep ways, forth art thou from the narrow. See there the sun, which is shining on thy front; see the young grass, the flowers, and the shrubs, which here the earth of itself alone produces. Until the beautiful eyes come rejoicing, which weeping made me come to thee, thou canst sit down and thou canst go among them. Expect no more or word or sign from me. Free, upright, and sound is thine own will, and it would be wrong not to act according to its choice; wherefore thee over thyself I crown and mitre."

4. Leah and Rachel are the types of the active and the contemplative life. Rachel contemplates the Divine mysteries; Leah works according to the Divine will.

CANTO XXVIII

*The Earthly Paradise. — The Forest. — A Lady gathering flowers on the bank of a little stream. — Discourse with her concerning the nature of the place.*

CANTO XXIX

*The Earthly Paradise. — Mystic Procession or Triumph of the Church.*

Singing like a lady enamored, she, at the ending of her words, continued: *"Beati, quorum tecta sunt peccata."* [1] And, like the nymphs who were wont to go solitary through the sylvan shades, one desiring to see and one to avoid the sun, she then moved on counter to the stream, going up along the bank, and I at even pace with her, following her little step with little. Of her steps and mine there were not a hundred, when the banks both alike gave a turn, in such wise that I faced again toward the east. Nor even thus had our way been long, when the lady turned wholly round to me, saying: "My brother, look and listen." And lo! a sudden lustre ran through the great forest on every side, so that it made me question if it were lightning. But because the lightning stays even as it comes, [2] and this, lasting, became more and more resplendent, in my thought I said, "What thing is this?" And a sweet melody ran through the luminous air; whereupon a righteous zeal made me reproach the hardihood of Eve, who, there, where the earth and the heavens were obedient, the only woman, and but just now formed, did not endure to stay under any veil; under which if she had stayed devout, I should have tasted those ineffable delights before, and for a longer time. While I was going on amid so many first fruits of the eternal pleasure, all enrapt, and still desirous of more joys, in front of us the air, beneath the green branches, became like a blazing fire, and the sweet sound was now heard as a song.

O Virgins sacrosanct! if for you I have ever endured hunger, cold, or vigils, the occasion spurs me that I claim reward therefor. Now it behoves that Helicon pour forth for me, and that Urania aid me with her choir to put into verse things difficult to think.

A little farther on, the long tract of space which was still between us and them shewed falsely in their seeming seven trees of gold. But when I had come so near to them that the common object, which deceives the sense, lost not through distance any of its attributes, the power which supplies discourse to reason [3] distinguished them as candlesticks, [4] and in the voices of the song, *"Hosanna."* On high the

1. "Blessed are they whose transgressions are forgiven." Psalm 22:1.
2. Its stay is but for the moment of its coming.
3. The faculty of perception or apprehension.
4. The imagery of the Triumph of the Church here described is largely taken from the Apocalypse.

fair array was flaming, brighter by far than the moon in the clear sky at midnight, in the middle of her month. I turned me round full of wonder to the good Virgil, and he replied to me with a look charged not less with amazement. Then I turned back my gaze to the high things, which were moving toward us so slowly that they would have been outstripped by new-made brides. The lady chided me: "Why art thou only thus ardent in gazing on the living lights, and dost not look at that which comes behind them?" Then I saw folk coming behind, as if after their leaders, clothed in white, and such whiteness there never was on earth. The water was resplendent on the left flank, and reflected to me my left side, if I looked in it, even as a mirror. When I had such position on my bank that only the stream separated me, in order to see better, I gave halt to my steps, and I saw the flamelets go forward leaving the air behind them painted, and they had the semblance of streaming pennons, so that it remained divided overhead by seven stripes, all in those colors whereof the sun makes his bow, and Delia her girdle.[5] These banners stretched to the rear beyond my sight, and according to my judgment the outermost were ten paces apart. Under so fair a sky as I describe, twenty-four elders,[6] two by two, were coming crowned with flower-de-luce. All were singing: "Blessed art thou among the daughters of Adam, and blessed forever be thy beauties."

After the flowers and the other fresh herbage, opposite to me on the other bank, were free from those folk elect, there came behind them, even as light follows light in heaven, four living creatures, each crowned with green leaves. Each was feathered with six wings, the feathers full of eyes; and the eyes of Argus, if they were living, would be such. To describe their forms, Reader, I scatter rhymes no more, for other spending so constrains me that in this I cannot be liberal. But read Ezekiel, who depicts them as he saw them coming from the cold quarter with wind, with cloud, and with fire; and such as thou wilt find them in his pages such were they here, save that as to the wings John is with me, and differs from him.[7]

The space between these four contained a triumphal chariot upon two wheels, which came drawn along by the neck of a Griffon.[8] And he stretched up the one and the other of his wings between the midmost stripe, and the three and three others, so that he did harm to no one of them by cleaving it: so high they rose that they were lost to sight. His members were of gold so far as he was bird, and the rest were white mixed with crimson.[9] Not Africanus, or indeed Augustus, gladdened Rome with so beautiful a chariot,[10] but even

5. Delia, the moon, and her girdle, the halo.
6. Cf. Revelation 4:4. These four and twenty elders symbolize the books of the Old Testament, according to St. Jerome.
7. Cf. Ezekiel 1:6; Revelation 4:8.
8. The griffon, half eagle and half lion, represents Christ in His double nature, divine and human.
9. The Song of Solomon 5:10, 11.
10. The Church.

that of the Sun would be poor to it, — that of the Sun, which going astray,[11] was consumed at the prayer of the devout Earth, when Jove in his secrecy was just. Three ladies,[12] at the right wheel, came dancing in a circle; one so ruddy that hardly would she have been noted within the fire; the next was as if her flesh and bones had been made of emerald; the third seemêd as snow fresh fallen. And now they seemed led by the white, now by the red,[13] and the others took their step both slow and swift from the song of her who led. On the left, four,[14] robed in purple made festival, following the measure of one of them who had three eyes in her head.

Behind all the group thus described, I saw two old men, unlike in dress, but like in demeanor, both dignified and staid. The one [15] showed himself one of the familiars of that supreme Hippocrates whom Nature made for the creatures that she holds most dear; [16] the other showed the contrary care, with a shining and sharp sword,[17] such that it caused me fear on the hither side of the stream. Then I saw four of humble aspect,[18] and behind all an old man alone, coming asleep with a keen countenance.[19] And these seven were robed like the first band; but they made not a crown of lilies round their heads, rather of roses, and of other red flowers. The sight at little distance would have sworn that all were aflame above their brows.

And when the chariot was abreast of me, a peal of thunder was heard, and those worthy people seemed to have their farther progress interdicted, stopping there with the first ensigns.

CANTO XXX

*The Earthly Paradise. — Beatrice appears. — Departure of Virgil.
— Reproof of Dante by Beatrice.*

When the Septentrion of the first heaven [1] (which never knew setting nor rising, nor veil of other cloud than sin, and which was making every one there acquainted with his duty, as the lower [2] makes him who turns the helm to come to port) stopped still, the truthful people who had come first between the Griffon and it,

11. When driven by Phaëthon.
12. Faith, Hope, and Charity.
13. Hope must always follow Faith or Love.
14. Prudence, Justice, Temperance, and Fortitude: Prudence has three eyes, as looking at the past, the present, and the future.
15. The book of Acts, represented under the type of its author, St. Luke, called "the beloved physicıan" (Colossians 4:14).
16. That is, Man.
17. The symbol of war and martyrdom, a "contrary care" to the healing of men.
18. Writers of the minor Epistles.
19. St. John, as the writer of the Revelation, asleep because he was "in the Spirit" when he beheld his vision.
1. The seven candlesticks, symbols of the sevenfold spirit of the Lord, whose abode is the first heaven, the Empyrean.
2. The lower septentrion, or the seven stars of the Great Bear.

turned to the chariot as to their peace, and one of them, as if sent from heaven, singing, cried thrice: *"Veni, sponsa, de Libano,"* [3] and all the others after.

As the blessed at the last trump will arise swiftly, each from his tomb, singing Hallelujah with reinvested voice, so, upon the divine wagon, *ad vocem tanti senis,* [4] rose up a hundred ministers and messengers of life eternal. All were saying: *"Benedictus, que venis,"* [5] and scattering flowers above and around, *Manibus o date lilia plenis.* [6]

I have seen ere now at the beginning of the day the eastern region all rosy, and the rest of heaven beautiful with fair clear sky, and the face of the sun rising shaded, so that through the tempering of vapors the eye sustained it a long while; thus within a cloud of flowers, which was ascending from the angelic hands and falling down again within and without, a lady, with wreath of olive over a white veil, appeared to me, robed with the color of living flame under a green mantle. [7] And my spirit which now for so long a time had not been broken down, trembling with awe at her presence, without having more knowledge by the eyes, through occult virtue that proceeded from her, felt the great potency of ancient love.

Soon as the lofty virtue smote my sight, which already had transfixed me ere I was out of boyhood, I turned me to the left, with the confidence with which the little child runs to his mother when he is frightened, or when he is troubled, to say to Virgil: "Less than a drachm of blood remains in me that does not tremble; I recognize the signals of the ancient flame." [8] But Virgil had left us deprived of himself; Virgil, sweetest Father; Virgil, to whom for my salvation I gave me. Nor did all which the ancient mother lost avail unto my cheeks, cleansed with dew, that they should not turn dark again with tears.

"Dante, though Virgil be gone away, weep not yet, weep not yet, for by another sword thou needst must weep."

Like an admiral who, on poop or on prow, comes to see the people that are serving on the other ships, and encourages them to do well, upon the left-hand border of the chariot — when I turned me at the sound of my own name, which of necessity is registered here, [9]

3. "Come with me from Lebanon, my spouse." The Song of Solomon 4:8.

4. "At the voice of so great an elder"; these words are in Latin apparently for the sake of matching the rhyme with that of the two following verses.

5. "Blessed, thou that comest," words derived from Psalm 118:26, and shouted by the multitude at the entrance of Jesus into Jerusalem (Matthew 21:9).

6. "Oh, give lilies with full hands"; words from the *Aeneid* vi. 884; supreme honor is paid to Virgil by their introduction in this sacred scene.

7. The olive is the symbol of wisdom and of peace; the three colors are those of faith, charity, and hope.

8. "Agnosco veteris vestigia flammae." *Aeneid* iv. 28.

9. The only mention of Dante's name in the poem.

— I saw the Lady, who had first appeared to me veiled beneath the angelic festival, directing her eyes toward me across the stream. Although the veil, which descended from her head, circled by the leaf of Minerva, did not allow her to appear distinctly, royally, still severe in her mien, she went on, as one who speaks, and keeps back his warmest words: "Look at me well: I am, indeed, I am, indeed, Beatrice. How hast thou deigned to approach the mountain? Didst thou not know that here man is happy?" My eyes fell down to the clear fount; but seeing myself in it I drew them to the grass, such great shame weighed on my brow. As to her son the mother seems haughty, so she seemed to me; for somewhat bitter tastes the savor of tart pity.

She was silent, and the angels sang of a sudden: *"In te, Domine, speravi";* [10] but beyond *"pedes meos"* [11] they did not pass. Even as the snow, among the living rafters upon the back of Italy,[12] is congealed, blown and packed by Sclavonian winds, then melting, trickles through itself, if only the land which loses shadow breathe, so that it seems as fire melting the candle: thus was I without tears and sighs before the song of them who always sing following the notes of the eternal spheres; but when I heard in their sweet melodies their compassion for me, more than if they had said: "Lady, why dost thou so confound him?" the ice that was bound tight around my heart became breath and water, and with anguish issued from my breast, through my mouth and through my eyes.

She, still standing motionless on the aforesaid side of the chariot, then turned her words to those pious beings thus: "Ye watch in the eternal day, so that nor night nor slumber robs from you one step the world may make along its ways; wherefore my reply is with greater care, that he who is weeping yonder may understand me, in order that fault and grief may be of one measure. Not only through the working of the great wheels, which direct every seed to some end according as the stars are its companions, but through largess of divine graces, which have for their rain vapors so lofty that our sight goes not near thereto, — this man was virtually such in his new life,[13] that every right disposition would have made admirable proof in him. But so much the more malign and wild does the ground become with bad seed and untilled, as it has the more of good earthly vigor. Some time did I sustain him with my face; showing my youthful eyes to him, I led him with me turned in right direction. So soon as I was on the threshold of my second age, and had changed life, he took himself from me, and gave himself to others. When I had risen from flesh to spirit, and beauty and virtue were increased in me, I was less dear and less pleasing to him; and he turned his steps along a way not true, following false images of good, which pay no promise in full. Nor did it avail

10. "In thee, O Lord, do I put my trust."
11. That is, the angels sing the first eight verses of Psalm 31.
12. The forests upon the Apennines.
13. In his youth.

me to obtain inspirations with which, both in dream and otherwise, I called him back; so little did he heed them. So low he fell that all means for his salvation were already short, save showing him the lost people. For this I visited the gate of the dead, and to him, who has conducted him up hither, my prayers were borne with weeping. The high decree of God would be broken, if Lethe should be passed, and such viand should be tasted, without some scot of repentance which may pour forth tears."

CANTO XXXI

*The Earthly Paradise. — Reproachful discourse of Beatrice, and confession of Dante. — Passage of Lethe. — Appeal of the Virtues to Beatrice. — Her Unveiling.*

"O thou, who art on the farther side of the sacred river," turning her speech to me with the point, which only with the edge had seemed to me keen, she began anew, going on without delay, "Say, say, if this is true: to so heavy a charge thine own confession must needs be conjoined." My faculties were so confused that the voice moved and became extinct before it had been released from its organs. A little while she waited, then said: "What thinkest thou? Reply to me; for the sad memories in thee are not yet injured by the water." Confusion and fear mingled together forced such a "Yes" from out my mouth that the eyes were needed for the hearing of it.

As a cross-bow breaks its cord and its bow when it shoots with too great tension, and the shaft hits the mark with less force, so did I burst under that heavy load, pouring forth tears and sighs, and the voice slackened along its passage. Whereupon she to me: "Within those desires of mine that were leading thee to love the Good beyond which there is nothing to which one may aspire, what trenches running traverse, or what chains didst thou find, for which thou shouldst thus have despoiled thyself of the hope of passing onward? And what satisfactions, or what advantages were displayed on the brow of the others, for which thou shouldst have lingered before them?" After the drawing of a bitter sigh, hardly had I the voice to make answer, and the lips with difficulty gave it form. Weeping, I said: "The present things with their false pleasure turned my steps, soon as your face was hidden." And she: "Hadst thou been silent, or hadst thou denied that which thou dost confess, thy fault would not be less known, by such a Judge is it known. But when the accusation of the sin bursts from one's own mouth, in our court the wheel turns itself back against the edge.[1] Yet still, that thou mayst now bear shame for thy error, and that another time, hearing the Sirens, thou mayst be stronger, lay aside the sowing of tears,[2] and listen; so shalt thou hear how my buried flesh

1. The edge of the sword of Divine justice is blunted by Divine mercy for the penitent sinner.
2. Cf. Psalm 126:5.

should have moved thee in opposite direction. Never did nature or art present to thee pleasure such as the fair limbs wherein I was enclosed, and which are scattered in earth. And if the supreme pleasure thus failed thee through my death, what mortal thing should afterward have drawn thee into its desire? Forsooth thou oughtest, at the first arrow of things fallacious, have risen upward after me, who was no longer such. Nor oughtest thou to have weighed thy wings downward to await more blows, either of some young girl or other vanity of so brief a use. The young bird awaits two or three; but before the eyes of the full-fledged, the net is spread in vain, or the arrow shot." [3]

As children, silent in shame, with their eyes upon the ground, stand listening and conscience-stricken and repentant, so was I standing. And she said: "Since thou art grieved through hearing, lift up thy beard, and thou shalt take greater grief from seeing." With less resistance is a sturdy oak uprooted by a native wind, or by one from the land of Iarbas,[4] than I raised my chin at her command; and when by the beard she asked for my eyes, truly I recognized the venom of the argument.[5] And when my face was lifted up, my sight perceived that those primal creatures were resting from their strewing,[6] and my eyes, still little assured, saw Beatrice turned toward the animal that is one person only in two natures. Beneath her veil, and beyond the stream, she seemed to me more to surpass her ancient self, than she seemed to surpass all others here when she was here. So pricked me there the nettle of repentance, that of all other things the one which most had turned me to its love became the most my foe.

Such self-conviction stung my heart that I fell overcome; and what I then became she knows who afforded me the cause.

Then, when my heart restored my outward faculties, I saw above me the lady whom I had found alone,[7] and she was saying: "Hold me, hold me." She had drawn me into the stream up to the throat, and dragging me after her was moving over the water, light as a shuttle. When I was near the blessed shore, I heard *"Asperges me"* [8] so sweetly that I cannot remember it, far less can write it. The beautiful lady opened her arms, clasped my head, and immersed me where I had perforce to swallow of the water. Then she took me, and presented me, thus bathed, within the dance of the four beautiful ones,[9] and each of them covered me with her arm. "Here we are nymphs, and in heaven we are stars: before Beatrice had descended to the world we were ordained unto her for her

3. Cf. Proverbs 1:17.
4. From the South; Libya.
5. Because indicating the lack of that wisdom which should pertain to manhood.
6. Of flowers.
7. Matilda, whom Dante met on his entrance to the Earthly Paradise.
8. "Purge me with hysop, and I shall be clean: wash me, and I will be whiter than snow" (Psalm 51:7).
9. The four cardinal virtues.

handmaids. We will lead thee to her eyes; but for the joyous light which is within them, the three yonder [10] who look more deeply shall sharpen thine own." Thus singing, they began; and then to the breast of the Griffon they led me with them, where Beatrice was standing turned toward us. They said: "See that thou spare not thy sight: we have placed thee before the emeralds, whence Love of old drew his darts against thee." A thousand desires hotter than flame bound fast my eyes to the relucent eyes which ever stayed fixed upon the Griffon. Not otherwise than as the sun in a mirror, was the twofold animal gleaming therewithin, now with one, now with the other mode of being.

Think Reader, if I marvelled when I saw the thing stay quiet in itself, and in its image transmuting itself.

While, full of awe and glad, my soul was tasting that food which, sating in itself, causes longing for itself, the other three, showing themselves of the loftier order in their bearing, came forward dancing to their angelic carol. "Turn, Beatrice, turn thy holy eyes," was their song, "upon thy faithful one, who to see thee has taken so many steps. Of thy grace do us the grace that thou unveil to him thy mouth, so that he may discern the second beauty which thou dost conceal." [11]

O splendor of living light eternal! Who has become so pallid under the shadow of Parnassus, or has so drunk at its cistern, that he would not seem to have his mind encumbered, trying to render thee as thou didst appear there where with its harmony the heaven hangs over thee, when in the open air thou didst thyself disclose?

CANTO XXXII

*The Earthly Paradise. — Return of the Triumphal Procession.*
*— The Chariot bound to the Mystic Tree. — Sleep of Dante.*
*— His waking to find the Triumph departed. — Transformation*
*of the Chariot. — The Harlot and the Giant.*

So fixed and intent were my eyes to relieve their ten years' thirst, that my other senses were all extinct: and they themselves, on one side and the other, had a wall of indifference, so did the holy smile draw them to itself with the ancient net; when perforce my sight was turned toward my left by those goddesses, because I heard from them a "Too fixedly." And the condition which exists for seeing, in eyes but just now smitten by the sun, caused me to be for a while without sight. But when my vision reshaped itself to the lesser sensation (I say to the lesser, in respect to the great one

10. The evangelic or Christian virtues.
11. "The eyes of Wisdom are her demonstrations by which one sees the truth most surely; and her smile is her persuasions in which the interior light of Wisdom is displayed without any veil; and in these two is felt that loftiest pleasure of Beatitude, which is the chief good in Paradise." *Convito* iii. 15.

wherefrom by force I had removed myself), I saw that the glorious
army had wheeled upon its right flank, and was returning with the
sun and with the seven flames in its face.

As under its shields to protect itself a troop turns and wheels with
its banner, before it all can change about, that soldiery of the
celestial realm which was in advance had wholly gone past us, before
its front beam had bent the chariot round.    Then to the wheels
the ladies returned, and the Griffon moved his blessed burden, in
such wise however that no feather of him shook.    The beautiful
lady who had drawn me at the ford, and Statius and I were following the wheel which made its orbit with the smaller arc.    Thus
passing through the lofty wood, empty through fault of her who
trusted to the serpent, an angelic song set the time to our steps.
Perhaps an arrow loosed from the string had traversed in three flights
as great a distance as we had advanced, when Beatrice descended.
I heard "Adam!" murmured by all: then they encircled a plant
despoiled of flowers and of other leafage on every bough.[1]    Its tresses,
which the wider spread the higher up they are, would be wondered
at for height by the Indians in their woods.

"Blessed art thou, Griffon, that thou dost not break off with thy
beak of this wood sweet to the taste, since the belly is ill racked
thereby."    Thus around the sturdy tree the others cried; and the
animal of two natures: "Thus is preserved the seed of all righteousness."    And turning to the pole which he had drawn, he dragged
it to the foot of the widowed trunk, and that which was of it [2] he
left bound to it.

As when the great light falls downward mingled with that which
shines behind the celestial Carp,[3] our plants become swollen, and
then renew themselves, each in its own color, before the sun yokes
his coursers under another star, so, disclosing a color less than of
roses and more than of violets, the plant renewed itself, which at
first had its boughs so bare.    I did not understand, nor here [4] is
sung, the hymn which that folk then sang, nor did I bear the melody
to the end.

If I could portray how the pitiless eyes [5] sank to slumber, while hearing of Syrinx, — the eyes to which much watching cost so dear, —
like a painter who paints from a model I would depict how I fell

1. By the disobedience of Adam the Tree of the Knowledge of Good
and Evil, the type of the law of God, was despoiled of virtue until the
obedience of Christ restored it.    Cf. Romans 5:19, 21.

2. The pole, the mystic type of the cross of Christ, which was, according to an old legend, made of the wood of this tree.

3. In the spring, when the Sun is in the sign of the Ram, which follows
that of the Fishes, here termed the Carp, and its great light is mingled
with that of the constellation.

4. On earth.

5. The hundred eyes of Argus, who, when watching Io, fell asleep
while listening to the tale of the loves of Pan and Syrinx and was then
slain by Mercury (Ovid *Metamorphoses* i. 568–721).

asleep; but whoso would, let him be one who can represent slumber well. Therefore I pass on to when I awoke, and I say that a splendor rent for me the veil of sleep, and a call: "Arise, what doest thou?"

As, to see some of the flowerets of the appletree which makes the Angels greedy for its fruit, and makes perpetual marriage feasts in Heaven, Peter and John and James were led,[6] and being overcome, came to themselves at the word by which greater slumbers [7] were broken, and saw their band diminished alike by Moses and Elias, and the raiment of their Master changed, so I came to myself, and saw that compassionate one standing above me, who had before been conductress of my steps along the stream; and all in doubt I said: "Where is Beatrice?" And she: "Behold her under the new leafage, sitting upon its root. Behold the company which surrounds her; the rest are going on high behind the Griffon, with sweeter song and more profound." [8] And if her speech was further poured forth I know not, because already in my eyes was she who from attending to aught else had closed me in. She was sitting alone upon the bare ground, like a guard left there of the chariot which I had seen bound by the biform animal. In a circle the seven Nymphs were making of themselves an enclosure for her, with those lights in their hands which are secure from Aquilo and from Auster.[9]

"Here shalt thou be a short time a forester; and thou shalt be with me without end a citizen of that Rome whereof Christ is a Roman. Therefore for profit of the world which lives ill, keep now thine eyes upon the chariot; and what thou seest, mind that thou write when thou hast returned to earth." Thus Beatrice; and I, who at the feet of her commands was all devout, gave my mind and my eyes where she willed.

Never with so swift a motion did fire descend from a dense cloud, when it falls from that region which stretches most remote, as I saw the bird of Jove swoop down through the tree, breaking the bark, as well as the flowers and new leaves; and he struck the chariot with all his force, whereat it reeled, like a ship in a tempest beaten by the waves now to starboard, now to larboard.[10] Then I saw a she fox,[11] which seemed fasting from all good food, leap into the body of the triumphal vehicle; but, rebuking her for her ugly sins, my Lady turned her to such flight as her fleshless bones allowed.

6. Matthew 17:1–8.

7. Those of the dead called back to life by Jesus.

8. Christ having ascended, Beatrice, the type of Theology, or the knowledge of the things of God, is left seated by the chariot, the type of the Church on earth.

9. From the north wind or the south; that is, from any earthly blast.

10. The descent of the eagle symbolizes the disobedience of the emperors to the law of God; and the attack on the chariot their persecution of the Church.

11. Heresy.

Then, from there whence he had first come, I saw the eagle descend down into the ark of the car and leave it feathered from himself.[12] And a voice, such as issues from a heart that is afflicted, issued from Heaven, and thus spoke: "O little bark of mine, how ill art thou laden!" Then it seemed to me that the earth opened between the two wheels, and I saw a dragon issue from it, who fixed his tail upward through the chariot: and, like a wasp that retracts its sting, drawing to himself his malignant tail, he drew out part of the floor, and went wandering away.[13] That which remained covered itself again, as lively soil with grass, with the plumage, offered perhaps with sane and benign intention; and both one and the other wheel and the pole were again covered with it in such time that a sigh holds the mouth open longer.[14] Thus transformed, the holy structure put forth heads upon its parts, three upon the pole, and one on each corner. The first were horned like oxen, but the four had a single horn upon the forehead.[15] A like monster was never seen before. Secure, as a fortress on a high mountain, there appeared to me a dishevelled harlot sitting upon it, with bold brows glancing round. And, as if in order that she should not be taken from him, I saw a giant standing at her side, and now and then they kissed each other. But because she turned her lustful and roving eye on me that fierce paramour scourged her from head to foot. Then full of jealousy, and cruel with anger, he loosed the monster, and dragged it through the wood so far, that he made of that alone a shield from me for the harlot and for the strange beast.[16]

CANTO XXXIII

*The Earthly Paradise. — Prophecy of Beatrice concerning one who shall restore the Empire. — Her discourse with Dante. — The river Eunoë. — Dante drinks of it, and is fit to ascend to Heaven.*

"*Deus, venerunt gentes,*" [1] the ladies began, alternating, now three now four, a sweet psalmody, and weeping; and Beatrice, sighing and pitiful, was listening to them with such aspect that scarce was Mary at the Cross more changed. But when the other virgins gave place

12. The donation of Constantine — the temporal endowment of the Church.
13. The schism of the Greek Church in the ninth century.
14. Fresh endowments of the Church.
15. The seven heads have been interpreted as the seven mortal sins, the result of its wealth and temporal power.
16. The harlot and the giant stand respectively for the Pope and the king of France. The dragging of the car through the wood may be taken as typifying the removal of the seat of the Papacy from Rome to Avignon in 1305.
1. The first words of Psalm 79, which pictures the actual desolation of the Church, but closes with confident prayer to the Lord to restore His people.

to her to speak, risen upright upon her feet, she answered, colored like fire: *"Modicum, et non videbitis me, et iterum,* my beloved Sisters, *modicum, et vos videbitis me."* [2] Then she set all the seven in front of her; and behind her, by a sign only, she placed me, and the Lady, and the Sage who had remained.[3] Thus she moved on; and I do not think her tenth step had been set upon the ground, when with her eyes she smote mine, and with tranquil aspect said to me: "Come more forward, so that if I speak with thee, thou mayst be well placed for listening to me." So soon as I was with her as I should be, she said to me: "Brother, why dost thou not venture to question me, now thou art coming with me?"

As befalls those who with exceeding reverence are speaking in presence of their superiors, that they drag not their voice living to the teeth, it befell me that without perfect utterance I began: "My Lady, you know my need, and that which is good for it." And she to me: "From fear and from shame, I wish that thou henceforth disentangle thyself, so that thou mayst speak no more like one who dreams. Know thou, that the vessel which the serpent broke was, and is not; but let him who has the blame thereof think that the vengeance of God fears not sops.[4] The eagle that left its feathers on the car, whereby it became a monster, and then a prey, shall not be for all time without an heir; for I see surely, and therefore I tell it, stars already close at hand, secure from every obstacle and from every hindrance, to give to us a time in which a Five hundred, Ten, and Five [5] sent by God shall slay the abandoned woman together with that giant who is sinning with her. And perchance my narration, dark like that of Themis and the Sphinx, less persuades thee, because after their fashion it clouds the understanding. But soon the facts will be the Naiades [6] which shall solve this difficult enigma, without harm of flocks or of harvest. Do thou note; and even as these words are uttered by me, so do thou teach them to those alive with that life which is a running unto death; and bear in mind when thou writest them, not to conceal that thou hast seen the plant, which here has now been twice despoiled. Whoever robs or breaks it, with blasphemy of deed offends God, who

2. "A little while and ye shall not see me: and again, a little while and ye shall see me." (John 16:16).

3. The lady, Matilda, and the sage, Statius.

4. According to old belief, if a murderer could contrive, within nine days of the murder, to eat a sop of bread dipped in wine above the grave of his victim, he would escape from the vengeance of the family of the murdered man. The meaning of the words is, Let not him who has carried away the chariot, now become a monster, fancy that any means he may take can avert the vengeance of God for the wrong.

5. In Roman numerals a DXV, which letters by transposition form DVX, "a leader," sent by God. Possibly written when Dante's hopes were high concerning the results of Henry VII's expedition to Italy in 1310.

6. According to the manuscripts of Ovid's *Metamorphoses* vii. 759, the Naiades solved the riddles of the oracles.

for His own use alone created it holy.  For biting it, the first soul, in pain and in desire, for five thousand years and more, longed for Him who punished on Himself the bite.  Thy wit sleeps, if it deem not that for a special reason it is so lofty and so inverted at its top.  And if thy vain thoughts had not been as water of Elsa [7] round about thy mind, and their pleasantness as Pyramus to the mulberry,[8] by so many circumstances alone thou wouldst have recognized morally the justice of God in the interdict upon the tree. But though I see thee in thy understanding made of stone, and thus stony, dark, so that the light of my speech dazzles thee, I yet would have thee bear it hence within thee, even if not written, at least depicted, for the reason that the pilgrim's staff is carried wreathed with palm."  And I: "Even as wax, which does not change the figure imprinted by a seal, is my brain now stamped by you.  But why do your desired words fly so far above my sight, that the more it strives the more it loses them?"  "In order that thou mayst know," she said, "that school which thou hast followed, and mayst see how its doctrine can follow my word; and mayst see that your way is distant so far from the divine, as the heaven which highest hastens on is remote from earth."  Whereon I replied to her: "I do not remember that I ever estranged myself from you, nor have I conscience of it that reproaches me."  "And if thou canst not remember it," she replied smiling, "now call to mind how this very day thou hast drunk of Lethe; and if from the smoke fire is inferred, this thy forgetfulness clearly proves fault in thy will intent elsewhere.[9]  Truly my words shall henceforth be naked so far as it is befitting to uncover them to thy rude sight."

And more flashing, and with slower steps, the sun was holding the circle of the meridian, which appears here or there according to the point of view, when, as he who goes in advance of people as a guide halts if he find some strange thing on his track, the seven ladies halted at the edge of a pale shadow, such as beneath green leaves and black boughs the Alp casts over its cold streams.  In front of them, it seemed to me I saw Euphrates and Tigris issue from one fountain, and, like friends, depart slowly from one another.

"O light, O glory of the human race, what water is this which here pours forth from one source, and from itself divides itself away?" To this prayer answer was made to me: "Pray Matilda that she tell it to thee."  And hereupon the beautiful Lady answered, as one who frees himself from blame: "This and other things have been told to him by me; and I am sure that the water of Lethe has not hidden them from him."  And Beatrice: "Perhaps a greater care, which oftentimes takes the memory away, has darkened the eyes of

7. A river of Tuscany, whose waters have a petrifying quality.
8. Darkening thy mind as the blood of Pyramus dyed the mulberry.
9. The having been obliged to drink of Lethe is the proof that thou hadst sin to be forgotten, and that thy will had turned thee to other things than me.

his mind. But behold Eunoë,[10] which flows forth yonder, lead him to it, and, as thou art wont, revive his lifeless power." As a gentle soul which makes not excuse, but makes its own will of another's will, soon as by a sign it is outwardly disclosed, even so, when I had been taken by her, the beautiful Lady moved on, and to Statius she said, with manner of a lady, "Come with him."

If I had, Reader, longer space for writing, I would in part at least sing of the sweet draught which never would have sated me; but, because all the leaves destined for this second canticle are full, the curb of my art lets me go no farther.

I returned from the most holy wave, reanimate, even as new plants renewed with new foliage, pure and disposed to mount unto the stars.


# PARADISE

### CANTO I

*Proem. — Invocation. — Beatrice, and Dante transhumanized, ascend through the Sphere of Fire toward the Moon. — Beatrice explains the cause of their ascent.*

The glory of Him who moves everything penetrates through the universe, and is resplendent in one part more and in another less. In the heaven which receives most of His light I have been, and have seen things which he who descends from thereabove neither knows how nor has power to recount; because, drawing near to its own desire, our intellect enters so deep that the memory cannot follow after. Truly whatever of the Holy Realm I could treasure up in my mind shall now be the theme of my song.

O good Apollo, for this last labor make me such a vessel of thy worth as thou demandest for the gift of the beloved laurel. Thus far one summit of Parnassus has been enough for me, but now with both [1] I need to enter the remaining arena. Enter into my breast, and breathe thou in such wise as when thou drewest Marsyas from out the sheath of his limbs. O divine Power, if thou lend thyself to me so that I may make manifest the image of the Blessed Realm imprinted within my head, thou shalt see me come to thy chosen tree, and crown myself then with those leaves of which the theme and thou will make me worthy. So rarely, Father, are they gathered for triumph or of Caesar or of poet (fault and shame

10. Eunoë, "the memory of good," which its waters restore to the purified soul.

1. Parnassus was supposed to have two peaks, and Dante here assumes that the Muses dwelt upon one, Apollo upon the other. At the opening of the preceding parts of his poem Dante has invoked the Muses only.

of human wills), that the Peneian leaf[2] should bring forth joy unto the joyous Delphic deity, whenever it makes any one to long for it. Great flame follows a little spark: perhaps after me prayer shall be made with better voices, whereto Cyrrha[3] may respond.

The lamp of the world rises to mortals through different passages, but from that which joins four circles with three crosses it issues with better course and conjoined with a better star, and it tempers and seals the mundane wax more after its own fashion.[4]

Almost such a passage had made morning there and evening here;[5] and there all that hemisphere was white, and the other part black, when I saw Beatrice turned to her left side and gazing upon the sun: never did eagle so fix himself upon it. And even as a second ray is wont to issue from the first, and mount upward again, like a pilgrim who wishes to return; so from her action, infused through the eyes into my imagination, mine was made, and I fixed my eyes upon the sun beyond our wont. Much is permitted there which here is not permitted to our faculties, by virtue of the place made for the human race as its proper seat.[6] Not long did I endure it, nor so little that I did not see it sparkle round about, like iron that issues boiling from the fire. And on a sudden,[7] day seemed to be added to day, as if He who has the power had adorned the heaven with another sun.

Beatrice was standing with her eyes wholly fixed on the eternal wheels, and on her I fixed my eyes from thereabove removed. Looking at her I inwardly became such as Glaucus[8] became on tasting of the grass which made him consort in the sea of the other gods. Transhumanizing cannot be signified in words; therefore let the example suffice him for whom grace reserves the experience. If I was only that of me which thou didst the last create,[9] O Love that governest the heavens, Thou knowest, who with Thy light didst lift me. When the revolution which Thou, being desired, makest eternal,[10] made me attent unto itself with the harmony which Thou

2. Daphne, who was changed to the laurel, was the daughter of Peneus.

3. Not far from the foot of Parnassus, and here used as synonymous with Delphi, of which it was the port.

4. At the vernal equinox the Sun rises from a point on the horizon where the four great circles, namely, the horizon, the zodiac, the equator, and the equinoctial colure, meet, and, cutting each other, form three crosses. The Sun is in the sign of Aries. It was the season assigned to the Creation, the Annunciation, and the Resurrection.

5. There, in the Earthly Paradise; here, on earth.

6. The Earthly Paradise.

7. So rapid was his ascent as he was drawn upward, following Beatrice, through the gleaming sphere of fire, which was supposed to be between the sphere of the air and that of the moon.

8. A fisherman changed to a sea-god (Ovid *Metamorphoses* xiii. 943–49).

9. The living soul.

10. "The Empyrean . . . is the cause of the most swift motion of the First Moving Heaven, because of the most ardent desire of every part

dost attune and modulate, so much of the heaven then seemed to
me enkindled by the flame of the sun, that rain or river never made
so widespread a lake.

The novelty of the sound and the great light kindled in me a
desire concerning their cause, never before felt with such keenness.
Whereon she, who saw me as I see myself, to quiet my perturbed
mind opened her mouth, ere I mine to ask, and began: "Thou
thyself makest thyself dull with false imagining, so that thou seest
not what thou wouldst see, if thou hadst shaken it off. Thou art
not on earth, as thou believest; but lightning, flying from its proper
site, never ran as thou who art returning thereunto."

If I was divested of my first doubt by these brief little smiled-out
words, within a new one was I more enmeshed. And I said: "Already I rested content concerning a great wonder; but now I wonder
how I can transcend these light bodies." Whereon she, after a
pitying sigh, directed her eyes toward me, with that look which
a mother turns on her delirious child, and she began: "All things
whatsover have order among themselves; and this is the form which
makes the universe like unto God. Herein the exalted creatures [11]
see the imprint of the Eternal Power, which is the end for which
the aforesaid rule is made. In the order of which I speak, all natures
are disposed, by diverse lots, more or less near to their source; [12]
wherefore they are moved to different ports over the great sea of
being, and each with the instinct given to it which bears it on.
This bears the fire upward toward the moon; this is the motive
force in mortal hearts; this binds together and unites the earth.
Nor does this bow shoot forth only the created things which are
without intelligence, but also those which have understanding and
love. The Providence that ordains all this, makes always quiet
with its own light the heaven [13] within which that one which has
the greatest speed revolves. And thither now, as to a site decreed,
the virtue of that bowstring is bearing us on, which directs to a
joyful mark whatever it shoots. It is true, that as the form often
does not accord with the intention of the art, because the material
is deaf to respond, so the creature sometimes deviates from this
course; for it has power, though thus impelled, to bend in another
direction (even as the fire of a cloud may be seen to fall), if the first
impetus, diverted by false pleasure, turn it earthwards. Thou
shouldst not, if I deem aright, wonder more at thy ascent, than at
a stream if it descends from a high mountain to the base. It would

***

of the latter to be conjoined with every part of that most divine and quiet
heaven." *Convito* ii. 4, 19–25.

11. The created beings endowed with souls — angels and men.

12. The likeness to God is participated by different things in different
modes, and their common inclination to the universal good varies with
their different modes of being.

13. The Empyrean, within which the crystalline heaven, the *primum
mobile,* the first and swiftest of the moving heavens, revolves.

be a marvel in thee, if deprived of hindrance, thou hadst sat below, even as quiet in living fire on earth would be."

Thereon she turned again her face toward heaven.

CANTO II

*Proem. — Ascent to the Moon. — The cause of Spots on the Moon. — Influence of the Heavens.*

CANTO III

*The Heaven of the Moon. — Spirits whose vows had been broken. — Piccarda Donati. — The Empress Constance.*

That sun which first had heated my breast with love had uncovered to me, proving and disproving, the sweet aspect of fair truth; and I, to confess myself corrected and assured, so far as was needful raised my head more erect to speak. But a sight appeared which held me so fast to itself, to look on it, that I did not bethink me of my confession.

As through transparent and polished glasses, or through clear and tranquil waters, not so deep that their bed be lost, the lineaments of our faces return so faintly, that a pearl on a white brow comes not less readily to our eyes, such I saw many faces eager to speak; wherefore I ran into the contrary error to that which kindled love between the man and the fountain.[1]  At once, as soon as I was aware of them, supposing them mirrored faces, I turned round my eyes to see of whom they were, and saw nothing; and I turned them forward again, straight into the light of my sweet guide who, with a smile, was glowing in her holy eyes. "Do not wonder that I smile," she said to me, "at thy childish thought, since thy foot does not trust itself yet upon the truth, but turns thee, as it is wont, to emptiness.  These which thou seest are real substances, relegated here for failure in their vows.  Therefore speak with them, and hear, and believe; for the veracious light which satisfies them does not allow them to turn their feet from itself."

And I directed myself to the shade that seemed most eager to speak, and I began, like a man whom an excessive desire confuses: "O well-created spirit, who in the rays of life eternal art tasting the sweetness, which if not tasted is never understood, it will be gracious to me, if thou content me with thy name, and with your lot." Whereon she promptly, and with smiling eyes: "Our charity does not lock its door to a just wish, any more than that which wills that

1. Narcissus conceived the image to be a true face; Dante takes the real faces to be reflections of persons behind him.  According to Dante's cosmology, derived from Pliny, the inferior planets (Moon, Mercury, Venus) are within the shadow of the earth (capable of being eclipsed by it).  Therefore the spirits *manifested* in these spheres appear to Dante in more material (earthly) form than those above, and these spirits in the Moon, as the lowest, are nearest to material form.

all its court be like itself. In the world I was a virgin Sister, and if thy memory look back well, my being more beautiful will not conceal me from thee; but thou wilt recognize that I am Piccarda,[2] who, placed here with these other blessed ones, am blessed in the slowest sphere. Our affections, which are inflamed only in the pleasure of the Holy Spirit, rejoice in being formed according to His order; and this lot, which appears so far down, is given to us, because our vows were neglected and void in some particular." Whereon I to her: "In your marvellous aspects there shines I know not what divine which transmutes you from our former conceptions; therefore I was not swift in remembering; but now that which thou sayest to me assists me, so that to reshape is easier to me. But tell me, ye who are happy here, do ye desire a more exalted place, in order to see more, or to make for yourselves more friends?" With those other shades she first smiled a little, then answered me so glad, that she seemed to burn in the first fire of love: "Brother, virtue of charity quiets our will, and makes us wish only for that which we have, and quickens not our thirst for aught else. If we desired to be more on high, our desires would be discordant with the will of Him who assigns us here, which thou wilt see is not possible in these circles, if to exist in charity is here of necessity, and if thou dost well consider its nature. Nay, it is the essence of this blessed existence to hold itself within the divine will, whereby our wills themselves are made one. So that as we are, from seat to seat throughout this realm, to all the realm is pleasing, as to the King who inwills us with His will; and His will is our peace; it is that sea whereunto everything is moving which It creates and which nature makes."

Then was it clear to me, how everywhere in Heaven is Paradise, even if the grace of the Supreme Good does not there rain down in one measure.

But as it happens, if one food sates, and for another the appetite still remains, that this is asked for, and thanks returned for that; even thus did I, with act and with word, to learn from her, what was the web wherein she had not drawn the shuttle to the end. "Perfect life and high desert enheaven a lady[3] higher up," she said to me, "according to whose rule, in your world below, there are who vest and veil themselves, in order that, even till death, they may wake and sleep with that Spouse who accepts every vow which love conforms unto His pleasure. A young girl, I fled from the world to follow her, and in her garb I enclosed myself, and pledged me to the pathway of her Order. Afterward men, more used to ill than good, dragged me forth from the sweet cloister;[4] and God

2. The sister of Corso Donati and a relative of Dante's wife, Gemma dei Donati.

3. Santa Clara, the friend of St. Francis, who, in 1212, established under his direction a religious order for virgins, of extreme austerity.

4. According to the old commentators, her brother Corso forces Piccarda by violence to leave the convent, in order to make a marriage which he desired for her.

knows what then my life became. And this other splendor, which shows itself to thee at my right side, and which is enkindled with all the light of our sphere, understands of herself that which I say of me. She was a Sister; and from her head in like manner the shadow of the sacred veil was taken. But after she too was returned unto the world, against her liking and against good usage, she was never loosed from the veil of the heart. This is the light of the great Constance,[5] who from the second wind of Swabia conceived the third and the last power."

Thus she spoke to me, and then began singing "Ave Maria," and singing vanished, as through deep water some heavy thing. My sight, that followed her so far as was possible, after it lost her, turned to the mark of greater desire, and wholly reverted to Beatrice; but she so flashed upon my gaze that at first my sight endured it not: and this made me more slow in questioning.

CANTO IV

*Doubts of Dante, respecting the justice of Heaven and the abode of the blessed, solved by Beatrice. — Question of Dante as to the possibility of reparation for broken vows.*

CANTO V

*The sanctity of vows, and the seriousness with which they are to be made or changed. — Ascent to the Heaven of Mercury. — The shade of Justinian.*

CANTO VI

*Justinian tells of his own life. — The story of the Roman Eagle. — Spirits in the planet Mercury. — Romeo.*

CANTO VII

*Discourse of Beatrice. — The Fall of Man. — The scheme of his Redemption.*

CANTO VIII

*Ascent to the Heaven of Venus. — Spirits of Lovers. — Source of the order and the varieties in mortal things.*

CANTO IX

*The Heaven of Venus. — Conversation of Dante with Cunizza da Romano. — With Folco of Marseilles. — Rahab. — Avarice of the Papal Court.*

5. Daughter of the king of Sicily, Roger I; married, in 1186, to the emperor, Henry VI, the son of Frederick Barbarossa, and father of Frederick II, who died in 1250, the last emperor of his line.

CANTO X

*Ascent to the Sun. — Spirits of the wise, and the learned in theology. — St. Thomas Aquinas. — He names to Dante those who surround him.*

Looking upon His Son with the Love which the one and the other eternally breathe forth, the primal and ineffable Power made everything which revolves through the mind or through space with such order that he who contemplates it cannot be without taste of Him.  Lift then thy sight, Reader, with me to the lofty wheels, straight to that region where the one motion strikes on the other; [1] and there begin to gaze with delight on the art of that Master who within Himself so loves it that His eye never departs from it.  See how from that point the oblique circle [2] which bears the planets branches off, to satisfy the world which calls on them; and if their road were not bent, much virtue in the heavens would be in vain, and well-nigh every potency dead here below; and if its departure were more or less distant from the straight line, much of the order of the world, both below and above, would be defective.  Now remain, Reader, upon thy bench, pursuing in thought that which is foretasted if thou wouldst be glad far sooner than weary.  I have set before thee; henceforth feed thou thyself, for that theme whereof I have been made the scribe wrests all my care unto itself.

The greatest minister of nature, which imprints the world with the worth of the heavens, and with his light measures the time for us, conjoined with that region which is mentioned above, was circling through the spirals in which from day to day he earlier presents himself. [3]  And I was with him; but of the ascent I was not aware, otherwise than is a man, before his first thought, aware of its coming.  It is Beatrice who thus conducts from good to better, so instantaneously that her act does not extend through time.

How lucent in itself must that have been which was apparent not by color but by light within the sun where I had entered!  Though I should call on genius, art, and use, I could not tell it so that it could ever be imagined; but one may believe it, and let him long to see it.  And if our fancies are low for such loftiness, it is no marvel for beyond the sun there was never eye could go.  Such was here the fourth [4] family of the exalted Father, who always satisfies it, showing how He breathes forth, and how He begets.  And Beatrice

1. The Sun in Aries is at the intersection of the ecliptic and the equator of the celestial sphere.
2. The zodiac.
3.            "Where the Sun rose to-day
   He comes no more, but with a cozening line,
   Steals by that point, and so is serpentine."
             Donne, *An Anatomie of the World.*
4. Dante is now in the fourth sphere, the Sun, having passed through the Moon, Mercury, and Venus.

began: "Give thanks, give thanks to the Sun of the Angels, who to this visible one has raised thee by His grace." Heart of mortal was never so disposed to devotion, and so ready, with its whole will, to render itself up to God, as I became at those words; and all my love was so set on Him that it eclipsed Beatrice in oblivion. It did not displease her; but she so smiled thereat that the splendor of her smiling eyes divided upon many things my mind intent on one.

I saw many living and surpassing effulgences make of us a centre, and make of themselves a crown; more sweet in voice than shining in aspect. Thus girt we sometimes see the daughter of Latona, when the air is so impregnate that it holds the thread which makes her zone.[5] In the court of Heaven, wherefrom I return, are found many jewels so precious and beautiful that they cannot be brought from the kingdom, and of these was the song of those lights. Let him who does not wing himself so that he may fly up thither, await tidings thence from the dumb.

After those blazing suns, thus singing, had circled three times round about us, like stars near to the fixed poles, they seemed to me as ladies not released from a dance, but who stop silent, listening till they have caught the new notes. And within one I heard begin: "Since the ray of grace, by which true love is kindled, and which then in loving grows multiplied, so shines on thee that it conducts thee upward by that stair which, without reascending, no one descends,[6] he who should deny to thee the wine of his flask for thy thirst, would not be more at liberty than water which descends not to the sea. Thou wishest to know with what plants this garland is enflowered, which, round about her, gazes with delight upon the beautiful Lady who strengthens thee for heaven. I was of the lambs of the holy flock which Dominic leads along the way where they fatten well if they do not stray. This one who is nearest to me on the right was my brother and master; and he was Albert of Cologne,[7] and I Thomas of Aquino.[8] If thus of all the rest thou wouldst be informed, come, following my speech, with thy sight circling around upon the blessed wreath. That next flaming issues from the smile of Gratian, who so aided one court and the other that it pleases in Paradise.[9] The next, who at his side adorns our choir, was that Peter who, like the poor woman, offered his treasure to Holy Church.[10] The fifth light, which is most beautiful among us, breathes from such love that

5. The halo on the Moon.
6. The poet is, therefore, certain of Heaven after death.
7. Albertus Magnus, styled *Doctor Universalis* (A.D. 1193–1280).
8. St. Thomas Aquinas, *Doctor Angelicus* (A.D. 1225–1274).
9. An Italian Benedictine monk of the twelfth century who compiled the *Decretum Gratiani*, composed of texts of Scripture, of the Canons of the Church, of Decretals of the Popes, and of extracts from the Fathers, designed to established the agreement of the civil and canon law.

10. Peter Lombard, a theologian of the twelfth century. In the proem to his work he says that he desired, "like the poor widow" (Luke 21: 1–4), "to cast something from his penury into the treasury of the Lord."

all the world there below is greedy to know tidings of it:[11] within it is the lofty mind wherein wisdom so profound was put, that, if the truth be true, to see so much no second has arisen.[12]   At its side behold the light of that candle which, below in the flesh, saw most inwardly the angelic nature, and its ministry.[13]   In the next little light smiles that advocate of the Christian times, with whose discourse Augustine provided himself.[14]   Now if thou leadest the eye of the mind, following my praises, from light to light, thou stayest already thirsting for the eighth.   Therewithin, through seeing every good, the holy soul rejoices which makes the fallacious world manifest to him who hearkens to it well.[15]   The body whence it was chased out lies below in Cieldauro,[16] and from martyrdom and from exile it came to this peace.   Beyond, see flaming the glowing breath of Isidore, of Bede, and of Richard who in contemplation was more than man.[17]   This one from whom thy look returns to me is the light of a spirit to whom, in his grave thoughts, it seemed that death came slow.   It is the eternal light of Siger,[18] who, reading in the Street of Straw, syllogized invidious truths."

Then, as a horologe which calls us at the hour when the Bride of God [19] rises to sing matins to her Bridegroom that he may love her, in which the one part draws and urges the other, sounding *ting! ting!* with such sweet note that the well-disposed spirit swells with love, so did I see the glorious wheel move, and render voice to voice in concord and in sweetness which cannot be known save there where joy is everlasting.

CANTO XI

*The Vanity of worldly desires. — St. Thomas Aquinas undertakes to solve two doubts perplexing Dante. — He narrates the life of St. Francis of Assisi.*

O insensate care of mortals! how defective are those syllogisms which make thee downward beat thy wings!   One was going after

11. Doctors of the Church debated whether Solomon was among the blessed or the damned.

12. 1 Kings 3:12.

13. Dionysius the Areopagite, the disciple of St. Paul (Acts 17:34), to whom was ascribed *On the Celestial Hierarchy*.

14. Paulus Orosius wrote at the request of St. Augustine his *History against the Pagans*.

15. Boethius, see above, pp. 45–57.

16. The church of S. Pietro in Cielo d' Oro — St. Peter's of the Golden Ceiling — in Pavia.

17. Isidore of Seville, died in 636; on Bede, see above, pp. 131–146; Richard, prior of the Monastery of St. Victor, at Paris, a mystic of the twelfth century.

18. Siger of Brabant in the thirteenth century gave instruction in the Rue du Fouarre.   The meaning of "invidious truths" is uncertain.

19. The Church.

the laws, and one after the aphorisms,[1] and one following the priesthood, and one to reign by force or by sophisms, and one to rob, and
one to civic business, one, involved in pleasure of the flesh, was
wearying himself, and one was giving himself to idleness, when I,
loosed from all these things, with Beatrice, up in Heaven was thus
gloriously received.

After each had returned to that point of the circle at which it was
at first, it stayed still, as a candle in a candlestick. And within that
light which first had spoken to me I heard, as making itself more
clear, it smiling began: "Even as I am resplendent with its radiance,
so, looking into the Eternal Light, I apprehend whence is the occasion
of thy thoughts. Thou art perplexed, and hast the wish that my
speech be explained in language so open and so full that it may be
level to thy sense, where I said just now: 'Where they fatten well,'
and there where I said: 'No second has been born;' and here is need
that one distinguish well.

"The Providence which governs the world with that counsel,
in which every created vision is vanquished ere it reach its depth,
in order that the Bride of Him, who with loud cries[2] espoused her
with His blessed blood, might go toward her beloved, secure in
herself and also more faithful to Him, ordained two princes in her
favor, who on this side and that should be to her for guides. The
one was all seraphic in ardor,[3] the other, through wisdom, was
on earth a splendor of cherubic light.[4] I will speak of one, because
in praising one, whichever be taken, both are spoken of, for to one
end were their works.

"Between the Tupino and the water[5] which descends from the
hill chosen by the blessed Ubald, hangs the fertile slope of a high
mountain, wherefrom Perugia at Porta Sole[6] feels cold and heat,
while behind it Nocera and Gualdo weep because of their heavy
yoke.[7] From this slope, where it most breaks its steepness, a Sun
rose upon the world, as this one sometimes does from the Ganges.
Wherefore let him who talks of this place not say Ascesi,[8] which
were to speak short, but Orient, if he would speak properly. He
was not yet very far from his rising when he began to make the
earth feel some comfort from his great virtue: for, while still a
youth, he ran into strife with his father for sake of a lady[9] such as

1. The Aphorisms of Hippocrates, meaning here, the study of medicine.
2. Matthew 27:46 and 50.
3. St. Francis of Assisi. The seraphs burn with ardent love.
4. St. Dominic. The cherubs shine with the splendor of the radiance
of knowledge of God.
5. The Chiassi, which flows from the hill near Gubbio, chosen for his
hermitage by St. Ubald.
6. The mountain makes it hot in summer, and cold in winter.
7. Little towns held in subjection by Perugia.
8. So the name of Assisi was sometimes spelled, and here with a play
on *ascesi* (as if from *ascendere*) "I rose."
9. Lady Poverty, to whom Francis vowed allegiance.

to whom, as unto death, no one unlocks the gate of pleasure; and before his spiritual court *et coram patre* [10] he was united to her; and thereafter from day to day he loved her more ardently. She, deprived of her first husband,[11] for eleven hundred years and more, despised and obscure, even till him had remained unwooed; nor had it availed to hear, that he, who caused fear to all the world, found her undisturbed with Amyclas at the sound of his voice; [12] nor had it availed to have been constant and undaunted, so that, where Mary remained below, she mounted on the cross with Christ.

"But that I may not proceed too obscurely, henceforth in my diffuse speech take Francis and Poverty for these lovers. Their concord and their glad semblances made love, and wonder, and sweet regard to be the cause of holy thoughts; so that the venerable Bernard first bared his feet,[13] and ran following such great peace, and, running, it seemed to him that he was slow. O unknown riches! O fertile good! Egidius [14] bares his feet and Sylvester bares his feet, following the bridegroom; so pleasing is the bride. Then that father and that master goes on his way with his lady, and with that family which the humble cord was now girding.[15] Nor did baseness of heart weigh down his brow for being the son of Pietro Bernardone,[16] nor for appearing marvellously despised; but royally he opened his hard intention to Innocent, and from him received the first seal for his Order.[17] After the poor folk had increased behind him, whose marvellous life would be better sung in the glory of the heavens, the holy purpose of this archimandrite was adorned with a second crown by the Eternal Spirit, through Honorius.[18] And after that, through thirst for martyrdom, he had preached Christ and the others who followed him, in the proud presence of the Sultan,[19] and because he found the people too unripe for conversion, and in order not to stay in vain, had returned to the fruit of the Italian herbage. On the harsh rock,[20] between the Tiber and the Arno, he received from Christ the last seal,[21] which his limbs bore for two

10. Before the Bishop of Assisi, and "in presence of his father," he renounced his worldly possessions.

11. Christ.

12. When Caesar knocked at the door of Amyclas his voice caused no alarm because Poverty made the fisherman secure (Lucan *Pharsalia* v. 515 ff.).

13. Bernard, a wealthy citizen of Assisi, was his first disciple.

14. The blessed Giles of Assisi.

15. The cord for their girdle, whence the Franciscans were called Cordeliers.

16. For being the son of a rich father.

17. In or about 1210 Pope Innocent III approved the Rule of St. Francis.

18. In 1223, Honorius III confirmed the sanction of the Order.

19. Francis, with some of his followers, accompanied the crusaders of the Fifth Crusade to Egypt in 1219.

20. Mount Alvernia, in the Casentino, the upper valley of the Arno.

21. The Stigmata.

years. When it pleased Him, who had allotted him to such great good, to draw him up to the reward which he had gained in making himself lowly, he commended his most dear lady to his brethren as to rightful heirs, and commanded them to love her faithfully; and from her bosom his illustrious soul willed to depart, returning to its realm, and for his body he willed no other bier.

"Think now what he was, who was a worthy colleague to keep the bark of Peter on the deep sea to its right aim! And this was our Patriarch:[22] wherefore thou canst see that whoever follows him as he commands loads good merchandise. But his flock has become so greedy of strange food that it cannot but be scattered over diverse meadows; and the farther his sheep, remote and vagabond, go from him, the more empty of milk do they return to the fold. Some of them indeed there are who fear the harm, and keep close to the shepherd; but they are so few that little cloth furnishes their cowls. Now if my words are not faint, if thy hearing has been attentive, if thou recallest to mind that which I have said, thy wish will be content in part, because thou wilt see the plant wherefrom they are hewn, and thou wilt see how the wearer of the thong[23] reasons — 'Where they fatten well if they do not stray.'"

CANTO XII

*Second circle of the spirits of wise religious men, doctors of the Church and teachers. — St. Bonaventura narrates the life of St. Dominic, and tells the names of those who form the circle with him.*

CANTO XIII

*St. Thomas Aquinas speaks again, and explains the relation of the wisdom of Solomon to that of Adam and of Christ, and declares the vanity of human judgment.*

CANTO XIV

*At the prayer of Beatrice, Solomon tells of the glorified bodies of the blessed after the Last Judgment. — Ascent to the Heaven of Mars. — Souls of the Soldiery of Christ in the form of a Cross with the figure of Christ thereon. — Hymn of the Spirits.*

CANTO XV

*Dante is welcomed by his ancestor, Cacciaguida. — Cacciaguida tells of his family, and of the simple life of Florence in the old days.*

22. St. Dominic. The speaker, St. Thomas, was a Dominican.
23. Distinguishing mark of the Dominicans.

"To the Father, to the Son, and to the Holy Spirit be glory," all Paradise began, so that the sweet song was inebriating me. That which I was seeing seemed to me a smile of the universe; for my inebriation was entering through the hearing and through the sight. O joy! O ineffable gladness! O life entire of love and of peace! O riches secure, without longing! [1]

Before my eyes the four torches were standing enkindled, and that which had come first began to make itself more vivid, and in its semblance became such as Jupiter would become, if he and Mars were birds, and should exchange plumage.[2] The Providence which here assigns turn and office, had imposed silence on the blessed choir on every side, when I heard: "If I change color, marvel not; for, as I speak, thou shalt see all these change color. He who on earth usurps my place, my place, my place, which is vacant in the presence of the Son of God,[3] has made of my cemetery a sewer of blood and of filth, wherewith the Perverse One who fell from here above, below there is placated."

With that color which, by reason of the opposite sun, paints the cloud at evening and at morning, I then saw the whole Heaven overspread. And as a modest lady who abides sure of herself, and at the fault of another, on only hearing of it, becomes timid, thus did Beatrice change semblance; and such eclipse, I believe, there was in heaven when the Supreme Power suffered.

1. Dante and Beatrice are in the sphere of the fixed stars, where the saints are manifested.

2. The pure white light becoming red, as if the planet Jupiter were to change color with Mars.

3. Dante held that Boniface VIII had no right to the papal throne, because his election to it lacked validity, having taken place while Celestine V, his predecessor, was still alive, and having been secured by bribery and deception.

Then his words proceeded, in a voice so transmuted from itself that his countenance was not more changed: "The Bride of Christ was not nurtured on my blood, and that of Linus and of Cletus, to be employed for acquist of gold; but for acquist of this glad life Sixtus and Pius and Calixtus and Urban [4] shed their blood after much weeping. It was not our intention that part of the Christian people should sit on the right hand of our successors, and part on the other; nor that the keys which were entrusted to me should become a device upon a banner which should fight against the baptized; [5] nor that I should be made a figure on a seal to venal and mendacious privileges, whereat I often redden and flash. Rapacious wolves, in garb of shepherd, are seen from here on high over all the pastures: O defence of God, why dost thou yet lie still! To drink our blood Cahorsines and Gascons are making ready; [6] O good beginning, to what vile end must thou fall! But the high Providence, which with Scipio defended for Rome the glory of the world, will succor speedily, as I conceive. And thou, son, who because of thy mortal weight wilt again return below, open thy mouth, and conceal not that which I conceal not."

Even as our air snows down flakes of frozen vapors, when the horn of the Goat of heaven is touched by the sun,[7] so I saw the aether become adorned, and flaked upward with the triumphant vapors which had made sojourn there with us. My sight was following their semblances, and followed, till the intermediate space by its vastness took from it the power of passing farther onward. Whereon my Lady, who saw me freed from gazing upward, said to me: "Cast down thy sight, and look how thou hast revolved."

I saw that, since the hour when I had first looked, I had moved through the whole arc which the first climate makes from its middle to its end; [8] so that beyond Cadiz I saw the mad track of Ulysses, and on the other side almost the shore [9] on which Europa became a sweet burden. And more of the site of this little threshing-floor would have been discovered to me, but the sun was proceeding beneath my feet, a sign and more removed.[10]

My enamored mind, that ever pays court to my Lady, was more than ever burning to bring back my eyes to her. And if nature or art has made bait in human flesh or in paintings of it, to catch the eyes in order to possess the mind, all united would seem naught compared to the divine pleasure which shone upon me when I turned me to her smiling face. And the virtue which that look vouchsafed to me,

4. Early Popes, martyred for the faith.
5. Boniface VIII waged war against the Colonna family.
6. John XXII, Pope from 1316 to 1334, was a native of Cahors; his immediate predecessor, Clement V, 1305–1314, was a Gascon.
7. In midwinter, when the Sun is in Capricorn.
8. Ninety degrees, a distance supposed to be comprised between Jerusalem and Cadiz, or six hours in the Sun's journey.
9. The coast of Phoenicia, whence Europa was carried off by Jupiter.
10. The region beyond it was in the shadow of night.

tore me from the fair nest of Leda,[11] and impelled me to the swiftest heaven.[12]

Its parts, most living and lofty, are so uniform that I cannot tell which of them Beatrice chose for a place for me. But she, who saw my desire, began, smiling so glad that God seemed to rejoice in her countenance: "The nature of the universe which holds the centre quiet, and moves all the rest around it, begins here as from its starting-point.[13] And this heaven has no other Where than the Divine Mind, wherein is kindled the love that revolves it, and the virtue which it rains down. Light and love enclose it with one circle, even as it does the others, and of that cincture He who girds it is the sole Intelligence.[14] The motion of this heaven is not marked out by another, but the others are measured by this, just as ten by its half and by its fifth. And how time can have its roots in such a flower-pot, and in the others its leaves, may now be manifest to thee.

"O covetousness,[15] which dost so whelm mortals beneath thee, that no one has power to withdraw his eyes from out thy waves! Well does the will blossom in men, but the continual rain converts the true plums into blighted fruit. Faith and innocence are found only in children; then each flies away before the cheeks are covered. One, so long as he lisps, keeps the fasts, who afterward, when his tongue is loosed, devours whatever food under whatever moon; and one, while he lisps, loves his mother and listens to her, who afterward, when his speech is perfect, desires to see her buried. So the skin of the fair daughter of him who brings morning and leaves evening, white in its first aspect, becomes black.[16] Do thou, in order that thou make no marvel of it, reflect that on earth there is no one who governs; wherefore the human family goes thus astray. But ere January be all un-wintered by that hundredth part which is down there neglected,[17] these supernal circles shall so roar that the storm which has been so long awaited shall turn round the sterns to where the prows are, so that the fleet shall run straight, and true fruit shall come after the flower."

11. From the constellation of Gemini, the twin sons of Leda.

12. The *primum mobile,* or Crystalline Heaven.

13. The properties inherent in the universe, by virtue of which its centre, the earth, is immovable while all the rest of the material creation revolves around it, have their origin here.

14. The angelic intelligences are the agents who move the lower heavens, but over the Empyrean, God himself immediately presides.

15. The transition is not unnatural, from the consideration of the Heaven which pours down Divine influence, to the thought of the engrossment of men in the pursuit of their selfish and transitory ends.

16. "The human race is the child of heaven . . . for man and the sun beget man according to [Aristotle *Physics* ii. 2]" (*De monarchia* i. 9).

17. Before January falls in spring, owing to the error in the calendar, corrected in 1582, by which the year was lengthened by about a day in each century.

CANTO XXVIII

## *The Heavenly Hierarchy*

After she who imparadises my mind had disclosed the truth counter
to the present life of wretched mortals; as one who sees in a mirror
the flame of a torch which is lighted behind him, ere he has it in
sight or in thought, and turns round to see if the glass tell him
the truth, and sees that it accords with it as the note with its measure;
so my memory recollects that I did, looking into the beautiful eyes,
wherewith Love made the cord to capture me. And when I turned,
and mine were touched by what is apparent in that sphere whenever
one gazes fixedly on its circling, I saw a Point which was raying out
light so keen that the sight on which it blazes must need close because of its intense keenness. And whatever star seems smallest
from here would seem a moon if placed beside it, as star with star
is placed. Perhaps as near as a halo seems to girdle the light which
paints it, when the vapor that bears it is most dense, at such distance
around the Point a circle of fire was whirling so rapidly that it would
have surpassed that motion which most swiftly girds the world; and
this was girt around by another, and that by the third, and the third
then by the fourth, by the fifth the fourth, and then by the sixth the
fifth. Thereon the seventh followed, so widespread now in compass
that the messenger of Juno entire [1] would be narrow to contain it.
So the eighth and the ninth; and each was moving more slowly, according as it was in number more distant from the unit. [2] And that
one had the clearest flame from which the Pure Spark was least distant; I believe because it partakes more of Its truth.

My Lady, who saw me deeply suspense in heed, said: "On that
Point Heaven and all nature are dependent. Look on that circle
which is most conjoined to It, and know that its motion is so swift
because of the burning love whereby it is spurred." And I to her:
"If the world were disposed in the order which I see in those wheels,
that which is set before me would have satisfied me; but in the world
of sense the revolutions may be seen so much the more divine as
they are more remote from the centre. Wherefore if my desire is
to have end in this marvellous and angelic temple, which has for
confine only love and light, I need yet to hear why the example and
the examplar go not in one fashion, because by myself I contemplate
this in vain." [3] "If thy fingers are insufficient for such a knot, it is
no wonder, so hard has it become through not being tried." Thus
my Lady; then she said: "Take that which I shall tell thee, if thou
wouldest be satisfied, and sharpen thy wit about it. The corporeal
circles are wide or narrow according to the more or less of virtue
which is diffused through all their parts. Greater goodness must

1. Iris, the rainbow.
2. These circles of fire are the nine orders of the angels.
3. The angelic circles are the example, or pattern; the spheres of the
material universe are the examplar, or copy.

work greater weal; the greater body, if it has its parts equally complete, contains the greater weal. Hence this one, which sweeps along with itself all the rest of the universe, corresponds to the circle which loves most, and knows most.[4] Therefore, if thou draw thy measure round the virtue, not round the appearance of the beings which seem circular to thee, thou wilt see in each heaven a marvelous agreement with its Intelligence, of greater to more and of smaller to less." [5]

As the hemisphere of the air remains splendid and serene when Boreas blows from that cheek wherewith he is mildest,[6] whereby the mist which before troubled it is cleared and dissolved, so that the heaven smiles to us with the beauties of its every region, so I became after my Lady had provided me with her clear answer, and, like a star in heaven, the truth was seen.

And after her words had stopped, not otherwise does molten iron throw out sparks than the circles sparkled. Every scintillation followed its blaze, and they were so many that their number was of more thousands than the doubling of the chess.[7] I hear Hosannah sung from choir to choir to the fixed Point that holds them, and will forever hold them, at the *Ubi* [8] in which they have ever been. And she, who saw the questioning thoughts within my mind, said: "The first circles have shown to thee the Seraphim and the Cherubim.[9] Thus swiftly they follow their own bonds, in order to liken themselves to the Point as most they can, and they can in proportion as they are exalted to see. Those other loves, which go around them, are called Thrones of the divine aspect, because they terminated the first triad. And thou shouldst know that all have delight in proportion as their vision penetrates into the Truth in which every understanding is at rest. Hence may be seen how beatitude is founded on the act which sees, not on that which loves, which follows after. And the merit, to which grace and good-will give birth, is the measure of this seeing; thus is the progress from grade to grade.

"The next triad, that in like manner bourgeons in this sempiternal

4. The ninth sphere, the greatest of all, corresponds in its superior virtue with the first and innermost circle of the angelic hierarchy, that of the seraphim.

5. Each sphere of the material heavens in proportion to its size corresponds to each circle of the angelic intelligences in proportion to the nearness of the latter to God.

6. The northeast wind was held to clear the sky of clouds.

7. A story that the inventor of the game asked, as his reward from the King of Persia, a grain of wheat for the first square of the board, two for the second, four for the third, and so on with successive duplication to the last or sixty-fourth square. The number reached by this process extends to twenty figures.

8. The *where,* the appointed place.

9. Beatrice is now describing the celestial hierarchy, popularized by the treatise generally ascribed to Dionysius the Areopagite (see *Paradise,* Canto x) to whom, it was believed, St. Paul communicated the knowledge concerning heavenly things which he had gained when caught up to Heaven (2 Cor. 12:2–4).

spring which the nightly Aries despoils not,[10] perpetually sing Hosannah with three melodies, which sound in the three orders of joy wherewith it is three-fold. In this hierarchy are the three divinities, first Dominations, and then Virtues; the third order is of Powers. Then, in the two penultimate dances, the Principalities and Archangels circle; the last is wholly of Angelic sports. These orders all gaze upward, and downward so prevail, that toward God all are drawn, and all draw. And Dionysius with such great desire set himself to contemplate these orders, that he named and divided them, as I. But Gregory [11] afterward separated from him; wherefore, so soon as he opened his eyes in this Heaven, he smiled at himself. And if a mortal declared on earth so much of secret truth, I would not have thee wonder, for he who saw it here on high disclosed it to him, with much else of the truth of these circles."

### CANTO XXIX

*Discourse of Beatrice concerning the creation and nature of the Angels. — She reproves the presumption and foolishness of preachers.*

### CANTO XXX

*Ascent to the Empyrean. — The River of Light. — The celestial Rose. — The seat of Henry VII. — The last words of Beatrice.*

The sixth hour is glowing perhaps six thousand miles distant from us, and this world now inclines its shadow almost to a level bed, when the mid heaven, deep above us, begins to become such that some one star loses its show so far as to this depth; and as the brightest handmaid of the sun comes farther on, so the heaven is closed from light to light, even to the most beautiful. Not otherwise the Triumph, that plays forever round the Point which vanquished me, seeming enclosed by that which it encloses, was extinguished little by little to my sight; [1] wherefore my seeing nothing and my love constrained me to turn with my eyes to Beatrice. If what has been said of her so far as here were all included in a single praise, it would be little to furnish forth this turn. The beauty which I saw transcends measure not only beyond our reach, but surely I believe that its Maker alone can enjoy it all.

By this pass I concede myself vanquished more than ever comic or tragic poet was overcome by crisis of his theme. For as the sun does to the sight which trembles most, even so remembrance of the sweet smile deprives my memory of its very self. From the first day when in this life I saw her face, until this sight, the following

10. At the autumnal equinox, the time of frosts, Aries, the Ram, is the sign in which the night rises.
11. Pope Gregory I differed slightly from Dionysius in his arrangement of the orders of the heavenly host.
1. Losing itself in the light that streams from the Divine point.

with my song has not been cut off for me, but now needs must my pursuit desist from further following her beauty in my verse, as at his utmost every artist.

Such, as I leave her for a greater heralding than that of my trumpet, which is bringing its arduous theme to a close, with act and voice of a leader whose talk is accomplished she began again: "We have issued forth from the greatest body to the Heaven which is pure light: light intellectual full of love, love of true good full of joy, joy which transcends every sweetness. Here thou shalt see the one and the other soldiery of Paradise; and the one in those aspects which thou shalt see at the Last Judgment." [2]

As a sudden flash which scatters the spirits of the sight so that it deprives the eye of the action of the strongest objects, so did a vivid light shine round about me, leaving me swathed with such a veil of its own effulgence that nothing was visible to me.

"The Love which quieteth this Heaven always welcomes to itself with such a salutation, in order to make the candle fit for its flame." No sooner had these brief words come within me than I comprehended that I was surmounting above my own power; and I re-kindled me with a new vision, such that no light is so pure that my eyes could not have withstood it. And I saw light in form of a river glowing with effulgence, between two banks painted with marvellous spring. From this stream were issuing living sparks, and on every side were setting themselves in the flowers, like rubies which gold encompasses. Then, as if inebriated by the odors, they plunged again into the wonderful flood, and as one was entering another was issuing forth.

"The high desire which now inflames and urges thee to have knowledge concerning that which thou seest, pleases me the more the more it swells; but thou must needs drink of this water before so great a thirst in thee be slaked." Thus the Sun of my eyes said to me; then added: "The stream, and the topazes which enter and issue, and the smiling of the herbage, are shadowy prefaces of their truth; not that these things are difficult in themselves, but there is defect on thy part that thou hast not yet vision so exalted."

There is no babe who so hastily springs with face toward the milk, if he awake much later than his wont, as I did, to make yet better mirrors of my eyes, stooping to the wave which flows in order that we may be bettered in it. And even as the eaves of my eyelids drank of it, so it seemed to me from its length to have become round. Then as folk who have been under masks, who seem other than before, if they divest themselves of the semblance not their own wherein they disappeared, in such wise for me the flowers and the sparks were changed into greater festival, so that I saw both the Courts of Heaven made manifest.

O splendor of God, through which I saw the high triumph of the true kingdom, give to me power to tell how I saw it!

Light is thereabove which makes the Creator visible to that crea-

2. Here the souls in bliss will be seen in their bodily shapes.

ture which has its peace only in seeing Him; and it spreads in circular shape so far that its circumference would be too large a girdle for the sun. Its whole appearance is made of a ray reflected from the summit of the First Moving Heaven, which from it takes its life and potency. And as a hill mirrors itself in water at its base, as if to see itself adorned, when it is rich with verdure and with flowers, so, above the light, round and round about, on more than a thousand seats, I saw mirrored, as they rose, all that of us have made return on high. And if the lowest row gather within itself so great a light, how vast is the spread of this rose in its outermost leaves! My sight lost not itself in the breadth and in the height, but took in all the quantity and the quality of that joy. There near and far nor add nor take away; for where God governs without intermediary the natural law is of no relevancy.

Into the yellow of the sempiternal rose, which spreads wide, rises in tiers, and breathes forth odor of praise unto the Sun that makes perpetual spring, Beatrice, like one who is silent and wishes to speak, drew me and said, "Behold, how vast is the convent of the white stoles! See our city, how wide its circuit! See our benches so full that few people are now wanting here. On that great seat, on which thou holdest thine eye because of the crown which already is set above it, ere thou dost sup at this wedding-feast, shall sit the soul (which on earth will be imperial) of the lofty Henry who, to set Italy straight, will come ere she is ready.[3] The blind cupidity which bewitches you has made you like the little child who dies of hunger, and drives away his nurse; and such a one will then be prefect in the divine forum that openly or covertly he will not go with him along one road;[4] but short while thereafter shall he be endured by God in the holy office; for he shall be thrust down there where Simon Magus is[5] for his deserts, and shall make him of Anagna[6] go lower."

CANTO XXXI

*The Rose of Paradise. — St. Bernard. — Prayer to Beatrice. — The glory of the Blessed Virgin.*

In form then of a pure white rose the holy host was shown to me, which, in His own blood, Christ made His bride. But the other,[1] which, flying, sees and sings the glory of Him who enamours it, and the goodness which made it so great, like a swarm of bees which one while inflower themselves and one while return to where their work acquires savor, were descending into the great flower which is adorned with so many leaves, and thence rising up again to where their love

3. Henry VII, elected emperor 1308, crowned at Milan 1311, died 1313.
4. The Pope, Clement V, for a time ostensibly supported Henry VII in his Italian expedition, but gradually in underhand fashion turned against him. He died in 1314.
5. In Hell, among the simoniacal Popes.
6. Pope Boniface VIII will be pushed down to make room.
1. The angelic host.

always abides.  They had their faces all of living flame, and their wings of gold, and the rest so white that no snow reaches that limit. When they descended into the flower, from bench to bench, they imparted of the peace and of the ardor which they acquired as they fanned their sides.  Nor did the interposing of so great a flying plenitude, between what was above and the flower, impede the sight or the splendor; for the divine light penetrates through the universe, according as it is worthy, so that naught can be an obstacle to it.  This secure and joyous realm, thronged with ancient and with modern folk, had its look and love all on one mark.

O Trinal Light, which in a single star, scintillating on their sight, dost so satisfy them, look down here upon our tempest!

If the Barbarians, coming from a region such that every day it is covered by Helicé,[2] revolving with her son of whom she is fond, when they beheld Rome and her lofty work, — what time Lateran rose above mortal things, — were wonder-struck, I, who to the divine from the human, to the eternal from the temporal, had come, and from Florence to a people just and sane, with what amazement must I have been full!  Truly what with it and with the joy I was well pleased not to hear, and to stand mute.  And as a pilgrim who is refreshed within the temple of his vow as he looks around, and hopes some day to report how it was, so, journeying through the living light, I carried my eyes over the ranks, now up, now down, and now circling about.  I saw faces persuasive to love, beautified by the light of Another and by their own smile, and actions graced with every dignity.

My look had now comprehended the general form of Paradise as a whole, and on no part had my sight as yet been fixed; and I turned me with rekindled wish to ask my Lady about things as to which my mind was in suspense.  One thing I purposed, and another answered me; I was thinking to see Beatrice, and I saw an old man, robed like the people in glory.  His eyes and his cheeks were overspread with benignant joy, his mien kindly such as befits a tender father.  And: "Where is she?" on a sudden said I.  Whereon he: "To terminate thy desire, Beatrice urged me from my place, and if thou lookest up to the third circle from the highest rank, thou wilt again see her upon the throne which her merits have allotted to her." Without answering I lifted up my eyes, and saw her as she made for herself a crown reflecting from herself the eternal rays.  From that region which thunders highest up no mortal eye is so far distant, in whatsoever sea it lets itself sink deepest, as there from Beatrice was my sight.  But this was naught to me, for her image did not descend to me blurred by aught between.

"O Lady, in whom my hope is strong, and who, for my salvation, didst endure to leave thy footprints in Hell, of all those things which I have seen through thy power and through thy goodness, I recognize

2. The constellation of the Great Bear: her son is Arctophylax or the Little Bear.  In the far north these constellations are always high in the heavens.

the grace and the virtue. Thou hast drawn me from servitude to liberty by all those ways, by all the modes whereby thou hadst the power to do it. Guard thou in me thine own magnificence so that my soul, which thou hast made whole, may, pleasing to thee, be unloosed from the body." Thus I prayed; and she, so distant, as it seemed, smiled and looked at me; then turned to the eternal fountain.

And the holy old man said: "In order that thou mayst complete perfectly thy journey, for which end prayer and holy love sent me, fly with thine eyes through this garden; for seeing it will prepare thy look to mount further through the divine radiance. And the Queen of Heaven, for whom I burn wholly with love, will grant us every grace, because I am her faithful Bernard." [3]

As is he who comes perchance from Croatia to see our Veronica,[4] who by reason of its ancient fame is never sated, but says in thought so long as it is shown: "My Lord Jesus Christ, true God, was then your semblance like to this?" such was I, gazing on the living charity of him, who, in this world, in contemplation, tasted of that peace.

"Son of Grace, this glad existence," began he, "will not be known to thee holding thine eyes only down here at the base, but look on the circles even to the most remote, until thou seest upon her seat the Queen to whom this realm is subject and devoted." I lifted up my eyes: and as at morning the eastern parts of the horizon surpass that where the sun declines, thus, as if going with my eyes from valley to mountain, I saw a part on the extreme verge vanquishing in light all the rest of the front. And even as there where the pole which Phaëthon guided ill is awaited,[5] the glow is brightest, and on this side and that the light diminishes, so that pacific oriflamme [6] was vivid at the middle, and on each side in equal measure the flame slackened. And at that mid part I saw more than a thousand jubilant Angels with wings outspread, each distinct both in effulgence and in act. I saw there, smiling at their sports and at their songs, a Beauty which was joy in the eyes of all the other saints. And if I had such wealth in speech as in imagining, I should not dare to attempt the least of its delightfulness.

Bernard, when he saw my eyes fixed and intent upon the object of his own burning glow, turned his own with such affection to it, that he made mine more ardent to gaze anew.

3. St. Bernard of Clairvaux, to whom, because of his fervent devotion to her, the Blessed Virgin had deigned to show herself during his life.

4. Shown at St. Peter's, on certain of the chief holy days.

5. Where the chariot of the Sun is about to rise.

6. That part of the rose of Paradise where the Virgin is seated.

CANTO XXXII

*St. Bernard describes the order of the Rose, and points out many of the Saints. — The children in Paradise. — The angelic festival. — The patricians of the Court of Heaven.*

With affection set on his Delight, that contemplator freely assumed the office of a teacher, and began these holy words: "The wound which Mary closed up and anointed, that one who is so beautiful at her feet is she who opened it and who pierced it. Beneath her, in the order which the third seats make, sits Rachel with Beatrice, as thou seest. Sara, Rebecca, Judith, and she [1] who was great-grand-mother of the singer who, through sorrow for his sin, said *Miserere mei,* [2] thou mayst see thus from rank to rank in gradation downward, as with the name of each I go downward through the rose from leaf to leaf. And from the seventh row downwards, even as down to it, Hebrew women follow in succession, dividing all the tresses of the flower; because these are the wall by which the sacred stairs are separated according to the look which faith turned on Christ. On this side, where the flower is mature with all its leaves, are seated those who believed in Christ about to come. On the other side, where the semicircles are broken by empty spaces, are those who turned their faces on Christ already come. And as on this side the glorious seat of the Lady of Heaven, and the other seats below it, make so great a division, thus, opposite, does the seat of the great John, who, ever holy, endured the desert and martyrdom, and then Hell for two years; [3] and beneath him Francis and Benedict and Augustine and others are allotted thus to divide, far down as here from circle to circle. Now behold the high divine foresight; for one and the other aspect of the faith will fill this garden equally. And know that downwards from the row which midway cleaves the two divisions, they [4] are seated for no merit of their own, but for that of others, under certain conditions; for all these are spirits absolved ere they had true power of choice. Well canst thou perceive it by their faces, and also by their childish voices, if thou lookest well upon them and if thou listenest to them. Now thou art perplexed, and in perplexity art silent; but I will loose for thee the strong bond in which thy subtle thoughts fetter thee. Within the amplitude of this realm a casual point can have no place, any more than sadness, or thirst, or hunger; for whatever thou seest is established by eternal law, so that here the ring answers exactly to the finger. And therefore this folk, hastened to true life, is not *sine causa* more and less excellent here among themselves. The King, through whom this

1. Ruth.
2. "Have mercy upon me" (Psalms 51:1).
3. The two years from the death of John to the death of Christ and his descent to Hell, to draw from the *limbus patrum* the souls predestined to salvation.
4. Children too young to have merit of their own.

realm reposes in such great love and in such great delight that no will dares for more, creating all the minds in His own glad aspect, endows with grace diversely according to His pleasure; and here let the fact suffice. And this is expressly and clearly noted for you in the Holy Scripture in the case of those twins who, within their mother, had their anger stirred.[5] Therefore, according to the color of the hair of such grace,[6] the highest light must need befittingly crown them. Without, then, merit from their own ways, they are placed in different grades, differing only in their primary keenness of vision.[7] In the early centuries, indeed, the faith of parents alone sufficed, together with innocence, to secure salvation; after the first ages were complete, it was needful for males, through circumcision, to acquire power for their innocent wings. But after the time of grace had come, without perfect baptism in Christ, such innocence was held back there below.[8]

"Look now upon the face which most resembles Christ, for only its brightness can prepare thee to see Christ."

I saw raining down on her such great joy, borne in the holy minds created to fly across through that height, that whatsoever I had seen before held me not suspended in such great wonder, nor showed to me such likeness unto God. And that Love which had before descended to her,[9] in front of her spread wide his wings, singing "*Ave, Maria, gratia plena.*" The blessed Court responded to the divine song from all sides, so that every countenance became thereby the more serene.

"O holy Father, who for me endurest to be here below, leaving the sweet place in which thou sittest by eternal allotment, who is that Angel who with such joy looks into the eyes of our Queen, so enamoured that he seems of fire?" Thus did I again recur to the teaching of him who was deriving beauty from Mary, as the morning star from the sun. And he to me, "Confidence and grace as much as there can be in Angel and in soul, are all in him, and we would have it so, for he it is [10] who bore the palm down to Mary, when the Son of God willed to load Himself with our burden.

"But come now with thine eyes, as I shall proceed speaking, and note the great patricians of this most just and pious empire. Those two who sit there above, most happy through being nearest to the Empress, are, as it were, two roots of this rose. He who on the left is next her is the Father because of whose audacious tasting the human race tastes so much bitterness. On the right see that ancient Father of Holy Church, to whom Christ entrusted the keys of this

5. Jacob and Esau. See Genesis 25:22, and Romans 9:11–12.
6. Jacob and Esau, who differed in color and skin.
7. In their innate capacity to see God, which is in proportion to the grace vouchsafed to them before birth.
8. In the limbo of children.
9. In the heaven of the fixed stars.
10. The angel Gabriel (Luke 1:26).

lovely flower. And he [11] who saw before his death all the grievous times of the fair bride, who was won with the spear and with the nails, sits at his side; and by the other rests that leader, under whom the ingrate, fickle and stubborn people lived on manna. Opposite Peter see Anna sitting, so content to gaze upon her daughter, that she moves not her eyes as she sings Hosannah; and opposite the eldest father of a family sits Lucia, who moved thy Lady, when thou didst bend thy brow to rush downward.

"But because the time flies which holds thee slumbering, here will we make a stop, like a good tailor who makes the gown according as he has cloth, and we will direct our eyes to the First Love, so that, looking towards Him, thou mayst penetrate so far as is possible through His effulgence. But, lest perchance, moving thy wings, thou go backward, believing to advance, it is needful that grace be obtained by prayer; grace from her who has the power to aid thee; and do thou follow me with thy affection so that thy heart depart not from my speech."

And he began this holy prayer.

## CANTO XXXIII

### Prayer to the Virgin. — The Beatific Vision. — The Ultimate Salvation.

"Virgin Mother, daughter of thine own Son, humble and exalted more than any creature, fixed term of the eternal counsel, thou art she who didst so ennoble human nature that its own Maker disdained not to become its creature. Within thy womb was rekindled the Love through whose warmth this flower has thus blossomed in the eternal peace. Here thou art to us the noonday torch of charity, and below, among mortals, thou art the living fount of hope. Lady, thou art so great, and so availest, that whoso would have grace, and has not recourse to thee, would have his desire fly without wings. Thy benignity not only succors him who asks, but oftentimes freely foreruns the asking. In thee mercy, in thee pity, in thee magnificence, in thee whatever of goodness is in any creature, are united. Now doth this man, who, from the lowest abyss of the universe, far even as here, has seen one after one the spiritual lives, supplicate thee of grace, for power such that he may be able with his eyes to uplift himself higher toward the Ultimate Salvation. And I, who never for my own vision burned more than I do for his, proffer to thee all my prayers, and pray that they be not scant, that with thy prayers thou wouldst dispel for him every cloud of his mortality, so that the Supreme Pleasure may be displayed to him. Further I pray thee, Queen, who canst whatso thou wilt, that, after so great a vision, thou wouldst preserve his affections sound. May thy guardianship

11. St. John the Evangelist, who witnessed and suffered from the persecutions that the early Church had to endure.

vanquish human impulses. Behold Beatrice with all the Blessed for my prayers clasp their hands to thee."

The eyes beloved and venerated by God, fixed on the speaker, showed to us how pleasing unto her are devout prayers. Then to the Eternal Light were they directed, to which it may not be believed that eye so clear of any creature enters in.

And I, who to the end of all desires was approaching, even as I ought, ended within myself the ardor of my longing. Bernard made a sign to me, and smiled, that I should look upward; but I was already, of myself, such as he wished; for my sight, becoming pure, was entering more and more through the radiance of the lofty Light which in Itself is true.

Thenceforward my vision was greater than our speech, which yields to such a sight, and the memory yields to such excess.

As is he who dreaming sees, and after the dream the passion remains imprinted, and the rest returns not to the mind, such am I; for my vision almost wholly departs, while the sweetness that was born of it yet distils within my heart. Thus the snow is by the sun unsealed; thus by the wind, on the light leaves, was lost the saying of the Sibyl.

O Supreme Light, that so high upliftest Thyself from mortal conceptions, re-lend to my mind a little of what Thou didst appear, and make my tongue so powerful that it may be able to leave one single spark of Thy glory for the folk to come; for, by returning somewhat to my memory and by sounding a little in these verses, more of Thy victory shall be conceived.

I think that by the keenness of the living ray which I endured, I should have been dazed if my eyes had been averted from it; and I remember that on this account I was the more hardy to sustain it till I conjoined my gaze with the Infinite Goodness.

O abundant Grace, whereby I presumed to fix my look through the Eternal Light till that there I consummated the seeing!

I saw that in its depth is enclosed, bound up with love in one volume, that which is dispersed in leaves through the universe; substance and accidents and their modes, fused together, as it were, in such wise, that that of which I speak is one simple Light. The universal form of this knot I believe that I saw, because, in saying this, I feel that I rejoice more spaciously. One single moment only is greater oblivion for me than five and twenty centuries to the emprise which made Neptune wonder at the shadow of Argo.[1]

Thus my mind, wholly rapt, was gazing fixed, motionless, and intent, and ever with gazing grew enkindled. In that Light one becomes such that it is impossible he should ever consent to turn himself from it for other sight; because the Good which is the object of the will is all collected in it, and outside of it that is defective which is perfect there.

1. Neptune wondered at the shadow of Argo because it was the first vessel that sailed the sea.

Now will my speech fall more short, even in respect to that which I remember, than that of an infant who still bathes his tongue at the breast. Not because more than one simple semblance was in the Living Light wherein I was gazing, which is always such as it was before; but through my sight, which was growing strong in me as I looked, one sole appearance, as I myself changed, was altering itself to me.

Within the profound and clear subsistence of the lofty Light appeared to me three circles of three colors and of one dimension; and one seemed reflected by the other, as Iris by Iris, and the third seemed fire which from the one and from the other is equally breathed forth.

O how inadequate is speech, and how feeble toward my conception! and this toward what I saw is such that it suffices not to call it little.

O Light Eternal, that sole abidest in Thyself, sole understandest Thyself, and, by Thyself understood and understanding, lovest and smilest on Thyself! That circle, which appeared in Thee generated as a reflected light, being awhile surveyed by my eyes, seemed to me depicted with our effigy within itself, of its own very color; wherefore my sight was wholly set upon it. As is the geometer who wholly applies himself to measure the circle, and finds not by thinking that principle of which he is in need, such was I at that new sight. I wished to see how the image was conformed to the circle, and how it has its place therein; but my own wings were not for this, had it not been that my mind was smitten by a flash in which its wish came.

To the high fantasy here power failed; but now my desire and my will were revolved, like a wheel which is moved evenly, by the Love which moves the sun and the other stars.

[tr. CHARLES ELIOT NORTON]

# DANTE'S CIRCLE

## SONNET TO DANTE

Interpretation of Sonnet I in *Vita Nuova*.

### Guido Cavalcanti

Unto my thinking, thou beheld'st all worth,
  All joy, as much of good as man may know,
  If thou wert in his power who here below
Is honour's righteous lord throughout this earth.
Where evil dies, even there he has his birth,
  Whose justice out of pity's self doth grow.
  Softly to sleeping persons he will go,
And, with no pain to them, their hearts draw forth.
Thy heart he took, as knowing well, alas!
  That Death had claimed thy lady for a prey:
  In fear whereof, he fed her with thy heart.
  But when he seemed in sorrow to depart,
Sweet was thy dream; for by that sign, I say,
Surely the opposite shall come to pass.

[tr. DANTE GABRIEL ROSSETTI]


## Sonnet: REBUKE TO DANTE

### Guido Cavalcanti

I come to thee by daytime constantly,
  But in thy thoughts too much of baseness find:
  Greatly it grieves me for thy gentle mind,
And for thy many virtues gone from thee.
It was thy wont to shun much company,
  Unto all sorry concourse ill inclin'd:
  And still thy speech of me, heartfelt and kind,
Had made me treasure up thy poetry.
But now I dare not, for thine abject life,
  Make manifest that I approve thy rhymes;
    Nor come I in such sort that thou mayst know.
  Ah! prythee read this sonnet many times:
So shall that evil one who bred this strife
    Be thrust from thy dishonoured soul and go.

[tr. DANTE GABRIEL ROSSETTI]

## Canzone: A DISPUTE WITH DEATH

### Guido Cavalcanti

"O Sluggish, hard, ingrate, what doest thou?
 Poor sinner, folded round with heavy sin,
  Whose life to find out joy alone is bent.
I call thee, and thou fall'st to deafness now;
 And, deeming that my path whereby to win
  Thy seat is lost, there sitt'st thee down content,
  And hold'st me to thy will subservient.
But I into thy heart have crept disguised:
 Among thy senses and thy sins I went,
By roads thou didst not guess, unrecognised.
Tears will not now suffice to bid me go,
Nor countenance abased, nor words of woe."

Now, when I heard the sudden dreadful voice
 Wake thus within to cruel utterance,
  Whereby the very heart of hearts did fail,
My spirit might not any more rejoice,
 But fell from its courageous pride at once,
  And turned to fly, where flight may not avail.
  Then slowly 'gan some strength to re-inhale
The trembling life which heard that whisper speak,
 And had conceived the sense with sore travail;
Till in the mouth it murmured, very weak,
Saying: "Youth, wealth, and beauty, these have I:
O Death! remit thy claim, — I would not die."

Small sign of pity in that aspect dwells
 Which then had scattered all my life abroad
  Till there was comfort with no single sense:
And yet almost in piteous syllables,
 When I had ceased to speak, this answer flow'd:
  "Behold what path is spread before thee hence;
  Thy life has all but a day's permanence.
And is it for the sake of youth there seems
 In loss of human years such sore offence?
Nay, look unto the end of youthful dreams.
What present glory does thy hope possess,
That shall not yield ashes and bitterness?"

But, when I looked on Death made visible,
 From my heart's sojourn brought before mine eyes,
  And holding in her hand my grievous sin,
I seemed to see my countenance, that fell,
 Shake like a shadow: my heart uttered cries,

And my soul wept the curse that lay therein.
Then Death: "Thus much thine urgent prayer
    shall win: —
I grant thee the brief interval of youth
    At natural pity's strong soliciting."
And I (because I knew that moment's ruth
But left my life to groan for a frail space)
Fell in the dust upon my weeping face.

So, when she saw me thus abashed and dumb,
    In loftier words she weighed her argument,
       That new and strange it was to hear her speak;
Saying: "The path thy fears withhold thee from
    Is thy best path.   To folly be not shent,
       Nor shrink from me because thy flesh is weak.
       Thou seest how man is sore confused, and eke
How ruinous Chance makes havoc of his life,
    And grief is in the joys that he doth seek;
Nor ever pauses the perpetual strife
'Twixt fear and rage; until beneath the sun
His perfect anguish be fulfilled and done."

"O Death! thou art so dark and difficult,
    That never human creature might attain
       By his own will to pierce thy secret sense;
Because, foreshadowing thy dread result,
    He may not put his trust in heart or brain,
       Nor power avails him, nor intelligence.
       Behold how cruelly thou takest hence
These forms so beautiful and dignified,
    And chain'st them in thy shadow chill and dense,
And forcest them in narrow graves to hide;
With pitiless hate subduing still to thee
The strength of man and woman's delicacy."

"Not for thy fear the less I come at last,
    For this thy tremor, for thy painful sweat.
       Take therefore thought to leave (for lo! I call:)
Kinsfolk and comrades, all thou didst hold fast, —
    Thy father and thy mother, — to forget
       All these thy brethren, sisters, children, all.
       Cast sight and hearing from thee; let hope fall;
Leave every sense and thy whole intellect,
    These things wherein thy life made festival:
For I have wrought thee to such strange effect
That thou hast no more power to dwell with these
As living man.   Let pass thy soul in peace."

Yea, Lord.   O thou, the Builder of the spheres,
    Who, making me, didst shape me, of thy grace,

In thine own image and high counterpart;
Do thou subdue my spirit, long perverse,
    To weep within thy will a certain space,
        Ere yet thy thunder come to rive my heart.
        Set in my hand some sign of what thou art,
Lord God, and suffer me to seek out Christ, —
    Weeping, to seek Him in thy ways apart;
Until my sorrow have at length suffic'd
In some accepted instant to atone
For sins of thought, for stubborn evil done.

Dishevelled and in tears, go, song of mine,
    To break the hardness of the heart of man:
        Say how his life began
From dust, and in that dust doth sink supine:
    Yet, say, the unerring spirit of grief shall guide
        His soul, being purified,
To seek its Maker at the heavenly shrine.
                              [tr. DANTE GABRIEL ROSSETTI]


### Sonnet: TO GUIDO CAVALCANTI

#### Cino Da Pistoia

What rhymes are thine which I have ta'en from thee,
    Thou Guido, that thou ever say'st I thieve?
    'Tis true, fine fancies gladly I receive,
But when was aught found beautiful in thee?
Nay, I have searched my pages diligently,
    And tell the truth, and lie not, by your leave.
    From whose rich store my web of songs I weave
Love knoweth well, well knowing them and me.
No artist I, — all men may gather it;
    Nor do I work in ignorance of pride,
        (Though the world reach alone the coarser sense);
But am a certain man of humble wit
    Who journeys with his sorrow at his side,
        For a heart's sake, alas! that is gone hence.
                              [tr. DANTE GABRIEL ROSSETTI]


### Sonnet: ON DANTE'S COMMEDIA

#### Cino Da Pistoia

This book of Dante's, very sooth to say,
    Is just a poet's lovely heresy,

Which by a lure as sweet as sweet can be
Draws other men's concerns beneath its sway;
While, among stars' and comets' dazzling play,
  It beats the right down, lets the wrong go free,
  Shows some abased, and others in great glee,
Much as with lovers is Love's ancient way.
Therefore his vain decrees, wherein he lied,
  Fixing folks' nearness to the Fiend their foe,
Must be like empty nutshells flung aside.
  Yet through the rash false witness set to grow,
French and Italian vengeance on such pride
  May fall, like Antony's on Cicero.
                         [tr. Dante Gabriel Rossetti]


### Sonnet: TO DANTE ALIGHIERI

#### Giovanni Quirino

Glory to God and to God's Mother chaste,
  Dear friend, is all the labour of thy days:
  Thou art as he who evermore uplays
That heavenly wealth which the worm cannot waste:
So shalt thou render back with interest
  The precious talent given thee by God's grace:
  While I, for my part, follow in their ways
Who by the cares of this world are possess'd.
For, as the shadow of the earth doth make
  The moon's globe dark, when so she is debarr'd
    From the bright rays which lit her in the sky, —
So now, since thou my sun didst me forsake,
  (Being distant from me), I grow dull and hard,
    Even as a beast of Epicurus' sty.
                         [tr. Dante Gabriel Rossetti]

# IX. LATE LATIN LITERATURE

In the eleventh century, Latin was the primary language of all literate western Europeans. The *culture* of western Europe was unified, and it was expressed in Latin. Latin was the living, active language of affairs, of nearly all laws and contracts, all negotiations, and all conferences. Moreover, poets and creative writers of all kinds wrote in Latin, for it insured a wider audience by far than any of the provincial dialects. But in the twentieth century, Latin is a living language only in the service of the Roman Catholic Church and among some of its clergy. The decline in use of Latin was not sudden, but a gradual decline, as one class or profession after another found it increasingly convenient to write in the vernacular.

Convenience primarily determines the language used. In the eighth century the Church encouraged its preachers to address congregations in the local dialect or language, but the clergy preferred to continue thinking in one language, and they chose that language in which all the ideas of religion were already expressed. In the next century the Carolingian rulers tried to cultivate vernacular poetry, but the audience was limited. To be sure, the *Hildebrandslied* was written down at Fulda, but not many of the monks could read it, for in the brotherhood were Bavarians, Franks, Saxons, Irish, and Lombards. Where sheepskin was expensive and copyists' time scarce, it was better to record Latin poetry which could be enjoyed by all. In the tenth century hymns were composed in the vernacular, but the language was hard for a congregation used to traditional tunes and images. Century after century Latin gave way to a younger language slowly; it gave way class by class. Until the eighteenth century, a scientist who expected an audience must write in Latin.

The greatest change came in the second half of the twelfth century, when popular, and therefore vernacular, poetry began with the towns. Urbanity was now a characteristic of French and Italian, where twelve centuries before it had characterized Latin. The agrarian barons who now became the courtly nobles created a new audience, not tied to an old language. Except for this one great change, the decline in the use of Latin has been gradual.

In the later Middle Ages — the twelfth, thirteenth, and fourteenth centuries — Latin was the primary language of all clergy, scientists and scholars, ambassadors and legates, and lawyers. Latin was the language of didactic and philosophical poetry, of epigram and epic, of satire and history, of science and, of course, of theology. Dante composed his *Comedy, New Life,* and some lyrics in Italian; but his prose tracts, which were scholarly, were all written in Latin, including his study of the vernacular, *De Vulgari Eloquentia.* Two generations later, Chaucer composed entirely in English, but his contemporary Gower composed three long poems, one each in English, French, and Latin. Authors chose Latin not only because it was international, but because they thought it would last.    The bulk of western literature in these three centuries was written in Latin.

It has been customary, since the humanists of the fifteenth and sixteenth century, to regard this medieval Latin as barbarous and decadent.    In fact, at regular intervals throughout the Middle Ages, humanists and classicists objected because the Latin used was not that of Cicero and Virgil.    In the schools of Charles the Great, Alcuin and his courtly contemporaries used every effort to restore the Latin of the Caesars and regarded all innovation as barbarity.    As we have read in the *Illustrious Vernacular*, Dante thought of Latin as unchanging, as always frozen in the mold that the writers of the Golden Age had cast.    Any variation from Cicero's syntax was thought a violation of grammar.    Only in the last century, since studies of the evolution of language have been rife, have we discarded this view and come to appreciate late Latin as a tongue capable of expressing, in a quite different way from the Roman classics, the fundamental struggles and emotions of men.    The Latin of the *Dies Irae* does not bow before the Latin of Virgil's eclogues.    In its author's hands it expressed an exaltation and nobility second to none.

# JACOBUS DE VORAGINE

The *lectio,* or reading, which formed an integral part of the hours of prayer, or office (*officium*), of the service of the Church spread with the cult of the saints to works composed to inform the congregation on the proper (*propria*) day about the saint honored in the calendar. This means of instruction, devised by the early Church, spread rapidly, particularly during the monastic period. Cathedrals and any churches of pretensions gathered these lives into a single volume, arranged according to the saints' days in the annual calendar. The volume was called a legendary (from *legere,* meaning variously to gather together, to instruct, and to read). The stories in the legendary were called *legenda,* or legends. According to the thirteenth-century Durandus of Mende, who composed the authoritative work on liturgy of the medieval Church, *Rationale divinorum officionum:* "That book is called *legendary* in which is brought together matter concerning the life and death of Confessors, which is read on their festivals" (*Legendarius vocatur liber ille, ubi agitur de vita et obitu Confessorum*). Durandus, like nearly all writers of the Middle Ages, used the singular for the lives of all the saints; for it was the common belief that all saints led a single life in God. Therefore, since "all things are common in the communion of saints," stories told of one saint might be attached to any other. The legendary, therefore, was not quite regarded as a book of biographies, but as a book of ethical instruction illustrating God's humanity and omnipotence and the godliness of saintly men. Historicity was not a concern of either author or audience. In this, it is identical with the monastic saints' lives already treated above.

These legendaries were very useful and popular in the Church; consequently, there are thousands of them in manuscript that differ according to local taste and authorship. But they had no real popularity in secular life until the *Golden Legend.* According to Caxton, "I have set myself to translate into English the legend of saints, which is called *legenda aurea* in Latin, that is to say the *Golden Legend.* For as gold is the most noble of metals, so is this legend held most noble of all works." There are more than five hundred manuscripts of the book still extant, and in the first century of the printing press, it was published in separate editions and translations more than one hundred and fifty times. According to Wyzewa, the modern French translator, "The catalogues mention nearly a hundred different Latin editions published between 1470 and 1500, not to count the innumerable translations into French, English, Dutch, Polish, German, Spanish, Czech, etc." It is impossible to love early modern art, from Cimabue to Rubens, Murillo, and Poussin, without falling under the spell of the *Golden Legend,* as did the artists.

A few notes from history will explain this great popularity of a work that has since fallen into almost complete obscurity. Its author,

James of Varazzio, a small town in Genoese territory, was himself
one of the most able and saintly men.   The son of poor parents, he
early joined the Brotherhood of Preachers (Dominicans) and, after
intensive education, taught theology in several houses of the Order.
For twenty years he supervised all the houses in Lombardy.   Then,
by a kind of popular demand, he became Archbishop of Genoa.   His
conduct as Archbishop accords with all the qualities of saintliness depicted in his book: He lived in abstinence that he might relieve the
poor, and he, temporarily at least, brought peace to the struggle between the Ghibellines and Guelfs which had raged unchecked in
Genoa for fifty years.

James finished the book in 1255, when he was still a teacher of
theology.   The Dominican Order was then but forty years old and
was filled with pristine enthusiasm.   It had been founded to carry
Christian doctrine by word of mouth to the common people in the
country and the teeming new towns, as the surest counteraction of
heresy, which had reared its head in Provence and Spain.   All the
arts were cultivated to this end of popular appeal.   The difference
between James' legendary and those that preceded it, bound to the
long and formal traditions of the Church, was the difference between
Gibbon and Scott.

Why, then, did James write in Latin, when these popular audiences
understood only vernacular?   They did not read any language.
They received the legends through the Blackfriars, who were working in every land.   Latin was still the universal language of the educated.   By writing in Latin, James could write for all his brothers,
who would then transmit the stories to the people by word of mouth.
But literacy spread in the late Middle Ages, and with the coming
of the printing press every family wanted a copy for itself.   These
were vernacular translations.   The *Golden Legend* became a by-
word in every home.

Eventually the reformers, the humanists, and the new science
destroyed its popularity.   The reformers objected to the cult of
saints because of the excesses it bred.   The humanists objected to
James' "Gutter-Latin," which they regarded as a degradation of the
tongue of Cicero.   And the new science revealed new marvels in the
universe that made the saintly miracles archaic.   From the seven-
teenth century, no English version of the *Golden Legend* appeared
until William Morris printed a small edition of Caxton's version in
1892.

The Life of St. Bernard, in the selections that follow, has been
somewhat abridged.

## THE GOLDEN LEGEND

Jacobus de Voragine (A.D. 1228–1298)

(James of Varaggio)

[From *The Golden Legend of Jacobus de Voragine*, translated by Granger Ryan and Helmut Ripperger; Longmans, New York, 1941.]

### THE SEVEN SLEEPERS

#### JULY 27

The Seven Sleepers were natives of the city of Ephesus. The Emperor Decius, the persecutor of the Christians, came to Ephesus, and built temples in the centre of the city, that all might take part with him in the worship of the idols. And when he ordered all the Christians to be sought out, bound, and forced either to sacrifice or to die, so great was the fear of his punishments that friend disowned friend, father betrayed son, and son denied father. And there were seven Christians in Ephesus, named Maximian, Malchus, Martianus, Dionysius, John, Serapion and Constantine, who were sore afflicted at seeing all these things. And although they were among the first men of the palace, they disdained to offer sacrifice, and remained hidden in their houses, fasting and praying. They were accused and hailed before Decius, and avowed that they were Christians; but he gave them the time until his return in which to renounce their faith. But they distributed their goods to the poor, and by common accord went to take refuge on Mount Celion, concealing themselves there. And each morning one of them, assuming the guise and seeming of a beggar, went into the city for provisions.

When Decius came back to Ephesus, and commanded that they be sought out and made to offer sacrifice, Malchus, who had gone into the town that day, returned in terror, to report the emperor's fury to his companions. And as they were overcome with fear, Malchus laid before them the bread which he had brought, that they might be strengthened by the food and made stronger for the combat. And while they sat at table and conversed with tears and sighs, the will of God caused all seven to fall into a deep sleep.

The following morning, when they were sought for and could not be found, and Decius was grieving at the loss of such youths, word was brought to him that they were in hiding on Mount Celion, and that they had distributed all their goods to the poor. Decius thereupon summoned their parents, and threatened them with death if they did not tell him all they knew. And the parents confirmed the accusations, and complained that their sons had given away their patrimony. And thinking what he should do in their regard, at the inspiration of God he commanded the mouth of the cave to be walled up with stones, that they might perish of hunger and need. This was done, and two Christians, Theodore and Rufinus, wrote down an account of their martyrdom and placed it secretly among the stones.

After three hundred and seventy-two years, when Decius and his whole generation had passed away, in the thirtieth year of the reign of Theodosius, there spread abroad the heresy of those who denied the resurrection of the dead. And the most Christian Emperor Theodosius was greatly aggrieved thereby, because he saw the faith of his subjects much disturbed; and he went into the inner chambers, put on a hair shirt, and knelt weeping day after day. Seeing this, God in His mercy willed to comfort those who mourned and to confirm their hope of the resurrection of the dead; and opening the treasures of His loving-kindness, He raised up the Seven Sleepers. He inspired a certain man of Ephesus to build sheds for his shepherds on Mount Celion. And when the stonemasons opened the cave, the Seven Sleepers awoke and greeted each other as though they had but passed the night in sleep; and then, recalling the anxiety of the day before, they asked Malchus, who had waited upon them, what Decius had decreed in their regard. But he answered, as he had said the day before: "We were sought for, that we might offer sacrifice. That is what the emperor plans for us!" And Maximian replied: "God knows that we will not sacrifice!" And when he had rallied his companions, he ordered Malchus to go down to the city to buy bread, and to come back with more loaves than on the previous day, and report what the emperor had commanded.

Malchus therefore took five coins and set out; and coming out of the cave, and seeing the stones piled up, he wondered, but thought little of it. Timidly he came to the city gate, and was surprised to see the cross above it; and he went from gate to gate, and his astonishment waxed the greater at seeing the cross over each, and the city changed. Signing himself, and thinking that he was dreaming, he came back to the first gate. Then he took courage, and covering his face, entered the city and came to the bread-sellers; and in the market-place he heard the people talking of Christ, and his wonder knew no bounds. And he said to himself: "How is it that yesterday no one dared to utter the name of Christ, and today all confess him? I would think that this was not the city of the Ephesians, for it is otherwise built, but I know of no other such like city!" And when he asked, he was told that this was Ephesus; and he thought that he must be wandering in mind, and was about to turn back to rejoin his companions. But he went to the venders of bread; and when he offered his coins in payment, the venders looked with wonderment, and said to each other that this youth must have discovered an ancient treasure. And when Malchus saw them talking to each other, he thought that they were about to drag him to the emperor: and terrified, he besought them to let him go free, and to keep the loaves and the coins for themselves. But they laid hold on him, and said: "Whence art thou? Surely thou hast found a treasure of the old emperors! Show us therefore where it is, and we shall share it with thee and shall conceal thee; for otherwise thou canst not remain hid!"

So great was Malchus' fear that he found naught to reply to them; and when he remained silent, they put a rope about his neck and dragged him through the streets to the centre of the city, and the rumour went abroad that some youth had discovered a treasure. And when the whole populace came together and looked upon him wondering, he sought to convince them that he had found nothing; but looking about, he saw no one that knew him, and seeking some of his kin, whom he in sooth thought to be alive, he found none; so that he stood like one demented in the midst of the townsfolk. And when Saint Martin the bishop and the proconsul Antipater had heard of all this, they ordered the citizens to bring him to them warily, with his coins. And when their servitors led him toward the church, he thought that he was being led to the emperor. Then the bishop and the proconsul, surprised at the sight of the coins, asked him where he had unearthed the unknown treasure. But he answered that he had found nothing, but had had these coins from his parents' purse. And when he was asked from what city he came, he replied: "Well I know that I am of this city, if indeed this be Ephesus!" And the proconsul said: "Summon hither thy kinsmen, that they may bear witness for thee!" But when he gave their names, and no one recognized them, all thought that he was making false pretense, in order to escape. And the proconsul said: "How shall we believe thee, that this is thy parents' money, when its inscription is more than three hundred and seventy-seven years old, and it comes from the first days of the Emperor Decius, and is in no wise like to our coinage? And if thy parents are of a time so long past, how canst thou seek to deceive the ancients and the wise men of Ephesus? Therefore shall I order three to be handed over to the law, until thou confess what thou hast found!"

Then Malchus fell down before them, and said: "In God's name, my lords, tell me what I ask, and I shall tell you what is in my heart! Where is the Emperor Decius now, who yesterday was in this city?" And the bishop replied: "My son, in the whole earth there is now no emperor called Decius. Only in olden times was there such a one!" And Malchus said: "Herein, my lord, am I sore bewildered, and no one believes me. But follow me and I shall show you my companions who are on Mount Celion, and believe ye them! For this do I know, that we fled from the face of the Emperor Decius, and yestereve I saw Decius enter this city, if forsooth this be Ephesus!" Then the bishop, thinking within himself, said to the proconsul: "There is some vision, which God wills to make manifest in this youth!" They therefore set out with him, and a great multitude of the people followed.

And first Malchus went in to his companions; and then the bishop, going in after him, found the scroll among the stones, sealed with two silver seals. And calling all the people together he read the writing to them, and all who heard were filled with awe. Then they saw the saints of God sitting in the cave, their faces like roses in bloom; and falling down they glorified God. And straightway the bishop and the proconsul sent to the Emperor Theodosius, asking him to come with all haste, and witness this new miracle of God. And he, rising at once from the ground where he lay mourning, came from Constantinople to Ephesus, glorifying God; and all went out to meet him, and together they went up to the cave. And as soon as the saints saw the emperor, their faces shone like the sun. And the emperor went in and threw himself before them, and gave glory to God; and rising he embraced them and wept over each, and said: "Seeing you, it is as if I saw our Lord raising Lazarus to life!" Then Saint Maximian said to him: "Believe us, that for thy sake God has raised us up before the day of the great resurrection, that thou mayest have unwavering faith in the resurrection of the dead! For we indeed have risen and are alive, and as an infant is in the womb of his mother and lives and feels no ill, so were we alive, lying asleep and feeling naught."

When he had said these things, the saints bowed their heads to the earth, in the sight of all, and fell asleep, and surrendered their souls according to the will of God. And the emperor arose and fell upon them, weeping and kissing them; and he ordered that golden coffins be made for them. But that very night they appeared to him, and said that as they had hitherto lain in the earth and had risen therefrom, so he should return them to the earth, until the Lord should raise them up again. The emperor therefore commanded that the cave be adorned with gilded stones. And he proclaimed that all the bishops who had professed the resurrection of the dead should receive indulgence.

The saints are said to have slept for three hundred and seventy-seven years; but this may be doubted, because they rose from the dead in the year 448, and Decius only reigned for one year and three months, namely in the year 252. Thus they slept for only one hundred and ninety-six years.

### ST. BERNARD

#### AUGUST 20

In the year 1112 of the Incarnation of Our Lord, the fifteenth from the founding of the Cistercian house, Bernard, the servant of the Lord, who was then about twenty-two years of age, entered the Cistercian Order with more than thirty companions. When Bernard was quitting his father's house with his brothers, Guy, the eldest, saw his youngest brother Nivard playing with other boys in the square, and said to him: "Ho there, brother Nivard, now all the land of our heritage belongs to thee!" But the child's answer was by no means childish. "So you would possess Heaven and leave me naught but the earth! That is surely not a fair division!" Nivard therefore dwelt for some time longer with his father, and then followed after his brothers.

Once Bernard had entered the Order, he was so wholly turned to God and absorbed in the spiritual life that he ceased to use the senses of his body. He lived for a year in the cell of the novices, and yet did not know that it had a vaulted roof. Although he went in and out of the chapel continually, he thought that there was but one window in its front wall, whereas there were three.

The abbot of the Cistercians then sent some of the brothers to build the house of Clairvaux, and appointed Bernard there abbot. There for a long time he lived in exceeding poverty, and many times made his meal from the leaves of the beech tree. The servant of God denied himself sleep to a degree that surpassed human powers, being wont to complain that no time was so wasted as the time spent in sleeping; and he compared sleep to death, saying that as, in the sight of God, dead men were as those asleep, so in the sight of men, sleeping men were as the dead. Moreover, if he heard anyone snoring rather loudly, or saw someone lying in an unseemly posture, he could scarce bear it with equanimity, and protested that such an one slept in a carnal or worldly manner. He took no pleasure in eating, but went to take food as a torture, led solely by the fear of fainting. It was always his custom, after eating, to examine how much he had eaten; and if perchance he had exceeded the usual measure even a little, he did not allow the fault to go unpunished. He had so quelled the disorders of the appetite that for the most part he no longer discerned divers tastes. Once when oil was put before him by an error and he drank it, he was unaware of it, and did not know it until someone marvelled that his lips had oil upon them. Another time raw blood was mistakenly offered to him in place of butter, and he is known to have eaten thereof for several days. He used to say that he tasted water only because, when he drank it, it cooled his mouth and throat.

He declared that whatever he knew of the Scriptures, he had learned through meditation in the woods and fields; and among his friends he was wont to say that he had no teachers save oaks and beech trees. Again he admitted that sometimes, while he was at prayer and meditation, the whole of the Sacred Scripture had appeared to him, spread open and explained. In his commentary on the Canticles he relates that once, preparing to speak, he was storing up in his mind certain of the thoughts which the Spirit suggested to him — not that he lacked faith in the Spirit, but that he feared to trust too far: — and as he was about to speak, a voice came to him, saying: "As long as thou keepest that thought in mind, no other shall be given thee!"

In dress, poverty pleased him always, uncleanliness never, for he said that it was evidence of negligence, or of inward vainglory, or of a desire to win the admiration of men. Often on his lips, and ever in his heart, was the proverb: "Whosoever doth what others do not, all men wonder at him." Hence for several years he wore a hair shirt, as long as he was able to keep it secret; but as soon as it was known to others, he put it off, and resumed the common usage. When he laughed, it was as though he had to force himself to laugh rather than to restrain his laughter, and needed a spur more than a curb.

He was wont to say that there were three kinds of patience, the first to bear insulting words, the second to bear damage to one's goods, and the third to bear bodily injury; and he showed that he possessed this threefold patience by the following examples. Once when he had written a letter to a certain bishop, admonishing him in a friendly spirit, the bishop, mightily angered thereat, wrote a most bitter reply, which began with the words: "Health to thee, and not the spirit of blasphemy," as though he had written with malice and irreverence. To this Bernard made answer: "I do not believe that I have the spirit of blasphemy, nor that I have spoken irreverently to anyone, nor wished so to speak, especially to a prince among my people."

Another time, an abbot sent him six hundred silver marks for the building of a monastery, but the whole sum was stolen by robbers in the way. When he learned of this, his only word was: "Blessed be God, Who has spared us this burden! And let us not think too harshly of the thieves, for man's natural greed drove them to this deed, and moreover, the size of the sum was a very great temptation to them."

Again, a certain canon regular came to him, and besought him earnestly to receive him as a monk. Bernard was unwilling to grant his request, and prevailed with him to return to his church. At this the canon said: "Wherefore then dost thou so highly commend the practice of perfection in thy books, if thou forbiddest it to one who yearns for it? Would that I might lay hands on those books, that I might tear them to shreds!" He replied: "In no one of them hast thou read that thou couldst not be perfect in thy cloister; for in all my books I have commended a betterment of morals, and not a change of place!" At this the canon was so enraged that he rushed at Bernard, and struck him so savagely on the cheek that redness and swelling ensued. Those present were about to set upon the author of the sacrilege, when the servant of God forbade them, calling out and adjuring them in the name of Christ, that no one was to touch him or to do him aught of harm.

To the novices who sought to enter his monastery he used to say: "If you are urged on by a desire for the things that are within, leave your bodies outside, which you have brought from the world! Let only the spirit enter, for the flesh profiteth nothing!"

His father, who had been left alone in his house, came to the monastery, and after some time, died there in the goodness of his old age. His sister, however, took a husband, and was endangered by the riches and delights of the world. Once she came to the monastery to visit her brothers, splendidly furnished and with a haughty retinue; but Bernard shrank from her as from a snare of the Devil,

set to trap souls, and refused for a time to go out to see her.   And seeing that none of her brothers came forth to meet her, and that one
of them, who was porter at the door, called her a bedizened dung-
hill, she burst into tears, and said: "Albeit I am a sinner, for such as I
Christ died!   For it is because I feel the guilt of my sins that I seek
the counsel and conversation of the good; and if my brother despises
my flesh, let not the servant of God despise my soul!   Let him come
and command me, and whatsoever he commands I shall do!"   Hearing this promise, Bernard went out to her with his brothers; and
being unable to separate her from her spouse, he first enjoined her
to abandon all worldly glory, and then, holding up the example of
their mother for her imitation, sent her away.   And she was so
suddenly converted thereby that in the midst of the world she led
the life of an anchoress, and lived a stranger to all secular concerns.
Finally she conquered her husband by force of entreaties, and, being
freed from wedlock by the bishop, entered a nunnery.

Once, being fallen sick, the man of God seemed about to breathe
his last; and at that moment, being rapt in ecstasy, he saw himself
before the judgement seat of God, and Satan standing opposite, pelt-
ing him with malicious accusations.   When he had come to the end
of his charges, and the saint was to speak in his own defense, fearless and unperturbed he said: "I avow that I am nothing worth,
and unable to obtain the Kingdom of Heaven by my own merits.
For the rest, my Lord has won Heaven by a twofold right, namely
by inheritance from His Father, and by the merit of His Passion;
whereof He is content with the one, and gives me the other.   Therefore, by His gift, I claim Heaven as my right, and shall not be
confounded!"   At these words the Enemy was overborne, the meeting came to an end, and Bernard returned to himself.

So great were the abstinence, the labours, and the watchings wherewith he mortified his body, that he suffered feeble health almost always, and was scarce able to follow the conventual life.   And once
when he fell ill of a dire sickness, and the brethren were persevering
in prayer for him, he felt himself restored somewhat, and said to the
assembled brothers: "Wherefore do ye cling to me, a miserable
man?   You are stronger than I and have prevailed over me; but
spare me, I beg of you, spare me, and let me go!"

The man of God was elected bishop by several cities, notably by
Genoa and Milan; but, being unwilling either to give his consent or
to refuse in an unseemly manner, he said that he was not master of
himself, but was destined to the service of others.   But his brethren,
at his own admonition, had foreseen this, and were armed with the
authority of the sovereign pontiff to prevent anyone from taking
away him who was their joy.

Once when he was visiting the Carthusian monks, and had given
them much edification in all things, there was one matter which
somewhat disturbed the prior of the monastery, namely that the
saddle upon which Bernard rode was of good quality, and made
little show of poverty.   The prior mentioned this to one of the

brothers, and he in turn to the saint, who was no less astonished, and asked what sort of saddle it might be; for he had ridden from Clairvaux to Chartreuse, yet knew not what kind of saddle he was using.

Another time he journeyed for a whole day beside the lake of Lausanne, yet did not see it, or did not see that he saw it. And when evening came, and his companions were talking of the lake, he asked where it was. Hearing this, they were filled with wonderment.

His lowliness of heart overcame the loftiness of his name, nor could the whole world exalt him as much as he alone humbled himself. He often said that when he was besieged with honours and favours by the people, it seemed to him that another man had taken his place, imagining, as it were, that he dreamt; but in the company of the simple brothers, he rejoiced to find himself again, and to return to his own person, where he might enjoy the friendship of the humble. He was always found either at prayer or in contemplation, or busy with reading or writing, or edifying his brethren by his words.

Once when he was preaching to the people, and all received his words with pious attention, a temptation crept into his soul, and he thought: "Now in sooth thou preachest most fairly, and all men gladly heed thy words, and hold thee learned and wise!" The man of God, feeling himself beset by such a thought, paused for a moment, and began to ponder whether he should continue or make an end: but instantly he was strengthened by the help of God, and silently said to the tempter: "Not for thee did I begin, nor for thee will I desist!" And unperturbed, he continued his sermon to the end.

A certain monk, who in the world had been a profligate and a gamester, was tempted by the Devil, and made up his mind to return to his worldly pursuits. When Saint Bernard was unable to dissuade him, he asked him how he would make a living. He answered: "Well do I know how to play at dice, and shall make my living thereby!" "If I give thee an initial sum," said Saint Bernard, "wilt thou come back once a year and divide the profit with me?" When the monk heard this he was overjoyed, and willingly promised to do as Bernard had said. He therefore demanded twenty sols, and went off with them. But the man of God had done this that he might be able to recall the monk, and so it befell; for the monk went and lost his all, and came back to the door in confusion. Hearing that he was there, the man of God went forth to him with joyful mien, and held his scapular spread out to receive his share of the money. But the monk said: "No profit have I made, father, but am stripped even of our capital: but take me back in its stead, an ye will!" And gently Bernard answered: "It is better so, that I should have thee back, than that I should lose both thee and the money!"

Once when Bernard was riding to a certain place, he chanced to speak sadly to a peasant about the heart's fickleness in prayer. The peasant straightway thought ill of him, and said that as for himself, he prayed with firm and steady heart. In order to convince him, and to curb his rashness, Bernard therefore said to him: "Go apart a little, and with all the attention in thy power begin the *Pater Noster;* and if thou art able to finish it without any wayward thought or distraction, thou shalt have the beast upon which I am mounted! But promise me on thine honour that if thou think of aught else, thou wilt not hide it from me!" Gladdened at the thought that he had already won the beast, the peasant went off boldly, recollected himself, and began to recite the prayer: but he had scarce finished the half of it when a question stole into his heart, whether he should have the saddle with the beast. Perceiving this he hastened back to the saint, and told him whereof he had thought in the midst of his prayer; and thenceforth he weened not so bravely of himself.

Brother Robert, a monk in his monastery and kin to him in the world, being easily misled, due to his youth, by the persuasions of certain men, had betaken himself to Cluny. The venerable father concealed his chagrin for some time, and then determined to recall him by letter. As he was dictating the letter in the open air, and a monk was taking it in writing, a shower of rain burst forth without warning; and the monk was about to roll up the paper, when Bernard said to him: "Thou dost the work of God; fear not to go on writing!" He therefore wrote the letter in the midst of the rain, and no drop fell thereon; for the power of charity warded it off.

An incredible multitude of flies once invaded a monastery which Bernard had built, and they vexed the monks sorely. The man of God then said: "I excommunicate the flies!" And on the morrow they were found dead, every one.

Bernard had been sent to Milan by the sovereign pontiff to reconcile the people of that city with the Church, and had already returned to Pavia, when a man brought his wife to him, she being possessed of the Devil. At once the demon, speaking through the poor woman's mouth, burst out in insults against the saint, and said: "This eater of leeks and devourer of cabbages shall not drive me from my little fool of a woman!" But the man of God sent her to the church of Saint Syrus; yet Syrus, wishing to do honour to his guest, wrought no cure upon the woman, and she was led back to Saint Bernard. Then the Devil began to babble through the woman's mouth, and said: "Not the little Syrus, nor the little Bernard, shall cast me out!" To this the servant of God replied: "Neither Syrus nor Bernard shall cast thee out, but the Lord Jesus Christ!" And no sooner had he begun to pray than the evil spirit said: "How gladly would I go out of this silly old woman, for I am sorely tormented in her! How gladly would I go out, but cannot, for the great Master is unwilling!" "Who is this great Master?" the saint asked. "Jesus of Nazareth!" the demon responded. "Hast thou ever seen Him?" the saint asked. "Yes!" said the Devil. "Where hast thou seen Him?" "In glory!" "Wert thou then in glory?" "Yes!" "How then art thou departed thence?" "Many were we to fall with Lucifer!" All these things he spoke through the old woman's mouth, in a gloomy voice, in the hearing of all. Then the saint said to him: "And wouldst thou now return to glory?" But the spirit, with a harsh laugh, replied: "It is too late for that!" Then, at the saint's prayer, the demon went out of the woman; but as soon as the man of God had gone away, he again entered into her. Her husband therefore ran after the saint, and told him what had befallen. Bernard then ordered him to tie about her neck a paper whereon were written the words: "In the name of Our Lord Jesus Christ I command thee, demon, dare no more to molest this woman!" This was done, and the Devil never again dared come near her.

In Aquitaine there was a woman who was tormented by a wanton incubus, who abused her for six years, and set upon her with incredible lust. It chanced that the man of God came that way, and the demon rudely warned the woman lest she go to him, saying that it would avail her nothing, and that after the saint's departure he, who had been her lover, would thenceforth persecute her most cruelly. But she went to Saint Bernard with all confidence, and told him the tale of her woe, with loud sobbing and weeping. He said to her: "Take this my staff and place it in thy bed; and then if he can do aught, let him do it!" When therefore she lay down in her bed with the staff beside her, the demon came thither forthwith, but could not do as he was wont, nor even draw near to the bed; but he threatened her again most harshly, saying that when the saint should be gone, he would wreak dire vengeance upon her. She related this to Bernard, who thereupon called the populace together, and bade them hold lighted candles in their hands; then together with all who were present, he excommunicated the demon, and forbade him to approach this or any other woman thereafter. And in this wise the woman was entirely freed of her possession.

When the saint went as a legate to the same province, in order to reconcile the duke of Aquitaine to the Church, the duke refused absolutely to be reconciled. Then the man of God went to the altar to celebrate the Mass, while the duke, as an excommunicate, stood without the doors. And when the saint had said the *Pax Domini,* he laid the Body of the Lord upon the paten, and taking It with him went outside the church, with fiery countenance and flaming eyes, and assailed the count with terrible words. "We have besought thee," he said, "and thou hast spurned us! Behold now there comes to thee the Son of the Virgin, He Who is the Lord of the Church which thou persecutest! Here is thy Judge, in Whose name every knee shall bow! Here is thy Judge, into Whose hands that soul of thine shall fall! Wilt thou despise Him as thou hast despised his servants? Withstand Him if thou canst!" Straightway the duke was bathed in sweat, and trembled in all his members; and he fell at the saint's feet. Bernard then touched him with his shoe, and ordered him to rise and hear the sentence of God. And the duke arose all atremble, and thenceforth did all that holy man commanded.

The saint went into the kingdom of Germany to bring peace out of some great dissension, and the archbishop of Mainz sent a cer-

tain venerable cleric to meet him.  And when the clerk said that he
had been sent by the lord archbishop, the man of God responded:
" 'Twas another Lord that sent thee!"  Wondering at this, the
clerk affirmed that none but the archbishop had sent him.  But the
servant of Christ persisted: "Thou art mistaken, my son, thou art
mistaken!  A greater Lord sent thee, for 'twas Christ Himself!"
Seeing the saint's meaning, the clerk said: "Thinkest thou that I
would become a monk?  Far be it from me!  The thought has not
entered my heart!"  And what then?  In that very journey the
clerk bade the world farewell, and took the monkish habit from the
saint's hands.

At one time Bernard received a soldier of high rank into his
Order; and after this man had followed the saint for some time, he
was beset with an exceeding grave temptation.  Seeing him so sad,
one of the brethren asked him the reason of his sorrow.  And he
answered: "I know, I know well, that never again shall I be happy!"
The said brother carried this word to the servant of God, who in turn
prayed the more earnestly for the soldier; and he who had been
so saddened by his temptations became more joyful and gay than the
others, by so much as before he had been more woebegone.  And
when the aforesaid brother reprimanded him gently for the sorrowful
words that he had spoken, the monk answered: "What though I then
said that I should never be happy again, now I say that nevermore
shall I be sad!"

When Saint Malachy, the bishop of Ireland, whose virtuous life
Bernard had written, breathed forth his soul to Christ in his monastery, and the saint was offering for him the Host of salvation, God
revealed Malachy's glory to him, and inspired him to change the
form of the Postcommunion, so that with joyous voice he sang: *Deus,
qui beatum Malachium sanctorum tuorum meritis coaequasti, tribue,
quaesumus, ut qui pretiosae mortis ejus festa agimus, vitae quoque
imitemur exempla:* which being put in English, means: O God,
Who hast made the blessed Malachy equal to Thy saints in merit,
grant, we beseech Thee, that we who celebrate his feast day may
also imitate the examples of his life.  And when the cantor signified
to him that he had erred, he said: "I have not erred, for I know
whereof I speak!"  Whereupon he went and kissed the bishop's
sacred remains.

At length Saint Bernard, tranquilly making ready for death, said
to his brethren: "Three things I leave for your observance, which
I mind me that in my own life I have observed as best I might.  I
have sought to give scandal to no one, and if another fell, I tried to
hide his fall; I ever trusted my own mind less than the mind of others;
being wronged, I never sought vengeance on the wrongdoer.  Thus
I leave you these three: charity, humility, and patience: these be my
testament!"

And finally, after he had wrought many miracles, and had built
one hundred and sixty monasteries, and had compiled a great number
of books and treatises, he came to the end of his days, being about

sixty-three years of age, and fell asleep in the Lord, in the arms of his brethren, in the year 1153.

After his death he manifested his glory to many. He appeared to the abbot of a certain monastery, and invited him to follow him; and when the abbot came with him, the man of God said: "Behold we are come to Mount Libanus, and thou shalt remain here, while I ascend thither!" Being asked for what reason he wished to ascend, he replied: "I wish to learn!" Wondering the abbot said to him: "What hast thou to learn, father, whom all hold second to none in knowledge?" He answered: "Here there is no knowledge, and no acquaintance of the truth; but above there is the fulness of knowledge, above is the true cognizance of all truth!" and with these words, he disappeared. The abbot therefore made note of the day, and then learned that Bernard had departed from the body at that time. Moreover, by His servant God has wrought other miracles almost without number.

### SAINT MICHAEL THE ARCHANGEL

#### SEPTEMBER 29

Michael is interpreted: "who is like unto God." It is said, as Gregory tells us, that as often as there is a work of wondrous power to be wrought, Michael is sent to perform it. Thus we are given to understand, both by his name and by his works, that what no other can do, the power of God can accomplish. Therefore many such works are attributed to Michael. Daniel attests that in the time of the Antichrist, Michael will rise and stand forth as the defender and protector of the elect. He it was that strove with the Devil over the body of Moses, when the Devil sought to conceal the body so that the Jewish people might adore Moses as a god. He fought with the dragon and his angels, and casting them out of Heaven, won a great victory over them. He receives the souls of the saints, and leads them into the Paradise of bliss. Of yore he was the prince of the Synogogue, and is now appointed by the Lord as the prince of the Church. It is said that 'twas he that inflicted the plagues upon the Egyptians, divided the Red Sea, led the people through the desert, and brought them into the Promised Land. He is held to be the bearer of the standard of Christ amid the host of the saints. At the Lord's command he will slay the Antichrist with great power, upon the Mount of Olives. At the voice of the Archangel Michael the dead will rise. In the Day of Judgement, he will present the Cross, the Nails, the Lance, and the Crown of Thorns.

The feast of Saint Michael the Archangel is called the Apparition, the Dedication, the Victory, and the Commemoration.

Michael has appeared many times. The first was on Mount Gargano, which is in Apulia, near the city called Sipontus. In this city, in the year 390, there was a man named Garganus; some say that he was named after the mountain, and others that he gave the mountain his own name. His wealth was great, and he possessed sheep and cattle in boundless numbers. And as they were feeding on the sides of Mount Gargano, it happened that a bull left the herd, and climbed up to the summit of the mountain. When this bull did not return with the rest, the master gathered a band of servants, and sought for him over the paths and byways, finding him at last at the top of the mountain, at the entrance to a cave. Being angry with the bull for wandering off alone, the master aimed a poisoned arrow at him, but at once, as if blown by the wind, the arrow returned and struck down him who had shot it. Much alarmed at this, the townsfolk went to the bishop and consulted with him concerning the astonishing event. The bishop imposed a three-day fast, and admonished them to seek an answer from God. At the end of the three days, Saint Michael appeared to the bishop, and said: "Know ye that it was by my will that this man was struck with his own arrow; for I am Michael the Archangel. I have chosen to dwell on earth in that place, and to keep it for my own; and I willed by this sign to make manifest that I watched over the place and guarded it!" At once the bishop and the townspeople went in procession to the cave, and not daring to enter, stood without in prayer.

The second apparition is one which is said to have taken place about the year of the Lord 710. At a place called Tumba, which is near the sea, a distance of six miles from the city of Avranches, Michael appeared to the bishop of the city, and ordered him to build a church in his honour, as had been done on Mount Gargano, and to celebrate his memory there. As the bishop was not certain of the place where the church was to be built, Michael instructed him to erect it at the spot where he should find a bull that had been hidden by thieves; and when the bishop knew not how large to build the church, the archangel commanded him to follow the lines traced by the bulls' hooves. At that spot two great stones were found, so heavy that no human strength could move them; but Michael appeared to a certain man, ordering him to go to the place and to remove the stones. He went, and moved the stones as easily as if they had no weight. And when the church was built, they brought thither a part of the mantle which Saint Michael had placed upon the altar at Mount Gargano, and a part of the marble whereon he had stood. And as there was a scarcity of water in the place, at the angel's bidding they made a crevice in a certain very hard rock, and straightway such a torrent of water gushed forth that they are still abundantly supplied therefrom. This apparition is solemnly commemorated at the aforementioned place on October 16.

In this same place a miracle worthy of being recalled is said to have occurred. The mountain was surrounded on all sides by the ocean, but twice on the day of Saint Michael a path opened for the people. Once when a great multitude was on its way to the church, it befell that a woman who was near to being delivered of a child went with them. Suddenly, with a great rush, the waters began to close, and the crowd, terror-stricken, fled to the shore. Only the woman was unable to save herself, and was caught by the waves. But the Archangel Michael preserved her unharmed, so that she brought forth her son in the midst of the deep, and held him in her arms to nurse him; and the sea opened once more to afford her a passage, and she came ashore rejoicing.

The third apparition took place at Rome, in the time of Saint Gregory the Pope. When Gregory had instituted the Greater Litanies, and was praying devoutly that the people of Rome might be delivered of the plague, he saw an angel of the Lord standing upon the castle which was once called the Tomb of Hadrian; the angel was drying a bloody sword, and putting it up into its sheath. From this Gregory understood that his prayers were heard, and erected a church at that same place in honour of the angel, whence the castle has since been called the Fortress of the Holy Angel. This apparition is commemorated on May 8, together with that by which Michael once gave victory to the people of Sipontus, at Mount Gargano.

The fourth apparition consists in the hierarchies of the angels themselves. For the first hierarchy is called the *Epiphania,* or upper apparition; the second is called the *Hyperphania,* or middle apparition; the third is called the *Hypophania,* or lower apparition. Hierarchy comes from *hierar,* sacred, and *archos,* prince, and means a sacred principate. Each of the hierarchies comprises three orders. The upper includes the Seraphim, the Cherubim, and the Thrones; the middle includes the Dominations, the Virtues, and the Powers, according as Dionysius assigns them; the lower includes the Principalities, the Angels, and the Archangels, according to the same author. This order and disposition of the angels can be understood by their likeness with earthly powers. For of the ministers who are in the service of a king, some are attached to the king's person, such as the chamberlains, the counsellors, and the assessors; and the orders of the first hierarchy are like to these. Some are in charge of the kingdom as a whole, not being assigned to this or that province, such as the commanders of the army and the judges of the curia; and the orders of the second hierarchy are like to these. Some, finally, are assigned to a particular part of the kingdom, such as the prefects and bailiffs and suchlike minor officials; and the orders of the third hierarchy are like to these. The first three orders are therefore set apart by the fact that they minister to God and are wholly turned to Him. For this service three things are required: the fulness of love, and this belongs to the Seraphim, whose name means ardent; the fulness of knowledge, and this belongs to the Cherubim, whose name means plenitude of knowledge; and perpetual possession and enjoyment, and this belongs to the Thrones, because in them God sits and rests, inasmuch as He causes them to rest in Himself. The three orders of the middle hierarchy are distinguished by the fact that they are set to rule and command the whole universe of men. This rule consists in three things: in presiding or commanding, and this is the office of the Dominations, whose office it is to command the lower angels, and to direct them in all divine missions, as is suggested in *Zacharias,* when one angel says to another: "Run, speak to this young man, etc."; in carrying out commands, and this is the office of the Virtues, to whom nothing that is commanded is impossible, and therefore miracles are attributed to them; and in warding off hindrances and attacks, and this is the office of the Powers, who combat the opposing powers, as is signified in *Tobias,* where it is said that the angel Raphael took the Devil, and bound him in the desert of upper Egypt. The three orders of the lower hierarchy are distinguished by their limited authority. Some of them rule over a particular province, and these are of the order of the Principalities, such as the Prince of the Persians, of whom it is spoken in Daniel. Others are assigned to rule over a certain group, as for instance the people of a city, and these are called Archangels. Still others are charged with the guidance of a single person, and these are called Angels. Hence the angels are said to announce things of lesser import, because their ministry is bourned to one man, whereas the archangels are said to announce greater things, because the good of a multitude is more important than the good of one. Thus Dionysius.

The fifth apparition is one of which we read in the *Tripartite History.* Near Constantinople there is a place where of yore the goddess Vesta was worshipped, but where there now stands a church built in honour of Saint Michael; whence the place is called Michaelium. Now there was a man named Aquilinus, who was stricken with a fever so violent that his face was flushed and red; and when the physicians gave him a potion to cure the fever, he vomited it out, and similarly vomited all that he ate or drank thereafter. Being thus brought near to death, he had himself carried to Michaelium, thinking that he would either die there, or be cured of his ail. There Michael appeared to him, and told him to prepare a mixture of honey and wine and pepper, and to dip all that he ate therein, and thus he would be cured. This he did, and was made whole, although it seemed contrary to the lore of medicine to give hot potions to one suffering of heats of the blood. This we read in the *Tripartite History.*

This feast is called Victory, for many have been the victories of Michael and the angels. The first is that which he granted to the people of Sipontus, in the following wise. Soon after the apparition on Mount Gargano, the Neapolitans, who were still pagans, attacked the inhabitants of Sipontus and Beneventum with a large army, Beneventum being at a distance of fifty miles from Sipontus. At the bishop's counsel, the defenders asked a three days' truce, during which they fasted and besought the aid of their patron Saint Michael. On the third night Michael appeared to the bishop, told him that the prayers were granted, promised victory, and bade him send the troops into the battle on the morrow at the fourth hour. As battle was joined, violent tremours shook Mount Gargano, and a black cloud hid its summit, whence lightning flashed continually, so that six hundred of the enemy fell, struck down by the sword and by flaming arrows. The rest, acknowledging the power of the archangel, abandoned the cult of the idols, and submitted to the yoke of the Christian faith.

The second is the victory which Michael won when he drove the dragon, which is to say Lucifer, and all his followers out of Heaven; of which victory we read in the *Apocalypse:* "There was a great battle in heaven, Michael and his angels fought with the dragon, and the dragon fought and his angels." For when Lucifer sought to be equal to God, the Archangel Michael, standard-bearer of the heavenly host, came forward, and cast the rebels out of Heaven, imprisoning them in the dark regions of the air until the day of judgment. They are not permitted to dwell in Heaven, which is the upper region of the air, and is bright and pleasant; nor with us on earth, lest they molest us excessively. They abide therefore between Heaven and earth, that they may suffer when they look upward to the glory which they have lost, and may be tortured with envy when they look downward, and see men ascending to the heights whence they themselves have fallen. But God's design permits them to come down to try us, whence, as has been revealed to certain holy men, they ofttimes fly about us like flies; for they are innumerable, and fill the whole air like flies. Hence Haymon says: "Philosophers have taught, and our doctors agree, that the air is as full of demons, and evil spirits as a ray of sun with specks of dust." Yet, according to the opinion of Origen, their number is lessened when we conquer them, so that when one is tempted to a certain vice and conquers the demon who tempts him, that demon can no longer tempt anyone to that vice.

The third victory is that which the angels daily wrest from the demons, when they fight against them in our defense, and deliver us from their temptations. This they do in three ways. They curb the power of the demons, as we see in the *Apocalypse* concerning the angel who bound Satan and cast him into the bottomless pit, and in *Tobias,* concerning the demon who was bound in the upper desert; for this is naught else than a curbing of the demon's power. They cool the fires of our concupiscence, as is signified in *Genesis,* where we read that the angel touched the sinew in Jacob's thigh, and forthwith it shrank. They impress the memory of Our Lord's Passion upon our minds, as is indicated in the *Apocalypse,* where it is said: "Hurt not the earth nor the sea nor the trees, till we sign the servants of our God in their foreheads." Likewise in *Ezechiel* we read: "Mark *Thau* upon the foreheads of the men that sigh"; for the letter *Thau* is formed like a cross, and those that are marked therewith fear not the destroying angel. Hence it is written in the same place: "Upon whomsoever you shall see *Thau,* kill him not."

The fourth victory is that which the Archangel Michael will win over the Antichrist, when he will slay him. For then, as we read in *Daniel,* Michael the great prince shall rise up, and shall stand staunch as the aid and protector of the elect against the Antichrist. The *Gloss* on the words of the *Apocalypse,* "I saw one of his heads as it were slain to death," says that then the Antichrist will feign to be dead, and after hiding for three days will appear again, and will say that he has risen from the dead; whereupon by the magic of the demons he will ascend into the air, and they will adore him, while all look on in wonderment.   Then, as we read in the gloss, on the words of *II Thessalonians,* "whom the Lord Jesus shall kill," the Antichrist will come to the top of the Mount of Olives; and while he sits enthroned in his tent, the Lord will go up against him, and Michael will come and slay him.

This feast is called the Dedication, because on this day the Archangel Michael revealed that he himself had dedicated the cave on Mount Gargano, whereof we have already spoken.  For when the men of Sipontus returned from the slaughter of their enemies and were celebrating their splendid victory, they began to wonder whether or not they should enter the cave, or dedicate it.  The bishop thought best to consult Pope Pelagius on this matter, and the pope responded: "If it be for man to dedicate this church, 'twere seemly that it be done on the day whereon the victory was won; but lest perchance Saint Michael's pleasure be different, his will must first be sought."  The pope and the bishop then joined with the people in a three days' fast, at the end of which Michael appeared to the bishop on this very day, and said to him: "There is no need for you to dedicate the church which I have built, for I myself have founded it and dedicated it!"  Then he ordered the bishop to go to the church on the morrow, together with the populace, and bade them honour him with prayers, and look upon him as their special patron.  The archangel also gave a sign of the aforementioned consecration, namely that they should climb up by a little-used path from the eastern side, and there they would find the footprints of a man impressed into the marble. On the morrow therefore the bishop and the entire populace came to the place, and going in they found a vast crypt, with three altars, of which two were on the southern side and the third toward the East; and this last was of awesome size, and covered with a red mantle.  The Mass was then celebrated, and all the people received the holy Communion, and afterward returned to their homes with great rejoicing.  The bishop then designated certain priests and clerks to celebrate the Divine Office there continually.  In this cave there flows a clear and exceeding sweet water, which the people drink after Communion, and divers ailments are healed thereby. And when the sovereign pontiff heard of all these things, he decreed that this day should be celebrated everywhere throughout the world, in honour of Saint Michael and all the blessed spirits.

Finally, this feast is called the Commemoration of Saint Michael, but in it we commemorate and honour all the angels.  For indeed we owe them praise and honour for many reasons.  They are our guardians, our ministers, our brothers and fellow citizens, they bear our souls to Heaven, they present our prayers to God, and they console the afflicted.

Firstly, we owe them honour as our guardians. To every man, indeed, two angels are given, one a bad angel to try him, the other a good angel to guard him. The good angel is deputed to guard him at birth, and in the womb, and immediately after his birth, and during his adult life; for in each of these phases of his life, man needs the wardship of an angel. While he is in the womb, he is yet subject to damnation. From the womb to adult age, he may be prevented from baptism. And when he is in adult age, he can be drawn into divers sins. For in his adulthood, the Devil beguiles his reason by subtilities, entices his will by allurements, and besets his virtue by violence. Thus it was needful that he have a guardian angel who might instruct and guide him against falsehood, exhort and hearten him against enticements, and defend him against violence.

Secondly, we must honour the angels as our ministers and servants, for as the *Epistle to the Hebrews* says, they are all ministering spirits. All are sent for our sake, the highest to those beneath, they to the lowest, and the lowest to us. This sending of the angels befits the goodness of God, for in this He shows His love of our salvation, that He sends His most noble spirits to assure our eternal well-being.

Thirdly, we must honour the angels as our brothers and fellow citizens; for all the elect are taken up into the angelic orders, some to the higher, some to the lower, some to the middling, according to the diversity of their merits; and the Blessed Virgin is over all.

Fourthly, we must honour them because they bear our souls to Heaven, and this they do in a threefold way. They prepare the way, as it is written in *Malachias:* "Behold I send my angel, and he shall prepare my way." They lead us to Heaven by the way which they have prepared, as is written in *Exodus:* "Behold I will send my angel, who shall go before thee, and keep thee in thy journey, and bring thee into the place that I have prepared." Finally, they give us our places in Heaven, as we read in *Luke:* "It came to pass that the beggar died, and was carried by the angels into Abraham's bosom."

Fifthly, we must honour them because they present our prayers to God, as it is written in *Tobias:* "When thou didst pray with tears, and didst bury the dead, and didst leave thy dinner, and hide the dead by day in thy house, and bury them by night, I offered thy prayer to the Lord." They likewise plead for us, as we read in *Job:* "If there shall be an angel speaking for him, one among thousands, to declare man's uprightness, He shall have mercy upon him."

Lastly, we must honour them because they console the afflicted, and this they do in a threefold manner. They comfort and strengthen him, as we find in *Daniel,* for when Daniel fainted away, the angel touched him and said: "Fear not, O man of desires, peace be to thee: take courage and be strong!" They preserve him from impatience, as the Psalm says: "He hath given his angels charge over thee, to keep thee in all thy ways; in their hands they shall bear thee up." And finally, they calm and lessen the affliction, as is signified in *Daniel,* when the angel of the Lord came down to the three children in the fiery furnace, and made the blast of the furnace like the blowing of a wind bringing dew.

[tr. GRANGER RYAN AND HELMUT RIPPERGER]

# HYMNS AND SEQUENCES

More than any other institution, monasticism brought western Europe out of economic and cultural chaos following the decline of Rome. For six centuries it controlled art, letters, and music. Its center was the office, or hours of prayer; its primary outlet for original composition was the hymn. Hymns in the Ambrosian tradition were militant and often directed against heretical doctrine. The ascetic professions of the monks colored the themes and imagery. The pattern was set by the hours of the day (vespers, matins, etc.) so that evening hymns and hymns at cockcrow were traditional.

But a new culture developed in the twelfth and thirteenth centuries. What we see clearly in the change from Romanesque to Gothic architecture is less obvious but no less real in other forms of art. The Franciscan and Dominican brotherhoods became as vital a force in ecclesiastical art as the Benedictines once had been. The service of the people was the Mass, with the Eucharist at its heart, not the hours of prayer; and the outlet for new composition in the Mass was the sequence (see above, pp. 247–248).

The sequence was tied to the calendar of proper feast days. It was intended for popular instruction in the fundamentals of the Christian story, as the Eucharist was the fundamental Christian sacrament. Christ, the Virgin, *Corpus Christi,* and the Christian virtues were constant themes. The sequence, as a newer form than the hymn, had a fresh vigor; in fact, hymn writers came to imitate the innovations of the sequence, and the only real difference in the thirteenth century lay in the liturgical use. Clerks and vernacular poets learned how to compose from the regular service and its music. The history of medieval lyrical composition is, therefore, to a considerable extent, the history of the sequence. By the middle of the twelfth century, composers had developed a strophaic pattern of accentual verse with complex two-syllabled end rhyme. The sequence reached its full bloom in the thirteenth century with the *Stabat Mater* and the *Dies Irae,* "the two supreme productions of the poetical genius of the Franciscan movement and the last authentic voices of Catholic hymnody" (Raby). Thereafter, the inspiration quickly disappeared before the growing taste of the humanists for classical Latin poetry.

Sequence: CONVERSION OF ST. AUGUSTINE (May 5)

Adam of St. Victor (fl. 1130–1172)

*Augustini praeconia*
  *Cuncti fideles personent!*
*Spiritali laetitia*
  *Lingua, mens, vita consonent!*

898

Let all the faithful tell around
  Augustine's praises publicly;
And tongue, heart, life, together sound
  In spiritual ecstasy!

Our father's solemn festal rites,
  Returning to us year by year,
Invite us to those pure delights,
  Which nevermore shall disappear.

Well-learned in all those arts was he,
  Which "liberal" we account to be;
And in all Scriptures equally,
  From which his thoughts were never free.

At first, puffed up with earthly lore,
  Which neither end nor object knew,
He wished unseen things to explore
  By light his senses on them threw.

Whilst he was still a Gentile youth,
  He falls into that error's snares,
Which would believe as very truth,
  That fig-trees, stripped of leaves, shed tears.

When there from Carthage he had come
  To lecture upon rhetoric,
Thou calledst him, O Lord! at Rome
  To the true faith, the Catholic.

When, by God's will and not his own,
  He comes to Milan to reside,
To Ambrose there becoming known,
  He straightway takes him for his guide.

When afterwards he was baptized
  By that blest prelate, throughly he
The pomp of this poor world despised,
  And changed his life most wondrously.

He, whilst his studies he directs
  Towards the words of Holy Writ,
The witness for all time collects
  Of many a writer touching it.

He 'gainst the Manichaean sect
  Proved an insuperable wall;
And by his preaching a respect
  Most wonderful obtained from all.

When Monica his mother, who
   Had come from Africa, first knew
Of the conversion of her boy,
   Her heart within her leaped for joy.

For she beholds that very son,
   Once as a Manichaean known,
Converted from his former state,
   Seeking his Lord to imitate.

Illustrious pastor! us, we pray,
   Who now thine endless praise declare,
From this world's ruin and decay
   Preserve thou by unceasing prayer.

Jesu! sweet refuge, where those slake
   Their griefs, who refuge with Thee take!
Grant us for this our father's sake
   A good departure hence to make.   Amen.
               [tr. DIGBY S. WRANGHAM]

## Sequence: ST. THOMAS OF CANTERBURY
### (December 29)

### Adam of St. Victor (fl. 1130–1172)

*Pia mater plangat Ecclesia*
*Quod patravit major Britannia*
   *Factum detestabile;*
*Pietate movetur Francia;*
*Fugit coelum, tellus et maria*
   *Scelus exsecrabile!*

Now let our holy Mother-Church bemoan
What was aforetime by Great Britain done;
   'Twas a deed detestable:
By pious feelings France is deeply stirred,
And in all horror from the guilt abhorred
   Flee heaven and earth and seas as well!

Ah! a crime beyond all telling,
One most hateful and repelling,
   Was at England's hands then done:
She prejudged her father, newly
To his home restored, and foully
   Murdered him upon his throne.

Thomas, all England's brightest flower,
The glory of the church, before

All others in exalted fame,
At Canterbury's temple door,
The laws of justice to secure,
    Both sacrifice and priest became.

'Twixt the temple and the altar,
  On the threshold, each assaulter
Doth rudely shake, but breaks him not;
Though with their swords in twain they cut
    In its midst the temple veil.
  Low Elisha's bald head lieth,
  Zacharias, slaughtered, dieth;
Peace, thus betrayed, dissolves away,
And the sweet organ now can play
    But the tearful mourners' wail.

Upon Childermas's morrow
Is this Innocent to sorrow
Dragged forth, and blows, and tortures' pain;
Whilst, on the earth outpoured, his brain,
    Lo! the sword's point bareth.
As that temple's chiefest glory,
Blushes still its pavement gory,
Which is o'ersprinkled with his blood,
As there this holy priest of God
    Robes of passion weareth.

Rages wrath, with fury fevered,
Just blood is to death delivered;
With a sword his head is shivered
    In the presence of the Lord:
  Consecrating, consecrated,
  Immolating, immolated,
  He to man a celebrated
    Type of virtue doth afford.

Holocaust, with marrow welling,
Known to earth's remotest dwelling,
Sacrifice to God sweet-smelling,
    This pontiff was selected;
  For a crown that maybe riven
  Two-fold robes to him are given
  On his primate's throne, in heaven
    Restored and re-erected.

Jews depreciate our fame, Pagans show derision,
Such as worship idols scoff, that our own religion
    Should to break its pledge have dared,
    Neither have that father spared,

Over Christians reigning,
Rachel weepeth for that son, nor finds consolation,
Who thus in his mother's womb meets assassination;
    Over whose untimely end
    Holy hearts their tears expend,
      Bitterly complaining.

This man is that pontiff bright,
Whom on heaven's supremest height
    Its supernal maker, God,
Stablished in great glory,
When with swords all-gory
    England's swordsmen smite him.
Since of death he felt no dread,
But surrendered up his head
    To welter in his blood,
When he hence was driven
God to highest heaven
    Did at once admit him.

Of his death indeed most precious mighty wonders testify;
Jesu! may he recommend us unto Thee eternally!
                    [tr. Digby S. Wrangham]

## HYMN TO THE HOLY SPIRIT

### Cardinal Stephen Langton?
### (d. *circ.* 1228)

*Veni, sancte Spiritus,*
*Et emitte caelitus*
   *Lucis tuae radium:*
*Veni, pater pauperum;*
*Veni, dator munerum;*
*Veni lumen cordium.*

Holy Spirit, Lord of light,
From thy clear celestial height
   Thy pure beaming radiance give;
Come, thou Father of the poor,
Come, with treasures that endure,
   Come, thou light of all that live!

Thou, of all consolers best,
Thou, the soul's delightsome guest,
   Dost refreshing peace bestow;
Thou in toil art comfort sweet,
Pleasant coolness in the heat,
   Solace in the midst of woe.

Light immortal, light divine!
Visit thou these hearts of thine
 And our inmost being fill:
If thou take thy grace away,
Nothing pure in man will stay:
 All his good is turned to ill.

Heal our wounds, our strength renew,
On our dryness pour thy dew:
 Wash the stains of guilt away.
Bend the stubborn heart and will;
Melt the frozen, warm the chill;
 Guide the steps that go astray.

Thou, on those who evermore
Thee confess and thee adore,
 In thy sevenfold gifts, descend;
Give them comfort when they die,
 Give them life with thee on high,
 Give them joys that never end.

[tr. EDWARD CASWELL]

## Hymn: VESPERS ON CORPUS CHRISTI

### St. Thomas Aquinas (1227-1274)

*Pange lingua gloriosi*
*Corporis mysterium*
*Sanguinisque pretiosi,*
*Quem in mundi pretium*
*Fructus ventris generosi*
*Rex effudit gentium.*

Sing, my tongue, the Saviour's glory,
Of his Flesh the mystery sing;
Of the Blood, all price exceeding,
Shed by our immortal King,
Destined, for the world's redemption,
From a noble womb to spring.

Of a pure and spotless Virgin
Born for us on earth below,
He, as Man, with man conversing,
Stayed, the seeds of truth to sow;
Then He closed in solemn order
Wondrously His life of woe.

On the night of that Last Supper
Seated with His chosen band,
He, the Paschal victim eating,

First fulfills the Law's command:
Then as Food to all His brethren
Gives Himself with his own hand.

Word made Flesh, the bread of nature
By His word to Flesh He turns;
Wine into His Blood He changes:
What though sense no change discerns?
Only be the heart in earnest,
Faith her lesson quickly learns.

Down in adoration falling,
Lo! the sacred Host we hail;
Lo! o'er ancient forms departing,
Newer rites of grace prevail;
Faith for all defects supplying,
Where the feeble senses fail.

To the everlasting Father,
And the Son who reigns on high,
With the Holy Ghost proceeding
Forth from Each eternally,
Be salvation, honor, blessing,
Might, and endless majesty.

               [tr. Edward Caswell]

## Sequence: FRIDAY AFTER EASTER

### Jacopone da Todi (1230?–1306)

*Stabat mater dolorosa*
*Juxta crucem lacrimosa,*
   *Dum pendebat Filius,*
*Cujus animam gementem,*
*Contristatam et dolentem,*
   *Pertransivit gladius.*

At the Cross her station keeping
Stood the mournful mother weeping,
   Close to Jesus to the last;
   Through her heart, His sorrow sharing,
All His bitter anguish bearing,
   Now at length the sword had passed.

O how sad and sore distressed
Was that mother highly blest
   Of the sole-begotten One!
Christ above in torment hangs:

She beneath Him holds the pangs
Of her dying glorious Son.

Is there one who would not weep
Whelmed in miseries so deep
  Christ's dear mother to behold?
Can the human heart refrain
From partaking in her pain,
  In that mother's pain untold?

Bruised, derided, cursed, defiled,
She beheld her tender Child
  All with bloody scourges rent;
For the sins of His own nation,
Saw Him hang in desolation,
  Till His spirit forth he sent.

O thou mother, fount of love,
Touch my spirit from above,
  Make my heart with thine accord!
Make me feel as thou hast felt;
Make my soul to glow and melt
  With the love of Christ my Lord.

Holy mother, pierce me through!
In my heart each wound renew
  Of my Saviour crucified;
Let me share with thee His pain,
Who for all my sins was slain,
  Who for me in torments died.

Let me mingle tears with thee,
Mourning Him who mourned for me,
  All the days that I may live;
By the Cross with thee to stay,
There with thee to weep and pray,
  Is all I ask of thee to give.

Virgin of all virgins blest!
Listen to my fond request:
  Let me share thy grief divine;
Let me, to my latest breath,
In my body bear the death
  Of that dying Son of thine.

Wounded with His every wound,
Steep my soul till it hath swooned
  In His very blood away;
Be to me, O virgin, nigh,

Lest in flames I burn and die
  In His awful judgment day:

Christ, when Thou shalt call me hence,
Be Thy mother my defence,
  Be Thy cross my victory
While my body here decays,
May my soul Thy goodness praise,
  Safe in paradise with Thee.

[tr. EDWARD CASWELL]

Sequence: MASS FOR THE DEAD

Thomas of Celano (*circ.* 1200–1255)

*Dies irae, dies illa*
*Solvet saeclum in favilla,*
*Teste David cum Sibylla.*

Hear'st thou, my soul, what serious things
Both the Psalm and Sibyl sings
Of a sure Judge from whose sharp ray
The world in flames shall fly away?

O that Fire! before whose face
Heaven and earth shall find no place;
O those eyes! whose angry light
Must be the day of that dread night.

O that Trump! whose blast shall run
An even round with th' circling sun,
And urge the murmuring graves to bring
Pale mankind forth to meet his King.

Horror of nature, hell, and death!
When a deep groan from beneath
Shall cry "We come, we come," and all
The caves of night answer one call.

O that Book! whose leaves so bright
Will set the world in severe light;
O that Judge! whose hand, whose eye
None can endure yet none can fly.

Ah then, poor soul, what wilt thou say?
And to what patron choose to pray,
When stars themselves shall stagger, and
The most firm foot no more can stand?

But Thou giv'st leave, dread Lord, that we
Take shelter from Thyself in Thee,
And with the wings of Thine own dove
Fly to Thy sceptre of soft love.

Dear, remember in that day
Who was the cause Thou cam'st this way;
Thy sheep was strayed and Thou wouldst be
Even lost Thyself in seeking me.

Shall all that labour, all that cost
Of love, and even that loss, be lost?
And this loved soul judged with no less
Than all that way and weariness?

Just mercy, then, Thy reckoning be
With my price and not with me;
'Twas paid at first with too much pain
To be paid twice, or once in vain.

Mercy, my Judge! mercy, I cry
With blushing cheek and bleeding eye;
The conscious colours of my sin
Are red without and pale within.

O let Thine own soft bowels pay
Thyself, and so discharge that day!
If Sin can sigh, Love can forgive:
O say the word, my soul shall live!

Those mercies which Thy Mary found,
Or who Thy cross confessed and crowned,
Hope tells my heart the same loves be
Still alive, and still for me.

Though both my prayers and tears combine,
Both worthless are, for they are mine;
But Thou Thy bounteous self still be,
And show Thou art by saving me.

O when Thy last frown shall proclaim
The flocks of goats to folds of flame,
And all Thy lost sheep found shall be,
Let "Come ye blessed" then call me!

When the dead He shall divide
Those limbs of death from Thy left side,
Let those life-speaking lips command
That I inherit Thy right hand.

O hear a suppliant heart all crushed
And crumbled into contrite dust!
My hope, my fear, my Judge, my Friend,
Take charge of me and of my end!
                              [tr. RICHARD CRASHAW]

# LATE LATIN LYRICS

As literature in the vernacular increased, Latin was more and more restricted to the professional classes: the clergy, the physicians, the lawyers, and the teachers. These were the professions for which the universities trained. Naturally enough, then, the authors of the lyrics in this section were university students or graduates. These scholars tended to move freely from one region to another; for learning knew no boundaries, and Latin was not confined to a province. Its users recognized no local allegiance.

As early as the seventh century, students and teachers wandered from one part of Europe to another, often against the edicts of governors. We have already read lyrics of such wandering scholars as Fortunatus, Walafrid Strabo, and Sedulius Scottus. Bishop Boniface and Emperor Charles each tried in his way to control such *vagantes* by regulations that were difficult, if not impossible, to enforce. As the cathedral schools grew in number and quality, and as the principle of primogeniture forced younger sons of barons off the land into the schools, the number of students who moved from school to school, seeking small preferments and living on their wits, grew. Then the universities began with the growth of towns. In students' quarters in overcrowded cities developed a Bohemian life with its own traditions. The students invented a living language, a Latin that mixed with rare abandon images from Horace, the classroom, and the tavern. The Parisian "Latin quarter" was no doubt duplicated in Oxford, Padua, Naples, Montpellier, Toulouse, Salamanca, Lisbon, and many other university towns. Germany had no universities until the fourteenth century (Prague, 1348; Vienna, 1365), but Germans studied in great numbers elsewhere.

For amusement, the impecunious students turned to wine, women, and song. The verses they composed exalted that trinity. They parodied what was familiar to them all — the classics and the liturgy; they satirized the pompous officials who were constantly badgering them. But not all the songs were humorous or impious. The love songs of Abelard have already been mentioned; Héloïse was by no means the only woman educated to a taste for Latin verse. Laments against cold and poverty ring true. And poets' welcomes to spring, when they could leave garret and hovel, are genuine enough. Many scholars caught up native tunes in their wanderings and composed noble verses for them. As a student moved from Cambridge to Bologna, he carried as his introduction to a new brotherhood the verses he had picked up on the way.

Apparently the students created their own saint — Golias — to whom they sang in much adoration. A typical academic poet is one not known by name, but is called simply the Archpoet. He composed some ten songs that have survived. We know from them that he was German, of knightly birth, that he failed to find preferment in the Church, lived long in poverty, and was patronized by Archbishop Rainald of Cologne, Archchancellor of Emperor Frederick I. The Archpoet's famous *Confession of Golias* has been sung and added to for nearly eight centuries. Its jingling line, consisting of a dactylic paeon and a dactyl followed by a dactylic paeon and trochee (or dactyl catalectic), is the so-called Goliardic line, which is older than the Archpoet and as good today as ever. The *carmina burana* composed by these *vagantes* are verses contained in a famous manuscript from Benedictbeuern in Germany, which also includes remarkable examples of early drama and vernacular lyric poetry.

The university songs have never died, and are still sung and imitated in European universities. But the hot breath of humanism and the Renaissance shriveled them; for in the new cultivation of good taste and "pure Latin," scholars regarded the medieval rhyme and rhythm as doggerel. The two poems of Jean Gerson, Chancellor of the University of Paris, which close this section, are produced in a Silver Age of decline.

## Strophes from THE CONFESSION OF GOLIAS

### The Archpoet (*circ.* 1165)

*Estuans intrinsecus ira vehementi*
*In amaritudine loquor meae menti.*
*Factus de materia levis elementi*
*Similis sum folio, de quo ludunt venti.*

Boiling in my spirit's veins
    With fierce indignation,
From my bitterness of soul
    Springs self-revelation:
Framed am I of flimsy stuff,
    Fit for levitation,
Like a thin leaf which the wind
    Scatters from its station.

While it is the wise man's part
    With deliberation
On a rock to base his heart's
    Permanent foundation,
With a running river I
    Find my just equation,
Which beneath the self-same sky
    Hath no habitation.

Carried am I like a ship
    Left without a sailor,
Like a bird that through the air
    Flies where tempests hale her;

Chains and fetters hold me not,
  Naught avails a jailer;
Still I find my fellows out
  Toper, gamester, railer.

Down the broad road do I run,
  As the way of youth is;
Snare myself in sin, and ne'er
  Think where faith and truth is,
Eager far for pleasure more
  Than soul's health, the sooth is,
For this flesh of mine I care,
  Seek not ruth where ruth is.

Prelate, most discreet of priests,
  Grant me absolution!
Dear's the death whereof I die,
  Sweet my dissolution;
For my heart is wounded by
  Beauty's soft suffusion;
All the girls I come not nigh,
  Mine are in illusion.

Who, when into fire he falls,
  Keeps himself from burning?
Who within Pavia's walls
  Fame of chaste is earning?
Venus with her finger calls
  Youths at every turning,
Snares them with her eyes, and thralls
  With her amorous yearning.

In the second place I own
  To the vice of gaming:
Cold indeed outside I seem,
  Yet my soul is flaming:
But when once the dice-box hath
  Stripped me to my shaming,
Make I songs and verses fit
  For the world's acclaiming.

In the third place, I will speak
  Of the tavern's pleasure;
For I never found nor find
  There the least displeasure;
Nor shall find it till I greet
  Angels without measure,
Singing requiems for the souls
  In eternal leisure.

In the public-house to die
  Is my resolution;
Let wine to my lips be nigh
  At life's dissolution:
That will make the angels cry,
  With glad elocution,
"Grant this toper, God on high,
  Grace and absolution!"

With the cup the soul lights up,
  Inspirations flicker;
Nectar lifts the soul on high
  With its heavenly ichor:
To my lips a sounder taste
  Hath the tavern's liquor
Than the wine a village clerk
  Waters for the vicar.

Nature gives to every man
  Some gift serviceable;
Write I never could nor can
  Hungry at the table;
Fasting, any stripling to
  Vanquish me is able;
Hunger, thirst, I liken to
  Death that ends the fable.

There are poets, worthy men,
  Shrink from public places,
And in lurking-hole or den
  Hide their pallid faces;
There they study, sweat, and woo
  Pallas and the Graces,
But bring nothing forth to view
  Worth the girls' embraces.

Fasting, thirsting, toil the bards,
  Swift years flying o'er them;
Shun the strife of open life,
  Tumults of the forum;
They, to sing some deathless thing,
  Lest the world ignore them,
Die the death, expend their breath,
  Drowned in dull decorum.

Lo! my frailties I've betrayed,
  Shown you every token,

Told you what your servitors
  Have against me spoken;
But of those men each and all
  Leave their sins unspoken,
Though they play, enjoy to-day,
  Scorn their pledges broken.

I have uttered openly
  All I knew that shamed me,
And have spued the poison forth
  That so long defamed me;
Of my old ways I repent,
  New life hath reclaimed me;
God beholds the heart — 'twas man
  Viewed the face and blamed me.

Thou Elect of fair Cologne,
  Listen to my pleading!
Spurn not thou the penitent;
  See, his heart is bleeding!
Give me penance! what is due
  For my faults exceeding
I will bear with willing cheer
  All thy precepts heeding.

Lo, the lion, king of beasts,
  Spares the meek and lowly;
Toward submissive creatures he
  Tames his anger wholly.
Do the like, ye powers of earth,
  Temporal and holy!
Bitterness is more than's right
  When 'tis bitter solely.
                    [tr. JOHN ADDINGTON SYMONDS]


## THE ORDER OF WANDERING STUDENTS

Anonymous, *Carmina Burana* (13th cent.)

*Cum in orbem universum decantatur: Ite*
*Sacerdotes ambulant currunt coenobitae*
*Et ab evangelio iam surgunt levitae,*
*Sectam nostram subeunt quae salus est vitae.*

At the mandate, Go ye forth,
  Through the whole world hurry!
Priests tramp out toward south and north,
  Monks and hermits skurry,

Levites smooth the gospel leave,
  Bent on ambulation;
Each and all to our sect cleave,
  Which is life's salvation.

In this sect of ours 'tis writ:
  Prove all things in season;
Weigh this life and judge of it
  By your riper reason;
'Gainst all evil clerks be you
  Steadfast in resistance,
Who refuse large tithe and due
  Unto you subsistence.

Marquesses, Bavarians,
  Austrians and Saxons,
Noblemen and chiefs of clans,
  Glorious by your actions!
Listen, comrades all, I pray,
  To these new decretals:
Misers they must meet decay,
  Niggardly gold-beetles.

We the laws of charity
  Found, nor let them crumble;
For into our order we
  Take both high and humble;
Rich and poor men we receive,
  In our bosom cherish;
Welcome those the shavelings leave
  At their doors to perish.

We receive the tonsured monk,
  Let him take his pittance;
And the parson with his punk,
  If he craves admittance;
Masters with their bands of boys,
  Priests with high dominion;
But the scholar who enjoys
  Just one coat's our minion!

This our sect doth entertain
  Just men and unjust ones;
Halt, lame, weak of limb or brain,
  Strong men and robust ones;
Those who flourish in their pride,
  Those whom age makes stupid;
Frigid folk and hot folk fried
  In the fires of Cupid.

Tranquil souls and bellicose,
  Peacemaker and foeman;
Czech and Hun, and mixed with those
  German, Slav, and Roman;
Men of middling size and weight,
  Dwarfs and giants mighty;
Men of modest heart and state,
  Vain men, proud and flighty.

Of the Wanderers' order I
  Tell the Legislature —
They whose life is free and high,
  Gentle too their nature —
They who'd rather scrape a fat
  Dish in gravy swimming,
Than in sooth to marvel at
  Barns with barley brimming.

[tr. JOHN ADDINGTON SYMONDS]

## TAKE THOU THIS ROSE [1]

*Carmina Burana* (13th cent.)

*Suscipe Flos florem quia flos designat amorem.*
*Illo de flore nimio sum captus amore.*

Take thou this rose, O Rose,
  Since Love's own flower it is,
And by that rose
  Thy lover captive is.

Smell thou this rose, O Rose,
And know thyself as sweet
As dawn as sweet.

Look on this rose, O Rose,
And looking, laugh on me,
And in thy laughter's ring
The nightingale shall sing.

Kiss thou this rose, O Rose,
That it may know the scarlet of thy mouth.

O Rose, this painted rose
  Is not the whole,

---

1. From *Mediaeval Latin Lyrics*, by Helen Waddell; Constable & Co., London, 1934. Reprinted by permission of the editor.

Who paints the flower
　　Paints not its fragrant soul.

　　　　　　　　　[tr. HELEN WADDELL]


## LET'S AWAY WITH STUDY[2]

　　　*Carmina Burana* (13th cent.)

*Obmittamus studia, dulce est desipere,*
*Et carpamus dulcia iuventutis tenere,*
*Res est apta senectuti seriis intendere.*
　*Velox aetas preterit studio detenta,*
　*Lascivire suggerit tenera iuventa.*


Let's away with study,
　Folly's sweet.
Treasure all the pleasure
　Of our youth:
Time enough for age
　To think on Truth.
*So short a day,*
*And life so quickly hasting*
*And in study wasting*
　*Youth that would be gay!*

'Tis our spring that slipping,
　Winter draweth near,
　Life itself we're losing,
　And this sorry cheer
Dries the blood and chills the heart,
　Shrivels all delight.
Age and all its crowd of ills
　Terrifies our sight.
*So short a day,*
*And life so quickly hasting,*
*And in study wasting*
　*Youth that would be gay!*

Let us as the gods do,
　'Tis the wiser part:
Leisure and love's pleasure
　Seek the young in heart
Follow the old fashion,
　Down into the street!
Down among the maidens,
　And the dancing feet!

2. Ibid.

*So short a day,*
*And life so quickly hasting,*
*And in study wasting*
  *Youth that would be gay!*

There for the seeing
  Is all loveliness,
White limbs moving
  Light in wantonness.
Gay go the dancers,
  I stand and see,
Gaze, till their glances
  Steal myself from me.
*So short a day*
*And life so quickly hasting,*
*And in study wasting*
  *Youth that would be gay!*

[tr. HELEN WADDELL]


## DANCE SONG

*Carmina Burana* (13th cent.)


*Late pandit tilia*
*Frondes, ramos, folia,*
*Thymus est sub ea*
*Viridi cum gramine,*
*In quo fit chorea.*

Wide the lime-tree to the air
Spreads her boughs and foliage fair;
  Thyme beneath is growing
On the verdant meadow where
  Dancers' feet are going.

Through the grass a little spring
Runs with jocund murmuring;
  All the place rejoices;
Cooling zephyrs breathe and sing
  With their summer voices.

[tr. JOHN ADDINGTON SYMONDS]


## A PASTORAL

*Carmina Burana* (13th cent.)

*Exiit diluculo rustica puella*
*Cum grege, cum baculo, cum lana novella.*

There went out in the dawning light
   A little rustic maiden;
Her flock so white, her crook so slight,
   With fleecy new wool laden.

Small is the flock, and there you'll see
   The she-ass and the wether;
This goat's a he, and that's a she,
   The bull-calf and the heifer.

She looked upon the green sward, where
   A student lay at leisure:
"What do you there, young sir, so fair?"
   "Come, play with me, my treasure!"
                [tr. JOHN ADDINGTON SYMONDS]

## STUDENTS' FAREWELL

*Carmina Burana* (13th cent.)

*Dulce solum natalis patriae,*
*Domus ioci, thalamus gratiae,*
*Vos relinquam aut cras aut hodie*
*Periturus amoris rabie*
     *Exul.*

Sweet native soil, farewell! dear country of my birth!
Fair chamber of the loves! glad home of joy and mirth!
To-morrow or to-day I leave you, o'er the earth
To wander struck with love, to pine with rage and dearth
              In exile!

Farewell, sweet land, and ye, my comrades dear, adieu!
To whom with kindly heart I have been ever true;
The studies that we loved I may no more pursue;
Weep then for me, who part as though I died to you,
              Love-laden!

As many as the flowers that Hybla's valley cover,
As many as the leaves that on Dodona hover,
As many as the fish that sail the wide seas over,
So many are the pangs that pain a faithful lover,
              For ever!

With the new fire of love my wounded bosom burns;
Love knows not any ruth, all tender pity spurns;
How true the proverb speaks that saith to him that yearns,
"Where love is there is pain; thy pleasure love returns
              With anguish!"

Ah, sorrow! ah, how sad the wages of our bliss!
In lovers' hearts the flame's too hot for happiness;
For Venus still doth send new sighs and new distress
When once the enamoured soul is taken with excess
                              Of sweetness!
                    [tr. JOHN ADDINGTON SYMONDS]


## THE VANITY OF THIS WORLD [3]

Anonymous (13th cent.)

*Cur mundus militat sub vana gloria*
    *Cuius prosperitas est transitoria?*
*Tam cito labitur eius potentia*
    *Quam vasa figuli quae sunt fragilia.*

Why does the world war for glory that's vain?
All its successes wax only to wane;
Quickly its triumphs are frittered away,
Like vessels the potter casts out of frail clay.

As well trust to letters imprinted in ice
As trust the frail world with its treacherous device,
Its prizes a fraud and its values all wrong;
Who would put faith in its promise for long?

Rather in hardship's uncertain distress
Trust than in this world's unhappy success;
With dreams and with shadows it leads men astray,
A cheat in our work and a cheat at our play.

Where now is Samson's invincible arm,
And where is Jonathan's sweet-natured charm?
Once-famous Solomon, where now is he
Or the fair Absolom, so good to see?

Whither is Caesar the great Emperor fled,
Or Croesus whose show on his table was spread?
Cicero's eloquence now is in vain;
Where's Aristotle's magnificent brain?

All those great noblemen, all those past days,
All kings' achievements and all prelates' praise,
All the world's princes in all their array —
In the flash of an eye comes the end of the play.

Short is the season of all earthly fame;
Man's shadow, man's pleasure, they both are the same,

3. From *Twenty-One Medieval Latin Poems,* edited by E. J. Martin; Scholartis Press,
London, 1931.   Reprinted by permission of Eric Partridge.

And the prizes eternal he gives in exchange
For the pleasure that leads to a land that is strange.

Food for the worms, dust and ashes, O why,
Bubble on water, be lifted so high?
Do good unto all men as long as ye may;
Ye know not your life will last after to-day.

This pride of the flesh which so dearly ye prize,
Like the flower of the grass (says the Scripture), it dies,
Or as the dry leaf which the wind whirls away,
Man's life is swept out from the light of the day.

Call not your own what one day ye may lose;
The world will take back all it gives you to use.
Let your hearts be in heaven, your thoughts in the skies;
Happy is he who the world can despise.

                    [tr. EDWARD JAMES MARTIN]


## SEQUENCE IN PRAISE OF WINE

### Anonymous (13th cent.)

*Vinum bonum et suave,*
*Bonis bonum, pravis praue*
*Cunctis dulcis sapor, aue*
    *Mundana laetitia!*
*Aue color uini clari!*
*Aue sapor sine pari;*
*Tua nos inebriari*
    *Digneris potentia!*

Wine the good and bland, thou blessing
Of the good, the bad's distressing,
Sweet of taste by all confessing,
    Hail, thou world's felicity!
Hail thy hue, life's gloom dispelling;
Hail thy taste, all tastes excelling;
By thy power, in this thy dwelling
    Deign to make us drunk with thee!

Oh, how blest for bounteous uses
Is the birth of pure vine-juices!
Safe's the table which produces
    Wine in goodly quality.
Oh, in colour how auspicious!
Oh, in odour how delicious!
In the mouth how sweet, propitious
    To the tongue enthralled by thee!

Blest the man who first thee planted,
Called thee by thy name enchanted!
He whose cups have ne'er been scanted
 Dreads no danger that may be.
Blest the belly where thou bidest!
Blest the tongue where thou residest!
Blest the mouth through which thou glidest,
 And the lips thrice blest by thee!

Therefore let wine's praise be sounded,
Healths to topers all propounded;
We shall never be confounded,
 Toping for eternity!
Pray we: here by thou still flowing,
Plenty on our board bestowing,
While with jocund voice we're showing
 How we serve thee — Jubilee!
[tr. JOHN ADDINGTON SYMONDS]

## WINTER AND LOVE [4]

### Anonymous (13th cent.)

*De ramis cadunt folia,*
*Nam viror totus periit,*
*Iam calor liquit omnia,*
 *Et abiit;*
*Nam signa coeli ultima*
 *Sol petiit.*

From naked boughs the leaves are gone,
 And all green things are perishèd;
That warmth which kept in unison
 The world is fled;
And in the heaven's last house the sun
 Has laid his head.

Now frost destroys all tender things,
 And winter to the birds gives pain;
The nightingale and all that wings
 Do have complain
Because the heat which summer brings
 They seek in vain.

4. From *Medieval Latin Lyrics*, by P. S. Allen; The University of Chicago Press, Chicago, 1931. Reprinted by permission of the publisher.

There's water in the stream no more,
  And no green grass on field or wold;
The sun doth stain some other shore
  Than ours with gold;
By day the snow is at my door,
  By night, the cold.

All things are ice from pole to pit,
  Only in me a flame leaps higher;
The heart that in my breast doth sit
  Is all on fire;
A maiden is the cause of it,
  Whom I desire.

My fire is nourished by her kiss,
  Her least light touch is ecstasy,
And on her eyelids hangs such bliss
  They're stars to me.
And time shall bring me naught like this,
  So heavenly.

Greek fire can be put out, they say,
  By pouring on it bitter wine;
Unhappy me!  How then allay
  This fire of mine?
Since it is fed, I swear, each day
  With fuel divine!

                              [tr. HOWARD MUMFORD JONES]


## FREE WILL AND FOREKNOWLEDGE

### Jean Gerson (A.D. 1363–1429)

Seest thou yon Sun in lustrous glory beaming,
  Shedding the rays of his unchanging essence
With the same tenor evermore outstreaming?
  How can he shroud him, niggard of his presence?

How can he choose, but with his force far-reaching,
  Shine on the world in plenitude supernal?
'Tis the same law the dreams of elder teaching
  Feign to coerce the Almighty and Eternal!

"Free," prate the Schools, "how free, the Force that acteth
  Even as it must, not wills, on mind and matter?
Free, when it never addeth nor subtracteth,
  Fixed in perpetual Law that nought can shatter?

If then Foreknowledge thus in Fate be folden,
   What thanks are due? and who is He that wants them?
What be His blessings?   Why are we beholden?
   'Tis but because He cannot choose He grants them!

What are thy prayers?   Wilt turn by supplication
   Him who remains the same from everlasting?"
Down, down, delusive doubt!   Faith's desolation,
   Sapping her fanes, her holy altars blasting!

Shall the Creator need in any measure
   Aught of the creature — praises or devotion?
'Tis enough praise that at His will and pleasure,
   He, without moving, giveth all things motion!

                        [tr. SEBASTIAN EVANS]


## HOC AGE!

### Jean Gerson


Whate'er the lot to which God calleth thee,
   There work, content!   Set not thy soul agape
In envious thirst thy life anew to shape!
      All things not thine let be!

Deal they with them to whom is given their care!
   Toil not to woo a doom that is not sent!
Prithee, to thine own self be competent,
      Nor grudge another's share!

Something of sorrow, pain, and weariness
   Each lot contains, to other lots unknown;
Trust thine experience!   Use and wont alone
      Can make that burden less.

His aching side the feverish sick man throws
   To right, to left, some place of ease to win —
Lies prone, supine.   In vain!   The hurt within
      Still bars him from repose!

Howe'er he lie, the bed feels hard and sore: —
   But let the fever in his bones be healed,
Health gives the quiet nought beside can yield,
      And he can rest once more.

God of His gifts enough is prodigal,
   So thou but use aright!   A thankful heart
Bring thou to Him, and bearing well thy part,
      Bestow a boon on all!

                        [tr. SEBASTIAN EVANS]

# X. DRAMA

Though many literary forms developed in the classical world fell into neglect in the Middle Ages and were only revived sporadically by antiquarians and humanists, no form so completely disappeared as ancient drama. *Representation* through dialogue on a stage was a lost art, never directly revived during our period. The very words, *tragœdia* and *comœdia* lost their meaning, and medieval writers like Dante and Chaucer used them in new senses to apply to forms of narrative to be read, not played. Though Hrotswitha of Gandersheim (see above, pp. 209 ff.) stands as a unique instance of an author who wrote drama according to classical precedent, it is doubtful whether she visualized her compositions as scripts for actors. Modern drama, which is a continuation of medieval drama, arose by steps from the liturgy of the Church, and was not influenced by classical dramatists until after the Middle Ages came to an end. According to Aristotle, ancient drama started in the market place and moved into the church, or temple; but modern drama started in the church and moved out to the market place.

The combination of poverty, governmental chaos, social breakdown, and revolt against pagan excesses that caused the disappearance of classical schools and the arts they fostered also caused the disappearance of the drama. Since drama depended not alone upon books, which would exist for centuries even in neglect, but upon the actors' art, which would disappear with loss of patronage, we can understand why, when the churchmen began to evolve dramatic forms, they did not realize that they were doing what had been done long before.

The Hebrews, from whom Christianity arose, were apparently not dramatic, if by drama we mean representation of one individual by another. Many attempts to show that, for instance, the Book of Job and the Song of Solomon are essentially dramatic scripts have not been successful. Like the Mohammedans who followed, there was a fear among the religious Hebrews that direct representation would lead to image worship. Yet the liturgy, as taken over from them by western peoples, contains certain dramatic elements — not drama itself, but the tools of drama. There are in a church service, for instance, music and a choir, a congregation, which in large churches tends to become an audience, an altar and appurtenances similar to stage properties, attachment of the notion of geographical position or locale to certain positions in the church (the orientation, for example), a calendar in which a historical or religious incident forms the center of attention, clerical robes and cantors' surplices, which are in one sense costumes, and scriptural texts, which contain here and there bits of dialogue. In the fifth and sixth centuries, when large basilicas like those in Ravenna were erected to take care of the many adherents to the state religion, acoustics were not good and the officiants had to introduce into the service certain gestures and motions, akin to mimicry, so that all might follow the service.

It is not, however, until the tenth century that clear elements of representation in the service emerge. Through hard work, gifts, and the patronage of the Carolingian emperors, monasteries had become substantial foundations with highly developed specialists in charge of separate tasks. The choir and choir school were in charge of artists who spared no effort to make the Hours as artistic as was conceivable. It was inevitable, therefore, that they should wish to introduce variations and niceties into the basic liturgy (the Roman rite). Some innovations took the form of *tropes,* that is, the insertion of words with music into a fixed sentence. For instance, the *Kyrie eleïson* might be troped as follows:

| Kyrie, *fons bonitatis,* | Lord, *font of goodness,* |
| *Pater ingenite,* | *Father without creator,* |
| *A quo bona cuncta* | *From whom all good* |
| *Procedunt* | *Proceeds* |
| Eleïson! | Have mercy upon us! |

Such tropes, of which the sequences already often referred to in this book are a primary example, gave ambitious choirs, their leaders, and composers an opportunity for displaying their creative power.

The famous *Quem queritis* trope was just such an addition, but it had two other qualities that stimulated development: (1) it was attached to the *introit* for the Mass on Easter Sunday and was therefore sung at that moment in the liturgical year when choirs were most anxious to refine and embellish the service; (2) it was written as question and answer and was therefore essentially dramatic dialogue. Since choirs had developed soloists and semi-choirs, which sang parts of a script, it took little imagination for a choirmaster to assign the question to one and the answer to another. In a large church, some gesture or action would accompany to aid the understanding of the congregation. The success of this trope, whose composer is unknown, stimulated imitation and addition. First were added words and music, then stage properties, and finally some distinguishing additions to the singers' robes that would identify the speakers. At this point, *representation* was established and drama had entered the liturgy.

The popularity of this dramatic means of instruction stimulated choirs to compose analogous representations for inclusion in the proper liturgy. Eventually, they were taken from within the rite and presented between Hours or before the Mass. Particular incidents in the life of Christ — the Nativity, the entry into Jerusalem, the Entombment, and Resurrection — were presented at the appropriate time of year. The entry into Jerusalem on Palm Sunday had already had a tradition of its own, for from apostolic days had developed a custom of marching from the town gates to the sanctuary while all joined in hymn singing. At Vespers on Good Friday, the clergy solemnly laid within a sepulchre built into the church or erected for the purpose, a crucifix and the consecrated Host, which were removed at Matins on Easter in preparation for the Mass. To this dramatic act was shortly attached a representation of Christ's Harrowing of Hell, drawn from the apocryphal Gospel of Nicodemus. In the same way, incidents from the Old and New Testaments, the Apocrypha, and even the legends of the saints, were dramatized for the instruction of the laity.

Eventually the great popularity of these actions and inevitable abuses drove the plays from the Church. A humorous or burlesque bit of mimicry that caught public fancy was repeated and developed; biblical characters like Noah, Balaam, and Herod became comic types. The irreverence was not in keeping with the holy Church, but was too generally enjoyed to be eliminated. The large congregations drawn by the plays could not easily be accommodated, and the solution was to present the dramas on the western porch that fronted the public square or in the churchyard. Once the plays were moved outdoors, the solemnity and restraint of the sanctuary were removed, and author and audience worked together in giving their imaginations free play — in the introduction of scenic devices, in the development of trained actors, in the composition of dialogue. Eventually, in many provinces dramatic entertainment was taken over by laymen — sometimes, as in England, for instance, by the guilds.

A number of transitional plays survive, in which the dialogue was written partly in Latin and partly in the vernacular. The introduction of vernacular composition brought greater secularity: The restraint of the ecclesiastical language was removed. In the thirteenth century, university students dramatized romances and other stories in common circulation. The first actors who earned a livelihood by drama formed bands who strolled from town to town, square to square, and inn to inn; for a building erected for the sole purpose of dramatic entertainment was not easily conceived. On the basis of evidence recently gathered by R. S. Loomis, Gustave Cohen says: "It seems sound and conservative to infer that, so far as theatrical art is concerned, the state of things in the thirteenth century was already about the same as in the fifteenth. Perhaps there was no permanent theatre, even in London, in the sense that the Swan theatre of Shakespeare's day was permanent, but there were some play-houses in the form of a circus, often in the ruins of a Roman amphitheatre (as at Douai and Bourges). A part of the structure was reserved for spectators, another part for the 'localities' and the actors sitting in front of them and waiting for the moment to appear before an applauding public."

# THE *QUEM-QUERITIS* TROPE

## Of the Lord's Resurrection

*Question* [*of the angels*]:
  Whom seek ye in the sepulchre, O followers of Christ?
*Answer* [*of the Marys*]:
  Jesus of Nazareth, which was crucified, O celestial ones.
[*The angels*]:
  He is not here; he is risen, just as he foretold.
  Go, announce that he is risen from the sepulchre.

## SEPULCHRUM

### *Regularis Concordia of Ethelwold* (10th cent.)

[From *Chief Pre-Shakesperian Dramas,* edited by J. Q. Adams; Houghton Mifflin Co., Boston, 1924. Reprinted by permission of the publisher.]

While the third lesson is being chanted, let four brethren vest themselves; of whom let one, vested in an alb, enter as if to take part in the service, and let him without being observed approach the place of the sepulchre, and there, holding a palm in his hand, let him sit down quietly. While the third responsory is being sung, let the remaining three follow, all of them vested in copes, and carrying in their hands censers filled with incense; and slowly, in the manner of seeking something, let them come before the place of the sepulchre. These things are done in imitation of the angel seated in the monument, and of the women coming with spices to anoint the body of Jesus. When therefore that one seated shall see the three, as if straying about and seeking something, approach him, let him begin in a dulcet voice of medium pitch to sing:

*Whom seek ye in the sepulchre, O followers of Christ?*

When he has sung this to the end, let the three respond in unison:

*Jesus of Nazareth, which was crucified, O celestial one.*

To whom that one:

  *He is not here; he is risen, just as he foretold.*
  *Go, announce that he is risen from the dead.*

At the word of this command let those three turn themselves to the choir, saying:

  *Alleluia! The Lord is risen to-day,*
  *The strong lion, the Christ, the son of God.*
  *Give thanks to God, huzza!*

This said, let the former, again seating himself, as if recalling them, sing the anthem:

*Come, and see the place where the Lord was laid. Alleluia! Alleluia!*

And saying this, let him rise, and let him lift the veil and show them the place bare of the cross, but only the cloths laid there with which the cross was wrapped. Seeing which, let them set down the censers which they carried into the same sepulchre, and let them take up the cloth and spread it out before the eyes of the clergy; and, as if making known that the Lord had risen and was not now therein wrapped, let them sing this anthem:

> *The Lord is risen from the sepulchre,*
> *Who for us hung upon the cross.*

And let them place the cloth upon the altar. The anthem being ended, let the Prior, rejoicing with them at the triumph of our King, in that, having conquered death, he arose, begin the hymn:

> *We praise thee, O God.*

This begun, all the bells chime out together.

[tr. J. Q. ADAMS]

### DEPOSITIO and ELEVATIO, including the HARROWING OF HELL

#### Barking Abbey (15th cent.)

*Depositio Crucis* (Good Friday, between Mass and Vespers)

Then, after the Holy Cross has been adored, the priests, raising the Cross from a stipulated place, should begin the antiphon:

> *Super omnia ligna*

and should sing the whole with the choir accompanying, the chantress leading. They should bear the Cross to the high altar and there, in the likeness of Joseph and Nicodemus, detaching the Image from the Cross, should wash the wounds of the Crucified with wine and water. And while this is being done, the convent should sing the responsory:

> *Ecce quomodo moritur iustus*

with the priestess leading and the chantress responding and the convent accompanying. After washing the wounds, they should bear Him to the sepulchre with candelabras and censers, singing these antiphons:

*In pace in idipsum.*
Antiphon: *Habitabit.*
Antiphon: *Caro mea.*

And when at the appointed place, hung with the pallium by the aurist and likewise properly arranged with rich linens, they should lay it in with reverence, and the priest should close the Sepulchre and begin the responsory:

*Sepulto Domino.*

And then the abbess should bring forward the candle, which should burn continuously before the Sepulchre and should not be extinguished until, on Easter night after Matins, the Image should be taken from the Sepulchre with candles and frankincense and procession and replaced in its position. These matters attended to, the convent should return to the choir and the priest to the vestry.


*Elevatio Hostiae*

Note that according to ancient ecclesiastical tradition the Lord's Resurrection had been celebrated before Matins and before any bellringing on Easter day. And since the gathering of people at that hour seems to have stultified devotion and greatly increased human indifference, the venerable Lady Katherine Sutton [Abbess of Barking, 1363–1376], then bearing the charge of pastoral care, desiring to root out the aforesaid indifference and to stimulate the most ardent celebration, with the unanimous consent of her sisters ordered that immediately after the third responsory of Matins on Easter Day the Lord's Resurrection should be celebrated, and the procession was fixed in this manner:

First should come the Lady Abbess with the whole convent and some priests and clerks clad in copes, with one priest and clerk carrying a palm and unlighted candle in his hand. They should enter the chapel of St. Mary Magdalene, in the manner of the souls of Christ, and should close the door of the aforesaid chapel on themselves. Then the hebdomadary priest, coming from above and approaching the chapel clad in alb and cope, with two deacons, one bearing the Cross with the Lord's banner hanging from it, the other bearing the censer in his hand, and other priests and clerks with two boys carrying candles, at the door of the aforesaid chapel should three times sound this antiphon:

*Tollite portas.*

Then the priest will represent the person of Christ descending to Hell and breaking down the gates of Hell, and he should begin each aforesaid antiphon in a high voice, which same all the clerks should repeat, and at each inception he should beat with the Cross at the aforesaid gate, in the guise of breaking down the gates of Hell; and at the third knocking the gates should fly open. Then he should enter with his ministers. In the meantime a priest within the chapel should begin the antiphon:

*A porta inferi,*

to which the chantress with the whole convent should add:

*Erue, Domine, etc.*

Then the hebdomadary priest should lead all the beings in the aforesaid chapel out, and at the same time a priest should begin the antiphon:

*Domine, abstraxsti,*

and the chantress should add:

*Ab inferis.*

Then all should leave the chapel, that is, the Limbo of the Fathers, and the priest and clerks should sing the antiphon:

*Cum rex gloriae*

processionally through the center of the choir to the Sepulchre, each carrying a palm and candle, designating victory gained over the Enemy, with the Lady Abbess, the prioress, and the whole convent following, like patriarchs.

And after they come to the Sepulchre, the hebdomadary priest should cense the Sepulchre and should enter the Sepulchre as he begins the verse *Consurgit.* Then the chantress should follow after *Christus tumulo.* Verse: *Quaesumus, auctor.* Verse: *Gloria tibi, Domino.* And during this the Body of our Lord shall be carried from the Sepulchre, at the beginning of the antiphon *Christus resurgens,* to a spot before the altar, with the face toward the people, the priest holding the Body of our Lord in his hands, enclosed in a crystal. Then the chantress subjoins *Ex Mortuis.* And after that antiphon, they should continue the procession to the altar of the Holy Trinity, with the appointed articles, singing the aforesaid antiphon with verse *Dicant nunc* and versicle *Dicite in nationibus.* Prayer: *Deus qui pro nobis Filium tuum.* And this procession should be in the manner in which Christ proceeded to Galilee after the Resurrection, with His disciples following.

[tr. CHARLES W. JONES]

## PROCESSION OF PROPHETS (*Ordo Prophetarum*)

Abbey of St. Martial, Limoges (*circ.* 1100)

[From *Sermon against Jews, Pagans and Arians,* edited by
E. N. Stone; The University of Washington Press, Seattle,
1928.   Reprinted by permission of the publisher.]

> *Omnes gentes*
> *Congaudentes*
> *Dent cantum leticie.*
> *Deus homo fit,*
> *De domo Davit*
> *Natus hodie.*

PRECENTOR: Let all nations, rejoicing together, raise a song of jubilee.   God is now made man; of the house of David He is born today.

O Jews, ye who God's Word deny: a man of your own Law, a witness of the King, hear ye now in order due.

And ye, Gentiles, who believe not that a virgin hath brought forth; by the teachings of your people scatter the darkness.

PRECENTOR: Israel, thou man of peace, tell what thou surely knowest concerning Christ.

ISRAEL: The chief from Judah shall not be removed, until He cometh who shall be revealed.   The saving Word of God the nations shall await with me.

PRECENTOR: Lawgiver, hither draw thou nigh, and utter worthy things concerning Christ.

MOSES: A Seer shall God give unto you; to him, as unto me, give ear.   Whoso heareth not this hearer shall be cast out from his people.

PRECENTOR: Isaias, thou that knowest what is true, wherefore dost thou not speak the truth?

ISAIAS: The Rod of Jesse from his root must needs exalted be; a flower thereafter hence shall spring, which is the Spirit of God.

PRECENTOR: O Jeremias, draw thou nigh, and speak thy prophecies concerning Christ.

JEREMIAS: Thus is it.   This is indeed our God, beside whom there shall be none other.

PRECENTOR: O Daniel, declare, with voice of prophecy, the doings of the Lord.

DANIEL: The Holiest One shall come, and the anointing fail.

PRECENTOR: Now, O Habakkuk, show what manner of witness thou art unto the heavenly King.

HABAKKUK: I also waited; soon was I sore dismayed, with fear of thy marvellous acts, at this thy work between the bodies of the two beasts.

PRECENTOR: Thou, David, of thy grandson tell the things that unto thee are known.

DAVID: The whole converted flock shall worship the Lord, whom all the race of men that are to be shall serve.

The Lord said unto my Lord: Sit thou at my right hand.

PRECENTOR: And now let Simeon draw nigh, who had the oracle received, that he should not come to his end until he should have seen the Lord.

SIMEON: Now let me go, O Lord, to end my life in peace, because mine eyes do now behold the one that thou hast sent unto this world for the salvation of the people.

PRECENTOR: Thither, Elizabeth, into the midst of these, bring forth thine utterance about the Lord.

ELIZABETH: What manner of thing is this, that the mother of my Lord doth visit me? For because of him the babe within my womb doth leap for joy.

PRECENTOR: Tell now, O Baptist, for what cause didst thou, shut up within the casket of the womb, give acclamation unto Christ? To whom thou gavest joy, to him thy witness bring.

JOHN THE BAPTIST: There cometh a shoe of such a sort that I am not even worthy to dare loose the latchet thereof.

PRECENTOR: Maro, Seer of the Gentiles, bear thy witness unto Christ.

VERGIL: Lo, from the heaven unto the earth is a new race sent down.

PRECENTOR: Come! Tell, winebibber, what thou dost truly know concerning Christ.

PRECENTOR: Nebuchadnezzar, with a prophecy confirm the author of all things.

NEBUCHADNEZZAR: When I returned to see the three whom I had sent into the flames, then saw I, joined unto those righteous ones all unconsumed, the Son of God. Three men into the fire I sent, but in the fourth God's offspring I behold.

PRECENTOR: Truly, O Sibyl, now reveal the signs that thou fore-knowest concerning Christ.

THE SIBYL: The sign of the Judgment: earth with sweat shall drip; from heaven shall come the King that through the ages is to be, present in flesh, forsooth, to judge the world.

O Judea, unbelieving, why dost thou shameless yet remain?

\*    \*    \*    \*

*Here let the Benedicamus begin*

Rejoicing, let us shout aloud; with diligence let us celebrate the birthday of the Christ. Joy supreme, with grace, he brought, and graciously all faithful minds illumed.

[tr. EDWARD NOBLE STONE]

## ST. NICHOLAS AND THE IMAGE

Hilarius (13th cent.)

[From *Representative Medieval and Tudor Plays*, edited
by R. S. Loomis and H. W. Wells; Sheed & Ward, New
York, 1942.   Reprinted by permission of the publisher.]

*First of all, the* BARBARIAN, *who has gathered together his goods, comes
to the image of* ST. NICHOLAS, *and commending them to his charge,
says:*

> All things whereof I am possessed
> I've put here, Nicholas, in this chest.
> Be thou their guardian, I request;
>     Take of them good care.
> Pray to my humble prayer give ear,
> Look well that robbers come not near,
> Unto thee I deliver here
>     Gold and vestments rare.
> To journey abroad is my design.
> I to thy ward my goods consign.
> When I return, see thou resign
>     All again to me.
> Now no more fears my mind beset,
> Since in thy ward my goods are set.
> Let me, returning, not regret
>     The trust I put in thee.

*When he has departed, some passing* THIEVES, *seeing the door open
and no guardian, bear everything away.   The* BARBARIAN *returns,
and not finding the treasure, says:*

> Out Harro!   Murder, theft!
> Here all my wealth I left.
> The more fool I — 'tis reft!
>     God! this is foul treason!
> If I be wroth, 'tis not without good reason.
> Treasures, at least a hundred,
> I placed here.   How I blundered!
> Money and all are plundered.
>     God! this is foul treason!
> If I be wroth, 'tis not without good reason.
> 'Twas here I left my store.
> But here it is no more!
> This saint must pay the score!
>     God! this is foul treason!
> If I be wroth, 'tis not without good reason.

*Then, approaching the* IMAGE, *he says to it:*

> Here all my pelf I brought,
> And unto thee betaught.
> How like a fool I wrought!
>     Nicholas, hear!
> Give up my goods, or thou shalt buy them dear.

*Taking up a scourge, he says:*

> To thee I'll now impart
> A most improving art.
> Not lightly shalt thou part.
> Thou'rt in my power;
> Therefore the goods I left with thee restore.
> I call thy God to testify:
> If me thou'lt not indemnify,
> Thy knavish back I'll scarify.
> Thou'rt in my power;
> Therefore the goods I left with thee restore.

*Then* ST. NICHOLAS, *coming to the* ROBBERS, *says:*

> Wretches, what is it ye do?
> Short will be the hours and few
> That ye gloat upon your prey.
> It was in my custody.
> Think not ye escaped my eye
> When ye bore the spoil away.
> Stripes I've suffered, without fable,
> Since through you I was not able
> To give back the treasure due;
> Borne the assault of tongue and lip;
> Nay, even more, the bite of whip.
> In this pass I've come to you.
> Speedily the goods restore
> O'er whose safety I presided;
> All was to my charge confided
> Which by stealth away ye bore.
> If ye do not this in sorrow,
> Ye'll be dangling on the morrow
> From the timbers of a cross;
> For I'll openly proclaim
> Your misdeeds and works of shame.
> Therefore, haste, repair the loss.

*The* ROBBERS *in fear bring back all, and the* BARBARIAN *on finding them says:*

> Unless my sight's declining,
>     They're mine once more;

Look, gold and jewels shining!
I marvel every moment more and more.
The lost are found again
      (They're mine once more),
Without expense or pain.
I marvel every moment more and more.
O true custodian,
      (They're mine once more)
Who hast returned each one!
I marvel every moment more and more

*Then approaching the* IMAGE *and kneeling he says:*

Humbly I come to thee,
      Good Santa Claus!
Thou hast restored to me
What in thy keeping was.
Awhile I've been a rover,
      Good Santa Claus!
I now entire recover
What in thy keeping was.
My soul has gained new health,
      Good Santa Claus!
Since naught lacks of the wealth
That in thy keeping was.

*Anon appearing to him,* BLESSED NICHOLAS *says:*

Oh, pray not, brother, unto me.
To God alone make thou thy plea.
The same it is by whose decree
Were fashioned heaven and earth and sea
That hath returned thy precious hoard.
Be then no longer what thou wast,
But praise Christ's name both first and last:
Thy trust on Jesu only cast,
Through whom thine own again thou hast.
Mine is no merit nor reward.

*In reply to him the* BARBARIAN *says:*

Thy counseling I do not need;
For I'm determined with all speed
Each cruel wrong and loathsome deed
      To cast away.
I'll trust in Christ, God's only Son,
Who wondrous miracles hath done,
And all the law of Apollon
      Abjure for aye.
For Christ it is who by His hand

Hath wrought the sky, the sea, the land;
And yet to those who make demand
    His grace doth bring.
For Christ, the Lord of high degree,
Hath blotted out my sin for me.
So may His kingdom ever be
    Without ending!

               [tr. ROGER S. LOOMIS]

## From *LE MYSTERE D'ADAM*

Anonymous (oldest drama in French, 12th cent.)

[From *Early Mediaeval French Lyrics,* edited by C. C. Abbott; Constable & Co., London, 1932. Reprinted by permission of The Oxford University Press.]

      *Diabolus: Eva, ça sui venuz a toi.*
      *Eva: di moi, Sathan, e tu pur quoi?*

DIABOLUS: Eve, now am I come to thee.

EVA:      Satan, for why? now tell it me?

DIABOLUS: I seek thine honour, good and fame.

EVA:      That comes of God!

DIABOLUS:               Be not afraid;
    A long time since I did surprise
    The secret thoughts of Paradise;
    A part of them to thee I'll tell,

EVA:      Begin now, I will listen well.

DIABOLUS: And wilt thou listen?

EVA:               Yes, in truth:
    In nothing will I cause thee ruth.

DIABOLUS: Wilt thou be secret?

EVE:             Yes, pardie.

DIABOLUS: Betray it?

EVA:         Never, not by me.

DIABOLUS: Unto thy faith I trust me now,
    I wish from thee no other vow.

EVA:      Thou can'st believe my word indeed.

DIABOLUS: Within a good school thou hast been;
    Adam I saw, too headstrong he.

EVA:      A little hard.

DIABOLUS:                    Soft he shall be.
He is more stern and fierce than hell.

EVA:      Most good he is.

DIABOLUS:                              A slave as well.
Though of himself no care takes he
Let him at least take care of thee.
Thou art a frail and tender thing
Fresher than is the rose in spring.
Than crystal is thou art more white,
Than snow that falls on lowland ice.
God did create you twain awry,
He is too hard, and thou too shy;
But nonetheless thou art more wise,
To wisdom hast thou raised thine eyes.
Therefore 'tis good to come to thee.
I wish to speak.

EVA:                          Thou may'st believe.

DIABOLUS: None must know it.

EVA:                          Who should know?

DIABOLUS: Not even Adam.

EVA:                          In truth, no.

DIABOLUS: Now will I tell thee, listen pray!
Only we two are in this way
And Adam there, who has not heard.

EVA:      Speak it aloud, he'll catch no word.

DIABOLUS: I tell you of a crafty snare
For you within this garden lair.
The fruit that God has given you
Has in it little goodness true;
What He has stern forbid you touch
Contains surpassing virtue, such
Therein is found the gift of life,
Of princely power and of might,
Of knowledge, good and evil all.

EVA:      What taste has it?

DIABOLUS:                          Celestial.
Thy lovely body and thy face
Desire thee this adventure take
To be earth's sovereign as well,
Mistress of heaven and of hell.
That thou may'st know all things that be,
And over all have mastery.

EVA:          Is the fruit such?

DIABOLUS:                    I speak aright.

*Tunc diligenter intuebitur Eva fructum vetitum, quo*
*diu eius intuitu dicens:*

EVA:          Only to see it brings delight.

DIABOLUS: If thou dost eat, what wilt thou do?

EVA:          And how know I?

DIABOLUS:                    Believest thou?
              First take of it, to Adam give,
              You shall have heaven's crown forthwith,
              Like the creator you shall be,
              From you no secret hidden be;
              When you have eaten of the fruit
              Straightway your heart it will transmute;
              You shall be godlike, without sin,
              In power and goodness equal Him:
              Taste of the fruit!

EVA:                    I am afraid.

DIABOLUS: Believe not Adam.

EVA:                    I will take . . .

DIABOLUS: When?

EVA:          Have patience with me pray
              Till Adam be in sleep away.

DIABOLUS: Eat it; fearfulness outfling,
              Delay would be a childish thing.
                              [tr. CLAUDE COLLEER ABBOTT]


### From the REDENTIN EASTER PLAY

Anonymous, Low German (A.D. 1464)

[From *Poet Lore, A Quarterly of World Literature,* Boston, Vol. XLVII, 1941.   Reprinted by permission of the publisher.]

[The following scenes come after the depiction of Pilate and the Roman Soldiers, the Resurrection, and the Harrowing of Hell, which depletes Lucifer's kingdom.]

(*Then the devils lead out* LUCIFER *in chains.   He laments*)

              Dear fellows, thank you from my heart
              That still you serve me in good part.
              What once was mine I'll have and keep,
              You hear me swear both loud and deep.

Very little news you've got —
Griping grief is not our lot:
Gone indeed is hell's front gate,
Smashed by Jesus, God so great.
That was indeed a doleful stroke!
He snatched away the souls of folk
That we, five thousand years and more,
Had tortured till their bones were sore.
Now we've lost them, every one,
Since Christ Jesus, God's own son,
Took them to His Father's house,
Whence we poor things like a louse,
Were shamefully kicked out, pell-mell;
Now we bite our nails in hell!
Let us never be afraid,
Keep our chins up, undismayed:
Though the saints escape our clasp,
We may yet the sinners grasp!
Since the Lord despises fools
Who love to sin and break His rules,
Since He runs the world this way,
Let's use His sun to make our hay,
Teach mankind such foul desires
That they'll fall into our fires.
Every imp in this be true —
Know that he'll his failure rue —
Trick alike the wise and dumb,
Fill hell up, so kingdom come.
Satan, servant tried and true,
Did you hear my orders through?

SATAN:          Oh, Lucifer, dear lord and star,
For us no road shall be too far!
Whoever lives and bears a sin,
We certainly shall rope him in.

LUCIFER:        So bring them in, the poor and rich —
Let none escape your tar and pitch —
The usurer, the robber chief,
Counterfeiter, small milk thief,
The pastry cook and the magician,
The dog trainer, the lie technician,
The maltster and the brewer ripe,
And fetch us all who deal in tripe;
The tinker, and him who loafs all day,
The fuller and him who drives the sleigh,
The flax-breaker and tanner smite,
And don't forget the false wheelwright,
The verger and the sexton bring,
The carp-roaster — we'll make him sing —

The writer and the one who reads,
The plowman, coachman — fill my needs;
Bring me the puppet-player, too,
For taking money — from fools, it's true;
Bring me the knight and the lord of the land;
Let not a one of them slip through your hand;
Bring me the tailor, bring me the smith,
Chain them all up with their kin and their kith;
Bring me the seer and the evil old wives,
Don't let the rascals escape with their lives!
What good does it do you to hesitate?
Begone from this place on your mission of hate!

SATAN:  Come gentlemen, be very wise;
Beware at all costs, I advise,
Dissention with Pope Lucifer.
Now on the road yourselves bestir
And labor for the lord of hell:
The last's a whoreson!   Fare thee well!

### SCENE

LUCIFER:  East, south, west, north!
Come here, from all my forts come forth!
Well done, well done, come here,
You Satan and Flop-ear!

SATAN:  What news, O Master dear?
You call so loud and clear.
I've run to you like fire,
Now what is your desire?

LUCIFER:  I don't know what I'd better say
Since your companions went away
And hid themselves and do not come!
Now tell me, don't you know of some?
Where they went and where they are,
What they're doing out afar,
Because they do not come? — for shame!
And yet I call each imp by name.

SATAN:  Lucifer, I'll tell, don't doubt it,
You won't have to ask about it.
Now the truth is, master dear,
Devils hide not far from here,
Huddled close together all,
Sore affrighted of your gall;
They've been gone a long time now;
Neither force nor love, I vow
Will bring them back to you this way
And make them dance when pipes you play,
Or let you lead them by the nose.

The reason why I shall disclose —
The people now in general,
If they be greater man or small,
Have changed themselves to please the Lord,
Are with their God in full accord,
And all our clever teachings flout.
Well, Lucifer, I've let it out
Why none before you dare appear.

LUCIFER:    Could that be true, my servant dear?
They should not flee the wrath of hell —
Already 'tis a bagatelle.
Now therefore hasten speedily:
Go say to them immediately,
That they may keep their honor bright
And come to me with all their might
Whenever they hear my voice resound,
And I'll try hard — that I'll be bound —
To teach them cunning like a fox
That they may make them heterodox
Who late my wicked will obeyed
But now from devil-craft have strayed.

SATAN:    Lucifer, dear lord, I'll do it
If they'll have no cause to rue it.
Now your voice they'll gladly hear
And run quickly without fear.

LUCIFER:    Welcome, my dear imps, and praise.
This is like the olden days;
You've all been to my school in hell
And learned your lessons passing well:
I thought you very clever men
But now I'll have to start again,
And as to little babies prattle
Who are as stupid even as cattle!
All this I freely now forgive
If you will more like devils live,
And strive alike with hoof and claw
To let no souls escape our maw.

THE DEVILS:    Lucifer, that's what we'll do,
More and more we'll work for you!

LUCIFER:    Let it be forgotten then!
But just hear me once again,
Now do at once the thing I say:
Make tracks for Lubeck right away;
Folks are dying by the score there,
Many souls I hope you will snare —

Bring them back with hullaballoo:
And this time come, when I call you!

ASTROT: Lord, we'll always do that now,
Even though it sweats our brow.

### SCENE

PUCK: Lord Lucifer, my name is Puck,
On many a thorn my tail has stuck;
Now don't be mad and twist your features
We've every one caught lots of creatures.

LUCIFER: Your speech has pleased me through and through
Now bring them for an interview!
And if the souls all look forlorn,
Then bring them up like sacks of corn.

PUCK: Rejoice, O Lucifer, dear lord!
Praise and honor us accord!
See how they stand before you here,
Who hearkened when we caught their ear!

ASTROT: Just see this beautiful parade;
With fried eggs now we should be paid,
And if you added ham and bread
Our drink would find a softer bed!

FLOP-EAR: We landed, lord, upon our feet;
These souls we garnered — aren't they sweet? —

LUCIFER: Let the souls step one by one,
While you say what each has done,
Then I'll make it more than plain
What we'll do to give them pain.

NOYTOR: Lord, this is the sort of trash
I'd contribute to your hash;
Here's a soul for the fattening pen!

LUCIFER: You may have this egg half-hatched by the hen!
(To BAKER)
The bran is dropping from your nose,
So you're a baker, I suppose!
Well, well, what have you to say
Since they hauled you in this way?
Now tell the truth, a lie's a sin,
Wouldn't heaven let you in?

BAKER: Mercy, lord, this is no lie,
Till this day a baker, I
But now, my God, a sorry oaf!
I used to hollow out the loaf;

I mixed my dough with so much leaven
One loaf would rise as high as seven;
And then when too much dough I had
I broke it off — now that was bad —
And threw it back into the trough,
Alas, that ever I broke it off!
I made my cakes with naught but bran,
The people cursed — my fall began;
I did not thoroughly bake the bread
And so I cheated those I fed.
If life were given anew to me,
I'd never again a baker be!

LUCIFER:

My clever devils, you've done well!
Go toss this baker into hell —
By the glowing oven make him a seat
He'll find it's hotter than bakehouse heat!
He baked bread with too thin a crust,
So beat him till you raise the dust!
He merits all that is to follow
For baking doughy bread and hollow.

PUCK:

My name is Puck; I'm number four.
My stomach's huge — just hear it roar!
My bellicose business I dare state —
In well-stocked cellars I lie in wait;
When the bar-maid blinks her eye
And does not fill the tankard high,
Then I usually touch her hand
And jostle the cup — you understand.
If she should fill a good full measure,
We'd lose her soul, the priceless treasure.
I think it's better that I should bring
Them all before you, Lucifer, king:
Into your power deliver them all.

LUCIFER (*to* PUCK):

You may have what the sow lets fall.
                (*To the* INN-KEEPER)
By wit I tell you your trade and sin,
You are a fellow who keeps an inn!
I read it plainly upon your face:
The mugs are never full at your place!

INN-KEEPER:

Why deceive you? I skimped the drink!
It seems you know whatever I think.
I always made a big batch of beer
Because of my method, expounded here:
I got my water right out of the slough,
Water is cheap — there's too much anyhow!
Also, whenever I sold beer or wine,

This was another old habit of mine:
I stuck my thumb in the glass — d'you follow? —
And served my beer with a three inch collar.
When measuring ale for a tippler or sot,
That was a lesson I never forgot;
With the second boiling I served a good many,
And thus I contrived to earn a fat penny.

LUCIFER:
You're a great fool from your head to your heel:
You smell as bad as a buzzard's meal!
You'll be disgraced when I tell the rest —
Half of your sins are unconfessed!
You told us all of the foam, in brief,
But did not mention the thumb of the thief
On top of the vat, where it served you well.
Over and over you've earned your hell!
Come, my servants, stand always pat:
His pay is ready, now give him that:
A barrel for home like a hot little hovel,
And give him to drink with a red hot shovel!
Hang him up by his thumbs to the ceiling —
Those thumbs were guilty in all his dealing.
Because he served so little beer,
Reward him hugely, servants dear!

LUCIFER (*to the* BUTCHER):
Unless my brains have turned to stones,
You busied yourself by cracking bones!
I can tell by your mouth that drips —
Many intestines have passed your lips!

BUTCHER:
The truth, my lord, you guess and tell:
I cooked cow mouths very well.
And when the sausages I fixed
Everything together mixed:
Intestines, lungs, scraps and all that,
But put in not a bit of fat.
When put into the pan to fry
Old shoes could not have been more dry;
When I wanted sausages myself,
I reached the fat down from the shelf.

DRUNK-AS-AN-OWL:
Lord, I'm Drunk-as-an-Owl, if you please;
I lay by the fence with a bottle to squeeze;
I listened at every crack and hole,
But I discovered no single soul,
Neither a priest nor a layman cheap;
So in my anger I went to sleep.
I sat there such a lengthy day,
Wolves might have gnawed my flesh away.
This is no joke, lord, no sirree.

You won't find many men like me!
If you hadn't called out so loud,
I'd have brought along a crowd.
You might give me a word of praise;
I'm puffing like a stove ablaze.

LUCIFER:

You shall suffer for it, wretch!
We'll see how far your neck will stretch!
When you hear me now, turn pale,
You shall climb an old wife's tail!
There you'll suffer from the stink;
Time shall slowly pass, I think.
You're good for nothing but to parch,
You're filthy as a cow in March!
You've failed and yet feel no remorse!
I never saw a worse plug horse;
Nor out among the lame and blind
Could I a greater sluggard find!
You chatterbox without a brain,
You stink like dog hair in the rain!
Since you don't like the rules I'm giving,
Go skin dead horses for a living!
You want to sleep, you want to shirk;
Even devils have to work!
Now let me be, go on, get out!
I'll have my other men about!

### SCENE

SATAN (*leading a* PRIEST):

Brace up, brace up, Pastor John,
Lucifer will scold anon!
Cut your prayer a little short!
I can't wait here for your sort.
Your prayers weigh less with me than shavings!
Now when I pipe dance on hot pavings!
You prayed right blithely with your mouth,
But, sir, your soul was dry as drouth!
And your heart was hollow, see!
Come on, Bald Head, follow me!

PRIEST:

By the Holy Jesus dear,
Who are you that leads me here!
You might well have let me be
To read my hours piously!
With holy thoughts I filled my head;
God won't allow me to be led
By you, nor can your wicked will
Do me the slightest bit of ill.

SATAN:

Oh, what's the use of so much talk?
Come on, old Bald Head mustn't balk!
You make yourself too pure a saint,
But I can see behind your feint,
It makes no difference what you read,
Your hours often slipped your head.
You like to live with a can of booze
And in the tavern take your snooze.
Beer, not water, is to your taste!
Your belly's big as an elephant's waist!

SATAN (*to* LUCIFER):

Watch, my dear lord, eyes this way!
Here's a clergyman today;

LUCIFER:

Is it possible, my dear?
Can a priest be drawn down here?
I vow you shan't escape, you monk,
Though you have holy water drunk.
He can teach us from his stock,
Since he led astray his flock,
If it is as I have heard,
You preach against us, preach God's word;
The people dance after your pipe,
And that's why they're so hard to snipe!
Hear me, hear me, Mr. Priest!
Listen to one word, at least;
Stand a little to one side,
A priest close by I can't abide!

PRIEST:

What was that I heard from you?
Here you are and your men too,
And here am I, but all alone,
And yet I do not quake and moan!
If to keep me here's your will,
Then I must come closer still!

LUCIFER:

Ah, Satan, you'll be hanged for fair!
This priest already burns my hair;
He does it with his words of grace.
If he should come into our place,
We could not stay another minute;
We'd have to leave hell, and him in it!

PRIEST:

Do you believe, dear Lucifer,
I am so dull a crucifer
That I myself could not defend
And into hell needs must descend?
Hell is not the home for me:
There are enough of lay-degree

Who well deserve to go ahead
Of me — I'll save my life instead!

LUCIFER:

Satan, let this priest retire!
I can't stand the scorching fire!
Perhaps he is a man God chose,
See, holy water tips his nose!
And incense is upon his back;
Oh, take away this praying hack!
He has read too many psalms;
Let him go and ease my qualms!

PRIEST:

Lucifer, you'd best take care!
Or you'll get another scare.
If Jesus storms your gates once more,
He will destroy you and your corps!
One thing alone I know is true,
My God's a better man than you!

LUCIFER:

You priests are all too debonair;
You scold us with too sharp an air!
The Lord has other occupations
Than to daily storm our stations!
Jesus of some souls has raped us,
But not nearly all escaped us!
It will not be long before
Spite the priests, we'll have a score!
My men and I can pull a trick
To catch a plenty of them quick!

SCENE

LUCIFER:

My pride has brought eternal scorn;
Oh, woe is me that I was born!
Ah, poor devils, led astray!
Who will pity me today
For my sins sinned in the past?
Could I now repent and fast,
I would suffer all these things
While time flew by on wooden wings!
There should be a monstrous tree
Standing here for all to see:
From the ground up to the top,
Shearing knives would never stop
Sticking out.  Upon my crup
I'd ride this tree, down and up
Until Judgment Day, my bane!
I would shriek with frightful pain!
That I cannot thus do penance
Is of pride the awful sentence!

Pride's the fire where sin is lit,
Pride has sunk us in this pit!
Men have now the pleasure got
Which we devils may have not!
But we want to rope them in
When they're loaded down with sin.
We shall wait for each and all
Till they join us in the fall!
(*To* NOYTOR)
You probably heard what this priest swore;
Christ Jesus is to come once more!
So it seems very wise indeed
To fly to hell and make full speed
That we may watch with greatest care
Those souls already chained down there.
Oh, my sorrow's beyond belief;
I am heavy, sick with grief!
Would you carry me off to hell?

NOYTOR:  Yes, my master, we'll do it well!

LUCIFER:  Oh, my servants, don't hurt me please!

NOYTOR:  Lucifer, lord, stretch out your knees!
Stretch them over my horny back;
Were you as great as a miller's sack
And had swallowed the whole of the miller's nag,
We'd carry you off like a bloated bag!
Come, my friends, take hold all round,
Lest his head roll on the ground!
Carry off the old fornicator!

### THE EPILOGUE

Hear a bit, I pray you all,
Men and women, great and small.
Quickly now without confusion,
We have reached our play's conclusion,
And if something's been forgot,
We implore you, blame us not!
From reading comes the recollection,
No man can ever reach perfection,
And seldom can a man of sense
Please each one in his audience.
Now for a final boon we ask
That you applaud our finished task;
And can it possibly be done,
We'll later play a better one!
In God above let us rejoice,
Divine commands fulfill by choice,
And with His holy grace to charm us

The evil spirit cannot harm us!
For He avenged us more than well
When for our sake He harrowed hell!
And Paradise He set apart,
Where peace awaits the heavy heart.
Rejoice, all men, rejoice and say
How Christ is risen on Easter Day!
[tr. A. E. ZUCKER, H. K. RUSSELL,<br>AND MARY MARGARET RUSSELL]

## THE BLIND MAN AND THE CRIPPLE

### Andrieu de la Vigne (A.D. 1496)

[From *Representative Medieval and Tudor Plays,* translated by R. S. Loomis and H. W. Wells; Sheed & Ward, New York, 1942. Reprinted by permission of the publisher.]

BLIND MAN: Alms for one penniless and blind,
Who never yet hath seen at all!

CRIPPLE: Pray, to the poor lame man be kind!
With gout he cannot trudge or crawl.

BLIND MAN: Alas, right here I'll fade away
Without a varlet to attend me.

CRIPPLE: I cannot budge, ah, welladay!
Good God, preserve Thou and defend me.

BLIND MAN: That rascal who led me astray
And left me here all empty-handed,
He was a goodly guide, ifay!
To rob me and then leave me stranded.

CRIPPLE: Alack, I'm in a pretty scrape!
How shall I win my livelihood?
I cannot from this spot escape,
However much I wish I could.

BLIND MAN: Meseems I here shall fast all day.
Unless I find a varlet faster.

CRIPPLE: Bad Luck has picked me for her prey,
And now she has become my master.

BLIND MAN: For this desirable situation
Can't I get even one application?
I've had one varlet in my day
I trusted. He was called Giblet.
Jolly he was and on the level,
Though ugly as the very devil.

I lost a treasure when he left me.
Plague on the plague that thus bereft me.

CRIPPLE: Will no one help me in my need?
For God's love, pity my estate.

BLIND MAN: Who are you that so loudly plead?
Good friend, betake you hither straight.

CRIPPLE: Alas, I'm planted in this spot,
Right in the middle of the street,
And cannot move. Saint Matthew, what
A wretched life!

BLIND MAN:                 Come stir your feet
Along this way: 'twill bring you luck.
Let's see what mirth we can discover.

CRIPPLE: Your tongue wags easily, my chuck.
But mirth and joy for us are over.

BLIND MAN: Come hither; we shall make great cheer,
An't please the Lord of Paradise.
And though like blunderers we appear,
We'll harm no man in any wise.

CRIPPLE: My friend, you throw your words away.
For hence I cannot budge an inch.
God curse them on the judgment day
By whom I got into this pinch.

BLIND MAN: If I could walk in your direction
I'd gladly carry you a bit —
(At least, if I had strength for it) —
To give you easement and protection.
And you could succor me in turn
By guiding me from place to place.

CRIPPLE: This is no plan to lightly spurn.
You've said the best thing for our case.

BLIND MAN: I'll walk straight towards you if I can.
Is this the right way?

CRIPPLE:                 Yes, don't stumble.

BLIND MAN: Methinks it is a better plan
To go on all fours and not tumble.
I'm headed right?

CRIPPLE:                 Straight as a quail.
You'll soon be here in front of me.

BLIND MAN: When I come near you, do not fail
To give your hand.

CRIPPLE:                                I will, pardee.
                Stop, you're not going straight, turn hither.

BLIND MAN: This way?

CRIPPLE:                       No, no!   Turn to the right.

BLIND MAN: So?

CRIPPLE:            Yes.

BLIND MAN:                    It puts me in high feather,
                Good sir, at last to hold you tight.
                Now will you mount upon my back?
                I trow well I can bear the pack.

CRIPPLE:       So much I must in you confide;
                Then I in turn can be your guide.

BLIND MAN: Are you well set?

CRIPPLE:                                By Mary, yes.
                Look well you do not let me fall.

BLIND MAN: If I should show such carelessness,
                Pray God may evil me befall.
                But guide aright.

CRIPPLE:                                Yes, by my troth.
                Look, here's my staff with iron shod.
                Take it.   And here I give my oath
                To guide you faithfully, by God.

BLIND MAN: Lord, had I known how much you weighed!
                Wherefore is this?

CRIPPLE:                                Plod on, good fellow
                And keep the bargain that we made.
                D'you hear?   Get up!

BLIND MAN:                                That's all quite well — Oh
                But what a load!

CRIPPLE:                       But what a lie!
                A feather's not more light than I.

BLIND MAN: Hold on, by God's blood; get a clutch,
                Or else I'll drop you!   Never yet
                Did blacksmith's anvil weigh so much.
                Get down; I'm in an awful sweat. . . .
                                [CRIPPLE *reluctantly gets down.*]
                Hey, what's the news?

CRIPPLE:                                What did you say?
                They tell a really sumptuous thing.
                A saint has lately passed away,

Whose works are most astonishing.
He heals the gravest maladies
Of which you ever yet heard speak —
That's if the sick are good and meek.
I here defy these powers of his.

BLIND MAN: What's that you're telling?

CRIPPLE: What's the joke?
It's said if the corpse comes this way
I should be cured all at one stroke,
And you too, likewise.  Now I pray,
Come hither.  If 'twere really so
That we were healed of all our woe,
Far harder then 'twould be to gain
Our livelihood than now.

BLIND MAN: Nay, nay.
That he may heal us of our pain
Let us go where he is, I say,
And find the corpse.

CRIPPLE: Were I assured
That we should not be healed by him,
Right well I'd go.  But to be cured
And strong, I will not stir a limb.
No, we had better find our way
Out of this place.

BLIND MAN: What's this about?

CRIPPLE: Why, when I'm cured, I'll waste away
Of hunger.  Every one will shout:
"Be off, and do some honest labor."
No, you'll not find me that saint's neighbor!
For if he fixed me up, they'll call
Me vagabond, and one would bawl:
"That brazen rascal, sound of limb,
The galleys are the place for him."

BLIND MAN: So glib a tongue I never saw.
Yet I confess it speaks good sense.
You have the gift of eloquence.

CRIPPLE: I tell you, I care not a straw
To go and have the corpse remove
My malady.

BLIND MAN: Yea, 'twould be folly
To seek it, and we will not move.

CRIPPLE: I dare pledge, if it cured you wholly,
In a short time you'd feel regret.
Folk would not give you anything

But bread, and never would you get
A tasty bit.

BLIND MAN:                     May heaven bring
Some great doom on my head, or let
Them strip from off my skin
Enough for two belts ere I'd set
My eyes on it!

CRIPPLE:                         Think, too, how thin
Your purse would be.

BLIND MAN:                               Yea, that I trow.

CRIPPLE:     Never a day but we'd be pining
And there'd be not a penny to show.

BLIND MAN: Yea, truly?

CRIPPLE:                     By the Cross, I swear
It will be even as I'm divining.

BLIND MAN: Since you have counseled me so fair,
Henceforth your word I'll never doubt.

CRIPPLE:     The body's in the church they say:
We must not venture thereabout.

BLIND MAN: If ever we are caught in there
May Satan carry us away!

                                         [*Pause*]

CRIPPLE:     Come, down this alley let us toddle.

BLIND MAN: Whither?

CRIPPLE:                 This way.

BLIND MAN:                          Let us not wait.

CRIPPLE:     My faith, 'twould show an empty noddle
To seek the saint out in his lair.

BLIND MAN: Let us be off.

CRIPPLE:                    Which way?

BLIND MAN:                                    Why, straight
Where this old toper winters merrily.

CRIPPLE:     A wise word have you spoken verily.
Where go we?

BLIND MAN:                    To the tavern.   There
Without a lantern I can totter.

CRIPPLE:     I tell you, even so can I.

Give me an ale-house when I'm dry
Before a cistern full of water.

BLIND MAN: Listen, I say!

CRIPPLE:                                Listen to what?

BLIND MAN: Whatever's making that to-do?

CRIPPLE:        If it's the body!

BLIND MAN:                        Horrible thought!
No longer we'd be catered to.
Hark!

CRIPPLE:                     After it the whole town chases.

BLIND MAN: Go look what's making all the pother.

CRIPPLE:        Bad luck is close upon our traces.
Good master, it's the saint, no other!

BLIND MAN: Quick, let's be off: we must not bide.
I fear he'll catch us after all.

CRIPPLE:        Under some window let us hide,
Or in the corner of a wall.
Look out, don't trip!

BLIND MAN [*falling down*]:

                                The devil's in it!
To fall at such an awkward minute!

CRIPPLE:        Pray God he do not find us here:
Too cruel then would be our state.

BLIND MAN: My heart is bitten through with fear.
We've fallen upon an evil fate.

CRIPPLE:        Lie low, my master, take good care,
And we'll crawl off beneath some stair.
                    [*Procession of clergy, bearing
                    body of saint in a reliquary,
                    passes, followed by crowd. Exeunt.*]

BLIND MAN [*looking at the reliquary*]:
I'm henceforth in this good saint's debt.
I see as never I saw before.
What a great fool I was to let
Myself be cozened into fleeing.
There's nothing, search the wide world o'er,
That to my mind's as good as seeing.

CRIPPLE:        The Devil take him in his chain!
He knows no gratitude nor grace.

Better if I had spared the pain
Of coming to this cursed place.
Alas, I'm quite at my wit's end.
Hunger will put me in my grave.
With rage I claw my face and rend.
Damnation on the whoreson knave!

BLIND MAN: I was a very dunderhead
To leave the good safe road and tread
The doubtful bypath, wandering.
Alas, full little had I guessed
That clear sight was so great a thing.
Now I can look on fair Savoy
And Burgundy and France the blest.
Humbly I thank God for this joy.

CRIPPLE: What an unlucky turn for me!
I never yet to work was taught.
This day has turned out wretchedly,
And I'm a wretch to be so caught.
So I am caught in Fortune's trap,
Not wise enough to dodge its snap.
Unfortunately I'm too wise
On my bad luck to shut my eyes.

BLIND MAN: The rumor of thy power to bless,
St. Martin, has been spread so wide
That folk crowd in from every side,
This morning, toward thy holiness.
I thank thee not in Latin tongue
But in live French — thou art so kind.
If to thy mercy I've been blind,
Pardon I beg for this great wrong.

CRIPPLE: Well, here I have a sweet new figure.
But you'll not have so long to wait
Before I'll manage to disfigure
This pretty form of mine once more.
I've stored up in this little pate
The use of herbs, and all the learning
I need to raise with oils a sore
Upon my leg, such that you'll vow
That with Saint Anthony's fire it's burning.
I'll make myself more sleek than lard, —
Don't think that I don't know the way, —
And there'll not be a man so hard
But will be melted with compassion.
Then too, I'm expert in the role
Of one whose body's one huge ache.
"In honor of the Sacred Passion,"
I'll quaver, "look at this poor soul,

And see these tortured members shake."
Then I'll tell how I've been at Rome,
How the Turks locked me up at Acre,
And how I'm here so far from home
On pilgrimage to St. Fiacre.

[tr. ROGER S. LOOMIS]

## THE WORTHY MASTER PIERRE PATELIN

### Anonymous French (15th Cent.)

[From *Poet Lore, A Quarterly of World Literature*, Boston, Vol. XXVIII, 1917. Reprinted by permission of the publisher.]

SCENE I: *On either side of the stage is a street scene. At the back, a curtain is partly drawn to each side showing the interior of* PATELIN's *house.* PATELIN *sits in bed reading a large folio; on a chair next to the bed* GUILLEMETTE *sits mending an old dress. On a bench a little to one side are kitchen utensils: a frying pan, a broom, etc. On the bed lie a nightgown and a cap.*

GUILLEMETTE: You have nothing to say now, I suppose, have you? . . . While I needs must mend rags a beggar would be ashamed to wear — and you, a member of the learned profession . . . a lawyer . . . !

PATELIN (*in bed*): There was a time when my door was crowded with clients . . . when I had plenty of work . . . and fine clothes to wear, too.

GUILLEMETTE: Of what good is that to-day — eh?

PATELIN: Wife, I was too shrewd for them. Men don't like people wiser than themselves.

GUILLEMETTE: Aye, you could always beat them at law . . . but that was long ago.

PATELIN: It hurts me truly to see you mending rags . . . and wives of men who are thick-skulled wearing golden-threaded cloth and fine wool. There is that draper's wife across the way. . . .

GUILLEMETTE: Cease the cackling. (*Silently working for a while*) I'd give something rare and costly for a new gown on St. Mary's day. Heaven knows I need it.

PATELIN: So you do and so do I as well. It is not fit to see one of the learned profession walking about like a beggar on the highway. Ah! If I could only get some clients! I know my law well enough yet. There is not many a one can beat me at the finer points.

GUILLEMETTE: A fig for it all. Of what good is it? We are all but starved . . . and as for clothes — look. (*Holds up the dress she is mending.*)

PATELIN: Silence, good wife! Could I but have some business and put my head with seriousness to it. . . . Who knows but the days of plenty would soon enough return!

GUILLEMETTE: There is not a soul in town but a fool would trust himself to you. They know too well your way of handling cases. They say you are a master . . . at cheating.

(PATELIN *rises indignant.*)

PATELIN: They mean at law . . . at law, good wife. Ha, I should like to see a lawyer beat me at it . . . and . . . (*Suddenly stops, thinks for a moment, then his whole face lights up.*) I am going to market. I have just thought of a little business I have there. (*Gets out of bed.*)

GUILLEMETTE: Going to market? What for? You have no money.

PATELIN: I am going to market . . . on business . . . to the long-nosed donkey, our neighbor . . . the draper.

GUILLEMETTE: What for?

PATELIN: To buy some cloth. . . .

GUILLEMETTE: Holy Saints! You know well he is more close-fisted than any other merchant in town. He'll never trust you.

PATELIN: Ah, that's just why I am going. The more miserly, the easier to gull; and . . . I have thought of something fine . . . that will get us enough cloth . . . both for you and me.

GUILLEMETTE: You must be mad.

PATELIN (*not heeding her*): Let me see. . . . (*Measuring her with his arm's length*) Two and one-half for you. . . . (*Measuring himself in the same way*) Three for me . . . and . . . What color would you want it? Green or red?

GUILLEMETTE: I'll be pleased with any kind. Beggars can't be choosers. But don't think I believe what you say. I am not a fool. You'll never get any from Master Joceaulme. He'll never trust you, I am certain.

PATELIN: Who knows? Who knows? He might . . . and then really get paid . . . on Doom's-day. . . . Ho, ho. . . .

GUILLEMETTE: Don't you think you had better make haste, lest all the cloth be sold?

PATELIN (*offended, walking off*): Wife, I forgive you. You are only a woman. I'll teach you a fine lesson now. If I don't bring home a fine piece of cloth — dark green or blue, such as wives of great lords wear, then never believe another word I say.

GUILLEMETTE: But how will you do it? You haven't a copper in your pocket.

PATELIN: Ah! That's a secret. Just wait and see. So . . . (*to himself as he walks slowly away*) two and one-half for her and three for me. . . . Look well to the house while I am away, wife. (*Exit.*)

GUILLEMETTE: What fool of a merchant'll trust him! . . . unless he is blind and deaf!

(*The back curtains are closed and now only the street scene is visible.*)

SCENE II: PATELIN *comes from his door and walks across to* THE DRAPER'S *table.* THE DRAPER *is just coming out with a pack of cloth and wools which he throws on the table. He busies himself arranging his goods.* PATELIN *looks on for a while and then goes right up to him.*

PATELIN: Ho, there, worthy Master Guillaume Joceaulme, permit me the pleasure of shaking your hand. How do you feel?

THE DRAPER: Very fine, the saints be thanked.

PATELIN: I am truly happy to hear that. And business?

THE DRAPER: You know how . . . one day one way, the other, altogether different. You can never tell when ill luck may blow your way.

PATELIN: May the saints keep it from your doors! It's the very phrase I often heard your father use. What a man he was! Wise! There was not an event in Church, State, or market he did not foretell. No other was more esteemed. And you — they say that you are more and more like him each day.

THE DRAPER: Do seat yourself, good Master Patelin.

PATELIN: Oh, I can well stand.

THE DRAPER: Oh, but you must. (*Forcing him to sit on the bench*)

PATELIN: Ah! I knew him well, your father. You resemble him as one drop of milk another. What a man he was! Wise! We, among the learned, called him the weather-cock. Well-nigh every piece of clothing I wore came from his shop.

THE DRAPER: He was an honest man, and people liked to buy from him.

PATELIN: A more honest soul there never was. And I have heard often said the apple has fallen nigh the tree.

THE DRAPER: Of a truth, good Master . . . ?

PATELIN: It's not flattery, either. (*Looking intently at him*) You do resemble him! No child was ever so like his father. Each marked the other. This is just his nose, his ears, nay, the very dimple on his chin.

THE DRAPER: Yes, they do say I look much like him.

PATELIN: Like one drop of water another. . . . And kindhearted! He was ever ready to trust and help, no matter who came along. The Lord knows he was ever the gainer by it. Even the worst scoundrels thought twice before cheating him.

THE DRAPER: A merchant must always take heed, good Master Patelin. You can never know whether a man is honest or not.

PATELIN: Aye, that's true. But he had a way of guessing whether it was an honest man he was dealing with that was a marvel to behold. Many a funny tale he told of it — when we sat over a bottle of wine. (*Feeling the cloth on the table*) What a fine piece of cloth! Did you make it from your own wool? Your father always used to weave his cloths from the wool of his own sheep.

THE DRAPER: So do I, sir. From the wool of my own sheep.

PATELIN: You don't say so! This is business in a manner I like to see it done. The father all over again.

THE DRAPER (*seeing the possibility of a sale*): Ah, worthy Master Patelin, it is a great hardship, indeed, to which I put myself because of this. And the loss and cost! Here a shepherd kills your sheep; I have a case against one of those scoundrels right now. The weavers ask pay like goldsmiths. But to me this is all of little account. . . . I'd attend to the making of each piece myself were it to cost ten times as much as I get in return. . . . So long as I please those who buy.

PATELIN: I can see this. It would make a fine gown.

THE DRAPER: You could not get a finer piece even in the city of Paris.

PATELIN: I am sorry I am not out to do any buying just now, though I am tempted to.

THE DRAPER: Business bad? Money scarce?

PATELIN: No, indeed not. I have a nice little sum of gold crowns even now, but I am about to invest them in something profitable. . . . It's as strong as iron, this cloth here. (*Examining it*)

THE DRAPER: You may take my word for it, Master, there is not a finer or stronger in town. What's more, it can be bought cheap just now. It's a fine investment. Wool is certain to go up.

PATELIN: Aye, it's a fine piece of cloth, Master Joceaulme. . . . But then I shouldn't . . . yet . . .

THE DRAPER: Come, Master Patelin, come. You need the cloth and have the money to buy. Then you'll invest a few crowns less. A man should always have a gown tucked away in the coffer. What would you say if some fine day, comes along the town crier shouting: there has been a new judge appointed and it is Master Pa . . .

PATELIN: You must have your little joke, worthy sir. Just like your father. I would pass his shop, a friendly chat . . . and then my purse was much lighter for it. But I never regretted it, never.

THE DRAPER: You wouldn't now, either. It's well worth buying.

PATELIN: It tempts me. . . . It would look well on my good wife, and I could use it well for myself.

THE DRAPER: It needs but your saying. Come, what's the word, Master?

PATELIN: Well . . .

THE DRAPER: It's yours even though you hadn't a copper.

PATELIN (*somewhat absent-minded*): Oh, I know that.

THE DRAPER: What?

PATELIN: I'll take it.

THE DRAPER: That's talking. How much do you want?

PATELIN: How much is it a yard?

THE DRAPER: Which do you like best? The blue?

PATELIN: Yes, that is the one.

THE DRAPER: You want a rock bottom price, no haggling. This is the finest piece in my shop. For you I'll make it twenty-one sous a yard.

PATELIN: Holy Saints! Master! What do you take me for, a fool? It isn't the first time I am buying cloth.

THE DRAPER: It's the price it cost me myself; by all the saints in Heaven.

PATELIN: That's too much — entirely too much.

THE DRAPER: Wool costs like holy oil now, and these shepherds are forever robbing me.

PATELIN: Well, there is truth in what you say. I'll take it at the price. I like to see every man make his honest penny. Measure it.

THE DRAPER: How much do you want?

PATELIN: Let me see. Two and a half for her, three for me, that makes five and a half.

THE DRAPER: Take hold there, Master, here they are. (*Measuring out*) One . . . two . . . three . . . four . . . five. I'll make it six. You'll not mind the few coppers more.

PATELIN: Not when I get something fine in return. Then I need a cap, too.

THE DRAPER: Would you like me to measure it backwards?

PATELIN: Oh, now, I trust your honesty. How much is it?

THE DRAPER: Six yards at twenty-one sous the yard — that's exactly nine francs.

PATELIN: Nine francs. . . . (*Under his breath*) Here it goes. Nine francs.

THE DRAPER: Yes, and a good bargain you got.

PATELIN (*searching his pockets*): No . . . I have but little with me, and I must buy some small things. You'll get your money to-morrow.

THE DRAPER: What!!! . . . No . . . No . . .

PATELIN: Well, good Master Joceaulme, you don't think I carry gold coin with me, do you? You'd have me give thieves a good chance to steal it? Your father trusted me many a time. And you, Master Guillaume, should take after your father.

THE DRAPER: I like my money cash.

PATELIN: It's there waiting for you, good Master Draper. You can come for it, I hope.

THE DRAPER: It's bad custom to sell on credit.

PATELIN: Did I ask you for credit: for a month, a week, a day? Come to my house at noon, and you'll find your money ready. Does that satisfy you?

THE DRAPER: I prefer my money cash, right on the purchase. . . .

PATELIN: And then Master Guillaume, you have not been to my house for I don't know how long. Your father was there many a time — but you don't seem to care for poor folk like myself.

THE DRAPER: It's we merchants who are poor. We have no bags of gold lying idle for investments.

PATELIN: They are there, Master, waiting for you. And my good wife put a fine goose on the spit just when I left. You can have a tender wing. Your father always liked it.

THE DRAPER: Perhaps. . . . It's true. I haven't been to your house for a long time. I'll come at noon, Master Patelin, and bring the cloth with me.

PATELIN (*snatching the cloth from him*): Oh, I would never trouble you. I can carry it.

THE DRAPER: But . . .

PATELIN: No, good sir, not for the wealth of the East. I would not think of asking *you* to carry it for *me*.

THE DRAPER: I'd rather . . . well . . . I'll soon be there, Master. I'll come before the noon meal. Don't forget the nine francs.

PATELIN: Aye, I'll not. And there'll be a bottle of red wine . . . and a fine fat goose. Be certain to come.

(*Exit* PATELIN.)

THE DRAPER: That I will right soon. Ho, ho, ho — ha, ha, ha — the fool! A good bargain he got! Twenty-one sous the yard. It isn't worth one-half that. And on top of it a fine dinner . . . Burgundy wine and a roasted goose! For a customer like that every day! Now I'll take in my cloth. I'll soon to his house. (*Takes up the cloth and leaves.*)

SCENE III: *The back curtains are drawn aside showing* PATELIN'S *chamber.*

PATELIN (*running in*): Wife, wife . . . (GUILLEMETTE *enters, the old gown in her hand.*) Well, Madam . . . now . . . I've got it . . . right here I have it. What did I tell you?

GUILLEMETTE: What have you?

PATELIN: Something you desire greatly. But what are you doing with this old rag? I think it will do well for a bed for your cat. I did promise you a new gown and get you one I did.

GUILLEMETTE: What's gotten into your head? Did you drink anything on the way?

PATELIN: And it's paid for, Madam. It's paid for, I tell you.

GUILLEMETTE: Are you making sport of me? What are you blabbering!

PATELIN: I have it right here.

GUILLEMETTE: What have you?

PATELIN: Cloth fit for the Queen of Sheba. (*Displaying the cloth*) Here it is!

GUILLEMETTE: Where did you steal it? Who'll pay for it? What kind of scrape have you gotten into now?

PATELIN: You need not worry, good dame. It's paid for . . . and a good price at that.

GUILLEMETTE: Why, how much did it cost? You did not have a copper when you left.

PATELIN: It cost nine francs, fair lady . . . a bottle of red wine . . . and the wing of a roasted goose.

GUILLEMETTE: Are you crazy? You had no money, no goose!!!

PATELIN: Aye, aye, that I did. I paid for it as it behooves one of the learned profession of law: in promissory statements. And the merchant who took them is no fool either, oh, no; not a fool at all; but a very wise man and a shrewd. . . .

GUILLEMETTE: Who was he? How . . .

PATELIN: He is the king of asses, the chancellor of baboons . . . our worthy neighbor, the long-nosed draper, Master Joceaulme.

GUILLEMETTE: Will you cease this jabbering and tell me how it happened? How did he come to trust you? There is no worse skinflint in town than he.

PATELIN: Ah, wife! My head! My knowledge of the law! I turned him into a noble and fine lord. I told him what a jewel his father was; I laid on him all the nine virtues thick as wax, and . . . in the end he trusted me most willingly with six yards of his fine cloth.

GUILLEMETTE: Ho, ho, ho, you are a marvel! And when does he expect to get paid?

PATELIN: By noon.

GUILLEMETTE: What will we do when he comes for the money?

PATELIN: He'll be here for it and soon to boot. He must be dreaming even now of his nine francs, and his wine, and the goose. Oh, we'll give him a goose! Now you get the bed ready and I'll get in.

GUILLEMETTE: What for?

PATELIN: As soon as he comes and asks for me, swear that I've been in bed here for the last two months. Tell it in a sad voice and with tears in your eyes. And if he says anything, shout at him to speak lower. If he cries: "My cloth, my money," tell him he is crazy, that I haven't been from bed for weeks. And if he doesn't go with that, I'll dance him a little tune that'll make him wonder whether he is on earth or in hell.

(PATELIN *puts on his nightgown and cap.* GUILLEMETTE *goes to the door and returns quickly.*)

GUILLEMETTE: He is coming, he is coming; what if he arrests you?

PATELIN: Don't worry; just do what I tell you. Quick, hide the cloth under the bedclothes. Don't forget. I've been sick for two months.

GUILLEMETTE: Quick, quick, here he is.

(PATELIN *gets into bed and draws the curtains.* GUILLEMETTE *sits down and begins to mend the old dress.* THE DRAPER *enters.*)

THE DRAPER: Good day, fair dame.

GUILLEMETTE: Sh . . . Speak lower.

THE DRAPER: Why? What's the matter?

GUILLEMETTE: You don't know?

THE DRAPER: Where is he?

GUILLEMETTE: Alas! Nearer to Paradise than to Earth. (*Begins to cry.*)

THE DRAPER: Who?

GUILLEMETTE: How can you be so heartless and ask me that, when you know he has been in bed for the last eleven weeks?

THE DRAPER: Who?

GUILLEMETTE: My husband.

THE DRAPER: Who?

GUILLEMETTE: My husband — Master Pierre, once a lawyer . . . and now a sick man . . . on his death-bed.

THE DRAPER: What!!!!!

GUILLEMETTE (*crying*): You have not heard of it? Alas! And . . .

THE DRAPER: And who was it just took six yards of cloth from my shop?

GUILLEMETTE: Alas! How am I to know? It was surely not he.

THE DRAPER: You must be dreaming, good woman. Are you his wife? The wife of Pierre Patelin, the lawyer?

GUILLEMETTE: That I am, good sir.

THE DRAPER: Then it was your husband, who was such a good

friend of my father, who came to my shop a quarter of an hour ago and bought six yards of cloth for nine francs. And now I am here for my money. Where is he?

GUILLEMETTE: This is no time for jesting, good sir.

THE DRAPER: Are you crazy? I want my money, that's all.

GUILLEMETTE: Don't scream. It's little sleep he gets as it is, and here you come squealing like a dying pig. He has been in bed for nigh twelve weeks and hardly slept three nights.

THE DRAPER: Who? What are you talking about?

GUILLEMETTE: Who! My poor sick husband. (*Weeps.*)

THE DRAPER: Come! What's this? Stop that fooling. I want my money, my nine francs.

GUILLEMETTE (*screaming*): Don't scream so loud. He is dying.

THE DRAPER: But that's a lie. He was at my shop, but a quarter of an hour ago.

PATELIN (*groaning from behind the curtain*): Au, au, au . . .

GUILLEMETTE: Ah, there he is on his death-bed. He has been there for thirteen weeks yesterday without eating as much as a fly.

THE DRAPER: What are you talking about? He was at my shop just now and bought six yards of cloth . . . blue cloth.

GUILLEMETTE: How can you make sport of me? Good Master Guillaume, don't you see how he is! Do speak lower. Noise puts him in agony.

THE DRAPER: It's you who are howling. Give me my money, and I'll not speak at all.

GUILLEMETTE (*screaming*): He is deadly sick. This is no time for fooling. Stop screaming. What is it you want?

THE DRAPER: I want my money, or the cloth . . . the cloth he bought from me only a little while ago.

GUILLEMETTE: What are you talking about, my good man? There is something strange in your voice.

THE DRAPER: You see, good lady, your husband, Pierre Patelin, the learned counselor, who was such a good friend of my father, came to my shop but a quarter of an hour ago and chose six yards of blue cloth . . . and then told me to come to his house to get the money and . . .

GUILLEMETTE: Ha, ha, ha, what a fine joke. You seem to be in good humor to-day, Master Draper! To-day? . . . When he has been in bed for fourteen weeks . . . on the point of death! (*She screams louder and louder all the time.*) To-day, hey! Why do you come to make sport of me? Get out, get out!

THE DRAPER: I will. Give me my money first . . . or give me my cloth. Where is he with it?

GUILLEMETTE: Ah me! He is very sick and refuses to eat a bite.

THE DRAPER: I am speaking about my cloth. If he does not want it, or hasn't the money, I'll gladly take it back. He took it this morning. I'll swear to it. Ask him yourself. I saw him and spoke to him. A piece of blue cloth.

GUILLEMETTE: Are you cracked or have you been drinking?

THE DRAPER (*becoming frantic*): He took six yards of cloth, blue cloth.

GUILLEMETTE: What do I care whether it is green or blue? My husband has not left the house for the last fifteen weeks.

THE DRAPER: May the Lord bless me! But I am sure I saw him. It was he I am sure.

GUILLEMETTE: Have you no heart? I have had enough of your fooling.

THE DRAPER: If you think I am a fool . . .

PATELIN (*behind the curtain*): Au, au, au, come and raise my pillow. Stop the braying of that ass! Everything is black and yellow! Drive these black beasts away! Marmara, carimari, carimara!

THE DRAPER: It's he!

GUILLEMETTE: Yes, it is; alas!

THE DRAPER: Good Master Patelin, I've come for my nine francs . . . which you promised me. . . .

PATELIN (*sits up and sticks his head out between the curtains*): Ha, you dog . . . come here. Shut the door. Rub the soles of my feet . . . tickle my toes. . . . Drive these devils away. It's a monk; there, up he goes. . . .

THE DRAPER: What's this? Are you crazy?

PATELIN (*getting out of bed*): Ha . . . do you see him? A black monk flying in the air with the draper hanging on his nose. Catch him . . . quick. (*Speaking right in the* DRAPER's *face, who retreats*) The cat! The monk! Up he flies, and there are ten little devils tweaking your long nose! Heigh, ho! (*Goes back to bed, falling on it seemingly exhausted.*)

GUILLEMETTE (*in loud lamentations*): Now see what you have done.

THE DRAPER: But what does this mean? . . . I don't understand it.

GUILLEMETTE: Don't you see, don't you see!

THE DRAPER: It serves me right; why did I ever sell on credit? But I sold it, I am certain of that, and I would swear 'twas to him this morning. Did he become sick since he returned?

GUILLEMETTE: Are you beginning that joke all over again?

THE DRAPER: I am sure I sold it to him. Ah, but this may be just a cooked-up story. Tell me, have you a goose on the spit?

GUILLEMETTE: A goose on the spit! No-o-o-o, not on the spit! You are the nearest. . . . But I've had enough of this. Get out and leave me in peace.

THE DRAPER: Maybe you are right. I am commencing to doubt it all. Don't cry. I must think this over for a while. But . . . I am sure I had six yards of cloth . . . and he chose the blue. I gave it to him with my own hands. Yet . . . here he is in bed sick . . . fifteen weeks. But he was at my shop a little while ago. "Come to my house and eat some goose," he said. Never, never, will I trust any one again.

GUILLEMETTE: Perhaps your memory is getting wobbly with age. I think you had better go and look before you talk. Maybe the cloth is still there.

(*Exit* THE DRAPER, *across the front stage and into his shop.*)

PATELIN (*getting up cautiously and speaking low*): Is he gone?

GUILLEMETTE: Take care, he may come back.

PATELIN: I can't stand this any longer. (*Jumps out.*) We put it to him heavy, didn't we, my pretty one, eh? Ho, ho, ho. (*Laughs uproariously.*)

THE DRAPER (*coming from his shop, looking under the table*): The thief, the liar, the liar, he did buy . . . steal it? It isn't there. This was all sham. Ha, I'll get it, though. (*Runs toward* PATE-LIN's *house.*) What's this I hear . . . laughing! . . . the robbers. (*Rushes in.*) You thieves . . . I want my cloth. . . . (PATELIN, *finding no time to get back into bed, gets hold of the broom, puts the frying pan on his head and begins to jump around, straddling the broom stick.* GUILLEMETTE *can't stop laughing.*)

THE DRAPER: Laughing in my very nose, eh! Ah, my money, pay. . . .

GUILLEMETTE: I am laughing for unhappiness. Look, how the poor man is, it is you who have done this, with your bellowing.

PATELIN: Ha. . . . Where is the Guitar? . . . The lady Guitar I married. . . . Ho, ho. Come, my children. . . . Light the lanterns. Ho, ho, ha. . . . (*Stops, looking intently into the air.*)

THE DRAPER: Stop your jabbering. My money! Please, my money . . . for the cloth. . . .

GUILLEMETTE: Again. . . . Didn't you have enough before? But. . . . Oh. . . . (*Looking intently at him*) Now I understand!!! Why, I am sure of it. You are mad . . . else you wouldn't talk this way.

THE DRAPER: Oh, Holy Saints . . . perhaps I am.

PATELIN (*begins to jump around as if possessed, playing a thousand and one crazy antics*): Mère de dieu la coronade . . . que de l'argent il ne me sonne. Hast understood me, gentle sir?

THE DRAPER: What's this? I want my money. . . .

GUILLEMETTE: He is speaking in delirium; he once had an uncle in Limoges and it's the language of that country.

(PATELIN *gives* THE DRAPER *a kick and falls down as if exhausted.*)

THE DRAPER: Oh! Oh! Where am I? This is the strangest sickness I ever saw.

GUILLEMETTE (*who has run to her husband*): Do you see what you have done?

PATELIN (*jumps up and acts still wilder*): Ha! The green cat . . . with the draper. I am happy. . . . (*Chases* THE DRAPER *and his wife around the room.* GUILLEMETTE *seeks protection, clinging to* THE DRAPER.)

GUILLEMETTE: Oh, I am afraid, I am afraid. Help me, kind sir, he may do me some harm.

THE DRAPER (*running around the room with* GUILLEMETTE *clinging to him*): What's this? He is bewitching me.

PATELIN (*trying to explain the signs to* THE DRAPER, *who retreats.* PATELIN *follows him, whacking the floor and furniture and occa-*

*sionally striking* THE DRAPER. *Finally* THE DRAPER *gets on one side of the bed, and* PATELIN *on the other. In that position he addresses him in a preachy, serious voice*): Et bona dies sit vobis magister amantissime, pater reverendisime, quomodo brulis? (*Falls on the floor near the bed as if dead.*)

GUILLEMETTE: Oh, kind sir. Help me. He is dead. Help me put him to bed. . . . (*They both drag him into bed.*)

THE DRAPER: It were well for me to go, I think. He might die and I might be blamed for it. It must have been some imps who took my cloth . . . and I came here for the money, led by an evil spirit. It's passing strange . . . but I think I had better go.

(*Exit.* THE DRAPER *goes to his shop.* GUILLEMETTE *watches, turning every moment to* PATELIN *who has sat up in bed, warning him not to get out. When* THE DRAPER *disappears, she turns around and bursts out laughing.*)

PATELIN (*jumping out*): Now, wife, what do you think of me, eh? (*Takes the cloth.*) Oh! Didn't we play a clever game? I did not think I could do it so well. He got a hot goose, didn't he? (*Spreading the cloth*) This'll do for both and there'll be a goodly piece left.

GUILLEMETTE: You are an angel. Oh, ho! And now let us go and begin to cut it up.

(*Both exit, and the curtain is drawn.*)


SCENE IV: *The street scene.*

(THE DRAPER *comes from the shop with a piece of cloth under his arm. He is much upset. Looks once more under the table for the cloth which* PATELIN *took.*)

THE DRAPER: These hounds. . . . I'll get them yet. Here's a fine piece of cloth! Only the fiend himself knows who took it — and then that shepherd. To think of it . . . robbing me for years. But him I'll get surely. I'll see him hanged, yet. (AGNELET *appears from the other side.*) Ah, here he comes. . . .

THE SHEPHERD (*stutters, thick voice; a typical yokel*): God give you a good day, sweet sir. I greet you, good sir. . . . I was not sure it was you, good sir. . . .

THE DRAPER: You were not, eh? You knave; but you will soon know for certain . . . when your head is on the gallows . . . high up. . . .

THE SHEPHERD: Yes, good sir . . . no . . . I saw the constable . . . and he spoke to me that you want to see me.

THE DRAPER: Oh, no! Not I, my fine thief . . . but the judge.

THE SHEPHERD: Oh, Lord! Why did you summon me? I don't know why. I never killed your sheep.

THE DRAPER: Oh, no, you are a saint. It's you, you mangy dog . . . all the while you were robbing me of my sheep. But now you'll pay for it with your head. I'll see you hanged.

THE SHEPHERD: Hang by the neck! Good Master, have pity.

THE DRAPER: Pity, eh? And you had pity when you were robbing me of my cloth . . . I mean my sheep. Thief, scoundrel, you robber . . . where is my cloth . . . my sheep?

THE SHEPHERD: They died of sickness, sir. . . .

THE DRAPER: You lie, you caitiff, you stole them, and now. . . .

THE SHEPHERD: It is not so, good Master. I swear. On my soul. . . .

THE DRAPER: You have no soul, you thief. By all the saints, I'll see you dangling this Saturday. . . .

THE SHEPHERD: Good and sweet Master, won't you please make a settlement . . . and not bring me to court?

THE DRAPER: Away, you thief. I'll make you pay for those six yards . . . I mean those sheep. You just wait. (*Walks off in a fury.*)

THE SHEPHERD: Oh, Lord! I must quickly find a lawyer. . . . I've heard of Master Patelin . . . they say no man is better at gulling. It's here he lives. (PATELIN *comes just then from his house. When he sees* AGNELET *he tries to get back, fearing it may be* THE DRAPER, *but on hearing his voice he stops.*) Ho, there, Master! Is it you who are Master Patelin, the lawyer?

PATELIN: What is it you want of him?

THE SHEPHERD: I have a little business for him.

PATELIN: Oh! is it that! Well, I am Master Patelin. Good man, tell me the nature of your business. Is it anything pertaining to the law?

THE SHEPHERD: I'll pay well. . . . I am a shepherd, good Master. A poor man, but I can pay well. I need a lawyer for a little case I have.

PATELIN: Come this way, where we can talk lower. Some one might overhear us . . . I mean disturb us. Now, good man, what may your business be?

THE SHEPHERD: Good Master Lawyer, teach me what to say to the judge.

PATELIN: What is it you have done, or has some one done you an injustice?

THE SHEPHERD: Must I tell you everything . . . exactly as it happened?

PATELIN: You can tell me the truth. I am your lawyer. . . . But, good friend, counsel is costly.

THE SHEPHERD: I'll pay all right. It's my master whose sheep I stole who summoned me to the judge. He is going to have me hanged because I stole his sheep. You see. . . . He paid like a miser. . . . Must I tell you the truth?

PATELIN: I have told you once. You must tell me how everything really happened.

THE SHEPHERD: Well . . . he paid like a miser . . . so I told him some sheep had the hoof sickness and died from it . . . and I buried them far . . . far . . . away, so that the others shouldn't get it. But I really killed them and ate the meat and used the wool for myself — and he caught me right so that I cannot deny it. Now I beseech you

... I can pay well — though he has the law on his side ... tell me ... whether you cannot beat him. If you can, I'll pay you in fine, gold crowns, sweet Master.

PATELIN: Gold crowns!!! H'm, what's your name?

THE SHEPHERD: Agnelet, a poor shepherd, but I have a few crowns put aside. You just ...

PATELIN: What do you intend to pay for this case?

THE SHEPHERD: Will five ... four crowns be enough, sweet sir?

PATELIN (*hardly able to contain himself for excitement*): Ah! ... Hm ... well ... that will be plenty seeing that you are a poor man. But I get much greater sums friend, I do. ... Did you say ... five?

THE SHEPHERD: Yes, sweet sir.

PATELIN: You'll have to make it six. I may tell you, though, that your case is a good one, and I am sure to win it. But now tell me, are there any witnesses the plaintiff can produce? Those who saw you killing the sheep?

THE SHEPHERD: Not one ...

PATELIN: That's fine.

THE SHEPHERD: But more'n a dozen.

PATELIN: That's bad. Hm, let me see now ... no ... (*He seems to hold a deep and learned debate with himself.*) No ... but. ... The book says otherwise. (*Suddenly his face lights up.*) I've got it ... aye, what a wonderful idea! Two ideas in one day! You can understand a sly trick, can't you, fellow?

THE SHEPHERD: Can I? Ho, ho, ho, ho. ...

PATELIN: But you'll pay as you promised.

THE SHEPHERD: Hang me if I don't. But I can't pay if I hang, ho, ho, ho. ...

PATELIN (*gleefully*): Now, first, you have never seen me; nor heard of me. ...

THE SHEPHERD: Oh, no, not that. ...

PATELIN: Silent until I have finished. Second you mustn't talk a single word but "Ba." (*Imitating the bleating of a sheep*) Only bleat like your sheep. No matter what they talk to you. Just say Ba. ... Even if they call you an idiot, or villain, or fool, don't answer anything but Ba. . Just as if you were a sheep.

THE SHEPHERD: Oh, I can do that.

PATELIN: Even if I talk to you, say nothing but Ba. ... And if they split roaring at you, just say Ba. ... The rest you leave to me. I'll get you out for certain.

THE SHEPHERD: I'll surely not say another word. And I will do it right proper.

PATELIN: Your case is as good as won. But don't forget the seven gold crowns.

THE SHEPHERD: I'll sure not, wise and sweet Master Patelin.

CRIER (*is heard from afar*): The court, make room. ...

PATELIN: Ah, here they come. Don't forget Ba. ... I'll be there to help you. And ... the money ... don't forget that.

(*Attendants, Constables, Town Clerks and Villagers enter. Two*

*Clerks carry a seat for* THE JUDGE, *which is placed in the center of the stage.* THE JUDGE, *fat and grouchy, comes to the front, looks about for a moment, then goes to his seat and sits down.*)

THE JUDGE: If there is any business to be done, come to it; the court wants to adjourn.

PATELIN: May heaven bless you and grant you all you desire.

THE JUDGE: Welcome, sir.  May the saints give you plenty of clients.

(THE DRAPER *now comes running in.* PATELIN *suddenly realizes that it is against him that* THE SHEPHERD *must be defended and expresses uneasiness.  He hides himself behind the crowd.*)

THE DRAPER: My lawyer is soon coming, Your Worship.  He has a little business elsewhere which is detaining him.

THE JUDGE: You must think I have nothing to do but to wait for your lawyer.  You are the plaintiff, aren't you?  Bring your complaint.  Where is the defendant?

THE DRAPER: Right there, Your Worship; that lummox shepherd, who has been hiding behind that good citizen there as if he couldn't say Ba. . . . But, Your Honor, it's in fear of justice.

THE JUDGE: Both being present!  I will examine you.  (*To* THE DRAPER)  Tell me all the facts of your case.  Was he in your hire?

THE DRAPER: Yes, Your Lordship.  He killed my sheep and after I treated him like a father. . . .

THE JUDGE: Did you pay him a good wage?

PATELIN (*edging up sideways, and covering his face with his hand*): Your Lordship, I have heard it said that he never paid him a copper for his work.

THE DRAPER (*recognizing* PATELIN): By all that's holy. . . . You. . . . !!!??? 'Tis he and no other.

THE JUDGE: Why do you cover your face, Master Patelin?

PATELIN: Oh, Your Lordship, I have a terrible toothache.

THE JUDGE: I am sorry for you, for I had one myself the other day. I'll tell you a fine cure, Master.  Hold your feet in cold water wherein are three hoofs of a red cow from Gascogne.  This'll draw the ache into the nails of your toes and you can then rid yourself of it with great ease by cutting them.  'Tis a sovereign remedy.  Try it and see, Master.  But let us go on.  Come, Master Draper, I am in a hurry.

THE DRAPER (*not heeding* THE JUDGE *but still staring at* PATELIN): It's you, isn't it?  It's to you I sold six yards of cloth.  Where is my money?

THE JUDGE: What is that you are talking about?

PATELIN: His mind is clouded, Your Lordship.  He is not accustomed to speaking clearly.  Perhaps the defendant will enlighten us.  You . . .

THE DRAPER: I am not speaking clearly!!  You thief . . . liar. . . .

PATELIN: Your Worship, I think I understand him now.  It's strange how incoherently those who have no legal training speak.  I think he means he could have made six yards of cloth from the sheep the shepherd is supposed to have stolen or killed.

THE JUDGE: Aye, so it would seem. Come, Master Guillaume, finish your tale.

PATELIN: Get to the facts as the judge directs you.

THE DRAPER: And you dare talk to me like that!

THE JUDGE: Master Guillaume, come to your sheep.

(*During the rest of the court scene* PATELIN *works always so as to attract the attention of* THE DRAPER *every time he tries to talk of his sheep, and so diverts his attention from that and leads him to talk of the cloth.  Whenever* THE DRAPER *talks of his case,* PATELIN *either sticks his face up to him or places himself in such a position that* THE DRAPER *must see him.*)

THE DRAPER: You see, Your Lordship . . . he took my six yards of cloth this morning . . . the thief. . . .

THE JUDGE: Do you think I am a fool?  Either you come to the point or I'll dismiss the case.

PATELIN: Your Worship, let us call the defendant.  He, I am sure, will speak clearer than this draper.

THE JUDGE: Yes, that will be wise.  Step forward, shepherd.

THE SHEPHERD: Ba . . . a . . .

THE JUDGE: What's this?  Am I a goat?

THE SHEPHERD: Ba . . . a . . .

PATELIN: Your Lordship, it seems this man is half-witted and thinks himself among his sheep.

THE DRAPER: He can talk, and he is not half-witted, either . . . but a thief like you.  It was you who took my cloth!

THE JUDGE: Cloth!  What are you talking about, anyhow?  Now, you either get back to your sheep or I'll dismiss the case.

THE DRAPER: I will, Your Lordship, though the other lies as near to my heart, but I'll leave it for another time.  That shepherd there . . . he took six yards of cloth . . . I mean, sheep.  Your Honor must forgive me.  This thief . . . my shepherd, he told me I would get my money . . . for the cloth as soon . . . I mean this shepherd was to watch over my flocks and he played sick when I came to his house. Ah, Master Pierre. . . . He killed my sheep and told me they died from hoof-sickness . . . and I saw him take the cloth . . . I mean he swore he never killed them.  And his wife swore he was sick and said he never took the cloth. . . . No, that shepherd there. . . . He took the sheep and made out that he was crazy. . . . I don't know what . . .

THE JUDGE (*leaping up*): Keep quiet; you don't know what you are talking about.  You are crazy.  I have listened to your idiotic talk about sheep, and cloth, and wool, and money.  What is it you want here?  Either you answer sensibly, or . . . this is your last chance.

PATELIN: There is surely something strange about this poor man's talk, and I would advise that a physician be consulted.  At times, though, it seems as if he were talking about some money he owes this poor shepherd.

THE DRAPER: You thief!  You robber!  You might at least keep quiet. Where is my cloth? You have it. . . . You are not sick.

THE JUDGE: What has he? Who isn't sick? Are you going to talk of your business or not?

THE DRAPER: He has it, certain. But I'll speak of this later. Now, I'll attend to this thief, this shepherd.

PATELIN: This shepherd cannot answer the charges himself, Your Lordship. I will gladly give my services to defend him.

THE JUDGE: You won't get much for your pains.

PATELIN: Ah, but the knowledge that I am doing a kind and honest deed, and then I may be able to stop this haggling which annoys Your Lordship so much.

THE JUDGE: I'd be greatly thankful.

THE DRAPER: You'll defend him . . . you thief . . . you . . .

THE JUDGE: Now, Master Guillaume, you keep quiet or I'll have you put in the stocks. I have listened long enough to your idiotic gab. Proceed, Master Patelin.

PATELIN: I thank Your Lordship. Now, come on, my good fellow. It's for your own good I am working as you heard me say. Just because I would do you a kind deed. Answer everything well and direct.

THE SHEPHERD: Ba . . . a . . .

PATELIN: Come, I am your lawyer, not a lamb.

THE SHEPHERD: Ba . . .

PATELIN: What's Ba . . . ? Are you crazy? Tell me, did this man pay you money for your work?

THE SHEPHERD: Ba . . .

PATELIN (*seemingly losing his temper*): You idiot, answer, it's I, your lawyer, who is talking to you. Answer.

THE SHEPHERD: Ba . . .

THE DRAPER (*who has listened open-mouthed and bewildered*): But, Your Lordship, he can talk when he wants to. He spoke to me this morning.

PATELIN (*severely*): Everything happened to you this morning, Master Joceaulme. Now it seems to me, it would be far wiser for you to send this shepherd back to his sheep; he is used to their company far more than to that of men. It does not look as if this fool had sense enough to kill a fly, let alone a sheep.

THE DRAPER: You . . . you . . . robber . . . liar!!!

THE JUDGE: I honestly think they are both crazy.

PATELIN: It seems as if Your Lordship is right.

THE DRAPER: I am crazy! You scoundrel! You robber! Where is my cloth? They are both thieves. . . .

THE JUDGE: Keep quiet, I say.

THE DRAPER: But, your Lordship!

THE JUDGE: All you get is vexation, in dealing with dolts and idiots, so says the law. To finish this wrangling the court is adjourned.

THE DRAPER: And my cloth . . . my money . . . I mean my sheep! Is there no justice? Will you not listen to me?

THE JUDGE: Eh, listen to you, you miser? You dare scoff at justice? You hire half crazy people, and then you don't pay them; then you bellow something about cloth which has nothing to do with the case and expect me to listen to you?

THE DRAPER: But he took my cloth . . . and he killed my sheep. I swear to you. There he stands, the thief. (*Pointing to* PATELIN)

THE JUDGE: Stop your bellowing. I discharge this half-witted shepherd. Get home and don't ever come in my sight again no matter how many bailiffs summon you.

PATELIN (*to* THE SHEPHERD): Say thanks to His Lordship.

THE SHEPHERD: Ba . . .

THE JUDGE: By all the saints, never have I come upon such a nest of idiots!

THE DRAPER: My cloth gone . . . my sheep. . . .

THE JUDGE: Huh! You. . . . Well, I have business elsewhere. May I never see your like again. The court is adjourned. Good day, Master Patelin.

PATELIN: A joyous day to you.

(*All leave except* PATELIN, THE DRAPER, *and* THE SHEPHERD.)

THE DRAPER: You thieves . . . you scoundrels! You. . . . You. . . .

PATELIN: Don't shout yourself hoarse, good Master Joceaulme.

THE DRAPER: You stole my cloth and played crazy . . . and now it was because of you that I lost my sheep. . . .

PATELIN: A fine tale! Do you think any one will believe you?

THE DRAPER: I am not blind. Didn't I see you dancing this morning? I saw you. . . .

PATELIN: Are you so certain? Good sir, it may have been Jean de Noyon. He resembles me very much.

THE DRAPER: But I know you when I see you. You screamed and acted mad, shouting a tale of dogs and . . .

PATELIN: Perhaps you imagined it all. Go back to my house and see if I am not *still* there.

THE DRAPER (*looks much puzzled*): I'll go to your house and if I don't find you there, I'll go to the judge and see to it that he listens to my story. I'll get a lawyer from Paris. (*To* THE SHEPHERD, *who has been standing at a safe distance*) You thief! I'll get you yet. (*To* PATELIN) I'll go to your house now.

PATELIN: That's a wise action.

(*Exit* THE DRAPER.)

PATELIN: Now, Agnelet, my fellow. What do you think of me? Didn't we do a fine piece of work?

THE SHEPHERD: Ba . . .

PATELIN: Yes. Ho, ho — wasn't it great!

THE SHEPHERD: Ba . . .

PATELIN: No one is near now; your master is gone. It was a great idea, wasn't it, this legal stroke? You may speak now without fear.

THE SHEPHERD: Ba . . .

PATELIN: I said you could speak without fear, no one is near. Where is the money?

THE SHEPHERD: Ba . . .

PATELIN: I can't stay with you all day. What is this game?

THE SHEPHERD: Ba . . .

PATELIN: How now? Come, I have business elsewhere.

THE SHEPHERD: Ba . . .

PATELIN: What do you mean? You are not going to pay?

THE SHEPHERD (*with a grin*): Ba . . .

PATELIN: Yes, you played your rôle well, good Agnelet. But now it's over. Next time you may count on me again. Now my money; the six crowns.

THE SHEPHERD: Ba . . .

PATELIN (*sees the game now, stops. In a somewhat pathetic voice*): Is that all I am going to get for my work?

THE SHEPHERD: Ba . . .

PATELIN (*getting furious*): I'll have a bailiff after you, you thief . . . you scoundrel . . . you robber. . . .

THE SHEPHERD: Ho, ho, ho . . . Ba . . . ! The judge said I need never come back. And — ho, ho, ho, I never knew you . . . Ba . . . a . . . ! (*Runs out.*)

PATELIN (*silent for a time, then grinning pathetically*): Alas! 'Tis only paying me in my own coin . . . Nevertheless 'twas a fine idea . . . (*Exit.*)

CURTAIN

[tr. MAURICE RELONDE]

# BIBLIOGRAPHY

The following works written in English explain the social, intellectual, political, religious, and artistic milieu of medieval Europe. Since many excellent books have not been translated, readers of foreign languages should consult the bibliographies of Paetow, Raby, and other authors named below, as well as the listings under special articles in a recent edition of the *Encyclopaedia Britannica*. References to fiction or fictionized reconstructions are marked by an asterisk (*).

## GENERAL

Baring-Gould, S., *The Lives of the Saints*, rev. ed., 16 vols., Edinburgh, 1914.

Batiffol, P., *History of the Roman Breviary*, translated by A. M. Y. Baylay, London, 1912.

Beazley, C. R., *The Dawn of Modern Geography*, 3 vols., London, 1897–1906.

Boissonade, P., *Life and Work in Medieval Europe*, translated by E. Power, London, 1927.

Britt, M., *The Hymns of the Breviary and Missal*, rev. ed., New York, 1936.

*Cambridge Medieval History*, 8 vols., Cambridge, 1911–1936.

Carlyle, R. W., and Carlyle, A. J., *History of Medieval Political Theory in the West*, 6 vols., London, 1903–1936.

Chadwick, H. M., and Chadwick, N. K., *The Growth of Literature*, Vol. I, Cambridge, 1932.

Chaytor, H. J., *From Script to Print: an Introduction to Medieval Literature*, Cambridge, 1945.

Clark, A. C., *The Descent of Manuscripts*, Oxford, 1918.

Coulton, G. G., *Five Centuries of Religion*, 3 vols., Cambridge, 1923–1936.

Coulton, G. G., *Life in the Middle Ages*, 4 vols., Cambridge, 1928–1930.

Crump, G. C., and Jacob, E. F., *Legacy of the Middle Ages*, Oxford, 1926.

Duchesne, L., *Christian Worship: Its Origin and Evolution*, translated by M. L. McClure, 5th ed., London, 1919.

Edwardes, M., *Summary of the Literatures of Modern Europe* (A.D. 600–1400), London, 1907.

Farrar, C. P., and Evans, A. P., *Bibliography of English Translations from Medieval Sources*, New York, 1946.

Gregorovius, F., *Rome in the Middle Ages*, translated by A. Hamilton, 8 vols. in 13, London, 1894–1902.

Holweck, F. G., *A Biographical Dictionary of the Saints*, St. Louis, 1924.

Julian, J., ed., *A Dictionary of Hymnology*, rev. ed., London, 1907.

Lagarde, A., *The Latin Church in the Middle Ages*, translated by A. Alexander, Edinburgh, 1915.

Medieval Towns Series (*Canterbury, Cambridge, Chartres, Padua, Paris, Venice*, etc.), 35 vols., New York, various dates.

Montalembert, C. F. R., Comte de, *Monks of the West*, authorized translation, 7 vols., Edinburgh, 1861–1879.

Morey, C. R., *Medieval Art*, New York, 1942.

Munro, D. C., and Sellery, G. C., *Medieval Civilization*, enlarged ed., New York, 1907.

Paetow, J. L., *A Guide to the Study of Medieval History*, rev. ed., New York, 1931.

Palaeographical Society, *Facsimiles of Manuscripts and Inscriptions*, ed. E. A. Bond and others, Series I–II, London, 1873–1901. New Paleographical Society, *Facsimiles of Ancient Manuscripts*, Parts I–X, London, 1903–1912. Second Series, 1913—.

Pirenne, H., *Economic and Social History of Medieval Europe*, translated by I. E. Clegg, New York, 1937.

Raby, F. J. E., *A History of Christian Latin Poetry . . . to the Close of the Middle Ages*, Oxford, 1927.

Raby, F. J. E., *A History of Secular Latin Poetry in the Middle Ages*, 2 vols., Oxford, 1934.

Reese, G., *Music in the Middle Ages*, New York, 1940.

*Reinhard, J. R., *Mediaeval Pageant*, New York, 1939.

Sarton, G., *Introduction to the History of Science*, 3 vols., Baltimore, 1927–1948.

Taylor, H. O., *The Medieval Mind*, 2 vols., London, 1911.

Thompson, S., *Motif-Index of Folk Literature*, 6 vols., Bloomington, Ind., 1932–1936.

Thorndike, L., *A History of Magic and Experimental Science*, 2 vols., New York, 1923. *Idem, 14th and 15th Centuries*, 2 vols., New York, 1934.

Tupper, F., *Types of Society in Medieval Literature*, New York, 1926.

Wendell, B., *The Traditions of European Literature from Homer to Dante*, New York, 1920.

## PART I, THE CHRISTIAN TRADITION

*Collins, W. W., *Antonina* (Sack of Rome, Alaric), London, 1852.

Dalton, O. M., trans., *Letters of Sidonius Apollinaris* (A.D. 430–483), 2 vols., London, 1925.

Delehaye, H., *The Legends of the Saints*, translated by V. M. Crawford, London, 1907.

Duckett, E. S., *Latin Writers of the Fifth Century*, New York, 1930.

Duckett, E. S., *The Gateway to the Middle Ages*, New York, 1938.

Dudden, F. H., *The Life and Times of St. Ambrose*, 2 vols., Oxford, 1935.

Dudden, F. H., *Gregory the Great: His Place in History and Thought*, 2 vols., London, 1905.

*Gissing, G., *Veranilda* (Theodoric and the Gothic Kingdom), London, 1904.

Haarhoff, T., *Schools of Gaul . . . in the Last Century of the Western Empire*, London, 1900.

*Hollis, G., *Leo of Mediolanum* (Ambrose, Augustine, Monica), London, 1909.

Labriolle, P. C., *History and Literature of Christianity from Tertullian to Boethius*, translated by H. Wilson, New York, 1925.

Laistner, M. L. W., *Thought and Letters in Western Europe*, 500–900 A.D., London, 1931.

Loomis, C. G., *White Magic: An Introduction to the Folklore of Christian Legend*, Cambridge, Mass., 1948.

Rand, E. K., *Founders of the Middle Ages*, Cambridge, Mass., 1928.

Smith, W., and Cheetham, S., *Dictionary of Christian Antiquities*, 2 vols., London, 1875–1880.

Smith, W., and Wace, H., *Dictionary of Christian Biography*, 4 vols., London, 1877–1887.
Wright, F. A., trans., *Fathers of the Church: A Selection from the Writings of the Latin Fathers*, London, 1928.
Wright, F. A., and Sinclair, P. A., *A History of Later Latin Literature*, New York, 1931.


## PART II, IRISH LITERATURE

Best, R. I., *A Bibliography of Irish Philology and Printed Irish Literature*, Dublin, 1913.
Cross, T. P., and Slover, C. H., trans., *Ancient Irish Tales*, New York, 1936.
Dillon, M., *The Cycles of the Kings*, Oxford, 1946.
Flower, R., *The Irish Tradition*, Oxford, 1947.
Gougaud, L., *Christianity in Celtic Lands*, translated by M. Joynt, London, 1932.
Hubert, H., *The Greatness and Decline of the Celts*, London, 1934.
Hull, E., *The Poem-Book of the Gael*, London, 1912.
Hull, E., *Textbook of Irish Literature*, 2 vols., Dublin, 1906–1908.
Jackson, K., *Studies in Early Celtic Nature-Poetry*, Cambridge, 1935.
Kenney, J. F., *Sources for the Early History of Ireland*, Vol. I (Ecclesiastical), New York, 1929.
*MacPherson, J., *The Works of Ossian*, 2 vols., London, 1765.
Zimmer, H., *The Irish Element in Medieval Culture*, translated by J. L. Edmands, New York, 1891.
(See also Chadwick above and Allen and Jones below.)


## PART III, OLD ENGLISH LITERATURE

Anderson, G. K., *The Literature of the Anglo-Saxons*, Princeton, 1949.
Atkins, J. W. H., *English Literary Criticism: The Medieval Phase*, Cambridge, 1943.
Brown, G. B., *The Arts in Early England*, 6 vols., London, 1903–1920.
Chambers, R. W., *Beowulf*, rev. ed., Cambridge, 1932.
Duckett, E. S., *Anglo-Saxon Saints and Scholars*, New York, 1947.
Hodgkin, R. H., *History of the Anglo-Saxons*, 2 vols., Oxford, 1935.
Jones, C. W., *Saints' Lives and Chronicles in Early England*, Ithaca, N.Y., 1947.
Kennedy, C. W., *The Earliest English Poetry*, New York, 1943.
*Kipling, R., *Puck of Pook's Hill*, New York, 1906.
Levison, W., *England and the Continent in the Eighth Century*, Oxford, 1946.
Sampson, G., *The Cambridge Book of Prose and Verse . . . from the Beginnings to the Cycles of Romance*, Cambridge, 1924.
Thompson, A. H., ed., *Bede: His Life, Times, and Writings*, Oxford, 1935.
Ward, A. W., and Waller, A. R., eds., *Cambridge History of English Literature*, Vol. I, Cambridge, 1907.
(See also Chadwick and Laistner above, and Routh below.)

## PART IV, ROMANESQUE LITERATURE

Allen, P. S., *Medieval Latin Lyrics,* Chicago, 1931.
Allen, P. S., and Jones, H. M., *The Romanesque Lyric,* Chapel Hill, 1928.
Bett, H., *Johannes Scotus Erigena,* Cambridge, 1925.
Breul, K., *The Cambridge Songs,* Cambridge, 1915.
Clark, J. M., *The Abbey of St. Gall as a Centre of Literature and Art,* Cambridge, 1926.
Deschamps, P., *French Sculpture of the Romanesque Period,* New York, 1930.
Gaskoin, C. J. B., *Alcuin: His Life and Work,* Cambridge, 1904.
Haskins, C. H., *The Renaissance of the Twelfth Century,* Cambridge, Mass., 1927.
*Kingsley, C., *Hereward the Wake,* 2 vols., London, 1866.
Morison, J. C., *Saint Bernard,* London, 1901.
Mullinger, J. B., *The Schools of Charles the Great,* London, 1877.
Poole, R. L., *Illustrations of the History of Medieval Thought and Learning,* rev. ed., London, 1920.
*Scheffel, J. V., *Ekkehard,* translated by S. Delffs, London, 1867.
Stephenson, C., *Medieval Feudalism,* Ithaca, N.Y., 1942.
*Waddell, H., *Peter Abelard,* London, 1933.
Webb, C. C. J., *John of Salisbury,* London, 1932.
(See also Laistner, Levison, Rand, Waddell, and Zimmer above, and Adams below.)

## PART V, ARTHURIAN LITERATURE

Brown, A. C. L., *The Origin of the Grail Legend,* Cambridge, Mass., 1943.
Bruce, J. D., *The Evolution of Arthurian Romance to* A.D. *1300,* 2 vols., Baltimore, 1923.
Chambers, E. K., *Arthur of Britain,* London, 1927.
*Clemens, S. (Mark Twain), *A Connecticut Yankee in King Arthur's Court,* New York, 1889.
Jones, W. L., *King Arthur in History and Legend,* Cambridge, 1911.
Lewis, C. B., *Classical Mythology and Arthurian Romance,* London, 1932.
Loomis, R. S., and Loomis, L. H., *Arthurian Legends in Medieval Art,* New York, 1939.
Reid, M. J. C., *The Arthurian Legend: Comparison of Treatment in Modern and Medieval Literature,* Edinburgh, 1938.
Spence, L., *A Dictionary of Medieval Romance and Romance Writers,* London, 1913.
Stubbs, W., *Literature and Learning at the Court of Henry II,* seventeen lectures, Oxford, 1886.
Ward, H. L. D., and Herbert, J. A., *Catalogue of Romances in the British Museum,* 3 vols., London, 1883–1910.
(See also Holmes, Kilgour, Prestage, Taylor, and Voretzsch below.)

## PART VI, TEUTONIC LITERATURE

Barraclough, A., *The Origins of Modern Germany,* rev. ed., Oxford, 1947.
Closs, A., *The Genius of the German Lyric,* London, 1938.
Craigie, W. A., *The Icelandic Sagas,* Cambridge, 1913.

*Harrod, F. (Frances Forbes-Robertson), *The Wanton* (Germany under Frederick II), London, 1909.

Hermannsson, H., *Old Icelandic Literature* (Islandica xxiii), Ithaca, N.Y., 1933.

*Lamb, H., *The House of the Falcon* (Teutonic Minnesang and Feudalism), New York, 1921.

Morgan, B. Q., *A Critical Bibliography of German Literature in English Translation*, Palo Alto, 1938.

Morgan, B. Q., *Nature in Middle High German Lyrics*, Baltimore, 1912.

Norman, F., *The Germanic Heroic Poet and His Art*, Oxford, 1938.

Phillpotts, B. S., *Edda and Saga*, London, 1931.

Richey, M. F., *Essays on the Mediaeval German Love Lyric*, Oxford, 1943.

Routh, H. V., *God, Man, and Epic Poetry*, Vol. II, Cambridge, 1927.


PART VII, ROMANCE LITERATURE (primarily of France)

Adams, H., *Mont St. Michel and Chartres*, Boston, 1913.

Aubry, P., *Trouvères and Troubadours*, translated by C. Aveling, New York, 1914.

Brunetière, F., *Manual of the History of French Literature*, Bk. I, authorized trans., New York, 1898.

*Davis, W. S., *"God Wills It!"* (First Crusade), New York, 1901.

Dickinson, C., *Troubadour Songs*, New York, 1920.

*Doyle, A. C., *Sir Nigel* (Battle of Poitiers, Black Death), London, 1906.

Fundenburg, G. B., *Feudal France in the French Epic*, Princeton, 1919.

*Hewlett, M., *Richard Yea-and-Nay* (Richard I, Bertran de Born), New York, 1900.

Holmes, U. T., *A History of Old French Literature*, New York, 1937.

*Hugo, V., *Notre Dame de Paris* (Paris under Louis XI), Paris, 1831 (various translations).

Huizinga, J., *Waning of the Middle Ages*, London, 1924.

Kilgour, R. L., *The Decline of Chivalry As Shown in the French Literature of the Late Middle Ages*, Cambridge, Mass., 1937.

Lawrence, W. W., *Mediaeval Story*, 2nd ed., New York, 1926.

Oman, C. W., *A History of the Art of War in the Middle Ages*, 2 vols., 2nd ed., London, 1924.

Painter, S., *French Chivalry*, Baltimore, 1940.

Paris, G., *Mediaeval French Literature*, translated by H. Lynch (Temple Primers), London, 1903.

Patterson, W. F., *Three Centuries of French Poetic Theory*, 2 vols., Ann Arbor, 1935.

Pope, M. K., *From Latin to Modern French*, Manchester, 1934.

Power, E., *Medieval People*, London, 1924.

Prestage, E., ed., *Chivalry: A Series of Studies to Illustrate Its Historical Significance and Civilizing Influence*, New York, 1928.

Rice, W. H., *The European Ancestry of Villon's Satirical Testaments*, New York, 1941.

Rosenberg, M. V., *Eleanor of Aquitaine, Queen of the Troubadours and of the Courts of Love*, Boston, 1937.

Saintsbury, G. E. B., *The Flourishing of Romance and the Rise of Allegory*, London, 1897.

Smith, J. H., *The Troubadours at Home*, 2 vols., New York, 1899.

Taylor, A. B., *An Introduction to Medieval Romance*, London, 1930.

Wright, J. K., *Geographical Lore at the Time of the Crusades*, New York, 1925.

Voretzsch, C., *Introduction to the Study of Old French Literature*, translated by F. M. DuMont, New York, 1931.

(See also ARTHURIAN LITERATURE above. and DANTE and Gaselee below.)


PART VIII, DANTE (and his Italian predecessors)

Chapman, J. J., *Dante*, New York, 1927.

Chaytor, H. J., *The Troubadours of Dante*, Oxford, 1902.

Gardner, E. G., *Sainte Catherine of Siena: A Study in the Religion, Literature, and History of the 14th Century in Italy*, London, 1907.

Gardner, E. G., *Dante's Ten Heavens*, 2nd ed., Westminster, 1900.

Gaspary, A., *The History of Italian Literature to the Death of Dante*, translated by H. Oelsner, London, 1901.

Grandgent, C. H., *From Latin to Italian*, Cambridge, Mass., 1927.

Hopper, V. F., *Medieval Number Symbolism*, New York, 1938.

Kantorowicz, E., *Frederick the Second, 1194–1250*, translated by E. O. Lorimer, London, 1931.

Little, K., *Saint Francis*, London, 1904.

Reade, W. H. V., *The Moral System of Dante's Inferno*, Oxford, 1909.

*Scudder, V., *Brother John* (the Franciscans), Boston, 1927.

*Stewart, N. V., *A Son of the Emperor* (Frederick II, Guelfs and Ghibellines), London, 1909.

Toynbee, P., *Dante Dictionary*, Oxford, 1898.

Toynbee, P., *Dante in English Literature from Chaucer to Cary*, 2 vols., New York, 1909.

Vernon, W. W., *Readings on the Inferno, Purgatorio, and Paradiso of Dante*, 6 vols., 2nd ed., London, 1906, 1897, 1909.

Vossler, K., *Mediaeval Culture: An Introduction to Dante and His Times*, translated by W. C. Lawton, 2 vols., New York, 1929.

(See also Grabmann and Pegis below.)


PART IX, LATE LATIN LITERATURE

(and the universities)

Burke, R. B., trans., *The* Opus Maius *of* Roger Bacon, 2 vols., Philadelphia, 1928.

Coulton, G. G., *A Medieval Garner*, London, 1910.

Foligno, C., *Latin Thought during the Middle Ages*, Oxford, 1929.

Gaselee, S., *The Transition from the Late Latin Lyric to the Medieval Love Poem*, Cambridge, 1931.

Gilson, E., *The Spirit of Medieval Philosophy*, translated by A. H. C. Downes, New York, 1936.

Grabmann, M., *Thomas Aquinas: His Personality and Thought*, translated by V. Michel, New York, 1928.

Lea, H. C., *A History of the Inquisition in the Middle Ages*, 3 vols., 1887 ff.

Lobel, E., *The Mediaeval Latin Poetics*, Oxford, 1932.

Neale, J. M., *Mediaeval Hymns and Sequences*, London, 1851.

Pegis, A. C., *St. Thomas and the Problem of the Soul in the 13th Century*, Toronto, 1934.

Rashdall, H., *The Universities of Europe in the Middle Ages*, rev. ed., 3 vols., Oxford, 1936.

Symonds, J. A., *Wine, Women, and Song*, London, 1907.

Waddell, H., *The Wandering Scholars*, 6th ed., London, 1932.


PART X, DRAMA

Chambers, E. K., *The Medieval Stage*, 2 vols., Oxford, 1903.

Coffman, G. R., "A New Approach to Medieval Latin Drama," *Modern Philology*, XXII (1925), 239-71.

Crosse, G., *The Religious Drama*, London, 1913.

Hastings, C., *The Theatre: Its Development in France and England*, London, 1902.

Mantzies, K., *A History of Theatrical Art in Ancient and Modern Times*, 6 vols., London, 1903-1921.

Rudwin, M. J., *A Historical and Bibliographical Survey of the German Religious Drama*, Pittsburgh, 1924.

Tiddy, R. J. E., *The Mummers' Play*, Oxford, 1923.

Young, K., *The Drama of the Medieval Church*, 2 vols., Oxford, 1933.

# INDEX OF PROPER NAMES

[In the main, the following list is comprehensive. Omissions include the word "Christian" and its variants, the names of the Christian Godhead, names for Satan except as indicating the fallen angel, names for knightly possessions like swords and horses, names for some regions, especially mythical, which occur but once in this volume and seldom elsewhere, and names of all authors or commentators who lived after the fifteenth century. Included are certain common personifications (e.g., Love, Death, Philosophy) and technical names for some typically medieval literary forms. The forms of the names entered are those of the translators represented in this volume; no attempt has been made to normalize their spelling or to reconcile it with the original texts.

A page number in roman type indicates that the name occurs in the translation; *italic* type indicates editorial comment.]